BECKWITH

IRISH AND SCOTTISH IDENTITIES IN A CANADIAN COMMUNITY

GLENN J LOCKWOOD

Frontispiece
Group of Beckwith inhabitants in front of Fred Scott's barns at Black's Corners as photographed by Eva Nesbitt ca. 1928. Rural school fairs in the 1920s and 1930s were one of the few attempts to bring inhabitants of Beckwith's disparate communities together. Although ethnic identities weakened with time, the geographic concentration of Irish and Scottish families that endured from the time of first settlement was transmuted into vying denominations, localities, villages and school sections. Photograph courtesy of Arthur Nesbitt.

BECKWITH

IRISH AND SCOTTISH IDENTITIES
IN A CANADIAN COMMUNITY

An account of two transplanted
cultural communities, their adjustment to Upper
Canadian frontier farming, their response
to demographic constraints and industrialisation,
and the transformation of their identities
between 1816 and 1991

GLENN J LOCKWOOD

Copyright © 1991
Glenn J Lockwood
in right of the Corporation
of the Township of Beckwith

All rights reserved

ISBN 0-9695758-0-7

The support of the Social Sciences and Humanities Research Council of Canada, the Summer Canada Student Employment Program, The Ontario Heritage Foundation, Wintario, the University of Ottawa and the Corporation of the Township of Beckwith is gratefully acknowledged. The Ontario Ministry of Colleges and Universities and Carleton University also offered funding in support of this work.

Printed in Canada on acid-free paper

Copies of this book can be ordered from
Beckwith Township Municipal Clerk,
R.R. No. 2
Carleton Place, Ontario
K7C 3P2
(613) 257-1539

CONTENTS

Introduction   vii

IRISH AND SCOTTISH TRANSPLANTS 1816-1824
The Military Plan   2
Scottish Beckwith   29
Irish Beckwith   52
Bush Life   76
Cultural Conflict?   96

PROTOTYPICAL BECKWITH 1825-1851
A Provisioning Economy   116
Family Ties   143
The Reverend William Bell's Beckwith   166
The Orange Anglican Polity   194
The Search For Order   225

RAILROADING BECKWITH 1852-1880
The People of Beckwith Township   252
The Maturing of Daniel McCuan   278
The Remaking of Beckwith   315
The Coming of the Mills   353

THE TRIUMPH OF SENTIMENTALITY 1881-1920
Edward Kidd and the Burden of Childhood   398
The Household of Faith   429
The Townward Rush   473
The Military Heritage   505

URBAN INFILTRATION 1921-1991
Not Dead! O No, She Only Sleeps   532
Commuting the Future   550

Appendices   576
Abbreviations   613
Index   614

For Corey Michael Reay

INTRODUCTION

This is two books in one. First, it is a comparison of the cultural adjustment and adaptation of equally large Irish and Scottish communities that settled in an eastern Ontario township. Second, it is a history of the municipality of Beckwith from 1816 to 1991, with particular attention paid to the century before 1920. Within the boundaries of these two considerations, the one informed by current scholarly debate and the other directed toward a popular audience, this study explores various aspects of regional society over a period of one hundred and seventy-five years. The balance in numbers of Irish and Scottish immigrants inhabiting Beckwith, arriving as they did at the same time, offers an excellent locality or laboratory within which to assess the comparative progress of these two immigrant groups in regional society, and to assess the comparative adjustment and financial strategies of their descendants as industrial towns emerged, as agriculture mechanised, as markets changed, and as eastern Ontario economically fell behind the rest of the province.

Recent historical scholarship has challenged previous assumptions about the experience of immigrants in Upper Canada simply echoing that in the United States, but there is still debate about the relative success of different ethnic groups in Canada. Interpretations of the Irish immigrant experience by Canadian historians range from the traditional view presented by Murray W. Nicolson of Irish Catholics in Victorian Toronto being a ghettoised and economically-troubled minority, to the evocation by Donald Akenson of the Irish in Leeds and Lansdowne townships being an economically, politically, socially and agriculturally successful community up to 1871. Marianne McLean has recently shown how early nineteenth century Scottish immigrants successfully made use of government immigration experiments to pursue their own goals by settling on poor lots near relatives in Glengarry rather than accept grants offered them by government. These differing interpretations reflect the very different communities used as case studies, with Nicolson addressing Irish Catholics in an urban setting, Akenson dealing predominantly with Irish Protestants in a rural setting, and McLean focusing on specific group migrations of Perthshire highlanders.

The lack of specific comparisons between various ethnic groups has been a major flaw of ethnic studies in Canada to date. Various interpretations are assisted by the vagueness with which the population interacting with the specific ethnic group being studied is delineated; hence Nicolson lumps all non-Irish Catholics together as British Protestants, and Akenson distinguishes only between Irish Catholics and Irish Protestants and compares them with the general population. It is not enough to say that the Irish fared well in regional society as compared with the non-Irish in a community such as Leeds and Lansdowne where the non-Irish listed in the census returns used by historians included United Empire Loyalists, American and French Canadian settlers, English and Scottish immigrants, and the Canadian-born children of the Irish immigrants themselves, not to mention other ethnic groups.

This volume flows quite naturally from my history of Montague Township immediately to the south of Beckwith, and from my doctoral dissertation "Eastern Upper Canadian Perceptions of Irish Immigrants, 1824-1868". As shall be shown in the course of this study, there were strong links between families in Beckwith and Montague, links that contributed to the creation of ethnic stereotypes. This study also flows from the work I pursued under the direction of Professor Julian Gwyn in 1980 at the University of Ottawa, in analysing the social structure of mid-nineteenth century

Montague from census returns as the subject of a Masters thesis. Another strong shaping influence guiding the preparation of this work was to attend a course on the writing of community history given by professor S.R. Mealing at Carleton University in 1981. I am grateful to professor Mealing for casting a critical eye over the fifth chapter. Co-teaching a course on eastern Ontario history with Bruce S. Elliott at the University of Ottawa in 1982 also benefitted the writing of this book.

The decade that has intervened since the Montague book was written has witnessed a new emphasis in Ontario on producing thematic professional community histories. The creation by The Ontario Historical Society of the Fred Landon Award for the best book on Ontario regional history in 1987 offers an opportunity to further the writing of better quality local history. In two sentences, the committee that created this award summarised what the worthy goals of a local historian in Ontario should be:

> The Fred Landon Award has been inaugurated to encourage the historical study of how Ontario people lived both in relation to their local environments and to one other within identifiable communities. This award recognizes books that represent a fresh and innovative approach to the study of community or regional history, demonstrating excellence in research, organisation, writing and production.

The most important aspect of writing a good local history, in my opinion, is to strive to capture the essence and the nature of a specific locality at a particular period of time. This is in distinct contrast with recent studies by scholarly historians who select localities as laboratories or case studies in which they examine minute evidence, produce a theory or explanation, and present it as applying to the rest of the province, if not, indeed, to the rest of the country or continent. The reluctance of these scholars to be identified as local historians notwithstanding, the contention that their work has application across Ontario has often not withstood the light of scrutiny for long. Michael Katz's study of Hamilton in the 1850s, for example, shows a high rate of mobility in the population of that city. Instead of that being the norm for either Canada generally or even for Upper Canadian cities, as Katz claimed, it is now perceived to have been exceptional. David Gagan's study of mid-nineteenth century Peel County's wheat economy, to take another example, claimed to be relevant for the rest of Upper Canada. Yet, recent research by Marvin McInnis reveals that Peel was exceptional in its production of wheat and in its proximity to urbanising Toronto. I am not for a moment suggesting that either Katz or Gagan have not produced good local historical studies. The point is, rather, that they have, but they refuse to accept that that is precisely what they have done—produced good local studies that explain the texture of life only in a particular locality.

* * * * * * * * *

The people of Beckwith Township have regarded their municipality as having a significant history for well over a century. There could be no more certain evidence of how seriously they have taken their history than when the municipal clerk in 1980 cited Section 242 of the Ontario Municipal Act which "empowers a Council of a municipality to pass by-laws and make such regulation for the health, safety, morality and welfare of the inhabitants of the municipality" as justification for funding the writing of an ambitious history. Although adjacent Montague Township began settling 25 years before Beckwith, and although it bordered on the Rideau Canal and on historical communities such as Burritt's Rapids, Merrickville and Smiths Falls, only a handful of publications contained straggling references to the history of Montague before 1980. In Beckwith, by contrast, between the 1870s and 1980 there was a succession of well over 100 articles, pamphlets, novels, books, historical plaques and promotional features celebrating the history of Beckwith and Carleton Place.

This local fascination with the past has developed because of the perceived mythic quality of Beckwith's history. The mythic perception of Beckwith's past has developed around or at least has been based on differing religious and ethnic world views that have persisted down through the years. For example, the *impasse* between the Reverend George Buchanan and most of his congregation in the early 1830s alone has inspired a number of books and articles with varying interpretations of what actually took place. The local study of Beckwith's past has become self-perpetuating by encrusting around recognisable, often remarkable points of interest. An 1818 Perthshire group settlement, along with Beckwith being part of the line of four military townships set up in 1816, have long been recognised as important events in local development. The Duke of Richmond first manifesting symptoms of hydrophobia at the site of Franktown during his 1819 tour of inspection as governor-in-chief of Canada was another point of interest. Similarly, the ancient crozier of St. Fillan being in the hands of a Beckwith family from 1818 to 1850, and Roy Brown being credited with shooting down the legendary World War One German flying ace Manfred von Richthofen, each provided a different and interesting focus inviting Beckwith inhabitants to explore their community's past.

The local tradition of eulogising and exploring the past began with the reminiscences of elderly inhabitants in the 1870s, marvelling in letters printed in Carleton Place newspapers about the transformation of Carleton Place into a town and the changing nature of rural society. The Lanark and Renfrew edition of the Belden *Historical Atlas of Canada* (1880) and Jessie Buchanan Campbell's *The Pioneer Pastor* (1900) were the major early monographs that instilled some sense of the worth of Beckwith's past. A host of brief newspaper articles sporadically appeared in the early twentieth century; George Edward Kidd's study of school section No. 6—*The Story of the Derry*—was published in British Columbia in 1943; and in the 1950s and 1960s the most prolific and resourceful of Beckwith's historians, Howard Morton Brown, published dozens of excellent articles and two books detailing various aspects of Beckwith and Carleton Place history. From the late 1960s on, with the raising of historical plaques, and due to the influence of Brown's work, interest in the history of the locality has increased apace. An influx of new inhabitants, most of them commuters to Ottawa, in recent years has further contributed to the growing interest in the past, as demonstrated by the movement to preserve heritage buildings and the establishment of a historical society and museum.

Although the amateur historians of Beckwith have focused on larger than life figures such as the Reverend George Buchanan and captain A. Roy Brown, it must be remembered that they were but two persons in a cast of thousands whose lives were acted out in the streets of Carleton Place and on the concession lines of Beckwith. In order to gain as true a sense of the larger group of people who called Beckwith and Carleton Place home from 1816 on down to our own day, it has been necessary to look at a vast collection of routinely-generated records such as ships' lists, settlement registers, census returns, land registry records, tombstone inscriptions, birth registers, marriage registers, death registers, obituaries, church registers, wills, assessment rolls, collectors' rolls, school attendance registers, township minute books and directories in addition to a wide variety of manuscript sources. To keep track of the vast amount of information that has been generated since 1981, the twelve thousand lines of information from the 1852 through 1881 census returns and the 32,000 lines of information from the Abstract Index to Deeds were computerised and analysed using the Statistical Package for the Social Sciences. In addition to the census and Abstract Index to Deeds, some 100,000 index cards containing vital statistics were assembled. An analysis of much of this information provides the basis for the text of this book.

This study has been prepared to provide an interpretive synthesis of Beckwith's development over 170 years, in the hope that it will spur local inhabitants to write their family histories as well as the individual histories of each school section, each village, each church, and every single social institution. The wealth of information available on Beckwith precluded giving a more detailed history of every institution and every vicinity. Local organisations such as the Carleton Place and Beckwith Historical Society and the Beckwith Women's Institute have already made a good beginning at both conserving records and writing the history of individual institutions. The growing popularity of genealogy alone ensures that Beckwith will long continue to be the focus of historical inquiry.

* * * * * * * * *

There are many people to thank for their contributions to the creation of this book. First, I must pay tribute to the Beckwith Township Council in 1981 which under the leadership of Reeve Stanley

Brunton commissioned the research and writing of this history, and to the successor councils which reaffirmed their support for this project. In addition to the substantial funding provided by Beckwith, I am grateful to the Social Sciences and Humanities Research Council of Canada, to the Summer Canada Student Employment program, to the Ontario Heritage Foundation, to Wintario, and to the University of Ottawa for additional funding which supported this project. I wish to thank professors Cornelius Jaenen, Fernand Ouellet, S.F. Wise, The Ontario Historical Society presidents Heather Broadbent and Alec Douglas, and Paul Dick, M.P., and Douglas Wiseman, M.P.P., who supported my application for funding. I owe an immense debt of gratitude to Howard M. Brown for his unstinting generosity in sharing the rich trove of research material he has gathered on Beckwith and Carleton Place over the past 25 years, and for various forms of support he has provided during some of the darker moments of this project. I am grateful to township clerks Arthur Hawkins and Yvonne Robert for their assistance and many favours over the past seven years. I am grateful to William C. Cox, head of the history department at Carleton Place High School for his generous assistance in providing the labour of dozens of Grade 13 students to help reconstruct families living in Beckwith and Carleton Place before 1925. I am grateful to Robert W.J. Moore for preparing plans and sketches. I wish to thank Leonard and Reva Dolgoy, Bruce S. Elliott, Geoffrey Ewen and Arthur and Vera Hawkins for both putting me up and putting up with me while conducting research in Beckwith, Kingston, Toronto and Carleton Place respectively. I am grateful to Robert Baker, Howard M. Brown and Arthur Hawkins for providing transportation.

The Beckwith Historical project attracted enthusiastic and diligent students to its summer projects. I an grateful for the computer skills of Rodney G. Swain and for the managerial skills of Jane P. Davis in directing fellow students so that I could pursue research at other locations. Students working on the project in 1981 included Jennifer Becherel, Thomas Kinch, Andre Levesque, Donald Smith and Russell Tattersall. Students in 1982 included Kathryn Brown, Lissa Buffam, Karen Fernback and Betty Jean Maennling; and students in 1983 included Linda Black, Debbie Brown, Lori Chamney, Betty Jean Maennling and Chris Tyson.

I am grateful to staff members Sandra Burrows, Jack D'aoust, Suzanne Chartrand, Ann Dunn (now Van Ulft), Franceen Gaudet, Diane Gauthier, Rick McSheffrey, Richard Patrie and Juanita Renaud at the now disbanded Newspaper Division of the National Library of Canada for their excellent service and infinite patience with my seemingly endless demands. I wish to express my gratitude to Patricia Kennedy and Marianne McLean at the National Archives of Canada; the staff at the Kingston Public Library; Reva Dolgoy at the Victoria School Museum Archives of the Carleton Place and Beckwith Historical Society; Barbara Walsh and Suzanne French at the Carleton Place Public Library; Ian Forsyth, the late William Ormsby, Cathy Shepherd, Leon Warmski and Ian Wilson at the Archives of Ontario; the Reverend Brian J. Price STB at the Archdiocese of Kingston Archives; Ruth Riggs at the Diocese of Ontario Archives; Soeur Marcelle Gratton at the Archdiocese of Ottawa Archives; John Francis at the Diocese of Ottawa Archives; Doug McNichol at the Perth Museum; George Henderson, Anne MacDermaid and Shirley Spragge at the Queen's University Archives; William F.E. Morley and Donna Dumbleton of Special Collections in the Douglas Library at Queen's University; and the staffs at the Royal Ontario Museum, the Baldwin Room at the Metropolitan Toronto Library, the University of Ottawa Morisset Library and the University of Toronto Robarts Library.

Finally, I wish to express my sincere gratitude to the many inhabitants of Beckwith who welcomed me into their home and generously shared their artifacts, photographs and documents with me for the ultimate benefit of this publication. Their individual contributions are duly credited under the various plates and in the endnotes. Despite the assistance I have received from many people in preparing this volume I must accept responsibility for any remaining deficiencies.

Glenn J Lockwood
University of Ottawa
19 November 1987

To plant a family! This idea is at the bottom of most of the wrong and mischief which men do. The truth is, that, once in every half century, at longest, a family should be merged into the great, obscure mass of humanity, and forget all about its ancestors. Human blood, in order to keep its freshness, should run in hidden streams, as the water of an aqueduct is conveyed in subterranean pipes.

Nathaniel Hawthorne
The House of the Seven Gables

As long as the lady is necessarily the most active member of her household she keeps her ground from her utility; but when the state of semi-civilisation arrives, and the delicacies of her table, and the elegancies of her person become her chief concern and pride, then she must fall, and must be contented to be looked upon as belonging merely to the decorative department of the establishment and valued accordingly.

Anne Langton
Journal

Plate 2
"The Battle of Waterloo". Beckwith was part of a military settlement established at the end of the War of 1812 to provide an inexpensive and viable alternative to shipping soldiers back to the British Isles. The military legacy and the counter-revolutionary rhetoric of such settlers had a profound impact on even the civilian settlers of Beckwith for generations to come. From Christopher W. Koch's History of Revolutions in Europe *published at Kingston, Upper Canada in 1840.*

IRISH AND SCOTTISH TRANSPLANTS

1816 - 1824

THE MILITARY PLAN

GEORGE THE THIRD BY THE GRACE OF GOD, of the United Kingdom of Great Britain and Ireland, King, Defender of the Faith" were the words to be found at the beginning of every indenture granting land to the very first settlers in Beckwith. These are appropriate words to open this narrative about an obscure backwoods community founded as part of an imperial, British, conservative, counter-revolutionary and military plan to prevent Upper Canada from being overrun by the United States of America. It was the same George III who had presided over the acquisition of New France in 1763 and who had championed the disastrous campaign to prevent American revolutionaries from wresting the thirteen North American Atlantic seaboard colonies out from under British control between 1776 and 1783. But by 1816 he was a sad mental remnant of the former influential monarch, locked away in the recesses of Windsor Castle during his lapses into madness. And yet legally he was still king when the triumph over Napoleon at Waterloo brought to end a quarter-century of war against revolutionary and Napoleonic France and incidentally brought into being the settlement of Beckwith.

Most Beckwith land patents were made in the 1820s in the name of the rakish George IV but the counter-revolutionary policy adopted in the 1810s and 1820s conformed to the earlier moral earnestness and Tory orthodoxy of George III's administrations. So horror-stricken were the members of British society generally by the initial bloodletting of the Terror during the late French Revolution, so exhausted were they by the scale of expenditure of both men and money in battling Napoleon, as to give renewed emphasis at war's end to a counter-revolutionary model of society, hierarchically ranked beneath the monarch, and in which church and state firmly buttressed one another.

Miraculously, the remote frontier colony of Upper Canada had survived intact against the campaigns of the United States. The straggling line of township clearings stretching along the St. Lawrence River and the Great Lakes from Cornwall to Sandwich had survived largely through luck. British strategists had played their part; Governor in Chief Major General Sir George Prevost employed a forebearance and subtlety which kept New England out of the war. Major General Sir Isaac Brock boldly used his temporary naval advantage on Lake Erie and seized on the enemy's mistakes. To this the added combined weight of British naval mastery on the oceans and an ability to compete on the lakes led to stalemate when peace suddenly was declared in 1815.[1] It was all too evident that Upper Canada had escaped by the skin of its teeth, and that the total dependence on the St. Lawrence River for supplies was recognised by the American high command. If Upper Canada were to be retained as a British colony, a second water route between Montreal and Lake Ontario would be needed, a waterway through the midst of the wilderness where it would not only be remote from American attack, but remote as well from the American-origin population of doubtful loyalty which clustered along the Upper Canadian shore of the St. Lawrence between Glengarry and Kingston.

Settlement in eastern Upper Canada had come to an impasse by the time war engulfed the colony in 1812, as shown by an overview of settlement in the Johnstown District (Leeds and Grenville counties). Recorded settlement in the region began in 1784 with the location of United Empire Loyalists in the St. Lawrence townships of Edwardsburgh, Augusta and Elizabethtown. These

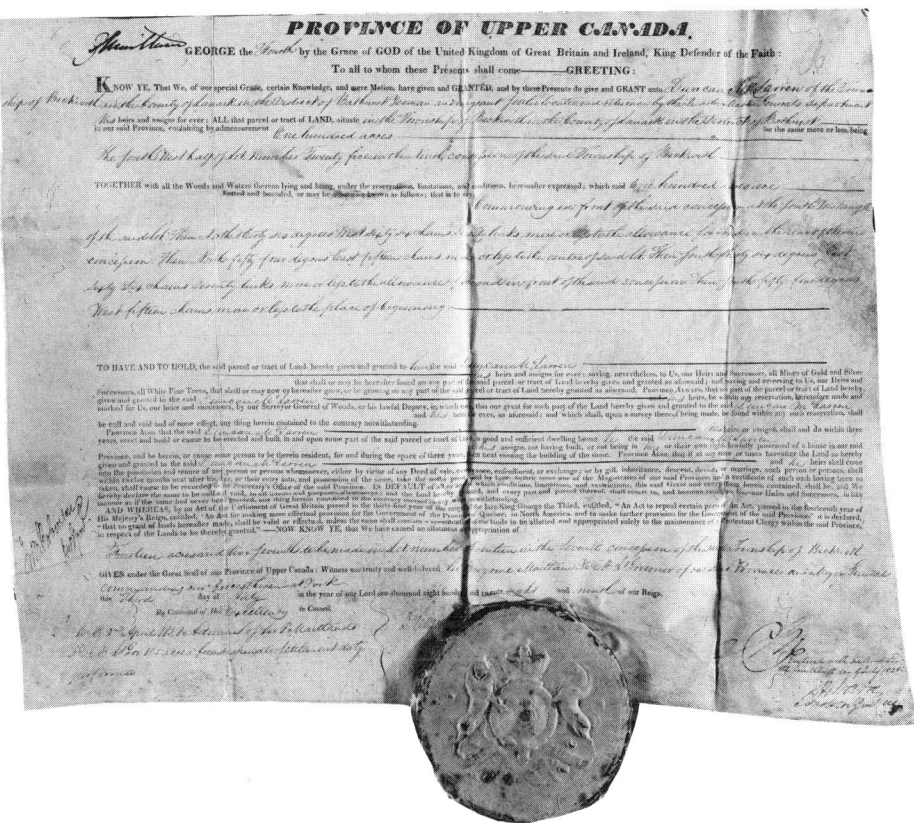

Plate 3
Land grant to Duncan McLaren, Beckwith, with the attached wax great seal of Upper Canada, dated 1828. Most Beckwith land grants were confirmed to settlers during the election years of 1824 and 1828. Although George IV was monarch during the 1820s, the legend in Latin on the seal reveals the pervading influence of the counter-revolutionary reign of George III. It translates "George the Third, by the Grace of God, King of the Britons and Defender of the Faith." Loaned courtesy of Arthur Hawkins.

Loyalists were largely frontier farmers and artisans from the Hudson valley, and largely English-origin in ethnicity, with natives of Scotland, Ireland, the German principalities and Holland among them. Many of these Loyalists were members of the Loyal Rangers, a regiment formed in 1781 from veterans of General John Burgoyne's disastrous 1777 campaign at Saratoga. These refugees received generous grants of land, varying in amount according to their military rank. Civilian heads of households received one hundred acre grants. Privates received one hundred acre grants; non-commissioned officers received two hundred acres; subalterns, staff officers and warrant officers were granted five hundred acres; captains were granted seven hundred acres; and field officers were favoured with grants of one thousand acres. An additional fifty acres was granted to every additional person in each family, giving rise to a baby boom as the Loyalist families sought to expand their acreages.[2] The combined population of Edwardsburgh, Augusta and Elizabethtown multiplied from 576 in 1784 to 4,800 by 1812.

In 1788 the already generous scale of grants to Loyalists was expanded. Civilian Loyalists and each of their sons and daughters now received two hundred acres apiece. Privates now received two hundred acres; corporals received four hundred acres; sergeants were given five hundred acres; subalterns, staff and warrant officers were granted two thousand acres apiece; captains were granted three thousand acres; and field officers saw their grants increased from one thousand to five thousand acres.[3] In addition to this, Lieutenant-Governor John Graves Simcoe issued a proclamation early in 1792 offering free grants of land to anyone who would swear an oath of loyalty to the King and pay the trifling fees of local officials to pass and record the patents. Simcoe at the same time arranged for one seventh of the land in each township to be reserved for the support of a Protestant clergy, and a further one seventh "for the future disposition of the Crown."[4] Copies of Simcoe's proclamation were extensively circulated in New York and Vermont by colonisers promoting group settlements.

The combined impact of a baby boom among the Loyalists, the expanded scale of grants, a flow of American settlers into the region, and reserving two-sevenths of all land placed pressure on the existing amount of surveyed land. This pressure was by no means allayed by opening four townships between Elizabethtown and Kingston for settlement in the late 1790s. The push for land led to fifteen townships bordering the Rideau River being opened for settlement in the 1790s. The fourteen hundred square miles of land surveyed in Oxford and Marlborough (1791); in Osgoode, Gloucester, Gower and Nepean (1793); in Montague, Wolford, Elmsley, Kitley, Bastard and Burgess (1794); and in North and South Crosby (1799) proved more detrimental than helpful to settlement for at least a generation. It was in these townships that the 1788 additional grants to Loyalists, disbanded soldiers and their children were located. Overwhelmingly, the people to whom these grants were made lived in the St. Lawrence townships and in more distant parts of Upper Canada, and consequently the fifteen townships remained almost empty. The few late-Loyalists and naturalised American settlers arriving from the 1790s through to the late 1820s found themselves in isolated sections of forest.

Inhabitants of the Rideau settlement townships of Wolford, Montague, Oxford and Marlborough complained that many incoming American immigrants who were given grants along the Rideau sold them and returned to the United States, and that the purchasers held the lots in speculation at such high prices that the poor could not purchase land in these empty townships.[5] Montague Township, immediately south of where Beckwith would be surveyed, 35 years after settlement began had a population of only 341 inhabitants in 1825.[6] Nepean, at the mouth of the Rideau River, as late as 1822 had only 191 settlers and was described by the Governor General as[7]

> almost wholly waste & wild woods, the property of absentees or Crown and Clergy Reserves, but generally in large grants made by the Government of Upper Canada which they can neither recall, nor force into settlement. This Township of Nepean...may be considered as a useless waste, a serious difficulty in the way of the prosperity of this part of the Country, and it is mortifying in a greater degree from its possessing the only harbour & approach — by which the great object of [new military] settlements can be attained.

The slow growth of population in the Rideau townships was not wholly due to most of the land being tied up in government reserves and grants to absentees and speculators. No new townships were opened for settlement in the region during the 1800s. Settlement during this decade focused instead on vacant and more fertile townships west of the Bay of Quinte. During the War of 1812 settlement was the furthest thing from most people's minds in eastern Upper Canada.

The experience of the war transformed the attitudes both of military administrators in Upper Canada and the predominant American origin population. In contrast with Simcoe's enthusiastic assumption that Americans would make loyal settlers, military leaders during the war had found the people listless and defeatist, with even legislators, magistrates and militia officers fully believing that their American cousins across the St. Lawrence must inevitably triumph.[8] Desertions in the

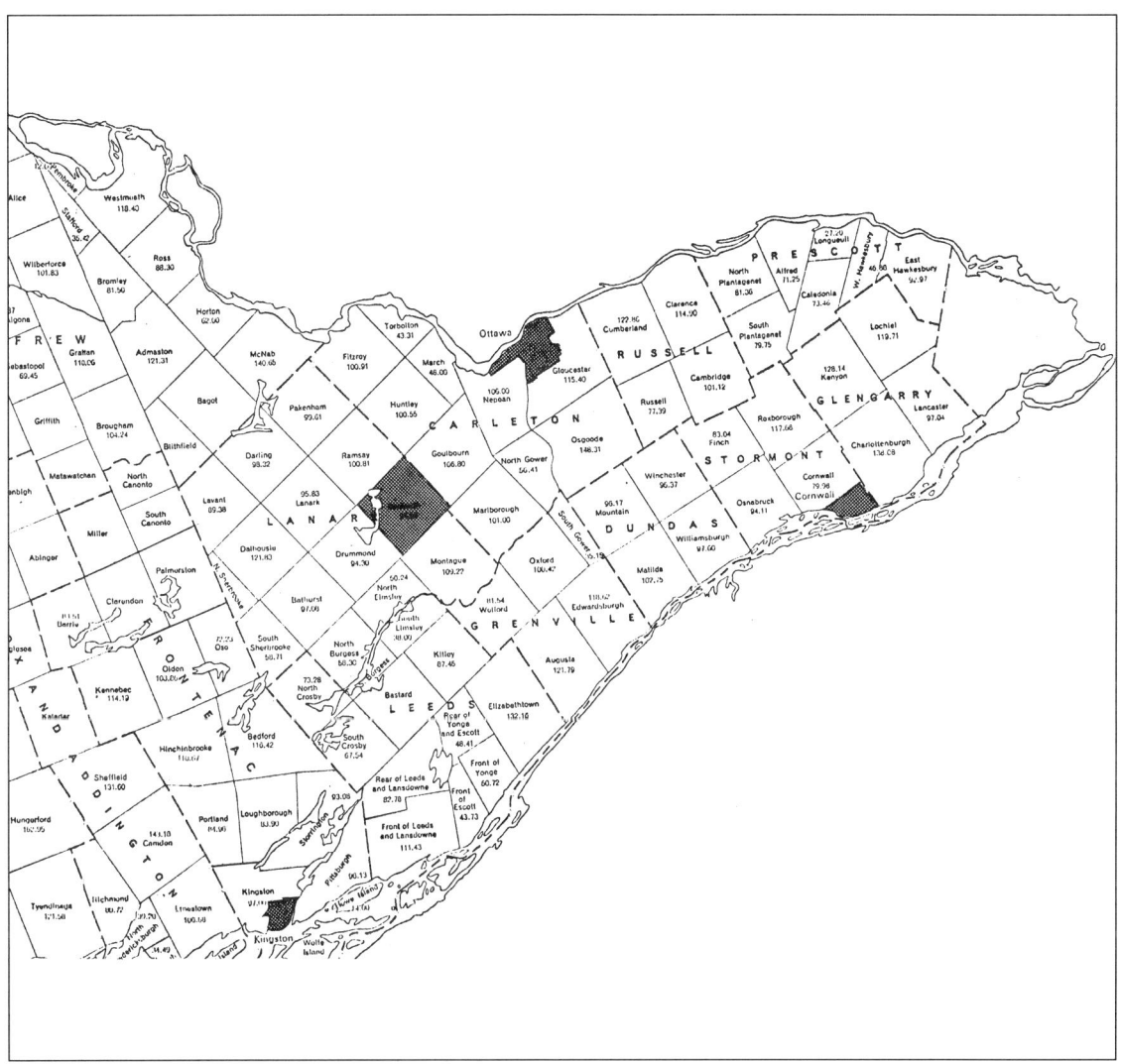

Plate 4
The location of Beckwith Township in eastern Ontario in relation to the cities of Ottawa, Kingston and Cornwall. When Beckwith was surveyed and settled in the late 1810s it was an isolated settlement of British immigrants on the frontier, remote from American-origin settlement along the St. Lawrence. Beckwith's proximity to Ottawa and the upper Ottawa valley was continuously important for its economy and development.

region were commonplace, and American raids were rumoured to be perpetrated with the connivance of local inhabitants.[9] The future of Upper Canada as a British colony simply could not be entrusted to people "speaking the same language, having the same laws, manners and religion" as the Americans, and whose open admiration of the republican "system of Government of the latter is the most favourable to the gratification of the passions of the Lower Orders of people."[10] Provincial chief justice William Dummer Powell described the inhabitants of the Brockville vicinity in 1820 as "Yankees [who] openly speak as such, [and who are] violent and disobedient to the Laws."[11] Military and civil authorities recognised that it clearly would be impractical and inhumane to remove the American-origin settlers in the St. Lawrence townships, but it was equally clear that arrangements had to be made for more secure lines of communication between Lake Ontario and Montreal.

The war awakened the local population to a new sense of the viability of Upper Canada. The colony was newly viable in their eyes not only because it miraculously came through the war, but because of the new infusion of cash into the economy. War's end found even inhabitants of recent American origin bragging about Upper Canadian exploits, glowing with pride in the heroism of Brock, and inevitably comparing and contrasting Upper Canadian feats with those of the Yankees. The emerging mythologising of the recent past, as much to mask the unheroic behaviour of many inhabitants as for any other reason, by no means meant that local society was suddenly pro-British. Insecure local inhabitants perceived British immigrants and British officials to "look with contempt upon everything which this country produces — there is nothing here as it is in England — even the eggs are not without contamination, they have neither the sweetness nor the nourishment of those produced by a British hen."[12] All the same, the war economy had produced a higher standard of living. Before the war cash was so scarce that even wealthy farmers found it difficult to raise their taxes, tea was rarely used, and coffee was made from peas. The economic change brought about by the war was evident to a Brockville area inhabitant.[13]

> The war furnished us with cash in abundance, and since the close of the War, such has been the unbounded munificence of our Government at home, in expending such vast sums in the formation of Canals, and in the encouragement given to a dislocated army and Emigrants to settle among us, that money has hitherto been plentiful, and in consequence, thank God, our farmers have obtained a much higher price for their produce than our neighbours in the State of New York.

The War of 1812 served to enhance the importance of North America in British eyes, so that rather than abandon Upper Canada to the United States, the King's colonial and military ministers deliberately adopted a policy of making the colony defensible. To do this they developed a three part program. First, they began to prepare for the construction of an inland military waterway between the Ottawa River and Lake Ontario, well away from the American frontier, and no less important, away from the American-origin inhabitants of the St. Lawrence townships. Second, in the vicinity of this military canal the imperial ministers planned to place loyal British immigrants to provide civilian resistance to American invasion and to provide a model of loyalty which, with any luck, the American-origin inhabitants might learn to emulate. Third, His Majesty's military advisors proposed to disperse British soldiers among the civilian settlers to solidify civilian resistance, and to form a second line of defence to protect the planned waterway.[14]

The imperial military plan had been devised without recognising that all the land in the townships bordering the Rideau save for Crown and Clergy reserves had been granted to American-origin settlers. The Military Settling Department, superintended by Sir Gordon Drummond, the commander-in-chief and administrator of Lower Canada (later Quebec), insisted on concentrating the military settlements together near the proposed Rideau route for the military waterway, refusing to scatter the disbanded soldiers and British immigrants on the Crown reserves checkering the eastern Upper Canada forest as Upper Canadian officials wished him to do. Civilian immigrants and disbanded soldiers began congregating in temporary camps stretching from Kingston to Montreal in late 1815 and early 1816, awaiting an end to the testy dickering taking place between Drummond and Upper Canadian Lieutenant-Governor Francis Gore over possible sites to place them. A compromise was reached in 1816 by ordering the four townships of Bathurst, Drummond, Beckwith and Goulbourn to be surveyed to the northwest of the Rideau (Plate 7).

In 1816 a military depot was established in the southwestern corner of Drummond Township

Plate 5
Portrait of Lieutenant-General Sir Thomas Sydney Beckwith, K.C.B., K.T.S., as painted by an anonymous artist ca. 1815. The cluster of medals on his chest, the firmly held sword and the billowing war clouds behind him allude to the name Beckwith made for himself fighting against Napoleon. He did so first by training and leading the 95th Rifle Regiment, then participating in expeditions to Denmark and Hanover, before serving in Spain and Portugal between 1808 and 1811. His military record in North America against the United States was less impressive, earning him the sobriquet from a fellow officer of being "a very clever fellow, but a very odd fish." As quartermaster general of British North America from 1813 to 1823, Beckwith was responsible for the encampment, quartering and movement of the army, and ultimately for settling soldiers in the military townships north of the Rideau River. There is no record that Sir Thomas Sydney Beckwith ever visited the township named after him. Reproduced by permission of the trustees of the Rifle Brigade Museum, Winchester, Hants, England. Credit E.A. Sollers.

8 THE MILITARY PLAN

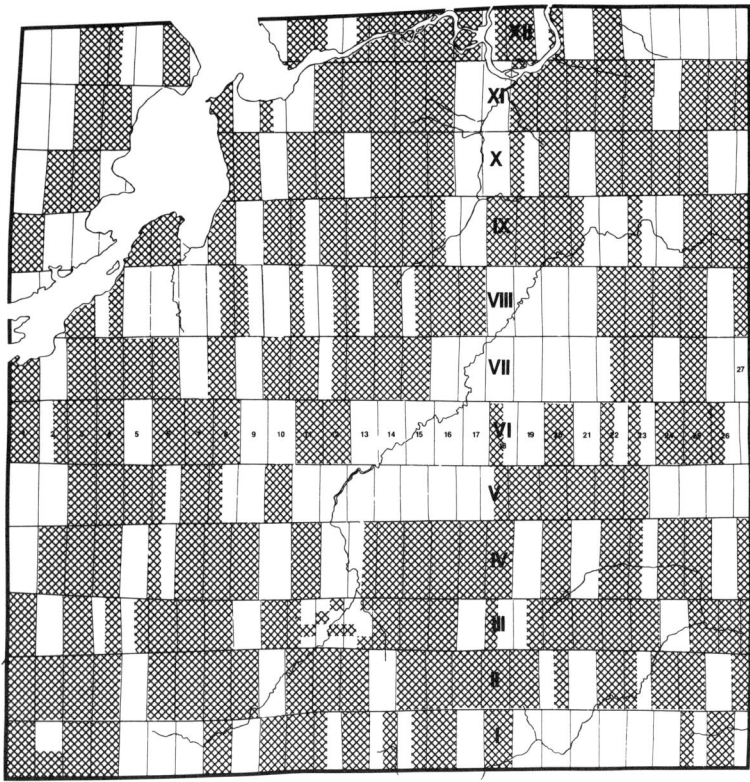

Land Grants Patented in the 1820s

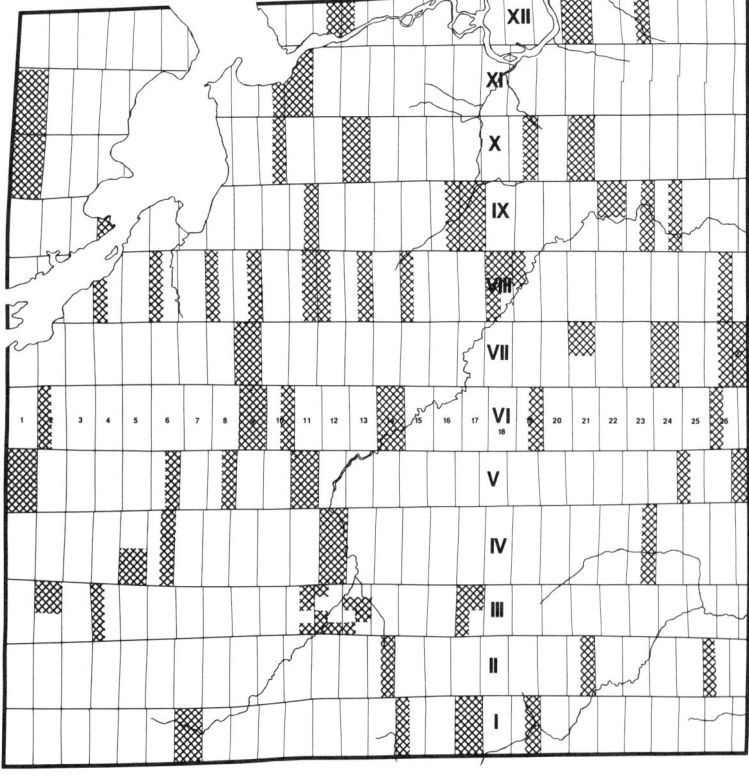

Land Grants Patented in the 1830s

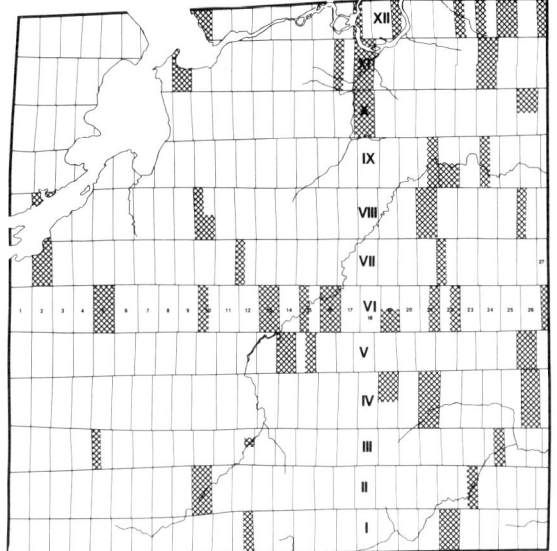
Land Grants Patented in the 1840s

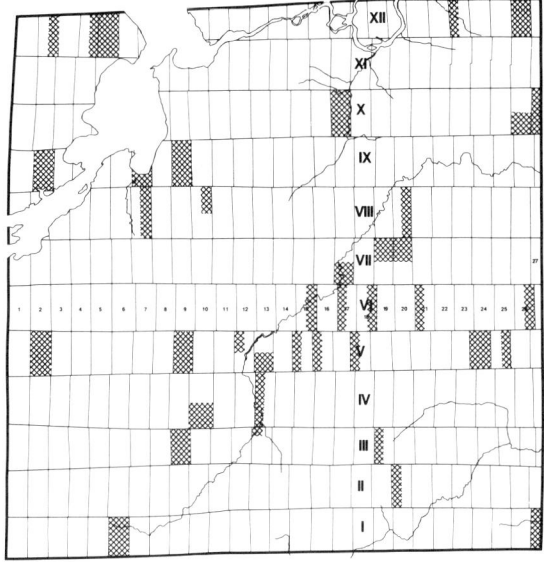
Land Grants Patented in the 1850s

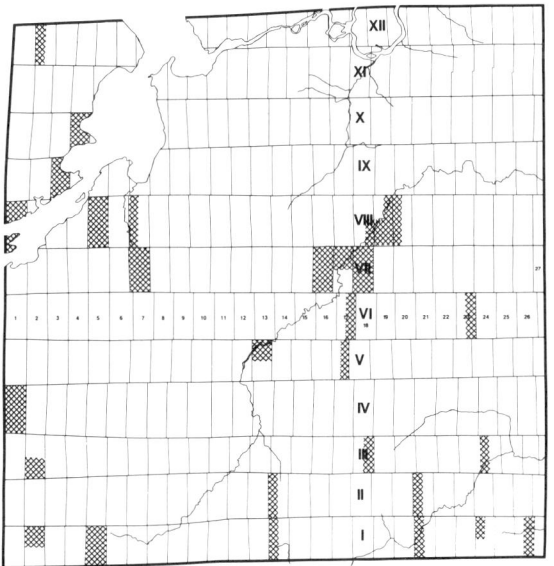
Land Grants Patented in the 1860s

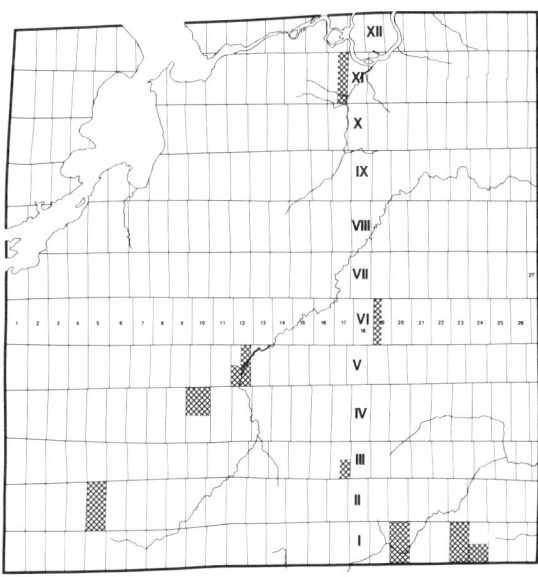
Land Grants Patented in the 1870s

and was named Perth. It was the administrative centre for the three townships of Bathurst, Drummond and Beckwith, and for scattered grants on reserves in adjacent townships to the south. From 1816 to 1822 one thousand discharged soldiers were settled in the Perth Military Settlement. They came from such varied troops as the Royal Newfoundland Regiment, the Royal Navy, the Royal Marines, the Royal Artillery, the Nova Scotia Fencibles, and two different Glengarry Light Infantry regiments — one a regular unit from Scotland and the other from Glengarry County, Upper Canada.[15] Of particular note were the DeMeuron and DeWatteville Swiss regiments, comprising men "recruited chiefly from the prison hulks, consist[ing] of all the nations of Europe, but all of [who]m had served in the armies of Napoleon, and all of [who]m had there learned to make the best of a bad bargain.".[16] In addition to the concentrated settlement of the three military townships, the military administration at Perth scattered disbanded soldiers and civilian immigrants on Crown reserves throughout the Rideau region.

In October 1812 while the war was at its height, the British secretary for war and the colonies, Lord Bathurst, began to promote the idea of diverting the tide of immigration flowing from the highlands of Scotland away from the United States to Upper Canada. By doing this, a loyal part of the British population no longer would add to the strength of a country with which Great Britain was at war, and "the male part of this population might be rendered in some degree valuable both for the present defence and the future protection of Upper Canada by offering to them grants of land...and a free passage for themselves and their families.".[17] The value of Scottish highlanders as a loyal population seemed all too clear in Upper Canada where those settled in Glengarry and Stormont Counties offered the only check to the disaffected settlers of American-origin in the other counties along the St. Lawrence between Cornwall and Kingston.[18] In late February 1815 Edinburgh and Glasgow newspapers carried notices of the new immigration scheme, soon followed by notices in the regional Scottish newspapers.

The scheme could not have been simpler, and it proved appealing. The government offered two thousand free passages to Canada with bedding and rations included. On arriving in Upper Canada, each family would receive a grant of one hundred acres of land and be put in possession of their grant immediately. Every male child continuing to reside in the colony would receive a similar grant upon reaching the age of 21. If a group of families wished to travel together and settle close to one another, the government offered to take pains to place their land grants as close together as possible, with additional grants of land for a church and for the support of a clergyman and a schoolmaster. To ensure that the government investment was safe, each adult male was required to make a sixteen pound deposit and every adult female was obliged to deposit two guineas. These sums were to be returned to the immigrants once they had fulfilled their settlement duties in Upper Canada. Ships bearing the immigrants were advertised as sailing from ports on the Clyde in April 1815.[19]

A total of 699 men, women and children immigrated from Scotland to Upper Canada in 1815 under the terms of this plan, half of whom came from some 48 lowland parishes, while most of the other half came from just four highland parishes.[20] The imbalance in the proportion of highlanders is noteworthy, considering that highlanders accounted for only twenty percent of the population of Scotland. The imbalance was due in part to Lord Bathurst appointing John Campbell Sr, a writer to the *Signet* at Edinburgh to superintend the immigration project. Campbell had been a longtime law agent for the Earl of Breadalbane whose extensive Perthshire estates he occasionally visited, and the condition of whose tenants he was familiar with.[21] The sizeable highlander component in the 1815

Plate 6 (previous page)
Maps showing sequence of land in Beckwith patented to settlers, 1820—1879. During the 1820s almost 60 percent of the township was given out in grants by the Crown, with 28 and 16 percent of the land area patented in the election years of 1824 and 1828 respectively. A decreasing proportion of land was patented in succeeding decades, 13 percent in the 1830s, 10 percent in the 1840s, 8 percent in the 1850s, 6 percent in the 1860s, and less than 2 percent in the 1870s.

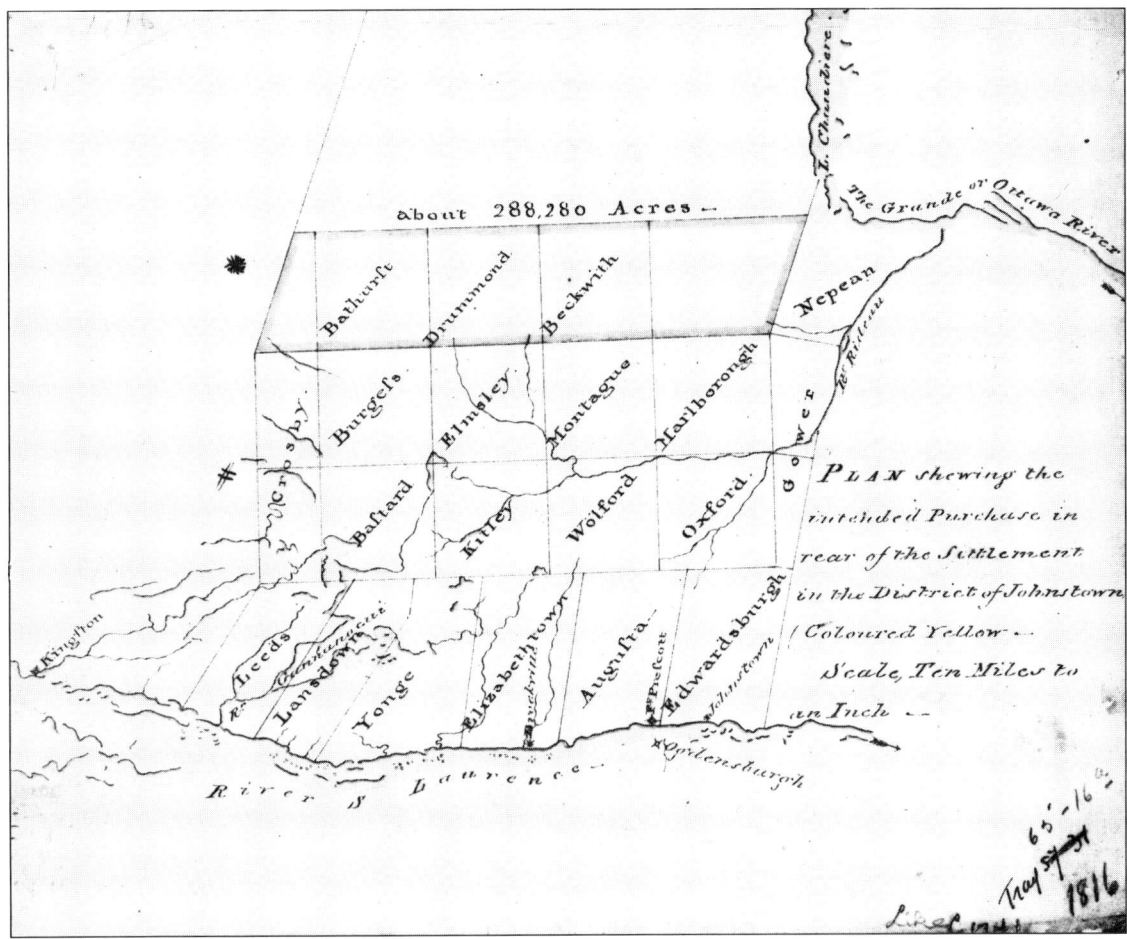

Plate 7
Plan showing the line of townships purchased for a military settlement at the rear of the Johnstown District, 1816. This was the closest government could settle a block of loyal British immigrants and disbanded soldiers to the proposed route of the military canal along the Rideau River. Most of the land in the townships bordering the Rideau was owned by absentee landowners of American origin living in the townships along the St. Lawrence. National Archives of Canada NMC 19505.

immigration from a mere four parishes was also due, as Marianne McLean points out, to groups of families too poor to otherwise afford immigration, taking advantage of a government policy to join the prior migrations to Glengarry in Upper Canada that had taken place in the mid 1780s, the early 1790s, 1802 and 1815.

Quite contrary to what the military plan had hoped to accomplish, the highlanders from Perthshire overwhelmingly chose to settle on poor land near kin and friends in Glengarry rather than be placed in the new military townships. The party of immigrants reached Upper Canada in October 1815, too late in the year to begin settling on the land, and before squabbling imperial military authorities and Upper Canadian officials agreed where they were to be settled, forcing the new arrivals to spend the winter in government barracks along the St. Lawrence. Military authorities in early 1816 agreed to make an exception to the plan of locating the Scottish immigrants in the military townships north of the Rideau to those who had been "promised the indulgence of settling with their countrymen" in Glengarry.22 The local American-origin population recognised that the Scottish immigrants huddling in the barracks had been brought in by the military authorities as part of a campaign to reduce American influences in the region, and to promote British settlement. Their resentment of the new arrivals spurred them to paint a gloomy picture of the climate and area where the grants in the new military townships were to be made. So effectively did American-origin inhabitants at Brockville describe the unattractiveness of the new military townships to the new arrivals, that the Scottish immigrants petitioned to be sent to a more westerly destination in Upper Canada. They had heard that.23

> The crops on the Radeau are subject to hurt from early frosts — the lands are badly watered for cattle — at an immense distance from the St. Lawrence and no water conveyance for their wood and produce — these are the reasons which chiefly preposssess them against the Radeau...

Despite the efforts of American-origin inhabitants to discourage British settlement, the Perth military settlement proceeded beginning with the construction of the Perth depot in March 1816. By October of that same year there were some fifteen hundred people in the settlement around Perth. Beckwith was more remote from Perth than either Bathurst or Drummond townships, and this made it the least attractive township to disbanded soldiers and civilian immigrants. Only seven out of 51 grants of land in Beckwith made out in 1816 from Perth were settled long enough for the inhabitants to qualify three years later as having completed their settlement duties and to recive a patent for their land. Barely a quarter of the 73 grants located in Beckwith in 1817 were followed through with to receive a land patent. These 27 families, with the exception of Etienne Roy on the west half of lot 24 in the sixth consession were located in the southwestern corner of Beckwith. Over half of the 1816 and 1817 Beckwith settlers were single men, and most of them had recently served in the military. In terms of country of birth or ethnic origin, these early settlers as a group did not reflect the ethnic profile Beckwith would develop by 1824; almost half of them (twelve) were from England, barely over a quarter (seven) were from Scotland, just under a fifth (five) were from Ireland, and two were from Lower Canada.

There were additional reasons for the slow settlement of Beckwith in 1816 and 1817. Not only was it more remote from Perth, hence requiring longer treks to the storehouse there for supplies, but southwestern Beckwith was hardly attractive for settlement. The eight southern concessions of Beckwith, and more particularly the southwestern corner of the township, proved to be an intermittent succession of swamps, beaver meadows, low lands, and stony patches of ground. There was a singular absence of arable, deep rich soil in southwestern Beckwith (Plate 9). Indeed, there were few stretches of concession line there that surveyor Reuben Sherwood did not pencil in with sections of swamp when he surveyed the concessions in January 1817.24 The unattractiveness of the land caused some grantees to abandon their locations or to request transfers to better land. Some of the early Beckwith grants were part of larger allotments to officers and administrators who chose either to live at Perth or to develop farms on better land closer to Perth. As a result, grants of land in Beckwith to officers in the Canadian Fencibles such as English-born Captain Josias Taylor, Lower Canadian Lieutenant Benjamin Delisle, and French-born Captain Tito Lelievre were not developed, but rather held in speculation.25 Ironically, the scale of grants of land to civilian and military settlers was significantly reduced from those given the United Empire Loyalists and late Loyalist or American settlers in a direct attempt to prevent any repetition of the empty tracts of land held in speculation by the Loyalists in the townships along the Rideau River.

Despite the small number of early settlers, in all totalling 54 by the end of 1817,26 the provisioning of the settlement by the quarter master general's department offered promise for the eventual success of developing Beckwith. How could it be otherwise, with the township named after Sir Thomas Sydney Beckwith (1772-1831), who had been quarter master general for Canada from 1815

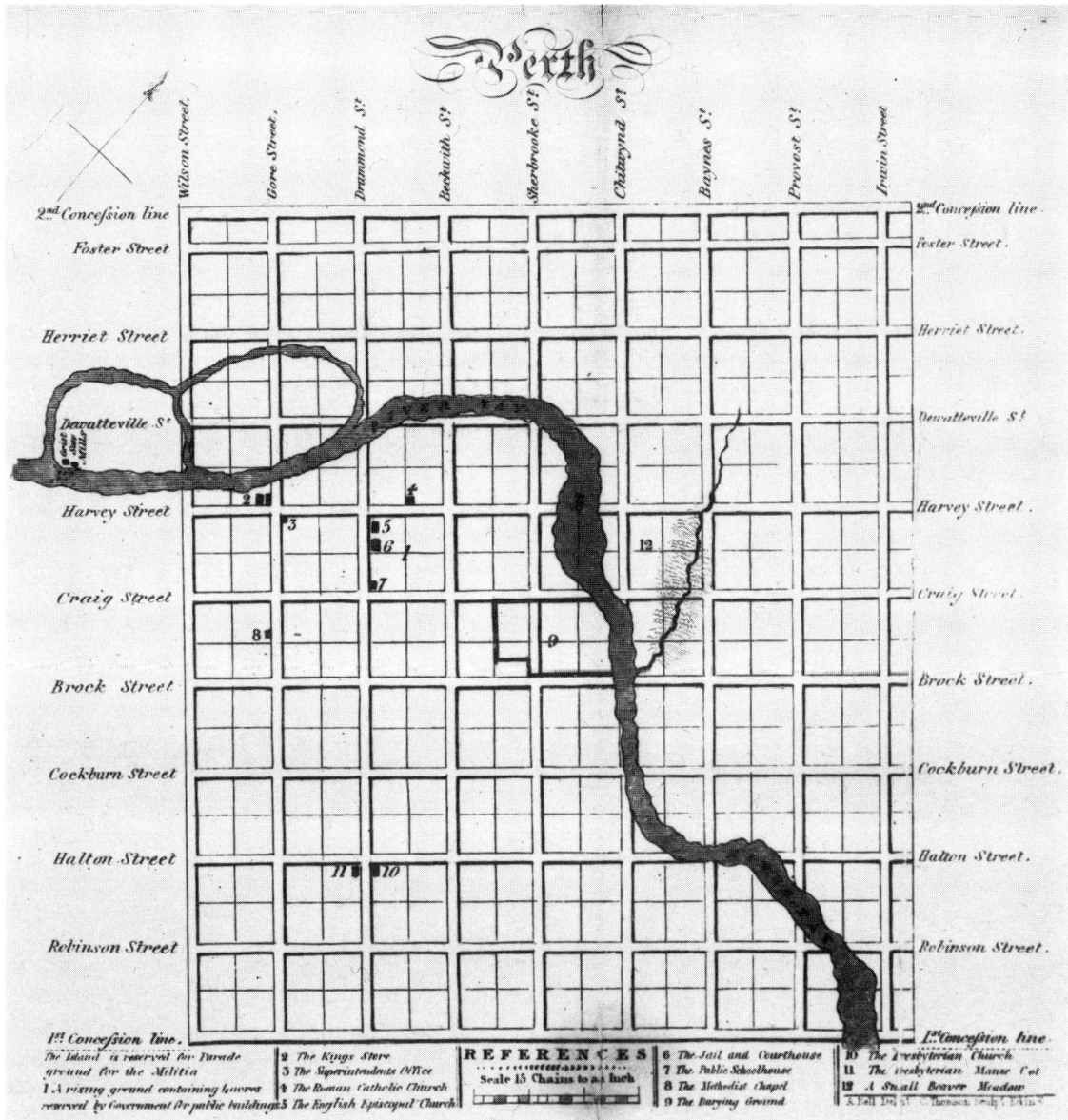

Plate 8
Map of Perth, Upper Canada, ca. 1824. Perth was described in October 1818 as being "one mile square, and regularly laid out: already there are about one hundred houses built in it, although it is little more than two years since the first tree was cut." From the Reverend William Bell's Hints to Emigrants *(1824), courtesy of the National Archives of Canada library.*

to 1823, and who made arrangements and personally superintended the arrival of the Scottish immigrants in 1816?[27] Moreover, it was widely known that the ultimate reason for settling the military townships with Scottish civilians and disbanded soldiers was "to throw a Consolidated Loyal Population upon the Communication between the two Great Rivers Ottawa & St. Lawrence by Montreal.".[28] Into the early 1820s there were even some who hoped that it might be the Mississippi

River flowing through Beckwith along which the military communication would be developed. In the autumn of 1822 it was reported that a party of settlers below Morphy's Falls (later Carleton Place on Beckwith's northern boundary) had built a boat, 24 feet long, in which they had descended the Mississippi, Ottawa and St. Lawrence rivers to Lachine in five days, and returned in seven days. As a result "the people in that quarter are in high spirits at the idea of the navigation passing that way to Montreal.".[29] But when an official party of commissioners seeking the best route for the military waterway in 1823 found themselves portaging around "numerous rapids, and cascades, as well as the falls at the Chats [Fitzroy Harbour], & Chaudiere, on the Ottawa, it was evident that the bed of the Mississippi was far too elevated, and that as the lockage to attain and descend from the Summit...would be enormously expensive, no Canal would be practicable in that direction."[30] By 1825 it was apparent that the less expensive Rideau route would be the military waterway.[31]

There were marks of the haste with which the range of military townships was laid out in 1816. So eager were Upper Canadian and military authorities to have settlers on their land as early in the year as possible that the lieutenant-governor, with the full concurrence of Sir Sydney Beckwith took the previously unheard-of step of having Bathurst, Drummond and Beckwith townships surveyed "without waiting to extinguish the Indian Title".[32] It was not until May 1819 that Captain John Ferguson, Resident Agent of Indian Affairs on behalf of George III signed a treaty with the chiefs of the Mississauga Nation, purchasing for a price of £642 10s in goods at the Montreal price the lands running northwest from the rear of the Johnstown District to the Ottawa River.[33] No purchase of land from Amerindians had been made in the region since 1783.[34]

The early surveys of the military townships betrayed great haste. The secretary of the Perth military settlement complained to the deputy assistant quarter master general's office on Christmas day 1816 that "many of the lines run are very erroneous," and recommended that they discontinue hiring the deputy surveyors in the settlement.[35] It was all too true. A brief glance at Plate 9, which is based on an aerial photograph, confirms the meandering rather than straight concession lines. As a result, some lots such as number ten in the fourth concession are twice the size of adjacent lots such as ten in the third concession. In 1823 the surveyor general of Upper Canada explained the disparate size of lots in Beckwith as arising from the township having "been Surveyed by several Dep[ut]y Surveyors, each admeasuring separate Lots and Concessions".[36] So poorly had they measured the width of lots that upon reaching the eastern limits of the first concession, they found there was land to spare, although hardly enough to make a full township lot. This mode of surveying the concessions one at a time hardly explains the discrepancies to be found in the lines between the lots in adjoining concessions. The surveyors had been instructed to mark each lot with a post at all four corners, and a post at each side of the centre side line.[37] Jean McGill tells of Reuben Sherwood's measuring chain breaking while he was surveying Beckwith, but it seems scarcely credible that the stretching of the pieces of willow used to repair the chain accounts for the irregular size of lots.[38] There is no explanation for the jogs which occur in side lines between lots 22, 23, 24, 25 and 26 in the eleventh concession.

There were strains between American-born surveyor Sherwood and the British-born administrators of the Perth settlement. Late in November 1816 the keeper of the King's store and secretary of the settling department at Perth, Daniel Daverne, wrote to the deputy assistant quarter master general, complaining that Reuben Sherwood without the local superintendent's "permission or order [had] been employed laying out a road from the Township of Beckwith to the Settlement [of Merrickville] at Wolford."[39] Sherwood denied laying out "a Road from Beckwith to the Settlements on the Rideau [as]...false," claiming only to have "purchased some pease for the use of the parties then five in number with me on that Township', and that he did not even mark the way he went.[40] The allegation and the denial marked the counter-revolutionary and anti-American vocabulary of the military settlement. This vocabulary was based on a concern for the disbanded soldiers and British civilian settlers keeping "up that spirit of loyalty and British feeling which exists

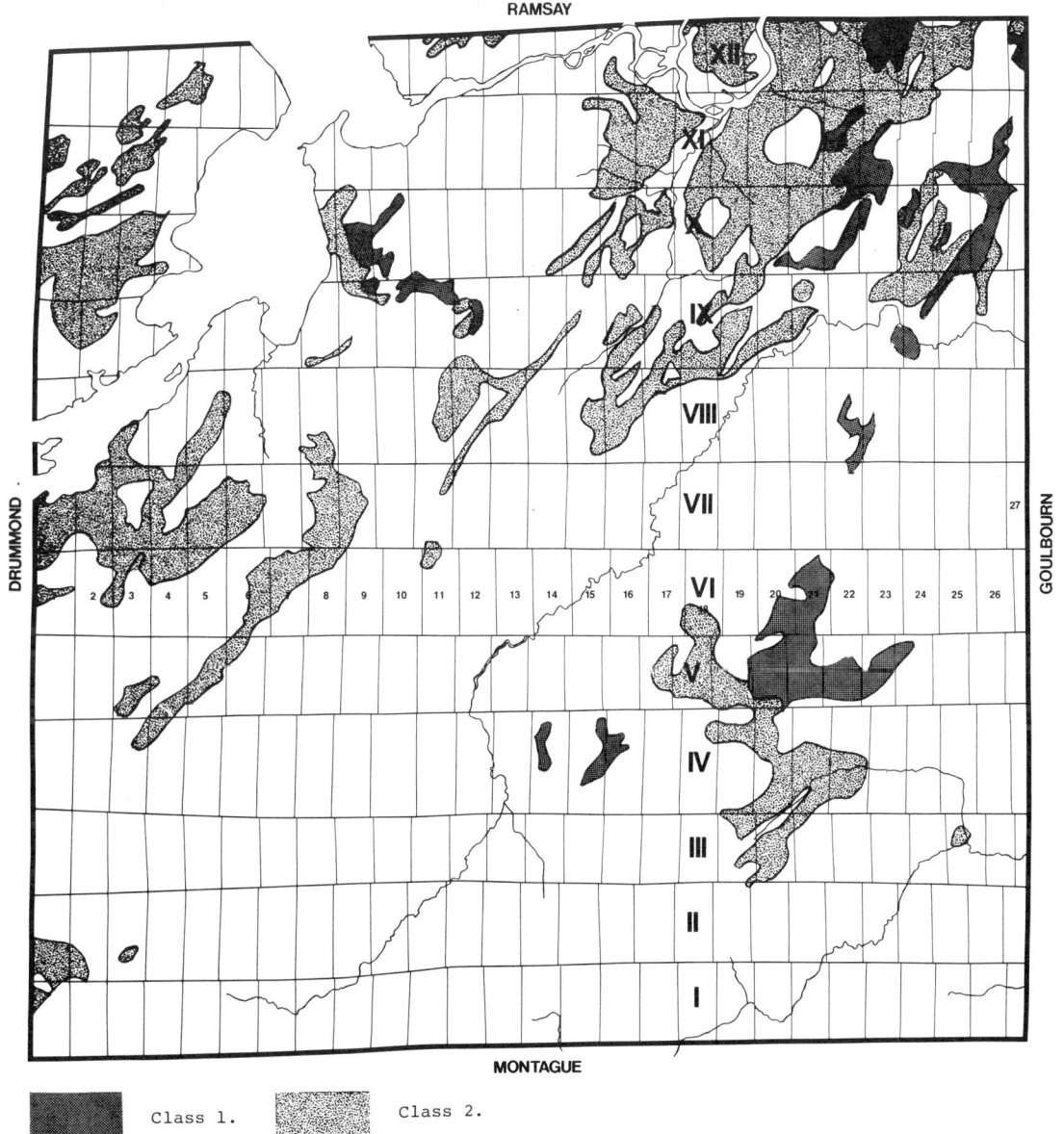

Plate 9
Soils of high and moderate capability in Beckwith. Most of the best land for agriculture in Beckwith was located in the northern half of the township where the Perthshire settlers were concentrated. Class 1 and class 2 soils are deep and hold moisture well, have moderate or no limitations, and can be managed and cropped with little difficulty to produce a fairly wide range of field crops. From Ontario Soil Survey Report No. 40, Lanark County.

now, but which might give way to evil communications with these Americans who really swarm in the woods near Brockville.".[41] Both Daverne and Sherwood recognised how sensitive an issue it was for the loyal settlers in Beckwith not to be exposed to the American settlement at Merrickville.

A second military depot east of Beckwith was established on the Jock or Goodwood River in the southeastern corner of Goulbourn Township in the summer of 1818. It was named Richmond in honour of the new governor general of Canada, the Duke of Richmond. Officers and men of the 99th

16 THE MILITARY PLAN

Regiment who wished to remain in Canada rather than return with the corps to England for disbandment were settled on grants of land in Goulbourn from the Richmond depot. These men from the western Irish counties of Ulster originally were raised in 1804 as the 100th Prince Regent's County of Dublin Regiment for colonial service.[42] The western half of Beckwith was closer to Richmond than to Perth, so it made sense to settle it from the Richmond depot. Despite the military concentration in adjoining Goulbourn, most of the immigrants settled in western Beckwith from the Richmond depot were civilians. But remote as Beckwith was from the comparative civilisation of Perth, Richmond was even deeper in the forest. In late 1817 when plans were being made to set up the Richmond settlement depot, military officials had decided against having settlers and suppliers of provisions make an extended journey along the trails that passed for roads from Brockville to Perth and then trek up to thirty miles through the swamps and forest between Perth and Richmond. Rather, the settlers destined for the Richmond depot were to ascend the Ottawa River from Montreal to a point just above the Rideau Falls on the Upper Canada shore opposite the flourishing American settlement of Wrightstown (later Hull). From this Richmond Landing, as it came to be called (now downtown Ottawa), the arriving immigrants would walk through the forest of Nepean to the Richmond depot. Philemon Wright of Hull was engaged by government in a substantial business of sending men, teams and wagons laden with provisions on the rough road opened up between the Richmond Landing and Richmond to supply the settlers provisioned from that depot between 1818 and 1822.[43]

The establishment of Richmond in 1818 marked the beginning of significant settlement in Beckwith. At the end of 1817 there was a total of 54 men, women and children settled on 26 farms in southwestern Beckwith. In 1818 a further 110 persons settled on thirty more farms in western Beckwith, totalling to 164 people on 56 farms. This compared with 252 immigrants settled from Richmond on 63 farms in eastern Beckwith in 1818 alone. In 1819, 115 settlers were placed on 37 farms in western Beckwith from the Perth depot, and 114 immigrants were settled on 35 farms in eastern Beckwith from the Richmond depot. Decreasing numbers of settlers were placed in Beckwith by officials at the two

Table 1. Numbers of Persons and Land Grants Settled, Beckwith Township, 1816-1822

	Emigrants Through Perth		Discharged Soldiers Through Perth		Total Settlers Through Perth		Emigrants Through Richmond		Total Settlers	
Year	Farms	Persons	Farms	Persons	Farms	Persons	Farms	Persons	Farms	Persons
1816	5	10	2	4	7	14			7	14
1817	6	17	13	23	19	30			19	30
1818	26	104	4	6	30	110	63	252	93	362
1819	31	99	6	16	37	115	35	114	72	229
1820	15	30			15	30	30	61	45	91
1821	18	53	2	4	20	57	23	65	43	122
1822	30	56	2	2	32	58	18	34	50	92
Totals	129	362	31	62	160	424	169	526	329	950

SOURCE: *Calculation of Howard M. Brown, based on NAC MG 9 (D8) Perth Military Settlement Book; NAC RG 7, G1, vol. 10, pp. 67-73; and NAC C.O. 384, vol. 3, pp. 57-69. Figures include men, women and children.*

Plate 10
Richmond on the River Jacques or Goodwood, 1830, as sketched by Thomas Burrowes. The eastern half of Beckwith was settled from Richmond between 1818 and 1822. In 1820 the Richmond military depot was described as "already a good large village, altho' not two years begun. Several excellent houses with good large gardens. The Inn kept by one Hill is very comfortable, the streets are laid off at right angles & fronting on the river, a deep & dull stream." With the removal of the seat of Carleton County to Bytown in the 1840s, Richmond declined. A visitor in 1852 found "most of the best houses...empty[,] almost all the old officers are dead and a great number of the young people left.... Captain Lyons' mills have been idle all winter, being without water...." Archives of Ontario.

military depots during the next three years. By 1822, only six years after the first grant had been made in Beckwith, save for the Crown and Clergy reserves, all of Beckwith's land area had been granted by the government. The total number of people located in Beckwith by the Perth military authorities between 1816 and 1822 was 424, whereas 526 were settled in Beckwith through the Richmond depot between 1818 and 1822 (Table 1 and Appendices 2 and 3).

The civilians located by the Richmond military depot in eastern Beckwith belonged to two distinct groups. The Colonial Office, as an immigration experiment, offered a new variety of assisted immigration. It offered to sponsor group settlements from Britain and Ireland if a responsible person organised a group of immigrants and paid a ten pound deposit for each settler which would be repaid by the settlers once they were located on their land. The first group to take advantage of this were 72 Tipperary Protestants from Ireland headed by Richard Talbot who were scattered among the military settlers in Goulbourn.[44] The second group consisted of 370 Perthshire Scottish Presbyterians from the estates of the Earl of Breadalbane, many of them from the same parishes from which immigrants had departed during the 1816 assisted immigration discussed earlier. Irish-born Captain George Thew Burke, superintendent at Richmond, placed the Perthshire immigrants together in a concentrated settlement in the northeastern quarter of Beckwith (Plate 35) on the rich soils of the Mississippi flood plain. In southeastern Beckwith, as another distinct group, Burke settled a block of Irish Anglicans and Methodists from Wexford and Carlow counties in southeastern Ireland. In November 1817 these prospective immigrants had been described as "Protestant families of most respectable character [and] tho' unable to bear the expenses of a removal, are unsettling themselves with the idea of being assisted with a free passage to British America".[45] Unlike Irish-born superintendent Colonel James Powell at Perth who mixed English, Scottish, Irish and Canadians together throughout western Beckwith, Irish-born Captain Burke at Richmond took pains to keep Perthshire highlanders separate from the Irish Anglicans and Methodists using the great swamp in the middle of eastern Beckwith to isolate the two ethnic groups, from one another. Burke clearly anticipated the possibility that a mixture of the two might lead to potential cultural conflict.

The influx of settlers in 1818 spurred government officials to provide more convenient access to supplies for Beckwith settlers. By late October of that year deputy quarter master general Colonel Francis Cockburn reported that a track was being opened between Richmond and Perth, running parallel with the southern boundary of Beckwith.[46]

> It is on this road [Cockburn noted], and as nearly as circumstances will admit in the centre of the township of Beckwith, that a provision store is to be built.
>
> The road will be sufficiently opened in the course of a month to admit of the sleighs passing over it during the winter, and I would earnestly recommend that an expenditure of three or four hundred pounds, exclusive of two or three months' rations and rum, might be allowed for the payment and subsistence of about eighty men to be employed in making it passable for waggons during the summer...
>
> [W]hen this road is opened and a provision store built in Beckwith, each of the new townships [Beckwith and Goulbourn] will be equally eligible for a settlement, and thus a very large proportion of land will be anxiously sought after which the settlers have hitherto been averse to being placed on.

The road for which Colonel Cockburn perceived a great need was not yet built, but a Beckwith storehouse was constructed in the winter of 1818-1819.[47] In September 1819 the village of Franktown, named somewhat jocularly in honour of Colonel Francis Cockburn, was surveyed around the storehouse on lots eleven, twelve and thirteen in Beckwith's third concession (Plate 36). The name of Franktown in all likelihood was bestowed by local settlers who were grateful for Cockburn's attempts to ease the burden of obtaining government provisions. The district surveyor, Josias Richey, placed the name of Franktown on his 1819 plan of the village, but as late as 1826 government officials and agents preferred to refer to "the village of Beckwith".[48] On paper Franktown presented the same orderly military grid as either Perth or Richmond, albeit on a smaller scale, with the Jock or Goodwood River flowing through to provide power for milling. The village site was divided into twenty-five 24-acre park lots. The military tidiness of the village plan was further shown by reserving lots for a church, a school, and a cemetery.

The few houses and taverns actually built at Franktown were concentrated along the sideline between township lots ten and eleven in the third concession. The Jock at Franktown was no more than a sluggish meandering creek, a torpid stream that barely moved its own water, let alone inspiring anyone who viewed it with the hope that it could move a mill wheel. The 25-acre park lots were meant to be large enough to allow each family settled on them to harvest sufficient subsistence crops and gardens for themselves and their livestock to supplement income from the trades that surely would be drawn to the central village of Beckwith. Franktown, as it turned out, was by no means the centre of Beckwith, and by 1824 it was clear that the milling hamlet of Morphy's Falls on the Mississippi was a greater magnet for attracting township business. Those village lots at Franktown

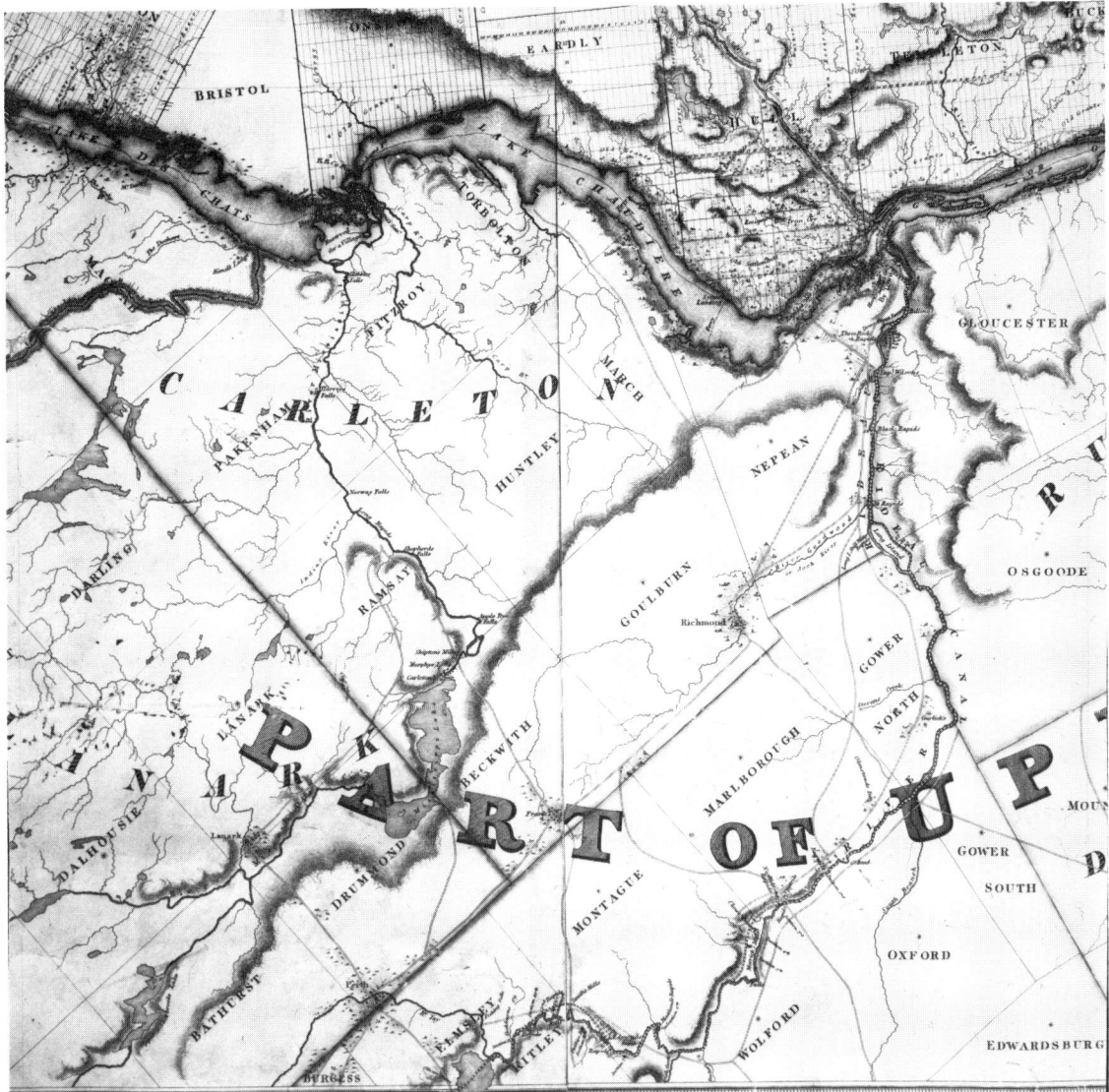

Plate 11
Detail of a topographical map of the district of Montreal drawn by Joseph Bouchette, 1831. This map "most humbly & gratefully dedicated...To His most Excellent Majesty King William IV" reveals the strong links between Beckwith and the Ottawa River. The Mississippi River linked Beckwith to the Gaelic-speaking settlement in McNab Township and to the timber camps and provisioning markets along the upper Ottawa, while a government road connected southern Beckwith with Perth and Bytown markets. National Archives of Canada NMC 16836 Section 1/3.

not located on a thin limestone plain were swampy, and only a corner of park lot number fifteen was deep enough to serve as a burial ground. Physician and surgeon Dr. George Nesbitt and surveyor Owen Quinn were two early inhabitants who along with disbanded soldiers Joseph Sutton, John Conboy, John Nesbitt, Peter and John Fullan, Daniel Ferguson, Stephen Redmond, Josiah Moss, John Moorhouse, Andrew Houghton and Thomas Armstrong were granted park lots in Franktown. Patrick

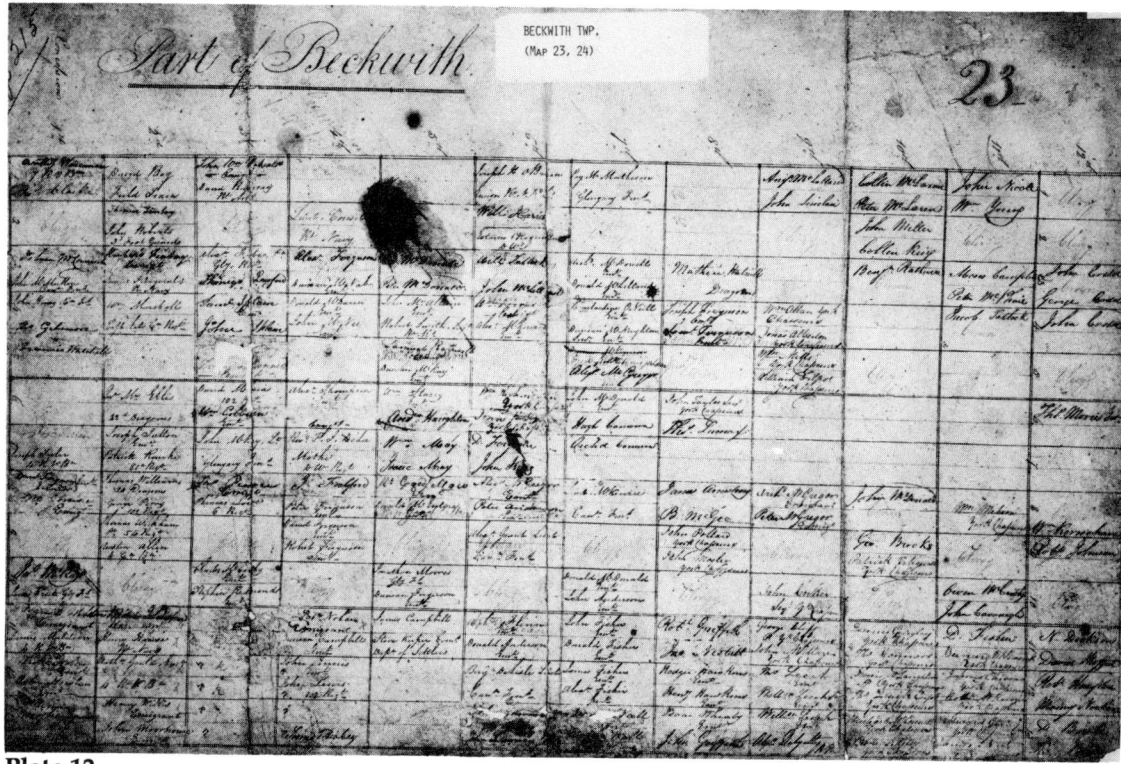

Plate 12
Map of patentees in western Beckwith. Lieutenant-Colonel Powell at the Perth military settlement office placed a mixture of Irish Anglicans, Irish Catholics, Irish Methodists, highland Scottish Presbyterians and Baptists, and military settlers throughout the western half of the township. Not all of the people whose names are shown on this map actually settled on these lots. Archives of Ontario, Drawer 20, Map 23.

Nowlan, who was in charge of the King's store opened the first tavern in Beckwith on part lot two, and next door on adjoining park lot one Thomas Wickham opened an inn at about the same time. Despite the numerous grants of park lots, Franktown as late as 1840 contained less than half a dozen houses.

In late August 1819, less than a month before Josias Richey surveyed the townsite, Franktown received the first of two notable visitors, the governor general of the Canadas. His Excellency the Duke of Richmond was in the midst of a trek to view the progress of the military townships, proceeding from Perth to Richmond, accompanied by Colonel Francis Cockburn. What should have been the proudest day for pioneer Beckwith turned tragic as the first symptoms of hydrophobia contracted by the duke from the bite of a soldier's pet fox became apparent. The man in chief command of his Majesty's military forces presented a pathetic figure to local settlers as he staggered distractedly to his death near Richmond, becoming "the subject of everyone's conversation" during the ensuing year.[49]

> It was at the Beckwith store...that the first appearance of the disease shewed itself; Major Burke, Superintendent of this settlement, and Col. Cockburn described it in the same way; that day the Duke had complained of pains in his neck and shoulders & Burke observed that at dinner he ate nothing at all, but played in his fingers a little bullet of soft bread. It escaped him once to give an involuntary scream, or nervous noise, like the snarl of a dog. He begged pardon instantly and afterwards muttered to himself "Shame, Charles Lennox, for shame Richmond, remem-

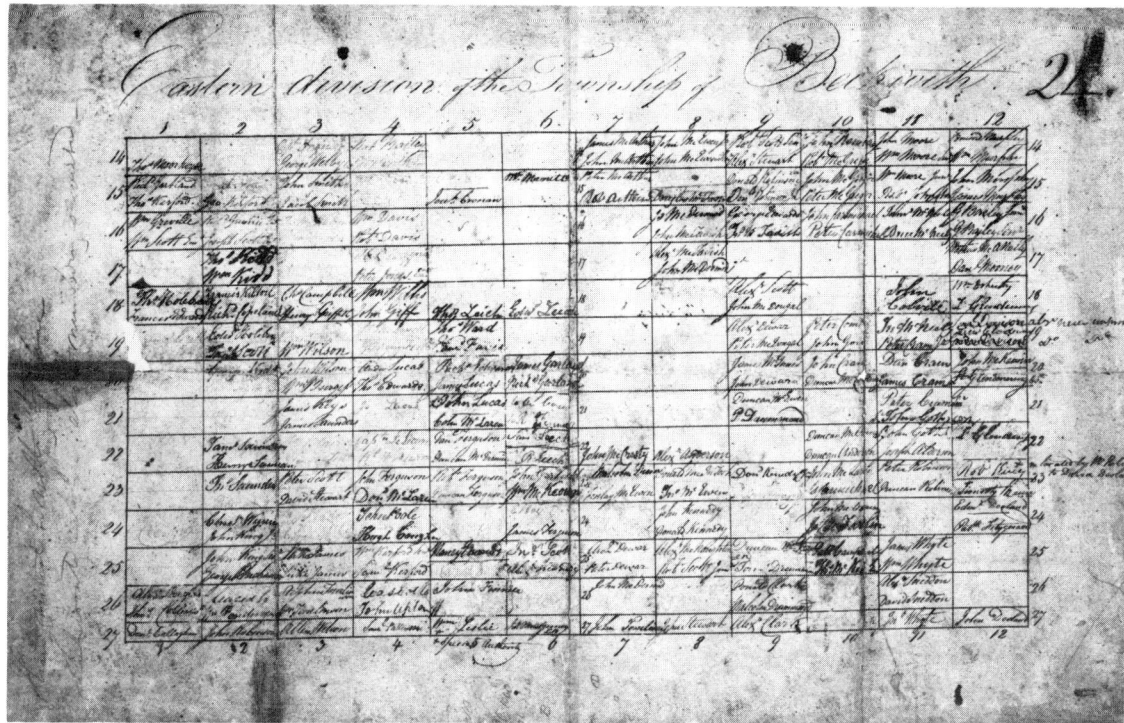

Plate 13
Plan showing names of patentees in eastern Beckwith. Captain Burke at the Richmond military settlement depot settled the six northern concessions of eastern Beckwith with a block of Perthshire highlanders. He filled the six southern concessions of eastern Beckwith with a block of Wexford and Carlow Irish immigrants, predominantly Anglicans. The lots without names were either unfit for farming or reserved by government. Archives of Ontario, Drawer 20, Map 24.

ber!" The next morning, having had a very restless night, the party proceeded to Richmond, but were obliged by fatigue to stop at the hut of Serg[ean]t Vaughn at the beginning of a great swamp about 5 miles broad. He became evidently greatly worse and weaker.

Exactly a year after the duke succumbed, Beckwith received a visit from Richmond's successor as governor general, the ninth Earl of Dalhousie. One of the chief reasons for Dalhousie's visit to the military settlements "was to see personally how they were conducted, in order to alter & improve the system if necessary".[50] Dalhousie's remarks during the Beckwith segment of his trek offer an invaluable record of conditions in southern Beckwith only a few years after settlement began:[51]

After breakfast this morning we left Richmond and arrived here at Beckwith about 2 o'clock, 17 miles. If the road yesterday was bad, this of today was a thousand times worse, in fact no road at all. The first 5 miles we were aware was thro' a swamp & we sent our servants & horses with baggage before us, accompanied by guides & axemen to help them through the difficulties;... Cockburn, Burke & I followed on foot, scrambling like squirrels along logs laid lengthways to one another so as to form a footpath, but only single logs; it required a long stick or balance pole to assist us, for in many places the slip of a foot would have taken us to the middle in black moss mud. At Serg't Vaughn's we stopt half an hour to cool after our very hot walk thro' the swamp, truly devoured by musquitoes & black flies. After that we got on horseback,

& when we again met the wet places in any of them a mile long we dismounted, & tying up the bridle reins let the horses go their way, two men being always on to stop them when thro'. It was really astonishing how they got thro' the deep holes & spreading roots of immense trees without breaking their legs; I rode a strong horse...that picked his step most sagaciously & marched thro' boldly, tho' up to the saddle girths. It was curious to observe the other horses, when by accident they were foremost, litterally trembling with fear, they constantly stopt & waited untill my horse took the lead & then they followed freely as if confident all was safe.

Dalhousie perceived the horrendous travelling conditions to be a major impediment to the development of the military townships. Despite the lack of roads he was persuaded that most settlers were bound to prosper. Dalhousie made note of the Beckwith storehouse at Franktown[52]

from whence Rations & implements of husbandry are issued to settlers. There are a great many settlers near, but chiefly soldiers, & as the great line of road is not yet laid out, the huts are scattered in the woods on the driest part of the land. I am much pleased however to find that tho' many have sad complaints to make and woeful stories made out of misfortune, yet the far greater part is satisfied, content & happy...

Governor-General Dalhousie found the most prosperous settlers in southern Beckwith to be those earliest located from Perth on grants west of Franktown.[53]

The people on this day's ride [from Franktown to Perth] have been settled now 3 years, & a fair idea of their exertions & success may be drawn from what they now generally boast of, that the poorest of them could this year spare half of their produce crop, after reserving enough for their family use, & for their seed time of next year, in Potatoes, Indian corn, wheat & barley.

Their houses or huts are yet poor. They have many wants, many complaints of hardship, but yet they confess themselves happy in their prospects after one or two years more.

Summing up his trip through the military townships, Dalhousie felt that " [a]ll those who have remained upon their lands are doing well, are contented and full of hope." He singled out Perth and Beckwith as already "shew[ing] what the whole of these townships severally will be, abounding in population and in produce."[54]

Dalhousie's visit inadvertently prompted a feud between Thomas Wickham and Patrick Nowlan at Franktown. Wickham, who was English and who had served in the 54th Regiment, in all likelihood already resented Nowlan, who as an Irish immigrant enjoyed higher military rank and had received the important post of being in charge of the King's storehouse at Franktown through the influence of another Irishman, Captain Burke, the superintendent of the Richmond military depot.[55] When Lord Dalhousie and his party (which included deputy quarter master general Colonel Francis Cockburn for whom Franktown was named) arrived at Franktown, Nowlan in the course of showing them the King's storehouse cannily cajoled them to spend the night at his tavern rather than at Wickham's inn. This naturally irritated Wickham, who felt aggrieved that a mere tavernkeeper should presume to entertain the governor general and enjoy the honour of putting up the King's representative. Wickham must have recognised that in years to come he stood to lose business to Nowlan because travellers naturally would prefer to stay at the same hostelry which had been patronised by the nobleman. His jealousy unsubsided, Thomas Wickham waited for a chance to retaliate. On the tenth of September 1820 he observed George Brooks picking up a grinding stone from the King's storehouse and also taking away from Patrick Nowlan's tavern "a small jug of Spirits...for the Nourishment of the men that was to Carry the Stone". Wickham immediately went to Perth, had Nowlan charged with "Selling Liquor as a Store Keeper and not as a Tavern Keeper"

Plate 14
Concession road between the first and second concessions in southeastern Beckwith, as photographed in June 1983. The undulations of this road reveal the absence of fertile and deep soil in southern Beckwith. Swamps, marshes and beaver meadows abounded, giving rise to the saying that southern Beckwith was "home to rock, swamps and mortgages."

and ultimately fined twenty pounds.[56]

Despite the animosity aroused between Thomas Wickham and Patrick Nowlan, Beckwith and other military townships generally benefitted from Dalhousie's 1820 visit due to the steps he took to provide a major road and to reinforce the military character of the settlement. Dalhousie wrote to the lieutenant-governor of Upper Canada that September:[57]

> I think it [a] matter of serious consideration, the increase of Americans into [Upper Canada] on the Brockville frontier. Some of the worthless [military] settlers are now disposing of their lots near Perth, and Americans are purchasing them. I was told of several near to Tollmans [in Kitley]...—cannot this be prevented?
>
> In the wish to encourage these new settlements I gave £200 at Richmond to open the great line of road to Beckwith store — £200 at Perth to open also towards Beckwith and £200 to clear it into the Lanark township from Perth, 12 miles of it being already fit for waggon in that direction. Next season I will repeat this, provided your Legislature shall vote us some efficient aid to that main line from Richmond landing place at the falls of Ottawa Chaudiere to Kingston. I also ordered 200 stand of Arms, & two light field pieces to be placed at Perth, & at Richmond, to induce them to form Volunteer Companies & to keep up that spirit of Loyalty & British feeling which exist now, but which might give way to evil communications with those Americans who really swarm in the woods near Brockville.

So it was that Beckwith and the other military townships were placed directly on a highway which eventually linked Kingston and the site of the future Bytown.

Dalhousie's grant of two hundred pounds for the road north from Perth marked the expansion of settlement in the region north of the military townships during the 1820s. Lanark was established in 1820 as the third settlement under military administration in the district. From the late 1810s immigration societies had been formed in Scotland to raise subscriptions to help pay the passage money to Canada of Lanarkshire and Renfrewshire weavers. This group of people had been particularly hard hit by the post war British financial depression. From the Lanark depot north of Perth nearly 3,500 men, women and children from the vicinity of Glasgow were located during the 1820s.[58] These Scottish lowland weavers were located in North and South Sherbrooke, Dalhousie, Lanark, Ramsay, Pakenham, Darling and Lavant townships.[59] In 1823 yet another experiment in government-assisted immigration brought 568 northern Cork immigrants to the region in hopes of reducing violent disturbances in southern Ireland by settling the "excess population" on land in Upper Canada. Only ten of the Irish immigrants were Protestants, the majority being Roman Catholics who were believed by the British government to be susceptible to violence only because overpopulation and unemployment in their native country had prevented them from having a fair opportunity to be productive and peaceful subjects.[60] These Irish settlers, brought to British North America under the superintendence of the Honourable Peter Robinson, were granted land immediately north of Beckwith in Ramsay, Pakenham, and in the northwestern corners of Huntley and Goulbourn townships. A few of the Robinson immigrants also could be found in Beckwith, Bathurst and Lanark townships (Appendix 11).[61]

In the early 1820s small settlements of former British naval and army officers were established along the southern or Upper Canadian banks of the Ottawa River above Nepean. In March Township the riverfront colonists were largely English, in Torbolton the few military settlers were Scottish, and in Fitzroy there was a combination of Scottish and American early settlers.[62] In the mid 1820s Archibald McNab, the seventeenth chief of McNab, in a bid to reestablish a feudal clan and rebuild his finances, colonised McNab Township with Perthshire Scottish Presbyterians from the same Loch Tayside vicinity Beckwith settlers had departed in 1818. These exploited Scottish settlers spilled over into southern Horton Township in the late 1820s and 1830s.[63] All told, fourteen new townships opened for settlement north of Beckwith in the 1820s. In the mid to late 1820s as construction of the Rideau military canal commenced, Irish Catholic and Protestant immigrant labourers were attracted by the promise of work. Scottish stonemasons and French-Canadian labourers also arrived in lesser numbers to work on the Rideau Canal.

The colonial and military authorities responsible for establishing the military townships arranged for the British state churches to buttress loyalty toward the mother country. The early piety and placing of clergy in Beckwith within only a few years was in complete contrast with American and Loyalist settlements along the St. Lawrence where there were virtually no congregations nor houses of worship built for at least a generation after settlement began. The irreligiosity in the St. Lawrence townships was due to the "older Settlers being almost all Soldiers in the American revolutionary War, and from their early manner of living, and the easy rate at which spiritous liquors may be had in this Province, added to the want of religious instruction, they have contracted careless and extravagant habits".[64] This created a climate which allowed American-trained Methodist and Presbyterian preachers to expound a gospel which was alleged to be tinged with republican and pro-American allusions. A Church of Scotland clergyman well acquainted with the American settlements along the St. Lawrence warned Governor General Dalhousie in 1822 that[65]

> the Methodist and Presbyterian Clergymen who reside in this Province from the United States must operate strongly in alienating the minds, and affections of his Majesty's loyal subjects. I have been told by a respectable English Methodist Preacher, that a preacher from the United

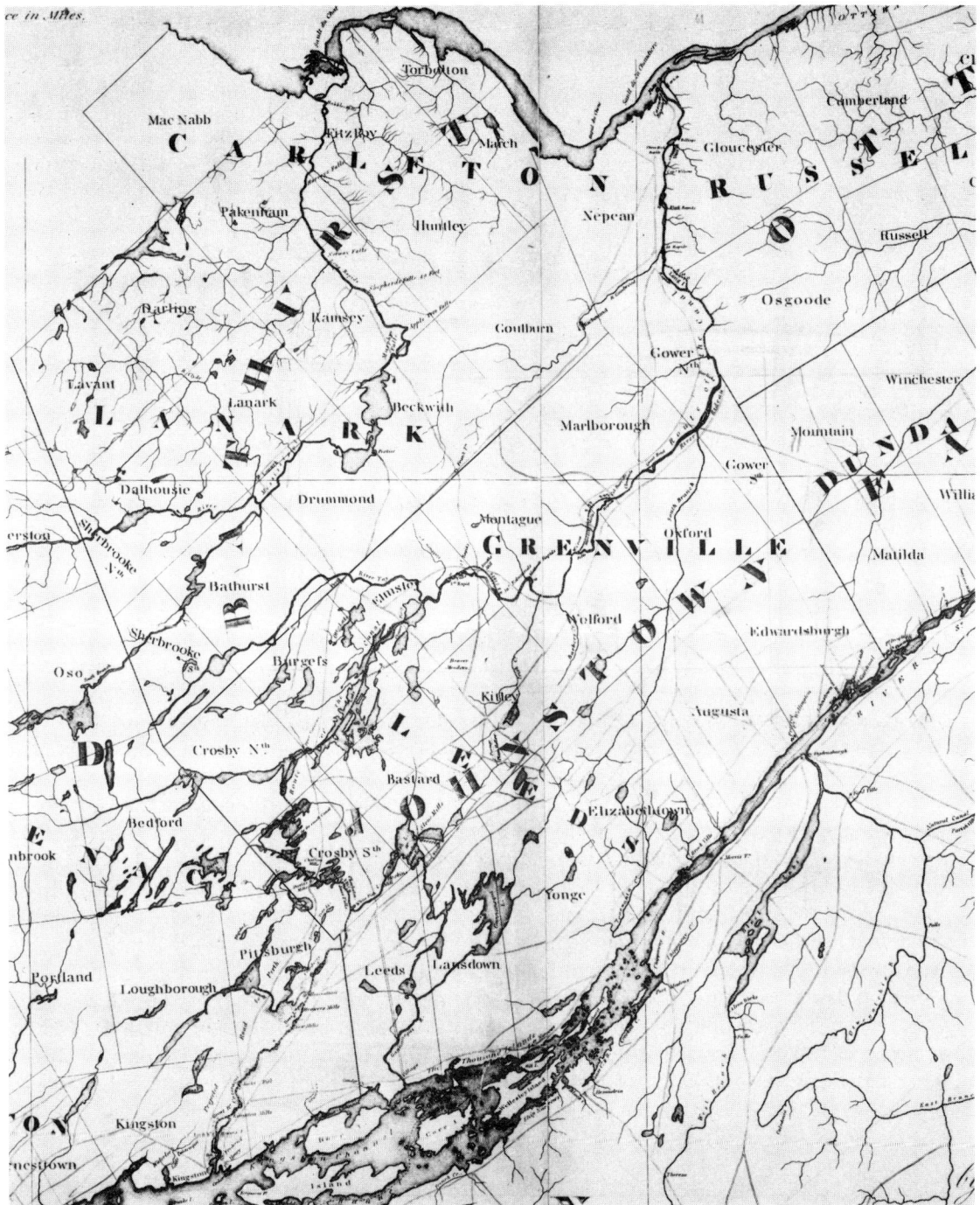

Plate 15
Detail of map "shewing the proposed route for a Canal to unite the waters of Lake Ontario with the Ottawa River", 1825, by James G. Chewett. Morphy's Falls (later Carleton Place, and here spelled Murphy) emerged as a milling hamlet in the early 1820s, but the rapids and waterfalls on the Mississippi discouraged human transportation. Early timber slides were built at major hurdles such as Shepherd's Falls (later Almonte) to send timber down the Ottawa River to Montreal. National Archives of Canada NMC 11233.

States harangued a large audience on a Sunday lately, on the probability of this Province's falling to the States in the event of war with Great Britain, and the beneficial effects which would flow to the Inhabitants of this Province from such an event.

By contrast, the clergy of the United Church of England and Ireland, the Church of Scotland and the Roman Catholic Church (the latter of which enjoyed official status in Canada but not in the British Isles) assured government that they "would give a direction, and an impulse to the minds of the rising generation — they would bind them to their King and Country in bonds of affection and love which would not easily be broken." The Reverend John McLaurin at Glengarry asserted in 1822 "that if the British Government wishes to retain this Province, Twenty Clergymen of known loyalty would be of more avail for this end, than many Regiments of Soldiers."[66] Beginning with the 1816 assisted immigration, military authorities promised to provide clergymen and school teachers for group settlements. Accordingly, the same link of civil and religious power which caused the Anglican, Church of Scotland and Roman Catholic churches to cluster about the court-house and government school at Perth, also dictated that the early clergy of Beckwith had military background as proof of their fitness to preach the Christian gospel in a British settlement. The Reverend Michael Harris of Perth who formed the Anglican congregation at Franktown in 1822 had previously been "an Ensign in one of the Reg[iment]ts, that have formed this settlement".[67] The first resident Presbyterian clergyman in Beckwith, the Reverend George Buchanan, in an 1822 petition informed Major Powell at Perth that "when our Mother Country was threatened with an Invasion your Memorialist raised a Company for the St. Andrews Reg[imen]t of Volunteers in one day, and in which he served in the rank of Lieutenant".[68] In addition to providing clergymen belonging to the established churches, by November 1823, as Robert Ferguson remarked in a letter home to his wife's parents in Kippen parish in Scotland, "their is plenty of S[c]hools all around us endowed with Governmint salarys".[69]

By 1824 it seemed on the surface that the British colonial policy of creating a military settlement out of a previously uncharted forest was an undoubted success. As early as 1821 members of Governor General Dalhousie's staff at Quebec routinely referred to Beckwith and the other military townships as "advancing with a progress far beyond the most sanguine expectations".[70] The success of Beckwith and other townships as a counter-revolutionary foil to the republican notions of the Americans settled in the St. Lawrence townships promised to be enhanced as British immigrants continued to pour into eastern Upper Canada. Even the empty townships along the Rideau River were beginning to attract British settlers, some of them squatting on the grants being held in speculation by absentee Loyalists and others leasing Clergy and Crown reserves. The largely empty Rideau townships only served to underline all the more fully the rapid settlement of Beckwith. Despite its isolation in the midst of the forest, despite the swamps and thin cover of soil, Beckwith only six years after settlement began had three to five times the population of any of the Rideau townships that had been open to settlement for a generation. The flourishing state of the new British military settlements inevitably led to disparaging contrasts with the older American settlements, as this excerpt from an 1819 editorial in the Kingston Chronicle shows.[71]

The very flourishing condition of the new townships in the interior, which have been recently surveyed and granted to actual settlers, is a circumstance highly encouraging to those who may be located in situations still more remote. Some of those townships which but two years ago were an entire wilderness, are now thickly settled, and the inhabitants abundantly supplied with provisions and other necessaries of life from the produce of their farms, which already begin to assume an appearance of neatness and comfort not always to be perceived in some of the older settlements, where much more might have been expected if the people had been equally industrious.

The creation of the military townships posed questions about potential regional disharmony in the future. It was all very well as late as 1824 for the loyal British population of Beckwith and the other military townships to be kept at a safe distance from the allegedly disloyal American-origin settlers along the St. Lawrence by a buffer of largely-empty Rideau townships. Once the Rideau townships did begin to fill, the possibility of cultural, ethnic, religious and ideological conflict as American and British settlers came into contact with one another was all too possible. How this would be prevented had not been prepared for, save for the placing of arms at Richmond and Perth. Despite positive reports about the development of the military settlements, local inhabitants knew all too well that many disbanded soldiers and immigrants had moved away rather than face up to the challenge of clearing poor land on remote grants. The sparring of Thomas Wickham and Patrick Nowlan posed the further question of how long the ethnic and national mixture even within British-settled Beckwith could be kept from coming into conflict.

After 1820 even the British Crown, which for as long as anyone could remember had symbolised order, continuity and the virtue of a state buttressed by a religious establishment in the face of immorality and revolution in Europe, was tarnished. The lives, loves and morals of George III's children made them the most unloved royal generation in English history. "In particular," observes David Cannadine, "George IV's extravagance and womanizing brought the monarchy to a low ebb, the nadir of which was reached in 1821 when his marriage to Queen Caroline became both public politics and public scandal ".[72] Upper Canadians, especially those in British settlements such as Beckwith, could not escape the irony of being a model British community under a King with such low morals. When Irish Methodists cautioned a newly-arrived American preacher in 1821 that he "would be expected in public worship to pray for the 'king and royal family'," he promptly responded that he "was willing to do that, and...had no doubt the King — George IV — *needed prayer as much as any one.*"[73]

Beckwith along with the other Upper Canadian military townships between 1816 and 1824 was a product of the counter-revolutionary British colonial and military policy which was deployed under the declining George III. Only time would tell if the one thousand Irish and Scottish settlers set down in the middle of the forest would fulfil the model of loyalty for American-origin Upper Canadians prescribed for them, or if like the wayward George IV they would wander off along a more flamboyant course.

Endnotes

1. W.A.B. Douglas, "The Precursors of Colonel John By" in F.C.L. Wyght, ed., *Archaeological Historical Symposium* (Lombardy, Ontario: F.C.L. Wyght, 1982), pp. 84-85.
2. Bruce Wilson, *As She Began: An Illustrated Introduction to Loyalist Ontario* (Toronto: Dundurn Press, 1981), p. 76.
3. Ruth McKenzie, *Leeds and Grenville: their first two hundred years* (Toronto: McClelland and Stewart Ltd., 1967), p. 24.
4. Gerald M. Craig, *Upper Canada: The Formative Years, 1784-1841* The Canadian Centenary Series (Toronto: McClelland and Stewart, 1963), pp. 24-25, 33.
5. Robert Gourlay, *Statistical Account of Upper Canada*, intro. and ed. by S.R. Mealing (Toronto: McClelland and Stewart Limited, 1974), p. 261.
6. Glenn J Lockwood, Montague: *A Social History of an Irish Ontario Township, 1783-1980* (Smiths Falls: Corporation of the Township of Montague, 1980), p. 88.
7. Marjory Whitelaw, ed., *The Dalhousie Journals* (Ottawa: Oberon Press, 1981) II:42.
8. Craig, *Upper Canada*, pp. 70-71.
9. Andrew Haydon, *Pioneer Sketches in the District of Bathurst* (Toronto: The Ryerson Press, 1925), p. 13.
10. Douglas, "Precursors of Colonel John By," p. 87.
11. Whitelaw, *Dalhousie Journals*, II:49.
12. *Kingston (Upper Canada) Gazette*, 5 February 1811, p. 1, col. 4.
13. *Brockville (Upper Canada) Gazette*, 5 April 1832, p. 1, col. 4.
14. Eric Jarvis, "Military Land Granting in Upper Canada Following the War of 1812," *Ontario History* LXVII No. 3, pp. 121-122.
15. Ibid., pp. 123-125.
16. William Dunlop, *Tiger Dunlop's Upper Canada* New Canadian Library (Toronto: McClelland and Stewart Limited, 1967), p. 39.
17. Haydon, *Pioneer Sketches*, p. 10.
18. Ibid., p. 13.

19 Ibid., pp. 16-17.
20 Marianne McLean, "Ach an Rhigh: A Highland Response to the Assisted Emigration of 1815" in Donald H. Akenson, ed. *Canadian Papers in Rural History* V (Gananoque: Langdale Press, 1986), p. 181.
21 Haydon, *Pioneer Sketches*, p. 15.
22 McLean, "Ach an Rhigh," pp. 187-194.
23 National Archives of Canada (hereafter NAC) RG 5, A1 Reel C-4546, vol. 25, pp. 11367-11369.
24 Ontario Ministry of Natural Resources, January 1817 plan of Beckwith surveyed by Reuben Sherwood, Deputy Surveyor.
25 NAC MG 9, D8 *Perth Military Settlement Book*, pp. 18, 20, 21.
26 This calculation is based on adding together the members of families listed in appendices 1 and 2.
27 NAC RG 5, A1 Reel C-4547 Upper Canada Sundries, vol. 30, pp. 13637-13640.
28 Ibid., Reel C-4546, vol. 26, p. 12100.
29 Ibid., Reel C-4609, vol. 58, pp. 30098-30100.
30 Ibid., Reel C-4612, vol, 63, p. 33632.
31 *Kingston (Upper Canada) Gazette*, 3 June 1825, p. 2, cols. 1-4.
32 NAC RG 5, A1 Reel C-4546 Upper Canada Sundries, p. 12102.
33 Jean S. McGill, *A Pioneer History of the County of Lanark* (Bewdley, Ontario: Clay Publishing Company Limited, 1979), p. 26.
34 NAC RG 5, A1 Reel C-4549 Upper Canada Sundries Vol. 32, pp. 15590-15591.
35 Ibid., Reel C-4548, vol, 31, p. 14396.
36 Ibid., Reel C-4609, vol. 58, pp. 29920-29924.
37 NAC RG 5, A1 Reel C-4547 Upper Canada Sundries, vol. 28, p. 12955.
38 McGill, *Pioneer History*, p. 13.
39 NAC RG 5 A1 Reel C-4548 Upper Canada Sundries, vol. 31, p. 14392.
40 Ibid., Reel C-4548, vol. 31, pp. 14394-14395.
41 Ibid., Dalhousie to Maitland, 22 September 1820, cited in Howard M. Brown, *Lanark Legacy: Nineteenth Century Glimpses of an Ontario County* (Perth, Ontario: Corporation of the County of Lanark, 1984), p. 214.
42 Bruce S. Elliott, "The North Tipperary Protestants in the Canadas: A Study of Migration, 1815-1880" (Ph.D. dissertation, Carleton University, 1984), pp. 117-118.
43 Haydon, *Pioneer Sketches*, p. 60.
44 This particular group of immigrants has been studied in remarkable genealogical and demographic detail by Bruce. S. Elliott in *Irish Migrants in the Canadas: A New Approach* McGill-Queen's Studies in Ethnic History no.1 (Montreal: McGill-Queen's University Press, 1988).
45 NAC Reel B-876 Colonial Office 384, volumes 1-2, vol. 3ff-60, printed pages 178-188.
46 Haydon, *Pioneer Sketches*, p. 66.
47 Brown, *Lanark Legacy*, p. 20.
48 NAC RG 5, A1 Reel C-4617 Upper Canada Sundries, vol. 77, p. 41190.
49 Whitelaw, Dalhousie Journals II:43
50 Ibid., p. 46.
51 Ibid., pp. 44-45.
52 Ibid., p. 45.
53 Ibid.
54 Brown, *Lanark Legacy*, p. 213.
55 NAC MG 9, D8 Perth Military Settlement Book, pp. 34, 96.
56 NAC RG 5, A1 Reel C-4605 Upper Canada Sundries, vol. 49, pp. 24422-24429.
57 Ibid., Reel C-4605 , vol. 49, pp. 24212-24218.
58 Brown, *Lanark Legacy*, p. 270.
59 Elliott, "North Tipperary Protestants," p. 214; McGill, *Pioneer History*, pp. 73-76.
60 Peter L. Maltby and Monica Maltby, "A New Look at the Peter Robinson Emigration of 1823" *Ontario History* LV No. 1 (1963), pp. 15,18.
61 Donald E. Read, Donald W. Kelly, James R. Kennedy and Bruce S. Elliott, *St. Michael's Roman Catholic Church Cemetery and Lists of Peter Robinson Settlers* (Ottawa: Ottawa Branch of the Ontario Genealogical Society, 1981), pp. 60-63.
62 Roger Hall, "Hamnett Kirkes Pinhey" *Dictionary of Canadian Biography* (hereafter DCB) (Toronto: University of Toronto Press, 1985) VIII:706-707.
63 [Dugald Campbell McNab], "History of the Settlement of the Township of McNab: Attempt to Establish the Feudal System" in *Perth (Ontario) Courier*, 1 October 1869 to 22 October 1869.
64 NAC RG 5, A1 Reel C-4609 Upper Canada Sundries, vol. 58, p. 30028.
65 Ibid., pp. 30030-30031.
66 Ibid.
67 Whitelaw, *Dalhousie Journals* II:48.
68 NAC RG 5, A1 Reel C-4609 Upper Canada Sundries, vol. 58, p. 30470.
69 NAC MG 55/24 No.199 Robert Ferguson, Beckwith, to John Moir near Kippen, West Stirling, Scotland, 10 November 1823.
70 NAC RG 5, A1 Reel C-4606 Upper Canada Sundries, vol. 51, p. 25148.
71 *Kingston (Upper Canada) Chronicle*, 17 September 1817, p. 3, col. 3.
72 David Cannadine, "The Context, Performance and Meaning of Ritual: The British Monarchy and the 'Invention of Tradition', c. 1820-1977" in Eric Hobsbawm and Terence Ranger, eds., *The Invention of Tradition* Past and Present Publications (Cambridge: Cambridge University Press, 1983), p. 109.
73 John Carroll, *Case and His Cotemporaries* (Toronto: Wesleyan Conference Office, 1869) II:321.

SCOTTISH BECKWITH

The group settlement of highlanders from Perthshire Scotland located largely in the northern quarter of Beckwith in 1818 immediately became the most visible and identifiable community of people in Beckwith. This was due in large part to their concentration together on some of the finest land to be found in eastern Upper Canada. It was also due to the fact that many Scottish inhabitants of Beckwith continued to speak Gaelic well into the late nineteenth century. In 1845 the Rev. Robert Burns from Scotland visited and found that a "large proportion of Beckwith is Gaelic; many of the settlers are from the Marquis of Breadalbane's country; and all of them more or less flourishing."[1] Quite apart from being distinguished by the use of Gaelic, the highland settlers of early Beckwith like immigrants in any age continued to live under the shadow of their own recent past in Perthshire. Other than for readjusting to the herculean toil of clearing the forest and learning the ropes of North American frontier farming, the Perthshire immigrants in Beckwith had readily departed Scotland to create in the midst of the forest a more prosperous version of their life back home.

The immigrants who arrived in Beckwith from the Loch Tayside vicinity of the Perthshire highlands in 1818 were the inheritors of various improvements that had been introduced by the second, third and fourth Earls of Breadalbane throughout the eighteenth century. In addition to starting lead mines in 1739, the second earl brought wool-workers from England to teach the people of Breadalbane the arts of spinning and weaving, and under the fostering care of the third earl spinning and weaving developed until they became a thriving industry in the region. In the decades before 1800 it was inevitable that the manufacture of cloth in Breadalbane became industrialised, but weaving continued to be done by the great numbers of handloom weavers in that region.[2] New roads were constructed, hamlets such as Kenmore were transformed into planned villages, and areas of waste ground were planted with forest.[3] The decline of clan battles and of war with England after the mid eighteenth century together with the coming of universal inoculation and vaccination against smallpox, typhus fever and other formerly fatal maladies, led to a considerable increase in population.[4] The increase in population was unremarkable when contrasted with the population explosion which took place at the same time in English and Scottish manufacturing towns, but by 1806 the population of Perthshire was at its highest point in history, and prompted contemporary observers to remark that the "principal misfortune of the Highlands at all times has been, that they contained too many inhabitants".[5]

The growth in population contributed to a deterioration in agriculture and food supply. The traditional run-rig system of farming prevailed, in which different tenants leased the arable land, lived in houses closely grouped together, and worked the different rigs of the land held together in common. The cultivated land under the run-rig system was divided into infield or croftland, and outfield. The croftland received practically all the manure, and was cropped annually. The outfield patches of poorer land were usually situated higher up the hillsides, were cropped without manure as long as they would bear, and then abandoned to weeds. As rigs changed tenants, there was little incentive to improve the land, and indeed the growing population led to the overstocking of the region with black cattle and horses, further draining the overtaxed land. In the 1780s and 1790s the fourth Earl of Breadalbane had the run-rig system done away with, and compact farms were laid out, removing the infield and outfield arrangement which had been the cause of many bitter disputes between tenants.[6] The strain of increasing population on the land by 1800 was shown by the new reliance on potatoes for food, and by importing other food supplies. In Comrie parish, from which a full third of the Scottish settlers in Beckwith came, the Church of Scotland clergyman reported in 1794.[7]

> The principal crops are oats and bear [or barley]. Potatoes are planted everywhere in great quantities, and, with milk, constitute the principal part of the food of the lower classes, for 8 months of the year. A good deal of meal is brought from the neighbouring parishes of Monzievaird, Crieff and Muthil. Those parishes also supply our small whisky stills with about 1200 bolls* of barley yearly.

The importing of meal to Comrie was due to the growth of the village of Comrie from "a small kirktoun beside the river, with a few cottar houses and their adjoining cow parks" in the mid eighteenth century to a centre containing about one thousand inhabitants. Comrie was a planned village when it was laid out in the late eighteenth century, with the houses deliberately built directly on the street frontage, with a mere space left alongside the roadway for pedestrians. This prevented households from continuing the traditional practice of placing dung heaps directly in front of their doors.[8] The staple manufacture at Comrie in 1794 was "linen yard, of which a great quantity is spun and sold every year.". Many of the spinners in 1794 were yet farmers, and most used the income from the yarn to "pay a great part of their rents."[9]

> From the tow of the lint, they spin harn yarn, which is made into cloth, that brings from 9d. to 1s. per yard. The finer sort is used for men and women's shirts; the coarser for sailors jackets and trousers. The women make also a great quantity of tartan, of which they make plaids and hose. These are partly for home use and partly for the market.

By 1824 cotton weaving was the staple trade carried on in Comrie village, and a substantial portion of the population had left farming behind, looking for mutual support by "forming themselves into an incorporation, or benefit society".[10]

Save for the gradual growth of Comrie as a manufacturing centre weavers in the other Perthshire villages and parishes of Balquhidder, Blair Athol, Callander, Dull, Dunblane, Fortingall, Kenmore, Killin, Kincardine, Little Dunkeld and Muthil maintained a close link with farming. Kenmore was developed as a picturesque estate village at the front gate of the Breadalbane estate, but it was Comrie which came closest to fulfilling the role of the ideal planned village by providing consumption for produce of the surrounding lands, by providing non-agricultural employment for tenants and sub-tenants who might otherwise find themselves cast out of the district by enclosure, and by industrious villagers providing an example and an inspiration to the rural tenantry without diminishing the landowner's hold over the countryside.[11]

The unprecedented increase in population, the various forms of improvement undertaken by landowners, the growth of planned villages, an increasing scarcity of fuel, growing dependence on spinning and weaving for a livelihood, and generally rising wages for servants and labourers[12] were all obvious marks of the age of improvement. Less obvious was the ease with which Scottish highland society began to crumble after 1746. As late as the time of the 1818 Beckwith immigration the established language of the Breadalbane highlands continued to be Erse, a dialect of Gaelic, but it did not promise to remain so for long. By 1806 the English language was reported[13]

* A boll was the equivalent of six bushels

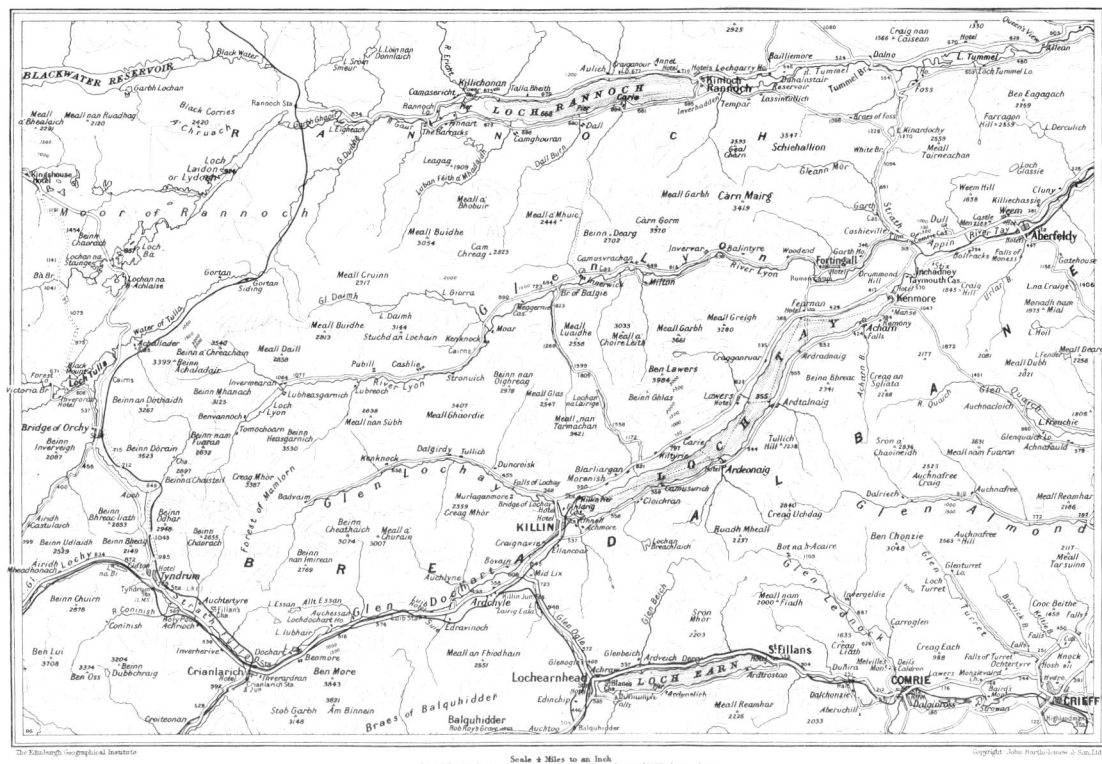

Plate 16
Map of the Breadalbane region of Perthshire, Scotland. The 1818 group migration to Beckwith was drawn from the parishes of Balquhidder, Blair Athol, Blair Drummond, Comrie, Dull, Dunblane, Fortingall, Kenmore, Killin and St. Fillan's. Additional family members migrated from this region to Beckwith in the 1820s and 1830s. Copyright © John Bartholomew & Son Limited MCMLXXXIX. Reproduced with permission.

working its way into the most inward recesses of the Highlands, and will, in a few years, probably supersede the use of the Erse; a circumstance which, whenever it may take place, will be fortunate for the country; as it will assimilate it more intimately with the neighbouring districts. It is now universally taught in the schools of the central Highlands. Hence it is spoken in greater purity here than in the Lowland districts. From the intercourse, however, which the Highlanders have with these districts, and from the teachers having the Lowland accent, the tone and many of the provincialisms of the Lowlands are in use.

The rapidity with which highland society crumbled in the late eighteenth century, changing language and dress, removing customs, transforming housing and villages, in turn transformed the popular British image of highlanders from despicable idle predatory barbarians to a romantic primitive people with the charm of an endangered species.[14]

By 1818, when the Beckwith group immigration took place, a highland revival was in full swing, the influence of which was clearly felt in the Comrie region. This highland revival was a romantic creation, and an invention which underlines all too firmly how thoroughly highland society had been demolished. Following the rebellion of 1746, the British government sought to divert the martial spirit of the highlanders away from Jacobite adventure to imperial war, and during the following seventy years Highland regiments covered themselves with glory in India, in America, and in Canada. Hugh Trevor-Roper has explained how the kilt was a purely modern costume, first designed and worn by an English Quaker industrialist about 1730 who bestowed it on his highlander employees in order not to preserve their traditional way of life but to ease its transformation as highlanders were brought out of the heather and into the factory. No such things as clan tartans existed before 1745.[15] The romantic novels of Sir Walter Scott at the beginning of the nineteenth century sparked widespread interest in the highlands and led to the formation of highland societies and to annual highland games such as those held in the village of St. Fillans beginning in 1819.[16] As highland society modernised, as it was integrated with the rest of Britain, the growing romantic fascination with fabricated traditional highland costume provided a desirable surrogate for the grim reality of traditional highland society which had been destroyed forever.

The dissolving of the Scottish parliament in 1707, the quashing of the 1746 rebellion, the integration of the Scottish economy with the rest of Britain, the importing of English notions about conducting agriculture and developing villages, and the replacement of the traditional clan system with a romantic legend of what highland society originally had been like, all effectively combined to leave religion the major if not the only activity in which there was significant continuity with the past and in which the majority of people concentrated their interest and intellect. Lacking a Scottish parliament, the Church of Scotland effectively became the national institution of Scotland in the eighteenth and early nineteenth centuries. Christianity had been part of highland society in the Breadalbane region for more than twelve centuries; it was first imported by a disciple of the Irish Saint Columba, Saint Fillan.[17] For twelve hundred years inhabitants of the Comrie vicinity venerated relics of St. Fillan such as his crozier, a holy well, a stone seat, a tree, remnant stones reputed to survive from a meal mill built by the saint, fragments of a font, and a chapel bell, all of which were believed to possess curative powers.[18] Following the Reformation, and more particularly after the quashing of Jacobite ambitions in the late seventeenth century, candles no longer were burned in front of images of St. Fillan in regional churches such as that at Killin,[19] as the established and Protestant Church of Scotland held sway. The dominance of the Church of Scotland in Breadalbane was effectively symbolised by the building of a church containing 1,026 sittings at Comrie in 1804 when less than a thousand people lived in the village.[20]

The Church of Scotland was the central institution in local life. The offices of elders and stewards were valued positions of status in every parish. The clergyman and elders administered funds from the parish poor box to those in need, arbitrated in domestic disputes, maintained moral standards by passing judgment on those suspected of adultery or fornication before marriage, and presided over the selection of the schoolmaster. Indeed, in smaller parishes the kirk minister was the schoolmaster.

To become a clergyman of the Church of Scotland was virtually the highest ambition of any gifted and intelligent young man not of noble or gentle birth. The ministry of that church provided the combined blessings of an assured good annual income, divine sanction, respectability to the point of being conversant with local gentry and nobles, and the prestige of being an important channel between the local population and Westminster. Consequently, the pulpits of the Church of Scotland attracted rigorously intellectual men who also knew the importance of serving the interests of either the nobility and government that substantially funded their livings. In Comrie and Dull parishes, which together provided 45 percent of the 1818 Beckwith immigration, the minister's salary was provided by the Crown, and substantial funding for schools in the Breadalbane region was provided by the Society for the Propagation of Christian Knowledge.[21] In Comrie the inescapable symbol of the importance of the Church of Scotland in harmonising local society to the wishes of the major landowners, was the 1804 church which became the visual focus of the town, especially with the construction of the substantial clock tower and steeple which was largely underwritten by a subscription from Henry Dundas, Viscount Melville.[22]

Plate 17
View from Killin at the head of Loch Tay, ca. 1770. This view reveals the intensive cultivation that took place during the late eighteenth century as the population rose to an unprecedented high. Robert Forsyth commented in 1806 that locally "the occupiers of the soil are too numerous, the farms are small, [and] the tenants consequently are poor.... But in these districts he who occupies no portion of the soil has no means of obtaining bread." Obtained courtesy of Bruce Elliott.

Comrie, of the dozen Perthshire parishes supplying immigrants to Beckwith in 1818, since the mid-eighteenth century was home to one of the few Presbyterian Secessionist congregations in the highlands. The Secessionists, as they were called, fully subscribed to the principles and constitution of the Church of Scotland, but broke away from the parent church in some three hundred parishes at different times throughout the eighteenth century because they refused to accept the interference of the Crown and nobility in the spiritual jurisdiction of the Church of Scotland.[23] The central argument of the Secessionists was that the Scottish church must be spiritually independent of the state, and that because the Church was headed by Christ, it could not submit to the intervention of a worldly government.[24] The small congregation at Comrie was remote from the concentration of Secessionists in central and western Scotland, especially Glasgow,[25] and although initially small, from 1791 through to 1826 Comrie was fortunate enough to be ministered to by an able and persuasive Secessionist clergyman, the Reverend Samuel Gilfillan. Among the small farmers, crofters and cottars who moved down into the village of Comrie from their farms to carry on with their secondary occupation of weaving, Gilfillan found a receptive audience. The abrupt transition from farming to village life, with many of the new inhabitants cleared off the Drummond and Breadalbane estates, spurred many to attend the preaching of Gilfillan rather than go to the Church of Scotland:[26]

> The tent at sacraments, where he preached, was surrounded by eager throngs; and when he left it to serve a table in the church the crowds pursued and even preceded him there. The orthodox admired him for his sound theology; the heterodox for his catholic spirit; the students for his historical allusions; and the children for his racy anecdotes.

The power of Gilfillan's oratory on the weavers of Comrie was assisted by one of some seventy earthquakes to hit the village between 1792 and 1814. On the 24th day of February 1799 he was preaching "on the power of Christ our Redeemer, and was arguing from His raising the dead at the Last Day that He has infinite power, when lo! the shock came [and following the] awfully loud and fully tremendous noise 'a deep sigh pervaded the congregation'."[27] Spellbinding oratory to one side, Gilfillan was revered as a "saintly minister"[28] and so lasting an impression did he have on some of the immigrants who left for Beckwith in 1818, that as late as 1856 his son, the Reverend George Gilfillan was cited in the Beckwith vicinity as an incontrovertible authority on the importance of keeping church and state separate.[29]

A pattern of migration from the Breadalbane region to eastern Upper Canada had already been well established, beginning with the settlement of Scottish Catholics in Glengarry in 1784 and 1785, followed by the government-assisted immigration of 1816 discussed in the previous chapter. Immigration to Canada flowed naturally enough from the highland clearances, but instead of being a cruel fate meted out to people forced off the land, recent scholarship suggests that the decision to go to Canada was an enthusiastic one on the part of ordinary people who took advantage of opportunity to improve their livelihood. J.M. Bumsted suggests how willing tenants were to leave Scotland between 1770 and 1815, how anxious landlords were to stop them from pulling up stakes, and that the threat or reality of mass emigration was used to counter the nobility's assumptions of economic and social hegemony.[30] Marianne McLean has demonstrated that the immigrants from Perthshire took advantage of a government-assisted scheme in 1815 to join relatives already established in Glengarry for a generation, rather than conform to the government plan of settling them in the dense forests of the military townships north of the Rideau.[31] Undoubtedly, letters home from the 1815 settlers extolling the generous land grants and the remarkable productivity of Upper Canadian soil whetted the appetites of those who had not the means to pay the sixteen pound deposit for each adult male, and the two guinea deposit required for every woman. Consequently, two years later when the Colonial Office offered to sponsor group settlements, John Robertson of Breadalbane agreed to organise a group of immigrants and paid a ten pound deposit for each settler, to be repaid him by the settlers once they were well settled on their land. A total of 444 Perthshire inhabitants sailed for Upper Canada in August 1818 on three brigs, the *Curlew*, the *Sophia* and the *Jane*. There is no record to suggest that they felt forced to leave Perthshire for the colonies.

The 1818 Perthshire immigration to Beckwith consisted of young families. Although many of the immigrants were related to one another, or were neighbours, the rules of the government scheme forbade couples or family heads above age 45 participating in the trip. Implicitly, older couples might not fare as well in the transition to frontier agriculture, they were less willing to leave their native country, younger people would be able to have the numerous children necessary to help clear the land, and, in any event the young people could readily raise the amount necessary to bring their aged parents to British North America once they could be persuaded to immigrate. For some couples, marriage was directly linked to the migration. Nineteen-year-old Christina McLaren, for example, "came in one day and told her mother that the meal kist was going to catch it today. Her mother asked her why. Well, she said, I'm going to make a lot of oatcakes. I'm going to marry Jamie Ferguson tomorrow, and go to America with him."[32] The ship's list for the *Jane* has not survived, but judging

Plate 18
Church at Balquhidder, Perthshire, as engraved ca. 1880. This small unpretentious Church of Scotland house of worship may well have served as a model for the church built in Beckwith in 1834. The Balquhidder congregation enjoyed the patronage of the Duke of Athol, and members of the congregation contributed to collections taken up for supporting the parochial poor roll. Obtained courtesy of Bruce Elliott.

from the Beckwith settlers on the *Curlew* and the *Sophia*, just over a quarter (26.5 percent) were male household heads, 28 percent were women, 7.6 percent were adolescents between the ages of twelve and seventeen, and 38 percent were children under the age of twelve.

The ocean voyage from Greenock to Quebec was uneventful. One of the children on the *Curlew* recalled their arrival in Canada.[33]

> We arrived in Quebec in seven weeks and three days from Greenock. There were but two steamboats then running between Quebec and Montreal, "The Car of Commerce" and the "Montreal." We got to Montreal in the first named, early in the month of October. The steamers then had to be drawn by oxen and horses past the current at St. Mary to the place of landing. There was no wharf at Montreal then. Long planks were used for a gangway....

At Montreal twenty of the passengers on the *Jane* and sixteen of those on the *Curlew* "became quite discouraged at the representation there made to them" about the Beckwith settlement. They "determined to go...to Cape Breton [instead, but] on their way being out of provisions and quite in distress they called at Prince Edward Island where [they] settled and [in 1820 described themselves as being] in a most deplorable state of poverty."[34] A smaller group headed by James and Archibald McFarlane, John Campbell and John Carmichael left the Beckwith party at Montreal for western Upper Canada. In May 1819 these four families published a letter in the York *Upper Canada Gazette*, addressed "To the Emigrants who arrived at Quebec in the summer of 1818...from the parishes of Comrea, Balyhidder, Weems and Killene in Perthshire, North Britain":[35]

> When we parted with you at Montreal for this part of the Country, we promised to inform you of the advantages which we might find it to possess. You are probably so scattered about now that we cannot inform you in any other way than by addressing you in a newspaper....
> We have been of the party of Colonel [Mahlon] Burwell, and assisted him to survey about 70,000 acres of Land in the township of London, which we have just completed, and Colonel [Thomas] Talbot has located us upon one hundred acres each.... The Land is of the finest quality we ever saw.... When we left Scotland, the Ministers of our parishes begged us to settle near each other, which we sincerely wish and hope, that such of you as are not settled to your satisfaction will come to this part of the Province.

Most of the immigrants who arrived at Montreal continued on to Beckwith, first being sent to Lachine in carts. One of the immigrants recalled.[36]

> Our passage up the Ottawa was by batteaux rowed by French Canadians. In three days we got to Point Fortune, and our luggage was transported mostly in ox-carts past the Long Sault, and the Rev. Mr. McKelligan preached to us. When the boats arrived we reloaded and started. We had to camp in the woods at night. One night we were surprised to see a large canoe putting [in] to our camp, with a numerous crew, all speaking Gaelic. These men were engaged in the trouble between Lord Selkirk and the Hudson's Bay Company. After three days' rowing we arrived at the Chaudiere Falls.... As our location was in the township of Beckwith, with no road to it, and as it was now late in the season the people built huts of poles covered with pine branches. When the men were absent choosing their land some of these huts caught fire and some valuable articles were burnt.

The initial settlement of Finlay McEwen's family was likely typical for most of the 1818 immigrant highlanders. He left his family in a small house he built at Hull, then set out for Beckwith with the oldest of his six children, located his lot, built a house, and moved his family from Hull in the spring of 1819. Colin McLaren, by contrast, rather than face the prospect of tackling the forest, located at Chatham, a small village east of Hull where he did business as a shoemaker until reports of developing prosperity from his countrymen in Beckwith induced him to homestead on the fifth concession in 1820.[37]

The reluctance of some of the 1818 Perthshire immigrants to locate in the forest reaches of Beckwith stemmed from a hope that they, like the 1816 immigrants from Perthshire, might settle near kin and old clan neighbours in Glengarry. Such hopes were dashed by the deputy quarter master general's office at Quebec, as shown in a letter from that office to D.N. McDermaid, one of the immigrants, informing him that "it was not the governor general's intentions to place any Emigrants in the Glengarry Settlement; and [that] directions have been given the Secretary at Perth to allot you Land at the Rideau Settlement".[38] Remote although Beckwith appeared from

Plate 19
Comrie Secessionist Presbyterian church, as photographed in 1985. The robust design of this house of worship reflected the strength the weavers in Comrie drew from the oratory of the Reverend Samuel Gilfillan in not compromising their faith by permitting worldly interference. The highlighting of window openings with darker stone was later echoed in the late Victorian church architecture of Beckwith congregations. Credit, Bruce Elliott.

Glengarry, the next group settlements from the same Perthshire vicinity were located yet further away from Glengarry. Eighty-four men, women and children were settled in McNab Township on the Ottawa by the exploitative Chief of McNab in 1825 and their numbers were supplemented by the arrival of another group in 1830. The McNab settlers quickly discovered, contrary to the chief's promise to furnish them with a year's provisions, that he could not supply them with even the necessaries of life. Instead, they would have to leave off clearing their land and go work out for provisions with settlers in other townships. Many of the McNab immigrants went to Beckwith and hired out to the settlers there, since it was the closest Gaelic-speaking settlement. In the process they helped to speed the development of the highland settlement in Beckwith and to build a communication between Beckwith and the upper Ottawa. From 1825 to 1827 the McNab settlers travelled the Madawaska, Ottawa and Mississippi rivers between Morphy's Falls (later Carleton Place) and inland McNab in crudely fashioned boats and canoes.[39]

The highlanders in Beckwith appear not to have been sentimental for the old life in Scotland. They had chosen to immigrate, as opposed to being forced out of Scotland, and some did not even give the appearance of missing their families in Perthshire. James McDiarmid on lot sixteen in the eighth concession was chided in 1820 by his brother back in Creag Ianaich, Perthshire, for not keeping in touch.[40]

Very Dear Brother,
We still feel it our imperative duty to write to you, and to solicit a letter from you; though you have denied us that favour, as yet, we feel thankful that we have the means of transmitting our thoughts to one another, from these distant climes. By these[,] Brother, you will know that we are all well at present; and greatly desiring to hear of your welfare, and situation in America. Brother, let not any thing in which we have failed of our duty, prevent you from writing to us. I sent a letter to J. Macdiarmid, by J. Macfarlane which he readily received[;] we got no word since from any of you[.] P. Campbell mentioned in one letter, to his cousin Boroyan, that John was once seeing them, but that you [all we]nt to see them, the distance being only 12 miles.

The plundering of the McNab settlers by their chief kept Beckwith inhabitants alive to the worst aspects of the old clan system as contrasted with the romantic image of traditional highland culture then enjoying currency in the transatlantic world. At the same time, the Beckwith highlanders revealed an innate conservatism which had only been strengthened by their passage being paid by government. This conservatism contrasted with the radicalism of the Scottish lowland immigrants in the northern townships of the Bathurst district, and especially those in neighbouring Ramsay Township. Most of the Scottish immigrants in Ramsay, Lanark, Dalhousie, Lavant, Darling and Pakenham townships were Lanarkshire and Renfrewshire weavers from the Glasgow vicinity who were thrown out of employment by the sluggish economy following the end of the Napoleonic wars. In their desperation these lowlander weavers engaged in radical activities and were further confirmed in their radical frame of thought by the repressive response of the British government.

The anti-administration mentality of these lowland weavers settled north of Beckwith is captured in an account by one of them detailing the heavy-handed measures taken against them by government.[41]

The spy system introduced by the tyrannical government sent many innocent parties to prison. Richmond, the principal of the spy department, had his emissaries among the people. These wretches deceitfully led men to give expression to their feelings against the government; the names were then forwarded to the officials, and imprisonment or transportation followed. Soldiers marched through the streets, while house to house examinations were made in search for "Radical pikes," and woe to the man in whose house an old rusty sword or bayonet was found. No one dared express an opinion in opposition to the Government, and all known to do so were imprisoned or hunted out of the country. Freedom of speech there was none.

A decade of radicalisation could not be readily forgotten. So accustomed had the lowland weavers become to both verbal and physical protest, that on one ship bringing them to Upper Canada in May 1821 there were numerous disputes among the passengers, and between the weavers and the ship's crew.[42]

The pattern of Scottish settlement in Beckwith consisted of a major concentration in the northeast quarter, a smaller settlement along the seventh line between concessions six and seven, and the remainder scattered among the Irish in the western half of the township. The inhabitants of the villages of Franktown and Morphy's Falls were mostly Irish and English. The Scottish highlanders concentrated their energies on agricultural development, and although most of them had further to travel to the King's storehouse at Franktown than the Irish majority in southern Beckwith, their more fertile soil soon compensated for this initial inconvenience.

In November 1823 Robert Ferguson wrote to his parents-in-law in Scotland, and in his letter revealed the positive view held by the highlanders of their new life in the forest. The opening lines

Plate 20
Loch Tay and Taymouth Castle ca. 1835, as engraved by Joseph Swan in Lakes of Scotland. *John Campbell, the agent selected to promote immigration from Scotland to the military settlement in Upper Canada, was already familiar with the tenants of the Earl of Breadalbane. Some 444 Perthshire highlanders left for Canada on three ships in 1818, taking advantage of the offer of transportation and grants made by government.*

indicated ongoing correspondence between Beckwith and Perthshire, a high birthrate, and an eagerness to learn the latest vital news.[43]

> [T]his comes to let you know that we are all in good health at preasant[,] thanks be to god for it[,] hopping these few lines will find you all the same[. W]e received your letter dated 19th May carried out by Helen McEwen and found great consolation to hear of all your welfare[.] Jean had a son and daughter born of the 29th of July[,] both doing well[. T]he daughter's name is Cathrine[,] the son's name is John[. T]he daughter is about 7 hours older than the son[,] so upon the whole you… will be ready to say whatever circumstances I am in I am increasing in family[. W]e heard you received my letter which I sent after Jannet's birth by a brother of John Ferguson who came out Last summer[;] he makes mention of James Dow's Death which Jean writ[.] Tis very sorry to hear[,] but who can prevent the orderings of providence[. W]e are very much surprised we did not receive a letter this summer[,] But out of sight is out of thoug[h]t[.]

Ferguson then proceeded to detail the abundance and prosperity of the Beckwith highland settlement, in an attempt to coax his parents-in-law to immigrate and settle near them.[44]

Jean has heer health very well at preasant and would find herself happy and comfortable if she had heer Father and Mother hear[,] as she knows you would be a great deal better hear than in Scotland[. Y]ou must allow me to know that knows the difference[:] a man has his own freehold property[,] no rent and but little taxes[.] I pay only 4 shillings a year of taxes. I can procure a handsome situation of 2 hundred acers of excellent land[,] well wattred and full of limestone on it about one half mile from the parish church and convenient to a mill for you and upon a very public highway that leads between t[w]o rivers[,] the [S]aint [L]aurence river and what is called the [G]rand [or Ottawa] river [—] two large rivers at an average four and five miles broad upon which their is a great trade car[r]ied on in the mercantile and Lumber business[.] I have seen about as much timber upon these rivers in one body as would cover 2 acers of land[.] I saw one body of it valued at two thousand pounds at Quebec[,] the place of landing it for the shipping; never think that we would ask you to come to America if we did not see that you would be a great deal Better hear[. I]f you will be convi[n]ced to come to America[,] your home is before you; you will not certainley form the idea we did that had no friends before us[,] but we found plenty of friends[,] we have a church of Scotland minister hear from Edinburgh…and their is plenty of S[c]hools all around us[,] all endowed with Governmint salarys[. I]f you take a thought of comming to America I will give you a sketch of what you should take…. [I]f you do not come the next sum[m]er, you will let John come to America as he is only losing his time[,] Let him be in any Situation whatever.

The eagerness of Robert and Jean Ferguson to have members of their families join them in Beckwith underlines their established sense of place a scant five years after immigrating. Compared with the confined prospect they had faced in Scotland, which Robert Ferguson described as "losing his time," frontier life in Beckwith posed no particularly daunting challenges. Indeed, one observant traveller through British North America, John M'Gregor, remarked that because highlanders had been used to a spartan life in Scotland, they adapted more easily than anyone else to the Canadian forest, and kept their cultural distinctiveness as a community much longer.[45]

Few people find themselves sooner at their ease than the Highland Scotch; no class can encounter difficulties or suffer privations with more hardihood, or endure fatigue with less repining. They acquire what they consider an independence in a few years; but they remain, in too many instances, contented with their condition, where they find themselves possessed of more ample means than they possessed in their native country…. I have observed, that whenever the Highlanders inhabit a distinct settlement, their habits, their systems of husbandry, their disregard for comfort in their houses, their ancient hospitable customs, and their language undergo no sensible change.

In Beckwith the transplanting and maintenance of highland culture centred on Presbyterian religious observance. Unlike most other pioneer settlements in eastern Upper Canada, Beckwith was remarkable for the religious observance of its early inhabitants. This piety may be explained in part by the fact that the Beckwith highlanders had in their midst one of the most powerful symbols of Scottish Christianity. Among the immigrants from Breadalbane to Beckwith was Archibald Dewar into whose custody the most precious of the relics of St. Fillan, the crozier, had descended from his forefathers. Compact in size, standing only nine inches high, and protected in a sumptuous case of silver, the crozier or quigrich was small enough to be brought to Canada. In spite of the Reformation and the opposition of the Reformed Church to the veneration of relics, the people of Breadalbane continued to believe in the virtues and curing powers of the quigrich. Before the eighteenth century an allowance of meal had been given from every piece of land in Glendochart in payment to the Dewar who had custody of the crozier, but after this had ceased still people came for water in which

Plate 21
Village of St. Fillan's, Perthshire, ca. 1844, as reputedly photographed by William Henry Fox-Talbot. The thatched roofs in the foreground were rare survivals amid the row of slate-roofed houses in this village. The local schoolmaster remarked in 1823 that if more highland proprietors developed villages in the way that St. Fillan's had been "the rage for emigration to the wilds of America...would...be done away". The building of log houses for a generation in Beckwith would remove all vestiges of traditional vernacular highland architecture. Photograph provided courtesy of Jim Mitchell and the late David B. McNaughton.

the holy quigrich had been dipped, and with which they hoped to cure sick friends and ailing cattle.[46] In Beckwith too, highlanders who knew of its healing virtues in Scotland came occasionally to the home of Archibald Dewar on the west half of lot 25 in the ninth concession to obtain water in which the crozier had been dipped to heal sick cattle.[47]

Although no clergyman regularly ministered to Beckwith before 1822, the Scottish highlanders attempted to preserve a rudimentary form of public worship. One settler recalled many years later:[48]

> Among the settlers were some pious men and women from the parish of Comrie, and meetings were got up for worship on the Sabbath, men taking turns in reading the Word and prayer. One Sabbath a couple of strangers made their appearance at the meeting, one middle-aged, the other a rather good looking young man. A hint was given that the elder of the two was a preacher. He was invited to engage in worship, but declined until all was over, when he took the Bible and read the third chapter of Paul's Epistle to the Galatians, in Gaelic, with strong Breadalbane twang, "O, a Ghalatianaich amaideach, co a chuir druidheachd oirbh?" "O foolish Galatians, who hath bewitched you?" on which he laid strong emphasis. It turned out that he was a Baptist

42 SCOTTISH BECKWITH

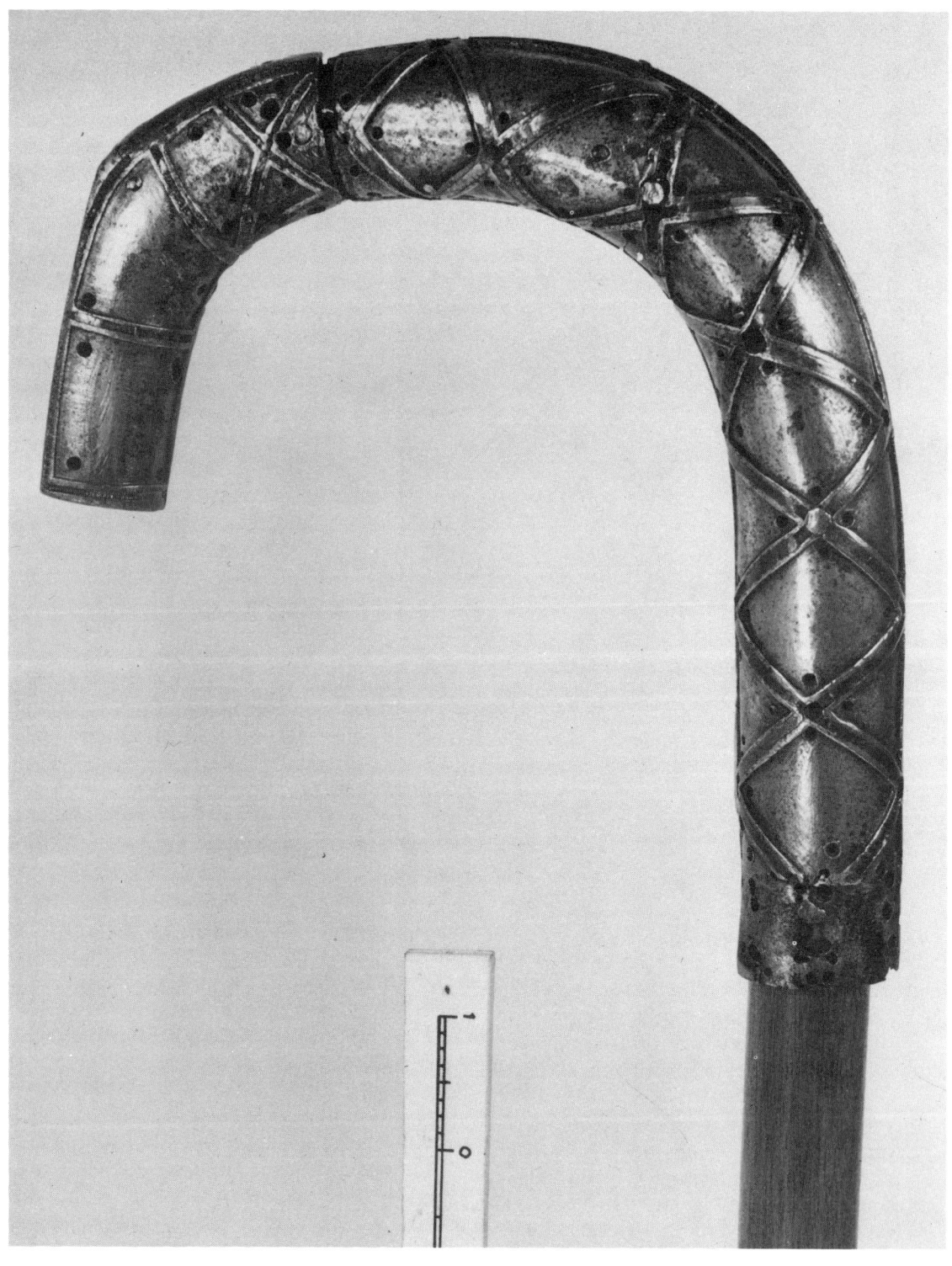

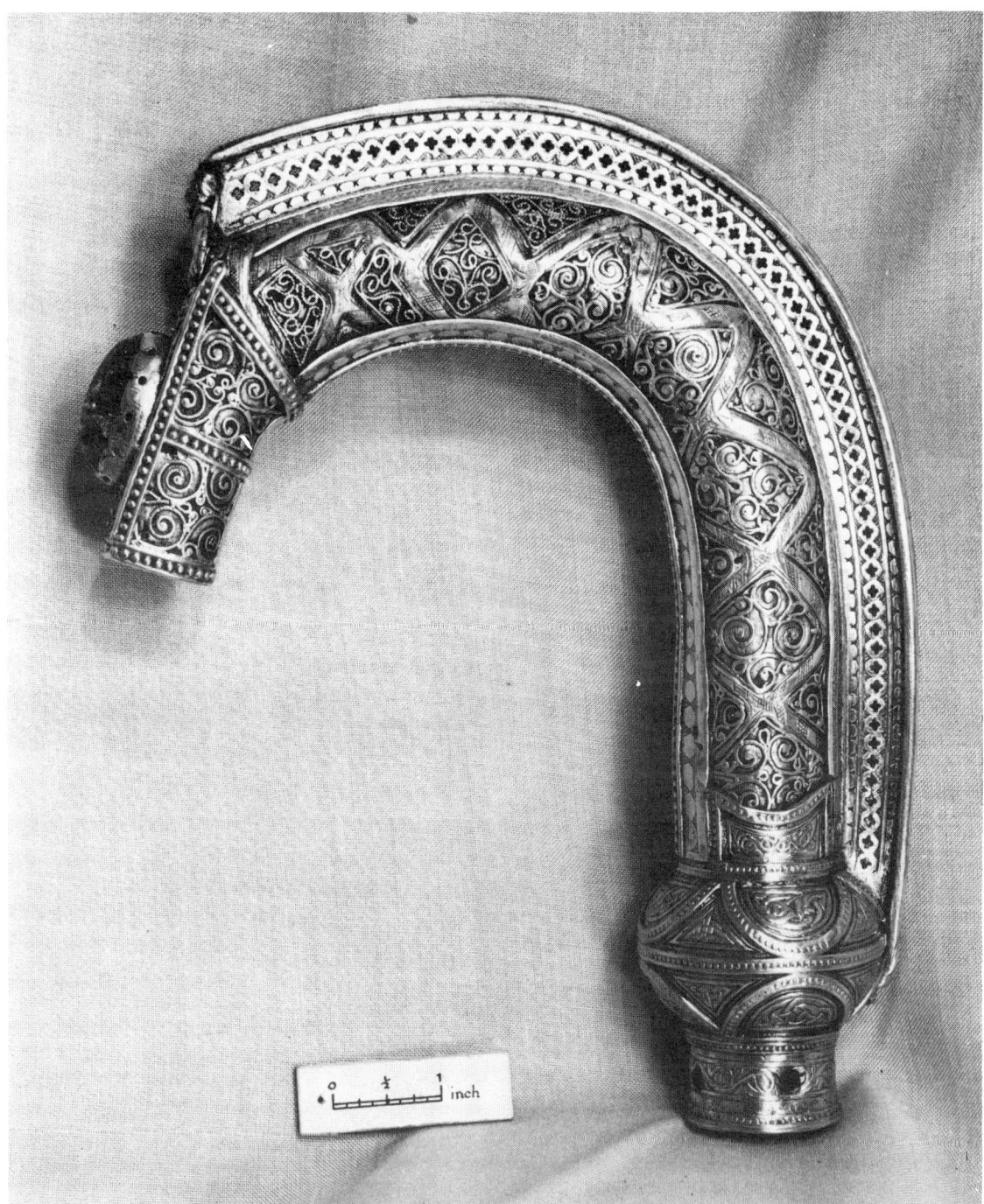

Plate 22
St. Fillan's crozier and silver outer case. This mediaeval relic was brought by Archibald Dewar from the Strathearn vicinity of Perthshire to Beckwith in 1818. It remained in Beckwith until the 1840s, when the Dewar family moved west to Plympton Township in Lambton County. This crozier or staff of St. Fillan is also called a quigrich, based on the Gaelic word Coigreach, which means stranger or foreigner, alluding to the relic being carried to distant places in Scotland for the recovery of stolen property. Courtesy of National Museums of Scotland, Edinburgh.

preacher from Glengarry, who having found out that a handsome young woman had arrived in Beckwith, had accompanied the young man to aid him in his efforts to get himself a wife. The next day they got Kate Maclaren persuaded to accompany them and become Mrs. John Fisher.

A few Beckwith settlers responded to the evangelising efforts of resident Baptist elder and weaver Duncan McNabb. The Beckwith Baptist congregation was founded in 1825 at McNabb's home with a membership of seven.[49]

The majority of the Beckwith Scottish settlers overwhelmingly were Church of Scotland in religious adherence. In late March 1819 a deputation of them called on the Reverend William Bell, the Presbyterian clergyman at Perth, and "inquired how they could get a minister".[50] Bell made preliminary inquiries, and beginning in April 1819 he occasionally preached in Beckwith.[51] In a letter to the Reverend James Peddie of Edinburgh, dated 28 June 1820, Bell enclosed a petition from the Beckwith highlanders for a Presbyterian clergyman.[52]

> I have preached and baptised children, at different times, in Beckwith [wrote Bell], and am of the opinion that a minister, who can preach in Gaelic, will be very comfortable. A fine gentleman however will not suit the people there. A plain, pious and diligent minister, is the one they want. Every minister coming to this country, must have a missionary spirit, or he will feel disappointed. Let him not therefore expect great things in the way of temporal support, for all here are making improvements on their land, and are consequently poor.

Bell had warned the Beckwith highlanders that even if the minister sent them was partly paid by the Crown, they would also voluntarily have to help support him. To this, he reported, "they readily agreed, and a bond I sent to them has been returned, with 54 names subscribed to it, each for two bushels of wheat yearly. This bond I shall deliver to the minister, on his arrival here".[53] From the early services held in a Mrs. Ferguson's shanty and in Hugh Spratt's kitchen in 1819, with no clergyman at Beckwith by 1821, the Reverend Bell in late February 1822 organised a congregation in a room over the barroom of Thomas Wickham's tavern at Franktown, agreeing to administer the sacrament and preach six times a year until a resident clergyman arrived. Finally, in mid August 1822 the Reverend George Buchanan arrived in Beckwith, sixty years old, with a large family, and able to preach in both English and Gaelic.

The importance of Buchanan being bilingual was evident in the affirmative response which he met when he first preached at Beckwith and in Perth. If we can believe the recollection of Buchanan's daughter, his first Gaelic service in Beckwith had an electric effect on the older members of the congregation: "Aged men and women shed tears of joy to hear the gospel once more in the language of their native glen — the language some Highlanders firmly believed 'the devils don't understand and the angels praise God in'."[54] After word went around Perth, ostensibly about Buchanan's ability to preach in Gaelic, his second service in Bell's large church attracted more people "than the church could contain. Some went away but others stood round the door."[55] Barely had Buchanan entered Beckwith before his parishioners, in the name of the "numerous Presbyterian Congregation of the Church of Scotland in the Township of Beckwith" petitioned governor general Lord Dalhousie to grant them "one of the vacant Lots of land in a centrical place of the Township for a Glebe to our Minister and to build a Manse and Church thereon."[56] The Beckwith Highlanders clearly had not yet discovered that the Rev. George buchanan was a Secessionist. It was enough for them in 1822 that he could preach in Gaelic as well as in English, and that he was available to minister to them on a regular basis.

A continuing trickle of relatives followed the 1818 immigrants to Beckwith throughout the 1820s and beyond. The correspondence back and forth between Perthshire and Beckwith prompted a flow

Plate 23
Kenmore estate village and the entrance gate to Taymouth Castle, as photographed in 1985. This village was created by the third Earl of Breadalbane in the 1760s as a picturesque estate village. The cottages built along the north and south sides of the square between the castle gate and village church were rented free by the earl in order to have tradesmen and artisans close at hand to the castle. The English appearance of the village suggests how readily traditional highland society was crumbling. Credit Bruce Elliott.

of information which enticed other family members and relatives to follow the members of the 1818 group settlement. James McDiarmid's brother wrote him from Creag Ianaich in June 1820, asking him to[57]

> write me directly on receipt, to inform us of your settlement there, and of our friends, and country people who emigrated to that country. Finlay Macpherson[,] Carnban[,] intends to emigrate this season, with whom, if he goes of[f] soon I [will] send this letter. I still retain the hope of a prosperous situation in America unless I be discouraged hereafter.

Peter Cram, his wife Janet Key, their five sons and two daughters immigrated from the parishes of Onzier and Strowan, adjacent to Comrie, in May 1820, and after "a tedious journey by sea and land, extending for over two months, they reached...Beckwith...where their eldest son John had settled two years before, and had prepared for them a primitive shanty in the woods."[58] With them the Cram family carried a certificate of character from the Secessionist clergyman at Comrie, the Reverent Samuel Gilfillan. It stated.[59]

> The Bearers of this Paper to America...have been in the communion of this Church for upwards

Plate 24
The Church of Scotland in Comrie, built 1804, as photographed in the early twentieth century. Comrie developed as a weaving town in Strathearn, immediately south of the Breadalbane lands. From this single parish came more than a third of the highland families that migrated to Beckwith. The large Church of Scotland with sittings for 1026 people was the visual focus of the village, with major funding to build the clock tower subscribed by Henry Dundas, Viscount Melville, Baron Dunira. The subscription by Dundas reflected the strong link between the established church and prominent landowners. Dundas as Secretary of State for War during the late Napoleonic era was profoundly admired in his native Perthshire, especially in a village that prospered from supplying cloth for uniforms, contributing to the counter-revolutionary mood of the immigrants leaving for Beckwith in 1818. Photograph courtesy of Elizabeth Alexander.

of twenty-five years[,] and their moral character has always entirely corresponded to their Christian character and Profession. They have been respected as neighbours, and have behaved in every respect as peaceable subjects. Peter Cram, himself, though chiefly employed as a Weaver, and some of his sons were brought up to this same employment, is not unacquainted with Agricultural affairs. He has occupied some land for many years—and his sons are willing to be employed in cultivating the soil.

The subscriber would therefore earnestly recommend this virtuous and industrious family to the notice of the Right Hon[our]able Government of Canada and trust that every encouragement will be given them in grants of Land and protection as shall correspond with the intentions of his Majesty in inviting settlers to go to that country.

Peter Cram and several of his sons selected locations in the eleventh concession of Beckwith. A late nineteenth century chronicle of the family stated, "The lots they selected were of good quality, and though heavily timbered, these sturdy Scotch pioneers did not feel the least dismayed, but soon succeeded in making a clearing in the forest, and establishing a comfortable home for themselves."[60]

Plate 25
The St. Fillan games, as engraved in the late Victorian period by W. Forrest from the drawing of D. McKenzie. As highland society crumbled from the mid eighteenth century onward, highland societies began to emerge from the 1780s on in a conscious attempt to retain some aspects of traditional culture. The St. Fillan's Highland Society Games began to be held in that village in 1819, and included piping, dancing and athletics. The 1826 games at St. Fillan's included playing highland reels on the bagpipe, dancing the ancient Scottish sword dance and highland reels, singing ancient Gaelic songs, throwing putting stones, and performing the highland broad sword exercise. Obtained courtesy of Bruce Elliott.

The ties that remained between Perthshire and Beckwith for a generation were simply based on persisting family connections. Despite the strong letter of recommendation the Crams had received from the Reverend Samuel Gilfillan, he did not appreciate losing substantial numbers of his flock to British North America. In an 1821 sermon Gilfillan observed that the Comrie "congregation has felt the vanity of the world equally with others... Forty-seven have left us during the last year to wander where they might find a place; some since leaving us have given their bones to moulder in the dust of America.[61] Despite such negative comments about emigrating, the flow of people out of the Comrie vicinity continued. In 1829 a petition from Comrie listed 79 persons from eighteen households who "in consequence of the pressure of the times...are inclined to emigrate,...all possessed of sufficient means to support themselves", and eighteen more persons from the St. Fillans area were listed about to take their passage, following seven people who had left for Canada the previous year.[62]

Plate 26
Loch Earn looking northwest ca. 1835, as engraved by Joseph Swan in Lakes of Scotland. *For over a generation before the 1818 migration to Beckwith, there was a movement of population down from farms on the higher slopes into villages in the valleys. James Robertson observed in 1813 that the soil along the Earn was in the highest state of cultivation and new villages were "rising in view and old ones extended." In place of mean hovels such as the one shown in the foreground "in which their fathers lived, without light and without air, in the midst of soot and smoke," by 1813 "many of the farmers now live in houses, substantially built with stone and lime, consisting of two floors and a covering of blue slate...tiles or straw, and few or none are built without glass windows."*

The persistence of correspondence between some Perthshire and Beckwith relatives even as late as the 1850s prompted a continuing trickle of migration to Upper Canada, such as "the Tenants of Craigelig, Keramore, Innerrich and Ard" who after losing the lease of their lands in 1845 "to others, some of them is preparing for America".63 In 1858 Allan McDiarmid of Glasgow wrote his uncle James McDiarmid in Beckwith to ascertain that his parents would adjust well to the Canadian climate, where he felt they would enjoy a happier life that as tenants at Creag Ianaich.64

> I have just returned from Craiganic a few days ago, after having spent a fortnight there, and it struck me very forcibly while there, how foolish it is for people to be wasting their time and labour in such a place, where they have nothing for what they do, and where they merely work for their Landlords. This made me speak to my friends about what they thought of leaving the place, and I found that all except my father and mother would be quite willing to go anywhere, where they could live more comfortable. I was telling them they ought to give up the place and start for America[.] After paying all his liabilities my father would have clear, quite sufficient to take them out and buy a piece of land there—and his and my mother's principal objection

to going, is simply that they would not like to leave their present home, because after all its disadvantages, they don't think they would ever like another place so well[.] This however is merely a notion of which they would very soon get rid.

The reports going back to Perthshire described a more prosperous life in Beckwith than that in the highlands. Allan McDiarmid continued:

From what I have read and heard of [Upper Canada] I have no doubt myself that farmers are in a condition there quite paradisiacal in comparison to what they are in the Highlands of Scotland, and the only thing that would make me hesitate in urging them to give up the place and go to Canada is my uncertainty, of how far the climate would agree with old people such as my father and mother—and I should feel obliged by your letting me know your opinion of this[.] At present in Slatich, they have no lease, merely getting their places from year to year—but it is expected that after next Whitsunday, there will be only two farmers in the place, and that these will get a lease of it—and I think that would be the best time for my father to give it up[.] I suppose there is plenty of land always to be got in Canada at moderate prices[.] I should not like uncleared land altogether however[;] a farm partly cleared, though higher in price would be preferable, and I suppose this can also be had at a reasonable figure[.] Would farther on [in] the country not be preferable to your part? I think in the direction of Georgian Bay is a better district[.]

It was only toward mid-century that Perthshire immigrants began to pass over Beckwith for more westerly settlement. The general reports that Perthshire relatives received from the Beckwith settlement during the late 1810s and early 1820s alluded to unprecedented prosperity. The most succinct contemporary assessment of Beckwith's Perthshire settlement within a few years of its founding was offered by the military superintendent at Richmond. In 1822 Captain George Thew Burke summed up the Beckwith highlanders as "a highly industrious and respectable people".[65] At that date he did not forecast impending ethnic violence in Beckwith.

Endnotes

1 R.F. Burns, ed., *The Life and Times of the Rev. Robert Burns, D.D.*(Toronto: James Campbell and Son, 1872), p. 294.
2 William A. Gillies, *In Famed Breadalbane: The Story of the Antiquities, Lands, and People of a Highland District* (Perth: The Munro Press, Ltd., 1938), pp. 187-188.
3 Ibid., pp. 189-193.
4 Sir John Sinclair, Bart., *The Statistical Account of Scotland, Drawn Up from the Communications of the Ministers of the Different Parishes* (Edinburgh: William Creech, 1794) VI:151.
5 Robert Forsyth, *The Beauties of Scotland: Containing a Clear and Full Account of the Agriculture, Commerce, Mines, and Manufactures of the Population, Cities, Towns, Villages, &c. of each County* (Edinburgh: Arch. Constable and Co. and John Brown, 1806) IV:252.
6 Gillies, *In Famed Breadalbane*, pp. 198-199.
7 Sinclair, *Statistical Account of Scotland* VII:182.
8 David B. McNaughton, *Comrie: Parish and Village in Upper Strathearn* (Comrie: Comrie Fortnight Association, 1981), p. 3.
9 Sinclair, *Statistical Account of Scotland* VII:182.
10 John Brown, *A Picture of Strathearn, in Perthshire; or, A Topographical Description of its Scenery, Antiquities, &c. Chiefly from Crieff to Lochearnhead* (Crieff: by the author, 1823), p. 62.
11 T.C. Smout, "The Landowner and the Planned Village in Scotland, 1730-1830" in N.T. Phillipson and Rosalind Mitchison, eds., *Scotland in the Age of Improvement: Essays in Scottish History in the Eighteenth Century* (Edinburgh: Edinburgh University Press, 1970), p. 75.
12 Sinclair, *Statistical Account of Scotland* VII:182-183.
13 Forsyth, *Beauties of Scotland* IV:252.
14 Hugh Trevor-Roper, "The Invention of Tradition: The Highland Tradition in Scotland" in Eric Hobsbawm and Terence Ranger, eds., *The Invention of Tradition* Past and Present Publications (Cambridge:

Cambridge University Press, 1983), pp. 24-25.
15 Ibid., pp. 21-23.
16 David Webster, *Scottish Highland Games* (Edinburgh: Reprographia, 1973), p. 11.
17 Samuel Carment, *Scenes and Legends of Comrie and Upper Strathearn* (Dundee: James P. Mathew and Co., 1882), pp. 49-50.
18 Gillies, *In Famed Breadalbane*, pp. 58-70. See also Donald K. Dewar, *St. Fillian's Relics: The Dewar Story* (Thorold, Ontario: by the author, 1981).
19 John Christie, *The Lairds and Lands of Loch Tayside* (Aberfeldy: Duncan Cameron & Son, 1892), p. 63.
20 John Marius Wilson, ed., *The Imperial Gazetteer of Scotland: or Dictionary of Scottish Topography Compiled from the most recent Authorities, and Forming a Complete Body of Scottish Geography, Physical, Statistical and Historical* (London: A. Fullarton & Co., n.d.) I:297.
21 Sinclair, *Statistical Account of Scotland* VI:153, XI:185.
22 Samuel Lewis, *A Topographical Dictionary of Scotland, Comprising the Several Counties, Islands, Cities, Burgh and Market Towns, Parishes, and Principal Villages, with Historical and Statistical Descriptions* (London: S. Lewis & Co., 1846) I:216.
23 William Gregg, *History of the Presbyterian Church in the Dominion of Canada* (Toronto: Presbyterian Printing and Publishing Company, 1885), pp. 38-39.
24 Thomas M'Crie, *The Story of the Scottish Church from the Reformation to the Disruption* (London: Blackie & Son, 1875), p. 469.
25 T.C. Smout, *A Century of the Scottish People, 1830-1950* (London: Collins, 1986), p. 184.
26 Carment, *Scenes and Legends of Comrie*, p. 16.
27 7 February 1986 letter from David B. McNaughton, Comrie, Scotland to Glenn Lockwood, Ottawa, Canada. I am grateful to the late David McNaughton for the many ways in which he provided assistance and information for this project.
28 Robert Ford, *The Harp of Perthshire: A Collection of Songs, Ballads, and Other Poetical Pieces Chiefly by Local Authors* (Paisley: Alexander Gardner, 1893), p. 464.
29 *Perth (Canada West) Bathurst Courier*, 28 March 1856, p. 2, cols. 6-7.
30 J.M. Bumsted, *The People's Clearance, 1770-1815* (Edinburgh: Edinburgh University Press, 1982; Winnipeg: The University of Manitoba Press, 1982).
31 Marianne McLean, "Ach an Rhigh: A Highland Response to the Assisted Emigration of 1815" in Donald H. Akenson, ed., *Canadian Papers in Rural History* V (Gananoque: Langdale Press, 1986).
32 Reminiscences of Bob Ferguson, 2 August 1910, noted in the back of the diary of William Livingston Kidd, 1908-1911. I am grateful to John and Leona Kidd for allowing me to read this diary and other family papers.
33 D., "Reminiscences of Sixty Years on the Ottawa" in *The Canada Presbyterian* (1879) p. 437. I am grateful to Bruce S. Elliott for bringing this article to my attention.
34 NAC MG 11, A15 40, enclosure in 15 March 1820 letter from Smith to Bathurst.
35 *York (Upper Canada) Gazette*, 17 June 1819, p., col..I am grateful to Howard M. Brown for providing a transcript of this letter.
36 D., "Sixty Years on the Ottawa," p. 437.
37 Jean S. McGill, *A Pioneer History of the County of Lanark* (Bewdley, Ontario: Clay Publishing Company, 1979), p. 33.
38 NAC RG 5, A1 Reel C-4601 Upper Canada Sundries, vol. 39, pp. 18369-18370.
39 Alexander Fraser [actually written by Dugald Campbell McNab], *The Last Laird of McNab* (Toronto: Imrie, Graham & Co., 1899; reprint ed.,: Renfrew: McNab Township Heritage and Museum Committee, 1982), pp. 19, 28-29, 48-49.
40 16 June 1820 letter from a brother in Creag Ianaich, Scotland, to James McDiarmid, Beckwith, provided courtesy Rosemary Wark, Beckwith.
41 Thaddeus W.H. Leavitt, *History of Leeds and Grenville* (Brockville: Recorder Press, 1879),pp.149-150.
42 Journal of Arthur Lang, published by Howard Morton Brown in *Lanark Legacy: Nineteenth Century Glimpses of an Ontario County* (Perth: Corporation of the County of Lanark, 1984), pp. 34, 36.
43 NAC MG 55/24 No. 199. 10 November 1823 letter from Robert Ferguson, Beckwith, to John Moir, near Kippen, West Stirling, Scotland.
44 Ibid.
45 John M'Gregor, *British America* (Edinburgh and London, 1832) II:449-450 cited in Jean R. Burnet, *Ethnic Groups in Upper Canada* Ontario Historical Society Research Publication no. 1 (Toronto: The Ontario Historical Society, 1972), p. 22.
46 Gillies, *In Famed Breadalbane*, pp. 65, 71.
47 Ibid., p. 73.
48 D., "Sixty Years on the Ottawa," p. 437.
49 Baptist Congregations of Canada Central Association, *Minutes of the Fiftieth Annual Meeting of the Canada Central Association of Regular Baptist Churches* (Ottawa: Canada Central Association of Regular Baptist Churches, 1879), p. 14.
50 Queen's University Archives (hereafter OKQAR) The Reverend William Bell, Perth, Journals I:77, entry for 24 March 1819.
51 Ibid., entries for 4 April 1819, 1 May 1819 and 16 January 1820.
52 Ibid., I:311, copy of letter from the Reverend William Bell, Perth, Upper Canada, to the Reverend Dr. Peddie, Edinburgh, 28 June 1820.
53 Ibid.
54 Jessie Buchanan Campbell and John J. McLaurin, *The Pioneer Pastor: Some Reminiscences of the Life and Labors of the Rev. Geo. Buchanan, M.D., First Presbyterian Minister of Beckwith, Lanark County, Upper Canada* (Franklin, Pennsylvania: John J. McLaurin,

1905), p. 20.
55 OKQAR, Reverend William Bell Journals II:142.
56 NAC RG 5, A1 Reel C-4609 Upper Canada Sundries, vol. 57, p. 29592. The petition is dated 19 August 1822.
57. 16 June 1890 letter from a brother in Creag Ianaich, Perthshire, Scotland, to James McDiarmid, Beckwith, provided courtesy Rosemary Wark, Beckwith.
58 George Maclean Rose, ed., *A Cyclopedia of Canadian Biography: Being Chiefly Men of the Time* Rose's National Biographical Series no. II (Toronto: Rose Publishing Company, 1888), pp. 117-118.
59 Copy of an 1820 certificate of character of Peter Cram and family, provided courtesy of Howard M. Brown, Ottawa.
60 Rose, *Cyclopedia of Canadian Biography*, pp. 117-118.
61 7 December 1913 letter from William Carey Cram, Raleigh, North Carolina, to his niece Gertrude H. Cram, Carleton Place, provided courtesy of Howard M. Brown, Ottawa.
62 NAC Colonial Office 384/22 Reel B-945. 1829, pp. 38, 60, provided courtesy of Bruce S. Elliott.
63 1 September 1845 letter from John McDiarmid, Osgoode, to his uncle James McDiarmid, Beckwith, provided courtesy of Rosemary Wark, Beckwith.
64 6 July 1858 letter from Allan McDiarmid, 28 Miller Street, Glasgow, Scotland, to his uncle James McDiarmid, Beckwith, provided courtesy Rosemary Wark, Beckwith.
65 NAC RG 5, A1 Reel C-4609 Upper Canada Sundries, vol. 57, p. 29704.

IRISH BECKWITH

The Irish immigrants in Beckwith formed no less identifiable and no less visible a community than the Scottish highlanders who arrived in 1818, although within eastern Upper Canadian society this was not how the Irish eventually came to be perceived. Like the immigrants from Perthshire they shared an origin largely in one county, Wexford in southeastern Ireland. If the Wexford immigrants in Beckwith did not all arrive together, they employed a process of chain migration similar to that used by the Perthshire immigrants, and a major block of them was planted in southeastern Beckwith in 1819. The Irish arrivals also shared with the Scottish highlanders in Beckwith a desire to settle close to one another, an innate conservatism, and an ardent attachment to their religion, but there all comparison between the two ethnic settlements in Beckwith ended.

The Wexford Irish settlement in Beckwith was one of the earliest plantations in an ongoing tide of immigration which would make the Irish an ethnic majority in eastern Upper Canada by the mid-nineteenth century. By contrast, the Beckwith highlanders were one of only a few concentrated Scottish highland settlements in Upper Canada. The Wexford Irish in Beckwith were predominantly Anglo-Irish in cultural origin, largely members of the United Church of England and Ireland with a generous sprinkling of Irish Roman Catholics and Methodists, English-speaking albeit with a distinct Irish accent, politically conservative, with a profound attachment to the British Crown, susceptible to joining illegal and paramilitary Orange lodges, and particularly emphatic in their opposition to republicanism or to revolutionary change either Napoleonic or Jacobin. Perhaps the most interesting aspect of the Irish settlement in early Beckwith was that it was less truly Irish in genetic ethnic descent, in its language, and in social and religious behaviour than the Scottish highlanders who became their neighbours—something which members of both groups would have adamantly denied.

Wexford and the adjacent portions of Wicklow, Kilkenny and Carlow in southeastern Ireland were the most unlikely counties to serve as a source of origin for immigration to British North America, at least within the traditional understanding of immigration proceeding from or among economically disadvantaged groups in society. Wexford as a source of immigration at the end of the Napoleonic wars is at first especially difficult to comprehend by an economic measure, when one considers that it was the Protestants as opposed to the Roman Catholic inhabitants who were most eager to leave the region in great numbers. Economically, why the more prosperous United Church of England and Ireland and Methodist inhabitants of Wexford and vicinity should choose to immigrate is all the more perplexing considering that they were in more prosperous circumstances than most other people elsewhere in the kingdom. When Arthur Young, a prominent English agricultural improver toured Ireland in 1776 he already was aware from the reputation that preceded them that the farmers of Wexford "were infinitely more industrious and better farmers than in any other part of Ireland."[1] The comparatively better agricultural economy of Wexford was evident in there being less subdivision of land there than in most other Irish counties.[2]

When Poor Law commissioners in the 1830s inquired around the countryside in various parts of Ireland as to whether the condition of the poor had improved since 1815, only in Wexford and Wicklow were the balance of responses affirmative.[3] The majority of holdings in Wexford in the

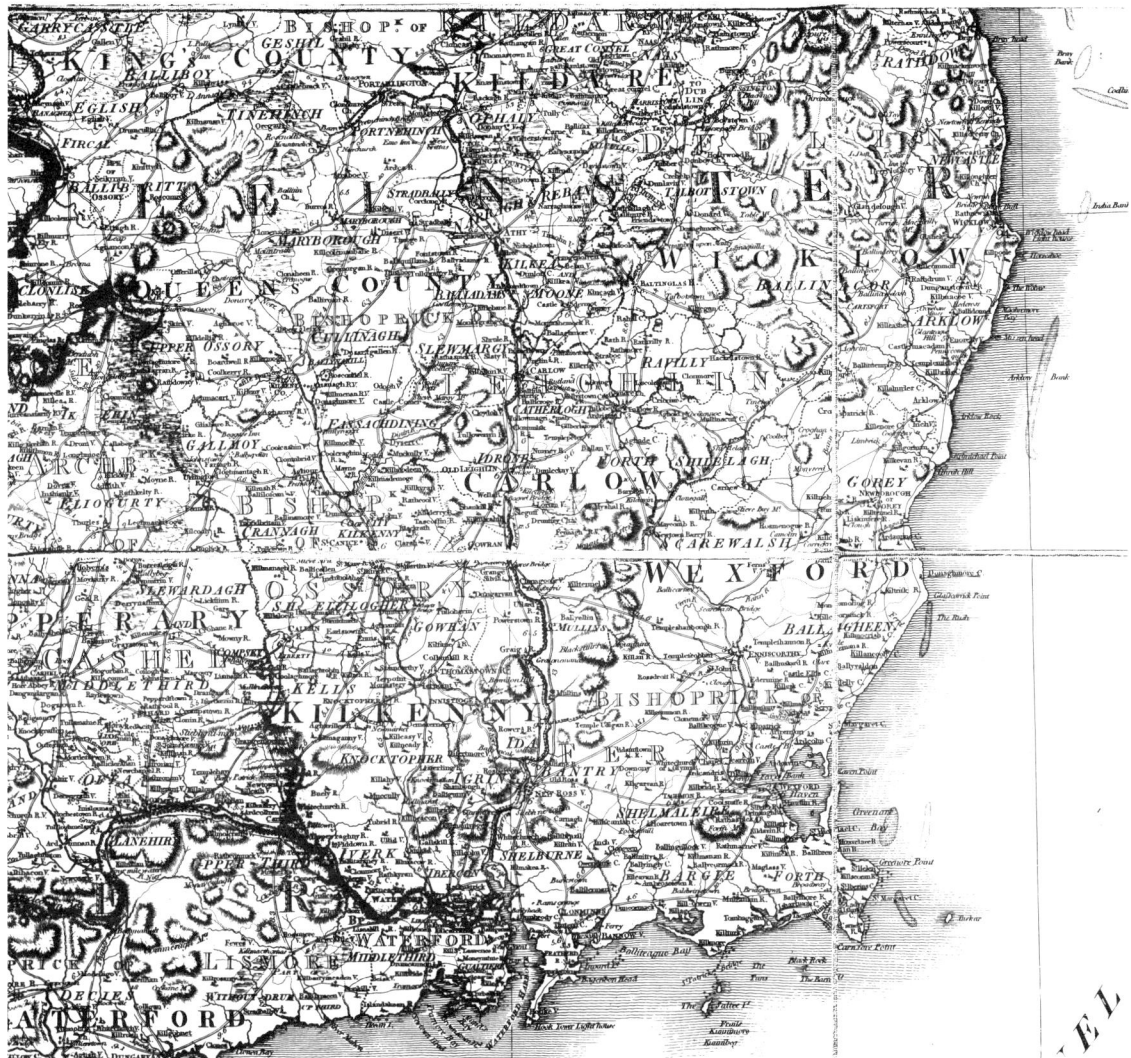

Plate 27
Southeastern counties detail of a map of Ireland, Civil and Ecclesiastical, prepared by the Reverend Daniel Augustus Beaufort, as published in 1833. The Irish Protestants who settled in Beckwith in the 1810s and 1820s were predominantly from Wexford, Wicklow and Carlow counties, with a particular concentration from Wexford. As descendants of English settlers in southeastern Ireland, they enjoyed a privileged position in eighteenth century Irish society as members of the established Church of Ireland and holders of government posts to the exclusion of the Roman Catholic majority and dissenting Protestants.

1840s were rated at a value over four pounds, a situation which existed nowhere else in Ireland save for the weaving areas of eastern Ulster and the more prosperous parts of the eastern Midlands. Landless labourers were almost non-existent.[4] Travel writers Samuel and Anna Hall just prior to the Irish Famine described Wexford inhabitants as enjoying a better standard of living than most of their compatriots:[5]

> The dwelling-houses and out-offices are far more convenient and comfortable than most Irish

houses. They are generally clay built, but dashed, or encrusted, without and within, with lime-mortar, neatly thatched, and have solid chimneys of masonry, not wicker-work plastered, so common and so dangerous elsewhere. Habituated to live dependent on their own resources, modern improvements were slower in gaining admittance among them than in other districts; and their customs being for ages superior to those of their neighbours, they were unwilling to hazard changes. Their industry is more uniform, not only throughout the day, but throughout the year—seldom breaking into fits of excessive action, and then as listlessly idling or resting.

The larger size of farms in the Wexford and Wicklow vicinity meant that the population in those counties was not as dependent on the potato for subsistence, and indeed more varied crops were grown.

The comparatively healthy economy of Wexford was partly due to its fertility, and due to most land capable of being made arable having been improved before 1800. Furthermore, few Wexford landlords were absentees, in distinct contrast with most of Ireland, which meant that there were no landlords' agents to antagonise or exploit peasants.[6] The improvement of most Wexford land and the lack of absentee landlords was largely due to Wexford and Wicklow possessing what Louis Cullen terms "the most successful Protestant settlements outside Ulster".[7] A large portion of northern Wexford, southern Carlow and the adjoining part of Wicklow had been planted with English settlers during the early Stuart monarchy. In emulation of the successful planting of loyal Scottish settlers in Ulster, the loyal English planted in northern Wexford were expected to provide a population loyal to English interests which would provide juries and other officers, elect the right sort of members of parliament, support the state church and introduce the English language, English methods of land-tenure, agriculture and so on to increase trade and industry, to populate the towns and to enlarge the King's revenues.[8] The battle of the Boyne in 1690 effectively ensured that the English-origin and Anglican ascendancy, socially, religiously and politically became securely established in Wexford as well as in the rest of Ireland for another century and a half.[9]

Despite the English-origin Anglicans of the Wexford vicinity enjoying privileges and special links with the English government, and despite their comprising a successful Irish settlement, they remained a decided minority. In Wicklow County just twenty percent of the population was Protestant in 1831, in Wexford only thirteen percent, and in Carlow a mere nine percent of the population was Protestant. Out of the 400,000 inhabitants of these three southeastern Irish counties, only 60,000 were Protestants.[10] This meant that the Irish Anglicans of the Wexford vicinity became very sensitive about their behaviour as a privileged minority linked to government. They honed basic diplomatic skills to survive among an overwhelmingly Irish Catholic peasant majority. Presbyterians in Ulster, by contrast, as a significant part of a Protestant majority there had never been continuously obliged to be diplomatic in dealing with Irish Catholics, nor had they been obliged to adopt the demeanour of members of a state church. The English-origin Anglicans in southeastern Ireland for over two centuries knew full well that their privileged position in society flowed from maintaining actual and rhetorical loyalty to Britain while at the same time they behaved discreetly toward the overwhelmingly Irish majority whose land the British government had given the English settlers in the late seventeenth century.[11]

The privileged position of the Anglican minority over the Roman Catholic majority, no matter how discreetly they learned to comport themselves, made religion especially visible and made it important for political and social reasons. In 1776 when Arthur Young attended worship at a Church of Ireland parish in Wexford, he was "surprised to find a large congregation [since] this is not often the case in Ireland out[side] of a [Roman Catholic] mass-house."[12] Ever mindful of how small their numbers were, the Anglican elite in southeastern Ireland had special reason to be visibly faithful attenders of the established state church, since it was through the mutual buttressing of church and state they came to enjoy their favoured place in society. As well, their outnumbering by Irish Roman

Plate 28
Captain George Thew Burke (1776—1854), superintendent of the Richmond military depot from 1818 to 1822, as photographed in the early 1850s. The medals on the lapel of his coat are testimony to Burke's impressive military record during the War of 1812 that gained for him the plum post of superintendent of the Richmond settlement office. He was responsible for keeping Wexford Irish and Perthshire highlanders in separate blocks of settlement in eastern Beckwith. Burke came from a Catholic gentry family in Tipperary, Ireland, but was able to overcome the restrictions placed against a Catholic pursuing a military career, by nominally converting to the United Church of England and Ireland. By settling Irish Anglicans on the poorest land in western Beckwith, as contrasted with placing Scottish highlanders on fertile land, Burke retaliated against the unjust policy of the British government that favoured Anglicans over Roman Catholics. National Archives of Canada negative no. C-54471.

Catholics added a particular fervency to Anglican prayers to maintain the existing state of affairs.

The Roman Catholic majority, naturally enough, resented the restrictions and penalties that had been placed on them by the notorious Penal Code for more than two centuries. Not only were they legally forbidden openly practising their religion, but they also were prevented from holding public office, civil government commissions, and positions in the military. Catholics were given the right to vote in 1793, but the qualification of owning forty pounds worth of property effectively prevented the majority of Catholics from voting. Moreover, the system of land tenure was so rigged that if one son in a Catholic family should convert to the state church, he automatically inherited all family property by law.

Elaborate means were taken by the older landed Catholic families to prevent losing their ancestral lands to disgruntled, reckless and impious younger members of their families. A favoured method was to have the son in whose hands the family lands could be most safely entrusted nominally convert to the state church, the Church of Ireland, while the rest of the family remained Catholic. This ensured that the family lands would be safely passed down from one generation to the next, without risking them falling into dissolute hands. By the same process a son who nominally became a member of the Church of Ireland also became eligible to fill public office, and became particularly eligible to purchase a commission in the military. Captain George Thew Burke, the superintendent of the Richmond military depot east of Beckwith, for example, had been raised in an old Tipperary Catholic gentry family, and nominally converted to the Church of Ireland to become an army officer. Most of Burke's family remained Catholic, and he was interred in the Richmond Roman Catholic cemetery in 1854 albeit under the ministrations of an Anglican clergyman.[13]

These defensive strategies employed by Catholic families occasionally backfired, with nominal adherence to the state church in many instances leading eventually to assimilation. Defections by leading Catholic gentry to the state church, whether deliberate or forced, only served to inflame the Catholic majority. Despite ongoing attempts to gain basic legal recognition, political rights and freedom of worship for Catholics, and despite local Protestant gentry and officials either blinking an eye at local Catholic worship and even giving them quarter in which to worship, in Wexford as well as in the rest of Ireland the Catholic faith was not formally recognized nor legally tolerated before 1829. By the late eighteenth century the anti-Catholic provisions of the Penal Code were not rigorously enforced, but Roman Catholics knew yet all too well how unequal they were in the eyes of the law in contrast with members of the state church.

The French Revolution of 1789 with its language of liberty, equality and fraternity spurred Whig radicals, Presbyterian intellectuals and Roman Catholic leaders to demand anew a radical reform of political representation and to limit English influence on Ireland. They felt that the creation of a nominally separate Irish parliament in 1782 had failed to satisfactorily limit English influence. During the late 1770s Ireland had been kept secure from the American revolutionary contagion by the Irish Yeomanry Volunteers. The Volunteers in the main were composed of Protestants of property and wealth, primarily motivated to protect Ireland from the French, and interested in the initiation of specific reforms to bring about a more efficient, just and egalitarian distribution of power among Irish Protestants.[14] Ireland by the early 1790s was a complex of militias, the Volunteers, protest organisations, Catholic committees, radical debating clubs and secret organisations. In 1793 the old Volunteers were disbanded by the Irish parliament, and in their place a government-controlled militia was created, a militia which permitted Roman Catholics to enlist at the lowest level. Though Catholics were now admitted to the militia, they were still not legally entitled to carry arms. Insecure Protestant working men, particularly in Ulster where Catholic and Protestant numbers were more closely balanced, launched raids into Catholic homes ostensibly to search for arms. Catholic secret societies cropped up in retaliation, and at Armagh in 1795 the Loyal Orange Order was founded and quickly became the largest and most effective Protestant secret society. Orangeism was an exclusively lower class and Anglican movement initially, though as the extent of its power and influence

Plate 29
Destruction of the Protestant church at Enniscorthy, County Wexford, May 1798, as drawn by George Cruickshank. Irish nationalist dissent was excited by the American and French revolutions, and the privileged place of Irish Anglicans became precarious in the late 1790s. Unlike the nationalist and political movement in the rest of Ireland, the rising in Wexford was more religious in tone, being led by a Catholic priest, Father John Murphy. With Methodist chapels as well as Irish Anglican churches destroyed by the Catholic peasant mob, the Methodists who migrated to Beckwith would remain politically conservative and closely aligned to their Irish Anglican neighbours. The Bettman Archive/BBC Hulton.

emerged Protestant landowners and men of substance joined to control and direct it.[15] Orangeism, it must be noted, was entirely a voluntary movement, and never received government support or overt encouragement.

Orange lodges flourished in Wexford in the late 1790s and beyond, offering as they did a form of assurance to local Anglicans in southeastern Ireland that despite the lax enforcement of the Penal laws and the growing clamour for Catholic emancipation, that their position in society would continue undisturbed. They were jolted by a rebellion led by Catholic priest Father John Murphy which broke out on 26 May 1798, and which was not fully quelled until the end of June. A country-wide rebellion instigated by the United Irishmen had been anticipated by the Irish administration, and government troops throughout Ireland indiscriminately flogged, burned, tortured, shot and hanged whomever they suspected of being complicit. In Wexford the disgraceful behaviour of the government troops was especially aggravated by the fact that they were largely Orange yeomen who treated the local outbreak as a religious war.[16] Despite being led by artisans and tradesmen who belonged to the United Irishmen, the rebellion in Wexford had a religious cast, being the rising of Catholic peasants many of who had as their principal aim "the avenging of years of interference and irritation by Protestant yeomen who served as government troops. Catholics slaughtered both innocent Protestants and yeoman troops", as they avenged themselves upon a local yeomanry, many of whom were their neighbours but upon whom they looked as immediate oppressors.[17] Fourteen hundred soldiers held off ten times that number of rebels in the most determined battle at New Ross only because the Catholics were for the most part mere pikemen, with some two thousand rebels left dead. With thousands of English militia on their way to the vicinity, the Wexford rebels made Vinegar Hill at Enniscorthy their headquarters, but this was stormed in late June by an army of thirteen thousand. Wexford town was recovered, and the rebellion in southeastern Ireland came to an end.[18]

Despite their loyalty to the Crown, despite their English roots, and despite their knowledge that the connection with England ensured their favoured place in society, the Anglican establishment and yeomanry in southeastern Ireland during the eighteenth century came to perceive themselves as more Irish than English. They resented Ireland being made a dumping ground for English politicians and divines, and kept under the legislative control of England. They grew contemptuous of all things English, and especially of English institutions that controlled and held back the development of the Protestants of Ireland. Moreover, Irish Anglicans recognised that the English looked upon them as Irish, that however loyal they remained to the Hanoverian seccession, their calls for greater autonomy for the Irish parliament only further strengthened the impression in England that the English-origin Anglicans in Ireland were a disloyal and turbulent people.[19] The Church of Ireland offered ready evidence of the evolving reluctant and tortured separate identity of Irish Anglicanism from the Church of England, with its strong evangelical emphasis and a reluctance to follow English ecclesiastical architecture in departure from the rationalist designs of Sir Christopher Wren's Restoration Churches. The evangelical emphasis of the Church of Ireland was a symptom of the growing and increasingly inescapable insecurity of an elite surrounded by the massive numerical superiority of the native Catholic Irish. At the same time they collected tithes from the native Irish majority to support the Church of Ireland, Irish Anglicans knew too well how deeply the Catholics resented this imposition; in contrast with religious indifference in late eighteenth century England they were only the more emphatic in their devotion to a church which in its link with the state ensured their otherwise precarious place in southeastern Ireland. Protestants in the Wexford region by the late 1810s found themselves in the psychologically frustrating position of simultaneously resenting English control of Ireland, recognising that the English link alone was the base for their own prosperity and the institutions that separated them from the Catholic and Gaelic-speaking majority.

The Wexford rebellion profoundly affected relations between members of the state church and Irish Methodists. In contrast with dissenters elsewhere in the British Isles, and particularly Presbyterians in Ulster who resented as heartily as Irish Catholics the privileges and the exclusivist claims of the Church of Ireland, Methodists in Wexford aligned themselves with the established church. Wesleyan Methodists in Britain at the turn of the nineteenth century looked upon Ireland as the centre of the world-wide conflict between heretical Catholicism and Biblical Protestantism. Irish Wesleyans were impeccably loyal to the "constituted authorities," and hence the rebellion in Wexford with its religious cast not only reinforced Irish Methodist opinion that Catholicism was disloyal and violent, but that if Ireland was to have peace then it must be converted to Protestantism. One Methodist preacher, George Taylor, published a history of the rebellion in 1800 in which he described his imprisonment by the rebels at Gorey and Wexford, and who emphasized "none of the rebels were so blood-thirsty as those who were most regular attendants at the popish ordinances..."[20] Another pamphlet, reproduced in the *Methodist Magazine* in 1799 vividly described the slaughter of Protestants in Wexford, detailing a rebel attack on a church at Gorey in which everything the Methodists held dear was brutally destroyed: the ten commandments over the communion table were broken

Plate 30
"The Massacre of Scullabogue". The burning of children in a barn at Scullabogue, County Wexford, by a peasant mob in 1798, as drawn by George Cruickshank for the St. Stephen's Review. *This particular atrocity of the rebellion in Wexford haunted the Protestant élite, and with the stagnating post-war economy there was growing interest in migrating to Upper Canada by 1817. Beckwith was one of the earliest concentrated Irish Protestant settlements to be found in Upper Canada. National Library of Ireland.*

in pieces, Bibles and prayer books were ripped up, and two Protestants were claimed to have been cruelly murdered. In the light of this reported carnage and because their numbers were weak in Ireland, Methodists in Wexford were committed to the religious and political support of the Church of Ireland as the best way of maintaining Protestantism.[21]

The Wexford Protestants who eventually immigrated to Beckwith found themselves in an increasingly untenable and tensing position. In addition to the Napoleonic threat, the memory of the violent uprising in 1798 only placed in deeper relief various problems that did not augur well for a continuing future in Ireland. Although there was not the same pressure on land in Wexford that could be found elsewhere in Ireland, the southeastern counties shared the same rapid growth in population which had been brought about by mass inoculation and vaccination in the late eighteenth century, and which had been enhanced by reliance on the potato as the nutritionally-balanced staff of life. The growth of population placed pressure on land, and added to violent confrontations. With the abolition of the Irish parliament in 1800, the merging of Ireland into a union with the British parliament, and with the Irish and English churches merged into the new United Church of England and Ireland, southeastern Irish Protestants began to sense that their world was in very real danger of crumbling around them. With Irish Protestants no longer in control of a nominally autonomous

Irish parliament, who could guarantee that the British parliament with its innumerable jostling interests might be prevailed upon to give Irish Roman Catholics civil and religious recognition? With the clamour for Catholic emancipation, should it ever be achieved, the outnumbered Protestants of southeastern Ireland in their paranoia believed that there was no future for them in Ireland.

The degree to which the violence of the Wexford rebellion haunted southeastern Irish Protestants can be shown by a couple of examples and by a sample of their rhetoric. Robert Davis, who settled near Franktown in Beckwith by 1820, had an uncle who fought "on the side of the crown" against the rebels at the battle of Vinegar Hill in Wexford. According to family legend, as he lay among the casualties on the field, he feigned death and allowed himself to be buried in a pit, by the victorious rebels, along with the dead bodies of many other soldiers. He eventually crawled out to safety, and his family in Beckwith commemorated his deliverance with the couplet:

> Shot and killed at Vinegar Hill,
> Dead, buried and alive still."

Several cousins of Robert Davis named Sutton and yet several other cousins named Hawkins, with relatives who immigrated to Beckwith were reputed to have been killed by the rebels on Wexford bridge in the massacre of 20 June 1798, and their bodies were thrown into the Slaney River.[22] Richard and Thomas Finley who settled on lots two and three in Beckwith's second concession handed down to their descendants a tragic account of their father, Thomas Finley, being "killed by 'The Green' during the Irish Rebellion and their home burned. The attackers shoved him back into the burning home to perish." Their mother "who was blind, made her escape to a pigpen only to die shortly after." Their brother Holland who went to England rather than accompany them to Upper Canada had narrowly escaped being killed by a Catholic mob at Scullabogue where a group of Protestant children had been herded into a barn and burned alive. According to family tradition, he was saved by a Catholic employee who stood up against the peasant mob, asserting "'If you kill Finley[,] you will have to kill me first'...[and] carried Holland to safety on his back."[23]

In the midst of a counter-revolutionary society, and with a downturn in the southeastern Irish economy at the end of the Napoleonic wars, the threat of continuing violence from a hostile majority made immigration an attractive alternative in 1817. The reactionary perception which Wexford Protestants had of themselves as reluctant and tragic Loyalists rooted out of Ireland was summed up in the following words by one of their clergymen a generation later:[24]

> [T]he Protestant farmers of Ireland were on every side, [e]specially in the eastern and southern counties, surrounded by the most bigoted and ignorant of the preponderating Romish population, who seized every opportunity of insulting, and injuring, and robbing them.... The rebellion of [17]98 was suppress[e]d, but still there was little peace or security for the Protest[a]nt farmers from their Romish neighbors, and in the first lull after the battle-storm, they left the shores of Ireland in numbers. They left their native soil, to look for some land in which they and their children might dwell without fear of the foe that was ever threatening the peace of their hearths and the purity of their faith....

The decision of Protestants in Wexford to immigrate in the late 1810s was influenced by a combination of economic, social, religious, political and demographic factors, but most of them were well enough off to consider immigration an affordable alternative to suffering the buffets of a decaying economy and a decaying society at home. Bruce Elliott has suggested that an earlier settlement of Wexford immigrants near Brockville in the Johnstown District of Upper Canada determined the destination of the postwar immigrants. In 1809 John and Nicholas Horton purchased land in Elizabethtown Township, and by 1815 there were at least ten families of Wexford and Carlow origin settled in Elizabethtown, Leeds and Lansdowne townships.[25] Following the war, there was a much greater movement of Wexford immigrants to Upper Canada, largely due to the efforts of two

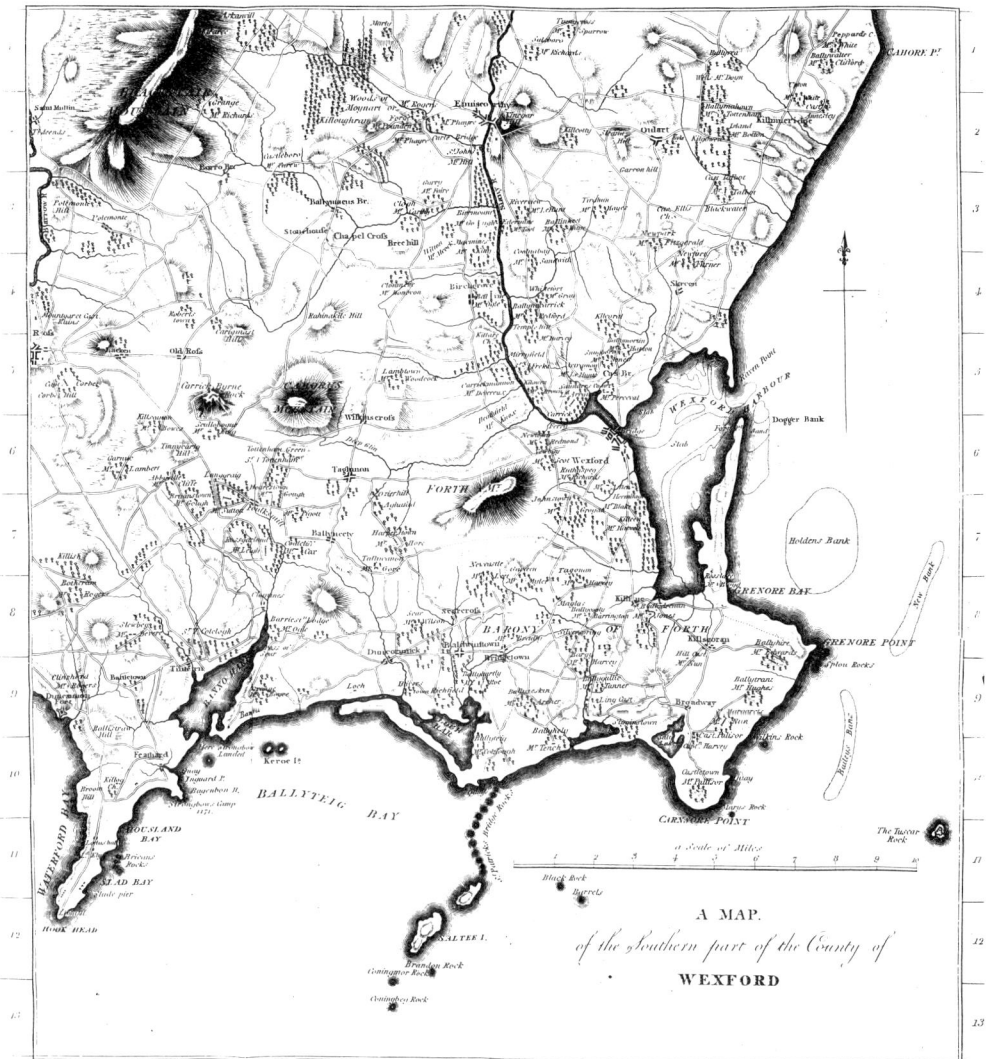

Plate 31
A Map of the Southern part of the County of Wexford, 1801. Many of the Irish Protestants who settled in Beckwith came from the vicinity of Ross and Old Ross shown on the upper left of this map. Scullabogue is just southeast of Old Ross. From Sir Richard Musgrave, Memoirs of the Different Rebellions in Ireland, *published in 1801, loaned courtesy of Bruce S. Elliott.*

brothers of Quaker merchant Samuel Elly Jr. who imported timber and staves from Quebec, and who commonly shipped out passengers to America in the returning timber vessels. Joseph Elly of New Ross, in Wexford, wrote the Colonial Office in 1815 seeking correct information to give people in his neighbourhood who applied to him for advice about newspaper articles telling of government-encouraged immigration to Upper Canada. By January 1817 his brother, Robert Elly, wrote that applications from the Wexford vicinity to go to Canada were "numerous beyond measure", that a great many neighbours had left for the United States which was "holding out baits" to get settlers from the region, and that most of the immigrants were "men of excellent character" whose loss to the British dominions was regrettable. Elly estimated that from 100 to 300 settlers who could not afford conveyance would go to Upper Canada, and who otherwise would have no choice but to immigrate to the United States since the passage there was less expensive.[26]

The Colonial Office in 1817 began to receive indications in letters from more distant towns that there was a more widespread interest in immigration to Upper Canada among the Protestants of southeastern Ireland than even the Ellys had recognised. A telling indication was provided by a September 1817 letter from the Reverend Mr. G.F. Vaughn, the curate of Enniscorthy, a town adjacent to Vinegar Hill, who wrote that both his clerk and sexton intended to immigrate the following spring. "To such an extent does *this spirit* prevail", Vaughn wrote, "that upwards of two thousand as I am informed are determined upon emigration from the Neighbourhood [of] Newtown[,] Barry & Carlow at the same time."[27] So besieged were Joseph and Robert Elly at New Ross by applicants wishing to go to Upper Canada, that they compiled a list in November 1817, and within one month their agents had collected the names of 710 Protestant heads of families and 281 Roman Catholic families, a total of 5,502 individuals including upwards of 1100 able-bodied Protestants capable of bearing arms. When Joseph Elly forwarded this list to the Colonial Office in December 1817, he explained that[28]

> The very great over population of this part of Ireland so severely felt last spring, and the extremely gratifying letters that have been rec[eive]d from the families who have settled in Upper Canada from these counties are the more immediate causes of the general and unprecedented desire to emigrate.

Elly observed that nowhere would the government find "a more loyal[,] brave[,] industrious and well regulated body of men" who in return for free passage to Canada "would gladly make [them]selves into a fencible Reg[imen]t to be called out to serve anywhere in the prov[ince]." Elly had with difficulty prevailed upon them not to dispose of their little property (insufficient to convey them to Canada) till 1 January 1818."[29]

The list compiled by the Elly brothers contained the names of the major block of Irish immigrants who settled in Beckwith Township (Appendix 4). Unlike the Perthshire settlers in Beckwith, and unlike the Tipperary Protestants in adjoining Goulbourn Township, these immigrants from Wexford and Carlow did not receive government assistance to immigrate. As early as 1816, 87 of the 199 Irish immigrants located on grants by the Perth settlement depot were from Wexford, and most of whom were settled in Drummond Township. In 1817 343 or more than seventy percent of the Irish immigrants located in the Johnstown District were from Wexford, and most of them were located by the Perth settlement office on reserves and vacant lots in townships near the families who had settled around Brockville before the war. Some 43 or a third of the 121 Irish immigrants who reached Perth in 1818 were from Wexford, and the 28 of these who had travelled on the *Henry* from Dublin were given grants in Beckwith. In 1819, 184 or sixty percent of the 307 Irish immigrants settled from Perth were from Wexford, and almost all of them were located in Beckwith, Drummond and Bathurst townships. Thirteen of the 37 Irish families settled from the Richmond military depot in 1818 were from the Wexford region, and nineteen of the 59 families that came to Richmond in 1819 were from Wexford. Captain Burke at Richmond settled a further sixteen Wexford families in 1820, fourteen in 1821, and 22 in 1822, most of whom he located in southeastern Beckwith and western Goulbourn.[30]

Relatives of the Wexford settlers in Beckwith continued to write the Colonial Office into the early 1820s, hoping to secure passages to join their kin in Canada, and when government assistance did not materialise, they immigrated all the same. William James petitioned in 1822 from Rosdelig in County Carlow for passage for himself, his wife and four children to join his parents and brother in Beckwith.[31] George Kidd of Knockabranar, Old Leighlin, County Carlow wrote the same year asking passages for himself, his wife and three children to join his parents and siblings who

Plate 32
An Irish immigrant at Long Island on the Rideau River ca. 1830 as sketched by James P. Cockburn. Construction of the Rideau military canal in the late 1820s attracted thousands of Irish Catholic labourers to the region. Although both the Perth and Richmond military settlements were inhabited by substantial numbers of Irish Roman Catholics, Beckwith had a singularly small Catholic population. The 477 largely Catholic Irish settlers settled north of Beckwith in 1823 by the Honourable Peter Robinson would also have worn the distinctive older style breeches that bind at the knee, stockings and porkpie hat shown here. The crude log shelter shown in the background was similar to those built by Beckwith Scottish highlanders in the earliest years of settlement. Royal Ontario Museum accession no. 924.48.11.

immigrated to Beckwith in 1821.[32] William Leech of Clinjordan, parish of Templeshanbo, near Enniscorthy, County Wexford, wrote that his three sons and two daughters and their families were in Upper Canada and solicited passages for the rest of the family.[33] Samuel Sutton of the same place wrote mentioning his "many relatives in Canada" and stated that he had received a letter from his brother-in-law, Robert Davis, encouraging him to immigrate.[34] George Wilson of Bilboa, County Carlow, wished to join his stepfather, William Kerfoot, his four brothers and his mother in Beckwith.[35]

The Wexford and Carlow immigrants were perceived by the Colonial Office and by the military authorities at Perth and Richmond to be an ideal ultra-loyal population needed to fill up the phalanx of military townships north of the Rideau River. Joseph Elly in November 1818 summarised the qualities that made these southeastern Irish immigrants suitable inhabitants for a military township:[36]

> The Protestant families of which this list is composed are remarkably sober, industrious, and well educated, can procure the most satisfactory recommendations and have generally [in] some of their branches members of yeomanry corps. Many of these families possess considerably more property than sufficient to remove them and [are] all fixed in their determination of joining their relatives and families who have so happily settled in Upper Canada upon land granted by the British Government within the last two years. Many other Protestant families of most respectable character tho[ugh] unable to bear the expenses of removal, are unsettling themselves under the idea of being assisted with a free passage to British America... Most of the men of these families capable of bearing arms in the Rebellion of 1798 were actually employed in the defence of their country.

Although the military superintendents at Perth, Richmond and Lanark were responsible in large part for the concentration of Wexford and Carlow immigrants in Beckwith and other townships in Leeds, Grenville, Lanark and Carleton counties, some southeastern Irish immigrants as early as 1816 were naturally attracted to the military settlements. Patrick K. Nowlan, the tavernkeeper and keeper of the King's storehouse at Franktown, on arriving at Montreal in September 1816 hoped "to procure a house and small farm near Brockville" but being "now on the point of commencing an industrious farmer's life" petitioned the lieutenant-governor to be located "near the late disbanded soldiers" since "in the event of another contest during my life some advantage may arise from my exertions in organizing them for service." Nowlan ambitiously asked to be granted "a commission in the Militia of this District" and stated that he "should feel happy in fulfilling the duties of Justice of the Peace—nothing shall be left undone on my part to induce my neighbours to industry, conciliation and true allegiance and esteem towards His Excellency's Government."[37] Settlers such as John D. Leslie were drawn to the Wexford settlement in Beckwith in 1821, when virtually all the available land in the township had been granted. Although he had neglected to make a formal application for a grant, Leslie with his family had confidently "proceeded to Richmond Settlement with the expectation of Receiving A bounty of lands simelar to other Irish emegrants," and as a squatter on lot twenty of Beckwith's fourth concession in October 1822 he applied "for A title of such lands as are Given for the incouragement of emegrants Settling in Canada...."[38]

A pattern of chain migration similar to that of the Perthshire Scottish immigrants in Beckwith attracted immigrants from Wexford in the early 1820s and in the decades beyond. John Garland, for example, at age 49 immigrated with his wife and ten of his thirteen children from Coolcullen in Kilkenny to Beckwith in 1819. The children remaining in Ireland included Nicholas who had arranged to be married, Thomas who was serving as a baker's apprentice, and Margaret, a girl in her teens who preferred to remain with her brother Thomas. Margaret came to Beckwith two or three years later, accompanying the William Kerfoot family, and her brothers followed soon after.[39] For

Plate 33
Gravestones of Robert Davis and Peter McGregor, respectively located on lot 16, concession 4, Beckwith and in St. Fillan's cemetery, as photographed in 1988 and 1981. The open Bible design on the Davis stone reflected the Irish Anglican emphasis on scriptural authority as the basis of their faith. The Davis stone was carved by J.H. Fulford, near Merrickville, reflecting the orientation of southern Beckwith toward the Rideau waterway. The Perthshire highlanders of Beckwith, in distinct contrast with their Irish Anglican neighbours, placed particular emphasis on recording the county and parish from whence they migrated. The McGregor stone was carved by Josiah Davies of Perth.

some Irish immigrant families it was not so direct a course from Wexford to Beckwith, although a Wexford connection alone explains why they ultimately settled in Beckwith. James Coleman, for example, had been born in County Cavan in southern Ulster. He is reputed to have been head shoemaker in the town of Cavan, but during the Napoleonic wars joined the British Army, and claimed to have served at the battle of Waterloo, after which he was stationed with the army in Lincolnshire, England. Coleman received a grant of 160 acres of land near what later became Bytown, the family immigrated in 1820, but not finding frontier agriculture to his taste he sold his grant and moved his family to the hamlet of Morphy's Falls (later Carleton Place) on the Mississippi River where he set up a successful shoemaking shop on the main street. It might seem at first that the family of this immigrant accidentally happened upon a community where there was a need for the services of a good shoemaker, but it was surely no accident that the Colemans came to Morphy's Falls, since Coleman was married to Elizabeth McCullough, a native of Wexford. The word had spread through the Wexford family lines even to this migrating family that a concentrated Wexford settlement was located in Beckwith.[40] Similarly, English-born Roger Hawkins who had emigrated from Devonshire to Enniscorthy, likely at the prompting of his Wexford-born wife, Elizabeth Griffith, joined the migration to Beckwith.[41]

The overwhelming majority of the Irish immigrants in Beckwith were from southeastern Ireland, but there were exceptions. Patrick McAlinden, for example, was a Roman Catholic from County Down in Ulster, and located on lot seven in the first concession in 1822.[42] James McNeely immigrated from Carneal in County Antrim in 1820 with a family consisting of two sons, four daughters and the wife of his eldest son. James and Bryce McNeely were granted the southwest half of lot nineteen in the eleventh concession in 1822.[43] The elder McNeely son was married to Jane Moore from Raloo in eastern Antrim, but she apparently was not related to the family of William Moore that immigrated from County Armagh in 1819 and located on lots fourteen and fifteen of the eleventh concession.[44] When the family of Edmond Morphy came through the forest from Prescott to settle their grants of land on lots fourteen and fifteen in the twelfth concession of Beckwith (the site of Carleton Place) in the summer of 1819, local tradition maintains that they were given lodging in the log house of William Moore.[45] All told, the immigrants from northern Ireland were a small fraction of Irish Beckwith, but because of their location on fertile land on or adjacent to the site of Carleton Place, families from Ulster such as the Moores and McNeelys enjoyed prominence in early Beckwith.

Many of the Wexford and Carlow families in Beckwith were either related to one another or had been neighbours in Ireland, but some of them belonged to ethnic and religious minorities as well as other groups that felt especially vulnerable in southeastern Ireland. Edmond Morphy, his wife Barbara Miller, their six sons and two daughters who gave their name to Morphy's Falls, had two different reasons for leaving Ireland. As Methodists they were descended from German Palatine settlers who had come to southern Ireland after fleeing as Protestant refugees from devastation and religious persecution which ravaged the Palatinate during the Thirty Years War. Edmond Morphy was born in King's County, his wife in Queen's County,[46] and at Littleton in Tipperary he had acted as an agent for a landlord, collecting rent, a role which hardly endeared him to either Roman Catholic or Anglican tenants.[47] Although his family had been in southeastern Ireland for over a century, Edmond Morphy did not enjoy the same sense of stability that came from tilling the same land generation after generation which most of the Beckwith Irish had enjoyed in Ireland. Another exceptional family was that of David Moffatt, who with his wife Elizabeth and most of their children were native of Northumberland, England. He was a millwright who at age forty hastily moved his family to southeastern Ireland after he was accused of killing a deer on the lands of the Duke of Northumberland. The Moffatts resided only briefly in southeastern Ireland before immigrating to Beckwith.[48]

Save for the Irish located on fertile land at Morphy's Falls, a small settlement to the west of Prospect and the occasional farm on the sixth and ninth lines, the Irish in Beckwith were largely located on some of the poorer land to be found in the township. The major concentration of Irish immigrants was in the four southern concessions. Perhaps because of the location of so many Irish on poor land, it is hardly surprising that all of the villages to develop in Beckwith were predominantly populated by Irish artisans. Franktown was the earliest, closely followed by Morphy's Falls. The nucleus of Prospect developed around the log Methodist chapel built on the farm of Kilkenny immigrant William Kerfoot in 1824.[49] The Ashton vicinity was a more ethnically mixed community, but the Irish Anglicans and Methodists easily outnumbered Scottish Presbyterians there. Arriving as many of the Irish settlers did a year or more later than the Perthshire immigrants, they found themselves located on the remaining poorer grants of land. For many of them a decent livelihood in the vicinity could only come from pursuing a trade rather than from any hope of profitably cultivating the swamp and thinly covered limestone plain. Hence the proliferation of Irish tradesmen in early Beckwith with James Burrows and Patrick Nowlan as innkeepers, Owen Quinn as surveyor,

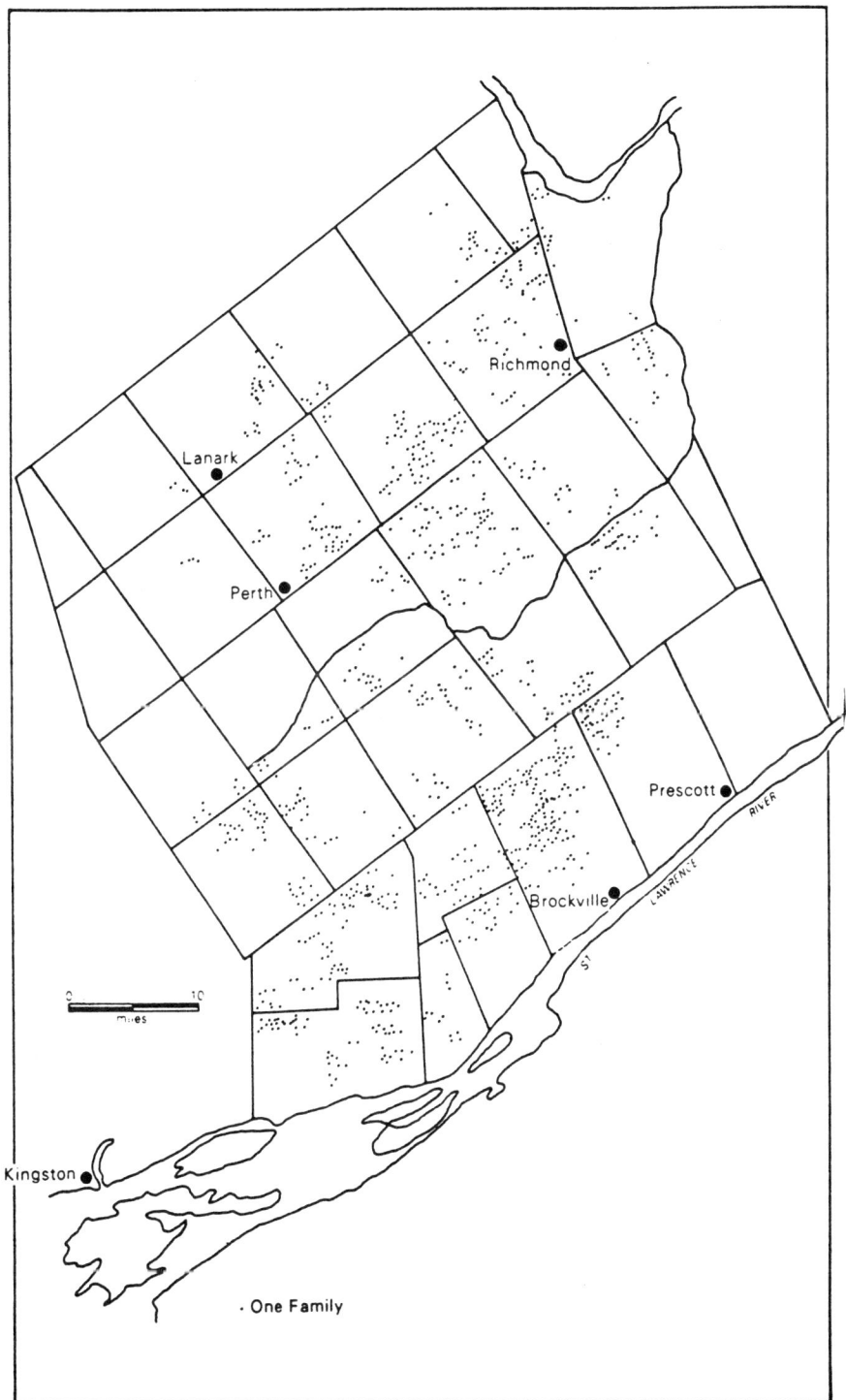

Plate 34
Map of families of Wexford area origin settled in eastern Upper Canada as of 1862—1863. Wexford immigrant settlement was concentrated in an axis between Kingston and Ottawa, with the concentration in southeastern Beckwith and northern Montague readily apparent. Adapted with permission from Bruce S. Elliott, "Emigration from South Leinster to Eastern Upper Canada" in Kevin Whelan, ed., Wexford: History and Society *(Dublin, 1987).*

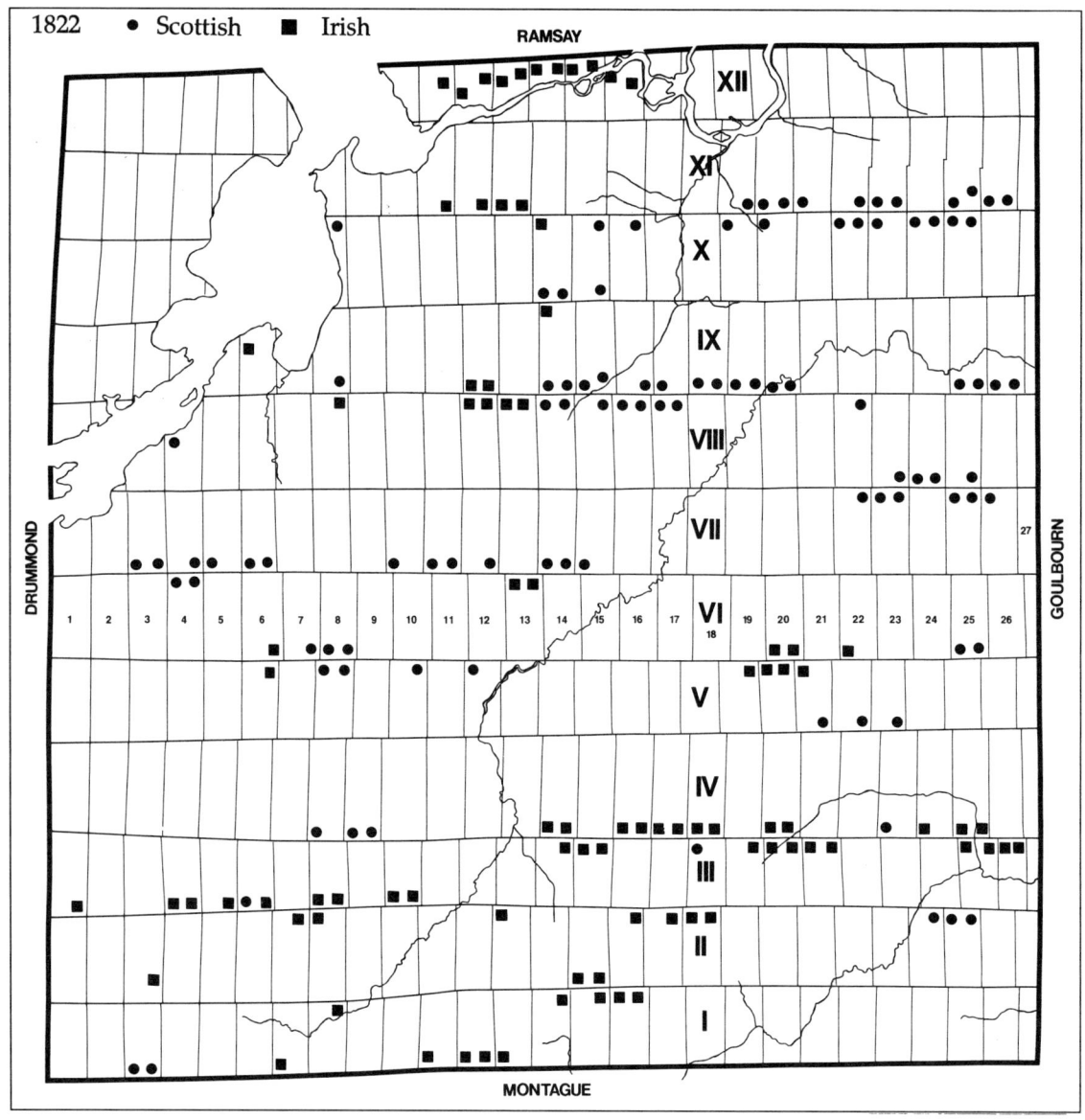

James Kent and William Poole as schoolmasters, William Kerfoot as stonemason, David Moffatt as millwright, George Nesbitt as physician, William Moore as blacksmith, and Robert Barnett as cooper.

The Irish in Beckwith, contrary to the biased report of some Scottish observers from a distance, became as adept at developing their grants as any other frontier farmers in Upper Canada. An 1825 petition from Edmond Morphy to the lieutenant-governor suggests how much one family had achieved within six years of arriving:[50]

> Your Excellency's petitioner is a native of Ireland[,] having immigrated into this county in eighteen hundred and nineteen with a large family (six of them being males, three of who being of age and married at that period) on the sole intention of becoming settlers and subjects under his Britannic Majesty. Consequently we made application to the land board in Richmond and

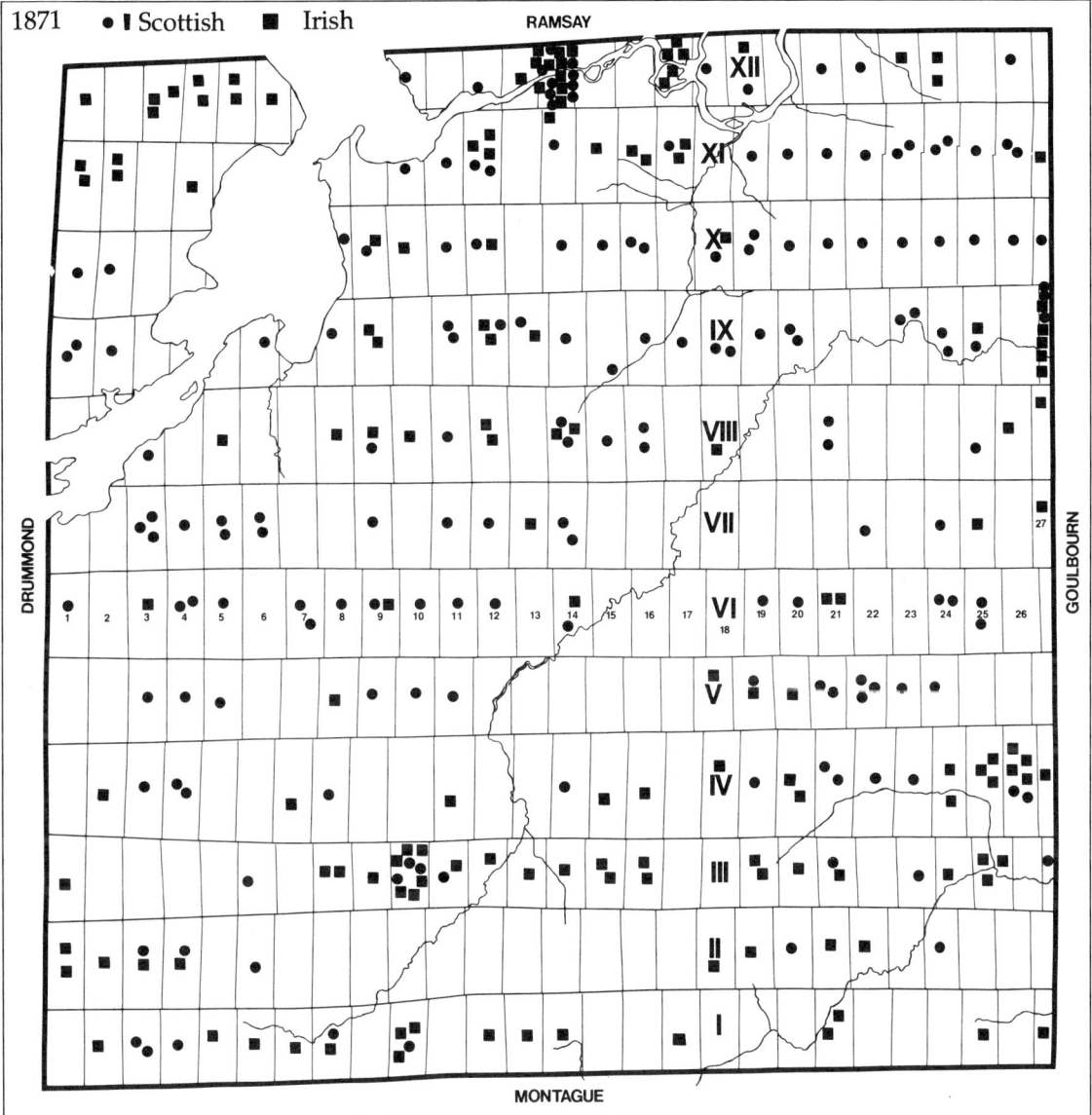

Plate 35
Maps of the pattern of Irish and Scottish settlement in Beckwith, based on the 1822 and 1871 census returns. Lots one to thirteen in all concessions were settled from Perth, while lots fourteen to 27 were settled from Richmond. Western Beckwith was a mixture of Irish and Scottish settlers, save for the concentration of highlanders along the seventh line in concessions six and seven. In eastern Beckwith, by contrast, the 1818 Perthshire highlanders were settled in a block on the fertile Mississippi floodplain in the six northern concessions, whereas Irish settlers were placed in a block on the swamp and thinly covered limestone plain of the six southern concessions.

received a grant of two double lots being lots No.14 and 15 in the 12th Conc[ession] of Beckwith but the deficiency in them being so great by means of a short survey that they scarcely consist of more than 240 acres; and having the most part of what good land is on that cleared, it is not near adequate to the support of our families...

    Your Excellency's petitioner being informed that government allows a grant of land to any person that erects the first mill in any new Township, I can get several respectable gentlemen (if requisite) to certify that I have caused to be erected on my premises the first mill in the aforesaid Township in case anything is allowed I hope your Excellency will grant it to me.

    What is striking in so many of the statements and petitions of the pioneer Irish in Beckwith was the confidence of their prose and their assumptions in expecting to enjoy a special relationship with the government. Edmond Morphy, for example, in requesting additional land in 1825 showed remarkable familiarity when he assured the lieutenant-governor that he did "not think it necessary to mention any compliment but will willing[ly] submit to your Excellency's generosity" and also took "the liberty of enclosing one of my sons' Orange certificate...hoping your Excellency will cause it to be returned".[51]

    The large size of early Irish families arriving in Beckwith was equally striking. The John Garland family with fifteen children, William Poole with "thirteen in family when embarking,"[52] Robert Moffatt and James McNeely with six children apiece, Edmund Morphy with eight children, and Roger Hawkins with nine in his family are not exceptional examples. The confidence of these early Irish settlers partly stemmed from the size of their families, surrounded as they were by people they knew and to whom they were related, and also from the close ties they had enjoyed with government in Ireland, ties that they expected to see continued in Upper Canada. In addition, many of them assumed that their arrival in the new land meant inevitable prosperity. The Rev. William Bell discovered that the Irish immigrants in the Beckwith vicinity "conceived themselves to be *Gentlemen* settlers not only entitled to, but actually living upon the bounty of Government and each now proceeding to take possession of a fine estate where he and his family would enjoy ease, affluence and independence for the remainder of their days."[53]

    The expectation of a comfortable future in Beckwith was partly due to the optimistic accounts the earlier immigrants settled on more fertile grants in other townships had written in letters back to Ireland encouraging kin and neighbours to immigrate. One immigrant:[54]

had left Ireland early in the spring of 1825 with his wife and an only daughter, expecting to settle in Canada, in peace and comfort. They had heard of others leaving their country, where they found nothing but hardships, and soon after finding themselves comfortably settled upon a farm in Upper Canada. These too had set out to push their fortunes, which like most people they concluded would be good. Their imaginations presented to them a beautiful picture, painted with the most brilliant colours.

But once familiar family faces disappeared, the heady confidence vanished. This particular family arrived at Quebec "in a sickly and uncomfortable condition" where the daughter soon died of consumption, and the grief-stricken parents proceeded on their way to the Beckwith region:

The wife, now deprived of the darling of her heart, struggled hard to bear up under an accumulated load of toil and grief, but it would not do. At the Rideau ferry she found herself worse, and unable to proceed. A few days more put a period to her sufferings on earth; for there she died, and was buried among strangers. The disconsolate head of the family being now stript of all that was dear to him, proceeded to one of the back townships where he obtained land, but what comfort could it afford him? He was now desolate, and a stranger in a vast wilderness, in which were a few unfeeling mortals, as unhappy as himself.

William Poole from Kilkenny "had thirteen in family when embarking for U[pper] C[anada in

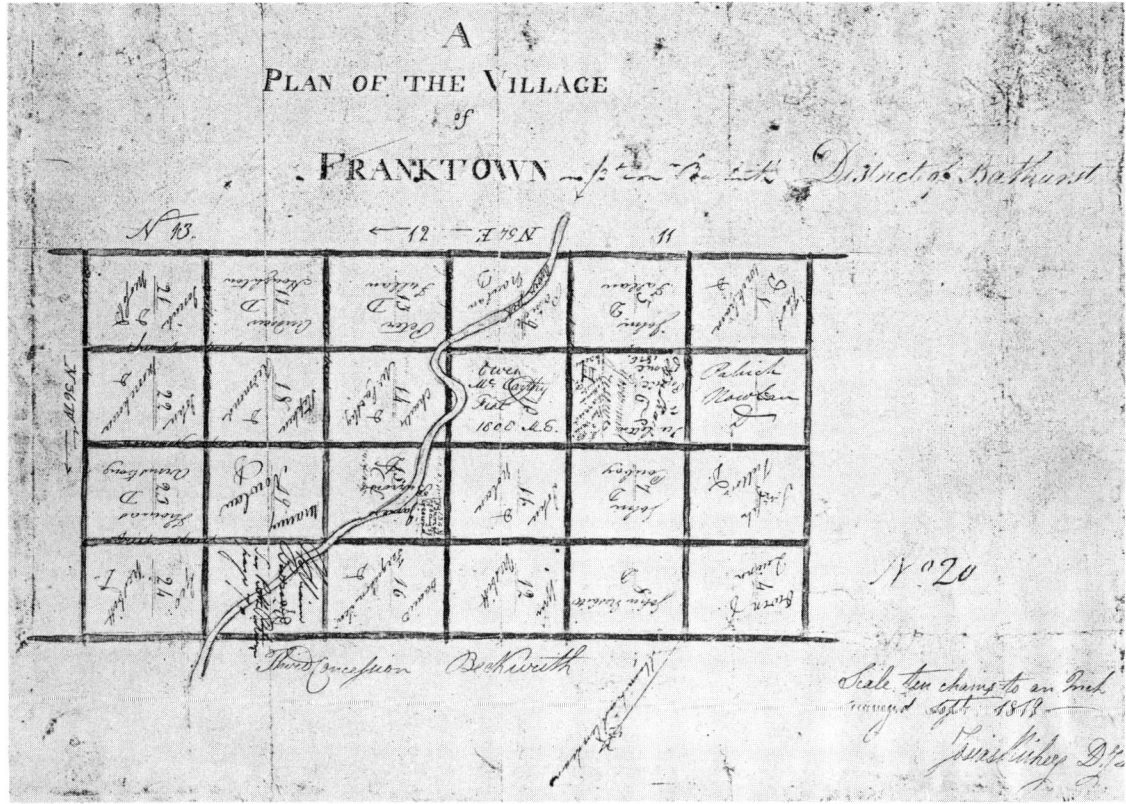

Plate 36
Plan of the village of Franktown surveyed in September 1819 by Josias Richey. Franktown failed to develop as a village before 1850, simply boasting an inn and tavern that catered to the stagecoaches clattering through between Perth and Bytown. A traveller observed of Franktown in the early 1840s that "there is no village at Franktown unless a mere scattering of three or four houses can boast the name." The royalist, loyalist, military and Irish emphasis of the population settled around Franktown is reflected in the street names. The east-west streets between the third and fourth concession lines from north to south were Irish Street, Barrack (sometimes called Barwick) Street, and Church Street. The north-south streets from west to east were named King Street, Maitland Street (after Lieutenant-Governor Sir Peregrine Maitland), Powell Street (after the Irish-born superintendent of the Perth military settlement), George Street, Francis Street (after Quartermaster General Francis Cockburn), Britain Street and Queen Street. Ontario Ministry of Natural Resources.

August 1831] but it pleased Providence to take two fine boys to himself while on Sea". Despite this loss, with five of the eight children who did make it to Beckwith being "orphans (Brother's children who were cast on me in 1821 when their Father and Mother died)...Providence", Poole optimistically "believe[d,] directed my Course to this part of U[pper] C[anada], where I expected to get land, but cannot."[55]

The Irish families combined with the Scottish highlanders to make Beckwith a predominantly Protestant settlement. The Irish from Wexford were largely members of the United Church of England and Ireland, but there were sufficient Irish Methodists to form classes at Prospect and at Carleton Place by 1824. The attitude of these Irish Anglicans and Methodists toward Irish Roman Catholics was aptly captured by Joseph Elly in his November 1817 description of 281 Catholic families in Wexford and Carlow who also wished to immigrate to Upper Canada:[56]

> The Roman Catholic Families which compose this list are generally respectable Farmers, have procured tolerable good recommendations for sobriety, industry, and good conduct, but as Farmers and work men they possess the want of order, neatness, and economy which generally designates the religious persuasion to which they belong. The Protestant immigrants look on their being accompanied by these families with a dissatisfied and jealous eye.

Beckwith Irish Anglicans and Methodists were equally as pious as their Scottish highland neighbours, and indeed lacking their own clergy attended worship services held by a Presbyterian clergyman, the Reverend George Buchanan, in 1822 and 1823.[57] In February 1823 the Reverend Michael Harris of Perth forwarded a petition to the lieutenant-governor from Beckwith Anglicans, requesting that the King's storehouse at Franktown, which no longer served as a distribution point for government provisions, be granted them to use "for a Church of the Established Religion of England."[58] Harris remarked:[59]

> I am in the habit of performing Divine Service there once a Month, & there is no place suitable for the purpose, therefore [I] am compelled to make use of the Tavern which...is not the most proper place. If his Excellency should grant their petition the people have pledged themselves not only to take care of it, but to finish it off for Divine Worship.

By April permission had been granted to use the storehouse as a house of worship.[60] Names of Methodists such as John Poole and William Kerfoot on this petition show the continuing Irish Methodist support of the United Church of England and Ireland, even in Upper Canada. The names of Presbyterians such as William McCuan on the petition is perhaps the earliest hint of impending dissatisfaction among Church of Scotland highlanders with the Secessionist ministry of the Rev. George Buchanan.

Robert Jeffers, who had been a local Methodist preacher in Ireland, may have visited the Irish Methodists in Beckwith from 1818 to 1820, as the most remote settlement on the Augusta Methodist Circuit.[61] In 1821 there was so warm a response to Methodist revival meetings in the back settlements of the Augusta circuit that a separate Rideau circuit consisting of Kitley, Wolford, Montague and Marlborough townships was created, but Beckwith was ministered to by James Griggs Peale stationed at Perth that year who was the first Methodist preacher to scour the woods of the military townships and to establish regular preaching places.[62] The first recorded mention of Methodist services in Beckwith was when American-born Ezra Healey from the Rideau Circuit on 6 September 1823 preached at Brother Kerfoot's and on 23 October preached at Brother Edmond Morphy's house at Morphy's Falls.[63] By 1824 Healey had the satisfaction of counting sixteen members in the Methodist class meeting at the home of George Kerfoot in Beckwith, while across the line in Goulbourn there were ten members in the John Poole society, and 22 in the Thomas Shillington class.[64] According to local tradition, a log chapel was built on a corner of the William Kerfoot farm (lot 25, concession 4) in 1824.[65]

There is not the least shred of evidence to suggest either ethnic or religious wrangling in Beckwith before 1824, numerically balanced as the township was between southeastern Irish Anglicans and Methodists on the one hand, and highland Scottish Presbyterians and Baptists on the other. The decision of early Irish Anglicans to worship with their Presbyterian neighbours in 1822 underlines the basic Protestant complexion of the entire population, and how compelling they found public worship as a constructive form of respite from the pioneer drudgery of clearing land. Whatever ethnic balance there may have been in Beckwith by 1824 did not reflect the overall pattern of settlement in the region. Bathurst and Drummond townships to the west were fairly balanced between Scottish and Irish settlers, the Lanark settlement to the north overwhelmingly lowland Scottish, while Goulbourn to the east was filled with Irish civilian and military settlers. Between

Plate 37
Entrance to Franktown public cemetery, as photographed in 1983. The placing of this burial ground at the centre of the 1819 plan of Franktown reflected an Irish emphasis on obeisance toward the dead in contrast with the neglected and disorderly burying grounds in the American settlements of Upper Canada. Local legend asserts that John Upton, an immigrant from County Carlow, Ireland, took a prominent part in laying out the Franktown burial ground, and upon completing the task, remarked, "Well, it is finished now. I wonder who will be the first in it?" Ironically, Upton himself is reputed to be the first person interred here, being killed by a tree falling on him in 1823.

these three ranges of townships filled with British immigrants and American settlements along the St. Lawrence there stretched two ranges of sixteen empty forested townships along the Rideau River. Before 1825 it is clear that in eastern Upper Canada American-origin settlers and British immigrants inhabited fairly well-defined regional settlements and were largely insulated from one another.

Whatever assumptions the Wexford immigrants settled in Beckwith may have had about Upper Canada being a haven for Irish Protestants as opposed to Irish Catholics, were shattered in 1823. Yet another experiment by the Colonial Office in government-assisted immigration brought 568 northern Cork immigrants to the Beckwith area that year. Colonial officials hoped to reduce violent disturbances in southern Ireland by settling the "excess population" in Upper Canada. Only ten of the Irish immigrants brought out by the Honourable Peter Robinson were Protestants. The majority were Roman Catholics who government believed to be easily susceptible to violence in a region and country where overpopulation and unemployment were perceived to be the two major barriers to domestic tranquility.[66] These Irish Catholics were settled on grants in Ramsay, Pakenham and in the northwestern corners of Huntley and Goulbourn townships. A few also could be found in Bathurst and Lanark Townships. Daniel Calaghan, Jeremiah Cronan, Denis Galvin, Timothy Mann and Patrick

Fitzgerald and their families from this migration were located on Beckwith lots (Appendix 11), but of these only Mann was still on his grant three years later. The families of David, Edmund and John Dooland moved to locations in Beckwith between 1823 and 1826, making a total of eighteen Irish Roman Catholics out of a population of more than a thousand in 1826.[67] All the same, the larger new Irish Catholic settlement immediately north of Beckwith caused Wexford and Carlow Protestant immigrants to question whether or not they had truly left behind them the ethnic and religious violence of Ireland.

Endnotes

1. Arthur Young, *A Tour in Ireland, 1776-1779*, ed. by A.W. Hutton and new intro. by J.B. Ruane (London: T. Cadell and J. Dodsley, 1780; reprint ed.: Shannon, Ireland: Irish University Press, 1970) I:86.
2. Bruce S. Elliott, "Emigration from South Leinster to Eastern Upper Canada" in Kevin Whelan and William Nolan, eds., *Wexford History and Society: Interdisciplinary Essays on the History of an Irish County* (Dublin: Geography Publications, 1988), p. 436.
3. Ibid.
4. S.H. Cousens, "The Regional Pattern of Emigration During the Great Irish Famine, 1846-51", *Transactions and Papers of the Institute of British Geographers* no. 28 (1960), p. 130, cited in ibid., p. 436, 549.
5. S.C. Hall and Anna Hall, *Ireland: Its Scenery, Character, &c.* 3 vols. (London: Hall, Virtue, and Co., n.d.) II:164.
6. Ibid. II:183-184.
7. Louis M. Cullen, *The Emergence of Modern Ireland* (New York, 1981), cited in Elliott, "Emigration from South Leinster,"p. 424.
8. Edmund Curtis, *A History of Ireland* (London: Methuen & Co. Ltd., 1968), pp. 232-233.
9. Ibid., pp. 270-271.
10. British Parliamentary Sessional Papers, H.C. (1835) XXXIII, First Report of the Commissioners of Public Instruction, Ireland, cited in Elliott, "Emigration from South Leinster," p. 424.
11. Glenn J Lockwood, "Eastern Upper Canadian Perceptions of Irish Immigrants, 1824-1868" (Ph.D. dissertation, University of Ottawa, 1988), p. 434.
12. Young, *A Tour of Ireland* I:90.
13. Bruce S. Elliott, *Irish Migrants in the Canadas: A New Approach* McGill-Queen's Studies in Ethnic History no. 1 (Montreal: McGill-Queen's University Press, 1988), p. 263.
14. Desmond McGuire, *History of Ireland* (London: Bison Books, 1987), pp. 86-87.
15. Ibid., p. 95.
16. Curtis, *History of Ireland*, p. 342.
17. McGuire, *History of Ireland*, p. 98.
18. Curtis, *History of Ireland*, pp. 342-343.
19. McGuire, *History of Ireland*, pp. 80-81
20. D.N. Hempton, "The Methodist Crusade in Ireland, 1795-1845" in *Irish Historical Studies* XX
21. Ibid.
22. James Beverley Craig, *The Craigs of Goulbourn and North Gower* (North Gower, by the author, 1929), p. 27. I am grateful to Bruce S. Elliott for this reference.
23. Mary Mackie, "Finley Family Tree" (unpublished manuscript), p. F-1. I am grateful to Bruce Elliott for bringing this to my notice.
24. Thomas Bedford-Jones, *A Sermon Preached in St. Thomas Church, Frankville, on the 12th of July, 1864* (Perth: by the author, 1864), pp. 3-4.
25. Elliott, "Emigration from South Leinster," pp. 424.
26. Ibid., p. 424–6.
27. Ibid., p. 426.
28. Ibid., p. 426–7, 439–45.
29. National Archives of Canada, Reel B-876, Colonial Office 384/1, ff. 170-171, 4 December 1817 letter of Joseph Elly, Ross. I am grateful to Bruce S. Elliott for this reference.
30. Elliott, "Emigration from South Leinster," pp. 430–34.
31. NAC Reel B-881, Colonial Office 384/8, f. 186, cited in Elliott, ibid., p. 435.
32. Ibid., f. 197.
33. Ibid., f. 204.
34. Ibid., Reel B-882, f, 367.
35. Ibid., f. 403.
36. NAC Reel B-876, Colonial Office 384/i, ff. 178-188, "Return of Protestant families preparing to emigrate from the Counties of Carlow and Wexford." I am grateful to Howard M. Brown of Ottawa for this reference.
37. NAC RG 5, A1 Reel C-4547 Upper Canada Sundries, vol. 30, pp. 13643-13644.
38. Ibid., Reel C-4609, vol. 58, p. 30077.
39. George Edward Kidd, *The Story of the Derry* (Ladner, British Columbia: by the author, 1943; reprinted.,: W. Livingstone Kidd and G.L. Halliday, 1977), p. 68.
40. Coleman family history, courtesy of Merrill Griffith, Carleton Place.
41. Dorothy Lewis and Irma Willoughby, "Hawkins Family History", unpublished typescript, courtesy of Arthur R. Hawkins, Carleton Place.
42. NAC RG 1, L3 M Bundle 16 Upper Canada Land Petitions, Reel C-2209, vol. 351(a) Petition no. 46, courtesy Mary Rayburn.

43 Howard M. Brown, "The James McNeely Family of Beckwith Township and Carleton Place," (unpublished manuscript compiled at Ottawa in 1978, and revised in 1983, based on a history of the family compiled by Elizabeth McNeely of Carleton Place and published by her niece M. Verne McNeely at Toronto in 1959).

44 The only source to suggest from where in Ireland the Moores came is the tombstone of William Moore in Franktown Public Cemetery who died in 1883 at age 85 which lists him as a native of County Armagh.

45 Howard M. Brown, *Founded Upon A Rock: Carleton Place Recollections* (Carleton Place: 150th Year Festival Committee, 1969), p. 3.

46 Douglas C. McGeachie, "The Morphy Family of Morphy's Falls," unpublished paper presented in a sociology course at Waterloo Lutheran University in 1969, p. 2.

47 Howard M. Brown, "The Edmond Morphy Family of Carleton Place," unpublished manuscript compiled at Ottawa in 1983, p. 2.

48 Idem, "The David Moffatt Family of Carleton Place, Ontario," unpublished paper compiled at Ottawa in 1976 and revised in 1983, p. 1.

49 J.M. Morris, *A Kerfoot History: Canadian Branch* (Smiths Falls: Winifred Morris Mair, 1953), p. 2.

50 McGeachie, "Morphy Family," pp. 8-9.

51 Ibid., p. 8.

52 Archives of Ontario (hereafter OTAR) RG 1 Series C-IV Crown Lands Department, Township Papers, Ramsay, Box 416, p. 872.

53 Queen's University Archives (hereafter OKQAR) Rev. William Bell Journals II:46.

54 Ibid. IV:86-88.

55 OTAR RG 1, Series C-IV Crown Lands Department, Township Papers, Ramsay, Box 416, pp. 872-873.

56 Elliott, "Emigration from South Leinster," p. 428

57 Jean S. McGill, *A Pioneer History of the County of Lanark* (Bewdley, Ontario: Clay Publishing Company, 1967), p. 199.

58 NAC RG 5, A1 Reel C-4612 Upper Canada Sundries, vol. 63, p. 33790.

59 Ibid., Reel C-4610, vol. 59, p. 31125.

60 Ibid., vol. 60, p. 31507.

61 John Carroll, *Case and His Cotemporaries* (Toronto: Wesleyan Conference Office, 1869) II:178-179, 244.

62 Ibid. II:294, 333.

63 Ibid. II:425, 430-431.

64 Ibid. II:482.

65 Morris, *A Kerfoot History*, p. 2.

66 Peter L. Maltby and Monica Maltby, "A New look at the Peter Robinson Emigration of 1823" *Ontario History* LV No. 1 (1963), pp. 15, 18.

67 Donald E. Read, Donald W. Kelly, James R. Kennedy and Bruce S. Elliott, *St. Michael's Roman Catholic Church Cemetery and Lists of Peter Robinson Settlers* (Ottawa: Ottawa Branch, Ontario Genealogical Society, 1981), pp. 57, 63.

BUSH LIFE

The forest loomed large in the minds and lives of the Irish yeomanry and Scottish highlanders who entered Beckwith between 1816 and 1824. From the decks of boats ascending the St. Lawrence and Ottawa rivers, they watched the cultivated plains and ranges of white houses in Lower Canada[1] give way to river banks "so luxuriantly wooded, that the foliage of the trees descended to the surface of the water, and completely concealed the bank on which they grew." Upon arriving at the Richmond landing opposite Philemon Wright's Hull settlement, the daunting scale of the forest became fully evident to the immigrants. As they trekked through Nepean and Goulbourn on foot, they experienced the darkness of the forest and the impossibility the immense trees posed to gauging distance. The Beckwith settlers found the "thick recesses of the shade around, were impenetrable to the eye, the limited prospect being closed by a rich green obscurity, except where a ray of the sun found its way through some distant interstice among the trees".[2] So overwhelmed was Colin McLaren of the Perthshire party by the forbidding forest that he initially chose to be a shoemaker at the village of Chatham east of Hull, rather than battle the great trees in Beckwith.[3] Save for the open area of the occasional beaver meadow and the smaller trees in swampy areas, the virgin forest had an awesome impact on the newly-arrived British immigrants:[4]

> There is something in the ponderous stillness of these forests—something in their wild, torn, mossy darkness, their utter solitude and mournful silence which impresses the traveller with a new aspect each time he sees them.... In Upper Canada the endless hills of pine give way at last, or at most stand thinly intermingled with gigantic beeches, tall hemlocks and ash, with maples, birch and wild sycamore, the underwood of these great leafy hills. Mile after mile, and hour after hour of such a route was passed—a dark black solitude, with here and there a vista opening up, showing the massive trunks, grey as cathedral ruins, which bore the rich canopy of leaves aloft.

The exultation of European travellers in "experienc[ing] the sublimity of a *real* forest"[5] contrasted with the exhaustion of early Beckwith area settlers "travelling through swamps and untrodden paths through woods." One local Scottish immigrant in 1821 described the loneliness and the impassability of the forest in terms of the countryside he had left:[6]

> The greater part of the forest, the underwood or bramble, is not so thick as at home but a great deal of it is worse to go through than the worst of Crucatone Wood.... [C]onceive Paisley Moors, for instance, all grown over with large trees, some fresh and green, others half rotten and a great many rotten from top to bottom, and almost as many lying in all directions as are standing, with not a living creature to be seen or heard except a bird or two, and the owl screaming in your ears at night.

The isolation of the forest was enhanced by the physical shape of the grants to settlers. Rather than divide each township lot into square northern and southern blocks, the settling departments

Plate 38
Swamp in the eastern part of Beckwith's first concession, as photographed in June 1983. When surveyor William Fortune surveyed what eventually became the southern boundary of Beckwith in 1794 he came across no less than ten swamps in as many miles. Thin soil cover and swamp prevented trees of any size from growing, effectively discouraging settlers from building houses and sowing crops on some lots. Thomas Rothwell of Prospect described the timber grown on swampy land as being "A useless description unless for firewood[,] it being chiefly composed of dwarf Tamarac, Water Elm, and Ash, with scarcely a Pole exceeding 9 inch[e]s in diametre."

at Perth and Richmond had split Beckwith lots lengthwise into narrow strips. This made each grant of one hundred acres approximately a mile in length and one quarter of a mile in breadth, and with this shape of farm most settlers decided to locate their houses and outbuildings in the centre, presumably to keep to a minimum the distance travelled from the buildings to the furthest field. When Governor General Lord Dalhousie came through Beckwith in August 1820 he assumed that because "the great line of road [between Richmond and Perth] is not yet laid out, the huts are scattered in the woods on the driest part of the land."[7] On some lots, it is true, the relative location of swamp and good land dictated where farmstead buildings were located, as was the case with John McRostie's grant on the northeast half of Lot 22 in the seventh concession; most of this grant was swamp save for a ridge of sandy soil in the centre which could be reached only by traversing on foot some two miles of swamp.[8] Even on lots located on fertile and firm land the preference for locating the homestead centrally on these "long hundreds" is evident 170 years later, giving Beckwith a distinction for an unduly high proportion of remarkably long lanes. Lacking as pioneer Beckwith did a system of roads, the tendency to centrally locate on lots meant that unless swamp or reserve lots intervened the nearest neighbour was only one quarter mile away, but neighbours whose lots were just across the concession line resided up to a mile away.

The isolation imposed by the forest setting is well illustrated by the unlikely experience of Donald Anderson and Peter McArthur who as friends from Perthshire crossed the Atlantic on the same ship, but at Quebec became separated. Anderson came via the St. Lawrence to Perth, and was settled on the northeast half of lot eleven in the sixth concession, whereas McArthur arrived by way of the Ottawa River to Richmond and was settled on the southwest half of lot fifteen in the seventh concession. The homesteads of both men faced onto the seventh concession line and hence were less than two miles apart, but because their clearings were in the middle of each grant[9]

> they lived there for over two years without either knowing that the other was there, till one Sunday McArthur heard there was beaver hay on the Jock [River] and went down to see. On the way he passed the other fellow's place and saw him out with an old knitted cap on his head that he used to wear in Scotland. McArthur knew the hat and went in.

The dense forest took its own tragic toll of the early settlers. Some discharged soldiers such as William Burrows from the 77th Regiment on lot thirteen in the fourth concession, already "worn out by a service of 21 years in His Majesty's Service" were unequal to the challenge of developing grants that were largely "barren swamp" and died awaiting transfers to better land."[10] Other disbanded soldiers, upon viewing grants such as lot three in the first concession on which "a heavy tamarac swamp cuts off all communication between the front and Rear of said Lot" threw up their hands in despair and never even attempted to settle.[11] Military and civilian settlers alike were without experience in swinging an axe. As they set about attacking the "dense jungle of brushwood" and "an endless array of huge tree trunks" it was inevitable that serious and sometimes fatal accidents befell the novice woodsmen as they initially hacked trees all around until they came crashing down where they might.[12] Some settlers, rather than clear every tree from the ground, attempted to plant crops around the large trees after clearing away the underbrush; the larger trees were then notched around the base and left to die, but as one settler pointed out in 1824 were therefore "apt to be blown down, and, besides spoiling the crop, they may, in their fall, kill cattle, or perhaps people themselves."[13] Even after the trees were felled, they posed a danger, for the house and barn-raising bees became reckless hair-raising social events, well-primed as they were with liquor and rivalry:[14]

> The foundation laid, and a few rounds added, on a set day the neighbours assembled. Corner men [—who as the best axemen in the community neatly dove-tailed the logs at the corners—] are chosen, the rest divide into two rival gangs, one at each end of the log to be hoisted. For the first few rounds there is little excitement; the logs are rolled in and slid up in a quiet, orderly manner. But, with the rising walls rises a rivalry, waxing fiercer and fiercer, till the "wall-plate" is placed, and all is over. It struck terror into the heart of the on-looker to see each gang wildly push to get their end up first. Pushed too fast and too far, it left the skid, then—sauve qui peut! Lives were lost in this way.

The roistering rivalry of these work bees among neighbours and families endured long after some inhabitants moved away from Beckwith. Angus McDiarmid at Kenmore in Osgoode Township wrote the following friendly challenge to his younger stepbrother John in Beckwith:[15]

> They tell me you have got to be a great big fellow now, that you are second best at the putting stone of all the men in Beckwith. [I]s that so, *Jack*[?] Wait till I go up, and then perhaps there will

Plate 39
Raising a log driveshed on the John McEwen farm, lot 9, concession 7, Beckwith, ca. 1932. The technique of building log barns endured in Beckwith for barely more than a century. Although a number of large frame dairy barns were built around 1900, the majority of Beckwith farmers made do with log barns and stables that were added onto from the earliest years of settlement. Teams of men shoved the logs up the sloping poles or skids to the top of the wall where the corner men fitted or morticed them at the corners to the logs of the two adjoining walls. Photograph courtesy of John and Verna McEwen.

be two better than you, at putting stone, Sledge or anything else you like to try. I entend giving you a settler to take that foolish conceit out of you[;] it will never do for young boys to think that they are better than their betters.

Now Jack, I am giving you the challenge in time, so as that you can get yourself prepared. [I]f you are not confident that you know enough about *Boxing*, you [had] best be practising with Duncan for it will take you to be a good deal better than him for to be a match for me. You young boys that was never half-a-mile from a cow's tail thinks you are everything.... I will go as soon as I can for I weary to see you all[.]...

Undoubtedly, the most poignant concern for many Beckwith parents was that very young children might venture into the forest, quickly lose their bearings, and either die of exposure or be attacked by wild animals. Community tradition asserts that a little girl belonging to a family named Dickson on lot 23 in the sixth concession wandered into the woods and was found dead on the banks of a stream running through that lot.[16] Tales of children going off into the forest never to return were commonplace in the region,[17] but the fate of Ellen Garland was unique. In the midsummer of 1824 Nicholas and Anne Garland who homesteaded on lot twenty in the sixth concession took their youngest child John to be baptised by the Anglican clergyman at the village of Beckwith (Franktown). They left the two older children, Thomas aged five, and Ellen aged three, in the care of a neighbour, Mrs. Fennel. This woman decided to pay a brief visit to Mrs. John Lucas. She gave each of the children a piece of maple sugar and left them alone in the house with the door bolted. Young Thomas managed with the aid of a broom to slide back the wooden bolt and to open the door. In company with Ellen he started in what he thought was the direction of home, but disoriented among the great trees, they instead took a path leading in the opposite direction. As Thomas later recalled, while they were passing through the heavy elm and ash woods on the south half of lot 21, they came to a large log which lay across the path. Thomas clambered over and turned to help Ellen, but she was nowhere to be seen. In frantically searching for her he became lost himself and remained in the woods all night. The next day he followed a wandering cow to the home of Samuel Leach. Here the neighbours who had organised a search party found him, but in such a condition of shock that two days elapsed before he could give a coherent account of what had happened.[18] Young Thomas received[19]

> such a fright that he was never right after, and sometimes he got so wild that his family had to tie him up. He was always looking for the girl, and a few years before he died in an asylum he heard of an old Indian up west in Bruce County who had confessed that he had stolen her, and told the number of the lot. He went up to see her, but as his sister was only three when she was lost and the woman was just like the Indians he did not know whether she was his sister or not.

Despite this particular episode, Beckwith's early settlers feared more for their children becoming lost and either dying from exposure or from being preyed upon by wild animals rather than coming to harm from Amerindians. Another traditional account from before 1825 relates that English-origin widower John Goth, obliged to leave his isolated clearing on lot 22 in the eleventh concession for three or four days to register his patent at Perth, locked his young son in their log house with sufficient food and water to wait out his father's return.[20] By implication, many settlers were obliged to lock their children in their shanties while away, rather than risk their becoming lost in the forest. There were few encounters between Beckwith settlers and Amerindians, and most early settlers were unaware "of any Indians being around at the time."[21] These encounters appear to have been amicable. John Cram settled on the southwest half of lot twenty in the tenth concession beside a beaver meadow where Amerindians came to trap. He recalled that once in a while "one of them would walk silently into the house, light his pipe, and as silently walk away. They were very harmless."[22] In the same vein, Morphy family tradition asserted that local Amerindians "loved to hear [Edmond Morphy] play the violin and one Indian, at least, took lessons from him," and that when Morphy shot a deer which a brave had been pursuing for a long distance "Edmond and the Indian settled the matter justly for both and established a rule to govern in like cases."[23]

The rare appearance of these Mississaugas in Beckwith during the late 1810s and 1820s contrasted with the numerous Amerindians that early settlers along the St. Lawrence to the south came across in the 1780s. A Brockville inhabitant in January 1825 deplored the "considerable diminution of these sons of the forest" and explained the reason for the decline of the few Amerindians left in the vicinity into "some of the most pitiful objects of humanity":[24]

> It is true [he wrote] they have greatly degenerated, through the excess of liquor, and I believe they have often been driven to desperation through the excessive cruelties of the English [or American-origin] inhabitants, who too often think it no harm to cheat and defraud the poor Indian of his hard earnings, for a little rum, or whiskey, and they can hardly associate in their minds that they form any part of the human family, and that they are not far removed from the Brutes, incapable of civilization, of improvement in knowledge, or of forming a religious character.

Plate 40
"Indian Hunters" as sketched by James P. Cockburn in 1830. The fire arms and dress of these Mississauga Amerindians reflect extended contact with Caucasian settlers. The Mississippi Lake region was never a place of fixed abode for any aboriginal peoples, simply offering a route of travel for nomads. In 1823 the Reverend William Bell observed Amerindians inhabiting islands on Mississippi Lake and hunting north of the lake. Although Bell found the Amerindians "far from being pleased with the encroachments our settlers are making on their territories," no accounts survive of enmity between Amerindians and arriving immigrants. Royal Ontario Museum accession no. 942.48.13.

This anonymous writer hoped to excite "some compassion for these unfortunate natives of our country," in contrast with the heartrending scene of seeing Amerindians who came into Brockville "made the objects of sport and derision" and insulted "by the rude boys."[25] The contrast between Brockville and Beckwith in the relations of Caucasian settlers with Amerindians can be explained by the newly-arrived Irish and Scottish immigrants having no legacy of relations with any North American indigenous peoples, unlike most people in the Brockville vicinity who were descended from American families of at least four or five generations' standing and who consequently inherited their bias from legends of colonial American encounters.

Irish, Scottish and military settlers, long before they arrived in Beckwith, had an "expectation of immediate Succour from Government by being placed on their Lands free of expense & with rations."[26] They were located on grants of one hundred acres on which they had to reside and a reasonable portion of which they had to cultivate for a period of three years before they could be granted legal title. During these first three years their crops were supplemented by provisions from government, and from the King's storehouse also came implements of husbandry, tools "and other comforts, according to the necessities of the individuals."[27] The families were provided with a regular allowance of army rations for the first twelve months, and each head of family received an axe, a broad axe, a mattock, a pickaxe, a spade, a shovel, a hoe, a scythe, a drawknife, a hammer, a handsaw, two scythe stones, two files, twelve panes of glass, a pound of putty, twelve pounds of wrought nails in three sizes, one camp bed, one bed tick and a blanket. To every five settlers Patrick Nowlan at Franktown was authorised to distribute from the King's storehouse a crosscut saw, a whipsaw and a grindstone.[28] These were the terms on paper with which the settlement of Beckwith began, and very quickly some immigrants found flaws in the plan. Allan Wilson, an Irish settler located on lot 27 in the third concession complained to Captain Burke at Richmond in 1822 "that his lot was very far short of 100 acres" and a measurement by surveyor Robert Currie confirmed that the lot contained only 35 acres. Burke recommended that a replacement grant be made to Wilson.[29] When the Reverend George Buchanan arrived in August 1822, the military administration of Perth had already come to an end, with the King's storehouses at both Perth and Beckwith closed, so that in late October he was obliged to request of Colonel William Marshall at Lanark Village "the remaining articles of Stores he could not obtain at Perth, particularly blankets, of which he is much in want. [H]e has a numerous family, and he is afraid it will suffer, on the approach of winter, from too scanty a supply of bedding."[30]

To Buchanan's family, arriving on the tenth day of August 1822 after a week-long fatiguing journey from Prescott through the forest in waggons heavily loaded with furniture and supplies, pioneer Beckwith presented a depressing prospect. One daughter recalled:[31]

> The first glimpse of Franktown dampened the ardor of the most sanguine of our party. [Wickham's] log-tavern and three shanties, in a patch of half-cleared ground, constituted the so-called village. Some of my sisters wept bitterly over the gloomy prospect, begging piteously to be taken back to Scotland... James Wall, a big-souled Irishman, not a Presbyterian, offered us the use of a small log-house he had just put up. His kind offer we accepted gratefully, moved into the humble tenement and occupied it six weeks.

The Buchanans arrived in the midst of the harvest in pioneer Beckwith, and during their six week stay in the Wall log shanty they gathered some initial impressions of "the privations and inconveniences of backwoods life":[32]

> During these weeks the settlers were busy harvesting from daylight till dark. Cutting grain with the old-fashioned sickle and scythe, on ground stumps dotted thickly, was slow, laborious work.... A cumbrous plough, hard to pull and harder to guide, a V-shaped harrow, alike heavy and unwieldy, a clumsy sled, in keeping with the plough and harrow, home-made rakes, weighty as iron and sure to blister the hands of the users, forked-stick pitchforks, first cousins of the awkward rakes, and gnarled flails, certain to raise bumps on the heads of unskilled threshers, with two or three scythes and sickles, represented the average agricultural equipment.

The crude implements of husbandry to the newly-arrived Buchanans reflected the larger lack of all amenities in Beckwith. "Not a grist-mill, saw-mill, factory, store, shop, postoffice, school, horse, chimney, stove nor even a chair could be found in Beckwith", the youngest daughter recalled.

The Buchanans, arriving as they did more than five years after Beckwith began settling, had escaped witnessing even more primitive and daunting conditions, particularly the disastrous harvest of 1817 when the twelve months of military rations were coming to an end. Many of the disbanded soldiers in the Perth settlement that year sowed from two to five bushels of wheat, and were confident of an abundant crop until a few weeks before harvest when "it was so much injured by rust, that the whole when collected, would barely compensate the reaper for his labour." An early frost rendered the 150 acres of Indian corn entirely useless. The potato crop alone was left for the settlers to depend on, and although the crop was prolific, the "impossibility of procuring seed last

Plate 41
"A First Settlement" as sketched by William H. Bartlett in 1838. No other image from early nineteenth century Upper Canada so effectively conveys the daunting visual and physical scale of the pillar-like pine trees that obstructed sunlight from penetrating to the forest floor. Although early settlers in Beckwith were provisioned from the military depots at Perth and Richmond, survival during the first years also depended on a steady supply of game. To the right of the half-completed log house a corner of the crude shanty in which this family started out can be glimpsed. To the left men are shown wielding axes, so intent on eliminating the forest that they neglected to leave shade trees near their homes. The National Gallery of Canada, Ottawa, negative no. 6587.

spring at any price" meant that the actual harvest was "far short of being adequate to the wants of the people". One settler observed in mid-December 1817:[33]

> Many large families have no other prospect of support through the approaching winter, but their supply of potatoes, destitute of milk, meat, or any other kind of nourishment. Now, Sir, to people who have seen better days, and many of them comfortable at home, the prospect is gloomy in the extreme. I know several families that have not a sufficiency to subsist on, for more than five or six weeks, and when famine forces them to abandon their farms, (which will soon be the case) they have not a sixpence in the world to convey them from the Settlement.

This combined failure of crops may help to explain why so few of the settlers located in Beckwith in 1816 and 1817 stayed to develop their grants, but the pride of some military settlers was a major handicap to their survival. When two of the Honourable Peter Robinson's settlers, John Barry and John Sullivan respectively located on lots in adjacent Ramsay and Goulbourn petitioned the lieutenant-governor in February 1825 for "a few Months Rations" to keep their large families from starving, they attributed their "Want and Distress" to "Coming So Late on our Respective Lots with all our industry" we "Could not Raise as Much Provesions as Would Put us over Half the year". But military vanity also hampered these veterans of the Limerick City and King's County Militia and His Majesty's 11th Regiment on Foot, as betrayed in the revealing remark, "We two Good old Soldiers are in Great Sperits, Heaving that Dependance in your Excellancys tinder Feelings for Men Who Can Not Work for others[,] Being Reared in the army."[34]

The majority of early settlers in Beckwith, once they recovered from their initial disappointment of finding the ground covered with large trees rather than with grass, began their battle against the forest.[35] One settler estimated that there were from eighty to one hundred large trees per acre in addition to a large quantity of small trees and brushwood. The smaller trees were cut first, close to the ground, and piled into large heaps. The large trees were then tackled, cut from two to four feet above the ground "and allowed to fall promiscuously over each other." The branches were chopped off as soon as the tree was felled, and thrown upon the heaps, and the tree trunk was cut into lengths of between twelve and fifteen feet.[36] These logs were then hauled together into heaps by teams of yoked oxen. "They all work with oxen instead of horses here", remarked Andrew Bell of Perth in 1819, "as they are better for going in the woods."[37] The culmination of removing each patch of forest was the grimy sociability of the logging bee where the great logs were rolled into heaps by teams of [38]

> two men against two, rolling, hoisting the logs, striving to be first! Grave fathers of families were boys again, as the logs swung in, and heaps arose. And when the sun was set, and the grime washed off, and supper over,...in came their wives and daughters, and out came a fiddle and the bottle, and "We'll not go home until morning!"

The great piles of logs and brush were burned off, the cleared land was then raked of chips and branches that had escaped burning, then fenced with wooden rails, before grain was "then sown and well harrowed into the scorched and blackened earth with a kind of harrow called a 'drag'." This implement was a triangular wood form containing nine large strong tines weighing from four to five pounds apiece and it served well the purpose of breaking up and tearing obstacles in the ground.[39]

The clearing of every Beckwith settler had at least three sections at different stages of development within the ring of forest, with land closest to the hut or shanty cleared, another section partially cleared, and land that was chopped but not cleared.[40] The chronology for a family of five to develop a clearing remained fairly constant in eastern Upper Canada for the next fifty years. The family upon arriving on their grant by the first day of May in year one, could have a rough hut constructed and two acres cleared and planted with potatoes before the end of June. By the end of August six more acres would be underbrushed and chopped:[41]

> It would take [the settler two months more] to log it, were he to do it alone, but the logging is usually done in a day by making a "bee" which means the calling together of his neighbours who gratuitously assist him, and he is naturally expected to go to each or many of them for a day upon similar occasions.

This exchange of labour lasted until the end of October, with November devoted to chopping firewood and making the hut as snug as possible for winter. The father then spent the four months from December through March working at a timber shanty on the Ottawa River or at other employment, earning up to ten pounds. His eight acres of cleared land would have produced about 480 bushels of ashes, and even lacking a kettle and the time to process them into potash, he could

Plate 42
The Roger Hawkins log house, lot 12, concession 8, Beckwith, as photographed in June 1983. The household of Roger Hawkins in 1820 included his wife Mary Griffith, five children, and his brother Henry Hawkins. The small dimensions of this early dwelling, 18 by 24 feet, kept these eight family members at fairly close quarters, but this was an advantage in the depth of winter when most of the heat generated in the fireplace went up the chimney. Cracks in the roof and loose spaces in the chinking caused by the green logs in the walls shifting permitted sufficient ventilation during the long winter nights. The small stone nine foot square structure was used to store ashes that could be sold as potash.

expect to sell these for six pounds. After paying for pork, flour and tea to use up to November of year two, the settler would have at least a pound of money left.

In the second year, after returning from employment elsewhere in early April, the settler would chop two more acres, bringing his total land cleared to ten acres, on which he would plant three acres of wheat, five of oats, and two of potatoes. From the wheat he could expect a yield of twenty bushels per acre, which in turn produced twelve barrels of flour. The surplus of two barrels not needed by the family would be spent on pork to supplement their own pig, supplying them with sufficient pork and flour to November of year three. The five acres of oats could be expected to produce 175 bushels and this sold at two shillings per bushel brought in £17 10s. The two acres of potatoes both in the first year and in the second year yielded four hundred bushels, and leaving half that quantity each year for home consumption both by his family and two or three hogs, the remaining two hundred bushels each year could be sold for a combined total of £25. After purchasing tea, herrings, salt, seed, seed wheat and oats, there would remain £34 5s from the sale of the surplus oats and potatoes made before the first day of May in year three. The summer of year two would be spent the same way as the first, but the winter of year two rather than working out for someone else or in a timber shanty was spent chopping, threshing and grinding his wheat and oats to have the surplus ready for market and his own seed ready to plant in year three.

By the first day of June in year three the family would have at least twenty acres ready to crop. Twenty pounds would be spent on a yoke of oxen and five pounds on a cow to provide milk for the children, reducing the £34 10s to £9 10s which was left for incidental expenses. Soap was not purchased because it could be made at home from ashes and grease, and dry pine was used for lighting rather than spend money on candles. Sheep, a horse and additional cattle could be added to the livestock from the larger profits of year three so that by the beginning of year four the settler could consider himself independent, and pay off without any inconvenience any capital which initially had been lent him.[42] Within five years of arriving Robert Ferguson on the southwest half of lot 25 in the fifth concession of Beckwith could boast in an 1823 letter back to relatives in Scotland that he had forty acres of land cleared of timber and the livestock he owned included "five milch cows and three yock of oxen[,]...sheep[,] and a good many young cat[t]le."[43] Once the land was cleared, the rich vegetable mould that had accumulated over thousands of years yielded bountiful produce. Larders were filled with Indian corn, peas, wheat, oats and ham. Thomas MacQueen at Pakenham, north of Beckwith, remarked in the mid 1840s, "Thousands of farms which have been under regular cultivation for ten, twelve or even twenty years have during that period been subject repeatedly to the same rotation of crops without ever having received one shovelfull of manure; and yet they are still yielding abundant harvests."[44] The rich early crops served to betoken to Beckwith's early settlers that despite the crudities of backwoods existence, they were building the base of a prosperous future for their families. As one Beckwith settler remarked, "There were many hardships but it was wonderful not to be under a Laird and to know that the land was one's own."[45]

There is no clear evidence apart from Robert Ferguson's incidental reference to viewing huge timber rafts on the Ottawa River that the first Beckwith settlers engaged in the timber trade during winter months before 1825 to earn extra income. Most of them were favoured with rations, provisions and tools from the King's storehouses at Perth and Beckwith village before 1823. The timber trade was not the only financial recourse of settlers. William Poole taught school at Carleton Place in 1832 "(as was my employment for twenty years in Ireland)" while the thirteen other members of his family took "the liberty of going to live on Clergy Lot No. 12—7th Concession, Ramsay, and...put in a little wheat and some potatoes to assist in the support of my large family, for we could get no land convenient for tillage near us." But Poole along with every other immigrant entering Beckwith was well aware that he could not "support his family in this Country as he expected without land to cultivate."[46]

With 57 percent of Beckwith lots patented in 1828, that is, located to inhabitants by 1825,[47] settlers were casting envious glances at empty Clergy and Crown reserved lots that accounted for more than 28 percent of township land. The rich deep soil on Clergy Reserve lot two in the seventh concession was irresistible to Irish immigrant William James, and in 1828 he wrote the Commissioner of Crown Lands at York (later Toronto) explaining that in partnership with his father he had held the lot[48]

> for the last past 5 years during which time we have cleared about 18 acres and built a Small Dwelling House & Barn thereon and at present has a considerable portion of the land under crop. Some time agoe I was informed that it was the intention of Government to have these Clergy Lands Sold, & on my being made certain of the matter I was resolved if it was in my power to be prepared with as much ready money as would meet the conditions that Government had presented (on the Lands being sold). I accordingly set out for the Rideau Canal, as being the most likely place, to earn ready money, but at the same time left my Father & children

Plate 43
Ruins of the Duncan McCuan homestead, lot 22, concession 10, Beckwith, as photographed in January 1987. Although the dimensions of this log house were only slightly larger than those of the Roger Hawkins house (Plate 42), the stone fireplace in it was larger, the logs in the walls were all flattened with an adze to provide a more uniform wall surface, and the walls rose higher above the rafters of the downstairs ceiling to provide more headroom upstairs than was available in the low loft of the Hawkins house. Later a still larger log house was built nearby, but only the fireplace and chimney survive. The cavity broken open above the hearth was probably a curing shelf where meat was left to cure in the smoke from the fire.

on the place, but previous to my going to the Canal I Call'd with the Rev'd Wm. Harris, Perth, & got my name enter'd as a person willing (either) to rent, or purchase the Lot.

William James, aware that Angus McLellan also was making a claim for this Clergy Reserve, pointed out that he had "Expended my little all that I brought from the Mother Country on this Farm, besides I have Suffer'd verry great Bodily Fatigue in the Culture of it, and I have a Large & Helpless Family to Support..."

The reliance by William James and William Poole on the labour of their families in developing their lots compared with the rest of Upper Canada, and indeed with the rest of frontier North America, but the active role of women in Beckwith agriculture appears to have been remarkable. From the beginning of settlement, government had promoted the settlement of families rather than of single settlers. Single women, unless they were the sisters of single men, were not allowed to immigrate from Scotland in 1816, and widows were not encouraged to immigrate either with or without their families,[49] whereas children under age sixteen were offered free passage.[50] It was an axiomatic rule of pioneer society that a large family made easier the endless round of chores that attended hewing down the forest, preparing the land for tilling, and growing crops. Selective immigration criteria favouring young families and the challenge of having as many strong backs and pairs of arms available combined to give Beckwith an astounding birthrate, to judge from the baptismal register of the Scottish Presbyterians. There were 19 births recorded in 1823, 25 in 1824 and

24 in 1825 among the Perthshire highlanders, giving Beckwith an estimated birthrate of between fifty and 67 births per thousand people.[51] The baby boom meant that the larger children working away at hoeing, piling brush, picking stones, raking hay and dropping potatoes were never far from the sound of a wailing infant. One of the Rev. George Buchanan's daughters, newly-arrived in August 1822, was impressed by all family members working together:[52]

> When obliged to help out-doors, young mothers took their babies with them—babies were by no means scarce in Beckwith—to the fields and laid them in sap-troughs, while they worked near by.... A fond mother near Franktown, hearing a strange noise at the trough holding her baby, ran to find a big snake crawling down the infant's throat! She caught the reptile by the tail and hurled it into the field, saving her child's life.

The pioneer women of Beckwith actively worked alongside their husbands, brothers and children in a way unknown in the American-settled regions of Upper Canada. Contemporary observers and authorities on the province agreed that it "is not so common... for women to be employed in field labour" as it was in the British Isles,[53] and that "[w]omen do not generally in U[pper] C[anada] work in the fields."[54] Many of the women from Perthshire were experienced in managing the homestead or infield part of their holding, while their husbands and brothers were off to the outfield. Still other women had actively been encouraged by improving landlords to participate in working at the cottage industries of spinning and weaving to augment the production of each household. The women from Wexford were used to making every acre of their limited acreages in the old country yield as much crop as possible. To the eyes of seven year-old Jessie Buchanan in 1822, accustomed as she was to her mother doing no work as a mark of the gentility to which she aspired, it was all too apparent that Beckwith "women bore their full share of the burden":[55]

> Besides attending to the children and household affairs, all spring and summer they worked in the fields early and late, burning brush, logging, planting and reaping. Much of the cooking, washing and mending was done before dawn or after dark, while the men slept peacefully. At noon they prepared dinner, ate a bite hastily and hurried back to drudge until the sun went down. Then they got supper, put the youngsters to bed, patched, darned and did a multitude of chores. For these willing slaves,...sixteen hours of constant labour would be a short day. They knew no respite,...nothing but hard work and child-bearing... Autumn and winter brought little relief, except to vary the style of work. The women carded wool with hand-cards and spun it on small wheels, for stocking-yarn and the weaver's loom. Knitting was an endless task, by the light of the hearth-fire or the feeble flicker of a tallow-dip, and everybody wore homespun.

The heavy labour of Beckwith women alongside their brothers and husbands is confirmed by a variety of sources. One of the children in the 1818 Perthshire party of immigrants recalled that the "settlers who had no teams [of] oxen exchanged work in logging; and it was not unusual to see the wife, with a handspike, helping her husband."[56] Accounts from nearby townships matter-of-factly refer to women sowing wheat,[57] to women being killed when lifting logs while constructing a shed,[58] to a mother and daughters stacking hay,[59] to a mother and children planting crops and harvesting thirty bushels of corn and 350 bushels of potatoes while her husband was away working on the Oswego canal.[60] The most poignant of these accounts tells of a woman burned to death after coming in from a hard day's work in the fields and drowsing off to sleep, as the pipe in her mouth fell to the floor and set fire to her house.[61] One Beckwith immigrant son recalled the women of his childhood making maple sugar[62]

Plate 44
Forest near Old Sly's Rapids, Rideau, ca. 1830, as sketched by James P. Cockburn. The landscape of Beckwith until the late 1830s was a seemingly endless succession of vertical tree trunks, relieved only by the tracks that passed for roads along the concession lines. With what anticipation must early Beckwith settlers inhabiting the forest shade have looked forward to the opening patches of sky as their clearings grew. National Archives of Canada negative no. C-12516.

with their pails, wading through snow thigh-deep from tree to tree, gathering the sap; struggling to lift and empty the ponderous sap-troughs, and wending their way back to camp, weary and be-drabbled to the knees, boots and stockings soaked! Then to the wearisome boiling again, pelted with rain, sleet, hail or snow; half blinded with smoke, and alternately chilled by the cold blast and fried by the licentious flame. Women did all save tap the trees and lay in the fuel. No roof save the leafless tree tops covered their heads; no friendly wall screen[e]d them from the blast.

Women too went out of Beckwith to earn additional money in other settlements. Catherine McEwen, for example, went to work for a Craigdarrach family from Scotland in an older settlement. Catherine was reputedly so industrious that after her employers went to bed "she would stuff the cracks of doors with cloth so that she could do her work without the family knowing that she was doing it late at night" since she did not feel "she was earning her wages unless she worked hard all day and half of the night."[63] Similarly Catherine McCuan worked as a domestic servant for Captain Burke at Richmond.[64]

The younger women working out as domestic servants in older settlements at least had the advantage of inhabiting better houses than their families back in Beckwith. The small log structures that a year or two into settlement replaced the first temporary huts offered very primitive accommodation. The interior of one such new log house offered by James Wall for the temporary accommodation of the Reverend George Buchanan and his family in 1822 was typical:[65]

What a contrast was this one-roomed cabin, with neither door nor window, to the pleasant home [in Edinburgh] we had left three months before!... Somehow our stuff was brought from Franktown and soon set to rights in the little shanty. We were not burdened with household effects, having sold the bulk of the furniture in Scotland... Quilts and blankets, hung over the openings and across the apartment, served as doors and windows and a partition. We cooked on the flat stone, at one end of the building, which did duty as a hearth in the chimneyless fireplace. More smoke stayed in than found the way out. Millions of mosquitoes and black flies added to our discomfort, obliging us frequently to exclude nearly every breath of air to shut out the pests.

Rock-elm was the favoured wood for building these early log houses and barns because it was a hard, tough, durable wood, cylindrical and clear of bough to a great height, and usually of moderate girth.[66] After the harvest in 1822, the Presbyterians of Beckwith "turned out in force to cut down logs and build...a large shanty "for the Buchanan family very similar to that of James Wall. "They roofed it with troughs, laid a big flat stone against the wall for a chimney, left a space at the ridge for smoke to escape, smoothed one side of split logs for a floor, and put in a door and two windows."[67] This was the standard of housing in early Beckwith, although early in 1823 the Rev. George Buchanan hired men to clear several acres of ground and take out timber for a more ambitious house:[68]

They worked hard until spring, hewing logs for a two story building and sawing lumber for floors and partitions with a cross-cut saw... The new house was ready for us in September, 1823. It had plank floors, a stone chimney, a number of good rooms and a cellar. Putting down the carpets brought from Scotland and arranging the furniture and father's library, we soon felt quite at home. A double stove and more furniture, hauled from Perth the next winter, added materially to our comfort. A year or two later, when Presbytery met at our house, the members spent the nights without unpleasant crowding.

The two-storey house of the Buchanans in 1824 with its fireplace, carpets, furniture and library

Plate 45
A pioneer homestead. Although this photograph dates from the early 1870s and shows a homestead on the Ottawa River, the atmosphere it represents rings true to bush life in early Beckwith. The stump-littered clearing, the chimneyless, windowless log shanty with a hole in the troughed basswood roof to allow smoke to escape, and the larger house that replaced it were familiar parts of the Beckwith landscape in the 1820s. The later date of this photograph is betrayed by the absence of fireplace chimneys on the larger house, but the carts in the foreground were similar in design to those the Beckwith highlanders used in Perthshire. National Archives of Canada negative no. C-8037

contrasted with the homes of all other Beckwith settlers in which "[s]plit logs furnished the materials for benches, tables, floors and roofs"; in which [s]awed boards, shingles and plastered walls were unattainable luxuries"; and all of which were simply "shanties chinked between the logs with wood and mud, often without a window" and with only a "hole in the roof [to] let out such smoke as happened to travel in its direction."[69]

The stove and furniture in the new Buchanan house were sleighed from Perth in 1824 along the first road to pass through Beckwith. According to the tidy geometric plan of Beckwith surveyed by Reuben Sherwood in January 1817 every concession line was to be a road, and there were to be roads crossing these at right angles every five lots, that is, there were to be roads between lots five and six, between lots ten and eleven, between lots fifteen and sixteen, and between lots twenty and twenty one in all concessions.[70] The priorities of forest life and the pervasive swamp in Beckwith prevented any such system of roads from ever realistically developing. The four hundred pounds granted in August 1820 by governor general Dalhousie[71] had initiated the construction of a road between Perth and Richmond which was in use by 1821.[72] This road ran along the second line between concession two and three of Beckwith from the Goulbourn border to lot eight, than ran directly south to the front of lot two of the first concession on the townline between Montague and Beckwith, and proceeded along the townline to Perth. This road "cut out by order of His Majesty's Government" was an impressive forty feet in width, but travel along it was better to Perth than to Richmond because the section east of Franktown was "from its extensive swampy wet parts completely deserted by Travellers" and a road commissioner by 1824 considered it "a great pity that the public money should have been so injudiciously expended."[73] Travellers between Perth and Richmond before 1824 had already abandoned this part of the road, preferring a route along the fourth line between lot nineteen and the Goulbourn border "opened by the Settlers[,] 20 feet Wide...over a generally solid foundation susceptible of being made an excellent Road at a trifling expense."[74] A causeway a quarter-mile long had yet to be built across swamp near William Wilson's house on lot nineteen in the third concession, but in 1824 the "frame of a log Bridge had been already laid" across the Jock or Goodwood River and Beckwith "people talk of finishing it this fall."[75]

In September 1823 the first road to be approved by the first assembly of magistrates in general quarter sessions for the newly-created county of Carleton was laid out from lot eight in Beckwith's first concession at the Montague border north through Franktown and skirting swamps to Morphy's Falls.[76] From Morphy's Falls this road continued north to Huntley Township, and south from Franktown it proceeded through Maitland's Rapids (later Kilmarnock) on the Rideau south to Brockville on the St. Lawrence. It was described as being "passable for Waggons" in 1824[77] and outclassed an earlier road which headed south through western Montague to Maitland's Rapids from the Perth Road at lot two in the first concession of Beckwith.[78] Despite there being two main roads through Beckwith by 1823, the majority of township inhabitants were remote from them, and found the local woods they inhabited filled with impediments to travel such as swamps. The Reverend William Bell of Perth, for example, on his way in mid July 1823 to visit the Reverend George Buchanan found "it impossible to get [his mare] Kate through the long swamp" and was compelled to go back to John Cameron's[,] leave her there[,] and walk the rest of the way."[79] The isolation of the forest continued to prevail well beyond 1824.

The isolation of the forest. There were efforts to combat it, of course, in the competition and revelry of logging, husking and barn-raising bees. The organisation of Anglican and Presbyterian congregations as well as Methodist and Baptist classes were attempts to provide more solemn and meaningful ways to combat the loneliness, drudgery and primitive life of the backwoods settler. It is true that the Wexford Irish and Perthshire Scottish settlers in Beckwith were fortunate in having so many kin and neighbours settled in the same township, but despite this there were still many relatives and friends who had remained behind in the old country. There can be no mistaking the length taken up in letters home describing the growth and appearance of children born in Beckwith to relatives who had never seen them, the fervent inquiries after numerous relatives and old neighbours, repeated assurances that members of family were in good health, and the inevitable request to "Give our best respect to all our friends and acquentances" breaking off with "No more at Preasant but be pointed in my Direction."[80] Despite their group settlement, despite the unceasing labour required to battle the forest, despite their boast of enjoying unprecedented prosperity and freedom, during the first years in Upper Canada the two communities of Beckwith settlers themselves in their thoughts were pointed in the direction of Perthshire and Wexford.

The isolation of the early settlers of Beckwith was a complete break from the greater concentration of rural population to which they had been used in the Scottish highlands and in southeastern Ireland. Rather than being located near one another on plots of four or five acres, families situated in the middle of their hundred acres tracts were most of the time kept physically separate by the demands of frontier agriculture. After the first year or two, providing they kept intent at developing their clearings, they enjoyed "all the animal necessaries of life without much trouble; that is, enough for back and belly, though but few comforts for the mind."[81] Liquor provided temporary escape. As early as 1816 John Campbell, the agent who arranged for the migration from the estates of the Earl of Breadalbane, apprehended the loneliness which might

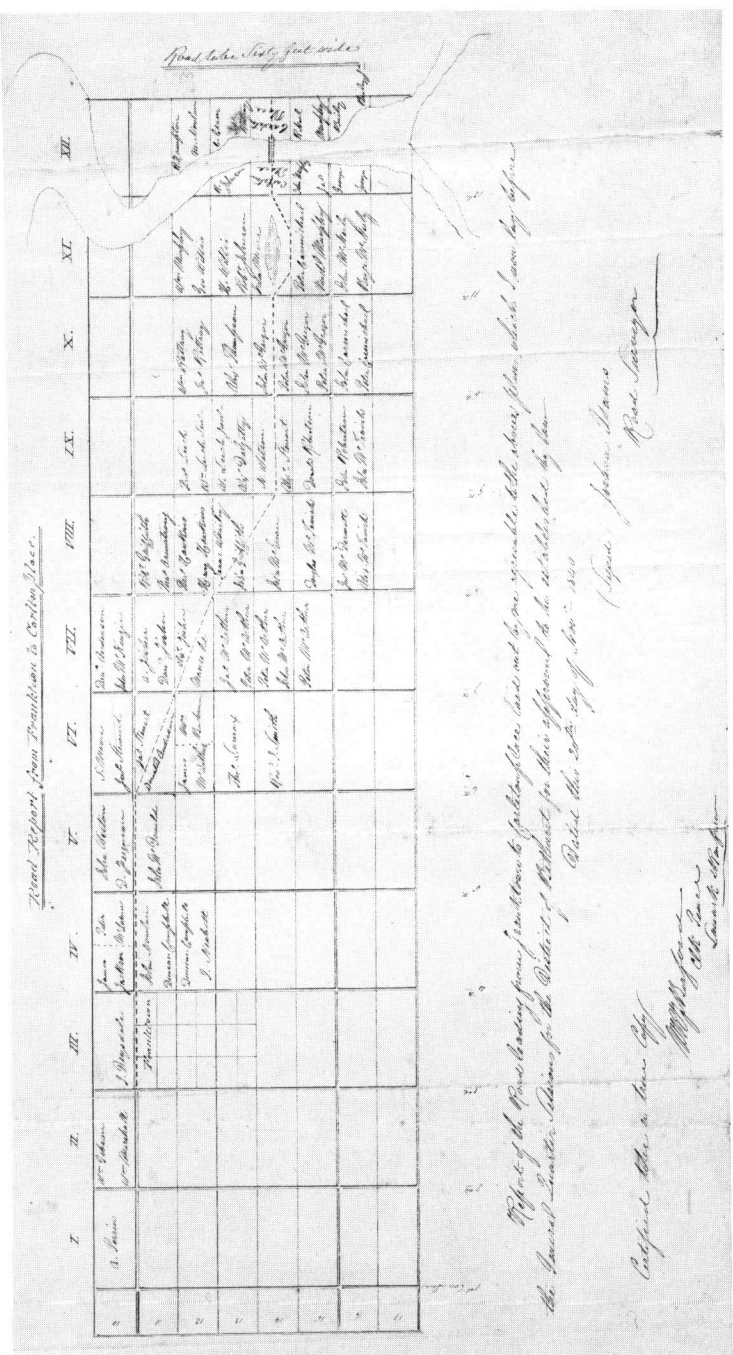

Plate 46
Plan of the road leading from Franktown to Carleton Place as laid out by Joshua Adams, road surveyor, 20 November 1840. This was the first road approved to be laid out by the first assembly of magistrates in general quarter sessions for the newly created county of Carleton or Bathurst District in 1823. The irregular route of this road departed from the original tidy surveyed plan of a road between lots ten and eleven in all concessions of Beckwith. This plan proposed widening the 1823 road to sixty feet, but as late as 1853 the road between Franktown and Carleton Place was described as a continuous tunnel of trees with endless seas of mud to plough through. Beckwith municipal records, Black's Corners.

overtake the highlanders in the Canadian backwoods and suggested to the Colonial Office that small stills might be legalised, as the immigrants would willingly pay for stills within reach.[82] Hence by 1824 the taverns of Patrick Nowlan and Thomas Wickham at Franktown and that of Alexander Morris at Morphy's Falls di
line of Beckwith and Francis Jessop at Morphy's Falls were operating distilleries.[83] From these taverns and distilleries Beckwith inhabitants emerged with the liquor which helped them forget temporarily the drudgery and loneliness of their daily lot. So constantly inebriated and so taken for granted was the need to drown the pain of their daily toil that William Morris at Perth in 1822 was "at a loss to find out many persons of sufficient information and respectability" who he could recommend to the lieutenant-governor to be resident magistrates in Beckwith.[84]

The Beckwith settlers who lurched home from the tavern either drunk or with a jug of whiskey had little concern with information or respectability. Unlike travellers touring through the more settled parts of Upper Canada they failed to be delighted by the brilliance of the autumn forest. They knew, after all, precisely the cost required in future years of toil to complete developing their tracts of forest into agriculturally productive farmland. What they did not know was how close they were to impending group violence.

Endnotes

1 Journal of Arthur Lang, published in Howard M. Brown, *Lanark Legacy: Nineteenth Century Glimpses of an Ontario County* (Perth: Corporation of the County of Lanark, 1984), p. 40.

2 John Howison, *Sketches of Upper Canada, Domestic, Local, and Characteristic* (Edinburgh: Oliver and Boyd, 1821; reprint ed., Toronto: Coles Publishing Company, 1970), pp. 11-12.

3 George Edward Kidd, *The Story of the Derry* (Vancouver: by the author, 1943), p. 50.

4 *Mirickville (Canada West) Chronicle*, 23 November 1860, p. 2, col. 6.

5 Howison, *Sketches of Upper Canada*, p. 11.

6 Brown, *Lanark Legacy*, p. 40.

7 Marjory Whitelaw, ed., *The Dalhousie Journals* (Ottawa: Oberon Press, 1981) II:45.

8 Kidd, *Story of the Derry*, p. 78.

9 Reminiscences of Bob Ferguson, 2 August 1910, noted in the back of the diary of William Livingstone Kidd, 1908-1911, provided courtesy of John and Leona Kidd, Beckwith.

10 OTAR RG 1, MS 658 Crown Lands Department, Township Papers, Beckwith, Reel 30, p. 282.

11 Ibid., p.11.

12 John May, "Bush Life in the Ottawa Valley Eighty Years Ago" in *Papers and Records of the Ontario Historical Society* XII (1914), p. 153.

13 William Bell, *Hints to Emigrants in a Series of Letters from Upper Canada* (Edinburgh, 1824), pp. 224-5

14 May, "Bush Life", pp. 161-162.

15 9 November 1860 letter from Angus McDiarmid, Kenmore, Osgoode Township, to his stepbrother John McDiarmid, Beckwith, provided courtesy of Rosemary Wark, Beckwith.

16 Kidd, *Story of the Derry*, p. 70.

17 For another example, see Lockwood, *Montague: A Social History*, p. 58.

18 Kidd, *Story of the Derry*, pp. 61-62.

19 Reminiscences of Mary Ann Kidd, aged 83, 11 December 1909, noted in the back of the diary of William Livingstone Kidd, 1908-1911.

20 Undated "Old time Stuff" clipping from the Ottawa *Citizen* of the 1920s, loaned by Audrey Renton, Kars.

21 Reminiscences of Mary Ann Kidd.

22 Howard M. Brown, *Founded Upon A Rock: Carleton Place Recollections* (Carleton Place: 150th Year Festival Committee, 1969), p. 10.

23 Ibid., p.11.

24 4 January 1825 letter from A FRIEND TO THE INDIANS, Brockville, to the *Brockville (Upper Canada) Recorder*, copied in the *Montreal (Lower Canada) Gazette*, 29 January 1825, p. 1, cols. 2-3.

25 Ibid.

26 NAC RG 5, A1 Reel C-4602 Upper Canada Sundries, vol. 41, p. 19730.

27 Andrew Haydon, *Pioneer Sketches in the District of Bathurst* (Toronto: The Ryerson Press, 1925), p. 34.

28 Ibid., p. 64.

29 NAC RG 5, A1 Reel C-4609 Upper Canada Sundries, vol. 58, p. 29920.

30 Ibid., pp. 30092-30094.

31 Jessie Buchanan Campbell, *The Pioneer Pastor* (Franklin, Pennsylvania: John J. McLaurin, 1905), p. 16.

32 Ibid., p. 27.

33 *Kingston Gazette*, 30 December 1817, p. 3, cols. 2-3, letter dated 14 December 1817 at Perth Settlement, from "A SETTLER."

34 NAC RG 5, A1 Reel C-4614 Upper Canada Sundries, vol. 70, pp. 37479-37480.

35 Extract from a letter written by Andrew Bell at Perth

35. in 1819, in Robert Lamond, *A Narrative of the Rise and Progress of Emigration, From the Counties of Lanark and Renfrew, to the New Settlements in Upper Canada, on Government Grant* (Glasgow: Chalmers and Collins, 1821; reprint ed., Ottawa: Canadian Heritage Publications, 1978), p. 73.
36. Thomas MacQueen, "Letters on Canada — No. IV — Settling On Land, Perth," *Perth (Upper Canada) Bathurst Courier*, 1 September 1846, pp. 2-3, cols. 7-1.
37. Andrew Bell, cited in Lamond, *A Narrative*, p. 73.
38. May, "Bush Life in the Ottawa Valley," p. 154.
39. MacQueen cited in Haydon, *Pioneer Sketches*, pp. 249-250; and Bell, cited in Lamond, *A Narrative*, p. 73.
40. OTAR RG 1 MS 658 Crown Lands Department, Township Papers, Beckwith, Reel 30, p. 443.
41. Ottawa (Roman Catholic) Archdiocesan Archives, Évêque Guigues, Registre des lettres, Vol. III (1854-1857), 5 April 1856 letter from T.P. French at Mount St. Patrick to Bishop Guigues, p. 312.
42. Ibid., pp. 312-313.
43. NAC MG 55/24 10 November 1823 letter from Robert Ferguson, Beckwith, to John Moir, near Kippen, West Stirling, Scotland.
44. MacQueen cited in Haydon, *Pioneer Sketches*, p. 251.
45. Jean S. McGill, *A Pioneer History of the County of Lanark* (Bewdley, Ontario: Clay Publishing Company Limited, 1979), p. 125.
46. OTAR RG1 Series C-IV MS 658 Crown Lands Department, Township papers, Ramsay, Box 416, p. 873.
47. Lanark County Registry Office, Perth, Ontario, Abstract Index to Deeds for Beckwith Township.
48. OTAR RG 1 Series C-IV MS 658 Crown Lands Department, Township Papers, Beckwith, Reel 30, p. 555.
49. Haydon, *Pioneer Sketches*, p. 19.
50. Ibid., p. 17.
51. The numbers of births are taken from the register for the Beckwith Presbyterian congregation at the United Church Archives at Victoria University in Toronto. An analysis of the 1822 census (Appendix 9) by Howard M. Brown places the Scottish proportion of the population at 374 persons, with an estimated margin of error at less than one percent. The birthrate per thousand among the Scottish highlanders was 50.8 in 1823, 66.8 in 1824, and 64.2 in 1825, which translates to a mean of 60.4 births per thousand during these years. Lacking comparable Irish Anglican figures, but recognizing equally large families among them, it is clear that pioneer Beckwith had an exceptionally high birthrate.
52. Campbell, *The Pioneer Pastor*, p. 28.
53. Samuel Butler, *The Emigrant's Hand-Book of Facts, Concerning Canada, New Zealand, Australia, Cape of Good Hope, &c.* (Glasgow: W.R. M'Phun; London: N.H. Cotes, 1843), p. 73.
54. NAC RG 5, A1 Reel C-6917 Upper Canada Sundries, vol. 260, p. 141905.
55. Campbell, *Pioneer Pastor*, pp. 27-28.
56. D., "Reminiscences of Sixty Years on the Ottawa" in *The Canada Presbyterian* (1879), p. 437.
57. *Brockville Recorder*, 28 June 1833, p. 1, col. 5.
58. *Bathurst Courier*, 17 November 1837, p. 3, col. 1.
59. *Perth (Ontario) Courier*, 25 December 1868.
60. Ibid., 15 March 1861, p. 1, col. 6.
61. *Bathurst Courier*, 25 August 1854, p. 2, col. 4.
62. May, "Bush Life,", p. 160.
63. [John A. McEwen], "Father's Father's Family," unpublished manuscript provided courtesy of Fred McTavish, Carleton Place, p. 11.
64. McCuan family correspondence, loaned courtesy of Alex and Jean McCuan, file 128, statement of Daniel McCuan, 7 May 1884.
65. Campbell, *Pioneer Pastor*, pp. 16-17.
66. May, "Bush Life,"p. 154.
67. Campbell, *Pioneer Pastor*, p. 29.
68. Ibid., pp. 29-30.
69. Ibid., p. 28.
70. Ontario Ministry of Natural Resources, Survey Map of Beckwith Township, January 1817, by R. Sherwood, Dpy. Surveyor.
71. NAC RG 5, A1 Reel C- Upper Canada Sundries, vol. 49, pp. 24212-24218.
72. This road is shown on an 1821 map of the Bathurst District from NAC, NMC(R) H1/409/Bathurst/1821 (Copy 2), reproduced in Nancy B. Bouchier, "'A Broad Clear Track in Good Order': The Bytown and Nepean Road Company — Richmond Toll Road, Ottawa, 1851-1875", in *Ontario History* LXXVI No. 2 (June 1984), p. 105.
73. NAC RG 5, A1 Reel C-4613 Upper Canada Sundries, vol. 67, p. 35768.
74. Ibid., p. 35768.
75. Ibid., pp. 35768-35769.
76. Bathurst District Quarter Sessions Roads Book, p. 2. I am grateful to George Bracken of Smiths Falls for allowing me to peruse and make photocopies from his copies of this volume.
77. NAC RG 5, A1 Reel C-4613 Upper Canada Sundries, vol. 67, p. 35769.
78. Bouchier, "A Broad Clear Track," p. 105.
79. OKQAR Rev. William Bell Journals II:125, entry for 13 July 1823.
80. NAC MG 55/24 No. 199. 10 November 1823 letter from Robert Ferguson, Beckwith, to John Moir, near Kippen, West Stirling, Scotland.
81. John MacTaggart, *Three Years in Canada: An Account of the Actual State of the Country in 1826-7-8* (London: H. Colburn, 1829) I:194.
82. Haydon, *Pioneer Sketches*, p. 24.
83. Brown, *Lanark Legacy*, pp. 203-204.
84. NAC RG 5, A1 Reel C-4609 Upper Canada Sundries, vol. 58, p. 30477.

CULTURAL CONFLICT?

The Irish and Scottish inhabitants of Beckwith were as shocked and astounded as the rest of Upper Canada by newspaper accounts of killing, gang violence and bludgeoning over a period of two weeks following a militia muster at Morphy's Falls in late April 1824. The Montreal *Herald*, for example, luridly described the violence as leaving "the floor and walls [of Alexander Morris's tavern] literally washed with blood."[1] Beckwith inhabitants were shocked not only because no such violence had previously existed in their vicinity, but also because it marred the second annual muster of the 4th Carleton militia. An orderly assembly of all younger able-bodied men of Beckwith and Ramsay townships to be put through various drills by officers on the birthday of George IV, somehow was transformed into a series of violent group skirmishes.

The beatings and bloodshed were remarkable for occurring in the midst of a British settlement which was intended by government to provide a model of loyalty and good order for Americans along the St. Lawrence. Somehow, rather than the Beckwith and Ramsay pioneers imposing order on their settlement, something in the nature of local society had prevented certain Irish and Scottish immigrants from peacefully coexisting. After all, had Captain Burke at Richmond not taken especial pains to keep the two ethnic groups separate in eastern Beckwith, by placing the Perthshire highlanders together in the northern quarter of the township, and the southeastern Irish immigrants together in the eastern quarter of the township? Even in domestic arrangements the mixture of Irish with Scottish could provide tensions as Perthshire immigrant John McDiarmid knew all too well. His Irish-born wife, Mary, invariably became indignant every time his Scottish neighbours visited and carried on a conversation with her husband in Gaelic, a language which she did not understand.[2]

The 1824 muster of militia at Morphy's Falls, at which the violence was precipitated, reminded Beckwith and Ramsay inhabitants of their ultimate military obligations as subjects of George IV, located though they were in one of the most remote corners of the British Empire. These men who journeyed up to fifteen miles from the more distant grants to spend an afternoon marching around under the gaze of company officers were part of a British settlement which was expected to set an example of loyalty and good order to American-origin inhabitants along the St. Lawrence. This was the second militia muster to be held in Beckwith, and it betokened the emergence of the Bathurst District. In April 1821 Beckwith along with Goulbourn, Drummond, Bathurst, March, Huntley, Ramsay, Lanark, Dalhousie, and North and South Sherbrooke townships became the county of Carleton. In November 1822 with the end of the military administrations at Perth and Richmond, Carleton County was proclaimed to be the separate administrative district of Bathurst. In January 1824 the Bathurst District was divided into the counties of Carleton and Lanark, with Beckwith, Drummond, Bathurst, North and South Sherbrooke, Dalhousie, Lanark, Ramsay, Lavant and Darling in the latter.[3]

Lanark and Carleton became separate counties both administratively and for electoral purposes, but Perth as the district seat boasted the court-house and gaol. The names Carleton County and Bathurst District were used interchangeably to refer to these united counties until the early 1830s, and it is possible that tavernkeeper Alexander Morris changed the name of Morphy's Falls to Carlton Place in the late 1820s to emphasize its comparative centrality in Carleton County. Carlton Place

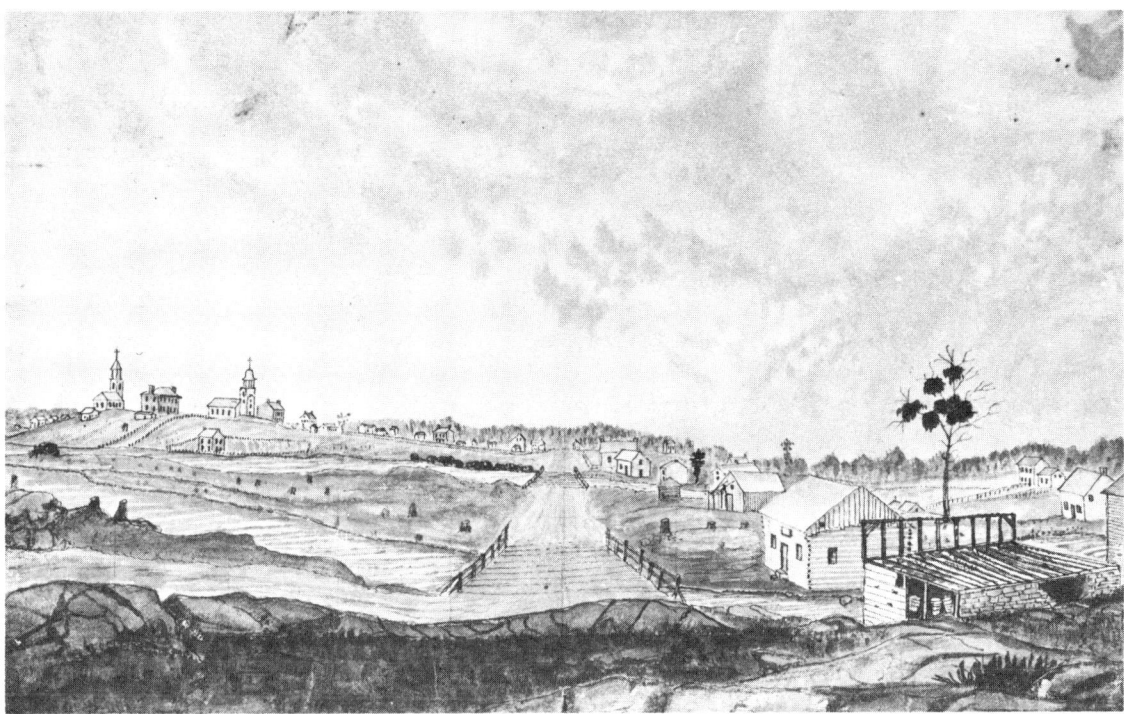

Plate 47
Perth, the Capital of the District of Dalhousie; from the North East bank of the River Tay: sketched 20th August 1828 by Thomas Burrowes. This view shows the emerging pretensions of the district seat twelve years after settlement began. On the far left is St. John the Baptist Roman Catholic church, next the brick mansion of barrister James Boulton, then St. James United Church of England and Ireland, and to the right of it the brick district court-house. The higher officers of the militia company of Beckwith and Ramsay men, save for Captain Thomas Glendinning, all lived in or near Perth. Archives of Ontario negative no. 22.

incidentally also was the name of a fashionable square in Glasgow in Morris's native Paisley,[4] but whatever the origin of the new name it served to give a more respectable name to a milling hamlet where murderous violence had briefly reigned.

The militia muster and the riots that followed it originated in the summer of 1822. That June, as preparations were being made to end the military administration at Perth, the second regiment of Carleton was divided into a new "Second Regiment to be composed of the Militia Residing within the Townships of Drummond and Lanark, and the Fourth Regiment of those residing within the Townships of Beckwith and Ramsay. The three highest officers in the fourth regiment did not reside in Beckwith. Under Colonel Josias Taylor, Lieutenant Colonel Ulysses Fitzmaurice and Major Donald Fraser there were ranked Captain Thomas Glendinning; lieutenants Thomas Wickham, William Moore, George Nesbitt, Duncan Fisher, Robert Ferguson and John Cram; ensigns Peter McGregor, John Nesbitt, Alexander Dewar, John Dewar, Manny Nowlan and Daniel Ferguson, and Sergeant John Nowlan, all from Beckwith.[5] The selection of these militia officers occurred in the midst of a severe drought in 1822, which fell particularly hard on the lowland Scottish immigrants in the range of townships north of Beckwith who had come to the end of the twelve months military rations supplied from the King's storehouses at Perth, Beckwith and Lanark.

The Scottish lowlanders who settled in Ramsay and the other northern Lanark County townships were radicalised, and pro-republican, who at the best of times had little love for the British government. When they first arrived in 1820 and 1821, many of the lowland immigrants were confident that they too could replicate the prosperity of the Perthshire settlers to be found across the line in Beckwith. A Ramsay lowlander asserted in November 1821 that he valued his new prospect so highly that he would not exchange it for the gift of a free horse, shop and one hundred pounds in Paisley. He perceived that the condition "of the weavers at home" hardly compared with "men here, who have not been more than two or three years on their land, who have now three head of cattle, and forty fowls about their doors, and living in the greatest plenty."[6] But as military provisions came to an end, as their poor efforts at husbandry were compounded by the drought in 1822 to yield insufficient crops, the radical and pro-republican spirit of the lowlanders came to the fore. As one of them admitted thirty years later, "In the hard times many men lost heart and left before they had cleared their lots", some going to the United States where they expected to find "liberty and Republican Government, but most of these when they had, through years of new sufferings and trials, scraped together their passage money, went home to Paisley or Glasgow." The men of the lowland families who determined to stay on their grants also went to the United States, working on the Oswego canal "to bring home some American cash." In their bitterness with the privations that befell them agriculturally and economically, the lowlanders who already were radicalised by the severe economic repercussions of the postwar economy on the woollen industry in Scotland, "thought much of the free country of America before we went to it, and little of Canada in which we saw what we called a tyrannical Royal Government."[7]

William Morris of Perth, a fellow lowlander, described the dilemma of his countrymen unsympathetically[8]

> The crops in Carlton have Suffered much from the drought, especially in the last settled townships (viz Dalhousie, Lanark and Ramsay)—The plan pursued in settling these townships has fallen short of the expectations formed by those connected with the department. The settlers are principally from manufacturing towns and not that hardy industrious race of beings, who only can surmount the difficulties of Settling a new country. In lieu of rations they received a certain sum of money, and I doubt in many instances were not very prudent in the management of it[. T]hey have long since been in want, many have gone away, some to return and some not[. T]hey are much to be pitied, altho' in most cases of distress the fault lies with themselves.
>
> The most part of their Corn and Wheat has been Cut off by the Grub, so that they have nothing to look to but their potatoes, and I fear ignorance of clearing the ground properly, will cause a failure in that crop also.

Radicalised as the Paisley weavers north of Beckwith were to begin with, deprived of their poor crops by drought in 1822, depressed and angry at being held up in developing their grants, with some of their friends and relatives departing for the United States either permanently or to raise money in 1823, they found a government agent preparing to settle hundreds of Irish Catholic immigrants among them. Initially, the Scottish superintendent of the Lanark settlement, Colonel William Marshall, attempted to have the Honourable Peter Robinson's Irish Catholic settlers placed on "land that is not so good as that which has already been conceded" to the lowland Scottish in North Sherbrooke, Dalhousie, Lanark and Ramsay townships,[9] but he was overruled by the Irish chairman of the Bathurst District land board, J.H. Powell, who preferred to place the Robinson settlers "on good land in townships advantageously situated and well settled."[10] As a result, the only overlap or mingling of Scottish lowlanders and newly arriving Irish Catholics occurred in Ramsay Township, immediately north of Beckwith.

The Robinson settlers arrived in the autumn of 1823, much too late in the year to make any kind of a beginning at settling grants of land. In the same way that the Lanark settlers before them were hauled in carts and waggons through the woods from Brockville in 1820 and 1821,[11] the 1823 Irish

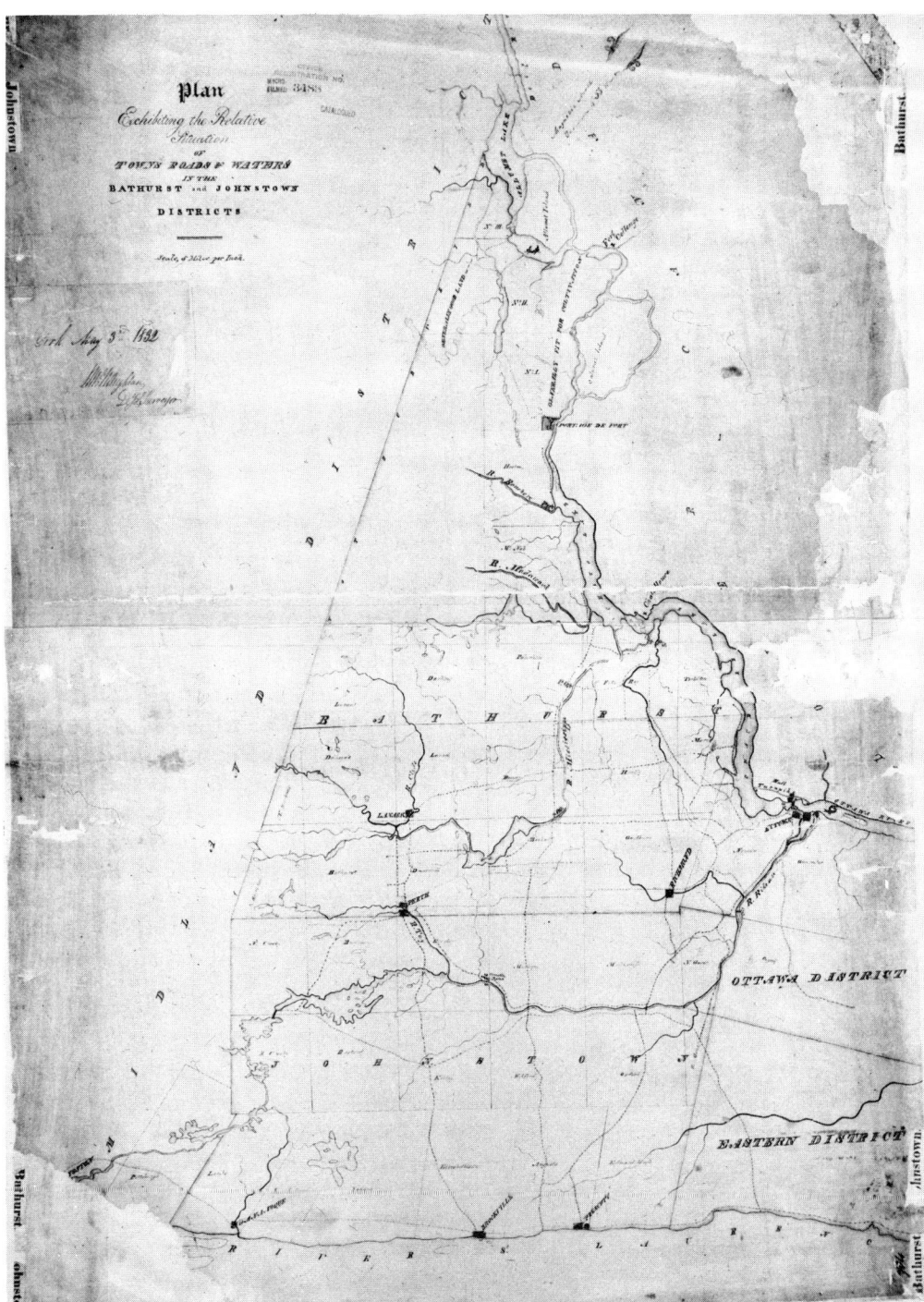

Plate 48
Plan exhibiting the Relative Situation of Towns, Roads & Waters in the Bathurst and Johnstown Districts, 1832, as prepared by J. McNaughton. This map suggests that there were more major roads cleared through Beckwith than was the case in most other nearby townships. The road system directly connected Beckwith to Perth on the west, Bytown to the east, the upper Ottawa to the north, and the Rideau and St. Lawrence settlements to the south. Archives of Ontario negative no. B-12.

Catholic arrivals were hauled by teams of oxen from Prescott to "Beckwith where...there is a large Government Store capable of containing most of them."[12] At Franktown, Robinson found at his disposal "many articles useful to settlers which remained in the King's Stores" which were distributed among the Irish settlers. Arriving at the Mississippi on 22 September, Robinson's first concern was to provide shelter for the immigrants against the oncoming winter. He reported:[13]

> As there were no Barracks or Government Buildings in the Neighbourhood and the whole party without shelter, my first care was to provide log houses for them, and that on their respective lots. Fortunately the autumn was unusually dry and warm and I completed this object by the First of September.
>
> To do this I was obliged to go to some additional expense, as the Settlers were not sufficiently acquainted with the use of the axe to put up log buildings themselves. However I feel well assured nothing tends so much to fix the attention of the emigrant to his newly acquired property and to ensure his becoming a permanent Settler as a little care and attention in placing him on his land.

In addition to helping the 568 Irish Catholic immigrants build houses, Robinson supplied them with 182 cows, farming utensils, guides to show the lands, seed corn and seed potatoes, medical advice, medicine, shoes and flannel all over and above what the Lanark Society settlers in Dalhousie, Lanark and Ramsay had received.[14]

The care taken by Peter Robinson in settling the Irish immigrants sent the lowland Scottish of northern Lanark County into alternating paroxysms of jealousy and paranoia. They had not been favoured with any of these extra benefits, and indeed had been charged three shillings each for survey expenses, and more than five shillings apiece for their patent grants. It would not have improved the mood of the lowland settlers to be told by a committee of the imperial parliament that even with these expenses and the extra provisions made for the Robinson settlers that the expenditure per person for both groups was nearly equal.[15] The cash advances that the lowlanders received upon arriving had been quickly frittered away,[16] followed by the drought of 1822 which reduced some of them to near-starvation and sent others away to the United States — all combined to intensify their jealousy of the newly-arrived Irish. It is likely that the Scottish weavers in Ramsay had hoped to acquire the empty lots scattered among them for their children to develop, and were piqued to find them suddenly granted to the Robinson settlers. Despite being in Upper Canada two to three years earlier than the newcomers, the lowland Scottish of Ramsay soon recognised that the different mode of settlement might even serve to advance the Irish ahead of them, and as a result not only would the lowlander settlement be behind the highlanders and Irish Anglicans of the Beckwith and Perth settlements, but it would endure the signal disgrace of falling behind a group of green Irish Catholic immigrants. The Scottish lowlanders brought an ingrained antipathy toward Irish Catholics with them as part of their cultural baggage. Their anger was rooted in the previous two generations as Irish Catholic weavers moved into the Glasgow vincinity and undercut lowland weavers in the cost of weaving cloth.

Jealousy quickly turned into paranoia, and coming as they did from the Orange stronghold of Glasgow, area lowlanders flocked to join Alexander Matheson[17] in founding a True Britons Orange lodge at Perth either in late 1823 or early 1824.[18] It was not mere coincidence that this lodge was founded immediately after the Robinson immigrants were settled north of Beckwith. The Perth settlement had existed for eight years with a large proportion of southeastern Irish Protestants and significant numbers of Irish Catholics without any need felt for an Orange lodge. Indeed what is surprising about the lowland weaver reaction to the Peter Robinson settlers is how ideologically close the two groups actually were had they somehow managed to communicate with one another before late April 1824. Many of the Catholic Irish, if grateful for being brought out to Canada, did

Plate 49
Log house in the village of Franktown, as photographed in 1982. The few older structures at Franktown testify to the limited commerce, lack of wealth, and limited early growth of this village before 1850.

not easily forget the burden of oppression and discrimination that the Protestant establishment of Ireland had inflicted on them for more than a century. Like Irish Catholics elsewhere in Upper Canada they could easily have become radicalised. Once the Orange lodge at Perth was organised, it refused to pass out of existence, although within a few years the Irish who replaced the lowlanders as the majority in the lodge expressed themselves "ready at all times to give the right hand of fellowship to our Catholic fellow subjects, and...to love them as men, though we cannot admit them as masters."[19] In the opening months of 1824 the lowland Scottish who formed the local Orange membership were of no mind to offer either fellowship or love.

* * * * * * * * * *

Initially, there was no outward sign of smouldering ethnic animosity nor of potential cultural conflict at the muster of militia at the straggling mill hamlet of Morphy's Falls on the 23rd of April 1824. All the witnesses present whose opinion later was considered worth consulting agreed that the muster itself had taken place "without any irregularity having occurred."[20] The four companies of the 4th Carleton militia all afternoon had paraded up and down an open piece of land on the north shore of the turbulent Mississippi across from the mills of Hugh Boulton and the store and tavern of Alexander Morris, "and the Men were dismissed without any appearance of a disposition to riot."[21] Sergeant John Nowlan from Franktown, a member of Captain George Nesbitt's company, had particular reason to be pleased with the drilling: Lieutenant-Colonel Fitzmaurice had called him over "and said that from his good behaviour he intended to recommend him for an Ensigncy". To celebrate this promise of promotion Nowlan joined Fitzmaurice and the other officers at the tavern of Alexander Morris to share a decanter of spirits and water.[22] Captain Nesbitt, who briefly had gone to attend a medical patient a short distance from the parade ground, joined Fitzmaurice, Nowlan, captains Thomas Glendinning, Duncan Fisher and William Moore, and lieutenants John Cram and Alexander Dewar in the comfort of the tavern.

The officers were not alone in seeking shelter from the occasional patches of rain. Some of the ordinary militia members also had crossed the river from the parade ground, but unlike the officers few had any money to purchase a drink, neither the newly-arrived Robinson settlers who had been given no cash nor the Ramsay Scottish lowlanders who long since had spent all theirs. The more resourceful of the lowland weaver settlers prevailed upon Captain Glendinning to give them a drink, for when Sergeant Nowlan went to find him some ten minutes after he had left the group of officers[23]

> he saw the Scotchmen having Capt[ai]n Glendenning on their shoulders, and huzzaing for the Scotch Captain "for he had treated his Company", and he saw the Men drinking the liquor. At this time there were about eight or nine of Capt[ai]n Nesbitt's Company standing by, of whom he thinks some were of Mr. Robinson's Settlers, namely, Teskey and his two sons, Serg[ean]t Brown, Mr. Armstrong, Buckley since Drowned, and Currin since shot. Then Teskey said "I never saw an Irishman worse than a Scotchman, and if Capt[ai]n Nesbitt was here he would treat his Company." This informant, John Nowlan, then said "Suppose I pay for it myself[.] Capt[ai]n Nesbitt's Company shall not be backward."

What Nowlan did not know was that earlier the Robinson settlers had asked Captain Nesbitt, "to give them some liquor, but he declined doing so, as he thought they had had enough already."[24] At this point the door opened, and Lieutenant Colonel Fitzmaurice and Captain Glendinning left to dine at the house of William Loucks one hundred yards west of the tavern.[25] Captain Nesbitt, overhearing Nowlan, ordered tavernkeeper Morris to give Nowlan half a gallon of spirits to treat the company. Morris replied that a quart was quite enough as there were not many of his company there. The quart was accordingly given, and Nesbitt carried it out to the men. Nowlan testified:[26]

> On going out Teskey[, one of the handful of Protestants among the Robinson settlers,] took the jug with the Spirits from Capt[ai]n Nesbitt and a glass, & told the Capt[ai]n he should drink a Toast, at the same time calling the men of Captain Nesbitt's Company together—when Captain Nesbitt took the glass and said he would drink the King and *all his loyal Subjects*—and then stood by until each man of his Company present drank the same Toast. They then took him up on their arms and harra'd for *an Irish Captain who never was backward* [emphasis added].

Nesbitt then rejoined the remaining officers inside the tavern without giving a second thought to what had taken place. His loyal toast was natural enough, given as it was at the end of a militia parade on the King's birthday. But from what was to follow it is clear that the insecure lowland Scottish who a minute before had cheered English-born Captain Glendinning as a "Scotch Captain" read the toast in quite a different light. Coming as they did from a radical stronghold in Scotland, favouring republican institutions over "a tyrannical Royal Government,"[27] and notorious for their first unproductive attempts at agriculture,[28] they misread the toast to "loyal Subjects" and the cheers for "an Irish Captain who never was backward" as an unflattering reference to themselves. One of the Scottish settlers immediately came up and struck an Irish Protestant settler named Benson "who however was not permitted to return the Blow, Nowlan and others interfering to prevent it."[29] Further blows having been avoided, Nowlan began to chat with a few Protestant Robinson settlers at the bar while the remaining men cleared out of the tavern. It was Captain Nesbitt sitting in the inner room who through the window witnessed two men outside striking one another. He ran out

Plate 50
An Irish wake as engraved for Samuel and Anna Hall's Ireland, Its Scenery, Character &c. *in the 1840s. The Peter Robinson Irish Catholic settlers who settled to the north of Beckwith brought with them customs such as the wake of which their lowland Scottish neighbours became either suspicious or intolerant. As late as 1860 an area inhabitant complained that the young who attended wakes "are exposed to the temptation of the 'inebriating cup,' and that 'great luxury' the pipe" and that there was "too much lightness manifested, too much trifling and frivolity displayed, so that persons became hardened, and to such a degree that they can jeeringly ask, who will next die?"*

but despite his best efforts was unable to either pacify or separate the two. Nesbitt later recalled:[30]

> [I know] that one of them was Irish and the other Scotch. ... One of these men threw the other down, and struck him with his Foot on the breast, when another who was looking on damned him, and asked him if he was going to Kill the Man, and immediately Knocked him down. A general attack was then made by all present.— [I believe] there were about Six of Mr. Robinson's Settlers then present, and perhaps twenty of the old [Scottish] settlers.

Realising that his efforts and those of the other junior officers to restore order were ineffectual "and hoping that L[t]. Col. Fitzmaurice would have more influence," Nesbitt ran toward the Loucks residence, arriving there just as Fitzmaurice and Captain Glendinning came running out.[31] Luckily for George Nesbitt's expectations, he did not hear an exchange which had just taken place between Fitzmaurice and Glendinning. As they were about to sit down to dinner in William Loucks's house, Glendinning looked out the window and "saw a great many people fighting at Morris's tavern

Door."³² Fitzmaurice saw no need to break up the riot. He said "Let them fight away; it will be soon over." Glendinning, looking out the window, insisted that he must go over, to which Fitzmaurice responded "You had better not. I will go and pacify them." Again, Glendinning stated that he must go over to the riot, adding somewhat tellingly, "This is all intended for me—and they must get it, for we are three or four to one"!³³ Coming as Fitzmaurice did from Ireland, he was not one to allow a little recreational violence to interrupt his dinner, and from his remarks it is clear he knew that Glendinning's presence would not stop the fighting. Still both men dashed out when they saw Captain Nesbitt running toward them.

Sergeant John Nowlan was deep in conversation with the handful of Protestant Robinson settlers in the barroom, when the "great noise of a hubbub" caused them to notice the riot gaining momentum outside. Nowlan, running out, heard Captain Glendinning urging the Scottish lowlanders on by saying "Since it is so Boys fight away like brave fellows". Nowlan ran over to where he "saw two or three men kicking a man who was down.... Nowlan caught hold of one of the three, a Scot named Hamilton, saying 'have you a mind to Murder the Man' "? Hamilton gave Nowlan a shove and said 'I would, him or you either'."³⁴ Fitzmaurice and Nesbitt "took from the rioters all the clubs they could, and threw them into the River".³⁵ Then Fitzmaurice went inside the tavern "where he found two more with sticks which he also took from them". The brutal fighting outside had resumed, and when Fitzmaurice rushed out "he saw a number engaged in fighting with their fists and among them Capt[ai]n Glendinning who he saw engaged in the affray"³⁶ exchanging blows with "an old settler who was also Irish".³⁷ Sergeant Nowlan at this point³⁸

> heard L[t]. Col. FitzMaurice desire Captn. Glendenning to go into the House, and he and Captn. Nesbitt would get more good of the People than he could. — The Irishmen at the Same time saying they did not want to have anything to do with the Scotchmen at all — Captn. Glendenning would not go in, but rather encouraged the men, when the Scotchmen began to hurra for an Irishman, for they were then a great many to one against the Irish. On turning [Nowlan] saw an Irish Settler, but not one of Mr. Robinson's, nor a Catholic, seize Captn. Glendenning by the collar and call him a Scoundrel adding that he ought to make peace, and not encourage the fight, —and that...he would fight him in any way a man could be taken. L[t]. Col. FitzMaurice then came between them and parted them, and said to Captn. Glendenning that it was a Shame for him to be encouraging such things instead of making Peace.

By the time that Fitzmaurice succeeded in restoring order, the number of Irish was increasing. The Scottish immigrants went into the tavern together, as Fitzmaurice with the assistance of Captain Nesbitt and another Irish settler succeeded in ferrying the Robinson settlers across the Mississippi to start them on their way home.³⁹ To prevent the Irish recrossing, Fitzmaurice "secured the Canoes below at the Beckwith side".⁴⁰

With order restored, Fitzmaurice returned to his dinner at the Loucks hostelry, but had only gotten as far as drying himself near the fire when a few of the settlers came to the door and requested him to come out to them. Fitzmaurice, suspecting that something was afoot, "bade them once or twice [to] come in but they would not and again begged of him to come out and speak to them, which he at length did, when they instantly raised him up on their shoulders and carried him to Morris'[s] where he desired Mr. Morris to give them some Rum".⁴¹ Fitzmaurice took care to order that "a glass of liquor...be given to each of the persons without distinction"⁴² but in his impatience to return to his dinner at William Loucks's he allowed Captain Glendinning to receive and divide the quart of liquor among the men.⁴³ The Robinson settlers, anticipating that Glendinning would pass them over and not wishing to incur ridicule from the Scottish, "took Capt[ai]n Nesbitt out of Mr. Morris'[s] House and begged of him to give them something to drink, and he ordered one quart of Rum to be given them."⁴⁴

Plate 51
The Captain Thomas Glendinning house, lot 20, concession 12, Beckwith, on Glen Isle, built ca. 1821, as photographed in 1984. This, the first stone house built in Beckwith, reflected the annual military pension received by Glendinning as a half-pay officer. His captain's rank provided him a grant of five hundred acres, five times the size of the usual land grant in Beckwith. Glendinning provoked a riot between lowland Scots and Irish Catholic settlers following a militia muster at Morphy's Falls in 1824.

Sergeant John Nowlan, who had gone off to saddle up his mare for the journey back to Franktown, returned to the Morris tavern to find the inner room "almost filled with Scotchmen" and two of the Protestant Robinson settlers, Teskey and Benson, in the outer barroom. When Nowlan entered the inner room, "Ensign Dewar[,] a Scotchman[,] asked him to sit down and drink with them, he Nowlan said he would not as he must set out homeward[,] having a good way to go."[45] Captain Duncan Fisher, a Beckwith highlander, immediately sensing that the insecure lowlanders would interpret this as social or ethnic snubbing of them as a group, sidled up to Nowlan, "took a hold of him" and skilfully appearing to identify with the lowlanders said to him "Sure[,] you are...not offended with us". Nowlan, catching the hint, decided it might be wise to stay put and sat down alongside Captain Fisher.[46]

One of the people in the room bĕgan to sing a Scotch song, saying he supposed...Nowlan would not be offended at his singing a Scotch Song, when Nowlan answered that *no song would offend him if it was not Treason* [emphasis added]. Then Benson came in with a Small Decanter of Liquor and a glass, in his hands, and asked [Nowlan] to drink — when the man who was Singing bade him begone for he wanted none of his company there. Benson said he did not want anything from him, for he had his own liquor, and he would not go out till he pleased. — Upon which the man who had been singing and another arose and Seized Benson by the hands and legs and flung him out through the door and Shut it.

This presented John Nowlan with the excuse he needed to leave. He went out, and he and Teskey together convinced Benson to head off in the direction of Ramsay. Captain Nesbitt came up, and asked Nowlan "if all was peaceable," and upon assurance that it was, they "went in and paid their Bill at Mr. Morris'[s] and took their Horses and rode home"[47] toward Franktown.

Nesbitt and Nowlan's horses had barely disappeared into the forest when Lieutenant Colonel Fitzmaurice discovered that all was not peaceable. He returned from treating the men at the tavern only to find that dinner at the Loucks residence had been cleared away. While waiting to have it replaced on the table, Fitzmaurice "was informed that a number of the New [Robinson] Settlers were assaulting on the other side and about to cross at another Ferry.... After crossing they went to Morris'[s] House and called for the people inside to come out, and struck at the Door and Window with Sticks & Stones." Through the window of the Loucks house Fitzmaurice saw with his own eyes the attack on the tavern and, as he later testified, "Knowing only one of these Settlers, and seeing them now so exasperated he did not think it safe to go among them. — He soon after heard the Report of a gun..." The Robinson settlers left the tavern and stopped in front of the Loucks house, where instead of receiving empathy from Fitzmaurice, "he spoke to them saying that they had behaved very ill, and deserved to have balls fired at them instead of slugs — and that if he had been in the House so attacked by them he would have killed as many of them as he could."[48] Temporarily chastened by these words the Robinson settlers crossed the Mississippi and themselves vanished into the woods.

The only eyewitness account of what occurred inside the tavern comes from the pen of Captain Thomas Glendinning, an individual who by his actions and words earlier in the day clearly egged on the Scottish lowlanders. Glendinning claimed to see "a great number" of the Robinson settlers running from the direction of the Loucks house toward the tavern[49]

> when instantly the Door was Shut and on the arrival of the Irish they instantly broke in one of the Windows, and threatened they would take every one's life then in the House. Some of the old Settlers who were without the Door when it was Shut were Severely beaten by the Irishmen before the Door, and they were taken into the House. In taking in one of the old Settlers, an Irishman named Benson ran after to strike him and they both fell into the House and were Shut in.

One of the Scottish lowlanders inside the tavern, John Fumerton, produced a gun and boldly went outside only to have the gun snatched from him by a Robinson settler named Leahy who the next day bragged "let me see the man who will own it." Once the gun was grabbed from his hands, Fumerton "was knocked down, after which he escaped into the House." At this point in his account of what took place, Glendinning painted himself as attempting to prevent bloodshed:[50]

> Then Mr. Morris loaded a gun and gave it to Fummerton, and ordered him to Fire, and he did fire out of the end window: Capt[ai]n Glendenning as Fummerton was about to Fire through the front window Stopped him, when the people inside complained loudly of this interference saying that he wished them to be Murdered, — and they all called to Fummerton to fire which he did out of the end window, and wounded some of those outside, two of whom named Leahy he saw next day wounded.
>
> Immediately after this the Irish settlers dispersed and he saw no more of them that night.

Glendinning himself then left Morphy's Falls, and it was left to Lieutenant Colonel Fitzmaurice

Plate 52
The kitchen of the Captain Thomas Glendinning house, Glen Isle, as photographed in the early 1980s. Glendinning, hotly pursued by the Peter Robinson Irish Catholic settlers who he had insulted after the militia muster at Morphy's Falls, successfully evaded capture by hiding in a recessed cavity or curing shelf up in behind the kitchen fireplace. Captain James Fitzgibbon, in investigating the riots at Morphy's Falls, reported "that the strong feeling which I witnessed in the minds of the new [Peter Robinson] settlers against Capt[ai]n Glendinning...convinces me that that officer is greatly wanting in that temper and discretion now so requisite in every officer belonging to the 4th Regiment of Carleton Militia."

to witness the final anticlimactic incident of the day. Three to four hours after the Robinson settlers dispersed, while Fitzmaurice was inspecting the damage to the tavern of Alexander Morris, three or four men bearing fire arms came in with a prisoner, Hugh Boulton.[51] Boulton, the miller at Morphy's Falls and son of Leeds County United Empire Loyalists, had played no part in the riot.[52] Upon Fitzmaurice inquiring why he was a prisoner, Boulton "replied he had been returning from training and met these drunken men who forced him along with them." The men who held him prisoner explained that they had been "sent out by Capt[ai]n Glendinning to patrole and having met this man they brought him in." Boulton at this point "supposed he might go away, but the armed men cried out No."[53] Fitzmaurice promptly rebuked them for detaining Boulton, and sent them all home. So ended the violence of the 23rd day of April 1824 at Morphy's Falls.

For two weeks the vicinity trembled with intermittent conflict which developed from the riots that followed the militia muster at Morphy's Falls. The following day twenty of the Robinson settlers arrived at the house of William Loucks, many of them threatening to have Glendinning's life, with one John French who was armed with a gun refusing to leave "till he had satisfaction of Mr. Glendinning."[54] Loucks was helpless in dissuading the group from going upstairs where he saw a man he believed to be Luke McGrath "knock down Captain Glendinning in my house, in the upper apartment, with a club."[55] Two days later on 26 April William Morphy at Morphy's Falls looked up, startled to see "a number of men which I believe were Mr. Robinson's settlers pass through the field in which I was working, rank and file, with a green flag in front of them, carried by Luke McGrath...[and] armed with guns and bludgeons." As they filed by in the direction of Morphy's Falls, some of the Robinson settlers explained to Morphy that they had just been at Glendinning's looking for him to fight a duel with one John Sullivan."[56] This was probably the occasion, celebrated in local legend, when Glendinning hid from the Robinson settlers in a cavity behind his fireplace.[57] At Morphy's Falls, if the somewhat exaggerated statement of district magistrates seeking justification for their own subsequent behaviour can be believed,[58]

> upwards of one hundred men of the same party assembled in a riotous manner and marched in seeming military order, and appeared regularly to obey the command of an individual; that they marched with music and displayed a green flag, and having arrived at the house of [Alexander] Morris, they repeated their violent conduct by breaking open the door, entering the house and destroying his property.

Alexander Morris fled to Perth with this story. The district sheriff, Colonel James H. Powell, believing the Robinson settlement to be "in a very disturbed state," sent his deputy Alexander Matheson accompanied by three magistrates" and an armed party of 100 of the Militia as Constables to "apprehend several people against whom he had warrants for riots and assaults."[59] Matheson as founder of the Orange lodge at Perth a few months earlier was alleged to be a poor choice for this mission, since his father had been murdered by Catholics in Ireland, and many of the men he selected as constables were members of the Perth Orange Lodge.[60] This large party stopped overnight at Morphy's Falls, and from there continued on to the settlement depot at Shipman's Mills (later Almonte). There they made a running charge at a group of Irish Catholics gathering for mass, and another branch of the deputy-sheriff's party fired on the house of William Roche, wounding several people, beating others, and killing one. After an armed occupation and search of Ramsay for several days, they escorted some nineteen prisoners back to Perth.[61] A Scottish onlooker at the trials of the Robinson settlers that June reflected the pervasive lowlander bias against "the rogues from Ballygiblon" in observing that "They were a savage looking set."[62]

****

What had taken place?

This was the question that preoccupied everyone in Upper Canada as news of the violence at Morphy's Falls and Shipman's Mills trickled out to the Brockville *Recorder* and was picked up in turn by the Kingston, York and Montreal newspapers. The publicity was one-sided, being heavily loaded against the Robinson settlers. The 5 May 1824 Montreal *Herald* told of "a party...principally Scots...drinking His Majesty's health" who were attacked so outrageously "by the Ballygibinet...Irish emigrants" as to cause Morris's tavern "floor and walls [to be] literally washed with blood."[63] The extensive newspaper publicity created a negative image which was cast on all Irish immigrants. John MacTaggart in his two volumes on eastern Upper Canada in 1829 noted that the Peter Robinson settlement north of Beckwith "did not very well succeed, his people, as all from Erin are, being so difficult to manage, so disposed to riot."[64] What more thoughtful people such as Lieutenant-Governor Sir Peregrine Maitland found both extraordinary and unfortunate was that rioting should have occurred "in a District possessing so effective a population", that is, a hand-picked British immigrant population which was intended to set a model of loyalty for the rest of the province. How could a riot have "originated among people assembled in obedience to the laws for the [order-instilling] purpose of militia training and in the presence of their officers"? Most mystifying of all, the magistrates accompanying the deputy-sheriff's party were not surprised that an armed posse of more than one hundred persons was preparing to shoot at people who had not even once used a fire arm.[65]

Plate 53
Sitting room of the Captain Thomas Glendinning house, Glen Isle, as photographed in June 1983. This was the most elegant room to be found in Beckwith before 1830. It was modest in size, but the Georgian panelling of the interior window shutters, the simple yet pleasing Georgian design of the fireplace mantel, the hexagonal stovepipe hole in the ceiling and the large windows combined to give the interior of this house a brightness and sophistication impossible to find in the log houses of all other Beckwith inhabitants.

In Beckwith there was little immediate impact. Following the beating of Captain Glendinning in the upper chamber of William Loucks's house at Morphy's Falls on the 24th of April, armed volunteer guards were placed on the road leading south to Franktown. Apart from this and from Captain Thomas Glendinning's role as agitator, it is significant that there is not a single scrap of evidence to suggest that the Scottish highlanders and Irish Anglicans of Beckwith were frightened by the events that occurred. In this respect they provided a distinct contrast with the inhabitants of Ramsay, described "as labouring under...fear for the lives of themselves and families, and the destruction of their property".[66] An example of the ease with which even a slightly insecure Scottish lowlander, no matter how well established he was, could blame the Robinson Irish Catholics for incidents is provided by the Reverend William Bell at Perth. A couple of days after the deputy-sheriff's party brought in nineteen prisoners from Ramsay, Bell discovered that during "the night the railing in front of our house had been pulled down and we suspected that some of the Ballygiblonites who had been liberated the night before had done it", only to discover later that a neighbour "had done [it] in a drunken spree."[67] In Beckwith, by contrast, even the guards of the Franktown road, who in all probability were placed there by Captain Glendinning, regarded with some levity their instructions to shoot down any of the Robinson settlers who might try to pass. Alexander Stewart, for example, who was posted as a guard on Sunday the 25th of April prayed that "none of the 'Giblans' might pass as he 'wudna like to shoot them on the Sabbath day'."[68]

The violence at Morphy's Falls served to provide remarkable evidence of the major cultural differences that existed between the highland Scottish settlement in Beckwith and the lowland settlers in Ramsay. Obviously, there were cultural differences between the Catholic majority of the Robinson settlers in Ramsay and the Wexford Anglicans of Beckwith, but these differences were of such minimal importance that these two groups instantly bonded in the face of what they perceived as a potential affront to their common nationality. Irish Anglican John Nowlan from Beckwith, for example, offered to purchase a round of drinks for the Robinson settlers rather than allow them to be shamed by Glendinning's exclusion of them in treating only the Ramsay lowlanders. There could be no more touching instance of Irish Catholics bonding with Irish Anglicans than when the Robinson settlers begged Captain Nesbitt to treat them so that they could hold up their heads in front of the Scots.

The violence following the militia parade also reveals that the Irish Protestants and Perthshire highlanders of Beckwith at this initial point shared an innate conservatism which manifested itself in various ways. Whereas many of the Ramsay lowlanders were from passionately Secessionist Presbyterian backgrounds, most of the Beckwith highlanders were from Church of Scotland backgrounds. The Robinson Irish Catholic settlers came out of a tradition in which they had been penalised for the sake of their religion, whereas Beckwith Irish immigrants belonged to the United Church of England and Ireland. The stability and obligations which came with membership in the two state churches of the British Isles obligated the Irish Anglicans and Church of Scotland highlanders to edge away from any activity which threatened social stability. Hence the few Beckwith Irish and Scottish settlers present at Morris's tavern after the militia muster were to be found separating combatants and striving to restore order. For example, John Nowlan prevented one Protestant Robinson settler from returning the blow of a lowlander and both Fitzmaurice and another Irish settler upbraided English-origin Captain Glendinning for encouraging the rioting. Significantly, the remarks of John Nowlan at which the Ramsay lowlanders took umbrage were matter-of-fact ordinary everyday expressions of loyalty to the King, exactly the kind of toasts one would expect from a loyal subject.

The Ramsay lowlanders and the Irish Catholic Robinson settlers shared an insecurity of equally massive proportions. The lowlanders as Secessionists from a radicalised section of Scotland particulary hard hit by the postwar economic depression had no especial reason to trust government, subject as they had been to searches through their Paisley homes by government troops. How could they be certain that the conventional loyal toasts and rhetoric against treason were not barbs intentionally aimed by Irish Anglicans at them, possessing as many of them did a pro-republican spirit? Hard hit by the drought of 1822, and with very little to show after more than two years on their land, they now were obliged to put up with a host of galling monarchist toasts that left them feeling no more established than the newly arrived Robinson settlers who belonged to their company. Perhaps that was precisely where the rub lay. While the much earlier-established and more prosperous Beckwith Irish and Scottish settlers worked well together as a militia company, the Ramsay lowlanders and Robinson settlers (both Catholic and Protestant) felt that their comparative newness as groups on the local scene was all the more emphasized by being paired with one another. The lowlanders, resenting their poor agricultural beginning feared that the newly-arrived Robinson settlers might possibly show them up. The Irish Catholic Robinson settlers, sensing the hostility of the lowlanders, insecurely assumed that this was a continuation in Canada of the Protestant intolerance to which they were used in Ireland for two centuries. As for the few Protestant Robinson settlers, when matters came to a head at the Morris tavern, they revealed themselves to be Irishmen first and foremost, especially when a group of twenty lowlanders began beating a handful of Irish Catholics.

Above all, the violence at Morphy's Falls reveals how intact the cultural baggage of all four groups remained. Despite their recent generous settlement by government, the Irish Catholic

ELDERS AND MEMBERS OF REV. GEORGE BUCHANAN'S CHURCH IN BECKWITH

DUNCAN CRAM AND WIFE.   ALEXANDER DEWAR AND WIFE.   ROBERT KENNEDY AND WIFE.

Plate 54
Three pioneer Beckwith couples, as later photographed in old age from left to right, Duncan Cram and his wife Sarah Agnes Wilson, Janet Kennedy and her husband Alexander Dewar, and Christina McDiarmid and her husband Robert Kennedy. The handsome dress of these six people suggests the prosperity achieved by the Perthshire settlers inhabiting the Mississippi floodplain in northern Beckwith. Robert Kennedy opened a burial ground on his farm on lot 24 in the eighth concession, and subsequently Alexander Dewar opened another nearby on lot 24 in the seventh concession. From Jessie Buchanan Campbell, The Pioneer Pastor *(1905).*

Robinson immigrants retained the mindset of a people deprived of political and religious fair treatment, and almost involuntarily responded to violence with more violence. The Scottish lowland weavers of Ramsay, living under the shadow of the counter-revolutionary persecution by British government troops against radicals in the Glasgow vicinity, insecurely misinterpreted loyal toasts and rhetoric against treason as veiled attacks on themselves. The Wexford Protestants in Beckwith believed themselves to still be the embattled minority with links to a distant British government that they had been in Ireland, surrounded by treachery and disloyalty which might erupt at any moment and which required their most winning efforts to check. The Scottish highlanders of Beckwith, by contrast were the most stable ethnic group in the region, but in this they too showed that they were living under the shadow of their recent past in Perthshire. The innately conservative Beckwith highlanders were horrified by the radical activities of lowland weavers and the threat it posed to established authority. This horror was reflected by the comments made in an 1820 letter from a brother in Perthshire to James McDiarmid in Beckwith:[69]

> We had very threatning times in this kingdom lately, on account of the death of our Sovereign king. The manufacturing and weaving companies, were suing for a new ministry; and to effect that by force if resisted. They made several attempts, and much mischief about Glasgow, and Paisley; but all to no effect. All is subsided at present, and trade is getting better:—but it is reported that they will make a final a[ttem]pt ere long. At London lately five men have been executed, and six banished, on account of an attempt made to destroy the ministers of

112 CULTURAL CONFLICT?

Plate 55
"The Rival Candidates", a cartoon showing William Morris and Alexander Thom on the hustings at Perth during the 1828 election, by Francis W. Consitt. The 1824 and 1828 elections were significant for Beckwith inhabitants in that many of them received their land patents during these two years. The military and aristocratic dress of the Thom supporters on the left as opposed to the highland dress of the Morris backers on the right suggests that religious and ethnic identification mattered more for Beckwith electors than did the political labels of Tory and Reformer used elsewhere in Upper Canada. Perth Museum.

parliament. The radicals have likewise done much mischief in Ireland.

The docility the Perthshire settlers previously had manifested under the highland landowners and the Church of Scotland clergy continued in Beckwith. This is shown by their behaviour during the second election for Lanark County held at Perth in June 1824. One of the candidates, the active Church of Scotland supporter William Morris, wrote to the Reverend George Buchanan at Beckwith, asking him to do something on his behalf. Buchanan[70]

answered that he would talk to the congregation at a meeting to be held the next week. He did so, advising all to support Mr. Morris, whom he commended as a Presbyterian and a capable man. The people heard this with evident satisfaction and promised to act accordingly. Every one in the county who wanted to vote had to go to Perth to cast his ballot.... [T]he Beckwith delegation appeared in sight, having walked the whole way, Highland pipers playing the bagpipes at the head of the procession. Every man voted for Morris, electing him by a large majority.

The conservatism of the Perthshire immigrants largely helps to explain the lack of cultural conflict in Beckwith, sharing this as they did with the Irish Anglicans of the township. What relations did exist between theses two transplanted communities could best be described as a type of amicable rivalry, a rivalry which developed out of the few social occasions that bush life provided such as logging bees, barn raising bees and corn husking bees. But apart from the teams of men attempting to rival one another at these gatherings, the isolation of the forest kept Irish and Scottish immigrants in Beckwith from mingling. With many of the highlanders speaking only Gaelic and all of the Wexford immigrants speaking English, it is hardly surprising that the two communities had minimal intercourse. Ironically, the large families that both Irish and Scottish inhabitants of Beckwith were rearing to help develop their forest lots offered the only significant seeds of future potential conflict. With over 85 percent of Beckwith land either patented or held in reserve by the end of 1828, many children growing up in pioneer Beckwith sooner or later faced landless futures and became increasingly susceptible to the radical rhetoric of the lowland weavers in Ramsay. The riots at Morphy's Falls, at it turned out, did not reflect cultural conflict in Beckwith itself. Friendly rivalry was the hallmark of relations between the transplanted Irish and Scottish immigrant communities in Beckwith. Only in the future might the possibility for conflict exist in Beckwith.

Endnotes

1. *Montreal (Lower Canada) Herald*, 5 May 1824, cited in Andrew Haydon, *Pioneer Sketches in the District of Bathurst* (Toronto: The Ryerson Press, 1925), p. 144.
2. George Edward Kidd, *The Story of the Derry* (Vancouver: by the author, 1943), pp. 53-54.
3. Thomas A. Hillman, "A Statutory Chronology of Eastern Ontario, 1788-1981" in Donald H. Akenson, ed., *Canadian Papers in Rural History IV* (Gananoque, Ontario: Langdale Press, 1984), pp. 284-285, 305.
4. Howard M. Brown, *Founded Upon A Rock: Carleton Place Recollections* (Carleton Place: 150th Year Festival Committee, 1969), p. 7.
5. Charles Fothergill, *York Almanac and Royal Calendar of Upper Canada* (York, Upper Canada: by the author, 1823), courtesy of Howard M. Brown.
6. NAC RG 5, A1 Reel C-4609 Upper Canada Sundries, vol. 57, pp. 29283-29284.
7. Great Britain, House of Commons Select Committee on Emigration from the United Kingdom, *Second Report, Minutes of Evidence* (London, 1827), p. 129.
8. *Perth (Canada West) Courier*, 15 March 1861, p. 1, cols. 4-6.
9. NAC RG 5, A1 Reel C-4611 Upper Canada Sundries, vol. 61, pp. 32354-32356.
10. Ibid., pp. 32629-32630.
11. Marjory Whitelaw, *The Dalhousie Journals* (Ottawa: Oberon Press, 1981) II:48.
12. NAC RG 5, A1 Reel C-4611 Upper Canada Sundries, vol. 61, pp. 32746-32747.
13. Maurice Denham Jephson, *An Anglo-Irish Miscellany: Some Records of the Jephsons of Mallow* (Dublin: Allen Figgis, 1964), p. 377.
14. Great Britain, House of Commons Select Committee on Emigration from the United Kingdom, *First Report, Minutes of Evidence* (London, 1826), p. 217.
15. Ibid.
16. Diary of Arthur Lang printed in the *Carleton Place Herald*, 2 February 1938, cited in Howard M. Brown, *Lanark Legacy: Nineteenth Century Glimpses of an Ontario County* (Perth: Corporation of the County of Lanark), p. 42.
17. NAC RG 5, A1 Reel C-6870 Upper Canada Sundries, vol. 100, p. 56511.
18. OKQAR Rev. William Bell Journals II:133.
19. NAC RG 5, A1 Reel C-6863 Upper Canada Sundries, vol. 83, p. 45231.
20. Ibid., Reel C-4613, vol. 67, p. 35301. Nesbitt testimony.
21. Ibid., p. 35291. Fitzmaurice testimony.
22. Ibid., p. 35305. Nowlan testimony.
23. Ibid., pp. 35305-35306. Nowlan testimony.
24. Ibid., p. 35303. Nesbitt testimony.

25　Ibid., p. 35295. Glendinning testimony.
26　Ibid., p. 35306. Nowlan testimony.
27　*Perth Courier*, 15 March 1861, p. 1, cols. 4-6.
28　NAC RG 5, A1 Reel C-4609 Upper Canada Sundries, vol. 57, pp. 29283-29284. Morris testimony.
29　Ibid., Reel C-4613, vol.67, pp. 35307-35308 Nowlan testimony.
30　Ibid., pp. 35301-35302. Nesbitt testimony.
31　Ibid., p. 35302. Nesbitt testimony.
32　Ibid., p. 35295. Glendinning testimony.
33　Ibid., p. 35294. Fitzmaurice testimony.
34　Ibid., p. 35307. Nowlan testimony.
35　Ibid., p. 35302. Nesbitt testimony.
36　Ibid., pp. 35292-35292. Fitzmaurice testimony.
37　Ibid., p. 35302. Nesbitt testimony.
38　Ibid., p. 35308. Nowlan testimony.
39　Ibid., p. 35308. Nowlan testimony.
40　Ibid., p. 35293. Fitzmaurice testimony.
41　Ibid., p. 35292. Fitzmaurice testimony.
42　Ibid., p. 35303. Nesbitt testimony.
43　Ibid., pp. 35292-35293. Fitzmaurice testimony.
44　Ibid., p. 35303. Nesbitt testimony.
45　Ibid., p. 35309. Nowlan testimony.
46　Ibid., pp. 35309-35310. Nowlan testimony.
47　Ibid., p. 35310. Nowlan testimony.
48　Ibid., pp. 35293-35294. Fitzmaurice testimony.
49　Ibid., p. 35296. Glendinning testimony.
50　Ibid., p. 35297. Glendinning testimony.
51　Ibid., pp. 35293-35294. Fitzmaurice testimony.
52　Brown, *Founded Upon A Rock*, p. 4.
53　NAC RG 5, A1 Reel C-4613 Upper Canada Sundries, vol. 67, p. 35294.
54　Andrew Haydon, *Pioneer Sketches in the District of Bathurst* (Toronto: The Ryerson Press, 1925), p. 150.
55　Ibid., p. 149.
56　Ibid., p. 150.
57　For references consult Courtney C.J. Bond, *The Ottawa Country: A Historical Guide to the National Capital Region* (Ottawa: The Queen's Printer, 1968), pp. 115-117; Brown, *Lanark Legacy*, p. 48; and the fictionalized account by David K. Findlay, *Search for Amelia* (New York: J.B. Lippincott Company, 1958).
58　Haydon, *Pioneer Sketches*, p. 147.
59　NAC RG 5, A1 Reel C-4612 Upper Canada Sundries, vol. 66, p. 35113.
60　Haydon, *Pioneer Sketches*, p. 156.
61　Ibid., pp. 151-161.
62　OKQAR Rev. William Bell Journals II:139.
63　*Montreal (Lower Canada) Herald*, 5 May 1824, cited in Haydon, *Pioneer Sketches*, p. 144.
64　John McTaggart, *Three Years in Canada* (London: Henry Colburn, 1829) I:281
65　Haydon, *Pioneer Sketches*, pp.151-153
66　Ibid., p. 148.
67　OKQAR Bell Journals II:138.
68　September 1892 obituary of Alexander Stewart, provided courtesy of Alexina Dakers, Beckwith.
69　16 June 1820 letter from a brother in Creag Ianaich, Perthshire, Scotland, to James McDiarmid, Beckwith, provided courtesy of Rosemary Wark, Beckwith.
70　Jessie Buchanan Campbell, *The Pioneer Pastor*, p.44.

Plate 56
Formal front entrance to the stone house of Dr. William Wilson, built on Bell Street in Carleton Place in the 1840s, as photographed in 1988. This was the most refined architectural statement that it was possible to find in Beckwith before 1850. The orderly Georgian panels of the door, the even size of the cut stone, the delicate glazing bars in the sidelights, and the gentle curve of the archway all bespoke a yearning for order and elegance amid a frontier agricultural settlement.

PROTOTYPICAL BECKWITH

1825 - 1851

A PROVISIONING ECONOMY

When the inhabitants of southern Beckwith sent a loyal address to lieutenant-governor Sir Francis Bond Head in early 1836, they declared themselves "to be occupied in attending to the practical duties of our station, converting the forest into green fields, and providing for our rising families."[1] With this admirable economy of words they accurately described the transition from subsistence agriculture amid the forest to a diversified cash crop economy which took place between 1825 and 1851. As early as 1827 a traveller riding through Beckwith referred to "the ripening grain, spread over many a smiling field" as giving "a look of plenty to the country,"[2] and in 1852 a census enumerator asserted that in Beckwith "the Farmer is in comfortable circumstances and making good improv[e]ments."[3] The comfort of Beckwith farmers stemmed from a combination of factors including the continuing fertility of the forest mould soil, the presence of a massive market nearby in the upper Ottawa valley timber industry, the opening of road and river transportation for quicker access to that market, a cultural emphasis on acquiring livestock that was heightened by holding cattle fairs, and the availability in the vicinity of an extensive and talented weaving population. Taken together, these factors combined to make Beckwith profit largely from the timber industry provisioning trade while at the same time setting in motion the beginnings of future agricultural and industrial diversity.

The forest of Beckwith continued to play an important initial part in helping settlers to raise money. Advertisements in regional newspapers for ninety and 110 gallon potash kettles in 1824[4] were followed as late as 1837 by reports of barges leaving Perth laden down with 220 barrels of potash for the Montreal market.[5] There were potash works located at Morphy's Falls (later Carlton Place*), Sumner's Corners (later Ashton) and Franktown. The latter of these was operated by Robert Cavanaugh on the banks of the Jock and consisted of long rows of leaching boxes and evaporating kettles. A barrel of potash could bring the farmer up to five pounds Sterling.[6] The farmers and landowners along the banks of the Mississippi were not the only inhabitants to send timber down river to the larger drive down the Ottawa.[7] Timber was floated out from central and southern Beckwith on the Jock or Goodwood River to join rafts containing 300,000 feet of timber on the Rideau.[8] Charles Rice from Drummond in December 1835 went to work[9]

> as book keeper with Aaron Chambers, who had a lumber shanty, taking out oak timber near Peter McArthur's [lot 16, concession 7].... He started on foot and walked to Franktown, fifteen miles [from Perth], and arrived there at dark only to find that he had five miles farther to go to reach the shanty, through a section of country and bush roads that he knew nothing about; but by following closely the directions given him, he succeeded in finding the place some two or three hours after dark. Chambers had hired him to keep his books, and on Sunday informed him that besides keeping the books he would have to cook for the men and chop the fire-wood. This he refused to do, and on Monday morning left the shanty and footed it for home.

---

* The post office established in 1830 was named Carleton Place, but before 1850 the common local spelling was Carlton Place, hence its use in this section.

Plate 57
Grain barn on the Ronald McDonald farm, lot 4, concession 6, Beckwith, as photographed in 1983. The provisioning of oats and wheat to the upper Ottawa timber industry in the 1830s and 1840s necessitated the construction of three-bay grain barns such as this. The large double doors opened to allow a load to be driven into the barn, and the unthreshed grain to be pitched into the mows on either side. In winter farmers threshed the crop on the floor of the central bay. The cracks were purposely left open between the logs to allow the unthreshed crop to further mature and dry out for threshing.

The profits from potash and timber were only fleeting and incidental, but as one of the few early sources of cash in Beckwith these two activities were pursued extensively to hasten converting the forest into fields. With a significant number of empty lots in Beckwith it was inevitable that timber was pirated off them, prompting farmers such as Douglas McTavish to post notices in the Perth newspapers "cautioning persons against trespassing on Lot 6 Con. 2, Beckwith, or cutting or taking away any timber thereof," by threatening to prosecute such timber pirates.[10] In the early 1840s the focus of timbering on the Mississippi moved upriver from Beckwith as the Gilmour Pollack company began cutting large quantities of timber from their limits along the river, but by opening a sawmill at Carleton Place[11] in 1842[12] and with the timber rafts of the Scottish company floating on Mississippi Lake, Beckwith farmers continued to have the timber industry in their midst.

The transition from forest clearings to waving fields of grain imposed changing obligations on Beckwith farmers. Instead of marking their cattle and allowing them to roam in the woods, increasingly not only did the crop fields have to be fenced, but the pasturelands and indeed the boundaries of each farm had to be fenced as well. The mark of a worthwhile farm offered for sale by the early 1840s was that it had a barn and over half of its acreage "cleared & fenced."[13] Not all farms were well fenced, and some farmers complained of local township officers making laws "preventing cattle from running at large",[14] inevitably leading to livestock, particularly horses, straying, being stolen[15] or being impounded.[16]

The economy of Beckwith moved from subsistence agriculture in the mid 1820s to supplying wheat to construction sites along the Rideau waterway in the late 1820s and early 1830s. Thus while farmers along the Mississippi may have been supplying wheat for the upper Ottawa timber industry this early, the farmers of southern Beckwith had a much closer and more immediately lucrative cash market. They supplied wheat to the largest concentration of building sites on the Rideau Canal directly south of them, drawing their crop along the road from Franktown to Maitland's Rapids (later Kilmarnock) to the sites between Smith's Falls and Burritt's Rapids where fourteen massive canal locks were being built.[17]

The emergence of Bytown in the late 1820s not only as the single largest construction site on the Rideau Canal but also as the regional commercial *entrepot* of the timber trade, attracted the farmers of southern and western Beckwith to make annual winter hauls of their crop to market there:[18]

> Threshing wheat and oats with the flail employed the men until plenty of snow fell for good sleighing. Then the whole neighborhood would go in company to Bytown — now Ottawa — to market their produce. Starting at midnight, the line of ox-sleds would reach Richmond about daylight, stop an hour to rest and feed, travel all day and be at Bytown by dark. Next day they would sell their grain, sometimes on a year's credit, buy a few necessary articles, travel all night to Richmond and be home the third evening. A night's lodging at Bytown, unless they slept on their sleds, was the total outlay, as they carried food and hay with them to last the three days and nights of the trip. When the small grist-mill was built at Carleton Place the farmers would grind their wheat, often watching by their sleds two or three days and nights in the open air, until their turn came. They sold the flour at Bytown, the nearest market. Four dollars a barrel for flour and eight for pork were the highest price....

The early link of southern Beckwith to Bytown was enhanced as they watched "red-toqued French [Canadians], wearing gay sashes, pass along the fourth line, driving in single file their one-horse sleighs, loaded with supplies" for Perth stores.[19]

For farmers in northern Beckwith the Mississippi River offered a turbulent route to send their crops to the timber trade market of the upper Ottawa. Lanark and Dalhousie farmers supplied the timber camps on the upper Mississippi, sending "provisions...up to the men who are at work in the Shantys...in Canoes...which...can carry but a small quantity in proportion to the number of hands required to man them...." Beckwith farmers endured similar difficulties in sending provisions down the Mississippi to the upper Ottawa that the Lanark and Dalhousie settlers faced in ascending the Mississippi. They complained in the early 1840s of "numerous portages occasioned by falls & Rapids where cargoes so heavy in proportion to their value as flour and salted provisions as well as the canoe which transported them are obliged to be carried over Roads steep and unimproved" which doubled the price of the provisions.[20] It was just as well for Beckwith farmers that they were provisioning the upper Ottawa rather than the upper Mississippi, for the difficulties faced by farmers taking crops to the shanties[21]

> is trifling compared to the delay occasioned in bringing the timber to Market[... I]n the numerous Falls over which it has to pass it generally happens that a raft is reduced to separate logs which have to be reunited at the foot of the fall[,] again to be disunited and reconstructed at the next (independant of the loss and damage on the timber which sometimes amounts to twenty per cent)[. B]y this[,] Rafts of timber which might easily be brought to Quebec in the month of June are delayed till the fall of the year at a great expense of labour which might otherwise be better employed in getting out more timber (for all the hands who originally forward the lumber are generally employed in floating it down) [. I]t not unfrequently happens

Plate 58
Upper Ottawa timber sleds and drivers, as photographed ca. 1890. Sleds such as these were used to haul timber to the Mississippi Lake in the 1830s and 1840s. The thousands upon thousands of men and teams of oxen and horses utilized in the upper Ottawa timber and sawn lumber trade from the 1820s right through to the turn of the century provided a huge market for Beckwith agricultural produce. The continuing local rural prosperity of Beckwith during the nineteenth century was based on this market. National Archives of Canada negative no. C-19837.

that from the frequent breaking up and putting together of a Raft, the Season is gone before it can be brought to Market always to the injury and often to the ruin of the proprietor.

Presented with the difficulty of navigating the Mississippi, and with most farms located inland, Beckwith inhabitants were anxious to gain better transportation to Bytown and to the upper Ottawa valley. Some of the earliest roads were built from points outside of the township by people who wanted access to the roads or mills already existing in Beckwith. Hence in 1826 there was a road from Freer's Rapids (later Innisville) in northern Drummond to Morphy's Falls because the mills of Hugh Boulton were closer than the mills at Perth. Similarly, between 1826 and 1840 the district magistrates approved roads connecting the inhabitants on the western section of the Huntley road in Ramsay with Morphy's Falls, and from Sumner's Corners (Ashton) to Appletree Falls (later Appleton), and spent district funds rerouting the Perth to Bytown road through Franktown, and revising the route of the road between Morphy's Falls and Franktown.[22] Some roads were opened by private individuals who hoped to attract business to their nascent centres. In 1827, for example, James Simpson of Smith's Falls "came on with about twenty men and with teams, and we opened a road from Smyths Falls to the By-town Road" at lot three in Beckwith's second concession, giving rise to the hamlet of Gillies Corners.[23] By 1832 there were four main roads in Beckwith. The road from Perth to Bytown and the road which crossed it at Franktown running north from Maitland on the St. Lawrence to Arnprior on the Ottawa were joined by a road along the ninth concession line, and another route which angled north from the future site of Tennyson to Morphy's Falls before heading east along the eleventh line toward Bytown.[24]

Roads in Beckwith were as bad as anywhere else in the Bathurst District, and there were many stretches of corduroy road with round cedar logs laid crossways side by side to traverse swampy sections.[25] The gowing number of roads and paths through Beckwith reflected the pressing need to get crops to market, but the quality of roads remained abysmal. The only improvement to the road between Franktown and Morphy's Falls in the quarter century following its construction in 1824 was the fencing of land on either side.[26] A description of this important Beckwith road by a Smith's Falls inhabitant in 1853 underlines how poor the quality of roads remained at mid-century. He reminded readers of the Carleton-Place *Herald* setting out for a journey between Smith's Falls and Carlton Place that[27]

> the road nearly all the way is a tunnel — a tunnel cut through the dense forest — that the thick foliage approaches close on either side, and arches high above, so as almost to defy the most persevering sunbeams in their attempts to penetrate it. Let him imagine here and there a flood of light beaming down upon his path, and an occasional view of the azure clouds above. The contemplation of such a "leafy temple"...is short-lived, — a certain rolling, plowing sensation is felt by the traveler.... The jolting corduroys have disappeared, except small patches at intervals, and their place is occupied by "great seas of mud," which seem almost ample enough to swallow up horse and driver. The stranger who first passes over this road, thinks himself very far in the back-woods, "and could scarcely believe that he is in the front Townships of a fine County, and in the midst of a most intelligent and enlightened community; while the new settlements are yet one hundred miles away north from him....
>
> Now, if the thick forest were prevented from "shutting out the day," the "seas of mud" would soon begin to disappear; as it is, "from morn to noon, from noon to dewy eve," the sun visits them not; and then they remain under the protection of the mighty arms and thick foliage of trees, the felling of which, would be of double advantage, — letting the road dry, and offering less danger to travelers who are passing under them during a gust of wind.

Construction of the Rideau Canal in the late 1820s prompted some impossible hopes in 1830 that it might offer access to the Mississippi River,[28] and in 1834 inhabitants of Beckwith joined Ramsay, Lanark and Dalhousie in petitioning the Upper Canadian legistature to have a canal some three miles in length connect Cockburn Creek with Mississippi Lake to feed into the Rideau Canal.[29] No such canal was constructed, but with the building of the Tay Canal from Perth to the Rideau, farmers in western Beckwith increasingly hauled their crops to Perth to be moved by barge from there to Bytown from 1832 on,[30] while their counterparts in eastern Beckwith continued to market their grain at Bytown. By the mid 1840s the Tay Canal was in a useless state, and although some of the more westerly Beckwith farmers continued to haul to Perth, the extra cost of ox-teams further hauling their crop along the road from Perth to Oliver's Ferry (later Rideau Ferry) increased the expense of transportation.[31] The rapids and portages of the Mississippi left the farmers of Beckwith and storekeepers at Carlton Place with no alternative but to use the rutted roads which they described as being in a "Desperate and Impassable state...by which teems from the Back Country from Carlton and Packenham could with the greatest Difficulty get through with their Merchandize"[32] to depots along the Rideau. At the same time the Tay Canal fell into disuse in the mid 1840s there was a push by regional inhabitants for an extension of the Victoria Macadamised Road (which

Plate 59
Entrance to the Rideau Canal, Bytown, 1839, as sketched by Lieutenant-Colonel Henry F. Ainslie. Construction of the Rideau Canal in the late 1820s of itself provided a market for the crops of southern Beckwith farmers, and the canal as a major route for moving timber to the Ottawa River made Bytown the commercial entrepôt of the upper Ottawa timber trade. The importance of the Bytown market drew Beckwith farmers to make three-day winter excursions to sell their crops for the high prices they commanded there. This view shows timber rafts being assembled from the timbers floated down the canal. National Archives of Canada negative no. C-518.

began construction from Brockville to Smith's Falls in 1837) northward to the Ottawa River.[33] A public meeting at Carlton Place in mid July 1845 sought to call the attention of the provincial board of works to the necessity of building a macadamised road from Smith's Falls through Carlton Place and Pakenham Mills directly north to the Ottawa. The province rather than the local inhabitants should fund such an ambitious thoroughfare, it was argued, because the Bathurst district paid large sums into the provincial treasury in the form of timber duties.[34] The route north from Carlton Place had been established by the early 1830s, but the road was upgraded and straightened in a piecemeal fashion by the district and later by the county council from the mid 1840s to the mid 1860s.[35]

Beckwith farmers in the 1830s and 1840s prospered from being on the doorstep of the best market for agricultural produce in all British North America. Government immigration agents in the early 1840s explained that because the Ottawa River was "the great lumbering depot of the country, the farmer is certain to find a ready sale and a good market at his door for all the surplus produce he may be able to raise."[36] By 1836 it was estimated that timberers paid out £15,000 in cash each year for agricultural products on the Bytown market, in addition to receiving large quantities of goods through bartering.[37] The rates for selling farm products on the Bytown market were from twenty to fifty percent higher than any other Canadian market, and right through the nineteenth century prices remained firm in Bytown at the same time they were unsteady elsewhere.[38] By being relatively close, but with poor river transportation, Beckwith farmers were close enough to sell in the Bytown market, but just remote enough to avoid the internecine conflict which flared up seasonally along the Ottawa and the Rideau in the 1820s and 1830s. A correspondent of the Perth *Bathurst Courier* in February 1841 summarised the importance of this agricultural provisioning of the Ottawa Valley timber trade to the rural Beckwith economy by remarking that "when the Lumber Trade ceases the Bathurst District will lose its main support" and "its prosperity will diminish."[39]

Provisioning the timber trade made oats the major cash crop in Beckwith between 1825 and 1851. Leeds and Lansdowne township on the St. Lawrence, by contrast, was typical of American-settled townships throughout Upper Canada in planting two acres of wheat for every acre of oats, whereas in Beckwith there were more than two bushels of oats harvested for every bushel of wheat.[40] In 1851 the harvest for the provisioning trade in Beckwith included 33,660 bushels of oats, 14,725 bushels of wheat, 50,441 bushels of potatoes, 65,652 pounds of butter, 999 barrels of pork and 190

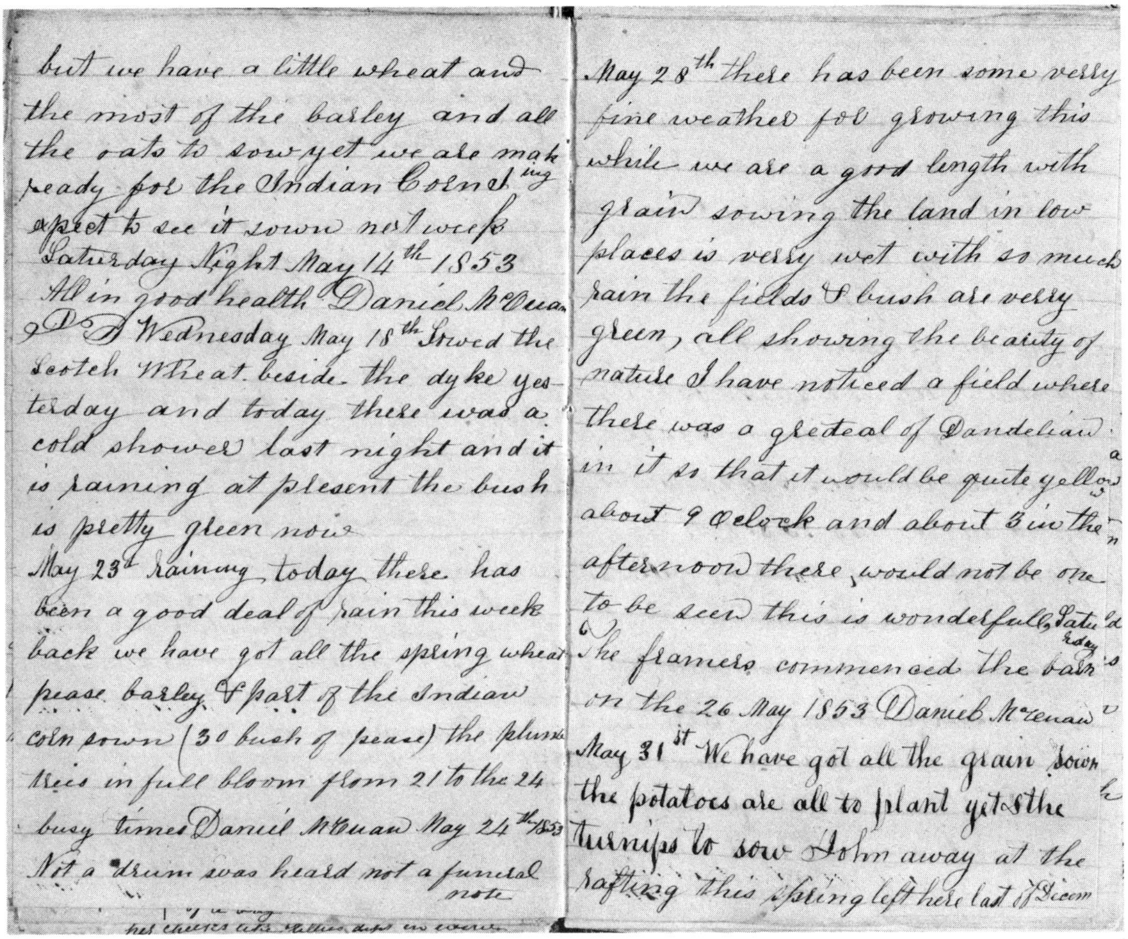
but we have a little wheat and
the most of the barley and all
the oats to sow yet we are mak ing
ready for the Indian Corn &c
expect to see it sown next week
Saturday Night May 14th 1853
All in good health Daniel McCuan
Wednesday May 18th Sowed the
Scotch Wheat beside the dyke yesterday and today there was a
cold shower last night and it
is raining at present the bush
is pretty green now
May 23d raining today there has
been a good deal of rain this week
back we have got all the spring wheat
pease barley & part of the Indian
corn sown (30 bush of pease) the plum
trees in full bloom from 21 to the 24
busy times Daniel McCuan May 24th 1853
Not a drum was heard not a funeral
note

May 28th there has been some verry
fine weather for growing this
while we are a good length with
grain sowing the land in low
places is verry wet with so much
rain the fields & bush are verry
green, all showing the beauty of
nature I have noticed a field where
there was a greatdeal of Dandelian
in it so that it would be quite yellow
about 9 Oclock and about 3 in the
afternoon there would not be one
to be seen this is wonderfull, Saturday
The framers commenced the barn
on the 26 May 1853 Daniel McCuan
May 31st We have got all the grain sown
the potatoes are all to plant yet & the
turnips to sow John away at the
rafting this spring left here last Decem

Plate 60
Pages from the 1853 journal of Daniel McCuan, Beckwith. These entries reveal the bustling pace of spring planting and the predominance of grain crops as late as the early 1850s. The McCuans along with other Beckwith highland families sowed peas as part of a dietary tradition they brought from Perthshire. Loaned courtesy of Alex and Jean McCuan.

barrels of beef.[41] Wheat may have been a more popular crop than oats in the late 1820s and in the 1830s, but by the early 1840s the wheat fly was reported destroying up to a third of the crop in the Brockville vicinity.[42] In late July 1844 the pest was in the Beckwith area and was expected "to prove a serious barrier to the raising of wheat."[43] By 1848 the vulnerablility of the wheat crop made the economic depression particularly acute. The editor of the *Bathurst Courier* remarked that the failures in the lumber market in 1848 "has caused more anxiety to be experienced about the incoming harvest than ordinarily — more particularly in the staple article — wheat".[44] By 1851 Beckwith farmers found their wheat crops attacked by smut and rust, futher evidence that wheat was in steady decline as a dependable crop.[45]

The diversified agricultural economy of Beckwith prevented bad wheat crops from ruining farmers. Bad years for the timber trade such as 1846 and 1848 meant lower prices for farmers provisioning the trade, but Beckwith farmers enjoyed a stable existence in contrast with the timberers withstanding the crashes of the timber market. By 1839 the *Courier* editor claimed that merchants at

Perth had moved from barter or credit to a cash economy following a number of prosperous harvests.[46] The earliest mention of a cash economy within Beckwith was when John A. Gemmill at Carlton Place in March 1845 offered "to pay CASH for any quantity of good merchantable Wheat".[47] In addition to oats, potatoes and butter, beef and more especially pork became important parts of the provisioning trade in the 1840s. In July 1838 Robert Bell, Ewen McEwen, Peter Comrie, J[ohn] McEwan, James Bell, John Sumner, Michael and John Morphy of Carlton Place successfully requested the lieutenant-governor to appoint Napoleon Lavallee inspector of beef and pork in that village.[48] In the first six months of 1839 Lavallee inspected two barrels of mess pork, 136 barrels of prime mess pork, and 42 barrels of prime pork.[49] Eleven years later, as the volume of pork sent to the timber shanties increased, Lavallee complained that a great deal of the pork killed and prepared for market was "reduced in value by being improperly bled and cut up." He provided minute instructions for butchering, cutting and packing the pork in barrels in order that "a great deal of pork, that is now obliged to be sold for prime, might be branded prime mess, which would command a cash market at an advance of at least two dollars on the barrel".[50]

Lavallee's helpful advice was part of a movement to improve local agricultural practice that began at the same time he was appointed an inspector. On the afternoon of 22 January 1840 subscribers from Beckwith and Ramsay held a meeting at which they drew up the articles for the County of Lanark Agricultural Society.[51] It was modelled on an agricultural society organised at Perth in January 1839.[52] By May 1842 when the society was offering premiums for its first competiton its name had changed to the Bathurst District Agricultural Society.[53] The name reflected the ambitions of members to make Carlton Place the centre of agricultural improvement in the district, but it was well known that "Beckwith and Ramsay have been the main support of the Bathurst District Agricultural Society."[54] The annual cattle show at Carlton Place by 1847 spurred the local production of excellent butter, cloth and wheat.[55] In August 1848 a copy of "the American Farmer's Encyclopedia (1165 pages)" was offered as " a Prize for the best Essay 'On the Theory and Practice of Agriculture, Philosophical and Chemical'...to be read at the close of the annual Cattle Show...and to remain the property of the Society."[56] This society imported Ayrshire bulls to improve the quality of local livestock,[57] and offered awards to both men and women at the annual cattle show.[58] The society's contribution to upgrading Beckwith agriculture throughout the 1840s was reflected in the comments of 1852 census enumerator James Duncan:[59]

> The valew of the land in this part is about one pound[,] ten shillings the acre[. T]he Farmer is in comfortable circumstances and making good improv[e]ments[. A]gricultural improvements and the stock genrely [are] greatly improved within these few yeares[,] particuler[l]y Horses, cattle and pigs[. O]ur sheep is not so good as theay should [be] but the Agricultural Society of thease United Counties [of Lanark and Renfrew] is dooing much to improve the Country general[l]y.

Livestock was important in Beckwith agriculture from the beginning of settlement. This was particularly true for the Perthshire highlanders who traditionally had raised livestock on the outfield, and who themselves had been replaced by sheep on the land after the improving landlords had moved them into villages such as Comrie to pursue cloth manufacturing. In the days before a cash economy developed, livestock was the best form of portable property to be found in the township. Duncan McDiarmid in making out his will in 1836 left "one sheep of the value of 10 shillings" apiece to three of his children; "cattle to the amount of ten pounds" to his daughter Christiana; "a yoke of oxen of the value of 15 pounds, a cow of the value of 4 pounds, and 4 sheep of the value of 10 shillings each" to his son Peter; and "25 pounds paid in cattle" to his daughter Ann.[60] In March 1837 72 inhabitants of Franktown vicinity petitioned the lieutenant-governor for a charter to establish a semi-annual public fair in that village (Appendix 16).[61] In January 1839 Patrick

Plate 61
Ruins of log barns on the Joseph Jacobs farmstead, lot 20, concession 2, Beckwith, as photographed in June 1983. On many Beckwith farms barns were added to one another to form barnyards that sheltered the farmer from the winter winds as he went around feeding livestock. This formation of buildings also facilitated the coralling of animals about to be slaughtered.

Nowlan posted a notice in the *Bathurst Courier* that the fairs at Franktown would be held on the second Tuesday of May and the second Tuesday of September. "The above fairs", he announced, "will be open for all kinds of Horn Cattle, Horses, Hogs, Sheep and Hawkers. Persons coming from other townships will get free pasturage for one night gratis".[62] Prominent men at Carlton Place, fearing that Franktown was attempting to steal a march on them gathered 57 signatures on a petition to the lieutenant-governor in November 1838 (Appendix 17). They anticipated that the establishment of a fair held in April, August and November "for the sale of goods, wares, merchandise, live stock and agricultural produce, would be of great advantage to the inhabitants of this village and neighbourhood in particular, and from its central location to the inhabitants of the District in general."[63] The Franktown fair with its emphasis on livestock fell behind the Carlton Place exhibition which in the 1840s encouraged the display and marketing of crops, cloth and manufactures.

Beckwith more than held its own with the rest of Lanark County in livestock and crop harvests. In 1851 it ranked sixth among the fourteen rural townships in the county in population (2,540 persons), in acreage cultivated (11,579 acres) and in acreage under pasture (4,860 acres). Beckwith ranked fifth in number of cows giving milk (1,173), in butter production (65,652 pounds), in wool production (10,296 pounds), in oats harvested (33,660 bushels), in Indian corn harvested (2,326 bushels), in hay cropped (2,713 tons), and in pork produced (999 barrels). Beckwith ranked fourth in number of pigs (2,114) in barley harvested (1,356 bushels), and in cheese production (5,122 pounds). The township ranked third in number of horses (708) and in harvesting of potatoes (50,441 bushels). It ranked a close second in numbers of calves and heifers (1,446), and in the harvest of rye (587 bushels) and buckwheat (2,698 bushels). Beckwith surpassed all other townships in Lanark

County in the harvest of peas (7,323 bushels), beans (1,062 bushels), and in the manufacture of fulled cloth (19,849 yards) and flannel (12,923 yards).[64]

The development of a textile industry at Carlton Place flowed natually enough from the weaving heritage of the Beckwith highlanders, but it devleoped only after the initial subsistence stage of pioneer agriculture had passed. One traveller through the vicinity in 1823 remarked that a major drawback to developing a clearing "is the want of clothes" and recommended that [65]

> none ought to come here but such as are well able to supply themselves with a sufficiency of that necessary article, for 4 or 5 years at least. In the course of that time, they may raise flax and breed sheep, which will produce wool that may be manufactured for family use, and thus their difficulties in that respect may be greatly removed. But a family going thither, poor, naked, and unfurnished with necessary clothing suited to that rigorous climate, and without the means of obtaining it, are really to be pitied indeed.

This was confirmed when Robert Ferguson of Beckwith, in urging his parents-in-law to immigrate to Beckwith in November 1823, urged that above all else they bring "plenty of good stout Cloth and blankets" with them.[66] Ferguson himself claimed to be keeping sheep in 1823, and the concentration of handloom weavers in the region meant that household cloth production was inevitable. It was spinning and weaving at which the Scottish highlanders in Beckwith and the lowlanders in Ramsay excelled, who rather than take up their time at home with carding small lots of wool between two brushes studded with wire teeth, took advantage of carding and fulling mills respectively established by Allan McDonald and the partnership of Robert Bell and Leitrim immigrant James Rosamond in 1835 and 1837.[67] The farmers took their carded wool home, spun it, then took it to neighbours such as Duncan McNabb,[68] James McNaughton,[69] Peter Cram,[70] William Bradley, Donald Buchanan, James Devlin, Ephraim Kilpatrick, Donald McDiarmid, John McEwen, William McKenzie, James McRorie, John Salter and Hugh Williamson[71] — all of whom were accomplished weavers. After the cloth was woven Beckwith inhabitants returned to Carlton Place to have it fulled, that is, soaked in warm soapy water, wrung out and stretched to produce a warm, thick, strong and pliable material with a consistent finish.[72] In Beckwith from the late 1820s to the early 1850s this "homespun" was what women and local tailors made all clothes from. It was not only worn every day but also at church, social gatherings and dances.[73]

So popular did the carding and fulling mills prove that six district owners met at Carlton Place in March 1838 and declared that in future they would accept "ready pay only" and agreed that "merchantable produce shall be taken in payment, at Cash price."[74] In June 1846 James Rosamond announced that his "WOOL MANUFACTURING, WOOL CARDING, AND CLOTH DRESSING establishment" was also fitted up with machinery for spinning and weaving, that he was "prepared to receive Wool to manufacture either on Shares or by the yard" and that he kept "constantly on hand Satinette Warps to accommodate any who may wish to have their Wool manufactured in that way." Effectively, this was as Rosamond claimed "the first attempt to establish any thing of the kind in this District,"[75] that is to take the raw wool, to card, to spin, to weave and to full it. Within a year, with three narrow looms, one spindle jack of 120 spindles, and one bolting roll, Roasmond printed this immodest notice in the Perth newspaper:[76]

> WOOL! WOOL! WOOL! THE Subscriber is now prepared to manufacture Wool into the different varieties, viz., Plain Cloth, either grey or dyed Cassimere, Sattinett, Flannel, all Wool or Cotton and Wool, Blankets, &c. He is also prepared to exchange Cloth for Wool. Wool Carding and Cloth Dressing done to order and with despatch. Prices reasonable. Persons at a distance will please call and see for themselves. Should Wool or Cloth be damaged in the manufacturing or dressing, it will be made good.
>
> JAMES ROSAMOND. Carlton Place, 1 June 1847.

Plate 62
The Allan McDonald house, Mill Street, Carleton Place, built in the 1840s, as photographed in 1983. The wealth to build this house came from the carding and fulling mill that McDonald built just west of this house in the mid 1840s. Continuing profits from a larger mill permitted the McDonald family to build a stone addition to this house either in the 1870s or 1880s. The narrow eave and large fireplace chimneys of the older house contrast with the wide eaves, finely cut Beckwith quoin stones, and small stove chimneys of the later addition.

Rosamond continued to prosper and to mechanise to the extent that by 1850 he boasted of reducing the price of manufacturing woollens by eight percent, and by 1851 his "cloth manufactory was valued at £1,500 and he employed fifteen men."[77]

The success of James Rosamond's woollen factory contributed substantially to the growth of Carlton Place from a mill hamlet containing only a few log houses in 1825 to a village of five hundred inhabitants in 1852. The thirty foot fall of water at Morphy's Falls atracted Hugh Boulton from Leeds County to build a gristmill on the south bank of the Mississippi and a sawmill on the north bank. The business attracted to Boulton's mills impelled William Moore to open a blacksmith shop, and Robert Barnett to open a cooper shop. Alexander Morris opened a general store of sorts, an inn and a potash factory on the south bank, and William Loucks opened a second store of sorts in 1822. In 1825 Caleb Strong Bellows, an American, purchased Loucks's shop and according to local tradition was "the first merchant to open a store really worthy of the name, having a general assortment of merchandise unmixed with offshoot enterprise."[78] In 1827 Bellows built a distillery which was operated by Fancis W.K. Jessop until 1832, and in 1830 Bellows became the first postmaster of Carlton Place.[79] Despite the Irish and Scottish numerical predominance in Beckwith and adjacent townships prominent settlers of American origin such as Hugh Boulton, William Loucks and Caleb Bellows succeeded in obtaining an American teacher for the school built at Morphy's Falls in 1825. The cultural tension this stimulated was evident to Alexander Wylie who stopped overnight at the tavern in the hamlet just as the school was nearing completion:[80]

> The teacher who was [a] Yankee from the front [Brockville vicinity], was treating them with a quart of whiskey, and at the same time boasting of his abilities as a teacher, and telling his audience with great exultation that he could teach all kinds of languages. Aye, said Mr. Wylie, you must be very useful in the neighbourhood. Can you teach French? No; I cannot teach French. Can you teach Latin? No; I do not understand Latin. I thought you said you could teach all languages? O yes, said the worthy pedagogue, but I meant all kinds of English!!! At this all who heard him burst out laughing. But he apologized by saying that many pretended to teach English who did not understand it themselves; but he could teach it properly!

Despite the deficiencies of the first teacher, the building of the 1825 school, the establishment of a post office and the selection of Carlton Place as a name marked the emergence of a village out of the milling hamlet. The new name proved enduring, an unusual feat in a region where most villages in the mid to late nineteenth century discarded early choices of names for those with more grandiose associations. The only critique of Carlton Place as a name came from a American visitor in 1865 who found it ironic that a bustling village should have such a rural-sounding name, in contrast with a few scattered houses that rejoiced in the urban-sounding name of Franktown some eight miles to the south.[81] Manny Nowlan became proprietor of Alexander Morris's tavern in the late 1820s,[82] and was listed as the Carlton Place agent of the Perth *Bathurst Independent Examiner* in September 1829.[83] In 1829 Carlton Place appeared to offer such a promising market that William and John Bell of Perth established a branch of their extensive Perth merchandising store. After constructing a building, John Bell "on the 20th July, set out for that place [from Perth] with three wagons loaded with goods. More were sent soon after, as the demand increased."[84] By early August their brother Robert was running the business, offering "a general assortment of goods, suitable for that part of the country",[85] and by December of 1830 he agreed to receive payment of debts by local settlers in wheat and barley.[86]

The opening of the Bell store in 1829 and of James Rosamond's mill in 1830 marked the end of any predominance by American-origin settlers which may have existed in the hamlet. Caleb Bellows advertised his distillery for sale by public auction in late 1829.[87] When his income as postmaster failed to make up for the customers he lost to the Bells, Bellows by late 1831 began mooting plans for "Establishing a Saw- and Grist Mill on an Extensive Scale on the Grand or Ottawa River about Seventy Miles above By Town" on a 2,000 acre tract he hoped to purchase there.[88] He actually did not give up the Carlton Place post office until 1834, moving to Westmeath Township in Renfrew County where he established mills and the community of Bellowstown.[89] As for Hugh Boulton, his property of four acres containing a gristmill, a sawmill and a distillery was sold at a sheriff's sale in 1830 to meet the demands of his creditors.[90] The growing British population of the village increasingly appears to have patronised British immigrant merchants and tradesmen over those of American origin. Caleb Bellows in particular "greatly an[n]oyed the Inhabitants of Carlton Place" in either 1829 or 1830 when he "h[o]isted the American Flag and Celebrated the Independance of his Country on the 4th of July".[91]

By 1832 "the Village of Carlton Place" was described as being "now much Improved" and "Containing three or four Stores, two mills, a distillery, and Several other us[e]ful works…and Mr. John McEwan[,]…a Tavernkeeper…."[92] James Kerr described himself in July 1835 as "a young man commencing a small Brewery in the Village of Carlton Place",[93] and further evidence of village inhabitants attempting to promote growth was provided by William and James Bell offering for sale in 1835 "a few first rate Building Lots in the flourishing village of Carlton Place.[94] A significant point in the village's development occurred in April 1837 when 37 inhabitants and nearby Beckwith and

Plate 63
View looking west along Bell Street toward Napoleon Lavallee's Carleton House hotel on Bridge Street in Carleton Place, as photographed ca. 1868 by George E. Willis. Lavallee, after building this as the Waterloo Hotel in 1846, briefly immigrated to Australia in 1853, and not long after this photograph was taken, added a third storey and an extra bay to his renamed Carleton House. The more modest hotel of Absolam McCaffrey on the north side of Bell Street could not compete. In 1860 McCaffrey was a wine merchant before setting up a bakery on the south side of the street in the summer of 1867. The pile of lumber on the left suggests the building boom just beginning to take place in 1868. National Archives of Canada negative no. C-547.

Ramsay farmers contributed money to cover the expense of ringing a morning bell at Carlton Place. Whether or not the bell in the Anglican church actually began to be rung on a daily basis at this time, it is significant that so many inhabitants felt a need for this way of marking time, to give a common hour at which employment in the village should begin, and that the previous practice of relying on daylight as determining the hours of work was no longer satisfactory. It is significant as well that Carlton Place in the 1830s was a commercial centre not only for northern Beckwith but for southern Ramsay as well, and that increasingly the move of Scottish lowland weavers and Peter Robinson settlers into the village made its outlook culturally and politically different from that of most inhabitants of rural Beckwith. Contributors toward the fund for ringing the morning bell included sawmill owner George Bailey Jr., carpenter Adam Beck, merchants James and Robert Bell, miller Hugh Boulton, shoemakers Joseph Bond and James Coleman, tailor William Fitzpatrick, distiller James Kerr, cooper Napoleon Lavallee, saddler William Morphy, innkeepers John McEwan and Manny Nowlan, carpenters John McLaughlin and David Pattie, schoolteacher William Poole, miller James Rosamond, and merchant's clerk John Sumner.[95]

Manufacturing based on the excellent waterpower and local agriculture attracted physicians and more ambitious buildings were constructed in the "beautiful and rising village of Carlton Place"[96] in the 1840s. At least as early as 1835 newspapers were available in the village, with Robert Bell carrying the Perth *Bathurst Courier*[97] until succeeded by John McEwan as agent in 1836,[98] and with William Morphy stocking issues of the Brockville *Statesman*.[99] Indeed, as early as 1830 an

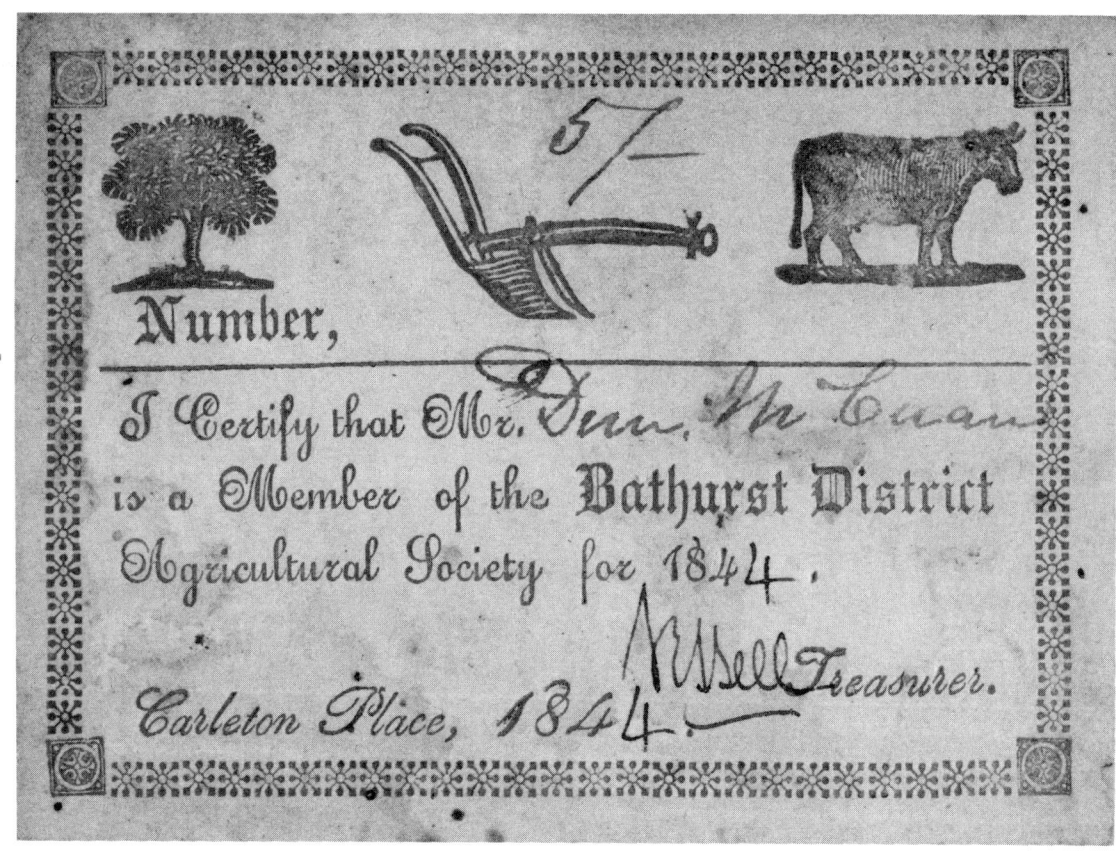

inhabitant of Carlton Place, writing under the pseudonym of Pat O'Shaughnessy jousted with William Tully of Perth in the columns of the *Bathurst Independent Examiner*.[100] In April 1841 William Wilson, a surgeon and "Licentiate of Midwifery" begged to "inform inhabitants he has opened apartments in Mr. Rosamond's building".[101] In late May 1841 Dr. Edward Barry placed an advertisement in the *Bathurst Courier* that having been "appointed Surgeon to the Lanark Militia by [Lieutenant-Governor] Sir George Arthur, he has now removed to Mr. Fitzpatrick's stone building, Carlton Place". He printed the testimonial of John Teskey in Ramsay whose sight had been restored under Barry's attendance.[102] In August 1846 Dr. Gavin Russell opened an office, and announced himself "duly qualified to practise Physic, Surgery and Midwifery".[103] Russell was described in 1848 as performing an operation using chloroform to remove a tumour from a patient's neck,[104] but during his five year residence he became noted as a passionate exponent of phrenology[105] and as a frenetic controversialist in local newspapers.[106]

A mark of the growth and prosperity of Carlton Place in the 1840s was the change from a hamlet in which all structures were built of log in the early 1830s to a village of sixty houses in 1851, thirty of which were frame and ten of which were stone.[107] The pride of village inhabitants in their new houses and the growth of their village was reflected in Ephraim Tweedy's reference in November 1842 to his "comfortable new Frame House and Shop, with out offices new, conveniently situated in the thriving village of Carlton Place."[108] Compelling testimony as to the buoyancy of the village's economic growth in the early and mid 1840s is provided in a 29 November 1841 letter from Matthew Houston, a newly-arrived Paisley weaver to a friend back in Scotland:[109]

ARTICLES OF THE

Bathurst District Agricultural Society, agreed to at a General Meeting of the Subscribers, held at Carlton Place, 15th January, 1845.

1st. This Society shall be denominated the *Bathurst District Agricultural Society*, to aid in effecting the views of the Provincial Legislature, for the improvement of Agriculture in this Province.

2d This Society shall be conducted by a President, three Vice Presidents, a Treasurer a Secretary and fifteen Directors, who shall form a Managing Committee, any seven of whom including the President or a Vice President, shall form a quorum; likewise three auditors whose duty it shall be to audit the accounts of the Society and give in a written report, prior to the election of office bearers at the general meeting in January.

3d There shall be an annual meeting of the Members of the Society held at Carlton Place, on the third Wednesday of January at eleven o'clock, A. M. at which time a new election of Officers shall take place, to serve for the ensuing year. There shall also be a general meeting of the members at Carlton Place, on the last Thursday of September in each year at eleven o'clock A. M. at which a Cattle Show shall be held, where all stock, implements of husbandry, &c. intended for Premiums shall be exhibited, which show shall be under the direction of the managing Committee.

4th An annual subscription of five shillings shall constitute the subscriber a member, and a donation of ten pounds a member for life.

5th The managing Committee may call meetings of the Society at any time and place, when they consider it necessary, giving notice thereof for 2 weeks, by notices put up at several public places in the different Townships.

6th No member in arrears shall have any privileges until his subscription is paid up.

7th The Treasurer shall keep an account of the receipts and expenditures of the Society, and the names of the Members who may have neglected to pay their annual subscriptions, to be exhibited at the annual meeting, and also a list of all the members of the Society; he shall also have charge of all the monies and property of the Society, subject to the orders of the managing Committee. All orders on the Treasurer to be signed by the President or presiding Vice President of the Committee, and counter-signed by the Secretary. The Treasurer shall exhibit a statement of the funds and property of the Society whenever required to do so by the managing Committee, and shall also give such security as may be approved of by the said committee or President, for the faithful discharge of the duties of his office.

8th The Secretary shall record the proceedings of the Society and exhibit the same when required by the managing Committee, and all the books and papers of the Society shall be open to the inspection of Members at said meetings.

9th It shall be the duty of the managing Committee to conduct the affairs of the Society agreeable to this constitution, and to make such further temporary rules and regulations as may be necessary for carrying its designs into effect, also to make out and advertise a list of Premiums, which in their opinion should be offered, within the limit of their funds, for any object tending to the improvement of domestic manufactures and the Agriculture of the country, also to purchase and import such valuable live stock, grain, grass seed, useful implements of husbandry, or whatever else may conduce to the improvement of the Agriculture of this country.

10th No Member of this Society shall be allowed to receive a first Premium for the same kind of crop or domestic animal, oftener than once in four years, but a Member taking a second or third prize, may compete for a higher; and persons competing for Premiums of crops, shall exhibit to the judges an account of the manner of cultivating the same, which account shall be considered as belonging to the Society.

11th A report of the proceedings of the Society, the state of its finances, and a general view of its affairs, shall be published, once in each year by the managing Committee, and be exhibited to the Society at its general meeting held in the month of January.

12th The President and Secretary shall have power to call meetings of the managing Committee, when they think it most advisable, and if the President and Secretary neglect or refuse to do so, any three of the managing Committee shall have power to call a meeting, due notice of which shall be given previous to its taking place.

13th This Constitution may be altered or amended at any general meeting where at least fifteen members are present, provided they are unanimous, twenty five or upwards three-fourths to carry, thirty five or upwards two-thirds to carry, and fifty or upwards a majority.

24th The Officers of the Society shall have power to fill vacancies, which may occur in their numbers by death or otherwise, until the next annual Meeting.

Plate 64
Duncan McCuan's membership ticket (opposite) and the articles of the Bathurst District Agricultural Society, Carlton Place, respectively dated 1844 and 1845. This agricultural society not only promoted more progressive ways of pursuing husbandry, such as improving the quality of livestock bred, but in the holding of an annual exhibition it promoted the trade of Carlton Place by attracting farmers from throughout the Bathurst District. Loaned courtesy of Alex and Jean McCuan.

I am very sorry to hear of your distress at home — so many going idle, and have no work to do. We may be thankful that we have left the place and have come here. We have all plenty of work to do here. I agreed to work at the oat-mill for the winter; my wages, are 10s. per week for board, and 8 dollars per month. I am to act as foreman of the mill. My wages run to 19s. 6d. per week, by the spring it will rise to 11 or 12 dollars per month, and no outlaid money out of it. My house rent is 5s. per month. I do not *rue* [regret] of coming to this country as yet. The people who are settled in this place for some time are quite happy. They have all plenty of work and plenty of provisions. For my part, we have three months' provisions on hand, and we know of more when we need them. You may know the state we were in when we left you — we had neither meat nor money, but we have plenty of everything that we need at present. How long it may last we do not know; but I am not afraid of dull trade as long as I am here. The provisions run not so high as at home.... Magdalen and James are out at country work, and are doing well.

The material prosperity of the "sprightly little village" of Carlton Place was attributed by a temperance lecturer passing through in March 1842 to its having "more churches than taverns,"[110] but liquor was available in the shops of Robert Bell, Lancaster Schofield and John A. Gemmill; in the inns of Manny Nowlan, John McEwan, Robert McLaren, Michael Murphy, and George Wardner during the 1830s and 1840s; and Orrin Pierce briefly operated a sixty gallon wooden still in the late 1830s.[111] As the village became home to the third division court for settling small claims in 1841,[112] and hosted meetings and exhibitions of the Bathurst District Agricultural Society, sufficient numbers of people and business were drawn into the village to set up John Graham in business as a vehicle and implement repairman in 1842 [113] and to spur Napoleon Lavallee to build an impressive two-storey stone "Waterloo Hotel" at the end of Bell Street in 1846. After the cattle show and exhibition held on the edge of the village on 24 September 1846, it was reported that fifty members sat down in Lavallee's new hotel to a "dinner conducted strictly on teetotal principles."[114] A native of Hochelaga, Lower Canada, Napoleon Lavallee was unique as a French Canadian inhabitant of Beckwith; his name proved so difficult for the Gaelic-speaking "canny Scotch Farmers of the neighbourhood, [that they] quietly but poetically metamorphosed Napoleon Laval[l]ee into plain '*Bonnie Lovely!*'"[115] The Founding of a library and Mechanic's Institute in 1846 was a further mark of sophistication.[116] By 1850 Carlton Place had the reputation of being a village "where every body knows Malcolm Cameron, and every body reads the newspapers",[117] and indeed in June of that year James Duncan presented an address from the Carlton Place library & Mechanic's Institute to Lord Elgin,[118] confirming the strong pro-Reform feeling that could be found in this Beckwith village.[119] Under Ulster immigrant Johnston Neilson the Carlton Place public school gained a good reputation in the late 1840s.

The significant economic partnership that developed in Carlton Place was that of Robert Bell and James Rosamond, following the dissolving in 1836 of the "partnership relating to Carlton Place Mills" between John McEwan and Rosamond.[120] Bell and Rosamond ran grist, oatmeal and sawmills in addition to the carding and fulling mill which Rosamond operated by himself. The productivity of their sawmill is indicated by an 1847 advertisement offering for sale "200,000 feet inch Boards, 12, 14, 16 & 18 feet long[;] 100,000 feet 1 1/2 inch plank[s;] ALSO 2 inch Planks, Clapboards, Lath, Scantling, Rafters & Joists."[121] By 1846, in addition to James Rosamond's new woollen factory, there was the carding and fulling mill of Allan McDonald; the blacksmith forges of Duncan McGregor and James Duncan; the carpenter shops of David Pattie, John McLaughlin and William Moffatt; the boot and shoe stores of James Morphy, Joseph Bond and James Coleman; the cooper shop of Absolem McCaffrey; the tailor shops of Walter Scott, Henry Fitzpatrick, a Mr. Laidlaw and Patrick Galvin; the harness shop operated by David McNab and Israel Webster for Bell & Rosamond; and the waggon shops of John Graham, Michael Walsh and Joseph Pittard.[122]

At the annual exhibition of the Bathurst District Agricultural Society in October 1848 a cooking

Plate 65
The hotel built for James Burrows at Franktown ca. 1852, as photographed in 1982. It was in this new hotel in December 1852 that prominent businessmen from Smith's Falls, Carleton Place, Ramsay and Beckwith came up with the proposal to build a railroad passing through their part of Lanark County from Brockville on the St. Lawrence to the upper Ottawa valley. This hotel was the most prosperous business in Franktown before railroad fever gripped Beckwith inhabitants in the 1850s.

stove was displayed which had been manufactured in the foundry of Samuel Fuller at Carlton Place.[123] In 1850 James Condle Poole established a newspaper entitled the *Lanark Herald* which served the political interests of and was subsidised initially by Robert Bell who in 1848 was elected member of the Legislative Assembly for Lanark County. By 1851 Carlton Place was deemed "a considerable village...contain[ing] about 500 inhabitants,"[124] but despite being "a business like village" whose merchants did a large trade based on supplying the provisioning trade, "with the exception of a Church and a Hotel", one visitor remarked disparagingly, "there are few good buildings in it."[125] Despite the change from a half dozen houses in 1825 to a village "containing some 60 houses" in 1847,[126] Carlton Place remained locked into backwoods life by roads that Upper Canadian travellers described as the worst they ever travelled.[127]

Travellers who proceeded south from Carlton Place in the 1830s and 1840s emerged from the eight mile "tunnel of trees" to discover the much smaller and less prosperous hamlet of Franktown. Local historians of the Beckwith region have consistently suggested that construction of the Brockville and Ottawa Railway in the late 1850s arrested the development of an otherwise thriving village, but there is no evidence to back up this theory of a "railroad-killed village."[128] Lord Dalhousie in 1820 found "the village of Beckwith" to consist of the King's storehouse, Thomas Wickham's inn and Patrick Nowlan's tavern,[129] two years later the Reverend George Buchanan's family described Franktown as a tavern and a couple of log huts,[130] and in 1840 Bishop John Strachan tersely observed "Franktown has no village unless three or four houses can claim that name."[131] A traveller passing through in May 1841 remarked:[132]

> The village of Franktown is at a dead halt, neither thriving nor 'vice verse.' Two or three attempts have been made to keep a store here, but [it] never was found profitable, being so near Perth (15 miles) or approximate to other more thriving villages — Carlton Place being about 9 miles from it, and Smith[']s Falls about the same distance in an opposite direction, where better stocks are always on hand for the buyer than [at] Franktown, [I] preferred resorting to these places.

It was only in the early 1850s, coinciding with the first mention of a railroad being built through the locality, that Franktown truly became a village, and by 1851 it was said to contain between fifteen and twenty houses.[133]

The log houses that predominated at Franktown[134] made the hamlet look more primitive, less prosperous, and certainly hardly worth comparing with Carlton Place in the 1830s and 1840s. The material out of which houses in a community were constructed was considered a measure not only of prosperity but also of worth and industriousness in regional society. A correspondent of the Brockville *Recorder* in 1839, for example, recommended anyone wishing "to see what honest industry *might* do, in a Canadian clime,...[to] take a ride along up the Scotch Line [the boundary between Drummond and Elmsley townships], and observe...the neat looking *Stone* houses on both sides of the road, in the midst of the respective farms" achieved by the combined virtues of "Scottish thrift, a willingness to earn daily bread, and piety".[135] The two main roads travelled in Beckwith, passing as they did through the poorest land, gave travellers a poor impression of Beckwith in contrast with the main road through neighbouring Ramsay which followed the fertile Mississippi floodplain from Carlton Place to Pakenham. A visitor passing through the two townships in 1841 concluded:[136]

> Beckwith has not improved as rapidly as Ramsay, there is not the same taste shown, nor acquaintance with neatness; but this is not always indispensably necessary to make a thriving settlement: and if we meet not with a display of taste, yet we see something, may be, that tells as well — good substantial log buildings with here and there a stone one, and well cultivated fields...There have been a few new clearances opened out, with log buildings placed on them, as if they were occupied by new settlers... On the way [from Franktown] to the village of Richmond there are no striking symptoms of prosperity worthy of notice, except an addition of a few new settlers, and the erection of another common school.

The log houses at Franktown were typical of Beckwith's larger population, with two-thirds of all houses in the township being constructed of log as late as 1852. It was Carlton Place which was exceptional in having two-thirds of its houses built either of frame or stone. The log houses built in Beckwith between 1825 and 1851 were larger and more comfortable than the temporary log huts that immigrants had first built upon arriving. The Perthshire highlanders in Beckwith, concentrated together as they were, and from force of cultural tradition neglecting comfort and being "careless, in many particulars, of cleanliness, within their houses"[137] contrasted with the lowlanders of Ramsay who by 1841 had a "great number of substantial stone buildings erected".[138] The Reverend William Bell described the interior of Alexander McGregor's log house (lot five, concession 7) on a sweltering August day in 1831:[139]

Plate 66
The John McEwen homestead, lot 11, concession 9, Beckwith, as photographed by Fritz Kuehn in 1904. This was a large log house by early nineteenth century Beckwith standards, in contrast with the small log structure at Franktown shown in Plate 49, and the early houses on the Roger Hawkins and Duncan McCuan homesteads (plates 42 and 43). The small size, scarcity and primitive sashing of the windows in this structure suggest the lingering influence of the traditional windowless cottages in the Perthshire highlands. The poor land on this farm prevented a more pretentious house replacing this structure until 1904, when from the profits of his Dominion Quarry, Findlay McEwen built a large brick house. Photograph courtesy of Findlay and Mary McEwen.

> There was only one door, and all the windows were fast. So that we were stewing with heat from the improper construction of the house, while we might have been comfortable, had there been an opening on each side, to allow a current of air to pass through. This error in the construction of buildings, I find very general in the houses of the highlanders... They have been accustomed to this, which is a sufficient reason for refusing to change.

These ambitionless second houses of the highlanders contrasted with the more comfortable log houses built by the Wexford Irish inhabitants of Beckwith. One of the finest of these, the residence of the Reverend Richard Harte at Franktown, was described in 1837 as "a squared log building of Oak," and built in the most substantial manner, with an extensive addition capable of affording spacious accommodation — the front building is divided into large sit[t]ing and sleeping appartments, lathed and plastered, and finished in a style to secure comfort, with open fire-places in each gable."[140]

Franktown, unlike Carlton Place had no water-power to attract milling and manufacturing, and the concentration of three-quarters of all shanties, that is, habitations too miserable to be called log houses in the four southern concessions underlined how little deep rich soil and how much swamp there was in southern Beckwith. The bleak subsistence farming of many southern Beckwith farmers was well described by an 1852 census enumerator for adjacent northern Montague in prose as inadequate as the soil:[141]

> [T]he people in general is very poor[. T]he most part of them gets their living by working out in the winter and raising a little crop in the summer[. T]hem that don[']t work out strives to make out there wants by getting out a little fire wood or hemlock bark [for tanneries] or [c]ooper stuff to Smyths falls or to Merrick[ville.]

Franktown had received its few advantages such as the King's storehouse, the location on the road from Perth to Bytown, funding for a stone church, and a post office from government. Franktown area inhabitants rehearsed these advantages, as for example when John McKay offered a farm for sale in 1829 which he described as "lying on the great road from Bytown to Perth, about a mile from the church at the Village of Franktown."[142] The only agricultural crop to be processed at Franktown was potash. The potash works at Franktown were described in 1837 as being "in thorough repair...(in which for some years past 60 or 80 Barrels of Potash have been annually boiled)."[143]

Franktown from the 1820s onward offered the services of a small group of professionals settled nearby to the inhabitants of southern Beckwith and northern Montague. These professionals included the Anglican rector, postmaster Ewen McEwen, surgeon George Nesbitt, surveyor Owen Quinn and schoolteacher James Kent. Tradesmen in the Franktown vicinity in 1842 included blacksmiths George Buchanan and William McFarland; shoemakers Christopher Wynn, George Cockle and Patrick Doolan; innkeepers James Burrows and Peter McGregor; merchant George Nowlan; tailor Moses Sheil; coopers Alexander McLaren and Nicholas O'Neil; carpenter James Bowles; and weaver James McNaughton.[144] Ten years later tradesmen at Franktown included blacksmiths Matthew Anderson and John Morris; cooper William Armstrong; tailors Samuel Carley and Moses Sheil; shoemakers Thomas Clark, John Lyons, Timothy Conboy, Michael Murray; carpenters John Edwards and Robert Leaver; and merchant John Hughton.[145] The emergence of increasing numbers of tradesmen at Carlton Place and to a lesser extent in the vicinity around Franktown in the 1840s reflected the prosperity that Beckwith families enjoyed in provisioning the upper Ottawa timber industry, and increasingly they preferred to produce crops for that market and pay for the services of local tradesmen rather than attempt to be self-sufficient on their farms.

Franktown and Carlton Place were the only two centres to develop in Beckwith by 1852. The only evidence of the future hamlet of Prospect on the eastern end of the fourth concession line was the stone Methodist chapel reputedly built in 1847, a log school, the store in which James Conn clerked, and weavers Donald McDiarmid, James McRorie and John Wilson. The only tradesman on the Beckwith side of Mount Pleasant (later Ashton) as late as 1852 was blacksmith Hugh Houston. The junction of the Perth-Bytown road with a road leading to Smith's Falls gave business to an inn which Archibald M. Gillies opened in 1836[146] and which was still licensed as a drinking establishment as late as 1849.[147] As befitted an agriculturally-based economy, many of Beckwith's coopers, blacksmiths, distillers, weavers, shoemakers, labourers, teachers and clergymen as late as 1852 did not live in villages or hamlets, but rather at rural locations where there was a demand for their services (Appendix 23). One of the more notable rural operations in Beckwith was a distillery operated by James McArthur and his son Peter from the late 1820s through to the 1850s, using a 33 gallon copper still.[148]

Provisioning the upper Ottawa valley timber industry through markets at Bytown and Perth was the predominant source of income for Beckwith farmers and the local tradesmen who serviced them in the 1830s and 1840s. Carlton Place emerged as a marketing centre in the 1840s. William Stewart, a lumbering merchant at Bytown, received fifty barrels of flour from Robert Bell in May 1840 which he forwarded to J. Egan & Co. upriver. Further shipments received by Stewart from Robert Bell & Co. included 35 barrels of prime mess pork and 27 of prime pork in July 1841, 97 barrels of prime pork and 37 of prime mess pork in May 1842, eight kegs of butter and three bales of harness

Plate 67
The Thomas Pierce farmhouse, lot 8, concession 4, Beckwith, believed built in the late 1830s or early 1840s, as photographed in 1982. This was probably the largest private house built in Beckwith during the period before 1850. Unlike other stone structures dating from the same period, the exterior harl or stucco that covered the stone has not been removed. The harl was scored or incised with a sharp implement so as to give the impression that one was looking at a house built of uniformly-sized cut stones rather than rubble construction. The visual illusion of a cut stone structure along with the classical design of the verandah pillars attempted to conjure up some basic sense of refinement in early Beckwith.

leather in October 1842, a barrel of potash in July 1843 and four barrels of potash in November 1843.[149] The demand for butter that had existed in Brockville since the early 1830s,[150] was echoed by merchants and forwarders at Perth in 1846 who respectively offered to exchange goods for butter and cheese,[151] and requested butter "of superior quality, for immediate shipment to London, for which an extra price will be paid."[152] By the late 1840s, as the timber industry experienced some of its most depressed seasons, the mining of the land by planting the same cereal crops for a generation without being manured was causing the soil to wear out and to become depleted.[153] The farmers of Beckwith as in the rest of Lanark County differed from farmers elsewhere in Upper Canada in keeping "an immense quantity of livestock", which was a cultural trait which the Perthshire highlanders brought with them. The editor of the *Bathurst Courier* commented in 1843:[154]

We have heard it stated frequently by many, that it would be wise economy in the farmer, to reduce

Plate 68
The William Rattray farm, lot 12, concession 10, Beckwith, as photographed in June 1983. Dozens of stone houses were built in Beckwith during the late 1830s and 1840s, following the construction of the stone United Church of England and Ireland rectory near Franktown in 1837 and the stone Church of Scotland manse on the seventh concession line in 1839. This house, probably built in the early 1840s, still features a fireplace flue.

> his stock — attend to his farm rather than that of raising a stock about him, which made no return to him for the expense of their feed, and cannot bring a remunerating value when sold... The keeping up of ten or a dozen cattle over winter, whether fodder be plenty of scarce, is a system upon which no farmer can expect to thrive.

Despite this pessimistic assessment, when the wheat crop began to fail at mid-century the tradition of keeping and improving livestock would stand Beckwith farmers in good stead as they developed a mixed farming and dairy economy.

The provisioning trade continued to remain important well past mid-century. The importance of agriculture to the incomes of the 500 inhabitants of Carlton Place was reflected in an April 1852 editorial in that village's new newspaper, the *Herald*:[155]

> The farmers are preparing for the pressure of the spring work, and anxiously looking for the time when they can get their plows a-going, which they will shortly be able to do, as there is scarcely any frost in the ground. There is a good market here, for Oats, Pease, Corn and Potatoes, both for consumption and for seed; the whole of which articles would readily command Cash at good prices; even wheat which has been a drug in the market the whole winter is now looking up, and flour is rather scarce. There is scarcely any business doing in the Merchant's Shops: but the Founders, Blacksmiths, and Wheelwrights are all busy preparing implements of husbandry. The Foundry is turning out large quantities of excellent Plow Castings, varied enough to suit all kinds of work.

Just as Carlton Place had visibly developed from the mill hamlet of the mid 1820s to a prosperous village by 1851, so Beckwith itself had been transformed from a collection of isolated subsistence clearings in the forest populated by under a thousand people to more than 2,500 people cultivating 11,579 acres.[156] Beckwith's population would not be this high again for another century and a half. A traveller passing through in 1852 remarked that "Beckwith is not settling up very fast".[157]

The peaking population of rural Beckwith in 1851 was due to the best land being entirely taken up. There was no prospect for new settlers at mid-century since even long-established farmers earned no more than a comfortable subsistence. Phineas Lowe on the east half of lot eight in the third concession just west of Franktown revealed the quality of comfortable subsistence that pervaded Beckwith in a letter he wrote back to his brother and sister in Lancashire, England, in March 1849:[158]

> We have many reasons to return sincere and hearty thanks to Almighty God for all His kind mercies to us. For my own part I have much cause of thanks; our family enjoy good health and many of the blessings of this life. Thank God we know not want nor distress. As yet we cannot command much money, but it is a very great blessing to have an abundance of good victuals, clothing and every other necessity of life.
>
> If I could send you provision I would do so but that is almost impossible and money, I have not. Our business in this country is carried on by barter or what they call trade; anything we have to buy in the shops we get on credit and we pay for them by returning wheat, pork or other produce, but we get no money. The shopkeepers or merchants send these away by steamers so that we have very little money excepting that which is brought from Britain.
>
> This country in many respects is very severe on immigrants, the winter extremely cold and the summer exceedingly hot. The land in this part of the country is all taken up and it is by many years of the hardest labo[u]r that a man will get a farm cleared. We have no roads but what we make ourselves and I don't know that your business would be suitable to this country; we have no factories as you have in England. People who came here about 20 or 30 years ago are well settled now, but at that time it was easy to get land. We have to fodder our cattle for five or six months; the snow mostly lies for five months and at the present time we have all [the] appearance of scarcity by reason of the great heat and drought.

By 1851 there already had been a trickle of migration leaving the township for over a decade. The growing agricultural productivity and prosperity of Beckwith during these years masked the fact that families were pulling up stakes and leaving.

Endnotes

1. *Bathurst Courier*, 3 June 1836, p. 3, col. 4.
2. OKQAR Rev. William Bell Journals V:94.
3. NAC Reel C-11731 1852 census of Beckwith Township, comments of enumerator James Duncan.
4. *Brockville Recorder*, 13 September 1824, p. 4, col. 5.
5. *Bathurst Courier*, 18 May 1838, p. 2, col. 5.
6. George Edward Kidd, *The Story of the Derry* (Vancouver: by the author, 1943), pp. 25-26.
7. The 18 May 1838 issue of the *Bathurst Courier* contains a notice of a child at Pakenham Mills drowning when he fell into the timber slide there. A timber slide was built at Shipman's Mills (later Almonte) by 1835.
8. *Brockville Recorder*, 19 July 1833, p. 2, col. 6.
9. George Maclean Rose, ed., *A Cyclopedia of Canadian Biography: Being Chiefly Men of the Time* Rose's National Biographical Series no. II (Toronto: Rose Publishing Company, 1888), pp. 75-76.
10. *Bathurst Courier*, 11 January 1839, p. 3, col. 3.
11. Most inhabitants of Carleton Place before 1852 spelled Carleton Place without an "E", and hence in this section of the book I have conformed the spelling

to the usage of the time. Editors of contemporary Perth newspapers tended to insert the "E".
12 Jean S. McGill, *A Pioneer History of the County of Lanark* (Bewdley, Ontario: Clay Publishing Company Limited, 1979), p. 169.
13 *Bathurst Courier*, 30 November 1841, p. 3, col. 3, notice of George Buchanan, Beckwith.
14 *Perth (Upper Canada) Bathurst Independent Examiner*, 15 January 1830, p. 2, col. 1.
15 *Bathurst Courier*, 16 September 1836, p. 3, col. 5, notice of William Marritt, Beckwith.
16 Ibid., 16 June 1837, p. 3, col. 4.
17 Glenn J Lockwood, "Irish Immigrants and the 'Critical Years' in Eastern Ontario: The Case of Montague Township, 1821-1881" in Donald H. Akenson, ed., *Canadian Papers in Rural History* IV (Gananoque: Langdale Press, 1984), p. 158.
18 Jessie Buchanan Campbell, *The Pioneer Pastor* (Franklin, Pennsylvania: John J. McLaurin, 1905), pp. 28-29.
19 Kidd, *Story of the Derry*, p. 15.
20 NAC RG 5, A1 Reel C-6916 Upper Canada Sundries, vol. 255, pp. 138565-138566.
21 Ibid., pp. 138566-138567.
22 Bathurst District Quarter Sessions Roads Book, pp. 8, 12, 23, 29, 51, 75 and 89.
23 Howard M. Brown, *Lanark Legacy* (Perth, 1984), p. 160.
24 This assessment is based on a perusal of an 1832 Plan *Exhibiting the Relative Situation of Towns, Roads and Waters in the Bathurst and Johnstown Districts*, Map B-12 from the Archives of Ontario.
25 John May, "Bush Life in the Ottawa Valley Eighty Years Ago" in *Papers and Records of the Ontario Historical Society* XII (1914), p. 158.
26 *Carleton Place Herald*, 22 October 1901, p. 7.
27 *Carleton-Place Herald*, 16 June 1853, p. 3, col. 2.
28 *Brockville (Upper Canada) Gazette*, 7 May 1830, p. 2, cols. 2-4.
29 McGill, *Pioneer History of the County of Lanark*, p. 117.
30 *Brockville Recorder*, 30 August 1832, p. 3, col. 2.
31 Ibid., 3 October 1844, p. 2, col. 5.
32 Glenn J Lockwood, *Montague: A Social History of an Irish Ontario Township, 1783-1980* (Smiths Falls: Corporation of the Township of Montague, 1980),, p. 219.
33 *Kingston (Upper Canada) Statesman*, 21 February 1844, p. 2, col. 5.
34 *Brockville Recorder*, 31 July 1845, p. 3, col. 2.
35 Samples of the piecemeal expenditures and improvements can be found in issues of the *Bathurst Courier* dated 26 March 1844, p.3, col. 5; 23 July 1844, p. 3, col. 5; 15 September 1846, p. 3, col. 4; 20 October 1846, pp. 1-2, cols. 4-1; 27 October 1846, pp. 2-3, cols. 7-2; 10 November 1846, pp. 1-2, cols. 7-4; 23 November 1847, pp. 1-2, cols. 6-5; and 24 November 1848, pp. 1-2, cols. 4-2.
36 Samuel Butler, *The Emigrant's Handbook of Facts, Concerning Canada, New Zealand, Australia, Cape of Good Hope* (Glasgow: W.R. M'Phun, 1843), pp. 95-96.
37 *Bytown (Upper Canada) Gazette*, 6 October 1836, cited in Michael S. Cross, "The Dark Druidical Groves: The Lumber Community and the Commercial Frontier in British North America to 1854" (Ph.D. dissertation, University of Toronto, 1968), p. 281.
38 *Bytown Gazette*, 12 September 1844, cited in Cross, "Dark Druidical Groves," p. 281.
39 *Bathurst Courier*, 12 February 1841, p. 2, cols. 4-5.
40 Canada, Department of Agriculture, Census Report of the Canadas, 1851-1852 (1852), :26-29.
41 Ibid.
42 *Bathurst Courier*, 2 August 1843, p. 2, cols. 5-6.
43 Ibid., 23 July 1844, p. 2, col. 6.
44 Ibid., 21 July 1848, p. 2, cols. 4-5.
45 *Carleton-Place Herald*, 22 August 1851, p. 2, col. 6.
46 *Bathurst Courier*, 22 November 1839, pp. 2-3, cols. 6-1.
47 Ibid., 25 March 1845, p. 4, col. 4.
48 NAC RG 5, A1 Reel C-6990 Upper Canada Sundries, vol. 199, pp. 110518-110519.
49 Ibid., Reel C-6907, vol. 227, p. 122696.
50 *Carleton-Place Lanark Herald*, 29 November 1850, p. 2 col.5
51 *Bathurst Courier*, 3 April 1840, p. 1, cols. 2-3.
52 Ibid., 28 February 1840, p. 2, col. 6.
53 Ibid., 24 May 1842, p. 1, col. 1.
54 Ibid., 7 July 1848, p. 2, col. 5.
55 Ibid., 5 October 1847, p. 2, col. 4.
56 Ibid., 18 August 1848, p. 3, col. 1.
57 Ibid., 6 October 1848, p. 3, col. 2; and 16 March 1849, p. 3, col. 4.
58 Ibid., 2 November 1849, p. 1, cols. 3-4.
59 NAC 1852 census of Beckwith, Reel C-11731.
60 Lanark County Registry Office, Perth, Ontario, 20 April 1836 will of Duncan McDiarmid.
61 NAC RG 1, E3 Upper Canada State Papers, vol. 31, pp. 47-54, provided courtesy of Howard M. Brown.
62 Bathurst Courier, 11 January 1839, p. 3, col. 3.
63 NAC RG 1, E3 Upper Canada State Papers, vol. 18, pp. 169-174, cited in Brown, *Lanark Legacy*, p 176.
64 1852 printed census II:28-31.
65 John M'Donald, *Emigration to Canada. Narrative of a Voyage to Quebec, and Journey from thence to New Lanark, in Upper Canada* (Edinburgh: by the author, 1823; reprint ed. Ottawa: Canadian Heritage Publications, 1979), p. 23.
66 NAC MG 55/24 No. 199. 10 November 1823 letter from Robert Ferguson, Beckwith, to John Moir, near Kippen, West Stirling, Scotland.
67 Richard Reid, "The Rosamond Woolen Company of Almonte: Industrial Development in a Rural Setting" in *Ontario History* LXXV No. 3 (September 1983), p. 267. An article on the early history of Carleton Place in the 14 December 1887 issue of the *Carleton Place Herald* indicates that Rosamond came to the

village as a chairmaker about 1830. Both this article and another in the 26 March 1887 issue of the *Toronto Mail* state that Rosamond built his first mill at Carleton Place in 1830, but do not state that it was a carding mill. Given the proud connection of the Rosamond family name with the woollen industry at the time these two articles were published, and given that the earliest carding mill in eastern Upper Canada was that of John Haggart at Perth in 1835, it seems unlikely that Rosamond's 1830 mill at Carleton Place was a carding mill. There is a notice in the 8 December 1836 issue of the *Bathurst Courier*, p. 3, col. 2, dissolving the partnership of John McEwan and James Rosamond in running the Carleton Place Mills, but there is no reference which clearly suggests that Rosamond engaged in carding and fulling before 1837.
68 Isabel Skelton, *A Man Austere: William Bell, Parson and Pioneer* (Toronto: The Ryerson Press, 1947), p. 152.
69 NAC Reel C-1345 1842 census of Beckwith.
70 Lanark County registry Office. In his will dated 31 May 1841, Peter Cram left his weaver's loom and all the utensils thereunto belonging to his sons James and Duncan.
71 NAC Reel C-11731 1852 census of Beckwith.
72 [Richard Reid], *The Development of the Woolen Industry in Lanark, Renfrew and Carleton Counties* (Almonte, Ontario: The North Lanark Historical Society, 1978), pp. 6-7.
73 May, "Bush Life," p. 158.
74 *Bathurst Courier*, 6 April 1838, p. 3, col. 3.
75 Ibid., 30 June 1846, p. 4, col. 7.
76 Ibid., 8 June 1847, p. 3, col. 3.
77 Reid, "Rosamond Woolen Company," p. 268.
78 William H. Allen, comp., "A Brief History of Carleton Place" in the *Carleton Place Herald*, 14 December 1887, printed in Howard M. Brown, *Founded Upon A Rock: Carleton Place Recollections* (Carleton Place: 150th Year Festival Committee, 1969), p. 16. According to the obituary of Bellows printed in the *Carleton Place Herald*, 10 June 1863, p. 2, col. 1, he was born in Walpole, New Hampshire in 1806, and was attracted to the Carleton Place vicinity by an elder brother who was in business at Nepean Point (later Ottawa).
79 Brown, *Carleton Place: Founded Upon A Rock* (Renfrew: Juniper Books, 1984), p. 75.
80 OKQAR Rev. William Bell Journals IV:139.
81 *Carleton Place Herald*, 2 August 1865, p. 3, col. 1.
82 Brown, *Founded Upon A Rock*, p. 5.
83 *Bathurst Independent Examiner*, 11 September 1829, p. 4, col. 4.
84 OKQAR Rev. William Bell Journals VI:125.
85 *Bathurst Independent Examiner*, 11 September 1829, p. 2, col. 3.
86 OKQ Douglas Library Special Collections, Canadian Broadsides and Posters,1830a 1 Notice of Robert Bell.
87 *Bathurst Independent Examiner*, 2 October 1829, p. 3, col. 4.
88 NAC RG 5, A1 Reel C-6873 Upper Canada Sundries, vol. 110, pp. 62656-62657.
89 Brown, *Carleton Place*, p.75.
90 *Bathurst Independent Examiner*, 19 March 1830, p. 3, col. 2.
91 NAC RG 5, A1 Reel C-6879 Upper Canada Sundries, vol. 130, p. 71697.
92 Ibid., p. 71698.
93 Ibid., Reel C-6887, vol. 155, p. 85219.
94 *Bathurst Courier*, 13 November 1835, p. 3, col. 3.
95 *Carleton Place Herald*, 17 April 1894. The document reproduced in the newspaper was probably from the papers of Robert Bell. I am grateful to Howard M. Brown for this reference.
96 *Bathurst Courier*, 22 November 1839, p. 3, cols. 1-2.
97 Ibid., 13 November 1835, p. 4, col. 5.
98 Ibid., 16 September 1836, p. 3, col. 3.
99 *Brockville (Upper Canada) Statesman*, 10 November 1836, p. 1, col. .
100 *Bathurst Independent Examiner*, 5 March 1830, pp. 2-3, cols. 4-2; and 26 March 1830, p. 3, cols. 1-2.
101 *Bathurst Courier*, 9 April 1841, p. 3, col. 3.
102 Ibid., 21 May 1841, p. 3, col. 1.
103 Ibid., 11 August 1846, p. 4, col. 5.
104 Ibid., 10 March 1848, p. 3, col. 4.
105 In May 1849 the editor of the *Bathurst Courier* received a copy of a pamphlet written by Dr. Gavin Russell, "On the operation of Physical Agencies in the function of organized bodies (*Bathurst Courier*, 25 May 1849, p. 2, col. 7). It was in dozens of letters to the Perth and Carleton Place newspapers that Russell promoted phrenology.
106 For some samples of Russell's writing see the *Bathurst Courier*, 1 September 1846, p. 3, col. 2; 8 September 1846, pp. 2-3, cols. 7-2; 15 September 1846, p. 3, cols. 1-2; 22 September 1846, p. 2, cols. 5-7; 10 November 1846, p. 1, cols. 5-6; and 8 December 1846, p. 1, cols. 6-7.
107 NAC Reel C-11731, 1852 census of Beckwith.
108 *Bathurst Courier*, 27 June 1843, p. 4, col. 4.
109 Butler, *The Emigrant's Hand-book*, pp. 85-86.
110 *Bathurst Courier*, 8 March 1842, p. 2, cols. 3-4.
111 Ibid., 19 February 1836, p. 4, col. 1; 3 March 1837, p. 3, col. 5; 8 February 1839, p. 3, cols. 2-3; 21 February 1840, p. 1, cols. 3-5; 27 February 1844, p. 3, col. 6; 23 July 1844, p. 3, col.4; 2 February 1847, p. 3, col. 3.
112 Ibid., 14 December 1841, p. 3, col.2; 27 February 1841, p. 3, col.4.
113 OTAR MU 4841 #7 Account book of Carlton Place vehicle and implement repairman John Graham, 1842-1865.
114 *Bathurst Courier*, 29 September 1846, p. 3, col.3. A notice by Lavallee in the 17 November 1846 issue of the Courier refers to opening his large stone building as a "TEMPERANCE HOUSE."
115 *Bytown (Canada West) Packet*, 6 April 1850, p. 3,

col. 1.
116 Carleton Place Public Library, Carlton Library Association & Mechanic's Institute subscription book, 1846-1851.
117 *Bytown Packet*, 6 April 1851, p. 3, col. 1.
118 *Bathurst Courier*, 1 June 1849, p. 1, cols. 5-6; 8 June 1849, p. 2, cols. 4-5.
119 Ibid., 13 July 1849, p. 3, col. 3.
120 Ibid., 8 December 1836, p. 3, col. 2. McEwan attempted a partnership with Francis W.K. Jessop, but this too was dissolved by April 1841 as shown by a notice in the *Courier*, 30 April 1841, p. 4, col. 5.
121 Ibid., 31 December 1847, p. 3, col. 4.
122 Recollections by Patrick Galvin, *Carleton Place Herald*, 9 June 1891.
123 *Bathurst Courier*, 3 November 1848, pp. 2-3, cols. 7-1.
124 W.H. Smith, *Canada: Past, Present and Future* (Toronto: Thomas Maclear, 1852; reprint ed. Belleville: Mika Publishing. 1973) II: 332.
125 *Bytown Packet*, 6 April 1850, p. 3, col. 1.
126 *Bathurst Courier*, 5 October 1847, p. 2, cols. 3-4.
127 Ibid., 22 November 1839, p. 3, cols. 1-2.
128 May, "Bush Life", p. 159.
129 Marjory Whitelaw, *The Dalhousie Journals* (Ottawa: Oberon Press, 1982) II:44-45
130 Campbell, *Pioneer Pastor*, p. 16.
131 OTAR MS 35 R9 Calendar of the John Strachan papers, 1794-1891, June [1840].
132 *Bathurst Courier*, 14 May 1841, p. 2, col. 4.
133 Smith, *Canada* II:333.
134 NAC Reel C-11731, 1852 census of Beckwith.
135 *Brockville Recorder*, 19 September 1839, p. 3, col. 2.
136 *Bathurst Courier*, 14 May 1841, p. 2, col. 4.
137 John M'Gregor, *British America* (Edinburgh and London, 1832) II:445, 447 cited in Jean R. Burnet, *Ethnic Groups in Upper Canada* (Toronto: The Ontario Historical Society, 1972), pp. 21-22.
138 *Bathurst Courier*, 23 April 1841, p. 3. col. 2.
139 OKQAR Rev. William Bell Journals VIII:11.
140 *Brockville Statesman*, 22 April 1837, p. 3.
141 NAC Reel C-963, 1852 census of Montague, general remarks of Montague enumerator, John Nowlan, cited in Glenn J Lockwood, "Success and the Doubtful Image of Irish Immigrants in Upper Canada: The Case of Montague Township, 1820-1900" in Robert O'Driscoll and Lorna Reynolds, eds., *The Untold Story: The Irish in Canada* (Toronto: Celtic Arts of Canada, 1988), p. 333.
142 *Bathurst Independent Examiner*, 2 October 1829, p. 4, col. 3.
143 *Brockville Statesman*, 22 April 1839, p. 3.
144 NAC Reel C-1345, 1842 census of Beckwith.
145 NAC Reel C-11731, 1852 census of Beckwith.
146 *Bathurst Courier*, 19 February 1836, p. 4, col. 1.
147 Ibid., 9 March 1849, pp. 1-2, cols. 7-3.
148 *Bathurst Courier*, 3 March 1837, p. 3, col. 5. The Carleton Place and Beckwith Historical Society has in its collection this copper still and the distillery journal dating from 1841 to 1852.
149 OTAR MU 1729 William Stewart Letterbooks, Bytown, 1834-1846, lumber merchant, 20 September 1832, p. 4, col. 2; ibid., 16 May 1833, p. 4, col. 6.
150 *Brockville Recorder*, 20 September 1832, p. 4, col. 2; ibid., 16 May 1833, p. 4, col. 6.
151 *Bathurst Courier*, 25 August 1846, p. 3, col. 3. Advertisement of Francis Holliday, Perth.
152 Ibid., 20 October 1846, p. 3, cols. 6-7.
153 Ibid., 23 February 1847, p. 3, col. 1.
154 Ibid., 18 July 1843, p. 2, cols. 4-5.
155 *Carleton-Place Herald*, 15 April 1852, p. 2, col. 4.
156 1852 printed census of Canada II:28.
157 W.H. Smith, *Canada: Past, Present and Future* (Toronto: Thomas Maclear, 1852), II: 333.
158 Beckwith Women's Institute, Tweedsmuir History of Beckwith.

FAMILY TIES

In early February 1851 John McEwen of Lochearnhead, in Perthshire sat down and wrote a remarkable letter to Duncan McLaren in Beckwith, Upper Canada. The content of the letter was not singular, detailing as it did the deaths and illnesses of family members, listing the children born, the state of local crops and markets, and the vicissitudes of employment and wages. What made the vital and intimate commonplaces of family news in this letter stand out was that it was written by one man to someone he had never met nor ever known, and at a time when links between Scotland and Beckwith were beginning to disappear. It was only at the end of the letter that John McEwen acknowledged[1]

> Now Duncan although we are personally unacquainted with one another, and although this is the first direct communication that has passed between us I wish it to be continued and our being unknown to each other ought to be an inducement to us to correspond fully and freely that we be not strangers[,] seeing the relation in which we stand one towards another... Our relations in Canada are so numerous that to mention them all would be a difficult task but tender to all of them within your reach our united and kindest regards. Margaret joins me in our best wishes to you, your wife and to each member of your family. *Write me on receipt.*

This attempt to keep in touch with relatives who had immigrated a generation earlier is poignant evidence of how strong a force family ties were in early Beckwith, or at least of how strong a force it was believed kinship should be between the old world and the new. Family ties, as this chapter will show, were very important, but in Beckwith they counted more for facing the future in Beckwith or facing moving to a more distant location than for looking backward to Ireland and Scotland.

The ties between relatives in the homeland and Beckwith inhabitants remained strong into the 1830s. When James McCuan, a private in the 79th Highlanders stationed at Montreal, wrote his uncle Duncan at Beckwith in December 1832, he was able to relay news about relatives in Scotland as handily as about relatives of various Beckwith families living in Montreal.[2] The intimate correspondence which bound family members in the mother countries and Beckwith together as late as the mid1830s is well represented by an excerpt from a letter written to Alexander Clark from his brother in Comrie in March 1834:[3]

> Dear brother, Wife and children[,] We received your letter about the 15 December which gave us no small pleasur[e] to learn that you were all alive and in health for which there is ground of thankfulness to the god of all our mercies and although you are in possession of abundance of the necessarys of life it appears that you maintain already that you have banished yourselves from god[']s ordinances and as you expressed yourself, no dou[b]t nor is it a want which the things of time will not make up.... John McLaren's son in Careglen is going[,...& James Carmichael [(]Comrie Donald Carmichael's son[)] & one Peter McIntyre from Lochearnside who learned the shoe making with James Mingas [(]a son of Alexr. Stirling's[)] and it is reported a son of Donald and Galech Cowan I thinke [are] all bound for Canada. As for the book you

wanted it has not been printed as no man could make out the writing[.] You may mention in your next letter what kind of a house you have and if you have furniture as good as [you] had in the [R]oss [and] what kind of Market you get for your [crops.].

As the number of letters crossing the Atlantic between Beckwith and Perthshire and between Beckwith and Wexford fell in the late 1830s and 1840s, the range of topics dropped from a discussion of health of family members, crops, religious practice and listing the people leaving for Canada to the sole topic of immigration itself. The only letters written after mid-century were from members of families who returned to Perthshire and Wexford[4] to improve their health. At mid-century, despite poor crops and a growing family, Alexander McEwen of Lochearnhead resisted letters from James McLaren "offering him some inducements to go to Canada."[5] When John McEewn at Lochearnhead wrote his brother Peter in Beckwith at about the same time, he was disappointed that "he never returned me an answer",[6] showing how faint the connection with the old country had become.

The dwindling correspondence and the decreasing inflow of immigrants from Perthshire and Wexford into Beckwith reflected the declining availability of arable land in Beckwith and the economic opportunity it represented. By the early 1830s there clearly was no good land left in Beckwith that squatters or farmers' sons were not already jealously guarding or developing. When Private James McCuan in the 79th Highlanders at Montreal wrote his uncle Duncan at Beckwith in December 1832 seeking his "advice whether you would advise me to stop in the Country" or return to Britain with his regiment, there was no suitable Crown land left in Beckwith for him to receive as a discharge grant.[7] The economic promise of Beckwith and of British North America was no longer quite as attractive from the mid 1830s to the mid 1840s as the Wexford and Perthshire economies picked up following the post-war slump and as the outflow of population to North America relieved the pressure of population on land. John McDiarmid of Tullimet in 1845 wrote family members in Beckwith and Osgoode that in Perthshire, "Trade and manufact[uring] are in a prosperous State at present[,] all hands employed more so than it has been for 20 years past."[8] Moreover, British North America was a distinct disappointment for some families. Allan McDiarmid from Creag Ianaich in Perthshire informed his uncle James McDiarmid in Beckwith that a neighbouring family of Mc-Callums who left for Canada in 1857 "from the accounts they send home they don't appear to be very well pleased with the place".[9] When a young Comrie cousin of Alexander Clark arrived from Scotland in the early 1840s, despite the many kindnesses of his relatives, he quickly perceived that there "was no economic future for him in the Beckwith vicinity and pursued employment in Montreal instead. In a letter to Alexander Clark he confided:[10]

> though Archibald [McArthur] used all endeavours to get me a situation he failed[.] I might have got work for the summer but there was little prospect for the winter.... I would feel very much obliged to you if you would write a few lines to Peter McArthur and let him know how I am circumstanced and I would feel very much obliged to you if you would send down my trunk with the first things that you send down. [G]ive my kindest respects to your parents and brothers and sisters[. I]t may never be in my power to recompence you all for your kindness to me but I sincerely wish you all prosperity, both spiritual and temporal, and that you all may [lead] holy lives in all goodliness and honesty.

Alexander Clark could hardly have been surprised at the poor employment opportunities in rural Beckwith during the early 1840s. He was seventeen years old when his parents Alexander Clark and Margaret Comrie immigrated from Perthshire in 1829. They found Beckwith so fully settled that they instead selected land near Kilmarnock in Montague some ten miles south of Beckwith to farm. Montague with its large Irish and American-origin population was not necessarily the most congenial environment for Scottish highlanders and young Alexander was drawn to the Perthshire

Plate 69
The William James house, lot 25, concession 3, Beckwith, at Prospect, as photographed in 1982. The graceful elliptical curve of the fanlight over the front entrance to this house was rare in Beckwith, and was based on a prevalent design used in houses built in the early 1830s along the Rideau Canal. The funds to build this house came from William James's sawmills at Prospect. The few touches of architectural refinement in Beckwith before 1850 were largely confined to the homes of Irish and English Anglicans.

settlement in northern Beckwith where he taught school in the early or mid 1830s. In an 1838 letter back to the family of Duncan McCuan with whom he had boarded, Alexander Clark confided that[11]

> often does my thoughts wander back to the many pleasing and agreeable days & nights which I have spent with you around your hospitable hearth in the Innocent and youthful amusements of your domestic circle [and he particularly asked] Miss Catherine [to] please receive this...token of Respect from your old teacher and when your eye happens to glance over this you will think on me when perhaps far away.

But congenial highland neighbours and even the attractions of Miss Catherine could not obscure the fact that teaching was the last resort for people who had failed at everything else and who preferred it to begging.[12] Ambitious young Alexander Clark could see that there was no place for a young man without family to help him make his way in rural Beckwith. So he returned to Montague and in 1840 launched a wholesale and retail business which eventually made him a leading merchant at Smith's Falls.[13]

The "youthful amusements" that Alexander Clark enjoyed in the McCuan household on the tenth line were appropriate in a population that was still remarkably youthful in profile. Immigration had appealed to younger married couples and to already large families, and the need for as many pairs of hands to assist in the drudgery of pioneer agriculture gave Beckwith a phenomenal birthrate of between fifty to 67 births per thousand in the early 1820s. The Beckwith birthrate fell to twenty per thousand in 1827 and remained constant until the early 1840s, when it rose to 27 births per thousand as the children of the 1818 and 1819 immigrants married and began raising families.[14] From 1822 on the Reverend George Buchanan and George Nesbitt served as doctors delivering children. There is no record of whether Beckwith women in the 1830s availed themselves of the services of midwives Margaret M'Caul[15] and a Mrs. Davidson at Perth. Mrs. Davidson, from Edinburgh, solicited the patronage of Drummond Township and vicinity, claiming that she had been regularly instructed by Dr. James Hamilton, M.D., Professor of Midwifery in the University of Edinburgh in 1816 and that she had studied the diseases of women and children under the most scientific teachers, and offered certificates attesting to her character.[16] Male doctors at Carlton Place in the 1840s also offered midwife services.

Exactly how the women of Beckwith lowered their birthrate to at least half of what it had been in the early 1820s is difficult to determine. There is no evidence that the widespread practice of infanticide by American-origin women in townships along the St. Lawrence was so much as even considered in the Beckwith region.[17] The repugnance with which both Irish and Scottish immigrants viewed infanticide is shown by the sentence of eighteen months imprisonment meted out in the rare instance of a domestic servant in the Bathurst District who was found guilty of drowning her illegitimate child in a well.[18] Along the St. Lawrence, by contrast, American-origin juries and judges invariably acquitted women of the charge, no matter how obvious the evidence. Numerous instances of masters getting domestic servants pregnant at Perth were dealt with not by strangling, hanging, concealing or burying alive the newly-born child, but rather by sending the servants away to Montreal where they discreetly gave birth.[19] In the closed society of Beckwith, where the members of the Irish and Scottish group settlements had known one another and whose ancestors had known one another, where the early establishment of churches kept sexual appetites within certain social bounds, infanticide appears not to have been tolerated.

Beckwith in many respects was a benign patriarchy in the second quarter of the nineteenth century, with the Presbyterian elders and United Church of England and Ireland vestries working fairly effectively to maintain domestic and social standards of marital behaviour. The influence of religion in reinforcing marital relationships is indirectly indicated in a verse of doggerel by a Perth man taking leave of his unfaithful wife Grace in 1831:[20]

> Christianity and Grace lived in one place,
> And the Angels kept the door,
> Christianity is gone and the Angels fled,
> And Grace is turned a W_____e.

Religious social control attempted to shield women from scorn in a society so paternalistic and male-oriented that it regarded as tragic the seduction of a woman in terms of other men: it rendered her useless, wronged her husband and dishonoured her father.[21] The strong sense of social control maintained by congregations in Beckwith before mid-century required guardians of orphaned young women such as Dorah Smith at Carlton Place in 1839 to give their consent before their charges could marry.[22]

Marriage provided the base of an economic partnership and was the foundation for the large families by whose labour farms were cleared and developed to produce wealth. Hence, when a daughter of Peter McEwan withdrew from a promise to marry William McCormack of Drummond in 1840, the young man hauled her parents up before the Bathurst District assizes.[23] His fiancée-to-be may have changed her mind after reflecting that she would be deprived "of many rights on entering the married state that she is entitled to enjoy when single," a conclusion which a judge offered a grand jury at Perth in 1851.[24] But most Beckwith women before mid-century were firmly in the grip of cultural tradition, working alongside their fathers, husbands and brothers in the fields, intent on developing the land which their men owned, and persevering at raising their large families. If anything, the local press they read gave new emphasis to the role of women as nurturers of their

Plate 70

Margaret Nelson Bell (1820—1906) as photographed ca. 1900. Margaret Nelson offers the example of a woman who dominated her family in Beckwith by claiming to come from a family of quality. According to family tradition, her husband, David Bell, immigrated from their native northern Ireland after the birth of their first child in 1842, settling in the Gillies Corners vicinity working for established farmers. Margaret and her child followed some two years later. Pridefully maintaining that she was closely related to war hero Admiral Horatio Nelson, she insisted that they set up house in a log hut on their own land, rather than live under their neighbours' roofs as David Bell had previously been willing to do. So successful was she in maintaining her family's pre-eminence in the Gillies Corners vicinity based on this fiction, that the post office there was named Bellcott. Photograph courtesy of Alex and Ina Bell.

Christina Anderson of Beckwith as photographed ca. 1875. The two directions in which Beckwith women felt themselves pulled after mid-century are well summed up in this photograph. According to what they read in newspapers such as the Carleton Place Herald, their role in life should be a domestic one, a role separate from the labour of their husbands in which they nurtured children; presided over household tasks such as preparing food, cleaning and mending clothes; performed acts of charity; and set a moral influence for the community. The weight of tradition, on the other hand, set them beside their men in the fields planting and harvesting crops. The dress and setting shown here suggest how attractive the new domestic role appeared to women, but the workworn hands betray the farm chores that women like Christina Anderson continued to perform. Photograph courtesy of the Carleton Place and Beckwith Historical Society.

husbands and children, as the following excerpt from the Perth *Bathurst Courier* reveals:[25]

> Great, indeed, is the task assigned to woman; who can elevate its dignity? Not to make laws, not to lead armies, not to govern empires; but to form those by whom laws are made, armies are led, and empires are governed, to guard against the slightest taint of infirmity, the frail yet spotless creature, whose moral, no less than physical being, must be derived from her; to inspire these principles, to inculcate these doctrines, to animate these sentiments which generations yet unborn and nations yet uncivilized shall learn to bless; to soften firmness into mercy, and to chasten honour into refinement; to exalt generosity into virtue, by a soothing care to allay

the anguish of the body and the far worse anguish of the mind; by her tenderness to disarm passion; by her purity to triumph over sense; to cheer the scholar sinking under his toil; to console the statesman for the ingratitude of a mistaken people; to be compensation for friends that are perfidious, for happiness that has passed away. Such is her vocation.... Such is her destiny; to visit the forsaken, to attend to the neglected; when monarchs abandon, when counsellors betray, when justice persecutes, when brethren and disciples flee, to remain unshaken and unchanged; and to exhibit in this lower world a type of that love, pure, constant, ineffable, which in another world we are taught to believe the test of virtue.

This image of angelic, uplifting women promoted in the popular press in the 1840s did not square with reality in Beckwith before mid-century, where paternalistic leadership included leading the family in worship as well as in every other activity. When seven year-old Andrew Cram lay on his deathbed in November 1851, for example, it was not his mother Agnes Wilson offering spiritual consolation, but rather his father Duncan Cram who "assured the dying Boy & his mother what the Lord would do for him. [H]e listened attentively, But said nothing. His Mother said, weeping, ["W]ell[,] if that be so we need not be sor[r]y in giving him up[. W]ill he not be well away out of this world of trouble — to which [her husband] replied he would."[26] The combined strain of helping with the outside work, of bearing numerous children, and of keeping their large households fed and in clothes preoccupied the married women of Beckwith. The only known instance of a wife leaving her husband before mid-century in Beckwith was Janet Anderson in 1838. Joseph Anderson immediately placed a notice in the Perth *Bathurst Courier* stating that she had "left my bed and board without any just cause or provocation" and forbidding "any person to give her any credit on my account as I will pay no debts contracted by her, from this date."[27] The only direct account of domestic violence in Beckwith before mid-century was noted by the Reverend William Bell in July 1823:[28]

Thomas Wickham, who kept a tavern in Beckwith...had beaten his wife in a shocking manner and turned her out of the house. He even denied their marriage although she had the certificate in her pocket which proved it. What many a poor female has to endure from the inhuman brute with whom she is connected!

Bell's comment implies that violence inflicted by husbands on wives was not rare. All the same, it must be remembered that Beckwith was remarkable in having clergy and congregations almost from the beginning of settlement. Thomas Wickham, it must also be pointed out, was part of the shrinking English population of Beckwith, and his tavern at Franktown was in decline by the mid 1820s.[29] Wickham's behaviour may have been exceptional since he belonged to no ethno-religious group settlement which might have modified his violence toward his wife. Even so, the social control of local congregations had little impact on Beckwith men after they became drunk, and recourse was occasionally taken to charivaris in which the abusing husband "would be seized and taken for a ride on a rail or perhaps tarred and feathered."[30] Increasingly, toward mid-century the regional temperance movement focused on the need "to defeat alcohol & make it a thing of the past" since through the violence it stimulated "Woman has suffered most of all."[31]

The women living in Beckwith before mid-century did not perceive themselves disadvantaged, despite the paternal mould of society which effectively made the men owners of property and placed them in control of all institutions and decisions. For the women it was enough that their husbands and brothers were acquiring land which they could call their own. In January 1824 only eight percent of Beckwith land was patented, but by 1850 over eighty percent of the land no longer was owned by the Crown.[32] Compared with the small plots of land they had leased in Wexford and Perthshire and on which they had barely subsisted, the importance which the Irish and Scottish families in Beckwith attached to becoming the owners of property cannot be emphasized too highly. By owning

Plate 71
The George Kerfoot house or the "Cuckoo's Nest", lot 15, concession 2, Beckwith, believed built in the late 1830s or early 1840s by his father, William Kerfoot of Prospect, as photographed in June 1983. This farm was dubbed the "Cuckoo's Nest" because of the folly of building such a fine early house on such agriculturally worthless land. By 1861 the Kerfoots were attempting to sell the 300 acre property, describing it as having "about 160 acres cleared, well fenced and well watered. Also a good STONE HOUSE, well finished, 26 x 36, and Stone Kitchen, a young Orchard, two Frame Barns, 30 x 42, good Stables, wood Shed and Carriage house, with 3 other Log Barns, and other outhouses." Another traditional account of how the Cuckoo's Nest came by its name was when Robert Saunders and his neighbours began clearing a lot to build a school ca. 1830. They spared a tree in which a small bird which they identified as a cuckoo was building a nest — a remarkable thing to do in a period when most area inhabitants were intent on eliminating the forest.

property they became freemen, no longer scraping to meet the payments on someone else's land, and as freemen they could vote at elections. It is significant that the two single years in which the largest numbers of Beckwith patents were given out, with 167 grants in 1824 and 98 in 1828, were election years. As the owners of their own land and as part of interrelated group settlements, most Scottish highlanders and southeastern Irish Protestants before mid-century believed they could settle their sons and daughters around them and that the farms they established would be passed down from generation to generation.

    The pride of Beckwith inhabitants at becoming owners of property was kept in focus as late as the 1840s by their intermittent contacts with Perthshire and Wexford. Some local inhabitants were sending money to relatives and friends in their place of origin. In 1843, for example, Colin King of Carlton Place sent three pounds through the Canada Company to Mrs. Janet McIntosh care of the Reverend James Gilfillan at Stirling, John Crowe of Beckwith sent £25 to Mr. Patrick Crowe at Roscommon in Central Ireland, Arthur Moore at Carlton Place sent five pounds to William Moore care of Bennett Rosamond at Ballinamore in County Leitrim, Ireland, and Thomas Hamilton of Carlton Place sent fifteen pounds to Mrs. Helen Hamilton care of Joseph Whitehead, a tanner in Paisley. In 1844 Colin King sent an additional three pounds to Mrs. Catherine McIntosh care of the

Reverend Mr. Gilfillan in Stirling, John McNaughton of Carlton Place sent five pounds to Miss Elizabeth Morrison care of Mr. Morrison at the Excise in Glasgow, and James McNeely of Carlton Place sent four pounds to Nancy Richey care of James Richey at Ballyligpatrick in County Antrim.[33] These remittances were made either in support of aged parents who refused to immigrate or in response to passionate appeals such as the following one made by William Hill at Mountalexander in Wexford to his brother in Upper Canada:[34]

> [W]hen I last wrote to you I had money in the Bank but since then I have been compelled by the failure of my crops to draw it all out and sell all my stock (but a cow & horse) to support myself and family[,] pay rent and other enormous expenses at present[. S]tock (even if I was possessed of it) is scarcely worth anything here[. W]e may take the cattle to fairs and never be asked the price[,] and yet Landlords are pressing for the rents as ever[,] and not only so but threat[e]ning such of their poor tenants that they find in distress and not able to pay them[.] I am sorry to have to tell you it is now the case with myself, not being able to answer my last halfyear[']s rent and I fear not likely to be able to answer the next and having no friend in Ireland to apply to[,] I must Dear Brother throw myself on your generosity and unless you be so kind as to consider me and it be in your power to send me some little m[ea]ns to enable me to meet my present necessities[,] I must confess that I fear the loss of my place and so what remains for me in my old days but the poorhouse[. Y]et if I had but a friend that would lend me 9 or 10 pounds I would not fear getting through with God[']s assistance as my rent is but light[.] I have not distorted or exaggerated anything[.... I]f I were not distressed I would not look for assistance to any one, and as I know you have a heart to feel for Irish woes and to throb for Irish friends[,] much more for a brother[,] I make my request to you with confidence.

The ties to kin that compelled Beckwith inhabitants to send money across the Atlantic to needy relatives in Wexford and Perthshire only served to reinforce their determination to establish permanent homesteads in Beckwith. Some 38 wills were made out by Beckwith inhabitants between 1828 and 1851, and although statistically it would be hazardous to base any generalisations on them, taken together they reveal the emphasis on keeping extended families together in the vicinity. Six of the wills did not mention the wife, effectively reflecting a high mortality rate for women bearing large families. Only four wills left property to the wife without placing any conditions, and only three wills left property to daughters. Most of the wills arranged for property to be left for the mutual benefit of widows and sons, with the ultimate object of having it passed on in the family name. Of the 32 wills made out by Beckwith men that referred to relicts, eleven or a third of them left their property to their widows to be passed on to their sons upon their deaths. Eight or a quarter of the 32 left their property to their sons provided that they pay an annual pension to and care for their mother. Seven men left their property to their wives only for as long as they remained unmarried, in which case it passed on to family members, usually the sons. In total, then, over three-fourths of the men making wills involving a widow, potentially gave their relicts varying degrees of control and security, especially if they furthered the objective of passing homesteads down in the family name. Undoubtedly, the majority of wills in Beckwith before mid-century reflected a patriarchal model of society, but in the very aim to preserve homesteads within the family name they unwittingly nurtured the seeds of future matriarchal ambitions.

The explicit directions in some wills reflect the general trend of concern with passing homesteads down from one generation to the next and of keeping the extended family of brothers and sisters and their wives and husbands together as much as possible in the same vicinity. Duncan McDiarmid in dividing his land among his three sons in 1836, for example, stipulated that if one of them wanted "to sell his share[,] it must be to his Brother or Brothers at a fair valuation of two persons mutually chosen."[35] John Carmichael in leaving his farm to his wife in 1840, directed that if his eldest

Plate 72
A photographic collage of John Nesbitt and his children (clockwise from the bottom left) Thomas, Edward, Anne (Pierce), John, Janet (Lett, and later Miller), James and George. This collage was based on photographs that were emphasized with charcoal, and coloured with water-based paint ca. 1885. It reflects two basic realities for most nineteenth century Beckwith families. First, the father was the central and dominant presence in the family. Second, the death of either a husband or wife took place before all children had grown to maturity. John Nesbitt's wife, Jane Pierce, died aboard ship on a trip to back to Ireland in hopes of recovering her health in 1875. As she lay dying in his arms the distraught John Nesbitt asked his wife "if she knew me, when she smiled and said, "O don't you know it is you, don't be crying, sure I will be well as soon as we get in". To his daughter Frances John Nesbitt wrote "I cannot describe to you the grief and desolation I feel and if I had my choice of all earthly wishes, my first wish would be, with all her waywardness, to have her back again. In this world there is no more happiness for me." Photograph courtesy of Arthur Nesbitt.

son "Robert continues to be obedient to his mother then the said property shall fall to his hand."[36] Donald McDonald in his 1849 will stipulated that if his son "John is not good to his mother" he would inherit a poorer tract than the homestead, and the homestead would revert to another son.[37] Peter Jones Sr. in 1849 left his farm and homestead to his son John, and to his wife Lydia he left the household goods, furniture, all moveable property, a bedroom and a sitting room in the farmhouse on lot seventeen of concession four, the use of the kitchen, yard, garden and outbuildings, a good and sufficient supply of firewood for her use by son John, and the payment of ten pounds annually in half-yearly payments due the first day of March and the first day of September. Above all else, Jones directed "The homestead and farm is not to be mortgaged or sold at any time",[38] and Thomas Leech in his 1851 will detailed how his land could not "be sold or mortgaged unless from one son to another":[39]

> If Edward shall die without lawful issue, his property shall be equally divided between Thomas and James. If James shall die without lawful issue, his property shall be equally divided between Thomas and Edward. If both James and Edward die without lawful issue, their property shall be inherited by Thomas. If Thomas dies without lawful issue, his property shall be equally divided among the then surviving children.

Further excerpts from these early Beckwith wills reflect the emphasis on posterity, on pre-arranging or preordaining the lives of widows and children, on having "lawful issue" rather than illegitimate children, on keeping land in the family, and as much as possible on keeping the family physically close together. James Fanning in his 1849 will, in an attempt to prevent his youngest son Robert from running wild, left him "20 pounds provided he works on the farm with his mother or brother until he is 21 years old."[40] Alexander McTavish in 1851 left his farm and livestock to his eldest son Alexander who in turn was directed to make cash payments to his five sisters; McTavish's younger son Donald was bequeathed £100 "and if he settles on the farm he is to have a yoke of oxen and 1 cow when 21 years old" whereas a younger daughter Ann "at leaving the house...is to have all the necessary equipments as are common with her equals in the neighbourhood."[41] John Kidd in 1850 did not have enough land to divide among his eleven sons, but attempted to encourage his youngest sons George and Wesley to remain near the rest of the family by stipulating that "if they settle in Beckwith[,] provisions and seed to the amount of 2 pounds, 10 shillings each" would be given them.[42]

The children of the immigrant pioneers needed all the encouragement they could receive. Beckwith by the early 1830s offered no new arable grants of land on which they might settle, and the homesteads that their labour had been exploited to help develop throughout the township could not accommodate all of them. Unlike the United Empire Loyalists in townships along the St. Lawrence who had received larger grants of land supplemented by grants in townships along the Rideau, the concentration of settlement in Beckwith and the other townships of the Bathurst District effectively meant that there simply was not enough land for the children of the Perthshire and Wexford immigrants to settle near their parents. So powerful and so compelling were the ties of family and the ethno-cultural ties of community that bound members of each group settlement together, that many families persisted against impossible economic and topographical odds either in settling their children around them in Beckwith or in moving as a group to a new settlement where they could remain together. It is an impressive measure of the cultural solidarity of both Irish and Scottish families in Beckwith that they placed their importance on being near one another far above any scramble for economic success.

There were no easy ways of dealing with the increasingly apparent shortage of land. Some settlers opted to move onto the empty Crown and Clergy reserve lots and the empty lots of military settlers who had moved away, some of them leasing these lots and others simply squatting on them. The land on many of these reserves was so poor that the development of these lots actually reduced the price of them. Thomas MacQueen near Pakenham remarked in 1846[43]

Plate 73
Robert Davis, his son Thomas, and his wife Mary Sutton, as painted by an itinerant artist, ca. 1845. These three portraits taken together reveal the emphasis on patrilineal impartible inheritance that held sway in Beckwith for a century and a half. The father and the eldest son are both shown holding the deed to property in Beckwith, whereas the mother is shown holding a book, possibly a prayer-book. No portraits were created of the two younger sons and five daughters in this family. Loaned courtesy of the late Hazel Davis.

> There are numerous lots in this District which have been occupied for ten or twelve years with the [Canada] Company, and are in a much worse condition and of less value than when in a state of nature, and yet the [Canada] Company has never received a sixpence nor adopted any means of ejectment.

By physically occupying a lot, even though he neither owned it nor made a payment on it, it was a commonplace of the period that the squatter enjoyed possession of the lot and had nothing to fear from government as long as he paid his taxes and performed statute labour "as if the fee simple of the property was vested in himself."[44] A gauge of the desperation of local inhabitants to balance their need to stay near their families with the demographic crisis that was emerging is shown by their interest in settling on reserve lots that had little to recommend them. Christopher Wynn in 1828 asked to purchase the east half of lot 24 in concession three after "having made considerable improvements" on land which a surveyor described as "one half...Cedar Swamp and the other half a light Sandy Soil."[45] John Salter, "a poor man with a wife & five children," after squatting for six years on the east half of lot fourteen in concession two which was described as "mostly swamp, and of a poor description" applied to purchase the lot in 1836 "fearing lest he should be put off the land".[46] Despite a surveyor's assessment of lot ten in the second concession as "almost unfit for cultivation...[with] about ten or twelve acres of bad rocky Land in the front[,] about one hundred and fifty acres of a bad Tamerock Swamp in the centre[,] about forty acres of thin Rocky Land in the Rear...[and with] not more than twenty acres of the whole Lot that can be Plowed", James Murray and William Gibson vied with one another to purchase it in the early 1840s.[47]

The scramble for reserve lots in Beckwith produced a number of struggles for the same lots between squatters. Phineas Lowe in 1837 claimed to "have been in occupation" of Clergy Reserve lot nine in the third concession for fifteen years and had improved about eighteen acres, eight of which were planted with wheat; Thomas Williams claimed that he had cleared twelve acres, erected a house and barn, was an occupant on the lot for seven years, "and the only one at present on the premises. Phineas Lowe...is no occupant, as he never built, or lived thereon, but cleared for his own convenience, that part adjoining his own Land."[48] William James and Angus McLellan fought for possession of the fertile soil on lot two of the seventh concession in the late 1820s and early 1830s.[49] A dispute between Allan Cameron and Thomas Clarke over the north half of lot thirteen in the fifth concession prompted the Crown Lands agent at Perth to remark about the squatters in general[50]

> that there is a good deal of the dog in the manger way among the present unauthorized holders of lands — they will not purchase themselves nor will they allow others to do so. If they are suddenly awoke from their dream of fancied security by some one purchasing, they instantly make all sorts of pretension to possession [and] intention to purchase &c.

One of these struggles for a reserved lot turned tragic, as recounted by John McDonell in 1833. When McDonell applied to purchase Clergy Reserve lot five in the sixth concession in the late 1820s he found that Peter Anderson already had applied for it and that the lot "was occupied by a widow woman named Read and her son who were not in circumstances to purchase". Anderson gave up his claim to the lot, and McDonell obtained a lease on the lot in 1833. In the interval[51]

> in the year 1830 one George Stone just arrived from Ireland came and forcibly turned out the poor old widow and her son who is an Idiot. [T]heir little effects were turned out of doors and exposed to the weather for several months, so that they became useless. [T]he widow and her son by this cruel and unjust treatment became objects of charity. [T]he former was supported by the people in the neighbourhood[;] the Idiot[,] her son[,] became a wanderer through the Country, and it is the same Insane person that was found nearly frozen to death on the shore of Lake Ontario near Couburg last winter. Stone [in] 1833 still keeps forcible possession of the Lot.

John McDonell was advised by government officials to try and ease George Stone off the lot by offering to "Pay for all that he had done according to the value placed on the Same by people in the neighbourhood[,] which conditions he refused to accept, and has been destroying the Land by Slashing down the Timber with a view to make [McDonell] pay for the chopping of it." In total perplexity as to how he should deal with the squatter on land he had paid for, McDonell addressed a letter to the Crown Land Commissioner at York:

> My object...is to obtain peaceable possession of the said lot, and that the said Stone should be sent off. I have been in the Settlement since the commencement and rearing a Large family; my name has been entered for the Lot...before the said Stone left Ireland[.... M]y labour had largely contributed to enhance the value of the Lot in Question. I live close by it, and wish to purchase it for my children.

Most reserved lots were purchased by adjacent farmers on which to settle their sons. Richard Fleming wished to purchase lot fifteen in the fifth concession "in consequence of the Lot adjoining my own."[52] Robert Edwards upon turning age twenty in 1827, after assisting his father Thomas "to make a clearance of nearly forty acres" during the previous nine years, was "very anxious to obtain land near his aged Parent in order to render him all the assistance in his power during the remainder of his life." He petitioned the lieutenant-governor to grant him lot nineteen in the fourth concession which was "situated alongside [his] father's farm" despite "it being nearly from one end to the other a Swamp in reality" and despite its not containing "more than about forty acres of land fit for improvement".[53] Similarly, Angus McDiarmid applied in 1828 for Clergy Reserve lot 24 in the fifth concession, on which he had already cleared about fourteen acres "as it was near my father".[54] Daniel Ferguson, also in 1828, applied to purchase Clergy Reserve lot ten in the fourth concession for which his deceased brother Robert earlier had applied because it was adjacent to his land:[55]

Plate 74
Map showing the names of Beckwith landowners believed drawn ca. 1850. By mid-century most land in Beckwith had either been developed or was being held for the children of adjacent families. Loaned courtesy of Alex and Jean McCuan.

[H]e has left four Children[,] the oldest onley nine years old, the mother being Dead also[,] explained Daniel,] & as the Care of the Children In a great measure Devolves on me[,] I am Desirous of purchasing Said lot that I may be near to my Brother's property while I have the Charge of my brother's Children[.]

Duncan McNie applied to purchase the southwest half of lot five in the fourth concession that same year because it was "the adjoining Lot to my Father's" and because he was "particularly anxious to purchase in order to keep our family together as much as possible".[56] In yet another instance,

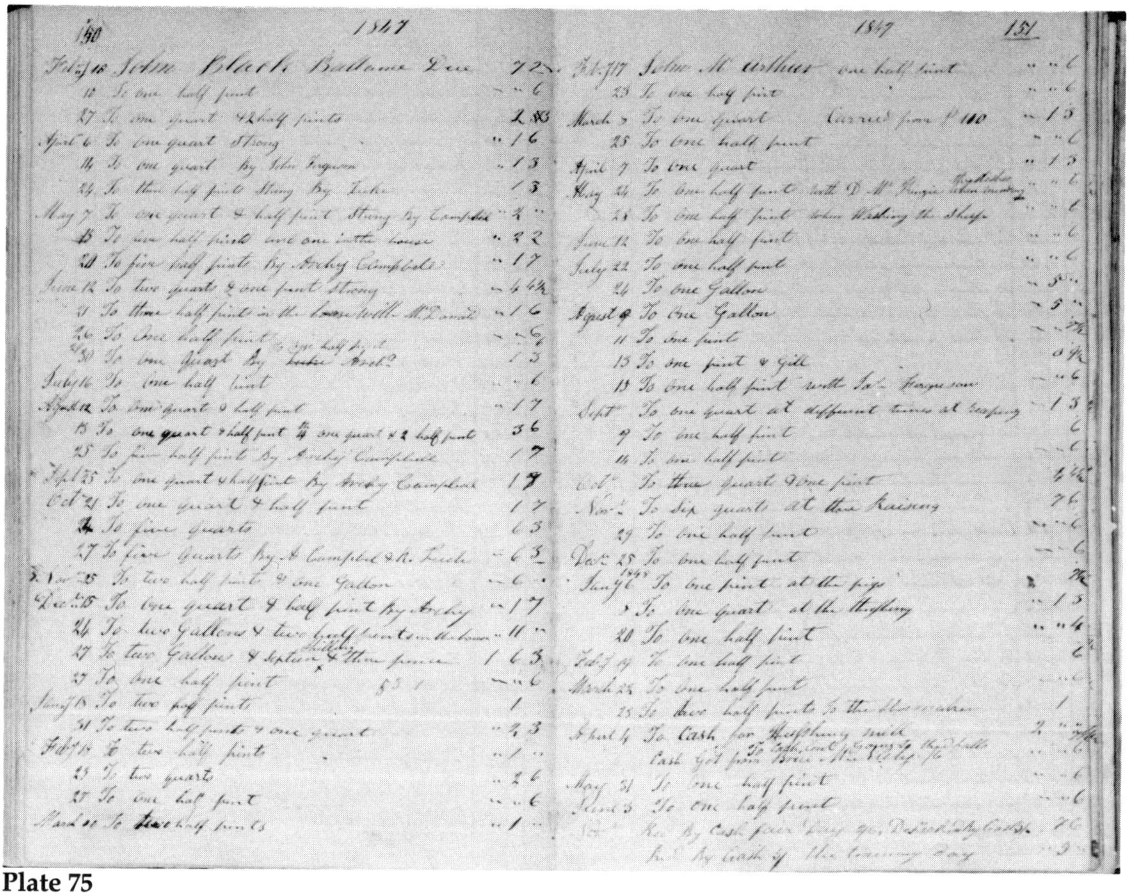

Plate 75
The distillery account book of Peter McArthur, lot 14, concession 7, Beckwith, 1847—1848. The accounts of John Black (the blacksmith after whom Black's Corners was named) and John McArthur show the steady but moderate amounts of liquor consumed in early Beckwith. The McArthur account shows the customary serving of liquor when neighbours came together working at shearing sheep, reaping crops, raising barns, slaughtering pigs and threshing grain. Loaned courtesy of the Carleton Place and Beckwith Historical Society.

Timothy Conboy sought to purchase the northeast half of lot thirteen in the second concession in 1843 "tho' the land is not good" because it was adjacent to his own grant.[57]

When empty lots no longer could be found in Beckwith by the early 1830s, families had to look beyond its boundaries. In townships immediately to the east, west and north there was settlement as concentrated as that in Beckwith. To the immediate south they beheld Montague Township, three-quarters empty and with a population in 1829 only one third that of Beckwith. More significantly, the 505 persons in Montague were concentrated in southern concessions on the more fertile tracts of land along the Rideau River. By contrast, the empty concessions in northern Montague adjacent to Beckwith consisted of such a gaunt and thinly-covered limestone plain that a census enumerator in 1852 doubted there were "ten families from [lot] No. 1 to 20 in the four con[cessions] that could live by the crop they could raise on these farms".[58] As Irish immigrants transported on the long-awaited and newly-opened Rideau Canal began squatting on empty Montague lots in the early 1830s, young men from Beckwith also began selecting lots in northern Montague as the closest they could realistically hope to settle to their parents and families on Beckwith homesteads. The popula-

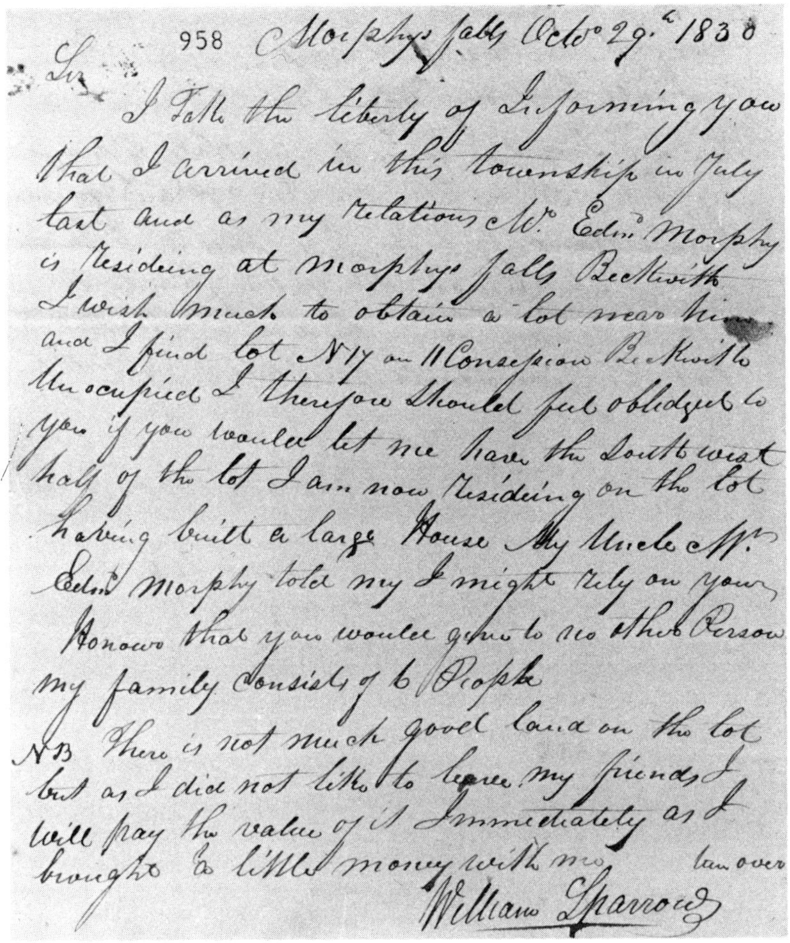

Plate 76
A letter from William Sparrow, Morphy's Falls, to the Honourable Peter Russell, Commissioner of Crown Lands for Upper Canada, York, dated 1830. The continuing trickle of immigrants into Beckwith in the 1820s and 1830s largely consisted of relatives of families already settled in the township before 1822. The obvious attraction of settling near kin was evident in the willingness of the later arrivals to settle for poor lots as long as they could be near other members of their family. Archives of Ontario, RG1 C-IV 40-2 Crown Lands Records, Beckwith Township Papers, p. 958.

tion of Montague jumped more than six hundred percent between 1829 and 1852, whereas that of Beckwith did not quite double from 1,330 in 1827 to 2,540 in 1852.[59] Because northern Montague was adjacent to the part of Beckwith where Wexford Irish settlement was concentrated, most of the Beckwith younger brothers and sons who settled there were Irish, significantly contributing to make Montague's population three-quarters Irish in ethnic origin while that of Beckwith was divided more evenly between Irish and Scottish.[60] The concentration of Beckwith families in Montague was evident in the family names scattered throughout the township;[61] in the names of new hamlets such as Comrie's Corners, Greville's Corners, Griffith's Corners, Nowlan's Corners, Pierce's Corners and Poole's Corners;[62] and in the Montague township hall being built by Robert Leaver of Franktown.[63]

The petitions requesting permission to purchase Clergy and Crown reserves in northern and central Montague during the 1830s further affirm the strong ties of family that compelled brothers, sons and relatives newly-arrived from across the Atlantic to settle on the inhospitable terrain. John Ferguson in 1830 sought to purchase Clergy Reserve lot 26 in Montague's tenth concession on which he had resided for a year after arriving from Ireland because he "had acquaintances settled in the immediate vicinity of the said Lot" in southern Beckwith. Ferguson's occupation of this lot was challenged "by a man of the name of Wynn, in Beckwith".[64] George Kerfoot applied to purchase lot ten in the second concession of Montague in 1831,[65] relinquishing it to "Richard Grevil an emigrant from Ireland" a few months later.[66] David Bennett at Franktown sought to purchase lot one in the ninth concession of Montague in 1838 "on the intention of settling on it."[67] Patrick Nowlan at Franktown a year later applied to purchase lot 28 in the third concession of Montague as he understood that "the owner has Gone to the states 14 years ago".[68] Patrick McAlinden of Beckwith in 1831 applied to purchase Clergy Reserve lot 21 in the tenth concession of Montague. Despite a surveyor's description of the lot as being "about Eighty or Nin[e]ty acres of a bad Cedar and Tamerock Swamp...[and] about one hundred or one hundred and ten Acres of poor thin hard soil nor farr from the Rock"[69] McAlinden explained that "the only reason I am anxious to purchase is, my own lot [in Beckwith] adjoins it and I have a number of Children growing up."[70]

As Montague filled up in the 1830s and 1840s, disputes every bit as nasty as those between contending squatters on Beckwith reserve lots developed between extended family members of old Beckwith families. An excerpt from an 1857 report on a dispute between the sons of William James and Edward Burrows over Clergy Reserve lot 21 in Montague's sixth concession reveals to what depths the hunger for land could push people:[71]

> William and Charles Jones, violent and bad young men, have taken possession of Clergy Reserve Lot 21 in the 6th Concession of Montague. [F]or some time back both of those men have cut and carryed away all the valuable Timber and yesterday grossly abused this lone woman. As her husband Edward Burr[ow]s is in a state bordering on Insanity, she therefore begs [the Crown Lands office's] protection.... I was in hopes when old James died there would be peace, but it appears the sons are if possible worse than the Father.

There were other local options for Beckwith sons and daughters who could not obtain land in Montague. Montague was just one of numerous townships along the Rideau that remained largely empty until the early 1830s. Osgoode attracted a concentration of Perthshire highlanders from northern Beckwith including members of the Campbell, Ferguson, Fraser, McCuan, McDiarmid, McDonald, McEwen, McLaren, McNab, McNie, Reid and Saunders families,[72] while others were drawn to land in Nepean. John Moorehouse moved to South Elmsley Township near Smith's Falls in 1839.[73] By the late 1840s there was no vacant land left along the Rideau. A clergyman at Smith's Falls commented in 1855, "Twenty-five years ago this land (lying between Bytown and Kingston) was a forest. It has been reclaimed by Irish immigrants."[74]

With land in nearby townships filled by the mid 1840s, Beckwith families began to face up to the necessity of settling at a distance, and looked north to land in townships along the upper Ottawa River. As early as 1831 Caleb Bellows of Carlton Place had proposed settling along the Ottawa, but his move to Westmeath in 1834 was exceptional at that early date.[75] By 1844 the number of people moving north from Lanark and Carleton counties into the newly named county of Renfrew was so visible that the editor of the Ottawa *Advocate* commented, "it is highly satisfactory to observe that there is an inclination among the youth of these parts to establish themselves within the limits of the Ottawa region, under all discouragements."[76] As early as 1832 the Crown Lands Office offered land in Ross, Pembroke and Westmeath townships to "indigent Settlers, on condition of actual residence".[77] Samuel May of Carlton Place by December 1841 claimed he had "made a small clearing and put up a shanty on the front half of lot 21, 2nd con[cession] Fitzroy,...a Clergy Reserve" and was "very anxious to purchase it".[78] James Kent, the first schoolmaster at Franktown, in 1845 stated that

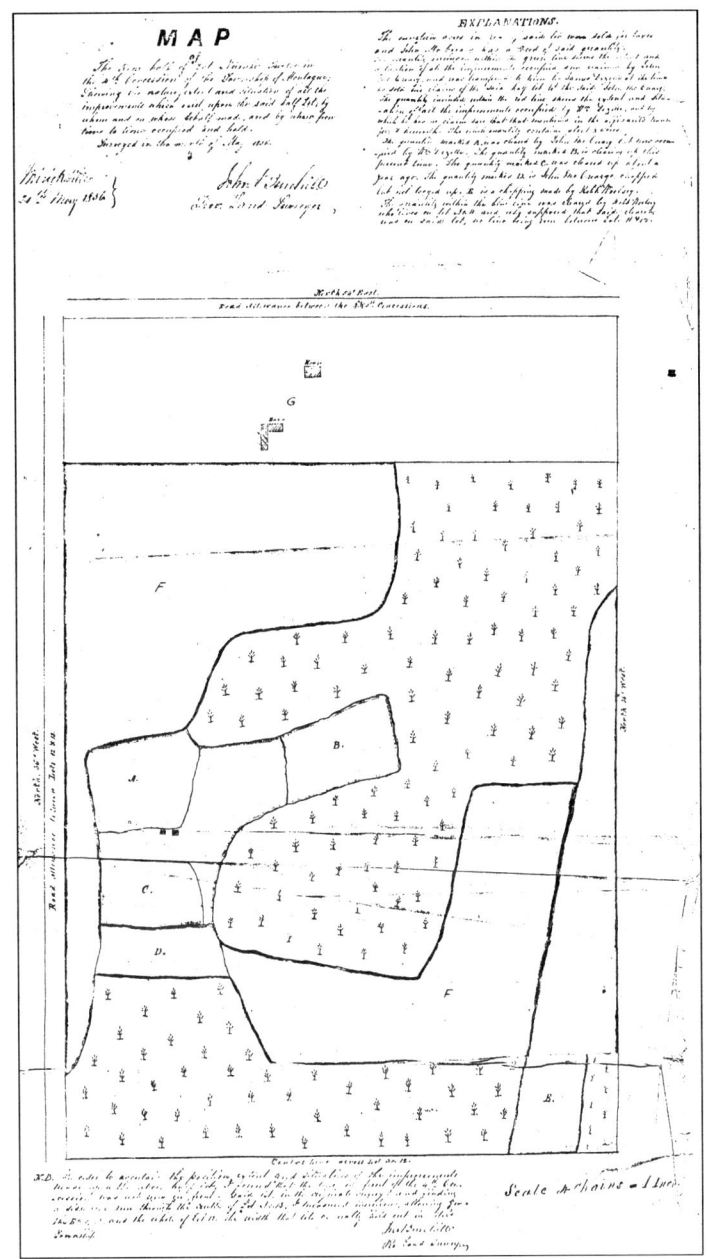

Plate 77
Map of the rear half of lot 12, concession 4, Montague Township, drawn by surveyor John Burchill in May 1856. This map illustrates the conflict that emerged between settlers in Beckwith and between their sons in Montague in attempting to clear and lay claim to ungranted Crown and Clergy reserve lots, and to lots which had been abandoned by the original person located on them. In this example two settlers developed farms at A and at G, while a settler on an adjacent lot cleared the wedge of land at E, all hoping to base appeals to the Crown lands office to purchase the lot on their investment of having cleared the land. In one such dispute over Clergy reserve lot 9 in the third concession of Beckwith, Thomas Williams claimed in 1837 that he was "an occupant, and the only one at present on the premises [whereas] Phineas Lowe (who no doubt, has already applied) is no occupant, as he never built, or lived thereon, but cleared for his own convenience, that part adjoining his own Land." Archives of Ontario Crown Lands Records, Township Papers.

he intended "to go up the Country to look for land" to replace his grant in Beckwith which Robert Edwards had taken over.[79] By 1852 the family of Duncan Ferguson had moved from Beckwith to Horton, and carpenter John Cameron of Beckwith was visiting in Horton.[80]

Instances of individuals moving on their own any distance from Beckwith were exceptional. So strong was the fostering influence of the Irish and Scottish group settlements, of families keeping sons and daughters as physically close by them as possible, that when the shortage of land in Beckwith became sufficiently acute groups of families migrated together. The earliest of these group or chain migrations took place in the 1840s when members of the Cram, Dewar, Edwards, Holbrook, Kerfoot, Kidd, Kilfoil, Leach, Lewis, Lett, Lucas, McKeown, Saunders, Shirley, Sutton, Taylor and Willoughby families moved west across the province to Brooke, Plympton and Warwick townships in Lambton County.[81] They responded to the inducements of Lanark Reform politician Malcolm Cameron who purchased land on the site of Sarnia in 1835 and encouraged Scottish families in Lanark County to migrate to fertile land in the vicinity.[82] A second chain migration from Beckwith to Stafford Township in Renfrew County during the 1850s included members of the Burgess, Code, Edwards, Hawkins, Hill, Jackson, James, Kenny, Kidd, Leach, Lett, Libby, Lumax, May, Rath, Sutton, Tennant, Tomlinson, Wallace and Warren families.[83] Another group settlement proceeded to Elma Township in Perth County during the 1850s,[84] and yet another chain of Beckwith and other regional families migrated to Paisley in Bruce County. Letters back to Beckwith from all of these areas only served to further the stream of migration, telling as they did of "no stones to obstruct the plow, and no swamps to absorb the richness of the ground, but [rather] a fine heavy, rich, loamy soil everywhere gives promise of an immediate reward to the labor of the husbandman and future comfort to his family."[85]

The movement of younger brothers and sons with their families out of Beckwith in group or chain migrations when there simply was no land left in the immediate vicinity is one of numerous traits examined in this chapter that testify to how compelling a hold family ties had on these people. There are other pieces of evidence testifying to the concern with having members of family settled nearby, such as the notice which Maria Saunders of Beckwith placed in the *Bathurst Courier* in 1835, inquiring after her sister Margaret Stephens whom she asked to write to her care of the Rev. Jonathan Shortt, Franktown. "The last I heard of her", she plaintively remarked, "was from the Rev. J. McGrath who only knew that he married her on 3 August 183_, to Thomas Lees, Blacksmith — he thinks they are Gone to the T[o]w[nshi]p of Ops."[86] The priority or emphasis on keeping family together helped the immigrants coming to Beckwith and those later leaving to psychologically cope with what otherwise was a traumatic experience. The children of the Perthshire and Wexford families, facing up to the implications of overpopulation as the large pioneer families matured in the 1830s and 1840s, remained tightly knit to their parents and neighbours, as they pondered remaining in Beckwith or migrating. The bonds of family were never better expressed than when Daniel McCuan wrote his brother John in 1857:[87]

> Father and Mother are much about the same way],] generally enjoying pretty good health though sometimes they are not so well, still, considering their age and the hardships and privations which they endured in their early days in Canada they stand well to their age. We can never be too kind to them for they have been the very best of parents to us[,] however they are now pretty comfortable and seem to be contented with us, we enjoy peace and a competent portion of the good things of this life, thanks to a bountiful Providence for it.

The various manifestations of maintaining family ties, the rhetorical yet genuine expressions of concern for keeping families together, admittedly were a form of paternalist social control. From the perspective of Beckwith inhabitants before mid-century it might be more accurate to say that the concern for maintaining these family networks stemmed from the crucial motive of survival, both social and psychological. Despite the pressure of maturing large families on available land, ties to

Plate 78
St. Patrick's Anglican church and cemetery, Stafford Township, Renfrew County, as photographed in 1987. Many of the founding members of this congregation migrated in a chain from Beckwith in the late 1840s and 1850s, as the lack of land in Beckwith made it difficult to keep the large families together located near one another. The round-headed windows in this church reflect the continuing Irish Anglican low church suspicions of what they considered the Catholic-looking Gothic Revival architecture and mediaeval liturgy being promoted by English Anglicans after mid-century. The front entrance to this church was exactly the same design as that of St. James Church at Franktown.

kin and a strong compulsion to remain within or close to their group settlements caused Beckwith inhabitants to do a number of things that were decidedly out of step with scrambling for economic success. They sent payments of money back to relatives in Ireland and Scotland as late as the mid 1840s. They cut their birthrate at least in half, perhaps even to a third by the late 1820s, effectively reducing their economic security should they wish to move to a new settlement. Fathers began arranging in their wills for farms to continue within the family name, even specifying on occasion that they could not be sold or mortgaged, and emphasizing that property be passed down to "lawful issue". Sons either purchased or squatted on Crown and Clergy reserves, often on lots that were mostly swamp, and many squatted on the inhospitable limestone plain of northern Montague to remain near family, awaiting the chance of moving onto more desirable local lots when the occasion arose. A few even resorted to violence to obtain control of property near family in Beckwith, but by the 1840s and 1850s the pressure on land was so intense that chains of families were moving from Beckwith to new settlements in Lambton, Renfrew, Bruce, Brant and Perth Counties.

The chains of families and neighbours moving from Beckwith to what can be called Beckwith colonies in southwestern Upper Canada endured on past Confederation. A letter written by James

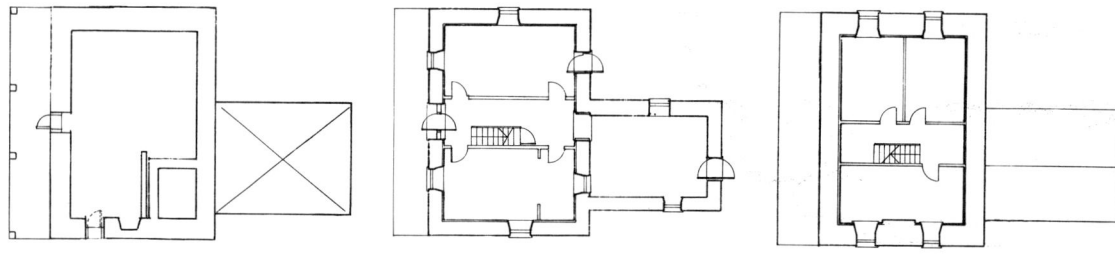

McRae of Brant County in late November 1869 to his uncle Alexander Stewart in Beckwith reflects the growing links between Beckwith and new areas of settlement at the same time ties with families in Ireland and Scotland dissolved:[88]

> We have written to you several times but have received no answer[,] not having had any letter from you since May[.] We would like to know what you are doing now as you last said that you had sold out[.] Mother wishes to know if you are living on the old place yet or if you have moved on to the nineteent[h.] Eli Kidd and John are well[.]... We should like to know if you think of coming up here[. T]here is a place for sale right beside us[;] the owner is offering it for 375/225 pound[s] (150 off)[.] We have lost Maggie[;] she has married a man by the name of Wm. Young[. H]e lives about 3 miles from us[.] Bob Nolan has left here for parts unknown[.]... We are going to have a railroad within two miles of us[;] it is to be finished in two years and a half so that it will not take long to go up [to Beckwith] and down[.]... Bella wants the girls to send up their pictures[.]

The most compelling proof of how real and how necessary these ties among family members and among groups of families were felt to be is offered by the William McKeown family when its links with the Beckwith group settlements were broken. William McKeown, who resided on the northeast half of lot 23 in the sixth concession of Beckwith, died in October 1827, leaving his pregnant wife Jane with two daughters, Jane and Elizabeth. Widow McKeown in April 1828 gave birth to a son named William. In his will, the father had directed "that in case his youngest child shall be a Boy he should have half...the...Land, and the other half [was] to be divided between his two daughters." The widow and her three children joined her father Andrew Lucas and other Beckwith families in migrating to Brooke Township in Lambton County in the 1840s, and she married James Kilfoil also from Beckwith. They briefly resided in Warwick Township in Lambton, before moving to a homestead near Council Bluffs, Iowa.

It was at this point that the links with Beckwith and with the Beckwith group settlement in Lambton County were broken, although at least one letter back to friends in Warwick urged "if you knew how much easyer a man can farm here than they can in the old countrys you would soon come

Plate 79
The William Kerfoot homestead on lot 25, concession 4 of Beckwith, at Prospect, as photographed in 1989. William Kerfoot (1776—1862) was a stonemason who built this house probably in the 1840s. Other stone buildings constructed by him included a house for his son George on lot 15 in the second concession (Plate 71) and the Methodist chapel at Prospect (Plate 107). This photograph was taken after a restoration of this house which removed an exterior coating of stucco or harl intended to hide the rubble construction of the walls. This house was exceptional for having a fireplace in the basement, for having paterae designs on the window frames, and for having the gable walls face north and south in conformity with the knoll the house was located on at an angle to the concession road. Line drawings (opposite) are by Robert W.J. Moore.

here". But when none of their old Beckwith neighbours joined them in Iowa, and the mother died in mid April 1853, the loneliness which most Beckwith families had warded off by remaining in a group settlement came crushing in on them. Young William McKeown revealed his sense of uprootedness in a pathetic letter back to Beckwith acquaintances in Warwick:[89]

> Dear friends[, M]y mind is so troubled that [I] don't know what to write to you. [W]e are here alone with out our friends to comfort us in this time of trouble and of mourning[.... Y]ou never saw a man take any thing so hard as [our stepfather] did Mother[']s death[. A] few minutes after Mother died he fainted away for a long time[;] he was most out of his senses[.... I] believe if he lives in the house or on the place where Mother died he would not live a year[,] yet [I] don't want him to go away from here for we are so lonesome now that we can hardly stand it[,] and if he goes we will be left here alone[.] Mother wanted us all to stay together if she died so that we could see after the children[.] Mother intended for us to take Martha and [R]achel and take care of them till they growed up[....T]he most of her trouble before she died was to see all of her children together.... [S]he wanted to see [B]etsy and gran[d]father and [J]ane. She talked about you all but she talked the most about them three[. M]any a time she would say ["]poor [B]etsy and my poor old father[." S]he wanted to see him verry bad before she died[.]

It was against this despair of loneliness among strangers that the family networks in Beckwith and the chain migration to and from Beckwith had worked. The breakdown of family ties was not totally complete for the McKeown children in that they wrote back to Beckwith acquaintances in Lambton, but the fear expressed by Elizabeth McKeown of being "left here alone unless some of you will move out here" revealed how ill prepared to face the future was this exceptional floating broken link from the chains of Beckwith families.

Endnotes

1. 6 February 1851 letter from John McEwen, Cartran, Lochearnhead, Scotland, to Duncan McLaren, Beckwith, Canada West. I am grateful to Arthur R. Hawkins of Beckwith for giving me a copy of this letter.
2. 13 December 1832 letter from Private James McCuan No. 246, 79th Highlanders, Montreal, to Duncan McCuan, Carleton Place, Beckwith, Upper Canada. This letter is in Correspondence file no. 2 of the McCuan family papers. I am grateful to Alex and Jean McCuan for allowing me to sort, file and read their collection of family papers.
3. 24 March 1834 letter believed addressed to Alexander Clark of Beckwith, which was with a volume of Scottish sermons owned in the eighteenth century by George Clark of Nisbet, a village in Roxburghshire, in the possession of Margaret Comrie Clark (Mrs. G.B. Farmer, Perth, Ontario), given by her nephew George Hugh MacCallum to Howard M. Brown, Ottawa, in 1961. I am grateful to Howard Brown for providing transcripts of these letters.
4. John McCuan of Beckwith went to Perthshire in 1857 to recover his health, and while in the Comrie vicinity he corresponded with his brothers back in Beckwith; 1 November 1874 letter from John Nesbitt, Coolnahorna, Enniscorthy, Ireland, to daughter, Frances, Beckwith, telling of wife's death aboard ship on voyage back to Ireland to recover health. I am grateful to Arthur Nesbitt for allowing me to have a copy of this letter.
5. 6 February 1851 letter from John McEwan to Duncan McLaren, provided courtesy of Arthur R. Hawkins, Beckwith.
6. Ibid.
7. 13 December 1832 letter from private James McCuan, Montreal, to Duncan McCuan, Beckwith, courtesy Alex and Jean McCuan, Beckwith.
8. 1 September 1845 letter from John McDiarmid, Osgoode, to his uncle James McDiarmid, Beckwith, provided courtesy Rosemary Wark.
9. 6 July 1858 letter from Allan McDiarmid, Glasgow, to his uncle James McDiarmid, Beckwith, provided courtesy of Rosemary Wark.
10. 1 May 1843 letter from D. Comrie, Montreal, to his cousin, A. Clark and Company, Merchants, Smith's Falls, Canada West, transcript provided courtesy of Howard M. Brown, Ottawa.
11. 16 July 1838 letter from Alexander Clark, Montague, to Duncan McCuan, Beckwith, provided courtesy of Alex and Jean McCuan, Beckwith.
12. John May, "Bush Life in the Ottawa Valley Eighty Years Ago" in *Papers and Records of the Ontario Historical Society* XII (1914), p. 162.
13. Howard M. Brown, "Clark Family of Perthshire" (unpublished manuscript), p. 3.
14. These figures are based on the baptismal register of the Beckwith Church of Scotland congregation at the United Church Archives in Toronto.
15. *Bathurst Courier*, 25 September 1835, p. 4, col. 3.
16. Ibid., 4 March 1836, p. 4, col. 5.
17. Examples of infanticide are found in the *Brockville Recorder*, 22 June 1830, p. 2, col. 2; 24 August 1830, p. 2, cols. 3-5 and p. 3, cols. 2-4; 17 November 1831, p. 3, col. 2; 27 September 1832, p. 3, col. 2; 5 August 1836, p. 2 col. 5; and 19 August 1836, p. 1 col. 2.
18. *Bathurst Courier*, 1 May 1840, p. 1, col. 4.
19. OKQAR Rev. William Bell Journals.
20. *Brockville Gazette*, 25 August 1831, p. 3, col. 4.
21. *Brockville Recorder*, 25 April 1834, pp. 2-3, cols. 6-1.
22. NAC RG 5, A1 Reel C-6909 Upper Canada Sundries, vol. 229, p. 125152, 17 September 1839 note from George Burroughs, Carlton Place to Robert Bell, Esq.
23. *Bathurst Courier*, 1 May 1840, pp. 1-2, cols. 4-1.
24. Ibid., 2 May 1851, p. 2, cols. 4-5.
25. Ibid., 21 July 1848, p. 1, cols. 4-5.
26. Carleton Place and Beckwith Historical Society, meditation written by Duncan Cram, Beckwith, on the death of his son Andrew on 4 November 1851, in manuscript folio bearing the title *Peter W. Cram's Book*.
27. *Bathurst Courier*, 16 March 1838, p. 3, col. 4.
28. OKQAR Rev. William Bell Journals III:2.
29. English-origin inhabitants declined from ten percent of Beckwith's population in 1822 to less than three percent by 1871.
30. Robert Lewis, "Ashton Village First Founded 117 Years Ago" in *Carleton Place Canadian*, 25 July 1935, p. 8, col. 4.
31. *Bathurst Courier*, 18 January 1850, p. 1, col. 1.
32. Lanark County Registry Office, Perth, Ontario (hereafter OPLRO) Abstract Index to Deeds for Beckwith Township. By the end of 1823, 8.1 percent of Beckwith land had been patented. By the end of 1849 81.2 percent had been patented.
33. Bruce S. Elliott, "Canada Company Remittance Books" in Ottawa Branch, Ontario Genealogical Society, *Ottawa Branch News* XIV No. 5 (September-October 1981), pp. 58-60.
34. 28 July letter from William Hill, Mountalexander,

County Wexford, Ireland, to his brother Thomas Hill, Jellyby, Leeds County, Upper Canada, in Leeds and Grenville Branch, Ontario Genealogical Society, *Families of Leeds and Grenville Counties* (Brockville: by the author, 1983), p. 6. The original of this letter is in the possession of Lorna Johnston, North Augusta. I am grateful to Bruce Elliott for bringing this article to my attention.

35 OPLRO 20 April 1836 will of Duncan McDiarmid, Beckwith.
36 Ibid., 28 August 1840 will of John Carmichael, Beckwith.
37 Ibid., 12 October 1849 will of Donald McDonald, Beckwith.
38 Ibid., 9 March 1849 will of Peter Jones Sr., Beckwith.
39 Ibid., 31 December 1851 will of Thomas Leech, Beckwith.
40 Ibid., 6 September 1849 will of James Fanning, Beckwith.
41 Ibid., 7 May 1851 will of Alexander McTavish, Beckwith.
42 Ibid., 19 August 1850 will of John Kidd, Beckwith.
43 *Bathurst Courier*, 1 September 1846, pp. 2-3, cols. 7-1.
44 Brockville (Upper Canada) *Antidote*, 2 April 1833, p. 3, col. 2.
45 OTAR RG 1 MS 658 Series C-IV Crown Lands Department, Township Papers, Beckwith, Reel 30, pp. 214-215, 223.
46 Ibid., p. 126.
47 Ibid., pp. 106, 110.
48 Ibid., pp. 163, 166.
49 Ibid., pp. 551-564.
50 Ibid., pp. 377-379.
51 Ibid., pp. 440-442.
52 Ibid., p. 406.
53 NAC RG 5, A1 Reel C-6863 Upper Canada Sundries, vol. 4, pp. 45998-45999.
54 OTAR RG 1 MS 658 Series C-IV Crown Lands Department, Township Papers, Beckwith, Reel 30, p. 417.
55 Ibid., p. 257.
56 Ibid., p. 238.
57 Ibid., p. 120.
58 NAC Reel C-963 1852 census of Montague Township, general remarks of enumerator John Nowlan.
59 The population figure of 1,330 for Beckwith in 1827 is taken from Howard M. Brown, "Franktown Was Once Village of 200 People" in Carleton Place *Canadian*, 13 May 1965. The 1852 figure is taken from 1852 printed census returns. Information on Montague's early population is found in Glenn J Lockwood, "Irish Immigrants and the 'Critical Years' in Eastern Ontario: The Case of Montague Township, 1821-1881" in Donald H. Akenson, ed., *Canadian Papers in Rural History* (Gananoque, Ontario: Langdale Press, 1984) IV:160.
60 Canada, Ministry of Agriculture, Census of Canada: 1870-71 (Ottawa: I.B. Taylor, 1873) I:276-277.
61 Glenn J Lockwood, *Montague: A Social History of an Irish Ontario Township, 1783-1980* (Smiths Falls: Corporation of the Township of Montague, 1980), p. 257.
62 Ibid., pp. 367, 569.
63 Ibid., pp. 212-213.
64 OTAR RG 1 Series C-IV Crown Lands Department, Township Papers, Montague, Box 334, 22 July 1830 letter.
65 Ibid., 1 April 1831 letter.
66 Ibid., 1 June 1831 letter.
67 Ibid., 19 March 1838 letter.
68 Ibid., 22 July 1839 letter.
69 Ibid., 23 June 1849 letter.
70 Ibid., 13 April 1831 letter.
71 Lockwood, Montague: *A Social History*, p. 206.
72 Osgoode Township Historical Society and Museum, *Pioneer Families of Osgoode Township* I:1,3,4; II:6; III:9; IV:9; V:1; X:6,8; XII:7; XV:4,6; XVIII:3,4. I am grateful to Elizabeth S. Stuart for the generous assistance she has provided over the past fifteen years.
73 James R. Kennedy, *South Elmsley in the Making, 1783-1983* (Smiths Falls: Corporation of the Township of South Elmsley, 1984), p. 56.
74 John Irwin Cooper, "Irish Immigration and the Canadian Church before the Middle of the 19th Century", *Journal of the Canadian Church Historical Society* II No. 3 (May 1955), p. 7.
75 NAC RG 5, A1 Reel C-6873 Upper Canada Sundries, vol. 110, pp. 62656-62657.
76 *Bytown (Canada West) Ottawa Advocate*, 30 July 1844, p. 3, cols. 1-2.
77 *Brockville Gazette*, 14 June 1832, p. 3, col. 2.
78 OTAR RG 1 Series C-IV Crown Lands Department, Township Papers, Fitzroy Township, Box 180, p. 310.
79 Ibid., Beckwith Township, MS 658, Reel 30, p. 295.
80 Bruce S. Elliott, ed., *1842 and 1851 Census of Renfrew County, C.W., Vol. 1 Horton* (Ottawa: Ottawa Branch, Ontario Genealogical Society, 1983), n.p.
81 OTAR RG 1 Series C-IV MS 658 Crown Lands Department, Township Papers, Beckwith, Reel 30, pp. 488-510; 26 October 1982 letter from Bruce S. Elliott, Nepean, to Elizabeth Cahill, Montreal.
82 Margaret Coleman, "Malcolm Cameron" in Marc La Terreur, ed., *Dictionary of Canadian Biography* (Toronto: University of Toronto Press, 1972) X:124.
83 Bruce S. Elliott, *Irish Migrants in the Canadas: A New Approach* (Montreal: McGill-Queen's University Press, 1988), pp. 316-317.
84 A series of letters back to Beckwith from Elma was published in the *Carleton Place Herald*, 20 August 1857, p. 2, cols. 3-4; 31 December 1857, p. 2, col. 4; and 2 September 1858, p. 3, col. 4.
85 *Perth Courier*, 13 September 1867, p. 2, cols. 7-8.
86 *Bathurst Courier*, 24 July 1835, p. 4, col. 5.
87 March 1857 letter from Daniel McCuan, Beckwith, to his brother John touring Scotland to regain his health, courtesy of Alex and Jean McCuan, Beckwith.
88 Beckwith Women's Institute, Tweedsmuir History of Beckwith.
89 OTAR RG 1 Series C-IV MS 658 Crown Lands Department, Township Papers, Beckwith, Reel 30, pp. 489-510.

THE REVEREND WILLIAM BELL'S BECKWITH

"The Reverend Iscariot Humdrum"[1] was the name that a mid-century satirist used to describe the self-righteous, self-justifying, cantankerous and moralising qualities that combined in the personality of the Reverend William Bell of Perth. This middle-aged pioneer Presbyterian clergyman was equally content to criticise and reprimand the members of his own flock as well as those of other denominations, and yet through his eyes it is possible to view the tempestuous course of early Presbyterian congregations in Beckwith. With the assistance of Bell's voluminous journals, it is possible to understand the social, sexual, moral and political texture of life for Scottish Presbyterians and Baptists in Beckwith between 1825 and 1851.

Bell was attracted to visit Beckwith from the outset because it was the closest and earliest Scottish settlement of any size near Perth. He was flattered by the warm response to his occasional preaching visits between 1819 and 1822. The Beckwith highlanders displayed a due regard for his position as clergyman in distinct contrast with American Methodists to whom Bell preached in 1817, most of whom "never having seen a Presbyterian minister before" stared at Bell "in a very clownish manner...as if I had been a bear, or some other wild beast."[2] Bell believed that as a minister he held a unique position in the community and that he should be recognised as the unquestioned arbiter of all moral standards. Bell himself religiously awakened at age nine after surviving a smallpox epidemic, at age fourteen he joined the Established Church of Scotland,[3] he trained for the ministry at a Congregational academy in London, then for the Presbyterian ministry first at Selkirk and later at the University of Glasgow. He was ordained by the Associate Presbytery of Edinburgh in March 1817, a month before he sailed for Perth in Upper Canada where he ministered for the rest of his life.[4] When fellow Scot, Governor General Lord Dalhousie visited Perth in 1820 he sized up Bell as "a troublesome fellow",[5] an assessment that was borne out by innumerable clashes with neighbours and associates prompted by Bell's "intense sense of divine mission coupled with an irascible disposition and sanctimonious temperament".[6] Bell's many visits to Beckwith between 1817 and mid-century may have been made as much to escape the various frays he waged in Perth as to visit the Perthshire highlanders.

Bell began his visits to Beckwith in the spring of 1819 and the warmth of reception he received can be judged from the entry in his journal for 16 January 1820:[7]

> I borrowed Mr. Cameron's horse, and went out to the gov[ernmen]t store, in Beckwith to preach. The morning was dry, but very cold, so I had to run and ride, while about. I preached in Mr[. Hugh] Spratt's kitchen, but the con[gregation] being large, and the place small, they completely crammed it. Besides, there being no seats for them, nor a stand for me, I was so crammed up in a corner, that I had scarcely room to breathe.

By February 1822 Bell had become more familiar with the Beckwith highlanders. He held examinations and services at the home of Duncan McNaughton[8] on lot four in the seventh concession and at the home of a Mrs. Ferguson,[9] but when he conducted the first communion service on 24 February 1822 "in the upper story of the inn, at Franktown; that being the largest room in the village;...the

Plate 80
The family of the Reverend George Buchanan as presented in the second edition of Jessie Buchanan Campbell's book, The Pioneer Pastor. *The conflict between the Secessionist Reverend George Buchanan and his pro-Church of Scotland congregation was heightened by the dominance his wife exercised over him. Alexander McGregor complained that Mrs. Buchanan "was both man and wife", a telling revelation of the patriarchal assumption that men were the moral, legal and economic heads of their households in early nineteenth century highland Beckwith.*

con[gregation] was too large for the place, and more came than could get in. There were three table services [which left Bell] very tired at night, but very happy to see a church formed, and the children of God fed with the bread of life."[10]

Bell's efforts to obtain a clergyman for Beckwith Presbyterians and the arrival of the Reverend George Buchanan with his large family on 10 August 1822 have already been described. The first Presbyterian service conducted by Buchanan in Beckwith in mid August was described decades later by his youngest daughter:[11]

> Word had been sent to every family that service would be held in the forenoon.... Men, women and children trudged many miles to be present.... Black flies and mosquitoes swarmed in myriads, seeking to devour the multitude.... A huge tree was cut down, the stump of which, sawed off straight, accommodated the big Bible and sufficed for a pulpit. On the trunk, drawn by oxen to one side, sat mother and her ten children. Other trees, stripped of their branches and hauled in front of the stump, seated the congregation. At the appointed hour father arose, spoke a few words of greeting and gave out a familiar psalm. John Cram, a talented musician, led the singing, which was devotional and inspiring....
>
> Standing with bowed heads, the attitude of deepest reverence, the people heard a fervent prayer. Another psalm and an exposition of the chapter of scripture followed. The sermon...entreated those out of Christ to "make their calling and education sure." The entire service was in English, with which a few of the oldest folks were not on very intimate terms. After a short intermission, to eat their simple repast and drink at the nearest well, the worshippers gathered again for Gaelic services.... It proved a notable Sabbath in the history of Beckwith. Late in the afternoon all returned home....

Despite his sixty years, the Reverend George Buchanan at first appeared to be an energetic individual who offered Beckwith Presbyterians the combined services of clergyman, schoolmaster and doctor. He was born at Cupar-Angus, Perthshire, in 1761, the baby in a household of twelve children, and if his daughter's account is to be credited he graduated from the University of Edinburgh with a diploma as a doctor and with a licence to preach.[12] Within six weeks of conducting his first service in Beckwith Buchanan selected lot fourteen in the sixth concession at the centre of the township to reside on. Members of the congregation built a shanty on this lot to house Buchanan's large family, which he replaced with a two-storey log house the following year. The congregation also built a rough log structure to serve as a house of worship on Buchanan's lot. At a meeting to fix the minister's salary it was agreed that each family would pay three dollars a year, or one dollar and two bushels of wheat. Alexander Dewar, John Carmichael, John Ferguson and Duncan McDonald were elected and ordained elders. It was arranged that families in each section of the township should meet together with Buchanan in one house to be examined and catechised as to their knowledge of the Bible, the catechism and Presbyterian doctrine.[13]

Buchanan's visits to the various sections of Beckwith revealed that "numbers of young people were growing up in comparative ignorance" because there were no schools other than those at Franktown and Carlton Place. Buchanan opened a school in "a small miserable structure" built by local parents in his neighbourhood, and once his large new log house was built in 1823 he moved the school into the shanty which his congregation had built for him a year earlier. Lacking textbooks, but with students apparently crowding his school, Buchanan initially used the Mother's Catechism, the Shorter Catechism and the Bible as readers:[14]

> In winter when the grown pupils attended, having to work in summer, grammars and geographies were procured from Perth. Mud, wolves, deep snow and storms would not keep the scholars at home. Some walked five or six miles every morning and evening and were never

Plate 81
Beckwith communion tokens, obverse and reverse faces, possibly dating from the late 1830s or 1840s. Communion tokens were issued to those adult members of the Beckwith Church of Scotland congregation who had no charges of immoral behaviour held against them before the church session. The church session, composed of the minister and elders, held the right to dispense or withhold these tokens from members of the congregation according to whether an individual's morals were perceived to qualify him or her to admission to sit at the Lord's table for communion. The token was exchanged by the communicant during the service at the point of being permitted by the elders to take communion at the table. Loaned courtesy of St. Paul's United Church, Franktown.

absent nor tardy.... From that unpretentious school, with its long benches and desks of split logs, its utter lack of maps and apparatus, its poverty and general wretchedness, young men went forth to prepare for the ministry, to acquire a profession, to engage in business and to fill positions of usefulness. Young women were equipped for teaching or other duties. In [Buchanan's] absence, visiting the sick or making pastoral calls, one of his [daughters] took charge of the school.

In summer the school was sometimes held in Buchanan's barn in which there was more room and better ventilation. According to his daughter's memoir, Buchanan "never received a penny for his years of teaching in Beckwith." Two of Buchanan's daughters, Helen and perhaps Catharine, opened a school in Perth.[15] Their sisters back in Beckwith taught the younger children in a Sunday School which Buchanan opened.

In addition to his duties as clergyman and schoolmaster, Buchanan was frequently in demand as a physician, being roused at night to walk miles along logs set lengthwise through swamp-mud and water by torch-light to attend pregnant women and those taken ill. Those patients belonging to Buchanan's congregation apparently felt no need to pay him for his medical services. "They took it for granted that his...salary as a minister entitled them to command his talents as a doctor and a teacher also. He was expected to officiate at births, baptisms, marriages and funerals, to heal the sick and educate the rising generation without charge."[16] Buchanan, after all, was fairly prosperous by Beckwith standards, occupying as he did a 200 acre lot in contrast with the standard 100 acre grant, and inhabiting a two-storey log house. In October 1829 Donald McGregor and John Campbell certified "that the Rev'd George Buchanan has built a good house, barn and Several Office houses on his Lot[,] No. 14th 6th Concession[,] Beckwith, cleared above thirty Acres, and also cleared the Road both in front and in rear of both Lot No. 14 and No. 9 in said Concession."[17] In 1831 Buchanan received legal title to his lot, to crown the initial success of his ministry to Beckwith Presbyterians. The Reverend William Bell when he assisted at a July 1823 service in Beckwith was pleased to see a large congregation and the pleasant services they enjoyed "under the care of a pastor."[18]

Beginning in 1824 Bell began to perceive problems in the Beckwith Presbyterian congregation. On the eighteenth day of July after Bell preached a sermon to Buchanan's congregation in the evening, "Old Mr. Cram made a grievous complaint against Mr. Buchanan for preaching erroneous doctrine."[19] Earlier in February John Alston's wife complained that he was induced to drink heavily at Buchanan's house.[20] A "somewhat tipsy" Alexander McGregor called on Bell in February 1825 and remarked that Beckwith "could not have got a worse minister" and that Mrs. Buchanan "was both man and wife."[21] In the late spring of 1825 Bell met another man from Beckwith who "complained bitterly of Mr. Buchanan's conduct; and among other things, said he charged 2/6 for baptising a child, which he was not able to pay"; he implored Bell to "establish a preaching station in his neighborhood".[22] Some people in Beckwith stopped making their annual payments to Buchanan by 1826. When the neighbours of a settler named Goodfellow chided him that his crops were destroyed that year by a swarm of caterpillars "as a judgement of heaven sent upon him for refusing to contribute for the support of the minister[, h]e replied that he probably might have been of that opinion himself had not the minister[']s crops been attacked."[23] By July 1828 the difficulties between Buchanan and part of his congregation were no secret, and despite a large attendance at services, the number of communicants was suspiciously low, revealing that only those loyal to Buchanan were willing to be fenced by him to partake of communion. To Bell who witnessed it, this was proof of disaffections and of rumours that minister and congregation "had not been on good terms of late."[24] By 1830 members of Buchanan's congregation openly complained to Bell of their minister "threatening to deprive of church privileges, those who did not pay him according to agreement."[25]

From the late 1820s on Bell watched Buchanan decline into a man who teetered between bouts of rage and morose depression. In the late winter of 1826 just when sleighing was breaking up, Buchanan attempted to make a strong impression before the Presbyterian congregation at Brockville, in hopes of being called to minister there so that he might leave behind the dissension in Beckwith. He "dressed himself in his best clothes, borrowed a better cutter than his own, and carried the best specimen of his daughters with him" and was seen by several people on the road "beating the poor animal with a stick. He reached Brockville with difficulty, and there the poor beast died".[26] On a trip to York in September Bell observed Buchanan's temper at closer range. While hurrying to escape a rainstorm, Buchanan lost his portmanteau and "had to go back a mile in the thickest of rain, by which he got completely drenched. This put the old man in such a passion with me", Bell noted, "because I had got in dry, that he could not again speak peaceably to me for some hours." Bell eventually became so shocked by "the very unreasonable and fitful disposition" he discovered in Buchanan that he attempted to part from him at York "for I found he was only an incumbrance, but he flew in a rage at the mere mention of it, so that I was forced to take him along with me."[27] At a presbytery meeting in York Buchanan prepared a petition complaining "that hymns contained dangerous errors," and mortified Bell in front of the other clergymen by complaining of his fellow traveller's conduct.[28]

Back in Perth Bell continued to receive discouraging reports from Beckwith. In early March 1830 Bell attempted to rouse both Buchanan and his congregation by proposing "the building of a church and the formation of a missionary society."[29] A new church certainly was needed. The structure hastily built in 1822 had deteriorated in less than a decade, causing Bell to expostulate:

> But what a place of worship! An old shanty in such a state of ruin that cats and dogs might pass between the logs.... Here [the Beckwith Presbyterians] were sitting in a miserable log hut, the wind whistling between the logs — the thermometer down to zero, and, at sunrise, 10 degrees

Plate 82
"Family Prayer" as painted ca. 1890 by George A. Reid, R.C.A. This was a familiar scene in many early nineteenth-century Beckwith homes, with the male head of the family addressing the Almighty, while the rest of the household bowed their heads in submission. It is important to recognize the genuine piety that predominated in family worship, but in not a few instances patriarchal authority in forcing children to do their fathers' bidding, even after children became adults, was only further reinforced by this tradition of moral dominance. Photo, courtesy Art Gallery of Ontario, from a painting in the collection of Victoria University.

below it. Yet they will neither repair the place nor send fire wood, lest it might make *the minister* comfortable....[30] Just in front of the building, in which the congregation met for worship, was the greatest mass of dung. Here it lay to the depth of a foot, and being now saturated with water, it resembled a soft peat bog.[31]

The congregation turned a cold ear to forming a missionary society, and "most of those present seemed unwilling to assist in building a church for Mr. Buchanan", leading Bell to conclude that "most of the people were very ignorant and they seemed to be influenced by one or two demagogues, who were personal enemies to Mr. Buchanan."[32]

By 1827 Buchanan and his congregation were worshipping in the barn on his lot,[33] and when Bell preached there in July 1830 he found it so "excessively crowded that, though very large, and having a free circulation of air, it became so heated that it was scarcely to be endured."[34] In early

May 1832 Buchanan left a pile of burning chips and rubbish unattended; when he looked up from his garden he discovered the church barn to be ablaze. "In half an hour the barn was consumed, together with the hay, grain, cutter, harness, saddle, seed potatoes, pulpit, seats...and every thing else it contained."[35] The barn had been "an excellent, large and useful building...erected for [Buchanan]...by his congregation",[36] but three months after the fire Bell arrived at the Buchanan farm to find that "no steps had been taken to provide another." At Bell's request[37]

> preparations were made for the services of the Sabbath in the adjoining pasturefield, as it was evident the shantie [built as a house of worship in 1822] would not contain one quarter of the people that would attend. With the assistance of the elders [Bell] erected a tent for preaching in; and there being plenty of building logs at hand, [they] placed them in parallel lines for seats.... [W]hen [Bell] went into the tent to begin the service, at least a hundred umbrellas were employed to protect their owners from the rays of the sun.

At this point the outdoor worship service, the building logs, and the people assembled who Bell believed "had never been as numerous on any former occasion" gave the appearance of a new beginning for the Beckwith congregation, but for Buchanan it was effectively the beginning of the end. In September 1830 Bell learned "that the people in Beckwith...were still endeavouring to get a minister from the Church of Scotland" and that notices of meetings by this Church of Scotland party were posted "on the very shanty in which Mr. Buchanan preached."[38] The burning of Buchanan's church through his own carelessness marked an opportunity to set aright an entire chain of events that was based on a muddle created by none other than the Reverend William Bell himself. The Beckwith deputation which had asked Bell in 1819 to forward their petition for a clergyman had no idea that the men in Edinburgh to whom he addressed it were Secessionists. After all, it was difficult to tell that Bell himself was a Secessionist. He accepted a government salary to teach the government school at Perth until ousted by the arrival of Anglican clergyman, the Reverend Michael Harris, he received £100 a year from government as resident clergyman at Perth,[39] and in a letter printed in the Brockville *Recorder* Bell even denied that the Presbytery of Upper Canada to which he belonged "is in connection with the Scotch Secession Church."[40] The highlanders of Beckwith in an 1831 letter to Glasgow claimed that from the beginning they had hoped for a Church of Scotland clergyman, that they had assumed Bell was helping them find just such a minister, and that back in 1819 they had not realised how readily the government would have supported a Church of Scotland clergyman in their midst. They pointed to the breaches that had taken place in the Beckwith congregation, and taking care not to mention his name, convincingly stated "The present minister is disesteemed and he cannot preach in Gaelic."[41]

There is no question that the Reverend George Buchanan was disesteemed by many members of his congregation, but to suggest that he was incapable of preaching in Gaelic was simply untrue. Had there been any truth to this charge, had Buchanan even had a poor command of Gaelic, the Beckwith congregation would have had justification for formally requesting a change of clergyman, and word of any lack of Gaelic language skills would almost certainly have drifted into the ears of the Reverend Bell who was most diligent in cataloguing Buchanan's shortcomings. The Beckwith congregation, as it turned out, simply had been unwittingly victimised by Bell's decision to introduce a Secessionist clergyman rather than one from the Church of Scotland. The Beckwith congregation had not recognised that Buchanan was a Secessionist until too late after he was settled among them, had drawn up an agreement with them, had made himself indispensable to them as physician, schoolmaster and clergyman, and legally owned the building in which they worshipped on his lot. Buchanan effectively controlled congregational life far beyond the limits normally set by the Church of Scotland. He effectively enjoyed the power known as "the fencing of the table" by which he could debar anyone from receiving communion. This only served to inflame feeling against him for not belonging to the Church of Scotland.

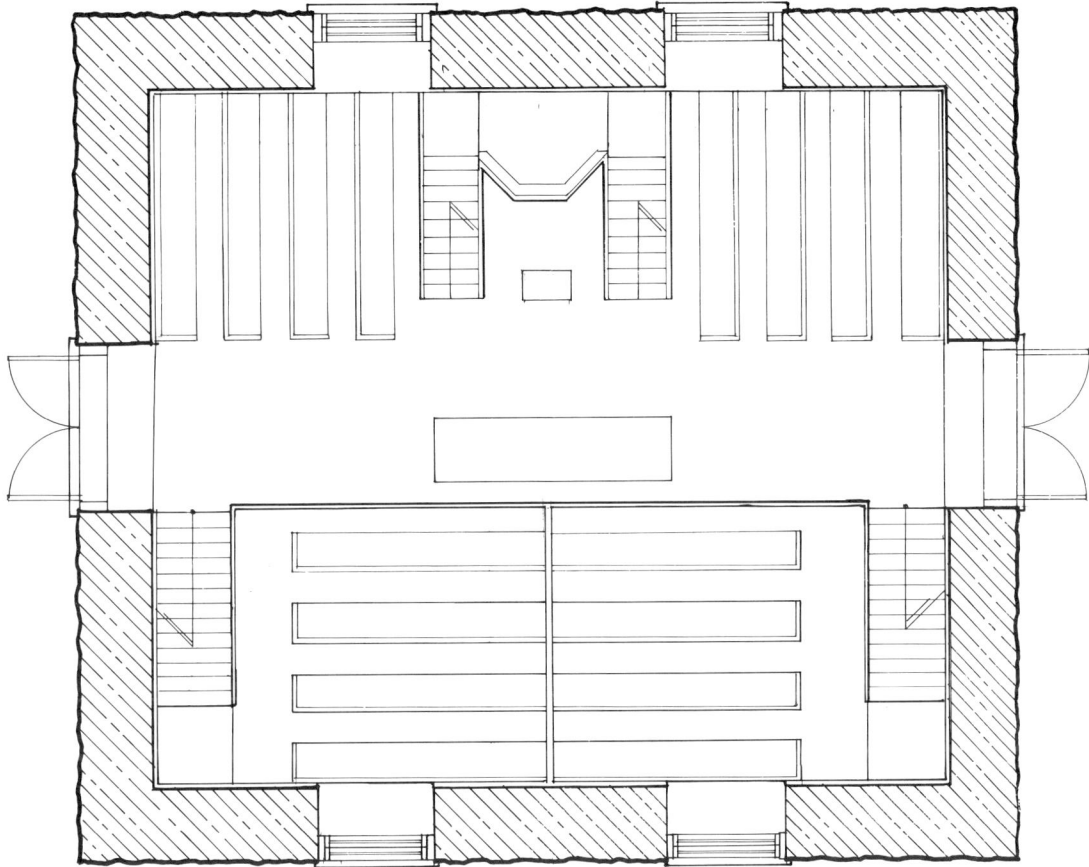

Plate 83
Conjectural floorplan of the Beckwith Church of Scotland house of worship constructed in 1834 as reconstructed by Robert W.J. Moore from contemporary descriptions. The communion table was at the centre of the interior, with the precentor's desk and the pulpit rising behind it. The height of the pulpit, mounted with the sounding board above it against the north wall, permitted the congregation on the ground floor and people sitting in the gallery to see the minister's face while he preached. This plan underestimates the number of benches.

Part of the disesteem felt for Buchanan by most of his congregation may have stemmed from the fact that he was effectively controlled by his wife, and from Ann Buchanan putting on too many airs in the middle of the backwoods. Most certainly she was not the only Beckwith woman who ran her husband, as shown by the example of Jane Hill who "had the management of" her husband Thomas Glendinning.[42] Rather than set a model for their parishioners worthy of emulation, Buchanan and his family with their empty vanity and lack of ambition were an embarrassment. In October 1831 Bell was unable to find "any mark of industry about the [Buchanan] place. Though the fields around were in great want of manure, it had never been removed during ten years, but lay about every where as made by the cattle."[43] When Bell and his wife called unexpectedly on the Buchanans in January 1833:[44]

> it was some *time* before we saw anyone, all having disappeared to *dress* so that they could be seen. After a while we got something to eat, fried in grease as usual. There was neither bread nor

wine in the house, but we had an abundance of apologies and had to take the word for the deed.

When the Bells called again in February 1836 [45]

> we found all in darkness, dirt and confusion, — yet the young ladies were out taking an airing, of which, if we may judge from the state of their apartments, they must have had some need. The room we were in being quite dark, Mrs. B[uchanan] called repeatedly to the servant girl to bring in a candle, but as the candle never yet appeared, we suspected there was none in the house....
> In order to escape from this squalid scene of misery, we groped our way out of the house....

The charges by members of the congregation that Mrs. Buchanan "was both man and wife" appeared confirmed in January 1833 when Bell invited Buchanan to discuss uniting with the Church of Scotland; Ann Buchanan also made an appearance, as Bell noted, "for on these occasions her ladyship always attended her husband, that he might enjoy the benefits of her counsel and advice."[46]

Between May 1832 when the barn church on Buchanan's lot was destroyed by fire and the appointment of the Reverend John Smith as the first Church of Scotland minister for Beckwith it is difficult to establish a precise chronology of what exactly took place. Members of the congregation had already applied in 1831 to the Glasgow Colonial Society for a bilingual Church of Scotland clergyman and through their member of the legislative assembly, William Morris, they applied for funds to pay his salary.[47] Logs were taken out to build a new church, debate followed about whether to build a less expensive log or frame structure or a more costly stone church, and it was decided to build the stone structure on nearby lot fourteen in the seventh concession owned by Peter McArthur. The Church of Scotland minister at Perth noted in November 1832 "that a good stone church has been erected at Beckwith"[48] and a clergyman in Scotland in January 1833 read a letter from Beckwith stating "that the Church was built, the windows and doors ready, if not on, and all the wood for the seating, etc., ready".[49] If, as Buchanan's daughter later wrote, when the walls neared completion a meeting of the congregation was held requesting Buchanan "to join the old Kirk, if he ever expected to preach in the new edifice" this may have reflected their despair at finding a bilingual Church of Scotland minister willing to venture out into the backwoods of Upper Canada.[50] Perhaps it was a tactical manoeuvre on the Church of Scotland's side, in that by anticipating Buchanan's refusal to give up his Secessionist allegiance the larger part of the congregation could claim that he had chosen not to serve them. If Buchanan was asked to serve as minister in the new Church of Scotland stone church he certainly refused, probably prompted to do so as much by his wife's pride and pride of family tradition as by conviction. The major issue on which Secessionists differed from the Church of Scotland, receiving money and patronage from government, did not prevent Buchanan from pocketing more than £31 of a half yearly allowance from the Crown in June 1835.[51]

The break between Buchanan and the larger Church of Scotland portion of his congregation was both emotional and rancorous. In May 1833 a Church of Scotland clergyman able to preach in both Gaelic and English agreed to accept the Beckwith charge, and by October the Reverend John Smith arrived in Beckwith. In a letter back to Scotland in April 1834 Smith reported:[52]

> On my arrival here, the divisions and party feeling existing among the people of my congregation were alarming; these in a great measure originated from the presence of the Scotch Burgher clergyman who was settled here before I came. And at this time also it was expected that he along with the list of his brethren in the province were about to be received into a connexion with our Synod. For various good reasons the portion of the people here who applied to your Society became discontented with Mr. Buchanan... — a number more were less displeased with him; a good many, including several respectable families related to himself continued to adhere to him, and wished that he should have got possession of the Church; much division had its origin in this.

Plate 84
Ruins of the Beckwith Church of Scotland house of worship, as photographed ca. 1950. Although a very plain structure, this was as close as the Perthshire highlanders in Beckwith came to transplanting any vestige of their traditional ecclesiastical architecture. Separate entrances for men and women in the gable walls, separate galleries along the south wall, and the elevated pulpit combined to give a traditional austere highland Scottish design to this structure. Most Church of Scotland churches built in Upper Canada were more picturesque in their treatment. City of Ottawa Archives, Harry Walker collection, CA17518.

The messy division of Beckwith Presbyterians splashed into the pages of the Cobourg *Reformer*[53] and the Brockville *Recorder*[54] in a series of unedifying letters between Church of Scotland clergyman the Reverend Matthew Miller and Buchanan's son-in-law Anthony Philip. In the few months before Smith arrived, as he later reported, "the feeling of party spirit and animosity reached its height" and this "induced a few to connect themselves as regular hearers of a Cameronian clergyman named McLaughlin" whose appearance in the spring of 1833 Smith believed "was an additional cause of disunion among the Presbyterians of Beckwith."[55]

The Reverend George Buchanan and his ministry rapidly declined following Smith's arrival; by early 1834 he had "entirely given up preaching" and "except for his own immediate relations" most local Scottish Presbyterians in numbers varying from 300 to 500 attended the new stone church.[56] Bell at Perth was pained to learn that[57]

> Mr. Buchanan, since Mr. Smith came to Beckwith, instead of exerting himself more than before, had become more careless, and some Sabbaths did not preach at all, so that all his congregation had left him but his own family. He and they both showed too much taste for travelling about the country, and visiting. They sometimes came to see us with a whole retinue of horses and dogs, when I thought they might have been better employed at home. They had got into debt too, and were forced to sell first one lot of land, and then another. At last they sold the house and land on which they lived, and for less than half their value. They carefully concealed the particulars from me, but I soon heard that Mr. Smith had not only possessed himself of Mr. B[uchanan]'s congregation, but of his house and land into the bargain.

Considering the land he possessed, that elders John Carmichael and Alexander Dewar remained faithful to his ministry,[58] and that he received an annual salary from government beginning in 1833, Buchanan could have persevered and lived very well off a farm twice the size of most farms in Beckwith. Instead, he became despondent at being deserted by most of his congregation, and by March 1835 he was described as having "been ill for some time." When Bell and his wife called on the Buchanans on the 26th "we found all in dirt and confusion, and scarcely any fire to warm us. [I] thought Mr. B[uchanan] was not so ill as he had been a few days before, yet it was evident he was going the way of all the earth. He was suffering from both dropsy and asthma; and anasarca was already spreading over his feet and legs."[59] Two days later Mrs. Buchanan arrived at the Bell home in Perth "with all her retinue of colts, dogs, and bundles.... She had brought a keg with her, as she said, to take home wine for Mr. Buchanan, but concluded to take gin, as *it suited his trouble better.*"[60] By June Buchanan was "dangerously ill" and "aware he was dying, but was quite resigned to the will of God."[61] He died on the twelfth day of September 1835.[62] To Bell at Perth "the news came like a thunderbolt" and perhaps feeling some remorse for his part in creating an untenable situation for Buchanan in Beckwith, Bell arranged for him to be interred "in the place where I had expected to lie myself" in the Perth burying ground.[63]

The demise of Buchanan and his ministry in Beckwith did not deter Bell from continuing to visit and preach throughout Beckwith. He had often taken pleasure in preaching to the attentive highlanders,[64] and from July 1829 on he had added inducement to visit northern Beckwith when his sons William and John opened a store at Carlton Place. Two other sons, Robert and James, eventually took charge of this store.[65] In July 1830 at Carlton Place Bell[66]

> preached to about 50 people, part of them Methodists. Some of these, afterwards, came...and shook hands with me; and one of them, an Irishman, told me that I must surely be a servant of the Lord, for I had preached a *sweet Methodist* sermon, sure. This was in consequence of an ignorant, but designing Methodist preacher, lately in that part, persuading his less informed hearers, that none preached the gospel but themselves.

This welcoming response from Carlton Place Methodists complemented a visit Bell had paid to Duncan McNabb, the Baptist itinerant preacher, two months earlier at his rural Beckwith home. He found McNabb "busy at his loom" and in the course of an amicable conversation and a comfortable meal Bell perceived that Mrs. McNabb "seemed the better preacher of the two."[67] In January 1836 at Mr. Kerfoot's in Beckwith" Bell "as usual met with a very kind and christian reception. [H]e preached in the Methodist chapel, to about 100 people, and baptised 3 children" there.[68]

By January 1831 Bell's congregation at Carlton Place had increased to 100 persons, but he had to fend off "a vile slander which some ill designed persons had circulated in the neighbourhood; namely that I had come there to preach in order to get money."[69] In October 1831 Bell recommended

Plate 85
Gravestones of the Reverend John Smith and Duncan Campbell in St. Fillan's cemetery, as photographed in 1981. The high regard in which Smith was held by his Church of Scotland congregation is evident in their publicly subscribing the funds to raise what in 1851 was the largest gravestone in Beckwith. Carved stone markers were rare in Beckwith before 1851, but Smith's memorial made commissioning a handsome gravestone a vogue from the 1850s on, as the similar design of stone for Duncan Campbell who died a month later shows.

that the congregation, meeting in the village school, build a church,[70] and in February 1832 a subscription of £100 was raised over the objections of members of the Cram family "who seemed to prefer a union with the Church of Scotland."[71] The construction of a Methodist chapel at Carlton Place later that year stopped the church building project, effectively revealing how cohesive the Scottish Presbyterians and Irish Methodists in the village vicinity had become. When Bell preached in the Methodist chapel in January 1833 he described it as "a new building, 40 by 50 [feet], but not yet finished. About 100 people attended, but the chapel not being plastered, we were very cold."[72] The Secession Presbyterians and Methodists at Carlton Place continued to worship together into the 1850s.[73]

Bell could not keep away from where he and Buchanan had preached together in central Beckwith. In January 1836 he called at the Buchanan household:[74]

> For half an hour the Ladies as usual were invisible, for they are never fit to be seen till they are dressed. Mrs. B[uchanan] I found entertained the usual quantum of visionary schemes. She talked about getting a pension from Government, to support her in the decline of life, — about sending her son David to Scotland, to college, — about getting a bursary for him there, &c. Then she talked of going to Scotland with him herself, and getting some of her friends, who she said

were well off, to pay for his education. Thus she went on building castles in the air, till I left her, wondering at her folly.

Bell found that he could get along with the Reverend John Smith. Even before Buchanan passed away, Bell called on Smith in June 1835 and "found him in a ragged suit of blue, the coat having one of its sleeves partly torn away from the body. He seemed to have a great talent for silence, so I made my stay short."[75] Smith also had a talent for diplomacy. The two elders who had remained loyal to Buchanan were welcomed as Church of Scotland elders in July 1838.[76] A year earlier Ann Buchanan had quietly joined the congregation.[77]

As late as April 1834 the new church remained unfinished although Smith optimistically hoped to have the roof, floors and pulpit finished by the end of the year's harvest.[78] The central feature of the new church interior was the pulpit placed high in the centre of the north wall:[79]

> The Beckwith church pulpit was so high as to be on a level with the gallery opposite; and its canopy, made of finely carved native wood, reached the top of the wall behind it. The precentor's stand was placed directly in front of, and below, the pulpit. It was reached by ascending three steps. There was a doorway in each end wall of the church. These doors were connected by a wide aisle which divided the floor in halves. The pews in the south half all faced north, while those in the other half were placed at right angles to the aisle, and faced the pulpit from the east and west respectively. The gallery was reached by two flights of steps, one at each end of the church. An impassable partition cut across its centre. A long table at which communicants sat while they partook of the Sacrament, stood in front of the pulpit, encroaching somewhat on the aisle space.

For Smith, as with Buchanan, the first years of his ministry in Beckwith were the most rewarding. In reporting back to the Glasgow Colonial Society in 1834, Smith claimed that upwards of 300 people regularly attended worship and that on "some favourable days during the sleighing season, the number attending could not have been less than 500." He reported going to preach in remote corners of the township, and that although "the places of preaching" were "not large, [they] hitherto have been crowded to excess." Smith regularly kept a Sabbath School and in addition to the many children between ages eight and fifteen who were enrolled in it there also were "many of every age who attend and listen to the instructions and explanations of the Scripture given to the scholars. Last Lord's Day for instance, from 50 to 70 were present besides our scholars." During the winter months Smith visited most of his parishioners "chiefly for the purpose of obtaining some personal knowledge of their characters and mode of living" and claimed in every instance to have "met with cordial welcome." Between spring and harvest seemed the best season for catechising the young adults of the congregation. All things considered, Smith concluded after only half a year in Beckwith, "as one called to minister in Holy things among them I have met with every mark of esteem and respect from my congregation; in every way also in which they can add to my personal comfort they have shown the utmost kindness — the most cheerful willingness to oblige."[80]

In addition to unceasing visiting, catechising, writing sermons which he committed to memory, baptising babies, exhorting, teaching Sunday School, leading worship, comforting the dying, and generally setting an uplifting moral example, Smith presided over the Kirk Session as moderator. Together with the elders he guarded the admission of members to the communion table below the pulpit. In February 1834 the number of "those desirous of admission to the Ordinance of the Lord's Supper" numbered 156 (Appendix 15). Elders and minister were obliged to examine any and all reports of morally reprehensible behaviour unbefitting a person sitting at the table of the Lord. Between 1837 and 1851 ten married couples came before the Beckwith Kirk Session and "confessed themselves guilty of the crime of ante-nuptial fornication", that is, of having sex before they married. They were suitably admonished by Smith as to the sin, and readmitted "to church Privileges".[81] Five

Plate 86
The Church of Scotland manse built for the Reverend John Smith on lot 12, concession 7, Beckwith, as conjecturally restored and photographed in the late 1960s. The graceful elliptical curve of the front entrance and the four fireplaces inside testify to the important status of the clergyman in the community. No other Beckwith house was so lavishly endowed with fireplaces, but in the 1840s many stone houses equally as large were constructed. Credit, Hy Fund Studio.

individuals confessed to fornication, two of them having done so while servants. Margaret Dickson, for example, in 1840 confessed that she was "guilty of the sin of fornication, in the first instance some years ago and a short time previous to her departure from Scotland for this country, and again more recently while employed as a Servant in the neighbouring Village of Richmond."[82] Schoolmaster Thomas Ferguson was summoned before the Session in 1839 for falling "into the abominable sin of fornication with...[two] females of unblemished character until seduced from the path of rectitude" by him. The Session agreed to absolve Ferguson from the sin of fornication "after submitting to rebuke from the Moderator on two several sabbaths in presence of the Congregation," but because "so much of immorality has been of late years exhibited in his conduct," church privileges were withheld "until by a course of consistent & good conduct he affords reasonable ground of belief that he can value and improve them."[83]

The Church of Scotland session meted out absolution and humiliation for greater and lesser sins. John Cram was investigated in 1840 for falling "into the sin of drunkenness,"[84] John Stewart was suspended from church privileges in 1842 "for almost entirely absent[ing] himself from Church,"[85] James McArthur was charged in 1849 "with the scandalous sin of adultery",[86] and in 1850 a woman in the congregation was "charged with the crime of incestuous fornication with her Uncle".[87] In exacting public penitence before the rest of the congregation, the Beckwith session under Smith was more rigorous than most others in Upper Canada. Smith explained in January 1839:[88]

Altho' the Law obliging those guilty of scandalous offences to profess publicly penitence for the same, has in many Parishes become obsolete in Scotland, & has not, so far as is known to the Session, been fully acted upon in any Scotch Congregation in this Province, still the Session being unanimously of opinion, that the observance of this Law would be beneficial, it was resolved that it should be enforced.

By implication, Beckwith had more than its share of "scandalous offences" and Smith felt that public chastisements were essential to affirm the session's authority over members of the congregation. The need to establish the session's authority seems to have stemmed from the personality of Smith himself who was both introverted and stern. William Bell in 1838 found that "Mr. Smith's was a cheerless abode; those qualities which form the charm of social life being sadly deficient."[89] A daughter of the deceased Buchanan recalled that Smith was "a very quiet, unassuming man" and "extremely sensitive".[90]

The Beckwith Kirk Session was a strong force in maintaining social stability among the Scottish inhabitants of the township before mid-century, especially for the women in the congregation. Although the session was adamant when occasion required for a profession of penitence to be made and for an admonition from the pulpit to be administered publicly before the congregation, they evidently recognised on other occasions that a more sensitive approach might be called for. In November 1839, for example, the session agreed that Margaret McDonald, who on two different occasions when engaged as a servant outside Beckwith's boundaries had "fallen into the sin of fornication...without a public rebuke & public confession of her sins, ...should not be re-admitted to the privileges of the Church". And yet, they further agreed, "considering that such public appearance might possibly induce an attack of hysterical or epileptic fits, to which she is represented as being usually subject...she is to be admitted to Church privileges on her confession of crime to the Session."[91] When the widow of George Buchanan "brought a very extraordinary charge against a young man named A[lexande]r Stewart whom she...accused of a criminal connection with her own girl Maggy[,]...the Session...did not believe the story. They thought it a malicious conspiracy altogether."[92] These tempered judgments in 1839 may partly have flowed from the Reverend John Smith marrying Jane Morson of Rockcliffe that August[93] for whom he built a stone house on lot twelve of the seventh concession. The Reverend William Bell from Perth in June 1839 described the "new manse" as "very neatly finished."[94]

Bell happened to be preaching in the Beckwith church one Sunday in July 1837 when an unusual event occurred which prompted him to leave a record of the type of service that took place. His account less directly indicates the growing importance of religion to women in Beckwith. A young Mrs. Scott who became mentally deranged following an attack of measles, went to the Reverend John Smith's house, next door to the church, well before the service, requesting him to baptise her again since she had subsequently "been born again, and ought therefore to be baptized anew". Upon being refused, she kneeled down and prayed for the minister. "Rising up, she requested that he would pray for her, which when he was about to do standing, she ordered him to kneel, for she would not accept of it standing."[95] When Smith and Bell went to the church to begin the service, "all endeavours to keep her in the house were vain, to the church she was determined to go." Bell recounted:[96]

> For some time she sat very quietly, but after I began the lecture, she advanced along the passage and up the pulpit stair. I expected she was coming with a mischievous intention, but this had not been the case, as she sat down very quietly on the uppermost step at the door of the pulpit. She occasionally now and then made some remark on what I said; for instance when I spoke of Satan tempting some to despair of the mercy of God she said in a low tone *He is not able*. During my second discourse she discovered more agitation, and towards the conclusion she became so much agitated, both in body and mind, that two of her female friends attempted to take her out, but she resisted, so they let her remain. When I was about to begin the last prayer she stood

Plate 87
Knox Free Presbyterian Church, Black's Corners, built 1845, as photographed ca. 1932. Only one of the three extensive drivesheds at Knox Church is shown in this photograph. Although a vernacular structure, this was not as outwardly plain a structure as the Church of Scotland (Plate 84) built a decade earlier. The pointed windows declared to the world passing by that this was a Christian house of worship. Photograph courtesy of Donna Fox.

up and said, I'll pray — for you, if you please, Mr. Bell' but without taking notice of her I went on, and she gave me no interruption. The precentor appeared to be more disturbed than I was, for when he stood up to sing at the concluding psalm, he could not catch the tune. She began singing to set him right, and probably would have succeeded, had he sung with her. But, instead of following her, he struck in anew, after she had got nearly to the end of the first line, so that there was some jarring between them.

Attempts to remove her only served to create disorder:

While the elders were taking up the collection, a woman, with whom she had formerly lived as a servant, came and very injudiciously attempted to take her away. This enraged her, and she repeatedly struck at her with her umbrella, and when she ran from her, chased her out at the door. On her way along the passage she encountered one of the elders, who offered her a seat, and asked her to sit down; but, pointing to the person next her in the pew, she said she would not sit beside a sinner like that! But she prayed fervently that every sinner might repent of his sin, come to Christ, and obtain salvation. While this was going on, the congregation was in a state of considerable excitement. Some advised to take her away by force, and others to let her alone and let her take her own way. I observed several females crying with alarm. Just as I was about to pronounce the blessing, the woman she had before struck at, having come near her, she again struck her with so much violence that she broke her umbrella, and then chased her out at the door. Her husband, and others of her friends...prevented her return.

Bell's account tells about unusual events taking place during a church service, but a careful reading of it together with contemporary session minutes reveals how important the polity of this Church of Scotland congregation was for local women. Although women enjoyed no offices in the congregation, and despite being legally and economically at the mercy of their husbands, fathers, brothers and sons, the church acted as a social vehicle in which they attained some sense of worth. The closest and the most obvious analogy to the congregation was the family. Although the model of society they imported from Scotland accorded women either within the family or within the congregation little legal recognition, through the agency of the church session a man could not commit adultery or cast his wife away to one side without drawing censure and humiliation from minister, elders and neighbours. Such censure did not necessarily have any legal implications, but the moral, ethical and social implications of such behaviour spilled over into the economic sphere. Members of the congregation "in consideration of the favour which the Almighty has shewn us as a people" were "anxious to avoid everything [and every person whose life was not morally conducted or] calculated to provoke His [that is, God's] frown."[97] Numerous charivaris at Perth revealed that this community concern for individuals not stepping beyond the boundaries of accepted behaviour was not wholly religious in origin.

Conducive though the emphasis on moral order was to protecting the position of women within a patriarchal society, its obverse effect was to stifle freedom of individual thought and behaviour. Scottish Beckwith was wholly Christian with everyone assenting either silently or vociferously that the universe was permeated with moral law and purpose. When a correspondent of the *Bathurst Courier* named John Freeman, not from Beckwith, dared to suggest in 1847 that people had the right to believe or not to believe in God, it drew an angry response from an inhabitant of Carlton Place who disagreed with such "semi-Infidel notions" that "men should have choice to worship God or not".[98] Similarly, J. L. Wilkie of Carlton Place in May 1851 berated the editor of the Lanark *Observer* as an immoral influence, "he being an Infidel."[99] For the local individual who might not necessarily have been religious, to stand in defiance of the church session effectively was to risk being ostracised by most of the highland Scottish Presbyterians for whom their good standing within the congregation was a matter of great pride and which they jealously guarded. Young Mrs. Scott chasing after her former mistress with an umbrella and bluntly refusing to sit beside a woman who she claimed was a great sinner, in her deranged condition simply stated aloud the type of concerns and suspicions that everyone else silently pondered. Of course, the acceptance of women within the church as equal partakers of the sacraments, of equally participating in congregational singing, of making the same individual struggle against worldly temptation that men in the church did, all combined to make the young women of Beckwith staunch members who would allow no one to prevent them taking their place at Sabbath worship services.

The influence and the piety of the session over which the Reverend John Smith moderated was such that when the disruption of the Church of Scotland occurred in 1843, the Beckwith congregation was severely rent. Smith commented, "In Beckwith order & discipline were for a time nearly suspended, the Elders without exception ceasing to officiate."[100] The number of people who left the Church of Scotland to form Free Church congregations was greater than the number who remained. According to the 1852 census there were 515 members of the Church of Scotland as compared with 564 Free Church Presbyterians. Whereas the Church of Scotland built in the early 1830s had been placed in the exact geographic centre of Beckwith, the large new stylish Knox Free Church was located in the middle of the Scottish Presbyterian population on the northern part of lot fourteen in the eighth concession at Black's Corners, and a mission called Melville Free Church was established at Mount Pleasant (later Ashton). In terms of simple accessibility the two new churches were convenient for the concentration of Presbyterians in the northern quarter of Beckwith to attend, but

Plate 88
Melville Free Presbyterian Church, Ashton, as photographed in the early 1970s. Melville church was originally constructed in 1844, and was enlarged and had a tower and spire added in 1879. Although built a year before Knox church (Plate 87), the large numbers of people from Carleton Place and central northern Beckwith attending at Black's Corners made the Ashton congregation a mission. The naming of this church after nobleman Viscount Melville, of Perthshire, is curious, in that the impetus for the Free Church disruption of 1843 was to resist the worldly influence of wealthy patrons such as Melville on the Church of Scotland. National Archives of Canada negative no. C-80014.

convenience was hardly what had prompted the local disruption.

The Scottish highlanders and their children still followed events in Scotland very closely, and were able to do so in the extensive coverage of Scotland offered by the Perth *Bathurst Courier* and the Bytown and Brockville newspapers. They read of the dramatic withdrawal by Dr. Thomas Chalmers and a host of clergy in Scotland from the Church of Scotland. The controversy over whether or not the church should accept funds from the state was a matter of intense debate. When the Reverend Norman Macleod from Scotland toured through the settlements between Bytown and

Perth in August 1845 he found that the "angry spirit of Churchism which has disturbed every fireside in Scotland, thunders at every shanty in the backwoods."[101] When another visitor from Scotland, the Reverend Robert Burns from the newly formed Free Church, visited Beckwith a month later he discovered that "a call, signed by 240 members and adherents, had been drawn out in favour of the Rev. Mr. McMillan of Cardross", Scotland. Burns found the new Free Church congregations in Beckwith and Ramsay "in a matured and settled state — perfectly able to support the Gospel creditably, and presenting most promising situations for laborious and effective ministers. The rising village of Carleton Place, too, was not overlooked. An hour's notice brought out a respectable, though not a large, audience".[102] Whereas Burns was informed that five-sixths of the Scottish families in Ramsay were "decidedly Presbyterian and free", barely half the Presbyterians in Beckwith belonged to the new church. Burns observed that "A large proportion of Beckwith is Gaelic; many of the settlers are from the Marquis of Breadalbane's country; and all of them more or less flourishing",[103] implying that language and a sense of highland clan loyalty constrained many of the Beckwith congregation from departing the ministry of Smith in the old kirk.

What impelled half the Presbyterians in Beckwith to leave the Church of Scotland in 1844 was partly prompted by the timing of the disruption in Scotland. To it were added distinct political and moral concerns that were prompted by tensions in the large families looking for additional land on which to settle sons and daughters. It was no coincidence in the same decade that Beckwith families found their land insufficient to keep their families together, that their individual dilemmas as families were transmuted into religious protest. Theoretically, as an upright people favoured of God, the lack of land on which to settle sons and daughters comfortably around them in Beckwith showed that God was frowning on them. And with the example of the Free Church controversy in Scotland blazing as a beacon before them, Beckwith Presbyterians began to consider that the immediate future for them as members of the Church of Scotland under Smith was not as bright as it previously had been under the Secessionist Reverend George Buchanan who Providence had contrived to send them in 1822. Clearly, there was a moral to be drawn from the example of hundreds of congregations in Scotland where people withdrew to a separate place of meeting rather than accept interference from the state and thereby do dishonour "to Christ's crown, and [thereby] reject...his sole and supreme authority as King in His Church."[104] Was it possible that in receiving a salary from the government,[105] that the Reverend John Smith and by extension the Beckwith Church of Scotland congregation were exposing themselves to compromising their spiritual interests to whatever worldly policy the government might establish? In addition to doing "grievous injury to the cause of the Redeemer throughout the world" by accepting state pay "they have refused to discharge the obvious duty of lifting up a full and unambiguous testimony for the truth" and had "most seriously endangered the purity of the Church, and brought even her independence into peril, through the probable introduction of office-bearers prepared to submit to the same encroachments of the civil power by which the Church of Scotland has been enslaved."[106] The local source of funding from which government paid the salaries of Church of Scotland, Anglican and Roman Catholic clergy were the Clergy Reserve lots, tracts of land that government did not fully dispose of until the mid 1850s and that local inhabitants clamoured to purchase.

The religious protest against a link between church and state was part of a voluntarist movement with numerous utopian goals. The first clergyman of the Free Church congregation at Black's Corners copied into the session minutebook a paragraph that summarised the essence of the religious protest:[107]

> The Church, as the divinely constituted depository and guardian of revealed truth, is specially bound to lift up her testimony for those particular truths which are at any time endangered or overborne by the antagonist powers of this world... Those great and fundamental truths which respect the supremacy of Christ in his Church, — the spiritual independence of her rulers, their

Plate 89
William Muirhead and his wife Christina McEwan as photographed ca. 1867. William Muirhead was one of the founding members of Knox Free Church at Black's Corners. Although he ventured off to the California gold-rush with his uncle Alexander McLaren in 1851, he returned the following year. When at age fifty he married a woman twenty years his junior, he was reputed to be the wealthiest inhabitant of Beckwith. He was accused of impeding the development of Carleton Place by opposing the Brockville and Ottawa railroad and by keeping the water privilege he owned there "closed up in his selfish grasp, refusing either to let it at a reasonable price to more enterprising men or to put up machinery which would not only be remunerative to himself but beneficial to the community." As proof of Muirhead's wealth, when he died in 1870 his mother and stepfather, Agnes and Daniel McLaren falsely accused Christina with poisoning her husband. Photographs courtesy of Arnold Muirhead.

exclusive responsibility to her great Head, the rights and privileges of his people, and the proper relation which should subsist between the Church and State, — are at the present day endangered, and have actually been overborne in the Established Church of Scotland, through recent encroachments of the State upon the Spiritual province, and submitted to by her.

Closely connected with the religious protest of Free Church members against the link of church and state was their quest for political reform, their growing support of the temperance movement, a call for the abolition of Clergy Reserve lots, and demands for more strict observance of the Sabbath. Most Beckwith Free Church Presbyterians agreed with a correspondent of the *Bathurst Courier* in 1850 that "a great work remains to be done. Superstition and ignorance are still raging, infidelity is still fearfully common, Sabbath profanation is yet taking place; and intemperance with its dark train of evils is yet laying the fairest portion of our land in wild and sad confusion."[108] It was the Free

Church Presbyterians along with the few Baptists and Methodists in Beckwith who helped elect Reform candidate Malcolm Cameron in the 1840s. When Cameron brought the Honourable Robert Baldwin, former Reform premier to Carlton Place in August 1847 an address from eighty local inhabitants headed by the name of Robert Bell congratulated "the great champion of the Reform principles" for the prominent part he had taken "in support of the rights of the PEOPLE of Canada" and for "his unwavering opposition to any sectarian arrangement of the 'University Question'".[109]

The quest for political reform and for keeping church and state separate, however worthy goals they may have been, could not disguise the fact that the congregation of Knox Free Church at Black's Corners initially thrived on controversy. Whereas the congregation on the seventh concession had only two ministers between 1822 and 1851, Knox Church in 1850 was seeking its third minister within only six years of being established. The voluntarist spirit within the congregation at Black's Corners was positively manifested in early February 1850 when the members presented departing clergyman James Cameron with "a horse, cutter, and appendages, as a mark of their esteem and confidence."[110] Within the church the new minister the Reverend Peter Gray discovered that the zeal for purity among some members of the congregation knew no reasonable limits. At a 4 March 1851 congregational meeting William Muirhead "stood up publicly, and, without a previous intimation of his interest, did charge...the minister, with preaching various unsound doctrines."[111] The Free Church session after due investigation[112]

> unanimously agreed that Mr. Muirhead's conduct in bringing such charges against his minister at such a time and place was unchristian, offensive, and injurious both to the minister's influence, and the interests of the congregation, and therefore highly reprehensible: And further, Mr. Muirhead still expressing that he did not regret his conduct, they resolved to debar Mr. Muirhead...from the privileges of the Church until such time as he shall express his sorrow and repentance for this action.

Yet a third denomination of Presbyterians variously known as Cameronians, or Covenanters, or as Reformed Presbyterians began meeting at Carlton Place in 1830 when the Reverend James Milligan from Ryegate Vermont paid them at least two visits.[113] Many of those attending his services were from Ramsay, and he preached at two other stations in Ramsay. During his September 1830 visit, Milligan presided over the sacrament of the Lord's Supper, making it the first Reformed Presbyterian communion in Canada.[114] The Reformed Presbyterians were so named because they professed to adhere to the principles of the Church of Scotland in the purest terms of the second Reformation between 1638 and 1649. They were commonly called Covenanters because they believed that public covenanting was an ordinance of God, they held themselves bound by everything in the National Covenant of Scotland sworn and subscribed in 1638 and in the Solemn League and Covenant of the United Kingdom in 1649 which was of moral obligation.[115] The congregation at Carlton Place received occasional visits from licentiates of the Reformed Presbyterian Synod in North America, and in the absence of preachers prayer meetings were held on Sundays.[116] Many of the 28 members of the congregation apparently did not espouse the doctrines of the denomination,[117] but in an attempt to establish a congregation more formally, either in 1831 or 1832 together with the Ramsay congregations they applied to the Reformed Presbyterian Synod in Scotland for a minister. When the Reverend James McLachlan arrived in the autumn of 1833 there were only nine members in all of Ramsay, but within four years there were 125 members.[118] In 1834 David Moffatt of Beckwith was ordained as an elder of the Carleton Place congregation. In 1841 a frame house of worship was constructed on the east end of William Street[119] and a residence for McLachlan was built in Ramsay. In October 1851 the Carlton Place and Ramsay congregations returned to the North American Synod.[120] In 1852 there were seventy Presbyterians residing in Beckwith who belonged to neither the Church of Scotland nor to the Free Church.

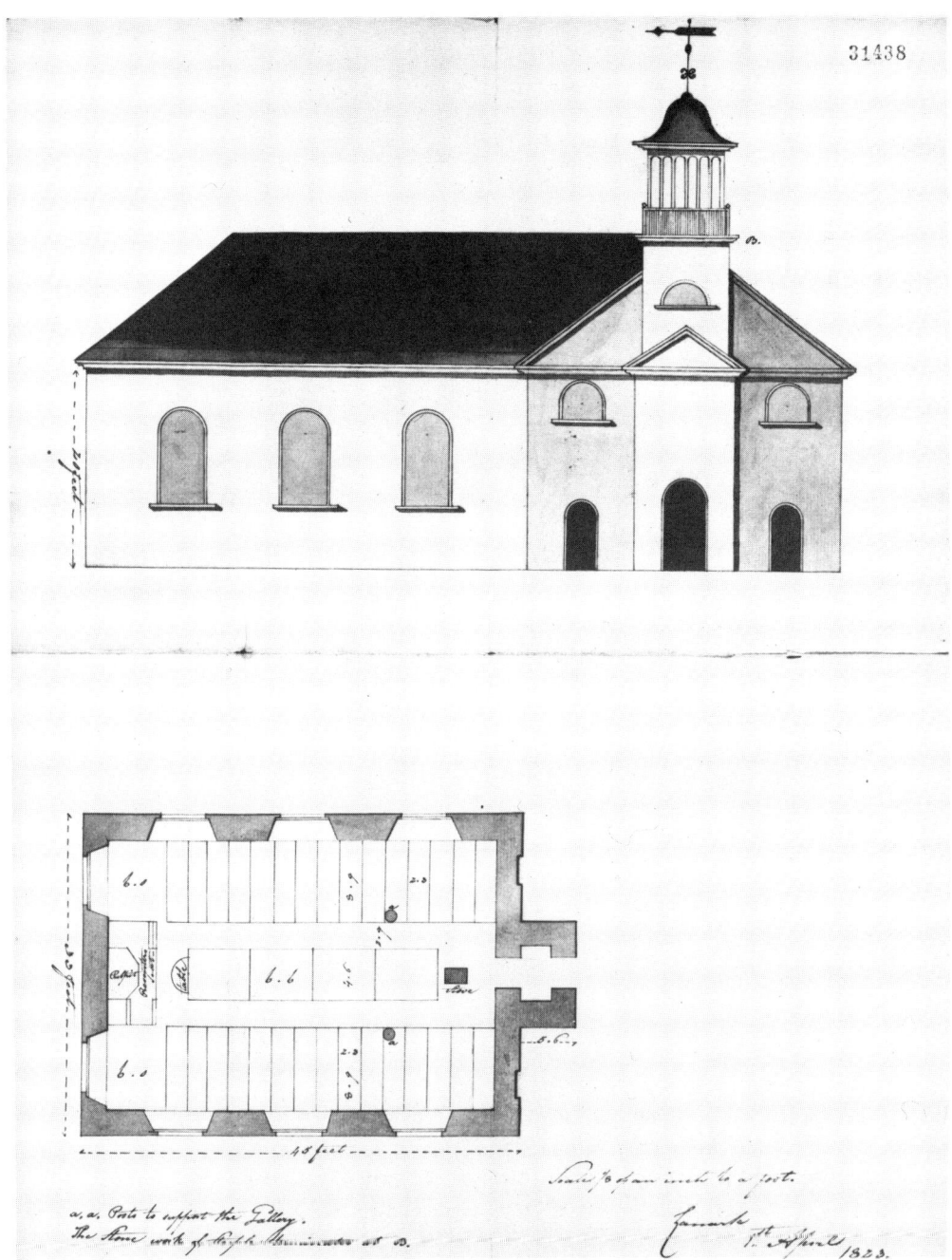

Plate 90
A plan proposed for the Presbyterian church to be built at Lanark village in 1823. This neoclassic design contrasts with the vernacular Presbyterian churches built in Beckwith before 1850 (plates 84, 87 and 88), but it may well have been the basis for the original design of St. James United Church of England and Ireland at Franktown (plates 100 and 101). The similar overall dimensions; the comparable size, shape and spacing of windows save for the addition of a large Palladian window over the altar in St. James church; the same slant of roof, the same height of masonry in the tower, the neoclassic pediment halfway up the tower, and the single round-headed entrance combine to suggest that the contractor from Perth who built St. James church had viewed this plan. National Archives of Canada Upper Canada Sundries, pp. 31435—8.

Plate 91
Susanna McDiarmid (left), as photographed ca. 1870. Born in Perthshire, Scotland, Susanna Malloch's family moved to the Perth vicinity where she married a McDonald of Drummond, and after his death she became the second wife of James McDiarmid of Beckwith. Their marriage in the Beckwith Church of Scotland offered Susanna and other Beckwith women assurance that their husbands would treat them with respect rather than suffer the indignity of being called to account before the church session. Photograph courtesy of Alan and Sharon Bullock, through Rosemary Wark.

The Scottish Baptists of Beckwith were organised into a congregation of seven members at the house of Elder Duncan McNabb in 1825. For the following eight years he preached to and exhorted believers in Beckwith and Drummond townships until he moved to the vicinity of Smith's Falls in 1833. No further Baptist services appear to have been held after McNabb's departure until early September 1840 when Robert Fyfe from the United States and Daniel McPhail from Osgoode conducted a missionary tour of Beckwith. McPhail described the Baptist revival that took place:[121]

> The Lord has mercifully visited the people of Beckwith with an outpouring of His Holy Spirit... We arrived there on Wednesday evening, and remained about twelve days with them. We held a prayer-meeting that same evening; and also kept meetings on Friday and Saturday evenings, at which time some interest began to be manifested among the people.
>
> On Sabbath the people gathered out well to hear — many having come ten miles to hear the Gospel preached, and some sixteen. They listened with profound attention, and some were even considerably affected. We continued public service every evening in some place or other

Plate 92
The James Ferguson farmhouse, lot 22, concession 5, Beckwith, as photographed in June 1983. This house, built in 1849 in the centre of the farm, was unusual in having the kitchen and woodshed wing extended to one side of the main structure rather than behind it. The large windows and detail of the transom above the front door reveal the growing ambition of the Perthshire highlanders by the late 1840s, although the upstairs bedroom windows remained small. The Georgian panelling of the door (opposite) reflects the slow adjustment of Beckwith to new designs.

of the settlement till the next Sabbath. When released from public engagements we were employed in private instruction or in visiting from house to house.

Toward the end of the twelve days it was evident how profoundly the Baptists of Beckwith had been reawakened. McPhail continued:

Our meetings were protracted to a very late hour; and sometimes it would be two or three o'clock in the morning before the people would retire. As often as we would pronounce the benediction, some of them would sit down, unwilling to depart.
    The last Sabbath we were in Beckwith will long be remembered. Early in the morning we heard a number relate their experience, and then proceeded to public worship. We had a crowded and an attentive audience, and many were deeply affected. Towards the evening we had a baptism in the Lake Mississippi. As soon as we could get in order we commenced public service again. We both addressed the people that night, and after we had done a number remained and spent the night till daylight in religious exercises.

The visit of Fyfe and McPhail spurred the four or five members at Carlton Place to build a chapel, and John McEwen of Beckwith led the congregation in the absence of clergy.[122] The Reverend Lawrence Halcroft, newly arrived from Scotland, was ordained Baptist pastor in April 1843 to serve the congregations at Carlton Place and on the town line between Beckwith and Drummond.[123]

Despite the strength of the Beckwith congregation being imperilled by the removal of Drummond members to found a new congregation at Perth,[124] Halcroft stayed on as clergyman at Carlton Place until 1856.[125] Halcroft shrugged off accusations made in September 1848 by a runaway slave lecturing on slavery that he in particular and Baptists in general sanctioned slavery.[126] In 1852 there were 143 Baptists in Beckwith.

During the 1840s the visits of the Reverend William Bell to Beckwith became less frequent, as the Baptist, Cameronian, Free Church Presbyterian and Church of Scotland congregations vied for the membership of Scottish-origin inhabitants. Despite disagreement between Baptists and Presbyterians over whether or not infants should be baptised,[127] these four denominations were similar in that they shared a largely Scottish-origin membership, and within their patriarchal structure individuals, women as much as men, participated in promoting and welding a moral structure that served their social welfare. Up until the Free Church disruption in Scotland reverberated in the Beckwith congregation in the mid 1840s, local Presbyterians including those who claimed to be Secessionists were content with the strong link between church and state that had underlain the ministries of Bell, Buchanan and Smith. William Bell in an 1828 address to Lieutenant-Governor Sir John Colborne opined, "Warmly attached as we are to the person and Government of our beloved Sovereign, we regard every arrangement he makes for our happiness, as a further proof of his paternal care."[128] Bell certainly had the patriarchal mentality. While breakfasting with his son John's family at Carlton Place in February 1832 he "saw some symptoms of carelessness, extravagance, and silly vanity, which [he] did not like; and threw out a few hints on the subject. After breakfast, [they] had worship, and [Bell] admonished the family never to neglect that duty."[129] Ten years later, alarmed at the drunken sprees of his son William, Bell commanded all his children to never again use intoxicating drinks as a common beverage, nor to offer them to others, "to enjoin the same upon your children" and forbade them "to make intermarriages, in all time coming, with any who refuse to join with them in following this example."[130]

Bell's daughter, Isabella, without waiting to consult her brothers at Carlton Place, promptly marched over to her father's house and bluntly refused to obey his commands "and much less would she enjoin them on her children.... She also said that she had as good a right to exercise liberty of conscience as he had and he was not justified in calling down the vengeance of Heaven, if she refused to obey."[131] This spirited response and the fear of drunkenness which prompted Bell's patriarchal edict in the first place reveal the healthy tension between the wish for societal order and individual freedom of expression that underlay the Scottish Presbyterian and Baptist congregations and their respective development in Beckwith. The Scottish Presbyterians of Beckwith as well as in the rest of the Bathurst District assumed that moral purity or lack of the same affected the prosperity and the quality of local society. Hence, when a Scottish Presbyterian in late 1849 offered as "a proof of the supreme intelligence and good moral character of the inhabitants of the Bathurst District their...[being] a Church-going people and ha[ving] temperance societies, and more circulating libraries than an[y] other District,"[132] he implied that moral virtue combined with political Reform caused Providence to smile on the Scottish settlements of the district.

The Reverend William Bell by the 1850s was not so sure about the moral and political perfection of the Bathurst District. By now in his seventies and rarely visiting Beckwith, Bell pondered the thievish propensities of youths robbing gardens and orchards in Perth,[133] the sad want of family government he witnessed around him,[134] Sabbath desecration,[135] and he lamented the lack of momentum in the temperance movement.[136] Still believing he was part of an age of progress, despite what he saw around him in Perth, Bell in 1851 was attempting to establish a Peace Society in hope of abolishing war.[137] The peace society never came to be, but Bell's memory remained prominent in Beckwith with the election of his son Robert of Carlton Place as a member of the Canadian legislative assembly from 1848 to 1864. The Scottish highlanders of Beckwith had divided into four denominations during the forty years that intervened between Bell's arrival in 1817 and his death in 1857, but at midcentury they remained firmly

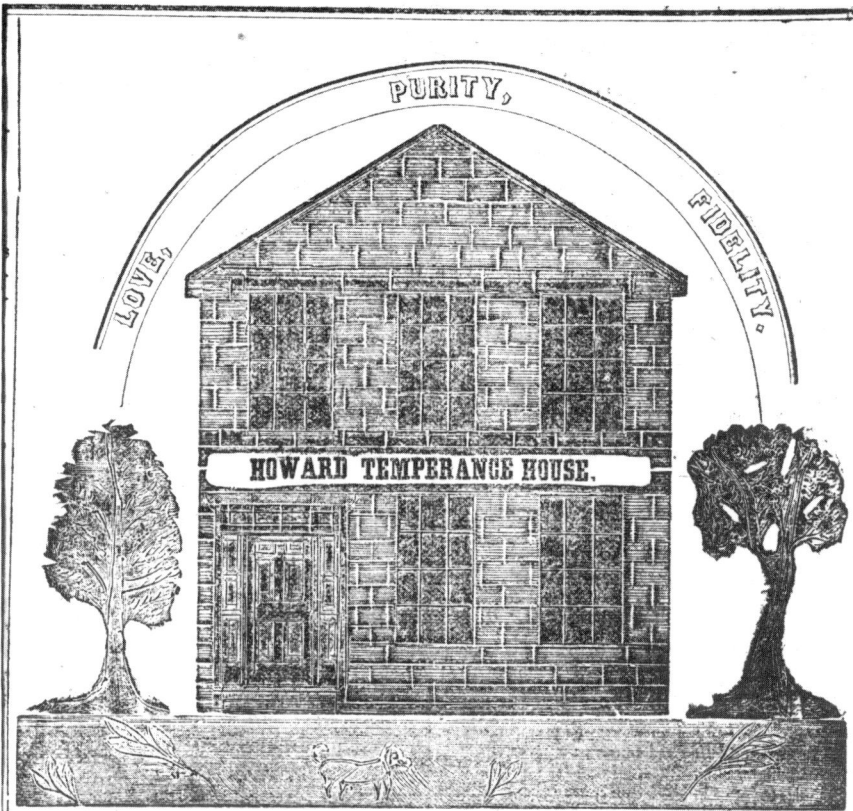

Plate 93
Woodcut of the Howard temperance hotel at Perth as printed in the Bathurst Courier *in 1852. From the mid 1830s to the early 1850s Malcolm Cameron, the mercurial Scottish Reform member for Lanark County zealously promoted temperance among the pro-Reform lowlanders in the county, particularly in the northern townships. The strong links of local Orange lodges with inns and taverns serving liquor made temperance hotels a refuge for lowlander Reformers, as a strong link grew between political Reform and the hoped-for social reform to be brought about by the temperance movement. National Library of Canada negative no. NL-16174.*

aware of their common Scottish origin which in some ways continued to keep them distinct from the Irish community alongside of whom they coexisted. In their strong denominational divisions the Presbyterians of Beckwith were largely the creation of the Reverend William Bell.

Endnotes

1. Nelson Dumbedykes [pseudonym for Dugald Campbell McNab], *The Annals of Trumpington* (Boston: 1854)
2. OKQAR Rev. William Bell Journals II:49-50.
3. Isabel Skelton, *A Man Austere: William Bell, Parson and Pioneer* (Toronto: The Ryerson Press, 1947), pp. 9-10.
4. H.J. Bridgman, "William Bell" in Francess G. Halpenny, ed., *Dictionary of Canadian Biography* (Toronto: University of Toronto Press, 1985) VIII:76.
5. Marjory Whitelaw, *The Dalhousie Journals* (Ottawa: Oberon Press, 1981) II:47.
6. Bridgman, "William Bell," p. 77.
7. OKQAR Bell Journals II:88.
8. Ibid., p. 107.
9. Ibid., p. 109.
10. Ibid., p. 108.
11. Jessie Buchanan Campbell, *The Pioneer Pastor*, pp. 19-20.
12. Ibid., pp. 10-11.
13. Ibid., p. 33.
14. Ibid., pp. 34-35.
15. OKQAR Rev. William Bell Journals II:123.
16. Campbell, *The Pioneer Pastor*, p. 36.
17. OTAR RG 1 Series C-IV MS 658 Crown Lands Department, Township Papers, Beckwith Township, Reel 30, p. 449.
18. OKQAR Rev. William Bell Journals II:126.
19. Ibid. II:140.
20. Ibid. II:161.
21. Ibid. II:159.
22. Ibid. IV:82.
23. Ibid. V:6.
24. Ibid. VI:32.
25. Ibid. VII:113.
26. Ibid. IV:152.
27. Ibid. V:113.
28. Ibid. V:169.
29. Ibid. VII:12.
30. Ibid. VII:140.
31. Ibid. VIII:43.
32. Ibid. VII:12.
33. Ibid. V:94.
34. Ibid. VII:66.
35. Ibid. VIII:94.
36. Ibid. VIII:112.
37. Ibid. VIII:112-113.
38. Ibid. VII:113.
39. NAC RG 5, A1 Reel C-6866 Upper Canada Sundries, vol. 91, pp. 50716-50717.
40. *Brockville Recorder*, 19 January 1830, p. 2, cols. 2-3.
41. Glasgow Colonial Society minutebook, 19 January 1832 entry. 28 September 1831 letter from unnamed Beckwith Presbyterian to Mr. Wilson, Glasgow, cited in Mabel Ringereide, *The Flourishing Tree* (Ottawa: Heritage House Publishers Ltd., 1979), pp. 38-39.
42. OKQAR Rev. William Bell Journals VIII:14.
43. Ibid. VIII:44.
44. Ibid. VIII:173.
45. Ibid. X:140.
46. Ibid. VIII:163.
47. NAC RG 5, A1 Reel C-6874 Upper Canada Sundries, vol. 114, pp. 63657-63658.
48. Glasgow Colonial Society III:141, 22 November 1832 letter from the Reverend Thomas Wilson, Perth, to Glasgow Colonial Society, cited in Ringereide, *Flourishing Tree*, p. 39.
49. Ibid. V:8, pp. 41-42.
50. Campbell, *Pioneer Pastor*, p. 41.
51. NAC RG 5, A1 Reel C-6886 Upper Canada Sundries, vol. 154, p. 84656.
52. Glasgow Colonial Society III V:28, April 1834 letter from the Reverend John Smith, Beckwith, to Archibald Young, Glasgow Colonial Society, cited in Ringereide, *Flourishing Tree*, pp. 66-67.
53. Ringereide, *Flourishing Tree*, pp. 60, 65-66.
54. *Brockville Recorder*, 15 November 1833, p. 3, col. 2.
55. Glasgow Colonial Society V:28, April 1834 letter from the Rev. John Smith, Beckwith, to Archibald Young, cited in Ringereide, *Flourishing Tree*, p. 66.
56. Ibid., pp. 65-66.
57. OKQAR Rev. William Bell Journals IX:73.
58. NAC RG 5, A1 Reel C-6881 Upper Canada Sundries, vol. 136, p. 74700.
59. OKQAR Rev. William Bell Journals X:25.
60. Ibid., p. 27.
61. Ibid., p. 49.
62. *Bathurst Courier*, 18 September 1835, p. 4, col. 1.
63. OKQAR Rev. William Bell Journals X:69-70.
64. Ibid. V:96; VI:32-33; VIII:66.
65. Skelton, *A Man Austere*, p. 326.
66. OKQAR Rev. William Bell Journals VII:66-67.
67. Skelton, *A Man Austere*, pp. 152-153.
68. OKQAR Rev. William Bell Journals X:124.
69. Ibid. VII:141.
70. Ibid. VIII:44.
71. Ibid. VIII:69-70.
72. Ibid. VIII:173.
73. *Carleton Place Herald*, 19 November 1862, p. 2, col. 4.
74. OKQAR Rev. William Bell Journals X:74.
75. Ibid. X:49.
76. OTAR MS 123 Minutes of the Kirk Session of the

Presbyterian Church, Beckwith Township, 1834-1889, p. 15.
77 Ibid., p. 12.
78 April 1834 letter from the Rev. John Smith, Beckwith, to Archibald Young, Glasgow Colonial Society, cited in Ringereide, *Flourishing Tree*, pp. 68-69.
79 George Edward Kidd, *The Story of the Derry* (Vancouver: by the author, 1943), p. 21.
80 Smith to Young, cited in Ringereide, pp. 66-67.
81 OTAR MS 123 Beckwith Kirk Session Minutes, 1834-1889, pp. 11-45.
82 Ibid., p. 21.
83 Ibid., p. 18.
84 Ibid., p. 24.
85 Ibid., p. 28.
86 Ibid., p. 44.
87 Ibid., p. 47.
88 Ibid., p. 15.
89 OKQAR Rev. William Bell Journals XI:47.
90 Campbell, *Pioneer Pastor*, p. 42.
91 OTAR MS 123 Beckwith Kirk Session Minutes, 1834-1889, p. 19.
92 OKQAR Rev. William Bell Journals XII:158.
93 Ringereide, *Flourishing Tree*, p. 101.
94 OKQAR Rev. William Bell Journals XII:157. Mabel Ringereide in her book about the stone house built by Smith cites the notebook of the Rev. James Croil who when making a survey of the Presbyterian Churches in Canada in 1867, wrote that the Beckwith Manse was built of stone in 1834. Croil evidently was not sure of the accuracy of this date, for he did not enter it in his published work. As documents cited on pages 69 and 70 of Ringereide, *The Flourishing Tree*, reveal, Smith could not possibly have afforded to begin building the stone house in 1834. When Bell visited Smith in June 1839, it is noteworth that "After dinner" they walked over to "his new manse," implying that it was not sufficiently finished to yet live in. Clearly, Smith built the house in 1839 for his bride.
95 OKQAR Rev. William Bell Journals XII:119-121.
96 Ibid., pp. 121-123.
97 OTAR MS 123 Beckwith Kirk Session Minutes, 1834-1889, p. 53.
98 *Bathurst Courier*, 22 June 1847, pp. 2-3, cols. 7-1.
99 Ibid., 23 May 1851, p. 2, col. 7.
100 OTAR MS 123 Beckwith Kirk Session Minutes, 1834-1889, p. 33.
101 Donald Macleod, *Memoir of Norman Macleod, D.D.* (Toronto: Belford Brother, 1876), p. 160.
102 Robert Burns, *Life and Times of the Rev. R. Burns, D.D., Toronto* (Toronto: James Campbell and Son, 1871), p. 294.
103 Ibid.
104 United Church of Canada Archives, Toronto (hereafter OTCC) Knox Free Presbyterian Church, Black's Corners, Session minutebook 1844-*1922*, pp. 8-9.
105 NAC RG 5, A1 Reel C-6883 Upper Canada Sundries, vol. 144, pp. 78947-78948.
106 OTCC Knox Free Presbyterian Session minutebook, 1844-18, pp. 11-12.
107 Ibid., pp. 9-10.
108 *Bathurst Courier*, 12 February 1850, p. 3, col. 1.
109 *Brockville Recorder*, 12 August 1847, p. 2, col.5.
110 *Bathurst Courier*, 29 March 1850, p. 2, col. 4.
111 OTCC Knox Free Presbyterian Session minutebook, 1844-18 , p. 25.
112 Ibid., p. 26.
113 William Gregg, *History of the Presbyterian Church in the Dominion of Canada* (Toronto: Presbyterian Printing and Publishing Company, 1885), p. 557.
114 R. More, "First Carleton Place Church Built in 1840" in the *Carleton Place Canadian*, 18 November 1965, p. 1.
115 Gregg, *Presbyterian Church*, p. 349.
116 Ibid., p. 557.
117 More, "First Carleton Place Church," p. 1.
118 Gregg, *Presbyterian Church*, pp. 557-558.
119 A vistor to Carleton Place in April 1841 stated "There are three Churches in Carlton Place — one Episcopal, (new), Presbyterian, and a Methodist church," in the *Bathurst Courier*, 23 April 1841, p. 3, col. 2.
120 More, "First Carleton Place Church," p. 1
121 J. E. Wells *The Life and Labors of Rev. R.A. Fyfe, D.D.*, (Toronto W. J. Gageand Company, 1885), p. 82.
122 T. Luckens, "Circular Letter: History of the Churches in our Association" in Canada Central Association of Regular Baptist Churches, *Minutes of the Fiftieth Annual Meeting* (Ottawa, Canada Central Association of Regular Baptist Churches, 1879), p. 14.
123 *Carleton Place Central Canadian*, 30 April 1925.
124 Wells, *Rev. K.A. Fyfe*, pp. 94-95.
125 Luckens, "Circular Letter," p. 14.
126 *Bathurst Courier*, 29 September 1848, p. 2, col. 6; and 6 October 1848, p. 2, cols. 6-7.
127 OKQAR Rev. William Bell Journals IV:122.
128 NAC RG 5, A1 Reel C-6866 Upper Canada Sundries, vol. 92, pp. 50881-50882.
129 Ibid. VIII:70.
130 OTAR MU 842 Judge John Glass Malloch Diary, 1841-1845, p. 51.
131 Ibid., p. 52.
132 *Bathurst Courier*, 9 November 1849, p. 2, col. 5.
133 Ibid., 19 August 1853, p. 2, col. 6.
134 Ibid., 22 September 1854, p. 2, cols. 5-6.
135 Ibid., 11 July 1856, p. 2, cols. 6-7.
136 Ibid., 26 march 1852, p.2, col. 7.
137 Ibid., 31 October 1851, p. 2, cols. 6-7; 7 November 1851, p. 2, col. 6; 14 November 1851, p. 2, cols. 6-7; 21 November 1851, p. 2, cols. 6-7; and 28 November 1851, p. 2, cols. 6–7.

THE ORANGE ANGLICAN POLITY

In the early 1830s the Irish inhabitants of Beckwith suddenly found themselves part of a much larger regional concentration of Irish immigrants. By 1851 the Irish were the largest immigrant group in Lanark County as well as in the adjacent counties of Carleton, Grenville, Leeds and Renfrew. Some 54 percent of the combined population of these five counties was of Irish ethnic origin according to the 1871 census.[1] Even in Lanark County which traditionally thought of itself as predominantly Scottish, two-thirds of the fifteen municipalities in 1852 had more Irish than Scottish inhabitants.[2] Most of the Irish families in Beckwith itself had arrived by the late 1820s. They along with the Wexford settlers in the Brockville vicinity acted as a magnet for the tide of southeastern Irish Protestants fleeing Ireland in the early 1830s following the passing of the Catholic emancipation Act of 1829. With the newly-opened Rideau Canal comprising the major route for transporting immigrants westward, many Irish immigrants left the boats and settled on the empty lands in the townships along the Rideau. By the late 1840s, with these townships full, Irish Catholics fleeing the Famine in Ireland found land in inland Renfrew County, but some of them were attracted to labouring and trades positions in villages such as Carlton Place, joining relatives who had earlier arrived as Peter Robinson settlers or as labourers on the Rideau Canal. The Irish in Beckwith were largely Protestant, with two-thirds of them members of the United Church of England and Ireland, sixteen percent Methodist, and seventeen percent being Roman Catholics. In some respects the Irish Protestants of Beckwith were reactionary in mindset, but comprising as they did a preponderant part of the regional population and enjoying privileges and special links with government, they proved less politically and religiously strident than many of their Scottish Presbyterian neighbours. Although by the late 1840s the links between Irish Anglicans and Methodists were beginning to weaken, the Orange lodge ultimately offered Beckwith Irish Protestants a means of retaining ethnic and cultural ties.

By the mid 1820s, as Daniel O'Connell mobilised the Roman Catholics of Ireland toward achieving political goals and as the British House of Commons rocked with debate over granting Catholic emancipation, Beckwith inhabitants read of the increasingly disturbed state of Ireland. The Montreal *Gazette* published a private letter in 1825 which stated: "A universal opinion prevails here, that a crisis is at hand. Go into company of any rank, high or low — of any party, Protestant or Catholic — and you will find a more intense political feeling, and more violent party animosity, than existed even in the year 1798."[3] With the passing of the Catholic emancipation Act in 1829, there was an immediate exodus of Irish Protestants from Ireland to colonies on the other side of the Atlantic. The numbers of Irish immigrants entering British North America jumped from an average of 10,000 per year in the late 1820s to an average of 37,000 in the early 1830s.[4] This surging exodus after 1829 betrayed a widespread fear among the Protestants of southeastern Ireland about the Roman Catholic majority around them gaining civil and religious recognition from government, a paranoia that sprang from ongoing tumult since before the turn of the century. With Catholics both in a majority and suddenly enjoying political power, the Protestants of the Carlow and Wexford region perceived they had no future in Ireland, and feared inevitable bloodshed. The editor of the Brockville *Gazette* in November 1831 reported, "by private letters, we learn that the emigration of Protestant families

Plate 94
Banner of Loyal Orange Lodge no. 48 at Carleton Place. This banner dating from the 1830s presents the Beckwith Irish Anglican perspective of their migration from southeastern Ireland to Upper Canada in the imagery of the Old Testament books of Exodus and Joshua. The centre image hearkens back to the defeat of James II by William of Orange when Protestant apprentices closed the city gates of Derry against the Earl of Antrim and his Catholic regiment. The Biblical images and symbols combine to suggest the sense of deliverance at having escaped the potential religious and political bondage and violence in the Egypt of emancipated Catholic Ireland to pitch their tents in the Canaan of Upper Canada. The confidence of Irish Anglicans in taking over regional society (symbolised by the seven priests blowing trumpets to bring down the walls of Jericho) did not permit them to forget their recent exile from a once-privileged position in Ireland (symbolised by Joseph's coffin). Loaned courtesy of Loyal Orange Lodge no. 48, Carleton Place through Eldon Henderson.

during the next year will be immense, as every person who can possibly dispose of his property for any thing like the value, hurries to do it, in order to escape the horrors of a war, which eventually must come, and which nothing can now avert."[5]

For Protestants of the Wexford, Kilkenny and Carlow region of southeastern Ireland the memory of the violence and atrocities committed by Catholic peasants led on by priests during the 1798 rebellion was still warm and inspired them with no confidence that they and their children would fare well at the political mercy of the Catholics by whom they were so hopelessly outnumbered. Prolonged agrarian violence during the 1820s by Catholic peasants aimed at the Protestant minority further confirmed the paranoia of the Irish Protestants who immigrated to Upper Canada, and by the time they arrived in the Beckwith region they had a reactionary perception of themselves as reluctant and tragic loyalist exiles hounded out of Ireland. They were attracted to eastern Upper Canada by the positive reports they received from relatives already settled in Beckwith and near Brockville. Thomas Graham posted a letter from the vicinity of Brockville in June 1827 describing the bounty of local agriculture to his mother back in Wexford:[6]

> With regard to the country, it is, in my opinion, a great deal better than Ireland. The land in general is very good, and not as hard to be cleared as you may think. I have seen as good corn and meadowing as ever I saw in Ireland; and mountains of dung not made any use of. Every stone you would see is limestone. And there is plenty of marl — and none made use of. They can plant potatoes, and have them excellent for table in seven weeks. — Barley in like manner. The apples, plums, cherries, gooseberries, currants, and grapes of all kinds, grow naturally in the woods.... Tradesmen of all descriptions ought to come here: a blacksmith, if he is able to work on his own account, can earn from 6 to 8 dollars a-day; otherwise a dollar a-day. Joiners, tailors, and shoemakers, 7s. 6d. a-day. Samuel Hendrick and his family are doing well; he has 200 acres of good land, and twenty of it cleared. He has 8 acres of wheat (and better I never saw) and 2 acres of potatoes, and kitchen vegetables, &c.

In a second letter to his mother a year later, Graham stressed how much more opportunity was available in Upper Canada in contrast with what he had left in the vicinity of Enniscorthy:[7]

> My master is a sober religious man, and he takes great pains to instruct me in my duty to God, as well as my trade; so I hope it was the Lord who put courage into my heart to leave Ireland. With respect to diet, it is always good here; no difference in this respect from one end of the year to the other.... Men must labour very hard here: but they are well fed and well paid; and what a man has is his own: there is no landlord or tyrant to reign over them. Men who came here some years ago, have large clearances now, and are taking their ease. The chief objection folks have to this country, is the want of pleasures, but these are vanities. This country answers well for young men, or men with grown up families; by industry they will have peace and plenty.... I am making great way in my trade, and if God spares me, I hope to do better than ever you could provide for me in Ireland. I am sorry that poor Sam settled himself there, for this is a better country for industrious people. Land is getting pretty dear here in the settled parts, but yet there is room, and many chances of which there are none in Ireland.... Dear Mother, I would be glad to see you all coming here, where you could nourish yourselves with the fruits of your labour: but choose for yourselves. If I was as Joshua and Sam, and knowing as much of this country as I do, I would sell out all, and stay no longer labouring under the heavy yoke. With a little money and my industry I could possess more property here in three or four years than I could ever have in Ireland, and I could call it my *own*.

Thomas Graham in his two letters betrayed the confidence characteristic of so many

Plate 95
Orange parade at Anderson's grove near Franktown in 1914. Orange processions became an annual sight in Beckwith from the early 1840s on as an overt protest by Irish Anglicans against legislation of the provincial Reform administration depriving them of the right to assemble in public and hold Orange processions. This scene of men, women and children marching along the dusty roads of Beckwith sporting scarlet sashes had become a familiar one during the previous seventy years, save for the addition of Scottish Presbyterians to their ranks such as Robert Ferguson shown here playing the fife. Orangeism gained pan-Protestant popularity from 1860 on. Photograph courtesy of Edna and John Porter.

southeastern Irish Protestants who settled in eastern Upper Canada in the 1830s. They believed they could pursue agriculture aggressively and do as well at it if not much better than the American-origin settlers around them who did not so much as trouble themselves to manure the soil. In Beckwith before mid-century the Wexford Irish Protestants noticed a similar unprogressive tendency among the highlanders not to manure their soil, if the ten-year accumulation of dung outside the house of the Reverend George Buchanan which assailed the nostrils of the Reverend William Bell in 1831 is any indication.[8]

The Irish in Beckwith related very well to the Scottish highlanders with whom they shared the township, even attending church services held by Bell and Buchanan alongside their Presbyterian neighbours before a United Church of England and Ireland clergyman was settled in Beckwith. Indeed, Irish Anglican James Wall offered the use of his new shanty to the Buchanan family when they arrived in 1822:[9] the Anglican rector at Franktown, the Reverend Jonathan Shortt, "was tireless in his kind ministrations" to Buchanan on his deathbed in 1833,[10] and conducted the funeral service in the Buchanan home.[11] As for the highlanders, they were jealous of the links with government that gave the Irish Anglicans of Beckwith a stone church and a resident clergyman at no cost at all. In November 1836 some 121 members of the Beckwith Church of Scotland congregation sent a petition to lieutenant-governor Sir Francis Bond Head. They pointed out that "as Members of the Established Church of Scotland in this British Colony" the treaty of union between England and Scotland gave them a claim to share "all Rights[,] Privileges and Advantages equally with Members of the Church of England."[12]

The Act by which Rectories have been Instituted and Endowed in this Province, according to

> the Establishment of the Church of England [the Beckwith Church of Scotland petitioners] conceive[d] to be an Infringement upon the claim in question, in as much, said Act places your Petitioners in the same relation to the Episcopal Body in this Province as Dissenters are in England, with regard to the Church of Scotland there.

The major grievance mentioned in the Church of Scotland petition was that the Act establishing the Anglican rectories invested the clergymen of the United Church of England and Ireland alone "with Power, which may be exercised in the way of Ecclesiastical Jurisdiction, which Your petitioners cannot conscientiously recognize." In other words, the Scottish highlanders of Beckwith considered themselves the equals of their Irish Anglican neighbours and demanded civil and religious recognition of the fact from the administration of Upper Canada.

While Irish Anglicans and Church of Scotland highlanders in Beckwith accepted one another as loyal British colonists, they did not flatter the American-origin settlers south of them in the St. Lawrence townships with holding any similar fealty to the British constitution. For the southeastern Irish Protestants of the region in particular, as they became a significant proportion of the population, the American settlers along the front seemed suspect; they reminded them of the United Irishmen at the time of the 1798 rebellion in their quest to remove the established church and to introduce republican institutions. It is significant that the petition of the Beckwith Church of Scotland members did not seek to remove privileges enjoyed by the United Church of England and Ireland, but rather to share them. A succession of newspapers issuing from under the hand of Orange editor and politician Ogle R. Gowan at Brockville worked to further excite the latent suspicion by Beckwith Irish Anglicans of their American-origin fellow-colonists. Despite becoming numerically important in the region during the 1830s and 1840s, the Irish remained overwhelmed by the psychological handicap of their past as a minority in southeastern Ireland and by the political handicap for the vast majority of them (the Irish in Beckwith and the other three military townships being significant exceptions) of not owning land and hence not being eligible to vote at elections.

Although most Irish inhabitants of Beckwith owned land by 1830, their mistrust of American settlers sprang from a variety of sources. The hundred acre grants they received in Beckwith paled in comparison with much larger grants given the Loyalists and late Loyalists, as shown by the thousands of empty and unclaimed lots in the two dozen townships along the Rideau waterway largely owned by American-origin settlers along the front. The Americans were settled on the finer tracts of land whereas the Irish were often located on less desirable lots. Those inhabitants of the St. Lawrence townships who were born in the United States appeared less than loyal to Beckwith Irish settlers due to the fuss they made during the late 1820s over having to pledge an oath of allegiance to the King. Furthermore, the quest by American-origin settlers to introduce republican institutions and to remove the privileges of the United Church of England and Ireland, appeared both disloyal and nothing less than an attack on Irish Anglicans. When the Irish of Beckwith read that Attorney General Henry John Boulton made anti-Irish remarks, they sent letters of protest to the Brockville *Antidote* in February 1833.[13] The nearest concentration of American-origin settlers was at Smith's Falls and in April 1833 a correspondent of the *Antidote* there reported that "Party spirit rages here to a great height...amongst Old Country people, Yankees and [French] Canadians." The old country people or British immigrants were not "inhabitants of Smith's Falls but [rather] the 'No Surrender Boys'...of Montagu[e] and Beckwith".[14] Beckwith Irish Anglicans were motivated to organise Orange lodges in the early 1830s as a form of collective protection for sons and daughters either renting or squatting on land owned by absentee American settlers in townships along the Rideau. The Orange lodges served to reassure them in the face of rumours that absentee landowners could coerce tenants to vote as they directed at elections.[15]

In their mistrust of American settlers and by their formation of Orange lodges, the Irish Anglicans of Beckwith revealed how weighted down they remained with the cultural baggage they

Plate 96
The James Rathwell house on lot 21, concession 1, Beckwith, as photographed in June 1983. The pervasive swamp on this lot discouraged settlement on it until the close of the nineteenth century when this modest log house was built. Irish-origin farmers on lots with a thin layer of forest mould soil could survive for a couple of generations until the soil was depleted. On swamp lots such as this, however, no crops could be grown and there was scarcely sufficient timber to build a house let alone provide marketable timber for sale.

had brought with them. In Ireland they had formed Orange lodges in response to the secret societies used by the Catholic peasant majority around them, and in eastern Upper Canada the Orange lodge offered mutual reassurance against being overwhelmed by the American-origin population and its republican notions. The failure of the attempted rebellion in 1837 and of the abortive invasion near Prescott in 1838 was heartening. Irish Anglicans and Catholics alike glowed with pride at the appraisal of their loyalty made by Chief Justice Sir John Beverley Robinson as printed in the Brockville *Statesman* and in the Perth *Bathurst Courier*:[16]

> I think it was universally felt throughout the Province that the conduct of the Irish, as a body, was pre-eminently good. They seemed not only to acknowledge promptly their obligations to support their government and laws, but they discharged their duty with an eager forwardness, and a fine hearty warmth of feeling, that it was really quite affecting to witness. Hundreds of these poor fellows came at the first summons, from remote settlements, in the depth of winter, half clothed, without other arms than hoes, pitchforks, axes or clubs; and...had to pass through the rich old settlements of the very persons who, under the influence of a feeling hardly to be credited or accounted for, had abandoned their homes and taken up arms against their Sovereign. These people [who rebelled] had lived in one of the very finest parts of Upper

Canada, and had enjoyed, for thirty years, the protection of good laws and a mild government; compared with the rugged wilderness these poor Irishmen came from, the land they inhabited is like the Garden of Eden: and to see these faithful emigrants pouring from the woods to support the government against the wicked attempts of the others was a spectacle really affecting.

Charges against American-origin settlers such as Daniel Shipman at Shipman's Mills (later Almonte) for being "actively employed sowing sedition"[17] and against Caleb S. Bellows at Carlton Place for hoisting an American flag on the fourth of July[18] only served to confirm Beckwith Irish Anglicans in their vigilance against American settlers and republican tendencies. Any unease they may have felt at the success Scottish Reform candidate Malcolm Cameron mustered among the radicalised lowlanders of northern Lanark beginning in the early 1840s was effectively offset in 1842 when Montague, North Elmsley and North Burgess were added to Lanark County, and the predominant Irish Anglican populations of which turned southern Lanark permanently into a Tory bastion.[19]

Irish Anglicans were the single largest denomination in Beckwith up until the last quarter of the nineteenth century, and enjoyed the benefits that came with being colonial members of the senior church linked with the British Crown. One of the earliest benefits was when the King's storehouse at Franktown was granted to Beckwith Anglicans as a place in which to worship when the Reverend Michael Harris from Perth came once a month to perform Divine Service. Harris had been educated at Trinity College, Dublin, was ordained to the diaconate in August 1819 and arrived at Perth early that autumn,[20] but there is no record to suggest that he held services in Beckwith before late 1822. Harris may have been impelled to visit Beckwith regularly to counteract the influence of a Presbyterian clergyman, the Reverend George Buchanan, who settled in Beckwith that August. Harris found the predominantly Irish congregation at Franktown congenial whereas he had "naturally given great offence to the Scotch congregation" to whom he ministered at Perth. Harris was sent to Perth by the Bishop of Quebec and his ministry was funded by the Society for the Propagation of the Gospel.

When Governor General Lord Dalhousie visited Perth in August 1820 he perceived Harris "an unwise appointment [as clergyman]...because the young man was only t[he] other day an Ensign in one of the Reg[imen]ts, that have formed this settlement, is known as such by almost everybody, & tho[ugh] perhaps a very good man, cannot be respected as a Clergyman".[21] The Reverend William Bell, the Presbyterian clergyman who lost his position and salary as schoolmaster at Perth to Harris, left an unflattering cameo of the soldier-turned-clergyman travelling out to Franktown in March 1824:[22]

> My neighbour Mr. Harris going to Beckwith one day this winter to preach[,] lost his sermon out of his pocket by the way. When he got there he told the people that he had lost his manuscript coming from Perth and consequently he could only read prayers! This intelligence caused many of the good folks in that neighbourhood to stare for they supposed that every minister could *preach* and therefore could be at no loss to make a sermon at any time. But what is still worse when this divine makes an excursion into the country in his sleigh he expects every one he meets to turn out of the road till he is past. If they do not show him this mark of submission he is said to swear at them very rudely; perhaps at the moment forgetting that he does not now wear a red coat, for he was once a soldier. The country folks however think a minister ought to set a better example before his people.

The Beckwith Anglican congregation requested the use of the King's storehouse in 1823, promising to finish off the interior for divine worship; but when the lieutenant-governor made a gift of the storehouse and the six acres on which it was located in 1826[23] together with the proceeds from

Plate 97
Detail from reverse side of banner of Loyal Orange Lodge no. 48, Carleton Place. The so-called 'No Surrender Boys' of southern Beckwith and northern Montague were actually groups of Irish Anglicans organised into Orange lodges in the early 1830s. They viewed the earlier-established American-origin settlers in the Smith's Falls and Merrickville vicinity as their political rivals and competitors for the same land they wished to acquire, particularly because most of northern Montague where Beckwith sons wanted to develop farms was largely owned by American settlers residing south of the Rideau River. Loaned courtesy of Loyal Orange Lodge no. 48, Carleton Place through Eldon Henderson.

selling the Perth lot on which the military settlement buildings were located,[24] the congregation decided instead to build a new church. Harris brought a contractor from Perth "to estimate the expense of repairing the Store in Beckwith, & fitting it up in a suitable manner for Divine Service". The contractor recommended that instead of spending seventy to eighty pounds on repairs to the storehouse, to "lay out whatever funds [they] could collect on a new building, as the money that would be expended on the old one would go far in putting up the walls &c. of a stone Church." Harris consulted with the Beckwith congregation in early April 1826; they enthusiastically offered "to put the whole of the Stone & Lime on the ground if His Excellency will permit the funds to be appropriated to that purpose, as they would much rather turn the old Store into a temporary Parsonage & to have a good Substantial place of Worship."[25] By November 1826 the congregation had stone and lime on the church site at Franktown "ready to commence operations in the Spring",[26] and in the spring of 1827 the construction of St. James Church began. Bishop Stewart at Quebec promised Harris "one hundred Pounds but we cannot touch that until the building is enclosed."[27]

Harris in an 1827 letter to Bishop Stewart argued the priority of having a resident clergyman placed among the concentrated Irish Anglican settlement in southern Beckwith over other locations in Upper Canada:[28]

> From letters I have received from York, I understand that Toronto and St. Catharines are to be opened immediately as mission stations. I should be sorry to remind His Lordship of his promise concerning Beckwith, but I must be allowed to say that, whatever claim both these places may have as to priority of settlement, still in point of church population I will not give in to them, both put together. Besides Beckwith is a station where it is not necessary to build up the church but to preserve that where it is already established.

Like Lieutenant-Governor Sir Peregrine Maitland who in 1826 recognised the "great importance of erecting a suitable place of Worship for the Congregation of the Church of England which is in the habit of assembling in…Beckwith, to the number of above 500 persons" by granting the Perth and Franktown properties to them,[29] Bishop Stewart yielded to Harris's entreaties. He appointed the Reverend Richard Harte in 1829, an ordained missionary of the Society for the Propagation of the Gospel from the diocese of Limerick as the first resident clergyman of the Rectory of Beckwith.[30] In an undated letter from Perth believed written in the late autumn of 1827, Michael Harris reported to Bishop Stewart that the Beckwith church was "completely inclosed, with the exception of the windows, which are now ready to be put in. They are being made at this place [Perth]. In the meantime we are going on with the inside. In consequence of the roads being bad we are not able to send the windows out."[31]

The Reverend Richard Harte had an extensive ministry at Franktown from 1829 to 1833. At the end of his first year in Beckwith Harte had the satisfaction of seeing Bishop Stewart from Quebec administer the rite of confirmation to 106 persons in the new church on 1 August 1830.[32] As a missionary, Harte travelled beyond the boundaries of Beckwith to other newer settlements. The Brockville *Antidote* reported that on the ninth day of January 1833 "the Rev. R. Hart[e] of Franktown, visited Smith[']s falls, preached to upwards of 150 people, married one couple, and baptized 15 children" and added, "We hope Murphy's Falls on the Mississippi, will be shortly looked after. It is a new settlement, principally members of the church, and well deserving encouragement and assistance."[33]

In a June 1833 report Harte summarised his four years of ministry in Beckwith. He stated that of the 323 heads of families in Beckwith, 150 belonged to the United Church of England and Ireland, 147 were Scotch Presbyterians and 26 were Roman Catholics. Of the approximately 750 Anglicans in Beckwith, Harte estimated that "a very few may be Methodists but they consider themselves members of the Church of England with only two or three exceptions." Harte stated that he held

Plate 98
Fireplace on the Richard Fleming farm, lot 15, concession 4, Beckwith, as photographed in 1981. The substantial stone fireplaces built onto the larger log houses of the 1830s and 1840s reflected the comfortable yet unpretentious lifestyle of the majority of inhabitants during these decades. With Irish Anglicans concentrated on the poorer land in southern Beckwith, their concern with the depleting soil on their farms was partly vented in the rhetorical protest of Orangeism. Local historian, Howard M. Brown, indicates the scale of this chimney.

services at the church in Franktown every Sunday morning at eleven o'clock with the[34]

> exception of about 12 Sundays in the year when I perform service [in a log building not yet finished] at Carlton Place in Beckwith — every Sunday evening at a Log Building put up for the purpose about 4 or five miles from Franktown towards Richmond [the site of Prospect. L]atterly I have gone once a month (Week days) to Smith's falls — and I have visited Packenham and Fitzroy once a year in [F]ebruary since I took charge of this mission.

The average number of persons attending services at Franktown varied from 150 to 250, from sixty to 120 at the Prospect log chapel, and 160 people attending at Carlton Place. The Franktown church with the aid of its balcony was capable of holding 250 to 300 persons, the Prospect log chapel 130 and the Carlton Place house of worship held about 150 people. The number of communicants at Franktown ranged from 35 to seventy and from thirty to forty at Carlton Place. The Franktown church was able to hold so many people because pews still had not been built by mid 1833, and neither was there a book of banns, nor linen cloths to cover either the communion table or the consecrated elements. There also was no baptismal font.

The austerity of the church interior at Franktown did not detract from its religious significance as a house of worship. It is impossible to ascertain what proportion of the ninety baptisms Harte performed in 1832 were held in Beckwith itself, but he was emphatic in stating that "the children are in allmost all instances brought to the church — very few indeed [are] baptized in Private Houses." Harte claimed never to "have omitted visiting the sick in a single instance when called on" and that whenever he heard of anyone being sick he went to their houses "without being sent for." As for preparing children for confirmation, Harte reported, "The children at the School in my immediate neighbourhood are regularly catechised on every Monday by the Master [James Kent] who is well qualified for that purpose. I frequently attend there myself — tho[ugh] perhaps not every Week[. T]here are about 25 in the School who attend."

Harte attempted to run a Sunday School before the church service at Franktown but found it "inconvenient for children to come at that Hour as they resided at a distance" and that the few who regularly came were chiefly girls from his immediate neighbourhood. He noted that some members of his congregation had Bibles and prayer books while others did not, and that in the church itself there was only "a small Prayer Book and a small bible — not the folio size generally in churches." Harte "at different times both in Conversation & in [his] discourses pointed out the propriety of the Congregation joining in the responses [from the Prayer Book] without effect." The burial ground down the road from the church had been fenced in although not consecrated, and in response to Bishop Stewart's question "are pigs or cattle admitted therein?" Harte responded with an answer that belied some weariness with the limitations of Beckwith, "No pigs — there may be a few sheep."

Harte's human flock in Beckwith did not allow him to take his leave of them in June 1833 for Ireland without expressing their own mixed emotions about the land from which so many of them had migrated. Church wardens James Hume and Robert Davis in the course of a congregational address reminded Harte that he was departing "for that country to which a very great majority of us owe our birth, and to which our affections shall ever cling with unalterable tenacity". They trusted that he would "experience that hospitality which is the national and distinguishing characteristic of Ireland" and that the sanctity of his office together with the suavity of his disposition would shield Harte "from the dangers which {Ireland's] agitated and distracted condition might present."[35] So numerous were the Irish Anglicans in the mission of Beckwith, that Bishop Stewart sent two clergymen to replaceRichard Harte. To Franktown he sent the Reverend Jonathan Shortt, a native of Jersey, who made no particular impression during his two year stay.[36] Carlton Place in November 1833 was made a separate mission under English-born Reverend Edward Jukes Boswell who

Plate 99
Detail from obverse side of banner of Loyal Orange Lodge no. 48, Carleton Place, showing priests carrying the ark of the covenant over the Jordan River. Beckwith Irish Protestants conceived of themselves as a chosen people comparable to the Israelites of the Old Testament. So strong was this notion that William H. Poole, the son of an Irish Methodist at Prospect, published a book entitled Anglo-Israel or The Saxon Race Proved to be the Lost Tribes of Israel *(1889) in which he alluded to the ongoing hostility of the native Celtic Irish as descendants of the Canaanites toward the Anglo-Irish as descendants of the Israelites. Ongoing violence in Ireland, according to Poole, resulted from the English failure to obey the Biblical injunction, "When you shall have passed over the Jordan enter into the land of Canaan, destroy all the inhabitants, break...in pieces their statutes, and lay waste all their high places, cleansing the land, and dwelling in it. For I [meaning God] have given it unto you." Implicitly, if Beckwith Irish Protestants were to enjoy more permanent residence in Upper Canada, the original inhabitants such as the Americans and French-Canadians at Smith's Falls would have to be eliminated. Loaned courtesy of Loyal Orange Lodge no. 48, Carleton Place, through Eldon Henderson.*

remained there until 1844.[37] Boswell in a January 1834 letter to the bishop was "most happy in being able to say that in no part of the Province, and I have been in many parts of it, have I found the Inhabitants more firmly attached to our Church than these among whom I have been now officiating for nearly three months."[38]

After three months in Beckwith, Boswell anticipated making Carlton Place the centre of a mission with an outlying congregation where Ramsay, Lanark and Drummond townships converged, another station in northeastern Lanark Township, and yet another congregation in Fitzroy and Pakenham. Carlton Place itself Boswell described as "a very neat growing Village situated very beautifully on the River Mississippi, about half a mile from its outlet from a Lake of the same name as the River's. This in running thro[ugh] the Village falls over a bed of rocks." When Boswell administered the sacrament of Communion on Christmas day in 1833 he was "pleasingly gratified at having thirty three communicants" and confidently predicted that there were two hundred people in the vicinity of Carlton Place "who will attend Divine Service when they have been used to its regular performance for a short time and have been visited and spoken to on the importance and necessity of it." The only drawback Boswell found to Carlton Place was that he[39]

> had no room in which to officiate except the Methodist Meeting house and the School house. To the using the first there are...several strong objections. The latter is frequently occupied by Preachers of various denominations. The people have determined to build a Church and I have been desired to solicit Your Lordship's aid towards the effecting their intention. The Congregation is very poor, but they have contributed much more than I at all anticipated. It is our wish to build a Church which will hold comfortably four hundred persons — the building to be of stone — which is the least costly material in this part of the country.

Significantly, Boswell explained that he had "persuaded the Congregation to have no pews" in their projected new church in order that "strangers & dissenters will more readily attend at Church where the seats are free than where there are pews." In other words, while Boswell was unwilling to appear dependent on Methodist generosity by using their chapel, he hoped to entice some of them back into the Church of England.

At the same time Boswell requested a grant of £100 from Bishop Stewart, Caton Willis, William Morphy and Manny Nowlan as trustees for the nascent congregation at Carlton Place petitioned Lieutenant-Governor Colborne for funds to assist a congregation which "altho[ugh] numerous is composed of persons by no means wealthy but on the contrary poor." They took "the further liberty" of reminding his Excellency that "the Inhabitants of this part of the Country are principally those who were settled here by Government some years ago — since which time they have been almost without hearing the Service of their Church. Attached to it by every tie...they [were] most anxious to have a building in which a clergyman can officiate comfortably and decently."[40] Neither the bishop nor the lieutenant-governor provided financial assistance, but despite this by early April 1834 the Carlton Place congregation "entered into a contract for the erection of a Frame Church — to be finished, as regards the whole of the Carpenters['] work before the first of September." The dimensions of the new church were 64 by 32 feet, with a gallery inside and a tower forty feet in height. Whenever Boswell called upon members of the congregation "to come out to work upon the Church themselves [with] their horses and oxen, they have most cheerfully attended". This prompted him to reiterate "there is no Congregation in the Province, more, if so attached to our Church, or so ready, according to, and even beyond their ability to do any thing, that as Members of the church they may be called upon to do."[41]

Boswell's praise of the Carlton Place congregation and his optimism about its growth were justified. Within less than six months of arriving he reported:[42]

> On Easter Sunday I administered the Sacrament, when there were Sixty Communicants belonging to the Congregation at this place. On the following Thursday I administered the Lord's Supper to an infirm old Woman at her own house, at which time there came forward three other females who were unable to come to Church — being obliged by their young families to remain at home, while their husbands attended, but who took this opportunity of shewing forth their belief in their Lord's death. Of this Congregation no one lived more than five miles from the village and the great majority, not more than two. Taking into account those who came forward on Christmas but not on Easter day I have administered the Sacrament to about eighty Communicants — and I have no doubt that at the next administration of it the number will be

Plate 100
St. James United Church of England and Ireland, Franktown, built in 1827, as photographed ca. 1895 after the original spire and neoclassic pediment were removed from the tower. This photograph was taken before the harl covering the stone walls was removed and before a belfry with pointed arches was placed atop the tower. Much later a stone bearing the erroneous date of 1822 was placed above the front door. Funds to build this church came from the sale of government property at Perth, revealing the continuing strong link with government to which Beckwith Irish Anglicans were accustomed in Ireland. Photograph courtesy of the late Stanley and Marguerite Hughton.

greatly increased.... The congregation on Easter Sunday was upwards of three hundred, and with few exceptions all of the persons, who composed it, belong to the Church.

When Bishop Stewart from Quebec visited St. James Church at Carlton Place on 24 August 1834 he confirmed 97 persons and promised a donation of fifty pounds from the Society for the Propagation of the Gospel to assist in completing the church. The bishop commented, "In some places such a gift is particularly well deserved, and profitably bestowed, and this is one of them."[43]

The Irish Anglican congregation at Franktown was temporarily weakened by the loss of parishioners in northern Beckwith to the new mission at Carlton Place. The movement of younger brothers, sons and their families to adjacent northern Montague together with the creation and endowment of the Rectory of Beckwith with public lands in January 1836 combined to offset the loss in parishioners. The Reverend Jonathan Shortt appears not to have been an impressive rector, for when in October 1837 the congregation at Franktown feared it was losing Clergy Reserve lot nine in the third concession as the glebe lot on which to build a new rectory, they turned to the Reverend

Michael Harris to plead with the Crown Lands office to secure it for them. Harris wrote government officials in October 1837, arguing that the two lots with which they intended to endow the Rectory of Beckwith were[44]

> of a very inferior quality [and] were selected to the serious injury not only [of] the Minister but [of] the Parish in general, as they are situated in a complete Swamp many miles from the Church, whereas the one I recommended [many years ago] was only a very short distance from it, not exceeding a mile and on which the Parishioners contemplated their Parsonage house. They have now made arrangements for that purpose, having subscribed largely toward the erection of it.

The congregation did not obtain full title to lot nine in the third concession until 1853, but the sale of the old oak King's storehouse which had served as a rectory in 1837 effectively shows that the stone rectory listed in the 1852 census as being inhabited by the Reverend James Padfield was built in the late 1830s.

Padfield, who was rector at Franktown from 1838 to 1852 deserves particular mention. Originally an English Methodist, he arrived in Canada in the early 1820s, taught at Upper Canada College in York (later Toronto), and in the mid 1820s became master of the Johnstown district grammar school at Brockville.[45] The Loyalist and Anglican trustees by July 1827 were dissatisfied with Padfield[46]

> because he represented himself upon his application for the appointment as being attached to the Church of England and desirous of breaking off the connexion... between himself and the Methodists of York; Because he had notwithstanding such representation adhered to the Methodists — had broken up his school for the purpose of attending a camp meeting and was himself a principal actor on that occasion. [They] further complained of Mr. Padfield keeping wholly aloof from the Trustees since his arrival and association with low people, alluding in particular to an individual who was reported to have deserted from the [A]merican army.

In the heat of the moment, Padfield retorted that he "was now again conscientiously attached to Methodism,...that he should feel it his duty when similar meetings took place to break up the school for the purpose of attending...and that he was desirous of giving up the school if the trustees were not satisfied with him." When this rash offer to resign was promptly accepted, Padfield at length regretted his hasty offer and when he recognised that the Methodist friends who he had defended "as being men who fear God, and work righteousness — and who are therefore accepted of God"[47] could not help him gain employment, he converted to the United Church of England and Ireland in 1831. He began studying for the Anglican ministry, was employed as a lay reader in York and in April 1833 he was ordained at St. Mary's Church in March Township on the Ottawa River. Before arriving at Beckwith, Padfield served March and Huntley as clergyman.[48]

In contrast with Padfield's renunciation of his youthful enthusiasm for Methodism, by the 1840s the link between Irish Anglicans and Irish Wesleyan Methodists in Beckwith remained strong. The log chapel on William Kerfoot's property in which Presbyterian and Anglican clergy preached in the 1820s and 1830s upon Padfield's arrival echoed only with the thunderings of Methodist preachers in the 1840s, and was replaced by a stone chapel built on land owned by the trustees of the Wesleyan Methodist Church.[49] Padfield, cautious about being seen fraternising unduly with Methodists, held Anglican services in a schoolhouse two miles west of Prospect during the 1840s and early 1850s [50] an appropriate setting for a clergyman who twenty years earlier had declared "from Inclination, Experience and Principle I love the profession of teaching."[51] Yet another Anglican congregation emerged in the early 1840s further north on the boundary between Beckwith and Goulbourn, under the care of the Reverend John Flood of Richmond who held services in the home of Jacob McFadden,

Plate 101
The interior of St. James United Church of England and Ireland, Franktown, as photographed ca. 1895, before a major attempt at gothicising was carried out. At the visual apex of the interior above the Palladian window was the Star of David, a reminder to Beckwith Irish Anglicans of their status as a chosen people comparable to the Israelites in the Bible. The austere interior reflects the Irish Anglican low church evangelical emphasis on a simple auditory hall where their reliance on scriptural authority could be emphasized. Despite the modesty of the furnishings, St. James Church was graced with a harmonium long before the Presbyterian churches of Beckwith. Photograph courtesy of the late Stanley and Marguerite Hughton.

a retired soldier. Early members of this congregation at Mount Pleasant (later Ashton) included Thomas Garland, Nicholas Garland, John Sykes, Hiram Sykes, John W. Shore, Stephen Enough [sic], Hugh Nesbitt, Andrew Fleming, John Garland, Edward Loney, James Fleming, James Douglas, Benjamin and Thomas Stanzel, Martin Switzer, George Bobier, George Jinkinson, John Sumner, Samuel McFadden and Denis Coogan.[52] Denominational rivalry appears to have prompted these families to voluntarily build a church of stone from the flat shallow bed of the Jock River. In August 1844 the Reverend William Bell from Perth "passed through the village of Mount Pleasant on the banks of a small river." He commented, "It is well named[,] for a more pleasant situation for a village I have seldom seen. The Presbyterian church was finished, but the Episcopalian one was but just begun."[53] Christ Church was completed in 1845, and in 1856 tenders were requested for constructing pews and a pulpit.[54]

Denominationalism came to Beckwith with a vengeance at mid-century when Wesleyan

Methodist preacher Benjamin Nankevill and the Anglican rector at Carlton Place, the Reverend John A. Mulock, clashed. Mulock was of English birth and had been pastor at St. James Church since 1844. Nankevill also was from England, and already had a reputation for controversy before he arrived at Carlton Place in 1849, as shown by a pamphlet he published while stationed in Augusta Township near Prescott in 1843 scourging Baptists for not baptising infants.[55] Nankevill perceived that links yet remained between Irish Anglicans and Methodists and he could hardly have helped noticing the free seats purposely placed in St. James Church to lure Methodists. Most of the Methodists meeting in the frame chapel built at Carlton Place in 1834 came from Ramsay, in the same way that most of the Methodists worshipping at the chapel at the site of Prospect came from Goulbourn. All told there were only 28 Methodist families in Beckwith as late as 1852, with four of them located at Gillies Corners, a dozen in the Prospect vicinity, and barely ten in or near the Carlton Place part of Beckwith. Some lowland Presbyterians from southern Ramsay and the immediate Carlton Place vicinity of Beckwith worshipped alongside Methodists in the Carlton Place chapel, effectively beginning to erode persisting ties of Methodists with the United Church of England and Ireland, but Methodists continued to attend Anglican services up until Nankevill and Mulock squared off in 1850.

Exactly who started the verbal fray is impossible to determine. A Methodist visitor to Carlton Place in December 1849 stated that Mulock was "engaged in a fierce crusade against dissenters — especially the Methodists". Mulock was reputed to be arguing "that the Methodist church was without a scriptural ministry, because its ordination was anti-scriptural — he said their church was bore in schism, cradled in error and continued in falsehood, and therefore it was a lying system — and he could prove its ministers liars." Moreover, Mulock was alleged to have chastised Anglican parents who kept "their children from grogshops, shanties, and other moral places but they would let them go to Methodist meetings which were much worse."[56] Mulock later explained that the controversy originated in a sermon he preached explaining the nature of confirmation, in which he quoted John Wesley "to show the estimation in which he held this ordinance of the Church of his vows — the Church of England". Mulock concluded his sermon "by inviting in the kindest and most christian manner the Methodists who were not confirmed to avail themselves of [Bishop Strachan's upcoming visit] of uniting themselves to the Church of their Founder."[57]

Mulock discovered how explosive this was for only the day after delivering the sermon he "was stopped on the road by a leader of the Methodist connexion and charged with 'attacking their body and giving extracts, as from Mr. Wesley, which he never uttered'."[58] Rumours circulated among Methodists and Anglicans about whether Mulock or Nankevill was the more astute clergyman, angry letters passed between the two clergymen, and ever angrier sermons were preached to mixed congregations. Either in January or February 1850 Nankevill published a lengthy pamphlet entitled *A Vindication of the Methodist Church* in which Mulock was appalled to discover "our pure and apostolic Church...assailed[,]...the rite of confirmation...declared popish and unscriptural[,]...the candidates for that rite...called hypocrites, and myself branded a Puseyite."[59] Mulock responded in a 54 page pamphlet entitled *Methodism Unmasked, In a Review of "A Vindication of the Methodist Church" (So Called)* published in late March 1850 at the urging of his churchwardens who wished for a printed refutation of Nankevill's "designed...slander[s]". To Mulock's detailed defence of apostolic succession and arguments that Wesley and other early Methodist leaders never left the Church of England, Nankevill retaliated with a 142 page pamphlet entitled *A Series of Letters to the Rev. J.A. Mulock, Presbyter, of the Church of England: Being a Reply to Certain Charges Against the Methodists in a Sermon Preached in the Different Churches in his Parish* which was printed by James C. Poole on the press of the new village newspaper, the *Lanark Herald*.

The mounting controversy between Nankevill and Mulock was the creation of two prickly personalities, but it also reflected the frustration of two non-Irish clergymen who did not know how to deal with the yet-strong ties between Irish Anglicans and Methodists. Reverend Padfield at Franktown, who also was not Irish, successfully separated Anglicans from Methodists at Prospect

Plate 102
The United Church of England and Ireland rectory on lot 9, concession 3, Beckwith, near Franktown, built in 1837, as photographed in 1982. The Rectory of Beckwith was created and endowed with public lands by a 15 January 1836 order-in-council of government, providing funding to construct this comfortable stone residence for the Anglican clergyman at Franktown. Denominational jealousy prompted the Beckwith Church of Scotland minister to build a stone manse two years later.

by using his power as school superintendent to commandeer a school two miles distant from the Methodist chapel. In vain did Mulock at Carlton Place plead with his congregation on 3 March 1850, "I hope I shall never hear of any of you, in this parish, entering a Methodist Meeting House, for it is a heinous sin, thereby, you would be encouraging the *sin of schism*, which is a sin as wicked as murder, if not more so for it is classed with murder, and other crimes." A week later he again petulantly implored:[60]

> My Brethren, — I hope this is the last time I shall have to warn you against going to Methodist Meetings: If it be a sin to go *once*, how much more, to go often!... They who contribute the smallest sum to *dissenters* are encouraging *schism*, are committing *sin!* In truth, I do not see how a man can go on his knees, day after day, and yet go to a Methodist meeting. You keep your children from Taverns, lest they learn to drink: from Shanties lest they learn to swear: and yet, you send them to Methodist meetings, where they learn *dissent*, which is worse! Oh let me intreat you to keep your children from the Methodist Sunday Schools.

Nankevill was equally paranoid, accusing Mulock of "selecting Methodist teachers to carry on your own Sabbath school? And what was your object? Why, you said: — *'I'll take them by guile!'*"[61] So common was the practice in Carlton Place as late as mid-century for Irish Anglicans and

Methodists to attend one another's services, that Mulock even after three years residence was often unsure exactly who were members of his own floack. At one point when Nankevill informed Mulock that two young men discussing the confirmation debate were members of the Anglican congregation, Mulock in amazement exclaimed *"Is not Rose a Methodist?"* and being informed that he never was, replied *"then I am deceived!"*[62] Nankevill ridiculed Mulock's insistence on the rite of baptism as practised in the United Church of England and Ireland alone being valid by pointing out that "at the last visit of the bishop to Carleton Place, two persons were presented to his lordship for confirmation, who had no other baptism than what they received from the hands of Methodist ministers."[63]

The controversy ended when Mulock was removed from Carleton Place, but not before Nankevill accused him of being a Puseyite, which accusation alone may have been enough to remove Mulock.[64]

What was Puseyism?

More than anything else it was a label. It was pejoratively applied by evangelical Anglicans and other Protestants to Church of England clergy reviving the mediaeval ritual and architecture of the pre-Reformation Anglican church. Beckwith Anglicans overwhelmingly came from the evangelical Church of Ireland tradition, and in Puseyism they feared that higher English clergy were weakening the United Church of England and Ireland by abandoning the form of worship established during the Reformation, especially the emphasis on Biblical authority. Beginning in the mid 1840s articles in the regional press warned against the new emphasis given by Puseyites to sacraments over the Bible. Beckwith Irish Anglicans were as uneasy as anyone, but the big Puseyite scare did not build steam until the late 1850s and 1860s. When Nankevill labeled Mulock a Puseyite in 1850, few Beckwith Anglicans were conversant with the term. Certainly, they did not anticipate any severing of the link between church and state.

Receiving as the Anglican clergy of Beckwith did a salary from government, with construction of their churches at Franktown and Carleton Place subsidised by friends in government and government agencies, and with their rectors established on lots specifically reserved by government, they also served as temporal and spiritual conduits between local inhabitants and those who governed them from afar. In addition to leading Beckwith inhabitants in praying for the King and for the lieutenant-governor every Sunday morning during public worship, Anglican clergy also circulated loyal petitions. One petition was signed by more than sixty inhabitants of Carleton Place in March 1832 protesting William Lyon Mackenzie's agitation "for the purpose of dissolving the Legislative Council and recalling our excellent Governor Sir John Colborne from the high station in which he is placed — the Guardian of a free and (for most part) loyal people."[65] Similarly, in early autumn 1836, the Reverend Boswell at Carleton Place drafted a petition assuring Lieutenant-Governor Sir Francis Bond Head "of our devoted and unalterable attachment to our revered Sovereign and the British Constitution and to express our heartfelt joy at the result of the late Elections [and hailing] with pleasure this visit of Your Excellency to this remote part of the Province".[66] Anglican clergy acted as local agents for the Crown Lands department and acted as clerks on the behalf of poorer immigrants such as John Salter in 1836 who were unsure about how to approach government.[67] The Reverend Michael Harris at Perth attempted to have the Reverend Richard Harte nominated a trustee of the district grammar school at Perth in 1831,[68] but it was the Reverend James Padfield who contributed significantly to the development of education in Beckwith, first as township superintendent in 1844[69] and then as superintendent of common schools for the Bathurst District from 1847 to 1850.[70]

Only in their tolerance of Orangeism were Anglican clergy of the Beckwith vicinity criticised for not fully encouraging a perfect loyalty to the Crown. This tolerance varied from one clergyman to the next. The Reverend Richard Harte at Franktown initially preached to Beckwith Orangemen on the twelfth of July, but by 1830 disapproved of the society and assured the Honourable William

Plate 103
St. James United Church of England and Ireland, Carleton Place, built in 1834, as photographed ca. 1880. The Irish Anglicans of northern Beckwith re-created at Carleton Place the Greek temple form of structure that was popular among Protestants in Ireland during the eighteenth century. The abrupt tower and pointed windows did not detract from the strength of the underlying classical temple design of this church. This was the most sophisticated building constructed in Beckwith before 1850. Anglican Diocese of Ottawa Archives.

Morris at Perth "that he will never again preach on such an occasion".[71] Roman Catholics at Richmond complained in an October 1838 petition to Lord Durham that on the twelfth of July "the Clergyman of the establishment performed Divine Service for [an assembly of Orangemen] with the Orange banner displayed over his head".[72] A correspondent of the *Bathurst Courier* in 1850 stated that the Reverend John A. Mulock at Carlton Place on the twelfth of July gave an audience of "men, women, and boys, dressed out with Orange ribbons and...armed with guns...a political harangue in [which] ...he puffed [up] the Orangemen as being everything that was good",[73] but Johnston Neilson the Carlton Place schoolmaster refuted this, claiming that Mulock had advised Orangemen against holding a procession in the village.[74] Church of Scotland and Roman Catholic advocates and clergy forwarded dozens of reports to the lieutenant-governor, complaining of the growth of Orange lodges in the Beckwith vicinity. As early as August 1825 William Morris at Perth warned of the unpleasant feeling developing between Irish Catholics and the members of an Orange lodge at Perth, and recommended if "respectable and influential Irish Protestants were to admonish those who are so far misguided as to [join Orange lodges]..., that a stop might be put to it".[75] In February 1827 Captain Burke at Richmond expressed alarm that the Orange lodges of the Bathurst District tended "to irritate and an[n]oy a very large portion of the community."[76]

Two Orange lodges developed within the boundaries of Beckwith in or about the year 1830. The earliest known reference to these lodges is a December 1832 notice in the Brockville *Antidote* advising members of the Beckwith and Carlton Place lodges among others to pay their debts due the Grand Orange Lodge.[77] In February 1833 Loyal Orange Lodge No. 31 at Franktown had 68 members who met on the first Monday of each month. The 32 members of L.O.L. No. 48 at Carlton Place met on the third Monday.[78] Undoubtedly, these lodges were organised under the influence of Ogle R. Gowan at Brockville, a recently-arrived Wexford immigrant who used the lodges as a political tool to boost his ambitions as a political candidate. Even before Gowan arrived in 1829, Sheriff Powell at Perth informed the lieutenant-governor in 1827 that offensive remarks made about Orangeism in the provincial house of assembly "produced much irritation and had the effect of giving vigour to a cause that would otherwise have died away, [and] from that period the society gained strength and...many persons of respectability and influence in the District are now members of it."[79]

Implicitly, Irish Anglicans and Methodists were aware that their actions were being carefully monitored and reported to the lieutenant-governor by Roman Catholic Clergy and local Church of Scotland members of the legislative assembly. The minuteness of these reports is suggested by the following aside in an 1827 letter from Catholic bishop Alexander Macdonell to the lieutenant-governor's secretary:[80]

> In justice...to the Rev'd. Mr. H[arris] of Perth I have been given to understand that altho[ugh] he preached three years successively to the orange lodges he did not dine with them, as I believe I mentioned to you & to His Excellency Sir Peregrine Maitland, & I beg you will have the kindness to correct my statement if I should unfortunately have said so to His Excellency that Mr. H[arris] had dined with the Lodge.

In 1830 William Morris reported that additional lodges had recently been formed by Alexander Matheson in the townships behind Perth.[81]

When the Orange lodges at Franktown and Carlton Place were formed either in 1830 or 1831, the Irish Anglicans and Methodists who joined were barely a decade out of Ireland. Before Ogle Gowan or Alexander Matheson exhorted them to form lodges, there had been little perceived need

Plate 104
Christ Church United Church of England and Ireland, Ashton, erected 1845, as photographed ca. 1925. This small unpretentious structure with its neoclassically-derived pediment on the front gable and the simple auditory box inside reflected the Irish Anglican congregation that built it. Lacking crosses, lacking a chancel, and lacking stained glass, it conformed to eighteenth century Irish Anglican low church tradition. The spacing of windows compares with Knox Free Church built at Black's Corners the same year (Plate 87). The orderly evenly-sized stone on the front facade (opposite) contrasts with the disparate stones in the side and rear walls taken from the streambed of the Jock River. National Archives of Canada negative no. C-9546. Line drawings by Robert W.J. Moore.

for Orangeism in Beckwith, considering the handful of Roman Catholics scattered among them and preoccupied as most of them were with clearing their land. Nonetheless, the rhetoric and the assumptions that had prompted them to form Orange lodges in Wexford during the late 1790s remained close to the surface as was shown by the readiness with which two lodges were organised in Beckwith during the early 1830s. An 1827 response by the Perth Orange lodge to an order by Lieutenant-Governor Maitland that their society be suppressed encapsulates the reactionary and ascendantist mentality that Beckwith Irish Protestants had transferred intact from Ireland:[82]

> Orangeism took its rise at a time, when threatened invasion from abroad and intestine commotions at home foreboded ruin to the very existance of the British constitution. The protestants of Ireland, bent on freeing their sinking country or finding a grave in the ruins of their glorious constitution, rose in their might — crushed the hydra headed monster of rebellion and insurrection and assisted by a handful of regular soldiers gave peace and harmony to the nation.

England has acknowledged them to be the salvation of Ireland, and for the prodigal waste of their lives in burying upon their young blood the triumphant Ark of British liberty in many a sanguine field, she has granted them several privileges which they have a right to claim in every country which is ruled by British laws.... We are ready at all times to give the right hand of fellowship to our Catholic fellow subjects, and [we are] free from all those asperities which some would falsely impute to us, to love them as men, though we cannot admit them as masters.

Unlike Perth, where violence between Orangemen and Irish Catholics from 1830 on removed any doubts about rhetorical claims of fellowship, there were no such incidents reported in Beckwith, in large part because the sparse Roman Catholic population was too small to in any way be considered a threat. The Beckwith Orange lodges from the beginning appear largely to have had political rather than religious objectives. John Doherty of southern Ramsay in late July 1833 withdrew from and renounced the Carlton Place Orange Lodge, of which he had been "a constant attendant for about two years past". Doherty claimed that "the moral principles of the institution have been perverted into combinations of a few depraved political aspirants for office."[83] No Orange parades took place in Beckwith during the 1830s, but when the Baldwin-Lafontaine Reform ministry pushed through a bill banning Orange processions in 1843 local lodge members were outraged. They perceived that their liberty was being tampered with. They who had taken a "noble part...in suppressing the rebellion of [18]37 and [18]38" in Upper Canada, echoing the chapter "in Irish history when treason and rebellion raised their heads in the ever memorable [17]98" and in which their fathers "were the foremost to rally round the Altar and the Throne,"[84] they were to be deprived of the right to assemble in public! The result, as the *Bathurst Courier* reported, was that "The 12th of July was celebrated at Carlton Place by a public procession." The *Courier's* Reform editor declined to print an "account of the day's proceedings...handed to us for insertion by one of the Orange party...[because it was] a proceeding which the Government of the country discountenance and condemn, and [one] which we, repeatedly, have expressed our hearty disapproval of."[85]

The processions at Carlton Place continued. On the twelfth of July 1850, a full year before the processions Act was repealed, Orangemen, women and children marched through the village "dressed out with Orange ribbons, and accompanied with a set of bagpipes and two or three drums.... A number of them were armed with guns, pistols &c., with which they kept up almost a continual volley. This band was led by...Thomas Griffeth, an Ensign in the Militia, dressed in uniform and carrying a drawn sword." One observer of this parade thought it strange that magistrates Rosamond, Houston, Conboy and Bowland "saw the whole of the proceedings, but did not in the slightest degree interfere to stop it" and wondered "How these gentlemen can reconcile their conduct...with their oaths of office."[86] In 1852, violence began to erupt between area Orangemen and Irish Catholics, as the latter came to comprise one sixth of the village population. The spring fair at Carlton Place in 1852 "was finished by one of those party fights between Orangemen and Catholics...which occasionally break out among [Ireland's] sons, in this, the land of their adoption." The editor of the *Carleton-Place Herald* commented:[87]

> The revengeful, rancorous and bitter spirit manifested by both parties exceeds any thing of the kind which has ever transpired here. And we know not to what length their passions would have carried them, had they not been checked by the prompt and decisive action of Mr. Rob[er]t Bell, who was called to the spot by the uproar, when there were about fifty actively engaged, and the whole crowd, which filled the street, were fast giving way to their passions.

The violence between Orangemen and Irish Catholics which emerged at Carlton Place in 1852 could well be attributed to heavy drinking, but it is significant that it occurred on the periphery of Ramsay with its uneasy balance of Irish Catholics and lowland Scottish and not in southern Beckwith

Plate 105
Gravestones of the Reverend John McNeely, St. Fillan's cemetery, and Catherine Bennett, St. Augustine's Anglican cemetery at Prospect, as photographed in 1981 and 1982. The detail on McNeely's stone suggests the wealth of his parents farming the fertile Mississippi floodplain who could afford to spare sending him off to Trinity College in Toronto and to erect this costly memorial. The modest wooden marker commemorating Bennett was typical of the perishable grave markers used in Beckwith before 1850. The use of wood as late as 1897 reflects the poverty of many farms in southern Beckwith.

where the larger concentration of Irish-origin inhabitants was to be found. The proportional increase of Irish Catholics in Beckwith was very small, rising from an estimated 26 heads of families in 1833[88] to 33 in 1852. Only in the 1840s did Roman Catholics become a significant part of the population of Carlton Place. In Beckwith as a whole Irish Catholics were eight percent of the population in 1833 and nine percent in 1852. In Carlton Place, by contrast, very suddenly in the 1840s Irish Catholics became one sixth of the village population. It is significant that with an equal number of Irish Catholic families in the immediate vicinity of Franktown as there was at Carlton Place in 1852, with a much larger concentration of Irish Anglicans at Franktown, and with an Orange lodge twice the size of that at Carlton Place, the odds for ethno-religious violence it would seem should have been greater at Franktown. Yet Franktown was free of violence, whereas Carlton Place had numerous Catholic-Protestant frays beginning in the mid 1840s.

The ethno-religious violence at Carlton Place is largely explained by the political division that occurred in adjacent Ramsay Township during the 1840s. The Scottish lowland settlers of Ramsay, true to their radical roots, were staunch partisans of political reform. They assumed that their Irish Catholic neighbours would join them in supporting their Reform candidate Malcolm Cameron in breaking up the strong links between the government and the United Church of England and Ireland. As it turned out, they assumed wrongly. A meeting of Roman Catholics on the eighth concession of Ramsay in mid March 1841 under chairman Dr. Edward M. Barry of Carlton Place resolved to support Irish Anglican Conservative John A. H. Powell instead. Ramsay Irish Catholics as proven "true and loyal subjects to our Queen and Country" chose Powell over Cameron because they "recollect[ed] the part he took when our holy religion was maligned, and ourselves denominated aliens, [and] we think him entitled to our everlasting gratitude."[89] Clearly Ramsay Catholics had not forgotten the part played by their lowland Scottish neighbours in attacking them at Morphy's Falls and in contributing to the attack by the deputy-sheriff's party at Shipman's Falls seventeen years earlier. The anger of Ramsay pro-Reform lowlanders was only further increased in 1842 when the predominantly Irish Conservative townships of Montague, North Elmsley and North Burgess were added to Lanark to make it a strong Tory riding.

Carlton Place until the mid 1850s was the largest village in the Ramsay vicinity, and with its cattle fairs, school, churches, mills and shops attracted business from a large section of southern Ramsay. As early as the late 1820s the Reverend John MacDonald, Roman Catholic priest at Perth, celebrated mass at Morphy's Falls in the shanty of a settler named Byms.[90] MacDonald continued to celebrate mass through to 1838 in the homes of Patrick McAlinden and John McDonell, and he collected tithes paid in cash, flour, butter, wheat and cheese from Beckwith Roman Catholics.[91] With the construction of a frame church at Almonte in 1842,[92] public worship no longer was conducted in Beckwith, with Catholics at Carlton Place travelling to Almonte, the four families south of Mississippi Lake going to Perth, and the ten families south of Franktown proceeding either south to Smith's Falls or east to Richmond. In the 1840s then, the Roman Catholic population of Beckwith was not only sparse, but was also divided among four congregations. The Roman Catholics at Carlton Place largely settled there during the 1840s and were part of an overflow from Ramsay, and those of them in trade certainly served the Irish Catholic farmers from Ramsay coming to do business in the village. It is significant that there were no brawls at Carlton Place during the decade Orange processions were held in the village illegally. Instead, the violent brawl in April 1852 occurred at the end of the cattle fair, an event which drew Ramsay Irish Catholics and Scottish lowlanders into Carlton Place in large numbers. Assisted by liquor, the latent hostility of the lowlanders for the refusal of Irish Catholics to support Malcolm Cameron and Reform surfaced. In return, Ramsay Catholics had by no means forgotten the attacks by the lowlanders in 1824 at Morphy's Falls.

It may seem remarkable that the embers of violence which took place in 1824 should yet be glowing at mid-century, but as late as 1872 the lowland Reformers of Ramsay described their Catholic neighbours as "most improvident and unruly" and "disposed to follow their old system in Canada, leading idle and dissolute lives."[93] James Poole, the Irish Methodist editor of the *Carleton-Place Herald* stated that the 1852 brawl at Carlton Place was "between Orangemen and Catholics" but it is very unlikely that Poole as mouthpiece for the Reform member of the legislative assembly, Robert Bell, would dare identify those pummelling the Irish Catholics as Ramsay Scottish lowlanders, since the massive concentration of lowlanders in northern Lanark not only had ensured Bell's election in 1848 but were the major subscribers to the *Herald*. Enjoying little support from either Irish Catholics or from Orange Anglicans, Poole had to be selective as to who he blamed for the violence for the sake of political expediency. Had the rioters at Carlton Place been Orange Anglicans, there is no question that James Rosamond as a prominent Orangeman and Anglican was the village magistrate who would have gone out to stop the fighting. Instead, it was the Scottish Presbyterian magistrate and provincial member Robert Bell "who was called to the spot", implicitly to separate his lowlander constituents from their Irish Catholic neighbours.

The role of James C. Poole from 1850 on in criticising the United Church of England and Ireland

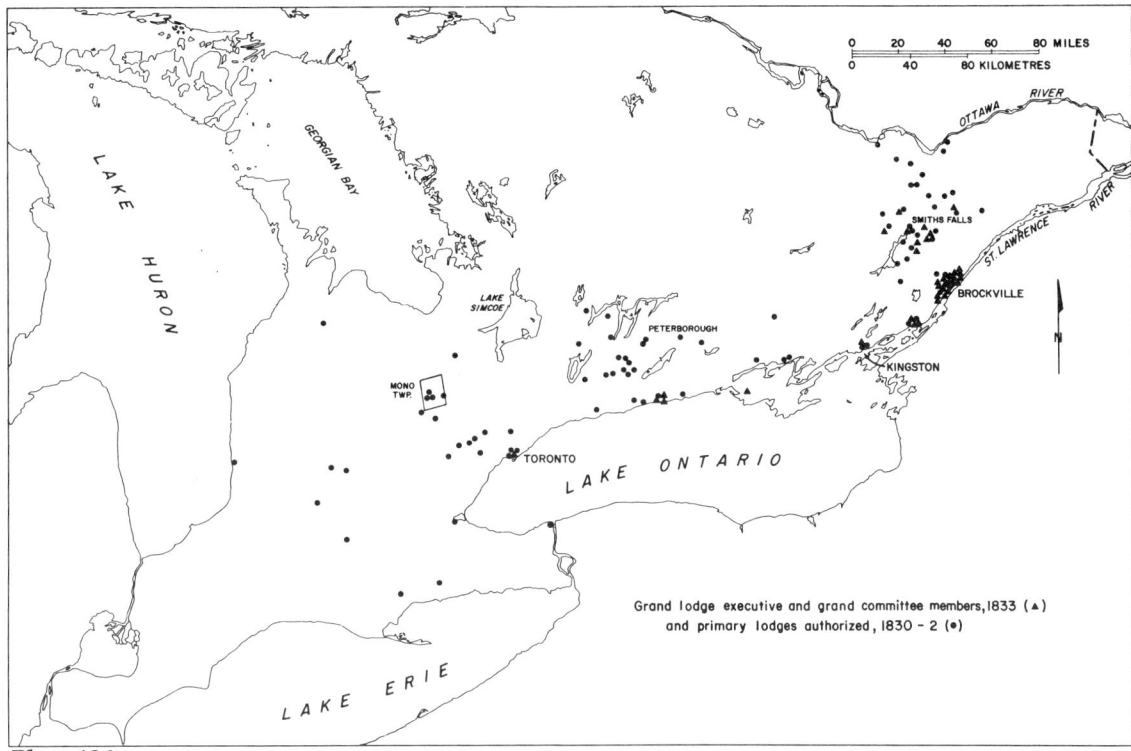

Plate 106
Early Orange lodges and officials of the Grand Orange Lodge of British America, 1833. The early concentration of Orange lodges in eastern Upper Canada follows the same geographic concentration of families of Wexford area origin shown in Plate 34. Members of the grand lodge executive and grand committee were concentrated among Ogle Gowan's associates at Brockville, with none residing in Beckwith. From Cecil J. Houston and William J. Smyth, The Sash Canada Wore: A Historical Geography of the Orange Order in Canada, *courtesy of Academic Press Inc.*

through the pages of the *Herald* partly reflected his role as a mouthpiece for Reform member Robert Bell against the Tory Anglican establishment in the region, and it also reflected emerging ties being fostered between Irish Methodists and lowland Presbyterians who worshipped together in the Methodist chapel at Carlton Place. More than half of Beckwith's 28 Methodist families in 1852 lived in southern Beckwith, and as a mission of the Richmond circuit from the 1830s on retained their Irish conservatism. The dozen or less Methodist families in the Carlton Place vicinity of Beckwith had few more members of their denomination in adjacent Ramsay to make them a strong congregation. The attendance of Presbyterians combined to make the congregations in the Carlton Place chapel substantial, but with Free Church congregations established at Black's Corners and Ashton in the mid 1840s much closer to Carlton Place than was the older Church of Scotland congregation, the number of Presbyterians attending the Methodist chapel declined, in turn prompting local Methodists to hold camp meetings.[94] Under its various names of the Mississippi Circuit, the Carlton and Pakenham Circuit, and the Carlton Place Circuit, Methodism in northern Beckwith struggled along, but as late as 1859 preachers John Howes and Henry Perdue claimed a total of 149 members in Beckwith, Ramsay, Lanark and Drummond townships and admitted that "the moral soil, is not very congenial to Methodism, the prejudices of a large proportion of the people being against it."[95] Despite its numerical weakness, despite the lack of sympathy the Irish members had for the

Plate 107
Wesleyan Methodist chapel and driveshed at Prospect, believed built ca. 1847—1850, as photographed in 1982. This chapel, built by William Kerfoot on a corner of his farm on lot 25 in the fourth concession, apart from its pointed windows and lack of a tower, could easily have been based on the 1823 plan shown in Plate 90. The outline of two windows later filled in can be seen in the rear wall. This was the site of a log chapel built in the 1820s. In March 1830 the Reverend William Bell from Perth preached in "the Methodist chapel, near Mr. Kerfoot's...to a congregation of more than 100."

American leadership of their church, Carlton Place had a high reputation within the Brockville district "because there is a spirit of the right kind in the people."[96] In 1839 Carlton Place contributed £76 to the Methodist centenary fund,[97] and in the 1840s William H. Poole and James Conn from the Prospect vicinity became Wesleyan Methodist clergymen.[98] All the same, the less than thirty Methodist families in Beckwith in 1852 and the growing influence of the lowland Presbyterians in adjacent Ramsay who worshipped with the Methodists at Carlton Place together help to explain the growing distance between Beckwith Methodists and Anglicans from mid-century onward, a distance that was forced by the anti-Anglican and anti-Orange editorials of James C. Poole in the service of his Reform patron, Robert Bell.

Between 1825 and 1851 it could be said that the large Irish Anglican community in Beckwith retained significant links with Irish Catholics and Irish Methodists. These bonds were not necessarily rational and they began to weaken during this quarter century under non-Irish clergy, with the formation of Orange lodges, and by the emergence of rigid political partisanship and denominationalism in the 1840s. Orangeism as a political organisation posed the biggest threat to the bonds between Irish Catholics and Anglicans, and yet when faced with choosing between the Orange Anglicans of Beckwith and the radical lowlanders of Ramsay, regional Irish Catholics chose the Orangemen as political allies. However unhappy Irish Catholics were with Orangeism reappearing in Upper Canada, their own experience in the region told them that they had more to fear from

Plate 108
Pulpit, kneeling step and communion railing in Prospect Wesleyan Methodist chapel, as photographed in June 1983. Up until the closing decades of the nineteenth century Methodists took communion kneeling at the railing around the pulpit at the front of the church. This reflected the Anglican heritage of Methodism, except that there was a pulpit inside the altar rail rather than an altar. The handsome massive pulpit reflects the importance given to preaching and Biblical exposition by Irish Methodists and Anglicans alike.

the lowlander Reformers who wished to crush the links of their church with the state along with those of the United Church of England and Ireland. Moreover, it is important to recognise that Irish Anglicans and Catholics were far from hostile toward one another. When the Irish Catholic priest at Richmond in 1853 regretted "to say that all those [Catholic girls] who come here, with few exceptions become [Protestant] perverts by marriage or some other way,"[99] he essentially was testifying to the camaraderie that existed between Irish Protestants and Catholics. The large Irish Anglican community and the sparse Irish Catholic and Methodist inhabitants of Beckwith in the late 1840s responded in concert to the shocking accounts of the great Famine in Ireland.

There could be no more striking testimony to the bonds of common nationality that bound Irish Anglicans and Irish Catholics together than a letter which Irish Anglican Joseph Doherty at Carlton Place received from Ireland in 1851. The letter was from Patrick Mulrony, a Catholic in County Clare, who was desperately trying to track down his brother Bernard who had been Doherty's servant in 1842 and 1843. Mulrony stated "Myself and my children must go in the poor house if [Bernard] does not send me some relief. [I] am holding the father[']s place yet[. T]here was 32 houses in [C]urraclone Butler[;] there is not in it but seven now[. T]here was farmers in the parish that was wort[h] 3 hundred pounds and the[y a]re in the poor house." Mulrony suggested that if Doherty needed a servant, that his sister Biddy would land at New York in August, and that "she will be as a servant as her Brother

Bernard M[ul]roney [was] in your [household] about six or seven years ago." Mulrony closed this letter to the former employer of a brother he had lost touch with with a revealing salutation, "no more at present but i am your affectionate Brother."[100]

An Irish Catholic addressing an Irish Anglican as an affectionate brother?

This is the key that helps to explain the behaviour of Irish Methodists and Irish Catholics and their relationship to the much larger Irish Anglican community in the Beckwith vicinity before mid-century. Despite the enmity that had existed in Ireland between Irish Catholics on the one side and Anglicans and Methodists on the other, they all were aware that they lived under vastly different circumstances in Upper Canada. For one thing, there was hardly the same competition for too little land that underlay much of the religious rancor in Ireland. Neither were there rents to pay to an established church, nor an aristocracy which was favoured because it belonged to a certain church. Equally important, regional Irish Catholics no longer belonged to an overwhelming numerical majority. It if had been frustrating to be politically impotent as members of an overwhelming majority in southern Ireland, it was equally unfulfilling to enjoy the franchise in Upper Canada yet to be only a fraction of the population. When it came down to making practical and pragmatic political and social alliances, Irish Catholics in the vicinity of Beckwith perceived that Irish Anglicans and even Irish Methodists might have some empathy for their interests whereas the lowlander Scottish Presbyterians of Ramsay had none. When Orange Irish Anglicans explicitly ridiculed or engaged in acts of violence against Irish Catholics, as was the case at Perth and Smith's Falls in the late 1820s and 1830s, the Irish Catholics soon became Reformers. Where the Orange lodge was more discreet, as appeared to be the case in Beckwith before mid-century, Irish Catholics sought to link up with their Irish Protestant brothers. It was the same type of uneasy alliance that Irish Methodists had made in Ireland decades earlier, and like the Methodists local Irish Catholics hoped to benefit from the stability which Irish Anglicans enjoyed as the single largest denomination and most firmly established church in early nineteenth century Beckwith.

Endnotes

1 Canada, Ministry of Agriculture, *Census of Canada, 1870-71* (Ottawa: I.B. Taylor, 1873) I:274-279.
2 Canada, Board of registration and Statistics, Census of the Canadas.2 (Quebec: John Lovell, 1853) I: 50-51.
3 *Montreal Gazette*, 23 April 1825, p. 2, col. 2.
4 Donald H. Akenson, "Ontario: Whatever Happened to the Irish?" in D.H. Akenson, ed., *Canadian Papers in Rural History* III (Gananoque: Langdale Press, 1982), p. 207.
5 *Brockville Gazette*, 17 November 1831, p. 3, col. 1.
6 10 June 1827 letter from Thomas Graham, Brockville, to Mrs. Elizabeth Graham, Clondaw, near Enniscorthy, Ireland, cited in Martin Doyle, *Hints on Emigration to Upper Canada, Especially Addressed to the Lower Classes in Great Britain and Ireland* (Dublin: William Curry Jr., 1834), pp. 71-72.
7 Ibid., 10 June 1828 letter from Thomas Graham to Elizabeth Graham, pp. 72-74.
8 OKQAR Rev. William Bell Journals VIII:43.
9 Jessie Buchanan Campbell, *The Pioneer Pastor*, p. 16.
10 Ibid., p. 49.
11 Ibid., p. 50.
12 NAC Reel C-6892 Upper Canada Sundries, vol. 172, pp. 94320-94321.
13 *Brockville (Upper Canada) Antidote*, 5 February 1833, p. 3, col. 5.
14 Ibid., 23 April 1833, p. 1, col. 4.
15 *Bathurst Courier*, 8 December 1836, p. 1, cols. 2-4.
16 *Brockville Statesman*, 10 September 1839, p. 1, col. 6. This article also was printed in the *Bathurst Courier*, 9 August 1839, p. 2, col. 3.
17 *Bathurst Courier*, 14 December 1838, p. 2, cols. 4-5.
18 NAC RG 5, A1 Reel C-6879 Upper Canada Sundries, vol. 130, p. 71697.
19 *Bathurst Courier*, 27 April 1847, p. 2, col. 5.
20 Thomas R. Millman, *Jacob Mountain: First Lord Bishop of Quebec: A Study in Church and State, 1793-1825* (Toronto: University of Toronto Press, 1947), p. 220.
21 Marjory Whitelaw, *The Dalhousie Journals* (Ottawa: Oberon Press, 1981), pp. 47-48.
22 OKQAR Rev. William Bell Journals III:114.
23 NAC RG 5, A1 Reel C-4617 Upper Canada Sundries, vol. 77, pp. 41189-41191, 41348.

24 NAC RG 1, L1 Upper Canada Land Book M, vol. 31, p. 647.
25 NAC RG 5, A1 Reel C-4617 Upper Canada Sundries, vol. 77, pp. 41348-41350.
26 Ibid., Reel C-6862, vol. 80, p. 43305.
27 Ibid., Reel C-6863, vol. 83, pp. 44890-44892.
28 Howard M. Brown, "St. James Church, Franktown, Oldest in Ottawa Valley" in *Carleton Place Canadian*, 26 January 1961.
29 NAC RG, L1 Upper Canada Land Book M, vol. 31, p. 647.
30 Thomas R. Millman, *The Life of the Right Reverend, The Honourable Charles James Stewart D.D., Oxon. Second Anglican Bishop of Quebec* (London, Ontario: Huron College, 1953), pp. 86, 203.
31 Brown, "St. James Church".
32 Robert Jefferson and Leonard L. Johnson, *Faith of Our Fathers: The Story of the Diocese of Ottawa* (Ottawa: The Anglican Book Society, 1957), pp. 60-61.
33 *Brockville Antidote,* 22 January 1833, p. 3, col. 4.
34 24 June 1833 report by the Rev. Richard Harte, Beckwith, to the Anglican Bishop of Quebec.
35 *Brockville Recorder*, 19 July 1833, p. 2, col. 1.
36 Millman, *Charles James Stewart*, p. 218.
37 Ibid., p. 191.
38 Society for the Propagation of the Gospel Archives, London, England, (hereafter SPGA) 27 January 1834 letter from the Rev. Edward Jukes Boswell, Beckwith, to Bishop Charles James Stewart, Quebec.
39 Ibid.
40 NAC RG 5, A1 Reel C-6881 Upper Canada Sundries, vol. 137, p. 75068.
41 SPGA 7 April 1834 letter from Boswell, Carleton Place, to Bishop Stewart.
42 Ibid.
43 C. Lionel G. Bruce, *History of the Parish of Carleton Place, 1834-1934* (Carleton Place: St. James Anglican Church, 1934), p. 5.
44 OTAR RG 1 Series C-IV MS 658 Crown Lands Department, Township Papers, Beckwith Township, Reel 30, pp. 160-161.
45 Millman, *Charles James Stewart*, p. 213.
46 NAC RG 5, A1 Reel C-6863 Upper Canada Sundries, vol. 85, pp. 46167-46175.
47 Ibid.
48 Millman, *Charles James Stewart,* p. 213.
49 George A. Neville and Iris M. Neville, *Prospect United Church Cemetery (A Pioneer Methodist Cemetery and Church of Lanark County)* (Ottawa Branch, Ontario Genealogical Society, 1976), p. 4.
50 George Edward Kidd, *The Story of the Derry* (Vancouver: by the author, 1943), p. 22.
51 NAC RG 5, A1 Reel C-6863 Upper Canada Sundries, vol. 85, p. 46172.
52 Freda Rajotte and Harry M. Preece, *The Story of the Churches: An Account of the histories of the various congregations, which now comprise the Mission of Ashton (Anglican) and the Ashton Charge (United), in the borderland of the Townships [of] Beckwith and Goulbourn, and of the Counties [of] Lanark and Carleton* (Ashton: mimeographed by the authors, 1964).
53 OKQAR Rev. William Bell Journals XIV:118.
54 *Carleton-Place Herald*, 21 February 1856, p. 3, col. 6.
55 Benjamin Nankevill, *Christian Baptism Scripturally Considered* (Toronto: Christian Guardian Office, 1844). I consulted a copy of this 53 page pamphlet in the Baldwin Room at the Metropolitan Toronto Library.
56 *Bathurst Courier*, 11 January 1850, p. 2, cols. 3-4.
57 John A. Mulock, *Methodism Unmasked, In a Review of "A Vindication of the Methodist Church" (So Called,) "In a Pastoral Address, by Benjamin Nankevill, Wesleyan Minister* (Carleton Place: by the author, 1850), p. 3.
58 Ibid.
59 Ibid., p. 4.
60 Benjamin Nankevill, *A Series of Letters, To the Rev. J.A. Mulock, Presbyter, of the Church of England: Being A Reply to Certain Charges Against the Methodists In A Sermon Preached in The Different Churches In His Parish* (Carleton Place: by the author, 1850), pp. 42-43.
61 Ibid., p. 73.
62 Ibid., p. 13.
63 Ibid., p. 92.
64 Ibid., p. 78.
65 *Kingston Chronicle*, 10 March 1832, p. 3, col. 1.
66 NAC RG 5, A1 Reel C-6891 Upper Canada Sundries, vol. 169, pp. 92691-92692.
67 OTAR RG 1 Series C-IV MS 658 Reel 30 Crown Lands Department, Township Papers, Beckwith, p. 126.
68 NAC RG 5, A1 Reel C-6872 Upper Canada Sundries, vol. 106, pp. 60450-60452.
69 *Bathurst Courier*, 12 March 1844, p. 2, cols. 1-4.
70 Lloyd C. Sutherland, *Yearning For Learning: The Story of Education in Lanark County, 1804-1867* (Smiths Falls: by the author, 1980), p. 119.
71 NAC RG 5, A1 Reel C-6870 Upper Canada Sundries, vol. 100, p. 56513.
72 Archives of the Archdiocese of Kingston (Roman Catholic), Bishop Macdonell Letterbooks III:626-627.
73 *Bathurst Courier*, 26 July 1850, p. 1, cols. 2-3.
74 Ibid., 9 August 1850, pp. 2-3, cols. 6-1.
75 NAC RG 5, A1 Reel C-4615 Upper Canada Sundries, vol. 73, pp. 39065-39067.
76 Ibid., Reel C-6862, vol. 82, p. 44617.
77 *Brockville Antidote*, 10 December 1832, p. 3, col. 6.
78 Ibid., 26 February 1833, p. 3, col. 5.
79 NAC RG 5, A1 Reel C-6863 Upper Canada Sundries, vol. 83, pp. 45226-45227.
80 Ibid., pp. 45298-45302.

224 THE ORANGE ANGLICAN POLITY

81 Ibid., Reel C-6870, vol. 100, p. 56512.
82 Ibid., Reel C-6863, vol. 83, pp. 45229-45232.
83 *Brockville Recorder*, 2 August 1833, p. 3, col. 5.
84 *Bytown (Canada West) Gazette*, 20 July 1848, p. 2, cols. 5-6.
85 *Bathurst Courier*, 26 July 1843, p. 2, col. 6.
86 Ibid., 26 July 1850, p. 1, cols. 2-3.
87 *Carleton-Place Herald*, 8 April 1852, p. 2, col. 5.
88 24 June 1833 report by the Rev. Richard Harte, Beckwith, to the Anglican Bishop of Quebec.
89 *Bathurst Courier*, 19 March 1841, p. 1, cols. 3-4.
90 Michael O'Donahue, "Historical Sketch of Carleton Place Mission" in parish register of St. Mary's Church, Carleton Place, 1 August 1886 cited in P.F. Murphy, *History of St. Mary's Church, Carleton Place* (Carleton Place: St. Mary's Church, 1969), p. 1.
91 Duncan W. MacDonald, *Interesting Notes and Comments from the Diary of Rev. John MacDonald, Catholic Priest for 14 Years (c. 1823-1837) at the Town of Perth* (Brockville: The Leeds and Grenville Branch, Ontario Genealogical Society, 1985), pp. 2-3, 5-8, 10-11, 32.
92 Hector Legros et Soeur Paul-Émile, *Le Diocèse d'Ottawa, 1847-1948* (Ottawa: Archbishop of Ottawa, 1949), p. 178.
93 Almonte Gazette Almanac, "Early Settlement of Ramsay Township" (Almonte: Almonte Gazette, 1872: reprint ed., Mallorytown, Ontario: Jack Brown, 1973) cited in Carol Bennett, *Peter Robinson's Settlers* (Renfrew: Juniper Books Limited, 1987), p. 15.
94 *Bathurst Courier*, 22 August 1843, p. 3, col. 3.
95 *Toronto (Canada West) Christian Guardian*, 18 May 1859, p. 78, col. 6. I am grateful to Howard M. Brown for giving me access to a transcript of this letter.
96 Ibid., 18 December 1850, p. 39, col. 1.
97 *Brockville Statesman*, 5 November 1839, p. 1, col. 6.
98 27 August 1846 letter from the Rev. William H. Poole, Kitley, to Richard Hammond, cited in Mabel Willows, *Anniversary of Boyd's United Church* (Boyd's Settlement: Boyd's United Church, 1973), n.p.
99 Archives of the Archdiocese of Ottawa (Roman Catholic), Évêque Guigues régistre des lettres, 1852-1854 V:331.
100 *Carleton-Place Herald*, 8 August 1851, p. 3, col. 5.

THE SEARCH FOR ORDER

Beckwith inhabitants between 1825 and mid-century in a variety of ways attempted to mould an orderly society out of the disorder that surrounded them on all sides in their forest setting. In their search for a more orderly version of society, most Irish and Scottish immigrant families in Beckwith moved beyond the stage of backwoods existence to which they became accustomed during the first decade of settlement. The previous four chapters have shown some ways in which local society became more orderly. Subsistence agriculture gave way to provisioning the Rideau Canal work camps and the upper Ottawa timber camps; these in turn provided a combined cash and barter economy that supported a variety of tradesmen such as weavers, shoemakers, storekeepers, waggonmakers and blacksmiths among others. Families became sufficiently concerned to ensure an orderly future for their children that they either moved in groups to new locations where there would be sufficient land or else dictated in their wills how Beckwith homesteads were to be passed down from one generation to the next. The formation of Presbyterian, Anglican, Baptist and Methodist congregations is evidence of concern for providing moral order in society, although schism among Presbyterians and the loosening of ties between Irish Anglicans and Irish Methodists and Catholics reveals that Beckwith inhabitants increasingly began to differ in their views as to how a more orderly society was to be created. This chapter discusses additional attempts to create a better society through emerging politicisation, municipal organisation, schools, temperance and agricultural societies, and domestic architecture. Beckwith inhabitants in the course of pursuing both pragmatic and utopian goals to create a more ordered society incidentally defined their place in Beckwith, and in turn, the place of Beckwith in eastern Upper Canada.

Beckwith from the late 1820s to the late 1840s remained politically conservative, but increasingly a Reform constituency developed in the Carlton Place vicinity. As early as 1830 a Carlton Place correspondent of the *Bathurst Independent Examiner* writing under the pseudonym of Pat O'Shaughnessy ridiculed the political ambitions of Irish and Orange Anglican candidate William Tully at Perth,[1] but this was exceptional in early Beckwith. Despite the large population of radicalised lowland weavers in northern Lanark, the combination of Irish Protestants, Irish Catholics, highlanders and military settlers in the Beckwith district gave pro-administration Scottish highlander William Morris of Perth a seat in the provincial legislature from 1825 to 1836. Morris appealed to Beckwith highlanders because of his ethnicity. He appealed to Irish Anglicans because he supported state funding for the established churches of the British Empire. A traditional account of a delegation of Beckwith inhabitants unanimously voting for Morris in their first election at Perth in 1824[2] was corroborated by Morris twenty years later when he expressed his gratitude for the unwavering support he had received in Beckwith.[3] By 1828 the population of Lanark County had so increased that it was entitled to two representatives in the Upper Canadian legislature. The radical lowlanders in northern Lanark were sufficiently numerous that Scottish Presbyterian ex-Army officer Donald Fraser ran as a Reformer, but after his election showed a conservative abhorrence for anything resembling rebellion against the Crown by moving that William Lyon Mackenzie be expelled from the legislative assembly.[4] Fraser was less discreet than Morris in his attempts to stop the growth of Orangeism, contributing to create a "raging party spirit in Montague and Beckwith" by April 1833[5] that led to Fraser being defeated by Perth English-born Anglican Tory Colonel Josias Taylor that year.

The growing rivalry between Reformers and Tories emerged in 1835, after William Morris was appointed to the legislative council, with the election of Irish Anglican Orange Tory John A.H. Powell and radicalised lowlander-supported Secessionist Presbyterian Reformer Malcolm Cameron to the provincial assembly. When Lanark was limited to only one assembly member beginning in 1839, it was the mercurial Cameron who was re-elected to represent Lanark until he permanently left the county behind in 1847. In February 1841 the majority of people at a political meeting in Carlton Place favoured Cameron, reflecting strong support for him particularly in adjacent Ramsay. The continuing conservatism of Beckwith was reflected by a minority at the meeting who stood up and denounced Cameron.[6] More tellingly, in December 1843 158 inhabitants of Carlton Place and vicinity sent an address to the Honourable William Morris at Brockville, thanking him for opposing moving the seat of government,[7] which spurred the editor of Cameron's organ, the *Bathurst Courier*, to argue that Cameron also deserved to be thanked.[8] Although both Morris and Cameron attempted to create a more orderly society, Cameron's passionate advocacy of temperance and endless tirades against Sir Francis Bond Head and the Tories generally produced much less than Morris's practical alignment with so-called "Compact Tories" and his skills as a parliamentarian. The Irish Anglicans and Scottish Presbyterians of Beckwith found in Morris:[9]

> the unflinching champion of civil and religious liberty, based upon the broad foundation of the British Constitution, and firmly believe[d] that while [he] would be the first man in the Province to uphold the supremacy of, and connexion with the British Government, still [he] would be the last to support that Government in any measure calculated...to injure the best interests of the Province, and of all its truly British inhabitants.

In the late 1840s Carlton Place challenged Perth as the Reform centre of Lanark County, after Beckwith reeve Robert Bell was unexpectedly elected warden of the Bathurst district council in 1847.[10] After being nominated at a Reform convention held in Napoleon Lavallee's Carlton Place hotel that June,[11] Bell went on in 1848 to be elected member for Lanark.[12] During the election campaign Bell encountered opposition from Perth area Reformers and the *Bathurst Courier* which obliged him to deny rumours "of ever having any wish to remove the Jail and Court House from Perth to Carlton Place, or ever having tried to".[13] The opposition Robert Bell encountered in the Perth vicinity was complex in its origins, and offers some insights into the political conservatism of Beckwith. An anonymous writer in the *Bathurst Courier* in March 1849, recognising that Bell's strength lay among the radical lowland weavers of northern Lanark, urged that Reformers in the military townships settled from Perth must learn how to organise. "The curse of Drummond and Bathurst has been, that they were *a military settlement*", he argued, due to the "deference...ex-military men required from those who once were under them—laggards in the march of mind, in liberality of sentiment, fags".[14] An additional cause for concern among Lanark County Reformers was the addition of Montague, North Elmsley and North Burgess townships to the Bathurst District in 1842,[15] filled as they were with Irish Orange Tories. Malcolm Cameron had hastily voted for this in 1838, because it gave Lanark County "commercial connections and water communications" through the Rideau Canal, and more importantly because it separated Lanark and Carleton counties so as to prevent Beckwith and other townships from becoming taxed and socially contaminated by the litigation and breaches of the peace committed by Irish rowdies at Bytown.[16] What Cameron did not anticipate was that the Irish in the three new townships provided enough Tory votes to allow Wexford-born James Shaw of Smith's Falls to success-

Plate 109
An engraving of Malcolm Cameron in 1876, as published in the Canadian Illustrated News. *First as editor of the Perth* Bathurst Courier, *as a zealous advocate of total abstinence from liquor, and then as a radical Reform politician, Cameron was familiar to Beckwith inhabitants in the 1830s and 1840s. Only in Carleton Place where lowlanders from adjacent southern Ramsay Township began to dwell was there political support for Cameron in Beckwith. The more significant influence of Malcolm Cameron on Beckwith was to attract families to migrate in groups to Lambton County in the 1840s and 1850s. National Archives of Canada negative no. C-64383.*

Plate 110
James Condle Poole, founding editor of the Carleton Place Herald *from 1850 to 1883, as photographed at Brockville ca. 1866 by A.C. McIntyre. The Napoleonic stance affected by Poole reflected his view of himself as a revolutionary agent of political and industrial progress amid the conservatively backward Perthshire highlanders and Wexford Anglicans of Beckwith. Poole's* Herald *was initially funded by Carleton Place Reform member, Robert Bell, but as the circulation grew from 600 in the Beckwith vicinity in the early 1850s to some 3,000 throughout the upper Ottawa valley by 1870 it became a source of wealth. For all his rhetoric about moral and social reform, the over-intent gaze of Poole belies his willingness to overwork apprentices, at least four of whom ran away from his printing office. National Archives of Canada negative no. PA-135218.*

fully wrest Lanark County away from the Reformers in the election of 1851.[17] Robert Bell countered the twin challenges of not receiving support from Perth area Reformers and an increased number of Irish Tory voters by establishing a newspaper at Carlton Place under editor James C. Poole entitled the *Lanark Herald*. The *Bathurst Courier* at Perth initially described it as "a neatly got up little sheet...issued weekly on the Reform, or rather we should say, on the Ministerial ticket",[18] and widely hinted that Bell as dispenser of Reform patronage in Lanark County[19] funnelled government funds into the operation of his Carlton Place newspaper.[20]

The establishment of a Reform newspaper at Carlton Place together with the addition of Irish townships along the Rideau to Lanark County, particularly Montague immediately to the south, served to emphasize the balancing position in which Beckwith found itself caught from the 1840s onward. To the north the lowlander weavers of Ramsay were confirmed in their radicalism and support of Reform by the rhetoric employed in the *Carleton-Place Herald*. To the south were the sons and daughters of Beckwith Irish Anglican Tories and the even more reactionary Irish Orange immigrants who arrived in the early 1830s. The radical influence from the north and the reactionary push from the south inevitably after mid-century served to make Irish Beckwith more conservative and induced a number of Beckwith highland families to become moderate Reformers. This trend emerged only in the mid to late 1840s as Robert Bell began to mould a constituency.

The emergence of partisan politics during the 1840s and the detailed coverage it received in the growing regional press coincided with the emergence of municipal institutions. No records have survived from before 1840, and yet incidental references in early documents suggest that meetings of townships inhabitants were held almost from the time settlement began. The 1820 census of Beckwith was conducted by town clerk Duncan Campbell, and the 1822 census was conducted by town clerk John Conboy (Appendices 8 and 9). An 1822 petition for a Church of Scotland glebe in Beckwith was signed by Beckwith town wardens Robert Davis and John Ferguson.[21] Town meetings of the inhabitants in adjacent Montague Township had been held as early as 1802,[22] and were also being held regularly in Drummond[23] and Ramsay townships well before 1830.[24] Without any doubt similar meetings were held in Beckwith, probably beginning about 1820, but there is no direct reference to township officers and meetings until inhabitants at a town meeting held on the third day of January 1831 sent a petition to their member William Morris. They enclosed a list of names which included the Reverend Richard Harte, the Reverend George Buchanan, Francis W.K. Jessop, Joseph Sutton, Manny Nowlan, Captain Thomas Glendinning, Peter Cram Sr., and William Kerfoot Sr. The Beckwith meeting requested the lieutenant-governor to select magistrates from these names to end "the great inconveniencies they rest under at present, as well as for some years past, in being obliged to go a great distance through bad Roads viz to be sworn in for the respective duties of the Township, together with the Adjustment of small debts".[25]

Repeated petitions to the lieutenant-governor from Beckwith inhabitants for the appointment of a resident magistrate during the 1830s revealed how little authority the township meetings and township officers possessed. As early as 1822 William Morris commented that the "inhabitants of Beckwith and Ramsay suffer much inconvenience owing to the want of Magistrates" and recommended John Ferguson as a "well informed, industrious farmer...bear[ing] an excellent character" to be appointed magistrate, to no avail.[26] Later in 1831 twelve Irish inhabitants of Beckwith petitioned lieutenant-governor Sir John Colborne to appoint Irish Anglicans Israel Webster and James Kent and Irish Methodist William Kerfoot from the southern concessions as magistrates. They claimed to:[27]

> labour under many disadvantages in consequence of the want of resident Magistrates in the above Township, that many of the Inhabitants who are pensioners, have to proceed to Perth, a distance of from Sixteen to twenty miles to make their aff[i]davi[t]s, not having a Magistrate residing in the Township.... [T]heir Township meetings for the purpose of Nominating and appointing officers Annually are seldom or never attended by a Magistrate, which causes great Irregularities and Inconvenience and in many instances, serious loss to the Inhabitants.... [The] appoint[ment of] a sufficient number of Magistrates — resident in the Township [would] enable [your petitioners] to hold a Court of request in some convenient place... which will prevent the necessity of going to Perth... on every trifling occasion.

Plate 111
The Robert Scott house, lot 20, concession 6, Beckwith, built in 1863, as photographed in 1983. The many large windows in this house reveal that all traces of traditional highland architecture had been totally obliterated during the 1850s. The sidelights and transom around the front door reflected a new emphasis on bright spacious interiors that had not existed in the log and stone houses built by Beckwith inhabitants of highland origin before the late 1840s.

Over a year earlier a public meeting of Ramsay inhabitants had been held to express their "alarm [at] the manner in which they have been treated...as far as concerns their Town Meeting" by the concentration of magistrates at Perth. The Ramsay lowlanders stated that His Majesty's magistrates were "obliged by Law to grant a warrant for calling and holding our Town Meetings" and to authorise "a Constable to preside at the same" since "without said Warrant, a lawful intimation and a presiding Constable, our meetings are illegal, and of course [so is]our whole procedure at said meetings." Ramsay inhabitants were alarmed "That some of our office bearers have been put to blush by those in authority, when applying to be installed in office, by being told they were not legally elected, as this town meeting was illegal." With magistrates no nearer than Perth, Beckwith and Ramsay office holders faced a trip of from twenty to 35 miles "for the express purpose of being sworn into office, under the penalty inflicted by law". Without such a trip, and without the approval of the Perth magistrates the Ramsay petitioners found their situation in January 1830 "not only unpleasant but disadvantageous, having neither overseers of roads, assessors, nor any office bearer whatever in the township."[28] Colonel Josias Taylor, after attending a militia muster at Carlton Place in June 1833 confirmed the feelings of anxiety and injury that the inhabitants of Ramsay and Beckwith felt they "are subjected to, in consequence of this want, particularly in holding their Annual Town Meetings, at which all the appointments of Town Officers is made, and at which by Law a Magistrate should preside."[29] By implication, the town meetings in Beckwith during the 1820s and 1830s were held regardless of whether or not the consent of Perth magistrates was received.

The radicalised lowlanders and Irish Catholics of Ramsay may well have faced more obstacles than the highlanders and Irish Anglicans of Beckwith in having their township officers sworn.

Certainly, Beckwith township officers were more discreet in that they forwarded their petitions to the lieutenant-governor through their members of the legislature rather than follow the Ramsay example of noisily publicising their complaints in the *Bathurst Independent Examiner*. The conservatism of most Beckwith inhabitants was well demonstrated in April 1832 when the American-origin Carlton Place postmaster Caleb S. Bellows "and some of his friends... circulated a paper for Signature recommending [John McEwan] and himself as being the most fit and proper persons for magistrates in the township of Beckwith." John Bell at Carlton Place commented, "I am aware that many of the people in Beckwith would be satisfied with the nomination of Mr. McEwan but I have reason to think that his name was used merely as a decoy to obtain Signatures for Mr. Bellows who by himself would not get more than twenty persons in the township to recommend him."[30] To prevent Bellows's petition from being taken seriously, Bell forwarded to the lieutenant-governor through the local member a counter-petition signed by 186 heads of Beckwith families a large proportion of whom were Irish who were of the "opinion that British born Subjects only should be appointed to fill [the] office [of magistrate], out of the many, more, or at least equally qualified with Mr. Bellows" (Appendix 14).[31] Bell explained, "The subscribers... wish it to be understood that they mean by 'British born Subjects,' persons who were actually *born* in the British dominions, and not Americans who may take the oath of allegiance on getting into some office of emolument."[32]

Donald Fraser, the Reform member for Lanark, in endorsing and forwarding the counter-petition on to the lieutenant-governor revealed why so many Beckwith inhabitants were opposed to Bellows being recommended as magistrate:[33]

> I cannot speak from any knowledge I have of him, nor of his Character and fitness for the Commission of the Peace but as far as my humble Judgment enables me to frame an opinion I deem an Alien (an American) more particularly to be [an] unfit person to be placed in the Commission of the Peace — I am induced to offer this Remark from the rapid Strides of Democratic Principles already avowed in this Province. It has been Stated, and I understand can be Satisfactorily Proved that Mr. C. S. Bellows h[o]isted the American Flag and Celebrated the Independence of his Count[r]y on the 4th of July some two or three years ago which greatly an[n]oyed the Inhabitants of Carlton Place.

The anti-American and anti-republican invective of Fraser shows how little in common the British-origin Reformers of Lanark County shared with the American-origin majority of Reformers elsewhere in Upper Canada. Fraser nominated John Bell, James Hume and John McEwan to be made magistrates, anticipating that McEwan would give up keeping tavern since he was "in every other respect well Qualified."[34] A year later Fraser again recommended Bell and Hume, but recommended Israel Webster in the place of John McEwan who "has again taken out [a] Tavern licence", arguing that they "will Strengthen the hands of the government and also administer the law impartially."[35]

As the 1830s proceeded, and Upper Canadian politics deteriorated largely into a fray between conservative British immigrants and American-origin and radical Scottish immigrants inflamed by the rhetoric of William Lyon Mackenzie, an address was circulated in Beckwith expressing loyalty to and satisfaction with the administration of Lieutenant-Governor Sir Francis Bond Head. Dr. George Hume Reade from Perth attended the Beckwith meeting in early May 1836, and was so gratified "to witness the feeling in favour of His Excellency evinced by the honest and intelligent yeomanry of this well settled Township" that he estimated a total of 400 signatures and recommended that John Drysdale and Israel Webster be appointed magistrates, especially since Head's successor Sir John Colborne had "promised to place Drysdale's name in the Commission of the Peace."[36] When still no magistrates were appointed, Captain Thomas Glendinning as foreman of the grand jury of the Bathurst District in June 1837 prayed that Head

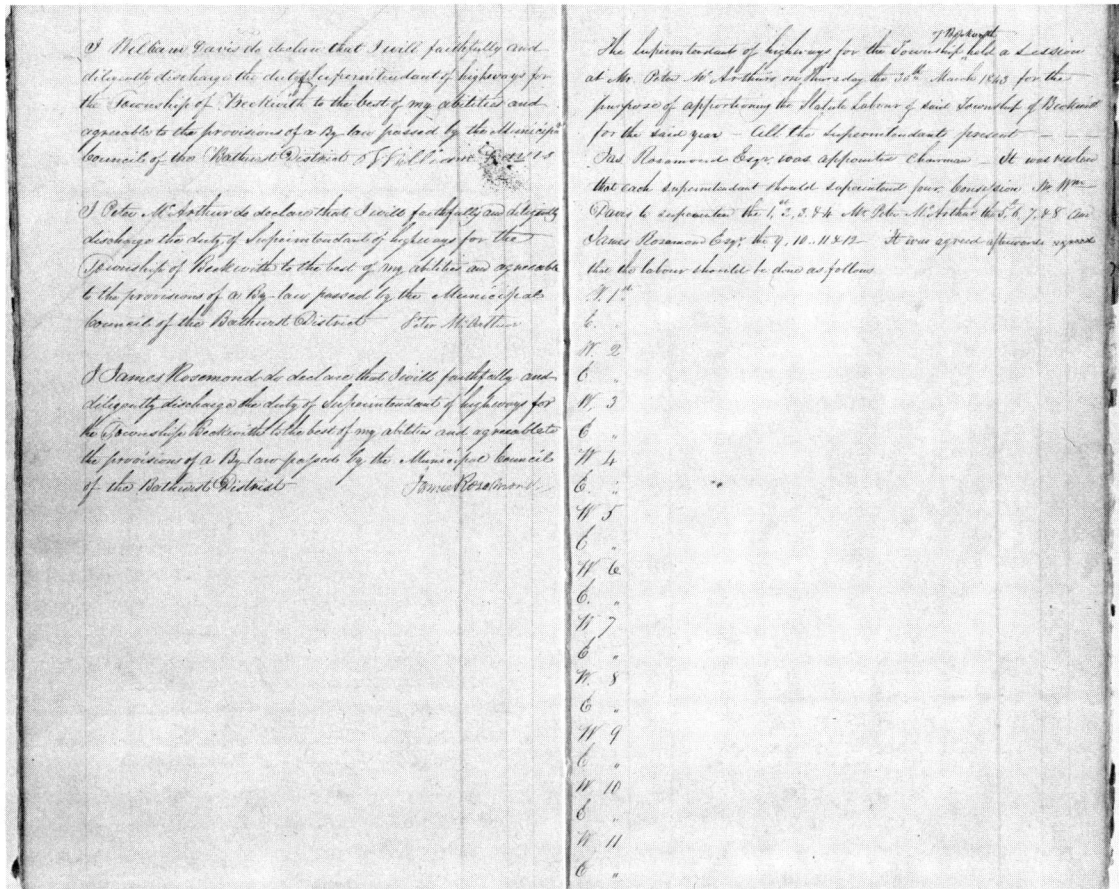

Plate 112
Beckwith municipal records for 1842 and 1843. The 1842 fenceviewers' oaths and 1843 resolution and by-law presented here reveal a transition away from forest agriculture that had allowed livestock to roam in the woods. In the new fenced landscape, fences not only surrounded crop fields to protect them from foraging livestock, but roads and pasture land, indeed entire farms, became fenced as part of a more orderly landscape emerging in the 1840s. Beckwith municipal records, Black's Corners.

would "be pleased to Select a few Gentlemen, resident in [Beckwith] to be included in the new Commission of the Peace." Glendinning pointed out that the population of "nearly two thousand three hundred Souls, chiefly respectable Yeomen, and faithful and loyal Subjects of His Majesty" in Beckwith felt "rather aggrieved that there does not reside a Magistrate nearer to them than fifteen Miles."[37] Glendinning's somewhat transparent attempt to have himself appointed magistrate seemed to work, for within a couple of weeks a reply from the lieutenant-governor's secretary assured him "that the wishes of the Grand Jury, shall be complied with",[38] but as late as 1840 there still were no magistrates in Beckwith.[39] By 1846, accompanying the emergence of district councils, Beckwith boasted six resident magistrates. They were Robert Bell, John Conboy, Robert Davis, Peter McGregor, Colin McLaren and James Rosamond.[40]

Despite the loss of all records concerning Beckwith township officers from the 1820s and 1830s, the list of officers for 1841 confirms that Beckwith was organised along the lines recommended by provincial law with the exception of not having a magistrate present (Appendix 19).[41] James Kent as township clerk was responsible for conducting annual nomination meetings, for acting as chairman of meetings in the absence of officials, for collecting fines, for keeping minutes of meetings, for posting one set of minutes up in a public place and delivering a second copy to the district clerk of the peace, for keeping a record of all township accounts, and for taking declarations from all other officers for promising to deligently carry out their duties.[42] Richard Finley as township assessor compiled a list of all the rateable personal property owned by inhabitants of Beckwith, presented the original to the district clerk of the peace, placed "a correct copy thereof in some conspicuous place within the township for the inspection of the inhabitants", and took a census of every inhabitant householder or head of family. Robert Davis as collector of rates was responsible for collecting the amounts entered on the assessment roll.[43] The six poundkeepers in Beckwith provided safe keeping, necessary food and drink on their own property for all animals unlawfully running at large, trespassing and doing damage delivered to them by residents within their respective divisions, and arranged for the sale of all unclaimed livestock.[44] The six fenceviewers upheld the height and description of lawful fences determined at the annual township meeting and arbitrated in disputes between neighbours over the building and upkeep of line fences.[45] Twenty-eight pathmasters, roughly one for each half of a concession, directed their neighbours in building, maintaining, bridging and opening roads. Any inhabitants neglecting or refusing to perform township offices to which they were appointed or giving an inaccurate return of their rateable property were liable to a fine ranging from one to five pounds.[46]

As the description of the duties of the town clerk, assessor and collector indicate, the annual meetings of township inhabitants and the officers they nominated were subservient to the magistrates and district officials in Perth who were appointed by the lieutenant-governor. From the end of the military settlement in 1822 until 1842 power in the district was concentrated in the hands of magistrates in the vicinity of Perth who in their meetings four times a year (the court of quarter sessions) exercised a great range of powers, administrative as well as judicial.[47] A general restructuring of Canadian government in 1842 brought district councils into being, with a warden appointed by the Governor General and councillors elected from the various townships. Before 1842 three town wardens had annually been nominated in each township to oversee the activities of the numerous other township officers. From 1842 to the end of the decade Beckwith was entitled to elect two district councillors because it had more than 300 inhabitant freeholders and householders.[48] The last town wardens for Beckwith were Thomas Kidd, Alexander Stewart and Peter McArthur in 1841. The first two district councillors elected from Beckwith were Robert Bell and Robert Davis in 1842. The district council in addition to its responsibility for constructing major district roads, managing property owned by the district and collecting assessments was responsible for establishing and supporting schools. In 1842 the Reverend James Padfield, the Reverend Edward Boswell, the Reverend John Smith, Thomas Kidd, John Conboy, John Ferguson, and John Whyte were appointed school commissioners in Beckwith.[49]

From the beginning of settlement Irish and Scottish immigrants in Beckwith gave priority to education, as reflected by Robert Ferguson's comment in 1823 that "their is plenty of S[c]hools all around us all endowed with Governmint salarys".[50] So widespread was the push for education in the Bathurst District in the late 1820s that no other district in Upper Canada had more schools. In Beckwith there were six schools by 1827, taught by Finlay McNaughton, the Reverend George Buchanan, Alexander Miller, John McLaren, Alexander McNabb and James Kent. Buchanan's school had the lowest number of pupils with the minimum number of twenty to allow it to qualify for a share of the grant received by the district from the provincial legislature. The school of Alexander McNabb had the highest attendance of any school in the entire Bathurst District, and indubitably was located at Carlton Place. Although less than half of all Beckwith children under the age of sixteen were male, they accounted for three-fifths of the 170 children attending school in the township in 1827.[51] A small log structure built by inhabitants near the residence of the Reverend George

Plate 113
Ewen McEwen (ca. 1810—1885) and his son Peter McEwen (1847—1911), successively township clerks of Beckwith from 1842 to 1911. The monopolising of the highest paid position in the municipality for over two-thirds of a century by this father and son provides striking evidence of the continuity in occupation from one generation to the next during the late nineteenth and early twentieth centuries in rural Beckwith. Photographs respectively loaned by Evelyn and William Scrivens and Jean McEwen, Ottawa, courtesy of Arthur Hawkins.

Buchanan in 1822 may well have been the earliest school in Beckwith. It was replaced a year later by the log shanty built for the Buchanan family when they arrived, and by 1825 inhabitants in other sections of the township such as Carlton Place were also building log schools.[52] The school over which Buchanan and his daughters presided may well have been as influential in the 1820s as his youngest daughter, Jessie, later recalled. She gave as an instance the story of one of Buchanan's early pupils, John McLaurin, whose Gaelic-speaking[53]

> parents urged father to take the boy into his house to do the chores for his boarding and attend school. The lad, who came next day, knew scarcely a word of English. He stayed with us for years, making fine progress as a student. He learned Greek, Latin and Hebrew, paid his way through Edinborough University by working morning and evening, was licensed to preach and returned to Canada.

Nor was McLaurin exceptional among Buchanan's students. In June 1830 the Reverend William Bell from Perth found himself "detained...at least an hour longer than [he] wished" by a doting Beckwith mother who "insisted that [he] should read...all [of]...a letter from her son, who had gone to Glasgow to attend university. It was nearly equal to a volume being the largest sheet that could be pressed and written very small and very close, and then crossed."[54]

Buchanan along with fellow clergymen John Smith, James Padfield and Johnston Neilson represented a high standard among the early teachers of Beckwith, benefitting as they had from higher education. Johnston Neilson who taught at Carlton Place from the early 1840s to the early 1850s described himself in 1836 as "a Licentiate of the General Synod of Ulster, Ireland, who has been 22 years employed in the Tuition of the youth in the north of Ireland, where he has taught respectable Classical and English Schools, having lately come to America on account of his family".[55] By virtue of their clerical training these clergymen "as truly Loyal subjects" considered it not only their duty but their inclination "to inculcate due attachment to the Government of that mighty and honoured Empire under whose protection we all have the happiness to repose — as labourers...in the field of Education — the handmaid of Religion".[56] Some of the other early teachers in Beckwith had background in teaching. Alexander Miller, for example, was reputed to be well educated, and who before immigrating to McNab Township on the upper Ottawa taught the village school of Nineveh, a small hamlet halfway between Loch Earn Head and Callander in Perthshire. Upon incurring the wrath of the notorious Laird of McNab who clapped him into the Perth gaol for six weeks, Miller left McNab in 1827 to teach school in Beckwith for many years.[57] William Poole, a retired British army officer who had followed in his father's footsteps as headmaster at Drysart School in County Kilkenny, Ireland, taught school at Carlton Place from his arrival in 1831[58] until 1843, when he was dismissed on a technicality for not attending a meeting of the local school commissioners.[59]

Many of the early teachers in Beckwith had little or no background in education and because of their bare literacy and their inability to do well at anything else had little alternative but to accept the meagre stipend offered by teaching. James Kent, for instance, who taught school at Franktown from the mid 1820's through to the mid 1840s[60] was an Irish-born discharged soldier from the Glengarry Fencibles.[61] The Reverend Richard Harte approvingly reported that Kent was well qualified to instruct students in the Anglican catechism, but Kent's salary as a teacher was so meagre that he was forced to supplement it by working as township clerk, and by 1844 "his famishing family" was described as being "in the greatest misery".[62] The poor qualifications of many early Beckwith teachers were recalled in later life by John May who had attended Kent's school at Franktown as a child in the late 1830s and early 1840s:[63]

> Young girls had not, as yet, begun to climb,
> In any number, to the Teacher's throne,
> Filled then by men, and almost men alone.
> Rare, curious specimens were most of these;
> Failures in other lines, and glad to seize
> On any lawful means to win their bread;
> The people glad to have their children fed
> On the best mental food that could be got
> Under the circumstances of their lot:
> The grim old soldier, on his wooden leg,
> Thus spared the dire necessity to beg:
> The broken merchant, sunk to penury:
> The sailor, battered on the stormy sea:
> And he who once had sat in college hall,
> But whom the wrestler, Drink, had given a fall.
> Such were the "dominies" of long ago[.]

The creation of the Bathurst district council composed of elected representatives in 1842 and the passing of the common schools Act by the provincial legislature in 1841 together gave promise of democratising and improving Beckwith schools. A meeting of teachers from across the Bathurst District at Carlton Place on 13 September 1842 expected better teaching conditions, substantially better pay and higher standards. They recommended to the provincial superintendent of education that no teachers be engaged who could not pass certain qualifications, that a teacher's salary "be no less than £50", that one of the commissioners in each school section be appointed "to collect quarterly wages when not paid to the Teacher", that rather than have the township appoint school commis-

Plate 114
Statute labour being performed near the southern boundary of Beckwith ca. 1902. Every male inhabitant between the ages of 21 and 60 was obliged to perform statute labour which basically consisted of building and repairing roads, bridges and drains. Beckwith was divided into 42 statute labour divisions. The large number of swamps necessitated that much statute labour was devoted to building corduroy sections of road, hauling stone and breaking up stone to fill in holes. In 1896 Andrew W. Cram purchased a stone crusher after Beckwith agreed to "give him a job of crushing 135 cords on the roadside" annually. It was not until March 1913 that Beckwith purchased a municipal stone crusher and three dump wagons, but by 1927 statute labour was abolished.

sioners "that *each* School District appoint *one*" and that no school district be formed "where there are *less* than *Fifty* children residing therein". Moreover, they recommended that "each School District be required to purchase Four acres of land and erect a House thereon for the use of the Teacher adjacent to the School house [with the] land to be obtained by any means the Legislators may devise — And the dwelling house furnished in a proper and comfortable manner." The final point agreed on by the convention at Carlton Place was that commissioners "be answerable to the District Council in *all* their transactions with regard to the management of Common Schools."[64] Clearly, local teachers were heartily tired of a situation where they were placed at the mercy of low standards, low status, and parents who did not pay their stipends of [65]

> Twenty or thirty pounds a year, eked out
> Precariously, by "boarding round about,"
> A fortnight with each family, or so.
> But the itinerant soon got to know
> The choicest places, and prolonged his stay;
> And few had heart to hasten him away.

The hiring of Johnston Neilson to replace William Poole as schoolmaster at Carlton Place in 1843 revealed the problems of the old system, and encapsulated the disparity between the idealistic rhetoric and the actual implementation of the 1841 Act. Neilson as an Irish Anglican teaching the common school at Smith's Falls for five years was unfairly dismissed through the connivance of the Church of Scotland clergyman and a Scotch Presbyterian trustee who replaced him with "John McPherson, just arrived from Scotland".[66] Neilson, in turn, agreed to replace Irish Methodist William Poole who had been unfairly dismissed for not attending a meeting of the Carlton Place school commissioners. Neilson was an idealist who looked forward to the day when "Education will...have free courses, [when] the condition of Teachers [will be] rendered comfortable and respectable, when the public [will be] well served, and the cause of Religion and Morals and National prosperity [would be] unspeakably promoted." He perceived that in contrast with the British Isles where there was "a more general thirst for education...in this land, the payment of even a trifling School bill...has deprived thousands upon thousands of children of that which, next to religion, is their best inheritance". Depriving children of an education in Neilson's opinion was "an evil" and would continue "unless some miraculous change be wrought in the selfish spirit of the people, so long as this payment is voluntary, or in other words, so long as the school fees tax is chargeable only for such children as actually attend school". In 1842, some seven years before anyone else in the Bathurst District advocated free schools, Johnston Neilson urged that all inhabitants "should be called upon to support [education], while they whose children receive it, should contribute a larger proportion" because of the benefits it provided not only to those being taught but also the general effect education had "on the public morals and happiness and prosperity" of society.[67]

Neilson's idealism was pulled down to earth by the disorder of the fledgeling Bathurst district council that in May 1843 moved to discontinue the new provincial school Act, and when subsequent attempts were made to reverse this decision, delays and lack of council quorums combined to militate against a district school tax being collected in 1843, and against the council receiving its share of the provincial grant. To add to the hardship this caused local teachers, their third source of income also dried up; many of the people who owed monthly school fees suddenly considered themselves exempt from paying them "in consequence of the District Council not having carried the School Act into operation this year". Johnston Neilson in December 1843 responded by drafting a petition to Governor General Metcalfe requesting relief for the teachers placed in jeopardy by circumstances, and had fellow Beckwith teachers James Kent, John W. Poole, James Conn, Thomas Ferguson,

Plate 115
Franktown village school with the stone 1848 school on the right and the larger 1868 structure that replaced it on the left. Local tradition has erroneously suggested that this structure was the government storehouse built to hold provisions for the early settlers in 1818. The school at Franktown was the only one in Beckwith built of stone before 1850, but in its design conformed to the log schools throughout the rest of the township in having students face the wall at a desk hugging the wall that ran around three sides of the room.

Alexander Miller, Archibald M. Young, Daniel Ferguson, and William Lindsay along with eleven other district teachers sign it,[68] to no avail.

The 1841 school Act in dividing Beckwith into eleven districts and providing for schools to be centrally located within each district angered some inhabitants, particularly a number of those in that most Scottish of school sections, S.S. No. 9 in the northern corner of Beckwith. John Whyte, an inhabitant of this school section wrote to the *Bathurst Courier* in late July 1842, and stated that inhabitants at a public meeting in the Church of Scotland on the seventh concession after trying the new system of education found it inadequate for the advancement of education. They complained that people remote from schools were deprived of their benefits, and yet they were required to pay so that other people might send their children, and the majority preferred the old system over the new.[69] A week later a Beckwith school commissioner responded to Whyte's letter, stating that there were only "two dozen...illiterate and contentious individuals 'half of whom' belonged to school district No. 9, a portion of whose inhabitants have been for some time up in arms...against the Commissioners, on the subject of the location of the school house for the district." A total of only 65 signatures had been gathered protesting against the new school Act, clearly showing that most Beckwith inhabitants either found no fault with it or knew nothing about it.[70] In 1842 ten schools were operating in Beckwith, and by 1845 453 or nearly two-thirds of all children between the ages of five and sixteen were attending school.[71]

Following the arrival of large influxes of Irish Catholic Famine immigrants in the late 1840s, a movement to establish free schools began to gain momentum. The free school system taxed all inhabitants the same rate of assessment on their property, and all children residing in the section, even of those who did not own property, were encouraged to attend school. This contrasted with the system introduced in 1841 which required parents of pupils to pay an additional fee above the educational assessment paid by all taxpayers. The movement for free schools gained impetus from 1849 on as arguments were made for the importance of educating all children so that the children of the Irish Catholic Famine immigrants flooding into Canada West could be trained to "grow up in the industry and intelligence of the country, and not in the idleness and pauperism, not to say mendicity and vices, of their forefathers."[72] A favoured argument of those advocating free schools was that if the state did not ensure virtuous education to young people, society eventually might have to pay a higher price for their incarceration as criminals.[73] Free schools, it was argued, would render unnecessary gaols, penitentiaries, sheriffs, penal colonies, hangmen and gallows.[74]

The moral order promised by free schools was especially needed in Carlton Place at mid-century where inhabitants perceived that knots of boys ran wild after dark, and young men used improper language and vented oaths on the public street. "This village", declared Johnston Neilson in March 1851[75]

> is the worst place I know for rearing boys.... It is beside the question now under consideration to require a line of demarcation to be observed between youth that have been longer resident and new-comers. The question is...are young persons hitherto unscathed by vicious habits, in danger of being corrupted, if playing in the streets with whatever sort of companions may offer,

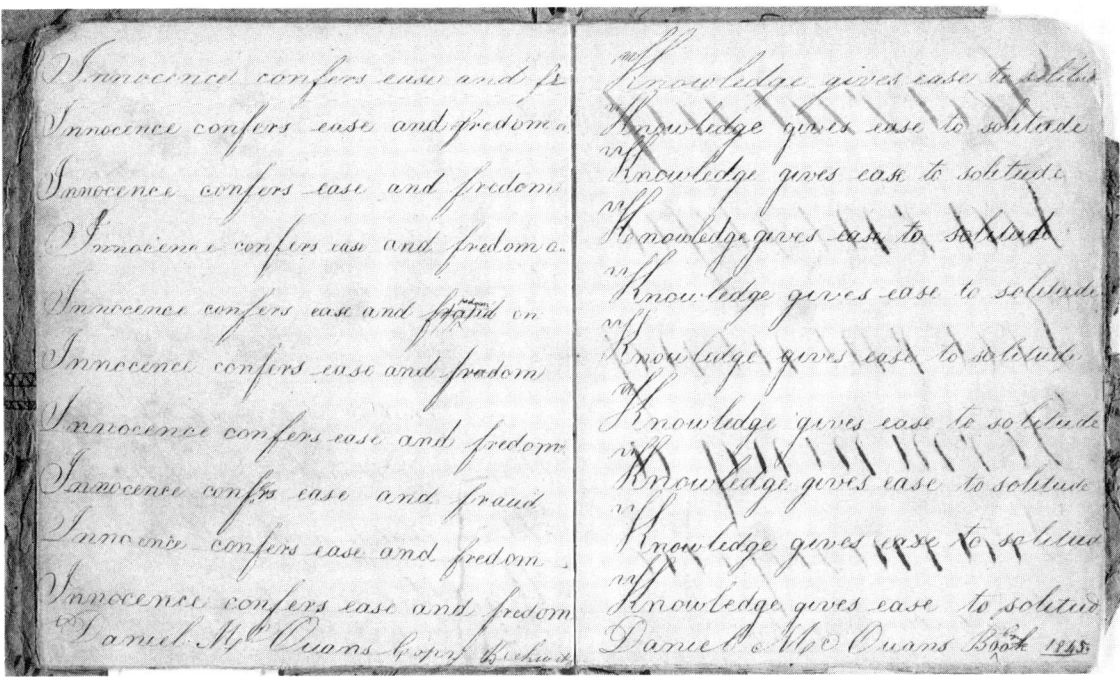

Plate 116
A collage of four pages from the 1845 copybook of Daniel McCuan, Beckwith. The children and grandchildren of Scottish highlanders attending school section number 9 in Beckwith's northern corner acquired a set of assumptions about industriousness and virtue being rewarded with happiness and prosperity. The repetitiveness of copying out these stock phrases caused Daniel McCuan to write that innocence conferred fraud rather than freedom. Loaned courtesy of Alex and Jean McCuan.

be allowed them any longer[?] — The inclination for street-playing is in this place so great, and the seducing arts of its devotees are so powerful, that I find...no inconsiderable watchfulness and rigor necessary to keep within doors one of my own children who has been of a harmless nature.

There was resistance in Beckwith to free schools, and particularly so from Presbyterian and Methodist Reformers. David Lawson, a Scottish merchant at Carleton Place, rejected the argument that education would eradicate criminality by observing that French Canadians were the worst educated part of the population, and who although comprising one third of Canada's total population, formed less than a sixth of its penitentiary inhabitants.[76] James C. Poole perceived no necessity for the state to educate the children of those who could well afford it, arguing instead that a direct tax should be levied to educate the children of paupers and criminals, because supporting a system of state paid schools was as intolerable a thought as supporting state paid churches.[77] The battle for free schools would persist on into the 1850s and 1860s in Beckwith, but for most Beckwith inhabitants it was achievement enough that ten schools were open and attended by 453 pupils by 1845. Only one other township in Lanark County that year could boast more students attending school.[78]

The establishment of libraries was another way in which Beckwith inhabitants attempted to create order in local society. Indeed, the inhabitants of the Bathurst District generally considered the fact that they had "more circulating libraries than an[y] other District" as "a proof of the[ir] supreme intelligence and good moral character"[79] and a Scottish correspondent of the *Bathurst Courier* averred that "the number of libraries and agricultural societies, of which this district can boast, attest that the inhabitants are *intelligent Scotchmen.*"[80] In Beckwith the first library was the Church of Scotland congregational library founded by the Reverend John Smith in 1833. It is possible to assess the growth and the strictly religious content of the books donated to and purchased for this collection from three surviving volumes. The *Select Remains of the Reverend John Mason...* "Containing A Variety of devout useful Sayings on divers Subjects...; religious Observations; serious Advice to Youth; occasional Reflections; and Christian Letters" (1798) was donated by a Mrs. McKay in 1834 as volume number 105.[81] *Familiar Letters to a Gentleman, Upon A Variety of Seasonable and Important Subjects in Religion* by Jonathan Dickinson (1772) was donated by Captain Anderson in 1836 as volume number 207. *Saint Indeed: or, The Great Work of a Christian Explained* by the late Reverend John Flavel (1840) was purchased in 1841 to become volume number 252 in the Beckwith Congregational Library.[82] The lagging number of acquisitions in the late 1830s suggest that this library was in decline by the early 1840s.

At a public meeting held in Robert Bell's company office at Carlton Place on the seventh day of March 1846 the Carlton Place Library Association & Mechanics Institute was formed. Mechanics Institutes were originally conceived at the beginning of the nineteenth century as an organisation to promote knowledge among radical artisans,[83] but by the time they migrated to Canada in the early 1840s they had been infiltrated by middle class manufacturers and businessmen who made sure that the volumes stocked in the libraries would not incite the labourers or mechanics* to riot or partake in radical activities, but rather inculcate middle class values. Significantly, not one of the three founding officers who drafted the constitution of the Carlton Place Library Association & Mechanics Institute in Bell's office was a mechanic; Robert Bell was a merchant and manufacturer, John A. Gemmill was a merchant, and Daniel Cram was a Beckwith farmer. They drafted a constitution stating that the foremost objective of the Mechanic's Institute was "the establishment and management of a Public Library, the acquisition of suitable Apparatus in connection with the Mechanic's Institute, and supply of Lectures on useful & interesting subjects."[84] A year later in April 1847 the committee and directors reported that the number of books increased from 23 to 144 and the membership grew from seven to 41 during the previous three months.[85]

When Johnston Neilson became supervisor in 1851, the library was moved from David Lawson's home to his residence. Neilson urged the general public to "consider the gratification...reading useful works affords to all members of the family" especially with an accession of new works expected from New York:[86]

> How pleasant, useful and improving to all in the house, would it be, were they to engage the young in reading aloud to the other members of the family while employed in sedentary occupations. The subscription to this Library being light, namely, 2s. 6d. entrance and 5s. annually, paid always in advance, none should deny themselves the benefit of it. To encourage apprentices and young men who may not be householders, they have been privileged to enjoy all the benefits of the shareholding members as far as it respects reading, on prepaying 5d. monthly.
>
> There is no restriction with respect to distance from the seat of the Library, except particular punctuality in returning the books by safe hands and regular pre-payment of subscriptions; so that persons at the distance of Franktown...may under these circumstances become entitled to the benefits of the Library.

The volumes in the Carlton Place library at mid-century offered a much wider variety of literary fare than had the Church of Scotland congregational library to appeal to the farmers, merchants,

---

* Mechanic is used here to refer to a worker with a manual occupation.

Plate 117
The Peter Anderson house, lot 8, concession 6, possibly dating from the late 1830s, as photographed in 1983. No effort was made to use uniformly sized or spaced stone even on the front wall of this early stone house in Beckwith. Despite the various sizes and shapes of stone used, the outer surface of the wall is uniformly flat. The porch is a later addition. The Perthshire highlanders in Beckwith began building ambitious houses as early as the 1840s thanks to the influence of Irish Anglicans and lowlanders, unlike the highlanders in Glengarry County who did not begin building ambitious houses until the late Victorian period.

artisans and clerks who comprised the membership. The 65 members between 1846 and 1851 (Appendix 20) read books such as *Renwick's Natural Philosophy, Eminent Zoologists,* the *Glasgow Mechanic's Magazine,* Dick's *Celestial Scenery,* Buell's *Farmer's Instructor,* Brewster's *Natural Magic,* the *Defence of Order, Locke on Government,* Scott's *Demonology,* Slade's *Phrenology,* Dick's *Improvement of Society, Camp on Democracy,* Russell's *Cromwell,* Franklin's *Life & Works, Wallace & Bruce, Canadian Brothers, Life of Sir Walter Raleigh, Plutarch's Lives, Marco Polo, Polynesia & New Zealand,* Russell's *Egypt, British India,* Millman's *History of the Jews, History of Palestine, Court and Camp of Bonaparte,* Taylor's *History of Ireland* and *Revolutions in Europe* among others.[87] The Scottish and Reform alignment of the first directors of the library was shown in 1849 after an extremist Tory mob set the parliament buildings at Montreal on fire and pelted the Scottish governor general, Lord Elgin, with stones. The library directors sent an address to Lord Elgin keenly sympathising that he had "been subjected to a series of cowardly insults and injuries by a portion of those who profess to be our loyal fellow subjects" simply for allowing an unpopular Reform measure to be implemented by the Canadian parliament.[88] By July 1850, Robert Bell as Reform member of the legislative assembly was advising local inhabitants how to establish township school libraries.[89]

The search for order was manifested in numerous other ways. The formation of the Bathurst District Agricultural Society, later the County of Lanark Agricultural Society, at Carlton Place in 1840 was one. The proposal to build a plank road from Carlton Place to Bytown (later Ottawa) in 1845 was another.[90] The very appearance of the rural landscape began to bear a more ordered appearance as clearings amid the forest gave way to stands of forest amid the cleared landscape, as fences surrounded not only the fields of crops but the pastureland as well, as grain barns and livestock stables joined other outbuildings on each homestead, and as the first gravestones were placed in the Mount Pleasant, Prospect, St. Fillan's, Cram, Kennedy and Franktown burial grounds. The concession lines of Beckwith were opened by local inhabitants under the guidance of local pathmasters so far as the prevalent swamps of the township would admit. The ten schoolhouses and nine churches either in Beckwith or on its periphery by 1851 reflected a more ordered landscape than had existed in 1825. The formation of Orange lodges at Franktown and Carlton Place in the early 1830s was the orderly means through which Beckwith Irish Anglicans attempted to politically organise and to align themselves with other conservatives in Upper Canada.

A decade earlier in 1822 a group of Carlton Place area men petitioned for a warrant to organise a Masonic lodge, but it was not until November 1842 that a second petition from Johnston Neilson, Brice McNeely, William Rea, James Robinson, William James, John More, Peter Carmichael, John McIntyre, Andrew Paul, and Peter McGregor was granted.[91] On the twentieth day of January 1842 St. John's Lodge was installed at Caleton Place, prompting one participant to coment:[92]

> We have every reason to expect that, from the good character of the officers of the New Lodge, and enlightened mind and good moral and religious reputation of the people of Ramsay and of that part of Beckwith with which Carleton Place is more immediately connected, the Lodge of St. John at Carlton Place will become one of the most flourishing in this Province.... We are happy to find that the Lodge of St. John have resolved to give enemies no handle against them on the point of spirituous liquors at their meetings, having resolved, as far as possible, to hold these in a private house.

The orderliness instilled by the Masonic fraternity among its members in Beckwith during the 1840s was shown by the emphasis to resolve disputes among the brethren, their benevolence to brother Ewen Cameron when he fell ill and care of his widow after his death, and reprimands to brethren who were intemperate on St. John's day.[93]

In the 1840s the temperance movement emerged in Beckwith as the ultimate means of producing order in local society. Temperance societies had existed in eastern Upper Canada from the late 1820s on, but most of them were organised by American immigrants to stave off potential assimilation by the tide of Irish Protestants pouring into the region during the 1830s. American-origin Methodists and Presbyterians in settlements besieged by a tide of Irish Anglican immigrants used temperance lodges as an ostensibly moral movement to offer an organisational base for the Reform political movement. It was hoped that they would counter the growing number of Orange lodges that were the active nuclei for the regional growth of Conservative power.[94] An attempt was made to organise a temperance society at Carlton Place in 1831,[95] but initially its appeal was limited largely to the radicalised Scottish lowlanders from Ramsay and the handful of American-origin inhabitants in the village. Among the Beckwith highlanders and Irish Anglicans there was no enthusiasm for temperance, as reflected in the 1829 boast of the Perth *Bathurst Independent Examiner*, "it has not been found necessary to establish, either here or in any part of the [Perth] settlement, that disgrace to humanity and certain mark of former debasement — a temperance society."[96] That drinking was not considered a moral issue by the highland Scottish inhabitants in the late 1820s was shown by the Reverend George Buchanan inducing Scottish immigrant John Alston to become a steady drinking partner at the Beckwith manse in 1825.[97] The distillery of Peter McArthur supplied liquor in the 1830s and early 1840s to funerals, to logging bees, to school building bees, to church meetings, and to men reaping grain.[98] Between eight and ten taverns, inns and shops dispensed liquor to Beckwith inhabitants during the 1830s and 1840s, and they operated without criticism before mid-century save for Franktown innkeeper Thomas Wickham who was charged by two Campbells at the Perth assizes

Plate 118
The parlour of the Peter Anderson house, lot 8, concession 6, Beckwith, as photographed in 1983. The downstairs of this compact stone house consisted of three rooms, a kitchen to the left of the box hall inside the front door, this parlour on the right hand side, and a downstairs bedroom or birthing room behind it that also opened to the rear of the kitchen. The downstairs birthing room was probably considered a practical arrangement at a time when the Beckwith birthrate remained high, but once the size of families consistently fell after mid-century, the birthing room simply became used as a guest bedroom. The simple yet pleasing neoclassic lines of the fireplace mantel testify to an emerging sense of taste among the Perthshire highlanders who were interspersed among the Irish Anglicans of western Beckwith.

in June 1828 with "keeping a disorderly house and allowing gaming [gambling] in it."[99]

The Irish community of Beckwith resisted the temperance movement even more resolutely than the Scottish highlanders. The connection being made between political Reform and temperance was evident in the relative numbers of members in the Beckwith vicinity. At the founding meeting of the Bathurst District Temperance Society in the Methodist chapel at Carlton Place in early March 1836 the Perth society reported 511 members, the Mississippi & Ramsay society 295 members, the Lanark society 187 members, the Richmond society 57 members, and the Franktown society reported only eighteen members.[100] By 1842 temperance meetings were being conducted at the Kerfoot settlement (later Prospect)[101] but as the political alignment of the temperance movement became more evident many Irish Methodists did not necessarily approve. Irish Methodists at Perth created a sensation in 1842 by refusing to allow their chapel to be used for temperance meetings,[102] in complete contrast with American-origin Methodists who gave the movement momentum by advocating it in the *Christian Guardian*. The poor prospects of the temperance movement were evident to Abram Duncan who travelled around the region as an agent of the Bathurst District Temperance Union in March and April 1847. He "had held three meetings in Carlton Place, the attendance at which he characterised as having been shabby in the extreme. The people appeared to take no interest in the subject. He was happy to say...that the two medical gentlemen of Carlton Place and 12 other respectable and influential individuals had at these meetings signed the pledge."[103] In early April 1851 seventeen boys were organised into a branch of the Cadets of Temperance at Carlton Place, pledging "not only to abstain from all that intoxicates, but to avoid these filthy and dangerous habits, the use of tobacco and snuff."[104] Before a month had passed the *Lanark Herald* editor was "sorry to learn that some of the bad boys of our village have behaved themselves in a very unruly manner towards the Cadets of Temperance by laying wait for and attempting to abuse them, on their way to and from their Section Room."[105]

A division of the Sons of Temperance was formed at Carlton Place either in late 1849 or early 1850,[106] but both it and the Cadets of Temperance did not gain the large membership that such lodges did in towns such as Prescott and Gananoque where there were large numbers of American-origin inhabitants. Those few inhabitants of Beckwith who belonged to the temperance movement perceived the domestic evil that heavy drinking produced. They could cite the example of James Fallon who under the influence of drink at the Perth Fair in 1838 was killed when his horse crushed him, leaving a young wife and family.[107] Another example was Franktown tailor John McNaughton, a native of Perthshire, who died in March 1851 after an extended drunken spree.[108]

Beckwith women, who otherwise relied on the social constraints of local congregations to uphold the bonds of marriage and family, occasionally reinforced by charivaris, felt vulnerable only when their husbands drank immoderately. The first support for temperance in Beckwith most likely came from women, flowing out of the concern of mothers and wives to have control of their husbands, as the Reverend William Bell discovered while preaching at Carlton Place in 1831:[109]

> In McEwan's [hotel], before preaching, [Bell remarked,] I met Captain Glendinning, He had been drinking, though he would not admit it—said he had been reading my published letters, and they contained the best account of the country he had seen,—praised my preaching, and the good conduct of my sons. After preaching he came to me with tears in his eyes, and begged I would go with him to his house and remain all night;—said the sermon he had just heard had determined him to break off his wild course, and begin a new mode of life. I exhorted him to adhere to this resolution, and gave him such further advice as his case required, but told him that I could not accept of his kind invitation, having to return to Mr. Buchanan's that night. A person of less experience might have been deceived by his professions and apparent repentance, but I knew how the matter stood. His wife had the management of him; and as he had been at the tavern for some days, he was sure of a lecture when he went home. This was what made him so anxious to have me along with him, as he knew that in that case the lady would restrain her wrath till another time.

The temperance movement made little headway in Beckwith before mid-century. Indeed, as Daniel McCuan pointed out in an 1858 letter to a neighbour who had been urging the cause of total abstinence on him, "Now I am afraid that there is a great deal of double faced dealing in your society and this is one of the worst faults I have to [raise against] it; I have seen numbers of your society drinking grog when none of their fellow brethren were in their company and still they were considered true members."[110] The strength of feeling against the temperance movement shared by the majority of Irish Anglicans and Scottish highlanders in Beckwith was evident in two letters John A. Gemmill wrote to the *Bathurst Courier* in early 1847, denying the suggestion by a Perth Reformer that the St. Andrew's Day dinner at Carlton Place in 1846 was connected with a temperance festival. The topic of temperance was not once mooted at the St. Andrew's Day celebration, remarked Gemmill, as "it would have been looked upon as an insult",[111] hardly comparable with teetotal dinners "where people guzz[l]es tea... and slander their neighbours.[112]

Plate 119
The kitchen fireplace and oven in the Peter Anderson house, lot 8, concession 6, Beckwith, as photographed in 1983. The rounded arch on this fireplace is similar to that in the John McEwen log house (Plate 66), confirming that this is one of the earlier stone houses built in Beckwith. Fireplaces remained in general use for heating and cooking into the early 1850s.

The few temperance advocates in Beckwith anticipated that the suppression of drunkenness would create a more orderly and a more prosperous society, permitting everyone to afford the large stone and frame houses beginning to be built. The log houses in which most Beckwith people lived between 1825 and 1851 were significantly larger and more comfortable than the log huts and shanties built during the first years of settlement. With glass windows, many of them with flattened or even squared logs in the walls, heated by cooking and box stoves, with staircases, shingle roofs, and divided into four or five rooms inside, and some of them with root cellars underneath, these moderate size log houses were inhabited by two-thirds of the population. Many of these larger log houses were symmetrical on the exterior, but it was the stone and frame houses built before 1852 that emphasized symmetry, order and a new sense of interior spaciousness with large windows, even-sized and evenly spaced stone on the facade, sidelights and transoms around front doors, joinery on fireplace mantels, numerous rooms, high ceilings, plank floors, plastered and papered interior walls, window sashes, panelled doors, door handles, private bedrooms, halls and ceiling mouldings. Beckwith had no distinctive architecture, save possibly for the small twin windows set closely together in upstairs end gable walls of stone houses built in the township. Without exception the 48 frame and the 44 stone houses constructed in Beckwith before mid-century with their symmetrical facades and gables were the most pervasive and enduring statement of the search for domestic and social order in Beckwith.

The new spaciousness, the new sense of light in the larger Beckwith houses built before

Plate 120
The Donald McDougall house, lot 21, concession 8, Beckwith, built in the 1840s, as photographed in June 1983. This stone house had more generous dimensions than the Peter Anderson house (Plate 117), but the continuing inhibition for some highlanders of putting sufficient windows in their houses to adequately admit daylight is clearly shown here. The distinctive small gable windows made the upstairs rooms dark and motivated later generations to add front gables with windows to these houses. Such a gable was added to this house in 1987.

mid-century, is a reminder that the search for order in Beckwith had been conducted within the all encompassing physical and visual context of one ongoing activity — what the son of one Irish immigrant described as "flinging the awful forest aside".[113] The rolling acreages of sun-drenched grain fields, the provisioning economy, the quest to settle children on nearby farms, the group migrations to Renfrew County and to the western part of Upper Canada, the organisation of congregations and building of churches, the emergence of regional politics, the organising of township officers and the holding of annual township meetings, the building of schools, the opening of libraries, the organising of Orange and Masonic lodges, the large new log, stone and frame houses, and the emerging temperance movement — all in various ways reflected a new concern with creating a quality of life far advanced beyond mere subsistence.

There is one additional piece of evidence that testifies to the success of Beckwith inhabitants of Irish and Scottish origin in creating a stable and ordered society. A Beckwith member of the 3rd Lanark Regiment described the inhabitants of Beckwith and Ramsay assembling at a militia muster at Carlton Place on 4 June 1841, revealing that the Irish Catholics and Scottish lowlanders had learned to emulate or at least simulate the mutual tolerance that Beckwith Irish and Scottish immigrants had always shown toward one another. The contrast with the riotous proceedings following the 1824 militia muster could not have been more complete:[114]

Plate 121
J. Murray stove advertisement in the 26 October 1849 issue of the Perth Bathurst Courier. *The few stoves in use in Beckwith up until the early 1850s were imported from Smith's Falls and Perth to the south. Even after the first stoves were manufactured in small Carleton Place foundries in the mid 1850s and early 1860s, agents from Perth and Brockville made the rounds of Beckwith, selling their stoves for lower prices. Stoves could provide more uniform heat from a smaller supply of firewood than could the fireplaces of earlier days. National Library of Canada negative no. NL-16173.*

At an early hour this morning I was awakened by the sound of a P[i]brock [or bagpipe], in an instant I was out of bed, and from the window perceived a body of most respectable looking young men marching into the village to the tune of "Patrick's Day," played by one of Scotia's sons, in Scotia's garb, on Scotia's national instrument — until about eleven o'clock the men were arriving in parties, equestrian and pedestrian, at which hour the Companies were ordered to "Fall in" and soon after we were all on the Parade ground in open column — when the Major (Alexander Frazer) ...addressed the Regiment in a short but pithy speech, stating the object for which the Flank Companies were to be formed, and his hopes that there would be sufficient volunteers... — this was received with enthusiasm, and "I'll Volunteer," was responded from all directions. We were again formed into open column, wheeled into line, the ranks opened, and three deafening cheers for Her Majesty made the forest re-echo the joyful chorus....

The 3d Battalion of Lanark militia is formed of the yeomen of the Townships of Beckwith and Ramsay, the sons of English, Scotch, and Irish Emigrants, and I do not think I exceed when I say, that four-fifths of the Regiment are under forty years of age, a finer or more orderly set of young men I never saw in a body.

The search for order, of course, like the militia formation at Carlton Place was more facade than achievement. A Scottish immigrant playing an Irish tune on a bagpipe had all the marks of a deliberate strategy by higher officers to keep relations civil between Ramsay Scottish lowlanders and Irish Catholics. And yet, facades have their importance as the members of the Church of Scotland congregation meeting on the seventh concession of Beckwith knew all too well. In church services the congregation was seemingly arranged in perfect order in the ground floor pews and galleries, but this was a necessary facade of order. Their orderly dress and the shoes they wore in church disguised the reality that many of them had walked from the Derry settlement in their bare feet through the swamp along a causeway of large cedar logs laid end to end and flattened on the upper side. Beneath an oak tree in front of the church those who walked through the swamp replaced their shoes and stockings that had been removed the more easily to wade through the wet places of the swamp.[115] For all the rhetoric and genuine hope for an ordered society, Beckwith inhabitants at mid-century yet perceived themselves mired in the mud of a backwoods swamp settlement.

The disparity between the reality of local everyday life and an emerging search for order would not have been difficult for most Beckwith inhabitants to recognise between 1825 and 1851. During this generation it is possible to identify the creation of what might be called prototypical Beckwith. Following the first decade of settlement, the Irish and Scottish settlers used religion as the most prominent aspect of life to distinguish and define their ethnicity or sense of belonging to a particular cultural community. Language remained an important distinction, with many of the highland families speaking Gaelic whereas all of the Irish immigrants spoke English, but it did not remain a barrier for most inhabitants past mid-century. To speak of a prototypical Beckwith emerging from the mid 1820s to the late 1840s is to recognise a local self-conception, partly real and partly mythic, that emerged and that endured for a long time. In the critical generation between getting established and the introduction of modernising forces such as railroads, compulsory education and municipal government, the Irish Anglicans and highland Presbyterians of Beckwith in coming to terms with one another developed a certain cultural competitiveness. If the Irish Anglicans constructed a stone church, then the Church of Scotland must also have one. If the Irish Anglican congregation could build a stone rectory for their clergyman in 1837, the Church of Scotland minister followed suit two years later.

These ethno-religious rivalries and loyalties would endure in many Beckwith families into the late twentieth century, long after the provisioning economy had disappeared and long after the highland families made up for the relative crudeness of their early houses by economically and socially outdistancing the Irish Anglicans in the next generation. Increasingly, with time both Irish and Scottish descendants would look back to the years before 1851 as the prototypical years in which the way Beckwith inhabitants increasingly chose to think about themselves was defined.

Endnotes

1 *Bathurst Independent Examiner*, 26 March 1830, p. 3, cols. 1-2.
2 Jessie Buchanan Campbell, *The Pioneer Pastor*, p. 44.
3 *Bathurst Courier*, 5 December 1843, p. 2, col. 2.
4 Jean S. McGill, *A Pioneer History of the County of Lanark*, p. 155.
5 *Brockville Antidote*, 23 April 1833, p. 1, col. 4.
6 *Bathurst Courier*, 5 February 1841, p. 3, cols. 1-2.
7 *Kingston Chronicle*, 13 December 1843, p. 2, col. 5.
8 *Bathurst Courier*, 5 December 1843, p. 2, col. 5.
9 *Kingston Chronicle*, 13 December 1843, p. 2, col. 5.
10 *Brockville Statesman*, 16 February 1847, pp. 1-2, cols. 7-1.
11 *Bathurst Courier*, 15 June 1847, pp. 2-3, cols. 7-1.
12 Ibid., 7 January 1848, p. 2, cols. 5-6.
13 Ibid., 31 December 1847, p. 2, cols. 5-6.
14 Ibid., 2 March 1849, pp. 2-3, cols. 7-1.
15 Ibid., 29 March 1842, p. 2, col. 6.
16 Ibid., 15 June 1838, p. 2, cols. 5-6.
17 Foster J.K. Griezic, "James Shaw" in Marc La Terreur, ed., *Dictionary of Canadian Biography* (Toron-

18 *Bathurst Courier*, 4 October 1850, p. 2, col. 5.
19 Ibid., 3 January 1851, p. 2, cols. 4-6.
20 Ibid., 31 January 1851, p. 2, cols. 3-5, 6.
21 NAC RG 5, A1 Reel C-4609 Upper Canada Sundries, vol. 57, pp. 29592-29593.
22 Glenn J Lockwood, *Montague: A Social History of an Irish Ontario Township, 1783-1980* (Smiths Falls: Corporation of the Township of Montague, 1980), p. 50.
23 *Bathurst Independent Examiner*, 15 January 1830, p. 3, col. 1.
24 Ibid., 12 February 1830, cited in Howard M. Brown, "Ramsay Objected to Justice Meted in 1830's" in the *Carleton Place Canadian*, 19 April 1962.
25 NAC RG 5, A1 Reel C-6872 Upper Canada Sundries, vol. 105, p. 59342.
26 Ibid., Reel C-4609, vol. 58, p. 30477.
27 Ibid., Reel C-6879, vol. 130, pp. 71692-71693.
28 *Bathurst Independent Examiner*, 12 February 1830, cited in Howard M. Brown, "Ramsay Objected" in the *Carleton Place Canadian*, 19 April 1962.
29 NAC RG 5, A1 Reel C-6879 Upper Canada Sundries, vol. 130, pp. 71677-71678.
30 Ibid., p. 71695.
31 Ibid., p. 71700.
32 Ibid., p. 71695.
33 Ibid., pp. 71697-71698.
34 Ibid., p. 71698.
35 Ibid., p. 71680.
36 Ibid., Reel C-6890, vol. 166, p. 90582.
37 Ibid., Reel C-6893, vol. 176, p. 97154.
38 *Bathurst Courier*, 21 July 1837, p. 2, col. 6.
39 NAC RG 5, A1 Reel C-6914 Upper Canada Sundries, vol. 247, p. 134837.
40 William H. Smith, *Smith's Canadian Gazetteer Comprising Statistical and General Information Respecting All Parts of the Upper Province, or Canada West* (Toronto: H. and W. Rowsell, 1846; reprint ed. Toronto: Coles Publishing Company, 1972), p. 267.
41 Beckwith Township Municipal Records (hereafter OBCMR) Beckwith Township Clerk's Book, 1840-1846, n.p.
42 W.C. Keele, *The Provincial Justice, or Magistrate's Manual, Being a Complete Digest of the Criminal Law of Canada, and a Compendious and General View of the Provincial Law of Upper Canada* (Toronto: H. and W. Rowsell, 1843), pp. 597-601.
43 Ibid., pp. 601-605.
44 Ibid., pp. 492-493.
45 Ibid., pp. 260-261.
46 Ibid., p. 605.
47 Gerald M. Craig, *Upper Canada: The Formative Years, 1784-1841* The Canadian Centenary Series no. 7 (Toronto: McClelland and Stewart Limited, 1963), p. 30.
48 Keele, *The Provincial Justice*, pp. 202-204.
49 OBCMR Township Clerk's Book, 1840-1846.
50 NAC MG 55/24 No. 199. 10 November 1823 letter from Robert Ferguson, Beckwith, to John Moir, near Kippen, West Stirling, Scotland.
51 Report on Common Schools in the Bathurst District in the Upper Canada House of Assembly Journals, 1828, cited in Lloyd C. Sutherland, *Yearning For Learning: The Story of Education in Lanark County, 1804-1867* (Smiths Falls: by the author, 1980), pp. 22-25.
52 OKQAR Rev. William Bell Journals IV:139.
53 Campbell, *Pioneer Pastor*, p. 34.
54 OKQAR Rev. William Bell Journals VII:47.
55 *Bathurst Courier,* 16 September 1836, p. 4, col. 1.
56 OTAR RG 2 C-6-C Education Department Records, Assistant Superintendent of Education Canada West, Incoming General Correspondence, 1843 Box 2, 12 December 1843 letter from the Common School Teachers of the Bathurst District.
57 [Dugald C. McNab], "History of the Settlement of the Township of McNab: Attempt to Establish the Feudal System" in the *Perth Courier*, 1 October 1869, p. 1, cols. 3-5; and ibid., 8 October 1869, p. 1, cols. 3-5.
58 Brown, *Founded Upon A Rock*, pp. 72-73.
59 Sutherland, *Yearning For Learning*, pp. 67-68.
60 The *Historical Atlas of Lanark County* published by H. Belden and Company in 1880, a source strewn with historical inaccuracies, suggests that James Kent was the "pioneer pedagogue" in the 1825 school built at Carlton Place. This is very unlikely, first because the Rev. William Bell from Perth recounted that the teacher at Carlton Place in 1825 was an American; second, because Kent was located on a township lot near Franktown where he was shown teaching school in the 1830s and early 1840s; and third, because James Kent in 1827 was shown presiding over 22 pupils whereas Alexander McNabb had 54 students. The larger number of students and a teacher with a Scottish name would more likely have been found at Carlton Place than at Franktown.
61 OTAR RG 1 Series C-IV Crown Lands Department, Township Papers, Montague, Box 334, 30 June 1841 letter from John McMullen.
62 Ibid., 20 April 1844 letter from Greenwell Dixon, Montague.
63 John May, "Bush Life in the Ottawa Valley Eighty Years Ago" in *Papers and Records of the Ontario Historical Society* XII (1914), p. 162
64 OTAR RG 2 C 6 Education Department Records, Assistant Superintendent of Education Canada West, incoming General Correspondence, 1842, Box 1, 20 September 1842 address from William Sommerville, Chairman, Perth.
65 May, "Bush Life in the Ottawa Valley," pp. 162-163.
66 OTAR RG 2 C-6-C Incoming General Correspondence, 28 November 1842 letter from Johnston Neilson, Smith's Falls.
67 Ibid., 3 August letter from Johnston Neilson, Smith's

Falls.
68 Ibid., 12 December 1843 address from Johnston Neilson and twenty other teachers to His Excellency Sir Charles Theophilus Metcalfe.
69 *Bathurst Courier*, 2 August 1843, p. 2, cols. 2-3.
70 Ibid., 8 August 1843, p. 2, cols. 6-2.
71 Sutherland, *Yearning For Learning*, pp. 79 112,
72 *Bathurst Courier*, 12 April 1850, pp. 2-3, cols. 7-2.
73 *Carleton-Place Herald*, 20 November 1851, p. 2, cols. 4-5.
74 Ibid., 1 January 1852, p. 2, col. 3.
75 *Carleton Place Lanark Herald*, 28 March 1851, p. 2, cols. 4-5.
76 *Carleton-Place Herald*, 1 January 1852, p. 2, col. 3.
77 Ibid., 23 October 1851, p. 2, cols. 3-5.
78 Sutherland, *Yearning For Learning*, p. 112.
79 *Bathurst Courier*, 9 November 1849, p. 2, col. 5.
80 Ibid., 18 May 1849, p. 1, cols. 4-5.
81 This volume is now in the collection of the Carleton Place and Beckwith Historical Society.
82 I am grateful to Mabel Ringereide for loaning me these two volumes.
83 E.P. Thompson, *The Making of the English Working Class* (Markham, Ontario: Penguin Books Canada Limited, 1979), p. 817.
84 Carleton Place Public Library (hereafter OCP), Carlton Place Library Association and Mechanic's Institute Subscription Book, 1846-1851.
85 *Bathurst Courier*, 6 April 1847, pp. 2-3, cols. 7-1.
86 *Carleton Place Lanark Herald*, 25 April 1851, pp. 2-3, cols. 5-1.
87 OCP Carlton Place Library Association and Mechanic's Institute, Catalogue ca. 1847. I am grateful to Howard M. Brown for providing a regrouped listing of the 140 books in the library.
88 *Bathurst Courier*, 1 June 1849, p. 1, cols. 5-6.
89 Ibid., 12 July 1850, p. 1, cols. 1-2.
90 *Bathurst Courier*, 1 March 1850, p. 2, col. 3.
91 Anonymous, "St. John's Lodge, A.F. & A.M., number 63 G.R.C. in Ontario, Carleton Place, Ontario" in the collection of the Carleton Place and Beckwith Historical Society.
92 *Bytown Gazette*, 16 March 1843, p. 2, col. 5.
93 Anonymous, "St. John's Lodge", p. 1.
94 For more detail consult Glenn J Lockwood, "Eastern Upper Canadian Perceptions of Irish Immigrants, 1824-1868" (Ph.D. dissertation, University of Ottawa, 1988), pp. 297-341.
95 M.A. Garland and J.J. Talman, "Pioneer Drinking Habits and the Rise of the Temperance Agitation in Upper Canada Prior to 1840" in F.H. Armstrong, H.A. Stevenson and J.D. Wilson, eds., *Aspects of Nineteenth-Century Ontario* (Toronto: University of Toronto Press, 1974), p. 193.
96 *Bathurst Independent Examiner*, 13 November 1829, p. 3, col. 1, cited in Howard M. Brown, *Lanark Legacy*, p. 66.
97 OKQAR Rev. William Bell Journals II:161.
98 Carleton Place and Beckwith Historical Society Museum and Archives (hereafter OCPAR) Peter McArthur, Beckwith, Distillery Account Book, 1841-1852, pp. 55, 59, 63, 93, 151.
99 OKQAR Rev. William Bell Journals VI:23.
100 *Bathurst Courier*, 4 March 1836, p. 3, cols. 1-2.
101 Ibid., 11 January 1842, p. 3, col. 2.
102 Ibid., 4 January 1842, p. 3, col. 1.
103 Ibid., 13 April 1847, p. 2, cols. 6-7.
104 *Lanark Herald*, 11 April 1851, p. 2, col. 4.
105 Ibid., 25 April 1851, p. 2, col. 4.
106 *Brockville Recorder*, 17 January 1850, p. 3, col. 1.
107 Ibid., 11 October 1838, p. 2, cols. 4-5.
108 *Bathurst Courier*, 28 March 1851, p. 3, col. 6.
109 OKQAR Rev. William Bell Journals II:161.
110 2 May 1858 letter from Daniel McCuan to an acquaintance, provided courtesy of Alex and Jean McCuan, Beckwith.
111 *Bathurst Courier*, 2 February 1847, pp. 2-3, cols. 7-1.
112 Ibid., 19 January 1847, p. 2, cols. 6-7.
113 May, "Bush Life in the Ottawa Valley," p. 163.
114 *Bathurst Courier*, 29 June 1841, p. 3, col. 1.
115 George Edward Kidd, *The Story of the Derry*, p. 20.

Plate 122

A Brockville and Ottawa Railway advertisement for an excursion to an Orange procession at Carleton Place, from the 8 July 1864 issue of the Perth Courier. *The railway enlarged the region within which Beckwith inhabitants regularly moved and worked. Orangemen could gather in the thousands on the 12th of July, families could go to see relatives across the province in a matter of a couple of days, they could visit relatives in Renfrew County or shop in Ottawa the same day, and men could catch the train for a quick ride to work in the timber camps of the upper Ottawa valley. National Library of Canada negative no. NL-16172.*

RAILROADING BECKWITH

EXCURSION,
12th JULY, 1864.

BROCKVILLE AND OTTAWA RAILWAY!

RETURN TICKETS AT ONE FARE.

IN addition to the regular trains leaving Brockville, Perth and Almonte, in the morning and evening, there will also be

2 SPECIAL EXCURSION TRAINS

TO CARLETON PLACE.

One leaving Perth at 9.30 a.m., and arriving at Carleton Place at 11 a.m.
" " Almonte, 10.30 a.m. and arriving at Carleton Place at 11 a.m.

In time for the

GRAND PROCESSION

All Tickets purchased to or from any Station on the 12th, at the usual price, will be good to return on, *if used the same day.*

GOD SAVE THE QUEEN!

R. P. COOKE,
Engineer and Superintendent.

Brockville, 1st July, 1864.   40-a

1852 - 1880

THE PEOPLE OF BECKWITH TOWNSHIP

On the evening of Sunday January 13th 1861 the 2,542 inhabitants of Beckwith Township, Canada West, went to bed as usual after having observed the Sabbath, fully expecting to awaken to the responsibilities and routine of a new week the following morning. The evening itself was of no particular importance, and yet despite protracted snowfall throughout January that made local roads either "very much drifted" or "entirely blocked up by enormous drifts of snow",[1] Beckwith families from the next day up to a month later received visits from census enumerators asking them to supply detailed information about the size and welfare of their households as they existed on that uneventful mid-winter Sunday evening.

The taking of the 1861 census marked a watershed in Beckwith's population. The township was more densely populated during the 1850s than at any other time during its first 150 years (Table 2).

Table 2. Population growth of Beckwith Township and the town of Carleton Place, 1816 –1991

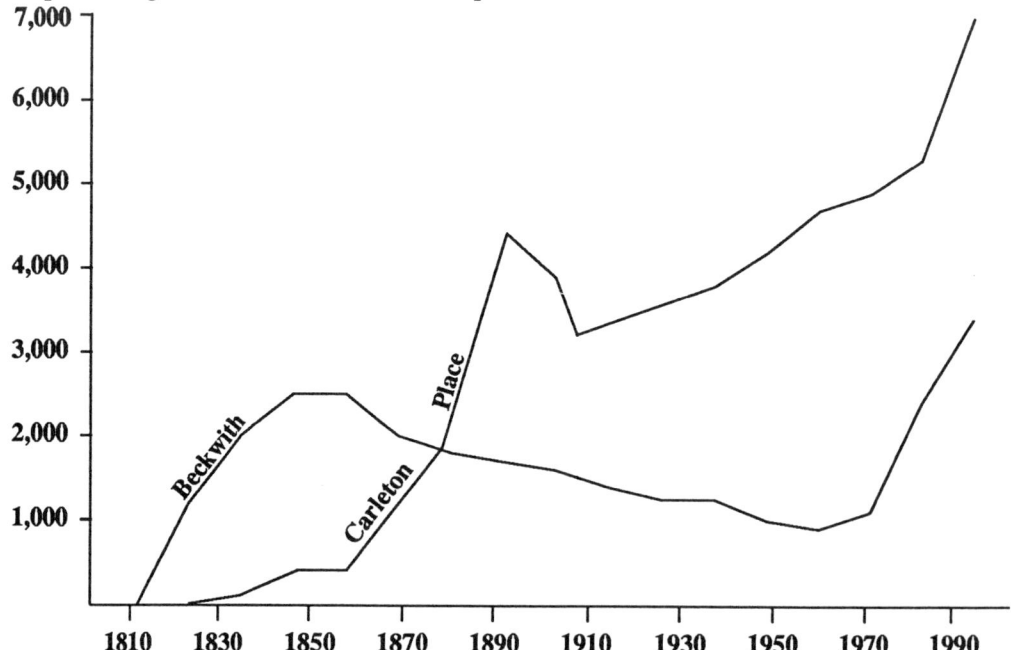

SOURCE: *Directors, gazetteers, decennial census returns and assessment rolls.*

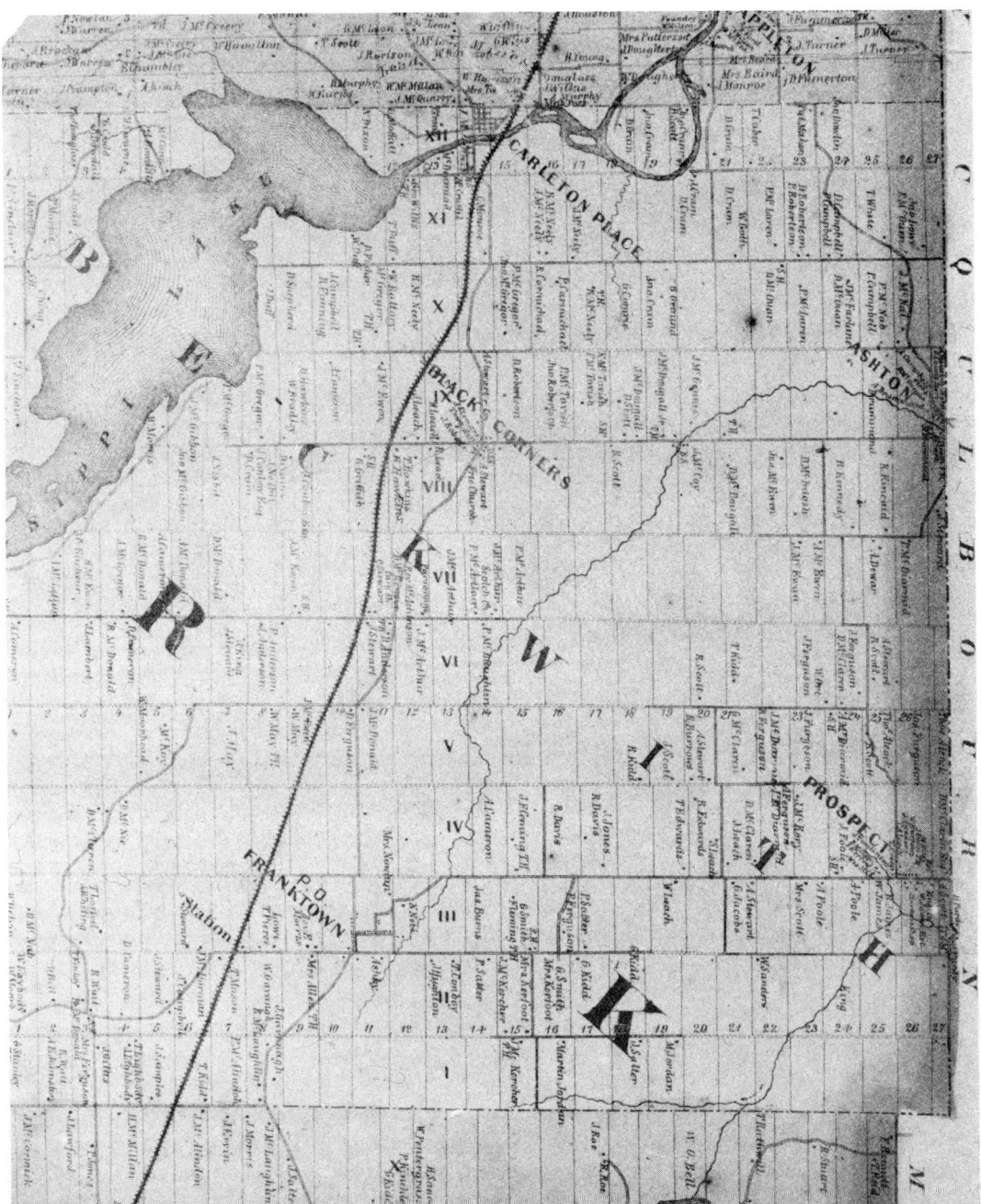

Plate 123
The Beckwith section of Henry F. Walling's map of the counties of Lanark and Renfrew, published in 1863 by D.P. Putnam at Prescott. James Poole remarked in the Carleton Place Herald *that "the more closely [this map] is inspected the more will it be admired.... [A]ll the public highways are most accurately represented...showing just their course relatively, with the lot lines, streams, &c... . The exact location of all dwellings is shown, telling the stranger at a glance, how the country is settled up, and who the owners of settled farms are, as every farmer's name is engraved on his lot. It shows also the location of all schools, churches, mills, and business places[, and t]he names and location of all Post Offices and prominent corners." National Archives of Canada NMC VR/420.*

From mid-century onward Beckwith's population began to decline as the township ceased to be a destination for immigrants and as Beckwith families continued to leave for Renfrew County, for western Upper Canada, and even for destinations in the United States. The population of Beckwith as a municipality in 1861 increased by only three persons from 2,539 in 1852, and then declined to 1,984 in 1871 and further to 1,929 persons in 1881. The dramatic growth of Carleton Place from a village with 500 inhabitants in 1852 to a centre boasting 1,975 people in 1881 and which became incorporated as a separate municipality in November 1870[2] obscures the gradual nature of the shift in Beckwith from an increasing to a declining population. If Carleton Place is taken away, the population of Beckwith would have increased slightly from something like 1,990 in 1852 to 2,000 in 1861, and then slightly decreased to 1,984 in 1871 and then to 1,929 in 1881. Had Carleton Place remained as part of Beckwith, the township's population would have climbed to 3,189 in 1871 and to 3,904 persons by 1881.[3] As it was, the decline of Beckwith's rural population was less than one percent between 1861 and 1871, and less than three percent between 1871 and 1881. Clearly, there was no demographic crisis in Beckwith between 1852 and 1880.

Despite the onset of modest population decline, Beckwith's population remained youthful in composition, although it was not as youthful as that in neighbouring Montague where so many Beckwith sons and daughters had settled in the 1830s and 1840s. It was nonetheless a population that was beginning to age, as age pyramids constructed from census returns clearly show (Table 3).[4] Over 53 percent of Beckwith inhabitants in 1861 were under twenty years of age in 1852, but the proportion fell to under fifty percent by 1881. In Montague there was a dramatic increase of fifteen percent in the age category of those most eligible to become parents (inhabitants between the ages of twenty and 24) whereas in Beckwith the increase was one-tenth of that in Montague.[5] The number of middle-aged inhabitants (aged 45 to 64) rose slightly between 1852 to 111. This increase in contrast with the decrease of those under the age of twenty underlines the decreasing birthrate which was evident in the 1870s and which probably dated from mid-century. Expressed as a crude birth rate,

Plate 124
Ambrotypes of Christina McEwen (opposite) and a man believed to be Donald Cameron taken ca. 1865. With land in the immediate Beckwith vicinity increasingly difficult for many farmers' sons to obtain by 1850, photographs became important mementos to keep family members in touch as sons and daughters migrated westward. The increasingly stylish dress captured in ferrotypes, ambrotypes and photographs reveals new levels of material prosperity and increasing sophistication in Beckwith. There was not sufficient demand for a photographer to set up shop at Carleton Place until 1868, but travelling photographers did stop in the village from mid-century onward. In November 1864, for example, N.J. Trenham arrived with his photographic car in which he was prepared to take photographs, cartes de visites, vignettes and ambrotypes of Beckwith inhabitants. Loaned courtesy of Findlay and Mary McEwen and Elsie Cameron and Jean Colburn respectively.

the birth of 26.8 children per thousand of population in 1852 fell to 23.2 in 1861 then rose to 28.2 in 1871, only to plummet to 6.2 children per thousand in 1881. Given the mortality rate of 4.0, 7.5, 6.6 and 10.9 deaths per thousand in these years respectively, the rate of natural increase was 22.8 per thousand in 1852, 15.7 in 1861, 21.6 in 1871 and -4.7 in 1881. Although Beckwith was yet a young society in 1881, the trend toward an older and less densely populated society was evident.

Beckwith by mid-century had the mark of a mature society, as shown by the declining population and the declining birth rate from 1852 onward. The fewer number of children born resulted from a changing male-female ratio and from shifting marital patterns. Where there had been 103 males for every 100 females in 1852, by 1881 females in Beckwith began to outnumber males. For the age category in which males and females were most eligible to marry (between twenty and 44 years of age) females continually outnumbered males. The gap separating the two sexes between age twenty and 44 slowly widened from 98.7 males per hundred females in 1852 to 94.9 by 1881. The range of ages at which Beckwith inhabitants actually did marry reveals that the ratio of men to women became more even, but the preponderance of women continued. Using the age cohorts of 21-59 for men and 14-44 for women, the ratio of 82.8 males per hundred females in 1852 consistently rose to 87.9 by 1881. Married women as a percentage of the total female population declined by a full nine percent between 1852 and 1881, and during these three decades the proportion of married

Table 3.   Age Pyramids for Beckwith Township, 1852-1881

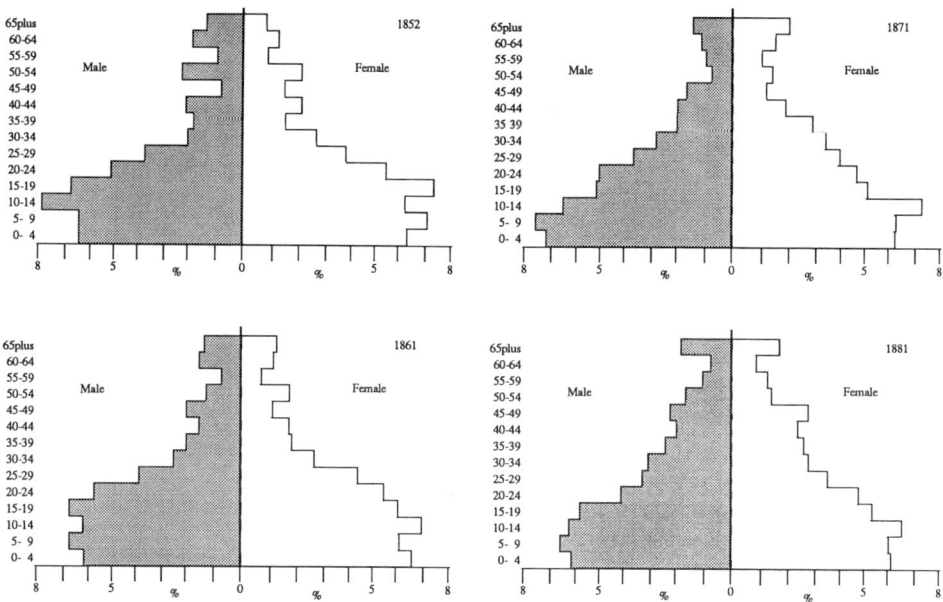

SOURCE: *Manuscript census returns for Beckwith for 1852, 1862, 1871 and 1881 at the National Archives of Canada.*

women among those between the ages of twenty and thirty declined from 8.3 percent to 5.7. Beckwith women increasingly were waiting until later to marry.

Both males and females appear to have deferred marriage, and increasingly many never did marry. The proportion of men between the ages of twenty and 24 who were married fell from 13.5 percent in 1852 to 4.9 in 1881, and the married proportion of men between ages 25 and 29 dwindled from 50 percent to 41.5. Even in the higher age groups there was an appreciable decline of interest in marriage. The proportion of married men among the Beckwith total between the ages of thirty and 34 declined from 67.3 percent to 62.9; the married proportion of those between 35 and 39 dropped from 87 percent to 67.3; and among those men between forty and 44 years of age the proportion of married men declined from 84.2 percent to 80.5 between 1852 and 1881. Many men waited until their late thirties or early forties to marry. There was a similar pattern of both deferring marriage and of not marrying among the women of eligible marrying age in Beckwith. Between 1852 and 1881 the proportion of women between the age of twenty and 24 who were married fell from 28 percent to 20.2; of those between 25 and 29 the proportion married fell from 61.4 percent to 47.8; of those between 35 and 39 from 87.5 percent to 69.4; and of those women between the ages of forty and 44 the married proportion declined from 89.4 percent to 75. The fifteen year age group in which men were most likely to marry shifted from 25-39 in 1852 to 30-44 in 1881. The fifteen year age group in which women were most likely to marry shifted from 20-34 in 1852 to 25-39 in 1881.[6] The declining numbers of men and women entering into marriage reflected the current population decline and were harbingers of long-continuing decline after 1881.

The deferral and decline of marriage enhanced an already declining fertility rate. Between 1852 and 1881 the number of children under the age of ten who called Beckwith their home declined from 651 to 485. The loss of Carleton Place in 1870 partly explains the decreasing number of children, but between 1871 and 1881 the number of children under age ten declined by eleven percent from 545 to 485. This was the same rate of decline observed in the number of women in age groups between

Plate 125
A photograph believed to be of the Neil Stewart farmhouse, lot 11, concession 7, Beckwith, built in the early 1840s, as photographed ca. 1900 before a 1915 fire and major alterations took their toll. The design of this house was largely based on the 1839 Church of Scotland manse a mile to the east built by the Reverend John Smith (Plate 86), except that glass panes filled the semi-elliptical fanlight rather than a blind transom. A later generation grew impatient with the low sloping ceilings upstairs. Archives of Ontario S.7450.

ages twenty and forty entering into marriage. Within the overall decline in the number of children, the number of children for every woman of childbearing age (15-44 years) remained constant at 1.1 during these three decades. The number of births per year fell from 58 in 1852 to less than twenty by 1880. For every 3.5 married women of childbearing age in 1852, one child was born, compared with 13.2 married women per child born in 1881. A significant decline in the Beckwith birthrate had already taken place before mid-century and was greatly in advance of the general population decline.

The decrease in fertility is but partially explained by an increasing proportion of Beckwith women deferring marriage until after age thirty. The later they waited to marry meant that there would be fewer children in a rural society. Beckwith like rural Peel County, in the words of David Gagan, "was a perfectly natural demographic regime in which women without the benefit of contraceptive devices or information produced children at regular intervals of thirty months, more or less, from marriage to menopause."[7] But, increasingly with all arable land cleared and with the mechanising of agriculture from mid-century onward, there no longer was the need for large families there had once been in Beckwith. Indeed, with decreasing economic opportunity in the vicinity because of the lack of farmland to accommodate all the children who had been raised in Beckwith before 1850, there was a very real concern to keep families small. As local society matured and grew more well-to-do; as women participated in social events connected with church, school and women's associations; as the first generation of young adolescent women began to work at non-domestic jobs such as schoolteaching, there were social pressures that both helped to delay marriage and to limit family size. Not a few deferred marriages awaited the slow acquisition of farmland, either by waiting to purchase when someone else moved away, or by awaiting a will bequest.

The deferral of marriage in turn forced many young men and women to repress their sexuality, and there was a toll in human lives as well. At least one prostitute plied her trade in Carleton Place during the 1850s,[8] but for many young men such a course ran contrary to every moral precept inculcated in a society which was growing more rigidly moral. Some couples were unable to ignore their passion, and the result was a number of abortions and infants either left to die or killed. In early December 1861 a group of boys found the body of female child nearly two years old in a swamp near Franktown, and an inquest conducted by Dr. William Wilson in John Hughton's hotel determined that the child "came to her death from exposure to inclement weather and the want of the common necessaries of life."[9] The few Beckwith inhabitants who subscribed to the Perth *Courier* were horrified to read in February 1868 of a pregnant young woman at Appleton who died following an abortion performed on her by her lover in her parent's house, after she earlier had implored him "in order to save them both from disgrace, to send her medicine" from Montreal.[10] The Carleton Place and Almonte newspapers refused to mention the affair, but they could not ignore the discovery two months later of "the dead body of a new-born infant...hidden under the floor of [Charles Tooley's stable in Carleton Place]...behind a wretched slum....Upon examination it was found that the child had been born alive, and had been dispatched either by the hand of the mother who bore it, or some one willing to undertake the horrid task of her behalf."[11] A local physician remarked in October 1868:[12]

> Abortion illegally, or in other words criminally induced, is, Mr. Editor, becoming so exceedingly common, in Canada, that the utmost exertions should be promptly used to put a stop to such an inhuman and outrageously wicked practice. A short time ago, a weaver, employed at a woolen factory in a small village, called upon me and stated that she had "met with a misfortune." Upon enquiry, I satisfactorily ascertained that her "misfortune" had been caused by her own folly; in short, she frankly acknowledged that she was several months advanced in pregnancy, and solicited me to give her medicine to produce abortion.... I...informed her that when medicine is administered in a dose sufficient to cause abortion, it generally eventuates in the death of the mother. Notwithstanding the foregoing remarks,...she was not only willing, but likewise extremely anxious to run all hazard, rather than her parents and the public should know that ere long she would give birth to an illegitimate child.

Few if any Beckwith women were willing to risk subjecting themselves "to the scorn and contempt of the community" either in having illegitimate children or obtaining abortions, but by deferring marriage until their thirties many placed their own lives at risk, as reflected by a pervasive genre of

Plate 126
Daniel Cram, his second wife Elizabeth Harkness, and their son George Dunnet Cram, as photographed ca. 1866. Daniel Cram with Bible in hand might affect the stance of patriarch and moral arbiter, yet by the date of this photograph women in Beckwith were beginning to take on the role of moral centre of their households. From the 1860s on, death notices and obituaries referred to the transformation of otherwise naturally timid local women into active, confident creators of a morally better world for their children. In promoting the temperance movement, Sunday Schools and singing schools they sought to offer Beckwith children a chastening and moral influence that contrasted with previous years when the streets of Carleton Place were "filled with children of tender years, with ears open to the ribald jest and obscenity of darkness — under no eye of care". Photograph courtesy of Elizabeth Alexander.

poetry in local newspapers with such titles as "I have No Mother Now".[13] Despite the ultimate perilous consequences, it is clear that a decision consciously had been made to give birth to fewer children.

Population decline along with a decreasing fertility rate contributed to a declining number of households and fluctuating family size. Initially, the number of households remained steady, increasing by only one in 1861 from 384 in 1852, but after Carleton Place became municipally separate, the number of households in rural Beckwith fell from 345 in 1871 to 323 in 1881. In Carleton Place, by contrast, the number of households increased from 191 in 1871 to 395 in 1881. The average family size of 6.6 persons per household remained constant from 1852 to 1861, but in rural Beckwith it only slightly declined to 5.8 in 1871 to rise back up to 6.0 by 1881, whereas in Carleton Place the average number of people per household declined to 6.4 in 1871 and then significantly fell to five per household by 1881. The average family size did not vary greatly during this period, but it is clear that smaller families were increasingly the rule. The mean number of married people per household during these thirty years was reduced from 1.8 to 1.6 persons. The deferral of marriage increasingly meant that an increasing proportion of households were being headed by a widowed female parent.

Household size varied according to ethnicity and according to the generation to which family heads belonged. The numerically significant statistics in Table 4 are for Irish-born, Scottish-born and Canadian-born heads of household. While the number of inhabitants in households headed by immigrants from Scotland progressively grew smaller, the number in households headed by immigrants from Ireland and by persons born in Canada grew only until the early 1860s, and then declined in size from the mid 1860s onward. This reflected the comparative lack of empty adjacent land onto which the Scottish-born inhabitants in northern Beckwith could settle their children, whereas Irish-born inhabitants and their children in the southern concessions by sending members of their families to squat in nearby northern Montague did not feel themselves under the same pressure quite as early to limit the size of their families. Indeed, the decline of the Scottish highlander birth rate can be traced back to the early 1830s at precisely the same time Beckwith Irish families were expanding into Montague. This early concern of Scottish-origin families to limit family size militated to produce such an abnormally low birthrate among the Scottish-origin inhabitants of Beckwith that when the younger children and older grandchildren of the Perthshire immigrants began having children and heading families in the 1860s and 1870s, the size of Scottish-origin headed households in Beckwith grew from an abnormally low 4.8 in 1871 to 6.4 in 1881. Beckwith households headed by persons of Irish origin, by contrast, slightly decreased from 6.2 in 1871 to 6.1 in 1881.

Religious affiliation only confirms the contrasting pattern between the household size of Irish and Scottish-origin household heads (Table 5). The significant figures are those of the United Church of England and Ireland and Presbyterians. The size of households headed by Anglicans consistently increased whereas the size of households headed by Presbyterians declined between 1852 and 1881. The 32 Roman Catholic, 29 Methodist and 22 Baptist households were numerically too insignificant to form the basis for comparing household size. It is significant that in 1852 there were 62 Church of Scotland, 83 Free Church Presbyterian and 26 Cameronian Presbyterian households, yet by 1881 all Beckwith Presbyterians had united to replace Anglicans as the single largest denomination in the township. Of all the denominations only the Methodists had a growing number of households between 1852 and 1861. Among the two denominations that accounted for more than three-fourths of Beckwith households the Presbyterians followed the average family size, whereas the Anglicans who in 1852 were below the average, by 1881 were above it.

The general decline of fertility at the same time marriage was being deferred until later meant that many children were raised by middle-aged parents. As Michael Katz in his study of mid-century Hamilton points out, "very few husbands and wives...had more than a few, if any, years to live together after their children had left home. In fact, many of the younger children in families could expect to lose at least their father through death before they reached maturity."[14] Although the mean

Plate 127
Canadian Pacific locomotive no. 997 with scheduled freight train heading south for Smith's Falls past Franktown station, as photographed by Omer Lavallée ca. 1950. The building of the Brockville & Ottawa railway in the late 1850s added to the migration of Beckwith families to increasingly distant destinations from the 1850s on. Half a generation would pass before the railway boosted the growth of Carleton Place, whereas Franktown experienced no growth at all following construction of the line. Photograph courtesy of the Smiths Falls Railway Museum.

number of children and adolescents in Beckwith declined from 3.5 to 3.0 per household between 1852 and 1881, the majority of households had between five and twelve members during this period. The number of households with four members or less increased from 26.2 to 32.7 percent, but large households remained common until the end of the century. Children and adolescents continued to comprise the majority of members in these larger households. Given the ongoing deferral of marriage by many men and women until their thirties and early forties, and the spacing of births approximately two years apart, this meant that many women were conceiving even in their final years of fecundity.

The decline of fertility and the deferral of marriage were caused by economic and demographic reality as much as by anything, but it was during the decades following mid-century that local women began to make their first social forays, to be regularly educated, and to leave their mark on public society. In some respects the thirty years between 1852 and 1881 were harmful ones for women due to the popular image promulgated in regional as well as transatlantic newspapers that their role in life was to soothe husbands retiring from the bustle of business filled with anxiety and turmoil. "Oh, how dear to the memory of man is the wife, who clothes her face in smiles", intoned one among thousands of similar articles, "who uses gentle expressions, and who makes her lap soft to receive and hush his cries to rest."[15] When news filtered in of women's rights conventions in the United States and of travelling women lecturers along the St. Lawrence advocating women's rights, local Reform editors ridiculed them as being incompatible with the new popular ideal of woman as an

Table 4.   Mean Size of Household by Birthplace of Head
(No. of persons per household)

Country of Birth	1852	1861	1871	1881
Ireland	6.4	6.8	6.5	5.6
Scotland	7.1	6.8	6.8	6.2
England	7.5	7.0	8.7	8.0
Canada	4.4	5.8	5.4	4.9
United States	9.0	8.5	5.5	9.0

SOURCE: 1852, 1861, 1871 and 1881 manuscript census returns for Beckwith township at National Archives of Canada.

Table 5.   Mean Size of Household by Religion of Head
(No. of persons per household)

Religion	1852	1861	1871	1881
United Church of England & Ireland	5.8	6.2	6.2	6.5
Roman Catholic	6.3	6.6	6.6	6.4
Presbyterian	6.6	6.7	6.2	6.0
Methodist	5.4	5.9	4.9	5.8
Baptist	6.7	6.5	7.7	5.7

SOURCE: The same sources listed in Table 4.

uplifting domestic nurturer of husband and children, a veritable "angel of the house". An article in the *Lanark Observer* in June 1852 mocked:[16]

> We at least go for women's rights, and are ready to do battle for them, with pen and ink, against every opposer. We hold in the first place, that women have a right to any number of babies. They have a right to any quantity of scolding. — They have a right to the domain of the kitchen — They have a right to make their husband's shirts, knit his stockings, and sew on a button that has dropped from his collar or wrist-band; and they have several rights which they do not always enforce. But that they have a right to put on the breeches, and do a great many other things which they regard as their province, we cannot admit. Their claim is so preposterous and absurd, that the rest of womankind ridicule it more effectually than men. All true-hearted women — all who have a right conception of the delicacy of their sex, and of their relation to the head of creation — disclaim the masculine pretensions of these viragos. Good women are too happy and too much at home in their domestic spheres, to have any taste for the din of the workshop, the publicity of the courts, the wrangling of Congress, the turmoil of politics, the carnage of the battle-field, and other scenes in which men play their appropriate part, but which are revolting to the finer sensibilities of lovely women.

Plate 128
The George McLaren farmhouse, lot 21, concession 5, Beckwith, built in 1877, as photographed in 1983. The larger houses built in Beckwith during the late nineteenth century were more vertical in look than the houses built before 1850. This verticality is emphasized by the dark brown cut limestone quoins which along with the cut stone door and window sills were likely purchased from Findlay McEwen's Dominion Quarry. The uniform size and shape of the building stone in the side and back walls as well as the front wall of this house contrasts with the stonework in the Peter Anderson house (Plate 117) built a generation earlier.

A major change which developed in the concept of woman's new domestic role was that increasingly she was expected to become a figure of moral authority in the household, effectively replacing the father in that role. Another article in the *Lanark Observer* in 1852 stated that God intended women to "occupy a subordinate, though an important place in the social relations of life", but only through going forward as a public leader even in enterprises of benevolence, or in associations designed to act on the public mind. *Her empire* is the *domestic circle*; her first influence is there; and in connection with that, in such scenes as she can engage in without trenching on the prerogative of man, or neglecting the duty which she owes to her own family."[17] In fulfilling her duty in the home, the wife exercised "those affections and...that authority which are essential to constitute a well-regulated family", remarked a correspondent of the Carleton Place *Herald* in 1853. "To[the mother] is committed especially the early discipline of the youthful mind, and the education of the infant has a most important bearing upon the future conduct of the adult. If any great moral change is to be effected in society, it must be brought about through the influence of maternal discipline."[18] Ten years later another *Herald* correspondent agreed, "We want mothers all affection within and all firmness without. Mothers to train themselves to such sufficient self-command as that they shall be equal to all the common events of life."[19]

> Woman's great mission is to be a wife and mother, and a good housekeeper [remarked the editor of the Perth *Courier* in November 1865]; and yet how few women know how to discharge their duties in this respect; and what the mother does not know she cannot teach her daughters. A young woman who thoroughly understands housekeeping in all its branches, who can economize and repair, who can keep her kitchen, and parlor and bedroom all clean, and neat, and tidy, and who has a place for everything, and everything in its place, would be worth her weight in gold as a wife to any young man of enterprise and industry commencing business in life. But where can such a helpmate be found?... What is wanted...is proper institutions for the education and training of women in women's proper business.

As early as April 1851 Johnston Neilson at Carleton Place recommended that a female school staffed by a female teacher be established in that village to teach girls in "accomplishments...which are peculiar to females, and in which they can be instructed only by a female teacher."[20]

The rhetoric about woman's role as housekeeper, and about the need to educate women to better fit within a domestic circle originated in the urban press, and within local society the reprinting of such articles in the Perth and Carleton Place weeklies reflected the urban ambitions of editors in these towns. This urban rhetoric had a curious effect on Beckwith women who previously had worked alongside husbands, brothers, fathers and sons at frontier agriculture during the early nineteenth century. As the provisioning economy began changing to either dairy or mixed subsistence farming during the 1860s and 1870s, the women of Beckwith found themselves in the hayfields helping to harvest crops, milking cattle twice daily every day of the week, churning butter, feeding poultry, collecting eggs, and making cheese among other chores. In winter with more and more children at school, and with the majority of husbands away in the lumbercamps earning additional income, most farm chores came crushing in on the women of rural Beckwith. On the fourth day of April 1881, for example, there were 247 married women and 28 married men in Beckwith; the other 236 married men were away elsewhere, presumably working in the lumber industry. At the same time they continued to be burdened down with various farm chores, the rural women of Beckwith had cause to fear that they were not keeping up with the women in Carleton Place socially.

In 1851 when Johnston Neilson urged that a female school be established at Carleton Place, he argued:

> In country places [it]...is not so much required, because the inhabitants are, in such situations, not so far advanced in refinements of taste and manners, however virtuous, as in towns or villages, where there are congregated within narrower bounds so many men of wealth, or that have themselves received a more liberal education, and have been accustomed to more polished society than the plain and laborious inhabitants of the country find necessary to their enjoyment.

In the face of this allusion to rural women being less polished than those in Carleton Place, the farmwomen of Beckwith all the more eagerly attempted to show that they were as refined, as fashionable, and as domestically graceful as their village counterparts. Sharing as they did in the farm workload, in running the farms while their men were away, with their places firmly ensured by the patterns of family inheritance, the women of Beckwith did not perceive that in honing their domestic skills as housekeepers along the lines suggested by local editors, they were putting into place the harness that would enshackle succeeding generations in a domestic ghetto. As early as 1851 an article in the *Carleton Place Herald* exhorted local women to subordinate themselves through domestic drudgery to serve others: "Everything in the education of women should tend to develope a spirit of self-devotion and self renunciation.... 'It is the true mission of women, to exhibit to mankind

Plate 129
The Thomas Cavers house, lot 22, concession 12, built in the 1860s, as photographed in June 1983. The patterned and finely-cut dark and light brown limestone in this house for a highland family farming the fertile Mississippi floodplain owed nothing to highland tradition. The front upstairs gable and window were incorporated as part of the original design of this house. The large windows in the new houses built in the 1850s and later reflected the more efficient heating offered by wood stoves as opposed to the fireplaces of previous years.

the mor[a]l beauty and power of that love which seeketh not her own, but the good of others, and finds its own highest honor and happiness in so doing'."[21]

The ideal of woman's true mission notwithstanding, the reality of married life for some Beckwith women proved intolerable. Violence by husbands against wives was not publicly tolerated as the *Carleton Place Herald* reported in August 1865:[22]

> A man named Thomas Lynch, in this village, distinguished himself on Monday last, by beating his wife with a club, and repeatedly knocking her down. He was brought up and fined $1 and in default of payment to get 10 days in gaol at hard labor. It is only a few weeks since he spent fifteen days in gaol and formerly three years in the penitentiary.

Out in rural Beckwith, with households more isolated from one another than in the village of Carleton Place, domestic violence was not as easily detected. Evidence of marital discord is provided by notices placed in the *Herald* by husbands refusing to be responsible for wives who left their bed and board. In an era when there were few economic alternatives for women to pursue outside of the home, there must have been something terribly wrong to induce some Beckwith wives to flee their husbands. The accumulated burden of chores under which they strained as much as overt violence may well have prompted some women to leave their husbands. Hence John Cram cautioned the general public in October 1852, "WHEREAS my wife, Janet Cram, has left my bed and board, without any just cause or provocation, I do hereby forbid any person or persons, from harbouring or trusting her on my account, as I will not be answerable for any debts of her contracting, after this date."[23] In March 1853 James Rattray had a similar caution published against his wife Catherine,[24] in July 1855 Hugh McGregor warned the public against harbouring his wife Eliza Ann Dack,[25] in 1858 Henry Hawkins cautioned against giving credit in his name to his wife Catharine,[26] and in 1864 John Cram again warned the public about his wife Janet having left him.[27] The few women who left their husbands may well have rebelled at the unfairness of working all their married life, doing farm chores and raising children, only upon their husband's death to have the homestead pass on to one of the children while the widow was left with scant provision as dictated in her late husband's will. Such women could not have failed to notice those widowed women who capably managed their farms when given the opportunity to do so. Ellen Rattray, whose husband William died in 1835, was one such woman, "left alone, with three of a family, to combat with many of the hardships of the sturdy pioneer." When she died at age ninety in 1864, the *Carleton Place Herald* paid tribute to her as having "braved the bleak, rigid frosts, the scorching heats and chilling damps, of many a long year".[28]

The children of Beckwith were the ultimate recipients of whatever self-abnegation their mothers came to practise increasingly between 1852 and 1880. The late age at which Beckwith women began to give birth to children meant that younger children in Beckwith lost at least one parent before they reached maturity. Notwithstanding the trend of deferring marriage, over two-thirds of married men were between 25 and 64 years of age in 1852, and the proportion increased to almost three-fourths by 1881. Three-quarters of all married women were between the ages of twenty and 49 throughout these three decades. Hence, many who waited until their thirties to marry faced the prospect that even their eldest children would not see maturity before one parent, usually the father, passed away. The mean number of married persons, or parents, per household declined from 1.8 in 1852 to 1.6 in 1881, while the number of households headed by women increased from nineteen to 25. Since in most cases women became household heads only after losing husbands and if a son had not yet attained maturity, the increase of women heading households from 5.1 to 8.2 percent of household heads between 1852 and 1881 is a fair gauge of the increasing number of children who lost at least one parent before gaining maturity. In those households where the male parent lived past age 54, advanced age increasingly made support of their families impossible. The trend toward deferring marriage increasingly forced women to face the prospect of raising children without a husband's assistance.

The aging of Beckwith's population was also evident in the increase of widowed inhabitants from 29.5 per thousand in 1852 to 33.2 in 1881. During these thirty years women accounted for two-thirds of all widowed persons, indicating the continuing greater likelihood of husbands dying before their wives. The ages of widowed women presented in census returns provides an indirect gauge of the longer life expectancy enjoyed by married men; the greater concentration of widowed women dramatically rose from between the ages of forty and 69 in 1852 to between ages fifty and 79 in 1881. The mean age to which married women could expect to live rose from 39.1 to 40.3 years, while that for men rose from 44.2 to 45.7 years between 1852 and 1881.

The aging population did not necessarily reflect a steadily increasing mortality rate. From 3.9 deaths per thousand of population in 1852 it almost doubled to 7.5 in 1861, then slightly declined to 6.6 in 1871, only to rise by fifty percent to 9.8 by 1881. The small number of deaths in the individual census years make it hazardous to deduce conclusions applicable to Beckwith, let alone to the rest of rural eastern Ontario society in general. Yet there are observable trends that accord with earlier findings in this chapter. Clearly, the first year of infancy was a critical period for survival, for it was

Plate 130
The John Campbell house, lot 6, concession 2, Beckwith, believed built in the 1860s, as photographed in June 1982. The original board-and-batten cladding of this house added to the verticality of the exterior. This was one of the few larger frame houses built in southern Beckwith during the mid-Victorian era.

within that year that between eight and thirteen percent of deaths occurred between 1869 and 1900. After the first year, however, the chances of surviving childhood and adolescence increasingly improved. The proportion of deaths between the ages of two and nineteen years declined from twenty percent of all deaths in the 1870s to 9.2 percent in the 1910s. Conversely, the number of deaths among middle-aged inhabitants rose from 18.3 to 29.1 percent of all deaths, but among the elderly the proportion began to fall from 35 to thirty percent between the 1870s and 1880s. Age pyramids in Table 3 indicate a continuing greater persistence of men as opposed to women after age 65. The aging of the population was reflected in the mortality rate, as Table 6 demonstrates. The most striking change was that almost half of all deaths in 1852 occurred before the age of fifteen, whereas three-quarters of those in 1881 occurred after middle age. Despite statistics collected by the Beckwith township clerk from 1869 onward that show the mortality rate in the township tripling during the 1870s, it is clear that Beckwith inhabitants enjoyed greater longevity with the passing years.

Longevity brought its own problems, especially when there were no children to help support parents. It happened in the best Beckwith families. Doctor George Nesbitt had been a physician at Franktown from the 1830s onward, and was deemed sufficiently respectable and competent to be appointed surgeon to the local militia regiment after Dr. Edward Barry left Carleton Place for Bytown in 1846.[29] By 1869 at age 70, unable to practise medicine any longer and with his only son ill, Nesbitt was reduced to having his neighbours petition the township council for a weekly allowance of one dollar to support his family, an allowance which was increased by fifty cents in 1871.[30] Similar assistance was given in April 1870 to "the family of John Nichol of Carleton Place who it appears are from the severe indisposition of the father and other accidental circumstances in the family in a very straitened position as [to] the means of life",[31] and to Richard Garland in August 1870 who had "spent all his means in efforts to recover his sight without effect, is now totally blind and reduced to poverty".[32] When "an infant child of three months" age was left at the door of John McNab in April 1868, the municipality granted him ten dollars to maintain the infant on condition "that no further claims for said Child be asked from this Council".[33]

The greater portion of Beckwith municipal relief between 1852 and 1881 went to elderly widowed inhabitants. In October 1862 widow Helen McKenna who was described as being "too old and infirm to help to support her" was granted a weekly allowance of five shillings;[34] this continued to be paid until October 1864 when it was cut in half because she was observed to be "so far recovered as to help herself to a certain extent"[35] only to be increased back to five shillings in November 1865.[36] Beckwith municipal council in October 1864 granted five dollars in relief to 73 year old "Mrs. Antwine Sansom who is laid on a bed of sickness with Dropsy."[37] In April 1870 the township council granted a weekly allowance of two dollars to Alexander Armstrong who was described in a petition signed by neighbours as being "laid up at his house very ill and without any means of support." In June 1870 this allowance was cut in half, in September Black's Corners merchant Alexander Stewart Jr. was authorised to spend the allowance on Armstrong's behalf, and in December the council resolved that the sum of twelve dollars be paid for the clothing and support of Alexander Armstrong out of the Funds of the Municipality and that Alexander Stewart[,] Merchant[,] be appointed to expend the same."[38] Many widows who refused to accept what was considered to be the indignity of municipal financial relief, petitioned to be exempted from municipal obligations and taxes. Margaret Salter, for example, in September 1869 prayed "to be exempted from Statute [Labour] and the payment of taxes" but only the first request was granted.[39]

For widows without children to support them and especially for those living on poor land, existence was a precarious balance of frugality and respectability as shown by the example of Catherine Griffith. Her husband had passed away in 1840, and yet as late as 1863 she had not yet obtained the deed for the east half of lot eighteen in the third concession on which he had been located. Ewen McEwen, the Franktown postmaster and Beckwith township clerk commented in February 1863, "All the benefit she gets just now is a few dollars for the pasture of it."[40] A year earlier McEwen stated:[41]

> It is assessed to her every year and she pays the taxes and Road work for it and is the only individual that has a claim upon it, and she hopes that the Gov[ernmne]t will without any longer delay cause the Deed to be issued to her. She has conducted herself most respectably ever since she became a widow and is well worthy of all the benefit derivable from said Lands which cannot be a great deal as it is of inferior quality.

The aging of Beckwith's population coincided with a declining number of inhabitants, depleting fertility of the soil, an emerging mixed farming and dairy economy, and the industrialisation of Carleton Place. In addition to a declining birthrate, the number of households within the general population was falling. The declining number of inhabitants meant that there was an increasing ratio of acres of land per household, and this was reflected in the increasing proportion of farmers heading households and in the increasing number of larger farms. Increasingly, Beckwith society by 1881 was becoming economically stable and more homogeneous. As late as 1866 the Church of Scotland clergy in Beckwith officiated both in Gaelic and English,[42] but Archibald McPhail at the time he moved to Carleton County in the 1850s was the last head of household to conduct family worship in Gaelic.[43] By the early 1880s Gaelic ceased to exist as a language in Beckwith. Stability was evident

Plate 131
The John Nesbitt farmhouse, lot 7, concession 8, built in 1857, as photographed ca. 1895. This, the largest house in rural Beckwith at mid-century, was built by Richard May, who probably also constructed the hotel of John Hughton at Franktown which has similar dimensions and a verandah of comparable design running in the same way along the front and along one side wall (Plate 165). The building of such a substantial house begs the question of how it was financed on a farm with neither first nor second grade soil. John Nesbitt's marriage to Jane Pierce who was raised in an earlier equally large stone house (Plate 67), their sons setting forth in professional life as lawyers and doctors, and a trip back to Enniscorthy in Wexford in 1875 combine to suggest that the Nesbitts and Pierces received income from property in Ireland and that they were part of the élite among the local Irish Anglican community. Photograph courtesy of Arthur Nesbitt.

in the composition of most households and in the persistence of families. In essence, economic stability was complemented by domestic stability and by a continuing attachment to the soil.

Beckwick's domestic stability between 1852 and 1881 can be measured by comparing relative household composition in the census returns and measuring the various proportions of widowed, married and single inhabitants living with one another. Considering that 77.2 percent of all single inhabitants in 1852 were under twenty years of age (and as the population aged the proportion fell to 72.8 by 1881), it is possible to associate single marital status with youth. It must be remembered that the decline in overall population between 1861 and 1871 was primarily due to the municipal separation of Carleton Place from Beckwith in 1870. Consequently, a comparison of proportionate changes, as opposed to actual numbers, within the declining population more accurately reflects the shifts in household composition in Beckwith.

Table 6.   Relative Mortality of Young and Aged

	1852		1861		1871		1881	
Age Cohort	No.	%	No.	%	No.	%	No.	%
1-14	5	45.5	5	20.8	4	30.8	2	9.5
15-40	3	27.3	7	29.2	5	38.5	3	14.3
40 plus	3	27.3	12	50	4	30.8	16	76.2
Total	11		24		13		21	

SOURCE: *The same sources listed in Table 4.*

Household composition remained relatively stable within the context of a declining and aging population, although there was a tendency toward smaller families. The number of households fell from 384 in 1852 to 323 in 1881, while the mean number of persons per household respectively fell from 6.6 to 6.0. The nuclear family or household (that is, a household containing two parents and their children) predominated, although it fluctuated slightly as a proportion of all households between 1852 and 1881. As Table 7 shows, the proportion of households containing two married and varying numbers of single people (the equivalent of the nuclear family) remained approximately two-thirds of all households. Although the proportion of households containing married, widowed and single inhabitants (the equivalent of the extended family in which relatives other than parents and children lived with them) increased overall only fractionally from 9.1 to 9.6 percent of Beckwith's population between 1852 and 1881, it is clear that the extended family was the exception rather than the rule. A more dramatic increase was that of households inhabited by widowed and singles, rising from 7.6 to 13.3 percent, and reflecting both the aging population and the contemporary deferral of marriage.

Table 7.   Household Composition

	1852		1861		1871		1881	
Household	No.	%	No.	%	No.	%	No.	%
Singles Only	15	3.9	11	2.9	35	10.5	25	7.7
Married Only	22	5.7	12	3.1	16	4.8	11	3.4
Widowed Only	4	1.0	2	0.5	3	0.9	9	2.8
Widowed & Married	2	0.5	0		0		0	
Widowed & Single(s)	29	7.6	49	12.7	41	12.3	43	13.3
1 Married & Single(s)	2	0.5	6	1.6	1	0.3	2	0.6
2 Married & Single(s)	245	63.8	254	66.0	193	58.0	186	57.6
3+ Married & Single(s)	30	7.8	21	5.5	17	5.1	16	5.0
Married, Widowed & Single(s)	35	9.1	30	7.8	27	8.1	31	9.6
Total	384		385		333		323	

SOURCE: *The same sources listed in Table 4.*

Plate 132
The John McArthur house, lot 14, concession 7, believed built in the 1870s, as photographed in 1983. The first brick houses were built in Beckwith during the 1870s and 1880s, and most of them followed the same plan that was used for stone houses in the 1850s and 1860s. The outline of an early verandah is visible on the brickwork.

Households containing two married and numerous single inhabitants do not alone reflect the predominance of the nuclear family. To these must be added the households containing widowed and single inhabitants, and those containing three or more married and varying numbers of single inhabitants. The sum of the three is presented in Table 8. Despite the crudeness of the measure, it is clear that the nuclear as opposed to the extended family was the prototype for the overwhelming majority of households in Beckwith. Indeed, if one were to consider that the households inhabited only by married people were primarily the homes of recently married people whose first child had not yet been born, and that the households inhabited by widowed people only were formerly the homes of nuclear families, it could be argued that up to ninety percent of all households followed the nuclear family prototype. This is hardly surprising since the selection criteria for the Irish and Scottish migrations that populated Beckwith in the late 1810s favoured young families and militated against the elderly, the widowed, and single householders.

The trend toward smaller families can be examined within the nuclear households in which two married and varying numbers of single inhabitants were present. A breakdown of family size within this group is presented in Table 9. The proportion of families with eleven or more members

Table 8. Nuclear Household Composition

	1852		1861		1871		1881	
Household	No.	%	No.	%	No.	%	No.	%
Widowed & Singles	29	7.6	49	12.7	41	12.3	43	13.3
1 Married & Singles	2	0.5	6	1.6	1	0.3	2	0.6
2 Married & Singles	245	63.8	254	66.0	193	58.0	186	57.6
3+ Married & Singles	30	7.8	21	5.5	17	5.1	16	5.0
Total	306	79.7	330	85.7	252	75.7	247	76.5

SOURCE: *The same sources listed in Table 4.*

Table 9. Nuclear Household Comparative Size

	1852		1861		1871		1881	
Household	No.	%	No.	%	No.	%	No.	%
2 Married & 1-4 Singles	110	44.9	123	48.4	93	48.2	90	48.4
2 Married & 5-8 Singles	107	43.7	101	39.8	81	42.0	85	45.7
2 Married & 9+ Singles	28	11.4	30	11.8	19	9.8	11	5.9
Total	245	100.0	254	100.0	193	100.0	186	100.0

SOURCE: *The same sources listed in Table 4.*

dramatically dropped to half at the same time there was a slight increase in the proportion of families with six members or less and in the proportion of families with between seven and ten members. To judge from these statistics alone, the decline in family size appears not to have taken place until after 1871. More precise statistics on the mean number of people in households headed by farmers indicate that the gradual decline in family size commenced in the 1860s. There were 6.6 persons per household from 1852 to 1861, a rate that decreased to 6.0 in 1871, and to 5.8 persons per household headed by farmers in 1881. Since farmers headed between two-thirds and more than three-quarters of all households in Beckwith between 1852 and 1881, this makes it impossible to compare decreasing farm household size with households headed by inhabitants engaged in other occupations. Notwithstanding this, on the whole Beckwith ceased to have the huge families that had been common in the early nineteenth century.

The decline of mean household size points to an increasing number of families that actually were not nuclear families, although their composition reflected the primacy of the nuclear family as a prototype. While the number of nuclear households either remained stable or decreased slightly, these "non-nuclear" families increased in number, as shown in Table 10. The few households in which widowed and married resided together complemented the larger number of widowed who

Plate 133
The Robert Kennedy house, lot 24, concession 8, Beckwith, as photographed in September 1987. The larger more ambitious stone and brick houses built during the 1850s and 1860s did not leave the older and more modest houses unaffected. The moderate-sized log house adjacent to the Dewar and Kennedy cemeteries had a front gable and upstairs window as well as a few extra tiers of logs added to conform to the new fashionable late-Victorian verticality. The spacing of doors and windows suggests that the downstairs ceilings after this alteration were not as high as those upstairs.

resided by themselves. Wherever circumstances permitted, widows apparently preferred to preside over their own households, rather than move in with married children, relatives or neighbours. The small number of households inhabited by one married person and varying numbers of single people points to a minor but continuing proportion of broken marriages that persisted. Whether abandoned, widowed, or remaining single, an increasing proportion, although still a minority of Beckwith inhabitants did not live within nuclear households.

The predominance of nuclear households and of the nuclear family prototype must be understood within the context of rural interdependence within a family and within a neighbourhood. It has been argued that the high rural birthrate that existed in the early mid-nineteenth century was the response of immigrants to the task of establishing farms and paying for them, by having numerous children to provide labour. This, asserts David Gagan in his study of Peel County, inevitably led to a crisis in the farm economy:[44]

> The real challenge in the long term was to solve the problem of those overpopulated rural households which had once depended for their standard of living on the labour of many

Table 10.   Non-Nuclear Household Composition and Growth

	1852		1861		1871		1881	
Household	No.	%	No.	%	No.	%	No.	%
Singles Only	15	3.9	11	2.9	35	10.5	25	7.7
Widowed Only	4	1.0	2	0.5	3	0.9	9	2.8
Widowed & Married	2	0.5	0		0		0	
Widowed & Singles	29	7.6	49	12.7	41	12.3	43	13.3
1 Married & Singles	2	0.5	6	1.6	1	0.3	2	0.6
Married, Widowed & Singles	35	9.1	30	7.8	27	8.1	31	9.6
Total	87	22.7	98	25.5	107	32.1	110	34.1

SOURCE: *The same sources listed in Table 4.*

children but could no longer compensate them adequately for their contribution and even victimized them in the interests of social security and stability.

The "crisis", claims Gagan, could only be circumvented by increasing the acreage of the land to be divided among sons, or by pulling up stakes and moving elsewhere. Only the last of these could be achieved within a short period of time.

Had a crisis indeed existed, more dramatic changes would have been evident in household composition. As Ian Winchester observes, "A *crisis* brought on by overpopulation should have led to more adults coming into one household, and more than one family unit appearing in a household.[45] But in Beckwith in 1852 less than eight percent of all households had three and more married as well as single inhabitant in the same household, and this proportion declined in subsequent decades. Similarly, in 1852 only nine percent of households had married, widowed and single persons residing together, and these declined in the 1861 and 1871 census returns as a proportion of all households. This insight must be kept within the context of recognising that more than one household existed on a farm where previously only one house had been located. It is unlikely that a son and his wife would choose to live with his parents in the same household, compared with the privacy and lack of domestic squabbles an adjacent house, often the older log house that had been replaced by a newer and more substantial structure, afforded.

Hence, two or three sons and daughters and their families resided near their parents' farm and worked together with one another and with fellow neighbours at farming, and at night each respectively returned to his own home. A sampling of the daily entries in the 1874 farm journal of George McLaren, aged 62, who farmed lot 21 in the fifth concession suggests the pattern of family and community interdependence that existed:[46]

[4] February [1874] — I am drawing wood today to Mr. Cam[p]b[e]l[l's] [5] I and Father in at Mr[.] Sincl[ai]r['s] child's funer[a]l [7] I am drawing wood to Carelton [Place] [19] I am at Alexander Duff[']s thra[s]hing clover [23] I am Drawing wood to McNab the schoolmaster....

John is chop[p]ing [27] I went to Ashton to see Dan Fanning for Mr. Fanning March — [5] I and John is cleaning up some grain.... we went to Carelton [Place] after Din[n]er.... I was at the mill[,] got the horses shod,... gave James Sterns 1 barrell of porke at 16 Dollers to be payed on the first of [April.] [6] I went out to Donald McL[are]n[']s[,].... gave Donald 5 bushels of peas for the 6 bushels of rye in the fall and got 2 bushels of buckwheat. [10] I went to Carelton [Place]... sold 126 pounds of pork to Mr. Hillfield.... John is not hear. [11] I am at home today attending to the Cattle. John is not hear[,] he is at home. [13] I am at home today[,] Drew 4 loads of sawed wood from the bush. John is not working here today[,] he came tonight. [14] I went to Mr. William Duff[']s[,] bought 2 cows... John is drawing wood home today. [20] I was at Dan McDoug[all]'s to see about a man. David Robertson came here today. John is chop[p]ing. [21] I am in the bush underbru[s]hing. [23] I went up to Mr. Nesbitt[']s in the forenoon to get one of them tomorrow and a horse [25] I and John is at Mr. Nesbitt's sawing [28] We are sawing today. David Robertson is with me and Thomas & James Nesbitt and Robert Dunlop. April [3] I am at Hue Robertson's sale on the 11 line[,] bought 1 roller for 4 dollers. [6] I was in Carelton [Place] to day. [T]his is fair day. [14] John Dell commenced to work today[;] he hired at the rate of 100 Dollers for 6 months [21] I went over to the counc[il] to get my Road work don[e] on the line [25] We are all taking of[f] stones till noon[.] I went to plow after din[n]er.

The residence of George McLaren's brother, John, was on lot 27 of the fifth concession, but despite the two farms being a couple of miles apart it is clear that the two brothers worked together despite George hiring a number of hired men. The close positioning of similar surnames within the census returns substantiates that this interdependent pattern existed on a substantial scale in Beckwith, and even those farmers without brothers and parents could join with neighbours in mutual chores and bees just as they did when performing statute labour.

The census enumerators who tramped up and down the roads of Beckwith in 1881, whether or not they were conscious of it, observed an intrinsically different society from the one recorded in detail by James Burrows, James Duncan and John McDiarmid thirty years earlier. A gradual albeit continuing population decline had set in, and although the population remained largely youthful in composition, by 1881 it was clear that it was aging. Nonetheless, by 1861 Beckwith was a mature society compared with other townships in the region, particularly those along the Rideau Canal. The population decline that began in the 1860s was one indication of this maturity. Other indications included the increasing deferral of marriage by both men and women, a declining fertility rate, the smaller number and size of families, the increasing number of native-born, the decline in proportion of married people per family, the increasing parenting of children at middle age, the loss of one or more parents before younger children reached maturity, the increasing number of households headed by women, the increasing number of widowed inhabitants, and the increasing mortality rate among the elderly as opposed to youth. The stability that developed in the face of Beckwith's declining population between 1852 and 1881 was reflected in the very gradual decline of family size in the general population. The nuclear family remained the prototype for the majority of households, notwithstanding an increasing number of extended family households. The small proportion of extended families clearly indicates that there was no crisis in the local farm economy. Within the context of co-operation among family members and neighbours, and the mechanisation of agriculture there was decreasing need for as large families as had existed before mid-century, and decreasing need as well for as many people to farm within the township's boundaries. As it turned out, Beckwith in 1861 was on the threshold of a century of continuous yet gradual population decline.

Endnotes

1. *Carleton Place Herald*, 30 January 1861, p. 2, col. 4.
2. Howard M. Brown, *Founded Upon A Rock*, p. 35.
3. Canada, Minister of Agriculture, *Census of Canada: 1870-71* (Ottawa: I.B. Taylor, 1873) I:26-27 and ibid., *Census of Canada: 1880-81* (Ottawa: Maclean, Roger and Company, 1882) I:62-63.
4. Most of the statistics in this chapter are based on an analysis of the 1852, 1861, 1871 and 1881 census returns for Beckwith Township. The procedure for analysing the census returns by computer is fairly simple. It began with an initial study of the manuscript census returns in order to recognise differences between censuses and enumerators, to note the variety of information contained in each census, to establish the quality of the microfilm copy as well as the handwriting of the enumerators. A codebook was then prepared, based partly on that devised by Julian Gwyn in his study of Huntley Township, Carleton County. Coding sheets were then devised to correspond to the codebook, and copies were printed; data from the manuscript census was then copied onto the coding sheets, beginning with the 1852 census and continuing to the end of the 1881 census. This was actually a transcription of written information into a numerical code, with only names allowed to remain in alphabetical characters. After double-checking this coded transcript of the census returns, the coding sheets were taken to a professional keypunch operator and entered upon a computer tape. Rodney G. Swain then took responsibility for transferring the information from the tape to a disc at the University of Ottawa Computing Centre. He then made a printout of the information entered by the keypunch operator and checked it against the codebook, then entered final corrections, and again checked this against yet another printout. Swain then took a list of formulated questions devised by Lockwood in a similar study of Montague Township and prepared a program based primarily on the Statistical Package for the Social Sciences (SPSS) modified computer packaged program to answer the questions based on the data in the disc. The printouts from this program provide the core of information for the second part of this chapter. I wish to commend Rodney Swain for his dedication in pursuing every step of this process, and for ensuring the accuracy of the data.
5. For similar detail on Montague Township consult Glenn J Lockwood, "The Irish in Eastern Ontario: The Social Structure of Montague Township in Lanark County, 1861-1881." M.A. Thesis, University of Ottawa, 1981.
6. In 1852, 34.6% of married men were between the ages of 25 and 39, and 43.5% of married women were between the ages of twenty and 34. In 1881, 40% of married men were between the ages of 30 and 34, and 39.5% of married women were between the ages of 30 and 44.
7. David Gagan, "Land, Population, and Social Change: The 'Critical Years' in Canada West" in *Canadian Historical Review* LIX (1979), p. 309.
8. *Carleton Place Herald*, 5 April 1865, p. 2, col. 5.
9. Ibid., 18 December 1861, p. 2, col. 6.
10. *Perth (Ontario) Courier*, 14 February 1868, p. 2, cols. 4-5.
11. *Carleton Place Herald*, 29 April 1868, p. 2, cols. 4-5.
12. *Almonte (Ontario) Gazette*, 16 October 1868, p. 2, col. 4.
13. *Perth (Canada West) Bathurst Courier*, 1 August 1856, p. 4, col. 1.
14. Michael B. Katz, *The People of Hamilton, Canada West: Family and Class in a Mid-Nineteenth-Century City* (Cambridge, Massachusetts: Harvard University Press, 1975), pp. 246-247.
15. *Bathurst Courier*, 21 March 1856, p. 4, col. 2.
16. *Perth (Canada West) Lanark Observer*, 18 August 1852, p. 1, cols. 2-3.
17. Ibid., p. 2, cols. 2-3.
18. *Carleton-Place Herald*, 27 December 1853, p. 3, cols. 4-5.
19. Ibid., 23 December 1863, p. 2, cols. 5-6.
20. *Carleton Place Lanark Herald*, 11 April 1851, p. 3, cols. 1-2.
21. *Carleton-Place Herald*, 30 October 1851, p. 4, cols. 1-2.
22. Ibid., 2 August 1865, p. 2, col. 4.
23. Ibid., 7 October 1852, p. 4, col. 2.
24. Ibid., 19 May 1853, p. 3, col. 4.
25. Ibid., 5 July 1855, p. 3, col. 8.
26. Ibid., 19 August 1858, p. 3, col. 6.
27. Ibid., 30 November 1864, p. 3, col. 7.
28. Ibid., 25 May 1864, p. 3, col. 3.
29. *Bytown (Canada West) Packet*, 17 January 1846, p. 2, col. 5.
30. OBCRM 13 May 1869 and 21 February 1871 minutes of Beckwith township council.
31. Ibid., 12 April 1870 minutes.
32. Ibid., 9 August 1870 minutes.
33. Ibid., 15 May 1868 minutes.
34. Ibid., 21 October 1862 minutes.
35. Ibid., 18 October 1864 minutes.
36. Ibid., 6 November 1865 minutes.
37. Ibid., 18 October 1864 minutes.
38. Ibid., 12 April, 14 June, 20 September and 13 December 1870 minutes.
39. Ibid., 21 September 1869 minutes.

40 OTAR RG 1 MS 658 Crown Lands Department, Township Papers, Beckwith, Reel 30, p. 204.
41 Ibid., p. 211.
42 James Croil, *A Historical and Statistical Report of the Presbyterian Church of Canada, in connection with the Church of Scotland for the year 1866* (Montreal: John Lovell, 1868), p. 90.
43 Jessie Buchanan Campbell and John J. McLaurin, *The Pioneer Pastor* (Franklin, Pennsylvania: John J. McLaurin, 1905), p. 34.
44 Gagan, "Land, Population and Social Change", p. 307.
45 Ian Winchester, "Review of Peel County History Project and the Saguenay Project" in *Histoire Sociale-Social History XIII* (1980), p. 201. The italics are Winchester's.
46 I am grateful to James I. McLaren of Ottawa for lending this journal for use in this publication.

THE MATURING OF DANIEL McCUAN

On the evening of October 20th 1858 before going to bed Daniel McCuan of northern Beckwith wrote in his notebook, "I heard the whistle of the locomotive tonight quite distinctly together with the rattling of the cars[. T]his is the first time ever I heard it in these diggings[.] I felt something delighted to hear it."[1] This was rather a remarkable statement in that the nearest railway on which trains ran was the Bytown and Prescott railway more than twenty miles distant at its closest point. It was not so remarkable a statement considering the railroad-building mania that gripped the inhabitants of Beckwith and most other Canadian municipalities in the 1850s. As early as August 1853 the *Carleton Place Herald* below its mast-head featured an illustration of a locomotive pulling a train of cars on the Brockville and Ottawa railway. Therefore it is hardly surprising that amid the frenzy of anticipation during the final months of construction that a young man from Beckwith should imagine hearing a train on tracks yet under construction.

Daniel McCuan was an impressionable adolescent when the mania for building railroads first gripped Lanark County in 1852, but his was the generation to ultimately reap the mixed harvest of benefits and higher taxes that accompanied railroads during the ensuing thirty years. The push to build railroads reflected the maturing of local society, and it particularly reflected a strong desire among local inhabitants to shake off their reputation of being stuck in the mud of the backwoods. Increased intercourse with the outside world, it was anticipated, would make markets more readily available both for local farmers and manufacturers, it would increase communication between northern and southern Beckwith, and it promised to facilitate a new push of settlement into the upper Ottawa valley and the western part of the province. In addition to the vast improvement the railroad offered as a form of transportation, as the ultimate symbol of progress it promised industrial growth for Carleton Place and the spread of agricultural, educational, religious and architectural advancement.

Daniel McCuan was only ten years old on the tenth of February 1844 when the way his family measured time changed. On that day his father, Duncan McCuan, purchased a clock from peddler Warren Herrick, a clock which in all likelihood was of American manufacture.[2] This purchase represented a significant departure in domestic life from a period when time was measured in daylight hours from sunrise to sunset to a new era when Beckwith inhabitants stayed up at night by firelight and candlelight to read their newspapers and pursue other activities. In their papers from the 1840s onward they read about the many ways in which Canada West lagged behind the United States in building railroads, in making education universally available, in giving the electorate control of municipal institutions, and in industrialisation. Daniel McCuan's family resided on the southeast half of lot 22 in the tenth concession in the very heart of the concentrated Perthshire settlement in the northern quarter of Beckwith. In 1852 the household consisted of his father Duncan aged seventy; his mother Catherine aged 55; his three older brothers John, Duncan and Alex; his younger brother Peter, his young sister Elizabeth, and a 29 year old spinster named Elizabeth McFarlane.

However much the members of this family felt their region suffered for lack of a railroad in the 1840s, the literacy of the children was sufficient testimony to the priority the Scottish immigrant

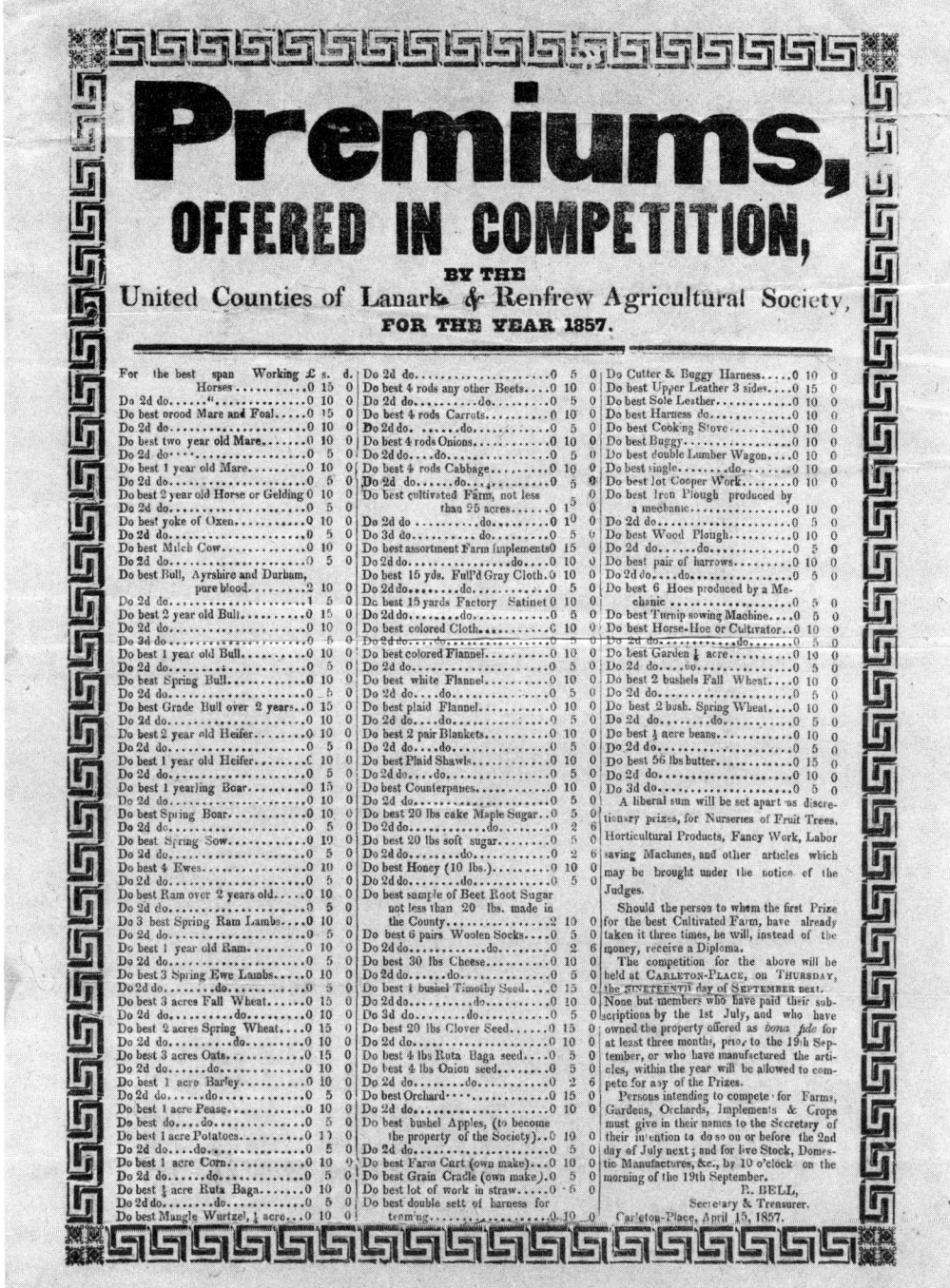

Plate 134
Broadside listing premiums offered in competition by the United Counties of Lanark & Renfrew Agricultural Society in 1857. The loss of the annual exhibition of this society to Almonte just a year before the railway arrived marked the first in a decade of setbacks for Carleton Place at a time when village inhabitants expected unprecedented growth to occur. The emphases on livestock and woollen cloth reflected a continuing highland tradition in Beckwith, and in the future would be important to the development of a dairy economy in Beckwith and a woollen industry in Carleton Place. Loaned courtesy of Alex and Jean McCuan.

parents placed on their obtaining an education. In his copy books Daniel McCuan progressed from tracing out inch-high words such as "Humility", "Remember" and "Unanimously" to short phrases such as "Avoid all vicious company", "Industry is the road to happiness", "Zealously strive to improve" and "Be assiduous in learning" to yet longer value-laden phrases such as "Wine is a mocker, strong drink is raging", "Gentleness ought to form our address", "Virtue exalts an empire, but sin is a disgrace" and "Procrastination is the thief of time".[3] By the time he was a young man of twenty in 1854, Daniel McCuan had received from the combined formative influences of parents, school, church, newspapers, neighbours frantically advocating railroads, the dispersal of his schoolmates, and the growing number of slabs in the nearby Cram burying ground a strong sense of how quickly time was passing such as no one half a generation earlier would have noted. In early September 1854 he wrote:[4]

> Surely a man's life is as a shadow or a dream that is soon passed away. I am now over twenty and when I look back I think it but short since I played merrily with my school fellows[. B]ut what a change has come over them[! T]hey are mostly engaged in the bustle of the world[,] a good deal scattered, and a few of them gone to their long home [in the burying ground].... Time is flying very fast and we will in a few short years be landed in eternity.

The railroad-building era for Beckwith began early in November 1852 with an editorial in the *Carleton Place Herald* calling for either a good macadamised or plank road to be constructed between Smith's Falls and Carleton Place.[5] Some 38 merchants from Carleton Place, Smith's Falls, Franktown and Ramsay[6] convened a public meeting of inhabitants interested in constructing such a road to form a joint stock company at the Franktown inn of James Burrows in late December 1852. Here they began seriously discussing "the project of a RAILROAD from BROCKVILLE *via* SMITH'S FALLS and CARLETON-PLACE to some point on the River Ottawa."[7] Perhaps a railway had been anticipated all along, but it was at this point that regional inhabitants began to wax euphoric about the benefits of railways. One advocate in the *Carleton Place Herald* estimated that there were a dozen sites along the line of the proposed railway between Smith's Falls and the Ottawa River where there was "a succession of water-power, perhaps, unequalled in the same extent, upon any other line of road in Canada" and which were surrounded "by forests where an almost inexhaustible supply of the raw material for lumbering purposes, could be easily procured". A railroad would lure capitalists to develop these sites, uged editor James Poole and "thousands would find empoyment in taking the timber from the woods, and preparing it for the market":[8]

> Flouring Mills of the first order would be erected upon our streams, and large quantities of Wheat [would] be annually imported from less favored spots, to be manufactured for distant markets; the ample resources of this fine agricultural section of our country would soon become fully developed; trade in all its ramifications would receive an impetus, that would astonish the most sanguine. Manufactories would be seen spring[ing] up on every available spot. — Carleton-Place, from an insignificant village, would soon become a thriving and populous market-Town, and other Hamlets [would] rise up, into respectable Villages "teeming with life and activity."

A railroad was argued as being beneficial to Beckwith farmers because the large and increasing number of mechanics and labourers in Carleton Place and local villages "would look to the farmer for a supply of life's necessaries" and consequently "a home market, AND CASH PAYMENT would be originated for many articles of farm produce now nearly unsaleable." The railway promised a profitable market for beef which as matters stood "rarely sells at a price equivalent to the expense of raising it" and for mutton "which is seldom calculated upon as an article of trade". The railroad

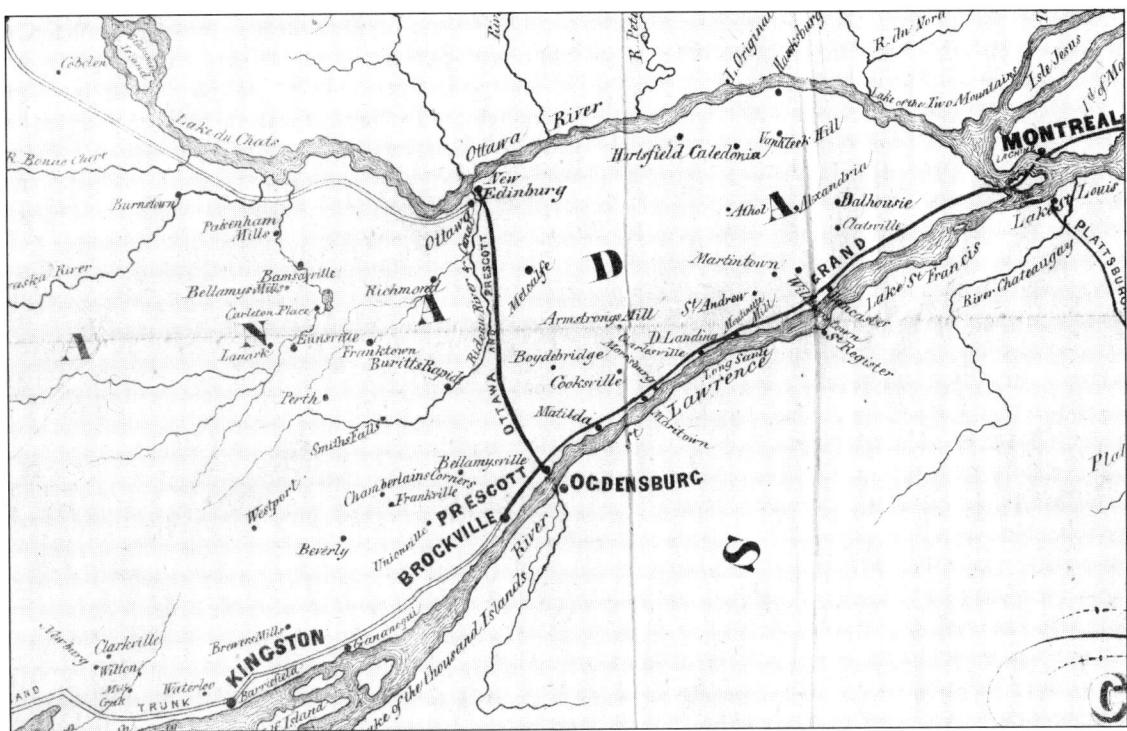

Plate 135
Detail from a "Map of Canada shewing the Railways Completed[,] in Progress[,] and Projected" in 1856, as published by Maclear & Co., Toronto. Three years after Beckwith and other area municipalities voted to back the Brockville and Ottawa railway, no line had yet been constructed, leaving Carleton Place and Franktown without good transportation to reach the outside world. Bankruptcy in 1856 would retard the arrival of train service in Beckwith for three more years. Loaned courtesy of Alex and Jean McCuan.

would attract speculators and purchasers from towns along the St. Lawrence and the neighbouring American states to purchase whatever extra produce farmers had to dispose of. By establishing a steady cash market for disposable produce of local farmers, a railroad would "abolish the crushing credit system" whereby local merchants, artisans and tradesmen exacted ten percent interest on purchases, and even "all goods purchased with Butter are charged credit price". The savings to local farmers if they were paid in cash was shown by the price of horse shoeing; "if cash is paid, on[e] shilling and three pence per shoe in the price, if charged, one shilling and seven pence halfpenny". Moreover, the railroad promised to reduce the prices of goods in local merchants' shops since they "would be placed in competition, not only with each other, but also with the merchants of Montreal, Boston, and New York, and in all heavy goods especially, the reduction would be sensibly felt". Not least among the arguments made to Beckwith farmers in favour of the proposed railroad was that it would remove the burden of winter travel to Bytown:[9]

> Farmers, the winter, instead of being looked forward to as a season of privation and hardship, which it now must be to numbers of us, who are necessitated to spend a great part of that time upon the road, (no matter how inclement the weather,) in conveying their own, or the produce of their neighbors to market, would then be hailed as a season of relaxation from severe labour, whose hours would be pleasantly and profitably devoted to increased attention to stock, mental culture and social enjoyment.

Beckwith inhabitants almost instantly became enthused. Public meetings held in schoolhouses on the fourth, seventh and eleventh concessions in early February 1853 unanimously agreed that the "railroad will benefit all classes"[10] and that "the Township of Beckwith should co-operate with the other Townships on the line, in carrying out the enterprise".[11] A poll was held in all the townships of the united counties of Lanark and Renfrew in July 1853 asking electors to vote their approval for a projected £200,000 loan to help finance the new railroad. Every municipality save for Admaston voted in favour of constructing the new railway.[12] Unlike nearby Montague where only 58 percent voted for the railroad at a poll [13] opponents of the railroad in Beckwith were unable to counter the effective oratory of Robert Bell, and the township meeting "carried the By-Law by acclamation".[14] If Beckwith generally was enthusiastic about the new railway, the inhabitants of Carleton Place were ecstatic:[15]

> [T]he inhabitants of this "city," elated at the success which had attended the Railroad scheme, thus far, turned out *en masse*, and had a regular rejoicing. The windows were illuminated; the old Cannon placed on the bridge and several shots fired by way of introduction; after which the party formed in procession, led on by the music of two drums and the Highland Bagpipes, with several flags floating in the breeze, marched round the town, stopping occasionally to let off some of the pent up gas, in the shape of hearty cheers....

The cheering proved premature when some three years later the Brockville and Ottawa Railway Company went bankrupt without so much as a railroad tie placed along the Beckwith section of the route. The stable financing expected from British investors dried up during the uncertain years of the Crimean War. The death of William Sykes, a prominent financier of the railway, brought its precarious financing tumbling down to reveal how little work had been done on it. The railway had squandered a vast amount of money in building a tunnel under Brockville, and yet three years after the undertaking had been funded, rails had not yet even reached Smith's Falls from Brockville. Although refinancing was arranged, construction dragged on for another three years before the first train travelled from Brockville to Smith's Falls and on to Perth in January 1859.[16] By April the Carleton Place *Herald* reported that trains "are now running regularly from Brockville to Perth" and enthused that "the establishment of our railway system appears as though it were the result of a miracle."[17] The track through Beckwith was not fully laid until mid July 1859, finally allowing a locomotive to chug into Carleton Place:[18]

> The streets presented a continued scene of commotion [James Poole reported in the *Herald*], from the western extremity of the village, to the eastern, the[re] were multitudes of men, women, and children, pressing rapidly along towards the railroad; and there stationed in groups, on either side of the track; watching the proceedings in profound astonishment. At intervals a prolonged exclamation simultaneously escaped from the multitude "behold the cars!" Many of the incredulous peasantry did gaze at the locomotive in contemplative amazement. Many of their countenances appeared contorted into the most frightful shapes as they beheld clouds of smoke intermingled with fire, emitted profusely from this fiery charge. Amidst the strange confusion and sound of many voice[s], could be at once distinguished the shrill roar of this furious stranger, conducting his train across the most formidable construction that has ever connected the south with the north shore of the Mississippi. It has now become a highway for this foreigner to pass over to Almonte; he is on his way to Pembroke, and it is very probable the the excitement will be as intense at that place, as was hitherto manifested at Perth, Smith's Falls, Franktown, and Carleton Place.

Plate 136
"Representation of the 'Iron Horse' on the way to Pembroke" beneath the mast-head of the Carleton Place Herald, *18 August 1853. Carleton Place merchants and landowners believed that the railroad would bring industrialisation, growth and ready access to the rest of the province. The contrast between the railway mania which prompted this illustration and the halting progress of construction on the Brockville and Ottawa railway is revealed by the interval of a generation before Beckwith inhabitants could travel to Pembroke by train. National Library of Canada negative no. NL-11921.*

The inhabitants of Pembroke would wait a long time for such a celebration. In 1859 the Brockville and Ottawa railroad only went as far north as Almonte,[19] in 1864 it was extended to Arnprior, and only by 1876 did it reach Pembroke.[20] Initially, there was little opposition to the railroad in Beckwith, save for a poem printed in the Carleton Place *Herald* in which a nymph bemoaned the laying waste of her ancient Beckwith woods:[21]

> The Iron Horse with thunder charged,
> Shall soon appear upon the rails,
> My frightened deer — with eyes enlarged,
> Will scarcely wait to cock their tails.
>
> The little birds whose plumage gay,
> So long adorned my silent walks;
> No longer can prolong their stay,
> Where such gigantic terror stalks.
>
> My wild flowers rich which gem the shade,
> And spread o'er hills a flowery cloak;
> At once will wither up and fade,
> Polluted by the poisonous smoke.

By April 1860 Beckwith inhabitants recognised that the Brockville and Ottawa railroad was incapable of making a profit. A public meeting in the township hall at Black's Corners viewed with alarm the increased taxation to be imposed on them to complete the railway and unanimously expressed their "disapprobation of the ensnaring manner in which we have been led and deceived by the Directors of the Brockville and Ottawa Railway Company" and suggested that they give the railroad "into the hands of some more efficient Company, that would be both able and willing to carry on and finish the said Railroad, thereby exempting us from the taxes which will otherwise be incurred."[22] The directors of the railway offered a pessimistic description of the railroad in 1862 as being 25 miles short of its river terminus, half-stocked, destitute of machine shops and therefore working at the maximum of expense. The question when it would become a dead loss to every *bona fide* interest concerned rested solely upon the time when rails and engines should wear out and heavy renewals would become necessary. Such renewals could not have been met by the limited income it earned, and to suppose that any interest owing to municipalities or bondholders could ever have been paid was simply preposterous.[23]

The boosterism generated by Robert Bell in the Carleton Place *Herald* was more than equal to the criticism of the railway that began to emerge. He accused Beckwith reeve Archibald McArthur in 1860 of maintaining a *"longstanding* enmity to the company, the directors and the Railroad", and argued that once the railway was completed to the Ottawa River it would generate profits.[24] Indeed, once the railway was extended to Arnprior, traffic on the railway increased substantially, so much so that a correspondent of the Ottawa *Citizen* in July 1865 complained that a "large portion of the trade of the city of Ottawa, has of late years been diverted" and recommended that a railroad be built from Ottawa to Franktown to connect with the Brockville and Ottawa Railway.[25] When surveys were completed in July 1868, the new Canada Central Railway as it was called linked up with the older line at Carleton Place, causing a Beckwith correspondent of the *Carleton Place Herald* to exclaim:[26]

> What an idea to think, that we in the County of Lanark shall be placed with[in] 26 miles or ¾ of an hour's ride by rail of the city of Ottawa, the capital of this great and large Dominion — the London of British North America. What the city of Ottawa shall yet be, and the influence it will have in this section of country, about to be so closely connected, it is hard to say, it must be great.

Construction of the new line began with a ceremonial sod-turning in late August 1868,[27] but lagged in the summer of 1869 due in part to a lack of interest by farmers living along the route in the tenth and eleventh concessions of Beckwith east of Carleton Place.[28]

The *Carleton Place Herald* exhorted Beckwith farmers to support the new railway since it offered "a new and extensive market opened out to them at all seasons of the year for almost everything, animal or vegetable, which their farms can produce, and they know it is a market, where they can always get cash for what they have to sell."[29] The farmers of rural Beckwith remembered all too well the debt on the Brockville and Ottawa Railway with which they had been saddled, into which they had been drawn by the intoxicated prose of the *Herald* in the 1850s. The Irish farmers of southern Beckwith had before them the example of their relatives in adjacent Montague who in 1865 stoutly refused to pay any further share of the accumulated debts on the Brockville and Ottawa Railway.[30] When a meeting of Beckwith ratepayers was called in late August 1869 to consider "whether the Township should take stock, or otherwise materially aid the construction of the Canada Central Railway" a large contingent from the Franktown vicinity showed up to defeat vigorously the proposal.[31] Despite Beckwith's disenchantment with railroads as an investment, the new line from Carleton Place to Ottawa opened in September 1870,[32] and by mid October the editor of the *Herald* was "most happy to learn that since the opening of the Canada Central railway...the business of the B. & O. Railway seems to have increased very much. It is surprising to see the trains passing at all hours of the day and night, and the quantity of freight which they carry. The passenger traffic is also very large and daily increasing."[33]

The protest by rural Beckwith inhabitants against aiding the Canada Central Railway reflected the little benefit they perceived themselves to obtain from the railways. Daniel McCuan and his

Plate 137
A Brockville and Ottawa railway broadside offering A Cheap Ride to the Montreal Exhibition, 1865. The coming of the railroad placed Beckwith inhabitants in more immediate contact with the rest of Canada, particularly the cities of Ottawa and Montreal. The integration of the railway lines running through Beckwith into the transcontinental Canadian Pacific railway in 1881 lured farmers' sons westward first on harvest excursions to prairie farms and eventually to develop farms of their own. National Library of Canada.

brothers still hauled crops to market in Ottawa over impossible roads in the early 1860s.[34] George McLaren in the Derry hauled livestock and crops to market in Carleton Place over rough township roads rather than ship them from Franktown on the train in 1874.[35] Even in the late 1870s when farmers such as Joseph Kidd began taking some crops to market in Ottawa on the train, he still continued to haul to Carleton Place.[36] In contrast with the enthusiasm with which they had embraced railroads in the 1850s, and in contrast with the ongoing boosterism of Carleton Place merchants such as Robert Bell who stood to prosper as the railway helped that village grow, Beckwith farmers found the railway too expensive a mode of hauling their crop to market. Initially some farmers profited from railway construction. Daniel McCuan and his brothers, for example, in early April 1855 contracted to provide the Brockville and Ottawa railway with "1,500 set[s] of caps[,] Bucks & stakes[,] each set to contane 1 cap, 1 Bunk & 2 stakes of cedar".[37] Farms that largely had been unarable swamps yielded railway ties, telegraph poles, fence posts and cordwood, for all of which the railway provided an immense appetite. Indeed, when the McCuan family was strapped for money in the autumn of 1862 and mulled over which section of the farm to sell, John McCuan advised against selling the hardwood bush and argued that "even part of the swamp is not dispensable."[38] For most Beckwith farmers the railway offered little or no benefit, and the burden it represented in taxes was made heavier by other negative developments such as the increasing failure of the wheat crop. Peter MCuan commented in January 1863, "Most people complain of the bad turn out of grain this winter[;] this along with the heavy Railway and Jail tax makes farmers grumble a good deal".[39]

Despite Beckwith farmers grumbling that the Brockville and Ottawa railway had been foisted on them by merchants in Smith's Falls, Carleton Place, Perth and Almonte ambitious to develop these villages into industrialising towns, and despite the heavy tax burden it imposed, the local rural economy remained remarkably stable from the 1850s through to the 1870s. Despite the decline in population which set in during the 1860s, the quality of life for the majority of Beckwith inhabitants improved for the better from that at mid-century. There were, of course, instances of poverty persisting in the twonship, but not to any extent to suggest that a rigid structure of inequality divided local society. This was due to the fact that most inhabitants were engaged in farming on land that they either owned or in which they felt they had some stake, and due to the absence of an extremely wealthy class of inhabitants at least until the late 1870s. Of course some farmers were more prosperous than others. They cultivated significantly greater acreages, they inhabited finer houses and they probably imagined themselves belonging to an elite compared with the majority of their fellow tillers of the soil. Still, there were no enormous inequalities, and failure was the exception rather than the rule after mid-century. Beckwith differed not only from urban settings such as Hamilton and Kingston, but also from rural communities such as Toronto Gore Township in Peel County as well, in its comparative economic stability during the 1850s, 1860s and 1870s.

Farming was the occupation of the majority of household heads in Beckwith, although the proportion was decreasing while Carleton Place remained a Beckwith village and after it became a separate municipality in 1870. As Table 11 demonstrates, the proportion of household heads employed in farming decreased by more than ten percent before Carleton Place left Beckwith, and continued to decrease by more than five percent between 1871 and 1881. The same trend was evident in the general population listed as having an occupation (Table 12). The proportion of Beckwith households headed by persons engaged in clerical and labouring work increased, but among the general population the pattern is less clear.

The family of Daniel McCuan offers a sense of the developments within numerous Beckwith families that combined to produce the diverging proportions of household heads and the general population employed at farming. Duncan McCuan was listed as head of this household in 1852 and again in 1861, but being over seventy years of age the farm was mutually operated by his sons John, Duncan, Alex, Daniel and Peter as they became mature men. In their copious correspondence during the 1850s and 1860s the brothers repeatedly referred to the homestead as their joint concern, as when

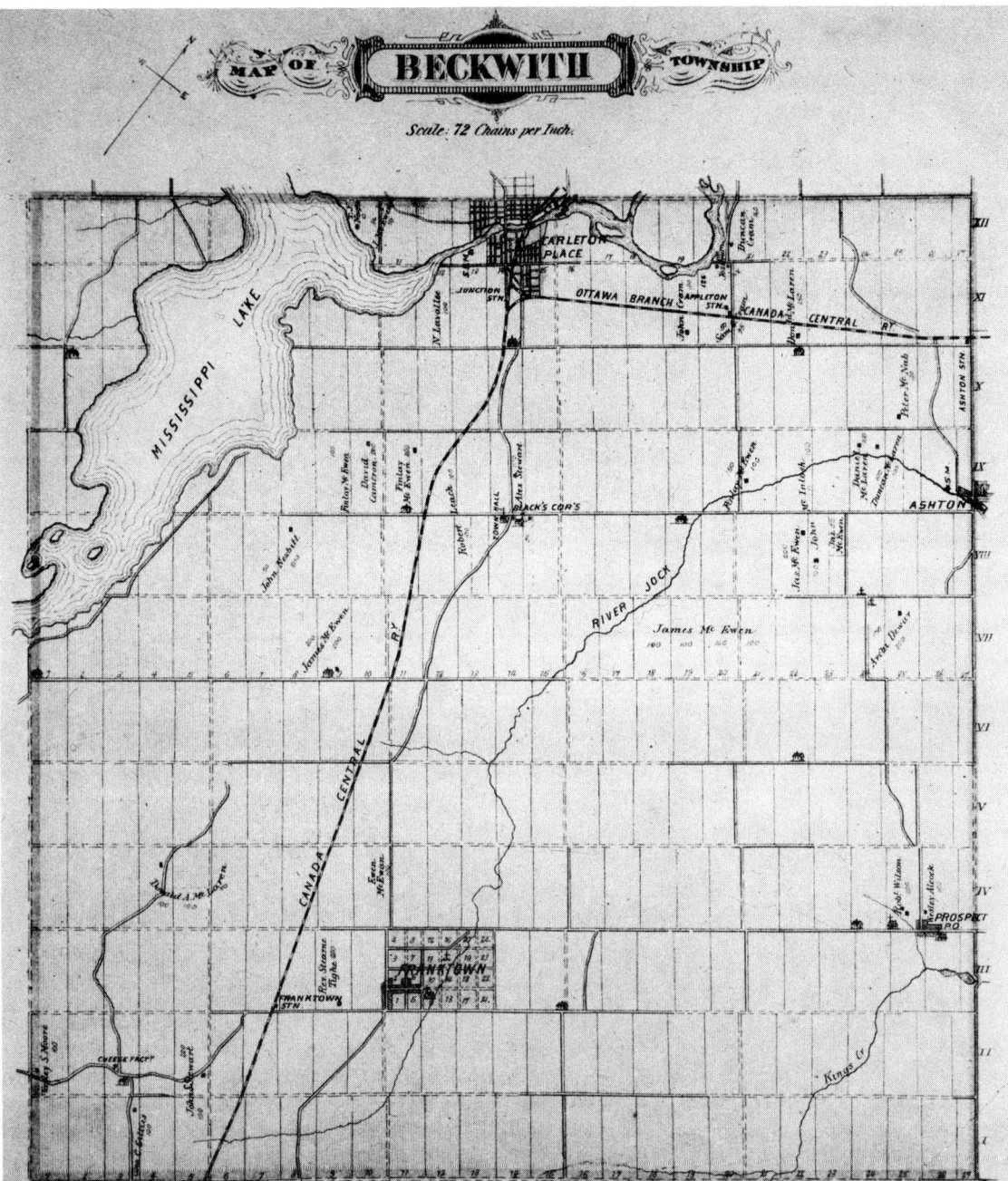

Plate 138
A map of Beckwith, 1880, from the Belden and Company Historical Atlas of the County of Lanark. *This map shows the Beckwith section of the Canada Central railway built between Ottawa and Carleton Place in 1870, and which was amalgamated with the Brockville and Ottawa railway in 1878. The quadrupling of Carleton Place in size between 1867 and 1880 contrasted with the fraction of Franktown's original plan that was built up as a village. The names of prominent inhabitants who subscribed to the atlas such as John Nesbitt and the Reverend Stearne Tighe are printed on the map, schools are represented by little buildings, churches are shown as little buildings with spires, and cemeteries are marked by crosses. The first cheese factory in Beckwith is shown at Gillies Corners.*

they agreed to purchase the northeast half of Clergy Reserve lot 21 in the tenth concession in March 1857 from John McEwen.[40] The feeling of mutuality among the brothers in developing and expanding the homestead was so strong and so taken for granted that the acquisition of the Clergy Reserve was accepted as sufficient excuse for Daniel's younger brother to lay aside attending school[41] in a family that valued education. As Catherine McCuan remarked, "My brothers...have taken a pretty heavy job in hand but as long as they stick together there is no fear but they will get over it."[42] This mutuality was real enough, but had its price, as Daniel put it, in that none of his older brothers "are like to get the woman in a hurry."[43]

Even with the acquisition of the adjacent Clergy Reserve, the McCuans did not have sufficient land to support all the sons once they married. As late as 1864 it was possible to find articles copied from American magazines in the Perth *Courier* claiming that fifty acres provided enough land for a farm,[44] but as early as 1852 knowledgable agents recommended that people seeking new farms in Renfrew County should not make do with less than two hundred acres.[45] Rather than risk the sort of sibling rivalry that in 1864 prompted James Leech to eject another brother off the east half of lot twelve in Beckwith's ninth concession,[46] the McCuan brothers purchased a lot in the western corner of Fitzroy Township on the Ottawa River where a number of Beckwith settlers were located. The Fitzroy lot contained 125 acres of good soil, a dwelling house, a tannery and a sawmill at the point where Waba Creek emptied into the Madawaska,[47] and there James and John McCuan proceeded to farm and mill, all the while keeping constantly in touch with the homestead in Beckwith, and betraying their sense of isolation or exile from home only by temporarily naming their Fitzroy property "St. Hellena."[48] When a change of climate was recommended to improve John McCuan's health, his brothers and sisters solicitously financed an extended trip to Perthshire in 1857.[49] Similarly, when Alexander was afflicted with prolonged ill health in 1862 his brothers and sisters placed him under the care of a doctor in Perth for many months,[50] and then in the Montreal General Hospital.[51] James McCuan, after leaving the sawmill and farm under John's control sought employment at Carleton Place in May 1862,[52] and by January 1863 he was working for John McIntosh[53] at Almonte, supervising some sixty carpenters and factory hands in building a large woollen factory.[54]

The example of the McCuan family underlines the lack of crisis in Beckwith farming between 1852 and 1881, and the gradual transition of family members from agricultural to nonagricultural employment. Unlike regions such as Peel County where the soil was mined repeatedly with wheat crops until the soil was depleted, in turn contributing to an agricultural crisis in the 1860s, there was no such sense of crisis in Beckwith. The crop viewers of the North Lanark Agricultural Society commented in July 1859:[55]

> The mixed system of agriculture practised by the farmers in the County of Lanark, where a fair proportion of the various grain and root crops are cultivated, and animals of different kinds kept for their products, is, we conceive, much superior to that in the western section of the Province, where many farms are devoted almost exclusively to the production of wheat, by which the soil must soon be exhausted, and where a failure of the particular crop is attended by the most disastrous consequences.

The absence of any sense of agricultural crisis in Beckwith was also due to the gradual trickle of sons and daughters out of the township. Those who left were headed to settlements where there were numbers of other Beckwith inhabitants. The McCuan brothers purchased the sawmill and farm in Fitzroy from John Whyte who was originally from Beckwith, and there were members of the Whyte, Conn and May families from Beckwith settled nearby.[56] When Daniel McCuan's childhood friend Francis May travelled west in search of employment in 1858, he ended up as schoolmaster in "a splendid log schoolhouse second to none in Beckwith...in the midst of the forest" of Brant County in a school section in which not only his sister resided but which he described as being "settled

Plate 139
Ambrotype of Daniel McCuan and photograph of James McCuan ca. 1880, the latter taken by J. Inglis, Montreal. Despite the McCuan farm being located on the fertile Mississippi floodplain and being judged one of the best managed in Lanark and Renfrew counties, it could not support all five sons of Duncan McCuan. The family purchased a farm and sawmill in Fitzroy that James and John developed, but in the late 1870s James McCuan sought a more prosperous future in Manitoba. Daniel as a younger brother remained on the family homestead in Beckwith, but control of the farm came only with his father's death in March 1864. He observed, "the funeral took place on the 18th and was very well attended[;] there was[,] I think[,] between 60 and 70 sleighs & cutters well filled & over 30 women attended[.] We have been very kindly attended in these troubles by our neighbours. Our life is as a shadow[;] it soon passes away." Photographs courtesy of Alex and Jean McCuan.

chiefly from Beckwith."[57] Similarly, schoolteacher William Taylor who boarded with the McCuans for a year wrote to Daniel in August 1857 to tell him of families from Beckwith he had visited in Grey County.[58] Another of Daniel's acquaintances from school, Margaret McCallum, wrote from Delnorte County, California in June 1858 where she had gone to live with relatives.[59] Despite continued coaxing from these and other correspondents that he leave Beckwith to possibly do better elsewhere, Daniel McCuan along with the majority of Beckwith inhabitants preferred to stay where he was.

The strong sense of belonging that kept most inhabitants as close to Beckwith as possible is hardly surprising. The structure of inheritance continued to reinforce the paternalist and patriarchal pattern of handing down property from one generation to the next to sons to ensure that the family name continued in Beckwith. Some 116 wills made out by Beckwith and Carleton Place inhabitants between 1852 and 1880 that have been located reveal the ongoing emphasis on continuity for Beckwith families. Ten of these wills were made out by women, but a whopping 33 wills did not mention wives, reflecting the high mortality rate among married women and

Table 11. Occupation of Household Head by Category

	1852		1861		1871		1881	
Type	No.	%	No.	%	No.	%	No.	%
Professional	16	4.6	21	6.0	8	2.6	6	2.1
Clerical	16	4.6	34	9.7	6	2.0	11	3.8
Farmer	226	64.8	196	55.8	256	83.6	224	78.0
Tradesman	58	13.8	63	17.9	27	8.8	25	8.7
Artisan	17	4.9	8	2.3	3	1.0	9	3.1
Labourer	16	4.6	19	5.4	6	2.0	8	2.8
Other	—	—	10	2.8	—		4	1.4
Totals	349	97.3	351	99.9	306	100.0	287	99.9

SOURCE: *The same sources listed in Table 4.*

Table 12. Occupation of General Population by Category

	1852		1861		1871		1881	
Type	No.	%	No.	%	No.	%	No.	%
Professional	26	4.0	27	4.6	8	1.5	10	2.5
Clerical	28	4.4	54	9.2	13	2.5	22	5.4
Farmer	249	38.7	209	35.5	422	81.3	281	69.4
Tradesman	125	19.4	103	17.5	36	6.9	34	8.4
Artisan	24	3.7	10	1.7	6	1.2	10	2.5
Labourer	186	28.9	158	26.9	26	5.0	30	7.4
Other	5	0.8	27	4.6	8	1.5	18	4.4
Totals	643	99.9	588	100.0	519	99.9	405	100.0

SOURCE: *The same sources listed in Table 4.*

the increasing proportion of inhabitants who either never married or were widowed. Only eleven wills left property to the wife without any restrictions, and only four wills left property exclusively to daughters as opposed to three wills in which property was bequeathed to servants. As was the case before mid-century, most wills continued to arrange for property to be left for the mutual benefit of widows and sons. Of the 73 wills made out by Beckwith men that referred to relicts, sixteen or 22 percent of them left their property to their widows to be passed down to their sons upon their deaths. Twenty-six or more than a third of the 73 left their property to their sons provided they pay an annual pension to or else kept their mothers comfortable for the rest of their lives. Eight men or eleven percent of the 73 left their property to their widows only for as long as they either remained unmarried or chose to live on the homestead, after which it passed on to the children, usually the sons. Over two-thirds of the wills mentioning spouses between 1852 and

Plate 140
Advertisements on the back page of the Carleton Place Herald, *June 1861. Rather than the railway bringing growth and industrialisation to Carleton Place in the early 1860s, Beckwith became a market for manufacturers in other larger regional centres who no longer were hampered by bad roads from bringing in their products. The Lanark and Renfrew agricultural society awarded premiums for the best home-made grain cradles as late as 1858, but the railway helped speed the pace of agricultural mechanisation by introducing mowers manufactured by Frost & Wood and G.M. Cossitt & Brother at Smith's Falls. National Library of Canada negative no. NL-16264.*

1880 reflected a patrilineal emphasis to preserve homesteads within the family name. At the same time, as William Duff made clear in his 1862 will in which he left the bulk of his estate to sons William and Alexander, as inheritors of the homestead they were to "remember that their house is to be the home or abode of all the family until such time as they get a home of their own."[60]

In addition to the structure of inheritance that encouraged all but a small fraction of Beckwith inhabitants to stay in the township, poems such as "DON'T LEAVE THE FARM" printed in local newspapers warned young men against going to the city where there was vice and sin, against the hazards of going into business, against being duped by bankers and brokers to pull up stakes and head west, and stressed that although profits might come in rather slowly, the "farm is the safest and surest" investment because "you've nothing to risk, boys, Don't be in a hurry to go."[61] Despite reports from former Beckwith inhabitants such as John Sinclair of being well satisfied with the fertile soil of Maryborough Township in the Queen's Bush, Daniel McCuan recognised the loneliness which impelled Sinclair to sit down and write "a letter to some one of his many friends in the East". The same loneliness caused William Taylor to admit "I wish I could spare time to visit Beckwith now that I might see you all", [62] and prompted F[rancis] May to confess in a letter from Brant Township in Bruce County "I thought I would write to you as I am anxious to hear how you are all getting along. I feel somewhat lonesome betimes when I think of the place of my childhood and the many acquaintances I had there."[63]

The decision of many sons and daughters to remain in or near Beckwith was possibly due to the mixed farming economy, due to increasing participation in the upper Ottawa valley lumber industry, due to the rapid growth of Carleton Place in the late 1860s and 1870s, and due to the increasing links with Renfrew County that allowed Beckwith inhabitants to recognise it as an accessible extension of Beckwith. The mixed farming economy of Beckwith remained largely based on provisioning the upper Ottawa lumber camps, unlike portions of Leeds County and Montague Township to the south where the establishment of cheese factories from the late 1860s onward already signalled a transition from a grain to dairy economy. As late as 1880 there was only one cheese factory in Beckwith, located at Gillies Corners. As early as 1851 smut and rust appeared in Beckwith wheat crops,[64] in 1852 a great deal of fall wheat was killed,[65] and in 1862 the crop of fall wheat was described as almost a total failure,[66] but with oats consistently a larger and more lucrative crop the difficulties of the wheat hardly amounted to anything resembling an agricultural crisis. Increasingly, as communications between Beckwith and the upper Ottawa improved with the extension of the Brockville and Ottawa Railway north to Sand Point, work in the timber camps of the upper Ottawa attracted Beckwith men to the extent that enumerators taking the 1881 census found only 28 married men as compared with 247 married women in Beckwith itself; the other 236 married men, it seems, were away in the lumber camps.

As early as May 1852 the editor of the *Carleton Place Herald* referred to "large rafts of White pine...lying on the river above the village" and to lumbermen being busy "fixing booms &c. preparatory to running the timber over the falls",[67] but it is unlikely if any or many of these workers were from Beckwith. An incident at Carleton Place in June 1860 suggests that the lumberers working at the lumber industry along the Mississippi were Scottish and French-Canadian inhabitants of Darling and Lanark townships; Bill Connell, an Irish Protestant from Goulbourn went "to the raftsmen's camp, and after sundry provocations, challenged the best man on the Mississippi to fight him. He was immediately taken up, and after the exchange of a few 'fair clouts,'" the *Herald* reported "our hero was glad to take shelter behind the counter in one of our merchant's shops, where he remained, in the greatest fear and trembling".[68] The move of Beckwith men into the lumber industry during the winter appears to have developed in the late 1860s, after the railroad had reached the Ottawa River and the Gillies and Caldwells established large sawmills at Carleton Place to transform the rafts of logs descending the Mississippi into sawn lumber to be shipped south on the Brockville and Ottawa railway to American markets. The flow of Beckwith men into Renfrew

Plate 141
A view from the air of the Fred Scott farmstead on lot 14, concession 8, Beckwith, at Black's Corners, as photographed in 1925. This view shows clearly the U-shaped court that developed as barns were added onto over the years. The main grain and hay barns were the larger buildings along the right side, the cow barn or byre was across the end, and on the left side an unusual outside stairway led up to a granary on the second floor above the sheep barn. The small buildings in the upper right of the photograph housed poultry. The log farmhouse on the upper left was also added to over the years. Photograph courtesy of Ellen Gardiner.

County through the aegis of winter work in the timber industry, and their gradual interest in settling there was mirrored in the growing coverage given Renfrew County in the *Carleton Place Herald* during the 1860s and 1870s.

The predominance of farming as an occupation in Beckwith is not sufficiently revealed by a comparison of the numbers and proportions of people employed within the categories of occupation used in Tables 11 and 12. Care must be taken not to accept at face value the terms used by census enumerators in listing Beckwith inhabitants within professional, clerical, farmer, tradesmen, artisan and labourer categories of occupation. Admittedly, the separation of Carleton Place from Beckwith in 1870 makes it difficult to assess any change between the 1861 and 1871 census figures, but the decline in proportion of farmers among the general population by twelve percent between 1871 and 1881 may well reflect a critical decade when many farmers' sons chose to work in industrialising Carleton Place rather than till the homestead acres. On the other hand, it must be remembered that most households were headed by farmers during this period, hence the majority of labourers listed in the 1852 and 1861 census returns were farmers' sons who worked either for their father or on a neighbour's farm as day labourers. In the 1871 and 1881 census returns enumerators distinguished farmers' sons, and these have been included in the farmer category in Table 12. The labourers also listed in these returns probably resided and worked in Carleton Place, and for the most part were not engaged in agricultural activity. Non-agricultural occupations in many instances were regarded by young men as a temporary or part-time form of employment that contributed to the general household income, but increasingly were regarded as insufficient for a household head to support a family. Hence, although there were eleven teachers employed in township schools in 1861, only one headed a household. Although sixteen blacksmiths were listed in 1861, only twelve of them headed households. Although the numbers of persons within specific occupations either fluctuated or were too small in themselves to offer significant patterns in occupational structure, it is quite clear that as large a proportion of young men who lived within their parents' households continued as avidly in 1881 as in 1852, to pursue nonagricultural occupations, while the proportion of household heads engaged in farming increased.

Beckwith was served by a thin layer of professionals, mostly teachers, a few clergy and the occasional doctor and magistrate. The number of individuals involved in clerical occupations fluctuated, doubling from 28 in 1852 to 54 in 1861, and then declining to a quarter that number by 1871. These clerical skills belonged to station masters on the railroad, to township officers, to merchants in the stores at Carleton Place who complained in the 1850s from the rigour of putting in sixteen-hour days,[69] and to telegraph operators, bookkeepers, printers and insurance agents. The number of tradesmen also fluctuated, including as this category did general merchants, grocers, travelling commercial agents and hotelkeepers among others. The proportion of artisans within Beckwith's boundaries between 1852 and 1881 fluctuated, arising in part from the mobility of many in this group such as Angus McDonald who resided with the McCuan family a number of weeks in 1863 "making shoes and boots and spinning yarns".[70] The principal artisans in Beckwith in 1861 included shoemakers, blacksmiths, cabinetmakers, carpenters, coopers, joiners, saddlers and weavers.

Census returns do not accurately reflect the role of women in Beckwith's economy. A married woman was not listed as having an occupation unless her husband had died or left, and his occupation was conveyed to the woman. Hence, the majority of women who toiled as homestead tenders, buttermaids and tenders of livestock while their men were away during the winter were not credited by census enumerators with having an occupation. When prizes were awarded at the annual exhibition of the Beckwith Township Agricultural Society in the 1860s, those awarded to women for items such as woven and pieced quilts, woollen stockings and dresses already were attempting to restrict women to the domain of housework rather than recognising the various types of farmwork they continued to perform.[71] The domestic production of 77,337 pounds of butter and 5,508 pounds of cheese in Beckwith homes in 1860 depended largely if not wholly on the work of Beckwith farm women. In 1852, of the 796 individuals listed with an occupation only 22 or three percent were women: two were farmers, ten were servants, two were teachers, along with two labourers, two seamstresses, one clothier, one weaver, and three unspecified occupations. The number of women listed as having an occupation in Beckwith were 52 in 1861, 28 in 1871, and 33 in 1881, representing respectively seven, five and nine percent of people listed with an occupation in those years. The proportion of servants declined from the 1860s on. Despite the small numbers of women perceived by the census enumerators to have an occupation worth noting on the forms they filled out, it is significant that the number of women listed as servants dropped by more than half from nine to four between 1852 and 1881. At the same time, it is equally significant that the number of women employed as teachers doubled from three to six, and the number of women listed as farmers tripled from three to ten during these three decades, reflecting an emerging sense of worth among women.

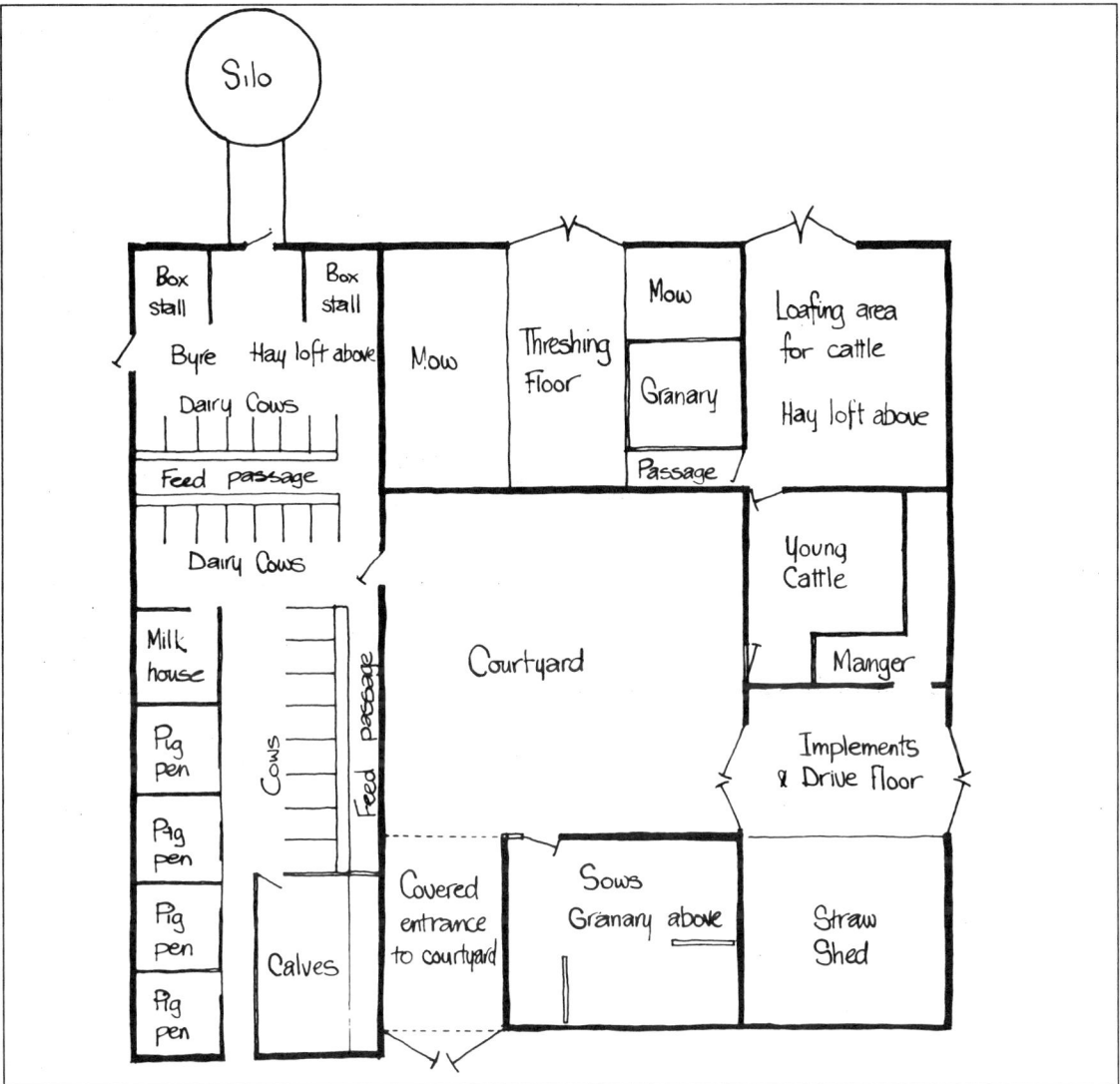

Plate 142
Layout of barns on the Alexander Cameron farm, lot 5, concession 7, Beckwith, as drawn ca. 1970 by Dudley Witney. This plan reveals the growing sophistication of Beckwith farming in the late nineteenth century as older grain barns and stables were added to or adapted to the mixed farming and dairy economy. In addition to this main group of buildings, there was stabling for workhorses, sheep and poultry. From Eric Arthur and Dudley Witney, The Barn: A Vanishing Landmark in North America, *by permission of Feheley Fine Arts Inc.*

Women comprised the majority of servants in Beckwith households although by 1881 there was an evening ratio of males to females as the number of servants declined (Table 13). It is striking how few servants there were in Beckwith in contrast with nearby Huntley Township in Carleton County. Although both townships were home to roughly the same number of people in 1861, there were 79 servants in Huntley as contrasted with only 34 in Beckwith.[72] The decline in number of servants was also more rapid in Beckwith, indicating either that the dislike of servitude was particularly pronounced, or else that the arrangements by which children were transferred from their parents' homes to work for neighbours were so amicable that it soon ceased to be thought of as servitude. Indeed, Elizabeth Bain who replaced her sister Jane as a servant in the McCuan household in 1856 clearly preferred to remain in service in Beckwith and resisted her parents' urging that she return to their frontier home in Admaston Township:[73]

> Dear Parents [she wrote] I received yours of the 15th and was...surprised to hear the hurry you are in for me[.] I have promised when Jane left to stay here till the fall but if you will not do without me till that time I suppose I must go.... However I cannot go till the road dries up[;] now if you will not allow me to stay here till the fall you must write again as soon as this will reach you[.] I am sorry to disappoint or offend you but I cannot see that this need be any cause for it[;] every body must look out for themselves to what they can consider the best and so must I.

Table 13.   Number of Servants in Beckwith and Huntley Townships

	1852		1861		1871		1881	
	B	H	B	H	B	H	B	H
Male	0	8	15	21	1	4	0	1
Female	9	31	19	58	7	33	4	22
Total	9	39	34	79	8	37	4	23
% of Total Population	0.4	1.5	1.3	4.0	0.4	1.5	0.2	0.9

SOURCE: 1852, 1861, 1871 and 1881 manuscript census returns for Beckwith and Huntley township; and Julian Gwyn, "The Irish in Eastern Ontario: The Social Structure of Huntley Township in Carleton County, 1851-1871" in Vrenia Ivanoffski and Sandra Campbell, eds., Exploring Our Heritage: The Ottawa Valley Experience (Toronto, 1980), p.27

The word "servant" by 1880 rarely was used in rural Beckwith, as farmers employed hired men, and as women such as Helen McCuan made arrangements for her niece to gain domestic experience in the posh home of Archibald and Margaret McArthur in Carleton Place. The neighbourly aspect of this domestic apprenticeship which was expected to prepare a girl for the duties of presiding over her own homestead, was reflected in Margaret McArthur's note of acceptance: "I think it best to engage your ni[e]ce at once and let the girl I have now go at the end of the month[,] that is if you think you can spare your friend[.] I suppose the Harvest work will be pretty well through by the first of September and I would like much to have her about that time[. T]ell her I will endeavour to make her as much at home with us as I can."[74] The greater number and greater persistence of servants in Huntley in contrast with Beckwith is one indication that there was less poverty in Beckwith, since those rural families that kept servants did so as much to provide employment for impoverished relatives and neighbours as to meet genuine needs for servant labour.

Localised communities of neighbours worked together at major projects such as building barns beyond mid-century, as Daniel McCuan's 10 June 1853 entry in a notebook reveals:[75]

Plate 143
Barns on the Duncan McNaughton farm, lot 4, concession 7, Beckwith, as photographed by Dudley Witney ca. 1970. This grouping of buildings shows the ways in which many Beckwith farmers readjusted older grain barns to suit the dairy economy in the late nineteenth century. The grain barn on the left had stable doors added and the lower tiers of logs chinked to become a cow stable. Doors were added to the upstairs lofts to permit hay forks to gather in hay, and a silo was added on to the far corner. Sheep husbandry was common in Beckwith from the beginning of settlement, but poultry were not kept in large numbers until the late Victorian era, when farmwomen began to keep flocks of hens as an independent source of income after losing the production of cheese at home to local factories. Photograph courtesy of M.F. Feheley Arts Company Limited.

[T]his is the day ap[p]ointed for the raising of the Barn[.] I hope none will be hurt. The frame was raised by 5 o'clock[,] I am glad to say[,] without any one being hurt[. T]he work went on very peaceably[;] not one cross word was to be heard the whole day[. I]t was pleasant to be this way[. E]very joint fitted well[;] this was [of] great satisfaction to the framers & owners[. T]here was preasent[:] Robert MacGregor[,] Robt[.] Carmichael[,] Peter Carmichael[,] Robt[.] MacGregor[,] John McLeod[,] John McDougall[,] James McEwen[,] James McInnis[,] Duncan McEwen[,] Donald McDougall[,] Donald McLaren[,] Peter McLaren[,] Peter Drummond[,] Malcolm Drummond[,] John McNab[,] Kenith McLeod[,] Peter McNab[,] William McFarlane[,] Donald Campbell[,] Peter Campbell[,] Thomas White[,] William McCuan[,] Duncan Robertson[,] James McNeely[,] Peter McLaren[,] John Goth[,] James Goth[,] David Cram[,] George Comrie[,] John McLaren[,] Donald McLaren[,] Duncan McCuan father[,] Duncan McCuan[,] Alexander McCuan[,] Peter McCuan and myself and Robert McLaren[,] George McLean[,] Framers[,] in all 38[. T]he day was warm[,] there was a liberal share of the cratur [or whiskey to drink. A]fter the raising was past and supper over some of the Boys tried their hand at Rifle and Musket shooting[.]

Beckwith farmers found less need for servants and for large families as agriculture increasingly mechanised from the mid 1850s onward. As early as 1858 the McCuan brothers purchased a reaping machine from an agent at Bell's Corners in Nepean,[76] and in late August 1863 a trial of reaping machines on their farm attracted some two hundred local farmers. The *Carleton Place Herald* reported:[77]

> There were three machines present and entered for competition, viz, 1, "Buckeye" manufactured by Cossitt & Bro., Smith's Falls; 2, "Buckeye." manufactured by Frost & Wood, Smith's Falls; 3, "Cayuga Chief," manufactured by Pattersons, of Belleville. The field selected to try the merits of the machines was a fine heavy field of Spring Wheat, and as the work progressed great interest was manifested by those who had come to witness the contest, which continued throughout until the whole plot of two acres was finished. Owing to the work being so well done and so nearly equal, it was from the most minute examination and observation as the work progressed that the judges were able to say really which done their part best. But taking time and the particular way that each machine laid off the sheaves into consideration, they awarded the first prize to Messrs. Cossitt & Bro., and the second to Frost & Wood.

Table 14.   Ratio of Males Aged 20+ to Land Occupied & Improved

Year	Acres Occupied	Ratio	Acres Improved	Ratio
1851	42,067	1:75	11,579	1:21
1860	48,385	1:83	16,924	1:29
1870	51,851	1:113	21,327	1:47
1880	50,201	1:106	23,905	1:51

SOURCE: *Canadian census returns in printed volumes for 1852, 1861, 1871 and 1881.*

By 1868 the inventory of farm implements used by the McCuan brothers included a double buggy, two double wagons, a double sleigh, large and small bobsleds, two pairs of harrows, a reaping machine, a fanning mill, a road scraper, a turnip cultivator, a grindstone, a grain cradle, an iron plough, two wooden ploughs, two bucksaws, four grainforks, two hoes, two dung forks, two scythes, two spades, a shovel, reaping hooks, axes, a broad axe, a pick axe, a pit saw, an iron kettle, an iron wedge, a maple sugar pan, two sets of lumber harness, a set of ploughing harness, two sets of whippletrees, one wrapping chain, one tozzling chain, and six horses — Joe, Tom, Bob, Jock, Mike and Bet.[78] As the variety of items listed suggests, many of the tasks on Beckwith farms remained unmechanised, but the saving in drudgery and time at harvest by the machines manufactured in the foundries at Smith's Falls compelled three-fourths of Beckwith farmers to use mowers, reapers and sulky rakes by 1880.[79]

The mechanising of Beckwith agriculture which continued in the 1860s and 1870s made it possible for fewer people to harvest larger crops from expanding acreages. As Table 14 indicates, the amount of land occupied and improved was maximised between 1851 and 1880. Table 14 also shows that the ratio of land to men aged twenty years and older increased as the overall population declined. Indeed, while the ratio of acres in general occupied per man over age twenty rose by 41

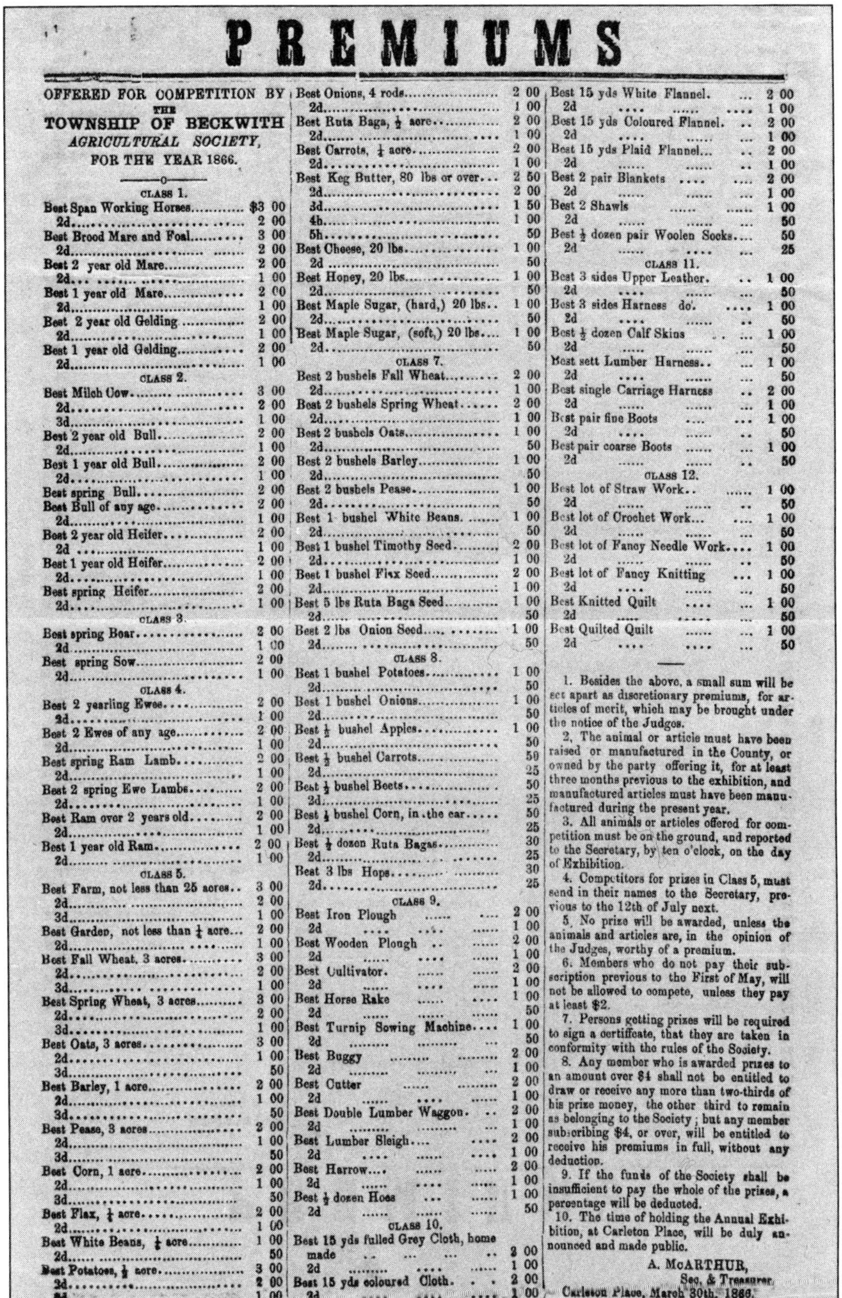

PREMIUMS

OFFERED FOR COMPETITION BY THE
TOWNSHIP OF BECKWITH
AGRICULTURAL SOCIETY,
FOR THE YEAR 1866.

CLASS 1.

Best Span Working Horses	$3 00
2d	2 00
Best Brood Mare and Foal	3 00
2d	2 00
Best 2 year old Mare	2 00
2d	1 00
Best 1 year old Mare	2 00
2d	1 00
Best 2 year old Gelding	2 00
2d	1 00
Best 1 year old Gelding	2 00
2d	1 00

CLASS 2.

Best Milch Cow	3 00
2d	2 00
3d	1 00
Best 2 year old Bull	2 00
2d	1 00
Best 1 year old Bull	2 00
2d	1 00
Best spring Bull	2 00
Best Bull of any age	2 00
2d	1 00
Best 2 year old Heifer	2 00
2d	1 00
Best 1 year old Heifer	2 00
2d	1 00
Best spring Heifer	2 00
2d	1 00

CLASS 3.

Best spring Boar	2 00
2d	1 00
Best spring Sow	2 00
2d	1 00

CLASS 4.

Best 2 yearling Ewes	2 00
2d	1 00
Best 2 Ewes of any age	2 00
2d	1 00
Best spring Ram Lamb	2 00
2d	1 00
Best 2 spring Ewe Lambs	2 00
2d	1 00
Best Ram over 2 years old	2 00
2d	1 00
Best 1 year old Ram	2 00
2d	1 00

CLASS 5.

Best Farm, not less than 25 acres	3 00
2d	2 00
3d	1 00
Best Garden, not less than ¼ acre	2 00
2d	1 00
Best Fall Wheat, 3 acres	3 00
2d	2 00
3d	1 00
Best Spring Wheat, 3 acres	3 00
2d	2 00
3d	1 00
Best Oats, 3 acres	3 00
2d	1 00
3d	50
Best Barley, 1 acre	2 00
2d	1 00
3d	50
Best Pease, 3 acres	2 00
2d	1 00
3d	50
Best Corn, 1 acre	2 00
2d	1 00
3d	50
Best Flax, ¼ acre	2 00
2d	1 00
Best White Beans, ¼ acre	1 00
2d	50
Best Potatoes, ½ acre	3 00
2d	2 00
3d	1 00
Best Onions, 4 rods	2 00
2d	1 00
Best Ruta Baga, ½ acre	2 00
2d	1 00
Best Carrots, ¼ acre	2 00
2d	1 00
Best Keg Butter, 80 lbs or over	2 50
2d	2 00
3d	1 50
4h	1 00
5h	50
Best Cheese, 20 lbs	1 00
2d	50
Best Honey, 20 lbs	1 00
2d	50
Best Maple Sugar, (hard,) 20 lbs	1 00
2d	50
Best Maple Sugar, (soft,) 20 lbs	1 00
2d	50

CLASS 7.

Best 2 bushels Fall Wheat	2 00
2d	1 00
Best 2 bushels Spring Wheat	2 00
2d	1 00
Best 2 bushels Oats	1 00
2d	50
Best 2 bushels Barley	1 00
2d	50
Best 2 bushels Pease	1 00
2d	50
Best 1 bushel White Beans	1 00
2d	50
Best 1 bushel Timothy Seed	2 00
2d	1 00
Best 1 bushel Flax Seed	2 00
2d	1 00
Best 5 lbs Ruta Baga Seed	1 00
2d	50
Best 2 lbs Onion Seed	1 00
2d	50

CLASS 8.

Best 1 bushel Potatoes	1 00
2d	50
Best 1 bushel Onions	1 00
2d	50
Best ½ bushel Apples	1 00
2d	50
Best ½ bushel Carrots	50
2d	25
Best ½ bushel Beets	50
2d	25
Best ½ bushel Corn, in the ear	50
2d	25
Best ½ dozen Ruta Bagas	30
2d	25
Best 3 lbs Hops	30
2d	25

CLASS 9.

Best Iron Plough	2 00
2d	1 00
Best Wooden Plough	2 00
2d	1 00
Best Cultivator	2 00
2d	1 00
Best Horse Rake	1 00
2d	50
Best Turnip Sowing Machine	1 00
2d	50
Best Buggy	2 00
2d	1 00
Best Cutter	2 00
2d	1 00
Best Double Lumber Waggon	2 00
2d	1 00
Best Lumber Sleigh	2 00
2d	1 00
Best Harrow	2 00
2d	1 00
Best ½ dozen Hoes	1 00
2d	50

CLASS 10.

Best 15 yds fulled Grey Cloth, home made	2 00
2d	1 00
Best 15 yds coloured Cloth	2 00
2d	1 00
Best 15 yds White Flannel	2 00
2d	1 00
Best 15 yds Coloured Flannel	2 00
2d	1 00
Best 15 yds Plaid Flannel	2 00
2d	1 00
Best 2 pair Blankets	2 00
2d	1 00
Best 2 Shawls	1 00
2d	50
Best ½ dozen pair Woolen Socks	50
2d	25

CLASS 11.

Best 3 sides Upper Leather	1 00
2d	50
Best 3 sides Harness do.	1 00
2d	50
Best ½ dozen Calf Skins	1 00
2d	50
Best sett Lumber Harness	1 00
2d	50
Best single Carriage Harness	2 00
2d	1 00
Best pair fine Boots	1 00
2d	50
Best pair coarse Boots	1 00
2d	50

CLASS 12.

Best lot of Straw Work	1 00
2d	50
Best lot of Crochet Work	1 00
2d	50
Best lot of Fancy Needle Work	1 00
2d	50
Best lot of Fancy Knitting	1 00
2d	50
Best Knitted Quilt	1 00
2d	50
Best Quilted Quilt	1 00
2d	50

---

1. Besides the above, a small sum will be set apart as discretionary premiums, for articles of merit, which may be brought under the notice of the Judges.

2. The animal or article must have been raised or manufactured in the County, or owned by the party offering it, for at least three months previous to the exhibition, and manufactured articles must have been manufactured during the present year.

3. All animals or articles offered for competition must be on the ground, and reported to the Secretary, by ten o'clock, on the day of Exhibition.

4. Competitors for prizes in Class 5, must send in their names to the Secretary, previous to the 12th of July next.

5. No prize will be awarded, unless the animals and articles are, in the opinion of the Judges, worthy of a premium.

6. Members who do not pay their subscription previous to the First of May, will not be allowed to compete, unless they pay at least $2.

7. Persons getting prizes will be required to sign a certificate, that they are taken in conformity with the rules of the Society.

8. Any member who is awarded prizes to an amount over $4 shall not be entitled to draw or receive any more than two-thirds of his prize money, the other third to remain as belonging to the Society; but any member subscribing $4, or over, will be entitled to receive his premiums in full, without any deduction.

9. If the funds of the Society shall be insufficient to pay the whole of the prizes, a percentage will be deducted.

10. The time of holding the Annual Exhibition, at Carleton Place, will be duly announced and made public.

A. McARTHUR,
Sec. & Treasurer.

Carleton Place, March 30th, 1866.

Plate 144

Broadside listing premiums offered for competition by the Township of Beckwith Agricultural Society, 1866. The Beckwith Agricultural Society was organized in response to the removal of the Lanark and Renfrew Agricultural Society to Almonte in 1858. The new society was not supported in the middle and southern concessions of Beckwith because its exhibition was held at Carleton Place and its executive was centred around that village. The cheese category on this list did not exist a decade earlier (Plate 134), reflecting an emerging recognition of the growing importance of the dairy economy long before the first cheese factory was built in Beckwith. Loaned courtesy of Alex and Jean McCuan.

percent between 1850 and 1880, the ratio of improved acres per man even more dramatically increased by 143 percent. Table 15 shows the trend toward larger farms that developed. The proportion of farms with more than one hundred acres more than doubled, while the proportion of farms with more than two hundred acres tripled. The number of farms containing between eleven and one hundred acres dropped by half. If it may be assumed that acreage size is an indicator of wealth, then clearly the number of prospering farmers increased by 1880.

Table 15. Land Holding in Beckwith, 1851-1880

	1851		1870		1880	
	No.	%	No.	%	No.	%
No. of Occupiers	377		293		287	
10 Acres & Under	73	19.4	7	2.4	14	4.9
11-50 Acres	34	9.0	15	5.1	21	7.3
51-100 Acres	162	43.0	94	32.1	74	25.8
101-200 Acres	81	21.2	114	39.2	116	40.4
200 Acres & Over	27	7.2	63	21.5	62	21.6

SOURCE: *Canadian census returns in printed volumes for 1852, 1861, 1871 and 1881.*

In the previous chapter a sampling of entries from the 1874 journal of George McLaren in the Derry settlement showed the variety of winter activities on the farm for those men not away working in the timber camps. The following entries suggest the bustle of activity which took place from spring planting through to autumn harvest:[80]

[1] May [1874]—I am plowing in the potatoland[.] John & David is raising stones till noon [2] David is gathering up some manure [4] David is picking roots [7] I am Drawing out manure[,] David Robertson[, the hired man] is filling[,] John is plowing till te[a]time[,] harrowing in wheat after tea [8] I am harrowing in some oats in the for[e]noon [9] I am sowing peas to day[,] John is harrowing the most of the day[,] sowed 9 bushels of wheat and 10 of oats[,] I am harrowing[,] David is shaking scutchgrass [13] John is rolling[,] I am putting manure on the garden[,] David is filling it [16] John is plowing[,] I am sowing oats[,] sowed 14 bushels[,] David is harrowing them to me. [18] this is a weat day[,] Dol[l]y is fo[a]led this morning...[,] I gave John Docherty 10 dozen of eggs [to take to Carleton Place, 21] David is planting potatoes[,] after Din[n]er I went down to James Duff's[,] hired him for 1 month at 12 doll[a]rs[,] I plowed after tea[,] paid John Dell for 30 Days[,] paid him 19.50 [22] James Duff and David is planting potatoes [23] David is fixing up a fence [28] I am harrowing and rolling in the forenoon[,] plowing in the afternoon[,] James Duff & David is planting potatoes. June [2] James Duff is put[t]ing up some fen[c]es, washed our sheep after tea. [4] I went to Careltom [Place] with 12 bushels of potatoes[,] gave 6 to Mr. Garner at 2 shillings & 6 mor[e] to P. Docherty at the same[,] gave him a Crock of butter[,] it weigh[ed] 38 lb[,] crock and all[,] received 5 doll[a]rs from him...[,] James Duff is shearing sheep [6] James Duff is not at work [9] gave J. Docherty 8 dozen of eggs...[,] James Duff is not here[, H]akey calved this morning [10] I am runni[n]g potatoes...[,] bought a washing machine for 4 doll[a]rs [12] went to Carelton P[lace]...sold 76 lb of wool[,] it came to 22.80 [18] I and James Duff is taking of[f] stone[,] gave John Docherty 10 dozen of eggs [22]

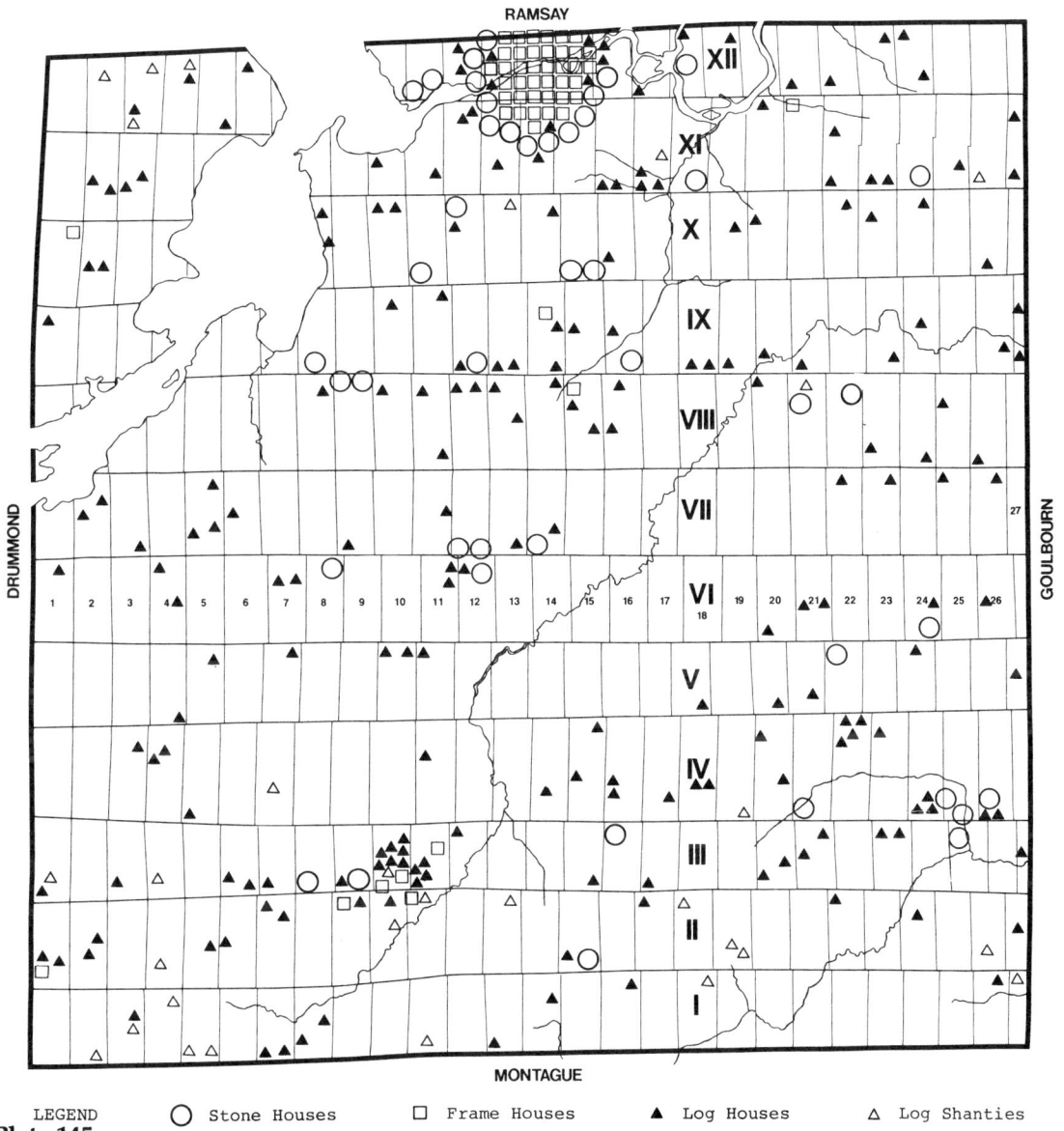

| LEGEND | ○ Stone Houses | □ Frame Houses | ▲ Log Houses | △ Log Shanties |

Plate 145

Map showing the pattern of house construction in Beckwith, 1852. Most houses in Beckwith were comfortable medium or large size log houses. The concentration of frame and stone houses in northern Beckwith reflected the fertile soil of the Mississippi floodplain. The concentration of miserable log shanties in the vicinity south of Franktown attests to the inhospitable terrain of swamp and limestone plain that settlers contended with in the southern concessions. With inhabitants of Irish origin located largely in southern Beckwith, while those of Scottish origin were concentrated in the north, the social image of the Scottish improved after mid-century while that of Irish inhabitants went into decline.

We are both drawing wood today [23] I am Howing potatoes. July [2] gave John Docherty 10 dozen of eggs [7] Mr. Docherty got 5½ bushel[s] of Ashes at 12½ cents [11] I made the Churn [13] went to Carelton after Din[n]er to look for a man[,] hired Thomis Duncan for 2 months at

20 Doll[a]rs per month [14] Killed a calve after Din[n]er[,] it weighed 80½ lb[,] gave John Docherty 21 of veal and 10 dozen of eggs. [15] I was at the great show [16] went to [Black's] Corners after din[n]er[,] got Dol[l]y shod all round[,]...paid Dani[e]l McGilvery for sho[e]ing and [for repairing] wagon and mower...[,] paid Alexander Stewart 2 doll[a]rs for sugar[,] 1.25 for scythe [17] I and Thomas Duncan is mowing till teatime[,] raking after tea [20] Drew in 4 loads after din[n]er [22] Thomis is mowing some and Raking today[,] I am cut[t]ing with the mach[ine 25] I gave Mr. John Docherty 11 dozen of eggs[,] raking till noon,... drew in 13 loads of hay this week [28] We are raking in the new land to-day...[,] Mr. Bradley is with us raking[. 29] I am cutting some with the Machi[ne,] it broke a g[u]ard[,] I got it mended. August [4] Mr. St[ew]art is cutting a piece of hay for himself[,] I sold it to him for 6 doll[a]rs [5] We are both cutting some rye and oats[,] gave John Docherty 11 dozen of eggs [6] killed a calve [7] Thomis Duncan is cut[t]ing peas [12] We drew in 2 loads of peas till noon[,] S[tew]art is binding at the old barn till noon[,] We are mowing oats in the squair field[,] after dinner drew in 1 load of wheat [14] Mr. St[ew]art is cradling Wheat up at the sideroad [15] Drew in 5 loads of oats and father's peas and 1 load of wheat[,] John Doherty got 10 dozen of eggs. [24] We are mowing some buckwheat till noon[,] Drawing in after Dinner[,] Thomis Duff is with us[,] after Dinner drew in 4 loads[,] finished our harvest [25 k]illed a lamb, [27] We are both picking stones today [28] gave John Docherty 12 lb of porke at 11 cents [30] killed 6 sheep and one pig. September [1] I am in Carelton today selling mut[t]on and porke. [7] killed 8 sheep [14] I killed a he[i]fer [19] I and James Duff is at Mr. Nesbitt's thra[s]hing [24] I am in Carelton with 4 lambs. October [10] I and James Duff is dig[g]ing potatoes [15] I am at Mr. Bradley's thra[s]hing [26] killed a steer [27] I am in Carelton selling beef.

Table 16.   Agricultural Produce of Beckwith Township

	1851	1860	1890
Oats (Bushels)	33,660	60,050	80,925
Wheat (bushels)	14,725	33,091	10,620
Potatoes (bushels)	50,441	99,202	53,635
Butter (pounds)	65,652	77,337	94,475
Pork (200 lb. barrels)	999	1,612	–
Beef (200 lb. barrels)	190	404	–
Wool (pounds)	10,296	11,328	12,568
Cheese (pounds)	5,122	5,508	1,317*
Fulled Cloth (yards)	19,849	1,690	–
Flannel (yards)	12,923	4,906	–
Peas (bushels)	7,323	15,338	16,790
Turnips (bushels)	50,441	15,501	15,135
Hay (tons)	2,713	2,498	5,726
Barley (bushels)	1,356	1,538	3,242

SOURCE: *The same sources listed in Table 14.*
* Cheese made at home rather than in cheese factories

Plate 146
The John King house, lot 24, concession 2, Beckwith, believed built in the 1850s, as photographed in June 1983. John King, as one of the few Scottish inhabitants to move into the southeastern corner of Beckwith, could not escape the rigorous limitations of his land being mostly swamp any more than could his Irish neighbours. The small size of his house and of the logs within its walls mirrored the relative poverty of many inhabitants in southern Beckwith.

George McLaren's journal confirms the mixed farming that continued in Beckwith, based as it was on supplying the timber camps of the upper Ottawa. Beginning in the 1860s this was supplemented by American agents purchasing livestock which was shipped to the United States by the rail links, and from the late 1860s on the rapid growth of Carleton Place provided an expanding local market. As Table 16 demonstrates, the agricultural productivity of Beckwith significantly increased as every available acre capable of growing crops was placed under cultivation. Although the number of acres occupied by Beckwith farmers increased by less than twenty percent between 1851 and 1880, the number of acres planted with crops more than doubled from 6,665 to 14,940 during these three decades. Census figures reveal that Beckwith's production of oats, wheat, potatoes, beef and peas doubled during the 1850s, while more modest increases developed in the cultivation of butter, pork, wool, cheese, cattle and horses. The 1851 figures may actually be somewhat low, as the editor of the *Carleton Place Herald* alleged, because inhabitants of northern Beckwith "have allowed their fears of taxation to step in between them and principle, and have made false returns, in the vain hope of escaping paying their quota of the taxation for the support of municipal institutions."[81] The increasing number of cattle as opposed to the declining numbers of sheep and pigs suggests a trend away from relying wholly on the provisioning trade, although it was not until the 1880s and 1890s that the dairy economy enjoyed precedence in Beckwith agriculture (Table 17).

The growing productivity, the diversity of crops, the mechanisation of sowing and harvesting, and the expanding size of farms in Beckwith were all in large part promoted by local agricultural societies and by articles in local newspapers advocating agricultural improvement. The Bathurst District Agricultural Society, renamed the United Counties of Lanark and Renfrew Agricultural Society, continued to hold fairs at Carleton Place until 1858 when it was moved to the by then larger centre of Almonte and its name changed to the North Lanark Agricultural Society.[82] Carleton Place continued to host cattle fairs[83] as contrasted with the fairs at Franktown which ceased to exist well before the mid 1870s, and in 1863 Carleton Place was the site of the first annual exhibition of the newly formed Beckwith Township Agricultural Society.[84] At the 1864 Beckwith Township exhibition the *Carleton Place Herald* reported that the quality of butter shown was superior to that of the previous year, but regretted "that the farmers in this neighbourhood would not pay a little more attention to the introduction of fine-wooled breeds [of sheep] which would assuredly repay the extra expense, by the increased yield and value of fleece."[85] In addition to the annual exhibition at Carleton Place, the Beckwith Agricultural Society like the Bathurst District Agricultural Society before it imported superior breeds of stallions, bulls, rams and boars to upgrade livestock in the township.[86] Crop viewers were appointed by the agricultural society to travel around the township to appraise the quality of crops generally and "to point out some of those improvements, which more particularly attracted [their] notice, so as to emulate others to follow in their wake." The crop viewers for the United Counties of Lanark and Renfrew Agricultural Society, for example, in their August 1855 report first singled out:[87]

> a small field of blade tartar — or, one-sided oats, on the farm of Mr. James Stewart of Beckwith, which would have stood a fair chance for the first prize, had there been enough of them in one plot. Next to that, in attraction, was a very fine field of club wheat, on the farm of Mr. James McFarlane, of Beckwith, which kept the lead as No.1, for some days — but was at last fairly beat, *"This farm shows the right man in the right place,"* a practical farmer, who understood his business. Next, comes the farm of Mr. Duncan Mc[C]uan, of Beckwith, which appeared in all directions to be groaning under the large fields of grain, looking most luxuriant. This farm is in good order, and in a fine state of cultivation, and taking the crop as a whole — both for quantity and quality, is the very best we met with.

Twenty-one year old Daniel McCuan was so delighted by this appraisal of his family's farm as the finest in all of Lanark and Renfrew that he copied it out word for word on a piece of notepaper.[88] And yet, for another ten years Daniel and his family continued to reside in a log house until finally in preparation for his marriage to Helen Whyte at age 33 Daniel built a large frame

Table 17. Livestock in Beckwith Township

	1851	1860	1890
Bulls, Oxen and Steers	179	52	–
Milch Cows	1,173	1,681	1,726
Calves and Heifers	1,446	1,683	1,761
Horses	708	954	980
Sheep	3,991	3,369	3,003
Pigs	2,114	1,544	625

SOURCES: *The same sources listed in Table 14.*

Plate 147
The Alexander Sinclair house, lot 1, concession 11, at Scotch Corners, built in the 1850s, as photographed in June 1983. A frame house is concealed beneath the late twentieth century aluminum cladding. The Sinclairs were from Argyllshire, unlike most Scottish immigrants in Beckwith who came from Perthshire. The width of Mississippi Lake and the marshy shoreline isolated the Scotch Corners community from the rest of Beckwith. The rambling knolls at Scotch Corners made its topography more varied than that in the remainder of the township.

house with stylish steep Gothic Revival gables, large windows and what probably was the first bay window in rural Beckwith. The McCuans were at least a decade behind many Beckwith families in building a large permanent house out of a material other than log, and one of few rural families to build such a house out of a material other than stone. In 1857 crop viewers William Smith, John Robertson Jr. and John Ferguson observed that "many new houses of a superior description, are in course of erection, giving evidence of substantial wealth and prosperity. It is quite evident", they continued, "that many persons in these Counties, who, a few years ago, had to live in log huts, and struggle hard for existence, are now reaping the reward of their toil, and enjoy not only the necessaries, but many of the luxuries of life, in great abundance."[89] Most of the 69 stone houses in Beckwith were constructed before 1852, and although they were larger structures than the log houses they replaced, they were very plain in design. Robert Bell, after travelling as a member of a railroad delegation in northern New York state in April 1853, commented:[90]

> [W]e could not but notice, both in the villages, and in the country, that Jonathan is decidedly ahead of us, in his taste for building. You cannot travel far without being convinced, that Downing's Rural Architecture, and other similar works are read and acted upon there. In Canada the farm houses are generally more substantial than they are in similar circumstances

Table 18. House Construction in Beckwith

	1852	1861	1880	1891
Brick	0	0	5	18
Stone	47	65	69	65
Frame	52	73	48	234
Log	235	245	201	
Shanties	36	–	–	–
Total Inhabited	–	383	323	317
Uninhabited	–	25	20	23
Houses Building	–	7	2	3

SOURCE: 1852, 1861 and 1891 manuscript census returns for Beckwith at the National Archives of Canada: and Ontario Agricultural Commission, Report (Toronto, 1881).

in the States, but they are deficient in something that gives beauty to the landscape, and pleasure to the eye.

But despite an advertisement for THE HOUSE: A Pocket Manual of Rural Architecture in the Carleton Place Herald in 1859,[91] most larger houses built in Beckwith before 1881 were strictly vernacular structures. As Table 18 clearly shows, two-thirds of Beckwith houses in 1880 remained log structures. It was quite evident that no stone, brick or frame houses would replace the "good flatted log dwelling house about 22 by 28 feet...all in one apartment" built by James Sample on lot five in the first concession which a surveyor described in 1859 as "a very wet tamarac swamp, utterly unfit for any purpose in agriculture, and worthless except for what little rail timber can be found upon it."[92] The late date at which Daniel McCuan built his frame house on the Clergy Reserve purchased a decade earlier had been dictated by the priority of acquiring the reserve and the property in Fitzroy as well as paying the costs of two ill brothers. By waiting as late as he did to build a house, ironically enough, Daniel McCuan's was one of the rare houses in Beckwith before 1880 that attempted to follow a popular architectural style.

If house construction is used as a barometer of relative wealth in Beckwith, it is clear that Scottish inhabitants were more prosperous than were the Irish.[93] This is hardly surprising considering the concentration of Perthshire highlanders who had been settled on the fertile northern quarter of the

Table 19. House Construction by Ethnicity of Household Head, 1852

	Irish	Scottish	English	Other
Log Shanty	22	8	2	–
Log House	91	119	7	31
Frame House	18	23	5	8
Stone House	20	25	2	2

SOURCE: 1852 manuscript census returns for Beckwith at the National Archives of Canada

Plate 148
Orena Villa, the house of William Duff on lot 10, concession 11, Beckwith, built in the 1850s, as photographed in June 1983. Although William Duff and his family immigrated from Paisley, Scotland to Beckwith in 1843, as a stonemason he was able to build this large handsome house a mere decade later. Some of the families building large new houses in the 1850s were loath to give up the traditional fireplace. A visitor to this house in the autumn of 1862 was "very politely introduced into the sitting-room, which, though rather antique in its appearance, yet possessed a good degree of moderate taste and comfort, being well furnished with varied articles of usefulness — the mantle-piece exhibiting a multiplicity of curious statuary, and the walls were gracefully hung with beautiful engravings and other ornamental appendages."

township. Evenly balanced though the numbers of Irish and Scottish inhabitants were in Beckwith in 1852, Table 19 shows that over two-thirds of the most miserable structures, commonly called shanties, were inhabited by people of Irish origin. Only a quarter of these shanties were inhabited by people of Scottish origin. The larger and more prestigious houses in Beckwith at mid-century were constructed of stone and frame, and in both categories the Scottish led the Irish. Whereas people of Irish origin inhabited a third of the frame houses, the Scottish inhabited over 42 percent; and the Irish inhabited 41 percent as opposed to the Scottish occupying 51 percent of stone houses. Clearly, as manifested in housing, Scottish-origin inhabitants taken as a group were enjoying greater prosperity than were their Irish neighbours.

Despite their relative greater prosperity, the Scottish-origin inhabitants of Beckwith from mid-century on slowly began to decline as a proportion of the township population, and the Irish proportion began to rise. By 1871 there were 980 people of Irish origin in Beckwith compared with 922 of Scottish origin. During the next decade the number of Irish inhabitants dropped by thirty and the number of Scottish fell by 56, resulting in the Scottish proportion of Beckwith's population dropping by a percentage point while the Irish proportion increased by half a percentage point. Surprisingly, although the Irish taken as a group were less prosperous and were located on comparatively poorer land than the

Scottish, they proved more reluctant to leave Beckwith. Some of the Scottish and Irish leaving Beckwith went to Carleton Place, but even as the population of that industrialising village jumped from 1,205 to 1,975 between 1871 and 1881, the Scottish-origin population of Carleton Place increased by only 223 or slightly more than half the Irish-origin increase of 419 persons. As a proportion of the population of Carleton Place, Scottish origin inhabitants declined by six percent from 43.5 to 37.8 percent of the village's population in contrast with Irish-origin residents who increased by five percent from 42.7 to 47.2 percent. Again, as in Beckwith, the Irish were more reluctant than the Scottish to leave the immediate vicinity.

Migration out of Beckwith had existed from the beginning of settlement, and yet by the late 1870s inhabitants such as Daniel McCuan began to perceive the movement of people out of the township differently. Why this changing view developed is not altogether clear. The number of people leaving Beckwith per decade could have been no more than one hundred or five percent. Nor was it a matter necessarily of people moving greater distances in 1880 in contrast with 1852, as shown by the example of John Thomson from Beckwith who migrated west to Plympton Township in Lambton County before mid-century and who in 1852 like many other young people went from Beckwith to California.[94] Daniel McCuan remarked in a letter to one of his friends who went off to the gold rush, "your going away caused considerable talk about here for a while[;] some thought that you would have been better in this country[,] others thought that you would get along better where you are now."[95] Napoleon Lavallee and his wife went to Australia in 1852, only to return to Carleton Place a year later.[96] Daniel McCuan's own brother John travelled to Scotland in 1857 for a change of climate,[97] and there were settlements of people from Beckwith in western Ontario to prove that distance had not been an objection for people in search of better land. The changing perception of the continuing trickle of migration out of Beckwith was due to the disappointed expectations that had been fed by the railway boosters, and which by 1880 were coming true for industrialising villages such as Carleton Place rather than for the farmers of Beckwith. Although Franktown actually had grown thanks to the construction of the Brockville and Ottawa railway past it in the 1850s, from the sour perspective of rural Beckwith inhabitants watching the population of their township decline while that of Carleton Place and distant regions grew in the late 1870s, Franktown appeared to be "now a railroad-killed village."[98]

By the 1870s the destinations of those leaving Beckwith became consistently more distant and fragmented as there ceased to be appealing agricultural settlement destinations along the upper Ottawa. When the Brockville and Ottawa railway came through Beckwith in 1859 the editor of the *Carleton Place Herald* predicted its extension to Pembroke "will induce hundreds and thousands of all nations to the inviting and fertile Valleys of the Ottawa."[99] During the 1850s letters printed in the *Herald* from Beckwith colonies out in western Canada West told of land still being available,[100] and as late as August 1861 blacksmith Duncan McGregor and his family left for Paisley in Bruce County.[101] By the late 1860s not only was there no arable land available for settlement along the upper Ottawa, but there was none near the Beckwith colonies in western Ontario. As the years passed and new generations took the place of those in Beckwith and in the colonies in western Ontario, it was inevitable that links between the two grew faint. When William Taylor from the distance of Oxford County opened an 1865 letter to Daniel McCuan's family by apologising for having "neglected — I can scarcely tell why — to keep up communication, I have not forgotten you"[102] it was but eloquent testimony to the inevitability of ties breaking down between Beckwith and its colonies. In the 1870s as local railways linked up with the transcontinental Canadian Pacific Railway and the American railway networks, there were few Beckwith families that did not have one or more members who lived half a continent away. Daniel McCuan, for example, in June 1973 received a letter from his nephew James McEwen in Clearwater Montana who variously inquired if he or the other boys had "any thought of seeing our prairie country this summer" and that "if any of the boys have a notion of investing out here I would sell my place reasonable" since he expected "I will likely go East for a while and I think they need me at home just now."[103] Daniel's own brother, James, when his sawmill in Fitzroy was rendered uncompetitive by the mills of Daniel

Plate 149
The Daniel McCuan house, lot 21, concession 10, Beckwith, built in 1864, as photographed in January 1987. This was a unique structure among the houses built in rural Beckwith before Confederation in that it was the only one the design of which was influenced by architectural currents in the outside world. The L-shaped floorplan, the dramatically steep gables, the use of dormer windows, the large windows and the first bay window in Beckwith combine to suggest that Daniel McCuan or the building contractor working for him had consulted a pattern book such as A.J. Downing's Architecture of Country Houses.

McLachlin in Arnprior in the late 1870s, decided to leave for the Canadian northwest[104] rather than attempt to survive in Fitzroy on "just enough of [a] farm here cleared for a person to starve on".[105]

The new way in which migration out of Beckwith came to be perceived was in part due to the decline of group settlement, partly due to a contrast of the reality of Beckwith with glowing reports sent back from the west, and perhaps most importantly it was due to local society acquiring a more profound sense of time passing by. The decline of group settlement was evident within the McCuan family itself, with Daniel's nephew James McEwen off by himself in Montana and his brother James going off to Manitoba alone to work for a logging syndicate, leaving his wife and children to run the farm in Fitzroy. Group or kin migration out of Beckwith declined as the railway whisked individuals off to seek their fortune in the west. When those who migrated sent reports back of "splendid country and good crops"[106] in Manitoba, the depleting soils and modest agricultural economy of Beckwith must have seemed even smaller in the eyes of those who remained at home. The railway as the principal form of transportation which conveyed the trickle of people migrating from Beckwith was obviously the most visible agent of change that many Beckwith inhabitants saw and that all of them heard on a daily basis from 1859 on. At the same time the railways were promoted, constructed and were perceived to quadruple the population of Carleton Place and to reduce that of rural Beckwith between 1852 and 1881, the people of Beckwith began to acquire a memory.

In one sense, to suggest that the people of Beckwith were acquiring a memory might seem overstated. Some of them, after all, had brought books with them from Wexford and Perthshire, and the McCuans had even brought with them from Scotland a sword which according to family tradition had been used at the battle of Culloden.[107] Most of them, if asked, could tell where their family came from in Ireland and Scotland. Many of them had corresponded with relatives back in the British Isles at least for the first generation. But that was exactly the problem with the memory of people in early Beckwith; it tended to die with its generation just as the links with relatives who migrated to distant parts from Beckwith died with the generation which moved. A combination of unprecedented change and the goal of universal literacy coincided to provide Beckwith inhabitants with a heightened memory and with an emerging sense of history between 1852 and 1880. The publishing of the *Carleton Place Herald* from 1850 on inspired one correspondent to write in 1858, "as the teacher of the history of our own times, let the newspaper be found in every dwelling. Let it be placed in our children's hands that it may beget in them a taste for literature."[108] Clocks began appearing in homes to ensure that children were off to school on time and that people were off to meet the train on time. The congregational libraries, school libraries, the Orange lodge library and the Mechanic's Institute library had played their complementary role in reinforcing the literacy inculcated in Beckwith schools. Beckwith burial grounds with rotting wooden slabs were transformed into cemeteries filled with handsome and enduring sculpted marble monuments.

People observed early humble houses, schools and churches replaced by spacious new structures. They noted the destruction of familiar landmarks to make way for the factories and railroads of a new era. Just as the pioneers who one by one were toppling into their graves were memorialised by handsome tombstones, prosperous inhabitants of Beckwith flocked to the studios of visiting daguerreotype and photographic artists to have their likenesses captured on glass, metal and paper. Correspondence was scattered with requests for photographs and copies of the Carleton Place *Herald* to be sent to those who had migrated. The rapid growth of Carleton Place in the late 1860s and 1870s, the declining fertility rate, the changing fashions of women gave Beckwith inhabitants a heightened sense that society was changing. Perhaps the ultimate recognition of change was a *Historical Atlas of Lanark County* published by H. Belden and Company in 1880 that included illustrations of the new factories in Carleton Place, a map of Beckwith, a history of the township, and brief biographies of prominent men who subscribed to the atlas. A few reminiscences of older inhabitants about earlier days in Beckwith began to be published in Carleton Place newspapers in the 1870s.

For those inhabitants of Beckwith who boarded the cars at Carleton Place for their first train ride, the greatest change of all was symbolised by the new perspective they were given of their familiar landscape at what to them was breakneck speed:[109]

> After a few minutes detention, and a few barrels rolled off, the Conductor gravely draws his watch out, says "all aboard" and the locomotive glides from the station, passes a crossing, and rushes away into Ramsay, past log houses, frame dwellings, stone dwellings, aged barns in the distance, past straight fences, crooked fences, log fences, and a variety of dilapidated fences enclosing dilapidated corners, now a patch of balsams, then a flying glimpse of a meadow with a bovine congregation with erected ears contemplatively eyeing the gusty fury which is flashing past; now a girl with a milk pail, 'tother side of the fence, with unkempt hair enveloping her shoulders in uncultivated luxuriance, and on [and] on, the sameness of scenery continues with here and there long vistas of farmlands, with the ripening grain shimmering with a golden tinge in the rays of the setting sun; a screech from the locomotive, a hurried view of the buildings in the distance, a ringing of the bell, an avalanche of smoke which eddies around you in fitful curves, a stop, and a row of inquiring mechanical faces, glowering with a dumb assurance that Almonte was the end of time — railway time....

Plate 150
A westbound Canadian Pacific passenger train crossing the Mississippi River at Carleton Place ca. 1900, as photographed by J.W. Hammond. The building of the Brockville and Ottawa railway through Beckwith in the 1850s had cost the township dearly, and, as it turned out, largely for the benefit of industrialising towns such as Carleton Place. As Beckwith farms were consolidated in the late nineteenth century, the transcontinental CPR carried the sons and daughters of Beckwith families westward over the old Brockville and Ottawa tracks to more arable land in the western United States and Canadian prairie provinces. National Archives of Canada negative no. C-3823.

The coming of the railroad had cost Beckwith dearly, both financially and in the exodus of inhabitants, and to become but a blur or trees, fences, houses and livestock between the industrialising centres of Smith's Falls, Carleton Place, Almonte and Ottawa seemed scant return of its investment. Still, despite the suspicions of many regional farmers that they had been railroaded into supporting an enterprise that benefitted only merchants and lumbermen, farmers also eventually began to make use of the railways to go to market. As a young man Daniel McCuan had only visited Bytown in winter during the long sleigh trips taking crops to market.[110] By the early 1860s he could take a trip to any town in eastern Canada West and return the same day. He was probably no less delighted to hear the actual whistle of locomotives on the railways passing through Beckwith in the 1870s than when he had imagined hearing one in October 1858. Like other young men who chose to remain farming family homesteads in Beckwith, he could appreciate that the years of waiting for the Brockville and Ottawa railway to complete construction along with the heavy taxes it commanded were the price to be paid for Beckwith and the rest of Lanark County to be part of a maturing Canadian industrial economy.

If Daniel McCuan understood anything, he recognised the value of pursuing realistic goals even if it required setting to one side his own immediate fulfillment. It had taken some thirteen years for the Brockville and Ottawa railway to be laid from the St. Lawrence to the Ottawa rivers. The maturing of Daniel McCuan had been delayed almost as long. Only after his father passed away in 1864 did he begin building a new house, and in 1867 at the age of 33 he married his 28 year old cousin Helen Whyte. On the occasion of his birthday in February 1882 Daniel McCuan appraised his life as a Beckwith farmer: "I am now 48 years old[,] in the enjoyment of good health and prosperity[.] My Helen & family are enjoying good health[.] Duncan & Thomas are upstairs learning their lessons[.] Alex & Nelly are frolicking through the house making a fearful din[.] upsetting chairs &c[.,] while Helen is washing up the supper dishes."[111] If Daniel McCuan felt that at last he was reaping the domestic rewards of choosing to stay in Beckwith, it yet remained to be proven that it ultimately was to rural Beckwith's benefit to have aided in financing the railroad three decades earlier. His children, like those in other Beckwith families, would in their turn have to face up to an eventual choice between leaving for increasingly distant destinations or face a future of diminishing personal expectations at home.

Endnotes

1. Daniel McCuan, manuscript journal, 1852-57. I am grateful to Alex and Jean McCuan, R.R. no. 2, Carleton Place, Ontario, for making the extensive papers of their family available for use in this book.
2. McCuan family correspondence, 10 February 1844 statement of Warren Herrick at Beckwith.
3. McCuan family school lessons, 1843, 1845-1846.
4. McCuan family correspondence, 21 October 1855 musings of Daniel McCuan, references 3.8, 3.8.2.
5. *Carleton Place Herald*, 11 November 1852, p. 2, col. 2.
6. Ibid., 25 November 1852, p. 3, col. 6 The merchants from Carleton Place were Robert Bell, William Peden, Archibald McArthur, James C. Poole, David Lawson, James Rosamond, William Wilson, Allan McDonald, George Dunnet and James Duncan. Those from Franktown were James Burrows, Ewen McEwen, John Edwards, Andrew and John Hughton, Thomas Griffith, Duncan Ferguson and James Stewart.
7. Ibid., 23 December 1852, p. 2, col. 5.
8. Ibid., 30 December 1852, pp. 2-3, cols. 7-2.
9. Ibid.
10. Ibid., 10 February 1853, p. 2, cols. 4-5.
11. Ibid., p. 2, col. 3.
12. Ibid., 21 July 1853, p. 2, cols. 3-4.
13. Lockwood, *Montague: A Social History*, p. 225.
14. *Carleton-Place Herald*, 21 July 1853, p. 2, col. 5.
15. Ibid., p. 2, col. 4.
16. *Brockville Recorder*, 3 February 1859, p. 2, col. 8.
17. *Carleton Place Herald*, 21 April 1859, p. 3, col. 2.
18. Ibid., 4 August 1859, p. 3, col. 4.
19. Leo Lavoie, *The Arnprior Story, 1823-1984* (Arnprior: The Arnprior and District Historical Society, 1984), p. 11.
20. Pembroke Centennial Committee, *The Pembroke Centennial Souvenir Book* (Pembroke: Centennial Publicity Committee, 1958), p. 18.
21. *Carleton-Place Herald*, 4 August 1853, p. 1, col. 1.
22. Ibid., 12 April 1860, p. 3, cols. 5-6.
23. J.M. and Edw. Trout, *The Railways of Canada for 1870-1* (Toronto, 1871; reprint ed. : Toronto: Coles Publishing Company, 1974), pp. 141–2.
24. *Carleton Place Herald*, 12 April 1860, p. 3, col. 1.
25. *Ottawa Citizen*, 20 July 1865, p. 2, col. 4.
26. *Carleton Place Herald*, 29 July 1868, p. 2, col. 7.
27. Ibid., 2 September 1868, p. 2, col. 2.
28. Ibid., 16 June 1869, p. 1, col. 2.
29. Ibid., 28 July 1869, p. 1, cols. 2-3.
30. Lockwood, *Montague*, pp. 227-228.
31. *Carleton Place Herald*, 25 August 1869, p. 2, col. 2.
32. Ibid., 28 September 1870, p. 2, col. 2.
33. Ibid., 12 October 1870, p. 2, col. 3.
34. McCuan family correspondence, 12 March (watermark 1861) letter from Peter McCuan, Carleton Place, to Alexander McCuan, Beckwith.
35. Diary of George McLaren, lot 21, concession 5, 14 September 1874, loaned courtesy of James I. McLaren.
36. Diary of Joseph Kidd, lot 21, concession 6, 20 January 1876. The late William Livingstone Kidd made this diary available for use in this study.
37. McCuan family correspondence, 1 April 1855 musing on scrap of paper by Daniel McCuan.

38 McGill, *A Pioneer History of the County of Lanark*, p. 30, and McCuan family correspondence, 22 November 1862 letter from John McCuan, Fitzroy, to Daniel McCuan, Beckwith.
39 McCuan family correspondence, 5 January 1863 letter from Peter McCuan, Beckwith, to Alexander McCuan, Montreal General Hospital.
40 Ibid., 9 March 1857 letter from Daniel McCuan, Beckwith, to John McCuan, Bridge of Allan, Scotland.
41 Ibid., 23 February 1857 letter from John McCuan, Bridge of Allan, Scotland, to Peter McCuan, Beckwith.
42 Ibid., March 1857 letter from Catherine McCuan, Beckwith, to John McCuan, Bridge of Allan, Scotland.
43 Ibid., 6 March 1857 letter from Daniel McCuan, Beckwith, to John McCuan, Bridge of Allan, Scotland.
44 *Perth Courier*, 11 November 1864, p. 1, col. 6.
45 *Perth Bathurst Courier*, 13 August 1852, p. 2, cols. 4-7.
46 *Perth Courier*, 21 October 1864, p. 2, col. 3.
47 McCuan family correspondence, June 1857 transcript of letter from Daniel McCuan, Beckwith, to William Taylor, Maryborough Township Wellington County.
48 Ibid., 12 February 1859 letter from John McCuan, St. Hellena, Fitzroy, to Duncan McEwen, Beckwith.
49 Ibid., 9 March 1857 draft of letter from Daniel McCuan, Beckwith, to John McCuan, Bridge of Allan, Scotland.
50 Ibid., 6 March 1862 letter form Peter McCuan, Beckwith, to Alexander McCuan, Perth.
51 Ibid., 19 December 1862 letter from Peter McCuan, Beckwith, to Alexander McCuan, Montreal General Hospital.
52 Ibid., 5 May 1862 letter from James McCuan, Beckwith, to Alexander McCuan, Perth.
53 Ibid., 23 January 1863 letter from Daniel McCuan, Beckwith, to Alexander McCuan, Montreal General Hospital.
54 Ibid., 9 March 1863 letter from James McCuan, Almonte, to Alexander McCuan, Montreal General Hospital.
55 *Carleton Place Herald*, 28 July 1859, p. 2, cols. 2-3.
56 H. Belden and Company, Illustrated Historical Atlas of the County of Carleton (Toronto: H. Belden and Company, 1879, reprint ed.: Stratford, Ontario: Cumming Atlas Reprints, 1976), p. 31.
57 McCuan family correspondence, 18 April 1858 letter from Francis May, Brant, to Daniel McCuan, Beckwith.
58 Ibid., 20 August 1857 letter from William Taylor, Maryborough to Daniel McCuan, Beckwith.
59 Ibid., 22 June 1858 letter from Margaret McCallum, Cresent City, Delnorte County, California, to Daniel McCuan, Beckwith.
60 Lanark County Registry Office (hereafter OPLCRO), 14 April 1862 will of William Duff of Beckwith, reference 2B-464.
61 *Carleton Place Herald*, 15 April 1868, p. 1, col. 3.
62 McCuan family correspondence, 20 August 1857 letter from William Taylor, Maryborough, to Daniel McCuan, Beckwith.
63 Ibid., 18 April 1858 letter from Francis May, Brant, to Daniel McCuan, Beckwith.
64 *Carleton-Place Herald*, 22 August 1851, p. 2, col. 6.
65 Ibid., 20 May 1852, p. 2, col. 2.
66 Ibid., 3 September 1862, p. 3, cols. 1-2.
67 Ibid., 20 May 1852, p. 2, col. 2.
68 Ibid., 14 June 1860, p. 3, col. 1.
69 Ibid., 1 July 1852, p. 2, col.7.
70 McCuan family correspondence, 17 August 1863 letter from Peter McCuan, Beckwith, to Alex McCuan, Beckwith.
71 McCuan family papers, file 102, 1866 prize list of the Township of Beckwith Agricultural Society.
72 The Huntley data is taken from Julian Gwyn, "The Irish in Eastern Ontario: The Social Structure of Huntley Township in Carleton County, 1851-71" in Vrenia Ivanoffski and Sandra Campbell, eds., *Exploring Our Heritage: The Ottawa Valley Experience* (Arnprior: Arnprior and District Historical Society, 1980), p. 27.
73 McCuan family correspondence, 21 April 1856 letter from Elisabeth Bain, Beckwith, to Alexander Bain, Admaston, Renfrew County.
74 Ibid., undated letter from Margaret McArthur, Carleton Place, to Helen McCuan, Beckwith, believed written in the 1870s.
75 10 June 1853 entry in notebook of Daniel McCuan.
76 McCuan family correspondence, 19 August 1858 letter from Duncan McCuan, Beckwith, to Frank Sargent, Bell's Corners.
77 *Carleton Place Herald*, 2 September 1863, p. 2, col. 6.
78 McCuan family correspondence, 8 April 1868 inventory of farm implements.
79 *Ontario Agricultural Commission, Report*, 5 vols. (Toronto: C. Blackett Robinson, 1881) II:279.
80 This journal was provided courtesy of James I. McLaren of Ottawa.
81 *Carleton-Place Herald*, 5 February 1852, p. 2, col. 3.
82 Ibid., 23 September 1858, p. 3, col. 3.
83 Ibid., 3 November 1859, p. 3, col. 1.
84 Ibid., 23 September 1863, p. 2, col. 5.
85 Ibid., 5 October 1864, p. 2, col. 3.
86 Ibid., 19 May 1853, p. 3, col. 4; and 16 November 1864, p. 3, col. 6.
87 Ibid., 16 August 1855, p. 2, cols. 3-4.
88 McCuan family correspondence, notes of Daniel McCuan, incorrectly dated as 18 April 1855,

89 *Carleton Place Herald*, 24 September 1857, p. 3, cols. 2-3.
90 Ibid., 14 April 1853, p. 2, cols. 4-5.
91 Ibid., 24 February 1859, p. 3, col. 6.
92 OTAR RG 1 MS 658 Reel 30 Crown Lands Department, Township Papers, Beckwith Township, p. 25.
93 Only the 1852 and 1861 census returns offer statistics on house construction material. The 1852 census was selected as a measure of wealth because most stone houses built in Beckwith were built before 1852, and this was the last census in which a number of shanties remained in the township.
94 *Carleton-Place Herald*, 7 April 1853, p. 2, cols. 3-4.
95 McCuan family correspondence, undated letter from Daniel McCuan, Beckwith, to unnamed friend in California, reference 2.13.
96 *Carleton-Place Herald, 28 July 1853, p. 2, col. 4.*
97 McCuan family correspondence, John McCuan, Bridge of Allan, Scotland, to Alexander McCuan, Beckwith, 3 February 1857, reference 3.2.
98 John May, "Bush Life in the Ottawa Valley", p. 159.
99 *Carleton Place Herald*, 4 August 1859, p. 3, col. 4.
100 Ibid.,

reference 3.6.

101 Ibid., 21 August 1861, p. 2, col. 6.
102 McCuan family correspondence, 14 August 1865 letter from William Taylor, Culloden post office, to Daniel McCuan, Beckwith, reference 8.3.
103 Ibid., 17 June 1873 letter from James McEwen, Clear Water, Montana, to Daniel McCuan, Beckwith.
104 Ibid., 30 May 1881 letter from James McCuan, Arnprior, to Daniel McCuan, Beckwith, reference 11.4.
105 Ibid., 20 April 1880 letter from James McCuan, Waba Mills, Fitzroy Township, to Daniel McCuan, Beckwith.
106 Ibid., 19 August 1880 letter from James McCuan, Brandon, Manitoba, to Daniel McCuan, Beckwith.
107 26 November 1883 letter from D.J. McCuan, Waba Creek, Fitzroy, to his or her uncle Daniel McCuan, Beckwith.
108 *Carleton Place Herald*, 12 August 1858, p. 3, col. 4.
109 Ibid., 11 September 1861, p. 2, cols. 6-7.
110 McCuan family correspondence,
111 Ibid., 3 February 1882 note of Daniel McCuan, reference 11.12.

THE REMAKING OF BECKWITH

No one watching the first meeting of the new Beckwith township council on the 22nd day of January 1850 could have guessed that the purpose behind its new municipal existence was the financing of railway construction. The first dozen official by-laws to which Beckwith's first reeve Robert Bell signed his name that evening suggested no particular departure from the business over which Beckwith wardens had previously presided, concerned as the by-laws were with appointing township officers, levying assessments for county purposes, building an extension onto the common school at Carleton Place, and regulating livestock and fences. The only unusual by-law among the dozen was one levying a prohibitively hefty tax "on Circus Riders, Wire Dancers, Puppet Shows and Jugglers coming into the Township of Beckwith for the purpose of exhibiting, practi[s]ing or performing".[1]

On the surface it seemed that Beckwith inhabitants finally controlled the funds for which they were assessed, a goal which appeared to fulfil the quest of Reformers and moderate Conservatives for responsible government. And yet, although it was true that between 1850 and 1880 Beckwith inhabitants enjoyed unprecedented control over their own roads, schools, agricultural standards, and even morals, they alternately gasped with shock at the cost and marvelled at the promise of these responsibilities. A Beckwith taxpayer who in one breath expressed horror that the Brockville and Ottawa railway with its debt of over three millions of dollars had shaken the credit of the municipalities backing it, in the next breath admitted "we like to see the magnificent carriages of the B. & O. Railway rushing past our doors. In it we behold the progress of science — the messenger of civilization."[2] In addition to creating an enhanced sense of township identity, improved schools and roads, Beckwith inhabitants discovered that the acquisition of local control also had a negative side. It fragmented the township, it gave rise to intense geographical jealousy between northern and southern concessions that culminated in Carleton Place becoming a separate municipality in 1870. By giving local municipalities the power to levy and spend taxes, provincial administrators and politicians made township officials accountable to Beckwith taxpayers at the same time they regulated, limited and manipulated them to do as they intended all along. The municipal remaking of Beckwith at mid-century simply served to make expensive railways and universally accessible education more palatable to local inhabitants.

An integral aspect of the remaking of Beckwith was its politicisation from the late 1840s on. From the mid 1820s Beckwith inhabitants had participated in elections, and often did so tellingly, with both Wexford Anglicans and Perthshire Presbyterians initially voting for Conservative William Morris. By the 1840s some Scottish Presbyterians in the township had shifted their support to Malcolm Cameron, the son of a highland Scottish sergeant who also was Presbyterian, a mercurial Reformer and an impassioned advocate of temperance. The Irish Anglicans of Beckwith, by contrast, identified all the more strongly with Conservative candidates, their support reinforced all the more by Tory candidates being members of the United Church of England and Ireland and of Irish birth. Save for six years during the 1830s, when one of the two members jointly representing Lanark County had been an Irish or English Anglican, all members of the provincial legislature from Lanark up until 1845 were Scottish Presbyterians. They were the largest franchised ethno-religious group in the county,[3] and even after a Conservative administration added Montague, North Elmsley and North Burgess with all the Irish Tories they contained in 1842, the riding of Lanark elected Scottish Presbyterian Reformer Robert Bell of Carleton Place as their member. Once Wexford-born James Shaw captured the riding for the Tories in 1852, local Scottish Reformers began to complain that the addition of Montague and the other townships had been a blatant Tory gerrymander. Accordingly, the Reform administration of Francis Hincks carved the huge riding into two new ones: North Lanark and South Lanark to confine the polical influence of the concentration of Irish Anglicans to southern Lanark. For the next sixty years Beckwith was part of the solidly Tory South Lanark riding whereas Carleton Place belonged to pro-Reform North Lanark.

The politicising of Beckwith from the 1840s on, then, had a number of components. First of all there was an innate conservatism handed down from highland and Wexford tradition that was reinforced by the Perth and Richmond military settlements. Ethno-religious ties were important, independent of tradition, causing many Scottish Presbyterians to vote for Reformers Donald Fraser and Malcolm Cameron after previously supporting Tory William Morris. Similarly, the ethno-religious identity of Irish Anglicans in Beckwith bonded them firmly to Conservative candidates, but the tension this generated appears initially to have been directed at the candidates, rather than lobbed back and forth between the two major ethnic communities in Beckwith. An anonymous Irish inhabitant of Beckwith, for example, wrote a letter to the Conservative Brockville *Statesman* late in 1846, chastising Malcolm Cameron for loaning a Beckwith settler money to purchase a farm for the sake of appearances prior to the recent election, but upon losing the election Cameron threatened to deprive the settler and his family of their home in mid winter.[4] Beckwith became increasingly politicised as public hustings eventually gave way to secret ballots, as the number of polling places increased, as candidates tramped around to address electors in local schools, as more and more people read newspapers, and as the Reform rhetoric of the *Carleton Place Herald* was matched by that of the Conservative *Carleton Place Central Canadian* founded by William W. Cliff in 1876.

There was a geographic aspect to the politicisation of Beckwith. The strong radical lowlander tradition in Ramsay had embraced the Reform rhetoric of Malcolm Cameron and infiltrated the Scottish concentration of settlement in northern Beckwith in the 1840s. Carleton Place, where many Ramsay lowlanders did their business, became a strong Reform centre, and became the base of Robert Bell's successful parliamentary career. To the south of Beckwith was Montague, a township whose Irish majority was so solidly Tory as to willingly harass Reform candidates on behalf of their candidate. In December 1857 the Perth *Courier* severely condemned:[5]

> the conduct of a lot of rowdies whom Mr. Shaw had brought up from Montague, evidently for the purpose of preventing his opponents from being heard. They appeared to fear neither God, Man nor Devil, and were the most savage, barbarous looking set of uncivilized ruffians we have ever set our eyes on. They call themselves Orangemen, we understand, and defenders of Protestantism. — From such defenders of Protestantism "Good Lord deliver us," must be the prayer of every man who witnessed their ruffianly conduct.... Richard Shaw, James Shaw, J., and George Shaw, all sons of the candidate, were round among the rowdy ruffians urging them on and telling them when to yell. Such conduct is disgraceful to civilization. A few missionary preachers should be sent to Montague without delay, to try and convert these barbarians to Christianity.

This along with countless other references in regional Reform newspapers to Montague as a backward, barbarous, unprogressive and liquor-ridden backwater[6] was not without its implications for the Irish in southern Beckwith, related as most of them were to the Irish in Montague. Undoubtedly, the Irish Anglicans of Beckwith resented the negative portrayal of their Montague kin, but as

Plate 151
Beckwith township hall, Black's Corners, built in 1857, as photographed ca. 1917. Black's Corners was the compromise location for the municipal hall of Beckwith between the warring sectional jealousies of Franktown and Carleton Place. Previously, township council meetings were held alternately at Franktown and Carleton Place. The frame construction of the hall in contrast with more substantial stone township halls in adjoining municipalities such as Montague suggest that this building was intended as a temporary compromise, and that eventually a stone hall would be built at one of the two vying villages. Photograph courtesy of Ellen Gardiner.

time passed and ethnic bonds dissolved, the negative stereotype became more particularly associated with Montague, and Beckwith inhabitants of Irish origin recoiled as readily as anyone from being identified with the people of Montague. As ethnicity receded as a form of electoral grouping between 1850 and 1880, Beckwith inhabitants increasingly identified with municipal or more localised community boundaries.

In the 1850s Beckwith returned to its Conservative roots, partly because Robert Bell was running in North Lanark and partly over religious issues. During the 1851 election members of the Church of Scotland in Beckwith "who heretofore had voted on the Reform side," alongside Irish Anglicans "voted for Mr. Shaw, being in favour of his scheme of supporting religion from the Clergy Reserve fund.[7] Shaw squeaked through with 54 percent of the Beckwith vote in 1851, and when Malcolm Cameron from the distance of Lambton County ran as a candidate in 1854 his majority in Beckwith was only 53 percent,[8] revealing how politicised and evenly divided Beckwith had become. When a three way contest developed in 1857, the Beckwith majority for English-origin Methodist Andrew W. Playfair was less than 52 percent.[9] But when Alexander Morris, the son of the Honourable William Morris, ran as a Conservative candidate against Irish Roman Catholic Reform candidate John Doran of Perth in 1861, a combination of innate conservatism, sentimentality for Morris's father and religious leanings brought together the Irish Anglican and Scottish Presbyterian majority in Beckwith to vote for Morris. Morris's opposition to further financial aid being given the Grand Trunk railway may have added to his popularity in Beckwith,[10]

but when even the pro-Reform *Carleton Place Herald* favoured Morris over Doran, it was clear that religion and ethnic ties were strong factors in backing a candidate.[11]

The Perth *Courier* chastised the Free Church Presbyterians of Beckwith for the train of calamitous results they set in motion by abandoning the Reform candidate:[12]

> The '*Secession*' of Beckwith...split the Reform party and defeated Mr. Doran. This unfortunate result was made a handle of by the Tories in North and South Leeds [ridings], who proclaimed that Mr. Doran had been "*sold*" by the Reformers of South Lanark, and the consequence was that numbers of voters who intended to vote for Smith and Richards, stayed at home, and both Reform candidates were defeated. The Beckwith "dodge" has therefore deprived the Reform party of Upper Canada of *three* votes in the House for the next four years....

In 1861 Alexander Morris received 93 percent of the Beckwith vote and in 1863 he received 78 percent.[13] Robert Bell of Carleton Place was the member for North Lanark from 1848 through to 1864 save for two years in the early 1850s. There was no other parliamentary representative from Beckwith or Carleton Place between 1852 and 1880. As the Irish Anglican-based majority in South Lanark acclaimed Alexander Morris as federal member in 1867 and again in 1869, followed by Scottish-origin Perth miller John Graham Haggart who was continuously elected federal Tory member from 1872 through to 1913, the number of Liberals in Beckwith among the Scottish population only gradually resurfaced.[14]

Beckwith was divided between Irish and Scottish inhabitants at its first municipal election held late in 1849,[15] and the ethnic divisions merged into geographic jealousies. The balance of Irish and Scottish is shown by Beckwith being presided over for seventeen of the 31 years by reeves of Scottish origin as opposed to reeves of Irish origin for fourteen years. In October 1850 Beckwith council divided the township into five "rural wards for the purpose of electing Township Councillors", essentially carving Beckwith into four equal geographic quarters, with Carleton Place as the centre

Plate 152
James McFarlane (ca. 1792—1864) and his wife Girsal or Grace McLaren (ca. 1792—1871) as ambrotyped ca. 1862 (opposite), and the stone house they built on lot 24, concession 10, Beckwith in the 1850s, as photographed in June 1983. If the highlanders of Beckwith initially inhabited less pretentious dwellings than their Irish neighbours, by the 1850s their fertile farms permitted them to build more ambitious houses. Despite the ample proportions, the large windows, the sidelights and transom around the front door, and the use of contrasting dark brown stone on the corners set off against the finely cut lighter-toned stone, there was one continuing influence on this house from the earliest days the lot was settled: it was located in the middle of the farm between a quarter and half a mile from the nearest concession road. Ambrotypes loaned courtesy of Donna and John McFarlane.

of a fifth ward running from lots ten to twenty in the twelfth concession.[16] Beckwith council received a petition from inhabitants protesting dividing the township into rural wards. It was perceived to encroach on "the necessity of the Municipal Electors meeting in one place that they may have an opportunity of a free and full discussion on many questions of paramount importance to the well being of the people, and of giving their Representative in the County Council an unmistakeable expression of their opinion on questions affecting the general interests of the Township". The rural wards consequently were done away with.[17] During the first three decades of Beckwith's municipal life, the northern quarter of the township in which Perthshire highlanders were concentrated dominated municipal life. The village of Carleton Place alone produced reeves for half of the thirty years, and all told the northern quarter of Beckwith produced reeves who presided over Beckwith ninety percent of these first three decades.[18]

It is not difficult to trace the reason why the other three-fourths of Beckwith produced only two reeves briefly before 1881. When Irish Catholic Franktown tavernkeeper James Burrows took over as reeve from Robert Bell in 1852, he was subjected to an onslaught of criticism in the *Carleton Place Herald*. An editorial in the first issue of 1852 alerted Beckwith inhabitants "to weigh well the characters of those [filling the office of councillor or tavern inspector]..., are they men, whose moral characters are such as to warr[a]nt us in leaving to their decision, the important questions which from time to time will be brought before them?"[19] The next issue of the *Herald* called loudly for an investigation of glaring inequalities of assessment:[20]

> The Township of Beckwith particularly requires investigation, as the assessment in certain localities in that Township, is altogether disproportionate; this will be evident to every candid man, who has any knowledge of the Township, when it is known that the Village of Carleton-Place, having only about sixty houses, none of which are over the ordinary value of the houses in the Township, has to pay one-fourth of the whole taxes; and this to[o], when the thriving Village of Franktown and a part of the Village of Ashton are in the Township.... Carleton-Place...inhabitants hav[e] been rated generally according to the true value of their property, whereas the rest of the Township has been valued at too low a rate, thereby causing Carleton-Place to pay over one-fourth of the taxes of the Township, independently of the tax levied to pay for their School House.

In late January 1852 the *Herald* accused the Beckwith council under Burrows of squandering time, "keeping parties, who had business before the Council, waiting on them till a late hour, whereas...they could have performed it in a fourth part of the time".[21] By mid February the editor of the *Herald* not only was flailing away with inconsistent facts at "the evil acts of our Council" but was throwing discreet slurs at the Irish concentration in southern Beckwith by suggesting that the house of reeve Burrows at Franktown was "by far the best Stand for a Tavern in the Township, having the advantage over Carleton Place, of a more drouthy set of neighbors".[22] The strident criticisms of the Beckwith council waned only after Robert Bell resumed his legislative career and after Beckwith reeves from 1856 onward came from the Carleton Place end of the township.

Beckwith municipal elections in the 1850s and 1860s were lively affairs, as a letter written by Peter McCuan in early January 1863 to his convalescing brother Alexander in Montreal General Hospital makes clear:[23]

> There has been considerable stir through the township this while back about the election[.] John Sumner through Dr. Hurd and other friends has been circulating all sorts of malicious reports about [Archibald] McArthur and others of the old councillors with the view of advancing his own cause in the township[. A[nother party again has been making vigorous efforts to put out John Roberts and to substitute James Conn. and Peter McGregor. McArthur then in a long speech defended his character and conduct from the slanders thrown upon them by Sumner and his satellites[. T]o this Sumner replied, bringing forward some paltry charges against Mac such as covering the sidewalk with cedar logs &c. Robert Bell then defended McArthur[,] made some remarks about railway matters, the late government &c[. T]hen Bryce McNeely's turn came. He, poor man, had while softened with drink been induced to commit some acts which in his more sober senses he would not own to; in trying to explain them (his memory being confused) he was contradicted at every word[,] so considerably humbugged he sat down[.] James Duncan next attempted to address the meeting[,] but was hissed[,] yelled[,] groaned and howled down. Polling of votes then commenced.... The council for Beckwith is the same as last year[,] only James Conn [is] in [the] place of John Roberts.

This filiopietistic account by a Scottish Presbyterian together with the rhetoric presented in the Carleton Place *Herald* show how firmly Beckwith came to be politically and municipally divided by ethnicity, religion and geography. Although John Sumner was of English birth, his prominence in the Irish Anglican congregation at Ashton garnered him support from the large Irish community of Beckwith.

Plate 153
Springside Hall, the residence built for William Morphy Jr., Carleton Place, in 1869, as photographed in 1982. William was a grandson of Edmond Morphy, the first settler at the site of Carleton Place, and he built this ambitious house from the profits he made selling building lots during the industrial boom of Carleton Place in the 1860s. This house marked a turning point from the earlier large houses constructed in Beckwith that had been vernacular variations on neoclassic plans. There was still a frontal symmetry to this house, but the projecting middle bay, the textured treatment of stone and the exuberant vergeboard all marked the dawn of a new romantic cast to local architecture. The circular driveway was repeated in front of the Archibald McArthur house (Plate 183).

The remaking of Beckwith between 1850 and 1880 was evident not only in the emergence of politics but in many other tangible ways. The two railways slicing through the township, the municipal separation of Carleton Place and the onset of continuous population decline were all major visible changes that took place in local society. The increasing numbers of frame and stone houses, the construction of the first brick houses, the financing of better quality schoolhouses throughout the township beginning with construction of a stone school at Franktown in 1848,[24] the establishment of the basic network of township roads that would remain in use for more than a century, the development of villages, and bringing under cultivation the maximum number of acres possible all took place during this period.

It has been noted earlier in this study that Beckwith was unusual among the townships of Upper Canada in being largely filled up by settlement within only six short years. It was for the other townships such as Montague immediately to the south of Beckwith, 87 percent of whose land area was either owned by absentee landowners or reserved by the Crown a generation after settlement began, that the Canadian government had instituted elective municipal district

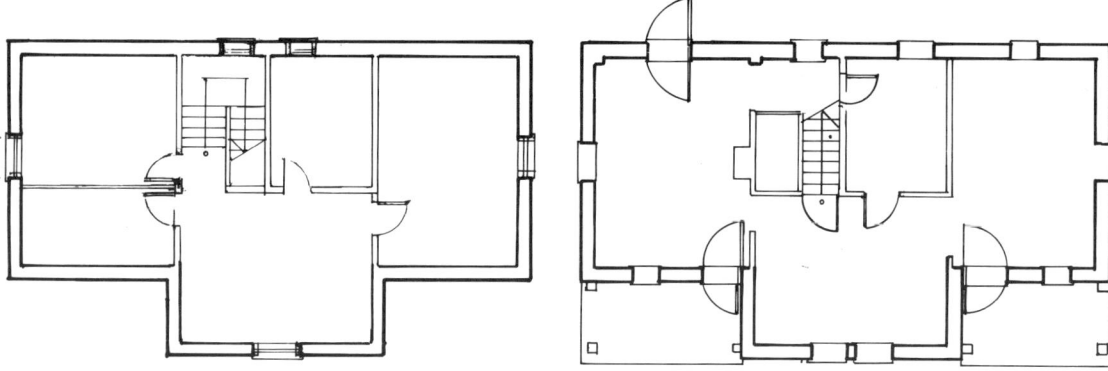

councils in 1842. The editor of the Bytown *Gazette* commented in 1843, "the great cause for the establishing of Municipal Councils, and empowering them with the authority of taxation to a certain extent, was with the view of imposing assessment on Wild Lands held by Absentees and Land-jobbers."[25] The augmented assessment increased the amount of locally-generated money and gave local inhabitants some illusion of control, when in reality the provincial government no longer had to contribute as large a proportion of the funds required for local projects while at the same time it directed local districts how to spend their assessments. Similarly, the municipal corporations Act of 1849 which Reformers such as Robert Bell vaunted as giving local township inhabitants control of their local institutions, was based on a more practical consideration. The Canadian provincial government in 1848-1849 was so heavily in debt that it was unable to borrow sufficient money to underwrite the construction of railroads necessary to make the Canadian economy competitive with the United States. By establishing local municipal government, the provincial Reform administration of Francis Hincks intended to shift financial responsibility for public works projects over to the municipalities. In 1852 the provincial legislature created a provincially administered Consolidated Municipal Loan Fund Act for Upper Canada which allowed municipalities such as Beckwith to raise money through the intermediary of the provincial government.[26] In effect, the meeting at James Burrow's Franktown inn in December 1852, ostensibly called to discuss building a macadamised or plank road between Smith's Falls and Carleton Place, in reality had been called by Bell and other railway promoters aware of the Municipal Loan Fund legislation who intended to make local municipalities pay for a railway which would boost their private businesses.

Only after construction of the Brockville and Ottawa railway had started, finding no market for their debentures, did Beckwith inhabitants fully begin to appreciate the cost of being railroaded by local capitalists. In November 1855 an additional assessment of three-fourths of a penny was levied on all assessed property in Beckwith to pay the interest due on debentures loaned by the provincial government to the United Counties of Lanark and Renfrew. Any person refusing to pay the additional assessment was liable to have his property seized and sold.[27] It is hardly surprising as late as 1863, with the Brockville and Ottawa railroad not yet reaching the Ottawa River that Beckwith inhabitants grumbled over the heavy railway tax they were obliged to pay.

Although the ulterior intention behind granting municipal status to townships such as Beckwith was to provide funding for railroads, it is clear from the spirited nomination meetings that municipal government gave inhabitants an illusory sense of being in control of their local institutions. Moreover, municipal government gave Beckwith inhabitants the first sustained sense of holding something in common other than sharing the name of inhabitants of the same township. True, the men of Beckwith had attended militia musters together previously, they had even

Plate 154
The Malcolm Whyte house, lot 26, concession 10, Beckwith, built ca. 1875, as photographed in June 1983, with a floorplan (opposite) drawn by Robert W.J. Moore. This house was one of four or five modest imitations of Springside Hall (Plate 153) to be built in rural Beckwith during the 1870s. From the mid 1870s to the 1910s brick replaced stone as the building material for the more ambitious houses in Beckwith and Carleton Place.

travelled in contingents to elections at Perth, and there had been an annual township meeting at which town wardens were appointed to look after local roads, schools and agricultural regulations. But in all of these Beckwith was simply a geographic contingent of a larger body whether it was the third regiment of Lanark militia, or the electoral riding of Lanark, or yet again the Bathurst district council. The new common interest that municipal government gave Beckwith inhabitants[28] was partly due to improved transportation between northern and southern concessions thanks to the railroad, due to the politicising of local council business by the *Carleton Place Herald*, and due to the real power which the municipal council wielded, even though it did so within the narrowly circumscribed bounds set by the provincial government. The strong jockeying between the geographic, religious and ethnic parties in the township indicates that Beckwith inhabitants gained a fuller recognition of the rest of the township. The unified focus that municipal government promised to give Beckwith inhabitants was shown by the unanimous vote in favour of the Brockville and Ottawa railway in 1853, the almost unanimous support of an 1863 nomination meeting granting four hundred dollars to the relief of starving cotton factory workers in Lancashire, England,[29] and the construction of a township hall at Black's Corners in 1857.[30]

The location of the township hall at Black's Corners reveals that municipal government in Beckwith was unable to overcome the various local divisions and indeed it may even have contributed to localise them further. Siting the township hall was a sensitive issue, with schoolmaster Johnston Neilson suggesting in February 1851 that if it were built in Carleton Place, it should be large enough to suit public needs so that it could be used as a news or reading room as well as a lodge room by various organisations in the village.[31] In September 1852 the *Carleton Place Herald* accused reeve James Burrows "no doubt with a view to his own profit as a Tavern Keeper {of] prevail[ing] on the majority of the Council to accept a building adjoining his Tavern for a Town Hall; so as to get the Town Meetings &c. to be held at Franktown."[32] The township council wisely continued to meet alternately at Franktown and Carleton Place until 1857 when John Roberts and Bryce McNeely, both from northern concessions, moved that a town hall be built "as near the centre of the Township as practible, taking roads and other conveniences into consideration.[33] The site at Black's Corners was by no means geographically central, but it was at the centre of Beckwith population. When the township was divided into two provincial electoral districts in 1869, subdivision one included the seven southern concessions and lots one through 22 of concession eight whereas subdivision two filled half the same area of land in the northern four concessions and the remaining five lots of concession eight.[34] Once Carleton Place separated from Beckwith in 1870, polling subdivisions reverted back to a more even geographical balance between the southern six concessions and the northern six concessions.[35] Despite the lack of overnight accommodation and despite not being the geographical centre of the township, Black's Corners was the only acceptable compromise between Franktown and Carleton Place. The inexpensive frame structure that was built contrasted with ambitious stone structures in neighbouring townships, suggesting that it was intended only as a temporary structure until a more permanent town hall might be built either in Carleton Place or Franktown."[36]

Around the Beckwith council table on a raised platform inside the new town hall, after the excitement of nomination meetings had died down, a certain unwritten, unspecified *modus operandi* took place. Unlike municipal elections in the twentieth century where separate candidates ran for the positions of reeve and deputy reeve, all candidates in Beckwith between 1850 and 1880 ran as councillors. The five candidates receiving the most votes were elected, and at their first meeting the councillors appointed a reeve from among themselves. Then, every year after the reeve and councillors were sworn in, a peculiar formality occurred. The newly-appointed reeve would nominate someone for office "on his part" and his recommendation without exception would be put down by one of the councillors. This ritual after every municipal election of defeating the reeve's inaugural motion appears to have been an enduring reminder to reeves that they were elevated to their position by the other councillors and, by implication, could just as easily be demoted. It may also have been a no less subtle reminder that if municipal government was going to work in Beckwith, it could only work through a consensus of councillors, divided as the township was otherwise by ethnicity, religion and geography. Hence, although northern Beckwith with its concentration of fertile soil and Carleton Place provided the majority of reeves, they enjoyed office at the discretion of councillors representing all parts of the township.

As a municipality Beckwith faced a greater variety of responsibilities than had the town wardens in the 1830s and 1840s. The municipality levied and collected an assessment on property, appointed pathmasters, pundkeepers and fenceviewers, but it also paid teachers' salaries, built schools, regulated the number of taverns and shops selling liquor, defined moral standards, surveyed new roads, built bridges, financed railways, laid down sidewalks in villages, controlled weeds, regulated fence standards, regulated and channelled drainage, took responsibility for health standards, declared public holidays, provided relief to the elderly and to indigents unable to earn their living or care for themselves, sought shelter in asylums for those with disabilities, opened streets in villages, financed school libraries, provided arms and a drill hall for militia

Plate 155
"Ross Dhu," the residence and newspaper printing establishment of James C. Poole, later the home of David Gillies, Carleton Place, built 1870, as photographed ca. 1913. It was at this location that the Carleton Place Herald was published between 1850 and 1883. Poole as an Irish-origin Methodist lived next door to the brick Wesleyan Methodist church built in 1871 that replaced an 1831 frame church on the same site. This church was purchased by the Baptists in 1889, after the Methodists moved to a larger stone church in the newer part of Carleton Place, south of the Mississippi. National Archives of Canada negative no. PA-135227.

volunteers and offered support to the families of the men away guarding the frontier from the Fenian menace. The common complaint that the cost of providing and administering these services gave rise to should not be readily discounted as a source of unity for the people of Beckwith after mid-century.

Despite its central control of finances, the appointment of a multiplicity of officers to local positions of authority may well have offset any unifying tendency of municipal government, and indeed bolstered the emergence of more localised identities. There were so many local and for the most part unpaid positions under the jurisdiction of the municipal council, that by no stretch of the imagination could one speak of a distance between those who governed and the electorate. Indeed, among the population of Beckwith by the early 1860s it was barely easier to find a household head who had not been appointed to fill some municipal station than to find one who had. After all, municipal stations included one reeve, four councillors, one township clerk, one assessor, one tax collector, one superintendent of education, three inspectors of houses of public entertainment, seven pundkeepers, six fenceviewers, 34 pathmasters, and three trustees in each of the dozen school sections — a total of ninety positions all found within a population in which there were only 381 heads of families in 1861. There is no question that all of these offices carried with them some degree of status, since the persons so appointed were implicitly competent, trustworthy, were esteemed by their neighbours, and somehow had attracted the notice of the township council.

The very subdivision of Beckwith into twenty or more statute labour districts and into a dozen school sections at the very same time the villages and hamlets of Franktown, Ashton, Prospect, Gillies' Corners, Black's Corners, Tennyson and Scotch Corners emerged, served to localise areas of the township. This was particularly true for the school sections, as schoolhouses provided a focus for community life in which activities ranging from political meetings to school concerts were held. As groups of men from each statute labour division worked together in groups on their local roads, in much the same way that they mutually harvested crops together, it was only natural that comparisons and contrasts with the work done in adjacent districts should occasionally spur sectional jealousies. Similarly, there were rivalries between school sections over the size and quality of schoolhouses, and over the land which belonged to each section. The concentration of Irish and Scottish-origin inhabitants was a significant component of these sectional jealousies, with Irish inhabitants predominating in school sections 2, 3, 4 and 10; the Scottish a majority in school sections 5, 6, 8, 9 and in the union section at Tennyson; and the two ethnic communities were evenly divided in school sections 1, 7, 11 (later 14) and 12 (Plate 157).

The concentration of Irish and Scottish inhabitants in Beckwith made it inevitable that one of the two ethno-religious groups would be predominant in most of the school sections. The township school superintendent, the Reverend Robert G. Cox reported in 1858, "Most of the schools under my charge are opened and closed with prayer. In some, the English church Catechism is taught, (that is where all are Church of England children); in others, where they are all Presbyterian the Westminster Catechism is taught, and in all, I think, without exception, the Scriptures are read and the Commandments taught."[37] The degree to which school sections reflected and possibly emphasized ethnic division in Beckwith is revealed by attempts to be removed from one school section to another. In February 1864, for example, Scottish-origin John Cram requested the township council to be detached from school section No. 11 which was evenly divided between Irish and Scottish inhabitants, and attached to S.S. No. 9 in which 25 of the thirty families were Scottish.[38] In December 1869 Scottish-origin inhabitants John, Duncan and Peter McGregor and John Carmichael petitioned to have their property removed from school section eleven and attached to section eight in which there were sixteen Scottish and three Irish families.[39] Further evidence of ethnic-based jealousy and division between sections is shown by the pattern of special assessments levied on sections, with Irish-dominated S.S. No. 4 in the eastern corner alone being levied a special assessment in the early 1850s, then followed by Scottish-dominated sections 8 and 9, so that by 1855 the municipal council was levying a special assessment in nine of the thirteen school sections.[40] The holding of an annual general public competition of all scholars in Beckwith schools in the late 1860s and 1870s for prizes in the form of books was a more positive aspect of the rivalry between school sections, but it contributed significantly to the localised identities that prevented a common community identity emerging in Beckwith.[41]

The emerging localised rivalries between school sections were in part due to the disparate wealth and population of each section. Despite the push by educational reformers for free schools, a system in which all property in a school section was taxed and education freely offered to all children, many Beckwith schools failed to live up to the improving influence that had been hoped for. A correspondent of the *Carleton Place Herald* in 1858 offered a tour of one such school:[42]

> It is about half past ten o'clock A.M. as we approach.... What is this? — half a dozen girls outside the house scampering round playing "hide & go seek." Their healthy faces and robust forms seem to indicate that their morning[']s mental exercise has hardly rendered such early relaxation necessary. We enter. We are greeted by an elderly man rather slovenly attired; and stared at vacantly by a couple of dozen pupils who are seated around indiscriminately without any apparent order or regularity. The[re] does not seem to be any definite plan of operations going on, for some are writing, others cyphering, some reading, several reading and we perceive that a crooked stick stationed near the door is in constant requisition as a passport for boys and girls who pass in and out by threes and fours, bearing the said stick with them as they retire, as a m[e]mento of their departure and replacing it on their return. We now turn our attention to the

Plate 156
The store, residence and outbuildings of Alexander Stewart on lot 14, concession 9, Beckwith near Black's Corners, as photographed in June 1983. 'Merchant Sandy' was just one of nine Alexander Stewarts who lived in Beckwith at the same time in the mid-Victorian era. The others, as locally distinguished, were the widow's Sandy, soldier Sandy, big Sandy, Sandy's Sandy, shoemaker Sandy (at Franktown), Sandy F., Sandy-on-the-hill (near Ashton), and blacksmith Sandy. Merchant Sandy ran a general store in the front room of his house, and brought in lumber from the sawmill operated by his sons in McNab Township. The ruins of a lime kiln on the property and a dry stone structure for storing ashes brought in as payment for goods suggest the varied operations Stewart presided over and the persistence of barter in rural Beckwith. See also Plate 220.

> furniture and find it not too liberally provided. We glance at an unusually dirty floor and enquire if a broom could not be provided, and are informed that there is a broom now on the premises which is presently dragged forth from its retirement beneath one of the desks. We perceive a heap of bonnets in one corner and a pile of caps and mittens in another and hint at the desireableness of procuring a few wooden pins or nails that they may be hung up with neatness and regularity.

The poor physical conditions of many Beckwith schools, it turned out, mirrored the miserable quality of instruction.

> We examine the reading classes, and find pupils in the fourth and fifth books, who would find it difficult to master the second and third. We find girls who will soon be young women, reading in the sixth book who are utterly unconscious of the uses of the comma, and do not know the name of the round dot placed at the end of a sentence. The pupils generally are intelligent and quick to learn, were they but properly directed, but left almost entirely to themselves, their progress is scarcely perceptible. They are quick at Mental Arithmetic, but know nothing of the principles on which its rules depend. The teacher excuses himself for not having taught them

Troy and other weights on the ground of their inutility, and has taught them very little of anything else. There is no grammar class[,] no geography class, no zeal or enthusiasm on the part of either teacher or scholars. They are a set of mere drones, drivelling away the glorious days of youth which should be diligently occupied in gathering rich stores of learning and knowledge. There is no exaggeration in this picture.

Many factors contributed toward these deplorable conditions. The very inadequacy of most schoolhouses and their furnishings was a significant handicap to good instruction. Many teachers suffered from drinking,[43] and when even the teacher at Beckwith's largest school in Carleton Place in 1853 was dismissed "in consequence of his immoral character",[44] the rural schools of Beckwith with their smaller assessment bases could hardly expect to escape hiring their share of incompetents. The ranks of those seeking to teach rural Beckwith schools included[45]

several young men who, after gliding through a shallow course of collegiate or grammar school studies, and finding themselves entirely unfit for any profession, impose themselves on the illiterate dupes of rural districts as shining ornaments to enlighten and direct the mental qualities of blooming youth. People whom accident or misfortune has deprived of means of subsistence, if able to read, write and calculate a little, according to a common expression, "are well adapted for school teaching." To these may be added dismissed clerks, superannuated tradesmen, drunken, hairbrained and immoral tailors; young ladies in their teens, too vain and stubborn for domestic callings, and old dames whose habits and culture furnish no special training, and whose tastes for youthful endearments have accompanied the delights of the past.

In addition to the poor influence of incompetent and immoral teachers, Beckwith schools were plagued with irregular attendance. At the Carleton Place common school in 1861 it was reported that there were "pupils who have not averaged more than three days in a week during the entire year, and we might say even *less* than that, with truth".[46] In 1852 only three-fifths of Beckwith children between the ages of ten and fourteen attended school, and as late as 1861 a full third of that age group still did not attend school. Even after the 1871 Ontario education Act made it compulsory for all children to attend school, over thirteen percent of children aged ten to fourteen did not attend school that year, and their proportion increased to sixteen percent by 1881 (Table 20).

Why so many children were not attending school was no particular mystery. The editor of the *Carleton Place Herald* in 1868 argued that it was only "the poor, ignorant, and vicious classes who systematically neglect the education of their offspring, even while living under the very shadow of the free school-house."[47] In rural Beckwith the seasonal demands and exigencies of farmwork, depending on the size and fertility of each homestead and the number of children, dictated the amount of time a child spent in school. Children between the ages of ten and fourteen while at the most likely age to be attending school, were large enough to be especially useful at various chores around the farm and yet sufficiently under the influence of their parents to be compelled to stay home. Despite the overall improving trend of a larger proportion of Beckwith children attending school, students between the ages of ten and fourteen declined as a proportion of those attending school before the 1871 education Act. The priority of farmwork in Beckwith meant that children were catching up with their lessons into late adolescence. In May 1857 sixteen year old Elizabeth McCuan alluded to the irregular attendance which was characteristic of the period, remarking "I have been going to school since the 1st of February" and added "there are a good many more big girls going to school too".[48] More than half of the children attending school consistently were under age ten or over age fifteen (Tables 20 and 21).

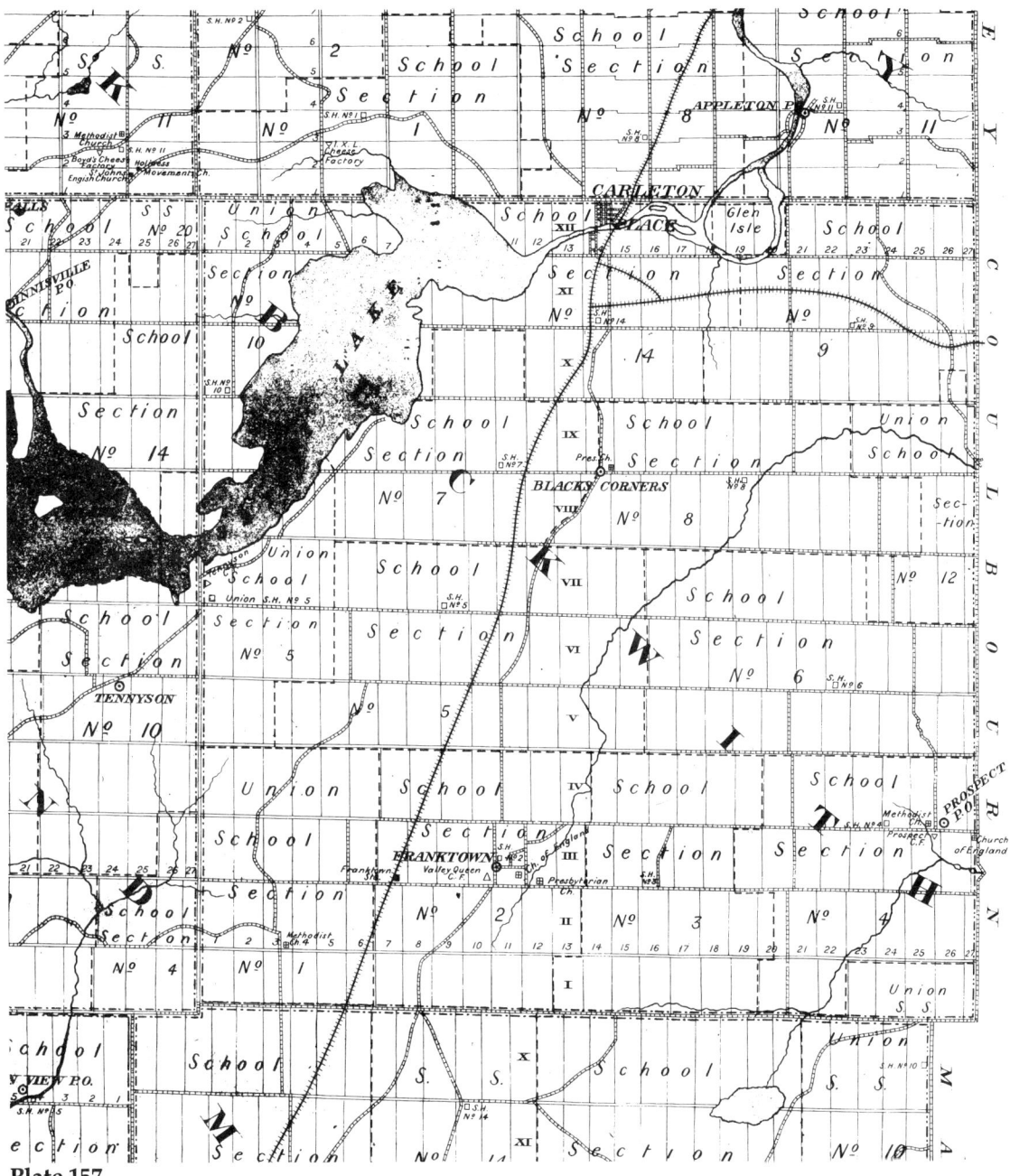

Plate 157
Detail from a map of the county of Lanark, ca. 1895 drawn by L. McMaster and published by the Perth Expositor, showing school sections, schools, churches, cheese factories, roads and railways. School sections and religious congregations increasingly defined the localised identities of Beckwith communities. Congregational identities emerged smoothly enough from the Scottish Presbyterian, Irish Anglican and Irish Methodist make-up of most Beckwith families. The predominant numbers of Irish-origin families in sections 2, 3, 4 and 10, and of Scottish-origin families in sections 5, 6, 8, and 9 and the union school at Tennyson, extended ethnic significance to local school section rivalries even as ethnic traditions were otherwise beginning to dissolve. Heritage House Museum, Smiths Falls.

Educational reformers pushing for compulsory attendance refused to recognise the economic and social constraints that kept many Beckwith parents from sending their children to school. For these reformers the establishment of good schools attended by all children ensured the prosperity of society and an absence of crime. In their view, compulsory attendance would compel children to submit to school discipline, it would create a sense of moral duties, obligation and rectitude among all classes of local society, the lowest as well as the highest. A generation which otherwise would grow up in ignorance and vice, successively gradating from reformatory to prison to penitentiary to gallows, through the influence of the common school could grow up to be an ornament to society. The editor of the *Carleton Place Herald* brooded in January 1868 over the "great mass of poor uneducated childhood of both sexes, who grow up in the worst kinds of debauchery, lewdness, profanity, and godlessness, and who, from their youth to their grave, are nothing but drunkards, loafers, vagabonds, and criminals."[49] There were strong practical reasons for keeping children at home working on the farm rather than attending school. The poorer farmers located on marginal land could not as readily afford to hire labour and needed their children to help them, particularly during spring planting and autumn harvest. Furthermore, some parents felt that the practical experience gained working around the farm was ultimately of greater benefit in preparing a child for life than was the average school curriculum. Moreover, the school as a public institution showed up disparities between wealthy and poor farmers. A teacher commented in the *Herald*, "The poorer a man is...the greater his necessity is to keep his child from school to help him and the less able he is to clothe his child suitably for school".[50] Perhaps the unspoken fear that prompted many parents to send their children to school only two or three months in the year[51] was that if they became too educated they would become dissatisfied with their lot as farmers and wish to move away.

Beckwith inhabitants proved resistant to adopting free schools, despite the enthusiastic description of one such local school presented in the *Carleton Place Herald* in 1858:[52]

[A]t the foot of the hill is to be seen the square walls and cottage roof which constitutes the child's first college and to many, their only one. Order and neatness reign within. The caps and cloaks are properly disposed of. The pupils are classified and arranged according to their proficiency. We find that the lessons are not merely read, mechanically, but that they are *taught*, and to a certain extent *understood* by the children. A large proportion of the school practices writing, and we are surprised at the improvement made even by the beginners. A special portion of time was allotted to this exercise; and the copy books were unusually exempt from blots, mistakes, or "dogs-ears" at the corners. We perceived that the females practiced a sharp running hand, while that of the boys was round and bold; and we were pleased at this mark of discrimination, which is too seldom practised in our country schools. We found a junior gramm[a]r class besides one more advanced and that nearly all the school were convertible into a geography class.... [A]lthough trustees are often at fault for supineness, the chief honor or the greatest blame is due to the teacher, for the success or failure of the school; as he is the mainspring upon which all its motions depends.

Even the most capable teacher could not hope to counteract the influence of family, argued a local superintendent in 1858, since it exerted "a stronger influence upon the youthful mind than any other; and parents mistake when they suppose their duty to be performed when their child has been sent to school a few hours each day."[53]

Most Beckwith parents looked upon attempts to introduce free schools as offering a substantial threat to local sectional control of schools. The Bathurst district council approved of free schools as early as 1848,[54] but for the better part of two decades most Beckwith inhabitants battled against the concept. So bitterly were township inhabitants divided over the question in 1854 that the local

Plate 158
S.S. no. 4 Beckwith schoolhouse at Prospect after conversion into a private residence, as photographed in June 1983. This stone school was built in 1868 to replace an earlier log structure. It is located on lot 24, concession 4, to the west of Prospect to be centrally located within the school section. The building of larger, more permanent schools such as this was one way by which municipal government remade Beckwith, although most of the newer schools were not built until the 1870s or later.

superintendent of schools, the Reverend Duncan Morrison, despaired of their ever being accepted voluntarily and recommended that legislators[55]

> make free schools the law, and no longer...leave the matter an open question. There can be no doubt that the free school system is the system best suited for us, and it is a pity that the friends of it should have to fight the battle annually. This causes more bitterness amongst the different neighborhoods than anything else I know, and before the feeling subsides another annual meeting comes round and the whole is acted over again. I feel assured that had the free school system been made law at first, everything would be going on most harmoniously now, and the country reaping the full fruits of our excellent system of public instruction; but as it is, the country is filled with complaints and almost every neighborhood in it has a minority smarting under real or imaginary grievances.

The Reverend Mr. Morrison could not have been more wrong. Even after Carleton Place, the largest of Beckwith's common schools, voted to adopt the free system in 1860, and after the township superintendent in 1864 reported that "Nearly all the schools have voted to be free," in the next breath he admitted "Lack of interest on the part of the parents has been cited as the chief reason for non-attendance in the Township."[56] A correspondent of the *Carleton Place Herald* in 1870 lamented

Table 20 School Attendance of 10-14 Age Group

	1852		1861		1871		1881	
	No.	%	No.	%	No.	%	No.	%
Males	125	59.0	117	53.9	106	45.5	110	52.3
Females	87	41.0	100	46.1	127	54.5	100	47.6
Total as % of Age Group	212	59.6	217	65.2	233	86.6	210	84.0

SOURCE: *The same sources listed in Table 14.*

Table 21 School Attendance of 5-18 Age Group

	1852		1861		1871		1881	
	No.	%	No.	%	No.	%	No.	%
Males	244	56.2	268	56.3	259	50.8	233	54.6
Females	190	43.8	208	43.6	251	49.2	194	45.4
Total as % of Age Group	434	44.2	476	51.4	510	71.3	427	63.5

SOURCE: *The same sources listed in Table 14.*

that on average only between a fourth and a fifth of school age children attended classes despite the fact that "in many of the sections they have good teachers employed, holding first and second class certificates, and generally kind to the pupils, with a comfortable schoolhouse, and most everything necessary in the school room, such as black-board and maps".[57]

By reputation Beckwith was not progressive nor did it offer leadership to the rest of Lanark County, but reputation alone did not reflect the pragmatic benefit that inhabitants received from local schools. Both Scottish Ramsay to the north and Irish Montague to the south built numerous frame and stone schools during the 1850s, but it was not until the 1870s and later that the log schools in Beckwith began to be replaced by larger more permanent structures. Ramsay not only led the rest of Lanark County but the rest of the province with the size of its school libraries, with over 8,000 volumes in thirteen schools by 1861.[58] In Beckwith, by contrast, the much smaller libraries were reported in 1864 as being little used and the books were in poor condition.[59] In contrast with Montague where 310 persons above age twenty or a tenth of the population either could nor read or write in 1871,[60] there were only twenty people in Beckwith that year who were illiterate. The quality of teachers in Beckwith was not as high as in Ramsay but not as low as in Montague on average. In 1867 three-fourths of the teachers in Ramsay had first class certificates, compared with less than a third in Montague and half the teachers in Beckwith. Parsimonious Beckwith trustees

Plate 159
Central School, Carleton Place, built in 1870, as photographed ca. 1910. Funding the construction of this school was a major issue that contributed to the municipal separation of Carleton Place from Beckwith the same year it was built. The consistent goal of education promoters in the Carleton Place vicinity was the creation of moral and social order among the population flocking into the boomtown in the late 1860s and 1870s. The stolid neoclassic facade of Central School with its dark brown Beckwith limestone quoining behind the jovial group of youths contrasts the grim intent of the education promoters with the immensity of their task. Archives of Ontario negative no. S.7447.

jumped at the opportunity to pay lower wages to women as school teachers. Half the teachers in Beckwith were women in 1867 as compared with two-thirds of Montague teachers that year. The average salary of $191 for male teachers in Beckwith was well below the average in both Ramsay and Montague, but the Beckwith average annual wage of $133 for female teachers in 1867 was midway between the average of $162 in Ramsay and $118 in Montague.[61]

If Beckwith did not share the educational zeal of Ramsay Scottish lowlanders, neither did it share the cultural paranoia which prompted it. A generation after the violence of the so-called

Ballyghiblin riots, the predominant lowlander community in Ramsay still regarded the large cluster of Irish Roman Catholics among them as an unruly and enduringly violent class who posed a continual threat to any hope of order in local society. Their longstanding fear of their Irish Catholic neighbours was further compounded by the arrival of thousands of destitute Irish Catholic Famine immigrants in the late 1840s and early 1850s, many of whom were settled in the interior of Renfrew County northwest of Ramsay. The Ramsay lowlanders listened to the warnings of provincial education superintendent, Egerton Ryerson, that the "physical disease and death which has accompanied [the Irish Catholic] influx among us may be the precursor of the worst pestilence of social insubordination and disorder." The push by educational reformers for free schools in the early 1850s and later for compulsory attendance grew from a concern "that every possible effort should be employed to bring the facilities of education within the reach of the families of these unfortunate people, that they may grow up in the industry and intelligence of the country, and not in the idleness and pauperism, not to say mendicity and vice, of their forefathers."[62] Clearly, while there was still time to act, the children of Irish Catholic settlers and immigrants must be assimilated to a more orderly Scottish Protestant standard of behaviour, and accordingly Ramsay inhabitants spared neither enthusiasm nor money in building and staffing the finest schools in the county during the 1850s. As one Ramsay lowlander pointed out in 1851, if the state "did not ensure virtuous education to youth it eventually might have to pay a higher price for their incarceration as criminals."[63] Carleton Place was the only Beckwith school section in which there was substantial zeal for free schools and compulsory attendance comparable to that in Ramsay, and this was based on the geographic proximity of Ramsay, the strong economic, market and electoral links between the two, and because the *Carleton Place Herald* was the organ in which the rhetoric favouring free schools was expounded.

Rural Beckwith with its sparsely scattered Irish Catholic population suffered from no such cultural paranoia. Indeed, the Irish Anglican and Scottish Presbyterian majority elected James Burrows, an Irish Catholic, to be the second reeve of the municipality in 1852. The lack of enmity towards Irish Catholics was in large part due to the lack of concentrated Roman Catholic settlement, rather than necessarily because the Irish Anglicans and Scottish highlanders were predisposed to be more tolerant of Irish Catholics than were the lowlanders of Ramsay. Just a few miles south of Beckwith's southern boundary, a group of Beckwith-origin Irish Anglicans and Irish Methodists in Numogate school section opposed retaining an illiterate Irish Catholic teacher. They complained to the provincial superintendent of education that the concentration of Irish Catholics in the section "like savages threatened to have the lives of all loyal people who dare oppose them and even beat one man, and had it not been that there was a justice of the peace in the house, they would certainly have done more harm". It is clear that the Irish Protestants of Beckwith had not lost their instinctive fear of Irish Catholic violence, as betrayed by the rhetoric of their sons at Numogate in northern Montague:[64]

> [N]ow sir[, they implored of superintendent Ryerson,] if we are to be trampled upon in this manner by a mob of uncivilized Papists, It is high time that we would be separated from them.... [A]t the annual meeting three of the most violent of the Papists called on the Trustees, and ordered them, not to allow any preaching being Protestant to be allowed in the school-house or they would prosecute them for so doing and If that failed they would pull down the house.

In Beckwith itself there was no more fear of the scattered Irish Catholic minority committing violence than there was of separate schools being built. By the mid 1850s as separate schools became a major issue, the Irish and Scottish Protestants of Beckwith became wary of the ultimate goals of Irish Catholics. Daniel McCuan noted on a scrap of paper in 1856[65]

Plate 160
Elmstone School, Beckwith school section no. 5, built in 1873 on lot 9, concession 7, as photographed ca. 1910. The stone and brick schools that replaced older log buildings from the 1870s on were overwhelmingly presided over by young unmarried women. The large windows in the side walls suggest the improved facilities in some Beckwith school sections, but well into the early twentieth century many children were kept home from school when they were needed to labour on the farm. Photograph courtesy of John and Verna McEwen.

(There is to be a convention at Buffaloe by the papists for the purpose of bringing papists from the United States to Canada. [I]t is carried on by them as if it were for the good of Irishmen in general but it is believed that it is only the Papists that they want[. T]here has been delegates nominated from Quebec, Montreal, Brantford, Hamilton and Toronto. I believe every one of them are Papists[.]) (They are getting on fast the sly papists.)

Although Beckwith lacked the concentration of Irish Catholics that fed the cultural paranoia of Ramsay lowlanders, and which in turn nurtured zeal for education reform, both municipalities purchased books for their school libraries through funds raised from tavern licence fees.[66] This was slightly ironic in that the Reform member for Lanark in the 1840s, Malcolm Cameron, who championed free schools in the provincial legislature,[67] was also the foremost advocate of total abstinence from drinking liquor to be found in all of Lanark County.[68] Moreover, Cameron was successful in inducing many of his supporters, especially among the lowlanders in northern Lanark, to become either teetotallers or at least more temperate drinkers. There had been a local temperance movement as early as the 1830s, but the new emphasis on total abstinence from drinking liquor in any form, stemmed from exactly the same cultural paranoia among Reformers about the influx of Irish Catholic Famine immigrants that had prompted the free school movement. A correspondent of the Lanark

Observer who signed himself "A TEETOTALLER" in 1853, argued that the two great causes of human woe were ignorance and alcohol."⁶⁹

> Alcohol produces a prolific crop on the soil of ignorance, because ignorance is most congenial to the growth of every evil; and no chemical combinations of gases could be applied as a profitable manure at all equal to alcohol — none which is so well calculated to excite, exh[i]l[a]rate, inflame and madden the ignorant mind, and none which is so well adapted to draw its victim on to the perpetration of the most deplorable, horrible crimes, which poor deluded man, in the wild delusion of his nature is capable of committing.

By applying tavern licence fees to purchasing books for school libraries, Beckwith and other municipal councils hoped to placate vocal anti-liquor forces, since the books offered a tangible benefit from the sale of liquor.

The campaign against liquor had little support in rural Beckwith in contrast with Carleton Place and Ramsay, but the stream of invective against intemperance continued unabated in the columns of the *Carleton Place Herald*. A succession of organisations including the Sons of Temperance, the Cadets of Temperance, the Independent Order of Good Templars, the British American Order of Good Templars and the Women's Christian Temperance Union along with church-associated groups attempted to induce members of society to stop drinking. The pervasive lack of interest in temperance by the rural Irish Anglican and Scottish highlander majority in Beckwith caused the township council to cease using tavern licence fees to purchase books for school libraries. In 1865 in adjacent Montague Township (largely due to inclement weather which made travel to the polls impossible for most Irish inhabitants) a vocal minority of American-origin inhabitants forced the municipal council there to enact a by-law forbidding the sale of liquor. The Reform editor of the Smith's Falls *Review* seized on this as proof "that the many charges brought against Montague for immorality and intoxication are but groundless aspersions" at Beckwith's expense:⁷⁰

> Comparisons may be odious, yet one strikes us which we cannot refrain from making. Here is old Beckwith, a township principally settled with Scotchmen professing to be a sober, temperate, church-going, God-fearing people, burning and shining lights in the mental darkness of the back-country, yet when the question comes before them of whether they will refrain or banish from their midst the demoralizing scourge, their answer is to this effect, Na, na. Shame on you Beckwith! Montague shines beside you in spite of all your pretended piety and morality.

Rural Beckwith did not begin to manifest any significant interest in the movement until the closing decades of the nineteenth century, but well before 1880 temperance had shifted from a Reform cause to a moral issue. When James Burrows of Franktown made out his will in January 1864, the scars of the repeated scourging by the *Carleton Place Herald* against a tavernkeeper acting as reeve were evident. After selling liquor for a generation, Burrows gave it as his "desire and wish that none of my Family or wife shall sell any spirituous liquors, in the Village of Franktown or vicinity, after my decease, and that no spirituous liquors be used at my funeral."⁷¹

As rural Beckwith attempted to resist the Reform-based agenda emanating from Carleton Place and Ramsay,, a major social transformation within the township was the emergence of villages and hamlets as service and retirement centres between 1851 and 1880. The growth of Carleton Place from a village of 500 persons to a separate municipality with four times the population is discussed in the next chapter, but at this point the development of Beckwith's rural villages and hamlets is briefly considered.

Plate 161
The James Scott farmstead, lot 20, concession 5, Beckwith, as photographed in June 1983. Beneath the respectable veneer of brick added ca. 1900 is a large mid-nineteenth century log farmhouse. The brick veneer like the vergeboard detail at the peak of the front gable was an attempt to make an older vernacular style of house fit in with the large brick houses being built locally in the late Victorian and Edwardian eras. Beckwith farmers became concerned to build as elaborate houses as their town cousins to keep their children interested in staying on the farm.

Franktown, of course, had been planned as the major centre in Beckwith from the beginning of settlement but was a signal failure at developing into a village before mid-century. A traveller remarked in 1850:[72]

> A most deserted looking, bleak, mournful spot is this village of Franktown. It is hard to conjecture what inducement was held out for the establishment of a village here. The few houses to be seen are built on the borders of an open common, which seems from its sterile appearance to have been brought to the surface since the command went forth to the earth to bring forth fruit. As if, however, to do work worthy of reward, a church steeple stands solitary and alone in its centre, like a ship among the breakers, erected doubtless by a faithful few in order to carry out the enthusiasm of the inspired ancient "Barren plains, and Mountains praise ye the Creator." This place as I am told, is one of the old military settlements, and its failure like most other military villages, is one more proof of the assertion, that man is in a great degree the creature of habit. "The tired soldier" in his youth, "bold and brave" — whose soul is wrapped up in the memory of the scenes, the toils and dangers of bye gone days makes not an energetic enterprising settler. It cannot be reasonably expected. — 'Tis true that occasionally there are some who gifted with stronger minds and more vigorous frame, become active citizens, but these form the exceptions.
>
> In Franktown there is a Post Office and a Store. There are also two Taverns, in which establishments there is the greatest possible room for improvement.

Lovell's *Canada Directory* of 1851 confirmed the seeming listlessness of Franktown, listing only Austin Allen, waggonmaker; James Bowles, carpenter; James Burrows, general store and hotelkeeper; John Hughton, general store and tavernkeeper; Robert Lever, waggonmaker and chair factory; George Nesbitt, medical doctor, and clergymen James Padfield and John Smith as the nonagricultural occupations.[73] In the vicinity of Franktown there was a larger variety of services available as the 1852 census readily reveals (Appendix 23). Behind doors in 1850 Franktown was not quite so listless. The proprietors of the Bytown *Orange Lily and Protestant Vindicator* ominously grumbled about "some irregularity in the transmission of the "LILY," through the Post office...at Franktown [and warned] if we hear any further complaints from our Subscribers, we will be obliged to lay the matter before the Post Master General."[74] In March 1850 an agent from the customs branch of the Inspector General's department at Bytown was sent to Franktown "to endeavour to put a stop to the large contraband trade carried on in this section, to the great injury of the honest trader."[75] At the shop of James Burrows he sized "Sundry casks of high wines, boxes of tea and tobacco...as smuggled Goods"[76] and hauled them to Bytown where "while passing through Upper Town, some person or persons obstructed the passage of the sleighs, which obstruction resulted in [the agent] Mr. McAlpine lodging an information against Mr. James Burrows,... charging [him] with assault and attempt to rescue."[77]

Franktown threw off its sluggishness in 1853 with the promise of being on the line of the Brockville and Ottawa railway. Charles Rice, the editor of the *Bathurst Courier*, approvingly commented on the change:[78]

> FRANKTOWN. — There has been a great improvement in this place since I visited it last — some ten or twelve years ago. — Quite a number of new houses have been erected, and it has quite a village-like appearance. The greatest improvement, however, has been made by Mr. Burrows, Jackson's stone house was the best in the village; but it is now completely eclipsed by the large and commodious two story Hotel erected by Mr. Burrows, and he has finished and furnished it inside in a style elegant enough to accommodate the Governor, if he should ever travel this way; and "mine host" is courteous and obliging, not forgetting "mine hostess." The traveller can here make himself as comfortable as at home.

When the railway came through in 1859 the inhabitants of Franktown included Anglican clergyman the Reverend Ebenezer Morris; physician George Nesbitt; cabinetmakers John Edwards and Robert Leaver: carpenters James Bowels and John Edwards; coopers Samuel Flagg and William Nesbitt; storekeepers Robert Cavenagh, James Burrows, Robert Ferguson and Catherine Jackson; hotelkeepers James Burrows and John Hughton; postmaster and township clerk Ewen McEwen; shoemakers Thomas Clerk, Michael Murray and Thomas Roche; blacksmiths Matthew Anderson and Thomas Griffin; tailors Duncan Stewart and a Mr. Duncan, and a tanner named Garvey.[79]

Unfortunately for the expections of Franktown boosters, when the railway came through it was built more than a mile west of the village. This gave rise to the myth that the railway had killed Franktown, or at least killed its chances of growing. In fact, it was only with the coming of the railway that Franktown blossomed into a village. Regardless of whether the Franktown railway station was located a mile from the village or on one of its few streets, Franktown as a landlocked location, lacking waterpower, with no mineral resources nearby, and surrounded by poor land had no realistic hopes of becoming a manufacturing centre and very limited prospects for growth as a service centre to the local farming population. The coming of the railroad put Franktown in touch with larger centres, and in the short run helped it to attract more business from the local population by being the local centre in southern Beckwith where horses were left when people took the train to local towns or to distant cities. As a result, as the focal point of local society, tradesmen and artisans increasingly moved into the village, contributing to its growth rather than residing scattered among the rural

Plate 162
Reverse side of banner of Loyal Orange Lodge no. 48, Carleton Place. This design, believed created in the 1860s, incorporates the motto 'In Memory of William the III, 1690, Aughrim, Derry and the Boyne.' The crown above William's head compares with those on contemporary St. Patrick's society banners, reflecting the common emphasis of Irish Catholics and Irish Protestants in the Beckwith vicinity on being loyal to the Crown. The lines beneath William's steed read
TO WILLIAM THE GOOD AND GREAT OUR CANADA OWES A MIGHTY DEBT.
May heaven still protect the sons of Roses
Whose Fathers ventured o'er,
For us they stood both fire and blood
Could mortal man do more?
This verse implies that Beckwith Irish Anglicans were aware of their seventeenth century English origins and increasingly identified themselves as being English rather than Irish from the 1860s on. Loaned courtesy of Loyal Orange Lodge no. 48, Carleton Place, through Eldon Henderson.

population. As the local population increasingly focused on going to Franktown to have horses shod, to carouse, to see physicians, to purchase barrels, and to ride the train, they increasingly purchased items. The increasing volume of purchases and the enhanced accessibility of Franktown merchants to suppliers in larger centres combined to increase the variety of general merchandise for sale in Franktown, which in turn led to increased local purchasing. Franktown became home to a number of retired farmers living in small houses who watched the world rumble by, with trains collecting and dispersing passengers while local traffic clattered along in waggons and carriages. In 1863 Franktown boasted some fifty buildings to only forty at Ashton, despite Ashton possessing water-power to drive a mill.

Franktown's development as a village during the 1850s and 1860s drew on a number of strengths. Its remoteness from larger centres on roads that were described as unfit for a corpse to travel meant that a large section of southern Beckwith and northern Montague naturally looked to it as a social centre. Ashton, by contrast, was half the distance that Franktown was from Carleton Place, which meant that although a farmer like Daniel McCuan went to the post office at Ashton because it was closer, his family marketed and shopped in Carleton Place because it was larger. Franktown was where every other Beckwith municipal council meeting was held from 1850 to 1857, and as the home of township clerk and treasurer Ewen McEwen from 1850 to 1880, a substantial amount of business and numbers of visitors were drawn to the village hotels. In the 1850s John Hughton built a large stone hotel to outclass that of James Burrows.

Efforts to make Franktown larger often served to emphasize its limitations. In May 1865 the township council initially complied with a petition from James Jackson and 23 other inhabitants "praying the Council to cause the Streets in the village of Franktown to be properly opened up according to the original Survey thereof.[80] A month later the council informed the Franktown delegation that since the opening of streets was a local improvement and was "not for the general convenience of the Rate payers within the Municipality" it recommended "that those parties who particularly desire that said improvement do voluntarily pay for the survey."[81] When 29 Franktown inhabitants petitioned Beckwith for $200 to build a sidewalk from the school to the centre of the village, the council refused to grant even a quarter of the amount.[82] Even when the Orange lodge at Franktown managed to attract a large twelfth of July celebration in 1859, it only served to show up the limitations of Franktown as contrasted with regional towns. The editor of the Perth *Courier* commented:[83]

> The County Procession was held this year at Franktown. Lodges...from Perth, took the [railway] cars, and were joined at Port Elmsley and Smith's Falls by large numbers of the brethren. — The cars were decorated by evergreens, and presented a very fine appearance. Some nineteen Lodges were represented at Franktown, and the beautiful banners gave the large procession a very animated and cheering appearance. The County Master appeared as King William, and was splendidly dressed, and looked well at the head of the men.
>
> At one o'clock the exercises were opened on the platform in the Grove at Franktown.... The addresses occupied over three hours, and yet the large audience kept its position, attentively listening to the various gentlemen who addressed them.... The day was oppressively hot, and the supplies of refreshments on the ground were in great request. Both Hotels at Franktown were crowded to overflowing, and not able to attend to all the numerous calls for dinner made by the members who visited Franktown. Such large gatherings of people require some place of meeting where there are better means of entertainment than Franktown affords — though all was done that could be done by Messrs Houghton and Burrows to accommodate.

The Orange hall and the hotels were not alone in making Franktown a service centre for much of southern Beckwith. In addition to the increasing concentration of tradesmen and artisans in the village, the church, the 1848 stone school which was replaced by a frame structure in 1868, a Presbyterian church built in 1870, and the post office operated by Ewen McEwen kept the village a

Plate 163
Certificate of membership in Victoria Temperance Loyal Orange Lodge, Kingston, 1861, for the Reverend John May from Beckwith. In contrast with the lack of interest in temperance among Beckwith Orangemen, when John May attended university in Kingston he found a new emphasis on limiting liquor consumption in lodges there. Within a decade even Beckwith Orangemen began to curtail liquor at lodge meetings, as they attempted to present a new image of Orangeism as a moral institution. They were responding to the Scottish-origin lowland Reformers of northern Lanark led by Malcolm Cameron who used temperance to lend respectability to their campaign and implicitly show up the violence and drunkenness of the Orange lodges that politically were an organisational base for local Conservatives. South March Loyal Orange Lodge, through Bruce Elliott.

vibrant local centre. Increasingly, as Carleton Place grew, and with the Franktown railway station a mile away, village inhabitants felt as if they had been passed by, and only briefly, accidentally attracted attention such as when two trains crashed outside Franktown in February 1880.[84]

The village of Ashton developed on the boundary between Beckwith and Goulbourn in the 1840s. It did not enjoy the advantage of Franktown of being planned by military authorities, and it did not benefit from being divided between two municipalities. Ashton did benefit from geography. On the southeastern half of lot 27 in the ninth concession of Beckwith the landscape dropped abruptly to make the Jock River a source of power. The location was sufficiently remote from central Beckwith and from Carleton Place to give rise to local stores and local churches, especially since there were no villages or hamlets in western Goulbourn to attract business away. Moreover, although the railway between Carleton Place and Ottawa passed as close to Ashton as did the Brockville and Ottawa railway to Franktown, it was constructed a decade later after Ashton had developed to its maximum possible size as a service centre. The Ashton vicinity was populated predominantly by Perthshire Presbyterians on the Beckwith side and by Tipperary Irish Anglicans in western Goulbourn. As late as 1914 a visitor to Ashton, noted the contrast between "the soft Irish brogue of the Irish voices of Goulbourne and the gutteral diction of the imperishable Scots from Lanark county".[85]

The emergence of Ashton as a local centre is generally agreed to begin with the arrival of English immigrant John Sumner in 1840. Sumner was born in 1814 near a village called South End on the banks of the Thames in Essex, and finished his education at Christ's Hospital, a school in London at age 16. In 1832 he migrated to Canada, clerked in stores at Montreal, Kingston and Bytown before coming to clerk at the stores of Robert Bell and Andrew Thompson at Carleton Place. Sumner and his family resided in Ottawa where he had other business interests during the 1840s, but from 1849 to 1859 he lived in Ashton.[86] According to local tradition, Sumner "erected the first mill in the place; engaged rather extensively, for that day, in lumbering,"[87] but his small water-powered mill did not operate long. "Mr. Neil Stewart built a small steam mill in its place but there was too little lumber to be much supply." Sumner operated a potash works[88] on such an extensive scale that at one time four labourers (Patrick Reilly, Sam Lyons, Patrick Hawthorn and George Douglas) were employed at a daily wage of fifty cents. A Mr. Doherty eventually took over the potash business,[89] but Sumner easily remained the most conspicuous inhabitant of Ashton. According to tradition, the hamlet at first was called Mount Pleasant,[90] and later Sumner's Corners, but when a post office was established in 1851 with Sumner as the first postmaster the village assumed the name of Ashton — reputedly based on Sumner's potashery business.[91]

John Sumner was a sharp-eyed postmaster, as was reflected by a comment in an 1857 letter from Daniel McCuan to his brother John in Scotland, "Beware when you send any more newspapers[;] if you write anything on them be sure and put it inside where it may not be detected by the postmasters. John Sumner observed what was in the last and said if he seen any more such like he would charge us with it ."[92] Sumner attracted attention in Ashton, and was described as "a man given to social splendors and who spent money like water.... He was a man of great natural strength, and...the people used to watch him handle barrels and carcasses of pork as a sort of amusement. He never drove less than a team, and never one that wasn't the best." Unlike James Burrows at Franktown, Sumner was never suspected of smuggling, although on one occasion while driving to Ottawa he met a Revenue officer. "The Colonel thought, after he passed the officer, that it might be his store he was seeking.... Wheeling his flyers around he soon overtook the officer, shot past him, and reached his store in time to get possession of his papers which demonstrated his complete innocence."[93] The success of Sumner's store in Ashton may well have stemmed from his exuberant advertising which gave inhabitants of northeastern Beckwith and western Goulbourn the sense that the latest fashions and best produce of the British Empire were imported into Ashton specifically for their benefit. An 1858 advertisement read:[94]

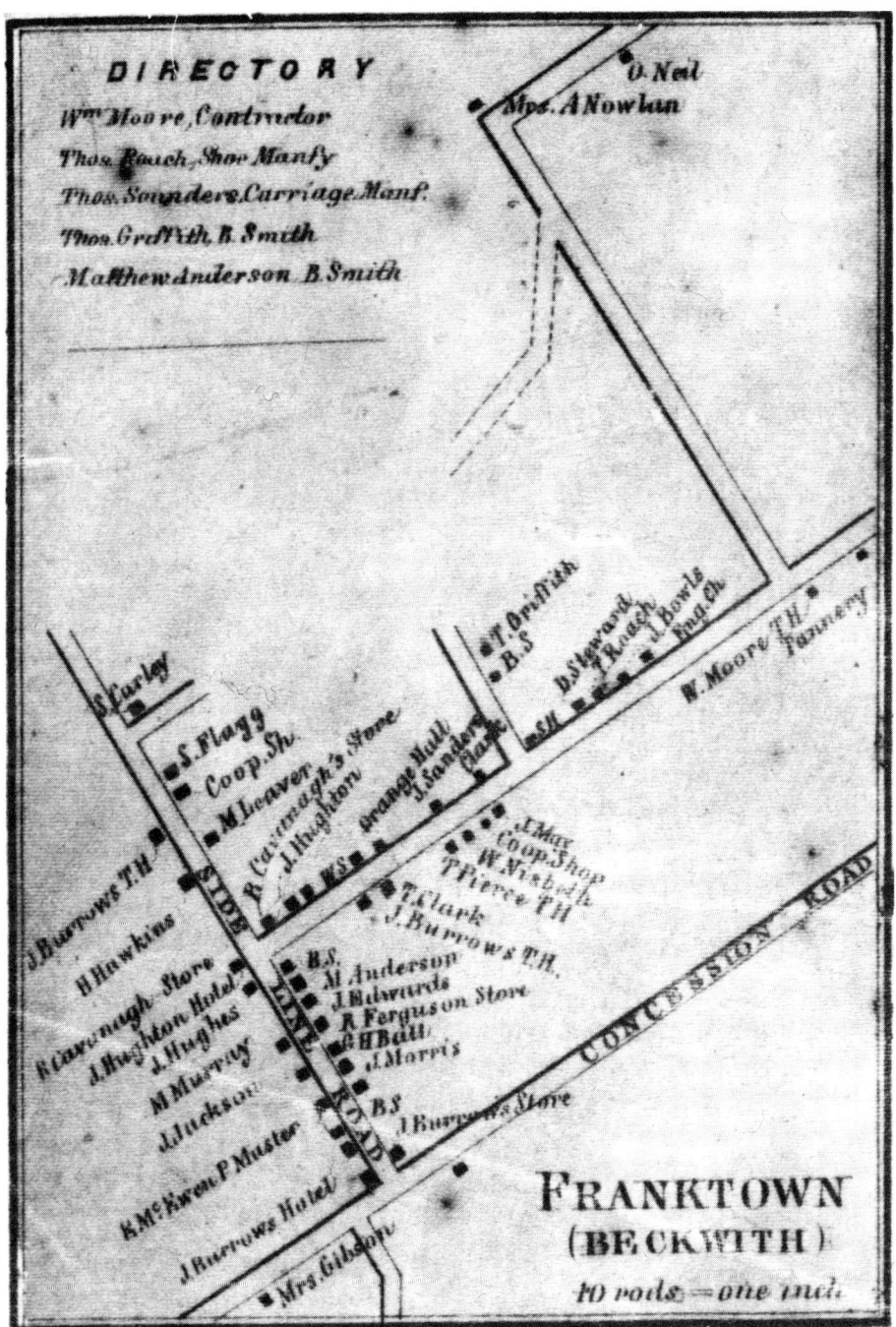

Plate 164
The Franktown inset from Henry F. Walling's map of the counties of Lanark and Renfrew published in 1863 by D.P. Putnam at Prescott. Most of the buildings and businesses shown here were set up in the decade before this map was drawn, ten years during which the Brockville and Ottawa railway was anticipated to run through Franktown, and which passed by in 1859 a mile to the west. The anticipated coming of the railroad had caused Franktown to develop, but the lack of growth after it came gave rise to the myth that Franktown was a railroad-killed village. The initials B.S. stand for blacksmith, S.H. for schoolhouse, and T.H. for tenant house. National Archives of Canada NMC VR/420.

> FIRST SPRING ARRIVALS!!! Per Steamers "EMEU" *and* "CANADA." AT BOSTON. The Subscriber has just received, per the above Steamers the first of his Spring Importations!!! IN LONDON BONNETS, (Latest Fashions,) Plain and Figured Ribbons, AND AN ELEGANT ASSORTMENT!OF PARASOLS, With a large variety of Dresses, and FANCY ARTICLES! Which he offers for sale LOW for CASH.
>
> He will also be receiving from the St. Lawrence River, on the opening of the Navigation, a full and complete assortment of all description of GOODS, Direct from LEEDS AND MANCHESTER, and from the facilities he possesses in buying in the English markets, he flatters himself, the Public on inspection will be satisfied they can buy from him 10 per cent lower than any Shop in this neighborhood.
>
> JOHN SUMNER[.] Ashton, April 18th, 1856.

Once the railway came through Carleton Place in 1859, Sumner left Ashton for the larger market offered by Carleton Place.

Other than for John Sumner's store, potash works and mills, Ashton was more a social than a commercial centre in the 1840s. When the Reverend William Bell from Perth passed through in August 1844 the "Presbyterian church was finished, but the Episcopalian one was but just begun."[95] The Melville Presbyterian Church was not finished inside until 1853,[96] and although named after the Perthshire nobleman who so munificently endowed the Church of Scotland congregation at Comrie, the Ashton congregation served Free Church members in northeastern Beckwith.[97] The congregation of Melville Church grew so significantly that the church had to be enlarged in 1879.[98] The interior of Christ Church Anglican Church was not completed until 1856[99] and it was largely attended by inhabitants of western Goulbourn. Ashton was the site of a log school by the late 1840s, and in December 1851 members of the Ashton Temperance Society proposed holding "one of those interesting meetings termed a 'Soiree'."[100]

With the establishment of a post office in 1851, tradesmen and artisans were attracted to Ashton. In September 1852 George Argue "prepared to commence Tanning on Mr. Shore's creek, near the village of Ashton", expecting to "Tan upon Shares and pay the Highest Price in Cash for Hides."[101] Donald McFarlane kept the only tavern in the village for many years which even the abstemious Reverend John Gourlay described as "a peaceable and quiet house." When John Sumner left for Carleton Place in 1859, his store was taken over by James Conn and his wife Janet Stewart[102] who already operated a store in competition against Sumner. James Conn in an 1856 notice requested those customers whose notes and accounts were due that he would take butter, hides and all sorts of merchantable produce at the highest market prices."[103] John Shore carried on a waggon and carriagemaking business.[104] By 1863 there were some forty buildings, in 1868 the Beckwith section of the village was surveyed,[105] and at its peak in 1879 Ashton was described as[106]

> quite a smart little country village, with many encouraging evidences of material prosperity and healthy improvement, and surrounded by many very fair farms and not a few really fine ones. The business portion of the place is represented by 3 general stores, 3 waggon-shops, 3 blacksmith-shops, 3 carpenter-shops, 1 harness-shop, 2 tailor-shops, 1 tannery, 1 steam grist and saw-mill, with shingle-mill attached. James Conn, the Postmaster, has just erected a very handsome and commodious stone building for a store, at a cost of $3,000. There are 2 fair hotels in the place, 1 school, 1 telegraph office, 2 churches (Episcopal and Presbyterian), and it has a daily mail both ways, off Ashton Station, which is 25 miles from Ottawa.

Some five miles southeast of Ashton on the Beckwith side of the Goulbourn border the hamlet of Prospect developed in the 1850s. Methodists had been meeting at the Kerfoot home since the mid 1820s and from the early 1840s a school gave added focus to the junction of lots 25 and 26 in the third and fourth concessions. Nearby King's Creek offered a seasonal supply of power, but the major

Plate 165
Ferrotype of John Hughton's hotel at Franktown, taken ca. 1867. This large stone structure was built in the 1850s in anticipation of the increased business that it was hoped the railway would bring to Franktown. This structure is similar in proportion and detail to the John Nesbitt house (Plate 131). The flat outcrop of limestone on the left in the foreground indicates the poor land that predominated in the Franktown vicinity, providing an increasingly impoverished hinterland for the village even as a service centre for local farmers. The two main roads and the railroad station provided some business for this hotel, as the group of people including the uniformed maid on the second storey gathered on the verandah suggest. The man framed in the front doorway in all likelihood was John Hughton. The ferrotype process does not use a negative, presenting the image backward, hence the downstairs door shown on the left in reality was on the right. Photograph courtesy of Donna and Robert Hughton.

reason for a hamlet emerging here was its location on the main road between Perth and Bytown, sufficiently remote from Franktown and Richmond, at the one point where a road pushed its tortuous course north past the Jock swamp in eastern Beckwith to link up with the northern quarter of the township. In 1853 a post office was established and operated by James Conn who soon left for Ashton. The post office was given the name Prospect, taken from an English plantation estate near Gorey in northeastern Wexford, Ireland, with which some Beckwith settlers were familiar.[107] By 1857 there were 75 inhabitants in the hamlet including postmaster, store and tavernkeeper John Burrows; sawmill owner William James; sawmill operator and carpenter John Scott; carpenters Patrick Devine, James Saunders and William Williams; shoemakers William Baxter and John Tomlinson; blacksmith Joseph Morris; tailor Peter Stewart; schoolmaster Fleming May and Wesleyan Methodist clergyman the Reverend William Coleman.[108] The sawmills of William James and brothers John and Donald Scott were located on King's Creek, southeast of the hamlet. They did sufficient business that Franktown postmaster Ewen McEwen in February 1856 was emboldened to offer for sale the northeast half of lot 25 in the second concession which he described as being "situated near James's and Scott's Saw Mills".[109] The waterpower of the mills was so poor that the upright saw in the Scott sawmill was unable to saw through to the end of a log, and the sawblade in the James sawmill was so slow that it was commonly joked about that it went up in the morning and came down in the afternoon.[110]

Prospect was at its peak in the 1850s and 1860s with two stone churches, a stone school replacing the former log structure in 1868, a post office, a store, tradesmen and a tavern. William Burrows took over the tavern from his brother John, but in 1861 it was destroyed. A correspondent of the Carleton Place *Herald* reported:[111]

> I have to inform you that the Hotel belonging to William Burrows, in Prospect, with sheds and stables, and a new dwelling house in course of erection, belonging to Wm. Reilly, blacksmith, were all destroyed by fire.... The fire was caused by a drunken, worthless character, which Mr. Burrows kept as stable boy, named Bill Simmons. On Sabbath, while he and some others of his bottle companions indulged rather freely, it appears there arose some dispute among them, which ended in a quarrel, and afterwards the fire occurred.

By 1871 Prospect had a peak population of one hundred persons. Nonagricultural occupations in the hamlet that year included innkeeper and postmaster William Burrows, saw and shingle mill owners William H. James and Duncan McGregor, carpenter John McLaughlin, storekeeper George Craig, blacksmith William Riley, shoemakers James Box and John Tomlinson, and justices of the peace Thomas Alcock and Adam Poole.[112]

Trailing in order of size behind the villages of Carleton Place Franktown, Ashton and Prospect were the crossroads centres of Black's Corners, Gillies' Corners, the Cross Keys and Scotch Corners and a number of other named locations that were more names than centres. Black's Corners emerged as a hamlet when early settler John Black opened a blacksmith shop, and endured after the township purchased a plot of land from John Roberts on which to build the municipal council hall.[113] Alexander Stewart is reputed to have opened his store as early as the 1830s. John Black did not remain long at the hamlet site, but Stewart's business flourished to the extent that he built a large stone house with extensive outbuildings. Although the stone house was not listed in the 1852 census, the style of its construction and the size of the kitchen hearth suggest that it was built in the 1830s. In 1855 Stewart advertised "a number of IRON PLOWS of the newest pattern" for sale,[114] and the ruins of a small lime-kiln and a stone building for storing ashes on the property suggest other ways in which he attempted to make money. An 1850 advertisement by Stewart shows how extensive a merchandising and milling operation over which he presided:[115]

> NOTICE. THE SUBSCRIBER, in returning his thanks to his customers, generally, for past favours, begs leave to inform them that he has received his usual supply. Self praise is useless. He invites judges to inspect for themselves. He expects a continuation of their former favours.
>
> He has at his MILLS in McNAB SEASONED PINE, That is, BOARDS *of all kinds* and qualities, fit to be used for any purpose. OAK, BIRCH, BAS[S]WOOD, and MAPLE. Also to his former Stock he has added about one hundred thousand Sawed Shingles, and a large quantity of SAWED LATHS. The whole will be sold very low for CASH or short Approved Credit.
>
> Having his BARLEY MILL new and in good order, he will exchange Pot Barley, and pay CASH for any quantity of good Barley.... All Country produce will be taken in payment till the 1st of February next.
>
> ALEXANDER STEWART. 9th Con. Beckwith, Dec. 4th, 1858.

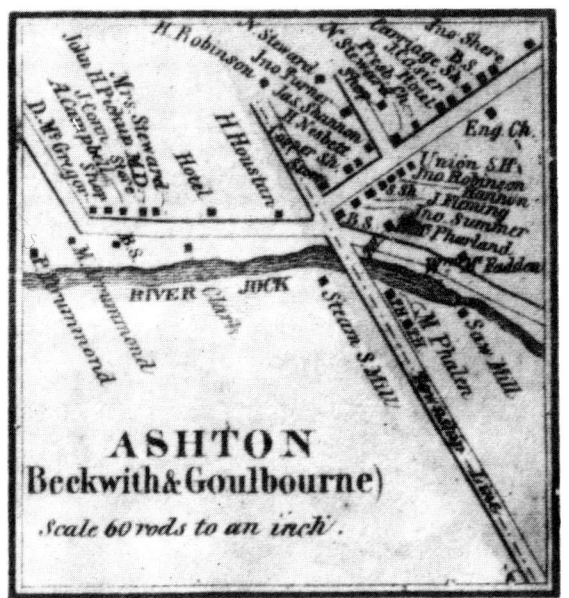 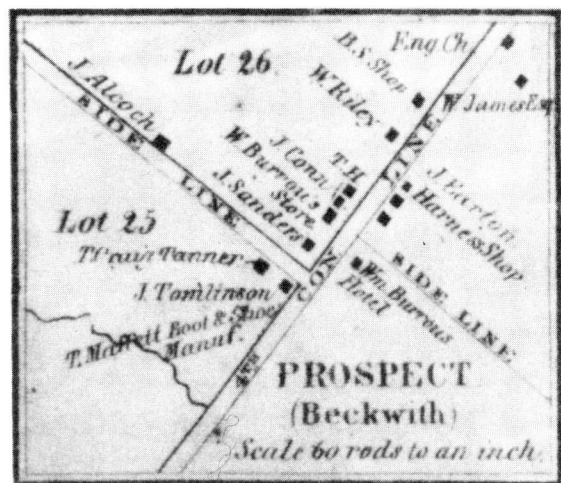

Plate 166
The Ashton and Prospect insets from Henry F. Walling's map of the united counties of Lanark and Renfrew published in 1863 by D.P. Putnam at Prescott. The Beckwith section of Ashton is shown to the left of the township line. Ashton was located in the midst of much more fertile country than was Franktown, and the Jock River provided power to drive one of the two sawmills in the village. The amount of business Ashton attracted as a service centre enabled more substantial residences to be built there than was possible at Franktown. Prospect was a midway stop between Franktown and Richmond, servicing farmers in southeastern Beckwith and southwestern Goulbourn townships. The school and Methodist chapel at Prospect were located slightly west of the hamlet whereas the sawmills were located to the southeast, as shown in Plate 123. National Archives of Canada NMC VR/420.

Stewart's business was so successful by 1852 that his neighbour across the Franktown-Carleton Place road, Newyear Watson offered his half lot (southwest half of lot fourteen in the ninth concession) for sale, extolling the "east corner of the lot joining the cross-road at McKay's Blacksmith's Shop, [a]s a good Stand for a Store, Tavern or other public business."[116] The construction of Knox Free Church at Black's Corners in 1845 not only made it a religious centre, but innumerable concerts and social evenings held in the church attracted other members of the general public.[117] Construction of the township hall for Beckwith across the street from the church ensured that Black's Corners became the municipal centre of the township, but because the hamlet was so close to Carleton Place no post office, no hotel, and no more tradesmen were established there, and consequently few houses were built at Black's Corners before the late twentieth century.

Similarly, the other crossroads centres, in contrast with the villages, were unable to attract a local population. Gillies' Corners with its tavern was joined by a school and boasted the first of Beckwith's cheese factories by 1880, but there was no other population at that crossroads. Isolated Scotch Corners, west of the Mississippi Lake, as late as 1880 boasted only a schoolhouse. The Cuckoo's Nest was simply the name for school section No. 3 east of Franktown; according to one account this name originated in the eccentricities of an early schoolteacher there. Tennyson was established as a post office in 1865 on the border between Beckwith and Drummond immediately south of Mississippi Lake because of the relative remoteness of the area from the post offices at Carleton Place, Perth and Franktown, and was named after the mid-Victorian British poet-laureate

Plate 167
John Porter Sr. standing in the doorway of his blacksmith shop at Prospect beside an American visitor as photographed in 1930. The blacksmith shop at Prospect would prove the second most enduring business in the hamlet, outliving the weaver, the harnessmaker, the shoemaker and the hotelkeeper who earned a living there in 1863. The squared chinked logs testify to the skill developed by Beckwith Irish Anglicans in building with timber, but the traces of whitewash on the exterior also betray the need to disguise the old-fashioned log construction. Note the sign on the far right for King George's Navy. Photograph courtesy of Edna and John Porter.

Alfred, Lord Tennyson.[118] As late as 1880 there was only a school and the post office at Tennyson. The locality where the seventh concession line crossed the Franktown-Carleton Place road in the geographic centre of Beckwith from 1822 until 1869 was a centre of Presbyterian worship but in 1870 the 1834 Church of Scotland stone house of worship there was abandoned for a new frame church at Franktown, after the Carleton Place and area part of the congregation rehabilitated the stone house of worship they had built in 1851 but left unused most of the 1850s and 1860s. The location of the seventh line church was reputedly known as the Cross Keys, a term of uncertain origin, possibly referring to its position at the geographic centre of the township, and known to some as "Ladies Corners" in reference to the genteel aspirations of the wife of the Reverend George Buchanan.[119]

Other names for localities in Beckwith included Elmstone for school section No. 5 on the seventh concession, Hillview for S.S. No. 7 on the western part of the ninth concession line, Ferguson's or S.S. No. 9 in the northern corner of Beckwith,[120] Arklan for the vicinity immediately south of Carleton Place and Glen Isle, and Dundurn for the locality on the tenth concession line east of the Franktown-Carleton Place road where members of the McGregor family built stone houses.[121] Finally, there was "the Derry", a name given to school section No. 6 which comprised the eastern portion of concessions five to seven, and the earliest written reference to which is found in an 1830 entry in the journal of the Reverend William Bell.[122] According to local tradition, when Robert Ferguson's widowed mother came from Perthshire to live with him on the southwest half of lot 23 in concession five, and viewed the groves of ash, oak and birch trees there, she was reminded of the

Plate 168
Black's Corners ca. 1900, as photographed from the west by Annie Elexey Duff. At the centre of this Beckwith hamlet was the stone Knox Presbyterian church built in 1845. To the left of the church can be seen the back wall of the frame township hall built in 1857, with sheds for road equipment to the left. The rural school fairs of the 1920s and 1930s were held in the open space between the township hall and the farmhouse and barns of Fred Scott on the far right. One of the few businesses in Black's Corners other than its cheese factory at the turn of the century was the woodworking shop of James W. Robertson. National Archives of Canada negative no. C-80013.

Gaelic word for a grove of trees — "Derry." A song heard in the vicinity in the late nineteenth century had this chorus:[123]

> Hame, Derry, hame; and it's hame we ought to be.
> Hame, Derry, hame; to our ain countree.
> Where the ash and the oak and the bonnee birchen tree,
> Are all growing green in our ain countree.

The Derry as a Gaelic name and as a rural grouping of farms was one of the few things in Beckwith to remain constant from the era of the first settlers. But even in the Derry, largely isolated as it was by the surrounding swamp, significant change occurred between 1852 and 1880, as local tradesmen left to relocate in villages, as farmers drove their teams either to Franktown or to Carleton Place to take trains to more distant towns and cities, as local post offices increased in number and as villages such as Franktwon, Ashton and Prospect emerged.

The remaking of Beckwith into a municipality at first had given many rural inhabitants a new sense of being in control of their affairs. But as northern Beckwith farmers dominated the township council, and as the initial enthusiasm for the railroad was transformed into a dawning recognition that the creation of municipalities such as Beckwith had simply allowed the Canadian government to tax the local population more heavily to build railways, Beckwith council itself wearily concluded in December 1864 that they "had no alternative but [to] levy and collect the Rail Road tax".[124] The railroad once built tended to serve the interests of Carleton Place rather than those of rural Beckwith, and increasingly township inhabitants found themselves drawn to the growing village on the Mississippi.

In 1867 yet a third level of government, the federal government at Ottawa, was created. Those inhabitants of rural Beckwith who wished to participate in the footraces and to watch the fireworks for which Beckwith council granted 25 dollars "to aid in making a Gala-day of the Birthday of the New Dominion of Canada"[125] on July 1st 1867 had to travel to Carleton Place. The *Herald* accordingly reported:[126]

> The...surrounding country poured its hundreds of people into the village; and enthusiasm, cheerfulness, enjoyment and harmony unmarred by any disturbance or strife were the order of the day. Early in the morning the inhabitants were startled out of their slumbers by the thundering of a cannon.... Footraces, sack races and wheelbarrow races, a torchlight procession and fireworks prolonged the amusement until a late hour, when all the people dispersed and the village sank again into its wonted quiet.

The industrial boom of Carleton Place was yet to come, and when it did the municipal remaking of Beckwith would be complete. It was the municipality of Beckwith that had paid for the coming of the railroad, but it was a separate municipality of Carleton Place that intended to reap the benefits after 1870. As it turned out, rural Beckwith had been thoroughly railroaded by the province of Canada, by local politicians, and not least of all by the ambitious denizens of Carleton Place.

Endnotes

1 OBCMR, By-law 110 of Beckwith township council.
2 *Perth Courier*, 6 March 1868, p. 3, col. 2.
3 Two different sets of statistics about the religious composition of the Bathurst District appeared in the *Brockville Statesman*, respectively on 22 June and 3 September 1839. The latter of the two is proabably more accurate, but both sets of figures serve to point out that Presbyterians and United Church of England and Ireland numbers almost balanced. Had Roman Catholics not been divided among themselves, being guided on the one hand by their clergy to vote for pro-administration candidates who happened to be Anglicans while on the other hand perceiving that these pro-administration candidates enjoyed support from local Orange lodges — a fact which prompted many Catholics to support Scottish Presbyterian candidates who fulminated against the existence of Orange lodges, Roman Catholics in Lanark County would have enjoyed a balance of power in deciding who the successful member of parliament would be.

Denomination	22 June 1839 Figure	3 September 1839 Figure
Presbyterians (including Kirk of Scotland, Seceders, United Synod, Independents, &c.)	8,660	8,933
United Church of England and Ireland	8,239	7,761
Roman Catholics	5,414	5,509
Methodists	1,745	1,802
Baptists	255	264
Other Sects	184	191
	24,497	24,370

4 *Brockville Statesman*, 16 February 1847, p. 3, col. 1.
5 *Perth Courier*, 24 December 1857, p. 2, cols. 1-3.
6 For a more detailed discussion, read Glenn J Lockwood, "Success and the Doubtful Image of Irish Immigrants in Upper Canada: The Case of Montague Township, 1820-1900" in Robert O'-Driscoll and Lorna Reynolds, eds., *The Untold Story: The Irish in Canada* (Toronto: Celtic Arts of Canada, 1988) I:319-341.
7 *Bathurst Courier*, 12 December 1851, p. 2, cols. 2-4.
8 *Bathurst Courier*, 4 August 1854, p. 2, cols. 1-4.
9 *Perth Courier*, 31 December 1857, p. 2, col. 1.
10 *Carleton Place Herald*, 3 July 1861, p. 2, col. 1.
11 Ibid., 17 July 1861, p. 2, cols. 5, 6-7.
12 *Perth Courier*, 19 July 1861, p. 2, cols. 2-3.
13 McCuan family correspondence, 15 July 1861 note of Daniel McCuan; and *Perth Courier*, 26 June 1863, p. 2, col. 5.
14 *Carleton Place Herald*, 8 November 1904.
15 *Carleton Place Lanark Herald*, 27 December 1850, p. 2, cols. 3-4.
16 OBCMR By-law no. 17 of Beckwith township council.
17 Ibid., By-law no. 33.
18 The northern quarter of Beckwith included the village of Carleton Place and can be defined as containing lots 14 to 27 in concessions 7 to 12.
19 *Carleton-Place Herald*, 1 January 1852, p. 2, col. 2.
20 Ibid., 8 January 1852, p. 2. col. 2.
21 Ibid., 22 January 1852, p. 2, cols. 3-4.
22 Ibid., 12 February 1852, p. 2, cols. 4-5.
23 McCuan family correspondence, 5 January 1863 letter from Peter McCuan, Beckwith, to Alexander McCuan, Montreal General Hospital.
24 Lloyd C. Sutherland, *Yearning for Learning* (Smiths Falls, 1980), p. 150.
25 *Bytown Gazette*, 28 September 1843, p. 3, col. 1.
26 Michael J. Piva, "Continuity and Crisis: Francis Hincks and Canadian Economic Policy" in *The Canadian Historical Review* LXVI No. 2 (June 1985), pp. 198-199.
27 OBCMR, By-law no. 82 of Beckwith township council.
28 McCuan family correspondence, 5 January 1863 letter from Peter McCuan, Beckwith, to Alexander McCuan, Montreal General Hospital.
29 Ibid.
30 OBCMR, By-law no. 90 of Beckwith township council.
31 *Carleton Place Lanark Herald*, 21 February 1851, p. 2, cols. 4-5.
32 *Carleton-Place Herald*, 30 September 1852, p. 2, col. 4.
33 Ibid., 14 May 1857, p. 3, col. 3.
34 OBCMR, By-law no. 130 of Beckwith township council.
35 Ibid., By-law no. 137.
36 The stone town hall built in Montague two years earlier was constructed by Franktown contractor, Robert Leaver.
37 *Annual Report of the Normal, Model, Grammar and Common Schools in Upper Canada, for the Year 1858* (Toronto, 1859), n.p., containing the report of the Reverend Robert G. Cox, Beckwith.
38 OBCMR, 25 February 1864 minutes of Beckwith township council.
39 Ibid., 7 December 1869 minutes.
40 OBCMR, By-law nos. 11, 26, 47, 50 and 80 of Beckwith township council.
41 OBCMR, 22 February 1867 and 1 April 1868 minutes of Beckwith township council.
42 *Carleton-Place Herald*, 11 February 1858, pp. 2-3, cols. 7-1.
43 Ibid., 12 February 1852, p. 3, cols. 1-2.
44 OTAR RG 2 Series C-6-C Education Department Records. Assistant Superintendent of Education, Canada West, Incoming General Correspondence, Box 16. 13 August 1853 letter from the Reverend Duncan Morrison, Beckwith, to Egerton Ryerson.
45 *Perth Courier*, 12 January 1866, p. 2, cols. 6-7.
46 *Carleton Place Herald*, 3 July 1861, p. 1, col. 1.
47 Ibid., 15 January 1868, p. 2, cols. 2-3.
48 McCuan family correspondence, 31 March 1857 letter from Elizabeth McCuan, Beckwith, to her brother John McCuan, Bridge of Allan, Scotland.
49 *Carleton Place Herald*, 15 January 1868, p. 2, cols. 2-3.
50 Ibid., 10 June 1868, p. 3, col. 1.
51 Ibid., 16 February 1870, p. 1, col. 2.
52 Ibid., 11 February 1858, pp. 2-3, cols. 7-1.
53 Ibid., 18 February 1858, p. 3, col. 1.
54 Lloyd C. Sutherland, *Yearning For Learning: The Story of Education in Lanark County, 1804-1867* (Smiths Falls: by the author, 1980), p. 163.
55 *Appendix to the Thirteenth Volume of the Journals of the Legislative Assembly of the Province of Canada* (Quebec, 1855), report of the Reverend Duncan Morrison of Beckwith.
56 Sutherland, *Yearning For Learning*, p. 264.
57 *Carleton Place Herald*, 16 February 1870, p. 1, col. 2.
58 Sutherland, *Yearning For Learning*, pp. 196-197.
59 Ibid., p. 264.
60 Lockwood, "Social Structure of Montague Township", p. 100.
61 Sutherland, *Yearning For Learning*, pp. 290, 292.
62 Susan E. Houston, "Victorian Origins of Juvenile Delinquency: A Canadian Experience," *History of Education Quarterly* XII No. 3 (Fall 1972), p. 256.
63 *Carleton-Place Herald*, 20 November 1851, p. 2, cols. 4-5.

64. Glenn J Lockwood, "Eastern Upper Canadian Perceptions of Irish Immigrants, 1824-1868" (unpublished Ph.D. dissertation, University of Ottawa, 1988), p. 392.
65. McCaun family papers, 1856 musing by Daniel McCuan in a notebook.
66. *Carleton-Place Herald*, 30 May 1851, p. 2, col. 6; and Bruce Curtis, "'Littery Merrit', 'Useful Knowledge', and the Organization of Township Libraries in Canada West, 1840-1860", *Ontario History* LXXVIII No. 4 (December 1896), p. 299.
67. Sutherland, *Yearning For Learning*, p. 157.
68. Margaret Coleman, "Malcolm Cameron" entry in Marc La Terreur and Francess G. Halpenny, eds., *Dictionary of Canadian Biography* (Toronto: University of Toronto Press, 1972) X:129.
69. *Perth Lanark Observer*, 30 March 1853, p. 1, cols. 1-3.
70. *Smith's Falls (Canada West) Review*, 9 March 1865, p. 2.
71. OPLRO, 8 January 1864 will of James Burrows, Franktown.
72. *Bytown Packet*, 16 March 1850, p. 2, col. 4.
73. John Lovell, *Canada Directory, 1851* (Montreal: John Lovell, 1851), p. 83.
74. *Bytown (Canada West) Orange Lily and Protestant Vindicator*, 1 March 1850, p. 134, col. 1.
75. *Bytown Packet*, 23 March 1850, p. 2, col. 4.
76. Ibid., 16 March 1850, p. 2, col. 4.
77. Ibid., 23 March 1850, p. 2, col. 4.
78. *Perth Bathurst Courier*, 25 February 1853, p. 2, cols. 3-5.
79. E.A. Copleston, *The Leeds, Grenville, Lanark and Renfrew County Directory, with the Names of the Principal Inhabitants of Upwards of Seventy Towns and Villages, including the Recent Settlements on the Crown Lands, and a Variety of Useful Local Information for the Year 1859* (Montreal: John Lovell, 1859), p. 23.
80. OBCMR, 16 May 1865 minutes of Beckwith township council.
81. Ibid., 6 June 1865.
82. Ibid., 15 May 1868.
83. *Perth Courier*, 15 July 1859, p. 2, col. 2.
84. Article entitled "A Bloodless Head-On Collision in Snowstorm at Franktown, 1880" in *Ottawa Citizen*, 24 December 1926.
85. *Carp Review*, 15 October 1914, p. 5, cols. 2-3, I am grateful to Bruce Elliot for this reference.
86. *Carleton Place Central Canadian*, 25 January 1894.
87. H. Belden and Company, *Historical Atlas of Carleton County*, p. xli.
88. J.L. Gourlay, *History of the Ottawa Valley* (Ottawa: by the author, 1896), pp. 84-85.
89. Robert Lewis, "Ashton Village First Founded 117 Years Ago" in *Carleton Place Canadian*, 25 July 1935, pp. 1, 8.
90. OKQAR Reverend William Bell Journals XIV:118.
91. Stittsville Women's Institute, *Country Tales* (Ottawa: by the authors, 1973), p. 84.
92. McCuan family correspondence, undated letter believed to date from 1857, from Daniel McCuan, Beckwith, to John McCuan, Scotland, reference 1.1.
93. *Carleton Place Central Canadian*, 25 January 1894.
94. *Carleton Place Herald*, 18 September 1856, p. 4, col. 6.
95. OKQAR Reverend William Bell Journals XIV:118.
96. *Carleton Place Herald*, 4 August 1853, p. 3, col. 6.
97. Gourlay, *History of the Ottawa Valley*, p. 82.
98. Stittsville Women's Institute, *Country Tales*, p. 44.
99. *Carleton Place Herald*, 21 February 1856, p. 3, col. 6.
100. Ibid., 25 December 1851, p. 3, col. 2.
101. Ibid., 14 October 1851, p. 3, col. 7.
102. Gourlay, *History of the Ottawa Valley*, pp. 84-85.
103. *Carleton-Place Herald*, 18 September 1856, p. 4, col. 2.
104. Gourlay, *History of the Ottawa Valley*, p. 85.
105. OBCMR, 15 May 1868 minutes of Beckwith township council.
106. Belden, *Atlas of Carleton County*, p. xli.
107. Rolf Loeber and Magda Stouthamer-Loeber, "The Lost Architecture of the Wexford Plantation" in Kevin Whelan, ed., *Wexford: History and Society* (Dublin: Geography Publications, 1987), pp. 196-197.
108. John Lovell, comp., *The Canada Directory for 1857-58* (Montreal: John Lovell, 1857), p. 532.
109. *Carleton-Place Herald*, 7 February 1856, p. 3, col. 7.
110. Wilda Porter, Kathy Makinson, Stephen Guetta and David Gall, *History of Prospect* (Prospect: by the authors, ca. 1975), p. 3. I am grateful to Edna and John Porter for making copies of this publication available for consultation.
111. *Carleton Place Herald*, 12 June 1861, p. 2, col. 5.
112. NAC Reel C-10018, 1871 census of Beckwith.
113. Carol Bennett, *In Search of Lanark* (Renfrew, Ontario: Juniper Books, 1982). p. 28.
114. *Carleton-Place Herald*, 19 April 1855, p. 3, col. 7.
115. Ibid., 9 December 1858, p. 3, col. 6.
116. Ibid., 18 March 1852, p. 3, col. 5.
117. Ibid., 17 March 1853, p. 4, col. 1.
118. *Perth Courier*, 14 April 1865, p. 2, col. 3.
119. Anonymous source
120. Sutherland, *Yearning For Learning*, p. 290.
121. 5 March 1988 interview with Audrey McRae, Beckwith.
122. OKQAR Reverend William Bell Journals, vol. 7, p. 13.
123. Kidd, *The Story of the Derry*, p. 52.
124. OBCMR, 1 December 1864 minutes of Beckwith township council.
125. Ibid., 15 June 1867.
126. *Carleton Place Herald*, 3 July 1867, p. 2, col. 3.

THE COMING OF THE MILLS

A visitor approaching the village of Carleton Place in 1853 at first glance beheld "a thriving village" with "a good well settled country around it." Although it was the largest village in Beckwith and the third largest centre in Lanark County, a closer look suggested that Carleton Place was just another isolated backwoods village. When Charles Rice from Perth visited in February 1853 he was impressed more with the industrial potential of the village rather than with what development already had taken place. He commented, "There is water-power here capable of driving a great amount of machinery, and could be used extensively for manufacturing purposes. There is a saw mill and a grist mill here, which are capable of doing a considerable amount of business." From the southern bank of the Mississippi visitors like Rice could see a dozen blocks of houses, shops and churches behind the few mills scattered along the river. Rice observed that there were "several good stores...which appear to be doing a good business; and any number of tradesmen's shops" inside of which he viewed "some handsome specimens of their handywork."

Two things that Charles Rice perceived lacking in Carleton Place were "a *good hotel* for the accommodation of travellers, and water for horses to drink" but this was simply retaliation for having been refused free lodging and stabling by Napoleon Lavallee in return for a glowing write-up in the Perth *Courier*.[1] Had Charles Rice visited the village in summer rather than in winter, he would have encountered the numerous pigs that roamed the streets and his nostrils would have been assailed by the stench coming from the "steaming monsters l[ying] beneath the sun, [and] wallow[ing] gloriously in kindred filth." At least one village inhabitant, fed up with the aggressive pigs and the smell of dung that crept through the streets of Carleton Place, complained in 1854:[2]

> We meet them on the side-walks — here and there,
> Along the puddled streets they run and squeel,
> Shoving their ugly muzzles every where,
> In search of something which will make a meal.

The majority of Beckwith inhabitants who clattered into Carleton Place in waggons loaded down with produce during the 1850s viewed the village from a different perspective. As their waggons rumbled over the wooden planks above the cumbersome stone butments of the bridge over the Mississippi into the village proper on the north bank, they inevitably considered the sixty houses and 500 inhabitants of Carleton Place as an improvement, as a sign of progressive growth from the collection of log buildings that it had been twenty years earlier. Carleton Place in the eyes of Beckwith inhabitants was a thriving village in 1853. What was more, they believed that much greater growth was inevitable in the very near future.

James Duncan made a brief description of the more prominent buildings and businesses in Carleton Place while taking the 1852 census of northern Beckwith. The village had five churches, the smallest of which were the Baptist and Reform Presbyterian meeting houses, two small frame structures worth about £150 apiece and each able to hold about 150 persons, the latter of the two measuring 28 by 38 feet. The old frame Wesleyan Methodist chapel measured forty by sixty feet, was

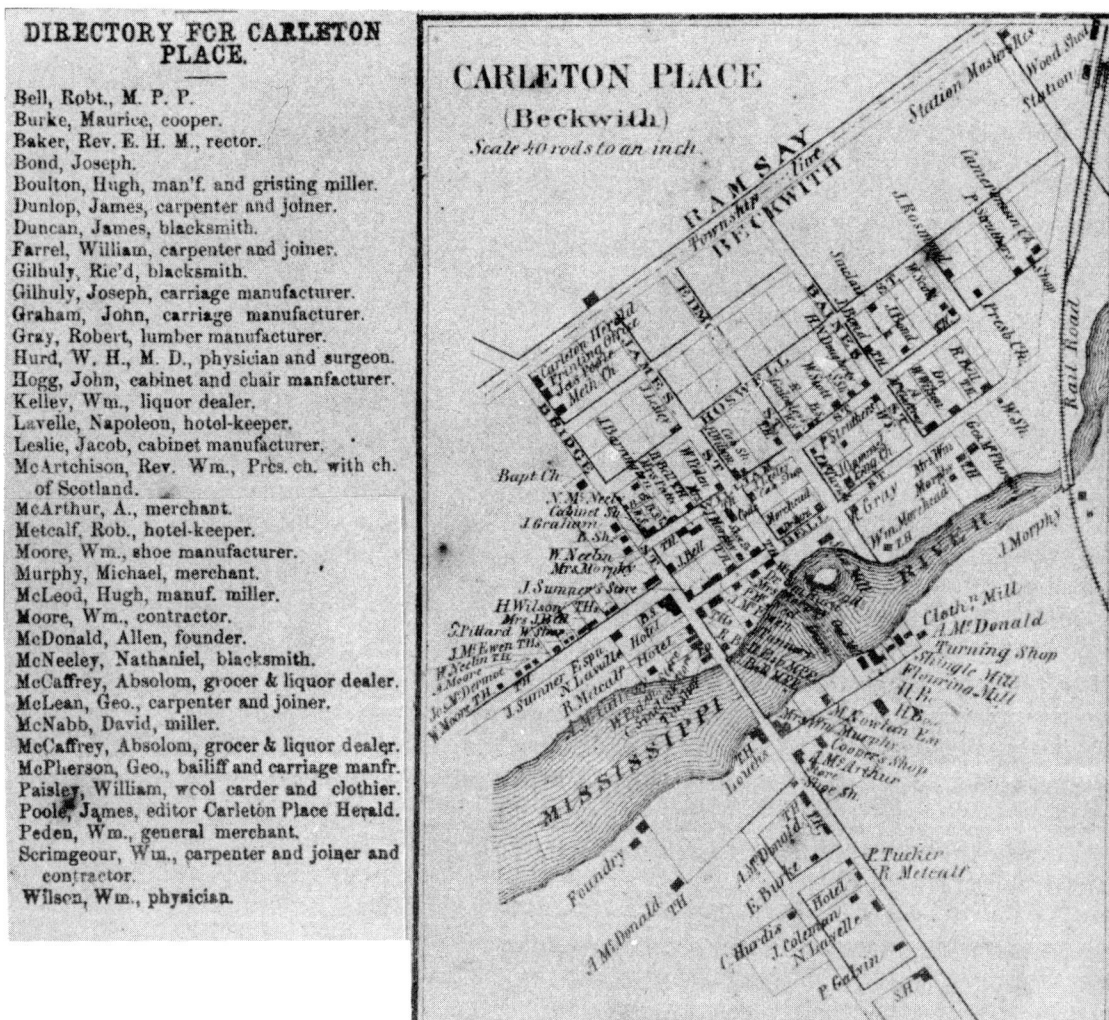

Plate 169
The Carleton Place inset from Henry F. Walling's map of the counties of Lanark and Renfrew published in 1863 by D.P. Putnam, Prescott. This map shows Carleton Place four years after the Brockville and Ottawa railway came through the village, failing to bring the industrialisation and rapid growth sought by local merchants. Bell Street on the north side of the Mississippi and what later was named Mill Street to the south were the oldest settled streets in the village, but between 1830 and 1860 the village proper developed between the Mississippi and the Ramsay town line. The initials S.H. stand for schoolhouse, P.O. for post-office, S.Sh. for shoemaking shop, W.S. for wagonmaking shop, T.H. for owner of tenant's house, B.S. for blacksmith shop, and Cab.S. for cabinetmaking shop. National Archives of Canada NMC VR/420.

valued at £200, and could hold approximately 300 persons. A stone Church of Scotland house of worship with dimensions of 48 by sixty feet at the east end of William Street was not finished when Duncan filled out his returns; its construction cost some £350 and it was expected to hold some 400 persons once completed. St. James United Church of England and Ireland was the largest of the five churches in Carleton Place, with seating for 450 persons, but because it was an older building and of frame construction it was valued at only £200. At the north end of Bridge Street on the boundary

Plate 170
Ferrotype showing shoemaker Patrick Tucker of Carleton Place with the tools of his trade and a customer, William Duff of Beckwith, taken ca. 1865. Tucker made and repaired boots and shoes beginning in 1857 in a shop at the corner of Bridge and Franklin streets, where he accepted sheep pelts and cow hides in return for his work. This rare view of a mid-nineteenth century tradesman in everyday dress, as the slogan at the bottom suggests, was made as a form of advertisement. Many of the tradesmen and artisans in Carleton Place such as Tucker were not considered the social equals of the more well-to-do farmers such as William Duff who dressed in finer clothes and inhabited more substantial houses (Plate 148). The Carleton Place and Beckwith Historical Society.

between Beckwith and Ramsay was the printing establishment of James C. Poole. The printing press and types were valued at £225 and every week some 600 issues of the Carleton-Place *Herald* were published. In the heart of the village was the inspection office of Napoleon Lavallee in which every year approximately 2,500 barrels of pork were inspected and graded before being sent off to market up the Ottawa. On the south side of the river, on the eastern section of Mill Street was the carding mill and cloth works of Allan McDonald, valued at £200. McDonald claimed that he and his two employees dressed about 900 yards of fulled cloth and carded some 8,000 pounds of wool in 1851. Nearby was the gristmill jointly owned by Robert Bell and James Rosamond under the name of Bell & Rosamond and operated by Hugh Boulton. This mill was valued at a whopping £1,600, was powered by water, and employed three persons. Bell and Rosamond also jointly operated an oatmeal mill worth £500 and a sawmill worth £200, both of which also were powered by the Mississippi.

The single enterprise in Carleton Place that consistently attracted praise from visitors was the cloth manufacturing establishment of James Rosamond which was described in 1852 as being worth £1,500, powered by water, employing some fifteen persons and producing 26,000 yards of cloth per year.[3] Charles Rice from Perth approvingly commented in February 1853:[4]

> Mr. Rosamond's Woolen Factory...was what particularly engaged my attention. I have visited some of the best factories in the State of New York, and Mr. Rosamond's is equal to any of them in improved machinery, although not on so extensive a scale. I examined several of his manufactured articles; his blankets are, without exception, the best that I have seen; and his cloths will stand a comparison with any manufactured in this country, or probably in this continent. Mr. Rosamond's enterprise should be liberally encouraged.

Rosamond's success at manufacturing cloth was partly due to introducing modern machinery, but it also stemmed from the simple fact that he cultivated the image of a good employer. There is no evidence that he paid better wages than anyone else in the Carleton Place vicinity, but the strong camaraderie he developed with his employees is shown by his treating them to an oyster supper at Newton's saloon in late January 1855. Following the main course and a fine dessert, the employees drank Rosamond's health with glasses of lemonade. An employee at Samuel Fuller's foundry enviously commented[5]

> Now, such acts of kindness as this, speaks volumes for Mr. Rosamond, it shows in what respect he holds his men, and long may that respect remain unsullied. I know the men fully appreciate the feeling, as an invited guest, I must say that I never spent an hour in better company. Such good feeling displayed between master and man I never witnessed before, let this occasion be a pattern to all employers.

Relations between most employers and employees in Carleton Place during the 1850s and 1860s were unrancorous, but even before large scale industrialisation arrived in the late 1860s and 1870s there was a strong local rhetorical tradition inveighing against exploitation by employers. It is difficult to attribute this growing sense of class grievance, certainly before 1869, to maltreatment by employers or to depersonalised or mechanised working environments. Rosamond's establishment with fifteen employees was the closest Carleton Place came to boasting a factory in the 1850s. Most labourers, apprentices and workmen were poorly paid. A few instances of cruel taskmasters could be found, such as James Poole, editor of the *Herald*, from whom at least four apprentices ran away between 1854 and 1870,[6] but evidence from employees and apprentices themselves makes it clear that the conditions under which they laboured in Carleton Place were far better than what they had left in Scotland and Ireland. In earlier chapters the evidence of Samuel Graham arriving at Brockville in 1828 and Matthew Houston arriving at Carleton Place in 1841 revealed how much better they

Plate 171
View looking south along Bridge Street from near the intersection of High Street, Carleton Place, ca. 1868. Only a section of the stone wall of John Sumner's store at the intersection of Bridge and Bell streets can be glimpsed on the left side. On the right a row of mostly frame buildings including livery stables and a tinshop stretches south of the Carleton House stone hotel of Napoleon Lavallee in the foreground past the bridge in the middle ground into the new blocks being built south of the Mississippi. National Archives of Canada negative no. C-551.

considered themselves to be treated by their masters in Upper Canada as opposed to those they had left behind in Wexford and Paisley. Similarly, John McCuan while visiting among his relatives in Perthshire in 1857, wrote back to his brother Peter in Beckwith, "An apprentice to the business you were at with [Archibald] McArthur would in this country have to pay an apprentice fee of four to six pounds[,] bind himself for four years[,] Provide his own clothing and board[.] All this time he gets nothing from his master[.] This you will find is somewhat different from Canada."[7]

The growing sense of class consciousness that emerged in the Carleton Place vicinity in the 1850s came from the radical tradition of the lowland weavers in adjacent Ramsay. It emerged as they perceived that Rosamond's factory staffed with Irish-origin inhabitants posed a threat to their livelihood of weaving with handlooms in their homes. In mid July 1854 a meeting of handloom weavers from neighbouring townships was held in Thomas Smith's hotel at Carleton Place, "for the purpose of taking into consideration the propriety and expediency of agreeing upon a scale of prices for their work", and by early August these Scottish weavers agreed to charge the following prices for work done:[8]

Cotton and Wool plain...	6 d per yard
Do. do. tweeled	7 d do.
Satinett	7 d do.
Do. Striped	1d 1st shuttle
½ d every extra shuttle	
All woolen warps plain,	7 d per yard

If striped and checked	1 d extra the 1st shuttle,
½ d for every extra shuttle.	
Shawls if one to be charged 5s, if 2, 4s[,] if 3 or more 3s 6d each.	
Woolen Quilts	9 d per yard
Figured Bedcover	9 s each
Rag Carpet	9d per yard

Although as late as 1865 handloom weaving continued to be done in the Beckwith vicinity,[9] many local handloom weavers in the mid 1850s suddenly recognised that they were newly vulnerable. They perceived that from their current state of practising a marketable skill they could very quickly be reduced to working as unskilled labourers tending power looms in factories such as that of James Rosamond in return for a mere pittance.

What hit some of the lowland weavers with even more impact was the realisation that more than a decade of agitation for political Reform had replaced the old aristocracy of the Upper Canadian Family Compact with a new aristocracy of politicians, railway promoters and capitalists.[10] What did it matter if politicians such as Malcolm Cameron and Robert Bell were part of a Reform wave in the 1840s and 1850s that brought about political Reform, universal education and railways, if in the process they also pursued the objective of setting into place the means of exploiting labourers? Of what practical significance were the paeans to the "Dignity of Labour"[11] and poetry about labouring men "wield[ing] a lofty power"[12] in local Reform newspapers, when these very newspapers were capitalised by manufacturers and merchants who had only their own ultimate economic interests at heart?

The continuing legacy of radicalised Scottish lowlanders fearing inevitable exploitation and betrayal is shown by an excerpt from an 1851 letter written by a Ramsay farmer for the *Carleton Place Herald*:[13]

> Wealth can take care of itself by purchasing physical power and by political influence; but legislation should give to the many their industrial rights, and declare men's earnings should not be needlessly diminished, either directly or indirectly.
>
> There is no property so sacred as that derived from bones and sinews — is it not our cunning fingers and assiduous industry which has made the country fruitful — who or what but our own want of energy and common sense prevents us from combining our entire strength and asserting our independence, that we may no longer be trampled on. It is the willing slave that makes the tyrant....
>
> It is to be regretted, should any empty headed debater, at the coming election, try to enlist any of the peasantry by any possible device in party array against each other; the dignity of our common nature rises superior to this insolence;...why should party enter at all into the coming election? [I]t will be sadly out of place at such a time as the present, when the masses are going to make a united effort to shake off the incubus of bad government and compel some wise legislation for the public good. Is there, Mr. Editor, any thing in the mere name of Whig or Tory which will cure the evils under which we have groaned so long[?]

Significantly, this was not written by a Carleton Place labourer nor an artisan nor an apprentice, but rather by a Ramsay lowlander farmer. It flowed from the routinised protest that was part and parcel of the intellectual make up of Glasgow area weavers from the time of their radicalisation during the post-Napoleonic economic slump.

Protest over labouring conditions in mid-nineteenth century Carleton Place came not from labourers and artisans. The rhetorical protest of the Ramsay lowlanders, notwithstanding their

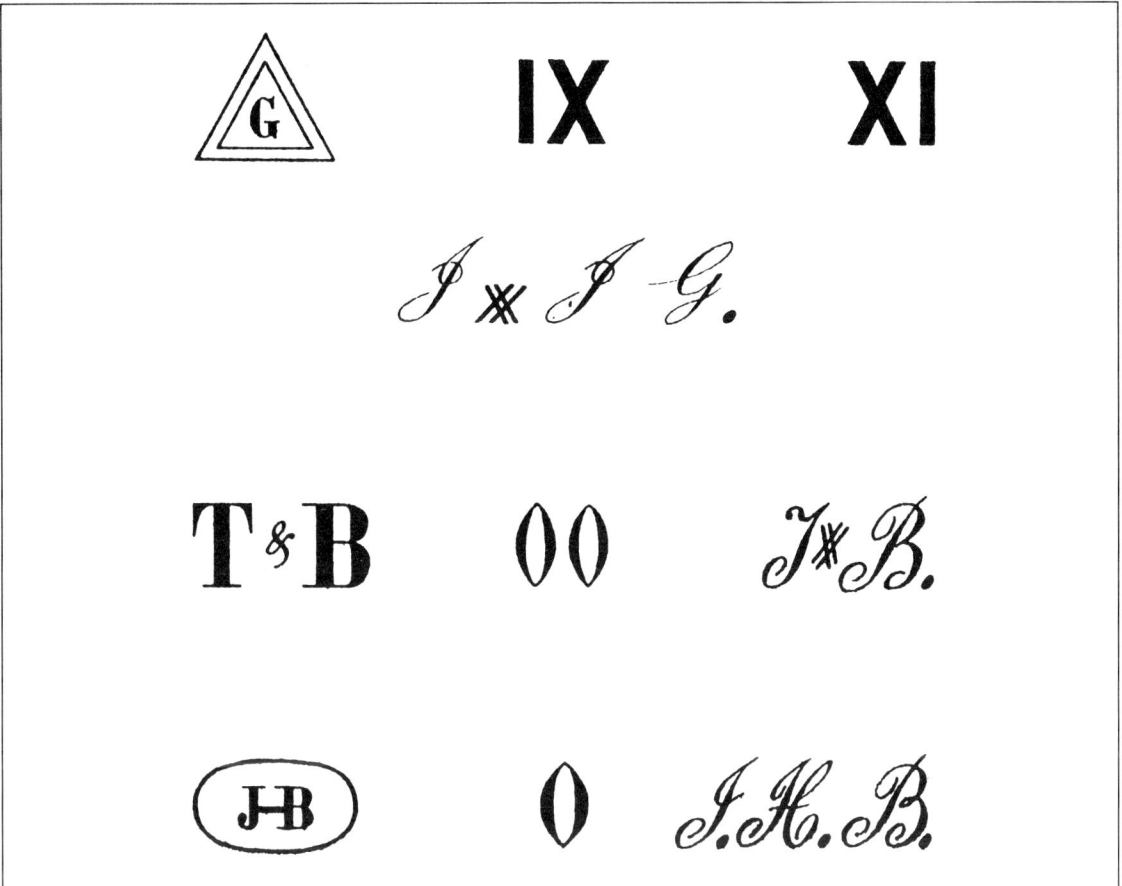

Plate 172
Hammer, stamp, bark and scrape marks used by lumber companies moving sawlogs down the Mississippi River to the mills at Carleton Place from the late 1860s onward. These were the marks placed on sawlogs to identify the property of the different lumber companies. The top row shows the hammer, bark and scrape marks patented by James and John Gillies in 1870, and below it the mark set up by the Gillies Bros. Co. Ltd. of Carleton Place in 1894. The two bottom lines respectively show the stamp, bark and scrape marks of the Teskey & Bredin and James Henry Bredin firms, all patented in 1872. From Diane Aldred, comp., Registered Timbermarks of Eastern Canada, 1870 to 1984.

agricultural self-sufficiency and comfortable homes, was supplemented by the more pragmatic complaint of merchants' clerks in the village. A letter to the *Carleton Place Herald* in early July 1852 signed by A FRIEND OF HUMANITY deplored the fact that merchants' shops in the village were left open from six in the morning to ten in the evening, whereas in most other towns and villages shops were open only until seven in the evening. "Surely it cannot be that the merchants of Carleton-Place are more hard and austere than they are in other places", he expostulated. "Even the laborer and the Mechanic have to work only eleven hours, while the merchant[']s clerk has to drudge for sixteen hours...." Such a long work day effectively deprived the clerks of any opportunity to gain an education. "Surely there must be a greater responsibility upon merchant masters towards their Clerks, for using them thus, in preventing them from improving their mind[s] as they ought to do, for no master is justified in allowing his servants to grow up in ignorance[,] much less is he justified who *compels* them to do so."¹⁴ Another *Herald* correspondent who signed himself PAGANUS argued that the clerks in Carleton Place stores "are all day on the move, yet never in exercise; always engaged in what wearies the body but never in that which invigorates", and with the lighting of lamps at dusk "young men in stores are compelled to breath[e] an atmosphere which gradually becomes more and more impure; until in the evening, and especially late in the evening, it becomes *positively and actively pernicious.*" PAGANUS lamented:¹⁵

> Alas! for the young men engaged in shops. Fields and walks can be of no avail to them, unless their hours of business are so curtailed as to allow them to share in the privileges of their fellow citizens! At present they are denied all such enjoyments.... The bright sun, the blue sky, and the *fresh air*, are blessings which God had bestowed upon the meanest of his creatures, but of which they, though among the noblest, are altogether deprived.
> "Not for them returns
> Day, or the sweet approach of ev'n or morn,
> Or sight of vernal bloom, or summery rose,
> Or flocks or herds!"
> But
> "Their unhappy lot
> Is the dull ceaseless round of business, toil
> And joyless rest."

Although the village clerks were tied down to the confines of the stores all year round, the amount of business in Carleton Place varied by season and by the vagaries of weather within each season. In the late winter of 1852, for example, the weather favoured the merchants of the village but not the millers. James Poole remarked in the *Herald* in early March, "A great deal of business has been transacted here this winter, and the roads have been peculiarly favorable for transporting the produce raised in this part of the district, to the Lumbering regions. A temporary check has been given to the trade by the snow and drift...which have...blocked up the roads but the unavoidable travel on them will make [them] passable for loaded teams in a day or two." Water for the moment was low in the Mississippi, forcing many of the village mills to remain idle. Poole reported that the market price of wheat and flour was advancing slightly while pork and coarse grains commanded a steady price, although prices were not as good in late February as they had been at the beginning of the winter.¹⁶ James Poole confidently predicted continuing good markets for local produce: "The high prices for timber last year, have induced manufacturers to get out an increased supply...; but there being but a very small supply on hand from the old stock, and there being a prospect of an increased demand from the United States, hopes are entertained that it will maintain its price." Over the winter of 1852 as a whole Poole reported that a "brisk business has been done in the Woolen Cloth Manufactures...by Mr. Rosamond in the Victoria Factory here, and...[a]n unprecedentedly large amount of business has been done this winter in the sawed lumber line, which has considerably reduced the stock on hand."¹⁷

The extent to which the change in weather affected the pace of business in Carleton Place is revealed in Poole's commentary in the *Herald* a week later:¹⁸

> We had a good deal of rain...which has raised the river enough...to allow the mills to drive a larger amount of work, this was much wanted, for a great portion of the wheat remains unground. However, it made the roads rather soft for teaming, till Tuesday night's frost hardened them up again. There still exists a difficulty to dispose of small lots of produce for cash; although large lots can command an advanced price.... The Merchants Shops have been

Plate 173
A lakeshore lumbering scene showing timber being prepared to be sent down the Mississippi to Abner Nichols's lumber mill at Carleton Place. Trees with as large dimensions as this could still be found in Beckwith as late as the 1890s, but were sufficiently rare to warrant having a photograph taken. The men in this photograph may have been largely Nichols employees, but many Beckwith farmers in the closing decades of the nineteenth century were familiar with lumbering on the upper Ottawa during the winter months every year. National Archives of Canada negative no. C-29319.

rather dull during the past week, but there appears to be no slack in the Mechanics Work Shops. The Hammer, the Plane, the Awl and the Needle being as busily plied as at the beginning of the season; and they work with more spirit now, as they sometimes see cash for their work, which was not always the case, as there was a time, which we hope is past, when tradesmen's bills were paid with Potatoes and Cedar.

Another week later Poole reported "There is a large lot of timber on the ice and on the banks of the bay below Teskey's [Appleton], there is also more than an average supply above this."[19] As late as early April the sleighing of produce into Carleton Place continued. "The water is now at a fine pitch for the machinery on the rivers, and the millers and manufacturers are taking advantage of it, and driving every wheel in their possession, which they can now do to advantage, as all repairs which were requisite were made when the water was too low to work the machinery."[20]

Carleton Place was constantly visited by the farmers of Beckwith and southern Ramsay all year round, save for the seasons when planting, haying and harvesting preoccupied their attention on their farms. George McLaren who lived on lot 21 in the fifth concession of Beckwith, for example, visited Carleton Place more than eighty times in 1874, bringing in firewood, grain, pork, cows, heifers, butter, eggs, calf skins, potatoes, wool, hay, mutton, veal, beef and lambs to sell, and purchasing horses, calves, pigs, sheep, steers and some dry goods.[21]

Excerpts from the letter-book of James S. Bangs at Pakenham in 1855 and 1856 reveal the delicate balancing role of local merchants acting as middlemen between Beckwith farmers and the large provisioning outfits at Ottawa and purchasers from the timber camps on the Ottawa. To one of his creditors, Bangs wrote in mid August 1855, "it is the dullest Season of the year with me for Cash — for the principal part of my Cash at this time is in Butter[,] which cannot be Stir[r]ed until fall[,] and in accounts with the farmers [who will make] pay[men]t in Butter & Pork in [the] fall and grain in Winter". The small cash sales he was making at the end of summer, Bangs admitted, "are inad[e]quate to the Many I have to trust...until fall" and although the greater part of his business was credit, he expected it to "be good in Winter for our farmers have great crops and are sure [to] pay as soon as they can dispose of their produce."[22] In a September 1855 letter to a Montreal firm Bangs confided "many of the best farmers here who own farms worth a Thousand pounds cannot pay their accounts now for their all is on the ground and must be marketed before they can pay — (money never was as scarce here) the crops are coming in abundantly here and all will soon be able to."[23] And although by November Bangs was shipping out potash, butter and lard,[24] on New Year's day 1856 he admitted that he was being squeezed by canny local farmers playing the market and foreign competition:[25]

> The season thus far has been very unfavourable to trade here in as much as the snow has held off very late thus preventing our farmers from getting to market with their produce and now when the Snow has come the Markets are on the decline and as yet unsettled, apparently waiting for further news from Europe, our farmers are holding back to see which way they will turn[.] T]hese Circumstances have made cash scarce in these parts, large quantities of produce are now Ready for market here and I expect soon to Realise from my accounts with the farmers what will relieve me from my present cramped up state — in a great measure.

But two weeks later it was all too clear that "our farmers are holding on to their grain so hard this season that it takes some time to draw it from them and convert it into cash."[26] Bangs attributed this reluctance to the fact that "the most of our farmers are Scotch — hard cases, for a price and when the markets opened so high in the fall they thought money was not good enough to buy their grain without a little beg[g]ing & preying along with it[,] and now they are loth to submit to the fall." The unfortunate consequence for both local farmers and middlemen of holding out for a high price was that many of the lumbermen brought in "large quantities of Pork from the States while there is plenty here to supply them."[27] To make matters worse for Bangs, in March 1856 "a party from Perth [began] auctioning off goods opposite my door at about half the prime cost and taking in about a hundred pounds per day."[28] Within three weeks the Perth pirates had "dr[ai]ned the country[side] of all the best part of the cash trade and Supplied them with a large amount of goods of every description at far below prime cost" and local farmers left their accounts with Bangs unpaid.[29]

Merchants at Carleton Place clearly perceived that the relative isolation of their settlement which in itself at one time ensured their viability increasingly made them vulnerable after mid-century. The poor transportation that hampered farmers bringing produce to them, and which in turn made it difficult for them to move it out to markets in Montreal, Ottawa and the timber shanties, was complicated by the vagaries of weather and farmers who speculated on market prices rising toward the end of winter. Poor transportation effectively placed village merchants at the mercy of area farmers, not only in their attempts to obtain the highest dollar for their crops, but in the unfair penetration of the local market by outsiders. In early March 1852 James Poole observed in the *Herald*, "There has been an immense traffic in Cooking Stoves this winter, persons from the front passing through here every day with loads of them, which they leave at the farmers' houses on trial, something similar to the manner the Clock Pedlars did some years ago with the clocks."[30] A month later, Poole observed, "Great dissatisfaction seems to exist among those who have purchased stoves, this winter, from the Pedlars from the Front, as the castings proved to be very thin, and there can be no doubt but that the dissatisfaction will increase as the time of payment approaches." And yet

Plate 174
Nichols lumbermen with a drive of sawlogs and a raft on the Mississippi River, in Beckwith in 1902, as photographed by Annie Elexey Duff. This photograph was taken from the north shore of the Mississippi looking across to the William Duff farm (Plate 148) on lot 10, concession 11. There had been lumber drives on the Mississippi at least as early as the 1840s and they continued a little past the turn of the century. The Nichols men are shown here using the pointer boats developed by J.R. Booth of Ottawa specifically for lumber drives on rivers. These boats drew so little water that it was claimed they could float on the dew. National Archives of Canda negative no. C-80023.

Beckwith inhabitants eagerly patronised the pirate merchants who swept through, at the expense of local merchant firms. "Money seems to be plent[iful]", James Poole caustically remarked in the *Herald* on April 1st 1852, "if we are to judge by the manner in which it is launched out at an Auction of *Goods* which has been going on here for four or five days, by persons who imagine that everything low priced is cheap."[31] Whereas Montague Township to the south in 1856 passed a stringent by-law for the licensing of auctioneers which effectively protected local merchants from outside firms,[32] no such by-law passed the Beckwith council to protect Carleton Place merchants.

Isolated as Carleton Place was from the major transportation routes of the St. Lawrence and Ottawa rivers and the Rideau Canal, it was accomplishment enough for village merchants to transport local crops to market and to bring in merchandise along the "Desperate and Impassable" road running from Smith's Falls to Carleton Place.[33] They would remain vulnerable to the depredations of pirating merchants from Perth, Brockville and the United States as long as they remained sufficiently mired in their slightly inaccessible position: — close enough to supply and profit from provisioning the upper Ottawa lumber industry, close enough to towns in which merchants and manufacturers kept their costs low by having access to cheap water transportation and who by purchasing and warehousing large stocks could quite handily undercut Carleton Place merchants, but far enough back in the woods and with such wretched roads as to offer no hope of competing with the towns along the front.

Competing with towns along the front? To even suggest the possibility for Carleton Place before 1850 would have been a laughable conceit for a backwoods village. But with railways being proposed across the province, local merchants and manufacturers quickly recognised that a railroad link with

other centres could transform Carleton Place "from an insignificant village [and it] would soon become a thriving and populous market-Town".³⁴ And so it was that the merchants and manufacturers of Carleton Place became the most enthusiastic and consistent promoters of the Brockville and Ottawa Railway to be found in the Beckwith vicinity throughout the 1850s. Not only would the railway permit the local mercantile economy to work more smoothly and to compete with larger centres, but Carleton Place inhabitants anticipated that it would substantially boost the sophistication and the urbanity of the village. The *Herald* reported in late 1850 that a substantial addition had been built onto the Carleton Place school "erected, in a style which will be a credit to the place." Moreover, James Poole reported, "It is the intention of the building committee to have a portico put up, with some other little architectural ornaments, which will give it a pleasing appearance, and take off the dead, barn-like appearance, which so many of our public buildings have in this country."³⁵ When the Lanark and Renfrew united counties council decided to hold one of its regular meetings at Carleton Place in May 1852, the *Herald* argued at length that the Beckwith village was a more central location than Perth for holding all counties council meetings:³⁶

> The *necessity* of a change in the place of meeting, must be evident to any person having a knowledge of the boundaries of the Counties; Perth being situated within five miles of the south line, and being upwards of SEVENTY miles from the northern extremity of the Counties; whereas the thriving and commodious village of Carleton Place is twenty miles nearer the centre as regards distance, and as near as possible in the centre of the population, so that there is a necessity for a change....

The desire for a more urbane community, one whose associations were more with distant cities rather than with the local countryside, was evident when the *Herald* argued in October 1853 that a newspaper reading room be added to the Carleton Place circulating library:³⁷

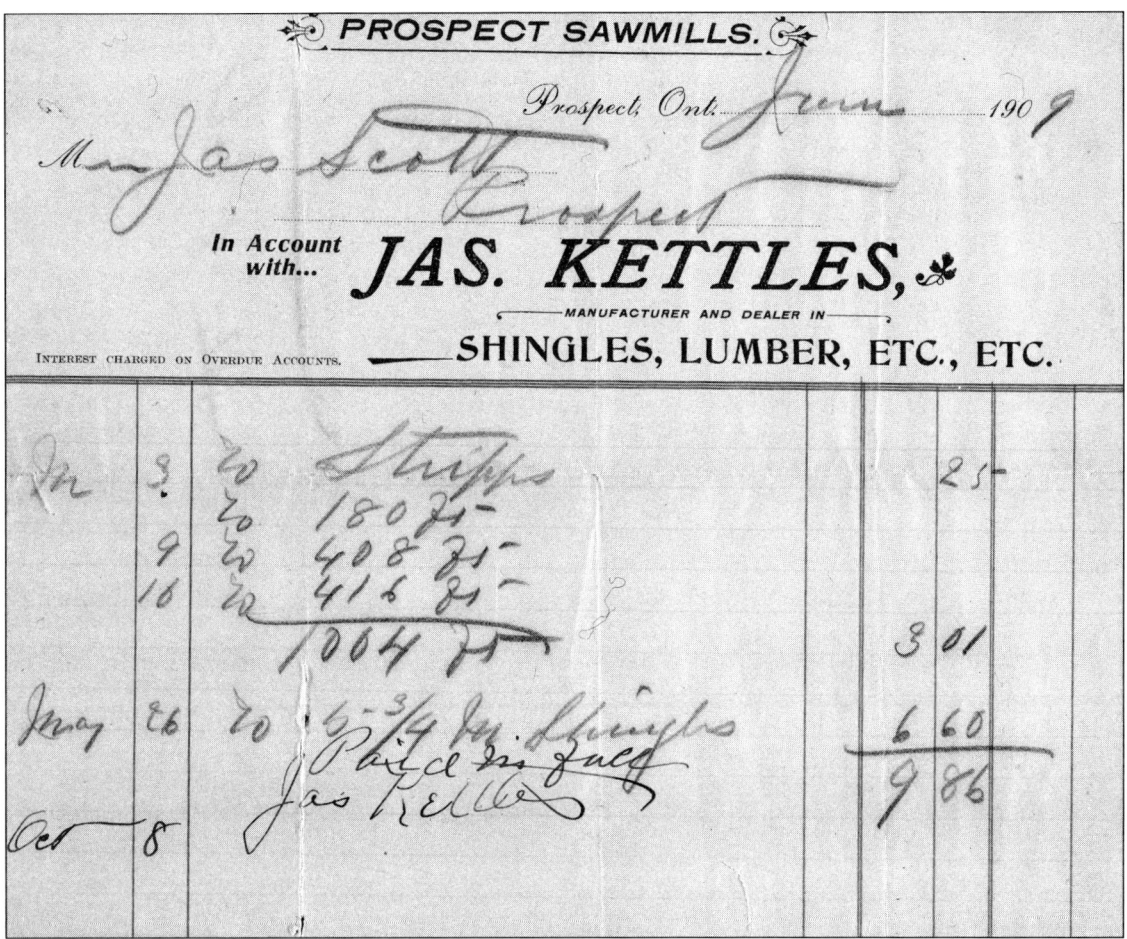

Plate 175
The Boyd Caldwell and Son sawmill at Carleton Place (opposite), built in 1869, as photographed ca. 1900, and an invoice from the Prospect sawmills of James Kettles, dated 1909. In October 1870 the Carleton Place Herald *reported "The Messrs. Caldwell of Lanark, have erected a steam sawmill of large capabilities. Unfortunately, the mill is stopped for want of logs, as the proprietors were disappointed in getting the logs floated down the river in consequence of the shallowness of the water caused by the want of rain. They have no less than eighteen thousand logs thus laid up and unless there are early rains, it will be impossible for them to get them down this season. The mill is capable of cutting 360 logs a day of eleven hours." By contrast, the Prospect sawmill was a small affair, servicing local farmers building large new farmhouses with lumber from their own woodlots. National Archives of Canada negative no. C-1344, and loan courtesy of Ruth McDiarmid, respectively.*

When a limited number of persons form themselves into a community, if their position, or any other circumstance, shut out, interrupt, or in any way obstruct their intercourse with the rest of their kind, the natural tendency is to degenerate into rude or unbecoming habits, into coars[e]ness of manner, or indifference to the tastes of the more polished and highly civilized inhabitants of cities — these are inevitable consequences, in a great measure, from the absence of that standard which emulation raises, which example upholds, and which constant intercourse improves. Now all small towns and villages are very much in this condition; but where the periodical literature of the day, (being a reflection of its manners and habits,) is introduced, it has the effect of materially elevating those who read its pages.

Bound together as were the hopes of Carleton Place boosters for the greater growth of their village with the promotion of the Brockville and Ottawa railway, they constantly slapped down criticism of its onerous cost by the rural inhabitants of Beckwith. A series of letters published in the *Herald* in 1853 purportedly written by a Ramsay inhabitant under the pseudonym of ANTI-LOCOMOTIVE, but which in all probability were penned either by editor Poole or Robert Bell, clearly parodied the unprogressive Beckwith highlander criticism of the railroad. The first of these letters criticised the "Radical bodies" of Ramsay "for ruining us, wa' their new-fangled schemes. If they get a Railroad, then the'll want a telegraph, an' steem engines, an' a' tha' dangerous kin' o' nonsense on the roads.... An' waur nor a' that, the Yankees will be in on us like a flood, and carry aff our timber an' our loyalty."[38] The last of the letters by ANTI-LOCOMOTIVE alluded to the superstition of the highlanders when it asserted, "I've heard o' fairies riding through the kintra on a winnale-straw; but is that ony mare daft-like or uncommon than some folk da on tha railroads." To ANTI-LOCOMOTIVE a picture of a locomotive "lucked, by a' the warld, like a great muckle tea-kettle, set on wheels, wi' a heap o' spoots and fal-de-rals aboot it." Upon learning that "they jist yoke the loco-motive to a wheen cars, an' when the kettle biles, awa they rin, at the rate o' sixty or seventy miles an hoor", the writer exclaimed "Ye may set me doon for a glaiket g[e]neral, when ye catch me gaun at that gait."[39]

When satire failed to dispel criticism of the cost overruns and delays in constructing the railway, Carleton Place promoters contrasted the slogging through muddy local roads with the railroads already completed along the St. Lawrence. Robert Bell wrote the *Herald* from Toronto in February 1857,[40]

After plowing through the mud...between Carleton-Place and Smith's Falls, at the rate of three miles an hour, and then riding to Brockville, in a common lumber waggon, (it was called the stage, because the mail happened to be carried in it!) O, how pleasant it was to get into the Railway cars, and travel more than two hundred miles in about half the time required to get over the first fifty miles of my journey.

The lack of growth, indeed the setbacks to growth in Carleton Place during the 1850s were perhaps the strongest argument for the railroad link. Among the few positive developments to which village inhabitants could point were the growth of the *Carleton Place Herald* to enjoy the largest circulation of any newspaper published in Lanark County,[41] the opening of a large RAILROAD HOTEL on Bridge Street by Robert Bell in 1855,[42] and the opening of a lead mine half a mile to the east in Ramsay.[43] When a man named Frank Hill returned in 1859 for a visit after a long absence from "the old village of Carleton Place on the Mississippi" which in earlier years he recalled it was believed "never would amount to anything" he paid it the rather backhanded compliment of being "somewhat pleased on entering the streets to see as much improvement as there is — places torn down and better buildings erected; also new shops, with new names quite strange and new to me over the doors." Hill "was also pleased to see by the preparation of a Railroad...ready for the cars to run here by the month of May, that [Carleton Place was] not altogether behind the times."[44]

The 1850s were full of setbacks for Carleton Place. The inability of the local economy to expand was mirrored by the ongoing migration of families elsewhere. "Every year", observed James Poole in 1855, "some persons of our acquaintance, who with good farms, and in comfortable circumstances, are not content, — but, longing for a home in some 'vast wilderness' — sell out their homes and their furniture and 'move to the West'."[45] Local merchants and farmers complained of "a great scarcity of servants and labourers, there not being enough to supply the demand of even th[e] usually dull

Plate 176
The grain mills and residence of Horace Brown, Mill Street, Carleton Place, as photographed in 1889. Mill Street with its grain mills was the destination for many Beckwith farmers from the mid 1820s through to the mid-twentieth century. On the extreme left is the oatmeal mill of Hugh Boulton, owned for a time by James Rosamond and Robert Bell, and known to have been operating in 1841 and possibly dating back to the 1830s. The second building to the right of it is the stone gristmill built by Hugh Boulton in the 1850s and enlarged by William Bredin. The brick building between the oatmill and the gristmill was a kiln built in 1888 by Horace Brown for roasting oats to make oatmeal and roasting peas to make pease brose — two staples of the Beckwith Scottish highland diet. The four-storey roller mill was built by Brown in 1885 in which rollers replaced grindstones in transforming wheat into flour. On the south side of the street the large stone house built by Hugh Boulton in the 1850s encroaches on the street, showing how closely the miller lived to his business. National Archives of Canada negative no. C-1345.

[w]inter season."[46] Fires took their toll. In late April 1853 the gristmill "burned almost to the ground" but "the lower floor and some of the machinery [were] saved and the fire [was] prevented from spreading to the adjoining buildings, by the prompt exertions of some of the neighbors."[47] A few months later another fire broke out in the barn of Dr. John Spencer, and again the prompt work of neighbours prevented "the destruction of a vast amount of property."[48] In early March 1858 "a fire broke out in the foundery and machine shop of Mr. Samuel Fuller...and before any assistance could be rendered, the building, with its contents, were totally consumed." A subscription was raised "to assist in getting up another building" since, as James Poole commented "This place cannot do without a foundery",[49] but no sooner was the money raised, than Fuller absconded with the profits. Carleton Place was left in need of an iron foundry and machine shop, and James Poole in a moment of unusual candour, admitted that Fuller's business "was only the name of a foundry...as the whole business was done on the credit of merchants and others who were desirous of giving the proprietor a chance, until he made off with the profits."[50] By implication, Fuller himself may well have set his own fire.

In late June 1859 an old frame building in the village owned by William Muirhead of Beckwith and "known as the 'Factory'" burned down. It was a telling reference to the lack of growth in the village that this building, although insured for $500 "contained no machinery" and "was used, for several months past as a place of common resort for the lower class of people, and [it was rumoured that the fire] might have taken place by a coal [dropping] from some drunken fellow's pipe."[51] Bad as the fires were, the worst blow to local hopes for village growth was when James Rosamond moved to Almonte to build extensive woollen factories hiring hundreds of labourers.[52] When the first locomotive chugged into the village in late July 1859, it represented the only realistic possibility for Carleton Place to shrug off its sluggishness and potential decline.

A few years later it was all too clear that the railroad was not bringing about new growth in Carleton Place, although at the annual fall fair in 1859 there "were several buyers from a distance, who took home large droves of cattle."[53] Not only was there no influx of investment and no new factories as local railway promoters had promised, but Carleton Place merchants quickly found their prices being undercut as local mechanics brought in flour on the railway at a lower cost.[54] Reeve Archibald McArthur of Beckwith hauled Carleton Place merchants and promoters of the railway before a public meeting in the township hall at Black's Corners, and alternately asked probing questions about the financing of the railway and blasted them, especially Robert Bell, for pushing the scheme, since no growth had been brought about since the railway came through.[55]

The lack of development was definitely a sore point, and James Poole slashed back with an editorial in April 1860 accusing William Muirhead, "the man who has the most money of any one in the Township" as being personally responsible for the undynamic state of Carleton Place. Muirhead, as the owner of the "splendid water privilege" there, Poole commented, "has kept it for years closed up in his selfish grasp, refusing either to let it at a reasonable price to more enterprising men, or put up machinery which would be not only remunerative to himself but beneficial to the community at large." As matters stood, Poole observed, many village inhabitants regretted "the vast daily loss of valuable motive power which is constantly running to waste, and which might long ago, have been turned to good account, in driving first-class mills and factories; and...have enriched [the] village and country round with remunerative employment".[56]

For the better part of a decade after the railway came through Carleton Place, descriptions of the village even by local boosters inevitably conjured up images of illness, advanced age and death. Robert Bell described Carleton Place in late 1861 as[57]

> rejoicing in stone buildings, clapboard buildings, with and without paint, three story high and new, down to the one-story cot[tage], verdant with ancient damp, and tottering to mother earth with lumbago in its back, rheumatism in its joints, and its optics sadly delapidated. Now the rattle of machinery keeps funny kind of time to the deep rumble of the pent-up waters escaping from its bondage, and churches make their appearance, and schoolhouses are thronged,...and bridges span the river, and the side-walks are — well — exactly where they were two years previously, the streets in wet weather get muddy, and in dry weather, dusty, and the trees on the outskirts are as brilliantly green as they were forty years ago.

A year later a correspondent of the *Herald* described the unharnessed power of the Mississippi at Carleton Place:[58]

> Below [the bridge]...is a dam, and on the South bank is a flume, which bears on its ancient ribs the time-honored marks of an antiquity anterior to the memory of the "oldest inhabitant" — weather-beaten, venerable old flume! troubled with the lumbago and racked with rheumatic gout,...and you are dropsical too...and pretty well "tapped," if I may judge from outward appearances, for jets of water are pouring from thy bursting body. A watery grave awaits thee,

Plate 177
St. James Anglican Church and the Gillies and McLaren sawmill, Carleton Place, as photographed ca. 1885. The Gillies and McLaren sawmill by 1871 employed more people than the ten next biggest industries and businesses in the town put together. The sawmills built at Carleton Place in the late 1860s were responsible for the population of the village suddenly multiplying and for scores of new houses being built on new blocks laid out south of the river. Since the sawmill operated only half the year, there was much misery and violence among the labourers who were unable to find work during the remaining months. The house to the left of the Anglican church is reputed to have been inhabited by prostitutes. National Archives of Canada negative no. C-20760.

thou toilsome servant of the public!...and...inexorable time, bearing in its arms perhaps a "spring flood," will scatter thy timbers on distant shores, rotting m[e]mentos of past prosperity. What a water-power is here running to waste, where a Canadian Lowell might be spreading around its branches of prosperity and stamping Carleton Place as a place of enterprise; but what is the cause?... [T]he water power is in the hands of a few who will not sell out, unless at a most exorbitant price, or who ha[ve] not the capital themselves to build or not possessed of sufficient enterprise to carry out any manufacturing scheme, but are quite content to sit there and allow a quarter of a century to roll over their heads with the hoarse murmur of wasted power singing a hymn of reproach in their ears.

The lack of industrial development and growth in Carleton Place during the late 1850s and early 1860s was all the harder for village boosters to accept when they contrasted it with the sudden growth of Almonte. In 1852 the population of Almonte was less than half that of Carleton Place, but by 1861 its population was almost double. Almonte's growth began well before the railway arrived and Almonte's population remained higher than that of Carleton Place as late as 1881. A three-storey gristmill was constructed in the 1840s and the Ramsay Woollen Cloth Manufacturing Company began business there in 1851.[59] When Almonte with its superior water-power was mooted as the temporary northern terminus of the Brockville and Ottawa railway in the late 1850s, James Rosamond of Carleton Place hastened to purchase strategic lots at Almonte and moved there in 1857. From the Beckwith perspective it was bad enough that Carleton Place had lost one of its leading

370 THE COMING OF THE MILLS

industrialists, with Almonte-manufactured goods being offered for sale in Carleton Place stores, [60] but when the meetings and annual exhibition of the United Counties of Lanark and Renfrew Agricultural Society were moved to Almonte in 1858[61] it was all too clear that Almonte had outstripped Carleton Place to become the leading industrial centre of the Mississippi valley. Needless to say, the promoters and merchants of Carleton Place were pea green with envy.

Once the railroad reached Almonte in August 1859,[62] the village experienced a building boom as its population quadrupled to one thousand. An advertisement in the Carleton Place *Herald* in January 1860 announcing a sale of Almonte town lots, boasted that Almonte had the reputation of being the handsomest village in Canada, and that its water privileges were second only to those at Ottawa:[63]

> Stone of the most beautiful and durable quality can be obtained in abundance for building purposes, while its several Saw Mills can supply at a moment's notice all the Lumber required for local consumption. Furniture of all descriptions can be made at its factories in abundance for building purposes, while its several Saw Mills can supply at a moment's notice all the Lumber required for local consumption. Furniture of all descriptions can be made at its factories in abundance, of a superior finish, and for durability unsurpassed, while its Woolen Factories have a reputation already that creates a demand nearly impossible to supply; and it is already in contemplation to erect a Cotton Mill on a large scale. In fact the water power is immense, and, with judicious management it may be made the "Lowell" of Canada. Its Grist Mills only compete with each other in the quality of their work. The Tannery, conducted and owned by Smith Coleman, Esq., is at once a market for all the hides brought in, and is known far and near for the superior quality of the leather made.

As if to emphasize the booming growth of Almonte at the same time Carleton Place languished, the Prince of Wales in the course of travelling across British North America in the autumn of 1860 made a lengthy stop and formally received addresses at Almonte as opposed to giving a passing nod to Carleton Place from the back of his railway carriage.[64] From the envious perspective of Carleton Place it was as if the triumphal arches erected at Almonte in honour of the prince's visit attested to the triumph of Almonte as opposed to Carleton Place in benefitting from railway construction.

Those Carleton Place inhabitants who scrutinised Almonte more closely noticed that rapid industrial growth had its cost. The editor of the Almonte *Gazette* admitted in 1867, "We have no deliberate stone or brick fulfilment of a paper plan, but a heap of spontaneously formed dwellings that have risen up impulsively just when, and where, and how the need of the moment required, altogether forming one inartistical and unattractive mass." And yet, although Almonte streets might "be irregular, its buildings flimsy, its trading inscriptions pretentious, its smoke dense, its mud ultra muddy, and its sidewalks meagre" there was no question of its quickly becoming a thriving town "or of its being at present, justly considered, *foremost of all its cotemporaries*." In 1867 the influx of people moving into Almonte was reported "so great that it was impossible to find a house or shop to rent. This season about forty or fifty new buildings have been erected, and yet the demand is undiminished."[65]

The lack of planning and irregularity of the hastily constructed mills and houses were not the only unfortunate consequences of Almonte's sudden industrial growth. Andrew Haydon of Perth argued that the business base of the town that sprang up gave Almonte a massive working class and a financially unsound middle class:[66]

> Some industries were started on insufficient capital and with too scanty a knowledge of the commercial outlook, and the town suffered as a result. A large part of the population is

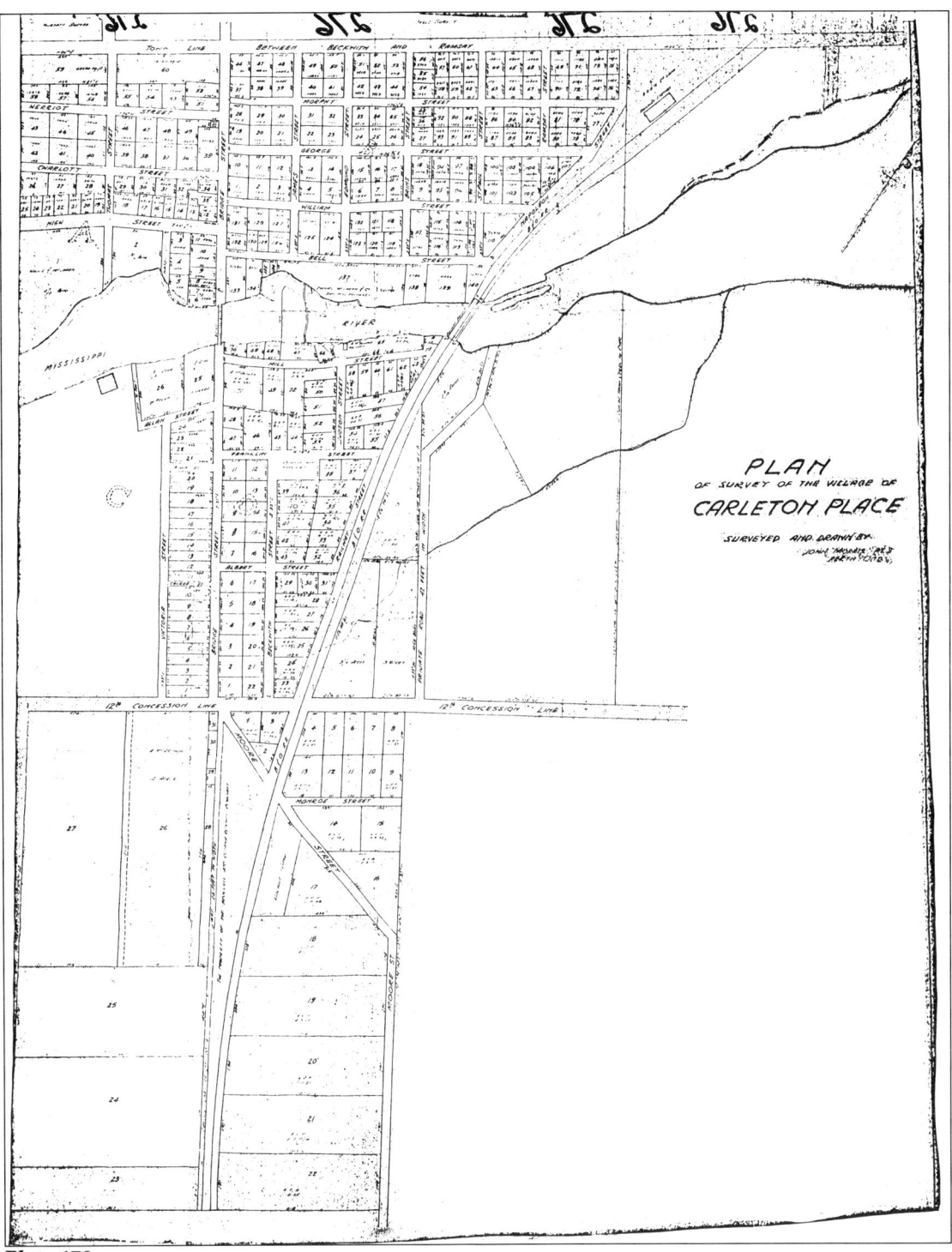

Plate 178
Map of Carleton Place in 1868, based on a plan of survey of the village of Carleton Place surveyed and drawn by John Morris, P.L.S., in October 1868. The sudden growth of Carleton Place within one year is shown by the dramatic expansion of blocks south of the Mississippi River. Lanark County Registry Office, Perth, plan no. 276.

composed of factory operatives, many of whom are constantly changing about from place to place, preventing the building up of steady citizenship.

The large labouring class component of Almonte's population was evident as early as 1861 to a Carleton Place inhabitant who, as his train pulled in to the Almonte station was struck by "a row of inquiring mechanical faces" that met his gaze.[67]

The somnolent state of Carleton Place in the decade before Confederation caused local inhabitants to wonder aloud whether or not Appleton, a few miles downstream, in its growth from a hamlet to a manufacturing village complete with a large woollen factory, shingle factory[68] and foundry[69] might yet rival Carleton Place. It is important to recognise that Carleton Place did not experience economic decline in the early 1860s. Indeed, William Paisley began operating a wool carding and cloth dressing mill,[70] Hugh McLeod took over the village oat mill,[71] and John McIntosh took over the village foundry and machine shop from the partnership of Dewar & McDonald, all in 1859.[72] Allan McDonald took over the foundry in 1860,[73] and in July John Sumner ambitiously opened his new store on the corner of Bridge and Bell streets by announcing he wished to purchase 10,000 pounds of wool and 500 kegs of good butter.[74] Similarly, the continuing importance of Carleton Place as a forwarding centre was shown by William Paisley's 1860 advertisement requesting 10,000 sheep pelts, 500 beef hides and any quantity of good wood in exchange for either cash or cloth.[75] In 1861 Allan McDonald offered for sale cooking and parlour stoves,[76] in 1862 John Sumner announced he no longer would give credit but rather only do business for ready pay,[77] William Paisley at his Wolverine Mills was seeking 200,000 pounds of clean wool and 30,000 sheep pelts,[78] and David Findlay arrived from Perth "prepared to execute all kinds of Castings, such as PLOUGHS, COOLERS of different sizes, STOVES, &c., of the most modern patterns."[79]

But if Carleton Place was not in decline, it seemed to be when compared with Amonte and Smith's Falls, and in contrast with the high hopes of local boosters. James Poole talked in vain about the natural advantages of Carleton Place, about its situation being "admirably adapted for business" by being centrally placed between the Ottawa River and Perth, and enjoying a "railroad connection with all parts of the civilized continent." The only thing lacking was "the introduction of two or three enterprising individuals, with the command of some capital."[80] A New York reader of the *Herald* suggested in 1865 that Carleton Place suffered from its rural sounding name, remarking "You will find Carleton Place occurring very seldom on maps, unless it may be a local one, while Franktown with probably half the inhabitants, and certainly with less advantages, is often mentioned. I think that those parties who got up the maps do not realize what an *important* position your little town occupies, from the name it bears."[81] The lack of significant growth at Carleton Place was so obvious in the early 1860s that another correspondent of the *Herald* advocated a trip on the railway to Brockville for those who "in the course of your mundane life in Carleton Place...may tire of its monotony and wish to drive off the 'blues'".[82] As late as the spring of 1866 the promoters of Carleton Place complained of the development that had failed to follow the railway into the village despite the excellent water-power available. "But of what avail are these natural advantages", exclaimed James Poole that January, "in view of the fact that...the splendid water power at this place, has unfortunately been kept in the hands of men who will neither sell nor rent, at a reasonable price; but instead of erecting mills and factories or allowing others to do so, prefer acting the part of the dog in the manger!!!"[83]

The industrialisation for which Carleton Place hungered began to materialise in 1866. John Gillies and Peter McLaren purchased the old sawmill in the village, fixed the machinery, and by August "an almost incredible quantity of sawn lumber is being turned out daily."[84] The partnership of Craigie and Stephenson from Peterborough that same month repaired the steam mill and began manufacturing shingles.[85] Before August was over the *Herald* happily predicted that Carleton Place "is destined at an early day, to become the most important point on the Mississippi river for the

Plate 179
The Mississippi Hotel, Bridge Street, Carleton Place, built in 1872 by Napoleon Lavallee, enlarged by Walter McIlquham in 1890, as photographed ca. 1920. A much larger structure than the Waterloo Hotel Lavallee built a generation earlier (Plate 63), this building reflected the growth of Carleton Place in the late 1860s and early 1870s. With a shortage of housing, and with a need for accommodation half the year while the sawmills were in operation, Lavallee recognised a market for rooms in the upper floors of his hotel. Better rooms with a promenade gallery were provided for discriminating travellers on the second floor. The Carleton Place and Beckwith Historical Society.

manufacture of sawn lumber" after learning that a major regional timberer, "Boyd Caldwell, Esq., of Lanark is said to have purchased...the site of a steam mill, to be erected next spring". There were further rumours of entrepreneurs arranging to purchase the water-power along the south side of the Mississippi in the village.[86] A year later, so optimistic was James Poole about the prospect of Carleton Place becoming "the largest town in the County of Lanark" that he ambitiously referred to sections of the village using the urban "upper town" and "lower town" designations found in the cities of Québec and Ottawa:[87]

> The steam mill is doing wonders in the way of making great numbers of good shingles. The steamboat is a great success, and is attracting many excursionists and pleasure parties. The large saw mill will be in motion in a few days, and with the other improvements in contemplation on the premises, and the line of railway to the station, will give profitable employment to a great number of men. Mr. [J.H.] Bredin's sawmill in Lower Town [Arklan] is also in successful operation, and is turning out large quantities of good lumber. He will soon require a railway track to connect with the iron horse.

By October 1867 Poole rejoiced[88]

> to say that our village has begun to show very marked symptoms of progress. The large lumber mills of Messrs. Gillies and McLaren are now in full and active operation, several gangs of men and several circular saws transformed the log in a few minutes into dressed lumber. Mr. Bredin, down the river further, has also an extensive saw mill in working order. Mr. All[a]n McDonald is engaged in erecting a large building to be used we believe as a Cloth Factory; and Messrs. Craigie and Stephenson are still employed in turning out shingles. All this has created a demand for house room for the large influx of population which these works have collected, and buildings are going up in every direction. Persons who are anxious to rent houses cannot obtain them, and we expect to see a good many buildings erected in the course of a year or two.

As the 1860s drew to a close the euphoria of Carleton Place promoters could hardly keep pace with their wonder at the growth of population and employment. "The manufacturing of lumber, and other business has brought in so many families of late", the *Herald* noted in November 1867, "that house accommodation is becoming scarce. Many old residents are surprised at the number of strange faces they meet in an evening's walk."[89] In the summer of 1868 the route of the Canada Central railway was surveyed from Ottawa to Carleton Place.[90] "Everywhere now are to be seen evidences of material prosperity, the result of busy enterprise" remarked James Poole in August 1868, "and we look forward for still further marks of progress."[91] In July 1869 a company was chartered, promising to canalise the Mississippi and to build a steamboat some 100 feet in length.[92] The steamboat, appropriately named the "Enterprise", was built, but construction of canal locks never went further than assigning contracts.[93]

The preponderant part of Carleton Place industrialisation in the late 1860s and early 1870s came from the sawn lumber industry. As James Poole remarked, "The B. & O. Railway, extending from the St. Lawrence to the Ottawa, and penetrating the lumber regions, in the great valley of the latter river, gives us the means of utilizing the millions of fine trees in our forests, which otherwise would be almost worthless". In the Gillies and McLaren sawmill in the summer of 1869 some "five hundred logs per day are 'chawed up'...into boards and lathe, and sent off to market" and at the Craigie shingle mill "about eighty thousand shingles are daily manufactured." That same summer Boyd Caldwell built a large steam sawmill "which will eat several hundred logs per day" and Allan McDonald began to install machinery in the woollen mill he had built a few years earlier.[94] The predominance of forest products in the Carleton Place economy is shown by the twelve major employers in the village in 1871 (Table 22). Over eighty percent of the employees working for the twelve largest employers in Carleton Place worked for the three big saw and shingle mills, and these figures did not take into account the large number of employees working at the Bredin sawmill just outside the Carleton Place village limits at Arklan.

Significantly, although the sawmills offered employment only seven months out of twelve, the monthly wage they paid was higher than that received by the employees of village artisans and tradesmen. Only the three employees of Caldwell and Brown's gristmill earned a higher monthly wage. As the population of Carleton Place jumped from 500 in 1861 to 1,205 in 1871, by July 1870 "the people in the streets might be counted by hundreds, all as busy as bees, over works of public or private enterprise".[95]

> Moreover [bragged James Poole in the *Herald*], our people are a united people.... We are not at cross purposes about our local improvements, but at this moment our mammoth saw-mills, our woolen factories, our large grist mills, our splendid school house, not excelled in the county, several large places of business worthy of any town in Canada, our steamboat "Enterprise," and forty or fifty buildings large and small rising in every direction, an unceasing clamour for

Plate 180
'Mapleleigh', the house built for James Gillies, Carleton Place, in 1883, burned in 1910, as photographed ca. 1895. When it was built this mélange of alternating wall surfaces, great chimney stacks, bay windows, polychromatic verandah posts and vergeboard finials, gables, cottage roof, shuttered windows and patterned shingles was considered the most fashionable house in town. The overall effect was one of substantial late-Victorian fussiness, of attempting to create some romantic sense of light and shade, and of an utter failure to create an overall pleasing effect. The major achievement for Carleton Place in the building of this mansion was for all future ambitious houses to be more subdued, and as a result, less ugly. National Archives of Canada negative no. PA-58041.

manual labour which cannot be satisfied...warrant us in inviting the...[County] Council to hold their next quarterly meeting at a place which promises to be a large town, when Perth has died of ancient respectability.

The sudden growth of Carleton Place in the late 1860s over which James Poole waxed rhapsodic in the *Herald*, also prompted a movement for the village to become municipally separated from Beckwith. Robert Bell and James C. Poole from the early 1850s had found their ambitions to promote Carleton Place opposed particularly by the Irish inhabitants of southern Beckwith, and as the costs of the Brockville and Ottawa railway mounted in the 1850s and 1860s, and as the railway contributed little to the development of Carleton Place before 1867, the criticism came from the Scottish highlanders of northern Beckwith as well, and particularly from Carleton Place merchant and Beckwith reeve Archibald McArthur. James Poole as editor of the village newspaper smarted at the defeat of a petition he presented Beckwith council in 1863 for a grant of fifty pounds to help build a drill shed for the local rifle company over which he presided in Carleton Place. He noted the large attendance of ratepayers from the southern and middle concessions of Beckwith voting against the measure and suspected that the matter had been "thoroughly canvassed in the neighborhood of Franktown and along the front of the township, and through some misconception of the proper motive embraced in the petition every man that could be drawn out filed his appearance in opposition to the measure, and felt they had done wonders when they had secured its defeat."[96] Three years later three Beckwith councillors opposed a second request for funds to build a drill hall[97]

on the ground of local feeling and seemed afraid some of their constituents would think that Carleton Place was getting too much of the Township money. One of the councillors said we ought to be satisfied since the Township had helped to build a bridge across the Mississippi river; another hinted that some of the people on the front of the Township would not be pleased

Table 22.   Carleton Place Major Industries in 1871

Firm	Annual Product Value	No. of Employees	Months Worked	Estimated Monthly Wages	Annual Total Wage Payments	Raw Material Costs
Gillies & McLaren Sawmill	$120,000	163	7	$30.7	$35,000	$75,000
Boyd Caldwell Sawmill	$100,000	40	7	$30.0	$8,400	$62,500
James & John Gillies Shingle Mill	$10,500	24	7	$23.8	$4,000	$6,600
Petty & McDonald Woollen Mill	$30,000	13	12	$34.6	$5,400	$13,500
John F. Cram Tannery	$20,096	7	12	$22.6	$1,897	$16,800
Joseph Cram Door & Sash Factory	$5,000	6	12	$34.7	$2,496	$2,000
William Patterson Cabinetmaker	$3,600	6	12	$17.4	$1,250	$1,200
Colin Sinclair Tailor	$4,715	6	12	$9.9	$718	$3,000
Andrew Walker Tailor	$2,700	5	12	$15.8	$950	$1,600
William Rorison Carpenter	$3,000	4	12	$31.3	$1,500	$1,200
James C. Poole Printing Office	$4,000	4	12	$16.7	$800	$1,600
Caldwell & Brown Flour, Barley & Oatmeal Mill	$15,000	3	12	$38.9	$1,400	$10,000
TOTAL	$318,611	281		22.58	$63,810	$195,000

SOURCE: 1871 manuscript census of Carleton Place, Ontario at the National Archives of Canada

Plate 181
The John McDiarmid farmhouse, lot 16, concession 8, Beckwith, built in 1904, as photographed ca. 1910. The overall structure of this house is similar to James Gillies's 'Mapleleigh' in Carleton Place (Plate 180), but was actually based on plans printed in the Farmers' Advocate. *John McDiarmid's sons, Daniel and Bob, hauled some 65,000 bricks by sleigh from Godfrey's brickyard in Carleton Place for the walls which were built three bricks thick. This was a more subdued and simpler treatment than the Gillies house, but it bears emphasizing that a brick house the same size as that built by the leading manufacturer at Carleton Place was built on a Beckwith farm where most of the barns were constucted of round logs and dated from the 1840s. The large new farmhouses may partly have resulted from the cheese economy, and from extended families of unmarried brothers and sisters pooling resources and living together with their parents in the same household, but the bottom line was to present a facade of sophistication equal to that found in Carleton Place. Photograph courtesy of Elizabeth and Norman McDiarmid, through Rosemary Wark.*

with him if he did not oppose everything that had for its object the improvement of Carleton Place.

The boosters of Carleton Place presented other instances of the humiliating treatment the village received at the hands of Beckwith councillors. In applying for funds to build new sidewalks to accommodate the new growth in 1868, James Poole reminded Beckwith "that the village pays about one-third of the whole taxes of the Township, and is now rapidly increasing in population, wealth and prosperity; and has never, at any time, enjoyed anything like its proportion of the expenditure of funds for public improvements."[98] In late August 1869 a meeting of Beckwith ratepayers was held at the township hall in Black's Corners to decide two questions, whether to loan $6,000 from the surplus funds of the municipality to build a large new school in Carleton Place, and whether to financially assist the Canada Central railway in constructing its line from Ottawa to Carleton Place. At the meeting James Poole observed that ratepayers from "the front and Franktown [were] there in full force, having been drummed up by those interested in defeating both measures."[99] Once again Poole perceived that the "jealous feeling which has frequently before been exhibited by the front of the Township with reference to Carleton Place again came into play, and a majority of the meeting refused to grant the reasonable request of the Trustees." Such treatment by Beckwith, Poole hoped, "will open the eyes of the people of this village to the necessity of at once separating from the township, and organizing a municipal government of our own."[100]

The campaign for the municipal separation of Carleton Place from Beckwith began with an editorial in the *Herald* in August 1868, listing numerous grievances of village inhabitants. Carleton Place was represented as paying almost a third of all Beckwith taxes because property in the village had for years been assessed at the highest possible value, whereas "the best farms in Beckwith are rated at an annual value, at which few of the proprietors would be willing to rent them, thus throwing the main bulk of taxation on the village people." What James Poole found galling was that whenever a grant was requested to make an improvement in the village, the Beckwith councillors became "afflicted with a retrenchment fit" and the people of Carleton Place were "regarded as a set of hungry creatures, whose desire is to prey upon the vitals of the township."

In 1868, without a representative from Carleton Place on the Beckwith council, there appeared to be "little to hope for in return for all they pay towards the township funds." If Carleton Place were to become a separate municipality, the village would not have to send[101]

> deputations of leading citizens out to the Town Hall to plead at "the bar of their honourable house" that the council should grant money for sidewalks.... The very statute labour would be better done, and the money expended to better account. Besides, our village would present a respectable appearance, and men and women would have some chance of walking our streets without having to divide the foot path with swine, which are now free commoners. We should have better regulations for the maintenance and direction of our village affairs, as the authority would be more centralized. We should be able to see the Reeve and Council, now and then, and if we had a little bill which required to be paid, it would not, as at present, require a day's journey to two villages, and a triangular expedition through the whole township to get a sight of our township officials.

James Poole held up the example of neighbouring Smith's Falls which fourteen years earlier had separated from North Elmsley Township, where there were "commodious streets, sidewalks with the planks *all nailed down*, (something we almost do not understand here,) and good wide ones into the bargain, as well as excellent roads for all vehicles."

The threat of municipally separating from Beckwith as late as December 1868 was simply a rhetorical weapon used to ensure that Carleton Place did not suffer unduly without a representative on the township council. James Poole was determined that Carleton Place would not be again caught without a representative on council, nor ganged up on by the rest of Beckwith at ratepayers meetings. In September 1868 Beckwith reeve Robert Crampton accused Poole of calling a separate meeting of Carleton Place electors so that they would not attend a township meeting at Black's Corners.[102] Sixteen freeholders residing in Carleton Place "highly dissatisfied with the manner in which the Councillors of the Municipality of Beckwith have, during the present year, discharged their duties" called a meeting in Napoleon Lavallee's hotel in December 1868 "to select, for nomination, freeholders to fill the offices of Reeve and Councillors during the year 1869".[103]

Plate 182
The Stages of Woman's Life from the Cradle to the Grave, a lithograph dating from the 1870s. Late nineteenth century Carleton Place and Ottawa newspapers increasingly promoted woman's role in life as being largely confined to the nurture of children, running a household, and also dispensing charity. For many small families on the poorer farms in Beckwith, women continued to labour in the fields, no matter how disdainfully the practice was regarded by women in Carleton Place who were introducing urbane rituals such as "at homes" and calling cards by the turn of the century. Most Beckwith women did not live to see their eightieth year, in contrast with the scheme of life presented here. Loaned courtesy of Nancy Adamson and Anne Molgat.

Even with a Carleton Place representative on the township council, the refusal of ratepayers from the southern eight concessions to loan money to build a large new school in the village or to help finance the Central Canada railway presented James Poole with just the evidence he needed to urge separation from Beckwith. "Though we contribute fully one-third of the revenue of the Township", he thundered after the meeting, "past experience has taught us that it is in vain to expect anything like justice from our neighbors of the front, and the sooner we obtain control of our own taxes the better." As one of twelve school sections in Beckwith, Carleton Place could only expect one twelfth of the school funds, whereas if it separated it would be entitled to an amount more in line with the one third of township taxes villagers paid:[104]

> The expense of carrying on a municipal government of our own would be very small, and we would have the satisfaction of seeing our revenue expended in our midst, and for our own benefit. Let a meeting be called and have the matter discussed, let a petition as required by law be presented to the County Council, and have the By-Law separating us passed at the October

meeting of that body, so that we may commence the next year as a separate corporation. Not till we "set up" for ourselves can we expect justice, or even that consideration which the growing wants of our flourishing village demand.

Throughout late 1869 and 1870 James Poole pulled out all the stops to bring about the incorporation of Carleton Place. He complained that municipal laws in Beckwith were "administered ignorantly, inefficiently and extravagantly, by a set of men who fritter away their time to very little purpose, leaving the points to be discussed and decided on in the hands of the clerk." It would be cheaper and the affairs of Beckwith inhabitants "would be more faithfully and justly transacted by the clerk alone", suggested Poole, "in the absence of councillors, attorneys, and other officials who hang round the board, impeding free access to the table, and interrupting all who may have business to bring before the CLERK."[105] The "ignorance and stupidity" of councillors kept Beckwith a "slow and behind-the-age township" as was shown by the disgraceful way tax money was squandered in breaking up stones for roads with "no benefit derived to the public." Breaking up stone to pave Beckwith roads, Poole charged, amounted to no more than "[h]eaping up along the roads *rocks* — obstacles in the way of carriage wheels — and then hav[ing] the audacity, the barefaced impudence to call them 'broken stones,' and paying men annually for a few yards here and there of this nuisance."[106]

In late August 1870, at the same time a great fire raged across nearby Carleton County, Poole stressed that Carleton Place was by no means free from danger, that a very slight spark "would in all probability envelop us in flames", and that the village fire engine was out of order and useless:[107]

What we want [Poole exhorted] is a good large fire engine, with a fire company regularly organized to work it. But before we can get that and many other things absolutely needed we shall have to get an Act of Incorporation for our village and shove off the burden of Beckwith which absorbs our funds and grumbles when we ask for our own in return. Carleton Place united with Beckwith at present is like a living being tied to a dead body.

In early October 1870 a public meeting of Carleton Place inhabitants in Dr. William Hurd's hall, chaired by Beckwith reeve Robert Crampton, was nearly unanimous "that the time had come when this village should be placed in its proper position, as to the township of Beckwith".[108] Accordingly, on the 13th of October 1870 Lanark county council enacted that Carleton Place "shall be a body corporate apart from the Township of Beckwith" as of the first Monday that November.[109]

Following incorporation as a village, Carleton Place continued to grow, with its population climbing from 1,205 in 1871 to 1,975 in 1881. In mid September 1870 traffic began moving between Carleton Place and Ottawa on the Canada Central railway,[110] and within a couple of weeks it was apparent that "large numbers of persons who were in the habit of passing up and down between Ottawa and the lumbering districts above Sand Point, instead of going by stage, steamer and tramway, now take the faster and most convenient route just opened."[111] David Wylie, the editor of the Brockville *Recorder* was so struck by the growth he beheld from his train window in early October 1870, that he stopped off in Carleton Place for a day "to note the improvements taking place in and around this thriving village." He exclaimed over the handsome new two-storey stone school built on Bridge Street as being "large enough to accommodate the children of the village for many years to come", and noted the newly completed Canada Presbyterian Church, and a new hotel being built by Mr. McIntosh of Perth. Wylie was impressed by the capacity of the Gillies and McLaren sawmill for sawing one hundred thousand feet of lumber a day, and observed that "the proprietors have built a branch railroad to the mill, which is of great service in the transmission of lumber." As for the steam sawmill of Boyd and Alexander Caldwell, Wylie found it temporarily shut down because the Mississippi was too low to bring down some 18,000 logs, but that ordinarily during each

Plate 183
The residence and woollen factory of Archibald McArthur, Esquire, Carleton Place, as lithographed in 1880 in H. Belden's Illustrated Atlas of Lanark County. *The rambling stone mansion started in 1872 and enlarged in 1877 and the stone woollen factory built in 1870 could not have been located further apart, unlike Hugh Boulton locating his gristmill and residence as close together as possible in the 1840s (Plate 176). The huge house, the shrubbery, flowerbeds, manicured lawns, winding driveway and stylishly-dressed men and women playing croquet were socially far removed from the dozens of labourers tending the looms in the factory. Beckwith farmers arriving with loads of wool might marvel at the size of the factory, but for much of the financially-troubled 1870s it remained closed. National Archives of Canada negative no. C-16905.*

eleven-hour workday it was capable of cutting 360 logs. He observed that the steam engine in the Caldwell mill "is furnished with a jacketted cylinder to keep the steam from condensing. The mill is also provided with machinery to carry the saw dust to the boiler fire, the machinery thus acting as a self feeder of fuel."[112]

Although sawmills remained predominant employers at Carleton Place until the turn of the century, the continuing growth of Carleton Place in the 1870s was fuelled by the construction of large woollen factories. The first of these was built for Archibald McArthur in 1870. David Wylie described the ambitious handsome stone structure built for McArthur by James McRorie as measuring[113]

> 95 x 55 feet, and will be five stories high, the dye house 40 x 50. The machinery is to be propelled by water power, and the labour to prepare a proper flume to convey a sufficient quantity of water has been so far, and will still be, a work of no small labour and expense, but when completed it is expected that a sufficient supply will be obtained to keep the factory in motion "all the year round." Of course the factory will be provided with all the et ceteras necessary, and the whole will probably not cost a less sum than $50,000 or $60,000. To the village it will be a boon of no small magnitude, giving employment...to hundreds of men, women and children, who must all be fed and clothed by the produce of the surrounding farmers and goods from the village merchants.

The success of McArthur's woollen factory was reflected in press announcements of 1872 that he was adding ten new looms[114] and building a huge stone house near the junction of the Canada Central and Brockville and Ottawa railways.[115]

In 1871 Abraham Code from Innisville requested tenders from contractors to build a stone woollen mill at Carleton Place,[116] but it was not until June 1875 that the completed mill opened. The editor of the Perth *Courier* was given a tour of the new woollen factory:[117]

> The building is a massive stone structure on the right bank of the Mississippi River, above the village proper and contiguous to Mr. Boyd Caldwell's steam sawmill.... [T]he upper flat of the factory rivals in height the lofty brick chimneys of the sawmill nearby.
>
> The size of the main structure is 55 x 70 feet, four stories and basement, with a dye and engine house 30 x 55 feet. The motive power is a steam engine manufactured by Goldie & McCulloch, Galt, 65 horsepower.... The building will be heated by steam throughout. The factory has a capacity for four sets of machinery.... [F]or the present only two sets will be put in the mill. When everything is in shape the building and outfit is not expected to cost less than $30,000.

The McArthur and Code woollen mills, despite the ambitious stone factories that were built, weathered the economic depression of the 1870s with some difficulty. In January 1876 Code suspended work at his Carleton Place mill for two weeks,[118] and yet by mid-December the Perth *Courier* presented as proof "that the woolen business is looking up in Canada Mr. Code's factory in Carleton Place is running to its full capacity on full time and Mr. McArthur's factory in that village will probably be in operation in the spring."[119] In May 1878 Code was forced to succumb to financial pressures, his mill closed,[120] and by March 1879 he was requesting a refund of his village taxes since his mill had made no profit,[121] but was refused.[122]

In February 1877 William Wylie of Almonte rented Archibald McArthur's empty factory[123] and began to manufacture tweeds. Wylie's success in part was due to hiring skilled men away from the Rosamonds at Almonte[124] and to the same canny ability to give the appearance of caring for his employees that James Rosamond had shown in the 1850s. In October 1879 Wylie threw a grand entertainment for his employees in the factory built by Archibald McArthur:"[125]

Plate 184
Abraham Code's woollen mill, Emily Street, Carleton Place, built in 1875, later the home of Leigh Instruments when photographed in 1982. The name of Hawthorne woollen mill that William Wylie bestowed on this factory upon leasing it in the late 1870s and purchasing it in 1881 remained connected with it. By 1880 Wylie was described as employing sixty labourers continually and turning out more than three thousand yards per week. This photograph was taken more than a decade after the brick smokestack of this woollen mill was torn down, and a few years before the belfry was dismantled.

> All his employees were present — also numerous friends and well wishers whom he had invited. The building was brilliantly lighted, and the road into the building was splendidly illuminated with Chinese lanterns.... The music was furnished by the Almonte String Band. The Carleton Place Brass Band was also in attendance and played a number of tunes at the outside of the main entrance. The evening was opened with a concert [including music, songs and recitations]. A grand supper was also given by Mr. Wylie and after dancing...and day was beginning to dawn they all started home.

The Wylie woollen factory was described in 1880 as being "fitted up with three sets of 48-inch cards, 16 narrow Crompton looms, five broad looms, and other machinery to correspond, all of the most approved patterns." Some 3,000 yards of finished cloth were produced every week by Wylie's seventy employees to whom on average he paid $21.42 every month.[126] In the autumn of 1881 Wylie purchased the mill built by Abraham Code, and proceeded to operate it as the Hawthorne Woollen Mill, and continued to lease Archibald McArthur's mill until his lease expired a few years later.[127]

During the summer and autumn of 1875 a stone factory was built on the north shore of the Mississippi across from McArthur's woollen mill for the firm of Gillies, Beyer and McLaren, headed by John Gillies. As machinery was moved into the factory in late October it was reported that the main bulding was "over 100 feet in length and will have a moulding shop, blacksmith shop and store room attached. The factory will manufacture steam-engines among other things, and will thus supply a want long felt in the section of country between Montreal and Toronto."[128] The Central Canada Machine Works as it came to be called was described in 1880 as "manufacturing the heavier classes of machinery for use in mills...including steam engines, water wheels, rotary pumps, presses, saw, grist and woollen machinery."[129] Among the products of this company was "a magnificent 120 horsepower engine which was shipped to Montreal for the Hochelaga cotton works" in late June 1879.[130] If there was any doubt about the coming of the mills transforming Carleton Place from a forwarding depot for provisioning the timber industry and servicing area farmers to an industrial town, the products of the Central Canada Machine Works being shipped to Montreal and as far west as Manitoba were substantial proof that Carleton Place had entered the industrial age.

The coming of the mills to Carleton Place in the late 1860s and throughout the 1870s caused the village to grow to five times its previous physical size. "We should very much like to have a few dozen good tradesmen in this village, — particularly Masons and Carpenters", remarked James Poole in the *Herald* in September 1870, "the demand for whose labour cannot at present be supplied. They could rely on constant work."[131] The houses constructed on the new blocks during 1870s were more ambitious structures than those built in previous decades. Carleton Place before incorporation had been the creation of two generations of Beckwith inhabitants attempting to escape the omnipresent forest, who inadvertently as a result had a visually unpleasant and physically uncomfortable place in which to live. Poole lamented in the summer of 1868:[132]

> In the majority of Canadian villages, where wooden houses prevail, they are generally put up in the most slovenly manner, without regard to order or neatness; and innocent of paint, they soon show the effects of the weather, and present anything but a respectable appearance. The mania for cutting down trees, has also been so thoroughly infused into the minds of the people, that many of them cannot bear to see a tree growing near their dwelling. If a young maple or elm tree has escaped in the general destruction of the forest, some urchin passing along with an axe on his shoulder, is sure to level it, out of sheer mischief. Our villages, therefore, have a bare and unsightly appearance.

Before Carleton Place was incorporated, Poole recommended in vain that if "every one would only set out a few trees in front of his own premises our streets would be more like avenues, and the trees

Plate 185
Employees at the Gillies woollen mill, Carleton Place, as photographed ca. 1885. In 1881 John Gillies purchased the woollen mill of Archibald McArthur (Plate 183) and continued manufacturing woollen cloth there. A quarter of the 41 employees posing for this photograph were women, and another ten were either children or young adolescents. The man in the three-piece suit at the centre was John Gillies. Most of the employees were decked out in their best clothes to have their photograph taken. The fancy hats and fine dresses of the women, the well-fitting suits, jaunty bowler hats and watch chains of the men combine to suggest the acceptable moderate standard of living the mills made available to many Beckwith farmers' sons and daughters for whom there was no farmland and who did not wish to move away any distance. The Carleton Place and Beckwith Historical Society.

besides affording a refreshing shade from the scorching heat of summer, would hide the deformities of the buildings, which...are generally of a poor class."[133]

One of the earliest by-laws enacted by the village of Carleton Place marked the end of disorderly streets, unkempt buildings and fire hazards. Privies no longer could be built near the streets, nor could piles of rubbish, firewood or timber be left indefinitely on public sidewalks. Animals could not be ridden or driven along or across sidewalks and people blocking the streets could be fined. Every proprietor of a house within two months was expected to provide a ladder reaching up to their chimneys, and fires were not to be made within ten feet of any building on the street and within 25 feet of any building on private property. Ashes could not be deposited within less than ten feet of any wooden structure, nor were stove pipes permitted to pass through the roof of any building. Fire arms could not be discharged within the village limits, nor could fireworks be set off among a crowd of people. Horses were not to be left untended, and not ridden nor driven any faster than at a moderate trot. Hand bills and advertisements could not be torn down, and no persons could "climb, bark, break, peel, cut, deface, remove, injure or destroy, the whole or any part of any tree or sapling". Streets could not be blocked up by anything having to do with the railway, and horses could not be trained or stud horses exhibited on any public street. Horses with vehicles could not stand too long along village streets, vehicles without horses could not appear on village streets, and horses and other animals could not be tied to trees or saplings.

Naturally, no disfiguring or defacing of public or private buildings was allowed, nor could stones and snowballs be thrown nor bows and arrows used on village streets. Excavations could not be left unattended, and "all steps, doorsteps, porches, railings, platforms, or other erections projecting into or obstructing any sidewalk, street, lane, or highway" had to be removed. All yards were to be kept "free from filth or offensive substances" and village inhabitants were required to "collect in one place [in their] yards all the house dirt or offal, and when the accumulation of such dirt or offal shall be equal to a load or become offensive" they had to remove it. Owners of dead animals were required to bury them at least three feet below ground, a distinct challenge in a village "built on a rock." Finally, "every person who shall keep any swine, horses, cows, dogs, goats, or other such animals on their premises in the said village, [must] maintain the...buildings, or pens...in such a clean state that the neighbours and passersby may not be incommoded by the smell therefrom."[134]

Substantial houses were built in the 1870s, with the stone mansion of Archibald McArthur setting the fashion with steep gables, L-shaped floorplan and set back from the street. As early as 1868 Robert Metcalf offered rough quarried or finely dressed stone window sills, quoins and base stones from his Beckwith quarry.[135] Lumber from the Carleton Place sawmills was as inexpensive as could be found anywhere in Ontario, and in an 1876 advertisement the firm of Pattie and Rorison announced that their planing mills not only made window sashes, doors and blinds, but also manufactured balusters, newel posts, terminals, scroll sawing, stair brackets, verandah brackets, barge boards, pine and hardwood hand rails, verandah roofing, verandah brackets, storm doors and shutters.[136] Napoleon Lavallee in 1879 built a large lime kiln on his farm on the southern outskirts of Carleton Place, after having previously burnt lime in adjacent Ramsay Township.[137] Brick, stone and frame houses of substantial proportions began to line the new streets of Carleton Place. The comfort and comparative sophistication of the interiors of these houses is reflected in the items that John Flett stocked in his store in 1880, including books, stationery, fancy goods, wall paper in great variety, pictures, picture frames, window blinds, fancy paper, clocks, watches, jewellery, silverware and lamps among other items.[138] As early as 1868 James Poole referred to village inhabitants "who would scorn to live in the old log houses which their fathers and grandfathers inhabited nearly half a century since, because they are now men of importance, squires &c," and who not only "improve their own dwellings [and] build new ones, [but even give] their sons and daughters broadcloth and silk to wear."[139]

The substantial houses built from the early 1870s onward reflected the prosperity that rapid industrialisation and incorporation brought to Carleton Place, but there were less attractive aspects to the sudden growth that made the village's population equal to that of rural Beckwith by 1880. Some of these social problems were simply extensions of situations that had existed in the village since before mid-century, such as gangs of young men congregating on street corners late at night. But if in 1851 David Lawson had argued that it was the more recently-arrived young men and boys who introduced foul language in contrast with "those who may be called natives of the village [who] are an orderly set of boys",[140] it was all the more tempting to draw distinctions between older-established families and the labourers flooding into Carleton Place during the late 1860s and 1870s. Despite the cleaning up of streets, the removal of wandering pigs, and the construction of large new private houses and public buildings, industrialisation also introduced a working class, industrial accidents, temporary employment, unemployment, starvation, rowdyism, social unrest, prostitution, abortion, infanticide, and crowded living quarters for workers. Not all of these things were entirely new, but from the local perspective it is important to recognise that many negative aspects of life were increasingly linked with the growing labouring population of Carleton Place.

Carleton Place inhabitants came to view the industrialists who brought positive growth to the village with increasing concern by 1880. The economic prosperity which the large sawmills alone had brought in the late 1860s was evident to a visitor from Perth in May 1867:[141]

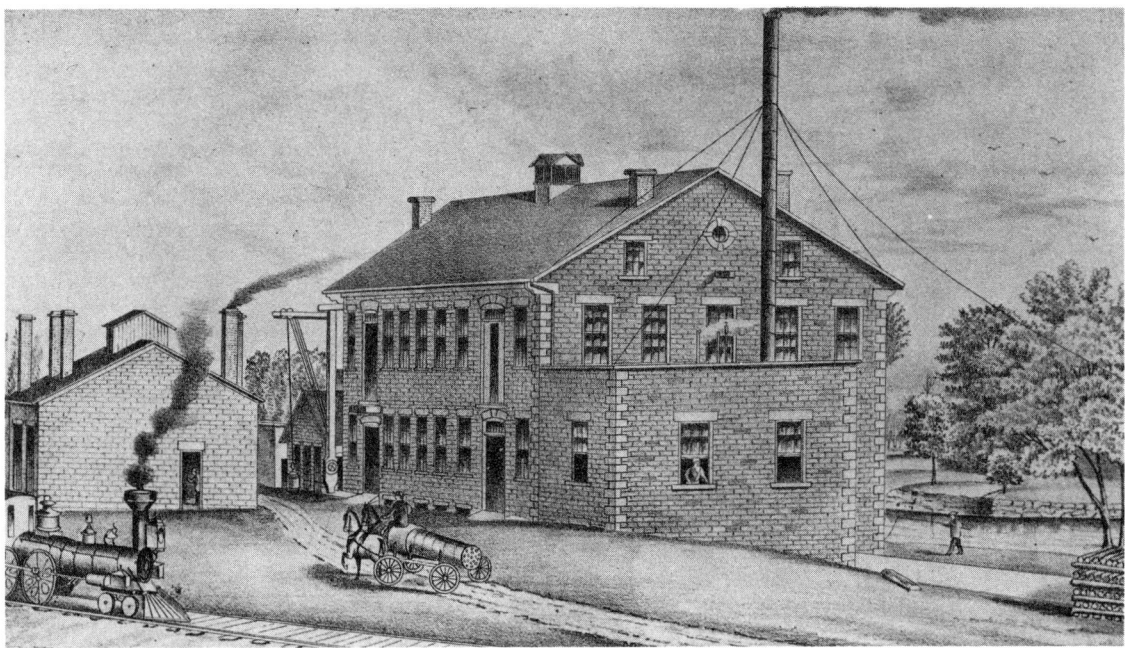

Plate 186
The Central Canada Machine Works of John Gillies and Ferdinand Beyer, built in 1875, as lithographed in 1880 for H. Belden's Illustrated Atlas of Lanark County. *This machine shop and foundry was built by John Gillies to set up his twenty-year-old son, Alexander, in business with an experienced partner. After Alexander's untimely death by drowning in 1878, his father carried on the business in his own name, manufacturing mill machinery and small marine engines. The smaller structure on the left was the forge. This business was located on the bank of the Mississippi to make use of the water-power, but during construction it was discovered that Archibald McArthur's deed of property on the opposite bank gave him control of the water privilege on both sides of the river. As a result, a forty horsepower steam engine was installed to run the machinery. National Archives of Canada negative no. C-16110.*

A year or two ago, Carleton Place exhibited many of the signs of p[re]mature decay that strike the eye so painfully in a ramble through the less-frequented streets of Perth. Dilapidated sidewalks, broken-down fences, empty-houses, whose broken windows alone indicated the p[re]sence of human beings, were the most prominent features of the "landscape." But now all this is changed; the sidewalks have been put in good walking order, the fences straightened up, the windows glazed and the houses filled with people. I am credibly informed that there is not lodging room for a cat left in the entire village, the result of which, though excellent for the property-owners thereof, is rather inconvenient for strangers. Every house, and every place fit to be converted into a house are occupied, so that all new comers are obliged to board out, and pay for the same whatever the conscientious villagers see fit to exact.

In addition to introducing economic prosperity, industrialists were at first positively viewed for substantially contributing to local worthwhile projects, as, for example, when Archibald McArthur headed the subscription list for building Zion Free Presbyterian Church in April 1868 with the hefty sum of £100.[142] In early April 1868, when two young men working in the Gillies and McLaren sawmill each broke a leg, their employer James Gillies "who is an example of benevolence and charity" headed up a subscription list circulated "among the generous-hearted workmen" to provide them with sufficient funds until they were well enough to work again.[143]

All too soon it became apparent that the industrialists did not necessarily share many of the goals of the longer-established village inhabitants. In January 1870 James Poole accused William Bredin of opposing "with all his energy, every public measure having for its object the prosperity and progress of our rising village...under the name of 'economy'", and particularly attacking one of Poole's pet projects, the building of a large new stone school.[144] In 1871, after a locomotive and four lumber cars ran off the track near the station, there were indeed grounds for suspecting that "operatives on railways are an overworked class, and that the long hours and broken rest tell upon the mental faculties of the employed, and leave them in no fit state for having care of the lives of passengers."[145] The sawmills as the major employers in the village offered only seasonal employment for seven months of the year from April to November when it was possible to bring timber down the Mississippi, and in a year such as 1868 low water in the river caused the Gillies and McLaren sawmill to close down before late October which the *Herald* deemed a calamity, as these fields of enterprise afforded maintenance to many families."[146] During the winter months many sawmill labourers went to work in the timber camps,[147] but numerous labourers remained without employment. When the Peter McLaren sawmill opened for the season in late April 1880, employing fifty men in night and day shifts around the clock, the *Herald* noted that this was "a great benefit to the labouring men of this town. A great many of them were idle for some time past and it was impossible for them to get work."[148]

The coming of the large mills also brought to Carleton Place the clash of capitalists competing with one another and of labourers battling exploiting employers. Between 1875 and 1884 the employees of Peter McLaren and Boyd Caldwell battled one another along the length of the Mississippi, as McLaren attempted to prevent other firms from using his dams and timber slides to move their logs downstream, and Caldwell responded by having his men cut passages through dams built by McLaren's men.[149] The ethnic rivalry for jobs which had existed in the upper Ottawa timber industry since the 1820s had sporadically emerged along the Mississippi at mid-century in fights among various raftsmen that occasionally touched individuals in the communities the lumber drives passed through. An inhabitant of Lanark Village complained in 1859 that if an "injured person complains he has a big cudgel with a Captain Rock like notice attached, advising him to keep silent else worse will befall him."[150] In early August 1880 when Peter McLaren "hired a gang of men...in Ottawa to work in his large sawmill...[,] most all of which were Frenchmen" the *Herald* reported that the "men who have been working in the mill all the summer up to the present date, are complaining of small wages and long hours which [are] considered almost unreasonable, and the new hands employed [are] getting higher wages than the old hands."[151]

In fact, the Franco-Ontarians were willing to work the long hours without grumbling for less pay, whereas the demand for wage labour in Carleton Place had driven local wages so high that "farmers are having to pay high wages for hirelings for harvest, much higher than for many years past."[152] In late October 1880 employees at the larger McLaren sawmill made a half-hearted attempt at striking for shorter hours:[153]

> It had been talked over for a few days before the strike was made, but at 6 o'clock on Friday evening they all stopped working and left the mill, vowing that they would work no longer from 6 in the morning till 7 at night. But on Saturday morning they were all at their posts at 6 o'clock. On being asked by the foreman of what had occurred on the previous evening they all promised to work the usual hours during the remainder of the season, and promised to make up the lost hour if required, but their foreman[,] manly enough[,] let them off on Saturday evening at six o'clock, as usual, being the rules of the mill. It is considered a foolish idea for all

Plate 187
View looking west along Elgin Street to the intersection of Victoria Street, Carleton Place, as photographed in 1982. Substantial frame houses were built along the streets of Carleton Place from the late 1860s on through to the turn of the century, reflecting the ready availability of cheap lumber in a town where most men were employed in the sawmills. Elgin Street was already laid out by the early 1860s, and the growing ambition of frame houses over the years is shown by the contrast in size of the single storey Edmond Burke house on the far right built in the late 1850s or early 1860s, the storey-and-a-half structure dating from the 1870s at the end of the street, and the full two-storey house on the left built in the 1890s.

the hands to have worked the full hours all summer to strike now when the mill is about to close down shortly for the season.

Apart from this feeble attempt at a strike, it is significant that there is no record before 1881 of any other organised protest by the labourers grinding away their lives during the thirteen-hour shifts in the mills at Carleton Place. As for the growing numbers of comfortably housed merchants, professionals and farmers, if as late as 1860 regional timber manufacturers feared that from among the Scottish lowland settlers Chartist agitators might arise exhorting raftsmen and bush farmers to restrict their powerful operations along the Mississippi,[154] by the mid 1870s middle class Carleton Place inhabitants were more inclined to criticise the labourers than the manufacturers. In April 1869 when James Poole at the *Herald* compared the "ruddy looks and hearty, healthy appearance" of young men in previous years with the "number of half poisoned looking specimens...to be seen, of from fifteen to twenty years of age, with their sharp-visaged, wrinkled, nervous-looking appearance, wearing unmistakeable evidence of care, anxiety and age", he attributed these cadaverous looks to the numbers of young men smoking pipes and cigars[155] rather than as the more obvious toll taken by thirteen-hour shifts in the mills.

The Carleton Place village council in April 1874 passed a by-law "prohibiting the keeping of billiard, bagatelle and pigeon-hole tables for public resort" because "Gambling is vice of a very aggravated nature, which encourages drunkenness, profane swearing and frequently causes the ruin of both body and soul of those addicted to it, and not unfrequently murder".[156] When in 1876 a French-Canadian labourer named Campeau "attempted to commit an indecent assault on a young woman named Gordon, [who although] reputed to be of light character,...in this instance rejected Campeau's approaches,...defend[ing] herself with a butcher's knife, inflicting an ugly wound on his left hand, nearly severing his fingers"[157] it was one of numerous violent incidents that justified the construction of a town hall and village lock-up in 1871.[158] It struck no one as unusual in the least that small boys as a matter of course were employed alongside men in the Gillies and McLaren sawmill,[159] but in 1879 the *Herald* editor was incensed by the village council's decision to deal with "the unfortunate poor who may call for a night's shelter and a meal's victuals" at the town hall by ordering the "chief constable to incarcerate these victims of poverty and want in their cold, damp cells without a particle of nourishment." James Poole termed this "a disgrace to civilized humanity."[160]

Poole's indignation at the treatment of the starving poor was not so much the sentiment of a charitably disposed person, but rather was a lashing-out at a party headed by manufacturer William Bredin which not only opposed some of the pet municipal projects of James Poole and Robert Bell, but gained control of the village council. Carleton Place in the 1870s became divided into two municipal factions each with sectional, religious and political overtones. With the Beckwith council no longer available to serve as a scapegoat for whatever ailed Carleton Place, Poole vented his wrath at the Bredin faction for opposing building a new school in 1870, a town hall and lock-up in 1871, a high school in 1878, and converting the 1871 town hall into a public school. As the village proper expanded south of the Mississippi so that the river evenly divided Carleton Place, strong sectional jealousies mounted as to the location of the schools and town hall, due to the value they would give nearby real estate. The construction of the new Free Presbyterian church south of the river in 1869 whereas the Church of England and Church of Scotland houses of worship were in the older part of the village added a voluntarist versus state church dimension to the sectional rivalry within the town.

The struggle between longer-established inhabitants and the newly-arrived manufacturers became so heated that William Bredin and his associates brought in William W. Cliff to run a newspaper in opposition to Poole's *Herald*. Cliff's Carleton Place *Central Canadian* became a Conservative organ, and served to politicise the strong sectional feeling.[161] As late as October 1878 the *Herald* loftily stated that the "organ of the Anti-School ring...is beneath notice" and refused to "trouble our readers with any lengthened notice of that ably edited, gentlemanly newspaper which is Printed in Napanee and circulated here as an industry of this town!"[162] But once the *Central Canadian* began receiving backing from the newly-restored Conservatives in Ottawa, Poole no longer could restrain his venom. An example of the politically-charged epithets hurled back and forth by the two editors is provided by Poole in June 1879: "That screeching sheet on the South side gave birth to an unmitigated falsehood in its last issue by publishing a report that our Brass Band received $30 for playing at the Reform celebration in Lanark."[163] So strong was the sectional feeling in Carleton Place by 1879 that when constables attempted to protect carpenters in carrying out the orders of the school board to convert the town hall chamber into two classrooms, a mob of north side inhabitants assaulted them and locked them up in the cells on the ground floor.[164] Clearly, north side inhabitants regarded the conversion of the town hall into a school as a pretext by the south side inhabitants to build a town hall on the south side.

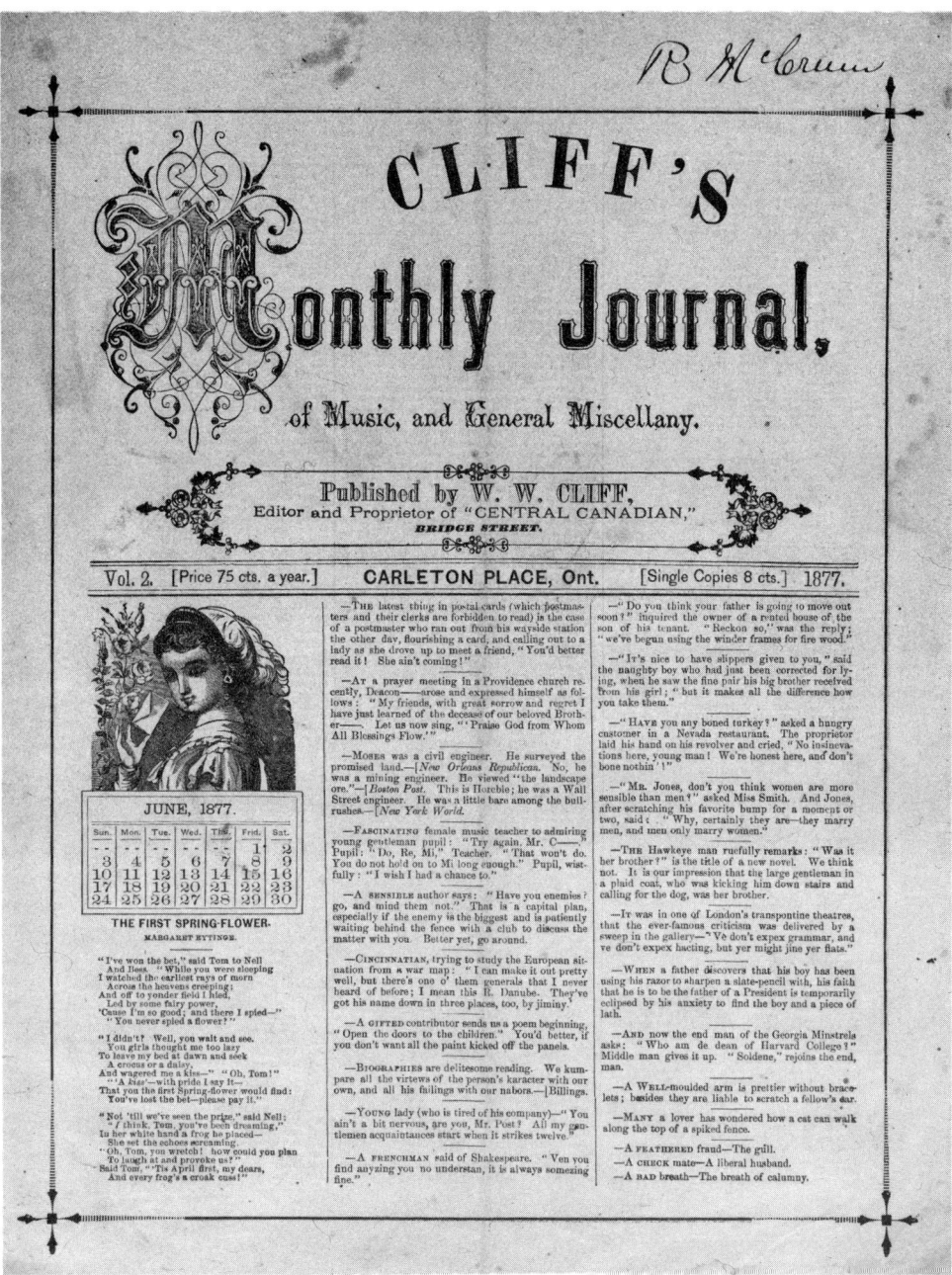

Plate 188
The title-page of Cliff's Monthly Journal of Music and General Miscellany *published by William W. Cliff, editor of the Carleton Place* Central Canadian, *1877. This briefly-lived periodical contained sheet music, poems, humour, designs for gowns and advertising, largely aimed at women readers. Save for the mast-head and local advertisements, this journal was an American publication, with appropriate blanks left to give it the look of a local publication. By the 1880s both the* Herald *and the* Central Canadian *newspapers at Carleton Place were using ready-print, that is, newsprint with one side of the sheet already preprinted either in Montreal or Toronto, and the blank side used to print local happenings and advertisements. The publishing of* Cliff's Monthly Journal *reflected a new awareness by local merchants of the growing influence of women as consumers and as the central figures in their households. Private collection.*

392 THE COMING OF THE MILLS

Plate 189
An unidentified camboose lumber shanty somewhere in the upper Ottawa valley, as photographed ca. 1900. Labourers from Carleton Place and farmers and farmers' sons from Beckwith up until the turn of the century sought to supplement their income by working in lumber camps on the upper Mississippi and the upper Ottawa. With most married men from Beckwith away in the timber camps, there was a growing social division between men and women. The 85 men in this camp shared the rough camaraderie of working, eating, drinking, dancing and sleeping together, away from the constraining influences of society in Beckwith that was growing increasingly sophisticated. Photograph courtesy of Pauline Wright.

The coming of the large mills to Carleton Place had not transformed the village quite in the way that its boosters had anticipated at the time they strove to leave Beckwith. Population growth, physical expansion of the village, and prosperity for some inhabitants came with industrialisation, but it also was accompanied by violence, poverty, sectionalism and bitter partisan division. The most profound change that industrialisation helped to bring about locally was to transform local attitudes toward social mobility, that is, toward the notion of improving one's station in life. A correspondent of the *Herald* in 1862 who signed himself TYRO argued against the weight of local tradition that militated against individuals raising their horizons:[165]

> A quarter of [a] century has passed away and the population has been probably twice renewed, and the differences which existed between the different families composing the population at that period are handed down as family heirlooms.... Every family has a chronicle of its own of the short-comings and peculiarities of its neighbors, and if Miss Blank on the head of her father's success in life tosses her feathers one-fifteenth part of an inch above the average, some small dormant speck on the escutcheon of the Blanks is unrelentingly poured on her devoted head. What a world of satisfaction is there in being able to say, "Pshaw! his father was only a

Shoemaker!" — although the respected cordwainer may have been one of nature's noblemen, still the speck is there undeniably, and the thermometer of pride consequently sinks.

A mere six years later, in the midst of Carleton Place industrialising, James Poole editorialised at length about pride of family distinction, won by the parents as "apt to poison the minds of the children, who, scorning those exertions which they think no longer necessary to subsistence, and to gratify lazy habits framed in youth, grow indolent, effeminate and, perhaps, vicious."[166]

But if there was concern about prosperity potentially leading to degeneracy, the antidote which James Poole recommended was one that everyone had agreed on since before mid-century, — teaching children to be industrious. As early as 1851 Poole had argued that indigent orphans, and the children of paupers and criminals should be educated by the state "to coerce these persons into industrial habits."[167] As for those children with parents, it was widely assumed that because "children are the property of their parents"[168] they would be sufficiently immersed in work to preclude becoming lazy and useless to society. The coming of the factories and mills to Carleton Place simply placed boys in an industrial setting performing the same lengthy hours of work that children did on farms in rural Beckwith.

The legacy of child labour that had existed in Beckwith from the earliest days of settlement continued in the factories of Carleton Place well past 1880. It was justified by local employers who argued that rather than allow boys to spend time on street corners "in frivolous amusements, or in inglorious inactivity" it would be better for them to "spend a few years of active earnest usefulness" benefitting themselves and others, even if it meant shortening their lives. This was preferable to drawl[ing] out four score years in sluggish indolence or dishonorable ease." Life was likened to a "march over a road beset on either side with ditches and quagmires, and he who is not active and enterprising will be either trodden down ignomin[i]ously, or shoved aside ingloriously."[169] It is tempting to speculate about the monotony, the drudgery, the long hours, the repetitive labour that turned the children into machines, the everpresent danger from whirring sawmill blades, gears, bolts and pulleys, and the coercion of parents working alongside the children to keep them at their tasks. All the same, it is important to recognise that children working in unmechanised environments in rural Beckwith also found the labour expected of them intolerable, as when apprentice Thomas Lumsden ran away from his employer at Franktown, cooper William Nesbitt, in 1855.[170] For all the growth and prosperity of Carleton Place that had taken place between 1867 and 1880, the coming of the mills enforced the same work ethic in that village which the children of Beckwith were pinioned under by their fathers.

Endnotes

1 *Bathurst Courier*, 25 February 1853, p. 2, col. 5.
2 *Carleton-Place Herald*, 8 August 1854, p. 1, col. 1.
3 NAC Reel C-11731, 1852 census of Beckwith, pp. 82, 94, 98, 101, 104.
4 *Bathurst Courier*, 25 February 1853, p. 2, col. 5.
5 *Carleton-Place Herald*, 1 February 1855, p. 3. col. 8.
6 Ibid., 15 August 1854, p. 3, col. 8; 30 November 1854, p. 4, col. 1; 13 July 1864, p. 3, col. 6; and 16 March 1870, p. 3, col. 3.
7 McCuan family correspondence, 23 February 1857 letter from John McCuan, Airthrey Cottage, Bridge of Allan, Scotland, to Peter McCuan, Beckwith.
8 *Carleton-Place Herald*, 18 July 1854, p. 3, col. 8; and 1 August 1854, p. 2, cols. 1-2.
9 Ibid., 24 May 1865, p. 3, col. 7.
10 *Bathurst Courier*, 12 December 1851, p. 4, col. 1.
11 *Carleton Place Herald*, 14 August 1861, p. 2, col. 5.
12 *Perth Lanark Observer*, 4 August 1852, p. 1, col. 1.
13 *Carleton-Place Herald*, 20 November 1851, p. 2, col. 1.
14 Ibid., 1 July 1852, p. 2, col. 7.
15 Ibid., 8 July 1852, p. 3, col. 1.
16 Ibid., 4 March 1852, p. 2, col.4.
17 Ibid.
18 Ibid., 11 March 1852, p. 2, col. 4.
19 Ibid., 18 March 1852, p. 2, cols. 3-4.

20 Ibid., 1 April 1852, p. 2, col. 3.
21 1874 diary of George McLaren, Beckwith.
22 OKQAR James S. Bangs, Pakenham, letterbook, 1855-1862, 14 August letter to J.H. Evans, Esq.
23 Ibid., 10 September 1855 letter to Messrs. Seymour, Whiting and Company, Montreal.
24 Ibid., 15 November 1855 letter.
25 Ibid., 1 January 1856 letter.
26 Ibid., 15 January 1856 letter.
27 Ibid., 21 January 1856 letter.
28 Ibid., 5 March 1856 letter to Messrs. John Henderson and Company, Montreal.
29 Ibid., 12 March 1856 letter.
30 *Carleton-Place Herald*, 11 March 1852, p. 2, col. 4.
31 Ibid., 1 April 1852, p. 2, col. 3.
32 Lockwood, *Montague: A Social History*, p. 242.
33 Ibid., p. 219.
34 *Carleton-Place Herald*, 30 December 1852, pp. 2-3, cols. 7-2.
35 *Carleton Place Lanark Herald*, 20 December 1850, p. 2, col. 5.
36 *Carleton-Place Herald*, 20 May 1852, p. 2, cols. 3-4.
37 Ibid., 27 October 1853, p. 2, col. 4.
38 Ibid., 3 November 1853, p. 2, col. 7.
39 Ibid., 24 November 1853, p. 2, cols. 5-6.
40 Ibid., 5 March 1857, p. 2, col. 6.
41 Ibid., 30 March 1870, p. 3, col. 3.
42 Ibid., 3 January 1856, p. 3, col. 7.
43 Ibid., 5 May 1859, p. 3, cols. 4-5.
44 Ibid.
45 Ibid., 19 May 1855, p. 2, col. 5.
46 Ibid., 26 February 1852, p. 2, col. 4.
47 Ibid., 28 April 1853, p. 2, col. 3.
48 Ibid., 30 June 1853, p. 3, col. 4.
49 Ibid., 11 March 1858, p. 2, col. 7.
50 Ibid., 30 June 1859, p. 3, col. 2.
51 Ibid.
52 Ibid., 12 March 1857, p. 3, col. 3.
53 Ibid., 3 November 1859, p. 3, col. 1.
54 Ibid., 19 April 1860, p. 3, col. 4.
55 Ibid., p. 3, cols. 3-4.
56 Ibid., 12 April 1860, p. 3, col. 1.
57 Ibid., 20 November 1861, p. 2, cols. 6-7.
58 Ibid., 19 November 1862, p. 2, col. 4.
59 Brown, *Lanark Legacy*, p. 136.
60 *Carleton Place Herald*, 2 June 1859, p. 3, col. 7.
61 Ibid., 23 September 1858, p. 3, col. 3.
62 Ibid., 25 August 1859, p. 3, col. 3.
63 Ibid., 26 January 1860, p. 3, cols. 5-6.
64 Ibid., 5 September 1860, p. 2, col 3.
65 *Almonte Gazette*, 11 October 1867, p. 2, col. 2.
66 Andrew Haydon, "History of Lanark County" in the *Almonte Gazette*, 26 January 1894, p. 1.
67 *Carleton Place Herald*, 11 September 1861, p. 2, col. 7.
68 Ibid., 5 May 1859, p. 3, cols. 4-5.
69 Ibid., 19 May 1859, p. 3, col. 7.
70 Ibid., 16 June 1859, p. 3, col. 7.
71 Ibid., 27 October 1859, p. 3, col. 5.
72 Ibid., col. 6.
73 Ibid., 8 March 1860, p. 3, col. 6.
74 Ibid., 5 July 1860, p. 3, col. 3.
75 Ibid., 24 October 1860, p. 3, col. 1.
76 Ibid., 23 October 1861, p. 3, col. 7.
77 Ibid., 29 January 1862, p.3, col. 6.
78 Ibid., 21 May 1862, p. 3, col. 7.
79 Ibid., 15 October 1862, p. 3, col. 7.
80 Ibid., 17 April 1861, p. 2, col. 5.
81 Ibid., 2 August 1865, p. 3, col. 1.
82 Ibid., 15 October 1862, p. 2, cols. 5-6.
83 Ibid., 17 January 1866, p. 2, col. 4
84 Ibid., 8 August 1866, p. 2, col. 2.
85 Ibid., 22 August 1866, p. 2, col. 4.
86 Ibid., 29 August 1866, p. 2, col. 3
87 Ibid., 21 August 1867, p. 2, col. 5.
88 Ibid., 2 October 1867, p. 2, col. 3.
89 Ibid., 13 November 1867, p. 2, col. 4.
90 Ibid., 1 July 1868, p. 2, col. 5.
91 Ibid., 12 August 1868, p. 2, col. 2.
92 Ibid., 21 July 1869, p. 2, col. 5.
93 Ibid., 28 July 1869, p. 1, cols. 2-3.
94 Ibid.
95 Ibid., 6 July 1870, p. 2, col. 4.
96 Ibid., 25 February 1863, p. 2, col. 3.
97 Ibid., 17 January 1866, p. 2, cols. 1-2.
98 Ibid., 1 April 1868, p. 2, col. 7.
99 Ibid., 25 August 1869, p. 2, col. 2.
100 Ibid.
101 Ibid., 19 August 1868, p. 2, col. 2.
102 Ibid., 9 September 1868, p. 2, col. 4.
103 Ibid., 16 December 1868, p. 3, col. 4.
104 Ibid., 25 August 1869, p. 2, col. 2.
105 Ibid., 3 November 1869, p. 2, col. 5.
106 Ibid., 6 April 1870, p. 2, col. 5.
107 Ibid., 24 August 1870, p. 2, col. 4.
108 Ibid., 12 October 1870, p. 2, col. 3.
109 Ibid., 7 December 1870, p. 2, col. 7.
110 Ibid., 7 September 1870, p. 3,col. 4.
111 Ibid., 28 September 1870, p. 2, col. 2
112 Ibid., 12 October 1870, p. 2, col. 3.
113 Ibid.
114 *Perth Courier*, 2 February 1872.
115 Ibid., 13 September 1872. The 6 July 1877 *Perth Courier* refers to McArthur completing a substantial addition to the house.
116 *Carleton Place Herald*, 3 May 1871, p. 3, col. 1.
117 *Perth Courier*, 4 June 1875.
118 Ibid., 28 January 1876.
119 Ibid., 15 December 1876.
120 Ibid., 17 May 1878.
121 Ibid., 26 March 1879.
122 Ibid., 12 November 1875.
123 Ibid., 2 February 1877.
124 [Richard Reid], *The Development of the Woollen Industry in Lanark, Renfrew and Carleton Counties* (Almonte: North Lanark Historical Society, 1978), p.

13.
125 *Perth Courier*, 15 October 1879.
126 H. Belden and Company, *Historical Atlas of Lanark and Renfrew Counties* (Toronto: H. Belden and Company, 1880; reprint ed. : Port Elgin, Ontario: Ross Cumming, 1972), p. 20.
127 *Carleton Place Herald*, 30 November 1881.
128 *Perth Courier*, 29 October 1875.
129 Belden, *Historical Atlas of Lanark and Renfrew*, p. 20.
130 *Carleton Place Herald*, 2 July 1879.
131 Ibid., 7 September 1870, p. 2, col. 3.
132 Ibid., 10 June 1868, p. 2, col. 3.
133 Ibid., 5 May 1869, p. 2, col. 5.
134 Ibid., 22 February 1871, p. 3, cols. 1-2.
135 Ibid., 22 July 1868, p. 3, col. 5.
136 Ibid., 12 April 1876.
137 Ibid., 27 August 1879.
138 Ibid., 31 March 1880.
139 Ibid., 18 November 1868, p. 2, col. 2.
140 *Carleton Place Lanark Herald*, 21 March 1851, p. 3, col. 1.
141 *Perth Courier*, 10 May 1867, p. 2, cols. 6-7.
142 Ibid., 24 April 1868, p. 2, col. 6.
143 Ibid., 17 April 1868, p. 2, col. 8.
144 *Carleton Place Herald*, 19 January 1870, p. 2, col. 7.
145 Ibid., 6 September 1871, p. 2, col. 3.
146 Ibid., 21 October 1868.
147 Ibid., 10 November 1880.
148 Ibid., 21 April 1880.
149 *Perth Courier*, 5 May 1882. For more detail consult Brown, *Lanark Legacy*, pp. 234-240.
150 *Perth Courier*, 28 October 1859, p. 2, col. 4.
151 *Carleton Place Herald*, 11 August 1880.
152 Ibid.
153 Ibid., 27 October 1880.
154 *Ottawa Citizen*, 25 August 1860, p. 4, col. 6.
155 *Carleton Place Herald*, 7 April 1869, p. 2, col. 7.
156 *Perth Courier*, 17 April 1874.
157 Ibid., 21 April 1876.
158 Ibid., 6 December 1872.
159 *Carleton Place Herald*, 21 April 1880.
160 Ibid., 2 April 1879.
161 *Perth Courier*, 14 January 1876.
162 *Carleton Place Herald*, 9 October 1878.
163 Ibid., 25 June 1879.
164 Ibid., 11 June 1879.
165 Ibid., 26 November 1862, p. 2, col. 6.
166 Ibid., 11 March 1868, p. 2, col. 6.
167 Ibid., 23 October 1851, p. 2, cols. 3-5.
168 Ibid., 20 November 1851, p. 2, cols. 4-5.
169 Ibid., 15 March 1855, pp. 2-3, cols. 8-1.
170 Ibid., 8 March 1855, p. 3, col. 7.

Plate 190
St. Paul's Presbyterian church, Franktown, built 1902, as photographed in June 1983. This whimsical yet picturesque essay in what was termed Scottish-baronial church architecture became the visual anchor for Franktown in the twentieth century. Despite the sentimentality of the architecture, rural churches such as this became the hub of local life, both devotionally and socially. Increasingly, christenings, weddings and funerals were held within churches, and women used the basement hall to hold annual church suppers. Despite the growing moral influence of women, the traditional patriarchal customs and vocabulary of Beckwith churches continued. When Dougald Ferguson of the Derry passed away in 1897, his lengthy obituary entitled "A Father in Israel" extolled this elder of St. Paul's church for having been "not once absent from the communion table and only once from the service preparatory to the sacrament."

THE TRIUMPH OF SENTIMENTALITY

1881-1920

EDWARD KIDD AND THE BURDEN OF CHILDHOOD

George Edward Kidd was only seven years old when his mother died in September 1889. He was much too young to remember her distinctly other than to occasionally view a *carte de visite* showing her, his father, himself as the baby of the family, and his brother Angus, taken a few years before her death. His father, Joseph Kidd, never remarried, so that Edward's older sisters Annie, Margaret and Elizabeth effectively attempted to mother their younger brothers, not only feeding and clothing them, but reading, talking to and singing with them. And yet, if there was a motherly or matriarchal image which ingrained itself in young Edward Kidd's consciousness it was one of a protecting Queen Victoria. From the vantagepoint of middle age he recalled, "My early days were lived deep in the Victorian age. The old Queen, of whom none dared ever to speak disrespectfully, seemed to have been living since the beginning of time, and would go on living forever. We had a framed picture of all of her family, together with their spouses; gotten through the *Family Herald*"[1] The extensive memoirs that Edward Kidd wrote in middle age offer a sense of what it was like to grow up in rural eastern Ontario during the closing decades of the nineteenth century and the opening years of the twentieth. Raised as he was near the centre of Beckwith, Edward Kidd was a product of the merging identities of Irish and Scottish families at a time when young people continued to leave the township seeking futures elsewhere.

Edward Kidd, or Ned as his brothers and sisters came to call him, was the sixth of eight children born to Joseph Kidd and Mary McDiarmid between 1870 and 1888. Eight children was a large family in Beckwith for the 1880s, but it paled before the family of fifteen children in which his father had been raised at mid-century. Edward Kidd's father, Joseph Kidd, was the son of John Kidd, who immigrated with his father, Andrew Kidd, from the village of Coon, in the parish of Leighlinbridge, county Kilkenny, Ireland, in 1818.[2] Joseph Kidd at mid-century was raised a member of the Anglican Church. Because the Kidd farm on Clergy Reserve lot 21 in the sixth concession was located in the Derry school section, a locality in central Beckwith isolated from the rest of the township by swamp that surrounded it on three sides, most of their immediate neighbours were of Perthshire highlander origin. Inevitably some of the Scottish influence rubbed off on the Kidd family. Hence Scottish expressions such as "cowbyre" crept into their vocabulary. Edward's mother, Mary McDiarmid, daughter of Perthshire immigrant Angus McDiarmid on Clergy Reserve lot 24 close by was raised as a Free Church Presbyterian. When she married Joseph Kidd in 1869[3] they compromised their differing religious inheritance by attending the Methodist church at Prospect, and while attending Methodist conferences Joseph Kidd gradually moved from the political Conservatism in which he had been raised to become a Liberal. The horror of the rest of his family at these defections was compactly stated by Harold Kidd of Burritt's Rapids, "It is bad enough for a Kidd to turn Methodist, but for one to be found in the ranks of the Liberals is terrible."[4]

Edward Kidd's father before him knew what it was like to lose a parent in early childhood. Joseph Kidd was only four years old when his father died in 1851, but in making out his will in 1850 John Kidd left his homestead to his sons Eli, James, Joseph and Edward, stipulating,[5]

> When my dear wife's time expires in giving up the said west and east halves of the beforename[d] LOT of land, it is ordered by me that she receive yearly during her natural life, 5 pounds from the

Plate 191
Interior of the Derry schoolhouse, lot 22, concession 6, Beckwith, built 1870, as photographed in 1913. Women predominated as teachers in this and other Beckwith school sections during the late nineteenth and early twentieth centuries. The large flag dominating the front of the classroom corroborates Edward Kidd's comment that "The imperialism of Kipling dominated all" at the turn of the century. Around the large woodbox and stove in the centre of the schoolroom were the new cast-iron seats purchased in the 1880s. The photograph of Queen Victoria on the upper left suggests her lingering influence more than a decade after her death. Taken together with the picture of an Edwardian beauty and a landscape, it suggests the importance placed by some teachers on creating a feminine environment. The chalkboards made of painted smooth planks indicate the financial limits placed on facilities even in a progressive school section. Photograph courtesy of John and Leona Kidd.

west half and 3 pounds from the east half besides the privilege of the Front Room on the first floor in the stone house to live in if my dear wife wishes to remain on the Farm.

Joseph Kidd's widowed mother chose to remain on the farm, but with numerous young children requiring her attention, in 1858 she married Thomas Kidd, a cousin of her late husband. One of her sons, Eli, moved to Huron County, and another son Edward went off to study medicine, leaving Joseph and James respectively to occupy the east and west halves of the homestead lot. There is no indication as to whether Joseph Kidd resented his stepfather running the family farm, but after marrying at the age of 24 he took over his part of the homestead, occupying the stone farmhouse his father had built in 1842 in the centre of the lot. In contrast with the majority of Beckwith farms, between half and two-thirds of Joseph Kidd's farm consisted of class 1 soil, but in conformity with agricultural practice in the rest of the township he practised mixed farming on it.

From the time he was able to toddle it seemed to young Edward Kidd that he was expected to make himself useful around the farm. At first his chores simply consisted of filling woodboxes, of laying in a double supply of firewood on Saturday nights, of tending gaps in the hay rack while

 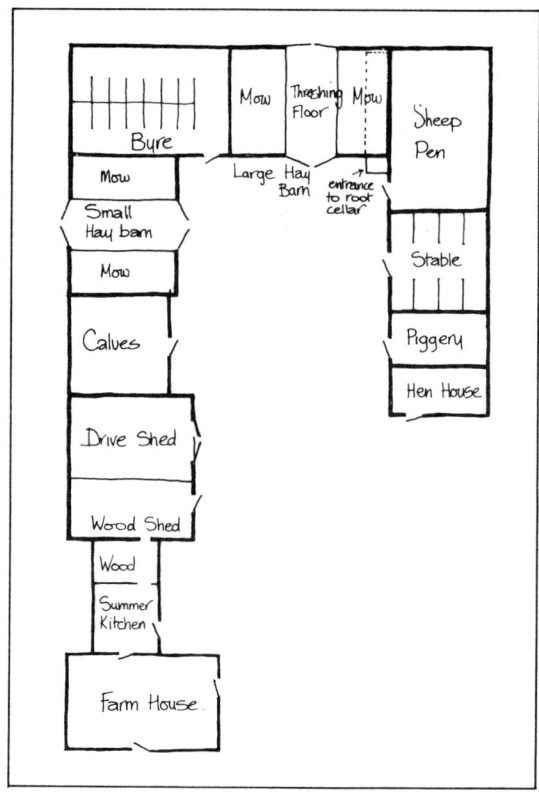

Plate 192
Joseph Kidd, his wife Mary McDiarmid, two of their sons, Angus and George Edward, as photographed ca. 1884 and their farm on lot 21, concession 6, Beckwith, (opposite) as photographed in June 1983. Joseph Kidd as the son of Kilkenny Irish Anglican immigrant John Kidd, and Mary McDiarmid as the daughter of Perthshire Scottish immigrant Angus McDiarmid, were evidence of the merging identities of Irish and Scottish families in Beckwith. The stylish clothes reveal the comfortable living possible from the dairy and mixed farming economy. Mary McDiarmid stopped teaching in the Derry school when she married Joseph Kidd in 1869, and the toll of raising eight children is evident in this photograph. Five years after this photograph was taken she died at the age of 46. Joseph Kidd at the time of their marriage described his rank as that of a yeoman. He was reeve of Beckwith in 1901.

loads of hay were being put on, and of bringing home cows for milking in the evening.[6] As he grew older the scope of his duties widened until Saturdays and other school holidays to him simply meant extra work days at home spent clearing fields of stones, filling mudholes in a road, rebuilding fences, and sawing wood in winter.[7] He recalled:[8]

> We were set to milk as soon as we could reach a cow. In flytime they bunched together for mutual protection and often the placing of a hoof on a bare foot would necessitate the sinking of one's teeth into her leg to induce her to remove it. On Saturdays we would weed the turnips, cut burdocks in the garden, or put a new plank in the stable floor.... The summer holidays opened with the great annual celebration of the First of July; but we soon settled down to work, putting Paris [G]reen on the potatoes being among the first jobs. Soon the mowing machine

The layout of the buildings (opposite) on the Kidd farm was drawn ca. 1970 by Dudley Witney. According to family tradition, John Kidd built this stone house in 1842, years before he acquired title to this Clergy reserve lot, and the barns were built between the 1840s and 1890s. There were no doors going from one barn to another, and the doors all opened into the sheltered barnyard. The connecting of house and farm buildings was common in early nineteenth century Beckwith, but became rare after 1850. The byre was for cows whereas the stable was for horses. The size of the sheep barn suggests the continuing importance of sheep in the mixed farming economy of Beckwith. Plan from Eric Arthur and Dudley Witney, The Barn: A Vanishing Landmark in North America, *by permission of Feheley Fine Arts Inc. Portrait courtesy of John and Leona Kidd.*

came out and haying was begun. Under protest we put on our boots and went to coil hay. The further apart the coils were the better we [children] were pleased and we envied the farmers around Prospect where there were only a half dozen rows across the field. Rainy days were welcome and we would either turn to and play more vigorously than we had worked the day before, or we would lie on the hay under the roof and listen to the patter of the rain, while we dreamed dreams and told stories, or made plans for the time when we should be grown up. No sooner would the last drop of rain fall than Father would announce: "Well, I guess the rain is over. Tell the lads."

Farm chores were so integral a part of growing up in rural Beckwith that fathers coerced their sons to participate in using the harvesting machinery at an early age, and the boundary between work and play was sometimes imprecise. Edward Kidd recalled riding around with his father on the iron seat of the grain binder, watching the rakes on the machine follow one another in circuit, each coming down on the table, threatening to sweep each accumulating sheaf off before gliding harmlessly over it. "Only when Father said 'Now', and I pressed my foot on the small lever", Kidd recalled, "would the rake dig into the sheaf and sweep it from the table, depositing it neatly on the ground where it was later tied with a band of straw."[9] Work and play were counterparts of each other, as a chore was made pleasant by turning it partly into a game. In wintertime when there was minimal work for children to do, curiously enough, their inside play imitated their farm chores. While older family members sat reading at the table, Edward and his younger brother Livingstone "could pretend that we were stall feeding steers, using two chairs for a stall and oatmeal for fodder. When well fattened, the process of killing, skinning and disembowelling had to be gone through. It was not fair to stick a pig until he was flat on his back, and getting him there was where the fun came in."[10]

At age four Edward Kidd started to school a scant half mile from his father's house in the stone Derry schoolhouse built in 1870.[11] Even before he learned to read, he had benefitted from a home atmosphere "such as to satisfy the cravings of the most inquiring mentality." His older sisters read to him, recited and told stories including such favourites as "Horatio at the Bridge", "Little Revenge", *Ivanhoe* and *Kenilworth*.[12] He learned to sing songs such as "Bonnie Dundee" as his sister Lizzie accompanied him on the organ in the evening.[13] The Derry school ranked highly among the schools of Beckwith. "We were fortunate in having good teachers", Edward Kidd later recalled. "Former scholars from our school had gone to university, and many had passed through high school. The Derry school already had a tradition to live up to."[14] During his early grades at school, in the late 1880s, new seats made of iron and wood that were bolted to the floor replaced ancient unpainted benches "which held four or five scholars, and every square inch of which [were] deeply cut with names of occupants of the years gone." Having spent considerable money on the new seats, to keep the Derry school in the forefront of educational improvement in Beckwith, trustee Sam Simpson told the students "in all seriousness that anyone found cutting his name on a new desk would go to jail." One of the teachers was a relative, Fred Kidd, who organised a school concert and raised sufficient money to purchase a bell, a belfry was constructed by Peter McLaren, and with much ceremony it was installed on the roof of the schoolhouse.[15] The interior of the school was renovated, with the old pencil-marked plaster replaced with walnut panelling, but on hot summer days the schoolroom was still cooled by throwing water on the floor.

Ten of the eleven teachers who taught Edward Kidd were women, since teaching afforded them the only locally available alternative to domestic drudgery or to working in the mills at Carleton Place, and also because women teachers could be hired for less than men. Two of these young single women teachers made very different impressions on the schoolboy. One, a Miss Code from Perth, "erected a flag pole on the school house one...24th of May. The folks all attended. She lined us up on the school floor and made us wave flags and sing patriotic songs to her heart's content. Father supplied an abundance of fire crackers and of candy. It was a big day." The other teacher, an extremely pretty and clever young woman named "Ortie McEwen was the most alive thing I ever knew",[16] Edward Kidd later recalled. In the "semipuritan atmosphere" of the Derry where the "uniformly high character of our neighbours tended to make community life slightly monotonous"[17] Miss McEwen definitely seemed exotic by comparison. She was fond of red dresses, could sing, play the organ, and twang a guitar at school concerts. She played a mouth organ accompaniment to gymnastic exercises which the students performed with wands, she taught them how to play baseball, she planted flowers on the school grounds, she held a picnic and a social, and even brought in two uniformed baseball teams who played in a nearby field. "This was the first occasion we had seen a game of this kind", Edward Kidd recalled.[18]

On a bright morning in late March 1894 just after he had turned twelve years of age, Edward Kidd was informed by his father that he would not go to school that day, but rather would replace his older brother Angus who was leaving to go to high school, as chief assistant on the farm. This effectively meant that he ceased to attend school between March and November.[19]

Plate 193
The Robert Scott Jr. farm, lot 25, concession 6, Beckwith, the house of which was built in 1856, as photographed by George Edward Kidd ca. 1913. Unlike the Kidds who adapted their old log barns to the needs of dairy and mixed farming, the Scott family built a modern frame barn atop a large concrete cow stable either in the 1900s or early 1910s. Older smaller log barns and the early log house on the property continued to be used to house sheep, swine and poultry, but the size of the cow stable and barn indicates the pride of place of dairying in Beckwith farm incomes by 1900. Photograph courtesy of John and Leona Kidd.

There had been no preliminary hints or discussions regarding this [Edward Kidd later recalled], — he simply announced it. We should proceed to clean up the barnyard. I accepted with mingled feelings of regret and of pride. Regret at leaving schoolmates without the privilege of saying to them, "Next week I am going to stop school and work at home." Pride that I was being called on to do a man's work.... I was still only twelve years old, and my heart sank a little when Jim and Livingstone left for school leaving me to face a big unknown world. When the boys came home in the evening my small muscles were aching. They brought my books and said that the teacher had intimated that she was sorry I was quitting school.

Neither Joseph Kidd nor his sons regarded this as an unusual step. It was standard practice in Beckwith, and had been since the beginning of settlement, to have large families as part of a planned agricultural and family economy since it assured abundant help in the fields and in the home.[20]

Joseph Kidd was at a relative disadvantage compared with many of his neighbours in taking over the management of his farm at a very early age. He had inherited one hundred acres from his father, but although the farm contained some of the finest soil to be found in Lanark County, because it was a Clergy Reserve and because Joseph's father had purchased it only a few years before his death at mid-century, much clearing of it remained to be done. "There was still land to clear, fences to build and buildings to be put up", Edward Kidd observed. By his own efforts Joseph Kidd erected two log barns, a frame woodshed and a frame sheep pen. As soon as his older sons were of an age to assist him he made improvements to the stone house, plastered it over, replaced the old stone chimneys with new ones, dug a well and cistern under the summer kitchen, built a woodbox into the kitchen wall, widened the long lane in from the sixth concession road, and strung wire fencing in front of the yard.[21] While Edward Kidd was a young boy his father purchased the west half of adjacent lot 22 from Dougald Ferguson, making for a farm with a total of 200 acres, although there was very little good cropland on the new acquisition.[22] The combined inheritance and purchase of land by Joseph Kidd was a microcosm of the general pattern of land tenure that took place between 1881 and 1920. The better farms, as a rule, passed from father to son, usually to the youngest son. As they grew up the older children left home, the girls marrying, while in most cases the boys moved away from the neighbourhood. The poorer farms proved unable to provide a basic income, particularly as local agriculture mechanised and the general size of farms increased, and eventually after a long succession of occupants, changing hands frequently, finally were absorbed into the holdings of neighbours.[23]

To assist in making his annual payments to Dougald Ferguson, Joseph Kidd bought cattle in the autumn from local farmers, and after feeding them all winter sold them. His expectations of his sons providing him with additional labour were successively frustrated by their academic ambitions. When Edward's eldest brother John reached the age when he might be expected to take his place as chief assistant to his father, he passed his entrance examinations with such a credible showing that school inspector Michell persuaded his parents to allow the boy to continue to high school, and in company with a neighbour's son, John S. McEwen, he went on to university. The next son, Angus, served as chief assistant to his father for three years until he too decided to continue his studies and go on to a professional career. Edward was next in line to work under his father's direction.

Their work together began with cutting wood for the next winter, then tapping the maple trees, boiling sap all day, wading through the deep wet snow gathering sap, before arriving back at the farm buildings cold and tired, with evening chores still to do. In the mornings, as the spring wind cracked his lips and burned his face a deep red, Edward Kidd walked on top of the morning crust of the snow drifts, with paper and matches to light a fire under a hanging pan and the two huge boilers slung between back logs, and with a piece of salt pork to prevent the sap from boiling over. The sap was gathered on bob-sleighs in barrels and cans, and in crossing running streams of melted snow, there was always the danger of an upset. Father and son went from tree to tree emptying the full buckets into gleaming tin pails, taking it all back to the arch where it was boiled down into syrup the colour of amber.[24]

From syrup-making they proceeded on to preparing for spring planting,[25] breaking in colts, building fences, and hauling in more firewood.[26] In the spring of 1895 Edward was given the impossible task of leading a cow with a vicious disposition through the streets of Carleton Place to the slaughterhouse. He recalled, "She did the leading, I followed. Going through the town she went completely berserk and the long rope by which I was trying to guide her, caught my foot. I was trailed along the street by a mad cow, but fortunately the rope broke.... When I think that I was only thirteen years old at the time, I wonder."[27] Edward Kidd then drove a team, ploughing, harrowing and rolling crops, milking cows night and morning, feeding calves and pigs, and washing the sore shoulders of tired, sweating horses. As summer went on there were drainage ditches to dig and fences to build. Father and son picketed every fence on the farm with a system of single pickets between the log ends which were held in place by wire.

In July, with his brothers home from school, Edward no longer was chief assistant and again became a part of the gang weeding turnips, putting ashes and Paris Green on the potato bugs, mowing hay, loading it onto the hay rack, operating the hay fork to haul bundles of hay from the wagon up to the hay mow where Edward alongside his father spread it where it fell, getting out the binder and replacing broken reels and canvas slats, binding the grain, and then stooking it. In September he was again alone, working with his father, while his brothers returned to school and his sisters worked in the house. He bound by hand a field of buckwheat, cut corn with a sickle, and ploughed through the beautiful autumn days. He recalled, "One handle of the plo[ugh] was broken, and when the point struck a stone this would catch me in the ribs. I would sit down and cry with pain and rage, or take it out on old Bill by throwing stones at him."[28] In late autumn as the ground began to freeze up and snow came, the sheep were driven home, the cows were shut up in the cowbyre and father and son boarded up all the cracks about the farm buildings and made things snug for the long cold winter. Only then was Edward permitted to return to school.

Plate 194
Interior of Wesleyan Methodist chapel at Prospect, as photographed in June 1983. The removal of the gallery and the installation of memorial stained glass windows in this chapel at the turn of the century reveal the trickle-down influence of innovations introduced into local Anglican congregations. Although Irish Methodists and Irish Anglicans gradually parted political company in the late nineteenth century, Beckwith Methodists could still be affected by the liturgical changes taking place in the Church of England. The removal of the gallery at the rear also reflected the declining population of Beckwith.

Under this state of affairs Edward Kidd was a very miserable child:[29]

I was unhappy [he later wrote] in that I never knew what the day's task would be until after breakfast. During family prayers in the morning I knelt at the bench behind the kitchen stove, with the sun streaming in through the open door, as it always did for an hour on summer mornings; and wondered what we should do that day. I waited anxiously for the dinner call, when I would curl up in the deep parlour window and read Dickens or Cooper until Father said it was time to get out the horses.

As spring changed to summer, and as summer turned to autumn the unrelenting round of chores continued. Young Edward thought "that surely everything which could be done, was done, and that we might have a rest tomorrow. That never happened." New projects materialised such as excavating a pond and blasting holes in the rock at its bottom, and sawing a huge pile of fence logs which for years had lain on top of a hill over in the fields purchased from Dougald Ferguson.[30] Edward Kidd later assessed his unhappiness at working as his father's chief assistant for four years as stemming from the fact that "I was neither boy nor man. I was doing a man's work with none of his responsibility

> **The Franktown Cheese and Butter Manufacturing Association.**
>
> ──── SEASON OF 1899 ────
>
> Milk furnished by Mr. *Richard Shirley* during the
> Week ending *Oct- 28th* 1899, *488* Lbs.
> Week ending _____ 1899, _____ Lbs.
> *Season's total = 19061 lbs*
> *add up the lbs on the weight* Total *488* Lbs.
> *slips and if not the same*
> *let me know at once* WM. McDONALD,
> SECRETARY.

nor his reward. My days were filled with yearnings for something unknown. There is something terribly wrong about this period of a boy's life, as I lived it."[31] He entertained no hopes of eventually taking over the farmstead, for by tradition the farmstead was left for the youngest son. The few months of the year in the depth of winter he was allowed to attend school were wasted. "I was a bad speller and a poorer writer", he admitted, "and should have taken occasion to improve both, but any seeds of ambition which might have been in my make up lay there as dead as a doornail."[32] As he grew into adolescence and began to wonder about the future, he frequently retreated to a hay loft. There he wept. [33]

Six days a week Edward Kidd laboured as his father's unpaid assistant, to take his rest as best he could find it within the narrow bounds of strict Sabbath observance. With his father a trustee of the Methodist church at Prospect, he was[34]

> brought up in a semipuritan atmosphere where dancing and card playing were contrary to the rules of the church. Even the violin was regarded with suspicion, due to its association with dancing. Objection to the church organ at service was just fading. I was born into a home where the fear of God dominated all else.... A puritanism coming down from the Scottish Covenanters was the standard of living in our community. In our home all newspapers were put away on Saturday evenings. There might be no whistling on Sundays. Shoes to be worn to church must be blackened the evening before. Going to church and prayer meetings was as much a part of our lives as was the eating of our daily bread. Alcohol was so far away that it seemed to be only an ugly myth, while the use of tobacco rated only slightly higher. The Bible was the most vital thing in the house, and the boy who used it to prop open a window was guilty of the greatest sacrilege. Providence was as real as our next door neighbor, supervising our daily lives.

Sabbath rigours notwithstanding, cows had to be milked, the milk carried to the cool cellar and placed in buckets which were in turn set in a huge pan of cold water awaiting delivery to the cheese factory the next morning, calves fed, breakfast eaten and family prayer conducted, all to be done before 8:30.

Five hours of time every Sunday morning for Joseph Kidd's family were taken up with the business of attending the Methodist church at Prospect. They climbed up into the carriage at 8:30, arrived at the church door for Sunday School at 9:30, stayed for regular church service which began at 10:30, and followed by a class-meeting at 12:15 so that it was 1:30 by the time they returned home,

Plate 195
The Richard Shirley farm, lot 3, concession 2, Beckwith, at Gillies Corners, as photographed in June 1983, and (opposite) a receipt of milk furnished to the Franktown cheese factory in 1899. This large brick L-plan farmhouse and substantial frame hay barn built atop a stone cow stable reflected the profits possible from the dairy economy at the turn of the century. Richard Shirley produced 19,061 pounds of milk in the summer of 1899 at a rate of 500 pounds a week on a farm of 200 acres of poor soil. The dairy economy and the growing mechanisation of agriculture promoted the consolidation of farms. Receipt loaned courtesy of Iva Shirley.

their heads light from empty stomachs. Once the family carriage turned off the much-travelled fourth concession line, up the side road, off came the shoes and stockings they had donned over five hours earlier. After a leisurely dinner most of the preparation of which had taken place the day before,[35] the whole family took an equally leisurely stroll in the woods, enjoying the beauties of the fields and bush[36] before supper. Church attendance was by no means over. Edward, his brothers and sisters had to dress up again, were bundled into the carriage, and trundled off to an Epworth League meeting, a service for young people in the Methodist church at which they recited verses they had committed to memory, followed by "a series of prayers, through which we children slept soundly."

One benefit of attending Epworth League for some young men, who unlike Edward Kidd were not accompanied by their father, was the opportunity to see a young woman home.[37] If regular weekly worship was an exhausting experience, Edward Kidd regarded revival meetings as the terror of his childhood:[38]

> Brought up as we were, surrounded by nothing but good influences, we knew little of evil [he later recalled]. Yet to my mind, the whole church conspired together and concentrated on getting me converted. Rev. [James] Simpson held revival meetings for weeks at a time. [Reverend W.H.]

Burnett...with his long black hair over his eyes, and perspiration streaming down his face, thundered directly at the poor little quaking figure in a back seat. When I was ten years old I carefully thought matters out. I decided that until I was sixteen I could safely risk dying and going to Hell. When I reached that age I should give in, renounce all pleasures and go to the penitents pew. In the meantime the very suggestion of a revival meeting filled me with dread, and I contemplated running away from home to escape them.

Edward Kidd experienced as restricting a childhood as it was possible to find in Beckwith at the close of Queen Victoria's reign, forbidden as he was from attending dances, and with even church socials and tea meetings frowned upon. These restrictions stemmed from the isolation of the Derry as a community, from his father being a trustee of the Methodist church, from the strict Sabbath observance expected by the predominantly Scottish neighbours in his school section, and from the lack of even such basic facilities as a swimming hole, a fishing stream, or a lake on which to row a boat. With no neighbours to the north and west, and confronted by a huge swamp which stretched for miles, Edward Kidd's childhood and early adolescence centred on his family,[39] and also on a well-stocked family library. Joseph Kidd would gather his children about him on winter evenings and tell them stories from the Bible that for Edward Kidd were imaginable only in terms of the world he knew — the family homestead. Hence in his mind "when the Lord walked in the garden in the cool of the day, He came around our house and reached the Siberian crab tree. Here he stopped and called for Adam. But Adam was hiding behind Lizzie's Apple Tree while Eve concealed her nakedness in the shelter of one of the sour apple trees at the bottom of the garden." In the library was a family favourite, a well illustrated story of the Bible entitled *The Beautiful Story* which was read and reread until it fell apart. "The awful pictures in Future Punishment", Edward Kidd later noted, "made one's hair stand on end." Works by Sir Walter Scott and Charles Dickens were pored over again and again until their covers were worn off and had to be recovered so they could be read again, whereas *The Great Irish Struggle* was never read by anyone.[40]

Had anyone dared take the unlikely step of reproaching Joseph Kidd for exploiting his son without remuneration at the cost of limiting his education, he would have vociferously denied it on both practical and moral grounds. After all, what he was doing in making Edward work alongside him was standard community practice across Beckwith. It provided him with a practical introduction to the various types of work he would face on his own farm in the future, whether it was located in Beckwith or on the Canadian prairies. For all the rhetoric of the school promoters since mid-century, formal education provided very few students for any kind of employment in Beckwith, save for the schoolteachers, and for the female majority of them teaching was a temporary step before they married and raised their own families. As for limiting his son's horizons by tying him down to farm labour all day six days a week, by morally and mentally imprisoning him by limiting what he could do on Sunday and taking up some seven hours of his Sunday in attending religious services, and by using daily religious worship to maintain a hold over him, Joseph Kidd could have argued that it was far more wholesome than the factories of Carleton Place and the timber camps of the upper Ottawa. One had only to read the Carleton Place *Herald* and the *Central Canadian* to note the copious drinking, smoking, cursing, suicide, abortion, infanticide and prostitution that took place among the lower orders in that town. As for the timber camps, they were legendary for their violence, roughness and heavy carousing, and even in the timber camps along the upper Mississippi what good influence could a young lad possibly derive from sleeping in a bunk with another full grown man, from dancing with other men, and from playing rough sexually-suggestive games with names such as "hit ass" and "pulling the stick"?[41] Far better for a maturing lad to live under his father's moral guidance, and under the gentling and feminine influence of his older sisters!

It was in 1898 during the fourth year of working as his father's chief assistant around the farm that Edward Kidd at the age of sixteen began to break away from his ambitionless unpaid labour. He was spurred to do so in part by a book in the family library entitled *Tact, Push and Principle* which

Plate 196
Promotional booklet on Manitoba as a home for agriculturalists, 1890. Booklets such as this lured young men from Beckwith westward on harvest excursions, with many of them returning permanently to establish homesteads from the 1870s through to the 1910s. This booklet published by the Manitoba government featured lithographs of comfortable houses, arable rolling acreages and healthy herds of livestock. Loaned courtesy of Alex and Jean McCuan.

after repeated readings he was able to quote at length, and which prompted him to start thinking about preparing to make his own way in the world. His brother Angus, after failing to pass his model school examinations to become a teacher, went west to look at farming prospects, and before he left Joseph Kidd "had a family group photographed at the time, as we never expected to see him again."[42] Eventually when they heard from Angus, he was working for a farmer in Manitoba, earning twenty dollars per month. Edward Kidd began to moot vague plans while he picked stones, and dreamed of future doings as he spread manure.

Then, in April 1898 he was offered two weeks work by Dougald R. Ferguson to replace Hugh Ferguson who had gone to work with Knox Ferguson making cheese at the factory in Prospect. By comparison, the work at home had been easy, but it was significant for Edward Kidd that the $6.50 he received was the first money he had earned in his life. As the sun rose he was milking cows, having already fed the horses, and as the sun set he was still working, with never a minute's rest all day except for meals. He later commented, "I worked at top speed, but never remember having been told 'You have done well'. This means a lot to a boy of that age."[43] He began to appreciate the drudgery and small pay for which hired men on Beckwith farms laboured. Back home that summer:[44]

> one forenoon, while stooking sheaves, the idea came into my head that I should go to school. I had never thought of it before, but before night [it] had taken such a hold on me that I could think of nothing else. Many grave doubts assailed me. I had never been a top scholar at school, was a poor writer and speller, and the bad boys like Hughie Ferguson, appealed to me more than the good ones. A review of all these things tended to discourage me, but fate drove me along, and that evening I persuaded Lizzie to ask Father if I might start to school after the holidays. The answer was that I might if I should promise to stick to it, and if [my younger brother] Jim would promise to stay at home and do the work.

With the help of a sympathetic teacher at the Derry school, a Miss Dunlop, Edward Kidd applied himself to his studies, making up for the four aimless years he had worked for his father in what amounted to a pre-high school year. In the summer of 1899 he bicycled to Carleton Place through a warm yet heavy summer rain to write his Senior Leaving examinations, and passed with honours. In November he started to attend the high school in Carleton Place, joined by his brother Angus who had returned from western Canada at New Year's. Their boarding house with a Mrs. Robinson was cold and cheerless, the beds were lumpy and their room without heat. They returned home every weekend for warmth and family camaraderie. Apart from a few chums such as Hastey McFarlane and Austin Gillies, Edward Kidd found few of his other fellow students either colourful or promising to amount to anything, just simply ordinary boys from town such as later would become druggists, insurance agents and clerks. The South African war made their winter in Carleton Place memorable. "Principal Patterson gathered us into one room where we sang 'Soldiers of the Queen.' We learned to hate Kruger and his Boers. Miss McNeely taught us to recite the just causes of the war. Later we celebrated the relief of Ladysmith during a two day blizzard."[45]

A smallpox epidemic struck Carleton Place in April 1900, and the high school closed indefinitely. Edward Kidd returned home and quickly found himself hired as a helper in the cheese factory at Munster, a hamlet in adjacent Goulbourn Township some five miles east of Ashton and north of Prospect. It is very likely that Joseph Kidd had made prior arrangements for his son to be hired there, not so much so that he could command an apprentice's wage of six dollars a month, but because the large Methodist church there was the centre of social life. If Edward was going to leave the isolation of the Derry, his father was determined to shield him from the impact of meeting up with worldly people as long as it was in his power. Accordingly, Edward Kidd found that the families in the Munster vicinity were for the most part of Irish extraction, the second and third generations from the original settlers, an earnest and God-fearing people. He observed: "It was a delight to hear Duncan Mcfarlane pray during the Sunday

Plate 197
The farm of William H. Graham and his widowed mother, Catherine Graham, lot 26, concession 1 dating from the 1890s, as photographed in June 1983. The undulations of the laneway and the cedar trees suggest the thin soil cover on this farm, with a backdrop of swamp behind the buildings. Even on this farm with a small patch of third grade soil, the pursuit of mixed and dairy farming at the turn of the century was possible where there previously had been no realistic hope of growing grain.

evening Epworth League meeting. He and Robert Wilson of Prospect had much the same style. Down on his knees, each prayed rapidly and earnestly, pouring out his whole soul; slowly at first, then rising to a crescendo of words; never hesitating, never halting for a phrase."[46]

The work at the cheese factory he found very hard, but there was a freedom about the work that he had never enjoyed working for his father:[47]

> Hours were definitely prescribed, with no chores to do afterwards. Each morning the milkmen came in with their loads of rich milk from the farms up and down the fifth and sixth concessions [of Goulbourn]. All day long went on the process of converting this milk into cheese. Only when the last vat was washed and scalded and the last cheese pressed down, were we at leisure to enjoy the long summer evenings.

To the day he died, a disturbing dream for Edward Kidd often would "take the form of a load of milk arriving at the factory while yet there [was] no steam in the boiler."

On the recommendation of two new acquaintances, Edward Kidd did not return to Carleton Place. Instead he attended high school at Kemptville where practically all the students were from out of town, and where the atmosphere not only of the school was different from Carleton Place but even the population of the town was friendly. He spent a second summer at the Munster cheese factory with his monthly salary raised to seven dollars, and in the course of the summer he attended a camp meeting conducted by the Reverend Ralph Horner in a grove near the village. He spent a second winter in the high school at Kemptville, a winter made pleasant and companionable among the predominantly Irish-origin student body by being elected captain of the football team and by the prospect of entering university the following winter.

In May 1902 he went to take charge of a cheese factory in which his brother Angus had worked two summers in an Orange Irish Anglican hamlet named Laurel some 24 miles north of the Ottawa River halfway between Ottawa and Montreal. He commanded the salary of 25 dollars per month, with his rent paid by the owner of the cheese factory. He made good cheese, and soon began to feel at home among the Irish families who were recent arrivals themselves, with the second generation beginning to marry and start families. It certainly was not the community his father would have chosen for him to stay in. He found himself invited to weddings where he was not expected to bring a gift, where three sumptuous meals were served, where anyone who wished might have become drunk on freely supplied liquor, and where people were insatiable in their love for dancing. At one wedding Edward Kidd "blundered into the spare bedroom and came across two couples stretched across the bed with their arms about each other." In nearby Lost River there was a dance hall where on the twelfth of July he helped his employer sell cold drinks in a stifling log building "filled with a mass of swirling, perspiring young men and women; yes, and old people too." At one wedding Edward Kidd was invited by one adventurous young woman who had gone as far afield as the United States to "pluck a Scotch pigeon" which he found "consisted of two persons each taking an end of a short string in his and her mouths, and chewing at it until there was no more string."

On Sunday mornings Edward Kidd:[48]

> attended the little Anglican church and was frequently alone in the responses. A student laboured through an artificial sermon; and struggled through the hymns at too high a key. There was always preserved that dignity of service, which the Anglican church never sacrifices to the commonplace. There were always those snow white robes of office. Always the intonations and proper postures — one could not help but be reverent in that little white church on the hill....

In September 1902 Edward Kidd wrote his entrance examinations at Queen's University in Kingston, then continued to work at Laurel until the cheese factory closed for the season in October. He spent the following four years taking an undergraduate arts course, and like many subsequent students, he came away from Queen's unimpressed, feeling that they "were rather stupid winters." He found making cheese each summer much more stimulating, and after experiencing Laurel he decided to move to a new factory each summer. He spent the summer of 1903 in Westport in the rear of Leeds County,[49] a locality where cheese production was so intensive that Bastard Township, for example, had fourteen cheese factories[50] in contrast with only four that operated in Beckwith.

The summer of 1904 he operated his old neighbourhood cheese factory at Prospect, which allowed him time to see his family after a protracted absence. The factory work at Prospect he found difficult because of the large territory it served, with milk coming from as far away as the vicinity of Dwyer Hill to the east and the Derry to the west, since the shaking drive of more than a few miles in hot weather threatened to lower the quality of the Cheese. "The quality of cheese had to be the highest to command the best price", he later noted, "and when on Monday mornings in the hot summer, the two days' milk poured into the vats — overripe from Sunday's milkings[,] it was no small task to keep up with the rapid development of lactic acid and ensure good cheese. A can of sour milk was ruinous, and I could smell one yards away."[51] In 1905 he made cheese at Admaston, some five miles southwest of Renfrew, and after graduating in 1906 he went to teach in a southern Manitoba district called Glendenning in the Pembina river valley.[52]

* * * * * * * * *

Plate 198
Carleton Place high school students at Queen's University in 1902. In the late nineteenth and early twentieth centuries Queen's was the university that most Beckwith students pursuing higher education attended. There were ethnic and religious ties from the founding of the college in the 1840s on, as Beckwith sons trained for the Presbyterian ministry. When Queen's teetered on the brink of bankruptcy after a Kingston bank failed in 1869, Beckwith farmers subscribed $750 toward an endowment fund. The higher subscription of $1,170 among Ramsay farmers together with the first women attending university coming from Carleton Place and Ramsay rather than Beckwith, suggest the continuing conservative and canny strain that persisted among the descendants of the highlanders. For names see appendix 34. Photograph courtesy of the late William Livingstone Kidd.

His sojourn at the Prospect cheese factory after having been out in the world for a few years gave Edward Kidd a new perspective of his native Beckwith. He recognised how relatively isolated the Derry was, even compared with the rest of rural Beckwith, and how comparatively puritanical had been his upbringing. He appreciated how poorly endowed southern Beckwith was with good soil, and the lack of a future within the township boundaries for most children raised locally. He had a new appreciation of the mixture of Irish and Scottish, and after listening to the speech of people in the outside world he noticed that there were traces of Irish and Scottish dialects in Beckwith even into the third and fourth generation.[53] Edward Kidd had been all of eight years old, after all, before he met an Englishman, a Yorkshire-origin hired man who worked for Jack Scott, and whose broad dialect caused him to double up with laughter."[54]

Edward Kidd also came to recognise how his Methodist upbringing had restricted him from mixing with people of other faiths, and from looking beyond the bounds of Prospect. He had been raised with the notion, somehow, that the local Methodist families such as the Wilsons, the Rileys, the Alcocks, the Pooles, and his own family comprised a patrician class of sorts:[55]

They formed an oasis of intelligentia on the borders of the great unknown desert beyond [to the south]. Here dwelt in ignorance the Finns and Bud[d]s — all barbarians to my youthful mind. On Sundays they came to the Anglican church on the hill [in Prospect], their women folk clad in costumes in which bright colors predominated. Billy Burrows was for many years the only Catholic of my acquaintance, and as such was a man apart. When I went alone for the mail and entered his tiny office, I always kept close to the door while he sorted it over, fearful that he might throw a knife at me, or shoot through the little window where letters were given out. This was the result of stories of the Fenian raids.

Now turned twenty, Edward Kidd recognised to what extent his father's Methodism and Liberalism had isolated his household from the larger extended family of Anglican Conservatives. Although his father's sister, aunt Eliza, lived a distance of only five to six miles from their farm after marrying Joshua Simpson and settling at Ashton, they visited only once or twice a year. Much rarer were visits to another of his father's sisters, aunt Margaret, who lived with her second husband James Robinson at Fallowfield in Nepean Township. As a child Edward found the few visits made to their large empty and spotless house forbidding, due, he felt, to the forceful and unbending aristocratic temperament of his aunt Margaret. In later life it seemed significant to him that "we never got beyond the kitchen." On one of these rare visits to Fallowfield, a severe snowstorm forced Joseph and his children to stay overnight, but so strained were relations between brother and a sister who had married well that despite impossible travelling conditions the next morning, Joseph Kidd set out through the drifts. "Any man other than Father would never have attempted the journey", Edward Kidd commented, "but he fought his way through, shovelling the drifts aside, breaking a path for the horses...until we reached the Long Swamp, where the woods prevented drifting. All day long it took to go home those 18 miles of misery".[56] Even within the farming community, and within the same generation of a family both religion and the quality of one's farm were used to socially distinguish layers of society. Edward Kidd, even as a child, dimly comprehended how much this distinguishing could hurt. Although his father's farm had a good section of top grade soil, like most other Beckwith farms with its old-fashioned grouping of log barns and old style of house, it compared poorly with the modern frame barns and large fashionable stone house of James and Margaret Robinson at Fallowfield.

From the opposite end of the social telescope Edward Kidd was raised with a similar condescension towards his Irish Anglican relatives in northern Montague, an entire community of people including members of the Tierney, Leeson, Kilfoyl, Kidd, Mills and Gourlay families with whom he shared a common ancestor. Edward Kidd was raised believing that "Montague was supposed to be an arid desert of a place, beyond the Pinery, where the rocks had no soil to cover them, and where the inhabitants grew only buckwheat and skinny horses." Estranged though they were from their Anglican and Conservative relatives in Carleton County and Montague by comparative wealth, by religion and by politics, one of the few continuing bonds was their sense of Irish heritage. Edward's cousin Irene during occasional visits to the home of uncle Joshua and aunt Eliza Simpson at Ashton rattled off tunes such as "The Irish Washerwoman.[57]

Joseph Kidd allowed his children to attend an Orange picnic at Ashton. As Edward Kidd recalled it,[58]

Dusty King Williams, on white plugs of horses, with white plumes on their hats and with very red faces rode into the maple grove at the heads of their perspiring lodges, past admiring crowds. A huge brass band made music and I went far into the woods to see how far away the big horn might be heard. I was proud to hold the music for the drummer, as I stood right in the middle of the band.

Plate 199
Prospect cheese factory as photographed ca. 1905 by Murray & Son, Brockville. Between 1880 and 1920 small cheese factories were established at most villages and hamlets as Ontario became the principal supplier of the English cheese market. The cheese factories at Franktown and Prospect were privately operated, with the owner paying local farmers a set rate. The cheese factories in the vicinity of Carleton Place at Ashton and Black's Corners were co-operatively run, with the return to farmers depending on the price their cheese commanded in the market from year to year. Photograph courtesy of the late William Livingstone Kidd.

Edward's sister Margaret even spent a week among her Montague relatives "and reported a hilarious time." One winter evening the family returned home tired and sleepy from a visit to the Simpsons at Ashton "to find the house filled with people from Montague...having supper at a long table" which Margaret had made by placing the dining room and kitchen tables end to end. To young Edward Kidd "there seemed to be dozens of them all eating from the good china which came out but rarely, and they were all fixed to rob us of our beds, and force a doubling up which meant all sorts of inconveniences."[59]

Edward Kidd's deprecatory references to northern Montague are worth considering for a moment because they were not simply a child's unthinking remark about poor relatives, but rather were an accurate reflection of the changing view of ethnic identity in regional society. By the late nineteenth century there was much mingling of the Irish and Scottish communities in Beckwith, as the marriage of Edward's Scottish-origin mother and Irish-origin father clearly demonstrates. But differing regional pockets of ethnic population, varying quality of soil from one locality to another, and political labelling combined to create blanket ethnic stereotypes that were applied to rural townships by regional town newspaper editors. These blanket stereotypes were often inaccurate and inappropriate, as, for example, when the Smith's Falls *Review* in 1865 praised Montague, an Irish township, for prohibiting the sale of liquor, whereas Beckwith, a Scottish township, refused to do so. Montague was rarely so praised in the nineteenth century, because as a Tory stronghold it was routinely criticised by the Reform - dominated press of nineteenth century Lanark County for its immorality, intoxication[60] and backwardness.[61]

Because most of northern and central Montague was shallow soil over a limestone plain, it was here that crops failed the earliest. Andrew Haydon, an Almonte Liberal lawyer of Scottish lowland descent, in his 1893 history of Lanark County explained the poor living in Montague as stemming from inherent Irish traits not found among people of Scottish origin.[62]

> The old Scotch settlers had brought to their new home the thrift and industry so characteristic of their nation, and these qualities were intensified under the new conditions of life in which the immigrants found themselves.... The Irish immigrants too have prospered. Industrious and frugal in the earlier years, they have not been quite so careful when a more comfortable existence was assured. Hence among many of them there is a disposition to live beyond their means.... In the southern part of the county, and especially in the township of Montague, more careless and less thrifty habits of life have developed.

The coincidence of poor land and a population three-quarters Irish in Montague made for a syllogism which equated the very name of Montague with Irish rural poverty. The editor of the Carleton Place *Canadian* in early May 1896 commented on the "great company of most odd-looking people" that attended the division court there: "You would take your solemn affidavit that a number of them were tramps, sundried, drunks, burglarious, revolver-bred. We were mighty glad when they returned to their own country — Montague, somebody said."[63]

The perception of Beckwith as being Scottish ignored the fact that there were more people of Irish than Scottish origin in the township after 1880. Save for the concentration of fertile first and second grade soil extending from the northern part of Joseph Kidd's farm in the sixth concession south into the third concession, the greater part of Beckwith's Irish-origin population was located in the southern concessions on very poor farms adjacent to northern Montague. Hence a locale such as the Cuckoo's Nest in southern Beckwith with its proximity to Montague, its poor soil, its Irish population with relatives living nearby in northern Montague increasingly became identified with Montague. With the Scottish-origin population of Beckwith largely concentrated in the northern concessions where many farms had better quality soil to a greater depth, and because they were fairly close to the prosperous lowland settlement in the adjacent Mississippi valley in southern Ramsay, they increasingly were the more well-to-do portion of Beckwith society.

The new melding of people of Beckwith highland Scottish origin with those of Ramsay lowland origin was furthered by the union in 1875 of the Church of Scotland and Free Church Presbyterians to create the Presbyterian Church in Canada. Although people of Irish origin remained the larger ethnic group in Beckwith, Presbyterians replaced Anglicans as the single largest denomination in the township. With Scottish Presbyterians for the most part located on better quality land than the Irish, they were able to profit from the dairy economy that emerged in the 1880s. On first glance at the distribution of cheese factories it might seem that the largely Irish farmers of southern Beckwith were served by as many cheese factories as their Scottish-origin counterparts in the northern concessions. Beckwith's first cheese factory at Gillies Corners by the mid 1890s was moved to Franktown where it was known as the Valley Queen factory. It and the cheese factory at Prospect in which Edward Kidd laboured both served the farmers of southern Beckwith. Although only two cheese factories were located in northern Beckwith, one at Tennyson and the other at Black's Corners, farmers there drew milk to a creamery in Carleton Place and to nearby cheese factories located just across township boundaries in Appleton, Ashton, and McCreary's Settlement. The large brick houses that began to line the ninth, eleventh and twelfth concession lines contrasted with the few built in southern Beckwith, effectively providing a visual gauge to the wealth that the dairy

Plate 200
Farmers delivering milk to the Black's Corners cheese factory ca. 1900, as photographed by Annie Elexey Duff. Milk could not be transported lengthy distances due to its perishable nature, due to the lack of refrigerated transport, and due to the poor quality of Beckwith roads. As a result cheese factories sprang up at every village and hamlet between 1880 and 1920. Cheese joined oats as a major Beckwith cash crop during these four decades. Photograph courtesy of Kathy Ogg-Moss.

economy brought to the better farms. Gradually, insidiously, with farmers of Scottish origin inhabiting the bigger, more substantial houses, Beckwith, certainly the part of Beckwith that people wanted to think about or look at, came to be thought of and perceived as a Scottish township. Edward Kidd somehow felt that the values and morals of Beckwith Scottish Presbyterians set the tone for the remainder of township inhabitants.

The Irish-origin population in southern Beckwith was perceived as an extension of unsavoury Irish Montage in contrast with the period of settlement nearly a century earlier when northern Montague settlement had been an extension of southern Beckwith. Increasingly in the late nineteenth century, as the farms of Beckwith Irish-origin families failed to compare with those of their Scottish-origin neighbours at the same time their Irish relatives in Montague became a byword for rowdiness and impoverishment, the Irish of Beckwith became silent about their ethnic origin. In the largest and earliest of the Scottish burial grounds in Beckwith, St. Fillan's cemetery, some forty gravestones pridefully referred to the Scottish birth of persons interred there. In the largest of the

Irsh burial grounds, Franktown public cemetery, by contrast, there were only nine gravestones that mentioned Ireland as the place of origin. Beckwith Irish-origin inhabitants in the late nineteenth and early twentieth centuries became less proud of their ethniciity as their economic situation and status dwindled.

The growing gap in visible agricultural prosperity between southern and northern Beckwith, and by extension between Irish and Scottish inhabitants, was evident in the numbers of large new brick houses constructed in a way it had not been visible previously in Beckwith's history when the majority of inhabitants of Scottish or Irish origin lived in similar log shanties and later in similar log houses. The prosperity came in large part from the cheese industry which throve in Beckwith as well as in the rest of Ontario between 1881 and 1920 because Canada was the major supplier to the British market during these four decades. The vulnerability of having a single market was evident in 1896 when the price of cheese dropped significantly. The Carleton Place *Herald* reported attempts to develop a home market for cheese since "little of our cheese is consumed in Canada.... We should be inducing people to become greater consumers of cheese."[64] Later that same year cheese prices rose, prompting the Ashton correspondent of the *Herald* to comment in November:[65]

> On Saturday last our cheese factory ceased operations for the season. The sales of late have been affected at a good figure, owing to the high market price of cheese. It is expected that the factory will resume operations next season with an increased number of patrons.

Beckwith cheese production was at its peak at the turn of the century. The Prospect correspondent of the *Herald* reported in June 1901 that the "delivery of milk at our cheese factory exceeds that of any previous year. At present prices the output is worth about $600 a week,"[66] The loss of the British market to New Zealand by the end of World War One meant that the cheese industry in Beckwith as in the rest of Ontario rapidly went into decline. Eastern Ontario reports in 1920 showed that the cheese industry was slipping. "There were fewer factories, fewer patrons, fewer cows, less milk delivered, less cheese made, and it required more milk to make a pound of cheese than the year before."[67] By implication, many farmers were watering their milk.

The dairy economy was responsible for changing the types of crops grown in Beckwith between 1881 and 1920 as those crops which could most easily be harvested by machine were increasingly favoured over those requiring manual labour. Oats remained the most significant crop, as local farmers continued to supply the timber industry market, with their crop increasing by more than eighty percent between 1890 and 1920 (Table 23). The crops of hay and mixed grains increased, the yield of barley tripled, and the amount of corn for fodder harvested jumped sevenfold during the same three decades. Turnips as fodder grew less popular, and the harvests of potatoes and rye fell by half. The harvest of peas, a reliable barometer of how well the Scottish cultural diet was faring, dropped by more than 93 percent between 1890 and 1920.

The forty years during which cheese production throve in Beckwith furthered the consolidation of farm holdings (Table 24). Dairy farming called for harvesting forage crops with the growing range of planting and harvesting machines increasingly available, and this mechanisation allowed larger acreages to be cultivated by one family. The Carleton Place *Herald* reported in 1901 that "entire farms of many hundred acres are devoted exclusively to" the dairy industry,[68] and in Beckwith by 1921 some 53 farms had 300 and more acres. As Table 24 shows, the number of farms with less than 100 acres declined, whereas the number with more than one hundred acres increased. Throughout the 1880s, 1890s, 1900s and 1910s the lure of vast holdings in the American west and increasingly in the Canadian west could not be ignored by local families. Edward Kidd observed in the 1880s and 1890s:[69]

Plate 201
The funeral of William Saunders, aged 21 years, lot 19, concession 10, Montague, in late September 1891, as photographed by Archibald Peden. The thin soil and omnipresent swamp in southern Beckwith and northern Montague made it impossible for many families to move up from their modest log houses to more prepossessing frame and brick structures. The walls of this house were whitewashed in an attempt to disguise the unfashionable out-of-date log construction. Many if not most of the people shown in the funeral carriages here were Beckwith relatives and friends of this Kilkenny-origin family. The funeral procession ended up in the Irish Anglican cemetery at Franktown, the village centre for the Irish Anglicans of southern Beckwith and northern Montague. Photograph courtesy of Jeanette Sansome.

People began selling off their farms and leaving for Dakota or Manitoba. The Stewarts first and then the Alcocks, each of whom had an unfertile farm. They came home occasionally, wearing calfskin vests, and laughed at our potholes of fields, each surrounded by a fence. They even felt smothered by the maple woods.

From the 1880s to the 1910s there was a constant stream of people leaving Beckwith. The birth rate in Beckwith doubled from a low of 9.1 births per thousand in 1871 to 19.4 births per thousand in 1901, and slowly declined to eighteen births per thousand by 1919 (Table 25). The mortality rate in Beckwith fluctuated almost in direct relation to the economy, rising from four deaths per thousand in the early 1870s to 10.4 deaths per thousand at the end of the recession in the late 1870s, falling to 7.9 deaths per thousand at the end of the prosperous 1880s, rising rapidly in the late 1890s to 15.2 deaths per thousand in 1899, to just as rapidly fall to an average rate of between ten and twelve deaths per thousand between 1906 and 1919 (Table 26). By subtracting the number of deaths that

Table 23. Agricultural Produce of Beckwith, 1890-1920

	1890	1910	1920
Oats (bushels)	80,925	127,265	148,051
Wheat (bushels)	10,620	6,487	11,168
Buckwheat (bushels)	9,519	17,711	8,459
Potatoes (bushels)	53,635	33,765	25,624
Hay (tons)	5,726	7,182	7,057
Turnip (bushels)	15,135	23,595	9,643
Peas (bushels)	16,790	2,781	1,029
Barley (bushels)	3,242	7,683	9,397
Corn (tons)	904	7,910	6,998
Rye (bushels)	2,794	1,877	1,500
Mixed Grains (bushels)	—	6,330	8,535

SOURCE: *Canadian census returns in printed volumes for 1891, 1911 and 1921*

took place in Beckwith each year from the number of births it is possible to construct a rate of natural increase of population. For Beckwith the rate of natural increase was somewhat fitful, especially between 1877 and 1881 when there were more deaths than births in the township, but the general trend or mean rate of the annual natural increase of population for Beckwith rose from 2.5 persons per thousand in the early 1870s to 8.5 per thousand in the early 1900s, and then fell to 5.7 per thousand by the end of World War One.[70] It is significant that there was an increase in the crude birth rate and in the natural rate of increase of population in Beckwith during the 1880s and 1890s, as the third generation of Beckwith inhabitants began to marry and to give birth to the fourth generation. It is equally significant that these increases were unable to offset the net drain of population migrating west out of Beckwith, so that census returns presented Beckwith's population as being in steady decline, dropping from 1,928 persons in 1881 to 1,766 in 1891, to 1,646 in 1901, to 1,402 in 1911, and to 1,221 in 1921.[71] Beckwith's population in 1920 was less than two-thirds of what it had been in

Table 24. Land Holding in Beckwith, 1881-1921

	1881		1901		1921	
	No.	%	No.	%	No.	%
Number of Occupiers	287		307		259	
10 Acres and Under	14	4.9	41	13.4	6	2.3
11-50 Acres	21	7.3	10	3.3	14	5.4
51-100 Acres	74	25.8	82	26.7	55	21.2
101-200 Acres	116	40.4	105	34.2	103	39.8
200 Acres and Over	62	21.6	69	22.5	81	31.3

SOURCE: *Canadian census returns in printed volumes for 1891, 1911 and 1921*

Plate 202
Gravestones of John McGregor and Peter McCuan in St. Fillan's cemetery and of Findlay McEwen and Mary McLaren in the Kennedy cemetery. From the late 1850s on, as Beckwith inhabitants began to develop a long term memory, those of highland birth in particular made a specific point of having their place of origin recorded on their gravestones. This custom among the Scottish-origin inhabitants of Beckwith reflected their growing prosperity. Irish-origin inhabitants were less likely to mention their country of origin as their economic and ethnic status declined in late nineteenth century Lanark County.

1881, but with the number leaving in the 1880s amounting to 8.4 percent of the 1881, population, the number leaving in the 1890s amounting to 6.8 percent of the 1891 population, the number leaving in the 1900s amounting to 14.8 percent of the 1901 population, and the number leaving in the 1910s amounting to 12.9 percent of the 1911 population, the movement of people out of township was quite gradual.

The flow of more than a third of the population out of the township between 1881 and 1920, however gradual it may have been, had a profound psychological effect in the communities of Beckwith. Every family that left whose property was added to another farmer's holding only served to make the local school section, the local congregation, and local rural businesses that much weaker. When Alexander F. Stewart and his family moved away from the seventh line in 1906, their neighbours in the school section expressed their "profoundest regret" since "[e]very phase of life in our community will miss you, for your best efforts were extended to all — church, state and the home."[72] Beckwith farmers endured boasting by those who went west about the unlimited acreages and the abundant crops that contrasted with local farmsteads, although many recognised that this was simply the bravado of relatives and old neighbours putting the best face on having to distance themselves so far from Beckwith. The suspicions of those who remained in Beckwith that life on the prairies was not all it had initially been cracked up to be, seemed confirmed by verses of doggerel sent back from Saskatchewan by a Presbyterian clergyman who previously had ministered at Franktown:[73]

Table 25. Birthrate and Rate of Natural Increase for Beckwith Township, 1869-1919.

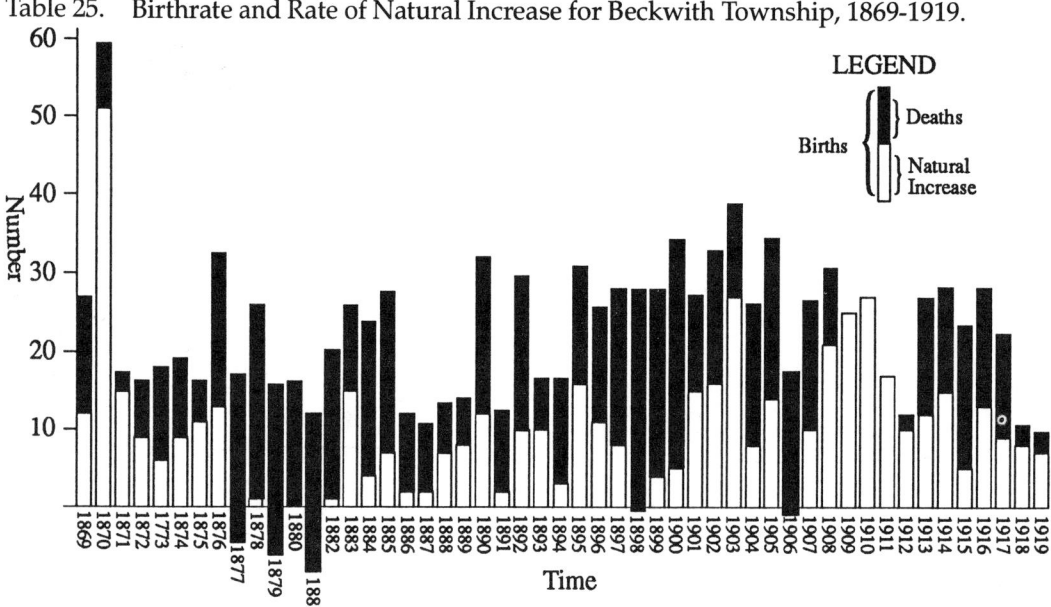

SOURCE: OBCMR Beckwith death registers, 1869-1919. *The statistics for the years 1908 through 1912 are incomplete.*

Table 26. Mortality rate for Beckwith Township, 1869-1919.

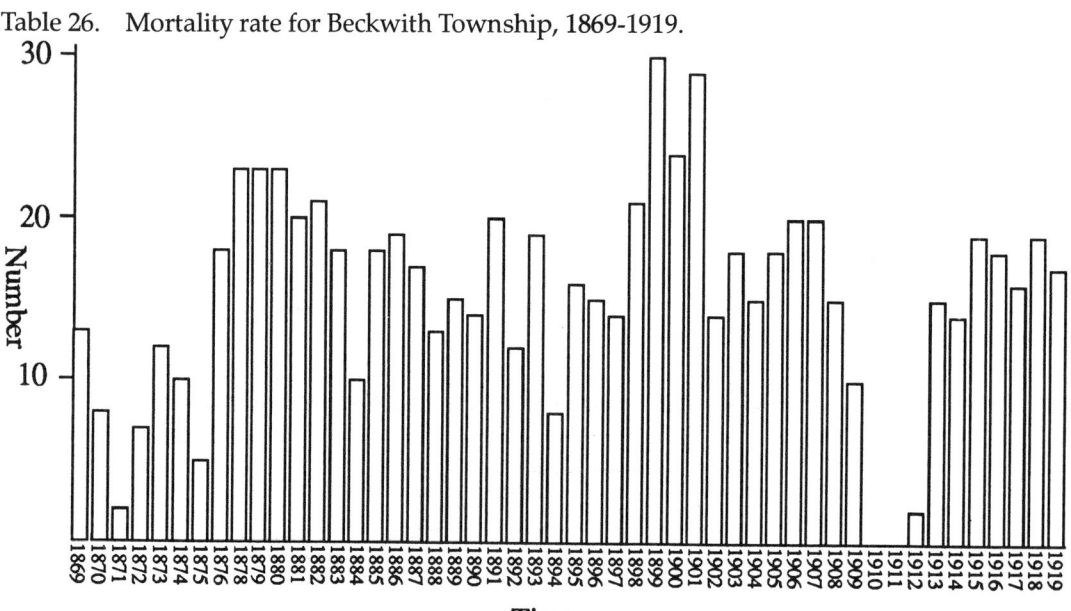

SOURCE: OBCMR Beckwith death registers, 1869-1919. *The statistics for the years 1908 through 1912 are incomplete.*

Plate 203
Arnold Griffith of Black's Corners and an unidentified Simpson child from Ashton ca. 1905, as respectively photographed by J.J. Kerfoot, Smith's Falls, and W.H. Hooper, Carleton Place. These two children were part of the peaking birthrate at the turn of the century. From a low average of fifteen births per year in the late 1860s, the birthrate in Beckwith rose to thirty per year by 1903, and then fell to seventeen per year by 1920. The dress of these children reflected the pervasive influence of mail-order catalogues in rural Beckwith homes. Photographs courtesy respectively of Pauline Wright and the late William Livingstone Kidd.

I'm weary of this Western life,
Its hurry and its bustle;
I'm tired of the wind and dust
The constant rush and hustle....
I'm tired of these prairie trails,
Of driving and of walking,
Of huge wheat fields and bigger deals
Their monstrous style of talking....

By Prospect heights, through Derry vales,
And old Black's Corners yonder,
I'd like to drive round there tonight,
As home in dreams I wander.
And feel the autumn breezes blow,
Where the Mississippi rushes,
And know I'm safe within the shades
Of Beckwith in the bushes.

The sentimentality for "Old Beckwith" by those families who migrated westward contrasts starkly with the refusal of some individuals who, rather than face up to the psychological impact of leaving Beckwith even after their homesteads had been sold by other family members, remained behind working at odd jobs and as occasional hired men for their old neighbours. One such person who Edward Kidd knew during his childhood was Dave McGregor at Prospect:[74]

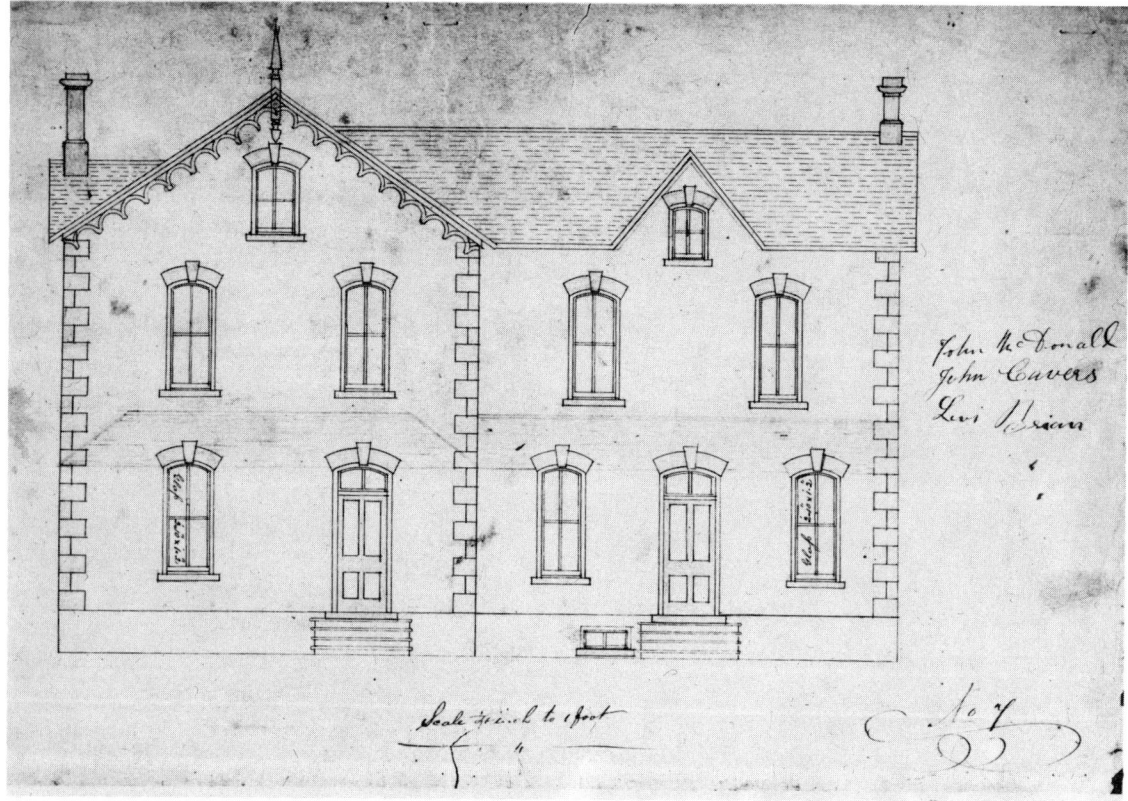

He rarely strayed beyond the limits of the immediate neighborhood. He lived from hand to mouth, earning only sufficient to keep him in clothes, tobacco, and an occasional bottle of whiskey. He made his headquarters at Burrows['s] and at Jack Scott[']s. If an emergency man were wanted to draw in hay or to go to the threshing, Dave would be sent for. With his long grey whisker[s] and his clay pipe, he was an excellent worker, being obliging and harmless. In the wintertime he made axe handles and sold them to the neighbors. He was a curiosity to me in that he drank whiskey.

A few of these remnants of old Beckwith families in their advanced years became the recipients of Beckwith municipal relief. From 1873 until his death in October 1881, Alexander Armstrong "as an old indigent and infirm individual" was provided with clothing and boarded by families who were paid a weekly rate for doing so by the township council.[75] As the number of individuals who remained behind in Beckwith rather than move west with their families threatened to place a growing number of indigent and elderly people as a burden on Beckwith ratepayers, the township council from the mid 1870s onward took pains to pay the passage of such persons often back to relatives in the British Isles. In March 1876, for example, Beckwith council voted fifteen dollars to send William Craig back to his friends in Ireland.[76] In 1888 reeve Archibald Dewar purchased a ticket for William John Hamilton to return to Belfast, and saw him off on the train at Carleton Place.[77] It was no worse than how the aged and infirm with families still in Beckwith were treated. When the Anglican clergyman at Franktown requested aid in 1872 to "support Mrs. [George] Nesbitt who has been insane for years", the township council granted ten dollars for temporary assistance "till her friends take the proper steps to support or provide for her or adopt proper means to send her to a

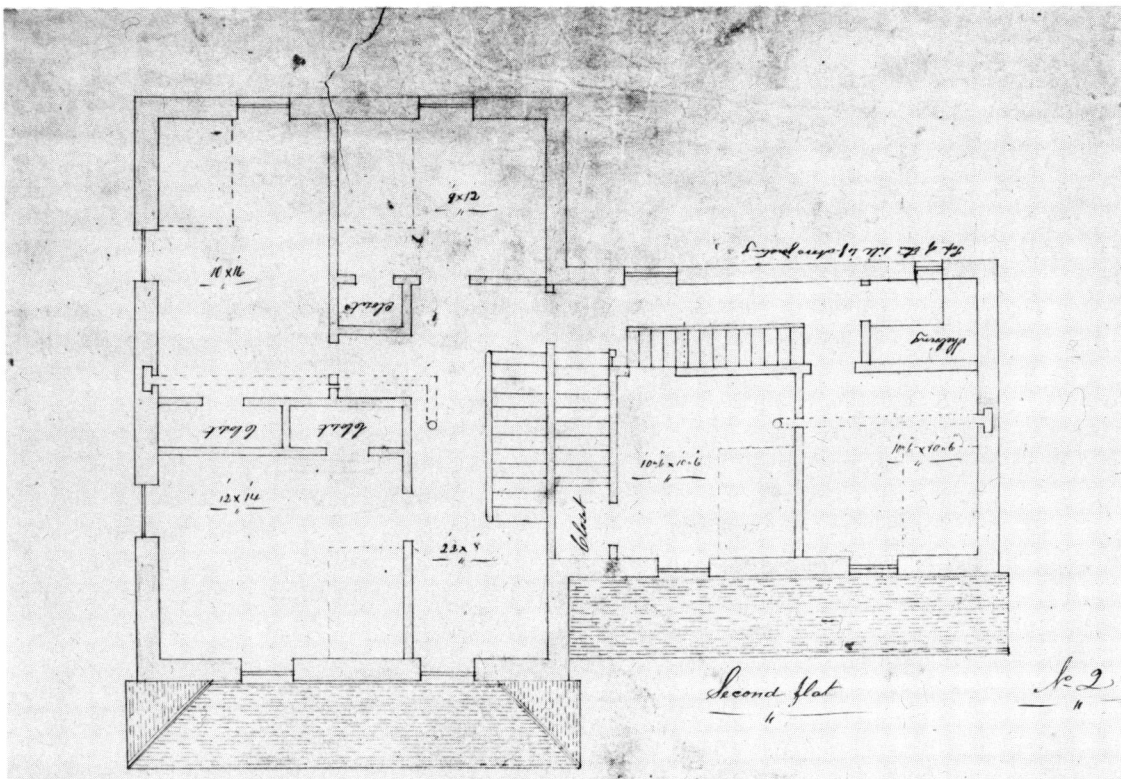

Plate 204
Elevation and floorplan of the second storey of an unidentified house in northern Beckwith sketched ca. 1890. Virtually all of the farmhouses built in Beckwith between 1880 and 1920 followed the L-shape of floorplan. The quoining, the tall windows, the transoms above doors, the attic gables, the tall ceilings and the finial at the peak of the gable all contributed to the new vertical look of Beckwith houses at the turn of the century. Four of the five bedrooms boasted clothes closets. The location of stovepipes is indicated by dotted lines. Archives of Ontario D1125, D1129.

Lunatic Asylum where all insane persons should be sent, that being the only hope of their ultimate recovery from such a state."[78] A year later Mrs. Nesbitt was housed in the Perth Jail, the only refuge available in Lanark County for elderly indigent persons who had no one to look after them.[79] For young Edward Kidd, oppressed as he was by the respectability of his own family, the small log house in which a neighbour known as "Old Bachelor Duncan and Crazy Colin, his brother" lived, seemed "a mystery, and [as] wonderful as a giant's castle." In later years when he stepped inside the humble structure, "it lost much of its glamour."[80]

* * * * * * * * *

Unlike most men his age from Beckwith, Edward Kidd's stay in the west was brief, the length of a year, before heading back to Queen's in the autumn of 1907, to take a course in geology, and for the first time he found himself really enjoying his work at university. In the spring of 1908 he was part of a geological expedition sent out by the Ontario government to open up the Montreal River area.[81] Here was an opportunity to visit the fabled Canadian north where, Edward Kidd had learned as a boy, two of his uncles had settled, and "who were rearing families in a district both isolated and romantic."[82] But just as the Canadian west from the Beckwith perspective "was looked on as a Promised Land", drawing his older brother Angus thither to study law and his younger brother Jim to homestead,[83] only to prove unfulfilling for Edward Kidd, so too the rigours of the north or "New Ontario" overwhelmed his interest in exploring its mineral splendour. One day while crossing a frozen stream on a slippery birch log, he fell into the icy water up to his chin. "As I made my way up the bank", he recalled, "I decided to change my profession to that of Medicine."[84]

Edward Kidd spent three years in the Queen's medical school, and passed his summers teaching school near Davidson, Saskatchewan, and boarded with Bob McConnell, a farmer from Beckwith who was in the process of completing his homesteading duties, breaking prairie with a team of four oxen. He graduated in 1910, became an intern at the Kingston General Hospital, and in the spring of 1911 was offered a position as head of the anatomy department at Queen's. He set off with his *fiancée* for a tour of American and European medical schools to "pick up the fundamentals of Anatomy teaching", visiting Harvard, Philadelphia, New York and Johns Hopkins, before embarking for Glasgow and visiting Edinburgh, London, Oxford and Paris. In the summer of 1912 Edward Kidd returned to Europe, visiting Hamburg before settling in Berlin to follow lectures by leading surgeons, pathologists and anatomists, before proceeding on to Amsterdam, Rotterdam, Antwerp and London.[85] In 1913 he married Lou Hastey, and in 1914 they returned to Europe.

In heading the anatomy department at Queen's University and in his trips to Europe, it might seem that Edward Kidd had come a long distance from his ambitionless rearing in the isolated Derry school section of Beckwith, but this was not the case. On the 22nd day of June 1911 very early in the morning he left the room he rented in London's Torrington Square to join the hundreds of thousands of people lining The Mall to view the coronation procession of King George V and Queen Mary. He recalled:[86]

> I lay on the grass in the midst of a good natured crowd. I rested against a man from Yorkshire, while a Birmingham girl slept with her head on my knee. The day was fine. I remember only a vague feeling of disappointment at not being impressed by the six white-cream color... horses, which drew the golden coach. The whole seemed like a huge opera, each one acting his part. Through the window of the huge coach I saw the blond elaborately coiffured head of the Queen, topped by a large blue hat. By her side was her much smaller, bewhiskered spouse.

The next day Edward Kidd again was in position viewing a second procession in which the King was formally given the Lord Mayor's permission to enter the City of London, and became absorbed in the "mixture of medi[a]eval pageantry and modern military units in full dress":[87]

> A few statesmen and heads of Dominion Governments were as unobtrusive as possible, and seemed to be rather apologetic for being there at all — in such gorgeous company.... There were Indian [p]rinces dressed in silken robes which glittered with precious stones. German cavalrymen in shining helmets and pale blue uniforms rode on splendid horses.... There were businesslike French curissures with tassels of black horsehair streaming from their golden helmets.... There were Canadian Mounted Police whose red coats looked somber in the company they kept. There were endless files of sailors and guardsmen, of Dominion and Colonial soldiers — the eyes grew weary of following them.... The procession passed, [and] again the city was left a seething mass of people which it took hours to scatter.

Edward Kidd in all likelihood was the only person raised in Beckwith who had the satisfaction of watching the splendid ceremony of the 1911 coronation procession of George V, the very same George who was shown as a young man in the portrait of Queen Victoria and her family which hung on a wall back home in the Derry. In viewing the procession, Edward Kidd affirmed the strong respect for empire and monarchy with which he had been raised by the succession of young women presiding over the Derry school. As he himself admitted, "Queen Victoria was over everything, and always would be — she was like God."[88] For Edward Kidd to view George V and Queen Mary on the way to their coronation was akin to watching a loved and respected relative being honoured by the community, in this case the community of the British Empire.

His Beckwith upbringing was never very far from Edward Kidd's mind, although he continued to roam far from eastern Ontario. During his visit to Scotland, he visited the battleground of Culloden, where some of his mother's ancestors had died. He was moved by the bleakness of the moor, the lack of houses around, the nearby forest of stunted pine trees, with the cold and cheerless Grampian mountains in the distance. He was saddened to view the row of mass graves, each some twenty feet long in which the highlanders were buried, each grave with a headstone designating which particular clan lay there, simple shallow mounds covered by long grass. But although moved, Edward Kidd was no sentimental romantic. He knew that the battle of Culloden was horribly mismanaged, and tersely commented, "Good men died for a lightheaded fop."[89] Within a matter of months of this visit the British empire was at war, and in the course of serving as a war surgeon overseas Edward Kidd was awarded the Military Cross and was mentioned in dispatches. During the war he was stationed in Egypt where he developed an abiding interest in Egyptology, and at war's end he returned to Canada with the rank of lieutenant-colonel. He resumed his Queen's professorship, but resigned to do postgraduate work in Edinburgh and Liverpool, and 1922 he made his own permanent westward migration to Vancouver, where he practised as an orthopedic surgeon, and died in 1947. Although his fascination with world civilisations led him to present an Egyptian mummy to the Vancouver museum and to research prehistoric and modern Amerindians on the Pacific coast, and although he was named a Fellow of the Royal Anthropological Institute, a Fellow of the American Geographical Society, and elected president of the Vancouver Arts and Historical Society,[90] he could not forget Beckwith. In 1943 he published a history of his childhood school section, *The Story of the Derry* that he dedicated "to the boys and girls with whom he went to school."

Edward Kidd never fully ceased to marvel at the isolation of his childhood, at the lack of ambition which frustrated him during the years he worked as his father's unpaid assistant, and at his eventual release into a larger more invigorating world. He never lost a certain affection for Beckwith, and returned to the family homestead to visit his brother Livingstone and his family on numerous occasions. He looked back on his strict semipuritan childhood "with a smile, but with what pride!"[91] But if he recognised that the combined influences of his father's control, his school section's isolation, his brothers and sisters, the strict religious standards of his Scottish neighbours, and the family library all had somehow positively contributed to fit him for a useful life, a nagging sense persisted that he had paid too high a price in prematurely being deprived of his childhood, of being kept home from school to be his father's drudge. How many other Beckwith children of his generation, especially those who were expected to continue on with family homesteads and who did not enjoy the advantage of a family library, like Edward Kidd found themselves working away on the farm "with never a minute's rest all day except for meals" and who despite working at top speed "never remember[e]d having been told, "You have done well".[92] As he mulled over the events of his childhood in Beckwith, Edward Kidd's ultimate assessment remained equivocal about what he considered the burden of his childhood. "It is a good thing to have learned how to work", he admitted. "Perhaps if I had not been set to the task of doing a man's work so early, I should have been happier in performing it."[93]

Endnotes

1. George Edward Kidd, "The Story of the Earlier Part of My Life" (unpublished manuscript written in 1935, made available courtesy of the late William Livingstone Kidd).
2. 22 July 1991 interview with John Kidd, Beckwith.
3. Kidd, *The Story of the Derry*, pp. 55, 64-65.
4. Idem, "Earlier Part of My Life", p. 62.
5. OPLCRO 19 August 1850 will of John Kidd, Beckwith.
6. Kidd, "Earlier Part of My Life", p. 59.
7. Ibid., p. 6.
8. Ibid., p. 59.
9. Ibid., p. 60.

10 Ibid., p. 63.
11 *Carleton Place Herald,* 2 March 1870, p. 3, col. 4.
12 Kidd, "Earlier Part of My Life", pp. 3-4.
13 Ibid., p. 66.
14 Ibid., p. 4.
15 Ibid.
16 Ibid., pp. 4-5.
17 Ibid., pp. 1, 2-3.
18 Ibid., pp. 4-5.
19 Kidd, "My Four Years On the Farm" (unpublished manuscript, made available courtesy of the late William Livingstone Kidd), pp. 1-2.
20 Ibid., p. 1.
21 Kidd, "Earlier Part of My Life", p. 59.
22 Ibid., p. 2.
23 Idem, *Story of the Derry,* p. 43.
24 Idem, "Four Years On The Farm", p. 1.
25 Ibid., p. 2.
26 Ibid., pp. 5-6.
27 Idem, "Earlier Part Of My Life", pp. 68-69.
28 Idem, "Four Years On The Farm", pp. 2-5.
29 Ibid., pp. 2-3.
30 Ibid., p. 7.
31 Idem, "Earlier Part Of My Life", p. 7.
32 Idem, "My Four Years On the Farm", p. 8.
33 Ibid., p. 10.
34 Idem, "Earlier Part Of My Life", pp. 1-2.
35 Idem, "A Summer Sunday at Home When We Were Children" (unpublished manuscript made available courtesy of the late William Livingstone Kidd), pp. 1-5.
36 Idem, "The Story of My Life", p. 58.
37 Idem, "Summer Sunday at Home", pp. 5-6.
38 Idem, "Earlier Part of My Life", p. 57.
39 Ibid., pp. 1-2.
40 Ibid., pp. 54-55.
41 James M. Hillis, "Life in the Lumber Camp: 1883" in *Ontario History* LIX No. 3 (September 1967), pp. 157-158.
42 Kidd, "My Four Years on the Farm", pp. 10-11.
43 Ibid., p. 11.
44 Ibid., pp. 11-12.
45 Idem, "Earlier Part of My Life", pp. 7-8.
46 Ibid., p. 8.
47 Ibid.
48 Ibid., pp. 8-15.
49 Ibid., pp. 17-18.
50 16 March 1874 letter from James Brown, Phillipsville, Ontario to his brother Asa Brown, Allendale, Michigan, provided courtesy of Howard M. Brown, Ottawa.
51 Kidd, "Earlier Part of My Life", p. 18.
52 Ibid., p. 19.
53 Ibid., p. 77.
54 Ibid., p. 3.
55 Ibid., p. 54.
56 Ibid., pp. 51-52.
57 Ibid.
58 Ibid., p. 64.
59 Ibid., pp. 51-52.
60 *Smith's Falls Review,* 9 March 1865, p. 2.
61 *Perth Courier,* 2 October 1868.
62 *Almonte Gazette,* 23 March 1894, p. 1, cols. 4-6.
63 Cited in the *Smith's Falls Echo,* 14 May 1896, p. 4.
64 *Carleton Place Herald,* 28 July 1896, p. 7, col. 2.
65 Ibid., 10 November 1896, p. 5, col. 2.
66 Ibid., 18 June 1901, p. 8, col. 3.
67 Ibid., 28 January 1920, p. 3, col. 3.
68 Ibid., 15 January 1901, p. 5, col. 3.
69 Kidd, "Earlier Part of My Life", p. 73.
70 OBCMR, birth and death registers for Beckwith Township, 1869-1919.
71 1931 printed decennial census of Canada.
72 1906 newspaper clipping in scrapbook loaned by the late Hazel Davis.
73 Excerpted from 1918 clipping of doggerel "Beckwith in the Bushes" written by the Reverend J.W.S. Lowry, Brownlee, Saskatchewan, in scrapbook loaned by the late Hazel Davis.
74 Kidd, "Earlier Part of My Life", p. 48.
75 OBCMR 10 June 1873, 21 April 1874, 11 June 1874, 4 August 1874, 18 September 1874, 10 November 1874, 8 December 1874, 26 May 1876, 27 June 1876, 1 August 1876, 31 October 1876, 12 December 1876, 24 November 1877, 11 February 1879, 27 May 1879, 17 February 1880, 7 June 1880, 31 May 1881 and 29 October 1881 minutes of Beckwith township council.
76 Ibid., 14 March 1876 minutes.
77 Ibid., 7 July 1888 minutes.
78 Ibid., 13 May 1872 minutes.
79 Ibid., 10 June 1873 minutes.
80 Kidd, "Earlier Part of My Life", p. 49.
81 Ibid., pp. 19-20.
82 Ibid., p. 52.
83 Ibid., p. 23.
84 Ibid., p. 22.
85 Ibid., pp. 22-42.
86 Ibid., p. 28.
87 Ibid., pp. 28-29.
88 Ibid., p. 73.
89 Ibid., p. 43.
90 Obituary of George Edward Kidd, provided courtesy of John and Leona Kidd, Beckwith.
91 Kidd, "Earlier Part of My Life", p. 2.
92 Idem, "My Four Years on the Farm", p. 11.
93 Ibid., p. 12.

THE HOUSEHOLD OF FAITH

The rigorously pious upbringing of Edward Kidd and other children raised in Beckwith between 1881 and 1920 did not necessarily flow from the religious inheritance brought from Ireland and Scotland in the 1810s and 1820s. A moral or devotional revolution took place in regional society from the 1860s on, a continuing crusade that maintained its vigour well into the twentieth century as religion was embraced by two generations of women as a form of release from the tedium of domesticity. Under the counsel of a growing supply of clergymen, Beckwith women sought to justify their domestic roles as increasingly they found themselves with fewer opportunities to participate in the economy, in agriculture, and even in the instruction of their own children. The new active participation of women in religious groups and collective activities not only made them feel that they were taking part in activities with international significance, but also that they were making Beckwith a morally better place in which to live. The feminisation of religion in Beckwith transformed the quality of denominational rivalries that had particularly existed at Carleton Place in the mid nineteenth century and it smothered the first tentative expressions of free thought in the 1850s. Denominational barriers became less rigid partly because of the growing social intercourse among women, partly because of the growing pan-Protestant influence of the Orange lodge, and partly because of the merging interest among members of most denominations in promoting the cause of banning liquor. Ultimately, the feminisation of religion in Beckwith served to disguise the fact that local farmwomen found themselves at an economic and social impasse.

Religion had been important in Beckwith from the beginning of settlement, providing as it did an intangible and emotional link with the homelands of Wexford and Perthshire. And, as has been shown in previous chapters, local congregations acted as powerful forces to maintain social order, for basing political careers, for providing occasions to socialise, to socially distinguish members of society, and to engage in public worship. In 1861 Robert Bell commented that society in the village of Carleton Place consisted of "ten distinct sets or circles, each moving in a social atmosphere of its own, and firing occasional shots of defiance at each other". In the next breath he remarked, "In religion there are numerous divisions, from the hard-shell Baptist...to the stern follower of John Knox, isolated in his asceticism — from the high Churchman of Apostolical succession dogma to the Wesleyan, who wanders at intervals to lowly and forgotten places to gather in the backsliders."[1] What Bell did not say, but broadly implied, was that religion was a major if not *the* major defining characteristic of these social sets. The continuing importance of religious observance in Beckwith was evident in the appearance of Carleton Place on a Sunday:[2]

> The Sabbath, generally wears the features of a day in which all the inhabitants prostrate themselves in penitence and humility, and the most rigid Puritan would glory in the deserted and sombre appearance of the streets, the only break in the churchyard-like stillness is the mel[l]ifluous tones of the Episcopal bell swelling out from its cathedral belfry and the flocking of worshippers to the different places of prayer, and then the most particular in regard to appearances and Sabbath propriety, could only mark the deep reverence which the different countenances bear.

By the 1870s many of the superstitions regarding ghosts and witches that the highlanders in particular had brought with them as part of their cultural baggage had gradually disappeared. In 1823 the Reverend William Bell observed that many ghosts were reported to be seen and that the highlanders were no less troubled with witches in Beckwith "than they were at home, among their native hills." He remarked:[3]

> These mischievous beings not only deprive them of their milk and butter in the summer, but even of their maple sugar in the spring. Last March, when the sap began to run, a decent old man told me that he set up a kettle and boiled sap for several days, but never got a grain of sugar from it. And what think you, said I, was the reason that you got no sugar? Indeed, said he, I ken the cause vera weel. I had a neighbour that was na counted vera cannie at hame, and I think she is nae better here. Surely, said I, you do not mean to say that your neighbour is a witch? If I sud na say that, I may at least think it, said he, for I'm sure my sugar could na gang awa without somebody that had a connection with witches.

The highlander fear of witches helps to explain the great store they placed on having St. Fillan's crozier in their midst from the late 1810s to the early 1840s, so that the curative powers of the water passed over it could dispel the power of spells cast by witches. Similarly, Bibles were invested with magical powers, as when a group of neighbours in 1841 held a "trial by ordeal" to discover the identity of a thief. They "sent Drysdale to borrow a riddle or sieve, which he balanced on a pivot, making it turn round, and with the bible open on the table, he called over the names of all the people in the line." The riddle continued to spin "till James Allan was named, when it turned round three times and fell to the ground. This, of course, was regarded as a clear evidence of his guilt by his superstitious neighbours.[4]

In the 1840s and 1850s as part of a general campaign for the moral, social and political reform of society, to free people from enslavement to custom and superstition, the Reform editor and correspondents of the Carleton Place *Herald* mounted an attack on continuing belief in witchcraft and the evil eye. When James Stewart of Beckwith's seventh concession was arrested by the sheriff of Lanark County in June 1856 with having murdered a young woman whose hacked-up body had been fished up from the depths of the Rideau River, James Poole at the *Herald* was astounded to learn that the sheriff had consulted a witch at Plum Hollow in Leeds County. "It is scarcely credible", he fumed, "that in this age of the world, a man, making pretensions to intelligence, respectability or honesty of purpose, would hire a witch to aid him in the discovery of a criminal".[5] As late as 1866 a correspondent of the *Herald* lamented "the superstition and ignorance that is often exhibited" in both Lanark and Carleton counties:[6]

> As an instance, a respectable and wealthy farmer contemplates selling off all his cows and stocking his farm with sheep because he believes that one of his neighbours has "*cast an evil eye*" on his cows, and his wife is unable to make butter. In the same locality there has been quite a number that has not been able to make butter during the very warm weather last summer, therefore their cows have also been bewitched. Their superstition does not stop there, for they believe and employ an ignorant and lazy fellow to remove the charm from the cows.

One of the most approved methods for removing a charm was "to get a little of the hair of the man of the '*evil eye*' and mix it with the hair of the cow, then burn it in a tin dish under the cow's nostrils". Other charm removers preferred passing the pan three times over the cow's back and under her belly. Similarly, to cure a bewitched gun, one had to put "in a crooked sixpence when loading the piece and then to draw the figure of [the] party with the 'evil eye' on some large pine tree, and blaze into it at a short distance and then the influence of the evil eye is removed for a time." That

BY-LAW,

To provide for the good Government and preservation of the streets and highways in the Municipality of Beckwith, and to provide for the safety of Her Majesty's subjects, and others travelling thereon.

BY-LAW to provide for the good Government and preservation of the Streets and Highways in the Municipality of Beckwith and to provide for the safety of Her Majesty's subjects, and others travelling thereon.

Passed the 8th day of Dec. 1874.

Whereas it is expedient and necessary to make provision for the Government of Streets and Highways in the Municipality of Beckwith, and to provide for the preservation of timber or other useful and needful material, growing, lying, or being thereupon, and to regulate travel, and provide for the safety of Her Majesty's subjects, and others travelling thereon.

Be it therefore enacted, under the authority of the Municipal Laws of the Province of Ontario, by the Council of the Municipal Corporation of the Township of Beckwith, in Council assembled.

1. That it shall be unlawful for any person or persons, to cut down, take away, sell, or appropriate for private purposes, or wilfully or maliciously to do any damage to injure or spoil any Timber, Stone, Sand or Gravel, or other useful and needful material Growing Lying and being in or upon any of the Streets and Public Highways of the said Municipality without leave or purchase from the Reeve and Council of the said Municipality.

2. That it shall be unlawful for any person or persons to place any obstructions such as timber, saw-logs, cordwood, stove wood, fire-wood cut into lengths, short-wood for railroad purposes, Railroad ties, fence timber, unless for immediate use, stones, or any other rubbish or material to the hinderance and endangerment of the safety of passengers, teams or vehicles on any of the Highways aforesaid.

3. That when any Public Highway or Government allowance for Road not heretofore opened or used, and is in the occupation of an owner or owners, occupant or occupants, shall be required for the public benefit, it shall be the duty of the occupants or occupants to open said Road to the full breadth required by law, when ordered to do so by the Council of the Municipality in time and manner, to be specified in a written order signed by the Reeve and addressed to the Pathmaster of the Section, whose duty it shall be to see such order properly executed.

4. That it shall be unlawful for any person or persons to injure break down, destroy, roll off, or remove, any railing or side safety logs, upon any bridge within the Municipality.

5. That no building material of any kind whatever shall be placed upon or suffered to remain on any Street or Highway within the Municipality without the permission of the Council, for a definite period to be stated in an order signed by the Reeve, and in such case or cases the materials aforesaid are to be laid in such a way as to secure a safe passage to persons and teams.

6. That it shall be unlawful wilfully or maliciously to cut down or injure any shade trees planted for ornament or spontaneously growing on the sides and within the limits of any Street or Highway in the Municipality.

7. That it shall be unlawful to throw place upon or leave any dirt, filth, carcases of animals, of any kind or species whatever, or any other rubbish, on any Street, Road, Lane or Highway within the Municipality.

8. That all persons travelling upon the Streets or Highways of the Municipality, whether in charge of Stage, Coaches, Waggons, Carriages, Sleighs or any other vehicle to which a horse or horses, or any other animal or animals shall be attached, or on horseback, shall when meeting each other on the said Streets or Highways turn out to the right hand from the centre of the Street and give each other one-half of said road.

9. That if from the extreme weight of any load the driver thereof shall find it impracticable so to turn to the right as aforesaid by reason of the centre rute or way-mark on said Road, he shall on meeting any Coach, Waggon, Sleigh, Carriage or other Vehicle, as aforesaid and immediately stop, and if required to do so, shall assist the person or persons so met to pass without damage.

10. That every person travelling with any vehicle, or on horseback as aforesaid, when overtaken by any vehicle or horseman travelling at a greater speed, shall quietly turn out to the right, giving one-half of the Road to the person so overtaking him, or if unable to turn out as aforesaid, the person so overtaken, shall stop and allow the other to pass, giving assistance if required or necessary to effect such passing.

11. That every person in charge of any Stage, Coach, Waggon, Carriage, Sleigh, or other Vehicle, Horse or other Animal, who shall be unable to ride or drive the same with care through drunkness shall upon due proof thereof be liable to the penalties imposed by this By-law.

12. That any person riding or driving on the Highways aforesaid shall on meeting or overtaking any person or persons on foot, carefully pass the same by giving them a portion of the track or otherwise.

13. That all Racing or Furious Driving upon any Street or Highway, in this Municipality shall be unlawful, and the persons so racing, or furiously driving, or shouting, swearing, and using blasphemous or undesent language, shall on due proof thereof be liable to the penalties imposed by this By-law.

14. That any person or persons, riding or driving any carriage or other vehicle, horse, or other animal over any Bridge in the Municipality, above the length of thirty feet, at any pace faster than a walk, shall be liable to the penalties imposed by this By law.

15. That no person shall leave any horse, team, or other animal upon any Street or Highway as aforesaid, whether travelling or standing, unless properly secured, or some one travelling with or in charge of the same.

16. That every person driving in a Sleigh, Cutter, or other Vehicle on runners in the Winter season, shall have a string of bells attached to the horse or team harnessed thereto.

17. And be it enacted by the authority aforesaid that any person or persons guilty of a violation of any of the provisions of this By-law, shall, upon conviction thereof before any Justice or Justice's of the Peace having jurisdiction in the said Municipality be liable to a fine of not more than Twenty Dollars with costs of conviction, to be collected by distress, and sale of the Goods and Chattels of the said offender or offenders, and in case sufficient Goods or Chattels cannot be found belonging to said offender or offenders as aforesaid on which to levy the fine and costs, as aforesaid it shall be lawful for any such Justice or Justice's of the Peace, to commit the offender or offenders to the Common Gaol or Lock-up within the County of Lanark for a period of not more than twenty days, with or without Hard Labour, as the said Justice's may determine, unless such fine and all costs be sooner paid.

18. And be it enacted by the authority aforesaid, that all fines and penalties imposed and collected by virtue of this By-law, shall be, when collected, paid to the Treasurer of the Municipality where the offence is committed, and shall form part of the Municipal Fund.

JAMES CONN, Reeve.

Plate 205
Printed copy of the Beckwith by-law for the preservation of public morals, December 1874. This by-law served as the basis for the moral revolution that developed in late nineteenth century Beckwith. Loaned courtesy of Alex and Jean McCuan.

such ignorance should yet be so common in the mid 1860s the *Herald* correspondent concluded, "says little for the teachings of the Clergy, the School Master, and the Press".[7] This was too pessimistic an assessment, for although superstitious observances such as casting spells to charm away warts continued well into the twentieth century, concern over the evil eye and witchcraft did not survive past the 1870s.

At the same time superstitious observance began to dwindle, religion in Beckwith at mid-century became transmuted into two ethno-political camps, with voluntarists in support of Reform on the one side, and churchmen in support of the Conservatives on the other side. The voluntarists included Free Church Presbyterians, Baptists and Methodists, whereas the churchmen included members of the United Church of England and Ireland, the Church of Scotland and Roman Catholics. But with Presbyterians and Anglicans numerically dominant in Beckwith, James Poole as editor of the *Herald* continually picked away at the privileges of the Church of England in an overt effort to polarise local inhabitants along an Anglican/Presbyterian split to the benefit of Reform candidate Robert Bell. This strategy worked to the extent that the old link between Beckwith Irish Anglicans and Methodists finally snapped, but initially Perthshire Church of Scotland members and local Irish Catholics refused to be budged, especially after Robert Bell in the summer of 1860 was rumoured to have "called the Blue Bonnet Highlanders of Beckwith a parcel of jackasses" and to have refused to send his own children to a school attended by Roman Catholic children.[8]

The rhetoric in the *Herald* against the United Church of England and Ireland, and the response it provoked from churchmen against dissenters and voluntarists inevitably served to distance Anglicans and Presbyterians from one another, and in Carleton Place particularly to polarise them sufficiently for a group of Presbyterian rowdies to thrust a pig in one of the windows of the Anglican church in August 1852.[9] By 1862 the ethnic and political polarisation of society in northern Beckwith was such that members of the five denominations worshipped in two churches. A Carleton Place inhabitant commented:[10]

> At a distance people have been informed of the highly religious character of its inhabitants, and yet the stranger opens his optics with surprise depicted therein to find that there are no fewer than three places of worship left to the ravages of the weather — fit habitations for colonies of rats. To look at one of them — a stone building — one would be apt to suppose that desolation had fallen on Christianity. Through the shattered window panes the November blast howls mournfully, while from the interior are evidences of husbandry peeping out, in the shape of straw; on [the] other two, wooden buildings, the doors are sealed, and the voice of prayer hushed. The Episcopal and Methodist buildings are the only edifices open for worship, and the walls of the latter ha[ve] echoed often to the impassioned language of some of the first orators on the continent, and for public worship it is the common ground for Methodist, Presbyterian Establishment, and Free Kirk, alternately.

The push by Reform politicians such as Malcolm Cameron and Robert Bell for religious liberty and for an end to the special privileges enjoyed by the United Church of England and Ireland and the Church of Scotland,[11] not only served to politicise religion, but transformed public worship into a facade of worship from behind which religious conviction grew diffident and church attendance fell. On the surface Carleton Place on Sundays was described as bearing the features of a Scottish village, with hardly a living creature to be seen on the streets except for the occasional pig. "A perfect stranger stopping over Sabbath in Carleton", commented a village inhabitant in 1862, "must either go the church or listen to interminable yarns from [hotelkeeper Napoleon Lavallee] on Sciences, Arts, Australian Sheep, state of the markets, Botany, Theology, &c." Attending church obliged one to pass through a knot of young men at the church door "who appear to be a self-appointed corps of observation to scrutinize most minutely the maidens who are entering the sacred building." Public

Plate 206
St. Augustine's United Church of England and Ireland, Prospect, built 1854, as photographed in 1982. This church was built by John May on land donated by sawmill owner, William James, as an Anglican response to the stone Wesleyan Methodist chapel built at the other end of the hamlet a few years earlier. This church was as simple a structure as the Methodist chapel and the early Irish Anglican churches built at Franktown and Ashton. Only the steeper slope of the roof and more vertical shape of the pointed windows in this church suggest the emerging interest in Gothic Revival architecture. A pointed window originally was on the front wall of the vestibule, with doors on either side wall.

worship being the major social public event of the week in Beckwith, the women who attended church were decked out in "quite a variety of costumes and fashions". On the surface, a visitor to Carleton Place in 1862 concluded that "the observance of the Sabbath is quite orthodox, although I have been informed some of the 'free-and-easy' muscular Christians slip away up to Allan's or McCann's Point, and cast longing eyes at the ducks as they fly within shooting distance".[12] A Beckwith inhabitant admitted that "freethinkers are numerous and silent, if we are to judge from their non-attendance at the sanctuary" but argued "that even the semblance of religion is beneficial to society."[13]

For the free thinkers, the political Reformers, and those who called themselves Chartists, the 1850s and 1860 appeared to bring about many of the reforms they had sought since the 1830s. The Clergy reserves no longer were to finance the old established churches of the British Isles, but rather to assist in financing free schools available to all children. The provincial university was to be nonsectarian, and members of voluntarist denominations were as eligible as members of the older churches for government positions and offices. James Poole enthusiastically editorialised in the

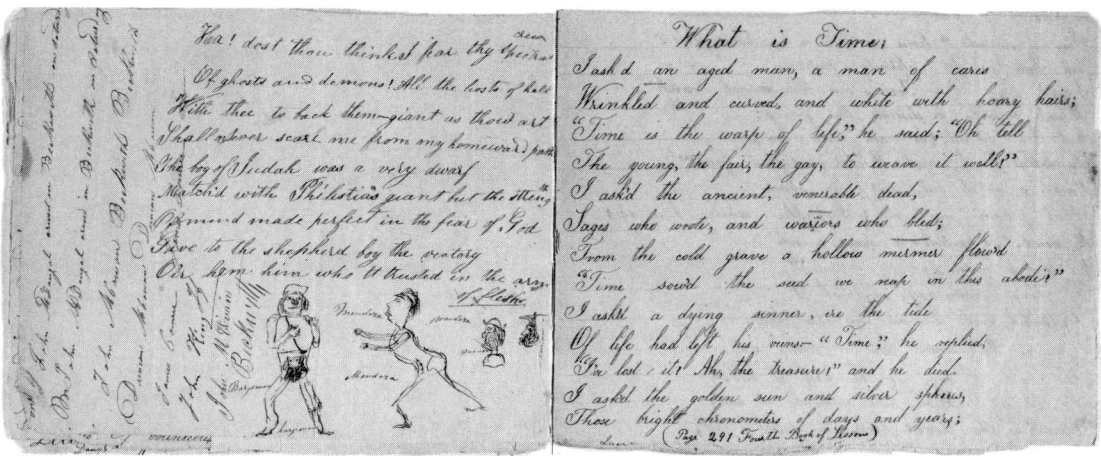

Herald in 1862:[14]

> We have the good fortune to live in an age of progress and development, and under a government that guarantees liberty and freedom of thought and action.... Priest craft, in the Reformed, as well as the old, Churches, is losing its hold upon the minds of the people. Common School education teaches men to read and think and act for themselves. And the result is, that the world is coming to a knowledge of the TRUTH, as it is beautifully exemplified in the books of Nature and Revelation. It is coming to a fuller appreciation of the sublime principles which form the true basis of all human happiness and social reform.... [T]he world of humanity, assisted by education, is advancing, constantly and rapidly, toward a higher degree of improvement.... It is coming to a state of more perfect harmony, and truer enlightenment than that which it has ever enjoyed in all by-gone ages.... Let the old land marks of bigotry and superstition go, if they are so frail as to be overthrown by the natural progress of the race and the light of Revelation; let even the old altars at which our forefathers worshipped crumble to dust if they are dissolved by the light which now streams from the unfolded heavens.

The confident expectation of a new enlightened and humanistic age over which Reformers would preside was premature to say the least. One of the major issues for which Reformers had particularly fought, the secularisation of Clergy reserves in 1854, served to bring about a new political and religious balance in local society. With the United Church of England and Ireland no longer favoured by government at the same time Roman Catholics were demanding separate schools, a new pan-Protestant identity began to emerge and was cemented by growing membership in the Orange lodge. Regional politics had always had a religious cast, but with Irish Catholic immigration in the late 1840s and 1850s following the union of Upper and Lower Canada into a single province, religion assumed a new importance which no one could ignore. In the Canadian legislature Irish Catholics allied with French Canadians were perceived to be a potentially threatening Catholic majority that could impose its wishes on Protestant colonists. The growing local fear of what was termed "Popish ascendancy" was initially promoted by Orangemen, but increasingly was subscribed to by all shades of Protestants and non-Catholics. When Irish Catholics in their quest for separate schools withdrew their support from Reform candidates in 1854, and in 1858 became allied with Orangemen in supporting Tory candidates, a curious realignment came into play. Orangemen and Irish Catholics pulled together in the Conservative harness, claiming that the blinkers on each prevented the other from seeing what the true goal was, while Reformers and voluntarists initially

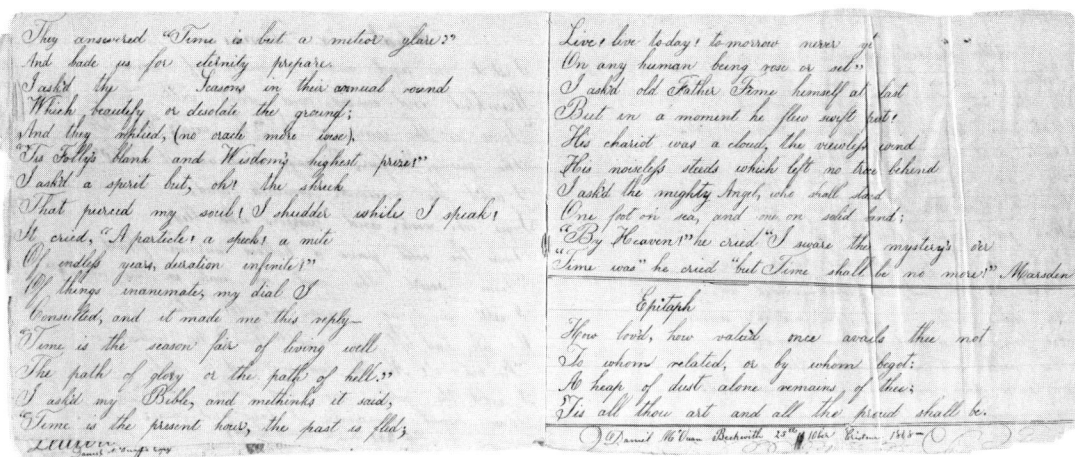

Plate 207
Pages from the 1848 copybook of Daniel McCuan. The decline of traditional superstition and the developing momentum of a moral revolution beginning in the 1850s and 1860s was brought about by religious instruction and value-laden readers in Beckwith schools. Penmanship exercises featured moral phrases such as "Avoid all vicious company", "Yield not yourself to vicious temptation", "Virtue the best treasure" and "Wickedness is the forerunner of misery" that were copied out repeatedly. The verses copied out allude to the decline of superstition, to a new consciousness of time quickly passing by, and to a need for spiritual consolation. Loaned courtesy of Alex and Jean McCuan.

blasted Conservatives for doing the bidding of the Catholic hierarchy. Within only five years, the growing strength of Conservatism forced the pro-Reform Perth *Courier* to admit that "what was once known as the Reform party of South Lanark, no longer exists".[15]

It seems ironic that there should have been a panic in Beckwith over Irish Catholic immigration into the region at mid-century, for the proportion of Roman Catholics in Beckwith and Carleton Place never rose above ten percent of the population, and from 1871 onward Irish Catholic numbers kept falling. In the larger vicinity, however, there was a significant influx of Irish Catholic immigrants, particularly noticeable in regional towns. Beckwith Irish Orange Anglicans were still heirs to the paranoia that had impelled their fathers and grandfathers to leave Ireland in the face of growing Catholic political clout in Ireland. This paranoia was fanned by Reform editors such as James Poole who printed anti-Catholic poems, arguments, stories of captive nuns, and accounts showing idolatry and superstition to be part of Roman Catholic ceremony. Most Beckwith Protestants were tremendously affected by what they read in the *Herald* during the 1850s and 1860s about reports of "priestly domination" coming from Europe, they became truly alarmed at what they perceived to be a threat to free speech when Irish Catholics used gang violence against Italian revolutionary lecturer Gavazzi in Montreal, and wondered at sensational charges of former provincial premier Sir Allan McNab being converted to Catholicism against his wishes on his deathbed. Suddenly, Reformers took note of the huge Catholic churches built at Bytown, Kingston, Brockville, Perth, Smith's Falls, Almonte, Westport, Fallowfield, Prescott and Gloucester, and began to fear that the Roman Catholic church had replaced the old United Church of England and Ireland as a threat to the liberty and equality of Protestant inhabitants. At first, Reformers were not at all worried by the incoming Irish Catholic immigrants, since they believed that the Upper Canadian common school system would be able to assimilate their children and prevent them from growing up to become barbarians, vagrants, thieves, incendiaries and murderers.[16]

The shock of Reformers at the refusal of Catholic clergy to allow Irish Catholic immigrants to send their children to the common schools, in favour of obtaining Catholic separate schools, was evident in James Poole's comment in the Carleton Place *Herald*:[17]

> Apparently afraid that the people will become too educated, intelligent and enlightened to receive as truth, the errors and dogmas of past generations, they curse our Common School system of Education, upon which mainly depend the hopes and prospects of our rising country, and pray, fervently, for the return of the gloom and ignorance of the "dark ages".

The push for Catholic separate schools, so it appeared to Beckwith Reformers, only served to weaken the common school as the central institution for breaking down all the ills which society suffered.

To James Poole in 1868, at the very moment when Carleton Place was finally beginning to industrialise and to attract a labouring population including Irish Catholics, there was cause for worry about attracting a pauper or criminal element. He observed that:[18]

> there are in every city in the Dominion a great mass of poor uneducated childhood of both sexes, who grow up in the worst kinds of debauchery, lewdness, profanity, and godlessness, and who, from their youth, to their grave, are nothing but drunkards, loafers, vagabonds, and criminals.... [He perceived that] the poor, ignorant, and vicious classes...systematically neglect the education of their offspring, even while living under the very shadow of the free school-house [,...allowing] our juvenile pauper population, our street Arabs, and our mischievous urchins, to grow up in ignorance and vice, and ultimately graduate from the Reformatory to the Prison, from the Prison to the Penitentiary, and from thence too often to the gallows.

If Reformers such as James Poole deplored the existence of separate schools, there was even greater consternation among Reform ranks at the new popularity of Orangeism among all stripes of Protestants from the 1860s on, while at the very same time Conservative candidates drew jointly on Orange and Catholic support at the polls. Certainly, among the Irish Anglicans of Beckwith Orangeism remained a defence against what they considered to be Catholic aggression. A younger lodge member from Beckwith asserted in 1857 that Orangemen were "the only true Protestants[,] the real Defenders of the faith". "What would become of this country without Orangemen", he asked. "We would soon be as bad as Ireland in its worst days."[19] As more and more Protestants generally began to fear that the Roman Catholic church was gaining increasing political influence, more and more they became attracted to Orangeism as a force that united the different Protestant denominations. The new popularity of Orangeism was due to it being considered a more respectable organisation, after the provincial ban on processions was lifted in 1851, and as the growing influence of the temperance movement was felt. A print of the Battle of the Boyne might grace Napoleon Lavallee's tap room as late as 1861,[20] but even James Poole, who professed no love for Orangeism, admitted in 1857 that the commemoration of the twelfth of July at Carleton Place by two thousand persons was a "most orderly gathering" in contrast with drinking sprees in earlier decades. Moreover, the temporary banning of Orange processions in the 1840s gave Orangeism additional legitimacy, seeming to corroborate fears that the Roman Catholic church enjoyed undue political influence, to the extent that people could be deprived of as basic a right as walking in a public procession.

The refusal of Beckwith Orangemen and their families to be thus circumscribed was evident to everyone who beheld them during the years of banning and beyond insisting on their right to form a public procession. Hence, despite a scorching July day at Carleton Place in 1857, "nothing daunted by the heat, the Orange men, Orange women, Orange boys, and Orange girls, from all parts of the country, met in our village and had a general parade."[21] When the Prince of Wales during his 1860 visit to Canada refused to visit either Kingston or Belleville in response to Catholic objections over

Plate 208
St. Paul's Church of Scotland, Franktown, built 1870, as photographed ca. 1900. The construction of this church across the street from St. James Anglican church in Franktown reflected the ability of Beckwith villages to attract institutions, services and tradesmen together into a concentration, rather than remaining scattered as they had been during the early nineteenth century. The relation of the window and doors in the vestibule was the same as in St. Augustine's church at Prospect (Plate 206), reflecting the continuing custom of men sitting on one side and women on the other during services. Photograph courtesy of St. Paul's United Church, Franktown.

Orangemen waiting to receive him with banners, it was the final proof needed by most Beckwith Protestants that only Orangeism offered a sufficient bulwark against Catholic ambitions. However genuine the fears that were expressed in the anti-Catholic rhetoric of the rank and file Orangemen, they did not recognise that shrewd political brokers such as James Shaw and John Haggart played upon these fears, yet at the same time courted the Catholic vote by supporting separate school bills and helping to incorporate other Catholic institutions. The Prince of Wales affair in 1860 was definitely a turning point, both politically and religiously for local society, and no one knew it better than editor James Poole. Initially, he had sided with the advisors of the prince, commending them for not tolerating an Orange demonstration.[22] Within a month, cowed by the surge of feeling supporting the Kingston Orangemen for not backing down in the "struggle between Protestant and Roman influences at work in the Province",[23] Poole changed his stance, saying instead that it stirred

Protestant principles to see the Prince advised to turn his back on the banners recording events that gave him his title to the Crown.[24]

Despite the growing popularity and respectability of Orangeism, there remained the problem of assimilating Irish Catholic Famine immigrants to Upper Canadian standards before the influence of their violent and crime-filled past in Ireland was felt by local inhabitants. From the time that the Famine immigrants arrived in the late 1840s onward Reform editors feared the social contamination they might spread among the longer settled population. They questioned whether or not the Peter Robinson Irish Catholic settlers had been fully weaned from their legacy of violence, more than a generation after they had emigrated from Ireland. When John Ryan in nearby Ramsay murdered his wife and then committed suicide in December 1851, James Poole moralised that it must "cause every reasonable person to reflect on the fearful consequences attending the indulgence of a depraved appetite; and the continuance of the custom of using liquor at Bees.[25] This was not mere rhetorical flourish for political ends. Reformers such as James Poole were genuinely fearful that Irish Catholics were naturally violent, and the disproportionate number of Irish Catholics incarcerated in Kingston penitentiary for crimes they had committed was offered as proof of the matter.[26]

In the 1850s and 1860s Reformers opposed anything which they felt would stimulate the inherent Irish Catholic thirst for violence. When James Poole in 1851 deplored the spectacle of a public hanging at Perth as "pamper[ing] the depraved appetites of those who delight in the horrible", he clearly was afraid that it might awaken or excite some latent violence among local Irish Catholics:[27]

> These Counties were, on Saturday last, disgraced by one of those semi-barbarous and brutalizing exhibitions, which occasionally mark and proclaim that we have not yet been able entirely to divest ourselves of the feelings and desires of a savage nature — one of those exhibitions which the authorities get up, to deter others from committing crime; but which have the effect of demoralizing and degrading the human race.... [N]or do we consider that it would answer any good end, to gorge the appetites of those who delight in the horrible, by depicting the agonies and convulsive throes of an erring fellow creature, prematurely hurried into eternity.

Reformers had anticipated that Irish Catholic Famine immigrants would be assimilated to the Upper Canadian way of life through the agency of public schools, but with Catholics granted the right in 1856 to form separate schools where there were sufficient numbers, hopes for assimilation were dampened. The only alternative response to the social threat posed by the Famine inundation was to be on one's guard and to pray for guidance. Almost by accident, Beckwith along with the rest of regional society stumbled onto a moral or devotional revolution as an effective means of countering a latent social threat. If Irish Catholics could not be assimilated to local society's standards in the public school, then local society must be made moral to the extent that it could not effectually be contaminated by the Famine immigrants. In due course the Famine immigrants and their children would come under the influence of their neighbours and lose all potential for violence which the poisoning atmosphere of Ireland had engendered. Moreover, there already existed a number of churches on which to base a wider all-embracing system of piety and morality.

To encourage widespread morality and piety, Lanark and Renfrew united counties council in 1860 passed a by-law restricting the kinds of activities permitted to take place on the Sabbath. It suddenly became unlawful to sell goods and merchandise on Sunday, and only mailmen, doctors and persons performing works of charity could engage in business on that day. Liquor no longer could be sold on Sundays, except to travellers lodging at inns, and profane language no longer was tolerated in public places. Children were now forbidden, under penalty of breaking the law, to play marbles, cricket, skittle, ball, racket and any other noisy games, to gamble, to run races, to dance and to play profane music on Sunday. It was forbidden to kill wild game or go fishing on Sunday.

Plate 209
The Reverend John May and the Reverend Charles Kidd as respectively photographed ca. 1870 and 1910, the latter taken by C.H. Baynes, Kingston. One of the more obvious results of the moral revolution was Beckwith sending out young men into the ministry, with Charles Kidd eventually becoming moderator of the Presbyterian Church of Canada. John May went on from the Irish Anglican congregation at Franktown, after graduating from Queen's University in 1854, to various careers as a clergyman, inspector of Carleton County schools, political candidate and land agent for Manitoba. In later years May returned to live with a sister in Beckwith, and in numerous pieces of doggerel he marveled at the great changes that had taken place in Beckwith rural society between the 1840s and 1890s. In his 1903 book What Ails the Church?, *he expressed concern that the Church of England instead of fulfilling its role as one of "the factories in which Christians are supposed to be made", had become infiltrated with Catholic ritual and sacraments, in contrast with the evangelical preaching he was used to hearing as a youth. The sacraments might be "good and wholesome food in its place...just as is cheese", May argued, "but who would make cheese his main diet?" The analogy was all too apt, since the prosperous cheese economy funded most of the new churches built after 1870. Photographs courtesy of Ottawa Anglican Diocesan Archives and the late Livingstone Kidd.*

Moreover, during the rest of the week, it became unlawful to post indecent broadsides on walls and fences. It was forbidden to be drunk on public property. It was illegal for a person to expose his or her body on public property. It was suddenly immoral to bathe on public property or within sight of public property between six in the morning and eight in the evening unless a person was properly dressed. Finally, it was unlawful to disturb public meetings by making any kind of noise.[28]

In 1874 Beckwith township council passed its own by-law "for the preservation of the Public Morals", reiterating the points in the 1860 county by-law, and tacking on some additional points to reveal how much the moral revolution had advanced in fourteen years. It no longer was "lawful to sell or give intoxicating drinks of any sort to a child, apprentice, servant, Idiot or insane person...without the consent of a parent, Master or Guardian of such person or child". It was also against the law "for any person to utter any profane oaths or any obscene, indecent[,] blasphemous or grossly insulting language or to be seen staggering from the effects of intoxicating Liquor, or to be guilty of drunkenness, or be guilty of Vagrancy or Mendicancy, or other disorderly conduct in any of the public Streets or public places". Already, tragically, there was assumed to be a connection between poverty and a lack of morality. It was also unlawful in Beckwith "to keep gambling or disorderly Houses", and "for any owner or person in charge of any Stud horse to allow or permit the trying or covering of any Mare or Mares in any offensively exposed place in this Municipality."[29] Any person caught contravening the morals by-law was liable to a fine of up to twenty dollars or confinement in gaol for up to twenty days.

The moral revolution gained momentum as Beckwith Protestants socialised together. At a March 1867 missionary meeting of the Church of Scotland congregation in the Carleton Place Methodist church, various speakers noted the tolerance that existed between the various Christian denominations. A guest speaker, James Croil, spoke to the meeting about "the duty of erecting places of worship in an elegant and handsome style and [he] trusted that in the course of a year or two he might see such structures occupying the place of the by no means creditable buildings used here as places of Worship."[30] The number of new churches built in Beckwith and Carleton Place between 1850 and 1920 reflected the growing momentum of the moral revolution, especially from the late 1860s onward. About 1850 a stone Methodist chapel was built at Prospect, in 1852 a stone Church of Scotland house of worship was under construction at Carleton Place, and in 1854 St. Augustine's Anglican church was built of stone at Prospect. In 1869 the stone Zion Free Presbyterian church was erected at Carleton Place, in 1870 the Beckwith seventh line old Kirk was replaced by a board-and-batten church across the street from St. James Anglican church in Franktown, and in 1871 the old 1832 Methodist church in Carleton Place was replaced by a brick church. In 1879 the old stone Melville Presbyterian church at Ashton was made larger.

Large churches were built at Carleton Place in the 1880s, beginning with the stylish stone Gothic Revival St. James Anglican church in 1881, followed by the brick St. Mary's Roman Catholic church in 1884, the huge stone Scottish baronial St. Andrew's Presbyterian church in 1887, and a new Methodist church built in 1889. In 1896 the brick St. John's Anglican church was built at Tennyson, in 1899 a brick Methodist church was constructed at Ashton, in 1901 a brick Methodist church and parsonage were built at Gillies' Corners, in 1902 the Scottish-baronial St. Paul's Presbyterian church was erected at Franktown, and in 1907 a brick Baptist church was built at Tennyson. In 1911 a new larger stone Zion Presbyterian church was constructed at Carleton Place, after the 1869 church burned down. In 1915 a new larger stone St. Augustine's Anglican church was erected to replace the 1845 house of worship at Ashton, and in 1925 a new brick church at Gillies' Corners replaced the old Methodist church there after it burned down.

The many substantial and stylish new churches that were built may partly be explained by the prosperous economic base offered by the dairy economy in rural Beckwith and industrialisation in Carleton Place. Denominational rivalry as to which church had the highest spire or most attractive appearance may also have been a reality, but there is no question as to the depth of spiritual conviction that underlay the moral revolution. James Poole commented in November 1866:[31]

> all will readily admit, that far above all men, spirits, and angels, there exists an intelligent Power, who is eternally cognizant of the whole and the minutest parts of the system of being; whose energies are ever exerted in favor of the most righteous cause, and whose omnipotent fiat, by mediate and immediate operations directs and controls all the events of creation, from the concurrent revolutions of many thousand worlds to the rustling of a leaf or the falling of a sparrow.

Plate 210
Beckwith Baptist church, Tennyson, built in 1907, with St. John's Anglican church in the distance, as photographed in June 1983. Denominational rivalry played a part in the moral revolution. The building of a brick Anglican church in 1896 spurred local Baptists to construct an equally sturdy house of worship. There was a log Baptist chapel on lot 27 of the sixth concession of Drummond Township at Tennyson built in 1847 that was also available to other denominations as long as they were "Calvinistic in belief". By the early 1870s worship services were discontinued and the log chapel fell into disrepair. In 1890 some twenty individuals reorganized a congregation at Tennyson. By 1901 under the influence of the large proportion of women members, attendance at weekly prayer meetings averaged 25 and there were fifty students in the Baptist Sunday School held during the summer. From the 1840s to the 1980s baptisms have taken place in nearby Mississippi Lake.

Regional politicians quickly recognised the growing power of the moral movement. When candidates John Doran, John Graham Haggart and Abraham Code addressed a public meeting at Carleton Place in late January 1869 "a good deal was said on religious matters, which" in the opinion of James Poole, "was quite out of place and uncalled for in a public political meeting."[32]

James Poole himself, it turned out, was not in the least adverse to discussing religion at length when it served to justify his growing personal wealth at the expense of overworked apprentices in his printing shop. He did not think it "degrading to the scriptures to look at them...as a civil code, and to show their economical and political bearings." In 1866 as he observed anniversary meetings being held, sermons preached, collections taken up and subscriptions put down — all for the purpose of sending missionaries to foreign lands, James Poole concocted a moral justification for exacting continual labour from employees. He claimed that as a general rule "the principles of Christianity are in harmony with the laws of nature; and that, in proportion as they are obeyed, [so] does the earth bring forth her fruits, and society advance in prosperity and in virtue." In a word, "pecuniary prosperity and happiness are ultimately connected with morals," and one had only to look at unchristian lands to see the proof:[33]

> In pagan lands, and even in civilized states where there is a want of religious principles, the masses generally labour irregularly and imperfectly, unless a constant fear, either of the rod or of starvation, renders their toil incessant. On the other hand, religion gives man a steady abiding motive to put forth his powers. The Christian is called to work; and he goes forth as a son at the voice of his father; he labours from gratitude, duty, and affection.... Labour is bound upon man by divine authority, and enforced by eternal sanction; while the energy of the laborer is greatly promoted by his belief that his toil is appointed for his welfare, and that his blessings are the tokens of divine goodness. A devoted Christian family is an industrious one. In a district of country thoroughly and generally imbued with Christian principles the people are industrious, the habitations comfortable and tasteful, the fields well tilled and consequently productive, the roads passable and even beautiful; in short, everything is indicative of pecuniary and physical prosperity and improvement.

Just as the sending of missionaries abroad would link Beckwith inhabitants "to the millions of Asia, to open resources which have long been buried to the world, and pour them into our bosom", so too could local farmers and labourers expect to eventually prosper from the outlay of their labour. Or, at least, so argued James C. Poole.

In all likelihood James Poole was hardly the only employer at Carleton Place who took advantage of the moral revolution to justify his own prosperity and the long hours of those working under him. As the previous chapter has shown, Beckwith farmers could use a pious upbringing to keep their adolescent sons and daughters under their control, to exploit them as unpaid labour, while maintaining their control through the daily rote of family prayers, grace before meals, family devotions, attending church-related meetings, and the weekly ordeal of the Sabbath itself — all the while maintaining a strong personal religious belief. By the 1880s and 1890s, when Edward Kidd was growing up, the emphasis on moral uplift was pervasive in Beckwith. From the vantagepoint of middle age, he felt that his pious upbringing had played a very wholesome part in forming his character. "The weekly prayer meetings at the school had a leavening influence, and very few of the Derry boys were lacking in reverence or were given to profanity", he later recalled.[34] Once when Edward Kidd overheard a neighbour "swearing lustily at a broken tooth in the cylinder of the threshing machine", another thresher admonished "Don't swear like that, Joe Kidd will hear you." It seemed to Edward Kidd in later years that during his Beckwith childhood, his neighbourhood "seemed always to be fighting sin in the abstract. No one smoked, but pledges were signed against the use of tobacco. There was never any tendency nor opportunity to experiment with drink."[35] But lest someone somehow should slip through the widely set moral net of local society, there were revival meetings that attempted to spear the loose fish. Edward Kidd recalled:[36]

> Crossley and Hunter came to Carleton Place, and we went to their meetings as often as four times a week. Hunter would have made a great tragedian. When he exhorted every sinner to come to the front, and they sang "There is a Fountain Filled with Blood", I shook like one with the ague and kept saying to myself over and over again: "They're not going to make me do it. It seems to me that I was convicted of being a great sinner, when in reality, with the bringing up which I had, I was not a very great one at all.

The moral revolution by the 1880s assumed a momentum of its own that continued until at least the end of World War One, and the effects of which continued to be felt well into the twentieth century. There was a crucial feminine dynamic underlying the moral revolution, as will be shown

Plate 211
Harvest festival decorations in St. James Church of England, Carleton Place, as photographed in 1882. The architecture of this new church marked an ebbing Irish Anglican influence as numerous English immigrants swelled this congregation in the 1870s and 1880s. The dropping of Ireland from the name of the church reflected the growing influence of English Anglicans in Canada, as English-origin clergy moved baptismal fonts from the front to the entrance, placed pulpit and desk to the sides, and made the altar the visual focus of the interior. Many local Irish Anglicans perceived the new liturgy and new emphasis on sacraments as threatening to "carry the church over bodily to the Church of Rome." Photograph courtesy of St. James Anglican Church, Carleton Place.

shortly, but the two chief emphases of the movement were on piety and morality. Contrary to the impression that often has been given of late Victorian religion being altogether cheerless and repressive, extracts from a journal of meditations by Duncan Cram in the 1860s and 1870 show his faith was cheerful, invigorating and inspired a creative imagination. On Sunday October 17th 1869 he wrote, "I enjoyed a very happy season of sweet refreshing communion at home while my family were worshipping in the house of prayer". On Sunday January 16th 1870 Duncan Cram "had the pleasure of being able to go up to the house of prayer & was much refreshed by the Baptist minister who preached a most exc[el]lent gospel sermon." Early in the morning of April 17th while in bed he "enjoyed a short but most delightful season of nearness to God". On January 7th 1871 in the evening he "found...in prayer the power of the Spirit", on March 5th during "our communion day in Beckwith...at home in secret it was given to me to serve God", and on the morning of March 30th "when engaged in family prayer [Cram found]great liberty in prayer while addressing God at the mercy seat." On May 19th he was "much refreshed by walking around looking at the works of God". On the communion day of June 11th Cram "sat down under [God's] shadow with great delight". During a sultry hot day on June 27th as he "was strolling through the fields [he] lighted at a spot under the shade of some trees where God used to meet with me". On the morning of July 11th "while engaged in family prayer [he] found much pleasure". On Sunday August 6th "while worshipping in the courts of God's house [he] was greatly refreshed & gladdened."[37]

A major component of the momentum of the moral revolution was the growing proportion of clergymen in the vicinity, as increasing numbers of young men regarded the Christian ministry as a respectable calling that could ultimately yield excellent financial and moral dividends. The train of clergymen who went out into the world from Beckwith between 1850 and 1920 included Duncan Morrison, John May, Charles Kidd, Walter Ross, George Nesbitt, William H. Poole, William Kidd, Peter Wilson Cram, Thomas Leach and John McNeely among others. The dozen or more clergymen who ministered to Beckwith and Carleton Place at any given time between the 1870s and the 1910s ensured that no one remained untouched by the pervading religious climate. Undoubtedly there were denominational rivalries, most particularly between the two largest denominations — Anglicans and Presbyterians, but these were informed by cultural background, political allegiance, and ethnic pride that had built up after three to four generations of living alongside one another. All the same, the intermarriage between different denominations as in the case of Joseph Kidd and Mary McDiarmid, and attending the services of other denominations as in the case of Presbyterian Duncan Cram attending the Baptist church as well as prayer meetings at the homes of his neighbours, show that denominational boundaries were not rigid barriers between Beckwith Protestants.

As the moral revolution gained ground by the early 1870s it became increasingly rare to find households inhabited by people who all did not have the same religion, as Tables 27 reveals. Whereas at mid-century there were nine households in Beckwith shared by Anglicans and Roman Catholics and eight shared by Presbyterians and Roman Catholics, by 1871 there were only two households in which Protestants and Roman Catholics cohabited. Obviously, there was a gulf of sorts between local Protestants and Catholics by the 1870s that had not existed in the early nineteenth century, and yet it is important to recognise that Beckwith Protestants felt that Roman Catholics would be better neighbours under the influence of a resident Catholic priest, rather than meeting twice yearly for services. In December 1880 James Poole remarked in an editorial, "We have plenty of Catholic citizens in Carleton Place to build a church and retain a priest.... There are lots of Protestants in town who would willingly aid [as]...it would add another adornment to the place."[38] Accordingly, when Archbishop Cleary confirmed and blessed the new St. Mary's church in September 1887, not only did the reeve of Carleton Place considerately appoint "this day as the Dominion holiday to enable the working classes to take part in the religious festivity of the Catholics"[39] but the church "was so crowded by Protestants that a large number of the Catholics had to stand outside the porch."[40]

Plate 212
St. John's Anglican church, Tennyson, built 1896, as photographed from the back in June 1983, long after it had been closed and turned into a residence. This was the first Anglican church in rural Beckwith to incorporate Gothic Revival architectural elements meant to accommodate the new liturgy. Despite the small size of the building and its brick construction, the Reverend Arthur Jarvis used pointed windows, a projecting apse, buttresses and a steep roof in his design to set this church apart from the Anglican churches built in Franktown, Ashton and Prospect. Local community loyalties would prove more enduring than denominational ties; upon this church closing in the 1960s, some members began attending the Tennyson Baptist church across the road.

Beckwith was hardly free of anti-Catholic sentiments, considering that local Orangemen in the lodges at Franktown, Carleton Place, Ashton and Prospect as a condition of membership swore never to marry Roman Catholics, and in their annual twelfth of July processions commemorated the triumph of William III over James II at the battle of the Boyne. At least one Carleton Place mother admonished her son to be careful about "these Catholic friends of yours[;] do not play on them too much [as] you know their treachery a little".[41] The majority of Beckwith inhabitants, both Irish-origin Orangemen and the Scottish highlanders some of whom became members of the Orange lodge, remained opposed to Catholic separate schools as an unwarranted privilege for one denomination, notwithstanding the support which Orange leaders and members of parliament gave to pushing through separate schools. In the 1870s, 1880s and 1890s the publicity given to Riel and the extension of separate schools into western Canada served to inflame fears that aggressive Catholic clergy and politicians were encroaching unduly on the rights of Protestants. In the early 1890s these fears were heightened by an economic recession, and Beckwith Protestants began listening to the rhetoric of the Protestant Protective Association. The P.P.A. claimed that Roman

Table 27   Religiously Mixed Beckwith Households, 1852–1881

	Church of England	Roman Catholic	Presbyterian	Methodist	Baptist
A		1852			
Church of England	97	9	29	8	1
Roman Catholic	9	25	8	—	1
Presbyterian	29	8	138	5	6
Methodist	8	—	5	22	—
Baptist	1	1	6	—	17
B		1861			
Church of England	112	9	26	10	4
Roman Catholic	9	27	4	1	—
Presbyterian	26	4	129	10	4
Methodist	10	1	10	20	—
Baptist	4	—	4	—	12
C		1871			
Church of England	104	2	6	—	—
Roman Catholic	2	25	2	—	—
Presbyterian	6	2	145	3	3
Methodist	—	—	3	30	—
Baptist	—	—	3	—	11
D		1881			
Church of England	99	2	12	4	—
Roman Catholic	2	18	—	1	—
Presbyterian	12	—	94	1	5
Methodist	4	1	1	34	2
Baptist	—	—	5	2	10

SOURCE: 1852, 1861, 1871, and 1881 manuscript census returns for Beckwith.

Plate 213
St. James Church of England, Franktown, as photographed in 1925 by Colborne P. Meredith. The new belfry with pointed openings, the removal of the coating of harl to reveal the stone construction of the walls, and the removal of the pediment halfway up the tower were the only exterior changes made when this church was gothicised in the mid 1890s. The cracks in the front wall betrayed this as Beckwith's oldest surviving church building. During the century between its construction and the taking of this photograph, this church had come down in status from being the centre of the rectory of Beckwith that included mission stations at Carleton Place, Smith's Falls, Pakenham and Fitzroy, to become the tail end of the parish of Montague with Franktown. The erroneous construction date of 1833 on the sign board would later be replaced by the equally wrong date of 1822 on a datestone. This church actually was built in 1827 and 1828. National Archives of Canada negative no. PA-26902.

Catholics were unfit to hold public office, because as a subversive element they owed their first allegiance not to the government of Canada, but to "a foreign ecclesiastical potentate" — the Pope, and by so doing effectively became aliens.[42]

In a February 1894 provincial by-election in the riding of South Lanark, James Ferguson of Numogate as a Protestant Protective Association candidate and known only in his end of the constituency,[43] polled 803 votes and obtained only 158 votes less than the Liberal victor, James M. Clark of Smith's Falls. In the general provincial election held four months later, Ferguson polled only half as many votes, but two years later his brother John ran federally, and polled 1,560 votes against the 1,939 of his Conservative opponent.[44] Unquestionably, many of the votes polled by the Fergusons came from Beckwith Scottish Liberals, from relatives, and from the membership of the Beckwith lodge of the Patrons of Industry which was predominantly Scottish. It was a commonplace locally that the Patrons of Industry, composed as it was of farmers grouping together to fight the high cost of agricultural supplies during the 1890s recession, strongly supported the Protestant Protective Association, and with the return of prosperity in the late 1890s both organisations faded away. If fleeting support for the Protestant Protective Association reflected a degree of induced anti-Catholicism, by implication the Irish Orange lodges of Beckwith were not considered sufficiently anti-Catholic. Increasingly, fighting supposed Catholic aggression was an abstract notion, as the Roman Catholic population of Beckwith fell from 181 persons in 1871 to 119 in 1881, and still further to only 42 persons by 1921.

Beneath the growing fear of Catholicism among regional Protestants in general, lurked an instinctive paranoia among Beckwith Irish Anglicans that the core institution of their ethno-religious identity, their church, was being subverted from within. This paranoia overtly focussed on separate schools and the perceived threat of a Roman Catholic ascendancy, but more subtly from the late 1840s onward there was the accompanying fear that ambitious clergy from the English church were stealthily at work to hand the United Church of England and Ireland over to Rome, following the lead of John Henry Newman who had converted to Catholicism and who had been made a cardinal for his example. Irish Anglicans were alarmed that higher English clergy were weakening the Anglican church by abandoning the form of worship established during the Reformation, especially the emphasis on Biblical authority, and by removing its links to the British government.

Regional Irish Anglicans were particularly uneasy at the emerging English emphasis on returning to the primitive mediaeval ritual of worship in the pre-Reformation Anglican church because it included practices similar to those of contemporary Roman Catholics. As early as 1845 in local newspapers Beckwith Irish Anglicans read warnings by clergy in Ireland against the new Tractarian emphasis and reliance on sacraments rather than on the Bible.[45] It did not help to read provocative statements in the Carleton Place *Herald* asking, "Is not the Episcopal Church of the present day, a depot, from which the Church of Rome is supplied with recruits to fill the place of those who have deserted her through disaffection or other cause?"[46] Beckwith Irish low church Anglicans for the remainder of the nineteenth century and beyond remained frozen at the same stage of ecclesiastical thought their parents had held at the time of their migration in the 1810s and 1820s.

Beckwith Irish Anglicans perceived both in the new liturgy and in the design of the new Gothic Revival architecture of the churches meant to accommodate ritualism that their Reformation heritage was ebbing. It was difficult for a population which for two centuries had relied on the link of church and state to accept the assurances of higher English-origin clergy that the separation of church from state was beneficial.[47] Beckwith Irish Protestants on the strength of their experience perceived hidden dangers and did not wish for change. They took note of the warning sounded by regional Irish-origin clergy that the new liturgy and architecture threatened to "carry the church over bodily to the Church of Rome", since in "England, churchmen were very confiding and very much d[i]sposed to take things as they were; while in Ireland they see the cloven foot."[48] Irish Anglicans throughout eastern Ontario in the late nineteenth century, and particularly during the 1860s and 1870s were up in arms at the new "ritualistic practices in this diocese" including the absolution of sins, Purgatory, the veneration of relics, praying to saints, the lighting of candles, the wearing of vestments, and the offering of masses for both the quick and the dead. All of these, it seemed, offered "unmistakeable proofs" to most Irish Anglicans "that the old landmarks of our faith and practice were fast passing away from among us"[49] and that "our beloved church is in danger of receiving at the hands of persons within her communion wounds and injuries which she could never suffer at the hands of external foes".[50]

Plate 214
The interior of Ashton Methodist church, built 1898, as photographed in June 1983. This church and St. Paul's Presbyterian church at Franktown featured floorplans with a semicircular grouping of seats facing toward a pulpit and choir placed in one corner. Ceiling, wainscoting and pews all featured stained and varnished natural wood, as Methodists and Presbyterians copied developments coming out of the Gothic Revival architecture in the Church of England. By the time this church was built, husbands and wives were sitting beside one another, rather than men sitting together on one side and women on the other as had been the tradition in Beckwith for most of the nineteenth century.

This fear among Irish Anglicans of treason within their own church was simply based on a cultural antipathy by a people used to low church evangelical worship toward "the attempts being made at introducing into our Church Services divers rites, and ceremonies calculated to estrange the people's thoughts from the great object of our frail worship, and instead...direct their attention to a gorgeous and unmeaning ceremonial."[51] To Beckwith Irish Anglicans the new St. James Church erected at Carleton Place looked suspiciously like a Roman Catholic house of worship. Few if any of them cared a fig for the symbolical meaning to the materials used and to the placement of furnishings. Instead of the baptismal font being placed in front of the congregation as it was in the older churches at Franktown and Ashton, in the new church it was placed near the entrance to symbolise that it was through baptism one entered the church. Whereas the pulpit and lectern were given pride of emphasis in the old Irish Anglican churches, in the new St. James Church the altar became the visual focus of the interior, the pulpit and lectern to the side to emphasize the new importance given to sacrament over preaching. The elliptical plaster vaults of the old churches which hid the true structural elements contrasted with the thrusting diagonal grained beams revealing the true structural force of the church as befitted a house of worship for the true Christian faith. The clear glass windows and simple auditory halls of the old Irish churches which were intended to ring with the exposition of Biblical truth, contrasted starkly with the stained glass images, flickering candles, elaborate clerical vestments, choral services and Gothic Revival arches of the new church.

The mingled anger and bewilderment of Beckwith Irish Anglicans with the new architecture and ritual which to them smacked of Catholicism, was summed up by a correspondent of the Carleton Place *Herald* in 1867:[52]

> Will the old Irish Churchmen allow themselves and their families to be dragged back into Popish superstition, by pretended ministers of the Church of England, while in very deed many of them are Jesuits in disguise.... I shall point out some things out of many that I believe to be contrary to our old Protestant usages. First, having a desk recently constructed in the form of a right angle, that part facing the congregation, on it the Bible is laid, the minister invariably reads it with his face to the east, and his side to the people. What is this for? Why not have the two books on a straight desk, side by side, as it has been heretofore[?}... Why not turn the back altogether with a large cross on it as some have already done, with crosses in abundance on books, crosses in the church and on the church, and on the headstones over the silent dead,...denying in the pulpit what they pray for in the desk.... [T]he introduction of what is called the little prayer book, and steps to the altar...are well calculated to lead the innocent youth with many of the old and simple ones in the way of Popery and the Mass... Neither do I sir, wish to make the impression that I am an enemy to Catholics; by no means, I respect many of my Catholic neighbours, though I despise the dogma of the[ir] religion, while we live on the most friendly terms.

As late as 1903 older Irish Anglicans in Beckwith such as the Reverend John May continued to flail away against the new Ritualist focus of the ceremony and architecture as a "deadly disease" which as prayer-book churchmen they regarded as "simply *Popery without the Pope*; a complete reversal of the English Reformation":[53]

> Our colleges, text-books, literature are saturated with the poison [May wrote]. In general the teaching is tainted, its trend being ever more and more towards Mediaevalism and away from the principles of the purest age. Its apostles repudiate the *Pope*, and would fain persuade the people that this is proof of their freedom from *popery*. This is a most *Jesuitical* falsehood. There is not a Romish tenet which they do not roll as a sweet morsel under their tongues.

As the growing number of English-origin Anglican clergymen ministering in Beckwith promoted the new liturgy and architecture, the younger Irish-origin Anglicans in the township became receptive. The Reverend Andrew C. Nesbitt as early as 1884 argued that the new ritual promoted study of the Bible, whereas the Sunday Schools used by most Protestant denominations "were a delusion and a farce [and]...had no power to hold the children of their own baptism":[54]

> The Roman Catholics had no Sunday Schools [Nesbitt observed] and still they retained their children. This was because they were taught to believe in Christianity as taught by the Roman Catholic church, a thing which had not been done in the Church of England. Don't fill your Sunday School libraries with those little goody-goody story books; they should be taken out and made a bonfire of. The children should be taught the history and purpose of the church. This would teach them to read the Bible properly.

The ritualist emphasis made no particularly physical impact on rural Beckwith until 1890 when a painted window bearing an image of Christ was installed in St. James church at Franktown.[55] In

Plate 215
Methodist church and parsonage at Gillies Corners, built in 1901, as photographed ca. 1913. Despite the relatively few Methodists who called Beckwith home, by 1901 there were Methodist chapels at Carleton Place, Prospect, Ashton and Gillies Corners. The antipathy of many Franktown vicinity Irish Anglicans to the English liturgy and Gothic Revival architecture infiltrating their church, swelled attendance at this church in the early decades of the twentieth century. The parsonage at Gillies Corners, served the Beckwith, Drummond and Montague Methodist circuit from the turn of the century up to 1922. Gillies Corners, which in the early nineteenth century was noted only for the carousing that took place at Archibald Gillies's tavern, from the 1870s on became a centre for pro-temperance activity. The mailbox indicates that there had been rural mail delivery for the better part of a decade by the time this photograph was taken. Photograph courtesy of Iva Shirley.

1896 the Franktown church was gothicised. The gallery was removed, the neoclassic pediment removed from above the entrance, the old tower top replaced with a Gothic Revival belfry, the exterior harl removed to reveal the natural stone in the walls, a bell was installed, a Gothic Revival rood screen replaced the earlier modest framework, a grained wooden ceiling was installed, and the altar was placed a number of steps above the rest of the interior. In 1896 the brick Gothic Revival St. John's Church designed by the Reverend Arthur Jarvis was opened at the hamlet of Tennyson as the first new rural church to be opened in the Anglican Diocese of Ottawa,[56] and in 1915 the 1845 house of worship at Ashton was replaced by an ambitious Gothic Revival structure.

The identification of Gothic Revival church architecture with Church of England congregations spurred the building committees for local Presbyterian churches to search for a style that would reflect their Scottish heritage. The builders of St. Andrew's Presbyterian church at Carleton Place appear to have been influenced by the Romanesque Revival design of St. Andrew's church in downtown Toronto, identifying along with many other late Victorian Presbyterians the visually peculiar Norman style of Romanesque architecture with mediaeval Scottish architecture.[57] St. Andrew's church in Carleton Place incorporated perpendicular Gothic windows, but it was the tower with its picturesque corner turrets that was perceived as giving a distinctively Scottish flavour to the church. In 1888 the Carleton Place Methodist congregation, containing as it did a good many Scottish-origin inhabitants, incorporated Norman Romanesque arches and windows and a tower capped by four turrets in their new church, generously scattering an additional four turrets along the facade. In 1899 the Ashton Methodist congregation used Romanesque windows and doors in their new church. In 1902 C. Edey of Ottawa designed St. Paul's Presbyterian church at Franktown, combining cruciform floorplan, Romanesque openings, and turret-crowned tower in what was perhaps the most fantastic of the Scottish Romanesque designs in the Beckwith vicinity.[58]

The Gothic Revival and Romanesque Revival design of churches built between 1881 and 1920 in Beckwith and Carleton Place were physical monuments to the triumph of the moral revolution. Initially in the mid 1850s the religious renewal of local society had been presented in the image of a railroad to heaven:[59]

> To Heaven the line by Christ was made,
> By his own hands the rails were laid;...
> You say you're poor, he's paid the fare,
> Accept his offer, trust his care;...
> Jesus himself is Engineer,
> And doth the Heavenly engine steer;...
> Abide in him — he'll never fail
> To keep the train safe on the rail;
> His love the fire, his truth the steam —
> His will gives motion to the train;....

The feeling grew in Beckwith during the 1860s that railways were not only fraudulent,[60] but served the interests of industrialists rather than of promoting morality. A Beckwith correspondent of the Carleton Place *Herald* in November 1866 was indignant to learn that the Brockville and Ottawa railway allowed cars to run on Sunday to convey "several parties...starting off on hunting or shooting excursions, with their dogs, boats and guns" and urged magistrates along the line "so far as they have the power, [to] enforce the laws for the proper observance of the sabbath."[61]

By 1870 editor James Poole was pained and annoyed to observe that the railway made "a common practice of running lumber, passenger, freight and other trains, and attending to their ordinary business, on Sabbath day,1 in defiance of all law, moral and Divine. It seemed as if in contempt of the "religious disposed portion of the community", Poole went on, "the rattling of the wheels of freight and lumber trains, the screaming of steam whistles, ringing of bells and all the other noise and confusion of running ordinary trains may be heard on the Sabbath day, and even during the hours of Divine Worship!" Poole argued that there was surely "moral power enough in the community" to prevent railway officials from profaning the Sabbath. If there was not, "it is clearly the duty of the authorities, in the towns and villages through which they pass, to have their engines, conductors and labourers arrested and placed in the Lock-up".[62] Already, the moral revolution as a creation of the local community, was seeking to obtain a wider influence over regional and provincial society.

The twenty congregations in Beckwith and Carleton Place provided people with an unparalleled opportunity for socialising, for pondering ancient theological messages, for gaining emotional nourishment, for displaying musical talent, for courtship, for socially distinguishing among themselves, and for wholesale sharing of gossip. George Edward Kidd's reminiscences of typical Sunday morning services at the Prospect Methodist church in the 1880s and 1890s convey the flavour of weekly worship at the height of the moral revolution:[63]

> When we heard the organ begin to play we went in [to Sunday School] and sat on the back seats

Plate 216
Laying the corner-stone of St. Paul's Presbyterian church, Franktown, 9 July 1902. At a time when scores of Beckwith families were lured to move westward or townward, building a substantial stone church was an attempt by local elders to affirm their belief in their community's future. The substantial stone basement of the new church and the fashionable clothes worn by the crowd reflect the prosperous dairy economy in Beckwith. Indeed, the steel vat for mixing mortar turned up on its side in the foreground may well have started out as a whey vat in the Franktown cheese factory. Unpainted fences and houses suggest the limited finances of some older people living in retirement in Beckwith villages. The background of rickety rail fences, an orchard, log sheds and trees confirms that Franktown remained a straggling village. The lines of telegraph and telephone poles passing by between Smith's Falls and Carleton Place were a reminder of the more invigorating outside world, and particularly of towns to which many of the young people attending this ceremony would inevitably be drawn. Photograph courtesy of John and Verna McEwen.

on the men's side. Later, after singing and reading of the lesson verse about, we boys went up to Mr. Wilson's class in the side seats at the front. He was an earnest, saintly old man, but I suppose there is no more thankless job than that of teaching a class of middle sized boys in Sunday-school. We watched Jim Conn with his bible class in the gallery, or the hornets that came out of the stovepipe hole high in the front wall.

After Sunday School, papers were given out and adults began to filter in for the main service. The children had a recess of five minutes, giving them just enough time to go to Alfred Poole's for a drink of water.

454 THE HOUSEHOLD OF FAITH

Then back to church where the congregation was singing the first hymn. Edna Wilson played the organ. (She and Florence McRorie were the belles of the countryside). We had good preachers in those days. [W.H.] Burnett was a powerful preacher who perspired freely with his long hair over his eyes.... After the hymn we all knelt down. Shortly before, a painter, one Williams, had done over the interior of the church. It was a terrible job. The paint never dried. When one sat down he simply stuck there, especially if the weather were hot. After a long sermon the order of service would call for all the congregation to stand. The sound of cloth separating from a sticky surface was heard all over the church. Some with delicate dresses could not struggle free. Others were wise enough to sit on a newspaper, which became firmly embedded in the paint.... As we listened to the sermon with our eyes on the windows open to the lazy summer day, and piled high with hats, we heard the horses restless in the sheds.... The choir rendered an anthem. The collection was taken on wooden plates lined with red cloth. These plates would be well lined with coppers by the time they got back to where we were sitting.

After the benediction of this main service came yet a third service, the fellowship or experience meeting. It seemed strange to young Edward Kidd:

that the congregation must be divided before this [experience meeting] was held. The more worldly went out and proceeded homewards, others stayed behind. Sometimes families were split, the husband waiting in the shed while his wife remained in church. During an experience meeting different members of the congregation in turn stood up and said a few words. This program was punctuated by snatches of old Methodist revival hymns, led by the preacher.

It is in this reference to the division of families, of women remaining behind at experience meetings while their husbands awaited them outside that it is possible to consider the crucial role of women in fuelling and promoting the moral revolution.

Exactly why there should be a strong underlying feminine dynamic to the moral revolution was no more apparent to contemporary observers than to subsequent historians of religion in late nineteenth century Ontario. As previous chapters have suggested, women in early Beckwith benefitted from the general moral environment promoted by strong Anglican and Presbyterian congregations almost from the beginning of settlement. At mid-century, before the moral revolution began, beneath the facade of a Christian community, Beckwith women filled their spare moments with slandering one another[64] and wolfing down light novels. A correspondent of the Carleton Place *Herald* in 1861, as proof that the women of the village were "vitiating their minds", invited fellow readers to[65]

Enter the parlour of our acquaintances, and there laid around in graceful carelessness are works of sterling value glittering in gilden morocco overcoats, but mark how refreshingly spotless the edges of the leaves are, what tell tale monitors they are? but should the spirit of investigation prompt one to look beneath the drapery of that ottoman, a specimen of yellow covered literature will probably meet the eye, "Eugene Sue's last and best," with all its bewildering and intoxicating scenes of Parisian life, fascinating and dangerous.

Numerous factors combined to spur the women of Beckwith on to become the front ranks of the moral revolution. Mid-century education reformers such as Johnston Neilson and Robert Bell had stressed the importance of girls attending school to become more generally knowledgable mothers and to produce a "greater refinement of manners."[66] In January 1851 the first women's group in Beckwith, the Carleton Place Female Association, Auxiliary to the French Canadian

Plate 217
A photograph of William Drummond and his wife Mary Hunter taken at their farm on lot 14 in the sixth concession of Beckwith with John McLaurin (centre) visiting the farm where his grandfather the Reverend George Buchanan had once resided. This 1902 photograph is unusual for showing a Beckwith couple in everyday dress. At the turn of the century a few older Beckwith women could be found doing fieldwork, resisting the growing emphasis on women's work and role in life being confined to the domestic sphere. The strong patriarchal legacy of Beckwith did not hamper canny township leaders when asked by the province in 1921 if women should be given the municipal vote. Beckwith municipal council was "quite in favour of the municipal franchise being granted to the ladies of this Province" and added in the same breath "that 300 additional electors be required to entitle municipalities to an extra representative at County Council". From Jessie Buchanan Campbell, The Pioneer Pastor *(1905).*

Missionary Society, met at the home of Margaret and Archibald McArthur with the avowed goal of collecting funds "to improve the religious and moral condition of the French Canadians".[67] In 1852 Robert Bell's daughter, Margaret, opened a private school for young ladies in which she taught reading, spelling, geography, grammar, history, writing, arithmetic, plain and fancy needlework, French and drawing.[68] At the same time James Rosamond imported a Miss Ray from Toronto (who later married his son Bennett) to open a "DAY SCHOOL, for the instruction of YOUNG LADIES, in all the branches of a sound English education" as well as "in French, Music, Drawing and Ornamental Needlework."[69] In adjacent Ramsay by 1855 a lodge of the Daughters of Temperance was holding patriotic tea meetings "to show their sympathy for the suffering widows & orphans" of soldiers killed in the Crimean War.[70]

Sunday schools had existed in Beckwith from the early 1830s on, but as late as 1861 there is no evidence that women participated in the running even of the large united Methodist and Presbyterian Sunday School at Carleton Place other than to prepare and lay out the "great trays of cakes, large baskets of apples, and huge boilers, steaming with coffee" consumed at the annual anniversary celebration.[71] By 1865, however, as a union Sunday School for Church of Scotland, Canada Presbyterian, Methodist and Baptist children was formed at Carleton Place, the rising role of women in the moral revolution was evident. Although there was the risk of denominational differences arising to frustrate instilling "an evangelical, unsectarian, Christianity", organisers expected "Mothers [to] come to the rescue" through the power of their maternal influence "in planting the first seedlings of thought, in shaping the first actions of childhood" by encouraging their children to attend.[72] Poems and essays with titles such as "WIVES SAVE YOUR HUSBANDS"[73] from the early 1850s onward urged upon women the need to win their husbands to Christ. No less a woman than Queen Victoria was cited as avowing that the greatness of the British empire was "not owing to her large and disciplined army or navy, nor to commerce or agriculture, or progress in arts and science, but, above all, to the BIBLE."[74]

Against this background of growing evangelical fervour among members of the Presbyterian, Methodist and Baptist churches, the very vocabulary of which permeated the pages of regional newspapers, increasing numbers of Beckwith women experienced conversion, often in response to the ministry of neighbours. Duncan Cram of Glen Isle described the conversion of one of his neighbours suddenly taken ill in the early 1850s:[75]

> After asking her a few questions reguarding her bod[i]ly trouble[,] I learned from her that there was little or no hope of her recovery — [b]ut, [rather,] shortly the prospect of being removed by Death to the Eternal world. "Well[,] if this is so [", I responded] asking her by name[,"] how is it in reguard to your soul in looking forward to the other world[?"] And in words as nearely as I remember...she [said], "Duncan", grasping my hand firmly in hers [as] a flood of tears burst & continued to flow from her eyes as she gave utterance to the following words, "Oh I have not attended to my soul but I have neglected that. But I have attend[ed] faithfully & given my strength [and] time to the world & oh how well would it be with me now if I had given that to God in serving him. But these opportunities are gone & I have not don[e] it, & this is how it is with me.["] These words spoken by her at such a time & [in] so feeling a manner sho[w]ed they proceeded from her very h[e]art & planely indicated the sad mistake she had made & sore disappointment she felt under it[.] I d[i]rected her as God was pleased to give me strength to that long neglected Saviour & day of salvation who was able & willing to save to [the] uttermost all who came to God by him, remembering to h[e]r for h[e]r encouragement the case of the thief on the Cross & as long as the lamp holds on to burn the greatest sinner may return. [A]fter reading a portion in God's word & prayer I took my leave of her & shortly after I again had another interview with her & found her a good deal composed in mind but cannot tell if it was all well with her at last or not. ...There was no Minister then in this neighbourhood. I was very willing to be useful to her. These interviews have left a deep impression on my own mind, I think never to be forgotten....

The deathbed conversions of dying women at first glance might hardly seem to be the stuff out of which revolutions, moral or otherwise, are made, but as the mortality rate generally tripled between 1870 and 1900, Beckwith inhabitants looked upon deaths or even the threat of death in their midst as personal warnings from God to lead better lives. When Daniel McCuan's eight-year-old son Alex narrowly escaped dying in March 1881, the anxious father placed in writing his firm belief in the redemption of Christ and also copied out this verse:[76]

> Such pity as a father hath
> Unto his children
> Like pity shews the Lord to such
> As worship him in fear.

Plate 218
A meeting of St. Augustine's Anglican Women's Association at the home of John and Mary Porter, Prospect, in 1918. Church groups were the only women's organisations formed in rural Beckwith before the mid twentieth century. The moral revolution brought women together to pursue religious objectives and to participate in local congregational life more actively, but beneath the elevating topics discussed and the mission projects undertaken there was an undercurrent of conversation about women in the vicinity suspected of having been beaten by their husbands and about suspected abortions that had taken place. Photograph courtesy of Edna and John Porter.

Similarly, Daniel McCuan's sister Elizabeth, upon hearing that their brother James had died in 1894, wrote "It is a very solemn warning to us all[.] May God in his mercy grant that we may all meet in that home above where their is neither sorrow nor suffering."[77]

The death of Duncan Cram's 23-year-old daughter Agnes in December 1871 reveals how dramatic the deathbed exhortations proved to be:[78]

> During a protracted & sever[e] illness she was taught to renounce all dependence in herself & to come to Jesus as a lost & undone sinner for salvation.... In taking farewell of her Dear relations gathered around her, she admonished her brothers & sisters to seek immediate preparation for Death & expressed her expectation & desire that they all would strive to meet her in Heaven. ["]Dear Father[, she said to me,] "you have been a kind father to me & you have been instrumental in leading me to Jesus the Saviour — you will soon follow me into His Blissful presence. [W]hen her work was done...she calmly shut her eyes as if going to sleep & without a struggle or a groan or a distorted feature she breathed her last.... Her countenance was the image of sublime repose & tranquility. The large concourse of sympathising friends & acquaintances which gathered to pay the last tribut[e] of respect by conveying to the tomb the mortal remains of the dece[a]sed testified the reguard in which she & her family were held. The funeral services were appropriately & impressively conducted by Rev. Messrs. McKenzie & Carswell.

The increasingly frequent wakes and funerals in Beckwith during the closing decades of the nineteenth century, the growing numbers of carved marble and granite gravestones and obelisks that transformed township burial grounds into cemeteries, and the exhortations at deathbeds to families and friends contributed to the moral revolution as Beckwith began to absorb its share of the glut of clergymen turned out by the theological colleges of Ontario from the late 1860s onward. The clergymen among their other duties went around the township visiting parishioners as well as those who did not regularly attend church. In these visits they more often than not found the women at home in rural Beckwith, while their husbands were either working out in the fields, on adjacent farms, or away from home altogether, and boys were either working alongside their fathers or were away at school. The women and daughters of rural Beckwith in this fashion became particularly vulnerable to evangelising and conversion, as they came under the influence of clergymen.

Certainly, the clergymen who exhorted the women of Beckwith were seriously in quest of winning their souls. A Methodist clergyman, the Reverend D. Winter, for example, in writing up a brief death notice about Edward Kidd's mother, Mary McDiarmid, in 1889 recalled that four years earlier she had heard him preach in the Prospect church from the words "Have ye received the Holy Ghost since ye believed?" and "[u]nder the sermon, our sister saw her exalted privilege in Christ Jesus of being filled with the Holy Ghost, and after that lived in the enjoyment of 'full salvation.'"[79]

The ease with which clergymen ingratiated themselves with the women of Beckwith is shown by the Reverend Joseph Little as pastor of the Franktown Methodist mission going around southern Beckwith and northern Montague, "visiting and seeking out the backslidden ones":[80]

> He introduced himself as a man "hunting for lost sheep." One good sister assured him that there were none at her place, for the bars had not been down. He was not satisfied with her explanation, and so led her on until her curiosity was fully aroused, and then he told her that it was "the lost sheep of the house of Israel" that he was seeking. She soon admitted that she was one of them, and they had a good time in fellowship and prayer.

Beckwith husbands were less enthusiastic about ministers' visits. Edward Kidd recalled that "Preachers had a reputation for being huge eaters, and [even his devout] Father said that they gave their horses a double supply of oats."[81] The new presence of women in the churches of Beckwith after these visitations by an increasing ratio of clergymen was evident in the contrast between 1834 when "females...were unable to come to Church — being obliged by their young families to remain at home, while their husbands attended"[82] and 1868 when Daniel McCuan's wife and sister left him at home to tend the baby while they went to church.[83]

The special relationship between Beckwith women and their clergymen developed as a result of the profound domestic ghetto into which women generally found themselves relegated. The clergymen who came round to visit them in their homes found the women torn between the tradition in rural Beckwith of sharing in the work with their men out in the fields, and the urban message imparted through newspapers and magazines that they should concentrate on keeping house. According to what they read, and to what they viewed in Carleton Place and other regional towns, women enjoyed a new and distinct calling, a separate sphere from men that centred in the running of their households. The mechanisation of Beckwith agriculture made women's labour in the fields no longer the necessary help it once had been. Where once women had churned butter and made cheese at home, earning their own money into the bargain, the cheese factory system that emerged in Beckwith beginning in the late 1870s effectively concentrated the management and profits coming from the dairy herds in the hands of their husbands,[84] although some farmwives continued to milk cows morning and evening.

Increasingly, it was stressed "that *physically* woman was not equal to man" and hence should not be expected to perform the same labour alongside him outdoors. Instead, "*intellectually* — while

Plate 219
Cast of the theatrical performance "Joseph" as photographed on the stage of the Carleton Place town hall, 27 February 1902. The large auditorium of the new town hall provided the women of Carleton Place churches with the best-equipped stage in Lanark County for mounting musical productions to raise money for their various charitable, missionary and church-building projects. Such lavish productions were beyond the means of rural Beckwith congregations, adding to the attractions that drew township women into town.

in some respect[s] inferior — she might on the whole be reckoned his equal; and that *morally*, she was his superior."[85] In the ideal Christian household, the Reverend Arthur Jarvis recommended in an 1884 sermon at Carleton Place,[86]

> you see a father supporting and defending — a father and mother together, by precept and example, guiding and teaching, leading those committed to their care, whether children or servants, with parental authority, care and affection. You see children and dependants looking up to those who are set over them with love and confidence.

The new separate sphere advocated for women when stripped of its fine words simply amounted to women concentrating their lives on making home as attractive and as alluring as possible in order to enhance the moral upbringing they gave to children. The foremost right of woman, the Carleton Place *Herald* affirmed in 1909, was "the right to make home happy."[87] Certainly, this was the message that Beckwith women took on as their lot, if the praise in obituary notices is any indication. When Jane Carmichael died in 1919 she was praised for having "spent a very active and unselfish career, loyally devoted to the best interest of her household and of the community as well."[88] The obituary of Margaret McArthur in 1903 emphasized that "Home to her was Beulah-land

— sweet and sacred; but she took deep concern in her husband's prosperities as well.... Her benevolences knew no bo[u]nds. Sick rooms were blessed by her radiant presence, or brightened by some pleasant gift."[89]

The homes that Beckwith women made pleasant were much larger as dozens upon dozens of full two-storey brick houses were built, particularly in the 1890s, 1900s and 1910s. The new houses with their high ceilings, large numbers of bedrooms and grooved mouldings required more time to clean and keep up than had the older more compact houses. Just as these new houses were built in emulation of the large houses going up in Carleton Place, so too the women of rural Beckwith found themselves emulating the furnishings, the decorations, and new customs such as receiving other respectable women to tea in their parlours. It is significant that the home in which Edward Kidd was raised during this period had neither a mother presiding nor was there a parlour. In coming across a parlour in a small log house, Edward Kidd recognised that this was a woman's domain:[90]

> This had a rough floor, scrubbed spotlessly white. In one corner was a table on which there were a few trinkets and ornaments, such as an album, a bunch of artificial flowers under a glass dome; and a [B]ible. On the wall was a picture of Queen Victoria — none other.... I never once saw [the parlour] used during the summer. A woman seems to demand such a room, to be a sanctuary, free from dirty feet, where she can keep the floor bleached and spotless; where she can segregate her more cherished possessions, and where she may have a show place removed from the everyday life of the family.

Despite the large new attractive houses, despite the parlours in which they entertained one another and their clergymen, and despite their new separate sphere as nurturers of a moral environment in which to raise their families, it was evident that many Beckwith women found themselves living in a legal and financial limbo. An astonishingly high percent of the wills involving Beckwith property made out by men whose wives were still alive between 1881 and 1925, were so arranged that the property ultimately went to a son. The continuing pattern of inheritance in Beckwith allowed widows no effective control over the land that supported them, they could look forward at best to enjoying control over only a couple of rooms in their houses following the death of their husbands, and had to look to the inheriting son for food, firewood and a dribble of an allowance. The disgrace of receiving municipal relief was to be avoided at all costs.

The mutual frustration for widows and sons in coping with dower specifications of wills was presented in the Carleton Place *Herald*:[91]

> A farmer dies, leaving a valuable lot of land under cultivation. His wife survives, and becomes his widow. His son inherits it, subject to the dower of the widow. She claims it. He offers no resistance. On the contrary he pleads that he is and always had been ready to assign the dower. Why, then, does not the widow accept what she apparently claims? Simply because though apparently claiming one thing, she, in truth, seeks another. She claims dower. What is that? The third part of the husband's land for life. Of what use is the third part of one hundred acres without a house upon it, to a widow without means? Sell it — she cannot. Till it — she cannot. Eat it — she cannot. Truly the widow asks for bread: but the law gives unto her a stone. What then does the widow want? She wants "sustenance," or that which will purchase sustenance for her — in other words, she wants money. The law does not provide that she shall recover money. It provides that she shall recover an estate in land, which is not convertible into money!

It is within the context of their relative actual economic powerlessness that Beckwith women received the ministers who visited them and embraced religion as the sole vehicle that offered them potential for wielding a different type of power — moral influence. The women quickly came to see

Plate 220
John Stewart and his daughter in front of their home at Black's Corners, as photographed by S.A. Smyth ca. 1895. This photograph shows the son and granddaughter of "Merchant Sandy" Stewart enjoying the small patch of garden and lawn in front of the stone structure built both as a residence and store (Plate 156) before 1850. The sun-bonnet and stylish dress on the daughter reveal that Beckwith women were keeping careful watch of the fashions being worn in the local towns of Carleton Place and Smith's Falls. At the time this photograph was taken, this substantial house was considered out of fashion. Photograph courtesy of Alexina Dakers.

that they could have a powerful influence in promoting Christian values, and in the process not only would they transform regional society into a better place, but they might even have an international influence. There were six areas in which women wielded their newfound moral power.

First, they could teach and persuade their children to be Christians. Although the public school removed children from under the mother's influence six days a week in the earliest years, in family worship and by encouraging children to attend Sunday School she could ensure that a child would grow up to be the type of person she could trust to look after her in old age. Besides, the work of men made it impossible for men to spend a great deal of time with their children. The Anglican *Canadian Churchman* published at Merrickville in 1863 argued that "women are admirably fitted for training their offspring in the nurture and admonition of the Lord. They have remarkably quick insight into character, and a warmth of affection, a tenderness and a delicacy, which win the affection of others, and enable them to correct faults without giving offence, and to present Christian principles and virtues to their children in their most amiable form."[92] Women in many Beckwith households effectively were thus encouraged to replace their husbands as the moral authority to whom children looked up.

The second area of moral influence was the area of domestic charity, with women clubbing together, holding bazaars and teas to raise funds, performing personal acts of charity, and in Presbyterian congregations such as that of St. Paul's church at Franktown forming a Women's Home

Missionary Society. Home missions tended for the most part to raise funds for the conversion of French Canadians to Protestantism, rather than assisting the indigent in local society.

The third area of moral influence was foreign missions, and it was particularly appealing not only because it gave Beckwith women the satisfaction of influencing affairs in foreign lands, but also because it focussed on women as missionaries working to remove foreign women from enslavement. As a measure of the commitment among women to the cause of missions, the Women's Foreign Missionary Society at St. Paul's church in Franktown alone between its founding in 1892 and 1925 raised some $5,732. At special meetings women missionaries returned from India, Africa and China described their work to Beckwith women. One woman summarised the interest of Beckwith women in foreign missions in these words:[93]

> The beautiful communion of women with each other, who have driven long distances year after year to these meetings, the prayers offered, the longings for a better world, and the heart interest for others have left an effect on their generation, and we who "Follow in Their Train" feel that we are treading on sacred ground. We catch their banner flung to us — "The World for Christ" — and hope that their mantle of devoted service may fall upon us.

The fourth area of influence was for women to become a financial force to be reckoned with in local congregations. Initially, fund raising by women's church groups was limited to specific projects such as the Young Ladies Sewing Society holding a "Juvenile Missionary Soiree" in the Carleton Place Methodist church "for the purpose of raising funds for the French Canadian Mission" in 1864.[94] Similarly, the ladies of St. James Church at Carleton Place held a CONCERT and CHRISTMAS TREE at Dr. Hurd's Hall" with the "proceeds to be devoted to the debt on the Harmonium and to the Parsonage Fund" in 1866.[95] The building of many new churches only served to extend the fund raising activities of women, as in the example of Zion Presbyterian Church in Carleton Place drawing the women of the congregation together in the winter of 1870-1871 "giving a number of Socials...for the purpose of aiding in the completion of the Church."[96] Some of the more rigid Baptists and Methodists were firmly opposed to the social occasions such as teas, bazaars, soirees, recitations and concerts, but for most women in most congregations these became regular activities that helped raise money for the congregation and provide vital social activities for the local community. One women's group at Zion Presbyterian church in Carleton Place called itself by the revealing name, the Willing Workers Society.[97]

The fifth area where women wielded moral influence in Anglican, Presbyterian and Roman Catholic congregations was the new feminising look they gave to church interiors. Even before women organised themselves into missionary societies, altar guilds, choirs, women's aids and auxiliaries, the furore over the new emphasis on liturgy in local Anglican congregations stemmed from the feminine look of the surpolices worn by rectors. One local wag commented in verse in 1867:[98]

> For me — I neither know nor care
> Whether a parson ought to wear
>   A black dress or a white dress:
> Filled with trouble of my own —
> A wife who preaches in her gown
>   And lectures in her night-dress!
> A very pretty embroglio
> Is making in Ontario
>   About the surplice fashion.

Within the new churches the majority of memorials donated and subscribed were presented by women, including Bibles, hymnbooks, prayer books, altars, fonts, bishops' chairs, sconces, alms plates, candle snuffers, bells, crosses, cushions, cruets, candlesticks and lamps. The most feminine touch of all were the painted and stained glass windows installed bearing representations of Christ and the apostles as rather feminine long-haired persons, and looking decidedly unlike any man who

Plate 221
The family of Duncan McEwen and Catharine Anderson with their children (left to right) Jessie, Mabel, Robert, Olive, Edie and Ethel ca. 1905, as photographed by C.C. Pelton of Carleton Place. Family group photographs taken before and after 1900 show women as central figures in their households in a way unthinkable a generation earlier, even though the local legal, economic and electoral clout of women had not advanced. Beckwith women through fuelling the moral revolution expected not only to secure their own future by creating a more moral environment, but actually replaced men in most families as the moral head. As early as 1862 a poem in a local newspaper extolled the two lives sacrificed when a child was born:
One was thy sainted mother's when
She gave thee mortal birth;
And one thy Saviour's, when in death
He shook the solid earth.

Photograph courtesy of Edna and John Porter.

ever drew breath in Beckwith.

The sixth and most political area in which women wielded their moral power was in their campaign to destroy the liquor traffic. In 1865 some 45 Beckwith electors petitioned the township council for a municipal poll to bring the 1864 Dunkin Act into effect, to effectively prohibit the "sale of intoxicating liquors and the issuing of licences, therefor".[99] The majority of Beckwith's male electors refused to pass the measure,[100] prompting James Poole to comment on there being "tavernkeepers who will sell poor inebriates liquor as long as they have money to pay for it, and when the last penny is in the till, kick their customer out of the door." Poole concluded that despite "the cup of misery of many a poor unfortunate, who has not moral power enough left to reform his bad habits", it was "useless to make laws, unless there is moral power enough in the community to enforce them."[101] The failure to prohibit liquor sales, however, served to spur new interest in the temperance movement in the late 1860s, more than a decade after the various temperance lodges founded at Carleton Place and Ashton in the early 1850s had faded away. Much of the impetus for the revival of interest in temperance can be traced to the Baptist, Methodist and Free Church Presbyterian congregations, but increasingly the women of the larger Anglican and Presbyterian congregations were attracted to the cause as both men and women were permitted to join the main organisational vehicle, the Independent Order of Good Templars. When a division of the I.O.G.T. was formed in the Baptist church at Carleton Place in 1865, Temple No. 122, it welcomed "young persons of both sexes".[102] Another I.O.G.T. temple, believed to have been located at or near Black's Corners, held a temperance soiree in Knox Free Presbyterian church there in January 1866,[103] and a picnic in Dr. Wilson's grove near the tenth concession that June.[104]

In early 1868 a temperance lecturer addressed meetings at Gillies schoolhouse, Franktown, Prospect, Ashton and in the Beckwith township hall at Black's Corners,[105] which led to the forming of Prospect Banner Temple of the I.O.G.T. in the Wesleyan Methodist church there. Under the superintendence of Beckwith reeve James Conn, 24 people at the meeting in the Melville Presbyterian church at Ashton gave their names to institute Ashton Star Lodge of I.O.G.T. Significantly, many of the people signing were women.[106] Another new I.O.G.T. temple, the Star of Beckwith, was formed at Gillies' Corners with twenty members, and even had a woman, Janet Lawford, among its officers — a remarkable step which did not occur in any other nineteenth century organisation in which men were members in Beckwith.[107] Yet another division of the I.O.G.T., Maple Grove Temple No. 588 held its annual picnic in Carmichael's grove on the seventh line of Beckwith in June 1869.[108] The annual concert of the Ashton Star Lodge by 1871, despite unfavourable roads, packed Mr. Fanning's hall in that village with a ready audience for the programme of dialogues, recitations, readings, songs, duets, solos and choruses.[109] Throughout the 1870s the momentum for temperance grew, with women adding their voices, and in September 1877 the Dunkin Act was put into effect across Lanark County, except for the town of Perth.[110]

The resurgent temperance movement placed local hostellers and the many men in Beckwith who drank regularly on the defensive. In 1865 the Carleton Place *Herald* censured the Reverend J. Masson for indulging "in extravagant statements against the vendors and consumers of intoxicating liquors at a temperance picnic held in McRostie's grove on the west side of the village:[111]

> There are some mean and some respectable men in the hotel business, [James Poole admitted], but we submit, that it is unfair, to class all public houses as *"sinks of Iniquity."* There is no accounting for tastes, but we do not admire that of the gentleman who would prefer as a partner for life a black wench from a nigger's hut in the South, to the daughter of an hotelkeeper.

Rumours were circulated about the untoward goings-on taking place within the secret society atmosphere of the Independent Order of Good Templars lodges, forcing the Carleton Place division to present an open temple in May 1866 to allow the public to judge for itself.[112] By early 1868 Ontario tavernkeepers were sufficiently worried about the temperance threat to form a society called the Licensed Victualler's Association, fighting against being excluded from holding municipal council seats.[113] Within eight months of the Dunkin Act being brought into effect across Lanark County in 1877, petitions were circulated and widely signed, demanding that the Act be repealed since "it had not served the purpose expected of it",[114] and by the late spring of 1879 it no longer was in effect.[115]

In 1878 the federal government passed the Scott Act, allowing the inhabitants of each municipality separately to determine what their local option would be, whether to allow the sale of

Plate 222
A young woman playing the piano in a Carleton Place parlour, ca. 1911. The moral revolution prompted growing interest in music as melodeons were installed in the rural Beckwith churches and pipe organs filled the large new churches of Carleton Place with hymns and voluntaries by classical and romantic composers. From the 1880s on it became a mark of social prestige to have either a piano or a reed organ in one's parlour, and they became the items of furniture most often mentioned in Beckwith wills between 1880 and 1920. Music teachers were in demand to give piano lessons particularly to daughters to permit them to grace concerts and preside over church choirs. National Archives of Canada negative no. PA-135225.

Plate 223
Denysa Duff at Orena Villa ca. 1905 as photographed by her sister Annie Elexey Duff. Rural mail delivery brought mass circulation magazines and urban newspapers such as the Ottawa Citizen *and* Ottawa Journal *to all Beckwith inhabitants. Magazines for women such as* Ev'ry Month *introduced Beckwith women to a wider world, and while in some instances they served to help push many of them even further into a domestic ghetto, a number of young women were encouraged to go to cities such as Montreal, Ottawa and Stamford to train for careers in nursing and stenography. Photograph courtesy of Kathy Ogg-Moss.*

liquor locally or not. An 1890s petition from 55 ratepayers respectfully begged the Beckwith township council to pass a by-law allowing no more liquor licences to be granted because "the liquor traffic is every where recognized to be one of the greatest evils in the world and all civilized nations and people are now endeavoring to curtail or suppress it" and because "liquor licenses in Ontario have been reduced in number to less than half what they were twenty years ago and are being still further reduced with the best results".[116] The growing numbers of women enrolled in the temperance movement, regrouping in the 1870s to form the Women's Christian Temperance Union, played a significant part in convincing many Ontario municipalities to go dry. A plebiscite of Beckwith ratepayers was taken on January 6th 1902[117] but it was not until a second plebiscite was taken on January 3rd 1910 that the sale of liquor was banned in the township.[118] In the midst of World War One the government sought to maximise resources by temporarily prohibiting the manufacture of liquor, and following the war a provincial plebiscite finally introduced the total prohibition of manufacturing and selling liquor across Ontario. It was the culmination to decades of effort that women in Beckwith and hundreds of other municipalities had poured into their fight against the liquor traffic.

The long struggle by Beckwith women to stop the liquor traffic reflected their political power-

Plate 224
James and Catherine Moore and their children (left to right) Ernest, Herbert, Ida and Clara in front of their grocery store and residence on Moore Street in Carleton Place, as photographed ca. 1890. Beneath the clapboards was the second log house of the William Moore family, the first Caucasian family settled at the site of Carleton Place. The photographer grouped the father and sons in front of the store and the mother and daughters in front of the reidence in conformity with the fashionable notion of separate spheres for the two sexes, that is, the idea that women's role should be confined to the household while men went out in the world to work. Despite the business being named J.P. Moore Groceries and Confectionery, Catherine Moore operated the business alongside her husband. There were a dozen such family groceries in Carleton Place in 1900, but the coming of chain stores and supermarkets closed all of these businesses by the early 1980s. Photograph courtesy the Carleton Place and Beckwith Historical Society.

lessness. They believed that by doing away with liquor, they would prevent the violence that they perceived to be committed by some men against their wives under the influence of drink, and which threatened the quality of life for women in old age when placed in the care of their sons. It was all very well for the women to enjoy official status in the various temperance lodges, to provide soirees, lectures, entertainments, picnics and socials to promote the cause, to coerce their husbands into signing petitions asking the township council to hold plebiscites. What they could not do was vote, and the vote when left to the men, with the names left unrecorded, took a long time to go dry. Even a devout non-drinking Methodist farmer such as Joseph Kidd, who campaigned in favour of banning liquor sales in Beckwith, was not above growing a bumper crop of barley that eventually was sold

Plate 225
The George Shail farmhouse on lot 1, concession 7, Beckwith, at Tennyson, built in 1916, as photographed in October 1988. This ambitious house with its handsomely bracketed eaves and fine Palladian attic windows was among the last of the large brick houses financed by the cheese economy of Beckwith, built as it was in the midst of World War One. The L-plan layout is similar to that of the Alexander McTavish farmhouse (Plate 226), although the verandah originally intended for the front appears never to have been built, leaving a suicide door in the upstairs hall. Houses of this size required intensive labour from women to keep them clean and to keep them heated. Most of the lumber to build such houses came from the farms they were located on, with brick carted out from the brickyards at Carleton Place. The building of ambitious houses such as this suggest the combination of social rivalry and gracious social entertaining that required numerous upstairs bedrooms, a formal parlour and dining room downstairs. All the same, numerous Beckwith families in their large new houses confined their winter activiies to the kitchen and a couple of bedrooms.

to distilleries at a distance.

Increasingly, the growing sentiments of women against liquor banned it from most Beckwith homes, the ultimate social result being that most Beckwith men hid their bottles in some strategic location in grain bins, safe from the eyes of the women. This covert behaviour gave liquor the added allure of somehow being equated with manliness, free from feminine influence. One of Joseph Kidd's neighbours who was fond of drinking was shown the family pet dog named Whiskey in the farm kitchen just after he had been shown a loft full of barley. "That is bad." he said, alluding to the common habit of hiding bottles in the barn away from the women, "Whiskey in the house and barley in the bin.[119] James C. Poole, the editor of the Carleton Place *Herald* who backed the efforts of women in organising temperance campaigns, in his declining years was described by a female neighbour as "raving up & down for whiskey. I do not think he does a thing else."[120] But even once women had the vote, and with prohibition in place, Beckwith was hardly free of liquor. The young woman who wrote the Franktown social column in 1920 on the one hand was "glad to see that the three prairie provinces of the West and Nova Scotia...have voted so overwhelmingly to prohibit the importation

Plate 226
The Alexander McTavish farmhouse, lot 16, concession 8, Beckwith, reputedly built between 1870 and 1873, as photographed in June 1983. The L-plan layout of this farmhouse and the sashes with large double panes give this house the appearance of a structure built closer to the turn of the century than the early 1870s date handed down in family lore, but the stone construction material was a rarity in rural Beckwith after 1880. The large frame dairy barn to the right was built in 1877. In 1881 Alexander McTavish captured a swarm of wild bees, and if family tradition can be believed, this was the first commercial swarm of bees in eastern Ontario. In the late 1910s McTavish was on the executive of the Ontario beekeepers association.

of liquor within their boundaries" and even hoped "now for a real 'dry' Ontario when the time arrives next spring".[121] She eventually found herself asking, "Who is it that circulates all the free flowing booze about our village and vicinity lately? We are beginning to think that there is a well-known source of supply not very far away."[122]

The moral revolution was at its peak in Beckwith from the early 1870s through to the late 1910s, in large part because churches offered the only outlet other than their families for local women to exert their energies. Save for the temperance movement in which a few of them were allowed to hold office, the churches along with fraternal societies, the municipal council, boards of school trustees and other organisations did not permit their holding office. Local churches, however, could not prevent women from organisationally building on the strong reliance they had long placed on congregations to safeguard their relative status in local society. Beckwith women used local churches increasingly between 1881 and 1920 to make local society a better place in which to live, which they assumed would naturally follow from it becoming more moral. During these decades there were some positive career outlets for women that fitted in well with the ideal of creating a nurturing moral world. Young women dominated Beckwith schools, albeit for much smaller salaries then men. A very few such as Jessie Comrie as early as 1885 went to Montreal and took a course in nursing in a maternity hospital, returning to nurse in Carleton Place and Beckwith.[123] In the 1910s Miss Evelyn Wilson, herself originally from Carleton Place, recruited many local women to train as nurses in Stamford, Connecticut.[124] Still other young Beckwith women such as Lena Hawkins by the 1910s were going to Ottawa to train as stenographers.[125]

The majority of young women raised in rural Beckwith before 1920 did not go off to train for careers. Their ultimate destination was marriage and motherhood, although the pattern of inheritance dictated that many of them ended their days as spinsters, either keeping house for a single brother or parents on the family homestead or, much less desirable, being provided with room and board by a married brother on the homestead. The simple central truth for all women growing up in late nineteenth century Beckwith was that they did not enjoy the range of options that men did. The traditional nature of local society worked to the advantage of brothers rather than sisters. If there is one type of judgment historians strive to avoid making, it is the presentist judgment, the erroneous notion that people in the past can be judged by the standards of the historian's own day. Undoubtedly, many women lived fulfilled and contented lives in Beckwith and Carleton Place between 1880 and 1920, but for other women local society offered too constricting a vision, as the action of Bertha Sumner reveals. In 1892, after having been missing for more than a week from her comfortable home, the body of this nineteen year old woman was found near the old lead mine at Carleton Place, and beside it a vial two-thirds full of carbolic acid. A newspaper reporter wrote, "There was also a note in clear, peaceful characters, in which she intimated her intention to destroy herself with the poison as life to her had lost its charm. She did not wish to live a day longer, and thought that the grave might be the end-all."[126]

Bertha Sumner's drastic step was in distinct contrast with the majority of Beckwith women participating in the moral revolution, who in the face of the limitations they faced in the vale of Beckwith, looked up to the more rewarding "Household of Faith" promised by local clergymen such as the Reverend Arthur Jarvis in an 1884 sermon below the Gothic Revival arches of St. James Anglican church in Carleton Place:[127]

> And when all is over and your chair in your family circle is vacant, and your place in this church knows you no more, do not think you will be forgotten even then. Your body will not be hurriedly cast away, but your brethren, who used to rejoice to come here with you in the days of your health, will now bear your remains and lay them tenderly at these altar steps and let them rest here awhile whilst they pray. And so, for the last time, you will enter God's house — the family home — and then be taken and laid in hallowed ground side by side with your brothers that sleep till the angelic herald shall call us to join the united family in the Heavenly Household, where there shall be no more parting forever.

Endnotes

1 *Carleton Place Herald*, 20 November 1861, p. 2, cols. 6-7.
2 Ibid.
3 OKQAR Reverend William Bell, Perth, Journals, II:120.
4 Lockwood, *Montague: A Social History*, p. 132.
5 *Carleton Place Herald*, 10 July 1856, p. 2, cols. 4-5.
6 Ibid., 14 February 1866, pp. 2-3, cols. 7-1.
7 Ibid.
8 Ibid., 15 August 1860, p. 2, cols. 2-3.
9 Ibid., 26 August 1852, p. 3, col. 3.
10 Ibid., 19 November 1862, p. 2, col. 4.
11 *Lanark Observer*, 9 December 1851, p. 3, col. 1.
12 *Carleton Place Herald*, 19 November 1862, p. 2, col. 4.
13 Ibid., 20 November 1861, p. 2, cols. 6-7.
14 Ibid., 23 July 1862, p. 2, cols. 4-5.
15 *Perth Courier*, 26 June 1863, p. 2, col. 4.
16 *Bathurst Courier*, 23 November 1847, p. 2, cols. 5-6.
17 *Carleton Place Herald*, 23 July 1862, p. 2, cols. 4-5.
18 Ibid., 15 January 1868, p. 2, cols. 2-3.
19 Ibid., 23 July 1857, p. 2, cols. 5-6.
20 Ibid., 18 December 1861, pp. 2-3, cols. 7-1.
21 Ibid., 16 July 1857, p. 2, col. 5.
22 Ibid., 12 September 1860, p. 2, col. 3.
23 *Brockville Recorder*, 13 September 1860, p. 1, col. 8.
24 *Carleton Place Herald*, 3 October 1860, p. 4, col. 1.
25 Ibid., 25 December 1851, p. 3, col. 1; and 25 March 1852, p. 2, col. .3
26 Ibid, 1 January 1852, p. 2, col. 3.
27 Ibid., 23 May 1851, p. 2, cols. 3-4.
28 *Smith's Falls Rideau Gleaner*, 17 May 1860, p. 2.
29 OBCMR, By-law no. 146 of Beckwith township council.
30 *Carleton Place Herald*, 13 March 1867, p. 2, col. 3.

31 Ibid., 28 November 1866, p. 2, cols. 2-3.
32 Ibid., 3 February 1869, p. 2, col. .2.
33 Ibid., 17 January 1866, p. 2, cols. 1-2.
34 George Edward Kidd, "Earlier Part of My Life", p. 56.
35 Ibid., p. 3.
36 Ibid., pp. 57-58.
37 OCPAR, Peter W. Cram's Book (a manuscript consisting of the religious meditations of Duncan Cram of Glen Isle).
38 *Carleton Place Herald*, 15 December 1880.
39 P.F. Murphy, *History of St. Mary's Roman Catholic Church, Carleton Place* (Carleton Place: mimeographed by the author, 1969), p. 11.
40 Ibid., p. 13.
41 17 March 1881 letter from Harriet Amelia Brown, Carleton Place, to her son James Morton Brown, Belleville, provided courtesy Howard M. Brown, Ottawa.
42 James T. Watt, "The Protestant Protective Association of Canada: An Example of Religious Extremism in Ontario in the 1890s", in Bruce Hodgins and Robert Page, eds., *Canadian History Since Confederation: Essays and Interpretations* (Georgetown, Ontario: Irwin-Dorsey Limited, 1972), p. 248.
43 Louis Aubrey Wood, *A History of Farmer's Movements in Canada: The Origins and Development of Agrarian Protest, 1872-1924* (Toronto: Ryerson Press, 1924), p. 138.
44 Lockwood, *Montague: A Social History*, p. 364.
45 *Brockville Statesman*, 4 November 1845, p. 1, cols. 2-6.
46 *Carleton Place Herald*, 25 November 1852, p. 2, cols. 2-3.
47 Ibid., 8 July 1868, p. 1, cols. 3-7.
48 Ibid., 5 December 1866, p. 1, cols. 3-7.
49 *Brockville Recorder*, 6 December 1866, p. 2, cols. 1-2.
50 Ibid., 16 May 1867, p. 2, cols. 1-4.
51 Ibid., 2 May 1867, p. 2, col. 3.
52 *Carleton Place Herald*, 10 April 1867, p. 3, cols. 1-2.
53 John May, *What Ails the Church?* (Toronto: William Briggs, 1903), p. 37.
54 *Carleton Place Central Canadian*, 23 October 1884, p. 2.
55 Ibid., 9 January 1890, p. 3.
56 Robert Jefferson and Leonard L. Johnson, *Faith of Our Fathers: The Story of the Diocese of Ottawa* (Ottawa: The Anglican Book Society, 1957), pp. 66-67.
57 Ontario Ministry of Culture and Recreation, *Historical Sketches of Ontario* (Toronto: Ontario Ministry of Culture and Recreation, 1976), pp. 104-105.
58 1904 clipping in scrapbook loaned by the late Hazel Davis, Beckwith. The fantasy aspect of the Franktown church tower and spire has inspired some late twentieth century viewers to refer to it as "Disneyland on the Jock".
59 *Carleton Place Herald*, 21 July 1853, p. 2, col. 6.
60 *Perth Courier*, 19 October 1860, p. 2, cols. 1-2.
61 *Carleton Place Herald*, 14 November 1866, p. 2, cols. 5-6.
62 Ibid., 11 May 1870, p. 2, col. 7.
63 Kidd, "Summer Sunday at Home", pp. 3-5.
64 *Carleton-Place Herald*, 11 January 1855, p. 2, col. 5.
65 Ibid., 27 November 1861, p. 1, cols. 6-7.
66 *Carleton Place Lanark Herald*, 11 April 1851, p. 3, cols. 1-2.
67 Ibid., 24 January 1851, p. 2, col. 5.
68 *Carleton-Place Herald*, 25 December 1851, p. 3, col. 5.
69 Ibid., p. 4., col. 4.
70 Ibid., 15 March 1855, pp. 2-3, cols.
71 Ibid., 23 October 1861, p. 2, cols. 4-5.
72 Ibid., 17 May 1865, p. 2, col. 5.
73 Ibid., 28 July 1853, p. 1, col. 4.
74 Ibid., 17 May 1865, p. 2, col. 5.
75 OCPAR Peter Cram's Book, reminiscences of Duncan Cram.
76 McCuan family correspondence, 20 March 1881 statement of Daniel McCuan.
77 Ibid., 8 January 1894 letter from Lizzie McEwen, Red Deer, to Daniel McCuan, Beckwith, reference 14.1.
78 OCPAR Peter Cram's Book, 9 December 1871 entry of Duncan McCuan.
79 Death notice of Mary Kidd, Prospect, 1889, presumed to have been clipped from the *Christian Guardian*, provided courtesy of John and Leona Kidd, Beckwith.
80 L. Bartlett, *"Uncle Joe Little": Life and Memoirs of Joseph Russell Little* (Toronto: William Briggs, 1903), p. 203. I am grateful to Iva Shirley for bringing this reference to my attention.
81 Kidd, "Earlier Part of My Life", p. 58.
82 SPGA 7 April 1834 letter from Edward J. Boswell, Carleton Place, to Bishop Stewart, Quebec.
83 McCuan family correspondence, 3 July 1868 letter from Daniel McCuan, Beckwith, to his brother Peter, reference 8.21.
84 For further detail consult Marjorie Griffin Cohen, "The Decline of Women in Canadian Dairying" in *Histoire sociale-Social History* XVII No. 34 (November 1984), pp. 307-334.
85 *Carleton-Place Herald*, 17 January 1856, p. 2, col. 7.
86 OCPAR Arthur Jarvis, *"The Household of Faith": A Sermon Preached in St. James Church, Carleton Place on the XXII Sunday After Trinity, November 9th, 1884* (Carleton Place: St. James Anglican Guild, 1884), p. 4.
87 *Carleton Place Herald*, 9 February 1909, p. 6, col. 1.
88 Ibid., undated obituary of Margaret McArthur.
90 Kidd, "Earlier Part of My Life", p. 12.
91 *Carleton-Place Herald*, 3 December 1857, p. 2, cols. 3-4.
92 *Merrickville Canadian Churchman*, 16 July 1863, p. 1, cols. 1-2.
93 Undated newspaper clippings in scrapbook loaned by the late Hazel Davis, Beckwith.

94 *Carleton Place Herald*, 9 March 1864, p. 2, col. 4.
95 Ibid., 19 December 1866, p. 3, col. 6.
96 Ibid., 7 December 1870, p. 2, col. 6.
97 Howard M. Brown, *Carleton Place: Founded Upon A Rock* (Renfrew: Juniper Books, 1984), p. 73.
98 *Carleton Place Herald*, 16 January 1867, p. 1, col. 1.
99 Ibid., 25 January 1865, p. 3, col. 3.
100 *Smith's Falls Review*, 9 March 1865, p. 2.
101 *Carleton Place Herald*, 3 May 1865, p. 2, col. 3.
102 Ibid., 21 June 1865, p. 2, col. 3; and 6 September 1865, p. 3, col. 5.
103 Ibid., 3 January 1866, p. 3, col. 5.
104 Ibid., 27 June 1866, p. 3, col. 5.
105 Ibid., 29 January 1868, p. 2, col. 7.
106 Ibid., 12 February 1868, p. 3, col. 1.
107 Ibid., 18 March 1868, p. 2, col. 6.
108 Ibid., 16 June 1869, p. 2, col. 7.
109 Ibid., 22 March 1871, p. 3, col. 2.
110 *Smith's Falls News*, 14 September 1865, p. 2, col. 3.; and 28 September 1877, p. 3.
111 *Carleton Place Herald*, 13 September 1865, p. 2, col. 3.
112 Ibid., 9 May 1866, p. 3, col. 5.
113 Ibid., 12 February 1868, p. 2, col. 7.
114 *Smith's Falls News*, 27 December 1878, p. 3.
115 *Carleton Place Herald*, 11 June 1879.
116 OBCMR Undated loose temperance petition from 55 ratepayers of Beckwith.
117 Ibid., By-law no. 328 of Beckwith township council.
118 Ibid., By-law no. 382.
119 Kidd, "Earlier Part of My Life", p. 48.
120 27 April 1881 letter from Harriet Amelia Brown, Carleton Place, to her son James Morton Brown, Belleville, provided courtesy of Howard M. Brown, Ottawa.
121 *Carleton Place Herald*, 27 October 1920, p. 5, col. 1.
122 Ibid., 22 December 1920, p. 7, col. 1.
123 1928 obituary of Jessie Comrie in scrapbook loaned by the late Hazel Davis, Beckwith.
124 *Carleton Place Canadian*, 10 December 1986, p. A1.
125 McCuan family correspondence,
126 Undated death notice for Bertha Sumner in scrapbook loaned by the late Hazel Davis.
127 Jarvis, *"The Household of Faith"*, p. 8.

THE TOWNWARD RUSH

It was the women of southern Beckwith, tied down as they were to their domestic chores, who were struck most by the dramatic growth of Carleton Place during their rare forays into town in the 1880s. As their trips into Carleton Place increased in frequency during the following generation, they also noticed various signs of economic decline, particularly the dramatic fall in town population during the 1890s and 1900s. Despite an inability to attract new industry from the 1890s onward, Carleton Place increasingly was perceived to offer its inhabitants a variety of conveniences and luxuries unattainable in rural Beckwith. Most Beckwith families had relatives and acquaintances living in Carleton Place, and they very quickly became acquainted with the advantages of town life, envying their town cousins their telephones, electric light, varied shopping, doctors, fine houses, automobiles, running water, indoor bathrooms, high school, varied social entertainment, cottages, moving pictures and various forms of recreation. At the same time Beckwith's own ongoing gradual population decline continued, the township birthrate grew and the size of families increased slightly, to effectively underline that the decline was due to people choosing to move away. Beckwith villages underwent their own transformation, beginning to survive less as service centres and more as social centres. More and more farm families made regular weekly visits to Carleton Place to market their produce and to purchase goods, but the growing dependence of the farmers on numerous store-bought products also ensured that local villages maintained viable general stores. Despite the continuing decline of Beckwith's population, despite the end of local village growth, and despite the attractions of town and city life as presented in the mass-circulation magazines and local newspapers, as late as 1920 there remained strong local identities in rural Beckwith based on ethnic concentration and on an emerging sense of township history.

Carleton Place boomed in the 1880s. Following the financial recession of the late 1870s, the bankruptcy of Abraham Code's woollen mill in 1878, and an 1879 fire which destroyed some thirteen million feet of sawn lumber in the Gillies and McLaren lumber yard, Carleton Place enjoyed a decade of remarkable growth. The empty woollen mills of Abraham Code and Archibald McArthur were respectively purchased by William Wylie and John Gillies, and set into production in 1881, and the following year the Gillies mill received a gold medal at the Toronto exhibition for tweed cloth.[1] In June 1881 the Canada Central railway was incorporated into the Canadian Pacific railway which when fitted together with other lines provided the infant transcontinental company with a main artery from St. Thomas to Montreal with the transcontentinental line to the Canadian west branching up from Smith's Fall's through Beckwith and the upper Ottawa valley.[2] The previous year the Canada Central railway changed the width of the tracks running through Carleton Place from the old Provincial gauge to the narrower standard gauge used by all other Canadian railroads.[3] In 1882 the C.P.R. moved its machine shops for eastern Ontario from Brockville and Prescott to Carleton Place, building the shops for servicing railway cars at the junction of the railways near the southern village boundary. Canadian Pacific was attracted by the Carleton Place village council offering municipal tax exemptions on machinery, buildings and grounds. They were also attracted by the Central Canada Machine Works which, the *Herald* announced in January 1882, was constructing a very large steam engine for the C.P.R.[4] In 1884 Carleton Place became the eastern terminus of the

Ontario and Quebec section of the railway, prompting the *Herald* to spell out the benefits for the village:[5]

> Now the trainmen and locomotives of the passenger trains between Toronto and Carleton Place will stop here, and the trainmen and locomotives of the freight trains between here and Havelock, will stop at this point. This will likewise be the stopping point for trainmen and locomotives on the other branches.... [W]e are likely to have fifty or sixty more men, some of them with families, living in our town.

The actual growth brought by the C.P.R. railway car repair shops upon Carleton Place being made a terminus was even more dramatic than the *Herald* had projected. Three years later the *Herald* editor commented:[6]

> The extensive repair shops of the railway established here in 1882 and employing at different times from 100 to over 200 men, with accessions to the town's trade by reason of the railway traffic and the many railway employees outside the shops, were a large element in the town's progress. In the five years to 1887, not yet incorporated as a town, the population has doubled to an estimated 3,780.

Carleton Place paid heavily for its growth. It followed the prevalent custom of bonussing that many towns and cities practised in the 1880s and beyond, offering large tax breaks and even cash grants to lure industrialists to locate in their midst, rather than in some other centre. In 1896 the ratepayers of Carleton Place voted a bonus of $20,000 to assist the C.P.R. in rebuilding their workshops on a larger, grander scale and more permanently in stone at an estimated total cost of between forty and sixty thousand dollars.[7] A handsome stone railway station was built in 1921,[8] but in 1908 the civic leaders of Carleton Place already began to appreciate the continuing cost of the Canadian Pacific railway as a corporate citizen. When the town made a demand on the railway for $500 as taxes for the year 1907 upon the property and works of the company, the C.P.R. took out an injunction against Carleton Place restraining them from collecting the taxes, and asked from the town "a declaration that their property which includes the machine and repair shops is exempt for the period of fifteen years from June 1, 1897."[9]

Canadian Pacific was not alone in insisting on bonussing inducements to remain in Carleton Place. The Findlay stove manufacturing foundry had significantly expanded from the cupola of stones that David Findlay built in the 1860s, and from a local community-based operation involving Beckwith farmers. His grandson recalled:[10]

> His cupola blower [at first] was operated by actual horse power. When he wanted to take off heat he sent out a call and the farmers in the vicinity came with their teams and took turns on a type of merry-go-round horse power. Casting day was like an old fashioned threshing bee on the farm. His trade was chiefly with the farmers and often the yard behind his foundry was filled with sheep, pigs or sacks of grain brought in payment for castings.

Under David Findlay's two sons, David and William, the firm expanded from an operation employing 25 men and producing a capacity of 4,000 stoves per year in 1895[11] to one with 75 hands on the payroll producing between 25 to thirty stoves a day in 1902. Upon building a new brick plant measuring 50 by 228 feet in 1902, the *Herald* reported that the new "moulding room will accommodate thirty moulders and their assistants, and although the firm want that many hands they cannot obtain them."[12] In 1905 another large new building was added to the Findlay plant and a catalogue issued that year setting forth the prices and designs of the various stoves manufactured

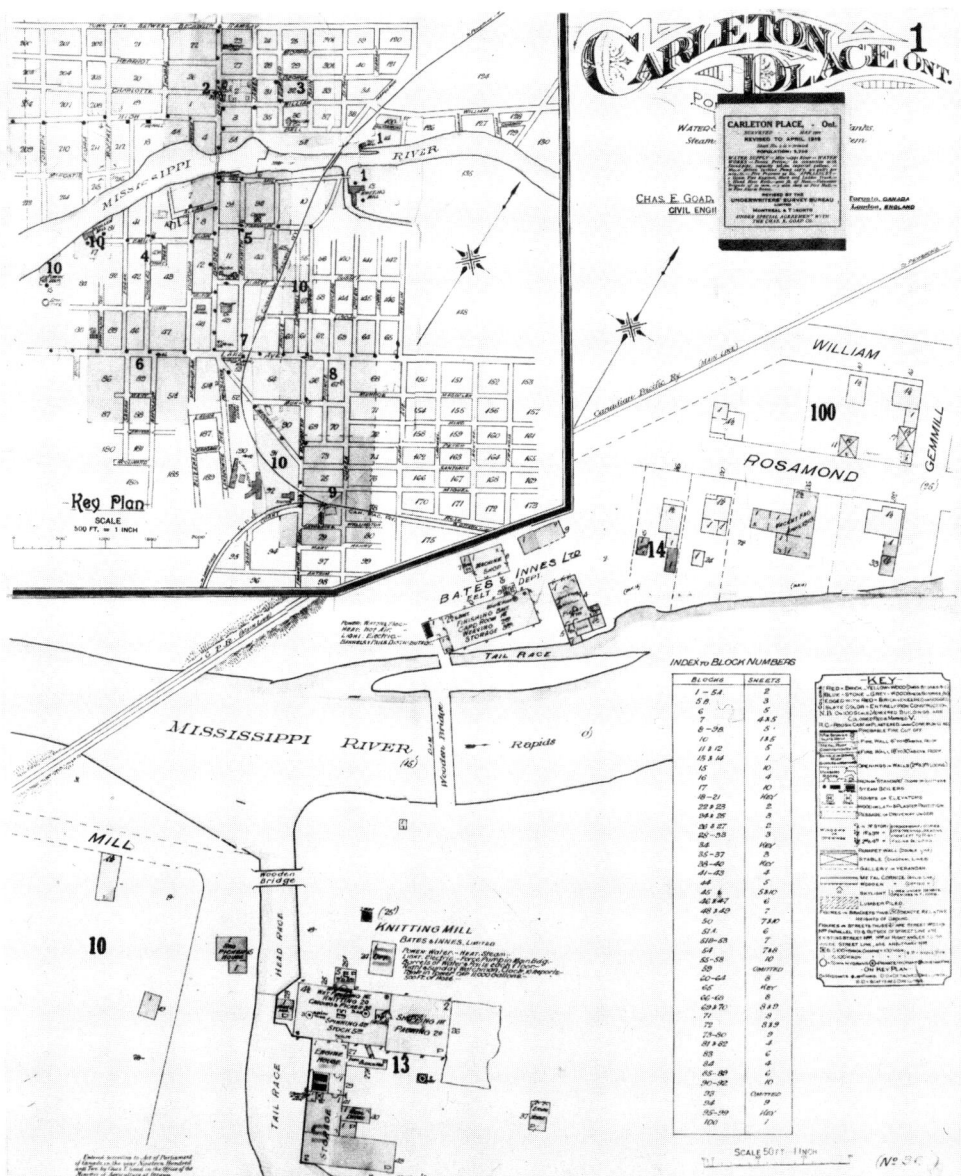

Plate 227
A fire insurance plan of Carleton Place showing in detail the Bates & Innes woollen mills, as prepared by Charles E. Goad for the Underwriters' Survey Bureau in April 1919. This map, updated from a 1902 fire insurance plan, shows the Canadian Pacific railway station adjacent to the railway shops. The Findlay foundry is not shown on blocks 18 and 4A on the north shore of the Mississippi River. The major employers in Carleton Place from the 1880s until the mid twentieth century included the woollen mills, the CPR shops and the Findlay stove foundry. When this map was updated a generation later, Carleton Place displayed virtually no physical growth. National Archives of Canada NMC-9881.

amounted to no less than forty pages.[13] In December 1911, some eight months after David Findlay Jr. moved into his new stone mansion on High Street,[14] the town fixed a modified assessment on the Findlay foundry at $20,000 for the following ten years, whereas for the previous ten years the foundry had been exempt from all taxation.[15] Yet again, in 1925, a ten year fixed assessment was granted the Findlay firm by the town.[16]

The bonussing of the 1890s and 1900s reflected the fear of Carleton Place inhabitants at losing major employers in the midst of a recession. 1888 was the peak year of sawmill construction along the Mississippi River,[17] and in Carleton Place that same year the former Gillies and McLaren sawmills were rebuilt by Peter McLaren's Canada Lumber Company to double their capacity.[18] In 1895 the Canada Lumber Company produced 25 million feet of sawn lumber[19] but the following ten years witnessed the demise of this industry at Carleton Place. During the depression of the 1890s the town's population fell from a high of 4,435 in 1891 to 4,059 in 1901, and fell still further to 3,621 persons by 1911, then managed a slight rise back to 3,841 by 1921. By the turn of the century both William Wylie's Hawthorne Woollen Mills and the John Gillies, Son and Company woollen mill were bought out by the huge Canadian Woollen Mills syndicate, reflecting the growing ascendancy of Montreal financial interests in the capitalising of woollen mills in the Mississippi valley.[20] In 1904 the Canadian Woollen Mills were declared insolvent, and the two large stone mills lay idle, further contributing to the recession of the 1900s in Carleton Place.

In 1907 two young men, Charles W. Bates and James A. Innes as managers in the Penman mill at St. Hyacinthe, Quebec, purchased the old McArthur mill in Carleton Place. Bates had a background in weaving mills and paper felt making whereas Innes's experience had been in knitting. Together they saw the potential in the empty stone woollen mill not only to make tweeds and other domestic cloths, but particularly to manufacture pulp and paper maker's felts, a product then largely imported from Britain and the United States. They negotiated a $10,000 loan from the town of Carleton Place, without interest, to be repaid by 1916, with the town's security being a chattel mortgage on the new machinery purchased by the firm. The new machinery included knitting and sewing machines, winders, fulling and scouring mills, dryers and a 220 inch-width felt loom. The old mill already contained four sets of 48-inch cards, four mules, and 25 Crompton and Knowles looms.[21] Bates and Innes initially manufactured heavy ribbed underwear, and their product found such favour that eventually they had a peak annual production of 360,000 pairs. In 1910 the firm purchased the old Central Canada Machine Works stone building on the north side of the Mississippi from the John Gillies Estate due to the expanding space requirements of making pulp and paper makers' felts. During World War One the production of blankets, underwear and cloth necessitated further expansion into other premises such as the old McDonald and Brown woollen mill on Mill Street. Charles Bates in a separate venture opened up William Wylie's old Hawthorn mill which had lain empty since 1904 for further war production. To meet the increased need for woollen mill workers, and because they were willing to work for lower wages, some French Canadian families were brought in and remained settled in the community. In 1918 company sales hit a record $1,200,000,[22] spurring Charles Bates to build a mansion next door to that of David Findlay on High Street,[23] and to construct a brick extension onto the old McArthur mill at a cost of $175,000 just before wool prices fell from about a dollar per pound to twenty cents in the autumn of 1920.[24]

The Central Canada Machine Works of Gillies, Beyer and Company in which John Gillies had set up his sixth son Alexander in the mid 1870s continued despite Alexander Gillies's untimely death by drowning at the age of 22 in 1878. John Gillies carried on the business under his own name, manufacturing mill machinery and small marine engines, and after his death the business was continued as the John Gillies Estate Company, Mechanical Department[25] until it was purchased by Bates and Innes in 1910. The manufactures of the Gillies machine shop included stationary and marine gasoline engines, gasoline and steam launches, steam engines, water wheels, sawmill

Plate 228
A group of moulders in the moulding shop at Findlay Brothers stove factory, Carleton Place, as photographed in 1909. The men who worked at the Findlay factory and the various woollen mills in Carleton Place belonged to weak unions that were unable to mount effective strikes for higher wages. By contrast, workers at the Canadian Pacific railway shops, backed by the strong larger national unions to which they belonged, mounted a successful strike for higher wages in 1907. The number of men employed at Findlay's steadily rose from 75 at the turn of the century to some 300 in the 1930s. Workers at the Findlay plant were paid as comparatively poor a wage as labourers in the local woollen mills, but their work was much more steady as extensive promotion and advertising created a growing demand for Findlay stoves. For names see appendix 34. National Archives of Canada negative no. C-369.

machinery, lath and resawing machines, shafting pulleys and gearing.[26] The firm employed up to fifty mechanics.

The dramatic growth of the 1880s gave Carleton Place a new urbane sense of itself. The *Herald* boasted in July 1887:[27]

> Carleton Place now has 27 business places with plate glass fronts and 48 without, i.e. 75; and two foundries, two machine shops, three woollen factories, two sawmills, two planing mills, a roller flour mill and a custom grist mill, three tanneries, three blacksmith shops and two carriage shops. We have two boat liveries, three billiard halls, seven hotels, three schoolhouses with twelve teachers, and six churches and two printing presses. We have four doctors and two lawyers, two telegraph offices, the telephone and the electric light.

As Carleton Place grew, so did the boosterism of its promoters. When the *Herald* in comparing the village's growth with that of other Ottawa valley centres in 1884, came up against the electric street lights that had been installed in Pembroke, it commented, "We had electric lights here in one of our great saw mills long, long ago and there is little doubt but it will be in use on our business streets in a short time."[28] Accordingly, in 1885 a system of electric street lights was installed in Carleton Place,[29] and seven years later an improved power system, utilising alternating current, was installed by the private firm of Horace Brown and Sons, illuminating some 400 electric lights on the streets and in some homes.[30] In 1885 the Bell Telephone Company constructed a line between Ottawa and Brockville, passing through Carleton Place, Perth and Smith's Falls.[31] When the Carleton Place exchange opened in November 1885 there were ten subscribers, this increased to seventeen a year later, to nearly sixty in 1892, and by 1928 there were some 800 town and rural telephones directly connected to the town exchange.[32] Further major improvements in Carleton Place included the construction of concrete sidewalks in 1906, the construction of a new hydro-electric power generating plant by Horace Brown and Sons in 1911, leading to the excavation and installation of municipal waterworks and sewers from 1912 to 1915.[33] By 1920 there were numbered street addresses for town inhabitants.

The dramatic growth Carleton Place enjoyed in the 1880s nourished a hunger for urbanity that sustained town boosters during the 1890s and 1900s when the municipality's population fell by more than 800 people. In 1884 a group of citizens petitioned the village council to prevent cows from running at large.[34] When Robert McDiarmid in 1885 refurbished the old Newman Hall at the corner of William and Bridge streets with seating for up to 500 people and a fully equipped stage, the *Herald* approvingly noted that "The drop curtain presents an excellent view of placid waters, of rugged mountain rocks, and ancient castles."[35] During the 1880s an annual four day musical convention was held in the town, featuring conductors from as far away as Boston, and an array of both local and imported singers and musicians.[36] So caught up were village inhabitants in making Carleton Place as urbane as possible that they contemplated even changing the municipality's name in 1885. Among the 75 proposed names were Gilliesburg, Wanburo (Amerindian for "the moving light"), Withram or Beckram (a combination of Beckwith and Ramsay), Bellrobert, Bellbay, Rapidsdale, Morphysburg, Alberta, Gilliestown, Lanarkboro, Gilliesville, McArthur, Lajuna and Beckwith.[37]

In January 1890 Carleton Place was incorporated as a town[38] and in October 1891 a prime Bridge Street lot on the southern riverbank was purchased as the site for a town hall and fire station. The 1891 census showed that Carleton Place was not only the largest town in Lanark County but also the largest incorporated town in the Ottawa valley and the largest town apart from Winnipeg on the continental line of the Canadian Pacific railway between Montreal and Vancouver.[39] The growing wealth of the town was reflected by massive rambling brick houses that began to be built from the 1880s on through to the 1910s. Bridge Street south of the river became the merchandising heart of the town, lined with two and three storey brick buildings. The brickyards of William Willoughby and William Taylor supplied local builders in 1896,[40] and were joined by yet a third brickyard operated by George Authur Burgess in which up to twenty people worked. Carleton Place brick was shipped to Perth, Smith's Falls and Almonte and to more distant larger centres.[41] In the planing mills and sawmills of W.A. Nichols between 30 and 35 men were employed in manufacturing rough and dressed lumber, sashes, doors, blinds, cheese boxes, shingles, mouldings, surface oak doors, wood trimmings and fixtures of every description, fretwork, and verandah materials.[42]

Many of the large new brick houses and brick business blocks featured as trim the distinctive Beckwith limestone that was extracted from the Dominion quarries of Findlay McEwen on the east halves of lots nine and eleven of the ninth concession and from the quarries owned by Daniel McNeely on lot twelve in the tenth concession. The stone in these Beckwith quarries lay just below the soil in a ridge some three and a half feet thick and consisted of a brown crystalline dolomitic limestone, the darkest colour of brown met with in any stone in Ontario. On weathering, the stone

Plate 229
Calendar of the Bates & Innes woollen mills, Carleton Place, from 1921. This was one of a series of large handsome calendars commissioned by Bates & Innes in the 1920s featuring sentimental old English scenes to draw attention to their woollen knitted goods. The calendars proved successful in gaining entry for Bates & Innes products in stores across Canada, particularly the prestigious Eaton's chain, after the wholesale firm in Montreal which previously had distributed the firm's goods from 1907 to 1919 proved ineffectual during the depressed woollen markets at the end of World War One. The OV trademark of Bates & Innes stood for their Ottawa Valley brand of products. Loaned courtesy of the Carleton Place and Beckwith Historical Society.

became still darker, melding with the red brick of the buildings in which it was used as trim. These quarries had supplied building stone as early as 1869 for Zion Presbyterian church and the 1871 town hall in Carleton Place. By 1912 it was shipped to Pembroke, Renfrew, Arnprior, Almonte, Perth, Smith's Falls and other places and was largely used for quoins, sills and accent stones on buildings.[43]

The rich dark Beckwith limestone was called into use by Toronto architect George King in his design for an ambitious new town hall at Carleton Place in 1896.[44] It was the spirit of boosterism above all else that prompted the Carleton Place town fathers to vote $26,000 in 1896[45] for the construction of a fantastic structure to match their hopes for the future rather than the economic recession in which they were mired. Here under one roof were to be housed the various municipal offices of the town, the public library, the fire hall, and a public meeting hall, with more space provided than even the inventive turn-of-the-century civic mind knew what to do with. The architecture, a stripped-down Richardsonian Romanesque, exactly suited the robust ambition of the town fathers, amalgamating as it did a variety of picturesque eclectic elements. From the opposite riverbank one beheld a French chateau. The tower for drying firehoses conjured up visions of the minaret balconies from which the imams of Islam exhorted the faithful to bow toward Mecca in prayer. The front entrance suggested, albeit tenuously, a provincial French Romanesque influence, while the municipal chamber with its elliptical bay window and casements filled with leaded glass bespoke a Renaissance Venetian court chamber.

If some Carleton Place ratepayers were overwhelmed by the cost of the town hall, their eyes were nonetheless dazzled by the grand staircase that swept crowds up to the concert hall on the second floor in a blur of black ash balustrade joinery to the official opening in late October 1897. To most town inhabitants there was simply no question that it was the most magnificent municipal building ever constructed in Lanark County, an architectural pot-pourri whose exuberance outdistanced by far the dreams for as well as the actual future of Carleton Place as a town. A half-century would pass before Carleton Place would again reach the level of population it had in 1891. The steep gables and turrets on the new town hall might be capped with jaunty iron pennants, but the walls were still of sombre dark Beckwith limestone, pulling the town back down to earth with the problematic growth of the 1890s and 1900s.

Despite the fantastic architecture of the new Carleton Place town hall, despite the increasing numbers of ambitious brick residences, despite the mansions beginning to line High Street, despite the handsome large churches and despite the varied shopping and modernisation of the town in the 1880s and 1890s, the majority of inhabitants were members of labouring families. They worked long hours in poorly-ventilated mills filled with fast-moving, deafening equipment, sawblades, pulleys and belts; were subject to layoffs when sales were slack,[46] and when log drives failed to arrive at the sawmills upon schedule.[47] Labourers in the woollen mills of Carleton Place were particularly vulnerable. Their employers cut wages or stopped production altogether when business periodically slumped, and also forced workers into long overtime hours when markets picked up. When workers at one woollen mill tried to organise a general strike for better wages, they were immediately fired.[48] In the late 1880s between forty and fifty Carleton Place workers formed a local assembly of the Knights of Labor, a North American organisation that opposed what it called class privilege and the exploitation of labour. The utopian goals of these workers in seeking to "secure to the toilers a proper share of the wealth that they created; more of the leisure that rightfully belongs to them; more society advantages, more of the benefits, privileges and emoluments of the world" did not materialise, and the local assembly of the Knights of Labor dissoved in 1889.[49] The unions in Carleton Place woollen mills and Findlay's foundry were weak affairs, incapable of organising effective strikes for higher wages. By contrast, the strong union at the Canadian Pacific railway shops, with backing from the larger union across Canada, mounted a successful strike for higher wages in 1908.[50] Many labourers rented rooms, lived in boarding-houses, built their own modest houses, and those who were least well off subsisted in shacks north of the town limits in a locale euphemistically called "Happy Valley".

Plate 230
Title page of The Chimes of Carleton Place, *published by the Carleton Place Mechanics Institute in 1885, promoting a musical convention. The Carleton Place mechanics institute, rather than providing town labourers with a forum for reducing their long working hours and low wages, instead promoted forms of sentimental escape including the town library and annual musical conventions during the 1880s. In 1885 a local assembly of the Knights of Labor was formed at Carleton Place, as part of a larger movement seeking to improve the quality of life of local workers, but its membership never rose above fifty and it ceased to exist in 1889. The musical conventions drew people from across the Ottawa valley. The growing influence of the moral revolution and the growing sophistication of Beckwith society generally is evident in the objectives of improving church choirs, cultivating the voice and forming an elevated musical taste. Private collection.*

Even the poor paying jobs in the woollen mills were better than to be left unemployed in the 1890s, as the Mississippi valley was logged out and as the woollen mills of the town succumbed to the depression. William W. Cliff, editor of the *Central Canadian*, reported in late 1897 that two young men from the town travelled north, only to find "parties of young men with bags either camping by the roadside or plodding along on the same hunt as themselves." In the Carleton Place vicinity, Cliff observed,[51]

> Trying to find employment seems...to engage the energies of a large proportion of all classes except farmers and capitalists. The lives of foremen in public works or factories are made a burden by the solicitations of people begging for work. They are met at all hours and in all places, and besieged with a pertinacity engendered by despair or actual starvation.
>
> Men supposed to have influence with employers are constantly beset by work hunters, and every influence is brought to bear to influence them in a good but almost hopeless undertaking.

Those unable to find work drifted away from Carleton Place, while town labourers found various outlets for the frustration and tension that accumulated from endlessly performing the same monotonous, often dangerous tasks, that paid poorly and provided them with little sense of worth. For men working on the river drives and in the sawmills there was the occasional skirmish with the men of a rival firm. Others sought religious solace. One labourer, Trevor McGuire, after shaking the dust of Carleton Place off his boots became one of the few native-born founding members of the Canadian Communist party and he was the first Communist in Canada to be jailed for sedition. Many Carleton Place labourers simply settled for cursing the men for whom they worked behind their backs. "Some people in town called us the damned Findlays", William F. Findlay later recalled, "and some called us the God-damned Findlays!"[52] Desperate as some men were for employment, still others could not face up to the thought of performing the same repetitive drudgery for a lifetime. Cardy Miller, for example, after moving with his mother from Ramsay Township into Carleton Place, and working for two years in the moulding department at Findlay's, could take it no longer. On an October evening in 1905 the nineteen-year-old man, who otherwise led an exemplary life, purchased a revolver, hired a horse, drove out to the tenth concession of Beckwith, and shot himself fatally in the heart.[53]

The population of Carleton Place continued to decline in the early 1900s, but as Table 28 reveals, following the turn of the century there were increases in nearly everything relating to manufacturing industries in the town. The number of firms increased, the capitalisation of firms grew more than sevenfold, the number of employees grew by more than fifty percent, and the value of Carleton Place factory products increased more than fivefold between 1901 and 1921. During these twenty years the amount of wages paid out increased fourfold in dollars, as the average worker's annual earnings grew from $351 in 1901 to $480 in 1911 to $1,042 in 1921. The growth of Findlays and of Bates and Innes in the late 1900s, followed by the strong war economy contributed to this growth, but Carleton Place industrial development remained hampered by innate weaknesses. Even when compared with other towns with more than 3,500 inhabitants in the comparatively sluggish eastern Ontario economy, Carleton Place industries had the consistently lowest capitalisation, the consistently second lowest value of products, and it was only in 1921 that the town broke out of paying the second lowest average annual wage to workers.

There were temporary forms of escape from the grind of Carleton Place mills and shops. A correspondent of the *Herald* observed as early as 1862:[54]

> The different Points, Bays and Islands afford pretty sylvan neuks for a Summer day's amusement, and whenever the younger branches of Carleton Place society wish for a day[']s relaxation

Plate 231
The Carleton Place town hall built in 1897 and the view looking south along Bridge Street, as photographed in 1908. Town life proved attractive to many Beckwith women from the 1880s on, offering them various opportunities to socialise together in the various large church groups, women's sports groups, and in emerging sororial groups such as the Captain Hooper branch of the Imperial Order of Daughters of the Empire. It contrasted with the relative isolation of women in rural Beckwith, separated as they were by distance until the Goodwood and Beckwith-Montague rural telephone systems were set in operation in 1915. National Archives of Canada negative no. PA-135226.

from the fatiguing duties of their daily labor, they collect a fleet of boats and canoes at McCaffrey's landing, and having prepared a commissariat of eatables and a proportionate quantity of the daughters of Eve, and secured perhaps a bagpipes and fiddle, they are able to consume a day at Allan's Point with quite an advantage to their physical health and mind.

The thickly wooded grove at Allan's point was a popular spot for picnics and outings from the 1860s onward, not only because the depth of water was suitable for swimming and the point had an excellent view of the lake not available in Carleton Place, but also because it was only a couple of miles away. The steamer *Enterprise*, a paddle wheeler capable of carrying 300 people that travelled Mississippi Lake in the service of the McLaren sawmill and later the Canada Lumber Company, also carried picnic and sporting parties to Allan's Point and Prettie's Island for outings in the 1870s and 1880s.[55] Town churches, clubs, societies, the fire brigade, railwaymen and industries increasingly held picnics at Allan's Point, the Carleton Place Boating Club hosted regattas there in 1880 and 1881, and during the 1880s it developed as a family tenting centre for the town. A small two-storey hotel was built in 1887. Carleton Place was preparing to purchase the property as a publicly owned picnic and regatta park for the town, hence the new name Lake Park, when a local syndicate of prominent town inhabitants incorporated as the Lake Park Company Limited bought it to develop as a lively commercial summer resort. The John Gillies boat works was commissioned to build an eighty by sixteen foot side-wheeler steamboat for the Lake Park Company. The new steamboat, named the *Carleton*, was launched in 1893 and carried life preservers for 200 people.

The opening celebrations for Lake Park in 1893 featured the Princess Louise Dragoon Guards from Ottawa, who in their dress uniforms and dazzling metal helmets put on a Dominion Day musical ride with forty horses before a gathering of two thousand spectators. Peter P. Salter built a four storey hotel at Lake Park named the Queen's Royal Hotel, an extension of his Leland Hotel on Bridge Street in Carleton Place, in the 1890s. A steamboat named the *Lillian B.*, owned by Salter

Table 28. Manufacturing Industries in Eastern Ontario Towns, 1901-1921

	Almonte	Carleton Place	Gananoque	Perth	Smith's Falls
Population					
1901	3,023	4,059	3,526	3,588	5,155
1911	2,452	3,621	3,804	3,588	6,370
1921	2,426	3,841	3,604	3,790	6,790
Establishments					
1901	10	15	16	20	11
1911	10	31	19	27	13
1921	18	21	27	28	16
Capital					
1901	$995,167	$357,760	$1,030,412	$379,138	$2,164,003
1911	1,000,376	659,138	1,676,462	701,711	4,243,500
1921	1,650,854	2,570,895	4,090,185	3,863,062	3,825,411
Employees					
1901	671	368	674	303	793
1911	483	577	787	496	958
1921	376	565	631	623	490
Salaries and Wages					
1901	$211,210	$129,226	$281,380	$90,910	$376,500
1911	103,907	276,700	400,748	180,851	592,887
1921	321,699	588,775	582,582	624,362	547,365
Value of Products					
1901	$845,800	$392,735	$863,079	$273,369	$1,397,075
1911	824,760	851,559	$1,453,467	971,505	1,680,909
1921	$1,413,896	$2,072,179	2,379,414	2,445,803	1,978,172

SOURCE: Craig Heron and George De Zwaan, "Industrial Unionism in Eastern Ontario: Gananoque, 1918-21" *Ontario History* LXXVII, No. 3, September 1985, p. 161; *Canada, Census* (Ottawa, 1911), vol. 3, Tables XI and XII; *Canada Year Book* (Ottawa, 1924), Table 23.

Plate 232
The Central Canada Machine Works of Messrs. John Gillies and Ferdinand Beyer, Carleton Place, as lithographed in the 15 February 1879 edition of the Canadian Illustrated News. *Despite the inaccurate scale of the train in the foreground, this lithograph indicates the large size of steam engines being manufactured in this factory within four years of being built. The extensive stocks of firewood to the left suggest that the steam engines in the various mills and factories of Carleton Place provided a large market for wood from Beckwith bush lots. The financial backing for this enterprise came from profits that John Gillies had built up from more than a generation in the timber industry. National Archives of Canada negative no. C-71890.*

carried guests back and fourth between the resort and Carleton Place. The Lake Park hotel featured a race track, band and dance pavilions, steamboat docks, and a picnic dining room capable of seating several hundred people at a time. Team, track and water sports, firework displays over the water, even circus acts were presented to bring in summer crowds by railway and steamer. The first canoe club at Carleton Place, the Ottawa Valley Canoe Association, was formed in 1893 and held its first regatta that same year at Lake Park.[56] It later became known as the Carleton Place Canoe Club. To further boost the popularity of the resort, a petition from 32 landowners along Beckwith's eleventh concession supported a plan by Peter Salter to construct an electric railway from Carleton Place to Lake Park along the Canadian Pacific railway tracks and the eleventh concession line, but it never came to be.[57]

Excerpts from a piece of doggerel written about Lake Park by Anna Elexey Duff and Denysa Duff who resided on a nearby farm about 1900, further testify to the attractions of the resort:[58]

Where do some folk go to dance?
Over at Lake Park.
Where do they flirt when they get a chance?
Over at Lake Park....

Where do they drink so much beer?
Don't say at Lake Park.
Where do they feel and act very queer?
Over at Lake Park....

Where do some travellers pass you by?
Over at Lake Park.
Where do they get a bottle on the sly?
Over at Lake Park.

Chorus: O, they like Park Lake,
It's the place that takes the cake,
O, they like Lake Park, they do,
O, they like Lake Park, pretty little Lake Park,
And they like the stuff that's sold there too.

    The days of Lake Park as a popular public resort from which the town of Carleton Place in particular benefitted were numbered. In January 1902 Beckwith ratepayers voted in favour of a by-law prohibiting the sale of liquor,[59] that was subsequently overturned in 1903;[60] but when 208 out of 273 Beckwith inhabitants voted in favour of local option in January 1910[61] the flow of liquor went underground and the Lake Park resort languished. In addition, as more and more Carleton Place merchants built cottages at Lake Park after 1895,[62] they viewed with increasing disfavour the noisy crowds and surreptitious drinking attracted by the resort, preferring a quiet cottage community to match the street names of Birch, Poplar, Cedar and Elm avenues set up in 1894 by the Lake Park Company of Carleton Place Limited.[63]

    The demise of Lake Park as a public resort left the young men of Beckwith and Carleton Place little form of escape from the rigours of factory life other than in a variety of sports. Cricket and lacrosse were popular from the 1860s onward, and were joined by football, baseball, hockey, the Carleton Place Canoe Club, ice skating, roller skating, YMCA athletics, bicycling and curling. There were fraternal organisations such as the Orange lodge, the Masonic lodge, the Oddfellows, the Foresters; there were women's church groups and the Imperial Order of Daughters of the Empire; and other activities such as the town brass band. In 1912 James Johnson and his brothers purchased a kinetophone, an Edison invention, and after experimenting, they succeeded in presenting talking pictures. Otherwise inanimate forms were made to move about a stage, run, walk, stand, sit down, speak and sing. Johnson's first theatre was located in the Masonic block, but in 1920 he opened a larger theatre on Bridge Street, before eventually moving to New York where among his pioneering moving picture achievements was the three dimensional screen in 1953.[64] Within the Carleton Place Roxy Theatre the workers in town mills sought escape from oppressive working environments.

    To the young people growing up in rural Beckwith between 1880 and 1920 the sports teams, the companionship, the attractions, the varied social entertainments, and the picnic excursions to Prettie's Island and Lake Park contrasted with the unending drudgery of farm work. If the mills and factories in Carleton Place were unventilated dismal places, at least there was a limit to the number of hours worked, even if it was an unreasonable limit, in contrast with farm work which went on forever, broken only by church and death, as entries from Joseph Kidd's journal in May 1880 reveal:[65]

May A.D. 1880. Sat. 1...Drew stones in forenoon[,] fenced after.... Mon. 3... Sowed 5 bu[shels] wheat with grass and clover[.] Tue. 4[.] Harrowed....Sowed 20 bus. oats.... Wed. 5...finished harrowing... Drew stones[.] Thu[.] 6 Went to sale at John McKercher's[.] Fri. 7 Finished ploughing pea[.] Sowed and harrowed one bus. oats[,] 21 in all[.] Sat. 8[.] rolled.... Sun[.] 9[.] Stopped at home. Quarterly [church] meeting at Stittsville[.] Mon[.] 10[.] Sowed 10 bus. peas and oats...and harrowed it Tue[.] 11[.] Went to C.P. Sold 21 bus. potatoes at 35-40 c[ents] e[ach]. Wed[.] 12[.]... Drew stones all day to drain.... Thu[.] 13...Finished fence. Fri[.] 14[.] Drew manure...for potatoes.... Sat[.] 15[.]... Drew manure for roots.... Sun[.] 16[.]...Walked to church[,] Reid preached. ... Mon[.] 17[.] Finished drawing manure[,] spread some... Tue[.] 18[.] Rained some. Mag had foal[,] cut potatoes in cellar[.] Wed[.] 19[.] Rained some[,] finished cutting potatoes. ... Thu[.] 20[.] Sorted potatoes in cellar[,] some rain[,] crops growing well[.] Fri. 21...fixed drain and cleaned it. Went to Prospect. Sat[.] 22[.] Finished picking potatoes[,] helped to wash.... Sun[.] 23.... Went to funeral [of] James Ferguson[.] Mon. 24.... Ploughed for potatoes and roots. ... Tue[.] 25.... Ploughed all day.... Wed[.] 26.... Ploughed[,] clipped some sheep....

Plate 233
The gold medal awarded to John Gillies at the Toronto industrial exhibition in 1882 for the manufacture of tweed at his woollen mill in Carleton Place. This rare accolade is significant testimony to the high quality of goods produced in Carleton Place woollen mills in the late nineteenth century, but the competition of hundreds of mills made the industry notoriously unstable and paid employees poorly. All the same, Beckwith farmers' sons and daughters increasingly looked to Carleton Place for employment, preferring the vitality of town life to the quiet countryside. National Archives of Canada negative no. C-61740.

Thu[.] 27.... Ploughed. Clipped some sheep.... Fri[.] 28[.] Went to J. Simpson[']s[.] Went to funeral [of] Jameses child[.] Sat[.] 29.... finished clipping sheep. ... Sun[.] 30[.] Rained all day[,] stopped at home[,] fine growing[.] Mon[.] 31.... Harrowed potato ground[.] Drew off stones[.]

488 THE TOWNWARD RUSH

The dairy economy that emerged in Beckwith in the 1880s only added to the length and routine of each day, as the twice daily milking of cows tied down families all the more firmly to their farms. The entries in Joseph Kidd's journal in May 1899 emphasize the added daily regime imposed on farmers in drawing milk to the cheese factory:[66]

> May 1899[.] Mon[.] 1[.] Sowed 5 bags barley.... Sowed 5 bags P[eas] and B[eans].... Tue[.] 2. Sowed 10 bags peas[,] oats and barley.... Wed[.] 3[.] Rolled.... James [his son] harrowed.... Thu[.] 4. Rolled.... Mare foaled. James harrowed[.] Fri[.] 5[.] Planted potatoes in garden[,] drew out manure.... Sat[.] 6[.] Clipped sheep, boys drew off stones.... Sun[.] 7[.] Went to quarterly meeting and P[rayer] meeting[.] Burnett preached[.] Mon[.] 8[.] Drew milk to factory[,] went to [cheese] business meeting.... Tue[.] 9[.] Drew milk[.] Sowed 4 bags peas-oats.... Wed[.] 10[.] Drew milk[.] Sowed 5 bags peas and oats.... Thu[.] 11[.] Drew milk[,] drew out manure.... Fri[.] 12[.] Drew milk[,] drew out manure.... Sat[.] 13[.] Drew milk[.] Put up fence...[,] drew out manure. Sun[.] 14[.] Went to church and P[rayer] meeting[.] Burnett preached.... Mon[.] 15[.] Drew milk[,] spread manure...[,] roads soft now[.] Tue[.] 16. Drew milk[,] put up fence at bush on east place[.] Wed[.] 17[.] Drew milk[,] spread and drew out manure.... Thu[.] 18[.] Rained[,] drew milk, read papers[,] spread manure. Fri[.] 19. Drew milk[,] drew and spread manure[.] Went to Prayer meeting.... Sat[.] 20[.] Drew milk[,] made drills[,] sowed turnips.... Sun[.] 21[.] Went to church[,] roads bad[,] Burnett preached[.] Mon[.] 22[.] Made drills for potatoes[,] sowed carrots and mangolds[.] Tue[.] 23[.] Drew milk[.] Made drills for potatoes.... Wed[.] 24[.] Drew milk[,] planted potatoes[,] harrowed ground.... Thu[.] 25[.] Drew milk[,] worked at fence at bush.... Fri[.] 26. drew milk[,] went to C.P. with wool[,] went to P[rayer] meeting[.] Sat[.] 27.... Ed [another son] drew milk[,] went to council meeting[.] Sun[.] 28[.] Went to church[.] A. Morton preached...[,] roads muddy. Mon[.] 29[.] Drew milk[,] split wood in yard[.] Went to Prospect[.] Tue[.] 30[.] Drew milk[,] put up fence[,] went to Prospect.... Wed[.] 31....Drew milk[,] picked up logs....

The dairy economy brought sufficient prosperity for many Beckwith farmers to build large rambling brick L-shaped farmhouses that echoed the large houses built in Carleton Place right down to the dark brown limestone quoins purchased from the McEwen and McNeely quarries. The dramatic growth of Carleton Place and Smith's Falls into towns during the 1880s provided Beckwith farmers with a growing cash market in the sale of firewood from the bush and swamp lots. They "cut and split trees into four-foot lengths and brought the wood into towns and villages on horse-drawn sleighs."[67] The procession of wood sleighs attracted discriminating buyers in Carleton Place, and every load was inspected carefully for dryness and freedom from knots. Good, clean dry maple was particularly sought after.[68] Between 1880 and 1920 Carleton Place increasingly replaced Ottawa as the major market for all the various kinds of farm produce other than cheese that Beckwith grew. The mills of Horace Brown and Sons from the 1870s through to the 1920s, and particularly after expansion in the late 1880s, drew Beckwith farmers with grain both to grind and to sell. James Morton Brown in a July 1882 letter to his father, Horace Brown, described the types and sizes of purchases made from individual farmers:[69]

> I bought Goth[']s oats (187 bus[hels]) had them delivered last Friday. Got about 43 bus[hels] from Jno. Cameron. Paid 46¢ for both lots but they were well worth it. Got a lot of little jags at 45. Tried to buy Goth[']s peas (about 100 bus[hels.]) He wanted 85¢. I thought it was a little too steep so I let them alone. Have been gristing on wheat almost all last week. Farmers think it kind of curious that Brown can't buy wheat this weather. Don[']t like to be sent to [Samuel Starr] Merrick's [, a flour and feed dealer,] with it. Merrick has come down 10¢ on the bushel.

Plate 234
View looking northeast along Bridge Street from the intersection of Albert Street, Carleton Place, as photographed in August 1983. In contrast with the largely frame structures built in Carleton Place before 1870 (Plate 171), most of the business blocks built along Bridge Street south of the Mississippi River between 1880 and 1920 were brick. Behind the proud range of late Victorian commercial facades rose the balconies and spire of the 1897 town hall tower.

Numerous farmers' sons and daughters who accompanied their parents to sell produce in Carleton Place, Smith's Falls and Perth found the attractions of town life irresistible, prompting the Reverend John May at Franktown in sardonic verse written in 1912 entitled "The Town-ward Rush" to appraise the ultimate cost of leaving the farm behind:[70]

> The world is streaming into Town,
>   The Farm is lone and bare;
> What is the bearing — up or down? —
>   On him who tarries there?
>
> No longer has he help enough
>   To fill the barn or byre;
> But bigger markets take his stuff
>   At prices ever higher.
>
> The more the rustics run away
>   The higher run these prices;
> And smaller acreages may
>   Give wealth in bigger slices.
>
> At any rate, away they run,
>   Sick of the homestead acres,
> To see the world and share the fun
>   Among the merrymakers.
>
> Where is the fun in "seeding down?"
>   In harrowing and hoeing?
> The lads and lasses of the town
>   Have all the pleasure going.
>
> All efforts made, or to be made,
>   To check this mad migration,
> Are vain. An evening promenade
>   Is worth a week's privation.

> Amusement is the winning card;
>   Let him who wants it win it;
> Yet months of farm are not so hard.
>   As is one city minute.
>
> To those distracted night and day
>   Concerning bread and butter;
> Some clad in rags or scant array,
>   Some in starvation utter.
>
> Staid farmer plodding after plow,
>   Say, isn't it a pity
> That no one ever showed you how
>   To frolic in the city?
>
> Though heaped your table, rich your clothes,
>   Your wallet big with bills,
> How poor your life, compared with those
>   Who live on throbs and thrills!
>
> Hurrah for poverty with fun!
>   Hurrah for pain with pleasure!
> Though some who to the city run,
>   Repent it at their leisure.

If there was one motive above all others that prompted the townward rush of Beckwith farmers' sons and daughters, it was the promise of having the freedom of thinking and acting for themselves, rather than being under their father's control as long as he was alive and subject to the restrictions of his will after he died. The pattern of patrilineal inheritance in Beckwith, if it ultimately favoured sons over widows and daughters, also placed financial burdens and social responsibilities on the shoulders of young men who in many instances were either loath or ill equipped to bear them. The unglamorous isolation and monotony of most farmwork, the dwindling pool of rural young men and women their own age to interact with, and the relative isolation from even viewing modern inventions such as telephones, automobiles, phonographs and the like was bad enough. But to be under one's father's control and direction in running a farm until his death, and then to be obligated by the terms of the father's will to look after his mother, to pay off brothers sums of money as their share, and to provide unmarried sisters with a home, became increasingly an unattractive proposition. Enough Beckwith men continued to do it for Edward Kidd to claim as late as 1943 that most of the better farms in the township "as a rule, passed from father to son — usually the youngest son".[71] By the time they inherited the property these sons who stayed on in Beckwith possessed but a fraction of their original drive, carrying on as best they could using the agricultural methods with which they had been raised.

A sampling of Beckwith wills between 1881 and 1920 reveals the burdens inheritance placed on younger sons. Duncan McLaren in leaving the homestead on lot six in the fourth concession to his son William in 1885, asked him, "as I know he will[,] to give to my daughters [Margaret, Janet and Christina] a pleasant and cheerful home as long as they remain unmarried", to make payments of money to four brothers and three sisters within three years, and asked the daughters "to assist their brother in the household work while they live with him in the same manner that they would have assisted me" in return for ten dollars paid each sister yearly "for their dress as long as they remain unmarried."[72] George McLaren (whose 1874 journal is excerpted in previous chapters) in his 1886 will divided his extensive farms among his four sons Colin, Donald, Duncan and Peter, and directed that cash payments and livestock be given to his daughters Mary Ann and Margaret. McLaren's widow was given use of the homestead dwelling house and the outbuildings, paid fifty dollars annually, and was further given "1 mare, 1 cow, 2 sheep, 2 pigs, all poultry, beds and bedding, household furniture, [and] a way to Church as often as she desires to go there."[73] James McFarlane in 1891 left his farm on the east half of lot 24 in the tenth concession to his nephew John McFarlane provided he pay his widow "Agnes $120/year & shall allow her the full & entire use of the dwelling,...and he shall also supply her with all necessary fuel & [a] sufficient share of the farm produce for her household use".[74] Abraham Dowdall in his 1900 will left the homestead on the east

Plate 235
A photograph of some eighty labourers and children at the Canada Lumber Company sawmill, formerly the Gillies and McLaren sawmill, at Carleton Place, taken ca. 1888. It is unlikely that the young children shown with bare feet in the front row of this group actually were allowed to work in this large sawmill. It is equally unlikely that these labourers wore vests, jackets and bowler or boater hats to work, instead donning them and bringing children along for the novelty of having their photograph taken. Behind them, in the distance on the south bank of the river can be seen the frame woollen mill of John McDonald and John Brown on the left and the new four storey roller mill of Horace Brown on the right. Private collection.

half of lot four in concession twelve to be passed on by his wife Ann to his son George, provided George pay cash sums to his eight brothers and sisters, and provided he give his widowed mother and sisters Dora and Mary "a home on the farm...while they remain unmarried and desire to remain on said farm...with necessary meat, drink, clothing, lodging and attendance."75

The examples are numerous, of farmers leaving sons with the responsibility of caring for their widowed mothers and unmarried sisters. Duncan Scott in 1905 had a "house in town" to leave his widow, but left his son Robert along with the homestead on lots eighteen and nineteen of the eighth concession and lot eighteen in the ninth the responsibility of providing "a home for my daughters Lizzie & Mary on the farm as long as they remain single,...furnish[ing] them with food...[and] giv[ing] them the lifestyle to which they are accustomed."76 William McNeely left his property on lot sixteen in the eleventh concession to his son William in 1908 provided he allow his widowed mother to use half the dwelling house, half the orchard and garden, "provided he supply [her]...with all the good dry, split wood she should need for cooking & heating..., vegetables & milk, butter &

other provisions which she may be used to."[77] William Duff in 1910 left the family farm on lots nine and ten in the eleventh concession jointly to daughters Annie Elexey and Denysa rather than to his sons Alexander and William.[78] In leaving all the homestead to his son Robert in his 1911 will, Thomas Nesbitt not only charged him with boarding, lodging, keeping, clothing and giving his daughter Eva medical attendance as long as she remained unmarried, but she was also to be allowed "the privilege of continuing to keep fowl in the same manner as she has been doing."[79] Franktown blacksmith James Anderson in his 1916 will directed that his sister "Zelda Kathleen Anderson shall have her home with my wife as long as she wishes to remain a member of the household, as heretofore, and to have the sheep out at Mrs. Currie's and John Roe's".[80]

As these examples reveal, the structure of inheritance in Beckwith between 1881 and 1920 not only placed financial burdens on sons, but also created numerous extended households in which widowed mothers jealously guarded their control of their rooms, and presided as matriarchs, especially in those homes where inheritance of the homestead passed through their hands to the son. The social significance of the lithographed portraits of Queen Victoria that hung in many Beckwith parlours may well lie in the image of the reigning widow monarch serving to justify attempts by widows to maintain preeminence in the household as farmsteads passed from fathers to sons. If despite the patrilineal bias of monarchical succession, Victoria presided over the British empire at its zenith, the widows of Beckwith in their relative actual powerlessness in the patrilineal handing down of homesteads, used the image of Victoria in tandem with the role prescribed for them by the moral revolution to cement their own sense of matriarchal precedence in their own households within local society.

The townward rush of sons and daughters seeking to escape parental control and influence was augmented by the visible physical evidence of decline in Beckwith from the 1880s onward. The declining population and the consolidation of farms left some 21 uninhabited houses in 1891 and the ruins of past enterprises. "Go into Ramsay or Beckwith in any direction", remarked William Cliff in the Carleton Place *Central Canadian* in 1890, "and your eye will soon catch sight of tottering stone structures with immense chimneys still standing."[81] In the Derry vicinity, for example, there were numerous reminders of the declining number of people the land now supported:[82]

> There were the remains of the log causeway leading along the seventh line to the ancient stone church within whose roofless walls Derry people of other days had worship[p]ed. There were the remains of a log house where once a man named McDonald had lived and who had made whiskey on a large scale. There were traces of an old schoolhouse on the McDiarmid place. There was a hill on [Joseph Kidd's] farm...on which grew a few plum trees, and which was strewn with whitened limestone slabs. Here had once stood a house, burned to the ground before it was occupied, and here there had later been a limekiln. A deserted home is a ghostly place. A few apple trees run wild; traces of furrows in [land now fit only for] pasture; an occasional broken down fence. All these told of some hardy pioneer who had once bravely started out to make a place for himself and his family. Finally defeated by repeated years of unrecompensed toil, he had to give it all up and find a home for himself elsewhere.

The small villages and hamlets of Beckwith felt the influence of the declining rural population, and particularly so in the southern concessions where four generations of cultivation had effectively depleted the shallow layer of vegetable mould once covering the patches of limestone plain interspersed between swamps. The cheese factories at Ashton, Black's Corners, Franktown and Prospect were the only forms of manufacturing left in these villages by the turn of the century, apart from the gristmill which continued to operate at Ashton, a stockyard at Franktown where horses and livestock were loaded onto railway cars, and a small tannery at Prospect operated by James Box.[83] The potashery at Ashton was only a memory by 1894,[84] and the large old tan

Plate 236
A group of women members of the Carleton Place Canoe Club paddling away from the town upstream toward Lake Park, with the new Findlay stove factory in the background, as photographed ca. 1903. Even as late as the turn of the century the streets of Carleton Place presented a fascinating blend of stylish large new brick houses and pioneer Beckwith homes. In the distance on the left in this photograph can be seen one of Carleton Place's earliest houses, a log building which appears to have a fireplace chimney in one of the gables. The long storage shed on the Findlay premises testified to the growing volume of stove production, but increasingly by the 1890s and beyond town inhabitants sought to escape from their industrial environment to a more pastoral locale. Forms of recreation such as this were unknown to the women of rural Beckwith. National Archives of Canada negative no. PA-58045.

bark pits at Prospect were a mystery to young people growing up in the 1880s and 1890s.[85] The numerous shoemakers, weavers and other artisans, the doctors and tradesmen who had conducted business in these villages at mid-century became unable to compete with larger establishments and specialists in regional towns and against mass production in distant cities producing a wider variety of consumer goods that sold locally at a lower cost. There was the occasional holdout such as Andrew Dunlop on the twelfth line of Beckwith who in an 1888 advertisement informed Beckwith, Ramsay and Huntley inhabitants that he was "prepared to do all kinds of country and custom work" weaving.[86] Villages increasingly became centred on cheese factories, post offices, general stores, schools, blacksmith shops and churches, with the occasional extra carpenter and tradesman employed at building the large new brick houses that were replacing the older log structures.

The depopulation of southern Beckwith caused the village of Franktown in particular to become but a shadow of the village it had been in the 1850s and 1860s, as excerpts from a piece of verse entitled "Franktown Past and Present" written along the lines of Goldsmith's *The Deserted Village* by the Reverend John May about 1910 suggest:[87]

The decline of business in Franktown and Ashton is shown by the contrasting directory entries in 1869 and 1898 (Appendices 26 to 31). The Franktown correspondent of the Carleton Place *Herald* in 1898 attempted to imitate the boosterism of regional town promoters by boasting that the village had "at least two of a kind of almost every kind of business known among us", including the smithies of James Henderson and Robert White, the carpenter shop of William Pendergast, the hotels of William Murdock and Mrs. Elizabeth Loney, the Valley Queen cheese factory; Peter McEwen's

This village saw a lively rush
When Ottawa was still a "bush."
Two highways intersected here:
Stage coaches crossed from far and near
Discharging passengers and freight:
Flourishing stores kept open late:
Two fine hotels, aglow with light,
Were vocal far into the night
With song, and glee, and rustic dance,
Toned with a "scrap" or two, perchance,
A jolly frolic place as yet,
For then the village still was "wet."
Two or three lively business men
Made tidy little fortunes then:
Labourers had enough to do:
Good wages for their labour, too:
Mechanics, artisans, and such
Had work enough, if not too much.
The tailor stitched with all his might:
The cooper thumped his barrel tight:
The brisk shoemaker pegged away
More than a dozen hours a day:
All were as busy then as bees
Until the RAILWAY banished these.
The engine crushed the Village legs
Much as the house-wife mashes eggs;
And left it moaning nigh to death,
With feeble pulse and gasping breath.

O for the golden days of yore! —
The Church was crowded to the door:
Two doctors fired their dead-shot pills
Full fifty miles, at mortal ills;
The great Van Amburgh brought his Show
To Franktown, sixty years ago:...
He halted at no other town:
All mustered here to see the clown,
The lion, elephant, chimpanzee,

And lots of things that tickle fancy.
As for the fairs on village green,
Their match could nowhere else be seen:
One deafening din of bullock roar!
Buyers and sellers by the score....
The buyer "settles," and departs:
Settlers go home with joyous hearts
And swollen pockets. Night sets in,
And ends the fair, the fight, the din.

Those days are gone. Those scenes are fled.
Poor dear old Franktown hangs her head.
Not hers the fault. Her sons are grand:
Her daughters, best in all the land!
Yet, still she droops and fades away:
Sad contrast to her early day.
No Amburgh now unfolds his tent:
No tavern rings with merriment:
No stage-coach blows its rousing horn:
The Fair, of all its splendours shorn;
The tailor, cooper, cobbler gone!
Two doctors? — No! nor even one!
In the still necessary store
One customer for ten of yore!
The streets are silent as the grave:
The whole place darksome as a cave:
The houses stand; but, on the street
You're startled if a face you meet!
The Agent now avoids the place:
Seldom a stranger shows his face:
The traveller likes it not a bit —
No place to eat, or sleep, or sit!
No provender for man or beast
Where once* was spread a DUCAL feast!
Wayfarers give it the "go-by;"
For Franktown, once so "wet," is "dry."...
For be it clearly understood
This wild old place, at last, is GOOD.

---

* An allusion to the Duke of Richmond passing through in 1819.

Plate 237
An encampment of women and children at the Lake Park tenting and picnicking grounds on Mississippi Lake in Beckwith, two miles upstream from Carleton Place, as photographed ca. 1890. As Carleton Place grew more sophisticated in the late nineteenth century, a corresponding need was felt by members of the town's middle class to escape to a more rustic setting. While their men and older boys remained at work in Carleton Place, the women set up camp complete with chairs, tables, cookstoves and even formal clothing brought out from town. By secluding their young daughters from the children of labourers in Carleton Place, these middle class women were contributing to the social stratification of town society and also to the moral revolution. The rustic pleasures of camping included improvising a hammock from barrel staves. National Archives of Canada negative no. PA-135193.

combined post office, stationery store and flour and feed business; and Robert Ferguson's shoe repair shop. "We have no resident physician", the Franktown booster was forced to admit, "which is sometimes inconvenient[;] notwithstanding the disadvantage we are a healthy people, and we might add in this connection, that we are not yet in a position to support an undertaker.

Despite protestations "that altogether we are a well-to-do thriving community and we know it",[88] the patterns of parish boundaries and school attendance between 1891 and 1921 reveal how much more rapidly southern Beckwith was depopulating than were the northern concessions. The Franktown-centred Methodist mission of Beckwith, Montague and Marlborough in 1875 was one of the poorest missions in the Perth District.[89] Even with the building of Poole's chapel in northern Montague and another in southeastern Drummond followed by a brick church and parsonage at Gillies' Corners in 1901, the Beckwith, Drummond and Montague Methodist circuit did not survive past the 1920s.[90] By 1919 the attendance at St. James Anglican Church at Franktown had fallen to the extent that it was grouped with three parishes in northern Montague as the "Parish of Montague with Franktown, and the 1837 rectory at Franktown was abandoned in favour of a newer 1907 rectory built at Nowlan's Corners in Montague.[91]

A comparison of attendance in school sections four and nine underlines the more rapid outflow of population taking place in southern Beckwith during the 1890s, 1900s and 1910s. S.S. No. 9 was located in the northernmost corner of Beckwith and was almost wholly attended by students of Scottish origin. The number of students attending school in this section declined by between one-eighth to one-third between 1893 and 1920.[92] A school inspector in 1905 referred to this as "One of the richest sections of [Lanark] County,"[93] Other school sections in which most pupils and parents were of Scottish origin and in which there was a supply of fertile land were similarly complimented. The attendance at S.S. No. 5 on the east section of the seventh line was small in 1905, "but few schools in the county have to their credit a larger number of graduates who have taken prominent positions in our land", commented inspector F.L. Michell. Similarly, the Derry school was judged "an excellent section, and like No. 5 it has sent out numerous young people to lives of usefulness."[94] By contrast, the number of students attending S.S. No. 4 at Prospect in the easternmost corner of Beckwith, most of whom were of Irish origin, by 1920 fell by between half and three-quarters the number attending in 1891.[95] The Franktown school section, which also was predominantly Irish in origin, was reported in 1905 as suffering from irregular attendance, and having rough unfenced grounds, while in yet another Irish school section (the Cuckoo's Nest) the schoolhouse was small and worn out.[96]

Despite the aura of declining population; declining villages; declining local trades; and of losing the best and brightest sons and daughters to local towns, to distant cities and to the remote Canadian west; the quality of life for many rural Beckwith inhabitants who remained continued to improve. Through the local post offices at Carleton Place, Ashton, Ashton Station, Franktown, Prospect, Scotch Corners, Tennyson and Gillies' Corners (named Bellcott)[97] Beckwith families began to purchase goods from the mail-order catalogues of Montreal and Toronto department stores. The mass advertising of agricultural implement manufacturers, seed nurseries, patent medicine concocters, religious publishers and temperance crusaders went through the Beckwith post offices along with such American magazines as the *Youth's Companion* and the *Saturday Evening Post* and such Canadian publications as the Montreal *Family Herald and Weekly Star* and the London *Farmer's Advocate*. In 1912 rural free mail delivery was set up in Beckwith, further placing township inhabitants in contact with city stores and manufactures, and in the process not only bypassing the stores and tradesmen of rural Beckwith villages but those of Carleton Place and Smith's Falls as well.[98] Carleton Place merchants responded to this urban competition by introducing the rural telephone to Beckwith.

The coming of the telephone to rural Beckwith in 1915 was initially a project of the Carleton Place board of trade, holding meetings in the Carleton Place town hall and at Ashton and Franktown in early February "of all [persons] interested in a Rural Telephone." It was in the Carleton Place town hall on the 26th day of February that the meeting "to organize a Rural Telephone Company and appoint provisional directors" was held.[99] Very quickly the rivalry that had existed between Franktown and Carleton Place, effectively between southern and northern Beckwith, surfaced to bring about the creation of two telephone companies serving the greater part of rural Beckwith. The Goodwood Rural Telephone Company Limited, with its central at Carleton Place was by far the larger of the exchanges, covering as it did the eight northern concessions of Beckwith,[100] the west end of Goulbourn, and southern Ramsay. It was not until the 1960s that telephone lines were run in to serve cottagers summering at Lake Park. By late September 1915 the Goodwood company had installed some 1,100 poles and was preparing to string the wires along the 44 miles of the route it covered.[101] By contrast, the Beckwith and Montague Rural Telephone Company, with its central at Franktown, was one fifth the size, with only sixty subscribers to match the 309 on the Goodwood

Plate 238
The log cottage of Peter Salter at Lake Park in Beckwith, built in the early 1890s, as photographed ca. 1895. This view shows the natural setting that attracted Carleton Place inhabitants to Allan's Point as a picnicking ground, and later to the summer resort of Lake Park. Salter as the major proprietor of the Lake Park resort and proprietor of the Leland Hotel in Carleton Place built the earliest substantial cottage at Lake Park. As more and more cottages were built in the 1890s and 1900s, including three fanciful octagonal ones, Lake Park became less and less a public resort and increasingly a private retreat for the more well-to-do families of Carleton Place. National Archives of Canada negative no. PA-58042.

exchange.[102] The Beckwith and Montague system served the entire first and second concessions, and those portions of concessions three and four in Beckwith west of lot eighteen.[103] In early January 1916 the Franktown correspondent of the Carleton Place *Herald* reported, "Some telephone messages have been passing over the Beckwith and Montague line and the Goodwood Rural, since the latter was brought into commission by connection with the Bell Central at Carleton Place. The phone is now the most popular and most serviceable institution in these parts."[104]

The telephone, rural-free mail delivery, mass-circulation magazines and rural editions of the daily Ottawa newspapers were all strong modernising influences in Beckwith, but from the 1880s on the many changes in society spurred a sentimental nostalgia about the township's early years. In 1887 a subscriber to the Carleton Place *Herald* urged the first settlers of the vicinity to write down their reminiscences of the early days:[105]

> That brave and hardy generation will soon all be gone. The history of their trials and triumphs will in many cases die with them. At this late date we know very little of the vicissitudes through which they passed. I think it would be well if many of their experiences were placed on record. No doubt, to themselves, some of these experiences — associated as they were in many cases with hard, grinding work — may seem commonplace, but, to the present generation, time has thrown over them a halo of romance, which tends to make them alike profitable and entertaining.

Numerous reminiscences were published in the Carleton Place newspapers, and in 1900 the lone surviving daughter of the Reverend George Buchanan published *The Pioneer Pastor*, a book detailing her father's accomplishments and tribulations as Beckwith's first resident clergyman. A second edition, profusely illustrated, was issued in 1905, and like the first not only sold well in Beckwith but was mailed to relatives in western Ontario and the prairie provinces, stimulating interest in individual family history. Elizabeth Code at Red Deer, Alberta, "was greatly pleased" with the copy sent her by her brother Daniel McCuan in 1901, noting "It brought to mind many a story Mother used to tell about the early days in Beckwith."[106] If township inhabitants had acquired a new sense of time and of short-term memory at the time the railroads were built through the township in the 1860s, from the 1880s to the 1910s Beckwith acquired a long-term memory. Relatives who had settled out in the prairies wrote back home noting "a good many changes in old Beckwith since we left it a year ago" according to the news items they read in the copies of the Carleton Place newspapers they received.[107] These repeated references to "old Beckwith" together with the reminiscences and detailed obituaries published in newspapers, the ruins of old houses and businesses, and the growing emphasis on having memorial gravestones put up in local cemeteries gave Beckwith inhabitants a new appreciation of their local history. In 1914 the Reverend John May published an article entitled "Bush Life in the Ottawa Valley Eighty Years Ago" in the *Papers & Records of the Ontario Historical Society*, based on his own youth in Beckwith[108] which was awarded a medal.

Sentimentality rather than historical accuracy marked this looking back to the past, as shown by the following description in the Carleton Place *Herald* of how the name Goodwood was chosen as the alternative name for the Jock River and for the Goodwood Rural Telephone Company:[109]

> As many of you know the early settlers of Beckwith were Scotch people. When the first settlers wrote home they described the country as "good land". The Scotch for good land is "jock", and hence the origin of Jock as applied to the little stream that flows through [this]...township. In looking for a name for the new rural [telephone] line that is to run in the vicinity of the Jock the English fitted the situation, hence the name Goodwood.

Plate 239
Three cottages at Lake Park as photographed in the summer of 1904. In the 1890s and 1900s the more prominent inhabitants of Carleton Place built private summer cottages at Lake Park. At the time this photograph was taken the single storey octagonal cottage on the far left was owned by William H. Allen, editor of the Carleton Place Herald. *The middle cottage was built for John A. Bangs, manager of the Bank of Ottawa in Carleton Place. The cottage in the foreground belonged to Robert Haldane Cram who was employed by the Canadian Pacific Railway. The Allen cottage was called "Ingle Nook" and the Cram cottage was named "Idle Wyld". The foliage on the Cram cottage obscures the turret on the far right. Photograph courtesy of Elizabeth Alexander.*

Similarly, when a wooden plaque was placed above the front entrance of St. James Anglican church at Franktown in 1913, it erroneously suggested that the church was built in 1833, and when it was replaced by a datestone in the 1920s the date of the congregation's founding, 1822, rather than the year in which the church was built was incised into it.

Historic commemorations were held. In early September 1915 hundreds of Beckwith inhabitants gathered at the ruins of the 1934 Church of Scotland house of worship on the seventh concession line to commemorate the arrival of the Reverend George Buchanan almost a century previously. The heroic prose of the occasion masked Buchanan's unhappy fate in the 1930s, as the following excerpt shows:[110]

> Commissioned by the Edinburgh Presbytery of the Church of Scotland, to be the first ambassador to unfurl the old blue banner of the covenant and to plant the standard of Zion in the new

Plate 240
The Queen's Royal Hotel, Lake Park, built in the 1890s and operated by Peter P. Salter as the centre-piece of a summer resort, as photographed ca. 1900 by Annie Elexey Duff. This summer resort attracted large crowds from towns throughout the Ottawa valley, and particularly the city of Ottawa throughout the 1890s and 1900s. Most inhabitants of rural Beckwith during these two decades were tied down to their farms by the dairy economy, with two milkings every day, and little opportunity or inclination after their labours to slip away to a resort. In 1910, following a plebiscite, Beckwith forbade the sale of liquor within township boundaries, bringing the Lake Park resort into decline. Photograph courtesy of Kathy Ogg-Moss.

country, then a wilderness, wild, the brave servant of God made his way to Beckwith and for many years laboured faithfully among the early settlers.

In May 1919 a meeting was called in the township hall at Black's Corners "to discuss the advisability of holding a Centennial to commemorate the *one hundredth* anniversary of the coming of the first settlers to the Township of Beckwith".[111] Professor Edward Kidd from Queen's University recommended that a history of early Beckwith be prepared,[112] but instead a day of festivities including

Plate 241
Boiling maple sap on the John Ferguson farm, lot 22, concession 4, Beckwith, as photographed ca. 1915. In distinct contrast with American-settled Leeds County to the south where most evaporators were placed in sugar houses, many Beckwith farmers retained the custom of boiling sap outdoors. The Reverend John May in 1912 reminisced about the role of women in making maple syrup in early nineteenth century Beckwith:

The tapper's clink rings joyous in my ears	But now I marvel when I think of men
Across the mottled intervening years...	Leaving a task to daughter or to wife
Whether the WOMEN of the family	So like to shatter health, or shorten life...
Relished that note, must ever doubtful be.	Her face half-blistered, but her shoulders cold —
It heralded for them a slavish moil,	Such was sap-boiling in the days of old:
A time for boys to sport, for girls to toil!	No cozy structure sheltered from the blast:
How little recked we of their labours then!	No sleigh, sap-laden, thro' the forest passed.

Photograph courtesy of Mary and Victor Shail.

picnicking, swimming, races, and speeches was held along McCreary's shore on the Mississippi near Lake Park.[113]

Beckwith's new romantic historical sense of itself developed out of its experience of decline in the face of urban pulls and urban growth, and from the perceptions of sons and daughters out west who looked back to Beckwith as an old settlement or homeland. The sense of Beckwith as a historic place of origin was also the creation of the editors of the two Carleton Place newspapers, the *Central Canadian* and the *Herald*, featuring as they did reminiscences of early days in the township and lengthy obituaries from the 1880s on into the 1920s. A substantial proportion of the readers of these papers were the brothers and sisters, sons and daughters who had migrated west, and with this in mind, local editors described local events in sufficient detail and in such sentimental prose as to make the locality even more cherished by former inhabitants spurring them to continue subscribing to keep abreast of contemporary events. They wrote back to Beckwith requesting photographs of various relatives, and many of them returned to visit, including young men and women who had been born and bred out west, who had been raised to look upon Beckwith as some half-familiar homeland to which they had some undefineable tie. The local reality was viewed with equal sentimentality despite men and women leaving for futures elsewhere, and most visibly to go to live in Carleton Place. The triumph of sentimentality extended even through the years of World War One in Beckwith, but the depleted ranks of returning men marked the decline of even sentimentality in local society during the 1920s and beyond.

Endnotes

1. Brown, *Founded Upon A Rock*, pp. 103-104.
2. Donald M. Wilson, *The Ontario and Quebec Railway* (Belleville, Ontario: Mika Publishing Company, 1984), p. 18.
3. Ibid., p. 33.
4. *Carleton Place Herald*, 11 January 1882.
5. Ibid., 26 November 1884.
6. Ibid., 14 December 1887.
7. Ibid., 22 December 1896.
8. Glenn Lockwood, "Former Canadian Pacific Railway Station, Carleton Place, Ontario," Agenda Paper, Historic Sites and Monuments Board of Canada, 1991 n.p.
9. *Carleton Place Herald*, 8 February 1908.
10. George E. Findlay, "Findlay Stoves Answer Energy Crisis" in *Early Canadian Life* (January 1980), p. 6.
11. Eric Arthur and Thomas Ritchie, *Iron: Cast and Wrought Iron in Canada From the Seventeenth Century to the Present* (Toronto: University of Toronto Press, 1982), p. 189.
12. *Carleton Place Herald*, 23 December 1902.
13. Ibid., 1 August 1905.
14. Ibid., 11 April 1911.
15. Ibid., 19 December 1911.
16. Ibid., 30 December 1925.
17. Brown, *Lanark Legacy*, p. 244.
18. Idem, *Founded Upon A Rock*, p. 105.
19. Idem, *Lanark Legacy*, p. 244.
20. Reid, *Development of the Woollen Industry in Lanark*, p. 25.
21. Earl H. Ritchie, "Bates and Innes, Limited: The First Fifty Years, 1907-1957" (unpublished manuscript provided courtesy of Agnes Iveson, Carleton Place), pp. 1-4.
22. Ibid., pp. 4, 6-7.
23. Marina Quattrocchi, "The Old Bates Home: Review Home of the Week" in *Carleton Place Review*, 19 June 1975, p. 2.
24. Ritchie, "Bates and Innes, *pp. 6-7.*
25. Charlotte Whitton, *A Hundred Years A-Fellin'* (Braeside, Ontario: Gillies Brothers Limited, 1943), pp. 64, 70.
26. Arnold Gillies Muirhead, "John Gillies' Businesses after 1874" (unpublished paper written in September 1985, provided courtesy Howard M. Brown, Ottawa), p. 3.
27. *Carleton Place Herald*, 13 July 1887.
28. Ibid., 29 October 1884.
29. Ibid., 11 March 1885; and 20 May 1885.
30. Brown, *Founded Upon A Rock*, p. 106.
31. *Carleton Place Herald*, 25 March 1885.
32. Howard M. Brown, "Story of the Telephone in Carleton Place District" in *Carleton Place Canadian*, 18 October 1962.
33. Idem, *Founded Upon A Rock*, pp. 109-111.
34. *Carleton Place Herald*, 6 August 1884.
35. Ibid., 11 February 1885.
36. Ibid., 18 July 1883; and 23 July 1884.
37. Ibid., 18 March 1885.
38. Thomas A. Hillman, "A Statutory Chronology of Eastern Ontario, 1788-1981" in Donald H. Akenson, ed., *Canadian Papers in Rural History* (Gananoque: Langdale Press, 1984) IV:308.
39. *Carleton Place Herald*, 15 September 1891.
40. Ibid., 22 December 1896.
41. Dianne Tysick, "Manufacture of bricks once booming business" in the *Carleton Place Canadian*, 7 October 1981, p. B1.
42. *A Review of Prosperous Towns in the Counties of Lanark and Grenville*, (published in 1909), loaned courtesy of the Carleton Place and Beckwith Historical Society, Carleton Place.
43. Canada Department of Mines, William A. Parks, *Report on the Building and Ornamental Stones of Canada* (Ottawa: Government Printing Bureau, 1912) I:180-181.
44. Marion MacRae and Anthony Adamson, *Cornerstones of Order: Courthouses and Town Halls of Ontario, 1784-1914* (Toronto: Clarke Irwin, 1983), p. 246.
45. *Carleton Place Herald*, 22 December 1896.

46 Ritchie, "Bates and Innes", p. 9.
47 *Carleton Place Herald*, 6 August 1884.
48 Reid, Development of the Woollen Industry in Lanark, *p. 22.*
49 Gregory S. Kealey and Bryan D. Palmer, *Dreaming of what Might Be: The Knights of Labor in Ontario, 1880-1900* (New York : Cambridge University Press, 1982), pp. 88, 399.
50 14 October 1988 interview with Willard Hawthorne, Almonte.
51 *Carleton Place Central Canadian,* 23 December 1897.
52 24 August 1981 intervview with William F. Findlay, Carleton Place.
53 26 October 1905 Carleton Place newspaper clipping in scrapbook loaned by the late Hazel Davis.
54 *Carleton Place Herald*, 26 August 1863, p. 2, cols. 6-7.
55 Ibid., 15 June 1870, p. 2, col. 5.
56 Howard M. Brown, "Writer Tells How Lake Shores and Bays Named" in *Carleton Place Canadian*, 12 April 1956.
57 OBCMR, Undated petition from Peter P. Salter and others promoting the construction of an electric railway from Carleton Place to Lake Park.
58 Doggerel "Lake Park" written by Annie Elexey Duff and Denysa Duff, Orena Villa, Beckwith, in 1900, provided courtesy of Howard M. Brown, Ottawa.
59 *Carleton Place Herald*, 11 February 1902.
60 Ibid., 28 April 1903.
61 Ibid., 4 January 1910.
62 *Carleton Place Central Canadian*, 26 April 1894, 15 May 1894, and 28 May 1894.
63 OBCMR, By-law no. 278 of Beckwith township council.
64 "Jimmy Johnson Was A Man of Varied Interests" in Carleton Place Canadian, *31 March 1955.*
65 Journal of Joseph Kidd, excerpted entries for May 1880, loaned courtesy of the late William Livingstone Kidd, Beckwith.
66 Ibid., excerpted entries for May 1899.
67 George E. Findlay, "From Farmyard to Farmhouse: The Findlays of Carleton Place" in Vrenia Ivanoffski and Sandra Campbell, eds., *Exploring Our Heritage: The Ottawa Valley Experience* (Toronto: Arnprior and District Historical Society, 1980), p. 71.
68 Idem, "Findlay Stoves Answer Energy Crisis", p. 6.
69 17 July 1882 letter from James Morton Brown, Carleton Place, to his father, Horace Brown at the Ashland House, New York, loaned courtesy of Howard M. Brown, Ottawa.
70 *Carp (Ontario) Review*, 6 March 1912. I am grateful to Bruce S. Elliott for bringing this item to my attention.
71 Kidd, *The Story of the Derry*, p. 43.
72 OPLCRO, 25 June 1885 will of Duncan McLaren, Beckwith.
73 Ibid., 18 September 1886 will of George McLauren [sic], Beckwith.
74 Ibid., 17 April 1891 estate document of James McFarlane, Beckwith.
75 Ibid., 27 April 1900 will of Abraham Dowdall, Beckwith.
76 Ibid., 16 August 1905 will of Duncan Scott, Beckwith.
77 Ibid., 14 March 1908 will of William McNeely, Beckwith.
78 Ibid., 29 April 1910 will of William Duff, Beckwith.
79 Ibid., 5 April 1911 will of Thomas Nesbitt, Beckwith.
80 Ibid., 29 February 1916 will of James Anderson, Franktown.
81 *Carleton Place Central Canadian*, 6 November 1890.
82 Kidd, "Earlier Part of My Life", p. 50.
83 Ibid., p. 53.
84 OPLCRO, 22 November 1894 will of Peter Gow, Beckwith.
85 Kidd, "Summer Sunday at Home", p. 2.
86 *Carleton Place Herald*, 11 July 1888.
87 Undated newspaper clipping in scrapbook loaned by the late Hazel Davis, Beckwith.
88 *Carleton Place Herald*, 26 July 1898, p. 8, col. 1.
89 L. Bartlett, *"Uncle Joe Little"*, p. 201.
90 NAC reel M-2209 1896-1922 marriage register for the Beckwith, Drummond and Montague Methodist Circuit.
91 Jefferson and Johnson, *Faith of Our Fathers*, p. 62.
92 OBCMR School attendance registers, S.S. No. 9, Beckwith, for 1893 and 1920.
93 Howard M. Brown, "Teaching School Once Hazardous Occupation" in *Carleton Place Canadian*, 9 January 1958.
94 Ibid.
95 OBCMR, School attendance registers for S.S. No. 4, Beckwith, for 1891 and 1920.
96 Brown, "Teaching School".
97 27 February 1988 interview with councillor Alex Bell, Beckwith.
98 McCuan family correspondence, 26 June 1912 letter from Thomas McCuan, Beckwith, to his brother Alex McCuan, Davidson, Saskatchewan; and December 1912 letter from Duncan McCuan, Davidson, to his brother Alex, Beckwith.
99 Ibid., 12 February and 23 February 1915 notice of meeting cards from C.F.R. Taylor, Carleton Place Board of Trade, to Alex McCuan, Beckwith, references 32.5 and 32.6.
100 OBCMR By-law no. 417 of Beckwith township council.
101 *Carleton Place Herald*, 21 September 1915, p. 1,

col. 3.
102 Thomas Grindlay, *A History of the Independent Telephone Industry in Ontario* (Toronto: Ontario Telephone Service Commission, 1975), pp. 257, 272.
103 OBCMR, By-law no. 419 of Beckwith township council.
104 *Carleton Place Herald*, 11 January 1916, p. 5, col. 2.
105 Ibid., 21 December 1887.
106 McCuan family correspondence, 8 April 1901 letter from Elizabeth Code, Springvale farm, Red Deer, to Daniel McCuan, Beckwith.
107 Ibid., 8 January 1894 letter from Elizabeth Code, Red Deer, to Daniel McCuan, Beckwith.
108 May, "Bush Life in the Ottawa Valley", pp. 153-163.
109 *Carleton Place Herald*, 21 September 1915, p. 1, col. 5. The name Goodwood actually comes from the name of the country estate in England of the Duke of Richmond who died on the banks of the Jock in 1819. For more detail on the duke's death, consult the first chapter of this book.
110 Undated clipping in scrapbook loaned by the late Hazel Davis, Beckwith.
111 *Carleton Place Herald*, 20 May 1919, p. 5, col. 1.
112 Undated clipping in scrapbook loaned by the late Hazel Davis, Beckwith.
113 Ibid.

THE MILITARY HERITAGE

Despite the century of peace that Beckwith enjoyed from the time it was created as part of a military settlement, it remained strongly influenced by military events. Although only a small proportion of Beckwith's early settlers were military veterans, and although only a fraction of those given grants in Beckwith after the War of 1812 actually stayed on to settle them, the lingering influence of the Napoleonic wars was distinctly felt. Those immigrants from Perthshire and Wexford who had not actually served in some military capacity against Napoleon in the reactionary atmosphere of counter-revolutionary Britain knew full well the importance of appearing prominent in furthering war production, in recruiting soldiers, and in putting down anything remotely smacking of treachery. Both in oral legend and in printed school lessons the influence of the Napoleonic wars continued. As the decades of peace followed one another, rare events such as William Lyon Mackenzie's fizzle of a rebellion in 1837 and the equally harmless Fenian panics of 1866 and 1870 only served to emphasize the pervasive peacefulness of local society. Beckwith inhabitants looked out upon the rest of the world for military excitement. As the decades wore on, as the militia musters and rifle companies continued to parade, and as the memory of what war actually was like receded, a romantic conception of military valour came to be accepted, culminating in local participation in World War One.

The Crimean war of the mid 1850s and the American civil war of the early 1860s awakened Beckwith inhabitants to the possibility of their welfare being threatened. On the economic level alone, the outbreak of the Crimean war in 1854 crippled the financing of the Brockville and Ottawa railway, leading to bankruptcy in 1856. There was something more than patriotism alone underlying the jubilation at Carleton Place in October 1855 upon learning that the British had captured Sebastopol. James Poole at the *Herald* within "the short space of two hours after the arrival of the telegraphic despatch...had turned out 3,000 copies which were immediately forwarded to the several post-offices in this and the adjoining counties":[1]

> The news of the capture of Sebastopol was received by the inhabitants of our "rising city" with the greatest joy [Poole observed in the next issue of the *Herald*].... In the evening the several buildings were brilliantly illuminated, and a large bonfire lit up the "city park," which was literally covered with parties vieing with each other in throwing fire balls in imitation of the nightly practice of the besiegers and besieged. The "Victoria" fire brigade — a company of boys, — turned out in their uniforms, and conducted themselves in a manner creditable to riper years. Mr. Willis also added something to the pleasure of the evening, by the enlivening music of the highland pipes.

The American civil war in particular spurred concern among regional inhabitants that the infrequent muster of local militia that had taken place annually since the early 1820s was not sufficient protection from potential future invasion, particularly as the imperial government began to reduce the number of British soldiers stationed in Canada. In August 1861 the Carleton Place *Herald* detected "a desire fomenting among the people for military organization" and copied from the Ottawa *Citizen* a warning "that late events in the United States have proved that a raw volunteer force, however gallant, proves ineffective in the field, when called suddenly to take part in the stern realities of war." It was clear that the provincial militia had to be newly organised in preparation for a sudden call to arms. "Far distant be that day when the armed yeomanry of this young nation may be required", James Poole commented, "but in th[e]se days of Revolutionary upheaving within a gunshot of our boundaries, we had better be prepared."[2]

> We have a national existence to sustain, as Canadians [continued Poole], and we have the honor of that Red Cross flag, which waves unassailed and in triumph in every quarter of the globe, to uphold. In view of the tribulations which are fast destroying all constitutional lines in the neighboring Republic, we cannot tell what a day may bring forth, and the quicker the young men of Canada are imbued with a military spirit, the better for our future success as a nation.

James Poole's prose echoed the counter-revolutionary and reactionary attitude of the yeomanry of his grandfather's generation in Ireland who during the late 1790s had quelled the United Irishmen and had staved off invasion by the French. Indeed, in November 1861 Poole stated that the imperial government wished to encourage a military in Canada "so as to make the yeomanry of our land a great wall of defence against which the waves of future invasion may roll in vain."[3] Despite the Reform rhetoric James Poole and Robert Bell presented in the *Herald* advocating representative government, decrying curtailed liberty, and denouncing the privileges of the United Church of England and Ireland, at heart they themselves were products of a counter-revolutionary society. Despite the emphasis on defending the interests of Canada, it is very clear that remaining within the British empire for James Poole was emotionally and militarily important.

It could hardly have been otherwise, with veterans of the Napoleonic campaigns who lived in Beckwith continuing to draw pensions as late as the 1870s and 1880s. James Poole observed in 1862:[4]

> The nucleus of fighting men, if necessary, is among us — soldiers of half a century ago stride on our humble streets, with all the *vihm* of younger days, and their fading orbs of vision flash with a renewed electricity as they listen to brilliant deeds of arms among our American cousins. Where is the resident of our village but can point out that aged soldier — nearly a century old — as he grimly slides along the footpath. He has snuffed the sulphur of twenty battles, and time is almost tired of trying to make inroads on his seasoned frame, and there is another of a younger date, whose rapid locomotion to and from his home in the vicinity tells of a high animal spirit of sufficient volume to supply two average recruits, and again there steps along a pale nervous-looking man, of slight build, whose reminiscences of the Peninsula whiles away the otherwise dull tedium of a winter evening.... [T]here they are, the veterans of a few immortal pages of England's history, with physiognamies like mahogany, and a forty-horse power of willingness to stand in the breach.

James Poole argued in the *Herald* that it was "a useful and beneficial thing for our rising generation to have such venerable vestiges of former deeds of arms among them...at the present time, when both the Imperial Parliament and our local rulers are anxious to foster a military spirit among our young men".[5]

To Poole's horror most Beckwith farmers in 1862, caught up as they were in the cycle of planting, harvesting and threshing, appeared more tentative in their support of a stronger, more active local militia. In late January 1862 when the 5th battalion of Lanark militia (which by that date consisted of Beckwith alone) were paraded by Captain Alexander Fraser, half of them at Franktown and the other half at Carleton Place, it proved impossible to coax "the Beckwith yeomanry to leave agricultural pursuits, shoulder the rifle and knapsack, and rush, thoughtlessly, into the hardships and

Plate 242
A group of neighbours preparing to march in an Orange procession on the outskirts of Franktown, as photographed ca. 1914. Beckwith Orangeism with its annual processions re-enacting the seventeenth century military triumph of William III over James II contributed to the military memory of Beckwith, despite the century of peace the township enjoyed after its settlement. Among the paraphernalia to be found in the Orange halls of Beckwith were swords, banners recalling "the glorious and immortal memory" of battles in 1688 and 1690, and prints of the Battle of the Boyne. Despite the rhetoric of loyalty to King and country and the young man shown here bearing the flag, Orangemen did not strongly press their membership to go overseas. To the contrary, military police apprehended men from local Orange processions to send them off to World War One. Those overseas held 12th of July celebrations in the trenches. Photograph courtesy of Edna and John Porter.

Plate 243
Five Carleton Place area militia members armed against Fenian invasion, as photographed in Brockville at A.C. McIntyre's International Gallery in 1866. These men, James Story, William Dack, Donald Stewart, William Duff and Patrick Tucker, despite their differing ethnic and religious backgrounds, in the face of potential Fenian invasion gave the appearance of being united in the defence of their country. While stationed at Brockville to defend the border, Tucker, the one Irish Catholic in this group, "imbibed rather freely [and] foolishly gave utterance to treasonable language, denouncing our good Queen, in very ugly and unmanly terms, and wishing success to the Fenian cause." He received a sentence of three months imprisonment for his behaviour which the Brockville Recorder trusted, would "teach him and all others of his class to be careful what they say in these troubled times." The Carleton Place and Beckwith Historical Society.

dangers of a soldier's life" in forming an active service company. Only "about twenty or thirty men, after some coaxing and promises of being 'left at home to drill,' stepped out of the No. one Company, and only two out of [the] other 3 Companies, as volunteers, [only after receiving] the pledge of the Lieut. Colonel that they were *not to be called away from home.*"[6] James Poole and Robert Bell, both of whom had ambitions of rising in the military ranks, did not believe "that there is any lack of loyalty, or willingness to defend their country on the part of Beckwith people" but rather had a different approach been taken "a company of GRENADIERS might have been raised here, second to none in Canada for looks, courage and bravery." As proof of this point, they held a public meeting at Carleton Place on January 25th to organise an independent rifle company at which some seventy volunteers signed the muster roll.[7]

The ambivalence of Beckwith farmers toward joining an active service company stemmed in large part from the reports that came back to them from a few local men taking part in the American

Plate 244
Robert H. Cram and Raymond Bangs planting potatoes on the Daniel Cram homestead on Glen Isle, lot 18, concession 12, Beckwith, as photographed by Gertrude Cram in 1916. Carleton Place inhabitants went out to Beckwith farms to assist in planting and harvesting larger crops to supply the war effort. The fine clothes worn by Cram and Bangs belie their more urbane regular employment respectively as railroader and civil engineer. The ca. 1840 stone farmhouse in the background was uninhabited between 1900 and 1910 until Robert Cram purchased it as a summer home. His decision to take responsibility for the house his father had built three generations earlier is a measure of the growing sentimentality with which Beckwith inhabitants viewed themselves and their past. Photograph courtesy of Elizabeth Alexander.

civil war. One anonymous volunteer from Carleton Place wrote a letter to the *Herald* in May 1862 from his military camp in the state of Mississippi, describing the desolation and futility of agriculture in a countryside where the "rebels have stolen all the poultry, hogs, sheep, and everything in the eating line." If Beckwith farmers did not appreciate stories of agricultural land turned to waste, of houses emptied of inhabitants, of men impressed into armies against their will, and of women and children fleeing in terror, neither were they impressed by accounts of inept officers:[8]

> If you want the personification of pure know-nothingism, [the anonymous correspondent from Carleton Place serving in the American federal army continued], you will find it in a soldier of any rank from High Private to Brigadier General. Ask a man mounted on a fiery steed, covered with feathers, epaulettes, and sword, at the head of a mile and a half of glittering bayonets and muskets, all marching in one direction, "Which way General?" he will answer, "I don't know, Sir; was ordered to take the rear of this Division, that is all I know."

What was most disturbing to the sensibilities of Beckwith inhabitants after half a century of peace were the gruesome battlefield reports. The most haunting of these was written by Dr. Willard Hurd, younger brother of Dr. W.H. Hurd at Carleton Place, who left in late July 1863 "to enlist as a soldier in one of the Regiments of the Northern army" in his native country who "could not be persuaded to remain."[9] It was a sadder and disillusioned young man who wrote back to friends in Beckwith from amidst the carnage of the campaign in Virginia two years later. "O! it is horrible to think that within a few days or even hours, very many of our friends...now rejoicing in health and strength, will be ghastly, mangled and bleeding heaps of clay", he wrote, adding, "I often shudder to think that my example of coming here came near inducing others to do so:"[10]

> The nearest human imitation of Hell is a battle-field. Men, in every attitude possible for the human body to assume, and exhibiting every variety of wound, from the small round hole of the rifle ball...to the frightfully mangled remains of one struck by a shell or solid shot. A leg here, an arm there, a head or portion of one yonder, while at one side may be seen a portion of mangled flesh and crushed bones, which the most careful examination would fail to discover what was its position in the body. Guns, some broken or bent by shot, equipments, knapsacks, haversacks, canteens, swords and bayonets, drums, cannon, the carriage broken or otherwise disabled and the piece abandoned — cannon balls and shell, whole or in fragments — the earth torn up, fences overturned and perhaps on fire, everything broken or bent, crushed, smashed, splintered, trod upon by horses or the feet of men, or run over by the wheels of the ponderous cannon and crushed into the earth, — even the bodies of men, the dead and wounded alike — horses, dead and dying, the wounded shouting, screaming, praying and cursing, singing and moaning, and all, at times, crying for 'water,' 'water.' Blood is usually more plent[iful], for almost every step of ground is slippery with gore; every few feet having its separate pool of blood.

Willard Hurd attempted also to convey to his friends back in Beckwith the terrible deafening layers of sound that enveloped the ongoing butchery:[11]

> The one continuous roar or roll of musketry — now almost dying away to a few scattered shots — then more and more rapid become the discharges until it again breaks into [a] long low roar.... The loud and sullen "boom" of the cannon, followed by the hissing, shrieking, unearthly sound of the shell as it flies upon its deadly mission, or the duller, rushing and less terrifying sound of the round shot. A few stray rifle balls may pass within a few feet of you with a peculiar "bizz" which is not to be described.... And still, above all this almost deafening noise and tumult, can be always heard the shouting and yelling of the combatants, and when upon a charge the cheering of the attacking party drowns almost every other sound, and if the charge fails the victors will set up a counter shout, to which the previous shouting and cheering was nothing. This is as I have seen many battlefields. Many much less terrible than I have described, and *many far, far* more so. Yes, upon every battle-field, when seen immediately after a fight, there is something so indescribably terrible that no words that I or any one else can make use of can describe it. What destruction and desolation.

With reports such as this coming from the American battle lines in the early 1860s, it is hardly surprising that many Beckwith farmers wavered between their traditional loyalty to military superiors and a quite understandable dread of similar carnage laying waste the farms that had been developed for two generations. James Poole's ability to enlist local farmers to form a volunteer company is a telling indication of the transformation that already had taken place in Beckwith society. Previously, the leadership and control exercised by superior officers appointed by the

Plate 245
The junior war canoe of the Carleton Place Canoe Club paddling upstream away from the heart of the town, as photographed ca. 1905. The term "war canoe" partly alluded to the fierce rivalry that existed between canoe clubs from various regional towns, but it also reflected the growing use of military terms in the local vocabulary as school readers, church hymnbooks, newspapers and even children's books became suffused with military references. When the Carleton Place war canoe competed before the Duke and Duchess of York (later George V and Queen Mary) at Ottawa in 1901, H.C. Small and W.H. Hooper of Carleton Place were presented with their South Africa war medals by the duke. Military service was perceived to confer social status in the years leading up to World War One. For names see appendix 34. National Archives of Canada negative no. C-29322.

provincial administration reflected the strong role of government in establishing Beckwith as a settlement, in feeding and providing the first settlers with implements during the initial settlement period, in settling clergymen, funding churches, building schools, in eventually appointing magistrates, and paying military pensions. The ability of Robert Bell and James Poole to recruit a large number of local farmers where local militia officers had failed is striking testimony as early as 1862 to how local society had been wrested away from its strong reliance on government for leadership and came to be more voluntarist in spirit under the leadership of local merchants and capitalists instead. Despite the anger of many Beckwith farmers at the high price they continued to pay for the Brockville and Ottawa railway to the profit of Carleton Place entrepreneurs such as Robert Bell and James Poole, Bell's strong financial clout as a major forwarder in the local provisioning trade in particular explains his ability to persuade Beckwith inhabitants to form a rifle company. Hence when members of this company assembled on New Year's day 1863, "dressed in the coats and accoutrements forwarded by Government from Quebec" they were drilled in front of James Poole's Carleton Place *Herald* printing office by Robert Bell Jr., Esq., nephew of Robert Bell. These "exercises were particularly admired by several old veterans who were on the ground", the *Herald* reported,

Plate 246
Herb Griffith (kneeling on the left) and his brothers (left to right) Jack, Robert and Fred and an anonymous friend, from Black's Corners posing as military looters in a ca. 1900 photograph taken by C.C. Pelton of Carleton Place. This jovial group photograph was the obvious product of a generation that had not known war, no more than had their parents or grandparents. In part the new romanticism of things military increased proportionally to the distance in time from the Napoleonic wars. The Bytown Gazette *suggested in 1838 "that the farms in the worst state of cultivation had been in general free grants to men for their military or naval services," but a scant generation later Malcolm Cameron extolled the old soldiers as "a superior class of settlers." Photograph courtesy of Pauline Wright.*

"and the men who composed the company being, generally speaking, in the prime of youth, performed the evolutions with great credit."[12]

The new rifle company was no sooner created, than the Reform political connections and Carleton Place residence of its two main promoters, James C. Poole and Robert Bell, created problems. When backers of the rifle company requested a grant of fifty pounds from Beckwith council to help build a drill shed at Carleton Place, the councillors called a meeting of township ratepayers on February 20th 1863 "very largely attended by the inhabitants from the front and middle of the township." James Poole commented in the *Herald*:[13]

> We believe the matter was very thoroug[h]ly canvassed in the neighborhood of Franktown and along the front of the township, and through some misconception of the proper motive embraced in the petition every man that could be drawn out filed his appearance in opposition to the measure, and felt that they had done wonders when they had secured its defeat.

Plate 247
Private Andrew T. Hughton from the vicinity of Franktown, and Captain Stearne Tighe Edwards, originally from Franktown, as photographed in their uniforms. Hughton, shown here in the setting of his family farm east of Franktown, was one of numerous recruits from rural Beckwith who managed to survive the warfare of the trenches. Edwards, by contrast, as a pilot in the Royal Naval Air Service showed singular skill to merit him the Distinguished Service Cross in 1917. Tragically, both men shared a similar fate, Hughton dying two weeks before the armistice, and Edwards the day after, neither of them from military wounds. From a private collection and the National Archives of Canada, negative no. C-88238, respectively.

Three years later in 1866 a second deputation requested the Beckwith council to help fund the construction "of a large shed, to serve the double purpose of a drill shed and a hall for...exhibitions" of the Beckwith Agricultural Society. "Will our readers believe it", Poole exclaimed in the *Herald*, "Messrs. [James] Conn, [Alexander] Ferguson, and [Thomas] Kidd opposed the notion, on the ground of local feeling and seemed afraid some of their constituents would think that Carleton Place was getting too much of the Township money." If Poole's account is to be trusted, one of the township councillors candidly admitted "he would like to encourage the Rifles, as he was somewhat afraid of an invasion of our soil by the Fenians; but he was afraid to vote for a copper towards their encouragement without asking leave from the people who voted for him to be councillor."[14]

The Beckwith council was not in principle opposed to a drill hall being built, as James Conn made clear in a letter to the *Herald*, but rather simply wished to consult with the electorate[15] in a township severely polarised between Carleton Place and southern Beckwith. But if the occasional councillor worried about a Fenian invasion, clearly most Beckwith inhabitants did not:[16]

> In our own township [James Poole warned in 1863] the rich farmers who object to pay a dollar out of their gains for the shelter or encouragement of volunteers should be taught that a part of the defence of their homes and their hearths depends upon themselves and upon their sons; and that instead of sneering at volunteers for their sacrifice of time and labor, they, themselves must be prepared, by a regular course of drill, for the defence, in case of need of our common country.

What many Beckwith inhabitants actually were sneering at, if they sneered at anything, were Poole's own transparent efforts to use the rifle company to boost his own respectability by being made a captain, notwithstanding the thinning out of the ranks and the difficulty of maintaining a semblance of order. In July 1863 Poole denied a report that the Carleton Place rifle company had been disbanded, but admitted that "a few of the volunteers have withdrawn from the Company, and have absented themselves from drill because the Captain refused to receive their overcoats which were *much damaged*, and to certify that they were in good condition." Furthermore, Poole continued, another member of the company resigned "because he would not be allowed to disturb the Company while at drill." Still other members of Poole's company "of high political mettle, have scarcely got over the excitement of the late election", he remarked, "and do not attend drill because the Captain voted against the candidate of their choice!"[17] In January 1865 Carleton Place school trustees passed a resolution "forbidding the Rifle Company having the use of the School House, in the evenings for drill."[18] Even shortly after its founding, there were only 29 members in this rifle company (Appendix 24) drawn from both Beckwith and Ramsay[19] as contrasted with 64 militia members in Beckwith alone (Appendix 25).[20]

Up until early June 1866 the Carleton Place rifle company was regarded by most Beckwith inhabitants as a group of young men swaggering around to the orders of the self-important James C. Poole. They were perceived to enjoy the masculine camaraderie and competition of friendly shooting matches with the Almonte company of infantry, the young men somewhat self-consciously proud of the dark uniforms they paraded around in.[21] One member of the company, "although repeatedly cautioned by the officers,...persisted in wearing his uniform clothes for days together and even [was found] sleeping in them" until fined for doing so. "The clothing, if not...taken care of, will soon become soiled and unfit for service", commented James Poole.[22] The inhabitants of Carleton Place were sufficiently proud of the rifle company to treat the officers and men to an oyster supper at William Kelly's British Hotel in late March 1866.[23] By contrast, a petition to Beckwith council for a grant of fifty dollars "to be divided in prizes for competition for the best marksmen amongst the members of the Carleton Place Rifle Company" a year earlier was turned down.[24]

The refusal of Beckwith council to take the Carleton Place rifle company seriously suddenly changed after midnight on June 3rd 1866. After having been placed on alert for the previous 24 hours, a hurried despatch was received, ordering the Carleton Place and Almonte volunteer companies to repair to Brockville on a special train at 2:30 in the morning. James Poole described the scene:[25]

> The Carleton Place Rifle Company, commanded by Captain Poole and Lieutenant Brown, were...accompanied to the station by more than 100 of our citizens. At the reqest of Captain Poole, the Rev. J.A. Preston addressed the men.... He urged upon them as they had assumed the uniform and the responsibilities of the British soldiers, to remember two marks which always distinguished the soldiers of the army of Britain, *discipline* and *duty*....

Plate 248
A Beckwith woman and girls humorously posing for a photographer in a haying field near Prospect ca. 1915. In contrast with the 1820s and 1830s when Beckwith women worked alongside men at planting and harvesting crops, by 1910 a new domestic ideal largely confined women to household work. With a large proportion of men off to World War One, many Beckwith women returned to the fields to assist agricultural production for the war effort. In 1900 Jessie Buchanan Campbell commented: The world owes a debt beyond human computation to the patient, industrious, unselfish women who have stood side by side with fathers, husbands and brothers in the stern battle for existence. The pioneer women of Beckwith were noble helpmeets, kind, hospitable, self-forgetful and trustworthy..[and yet] the public has heard little of their struggles, their trials and their achievements. Photograph courtesy of Mary and Victor Shail.

It was a solemn and moving sight, the moonlight giving a dim view of the outline of the ranks, and the friends and relatives moving to and fro as they took leave of those near and dear to them. The conduct of the ladies was particularly worthy of remark; while without doubt there was deep feeling and tears were shed at parting with husbands and brothers, yet the feeling of resignation appeared as deep as that of grief, and they felt, we doubt not, proud that their relatives were discharging their duty in joining the forces who had gone before them at the call of the Government to defend our hearths and homes against the invasion of a lawless band of marauders. As the train left the station, three hearty cheers from the citizens rang the air, which were lustily re-echoed by the true men whom we hope to welcome soon again, back to their peaceful homes.

For Beckwith it was a dramatic leavetaking with an undramatic conclusion, prompted by a raid of Irish-American nationalists or Fenians across the Niagara frontier at Ridgeway where they temporarily defeated Canadian militia. No such Fenian raids transpired at Prescott or Brockville. James Poole wrote from Brockville:[26]

> We parade three time a day, at 6 o'clock in the morning, at ten, and at four. The men are drilled from one to two hours each time. Guard is mounted at 11 o'clock, and in addition to the regular sentries the town is patrolled during the night by a non-commissioned officer. One party goes east, the other west of the guard room.... There is also a gun boat here which cruises up and down the river, so that you see the Fenians can hardly take us unawares.

The only thing remotely resembling an incident was when Patrick Tucker, an Irish Catholic from Carleton Place, "imbibed rather freely [and] foolishly gave utterance to treasonable language, denouncing our good Queen, in very ugly and unmanly terms, and wishing success to the Fenian cause." Apart from receiving a sentence of three months' imprisonment, the Brockville *Recorder* dismissed Patrick Tucker as a "foolish fellow" and no serious threat.[27]

Despite the failure of Fenians to mount a raid at Brockville, back in Beckwith township councillors like most other regional inhabitants finally were beginning to take the Fenian threat seriously. They were shocked to learn that John Hermann Mewburn, the son of H.C. Mewburn, the principal of the Carleton Place grammar school, as a member of the University Rifles from Toronto" was one of those who fell in the engagement with the Fenians, near Ridgeway."[28] James Poole took particular pleasure "in noticing the prompt liberality of the Municipal Council of Beckwith, in setting aside the sum of two hundred dollars towards the fund for the families of the Carleton Place Rifles, now at the front, with the assurance that, if required, two hundred dollars more will be granted."[29] By mid-June the rifle company volunteers had "all returned unscathed to the comforts of home, and the society of their relatives and friends".[30] A public meeting in the Beckwith township hall organised a committee to collect contributions in aid of the monument erected at Toronto to the memory of the men who fell at Ridgeway."[31] In mid-September 1866 the women of the Carleton Place vicinity held a picnic at the new village drill hall to honour the returned volunteers that culminated in a ceremonial flag and drum which the women had purchased being presented to the rifle company.[32]

For the next half century Beckwith's links with warfare grew increasingly remote and romantic. When George Bailey died at age ninety in early August 1865 he was described as one of the oldest settlers in the township, having joined the yeomanry militia in the 1798 rebellion in Ireland at the age of 23,[33] effectively testifying to the depleting numbers of Napoleonic veterans. The occasional young man still ran off to war, such as James McMillan who joined the Egyptian expedition.[34] Even in the isolated Derry school section as late as the 1880s and 1890s, Edward Kidd grew up with a strong sense of military tradition. One of the people he frequently met was old "Soger Sandy", as he called him, a small man with white hair, who drove a team of white horses, and who once had been a soldier. "He suffered from an eversion of the lower eyelids, which gave to his face a sinister expression", Edward Kidd recalled. "We understood that this had been caused by a powder explosion while he was at war."[35] The military influence of the Napoleonic settlers even continued beyond the grave. During Edward Kidd's childhood in the 1890s:[36]

> Older members of the family told me of one Sandy Archer who had been a soldier in his youth and had fought against Napoleon. We saw and wondered about his war medal set behind glass in a niche cut into his tombstone which stood at the head of his grave in Dewar's Cemetery. Some of the tales which he had told came down to us; how he had thrown a man over his shoulder, impaled on the point of his bayonet. A soldier who had fought in an actual battle was a wonderful thing.

Plate 249
A commemorative service held at the ruins of the 1834 Church of Scotland on lot 14, concession 7, Beckwith in mid September 1916. This service betokened much more than simply a congregational anniversary. The huge union jack flag mounted behind the speaker's platform suggests that this service was held to draw attention to the need for new recruits in the midst of World War One. The crude benches assembled in front of the platform were reminiscent of the first services conducted by Beckwith's first resident clergyman, but the crumbling walls of the old church testified to the disintegration of local rural society as automobiles permitted sons and daughters to range out more widely within the region and to move to town. Photograph courtesy of Jean McMillan.

The romanticising of military endeavours in the late Victorian and Edwardian eras was furthered by newspapers, magazines, churches, schools and libraries. In the Carleton Place Herald as early as 1863 stories and poems such as "The Soldier's Experience" presented the battlefield as a moral place where the soldier could find Christ,37 and where young men proved their valour, their patriotism, and their manliness. Many a Beckwith parlour was lined with large framed prints of "Field Marshall Frederick Sleigh, Lord Roberts", "The Roll Call", "The Thin Red Line" and "Home From the War" — all offered as supplements for subscribers to the Montreal *Family Herald and Weekly Star*. Military imagery and allusions suffused the hymns that Beckwith churchgoers sang, as revealed by hymn titles such as "Onward Christian Soldiers", "Soldiers of Christ, Arise", "Equip me for the War, and Teach my Hands to Fight", "Soldiers of the Cross, Arise!", "Go Forward Christian Soldier" and "There's a Fight to be Fought". To rousing marching music Beckwith congregations lustily sang:38

> Urge on your rapid course,
> Ye blood-besprinkled bands;
> The heavenly kingdom suffers force;
> 'Tis seized by violent hands.

The Reverend John May in his 1903 book *What Ails the Church*? did not hesitate to use military imagery. He wrote, "On Sunday we replenish our lamps for a week's trudge through the dim lanes of existence; we whet our swords anew for its battle; we drink fresh draughts of the strength divine, bracing up afresh for the awful struggle."39

In Beckwith schools students found their readers filled with an extensive variety of essays and poems that gloried in historical accounts of military conquest and battle such as the "Death of Montcalm", "The Taking of Gibraltar", "The Death of Keeldar", "Conquest of Wales", "The taking of Edinburgh Castle", "The Battle of Clontarf" and "After Blenheim" among others. The glory of war was hard for even the dullest school child to miss in Goldsmith's "Lines On the Death of Wolfe", as the following verse shows:[40]

> Alive, the foe thy dreadful vigor fled,
> And saw thee fall with joy-pronouncing eyes;
> Yet they shall know thou conquerest, though dead,
> Since from thy tomb a thousand heroes rise.

Similarly, the closing verse of Browning's "An Incident at Ratisbon" extolled military valour and obedience to one's superiors:[41]

> The chief's eye flash'd; but presently
> Soften'd itself as sheathes
> A film the mother eagle's eye,
> When her bruised eaglet breathes:
> "You're wounded!" "Nay," his soldier's pride
> Touched to the quick, he said:
> "I'm kill'd, sire!" And his chief beside,
> Smiling, the boy fell dead.

In the Carleton Place Mechanics' Institute library it was possible to read such books as *The Royal Regiment*, *The Captain of the Guard*, *The Scottish Cavalier*, *The Great Sieges of History*, *Great Battles of the British Army* and *The Great Northwest Rebellion* among many others,[42] and by the Edwardian era there were the popular Henty books for boys presenting battlefield exploits as romantic fare.

The combined influence of a century's peace and the glorification of military exploits was to conjure up an illusion of continuing peace, and of war as an adventure. Young Edward Kidd, growing up in the 1880s was particularly impressed with a print of the "Roll Call" that hung on the wall at home beside the portrait of Queen Victoria and her family. It was[43]

> a picture of the Crimean war — a picture of men with high fur caps and bandaged heads, all standing in the snow. A dead man lay face down in the snow. England ruled the world and there was no reason to think that it ever would be otherwise. We sang "Soldiers of the Queen" and "Rule Brittania" and believed every word we sang. War was a thing of the dark past and could never happen again. We shuddered as we read [in our school readers] of how old Kaspar plowed up the skulls of dead men after Blenheim, or of the sufferings of the soldiers on the "Road to the Trenches".... The imperialism of Kipling dominated all.

There were occasional glimpses for Beckwith inhabitants of the military splendour that took up so much space in the coloured prints, the newspapers, the magazines, the hymnbooks, the school readers and the boys' adventure series they read. When Governor General and Lady Lansdowne made a brief stop at Carleton Place in late May 1887 the fifth company of the 41st battalion formed a guard of honour at the train station.[44] On Dominion Day of 1893 a company of some 39 Princess Louise Dragoon Guards rode out from Ottawa and paraded in full dress before a crowd of 2,000 people at Lake Park. The Carleton Place *Central Canadian* reported, "Instantly on their appearance, their bright helmets glittering in the sun, and their handsome trappings and uniforms a cynosure irresistible, every sport was stopped."[45] The pervading military influences, the century of peace which promised to go on forever, the rousing martial music, the handsome military uniforms, and

Plate 250
A demonstration of the machine gun purchased with funds raised by the Beckwith Patriotic League, near Franktown in 1916. The crowd of people gathered around to view this demonstration included a couple of boys on the left dressed in the unmistakeable garb of boy scouts. The purchase of this gun to send overseas was but one of numerous activities and fundraising efforts sponsored by the Beckwith Patriotic League during World War One. There was no comparable Beckwith effort during World War Two, with programs and the war effort either being focussed on Carleton Place or taking place within township schools. Photograph courtesy of Edna and John Porter.

above all the quest for adventure attracted a few sons from the more affluent families to seek military situations and careers. One of the dragoon guards parading at Lake Park was one Corporal Code, son of A.B Code from Carleton Place. Austin Gillies, from the well-heeled Gillies family, went to Royal Military College at Kingston,[46] whereas English-born Major William Hooper came to Carleton Place from Ottawa as a commercial photographer in 1901, after having served with the Royal Canadian Regiment in the Boer War.[47] Military rank proved a means of socially distinguishing and advancing in local society before and after 1900.

The outbreak of World War One in the late summer of 1914 revealed to what extent Beckwith and Carleton Place inhabitants were suffused with the spirit and vocabulary of military adventure. The *Herald* reported in early August, "Quite a number of our young men are anxious to go to the front with the Canadian Contingent and have offered their services."[48] The editors of both Carleton Place newspapers, as was expected of them, maintained a jingoistic front in support of the war effort throughout the war, but even a private letter from Roy Brown to his father, James Morton Brown, reveals the idealism that impelled many Beckwith young men to volunteer:[49]

> I have never said so before, but my reason for wanting the military training was to go to the war. I have thought it over a long time and have come to the conclusion that it is my duty to go. This is no sudden burst of patriotism or a thirst for adventure or as you used to say "fightin' and killin' and things". This war is a terribly serious thing and if we are to win we have to get large numbers of men to enlist and do it voluntarily. We do not want any conscription if it can

be avoided. Of course I am only one but every one is needed. I know what this is going to mean to you at home there and have considered what it will mean to myself but where things like this are concerned self has to be put aside and we need to look a little wider and broader.... I cannot write down all the way I feel about it but I wish you would think it over carefully and write me your advice.

The war had an immediate profound effect on Beckwith, one already apparent before the first contingent pulled out of Carleton Place. If it is possible to pinpoint one psychological moment when Beckwith forgot its denominational divisions, its ethnic rivalries, and the polarisation of northern and southern Beckwith between Carleton Place and Franktown, it was the Saturday morning in June 1914 when the first company of local men to go overseas was seen off from the Carleton Place railway station. The *Herald* reported:[50]

> As the troops march through the town great crowds of people line the pavements. Cheer upon cheer sweeps along, the ladies clap hands and wave handkerchiefs.... The band starts up the notes of 'The Maple Leaf Forever', the troops take up the strain.... When they arrive at the station..., the colonel addresses his men.... He recalls the glorious traditions of the Black Watch.... [Following t]he Chaplain's address...the whole crowd of over 2,000 souls repeat aloud the Lord's Prayer.

As the war dragged on much longer than anyone had imagined possible, Beckwith inhabitants contributed to the war effort in various ways. Older men and women such as Margaret Ross McEwen and Alexander McKay purchased victory bonds.[51] A Beckwith patriotic league was formed, selling victory bonds, raising funds for the war effort, and mounting projects such as purchasing a machine gun to be sent to the Canadian volunteers at the front. In 1915 Beckwith township council made a grant of $150 in aid of purchasing the machine gun[52] and granted a total of $400 to the British Red Cross from 1915 through to 1917.[53] The various women's groups mounted their own war effort, raising funds for the Belgian Relief Fund,[54] sending parcels overseas to local men, and making bandages and clothing. Prices shot up in local stores, and in Carleton Place the Findlay and Bates and Innes factories expanded their production to fill military contracts in addition to supplying their regular markets. Perhaps the most significant development of the war in Beckwith was that some young women such as Jessie Mabel McDiarmid, Jean Ramsay and Caroline McClenaghan[55] went overseas as nursing sisters.

Other young women such as Violet McDonald and Jennie Lightbody who had trained as secretaries and stenographers in Ottawa, in their work within various government departments, were exposed to the despair and fear of the men leaving for combat. Violet McDonald, from the department of militia and defence wrote to Lena Hawkins in August 1914:[56]

> Well[,] Lena[,] everybody here talks war all the time. One of the members of Princess Patricia's Light Infantry men w[as] in here this morning. He says that three weeks from today, he will be in Belgium. He says he never expects to come back, [and] says only one man out [of] a thousand will come back. I don't see how he has the heart to go. He leaves a wife, and two little boys....

From the very beginning, the seriousness of the war was sufficiently realised for some inhabitants to attempt to blot it out of their minds. "What a *fearful* war this is, isn't it?", Jennie Lightbody wrote Lena Hawkins in September 1914. "Two or three times I have thought I wouldn't read any more about it, and then I do. We see so many soldiers around now all the time, and so many leaving for Valcartier" camp.[57]

Many people retreated into religious justification for the war coming to take place. "Oh! this terrible war.", wrote Maggie McEwen from Lambton County to her nephew Alexander McCuan in

Plate 251
Evelyn M. Wilson, registered nurse, and John Horace Brown of Carleton Place as photographed in the trenches at Bois Grenier, France in March 1915. Imbued with the romantic military ideals that saturated late Victorian and Edwardian Beckwith and Carleton Place, Horace Brown joined the Second Battalion when war was declared in 1914. He wrote his parents, "I hope you think it right that I should go...but what do we go to camp to train for if it isn't to be ready for a case like this...." Evelyn Wilson, granddaughter of Dr. William Wilson at Carleton Place, was one of a number of late Victorian women who trained for a career in nursing. As superintendent of the famed Stamford Hospital School of Nursing from 1905 to 1932, she trained numerous women from Carleton Place and Beckwith. For her services above and beyond the call of duty as a nursing matron with the Canadian armed forces in World War One, among other awards Wilson was presented with the Royal Red Cross by King George V. Photographs respectively courtesy of Marguerite Vontobel and the National Archives of Canada, negative no. PA-107240.

January 1916, "it is something wonderful the amount of money and stuff that is going out of this country, but it must be for some wise purpose that God is permitting the war to go on, perhaps to make us less selfish."[58] In the same vein Jennie Lightbody wrote to Lena Hawkins:[59]

> It seems to me, that when the Lord is permitting this war it is to draw His people near to Himself. So often when He allowed wars to come in days of old, it was because His people were backsliding. We know that He loves us with an *everlasting* love and that He can make "wars to

cease"...and He tells us over & over to "Call unto Him in trouble" — "God *is* our refuge and strength[,] a very present help in trouble."

Elizabeth Code of Springvale, Alberta, in a letter to her nephew Thomas McCuan of Beckwith in 1918 simply stated the ubiquitous sentiment of the time when she wrote "the War still continues and no signs of coming to an end very soon either[.] It surely has been a terrible time."[60]

It is possible to gain some sense of the war experience for men at the front from Horace Brown's daily journals, through various selected excerpts. A son of Carleton Place miller James Morton Brown, Horace Brown was ready to leave with the first contingent from the Beckwith vicinity in the early autumn of 1914 due to his previous cadet training and membership in a rifle company. The first excerpts begin at Bustard camp on Salisbury Plains in southwestern England during the winter of 1915:[61]

Jan. 7 — Was up to see the doctor several times today. Have a cold & blood bad. Jan. 8 — ... If I can I will go to the hospital.... I am tired of all this mucking around in the mud.... Saw a military funeral on the way down at Bulford.... Feb. 4 — Today all the contingent that are near here was inspected by the King, [general] Kitchener and some of the other high mugs. He inspected us, then we had a march past and then we lined the track he passed out on. When he passed by in the train right around where I was they gave an extra loud cheer and he saluted. He looked very worried and many of us thought there were tears in his eyes.... Feb. 19 — Part of the platoon went to the trenches.... Feb. 22 — We...marched to the trenches. We were put in a very wet trench. It had been occupied by the Royal Fusiliers. One of them got killed when we had been in just about five minutes.... June 27 — Church parade today. Moved on into the trenches near Ploegsteert. June 28 — We have fine trenches, dry and well built. I have a fine dugout, just about the size of a bed, and one can sit up in it. There are two of us in it. There is a board floor in it and tin roof.... July 13 — ... On the 12th we had an Orange march — pipers, bugles and tin pan drum and Jim Beatty on a nag for King Billy.... July 14 — ... It was rain[ing] all evening and night. I got soaked and mud to the ear, fell several times when going up to the front line, then got in a dugout that leaked, so had to stand all night.... July 18 — Just the same old thing, working at the front.... July 26 — Was out digging trenches in the afternoon.... July 27 — Some of the company went on pass to England.... How we all envied them.... Aug. 8 — ... Got so[me] wood and sandbags to fix my dugout. I put a couple of shelves in, filled a big bread bag with grass I cut, making a big tick out of it. I lined the wall next where I lie with sand bags so it is quite cosy.

In early August 1915 Horace Brown had a close brush with death:

Aug. 9 — Working last night on sniping plates. Put in a couple. I was out in front cutting brush and stuff that was in the way when they must have heard me. They sent up two flares and gave a little rapid [fire] for a few minutes. Although I had my shirt sleeves up and it happened to be a bed of nettles, I hugged the ground and the nettles like long lost friends. Early this morning an attack was made on our left.... One of our lads got killed last night and one wounded. This morning things reminded me of duck-hunting. We stood-to earlier, before dawn on account of the attack, and the sun coming up and the mists rising out of the long grass which looked like the rice, all made me think of being up in the hide [on the Mississippi].... Aug. 13 — Got a good sleep today, first for quite a while.... Sept. 2 — We moved into trenches [in Belgium] in the evening. We are in a new trench that has never been held before.... There are no boards in the floor of the trench, no floors in dugouts, five of us to one.... Sept. 3 — Raining all the time, soaked to the skin and all over mud.... Sept. 5 — ... We got a parcel from Carleton, with candy and all other kinds of things in it. It was nice to get it, alright.... Sept. 12 — Had a church service today.... Sept. 21 — ... A fellow got six months for firing at our own trench when he was on listening

Plate 252
Canadian Expeditionary Force Grenadier Guards in the trenches together at Armentiers, as photographed by Horace Brown. As photographic historian Andrew Roger has remarked, the photographs taken by Horace Brown provide a rare record of the war as seen from the level of the common soldier. "These are not propaganda photographs. They were taken in the reality of the trenches — unlike official photographer Ivor Castle's too-famous work, taken twenty miles behind the front in practice trenches. Although these photos had to pass through the hands of military censors and do not show anything that cannot be seen in the commissioned work of war photographers, they differ from commissioned war photography in that they show Canadian soldiers from the point of view of one of their own comrades." National Archives of Canada negative no. PA-107237.

patrol.... Sept. 22 — Had a bath today.... It was warm water, the first warm bath I've had for ages so I had a good one and feel a lot better now.... We dug four lines of dummy trenches to fool the Germans.... Sept. 23... The Allies are using gas and smoke now and are making advances on the left.... Oct. 3 — Had a church parade in the morning.... Oct. 8 — ... The trenches are just about thirty yards apart here [left of the Messines-Wulvergheim road].... We can light no fires but one for the platoon and it is well back. We are knuckling down to the Germans here. We haven't a sniping hole that can be used, and we can't hardly show a periscope or it gets sniped, and our friend Fritz exposes himself quite freely.... Oct. 11 — ... About six or seven in the morning our miners heard Germans working close to one of our saps, and by eleven heard a mine laid and set off.... Oct. 14 — I was told off for bomb throwers course....

Conditions worsened with the onset of winter:

Nov. 15 — ... We are having cold weather now, freezes hard every night. The trenches are in awful shape, just like a long string of shell holes. We all have long rubber boots while in the trenches now.... Dec. 3 — ... Everything is going on in the same old monotonous way. Some of our officers had a close call from getting into trouble for being drunk in the trenches. There are one or two drunk nearly all the time in.... Dec. 19 — ... During the night the Germans made a gas attack somewhere very close.... All morning we were going around with eyes smarting and running water.... 1916... March 20 — We are in these trenches for the last time as we move up to the left near Ypres. I do not know if the movement has any significance but it may be getting troops in position for something. But little as one would wish to be killed, there are very few who would not welcome something if it were going to hasten the end of the war.... March 27 — They began the same old round of parades as before.... April 6 — ... Buried a couple of Germans.... One of them was a young fellow and hadn't been dead long as he was hardly discoloured.... [Private C.] Dart was killed today.... April 27 — Fairly quiet today until about six o'clock...when everything trembled as though the trenches intended to come in. Fritz had put up a mine in our company. Then he opened up with everything on the list and we did the same, and for about a couple of hours it was the hottest I ever had the misfortune to be near. Shortly before eight, when it was just dusk and one could hardly see for the smoke, Fritz tried to come over at several different points but only a few ever reach our trench.... They kept on being nasty all night.... It seems strange that anyone should live through it all. We had quite a bunch of casualties.... The trench mortar is the worst thing as there is no protection, it drops straight in. The only thing is to watch for them, but in a bombardment one cannot hear or see them with everything else coming around.... May 2 — ... One of my sect[ion], [Private R.] Mullen got killed today.... May 24 — ... This is Empire day, the day of fireworks and picnics at home. We had abundance and to spare of the former but not much in the line of a picnic.... June 4 — ... I have been writing this in the place where we are dug in, and Fritz has been throwing some heavy stuff quite close and the gentle curves of my writing have been very erratic. You cannot by your own will power stop your hand from shaking.

After seriously hurting his knee by falling on a bayonet in a shell hole, Horace Brown found himself taken away from the front line, first to a field hospital, then sent to England, and finally discharged and aboard a ship bound for Canada. In his ship's cabin he marvelled, "My it is fine and comfortable to be living like a civilized person and having such a dandy bed."[62] After arriving home, being visited by numerous relatives and townspeople, and welcomed with a procession, he proceeded to go around the region, speaking at concerts, church meetings, and community events, recruiting additional men to volunteer for service. An example of one such recruiting meeting was one sponsored at St. Paul's Presbyterian Church in Franktown on September 22nd 1915. It was billed as a "great patriotic and recruiting meeting with free admission to a programme of vocal and instrumental music" culminating in taking an offering "on behalf of the Beckwith patriotic fund for the purchase of a *machine gun*."[63] In response to an appeal from the Imperial Order of the Daughters of the Empire in July 1916, local churches took up an offering "on behalf of those suffering from the war situation in France."[64] The Franktown correspondent of the Carleton Place *Herald* reported in February 1917, "The eight soldier boys of Franktown who are overseas are heard from regularly by their relatives and friends here."[65] The intensifying need for recruits in 1917 prompted three more Franktown men to go overseas during the next few months, in turn spurring the village correspondent for the *Herald* to remark in late April, "Well done, old Franktown! Who will be the twelfth one to go?"[66]

But finally at four o'clock in the morning of November 11th 1912 the fire alarm in Carleton Place began to ring with the news of peace. One town woman wrote her daughter a day later, "I cannot think or say anything but Peace Peace. We were out yesterday morning as soon as we got dressed[,] every one went crazy[,] had a big bon fire on the old market square and everything that would make a noise sang and shouted until daylight."[67] At Franktown the "old town was all en fete...and all night royally celebrated the declaration of victory." Most of the inhabitants of rural Beckwith went to Carleton Place to "take part in the great jubilations in that town" but those from Franktown "after returning home did justice to the occasion in their own village."[68] The old sectional jealousies

Plate 253
High school cadets marching along the Mississippi River in Carleton Place, as photographed ca. 1930. As early as 1913 cadet training took place at Carleton Place high school when principal E.J. Wethey took a group of nine high school and public school pupils to Barriefield Camp near Kingston to join some 1,200 to 1,300 boys assembled there. They were put through regulation military drill and exercises and participated in athletic contests. A cadet company was formed at the Carleton Place high school, and continued well beyond the end of World War One. Military preparedness was a major reason for cadet training, but there was the additional benefit of conferring military discipline on the young men. It was a distinct change from the irrepressible young men of previous generations in Carleton Place who while swimming had sported about naked on the town bridge, incurring the wrath of local editors for "being subversive of morality and common decency". Photograph courtesy of Edna and John Porter.

between Franktown and Carleton Place were revived as soldiers returned to Beckwith.In early April 1919 the Franktown correspondent of the *Herald* editorialised:[69]

> Well now, it was really bad that the loyal people of Carleton Place could not furnish those returning soldiers with something better than a mere "scrap of paper" in recognition of their services. We think Mr. G.A. Burgess'[s] protest a very timely and sensible one. If they would come to Franktown they would be better received than that, for here we give them gold, silver and precious stones, in addition to a nicely inscribed complimentary address. Say Boys — just arrive at Franktown next time and there will be no "scrap of paper" welcome either.

Similarly, ere a month had elapsed, the *Herald*'s Franktown correspondent criticised Carleton Place town councillors for "side tracking the returning soldiers by offering them jobs at sawing hardwood with the bucksaw, two cuts at $1.00 per cord" and suggested that "Our junction town might surely do better for them than that."[70]

The heroic aura with which Beckwith inhabitants enveloped their returning soldiers spoke well for the continuing sense of being a military settlement, at the very time when preparations were being made to "commemorate the *one hundredth* anniversary of the coming of the first settlers".[71] An example of the individual community celebrations across Beckwith was a gathering in the township hall at Black's Corners in early August 1919 "to greet and welcome home two of their soldier boys, Private [John M.] McDiarmid and Private [Arthur] Scott."[72] The Beckwith patriotic league as one of its final acts gathered contributions for a costly black granite war memorial to be placed on a plinth of dark brown Beckwith limestone near the entrance to the township hall. In early October 1920 a large crowd "attended the unveiling of the memorial to the fallen soldiers of the township".[73] The names engraved on the monument included privates David McLaren, Robert Boreland, Hugh McMillan, Jeremiah O'Shea, Herbert Dowdall, Andrew T. Hughton, Cecil Smith, Arthur Officer and nursing sister Jessie Mabel McDiarmid. Charles D. Tinkler of Carleton Place designed a scroll or honour roll listing the names of all soldiers and nursing sisters from Beckwith serving in the war. This scroll was placed on a wall of the council chamber the same day the war memorial was unveiled (Appendix 32).[74] In contrast with other nearby townships such as Montague that had no tradition of being a military settlement and that erected no war memorials either in stone or more perishable materials, Beckwith had done handsomely by the memory of its war dead and by its own continuing sense of its military past.

Charles Tinkler's design for the Beckwith war honour roll showed a formally designed scroll burst asunder by the impact of the war to reveal the names of those from the township who had gone overseas. The war truly had had a dramatic effect on Beckwith inhabitants. Their five years overseas for the fifty men and women from the township had effectively provided them with new perspectives and removed them from parental control long enough to become unwilling to accept the limitations of a future in Beckwith once the initial euphoria at peace had worn off. There were tragic stories and shattered lives that lay behind the names chiseled into the cold granite of the Beckwith war memorial. Nursing sister Jessie McDiarmid had been drowned in the sinking of the *Llandovery Castle* by a German submarine in the Irish Sea, and privates McLaren, Boreland, McMillan, O'Shea and Dowdall were all reported killed in action on the front.[75] Private Andrew Hughton from Franktown died of pneumonia at the Edmonton military isolation hospital less than two weeks before the armistice while on his way to the Pacific coast with the Siberian expedition. He was 21 years old.[76] A name not to be found on the Beckwith war memorial was that of Stearne Tighe Edwards who was born at Franktown but who had moved with his widowed mother to Carleton Place in search of employment before the beginning of the war.[77] Edwards was the only one among a half dozen flying ace heroes from Carleton Place not to come from a well-to-do family. By the time he received the Distinguished Service Cross in October 1917 he had shot down at least five enemy aircraft, and he would triple this number by war's end. Edwards like other men from Beckwith regarded the war "as a job to be done, but he had a real horror of killing" as shown by the prayer he inscribed in his prayerbook "asking forgiveness for taking the life of an enemy, and for the safe return of himself and his men."[78] Edwards, tragically, lived to see the end of the war, but the day after the armistice he crashed his plane and died ten days later.[79] His name was incised on the cenotaph raised in Carleton Place by the Imperial Order of Daughters of the Empire and on a brass plaque in St. James Anglican church across the river.

Carleton Place had its own longer list of war veterans, war dead, and war heroes, particularly a remarkable number of flying aces, the most prominent of whom was A. Roy Brown, then credited with shooting down Manfred von Richthofen — the legendary German "Red Baron".[80] Many of the men and women returning both to Beckwith and Carleton Place soon realised that the future for them lay elsewhere. Carleton Place offered few attractive jobs, as its population slowly began to inch back up toward the level it had enjoyed in 1891. As for Beckwith, not only did the number of people continue to decline, but the cheese factory economy began to fall apart at war's end, there no longer was an Ottawa valley timber market

Plate 254
The mansion built for Charles Bates on High Street in Carleton Place in 1918, as photographed in 1982. War production kept the woollen mills and factories of Carleton Place running at full capacity, with sales of Bates & Innes products reaching an unparalleled $1,200,000 in 1918. Following war's end, the demand for Bates & Innes products dropped sharply, prompting the firm to print a full page advertisement in the Herald *stating, "Many men and women are out of work, factories are closing or running short time, wages are dropping and will go on dropping. And why? All because the demand has dropped off. There isn't enough work to go around.... Every cent that you spend for a foreign made article that is made as well and as cheaply in Canada, postpones the return of good times and brings you nearer to personal unemployment."*

for Beckwith oats, and much of the land cleared for agricultural use was fully depleted. The war veterans who remained in Beckwith were reminded of their fighting service by annual armistice day ceremonies at Black's Corners every eleventh of November. In contrast with their Napoleonic counterparts and ancestors in nineteenth century Beckwith who had received annual pensions from the British treasury,[81] the soldiers returning from World War One received no comparable benefits. The soldier settlement Act of 1919 provided those of them who wished to farm with loans to purchase land, stock and equipment. But for women such as Stearne Edwards's widowed mother, who depended on him for support, the future would hinge on a mother's allowance paid by the provincial government. A neighbour commented:[82]

> Mrs. Edwards is bearing up very bravely. It certainly is a great loss and grief for her. Stearne was a good son and a great comfort to his mother as well as being a great help to his mother financially[,] and she needs it as she is physically not of the kind that are able to do for themselves sufficiently to maintain in comfort.

The families of the dead who remained, the veterans who either stayed on in Beckwith or left for destinations elsewhere, the neighbours and friends and relatives who attended the armistice day services took what scraps of emotional and sentimental comfort they could from the eulogies, the obituaries, the honour rolls, the last posts and the hymns beseeching:[83]

> O God, our help in ages past,
> Our hope for years to come;
> Be Thou our guard while troubles last,
> And our eternal home!

For only half a generation were they spared the realisation that the war would not prevent future hostility. In their own generation at least they were spared the ultimate pain of hearing their great-grandchildren taught that the great war to end all wars was an accident and served no good purpose.

Endnotes

1. *Carleton-Place Herald*, 4 October 1855, p. 2, col. 2.
2. *Carleton Place Herald*, 28 August 1861, p. 2, col. 5.
3. Ibid., 6 November 1861, p. 2, cols. 4-5.
4. Ibid., 10 December 1862, p. 2, cols. 5-6.
5. Ibid.
6. Ibid., 5 February 1862, p. 2, col. 4.
7. Ibid.
8. Ibid., 11 June 1862, p. 3, cols. 2-3.
9. Ibid., 29 July 1863, p. 2, col. 5.
10. Ibid., 19 April 1865, p. 3, col. 1.
11. Ibid.
12. Ibid., 7 January 1863, p. 2, col. 4.
13. Ibid., 25 February 1863, p. 2 col. 3.
14. Ibid., 17 January 1866, p. 2, cols. 1-2.
15. Ibid., 24 January 1866, p. 2, col. 7.
16. Ibid., 12 August 1863, p. 2, cols. 3-4.
17. Ibid., 15 July 1863, p. 2, col. 4.
18. Ibid., 18 January 1865, p. 2, col. 4.
19. Ibid., 19 August 1863, p. 2, col. 4.
20. Ibid., 4 January 1865, p. 2, cols. 4-6.
21. Ibid., 12 August 1863, p. 2, col. 4.
22. Ibid., 25 April 1866, p. 2, col. 3.
23. Ibid., 4 April 1866, p. 2, col. 3.
24. Ibid., 22 March 1865, p. 3, col. 3.
25. Ibid., 6 June 1866, p. 2, cols. 2-3.
26. Ibid., 13 June 1866, p. 2, col. 3.
27. *Brockville Recorder*, 29 March 1866, p. 2, col. 1.
28. *Carleton Place Herald*, 6 June 1866, p. 2, col. 4.
29. Ibid., 13 June 1866, p. 2, cols. 2-3.
30. Ibid., 20 June 1866, p. 2, col. 7.
31. Ibid., 15 August 1866, p. 2, col. 3.
32. Ibid., 19 September 1866, p. 2, col. 3.
33. *Carleton-Place Herald*, 16 August 1865, p. 3, col. 6.
34. Ibid., 11 March 1885.
35. George Edward Kidd, "Transients", an unpublished paper, loaned courtesy of the late William Livingstone Kidd.
36. Kidd, "Earlier Part of My Life", p. 48.
37. *Carleton Place Herald*, 21 January 1863, p. 1, col. 2.
38. Methodist Church of Canada, *Methodist Hymn Book* (Toronto: Methodist Book and Publishing House, 1884), No. 459.
39. May, *What Ails the Church?*, p. viii.
40. Ontario, Council of Public Instruction, *Canadian Series of School Books: The Fourth Book of Reading Lessons* (Toronto: Canada Publishing Company Limited, 1879), p. 90.
41. Ibid., p. 212.
42. OCPAR Carleton Place Mechanics' Institute, *Catalogue of Books in the Carleton Place Mechanics' Institute Library* (Carleton Place: Carleton Place Mechanic's Institute, 1893), pp. 18, 20, 34; reference 982.1.1.
43. Kidd, "Earlier Part of My Life", p. 1.
44. *Carleton Place Herald*, 1 June 1887.
45. *Carleton Place Central Canadian*, 6 July 1893.
46. 30 October 1987 interview with Ewan R. Caldwell, Ottawa.
47. Brown, *Carleton Place: Founded Upon A Rock*, p. 81.
48. *Carleton Place Herald*, 11 August 1914.
49. 11 April 1915 letter from A. Roy Brown, Edmonton, to his father James Morton Brown, Carleton Place, provided courtesy of Howard M. Brown, Ottawa.
50. *Carleton Place Herald*, 1 September 1914.
51. OPLCRO 14 July 1914 will of Alexander McKay and 21 October 1918 will of Margaret Ross McEwen, Beckwith.
52. OBCMR 16 October 1915 minutes of Beckwith township council.
53. Ibid., 28 October 1916 and 20 October 1917 minutes.
54. *Carleton Place Herald*, 20 October 1914.
55. Undated newspaper clipping entitled "Beckwith Soldiers Memorial" in scrapbook loaned by the late Hazel Davis, Beckwith.
56. McCuan family correspondence, 19 August 1914 letter from Violet McDonald, Department of Militia and Defence, Ottawa, to Lena Muriel Hawkins, Beckwith.
57. Ibid., 2 September 1914 letter from Jennie Lightbody, Ottawa, to Lena Hawkins, Beckwith.
58. Ibid., 13 January 1916 letter from Maggie McEwen, R.R. No. 2, Wyoming, Ontario, to her nephew Alex McCuan, Beckwith.
59. Ibid., 2 September 1914 letter from Jennie Lightbody, Ottawa, to Lena Hawkins, Beckwith.

60 Ibid., 15 January 1918 letter from Elizabeth Code, R.R. No. 2, Red Deer, Alberta, to her nephew Thomas McCuan, Beckwith.
61 J. Horace Brown diaries, 1912-1917, provided courtesy of Howard M. Brown, Ottawa.
62 Ibid., 4 September 1916 entry.
63 *Carleton Place Herald*, 21 September 1915, p. 1, col. 3.
64 Ibid., 18 July 1916, p. 5, col. 1.
65 Ibid., 6 February 1917, p. 5, col. 2.
66 Ibid., 24 April 1917, p. 5, col. 1.
67 12 November 1918 letter from Mary Elizabeth Brown, Carleton Place, to her daughter Margaret R. Brown, Salem Hospital, Salem, Massachusetts, provided courtesy of Howard M. Brown, Ottawa.
68 *Carleton Place Herald*, 12 November 1918, p. 5, col. 1.
69 Ibid., 1 April 1919, p. 6, col. 1.
70 Ibid., 19 April 1919, p. 5, col. 1.
71 Ibid., 20 May 1919, p. 5, col. 1.
72 Ibid., 12 August 1919, p. 4, col. 1.
73 Ibid., 13 October 1920, p. 5, col. 1.
74 Undated October 1920 newspaper clipping in scrapbook loaned by the late Hazel Davis, Beckwith. See also the 19 March 1921 minutes of Beckwith township council.
75 Ibid.
76 Ibid.
77 W. Brian Costello, *A Nursery of the Air Force: The Story of the Carleton Place Great War Airmen and the Brown/Richthofen Saga* (Carleton Place: by the author, 1979), p. 115.
78 Ibid., p. 122.
79 Ibid., pp. 126-128.
80 Costello on pages 158-181 argues at length that Brown shot down Richthofen, but virtually all historians at the Canadian Armed Forces directorate of history are convinced that Richthofen was downed by Australian gunners on the ground, and this view has been confirmed in 1988 with the discovery of a contemporary doctor's post-mortem on Richthofen's body.
81 *Perth Courier*, 12 January 1877.
82 1 December 1918 letter from James Morton Brown, Carleton Place, to his son lieutenant J. Horace Brown, Royal Air Force, London, England, provided courtesy of Howard M. Brown, Ottawa.
83 The Church of England in Canada, *The Book of Common Praise* (Toronto: Henry Frowde, 1909), p. 689.

Plate 255
"Three O'Clock", oil on masonite (39.4 x 45.7 cm.) painted by Christopher Pratt in 1968. Findlay Oval cookstoves manufactured in Carleton Place dominated the kitchens of many Beckwith farmhouses. This painting, based on a kitchen in Newfoundland, reflects the transcontinental markets that existed for Carleton Place manufactures. It also serves as an icon of life in mid-twentieth century Beckwith, reflecting a continuing use of the woods on township farms at the same time there was an increasing reliance on Carleton Place and Ottawa for services, manufactures and employment. The urban pull on rural Beckwith was so strong by the 1960s that farm families tossed out their wood stoves in favour of the oil furnaces they admired in Ottawa homes. In 1971, the Findlay factory in Carleton Place was sold, closed, and demolished. Private collection reproduced by permission of the artist.

URBAN INFILTRATION

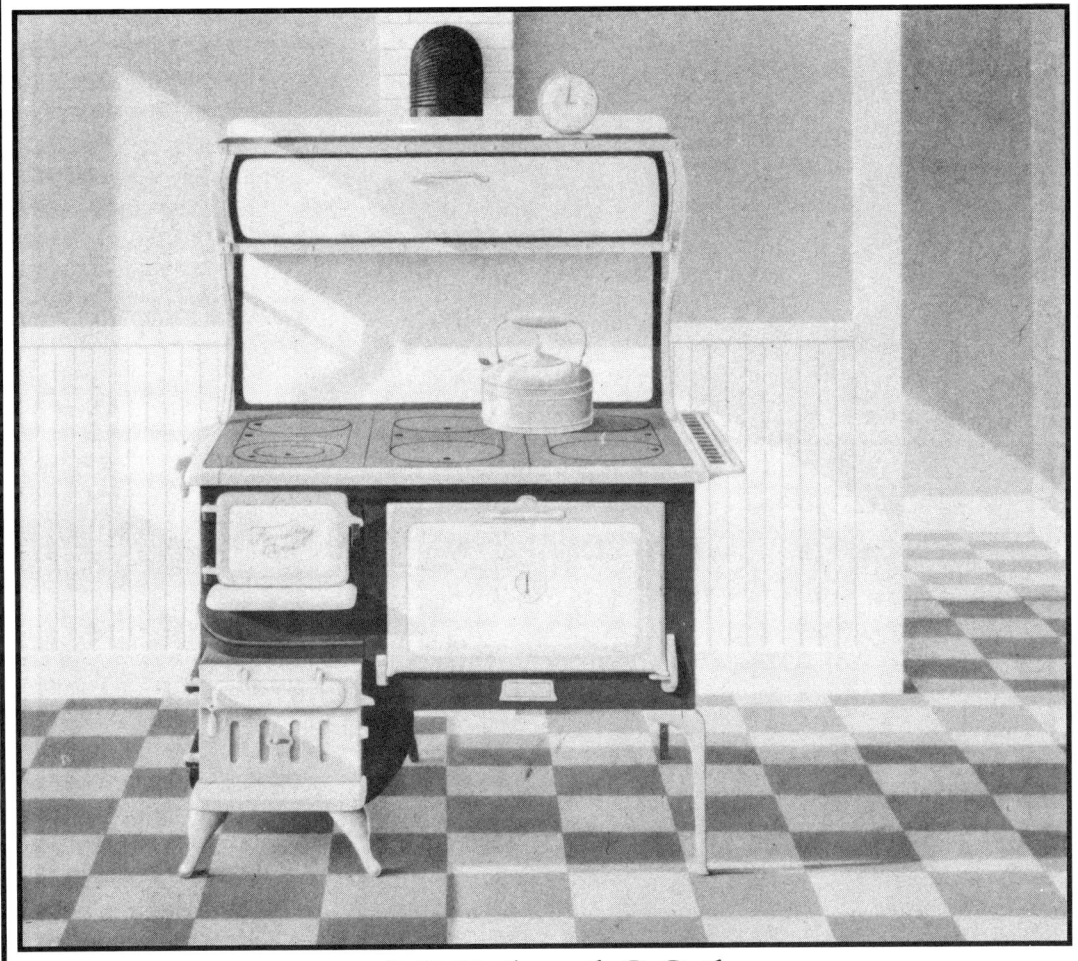

1921-1991

NOT DEAD! O NO, SHE ONLY SLEEPS

Beckwith society did not disintegrate during the 1920s, 1930s and 1940s as its population coasted to an all time low of barely one thousand people in 1951. If Beckwith did not roar during the 1920s, at least it did not find the 1930s unbearable in the same way that workers living in Carleton Place did. Despite the local sense of being comparatively backward, despite surviving the depression, and despite facing up to the demands and sacrifices of a second world war, Beckwith in 1951 was little changed from what it had been like in 1921.

On the surface it seemed that Beckwith along with most other regional rural townships was in constant decline during the 1920s, 1930s and 1940s. The township population remained frozen at 1,221 persons during the 1920s, then declined by 67 in the 1930s, and fell by 119 persons in the 1940s to only 1,035 people—the lowest population that had called Beckwith home since the mid 1820s. Three new houses built respectively by Livingstone Kidd, Berton Coleman[1] and John Sheil[2] in 1922, 1929 and 1944 were the only new houses apart from cottages to be built in Beckwith between 1920 and 1960, and the latter two were rebuilt from the timbers of older houses they replaced. The cheese factories at Appleton, Ashton, Black's corners, Franktown, Prospect, McCreary's Settlement and Tennyson all closed down, whereas creameries at Carleton Place operated into the 1960s. The post offices at Gillies' Corners, Prospect and Tennyson were closed down. Following the creation of the United Church of Canada in 1925, there was a spate of church closings during the next forty years that reflected the declining population. Gillies' Corners United church, despite being rebuilt after a fire in 1925, did not escape being closed in 1950. Before 1925 Gillies' Corners and Franktown had existed as separate denominations, respectively Methodist and Presbyterian, but following church union the larger congregation at St. Paul's church with its more ambitious building at Franktown made it inevitable that the Gillies' Corners church would close and be sold. At Ashton the former Melville Presbyterian and Methodist congregations used both houses of worship during alternate years to ease the adjustment of uniting, and finally they settled on the newer Methodist church building.[3] Knox United church at Black's Corners closed in 1941,[4] as its congregation increasingly was drawn into the larger church in nearly Carleton Place. St. John's Anglican church at Tennyson closed in 1967 for the same reason.[5] St. Augustine's Anglican church and the United church at Prospect were officially closed in the late 1960s,[6] and Zion United church at Carleton Place was sold out of church hands in the 1970s—all the result of pressures that began to be felt in the 1930s and 1940s.

With liquor no longer legally available in local hotels, and with more families purchasing cars in the 1920s and 1930s, there were no hotels and restaurants in Beckwith. Ashton and Franktown failed to grow, as their post offices, general stores and blacksmith shops offered only a fraction of the services and goods they had made available even in the Edwardian era. In 1921 the agent at Franktown station on the Canadian Pacific railway was removed over the objections of southern Beckwith inhabitants who protested the inconvenience, trouble and delay in business it would bring about.[7] In 1931 the C.P.R. closed Ashton station as a regular agency, installing a caretaker agency, but eventually even this was closed down.[8] As drastic as the decline in the number of children attending school had been between 1890 and 1920, it continued to fall corresponding to the general

Plate 256
Students at S.S. No. 1, Beckwith, Gillies Corners, as photographed in 1920. These eighteen students comprised a moderate attendance for a Beckwith school section, but as attendance continued to fall at many of the township one room schools throughout the 1920s, 1930s and 1940s, the weaker sections could not continue to pay a teacher. The Cuckoo's Nest school (S.S. No. 3) was closed in 1945 and its students attended at Franktown, S.S. No. 7 on the west half of the ninth concession line was closed in 1949 and its students taken to S.S. No. 8 on the east portion of the ninth line, and the Scotch Corners school was closed in 1959. Seven years later the eight remaining one room schools in Beckwith were closed despite the strenuous objections of two-thirds of township ratepayers. For names see Appendix 34. Photograph courtesy of Iva Shirley.

population decline. Both in the Prospect school section in the infertile southeastern corner of the township, and in S.S. No. 9 in the fertile northern corner of Beckwith, the number of students attending dropped by half between 1920 and 1930, notwithstanding the township's population remaining frozen during that decade. In 1925 the public school inspector reported so small an attendance at the Cuckoo's Nest school that he recommended it be closed and that the pupils attend Franktown school, a move which Beckwith council refused to make.[9]

Despite the many local closings the sense of local community in Beckwith endured throughout the 1920s, 1930s and 1940s. Indeed, community identities, based as they largely were on local school section boundaries, never before or again were so strong. As population continued to decline; as local stores, cheese factories and churches closed; and as rural inhabitants became increasingly dependent on area towns for services; local school section inhabitants drew together all the more closely and focussed their lives on their farms and local school affairs. The new harmony between farm and school was a distinct change from previous decades when fathers and teachers competed for the daily work of their children, especially in the poorer school sections and the smaller families. When Eva Gordon came to teach in union school section No. 13, 10 and 15 (which brought together pupils from the eastern part of Beckwith's first concession with children from northern Montague and northwestern Marlborough) in 1917, she found minimal supplies, a log school, and parents preoccupied with farmwork:[10]

> She was not nearly cynical enough to reflect that she was a bargain deal; they were paying her $400 instead of the $600 they would have paid a qualified person.
>
> She moved into her new district in September, finding a boarding place with an Irish family who fed her well for eighteen dollars a month. From well before nine o'clock each morning until at least five-thirty, her life was the little log schoolhouse, She had fewer than twenty pupils, ranging through the grades from one to eight. Facilities were stark—rows of double desks bolted to the floor, at the front the teacher's desk on a dais. There were blackboards, a globe, several wall maps, but no library. The children brought their own books, slates and squeaky slate pencils. There was no piano. When Miss Gordon staged a Christmas concert, accompaniment was provided by a local fiddler. Nor had any public money been wasted on such frills as a baseball or yard swings. The children amused themselves at recess and the noon hour with balls and bats and skipping ropes brought from home, or with snowballs in season.
>
> ... No music specialist arrived for regular lessons, no school nurse or doctor with vaccination shots appeared. She subscribed to no magazines, received no professional guides or journals, attended no seminars. If she met other teachers it was briefly and socially; no opportunity was given to compare notes. The inspector called twice a year; that was all....
>
> Because of her youth she was not an authoritative figure in the rural community. She knew the parents of all her pupils but they treated her with some condescension. Sometimes she was asked to social evenings in farm homes along with the family with whom she boarded. To the hard-working farmers and their wives the raising of crops and the care of livestock were the realities of existence.... At the end of December 1919 she left Union School, though her school board asked her to stay, and took a school close to Carleton Place at a slightly higher salary.

The new harmony of farm and school work in Beckwith from the early 1920s onward came with the creation of township rural school fairs. The need to make school relevant to farm children was recognised in the 1900s and 1910s, but education officials dithered along the paths of training agricultural specialists. In this vein the Carleton Place *Herald* in 1908 quoted the president of the Ontario Agricultural College at Guelph as saying:[11]

> The problem of successfully teaching Agriculture in the public schools has been long under trial and consideration and everyone admits the wisdom of instructing the children in the rural schools in the elementary principle of the science that relates to their life activities. The difficulty, however, of securing teachers specially trained for the work has hindered advancement.

By 1912 the Ontario department of education "fully set forth their plans and intentions regarding the teaching of Agriculture,"[12] The central practical feature of the new policy was the rural school fair. During the school year students were instructed on the raising and care of various crops, and in September a school fair was held in a central location in each township at which the students competed against one another with the crops and livestock they had raised. There were rural school fairs in neighbouring Montague as early as 1915,[13] but the earliest reference to one in Beckwith is

Plate 257
Drawing in hay on the John Porter farm, Prospect, ca. 1920. On farms where sons were few, women continued to assist at chores, particularly milking cows and helping with haying. The transition from growing grain to a dairying economy spurred some farmers to fill in the cracks between the logs in their grain barns to create comfortable cow stables in which to house their cattle. Hay forks were installed in the upstairs lofts to lift up the hay drawn in from the fields. Photograph courtesy of Edna and John Porter.

1923 when Beckwith township council granted ten dollars to the department of education for school fair purposes.[14]

The annual rural school fairs held behind the township hall at Black's Corners from the early 1920s until 1939 served to draw the people of Beckwith together in a way they never had been before. It is true that in the 1860s and 1870s there had been competitive examinations of students from across the township held in the hall at Black's Corners, but they were confined to reading, writing, spelling, arithmetic and general proficiency, and they had failed to attract parents as an audience.[15] Not so the rural school fairs! Photographs from the 1920s and 1930s show large crowds of onlooking parents dressed in their best, with even large tents set up some years to provide adequate exhibition space. In contrast with previous generations of Beckwith parents who had perceived that attending school was largely a waste of time, apart from acquiring basic skills in reading, writing and mathematics, the school fairs and the agricultural husbandry they promoted were seen to offer local children a practical preparation for farming. Moreover, the school fairs provided a welcome revival and replacement for the exhibitions of the Township of Beckwith Agricultural Society that had died out by the early 1870s, the Franktown fair which succumbed in 1902, the Carleton Place cattle and turkey fairs which did not survive past the 1900s, and the Carleton Place horse show which did not survive the 1910s.

The prize list of the rural school fair held at Back's Corners on September 10th 1937 reveals the variety of activities, and why they appealed to the youthful participants and the adult audience. The program of the day opened with the various schools arriving at Black's Corners. The various exhibits were placed in the tent between 9:30 and 10:30, following which they were judged. At 10:30 a weed naming and stock judging competition took place, followed by a sports program at 11:30 in which there were races for boys, girls, teachers and trustees. Lunch at noon was followed by school parade and Strathcona exercises, the description of which suggests that education officials were casting sidelong glances at Nazi Germany:[16]

> Parade of all Schools once around grounds, in order of school section number. Each school to be led by director carrying school flag with name and number of school section attached. Parade will not be judged this year but all pupils in all schools are required to take part. Decorations will add to the appearance of the parade but teachers and pupils may use their own judgment in this connection. No vehicle or horses allowed. Strathcona drill must be participated in by all schools. Drill in mass formations. No prizes will be awarded.

The Strathcona exercises were a set of prescribed pseudo-military movements that students performed in groups, in response to commands given out by the teachers. Following this drill the students sang in unison "God Save the King", followed by the distinctive school yell of each section.

From two to three o'clock the livestock of students was judged, followed by a discussion of the exhibits generally before the exhibit tent was opened for inspection by students, teachers and parents. At 3:30 there were public speaking and musical contests, and by 4:15 the school fair was over and exhibits were removed. The large attendance from across the township indicated how well these rural school fairs served to bring Beckwith inhabitants together who otherwise had few other social vehicles for coming together. In late May 1928 the township council sent its "congratulations to Miss Elsie McNeely for the splendid achievement she has obtained and the honour conferred on this township by receiving honours at the Provincial Public Speaking contest for rural schools held in Toronto to which she advanced from the Beckwith school fair.[17] Those students with the highest number of points at the school fair were respectively awarded a silver trophy, a geography book, and another book, *Salute the King*, all provided by the T. Eaton Company Ltd. of Toronto.

The ultimate purpose of the school fair was indicated by an often-ignored rule urging parents and teachers[18]

> to encourage the children to do all the work in preparing their exhibits without assistance. A word or two of encouragement and direction may be needed at times but *all the actual work must be done by the pupils*, otherwise, the purpose of the school fair which is to teach the boys and girls to do things, is defeated. The pupils will be more interested and show more pride in something prepared by themselves and will receive the benefit from such preparations.

The categories in which students exhibited included grain and corn; potatoes, roots and vegetables; fruit; flowers; special flowers; poultry; livestock; sewing (open to girls only); cooking (open to girls only); farm and home mechanics (open to boys only); collections of tree leaves and twigs, harmful weeds and weed seeds; writing (that is, the copying out of selections from readers, or composing business letters); art; and maps.

The continuing influence of the temperance movement and of imperial ties to Britain was evident in the three competitions listed under the maps category in 1937. Whereas students of the senior third class were set the challenge of drawing a "Map of Ontario with trade centers and routes", those in the senior fourth class were to draw a map of the "British Isles with trade centers and routes". There was a special competition sponsored by the Women's Christian Temperance Union to create a poster in pencil, ink or water colours, illustrating one of the five following subjects:[19]

    1. The Soberer the Safer.
    2. Building My House of Health.

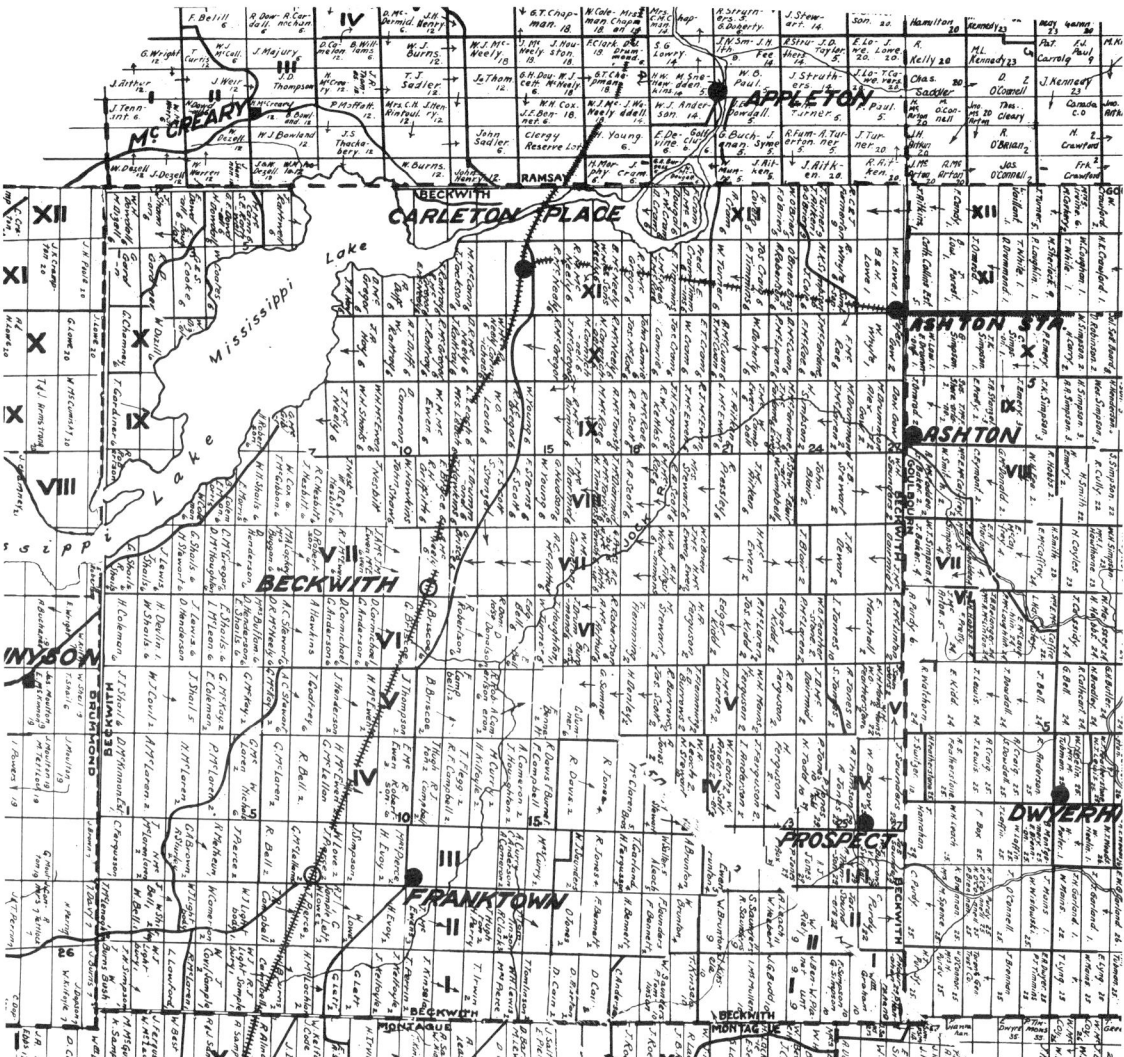

Plate 258
The Beckwith section of a Cummins Rural Directory Map of the vicinity published in 1924 by the Cummins Map Company of Toronto. The greater concentration of names in northern as opposed to southern Beckwith reflects the greater fertility of soil along the Mississippi floodplain. A comparison of this map with Plates 12, 13, 74 and 123 reveals that a high proportion of the Wexford and Perthshire families that settled in Beckwith beginning in the late 1810s were still locally resident a century later. On this map a round black dot represents a post office, a white dot a railway siding, and a black square a hamlet. The number below each landowner's name refers to his or her post office address, according to the following legend.

1	Perth	5 Ashton	11 Smith's Falls R.R. #1
2	Franktown	6 Carleton Place	22 Carsonby
3	Smith's Falls	9 Perth R.R. 5	25 Dwyer Hill
4	Prospect	10 Smith's Falls R.R. 2	29 Jasper

Loaned courtesy of Beckwith township council.

3. The Drinker—The Last Man Hired—The Soonest Tired—The First One Fired.
4. Money Waster—Alcohol and Tobacco.
5. Illustrate your own idea in regard to the use of alcohol or tobacco.

The restriction of sewing and cooking to girls and of farm and home mechanics to boys at the rural school fair is a fair measure of the emphasis on separate spheres for men and women in local society. Girls were trained and encouraged in the domestic arts of the farmhouse, of feeding and clothing their children and men, whereas the boys were encouraged to develop carpentry skills. It is equally significant, however, that all of the categories of husbandry were not restricted to either gender. There clearly was a continuing recognition that women actually contributed to the raising of crops, the milking of livestock and the general running of farms. But, notwithstanding women tending livestock and helping in the hayfield, the new wave of motorised mechanisation of farmwork that developed from the 1920s onward, with steam engines, gasoline engines and tractors coming into increased use meant that the teaching of farm and home mechanics only to boys served to place farmwork only the more firmly under men's control from the 1940s on. It added to a patrilineal inheritance system that favoured sons over daughters and a devotional revolution before the turn of the century that focussed women's energies on missionary activities and raising funds at the same time it kept the prestigious and controlling roles of clergy, elders, wardens and trustees firmly in the hands of men. The school system enshrined the inferiority of women teachers by paying them less than men and not requiring them to learn as many subjects. In the national and local press advertisers and editors promoted the idea that women's role in society was focussed on raising children and housekeeping. The motorisation of farm work in Beckwith by mid century prevented most women from contributing to the planting and harvesting process. The men had been trained in the use of the new machinery, whereas the women had been shown how to sew and cook.

There is no record that anyone in Beckwith protested the separation of male and female spheres as promoted and reinforced by most community institutions including the school system. It was taken for granted that men should earn a family's income while women performed a nurturing role. Those young women who in their late teens and twenties taught school and trained as nurses were regarded as developing skills in family management and nurture that would be useful when they gave up their careers, as inevitably it was assumed they would want to, to become full time mothers and housewives. As for those women who boarded in Ottawa, training to become stenographers and secretaries, their stints as working women were pragmatically viewed as a means of earning an income and not being a financial burden on their parents and brothers while awaiting marriage. When Nellie Hawkins died in early 1913 leaving a family of young children,[20] her husband's younger sister Lena gave up her stenography training in Ottawa to raise her nephews and nieces.[21] For most Beckwith women daily life during the 1920s, 1930s and 1940s revolved around cooking, sewing and caring for children as a letter from Bella Switzer at Ashton to Lena Hawkins reveals:[22]

> How are you getting along? How did your pies turn out. I wish I could step over and have a piece.... How are you and Jackie getting along. I miss him so much[;] it seems so quiet here without his chatter and after being used to him for a while. Tell Mother if you see her that I have the lining all basted in Bella McVean's coat. I got it in far easier then I expected.... Well Lena I am waiting on the potatoes to cook while I am writing. I am going to start at my dress after dinner.

Two trends developed for Beckwith women in the early twentieth century. While the lot of most women within the township became increasingly domestic, a growing number of them were going out into the world to earn money at some form of career. As early as 1900 there were three women among the twelve Carleton Place high school students attending Queen's University, and

Plate 259
A group of seventh concession line neighbours working together raising a log driveshed on the John McEwen farm, lot 9, concession 7, Beckwith, ca. 1932. The communal camaraderie of groups of adjacent farmers created strongly-knit local identities throughout Beckwith — identities that remained much stronger than any sense of township identity. In the western half of Beckwith localities such as the seventh line featured the mixing of Irish Anglicans and Scottish Presbyterians at work bees on farms and at statute labour, whereas in eastern Beckwith the two ethno-religious communities remained isolated until the late nineteenth and early twentieth century. Photograph courtesy of John and Verna McEwen. See Appendix 34 for names.

in the 1920s a gifted student such as Marjorie Davis could go on from the Cuckoo's Nest school to university and eventually become a surgeon at the Women's College hospital in Toronto. There is no question that gaining the right to vote in federal elections in 1917 provided Beckwith women with a new sense of worth, and if the weight of tradition and looking after their families kept most women in Beckwith firmly within the domestic sphere, many mothers were on the watch to make sure their daughters had careers or at least a means of making a livelihood rather than being left economically vulnerable or subject to the mercy of husbands and brothers who ultimately benefitted from the patrilineal order of life in Beckwith.

The women of Beckwith as their lives became increasingly confined to housekeeping, gardening and looking after their children's interests, created a larger sense of township identity beyond the boundaries of their school sections in their frequent use of the telephone. The first manager of the Beckwith and Montague Rural Telephone Company was Mary Lena Pierce who also ran her husband's store in Franktown.[23] Instead of being largely isolated from one another during the week as their mothers had been during the previous century; meeting only at rare school social events such as the annual Christmas concert and the school fair, Sunday church services and occasional meetings of women's church groups, and while shopping in Carleton Place; Beckwith women were now able to contact one another all over the township beyond the boundary of their school sections and concessions. Correspondents for each town and village with the aid of the telephone acquired a steady diet of information about visits and events that was presented in social columns in the Carleton Place and Smith's Falls newspapers.

There were limitations to the growing sense of Beckwith as a larger community beyond the limits of school sections. The rural school fair did not include children who lived in Beckwith but who attended union schools located in adjacent townships. Hence Beckwith children attending Ashton school went to the Goulbourn rural school fair, while those attending the union school in the northernmost corner of Montague attended the Montague rural school fair a dozen miles away at Roseville. Similarly, students living in Drummond township who attended the Tennyson and Scotch Corners schoolhouses inside Beckwith's boundaries went to the Beckwith rural school fair at Black's Corners. The division of most of Beckwith between the Goodwood Rural Telephone Company and the Beckwith and Montague Rural Telephone Company in 1915 determined the patterns of communication. The tolls charged for a connection between the two major exchanges served to isolate Franktown and the southern concessions from the rest of the township. The Scotch Corners section of Beckwith had always been isolated from the rest of the township both by the wide expanse of Mississippi Lake and by the tortuous lengthy route of the main road between Carleton Place and Perth, and it was further isolated from other Beckwith inhabitants by being placed under the Lanark and Ramsay telephone company exchange in 1922.[24] The northern corner of Beckwith was isolated from the rest of Beckwith by being placed under the exchange of the Lanark and Carleton Counties Telephone Company exchange.[25] The local news correspondents for Ashton, Black's Corners, the Derry, Glen Isle, Scotch Corners and Tennyson sent their reports exclusively to the Carleton Place newspapers, whereas the Franktown, Gillies' Corners and Prospect correspondents sent reports to the Smith's Falls and Perth newspapers in addition to the Carleton Place papers, reflecting a further fracturing that prevented Beckwith from developing any sense of a unified community.

The agricultural economy of Beckwith did not change between the end of World War One and the onset of World War Two, notwithstanding the closing of most local cheese factories by 1921. The number of landowners declined by only fifteen from 259 in 1921 to 244 in 1956, and yet the number of milk cows kept in Beckwith increased from 1,796 in 1890 to 2,395 by 1940. There still remained cheese factories outside Beckwith's boundaries to send milk to, and regional dairies required milk to supply Carleton Place, Smith's Falls and Ottawa inhabitants. The size of farms remained stable between 1921 and 1956 (Tables 24 and 29), and despite the arrival of sufficient numbers of automobiles in the late 1910s and 1920s to warrant the road along the eleventh concession line between Ashton Station and Perth and the road between Carleton Place and Smith's Falls respectively being designated and paved as the King's highways, numbers 15 (later 7) and 29 (later 15) by 1928, most farms continued to rely on horsepower. The number of horses in Beckwith only declined from 980 in 1890 to 824 as late as 1941. The amount of poultry remained the same, the number of sheep increased by more than half, and the number of hogs kept more than doubled at the same time (Table 30). Beckwith's population dropped by more than a third between 1890 and 1940. The crop acreages cultivated in Beckwith remained constant during the 1920s and 1930s (Table 31). The declining acreages planted in oats, wheat, rye and potatoes were offset by the increasing acreages of mixed grains, hay and barley cultivated. There remained a steady market for firewood from Beckwith bush lots. One winter in the 1940s John Sheil from the Tennyson vicinity hauled a thousand cords of firewood to Carleton Place, and he was just one of many farmers selling firewood in the local towns of Perth, Smith's Falls and Carleton Place.[26] Small sawmills continued to operate in Beckwith throughout the twentieth century doing custom work, and farmers occasionally continued to sell timber off their farms. Beckwith maple syrup continued to enjoy a ready market.[27]

Beckwith agriculture in the early twentieth century staggered away from the loss of the reliable upper Ottawa timber provisioning market it had enjoyed for a century and away from the British cheese market that Canadian cheese producers had lost to New Zealand by the early 1920s. Despite

Plate 260
Bringing in firewood on the Howard McRae farm, lot 18, concession 10, Beckwith, as photographed ca. 1932. The availability of firewood on even the poorest farms helped Beckwith inhabitants to comfortably survive the economic depression. The need for firewood to heat homes in Carleton Place continued to benefit Beckwith farmers throughout the 1930s. At the same time the mansion built of cut stone for Archibald McArthur in Carleton Place (Plate 183) was sold for taxes for a mere pittance, the rhythm of rural life continued in Beckwith, with children continuing to be used by their parents as a source of labour. Photograph courtesy of Audrey and Murray McRae.

depleting soil, Beckwith farmers continued to sow as large crops, but they no longer had the firm market prices that the timber provisioning economy and the cheese market had offered them in the late Victorian and Edwardian era.

As early as the 1890s Beckwith farmers were beginning to occasionally feel the effects of the declining market in the provisioning trade, and responded by politically supporting Protestant Protective Association candidates and forming a lodge of the Patrons of Industry, a fraternal organisation through which they ordered coal-oil, tea, sulphur, salt, plough points, machinery oil and other items.[28] In the late 1910s and early 1920s farmers from northern Beckwith in particular joined the United Farmers of Ontario. They along with farmers throughout the rest of Ontario had grown dissatisfied with the Liberal and Conservative political parties during World War One as a labour shortage developed and costs escalated. The short-lived provincial administration of the United Farmers of Ontario during the early 1920s prevented it from gaining further appeal, and indeed it is significant that very few of Beckwith's worst-off farmers, those of Irish-orgin in the southern concessions, became members of the United Farmers. Rather, it was Scottish-origin inhabitants such as Alexander McCuan to whom the promotional literature of the Farmer's Co-operative Harvesting Machine Company was sent,[29] and northern concessions inhabitants such as George Buchanan, Bert Hawkins, Robert J. McEwen and William McNeely who attended United Farmers of Ontario conventions at Toronto as late as 1928.[30] Despite the membership of mostly

Table 29. Land Holdings in Beckwith Township, 1956–1981

	1956		1961		1971		1981	
	No.	%	No.	%	No.	%	No.	%
No. of Occupiers	244		167		129		104	
9 Acres & Under	4	1.6	4	2.4	2	1.6	5	4.8
10–69 Acres	20	8.2	5	3.0	3	2.3	17	16.4
70–129 Acres	51	20.9	26	15.6	22	17.1	17	16.4
130–239 Acres	83	34.0	53	31.7	37	28.7	24	23.1
240+ Acres	86	35.3	79	47.3	65	50.4	41	39.4

SOURCE: *Canadian census returns in printed volumes for 1956, 1961, 1971 and 1991.*

Table 30. Livestock in Beckwith Township, 1890–1970

	1890	1940	1950	1970
Milch Cows	1,726	2,395	2,290	909
Horses	980	824	469	
Sheep	3,003	4,711	3,216	982
Pigs	625	1,292	1,415	630
Turkeys	1,608			
Geese	1,651	3,933	20,872	
Ducks	390			
Other Fowl	23			
Hens and Chickens	12,267	12,267	6,611	2,196

SOURCE: *Canadian census returns in printed volumes for 1921, 1941, 1951, 1956, 1961, 1966 and 1971.*

Scottish-origin farmers in the United Farmers, Beckwith farmers generally were reluctant to endorse the co-operative and collective programs they developed. Scottish lowlander-settled townships such as Ramsay and Pakenham, and even more conservative townships such as Bathurst and Ramsay and Montague contrasted with Beckwith in organizing local branches of the Lanark County Federation of Agriculture, taking out co-operative insurance, and forming local women's institutes and branches of the Lanark County Junior Farmers.[31] Beckwith farmers between the wars seemed locked into an economy of mixed and subsistence agriculture. Even during the economically depressed years of the late 1930s when Ewan Caldwell from Gillies Brothers lumber company at Braeside scouted around the Ashton vicinity for men to work in the lumber camps, he could not find a single man willing to leave Beckwith overnight.[32]

Beckwith looked inward on itself during the 1920s and 1930s, preferring to reflect on more prosperous days in the past rather than dwell on its falling population and undynamic economy. Hence when the old Church of Scotland manse on the seventh line changed hands in the early 1920s, the Black's Corners correspondent of a Carleton Place newspaper enthusiastically plunged into reminiscing about past glories:[33]

Plate 261
Sawing firewood at the John Porter farm, lot 26, concession 3, Beckwith, near Prospect, as photographed ca. 1935. Beckwith farmers found a ready market for firewood during the nineteenth and early twentieth centuries in the regional towns of Smith's Falls, Perth, and particularly in Carleton Place. The Mississippi River being commercially unnavigable between Carleton Place and the Ottawa River together with high freight costs on the CPR combined to keep coal as a domestic fuel out of Carleton Place. It is perhaps no accident that the rise of Findlay's as a major manufacturer of wood burning stoves occurred in a town where wood was the major fuel burned. Photograph courtesy of Edna and John Porter.

Table 31. Crop Acreages in Beckwith Township, 1920–1970

	1920	1940	1950	1955	1960	1965	1970
All Field Crops	14,838	14,659	12,178	11,765	10,583	10,761	9,969
Wheat	543	222	131	81	17	72	—
Barley	368	391	174	56	45	102	257
Oats	5,282	4,472	3,126	2,426	2,279	1,460	638
Rye	80	46	43	34	—	49	26
Mixed Grains	405	1,481	1,418	616	500	477	348
Hay Cultivated	6,306	7,078	6,376	5,973	6,899	6,888	6,223
Corn for Ensilage	710	—	—	505	334	1,127	1,885
Potatoes	246	185	66	67	36	24	—

SOURCE: *Canadian census returns in printed volumes for 1956, 1961, 1971 and 1991.*

If the bushes and stones about the old mansion of the Beckwith ministers could speak, what interesting stories they would tell of the days o' auld lang syne! Many are still living who recall with deep delight the by-gone days of the olden time when "Beckwith Manse" was the neatly kept residence of the "country clergymen" of the Church of Scotland in Canada, to which happy couples repaired to be united in wedlock in the old fashioned way, and where young men aspiring to professional life went to study the classics with the scholarly ministers of those early years in our township; and many still remember pleasant visits at their minister's home in their youthful days and the real old-time hospitality of the pastor and his family with the hearers who came to call. Many distinguished visitors from other parts were entertained at this renowned spot in the days gone by, among them being the Rev. Dr. Norman MacLeod, of Glasgow, Queen Victoria's royal chaplain and one of the most eminent ministers of the fatherland, whom the mother church of Scotland sent out to Canada to visit and confirm the churches in the faith of their fathers during the dark and anxious days of the disruption. Dr. MacLeod preached in the Seventh Line church on the occasion of his visit, and spent a few days among the Presbyterians of the locality, and was the guest at the parish manse with Rev. Dr. Smith, who was the minister of Beckwith at that time, now upwards of seventy years ago. But those incidents are now only a memory and everything is greatly changed. The long drawn out solitude of the old manse is now broken by the cheery ringing of the rural telephone....

By thus immersing themselves in prideful recollections of Beckwith's past, township inhabitants in the 1920s and 1930s could ignore their relative lack of modern conveniences, the lack of plumbing and flush toilets as contrasted with their relatives in Carleton Place, the lack of a hospital at Carleton Place as contrasted with other regional towns such as Almonte and Smith's Falls that had had hospitals since before World War One, the abandoned buildings that were torn down on farms being consolidated, and the rotting older buildings on the empty streets of local villages and hamlets. By burying themselves in their past Beckwith inhabitants did not have to dwell on the growth of Fascism in Europe and the growing possibility of yet another war that began to be mooted.

The escape of some Beckwith inhabitants into a romantic and heroic vision of their local past ignored the fact that many of the traditions their ancestors had brought from Wexford and Perthshire had either been transmuted or obliterated. For example, although Orange processions continued in

Plate 262
The store and residence of Thomas and Euphemia Featherston at Prospect, as photographed ca. 1928. General stores proved to be more enduring than many of the other services and businesses in the older villages and hamlets of Beckwith. At Tennyson after the cheese factory closed, it was converted into a general store. The gas pump inside the small structure built onto the shed at the Prospect store shown here helped attract customers to this store as Beckwith families began purchasing automobiles in the 1920s and 1930s. Patronage of these rural village stores also depended on customers being allowed to run up bills and barter for groceries with their own produce. Photograph courtesy of Emphemia Featherston.

regional towns, they were participated in by Beckwith Protestants of all denominations, whereas in the early Victorian era their membership in Beckwith was a tacit declaration of one's membership in an Irish Anglican congregation. Similarly, by the 1920s Beckwith inhabitants of Scottish highland descent routinely celebrated Christmas in complete contrast with the nonobservance of their ancestors, as William Cram recalled in 1928:[34]

> Christmas on Glen Isle wasn't observed as a day of much importance to our family—in fact the Crams and the people like them in the old times didn't observed Christmas as a holy day or holiday; the anniversary of this supernatural event did not appeal to the Scotch Presbyterians as it did to the Roman Catholics. And because the latter observed it as a Holy Day the Presbyterians wouldn't follow them in that respect. As an evidence of this, about the year 1856, Christmas Day, Father and Mother, took us children over to Uncle John's in a sleigh to spend Christmas Day (...near the Cram burying ground). When we got there we found his son Duncan hauling wood from the bush and he told us his father was in the bush chopping. When Uncle John came home for dinner, after speaking to...mother and we children, he said to...father "Dan, when did you turn to be a Papist?" that is what they called the Roman Catholics in those days. Of course he was only joking as he looked at...mother and winked....
>
> The next Christmas I remember was when we had a threshing mill in our barn.... Not

Plate 263
Sheep grazing in front of the John Ferguson farmhouse, lot 22, concession 4, Beckwith, as photographed ca. 1920. A century of intense cultivation left some Beckwith farms with land incapable of growing crops, and fit only for pasturing sheep. When the Canadian Co-operative Wool Growers opened a wool warehouse and grading station in the old Canadian Pacific railway shops at Carleton Place in 1941, there were some 4,711 sheep on Beckwith farms — more than at any other time in the history of the township. Photograph courtesy of the Carleton Place and Beckwith Historical Society.

> that...father wanted to thresh on Christmas Day, but as we were the last in our neighbourhood to have threshing done and the mill was going to move out the following day. Some of our neighbours refused to help because it was Christmas Day, and Mr. Nagle, who was a Catholic, told father he would rather work on Sunday than on Christmas Day. However the threshing was done on that day and we got help from the neighbourhood.

By contrast, Beckwith Irish Anglican families such as that of Benjamin Scott had always "believed in Christmas and always made great preparation for the two married daughters."[35]

The ongoing decline of cultural tradition in Beckwith was inevitable as increasing numbers of older inhabitants passed away. In July 1918 almost at the end of World War One when flight lieutenant Wilson D. Cram from Carleton Place was on leave from the Royal Air Force searching for living relatives in Comrie, Scotland, he found none in the vicinity. He reported to his sister:[36]

> There are still Crams living here and in Crieff, 6 miles south—but they are not of the same family. There are about 10 families still in Scotland but I think the only one who is any relation of ours is the family living in Edinburgh. I am certain of this now. I was talking to the postmaster of Comrie, an old man of 85 years and he told me the Crams around there are all new-comers and did not originally belong there. He remembers when a boy about 10 years of age, of an old Mr. Cram coming back from Canada to see his friends at Comrie but did not find them—[h]e supposed that they were all dead so he returned to Canada.

Plate 264
Students at Franktown school posing with bags of milkweed pods they picked, as photographed ca. 1943. Apart from the victory bond drives that took place in Carleton Place and the larger villages of rural Beckwith, the major focus of the domestic war effort took place in the one room schools of the township — the centres of its fractured identity. The students at Franktown school collected milkweed pods in order that the silk inside the pods could be used in the manufacture of parachutes. Photograph courtesy of Pauline Wright.

The decline of cultural tradition in Beckwith did not diminish local romanticism about the past. Wilson Cram, for example, undeterred by finding no relatives at Comrie, "climbed the hills and pulled a bouquet of heather off the hills behind the birth-place of Peter Cram" He "left Comrie satisfied [not only at having] found the exact spot from whence the Crams came" but also because "15 miles from Comrie is the home of the witches mentioned in MacBeth and...20 miles away to the west is Loch Katrine with Ellen's Isle where [Sir Walter] Scott pictured his 'Lady of the Lake'."[37] The romanticising of Beckwith's past was a response to the various changes that either accompanied or followed in the wake of celebrating Beckwith's centennial of settlement. These changes included the war, the telephone, the automobile, the building of the King's highways numbers 7 and 29 through the township in the 1920s.[38] In October 1937 the township council entered into an agreement with the Ontario hydro-electric power commission for power to be provided to rural Beckwith homes.

The outbreak of World War Two delayed the introduction of hydro-electricity to rural Beckwith by a decade. For all the romanticism with which Beckwith inhabitants regarded their past, they did not enter the new war with the same sense of military adventure that had prompted the previous generation to go overseas in World War One. Still, as late as the 1940s Beckwith's population overwhelmingly was composed of descendants of families that had been settled in the township for generations. A continuing sense of military duty was instilled by the remembrance day services that took place late every November 11th forenoon, and by the Strathcona drills that took place in local schools in preparation for the rural school fairs.

Altogether some 93 men and women from Beckwith volunteered to join the armed forces, with the women as members of the Canadian Women's Auxiliary Corps, participating in many non-combative roles in contrast with the nursing duties to which they were restricted in World War One.

Three men from Beckwith did not return from the war. Flight Sergeant Earl Rathwell died in England in June 1942, Private Earl Porteous was killed France in August 1944, and Private Thomas Hope was killed in Italy in December 1944. The war program on the domestic front in Beckwith was largely focussed in the schools, apart from the victory loan drives, the issuing of ration coupon booklets to conserve gasoline and foodstuffs, and drives for scrap metal, newspapers, animal fat and funds to support the war effort. Teachers in the one room schools across the township mobilised their students to go out collecting scrap metal, and to pick milkweek pods so that the silk inside could be used in the manufacture of parachutes. Posters on schoolroom walls kept the war ever before students, urging recruitment, telling of protecting freedom, alluding to the new gigantic war effort in Canadian factories, and constantly repeating the message of defeating Hitler. Little leaflets containing war news and war propaganda were distributed to inform students and their parents of recent developments. Students banded together collecting savings stamps to purchase war bonds. Red Cross programs were held weekly in the schools, at which skits, songs, recitations and general entertainment were featured, focussing on the war effort and collecting money for Red Cross work.

Beckwith township council played virtually no role in the war effort in direct contrast with its counterpart during World War One, assuming that the war effort was under the control of other levels of government, particularly the federal government in Ottawa. At the outset of the war the council was requested to conduct a canvas of the township for funds for the Red Cross. The council's response was to appoint each local school board to canvas their section, and to send the funds collected to the council. In November 1942 a public meeting of township inhabitants was called in an attempt to create greater interest in the Ottawa blood clinic, and a committee made arrangements for donors to be transported to Ottawa. Beckwith farmers grew larger crops, particularly increasing hog production, but the farm war effort only became substantial after 1941 and was not reflected in census returns. In August 1945 two members of the newly-formed Beckwith Women's Institute approached the council, offering the services of their group, should the council decide to hold a public reception for the returning Beckwith members of the armed forces. Accordingly, on October 25th 1945 the council and the Women's Institute held a public reception at Knox United Church across the street from the township hall at Black's Corners, with a number of higher military officials also in attendance.[39] A plaque was prepared listing the names of all the men and women who had seen service in the armed forces during the war and placed on the wall in the council chamber across from the honour roll listing those who had served in World War One (Appendix 33). The names of the three men killed during the war were incised on the lone remaining blank face of the grey granite war memorial.

The gathering of township inhabitants honouring those who had served in the war was smaller than the crowd that had witnessed the unveiling of the war memorial a quarter century earlier. By 1945 the township rural school fair had ceased to exist for six years, and the only opportunity for Beckwith inhabitants to come together otherwise were the annual remembrance day service and township council meetings. The war effort in Beckwith reflected the nature of local society in the township in being fragmented among the local school sections and congregations, notwithstanding the consolidation that was already beginning to take place.

Endnotes

1 28 March 1988 interview with Norma Coleman, Beckwith.
2 27 March 1988 interview with reeve John Sheil, Beckwith.
3 25 April 1988 interview with Arthur R. Hawkins, Carleton Place.
4 27 March 1988 interview with Arthur R. Hawkins, Carleton Place.
5 27 March 1988 interview with reeve John Sheil, Beckwith.
6 Porter et al., *History of Prospect*, pp. 6, 8.
7 OBCMR 2 April 1921 minutes of Beckwith township council.

8 Ibid., 4 July 1931 minutes.
9 Ibid., 14 November 1925 minutes.
10 Doris French, *High Button Bootstraps: Federation of Women Teachers Associations of Ontario, 1918-1968* (Toronto: The Ryerson Press, 1968), pp. 3-5.
11 *Carleton Place Herald*, 16 June 1908, p. 6, col. 3.
12 Ibid., 2 April 1912, p. 2, col. 2.
13 Lockwood, *Montague: A Social History*, p. 541.
14 OBCMR 26 May 1923 minutes of Beckwith township council.
15 McCuan family papers, 27 December 1878 prize list of Competitive Examination of Public Schools, Beckwith, file 107.
16 Ibid., Prize List, Lanark County Rural School Fairs, 1937, file 113.
17 OBCMR 26 May 1928 minutes of Beckwith township council.
18 McCuan family papers, 1937 Lanark County Rural School Fairs prize list, file 113.
19 Ibid.
20 McCuan family correspondence, 13 March 1913 letter from Laura Hawkins, Regina, Saskatchewan, to Henry Hawkins, Beckwith.
21 Ibid., 24 March 1913 letter from Grace Jordan, Kenora, Ontario, to Henry A. Hawkins, Beckwith.
22 Ibid., 20 March 1913 letter from Bella Switzer, Ashton, Ontario, to Lena Hawkins, Beckwith.
23 Undated obituary of Mrs. R.T. Pierce in scrapbook loaned by the late Hazel Davis, Beckwith.
24 OBCMR 30 September 1922 minutes of Beckwith township council.
25 Ibid., 17 April 1948 minutes; and Grindlay, *Independent Telephone Industry in Ontario*, p. 278.
26 27 March 1988 interview with reeve John Sheil, Beckwith.
27 *Lanark County Federation of Agriculture* (booklet published at Perth by the Lanark County Federation of Agriculture in 1950), p. 76.
28 Beckwith Association No. 1795 Patrons of Industry, *Minutes, 1893-1898*, provided courtesy of Victor and Mary Shail, Beckwith, pp. 5, 6, 10.
29 McCuan family correspondence, 1901 and 1903 advertisements for the Farmer's Co-operative Harvesting Machine Company.
30 25 April 1988 interview with Arthur R. Hawkins, Carleton Place.
31 *Lanark County Federation of Agriculture*, pp. 16-19, 28, 31-32.
32 30 October 1987 interview with Ewan R. Caldwell, Ottawa.
33 Undated newspaper clipping in scrapbook loaned by the late Hazel Davis.
34 30 December 1928 letter from Wilson D. Cram, Raleigh, North Carolina, to his niece Gertrude H. Cram, Carleton Place, provided courtesy of Howard M. Brown, Ottawa.
35 Ibid.
36 6 July 1918 letter from flight lieutenant Wilson D. Cram, Comrie, Scotland, to his sister Hilda Cram, Carleton Place, Ontario, provided courtesy of Howard M. Brown, Ottawa.
37 Ibid.
38 *Carleton Place Herald*, 29 July 1936, p. 5, col. 2; and 12 August 1936, p. 4, col. 2.
39 Beckwith Women's Institute, Tweedsmuir History of Beckwith (unpublished), made available through Mrs. Helene Eves.

COMMUTING THE FUTURE

Beckwith was never again the same after the end of World War Two. The jingoism of the war effort among other things had stressed removing the Fascist threat to make the world a safer and a better place in which to live than it had been before. For the men and women returning from service in the armed forces and for those other inhabitants of Beckwith working in the civil service at Ottawa, visiting back with their families, life in Beckwith could not much longer go on as it had. What sense did it make for men to have served in deadly combat with crack teams of engineers building good roads to further their advance, only to return to roads in peacetime Beckwith ninety percent of which were unfit for automobiles to travel most of the year? Who could be bothered returning to coal-oil lamplight, outdoor toilets, hand pumps and doing farmwork with horses in peacetime Beckwith, when the men and women who had served in the armed forces had for up to six years at various stages become used to electric lighting, flush toilets, running water and working with machinery. The men and women who had been in the armed forces, if they could not initially admit it in their intense relief at having come through the horrors of war alive, soon came to view Beckwith through the light of their recent experience as the equivalent of an underdeveloped country.

Even the closest local beacon of modernity, the town of Carleton Place, was an illusory mirage. For all its electric lights, sewer system, running water, and factories working to capacity supplying the war effort, Carleton Place did not offer any certain prospect of desirable future employment at war's end. With the exception of the Findlay foundry which had grown to employ 300 people and to produce 35,000 units annually,[1] Carleton Place industries were clearly unstable in the postwar decade. The woollen mills in the town had only enjoyed strong years of production during the two wars, but otherwise had suffered from periodic depressions and paid notoriously low wages. An article in the Carleton Place *Canadian* in 1951 looked forward to better days in the postwar economy:[2]

> Ottawa Valley...mills are soundly run and most are small. Machinery and equipment is modern and staffs are well trained. Many of the employees come from families with textile traditions— some are third generation descendants of the first workers in valley textile mills. During the past 20 years new ideas in labor-management relations have come into being and production methods are more efficient.... Products of these Valley mills have from the very beginning been of high standard, and with advances in technology and development of new machinery, the original quality has improved.

Despite such boosterism, without a protective tariff, the local textile mills were doomed. In 1950 the 300 employees at Bates and Innes mills at Carleton Place under their distinctive O.V. (Ottawa Valley) pure wool products label manufactured heavy rib woollen two-piece and combination underwear suits for men and boys; medium weight rib and spring needle wool two-piece and combination underwear for men and boys; all sizes and weights of white bleached pure wool blankets; all popular shades of fancy silk bound woollen bed covers, grey sports and camy blankets; red, blue and brown sporting blankets; travelling rugs; kitted cardigan style coats for men and boys;

Plate 265
Soldiers marching past the Carleton Place town hall in a Victory bond parade, as photographed in 1942 by Ronald Roe. With Beckwith's population at an all time low in the 1940s, and with most families possessing automobiles, Carleton Place became the major focus of shopping, entertainment and, increasingly, of employment. Many of the soldiers returning to Beckwith grew impatient with the limitations of the traditional structure of society. Photograph courtesy of Ronald Roe.

children's knitted suits and jerseys; woollen and knitting and hosiery yarns; and pulp and paper machine felts.[3] By 1959 Bates and Innes was "almost entirely devoted to blanket manufacturing", Renfrew Textiles in the old Code woollen mill had closed down,[4] with Bates and Innes following suit by the early 1960s.[5] The Canadian Pacific railway shops that once employed more than 120 men were closed in 1940, with most of the 35 remaining employees moved to the Angus shops in Montreal.[6] A year later the old roundhouse was purchased by the Canadian Co-operative Wool Growers as a warehouse on the main railway line to Montreal. The loss of hundreds of jobs in the railways shops and woollen mills contrasted with the skeleton staff of four or five persons who collected, graded and marketed Ontario wool.[7] As the industrial future of Carleton Place looked increasingly bleak in the late 1940s and 1950s, unlike the rest of Canada which was experiencing a baby boom, the town's population ceased to grow, after having continuously risen for the previous forty years.

Those Beckwith inhabitants unable or unwilling to become employed in agriculture increasingly looked to Ottawa for a livelihood. The growth of government in that city during World War Two and the expanded role of the federal government in planning economic development and developing social programs produced a remarkable increase in the size of the federal public service only a mere half hour's drive away. Morning and evening trains to and from Ottawa, later joined by buses, and carpools of those working in Ottawa became a daily sight in Beckwith. For the first time in a century, the population of rural Beckwith began to rise in the 1950s, increasing by 134 persons between 1951 and 1961, as the birthrate increased. Beckwith's population more dramatically jumped from 1,169 persons in 1961 to 1,712 in 1971, an increase of 543 or almost fifty percent brought about by younger people starting families and building new houses, and by the moving in of Ottawa commuters with no previous connection to the township. In the 1970s the attractiveness of Beckwith as a commuter residential area just over the boundary from the higher property taxes of the regional municipality of Ottawa-Carleton was apparent as the township's population jumped by two-thirds to 2,844 persons in 1981, and to a further new all time high of 3,975 inhabitants by 1991.

The postwar growth of Beckwith was due not only to its being close to employment in Ottawa. The township increasingly offered services and amenities that previously had only been available in Carleton Place or Ottawa, along with the added inducements of a lower assessment and a scenic countryside. Hydro-electricity was introduced to rural Beckwith inhabitants in the late 1940s, with the township hall wired for electricity in 1949.[8] In March 1945 Beckwith council agreed to share the expense with Goulbourn council of placing electric street lights along the street on the boundary between the two municipalities in Ashton village.[9] In August 1949 a deputation from Franktown applied to have street lights installed in that village,[10] but in 1958 council members were still opposed to installing street lights there.[11] Three property owners at Franktown threatened to submit their request for street lights to Toronto, requesting a public inquiry into the affairs of the township, in the meantime "holding the township liable for injuries received by persons on sidewalks caused by lack of proper and sufficient lighting."[12] Eventually a couple of street lights were put up along Church Street in Franktown, with power supplied and paid for out of private homes, but as late as 1991 there were no public street lights in Franktown, revealing how thoroughly the township remained under the control of local farmers most of whom had little empathy for the inhabitants of Beckwith villages. Certainly, the people moving into Beckwith were not attracted to the villages, but rather to lots severed off farms with sufficient room to accommodate septic tanks and wells. A number of older families did not have their houses wired for electricity until the mid 1950s.[13]

Beckwith villages, and particularly Franktown, drooped in the 1950s and early 1960s. Franktown was a village largely inhabited by older people, most of them retired, residing in old houses. Apart from the village store, apart from the post office, the two churches, the village school and the occasional dance in what once had been John Hughton's stone hotel, the village was redolent with decline. Few young people were to be found in Franktown, some of the few younger and middle-aged inhabitants to be found were known to have no occupation or work to do, and no new houses had been built in the village between 1905 and the early 1970s. People living at Franktown as in the rest of Beckwith who wished to make a living either travelled daily to Smiths Falls or Carleton Place.

The improvement of local roads was perhaps the major improvement that encouraged Ottawa commuters to start moving into Beckwith from the 1960s on. Statute labour was abolished in 1927 and township roads received little attention for the next twenty years. The only roads ploughed clear of snow in winter were the two provincial highways passing through. In 1946 several snow clubs were voluntarily formed in Beckwith, spurring the township council to encourage others to form, so that by October there were ten snow clubs or groups of men arranging to plough the roads in their respective localities. In 1958 Beckwith council discontinued the snow clubs, ordering the clerk "to advertise for tenders for the snow ploughing of part or all of the municipal roads." Before the winter of 1958-1959 was over, Beckwith purchased a grader with a snow plough and wing,[14] but substantial repair and rebuilding of townhip roads did not take place until the 1970s.[15]

As crucial as the year-round maintenance of roads and rural electrification became to Beckwith's postwar development, the most controversial change struck at the very heart of its scattered community identities. In June 1946 the county public school inspector J. W. Barber urged the township council to form a township school area whereby instead of having separate boards of trustees for each of the dozen school sections, ratepayers elected a board of trustees for the entire township who looked after all schools. The council complied with this request, and as a result more uniform standards existed in all the township schools.[16] Barber was able to report by 1950:[17]

Plate 266
Ruin of the Robert Scott Jr. farmhouse, lot 25, concession 6, Beckwith, as photographed in June 1981. Four generations of ongoing population decline and of watching generation after generation of young people moving west, into town, or into Ottawa had a profound impact on the psyche of Beckwith. Those left behind, although they would not admit it aloud, came to perceive themselves as relatively backward, less prosperous, and certainly more traditional or old-fashioned as contrasted with the more modern lifestyle of relatives in Ottawa and more distant centres. With farm consolidation, numerous old houses were left empty, and in this case the owner preferred to remove the roof rather than pay taxes on the structure. By August 1981, the township council, realising how much of Beckwith's heritage was destroyed, commissioned the writing of a detailed township history. Less than a month previously the ruin shown here was bulldozed. Note the contrast with Plate 193.

In Lanark County all of the townships except one have adopted the larger unit of administration for the elementary schools. The school buildings are being repaired and painted. Many wells have been drilled and electric lights are being installed wherever the power is available. All of the pupils in the school areas are supplied with notebooks, workbooks, pens, pencils and miscellaneous supplies. A few of the areas are also providing textbooks.

In May 1948 Beckwith applied to become part of the larger Carleton Place High School area, and that December Russell Craig was appointed the first Beckwith representative on the high school board as the township began to fund the high school and to bus students to it.[18]

Despite these advances, Beckwith township council in the late 1940s and 1950s was unwilling to face up to the inevitable question of school consolidation implicit in forming a township school area. Inspector Barber commented in 1950:[19]

We have reached an age of specialization in agriculture. Tractor farming is becoming common. Often the man with a tractor desires more land and this leads to larger holdings by one family. Thus the number of families per school section is decreasing. Furthermore, the size of each family is often smaller than in past decades. These factors have led to a small enrolment of only seventeen pupils per school. With the rising cost of education we will soon have to face the question of whether some re-organization of our rural schools should be made.

This was before Beckwith's population began to grow in the 1950s, but by the mid 1960s it was clear that the one room schools were hampering Beckwith's growth. The Ontario fire marshall's office informed the township council that the schools scattered across the township would have to be massively upgraded, probably replaced, to come up to acceptable safety standards. Some Beckwith parents by the early 1960s, convinced that their children were receiving a second class education in the one room schools with eight grades under one teacher, paid tuition to the Carleton Place school board in addition to paying their Beckwith school taxes, and transported their children to attend the larger schools in Carleton Place.[20]

The Beckwith township school area board recommended that a central seven room school for the township be constructed similar to the Montague Central School opened in 1964 to the south.[21] Unlike Montague where a majority of ratepayers approved building a new central school, the local village and community inhabitants of Beckwith were up in arms at the thought of losing the focus of their identities, the local schoolhouse. Despite arguments by inspector George Nobes and Beckwith school board officials that it would be less expensive to build and operate a central school rather than run a set of one room schools, a majority of Beckwith ratepayers refused to give up their local schools. When the township council held a plebiscite in July 1965, requesting ratepayer approval to apply to the Ontario Municipal Board to construct a large central school, as opposed to upgrading or rebuilding the local one room schools, 291 out of 435 or fully two-thirds of those who voted opposed the proposal.[22] A few months later, the result of the plebiscite notwithstanding, the Beckwith school area board again requested the township council to apply to the province for approval to construct a central seven room school.[23]

The township council found itself caught on the horns of a dilemma. It recognised the financial impossibility of building and maintaining new one room schools throughout the township at a time when the rest of the province had done away with them. If they kept the one room schools they would stifle the attractiveness of Beckwith as a residential area for Ottawa commuters spilling beyond the boundaries of Ottawa-Carleton. The plebiscite, on the other hand, effectively ruled out building a central school with Beckwith tax dollars. The only alternative for the council was to follow the recommendation of inspector Nobes in January 1966 to have a seven or eight room addition constructed onto Caldwell Street Public School in Carleton Place, and to have Beckwith pupils transported and educated there.[24] A special public meeting held in the Caldwell Street school in early March 1966 voted in favour of Beckwith and Carleton Place being amalgamated for public school purposes,[25] effectively ensuring that the larger number of town school supporters would handily be able to outvote the parochial ambitions of Beckwith school supporters. Within the year the one room schools of rural Beckwith were closed and sold off. There is no record of how many former township inhabitants revolved in their graves at the thought of Beckwith paying for a school in Carleton Place, but there was sufficient outcry among the living to remove reeve Stanley Brunton from office in the municipal elections that autumn.

The bussing of Beckwith children into Carleton Place beginning in 1966 truly marked the emergence of a new township identity, but it did so by means of a peculiar process. The loss of their local schools and the bussing of their children to Carleton Place united a majority of Beckwith inhabitants in a collective sense of loss in a way that construction of a new central school within Beckwith would have taken much longer to bring about. The bitter division of older Beckwith

Plate 267
Harrowing with horses and tractor on the Raymond Mains farm, lot 22, concession 5, Beckwith, as photographed in May 1944. Beckwith agriculture was never the same again once farmers began purchasing tractors from the late 1940s on. The acquisition of tractors contributed to the consolidation of large farms in the postwar period. Those farmers who did not enlarge their holdings, used tractors to do their field work more quickly, while holding down jobs in a nearby town. Photograph courtesy of Mabel and Raymond Mains.

families between those who wished to retain the old one room schools and those favouring a larger central facility was all too evident to the new families arriving in the 1970s. One of the new Ottawa commuters who came to reside in one of the old schoolhouses in 1975, observed:[26]

> Family life in the older farming community had changed dramatically just before we arrived. School consolidation and bus[s]ing represented an increased level of educational sophistication and urban social accessibility that was desirable for a number of families. Others saw it as too radical [a] break with tradition and loss of small community control. Families still do not speak to their neighbours and it is ironic that...the construction of a school at Black's Corners [in 1988] is the result of a strong demand by rural inhabitants (not only farmers) for a facility closer to home.

It was following the amalgamation of Beckwith and Carleton Place for public school purposes that significant population growth took place and new housing began to appear. Between 1951 and 1956 there was an increase of 151 people, but it was between 1966 and 1971 with an increase of 392 persons that Beckwith's population growth began to outstrip that of Carleton Place, Lanark County and even that of the entire province, leading to even more remarkable growth in the 1970s and 1980s.[27] In the ten years from 1975 to 1984 some 409 new dwelling units were built in Beckwith,[28] and in the late 1980s the township led all other Lanark County municipalities in the number of new housing starts.[29]

Beckwith relied on Carleton Place for a number of services long before it amalgamated with the town for public school purposes. Carleton Place had served as a market for agricultural produce from the beginning of settlement, and increasingly it was the hub for services and products that Beckwith inhabitants wished to purchase. There was an *ad hoc* arrangement for fire protection during the early and mid twentieth century whereby the Ocean Wave fire company responded to fires in Beckwith. In April 1955 the Carleton Place fire committee requested an annual grant equal to one mill on all Beckwith taxable property, This arrangement proved satisfactory until June 1963 when the Carleton Place council issued an ultimatum, threatening to remove all fire protection unless more satisfactory arrangements were worked out. In response, Beckwith decided to set up its own volunteer fire department, and that autumn a municipal firehall was built at Black's Corners and a water truck was purchased. Previously in the early 1950s Beckwith and Goulbourn councils jointly financed the construction of a dam across the Jock River at Ashton to provide a reservoir of water for fighting fires,[30] Beckwith inhabitants all along had individually made use of the Carleton Place public library, the high school and recreation facilities in the same way that town inhabitants had enjoyed Lake Park in Beckwith as a rural recreational facility at the turn of the century.

Since Carleton Place was town to the majority of Beckwith inhabitants, it was naturally expected and taken for granted that they had common interests. The importance of Beckwith rural inhabitants to the commercial exonomy of the town was shown by establishing a public rest room at Carleton Place in 1944 especially for the convenience of Beckwith and Ramsay women.[31] Carleton Place received other benefits from Beckwith. In October 1948 the township council granted the town permission to use a portion of an adjacent Beckwith property as the town dump. In 1953 Beckwith sold the town a portion of the McNeely property along the town's southern boundary for industrial expansion, and in 1954 Beckwith contributed to the new Carleton Place public hospital,[32]

The influx of Ottawa commuters into Beckwith from the late 1960s onward served to strain relations between the township and Carleton Place. The new arrivals expected, took for granted, and used extensively the town library and recreational services, and the children of the older Beckwith families sharing the buses with the children of the Ottawa commuters were drawn into sharing the same expectations. Carleton Place too found its population augmented by the arrival of Ottawa commuters from the late 1960s on, and invested heavily in arenas, community centres, parks, baseball diamonds, and an indoor swimming pool. Carleton Place town council members and the town public in general increasingly looked askance at the use of these expensive facilities by Beckwith inhabitants, and even after Beckwith began paying for the use of the town library and recreation services, Carleton Place complained that Beckwith did not pay a proportion equal to the use its inhabitants made of these facilities. By the mid 1970s Beckwith farm parents became dismayed at how thoroughly social and recreational life for their children had become focussed outside the township's boundaries. A perceptive newcomer noted:[33]

> The increased availability of activities in Carleton Place that would give children and adolescents more social skills had already turned farm parents into chauffeurs. Whereas in the past a trip to town was a once a week event[,] parents were often travelling nightly for hockey, skating and swimming and on weekends for riding, as well as driving to the suburban shopping malls for clothing.

The jump in Beckwith's population during the 1970s and early 1980s made recreation an important consideration in municipal services alongside planning, roads, fire protection and supervising building construction. The new population began "asking for community centres, public beaches, parks, sports facilities, new programs and recreation funds."[34] A 1986 recreation needs study and master plan provides numerous insights into the continuing fragmentation and changing quality of life in Beckwith. The study claimed that Beckwith's population was divided into five

Plate 268
The Patrick Watson house, lot 6, concession 2, Beckwith, as photographed in 1982. Located just outside the boundary of the national capital regional municipality of Ottawa-Carleton, the low real estate prices in Beckwith attracted new inhabitants looking for property within easy commuting distance of Ottawa. During the 1970s and 1980s there was a building boom along the concession roads of Beckwith, with more houses built during these twenty years than in the previous 150. Many of the new houses were large, handsome and sometimes innovative structures.

groups—seasonal cottagers, full time cottagers, commuters who recently had moved to Beckwith, commuters who had lived in Beckwith since the early 1970s, and a minority of farmers,[35] The study recognised that "[b]ecause of the real problems inhibiting neighbourhood communications on a Township wide basis" it was necessary "to use a decentralized approach to recreation in Beckwith." Accordingly, the township was divided for recreation purposes into five communities, with Franktown the focus of the five southernmost concessions, Scotch Corners the focus for the area west of Mississippi Lake, Black's Corners the focus for the remainder of concessions six to ten west of lot 21, Ashton the focus of lots 21 to 27 in concessions six to twelve, and Carleton Place the focus of lots eight to twenty in concessions eleven and twelve,[36] As late as 1986 Beckwith only had the municipal office, firehalls and church halls in which to hold social and sporting events in contrast with the arenas, tennis courts, soccer fields, community centres, canoe clubhouse, Royal Canadian Legion hall, Senior Citizens' clubhouse and school auditoriums in Carleton Place. Beckwith had only two private beaches and five different sports available to its citizens in 1986 in contrast with seven open maintained park areas and 22 different sports available in Carleton Place.[37] The construction of a new public school east of Black's Corners in 1988 promised to provide a venue for indoor recreation in Beckwith in the same way that Carleton Place inhabitants had used their school facilities for recreational purposes since the 1950s. In the mid 1980s Beckwith purchased a 43 acre plot on lot thirteen in concession nine to be ultimately used for recreation, and a smaller piece of undeveloped parkland in the Edey subdivision on lot 21 in concession nine.

The 1986 recreation study revealed numerous positive attributes to the new population moving into Beckwith. The growth in Beckwith's population was partly due to the postwar baby boom growing up, due to the lower cost of building and lower property taxes than in Ottawa-Carleton, and due to a lack of land in Carleton Place on which to build, but people also were attracted by a desire for open space and a rural atmosphere.[38] A 1985 recreation survey of Beckwith inhabitants revealed that because of its pleasant location they "would give a much higher priority to facilities which would allow them to get outdoors and enjoy nature, rather than structured facilities such as a ball diamond or outdoor arena."[39]

> The most remarkable level of support was found for the [establishment of a] public beach at Mississippi Lake, followed closely by the need for a boat launch at the same spot.... [A] substantial majority of residents [interviewed] said they desired a large outdoor space for get-togethers, barbeques and family outings.

The authors of the Beckwith recreation report further noted, "Current trends together with supporting requests from some residents indicate that hiking/cycling/skiing trails along the Jock River and King's Creek would be very popular. These areas have some very scenic views. The trails should be developed over the next twenty years."[40] The growth of Beckwith recreational resources in the closing years of the twentieth century was premised on a firm policy that all boards, committees, executives and instructors should be volunteers in order to keep recreation financially feasible and to create community spirit.[41]

The 1986 recreation report also revealed how fundamentally the nature of Beckwith society generally had changed. Among the reasons stressed for offering a wider variety of recreational activities in Beckwith was "the need for social interaction after a day spent with a computer", the "reality of shorter work weeks [that] allow... more discretionary time," and, more negatively, the "realization that many residents do not recognize Beckwith, or its parts, with any sense of community.[42] The authors of the recreation report were dismayed to discover "residents [who] don't even know they live in Beckwith [but] instead, they think they live in the nearest town or hamlet".[43] Most Beckwith inhabitants were unaware that well over half of Beckwith's recreation budget was paid over to the town of Carleton Place to ensure township inhabitants the right to use facilities such as the indoor pool and arena.[44]

The growing emphasis on recreation was simply one of many manifestations of major change in Beckwith during the postwar decades. Even before significant population growth began in the late 1960s, Beckwith had become redirected in its focus away from itself, away from Carleton Place, to Ottawa and to an urban perspective. The Ottawa *Farm Journal* and valley edition of the Ottawa *Citizen* had sufficiently infiltrated Beckwith and vicinity in the 1920s and 1030s that the Carleton Place *Herald* ceased publication in 1944, amalgamating with the *Central Canadian*. The *Canadian*, as it came to be called, successfully staved off competition from the briefly-lived Carleton Place *Review* in the mid 1970s,[45] but the *Canadian* itself in the 1970s simply became one in a string of valley newspapers owned and printed in Renfrew by D.F. Runge.[46] With effective control of the local paper removed from the immediate vicinity, the implications for the newspaper being a mirror of the local community memory were dire. Few copies of Carleton Place newspapers printed from the early 1950s on were preserved by the firm that took over the newspaper.

From the mid 1950s on the urban influence was even more directly felt with the arrival of television. Despite the best efforts of Ottawa television stations to give coverage to regional events, the television news focussed on Ottawa, putting Beckwith inhabitants instantly in touch with the latest daily developments in the city and making events in Beckwith and Carleton Place pale by

Plate 269
A service in St. James Anglican church, Franktown, as photographed ca. 1960. Beckwith churches in the twentieth century reflected the ongoing decline of population, as some were closed, and those that remained open had straggling attendance. With the closing of local rural one room schools in the mid 1960s, these churches became the major repositories of the continuing fractured local community identities of Beckwith. The Union Jack flag to the left of the Palladian altar window betrayed the persisting attachment to British institutions among descendents of the Irish Anglican settlers of southern Beckwith. Photograph loaned courtesy of Donna and Robert Hughton. Credit, United Press International Photo, Ottawa.

contrast. Television advertising cajoled Beckwith inhabitants to shop in the new shopping centre developments in Ottawa, and to enjoy the various forms of entertainment available in a city whose cultural sophistication was broadening. Carleton Place developers constructed small shopping plazas in the 1970s and 1980s, but not before the local cinema had folded before the brunt of television entertainment. It was not until 1990 that a cinema briefly opened its doors in Carleton Place. Even the imported American comedy and crime dramas featured on the Ottawa television stations emphasized the relative sophistication of urban life over rural rusticism, forcing Beckwith inhabitants to laugh along at rural characters in "Green Acres" and "The Beverly Hillbillies" and to view more seriously the street-smarts and moral drama in urban-based programs such as "Perry Mason" and "St. Elsewhere". And inevitably, every ten minutes there was the interminable succession of television commercials, wheedling *ad nauseum*, "Does your husband care about bathroom tissue?" "Strong enough for a man, but made for a woman!", "Would you believe over two million men are getting over their grey hair by using Grecian Formula?", "I don't believe in other soaps this

Plate 270
Members of the Beckwith Township Fire Department as photographed in front of the fire hall at Black's Corners in 1964. The establishment of the fire department was a significant development for Beckwith. In contrast with the fragmented associations and loyalties of school sections, church congregations, villages, and groups of neighbouring farmers working together, the fire department represented the first organization since the creation of the municipal council 115 years earlier to draw men together from across the entire township. The Beckwith fire department during its first quarter of a century was both voluntary and a male bastion. For names see Appendix 34. Photograph courtesy of Arthur Nesbitt.

strongly!", "Yours leaves your breath mediciney", "He's so good looking he deserves to be happy!", and "With Wintario we all win: twice the fun for a Buck!"

Television and newspapers were the two major forms of communication that increasingly channelled Beckwith's attention on Ottawa, but others followed. In April 1948 the Lanark and Carleton Counties Telephone Company sold out to the Bell Telephone Company,[47] the Goodwood Rural Telephone Company followed in 1960, then the Beckwith and Montague Rural Telephone Company sold to Bell in 1961, and finally the Lanark and Ramsay Telephone Company was purchased by Bell, in 1966.[48] Despite all of Beckwith being placed under the Bell system, the township was not only divided between the Carleton Place and Smiths Falls exchanges, but more fundamentally was divided between the Ottawa and Brockville/Smiths Falls telephone directories, thus maintaining a very strong division between southern and northern concessions. The closing of all the rural post offices in Beckwith had started much earlier than the consolidation of telephone exchanges. The Scotch Corners post office which had opened in 1889 was closed down in June 1907,[49]

Plate 271
An auction sale at the farmhouse of Donna and Robert Hughton, lot 14, concession 4, east of Franktown, as photographed on August 31st, 1985. Even those properties that were handed down from one generation to another in old Beckwith families witnessed the dispersal of various mementos with the passing of each successive generation. Despite being owned by the Irish-origin Hughton family for most of its history, the thistle design in the verandah vergeboard reveals that this house was built for the Scottish-origin James Fleming family. The older families of Beckwith became numerically insignificant among the sea of Ottawa commuters living in the township in the 1970s and 1980s.

the Bellcott post office at Gillies' Corners operated briefly from 1910 to 1913,[50] the Tennyson post office was closed in 1914, and the Prospect post office was closed in 1932.[51] The Franktown post office remained open with two rural routes operating out of it until it too was closed in 1970.[52] Thereafter eastern Beckwith was served by rural route three out of Ashton, northwestern inhabitants were served by rural route two out of Carleton Place, and southwestern Beckwith was served by rural route six out of Smiths Falls, and rural route one out of Perth. For a time in the late 1970s it seemed that Beckwith might be the location of a paved airport runway, as Beckwith joined Perth and other townships in a lobbying effort to cajole funding away from the Smiths Falls-Montague airport to a site more centrally located between Smiths Falls, Perth and Carleton Place, but to no avail.[53] A private airstrip was operated just west of Black's Corners from the early 1960s on.

The increasing urbanisation of Beckwith was most tellingly revealed by the diminishing proportion of township inhabitants who lived on farms. In 1941 over 85 percent of Beckwith's 1,154 inhabitants were to be found on farms, but this proportion declined slowly to 72 percent in 1956, then dropped to fifty percent in the next five years, then dropped again to 29 percent by 1971,[54] and finally in 1981 the 351 people living on Beckwith farms amounted to less than 13 percent of

Beckwith's 2,844 inhabitants. Only 91 of the 351, or slightly more than three percent of Beckwith's population in 1981 lived on farms with gross sales in excess of $25,000.[55] A couple from Ottawa moving into the Derry locality in the mid 1970s[56]

> discovered very quickly that John Kidd husbanded his cattle and sheep in a 19th C[entury] fashion with no electricity in the barn and no silo; his father William still ruling paternally from his widower's house. Raymond [Mains] ran a sophisticated beef and dairy enterprise while [Stanley and Keith] Brunton...exploited every possible piece of land (having purchased abandoned farmsteads) with corn growing for their pig "factory". In and amongst these three [operations] ranged marginal farms worked by part time farmers and the soon to be increased influx of urbanites....

The number of farms in Beckwith declined from 278 in 1941 to 202 in 1951, to 167 in 1961, and to 104 in 1981, and increasingly most of these were part time operations. Of the 104 Beckwith farms in 1981, only 27 or a quarter had gross sales in excess of $25,000 in a community where the average income in 1981 was more than $27,000.[57] The declining agricultural productivity of Beckwith is shown in tables 30 and 31.

By the late 1980s there were only ten full time dairy farms and a couple of dozen full time beef cattle farmers in Beckwith, in addition to a few other farmers specialising in honey and hogs. The move to part time farming for a number of farmers began when the bottom fell out of the cattle market in 1953,[58] and was heightened by the availability of better paying employment and better work hours both in Carleton Place and Ottawa in the 1960s. By the late 1960s those who wished to remain in farming had to greatly expand their operations and invest heavily in new technology to make their operations viable. When Jim Foster graduated from the Kemptville College of Agricultural Technology in 1970 he milked approximately 15 cows or what previously had been considered a decent-sized herd of dairy cows. He purchased 111 acres of land from his father, Boyd Foster, who owned the adjacent 250 acre farm, and they worked out an income-sharing arrangement. By 1986 the herd owned by Jim and his wife Lynda numbered almost sixty mostly purebred cows, and together with his parents' herd there was a total of 120 Holsteins on Jockbrae farm.

The heavy investment of time required by the few full time farmers remaining in Beckwith is shown by a reporter's description of a day on the Foster farm in 1986.[59]

> A typical day on the Beckwith farm begins at 5:30 a[.]m.... For the Fosters...it is out to the barn and milk the cows before returning to the house at 7:30 a[.]m[.] for breakfast.... [T]he Fosters milk between 52 and 56 cows at all times. The cows are kept in an open housing type of setup with milking being done on a pipeline system.... After an hour of brief relaxation indoors, there are more chores to do in the barn or outdoors, whether it be cleaning, feeding, maintenance, crop sowing or getting a cow that needs to be bred ready for the Eastern Breeders technicians.... [D]inner...brings another small break at noon. The afternoon period brings more work or perhaps a drive to town for additional supplies. The final milking starts at 4:30 p[.]m[.] with the Fosters generally being finished work for the day two hours later.

The large new farming operations required large crops and the participation of all family members in much the same way that Beckwith agriculture always had since the very beginning of settlement. Continuing with the example of the Foster farm, they sowed "approximately 100 acres of grain and silage corn and 50 acres in small grains (wheat, barley and oats) each year with the remainder of the 200 plus arable acres on the two farms and adjoining rented land used to produce hay. On the years that the corn is bountiful, the excess harvest is sold as a cash crop."[60] While Jim Foster did the majority of the heavy work, his father played a fairly active role in terms of tractor

Plate 272
Remembrance Day service outside the Beckwith municipal building at Black's Corners, as photographed on the eleventh of November 1986. The cenotaph commemorating men and women from Beckwith who died in the first and second world wars was moved from beside the front entrance of the 1857 township hall after it was destroyed by fire in 1961 to a similar position beside the entrance of the new municipal building constructed in 1962. During the twentieth century the solemnity of the annual Remembrance Day services has been one of the few things offering any sense of common identity to inhabitants across the township. Standing to the right of the lowered flag are reeve John Sheil and deputy reeve Mervyn Devlin. In the distance is one of the large new houses built in the 1970s and 1980s.

work and feeding calves. Boyd's wife, Vera, served as the farm accountant, insuring that farm finances were kept up to date, while Lynda maintained cattle records, herd books and some of the payroll as well as managing the hired help who lived in the back section of the house. Jim and Lynda's son, Greg, at age twelve already was helping with milking, haying and driving tractor.

Not only the minority of farm women but most women in Beckwith worked out at some form of paid employment by the 1970s and 1980s. It was a distinct change from the late 1930s when most married women in Beckwith did not work outside the home. The wartime call for women to enlist as CWACs, to work at war production in Carleton Place factories, to replace men in the farm workfields and stables jolted Beckwith women out of their isolation from one another. At war's end two organisations unconnected with church activities emerged, encouraging women to join. The first of these was the Beckwith Women' Institute which was organised by eleven women at the home of Mrs. James Reynolds in April 1945,[61] and the second was the Beckwith Township Federation of Agriculture formed in 1946 that encouraged both men and women to join. The federation did not last a decade, but during its brief existence carried out a campaign against the warble-fly and collected funds for the Canadian Appeal to Children.[62] The Women's Institute proved more enduring, attracting members from Carleton Place as well as all of Beckwith.

In a number of ways the Women's Institute reinforced the idea of women's traditional domestic role by offering courses to local women and girls in food preparation, working with cloth and

Plate 273
Beckwith Public School under construction, as photographed in September 1988. This structure stands as a monument to the new more unified municipality that developed in the 1980s. Before 1966 the elementary students of Beckwith were divided among eight school sections, reflecting the fractured local village and hamlet loyalties, interests and identities that divided township inhabitants. From 1966 to 1988 Beckwith students were lost among the larger numbers of students in Carleton Place schools, at the same time the old families of Beckwith became numerically swamped by an influx of new commmuting inhabitants.

handicrafts, but the institute also acted as a springboard for one township inhabitant, Audrey McRae, to join the Carleton Place and district public hospital committee and became chairman of the Lanark County Board of Education, the sole political achievement in the history of Beckwith women before Geraldine Robinson, the first woman member of the township council, was elected in 1991. Virtually one of the first acts of the Women's Institute was to organise a reception for the men and women returning from World War Two.[63] Members provided and installed name signs on township roads so that visitors and emergency vehicles could find the way more easily, they raised funds to help build and equip the hospital at Carleton Place, they helped establish and staff the North Lanark Museum at Appleton, they raised a cairn to commemorate the seventh line Church of Scotland after it was bulldozed, they compiled a Tweedsmuir history of Beckwith, and they made ongoing donations to worthwhile endeavours such as Alwood House — a centre at Scotch Corners for treating adolescent alcoholics, and Interval House — a county shelter at Carleton Place for battered women. Ultimately, the Beckwith Women's Institute was unable to bring women from all sections of the township together, and in 1982 under the leadership of Joan Irvine the Franktown — Numogate Woman's Institute was formed. The changing place of women in Beckwith society between the late 1940s and the late 1980s was most perceptively stated in the comment of Flo Barclay of the Beckwith Women's Institute in 1988 "that young women [today] have more demands on their time than was the case four or five decades ago."[64]

As commuters began to form a majority of Beckwith's population in the 1970s and 1980s, their values and needs began to form and shape the local landscape. As Beckwith became less a farming

Plate 274
The farm of Clarence and Dorothy Lewis, lot 25, concession 8, Beckwith, as photographed in September 1987. By the 1980s barely three percent of Beckwith inhabitants lived on working farms. This farm has a variety of buildings from the various phases of Beckwith agriculture, including a log grain barn from the early nineteenth century provisioning economy, frame barns and a brick house from the turn of the century cheese economy, and modern silos and stables suitable to feed, house and milk a large dairy herd in the 1990s. Increasingly, Beckwith farms resembled factories.

community and more a residential community, the need for planning the township's future growth became increasingly evident. The strip of commercial development that emerged along highway number 7 at the southern boundary of Carleton Place, although initially unattractive, provided motels, restaurants and 24-hour service stations to serve the motoring public. There were instances of older Beckwith families remaining insulated from the families moving in beside them, upset at having to pay high new insurance premiums on the property to guard against being sued by the families of children who crossed fences and risked being either trampled or gored by livestock. Conversely, some of the urban arrivals unrealistically expected to prevent Beckwith farmers spreading manure on their fields. Many of the old families, however, did not worry about the loss of sections of family farms to the strip development of new housing. They perceived the newcomers as a source of wealth for the community tax base and they replaced their emotional ties to the land with tracing their family history. For couples moving into Beckwith in the 1970s and 1980s,[65]

> Going into a farm house was no different than visiting a city home — all had contemporary kitchen and laundry equipment, [televisions] dominated the living rooms, bathrooms were being upgraded to catalogue standards and old family furniture heirlooms were mixing with modern pieces. Kitchen gardens still existed but no one was raising chickens and all bought eggs at the supermarket.... Properties were being advertised regularly as severance notices increased along the fence lines. A variety of housing appeared in the Derry [including] two old log houses dismantled and rebuilt on new locations to a new square cut timber [house] assembled by Forley Wells in a southwest Amercan ranch style. Contemporary bungalows in

wood, aluminum and brick facing now stretch out like rectangular mushrooms in open field or cedar bush.... There is little or no contact with the owners since most are still city workers.

Despite some of the urban refugees seeking isolation in a rural setting and despite the eagerness of old Beckwith families to cash in on their land's new value, even to the extent of selling the family home to build a sprawling bungalow beside it to keep up with the other lavish new homes being constructed, it was clear that growth was getting out of hand by the mid 1970s. Beckwith along with other municipalities rejected the recommendation of Donald King in 1976 that the seventeen municipalities in Lanark County be carved up into five town and village-centred municipalities by integrating, Almonte, Carleton Place, Perth, Smiths Falls and Lanark Village with their surrounding rural areas. The new Carleton Place-centred municipality that King recommended Beckwith be absorbed into included all of Beckwith, the eastern half of Drummond, a strip of southern Ramsay and southeastern Lanark township.[66] In 1977 Beckwith passed a zoning by-law "designed to regulate the use of land and the construction and use of buildings and structures" as part of an official plan for North Lanark.[67] The North Lanark official plan was generated on the premise of limited growth, but by the late 1980s as Beckwith attained the highest rate of severances and of housing construction of any municpality in Lanark County, it was clear that the original official plan for the township could not adequately deal with the new pressures of growth. A new official plan of Beckwith was developed beginning in 1986 to provide a plan along which dramatic population growth could be best handled. In creating such a plan in the late 1980s to set the base for future growth in the township,[68] Beckwith politicians and inhabitants sought to prepare for more orderly development, to improve the quality of the environment and to protect good agricultural land wherever possible.[69]

The new commuting inhabitants of Beckwith were among those most concerned with maintaining and improving the quality of the local environment and heritage. When Leonard and Reva Dolgoy moved to Beckwith in 1975,[70]

> Township meetings were still dominated by discussions about right of way, drainage and ditching, and the odd severance and the occasional petition. We participated in one [petition] regarding the illegal opening of a quarry off our 6th line. We also were part of a group requesting that Beckwith include the referendum on nuclear free zoning in an election year. Both these passed successfully because of the mixture of names reflecting old established families and newcomers. Now township meetings echo with many concerns that range from land use and pollution to culture and recreation.

The commuters moving into Beckwith in the 1970s and 1980s not only included nationally known broadcaster Patrick Watson and Ottawa Symphony Orchestra conductor Brian Law, but also gave the township a more highly educated population than either Carleton Place or the whole of Lanark County.[71] In addition to enjoying Beckwith's natural environment, some of the new arrivals began to figure prominently in the Carleton Place and Beckwith Historical Society founded in 1979, and they began to create museum desplays in the museum at Carleton Place such as the one in the summer of 1988 entitled "Homelands to Settlement: Scottish and Irish Immigration to Beckwith." In 1981 the township council under reeve Stanley Brunton commissioned the writing of an authoritative history of Beckwith. The construction of a large public school near Black's Corners in 1988 over strenuous objections from Carleton Place promised to provide a new centre and focus for community social life and events drawing participation from across the township such as Beckwith had not enjoyed since the demise of the rural school fairs in 1939.

Unprecedented development inevitably meant that the old fractured small community loyalties of Beckwith grew less important. The population growth and prosperity of the 1980s was capped by proposals to construct two large shopping malls at the intersection of highways 7 and 15. Many

Plate 275
An Orange procession marching north along Bridge Street in Carleton Place, as photographed on July 13th, 1983. Throughout much of Beckwith's history the survival of Orangeism reflected the insecurity of Irish Anglican exiles who had hurriedly pulled up stakes, afraid of the Roman Catholic majority in Ireland obtaining legal equality and political rights. Orangeism in Beckwith was transmuted into a successful political engine and fraternal organisation, but the legacy of insecurity lingered on, as reflected in slogans on banners such as "Defending our Heritage: Freedom of Religion." When local Irish Anglican Orangemen boasted of Wolfe's conquest of Quebec, it in effect was rhetorical overcompensation for their forefathers running out of Ireland in fear of Catholic emancipation. The first Orange processions in Upper Canada took place in the Beckwith vicinity in the 1820s, and as the ranks of the order dwindle in the late twentieth century it is likely that the last processions also will take place here.

Beckwith inhabitants hoped the new shopping malls would increase employment and expand the tax base.[72] The new malls and the new Beckwith Public School would serve in their respective ways to bring inhabitants from all corners of the township together as a more unified homogeneous population, in decided contrast with the fractured local identities that had persisted during the previous 170 years. With time, these identities were modified as ethnicity became transmuted by religion and politics, and eventually absorbed into local loyalites. These local loyalties survived into the 1960s and 1970s as shown by the overwhelming vote in 1966 not to close one room schools, and as also shown by some Anglicans at Tennyson switching to the Baptist church after St. John's Anglican church closed in 1967. Dwindling attendance at Orange parades betrayed the decline of traditional culture in Beckwith by the early 1980s. The growth of interest in tracing family history and the hosting of the North Lanark Highland Games at Almonte (where no highlanders had ever settled) beginning in 1983, only underlined how thoroughly traditional Beckwith had been demolished. It was comparable to the romantic highland revival in Perthshire 170 years earlier following the destruction of traditional highland society there.

Growth in general and the inflow of new population into Beckwith in the 1970s and 1980s was accompanied by a number of negative developments. If Beckwith enjoyed the highest rate of house construction in Lanark County by 1987, it also had the highest proportion of house robberies, as the large empty houses out along the rural roads became prime targets for theft.[73] With more than half of Beckwith parents away working in Ottawa, and up to 35 percent working in Carleton Place by the late 1980s,[74] children attending public school and high school in town left to their own devices inevitably experimented with illegal drugs, both soft and hard. Some town youths, in a combination of fear and anger at eventually having to face up to leaving the protective small town and rural ambiance of the locality, lashed out by breaking street lamps and in one particularly outrageous incident, setting the Carleton Place public library on fire in 1986.[75]

The introduction of Beckwith into the modern world was perhaps best illustrated by students at the Carleton Place High School being the first in eastern Ontario to visit the Soviet Union in May 1986.[76] But for all the many positive attributes that the commuters to Ottawa had brought with them to Beckwith, some of their children in being nourished and raised within the institutions and alongside the mentality of longer standing in both Carleton Place and Beckwith somehow imbibed the spirit of local decline and defensiveness that had built up during the economically troubled decades of the early to mid twentieth century. The population of Carleton Place like that of Beckwith increasingly depended on Ottawa for employment. The one major industry in town that had survived the 1950s, Findlay's, was sold out to a firm that moved the operation to Montmagny, Quebec, and the Carleton Place plant was torn down in 1971.[77] Fortunately for Carleton Place, Leigh Instruments, a local company that started up in the early 1960s and which was engaged in the design, engineering and production of high technology products largely for military markets,[78] by the 1970s was a major employer to fill the employment vacuum left by the Findlay closure. Employment at Leigh Instruments continued to grow; by the late 1980s half of its 800 employees worked in their Ottawa facility and a new head office was built in Kanata in 1988. In 1990 the company declared bankruptcy, its cash reserves squandered by the British multinational that purchased Leigh Instruments in 1987, but six months later Spar Aerospace of Mississauga resurrected Leigh as one of its divisions.[79] The other firms in the Carleton Place industrial park in the late 1970s and 1980s were much smaller, most of them without unions, a few offering attractive wages and good working conditions, but overall making the town less vulnerable than when the majority of Carleton Place labourers had worked for a few major industries.

The shortage of secure employment within the Beckwith vicinity, the growing dependence on Ottawa-Carleton for employment, and the daily toll of commuting 45 kilometres into downtown Ottawa and back produced various forms of paranoia. The commuters along with members of older families worked to keep the problems of the city away from their rural retreat. When an Ottawa facility for the treatment of emotionally disturbed children considered purchasing a farm near Franktown to house nine young people, concerned local inhabitants held a fiery public meeting and "presented a petition bearing 139 names against the proposed home to Beckwith Township Council".[80] In the early 1980s there was strong local opposition to arbitrary metrification being imposed by the federal Liberal government. A company owned by 37 Conservative members of parliament in 1982 set up a "Freedom to Measure" gas station on Highway 7 near Ashton in defiance of government orders making metrification mandatory rather than voluntary.[81] A leaflet produced locally stated, "We in Eastern Ontario, seeing our freedoms vanish through orders-in-council, have had enough!... We are a lot of little people, those who pay taxes, who are the victims of this senseless forced use of an alien system."[82]

Plate 276
Jehovah's Witnesses from across eastern Ontario building a Kingdom Hall on lot 11, concession 12, Beckwith, as photographed on September 13th, 1987. More than a thousand members of this sect constructed this house of worship in under four days. The dramatic growth of Beckwith's population in the 1970s and 1980s brought large numbers of fundamentalist church members into the vicinity. Photograph courtesy of the Carleton Place Canadian.

The most explosive issue of all for a population an increasing proportion of which depended on employment in Ottawa for its livelihood was the federal official languages Act of 1969 that declared French and English to be the official languages of Canada. Under this Act all federal institutions were obliged to provide their services in both official languages. Massive funding and special efforts were made by Ottawa to encourage, reward and facilitate anglophone civil servants learning French as a second language, all largely to no avail. The hysteria, the paranoia, the covert and blatant racism, the outright refusal of many civil servants who called Beckwith home in the 1970s and 1980s was one of the most depressing sights for anyone who had any hope for the survival of Canadian nationalism, let alone for those who believed that the soldiers who fought in the two world wars had fought to protect the continued existence of Canada. In the late 1980s as Ontario slowly lumbered toward guaranteeing French language services, the Lanark county council and Carleton Place town council revealed their continuing paranoia over bilingualism by asking the provincial government for a referendum on the issue. Some Carleton Place councillors conjured up scenarios of people hired to work at the Ministry of Natural Resources office at Carleton Place having to be fluent in both English and French as unfair. They stated that the need for a referendum on bilingualism was due to the "county being in the national capital region where bilingualism is a very vivid reality" and due to the "fact that residents here have a greater awareness of federal politics and policies."[83] Even at Queen's University, the university that most Beckwith students attended before the late 1960s, the majority of students showed "little interest in taking advantage of the many opportunities to learn French."[84]

It might be tempting to close this history of Beckwith by speculating on the similarities between the latterday anti-French reactionaries yet to be found in the vicinity and the military reactionaries who came to settle in the Perth and Richmond settlements 175 years previously. It might even be possible to weave a tenuous web of explanation, even tentative justification, for the anti-French attitude of Beckwith area inhabitants by pointing to the military settlers having fought against Napoleon's French troops, to the Irish Wexford settlers having been forced to fend off French invasion in 1798, to the competition of Beckwith farmers and lumbermen against French Candians working for lower pay in the provisioning trade and timber trade in the early nineteenth century. Continuing in this vein, it would be possible to point to the resentment against Peter McLaren bringing in French-Canadian labourers in the 1880s to drive local wages down, and later against Bates and Innes for importing French Canadian textile workers in the 1910s for much the same reason, to a pervasive feeling that French Canadians had not participated as fully as they might have in the two world wars, to losing Findlay's to a Quebec city, and finally to fearing that official bilingualism allowed unqualified French Canadians to take jobs away from English Canadians who otherwise were more qualified to fill them.

Tempting though such speculation might be, by the late 1980s it was possible to point to positive developments as increasing numbers of students attended bilingual Algonquin College and the University of Ottawa, as parents demanded[85] and received increasing French immersion programs for their children in local schools,[86] and as the Beckwith township council to its everlasting credit both refused to join other municipalities in requesting a referendum on whether French services should be provided by the Ontario government, and did not pass a motion declaring only English to be the official language of the municipality. Only six years after the "Freedom to Measure" gas station was opened near Ashton Station, another gas station a few miles west of it on Highway 7 was built in 1988, bearing the slogan "Mr. Gas avec/with Service". It testified to the growing realisation that if Beckwith's future was linked economically to Ottawa, sooner or later local inhabitants would have to face up to the reality of bilingualism in both the public service and in the private sector in the national capital region. Obviously, the passing of time together with watching political leaders and indeed no less a person than the Queen of Canada effortlessly switching back and forth from one language to the other on televised state occasions — all had a positive effect. Bilingualism for many Beckwith inhabitants represented the challenge of coping with a faster moving and changing country.

So much had changed in Beckwith and outside its boundaries in the forty years after the end of World War Two. Beckwith along with other townships had given up responsibility for administering general and child welfare, public health, public education and the revision court to the county council. Even the Beckwith assessment rolls were prepared outside the township by the late 1960s. In the late 1980s Beckwith along with other municipalities found itself handed sensitive issues such as Sunday shopping and Pay Equity to adminster as the Ontario government proved unwilling to offer leadership in these areas. In Beckwith's very physical appearance there not only were large new houses lining the concessions across the township, but there were subdivisions of houses, as planning arranged for the building of clusters of houses rather than continuing ribbon development. Mississippi Lake already was completely ringed with cottages and year-round homes. Most other changes that became apparent in the larger society proved liberating for some minorities at the same time they were challenging if not even worrisome to most other Beckwith inhabitants. These changes included the severing of all connection with Britain with the signing of the 1982 Canadian constitution, the loss of localised schools, striking teachers, locally available abortion, a profusion of quarries in Beckwith, the replacing in 1965 of the flag under which Beckwith men and women had served during two world wars, wife battering, closed gates and fences around some of the bigger houses built in the 1980s, the use of illegal drugs and their increasing availability, declining church attendance, female and male strippers in local hotels, the reputation of the intersection of highways

Plate 277
Beckwith township council as photographed in the municipal council chamber at Black's Corners on October 21st 1985. By the time this photograph was taken only a minority of township inhabitants were from old local families, and barely three percent of them lived on farms. Despite the new demographic reality, as late as 1985 three of the council members were full-time farmers, only one a commuter to Ottawa, and three of them were from old Beckwith families. In the large new municipal chamber built in 1984 the continuing importance attached to tradition was apparent in the prominent positioning of the honour rolls from the first and second world wars. Between the two lists of predominantly Perthshire- and Wexford-origin names, as if to corroborate that Beckwith inhabitants remained the models of loyalty they were expected to be, is a symbol of the single central institution that has maintained a hold on the hearts of a majority of inhabitants — the Canadian monarchy. For names see Appendix 34.

7 and 15 as the most treacherous in Lanark County, the new religious fundamentalism gaining ground as exemplified in the new Jehovah's Witness Kingdom Hall built on lot eleven in the twelfth concession in 1986, the continuing abuse of alcohol, bilingualism, multiculturalism, the ordination of homosexual clergy, and a high crime rate.

Amid the many changes that had taken place between the late 1940s and the late 1980s, Beckwith inhabitants in 1988 could also find comforting and not so comforting evidence of things that either had remained constant or gave the appearance of some sense of continuity. Even as older inhabitants continued to die, the continuing custom of the wake in the vicinity bespoke an enduring cultural custom of the Irish that survived in few other parts of Canada. The landscape endured in spite of the ravages of rapid development and blighting quarries. The enduring conservatism of the Beckwith vicinity was evident in the refusal of Lanark County to change from supporting a Tory candidate when the rest of Ontario turned Liberal in 1987 and New Democrat in 1990. The patriarchal legacy of Beckwith was perhaps no longer as intimidating as it had once been, but it was not until 1991 that a woman attempted to run for municipal office in the township. If only a fraction of the population attended church regularly in the 1980s, the major religious denominations in 1988 remained the same as they had been over the previous 170 years. The villages of Beckwith were regaining new strength, with new houses and subdivisions focussed around them. After the better part of two centuries passing, Franktown in the late 1980s finally began to measure up to the village plan set out for it in 1819.

* * * * * * * * *

The enduring conservatism of Beckwith inhabitants was quite in keeping with its establishment as one in a line of four military townships from which veterans of the Napoleonic wars could guard over the costly Rideau military canal. In addition to the veterans actually settled in Beckwith, the innate culturally-nurtured conservatism of the Perthshire highlanders and Wexford Irish Anglicans who formed the majority of settlers in the township served as a model of loyalty not only for American settlers to the south in the St. Lawrence townships, but for radicalised lowland Scots settled north of the military townships as well. The years of daily struggle against the frontier forest largely erased cultural traditions such as styles of house construction, but the strong loyalist heritage of Beckwith settlers was evident in their efforts to prevent the so-called Ballyghiblin riots breaking out in 1824.

Despite large families and agricultural practices that were not considered progressive before mid-century, Beckwith farmers were fortunate in their location adjacent to cash markets in the Rideau canal work camps and in provisioning the timber and lumber camps through markets in Bytown. As families grew and land to farm in Beckwith grew scarce, chains of families migrated to settlements in Carleton and Renfrew counties in the Ottawa valley and to western Upper Canada. By keeping together in chains of Irish-origin families and Scottish-origin families, migration from their base farms in Beckwith was robbed of any potential terrors. The strong denominational identities in early Beckwith contributed to the basic stability of families, those remaining behind as well as those moving on. Despite the existence of strong Orange lodges in Beckwith from 1830 on, there is no evidence of clashes with local Catholic inhabitants. Most Beckwith inhabitants resisted the temperance and free school movements spearheaded by Scottish lowlanders in northern Lanark who were attempting to develop orderly institutions to control the Irish Catholic famine immigrants they were alarmed to see streaming into the region at mid-century.

The perseverance of cultural identities among Irish and Scottish families was in part due to their group migrations by choice in 1818 and 1819, and due to their being settled in concentrated blocks in eastern Beckwith. During the late nineteenth century, although migration westward persisted, the population of Beckwith became older in profile, limiting the size of their families as new rural wealth flowed from the local cheese economy and from provisioning the timber industry. The development of Carleton Place into a town, the emergence of municipal government and the growth of stronger ties to the outside world with the building of railroads through Beckwith introduced new wealth and more economic opportunities. As a consequence, sons and daughters either moved away all the more quickly, or those who remained behind in Beckwith remained comparatively insular in their attitudes. Growing communications assisted a continuing stream of migration out of Beckwith to the northwestern United States and to the opening Canadian prairie provinces, and gradually lured Beckwith women away from their traditional participation in farmwork to become caught up in a moral revolution and preoccupied with domestic chores.

Industrialisation in Carleton Place allowed many Beckwith sons and daughters to stay close to their ancestral homes, although as industrial workers they came to share few things in common with their brothers and sisters on Beckwith farms. The local press in relaying the latest developments in Beckwith to town readers and to their numerous relatives scattered across the far west created an increasingly sentimentalised and mythic image of Beckwith as a romantic homeland. This contributed to a growing Scottish highlander image of Beckwith, as the Irish-origin population masked its identity, dismayed and dispirited by the much poorer land on which it was settled and by the negative image of adjacent Irish Montague relatives promoted in the regional Scottish Liberal press. As Beckwith gained a more romantic view of itself as a cultural homeland, it increasingly was drawn toward larger international and national movements such as the moral revolution and a heightened imperial military consciousness by 1900.

Despite continuous population decline in rural Beckwith from the 1850s to the 1940s, the ethnic concentrations of Irish and Scottish-origin inhabitants in the various school sections, added to congregrational loyalties, village loyalties and neighbours working together in groups at statute labour and harvesting. Together they combined to create and buttress scattered community identities that largely frustrated any collective unified township identity from emerging. Only with the dramatic influx of Ottawa-oriented commuters in the 1970s and 1980s did Beckwith begin to overcome the burden of its fractured ethnic and community loyalties, and the township landscape dramatically changed under the influence of rapid development.

* * * * * * * * *

Even the new economic reliance of the commuters who daily departed for Ottawa and returned to their homes in Beckwith in endless chains of headlights was not so new. The timber and provisioning trades, the early roads and railroads had all ultimately connected Beckwith to Ottawa and its markets — that site on the Ottawa River where settlers had gotten off the boats in 1819 to begin their trek through the forest to locations in Beckwith. If there was one location where tradition and change were compromised and commuted, it was the municpal council chamber at Black's Corners. A large modern new hall replaced the old 1857 township hall which burned down in 1961, but despite this change and despite the changes contained in the new by-laws and new issues introduced by municipal councillors and concerned citizens, there was an array of symbols testifying to a long and eventful past. The idle spectator awaiting his turn to speak to the council had only to look up around the chamber past the photographs of past clerks and reeves, past the current councillors around the big table, and up past the open windows (revealing new houses and green foliage in the distance). Up past the war honour rolls the eye could rest on a photograph of the single most enduring institution that had helped to shape Beckwith from even before its settlement and that could help cushion the brunt of change. The subject of the photograph was described in the 1982 Canadian constitution as Elizabeth the Second, by the Grace of God...of Canada and her other realms and territories, Queen, head of the commonwealth, defender of the faith.

Endnotes

1 Findlay, "Findlay Stoves Answer Energy Crisis", p. 6.

2 *Carleton Place Canadian*, 6 September 1951.

3 Ibid., 30 November 1950.

4   Ibid., 30 April 1959.
5   Courtney C.J. Bond, "Report on a Machine-Shop, associated with a Water-Driven Textile Mill in Carleton Place, Ont." prepared for the National Capital Commission Information and Historical Division, 16 April 1964. I am grateful to Howard M. Brown, Ottawa, for loaning a copy of this report to me.
6   *Carleton Place Herald*, 14 August 1940.
7   Betty Jean McHattie, "Background Information on the Canadian Co-operative Wool Growers" (unpublished report prepared for display in museum of the Carleton Place and Beckwith Historical Society, May 1987), pp. 4, 7-8.
8   OBCMR 6 August 1949 minutes of Beckwith township council.
9   Beckwith Women's Institute, Tweedsmuir History of Beckwith.
10 OBCMR 6 August 1949 minutes of Beckwith township council.
11 Ibid., 28 October 1957 and 16 June 1958 minutes.
12 Ibid., 21 July 1958 minutes.
13 30 June 1988 telephone interview with Arthur R. Hawkins, Carleton Place.
14 Beckwith Women's Institute, Tweedsmuir History of Beckwith.
15 27 March 1988 interview with reeve John Sheil, Beckwith.
16 Beckwith Women's Institute, Tweedsmuir History of Beckwith.
17 *Lanark County Federation of Agriculture*, p. 53.
18 Beckwith Women's Institute, Tweedsmuir History of Beckwith.
19 *Lanark County Federation of Agriculture*, p. 54.
20 2 July 1988 interview with Arthur R. Hawkins, Carleton Place.
21 Lockwood, *Montague: A Social History*, p. 547.
22 OBCMR 19 July 1965 minutes of Beckwith township council.
23 Ibid., 14 October 1965 minutes.
24 Ibid., 10 January 1966 minutes.
25 Ibid., 5 March 1966 minutes.
26 Reva Dolgoy, "Beckwith Society in the 1970s and 1980s" (an unpublished essay commissioned for the Beckwith Historical Project in 1988), p. 1.
27 Beckwith Recreation Committee, *Draft Study of Recreation Needs and Recreation Master Plan for the Township of Beckwith, 1986-1996* (Beckwith: Beckwith Recreation Committee, 1986), p. B-12, based on John Morris, *Beckwith's Recreation Master Plan* (unpublished report, 1985).
28 Ibid., p. B-2.
29 *Carleton Place Canadian*, 8 April 1987, p. A12, and 3 February 1988, p. 5.
30 Beckwith Women's Institute, Tweedsmuir History of Beckwith.
31 OBCMR 10 January 1944 minutes of Beckwith township council.
32 Beckwith Women's Institute, Tweedsmuir History of Beckwith.
33 Reva Dolgoy, "Beckwith Society", pp. 1-2.
34 Beckwith Recreation Committee, *Draft Study*, p. 1.
35 Ibid., pp. 10-11. Seasonal cottagers are not counted in population statistics used in this history of Beckwith.
36 Ibid., pp. iii, 17-19.
37 Ibid., pp. 38-40.
38 Ibid., p. 9.
39 Ibid., p. 30.
40 Ibid., p. 59.
41 Ibid., p. 51.
42 Ibid., p. viii.
43 Ibid., p. 61.
44 Ibid., p. 32.
45 J. Brian Gilchrist, comp. and ed., *Inventory of Ontario Newspapers, 1793-1986* (Toronto: Micromedia Limited, 1987), pp. 24-25.
46 Carol Bennett, *The Story of Renfrew* (Renfrew: Juniper Books and Heritage Renfrew, 1984), p. 166.
47 OBCMR 17 April 1944 minutes of Beckwith township council.
48 Grindlay, *Independent Telephone Industry in Ontario*, pp. 257, 272, 278.
49 Beckwith Women's Institute, Tweedsmuir History of Beckwith.
50 Carl and Madonna Bell, *Descendents of David Bell and Margaret Nelson, Past, Present and Future* (Franktown: mimeographed by the authors, [1983]), pp. 10, 15.
51 Beckwith Women's Institute, Tweedsmuir History of Beckwith.
52 5 July 1988 interview with Arthur R. Hawkins, Carleton Place.
53 *Smiths Falls Record News*, 15 February 1978, p. 5.
54 1941, 1956, 1961 and 1971 printed census returns.
55 Beckwith Recreation Committee, *Draft Study*, pp. 11, B-15.
56 Dolgoy, "Beckwith Society", p. 1.
57 Beckwith Recreation Committee, *Draft Study*, pp. 11, B-13.
58 27 March 1988 interview with reeve John Sheil, Beckwith.
59 *Carleton Place Canadian*, 12 March 1986, p. 20.
60 Ibid.
61 Beckwith Women's Institute, Tweedsmuir History of Beckwith.
62 *Lanark County Federation of Agriculture*, p. 83.
63 Beckwith Women's Institute, Tweedsmuir History of Beckwith.
64 *Carleton Place Canadian*, 27 April 1988, p. B12.
65 Dolgoy, "Beckwith Society", p. 2.
66 Donald King, *Restructuring of Municipal Government in Lanark Area: Final Report and Recommendations* (Perth: Corporation of the County of

Lanark, 1976), pp. VI-3-4.
67 OBCMR By-law no. 79-18 of Beckwith township council.
68 27 March 1988 interview with councillor Chris Tyson, Beckwith.
69 J.L. Richards and Associates Limited, *Official Plan of the Township of Beckwith* (Ottawa: J.L. Richards and Associates Limited, 1985), p. 2.
70 Dolgoy, "Beckwith Society", p. 2.
71 Beckwith Recreation Committee, *Draft Study*, p. B-14. Whereas 4.7 percent of Lanark County's population and 5.2 percent of Carleton Place inhabitants had university degrees, 7.5 of Beckwith residents had university degrees in 1981.
72 *Carleton Place Canadian*, 16 November 1988, p. 9.
73 *Carleton Place Canadian*, 8 January 1986, p. 5.
74 27 March 1988 interview with councillor Chris Tyson, Beckwith.
75 *Carleton Place Candian*, 27 May 1987, p.1.
76 1986 interview with William Cox, Carleton Place.
77 Findlay, "Findlay Stoves Answer Energy Crisis", p. 6.
78 *Toronto Globe and Mail*, 25 June 1983, p. B12.
79 *Carleton Place Canadian*, 29 June 1988, p. 1, col. 6.
80 *Smiths Falls Record News*, 18 September 1983, p. 1.
81 *Toronto Globe and Mail*, 12 February 1983, p. 1.
82 Leaflet "Measure Canadian" provided courtesy of Wilmer Campbell, Ashton.
83 *Carleton Place Canadian*, 4 November 1987, p. 1.
84 Julia Wilson, "The French Fact" in *Queen's Alumni Review* (September-October 1985), p. 9.
85 *Carleton Place Canadian*, 19 February 1986, p. 5.
86 Ibid., 9 March 1988, p. 1; 16 March 1988, p. 1; and 20 April 1988, p. A1.

Appendix 1

Demobilised Military Officers Given Land Grants in Beckwith from the Perth Settlement Office, 1816—1822.

Name	Country of Origin	Unit and Rank	Location Date	Con.	Lot
William Blair	Scotland	Lieutenant, Glengarry Fencibles	1816	3	22
Thomas Consitt	England	Lieutenant, Royal Navy	1817	4	2
Benjamin Delisle	Lower Canada	Lieutenant, Canadian Fencibles	1817	6	12
Mathew Gould	England	Ensign, 4th Royal Veterans Battn.	1816	2	12
Tito Lelievre	France	Captain, Royal Newfoundland Regt.	1816	4	22
Roderick Matheson	Scotland	Paymaster, Glengarry Fencibles	1816	7	1
William Marshall	Scotland	Captain, Canadian Fencibles	1816	2	4
John McKay	Scotland	Lieutenant, Glengarry Regiment	1816	3	7
John McKenzie	Lower Canada	Lieutenant, Canadian Fencibles	1816	7	8
Joseph H. O'Brian	Ireland	Ensign, Newfoundland Fencibles	1816	6	1
James H. Powell	Ireland	Major, 103rd Regt.	1818	2	13NE½
Josias Taylor	England	Captain, Canadian Fencibles	1817	2	20NE ½

Source: NAC MG 9 (D8) Perth Military Settlement Register of Located Persons, 1816—1822.

Appendix 2

Settlers Qualifying for Patents Located from the Perth Military Depot in Beckwith Township, 1816—1822.

SECTION A — MILITARY SETTLERS

Name	Country of Origin	Military Unit & Rank	Military Service Years/Days	Ship Landing	Location Date	Con.	Lot	Family
			1816					
Jonathan Moores	England	Private, Glengarry Regiment	15/22		30 Nov.	5	10SW	wife & son
Etienne Roy	Lower Canada	Private, Canadian Fencibles	6/119		30 Nov.	6	24NW	
James Campbell	Upper Canada	Storekeeper, Commissariat Dept.			9 Dec.	5	11	—
John Watson	Scotland	Quartermaster Glengarry Regt.			9 Dec.	3	16	wife
			1817					
John Henry	Lower Canada	Private, Canadian Fencibles	7/		28 Feb.	1	4SW	—

Name	Country	Rank/Regiment		Date			Family
James Kent	Ireland	Private, Glengarry Regt.	8/174	14 Apr.	1	10NE	—
David Bogg	England	Clerk, Field Dept.		17 July	2	1	wife & son & daughter
Anthony Wiseman	England	Private, 7th Royal Veteran Battn.	12/120	22 Aug.	1	1SW	wife
George Perry	England	Private, 101st Regiment	14/93	4 Sept.	2	8NE	—
Thomas Williams	England	Private, 20th Dragoons	11/85	4 Sept.	2	8SW	wife
Austin Allen	Ireland	Private, 4th Grenadiers	1/296	9 Sept.	2	9NE	—
Thomas Wickham	England	Private, 54th Regiment	7/250	9 Sept.	2	9SW	wife
Margaret Johnston (widow of Jacob)	England	Royal Navy		9 Sept.	2	11SW	son
John Roberts	England	3rd Regt. Guards	19/110	9 Sept.	2	2NE	wife, 2 sons, 2 daughters
James Fitzgerald	Ireland	Royal Navy	7/	9 Sept.	2	3NE	wife
Henry Hawse	England	Seaman	19/304	16 Sept.	2	11NE	—
Josiah Moss	England	Private, 38th Regt.	6/182	16 Sept.	1	13NE	wife
Alexander Dalgety	Scotland	Royal Navy	10/	16 Sept.	1	12NE	—
Alexander Bain	Scotland	Private, 10th Dragoons	22/183	16 Sept.	4	17SW	—
Phineas Lowe	England	Private, 6th Regt.	7/226	22 Sept.	3	8NE	wife
Charles Stewart	England	Private, 63rd Regt.	5/	25 Sept.	4	15NE	wife
James Whiting	England	Seaman	4/183	30 Sept.	3	3SW	wife, 2 sons, 2 daughters
David McCrea	England	102nd Regiment	23/	30 Sept.	3	6SW	wife
Rev. Abbé LaMothe	France	Chaplain, DeWatteville Regt.		31 Oct.	4	7	—
Robert Smith	England	Sergeant, Royal Marines	10/60	31 Oct.	5	4NE	—
John Ellis	England	Quartermaster, 22nd Dragoons		30 Nov.	2	6	wife & 3 children
James Muldoon	Ireland	Private, 4th Royal Veteran Battalion	10/90	1 Dec.	1	11NE	wife, 1 son, & 1 daughter

1818

Name	Country	Rank/Regiment		Date			Family
Baker Castle	England	Private, 4th Royal Veteran Battalion	16/30	ca. 1818	4	15SW	—
Patrick Rourke	Ireland	Private, 81st Regiment	3/40	14 June	2	7NE	—

1819

Name	Country	Rank/Regiment		Date			Family
Mathew Patrick	Ireland	Private, 3rd Dragoons		18 Sept.	8	3	wife
George Cliff	England	Private, York Chasseurs	6/200	22 Sept.	9	11SW	wife & 2 children
John Cocker	England	Sergeant, York Chasseurs		22 Sept.	9	10	—
Dennis Gingley	England	Private, York Chasseurs	5/205	22 Sept.	10	11SW	—
Thomas Connor	Ireland	Private, York Chasseurs	5/171	22 Sept.	10	11NE	wife & 2 children
John McDonald	Ireland	Private, York Chasseurs	5/57	22 Sept.	10	8	—
William Matson	Ireland	Private, York Chasseurs	2/79	22 Sept.	11	8	—
James Carson	Ireland	Private, York Chasseurs	5/207	22 Sept.	11	12SW	—
John Millage	England	Private, York Chasseurs	2/143	22 Sept.	9	11NE	—
Thomas Hays	Ireland	Private, York Chasseurs		21 Oct.	10	9NE	wife
Ranald McLellan	Scotland	Private, 37th Regiment	11/	28 Oct.	7	10SW	wife & 2 children

1821

Name	Country	Rank/Regiment		Date			Family
John Fallon	Ireland	Corporal, 12th Royal Veteran Battalion		3 Sept.	4	12SW	wife & 1 child
George Brooks	England	Sergeant, 41st Regt.	16/72	10 Dec.	10	9SW	wife
Thomas Lawford	Ireland	Private, 37th Regt.		21 Dec.	3	3NE	—

1822

Name	Country	Rank/Regiment		Date			Family
William Burrows	Ireland	Private, 77th Regt.	19/152	22 Sept.	4	13SW	wife & 1 child
Peter Fullan	Ireland	Sergeant, 27th Regt.	22/12	22 Sept.	10	13NE	—

SECTION B

CIVILIAN SETTLERS

1816

Name	Origin	Ship	Date			Family
John McDonell	Scotland	Morningfield	30 Nov.	7	6SW	—
Constantine O'Neill	Ireland	via United States	30 Nov.	7	4SW	wife, 2 sons, 3 daughters
William Stacey	Ireland	Betty & Nancy	30 Nov.	5	6SW	—
Archibald McDonell	Scotland	Morningfield	9 Dec.	7	3SW	—
Stephen Redmond	Ireland	Golden Grove	31 Dec.	3	10NE	—

1817

Duncan McNaughton Sr.	Scotland	Fame	31 Mar.	7	4NE	1 son, 2 daughters
Alexander McKenzie	Scotland	Hibernia	31 Mar.	6	4NE	—
Duncan McKercher	Scotland	Harmony	20 Aug.	2	15 SW	—
Francis Bennett	England	Maria	22 Sept.	3	5NE	wife & 2 daughters

1818

Donald Anderson	Scotland	Sophia	Nov.	6	11NE	wife & 2 daughters
John Anderson	Scotland	Jane	Nov.	7	10NE	wife & 2 daughters
Peter Anderson	Scotland	Sophia	Nov.	6	8NE	wife & 6 children
Duncan Campbell	Scotland	Curlew	Sept.	4	11NE	wife & 7 children
William Colbourn			Jan	3	6NE	—
Daniel Ferguson	Scotland	Sophia	Nov.	4	9SW	wife & 4 children
Duncan Ferguson	Scotland	Sophia	Nov.	5	10NE	wife & 3 male children
Peter Ferguson Jr.	Scotland	Sophia	Nov.	4	8NE	—
Robert Ferguson Jr.	Scotland	Sophia	Nov.	4	9NE	wife
Richard Findlay	Ireland			2	3SW	wife & 5 children
Thomas Findlay	Ireland			2	2SW	
Alexander Fisher	Scotland	Jane	Nov	7	12NE	wife & 1 daughter
Donald Fisher	Scotland	Jane	Nov.	7	11NE	—
James Fisher	Scotland	Jane	Nov.	7	12SW	—
John Fisher	Scotland	Jane	Nov.	7	11SW	wife
John Fulford	Scotland	Sophia	Nov.	4	8SW	wife & 2 children
John Kidd	Ireland			6	21NE	—
John McCallum	Scotland	Curlew	Nov.	5	4SW	wife & 2 daughters
Charles McCarthy	Ireland	Henry of Dublin	Sept.	3	10SW	wife & 2 sons
Alexander McGregor	Scotland	Curlew	Nov.	7	5NE	wife & 3 children
Alexander McGregor Jr.	Scotland	Sophia	Nov.	6	8SW	wife & 2 children
Duncan McKay	Scotland	Curlew	Nov.	5	5NE	wife & 2 children
Donald McLaren	Scotland	Sophia	Nov.	4	4SW	wife & 5 children
Duncan McNabb	Scotland	Curlew	Nov.	4	3NE	wife & 2 sons
John McNee	Scotland	Sophia	Nov.	4	4NE	wife & 4 children
Joseph Sutton	England	Lord Nidry	June.	2	7SW	—

1819

Name	Origin	Ship	Month	Day	Lot	Family
John Brown	Ireland		Oct.	6	6NE	wife & 7 children
Donald Cameron	Scotland	Speculation	Nov.	1	3SW	no family
Hugh Cameron	Scotland	Speculation	Nov.	7	6NE	no family
Moses Campbell	Scotland		Nov.	11	3SW	no family
Daniel Ferguson Jr.	Scotland	Sophia	July	1	8SW	—
Archibald Gillis	Scotland	Atlantic	Nov.	1	3NE	wife & 5 daughters
Robert Goodfellow	Scotland		Oct.	5	8SW	—
William Goodfellow	Scotland		Oct.	5	5SW	wife & 6 children
Henry Hawkins	Ireland	Maria	Aug.	8	12NE	—
Roger Hawkins	Ireland	Maria	Aug.	8	12SW	wife & 5 children
John James	Ireland	Maria	Aug.	9	6NE	wife & 1 son
				9	6SW	
William Jones	Ireland	Eolus	Aug.	1	8NE	wife & 2 sons
Thomas Leech	Ireland	Maria	Aug.	9	12SW	wife
William Leech Sr.	Ireland	Maria	Aug.	9	12NE	wife & 4 children
William Leech Jr.	Ireland	Maria	Aug.	9	13SW	—
John Lummox Sr.	Ireland	Maria	Aug.	6	13NE	wife & 4 children
John Lummox Jr.	Ireland	Maria	Aug.	6	13SW	—
George Merritt	England	Maria	July	4	14NE	wife & 4 children
John Moorehouse	Ireland	Eolus	July	1	13SW	—
John McDonnell Sr.	Scotland	Morningfield	Oct.	8	4SW	wife, 2 sons 3 daughters
John McDonnell Jr.	Scotland	Morningfield	Oct.	8	4NE	—
John McDougall	Scotland		July	9	18NE	—
Peter McDougall	Scotland		June	9	19NE	—
Archibald McGregor	Scotland	Sophia	July	9	8NE	wife & 2 children
Peter McGregor	Scotland	Sophia	July	9	8SW	wife & 2 children
James McKay	Scotland		Dec.	1	10SW	—
Finlay McNaughton	Scotland	Fame	Oct.	7	5SW	—
John Nowlan	Ireland	Atlantic	Oct.	1	12NE	—
Luke Nowlan	Ireland	Atlantic	Aug.	1	12SW	—
Patrick Nowlan	Ireland	Atlantic	Aug.	4	11SW	wife & 5 children
Thomas Pierce	Ireland	Eolus	Aug.	3	8SW	wife
Benjamin Rathwell	Ireland		Aug.	10	3	—
John William Roberts	England	William	May	3	1SW	—
James Wall	Ireland	Eolus	July	7	13NE	wife & 4 children
Moses Wall	Ireland	Eolus	July	7	13SW	—
Israel Webster	Ireland	Henry	July	1	11SW	wife & 2 sons
Isaac Whealey	Ireland	Maria	Aug.	8	13SW	wife & 1 son
Henry Willis	Ireland	Eolus	July	2	13SW	wife & 2 daughters

1820

Name	Origin	Ship	Month	Day	Lot	Family
Phillip Bayne	Ireland	Mary & Bell	May	12	13SW	—
William Bryan	Ireland	Atlantic	Oct.	6	2NE	wife & 3 children
Thomas Burns	Ireland	Eolus	Jan.	12	13NE	—
John Cameron Sr.	Scotland	Speculation	May	1	4NE	wife & 1 son

Name	Origin	Ship	Month	Day	Lot	Family
John Cavanagh	Ireland	Active	Aug.	11	10NE	—
Nicholas Dixon	England	X, Y & Z	June	12	11SW	wife & 7 children
John Griffith	Ireland	Maria	May	8	13NE	—
Robert Hampton	Ireland	Maria	May	12	11NE	—
Robert Johnston	Ireland	Mary & Bell	May	11	15NE	—
David Moffatt	England		May	12	12SW	wife, 6 sons, 3 daughters
Donald McDonald	Scotland		May	6	4SW	—
Manny Nowlan	Ireland	Atlantic	Sept.	12	12NE	—
John Shaw			Sept.	3	11pt	—

1821

Name	Origin	Ship	Month	Day	Lot	Family
Thomas Armstrong	Ireland	Ponsoby	Dec.	3	13pt	—
John Conboy	Ireland	Ponsoby	Dec.	3	11pt	—
Duncan Ferguson	Scotland	Duchess of Richmond	Dec.	6	7SW	wife & 4 children
Duncan Fisher	Scotland	Swiftsure	July	11	11SW	—
James Goldrick	Ireland	Ponsoby	Dec.	3	1NE	wife & 2 daughters
Andrew Hughton	Ireland		Dec.	5	6NE	wife & 1 son
John King	Scotland	Duchess of Richmond	Dec.	6	7NE	wife & 3 children
Joseph Morris	Ireland		July	9	5	—
Owen McCarthy	Ireland		Dec.	11	10SW	wife
Duncan McDonald	Scotland	Duchess of Richmond	Dec.	5	3SW	wife & 6 children
Bernard McGee	Ireland	Royal Edward	Feb.	8	8NE	—
John McLellan	Scotland	Morningfield	Feb.	6	3NE	—
Duncan McNee	Scotland	Duchess of Richmond	Dec.	6	6SW	wife & 2 children
George Nesbitt	Ireland	Ponsoby	Dec.	3	13pt	—
James Nesbitt	Ireland	Ponsoby	Dec.	4	12NE	wife
John Nesbitt	Ireland	Ponsoby	Dec.	8	11NE	—
Samuel Splain	Ireland	Martha	Dec.	3	4SW	wife & 3 children

1822

Name	Origin	Ship	Month	Day	Lot	Family
Thomas Clark	Scotland		Dec.	1	1NE	—
George Code			Dec.	12	3SW	—
John Code			Dec.	12	4SW	—
John Code Jr.			Dec.	12	3NE	—
Alexander Ferguson	Scotland	Sophia	Dec.	4	3SW	—
John Ferguson	Scotland		Nov.	6	6SW	—
John Goodfellow	Scotland		Sept.	5	8NE	—
Robert Griffith	Ireland		Nov.	8	11SW	—
Thomas Hatton	Ireland	Maria	June	10	12NE	—
Colin King	Scotland	Buckingham	Nov.	10	2NE	—
Thomas Lummox	Ireland		Nov.	8	6SW	—
Isaac May	Ireland		Nov.	5	7NE	—
William May	Ireland		Nov.	5	7SW	—
John Miller	Scotland	Buckingham	Nov.	10	2SW	—
Peter McDonald	Scotland		Nov.	5	3NE	—
Colin McLaren	Scotland	Buckingham	Nov.	10	1NE	wife
Peter McLaren	Scotland	Buckingham	Nov.	10	1SW	—
Angus McLellan	Scotland	Morningfield	Nov.	9	1SW	—
Patrick McLinden	Ireland	Assyria	June	1	7NE	wife & 4 children
Peter McPhail			Nov.	11	3NE	—
John Nichol	Scotland	Buckingham	Nov.	11	1SW	—
Owen Quinn	Ireland	Eliza		3	11pt	—
William Rattray	Scotland		Nov.	10	12SW	—
John Sinclair	Scotland	Pilgrim	Nov.	9	1NE	wife
John Splain	Ireland		Dec.	3	4NE	—

Name				April	11	4	—
Jacob Tatlock							
William Young	Scotland		Buckingham	Nov.	11	1NE	wife & 2 sons

Source: NAC MG 9 (D8) Perth Military Settlement Register of Located Persons, 1816—1822, and RG 1 (L3) Upper Canada Land Petitions, volumes P and M, R48 and R70

Appendix 3

Immigrants Located in Beckwith as Settlers by the Richmond Military Settlement Office, 1818—1822.

Name	Country of Origin	Parish	Date Located to Lot	Con.	Lot	Family
			1818			
Duncan Anderson	Scotland	Comrie	24 October	10	22NE	2 children under 12
George Buchanan	Scotland	Comrie	24 October	2	25NE	
Charles Campbell	Scotland		24 October	3	18SW	
Alexander Clark	Scotland	Comrie	24 October	9	27	1 child under 12
Donald Clark	Scotland	Comrie	24 October	9	26SW	
Peter Comrie	Scotland	Comrie	24 October	10	19SW	2 children under 12
John Cram	Scotland	Comrie	24 October	10	20SW	1 child under 12
Archibald Dewar	Scotland	Glenarlen	24 October	7	25SW	2 children under 12
John Dewar	Scotland	Glenarlen	24 October	9	20NE	
Malcolm Dewar	Scotland	Glenarlen	24 October	7	23SW	
Peter Dewar	Scotland	Glenarlen	24 October	7	25NE	
Alexander Douglas	Scotland	Dull	24 October	1	26SW	1 child under 12
Malcolm Drummond	Scotland	Comrie	24 October	9	26NE	2 children under 12
Thomas Edwards	Ireland		24 October	4	20NE	
Donald Ferguson	Scotland	Comrie	24 October	5	22SW	
Duncan Ferguson	Scotland	Comrie	24 October	5	23NE	2 children under 12
James Ferguson	Scotland	Comrie	24 October	6	24NE	Son of Donald
John Ferguson	Scotland	Comrie	24 October	4	23SW	Son of Donald
Robert Ferguson	Scotland	Comrie	24 October	5	23SW	Son of Donald
Luke James	Ireland		24 October	3	25NE	
William James	Ireland		24 October	3	25SW	
Alexander Kennedy	Scotland	Dull	24 October	6	25NE	2 children under 12
Donald Kennedy	Scotland	Dull	24 October	8	24NE	2 children under 12
John Kennedy	Scotland	Dull	24 October	8	24SW	2 children under 12
James Keyes	Ireland		24 October	3	21SW	
John Kidd	Ireland	Coolcullen	24 October	6	21NE	
John King Sr.	Scotland	Kincardine	24 October	2	25SW	2 children under 12 2 children 12—17
John King Jr.	Scotland	Kincardine	24 October	2	24NE	
Andrew Lucas	Ireland		24 October	4	20SW	
James McArthur	Scotland	Comrie	24 October	7	14SW	1 child, 12 to 17
John McArthur	Scotland	Comrie	24 October	7	14NE	2 children under 12
Duncan McCallum	Scotland	Comrie	24 October	10	20NE	2 children under 12
Duncan McCuan	Scotland		24 October	9	21SW	
John McCuan	Scotland	Dalinuck	24 October	10	24SW	2 children under 12
Angus McDiarmid	Scotland		24 October	5	24SW	
Duncan McDiarmid	Scotland	Comrie	24 October	5	22NE	2 children under 12
John McDiarmid Sr.	Scotland	Fortingall	24 October	8	17NE	2 children under 12
James McDiarmid	Scotland	Fortingall	24 October	8	16SW	
Finlay McEwen	Scotland	Balquhidder	24 October	7	23NE	5 children under 12 2 children 12—17
John McEwen Sr.	Scotland		24 October	8	14NE	
John McEwen Jr.	Scotland		24 October	8	14SW	

John McGregor	Scotland	Comrie	24 October	10	15SW	
Peter McGregor	Scotland	Comrie	24 October	10	15NE	
Robert McGregor	Scotland	Comrie	24 October	10	14NE	2 children under 12
James McInnis	Scotland	Callendar	24 October	9	20SW	1 child under 12
John McLaren	Scotland	Comrie	24 October	10	23SW	2 children under 12
Alexander McNaughton	Scotland	Dull	24 October	8	25SW	
Alexander McTavish	Scotland	Dull	24 October	8	17SW	
John McTavish	Scotland	Dull	24 October	8	16NE	
Donald Robertson Sr.	Scotland	Dull	24 October	9	15SW	
Donald Robertson Jr.	Scotland	Dull	24 October	9	15NE	
Duncan Robertson	Scotland	Dull	24 October	11	23NE	
Peter Robertson	Scotland	Dull	24 October	11	23SW	
John Robertson	Scotland	Killin	24 October	2	27	2 children, 12—17
James Saunders	Ireland		24 October	3	21NE	
John Scott	Scotland	Dull	24 October	6	25SW	2 children under 12
Robert Scott Sr.	Scotland	Dull	24 October	9	14SW	1 child, 12—17
Robert Scott Jr.	Scotland	Dull	24 October	9	14NE	
Peter Scott	Scotland	Dull	24 October	3	23SW	2 children under 12
Alexander Stewart	Scotland	Blair Athol	24 October	9	14NE	
David Stewart	Scotland	Muthil	24 October	3	22NE	2 children under 12
John Stewart	Scotland	Blair Athol	24 October	8	27	2 children under 12, 1 child 12—17
Stephen Tomlinson	Ireland		24 October	3	26SW	
William Tomlinson	Ireland		24 October	3	26NE	
Allan Wilson	Ireland		24 October	3	27	

1819

Joseph Alderson	England	20 September	11	22NE	
Nathaniel Bailey	Ireland	24 July	4	14SW	
William Burgess	Ireland	20 September	3	20NE	
Robert Davis	Ireland	24 July	4	16NE	
William Davis	Ireland	24 July	4	16SW	
Alexander Dewar	Scotland	24 June	9	19SW	
John Goth	England	1 December	11	{21NE / 22SW}	Yorkshire origin
Richard Greville	Ireland	24 July	2	16SW	
Peter Jones	Ireland	24 July	4	17NE	
George Kerfoot	Ireland	24 July	2	15NE	
Thomas Kerfoot	Ireland	24 July	1	15NE	
William Kerfoot	Ireland	24 July	4	25SW	
James Lucas	Ireland	20 September	5	20NE	
John Moore	Ireland	20 September	11	14SW	son of William Sr.
William Moore Sr.	Ireland	20 September	11	14NE	
William Moore Jr.	Ireland	20 September	11	15SW	
Edmond Morphy	Ireland	20 September	12	14SW	
James Morphy	Ireland	20 September	12	15NE	son of Edmond
John Morphy	Ireland	20 September	12	15SW	son of Edmond
William Morphy	Ireland	20 September	12	14NE	son of Edmond
John McDougall	Scotland	24 July	9	18NE	
Peter McDougall	Scotland	24 June	9	19NE	
Donald McIntosh	Scotland	24 July	8	23SW	
Samuel Patterson	Ireland	24 July	4	27	
Alexander Scott	Scotland	20 September	9	18SW	
Joseph Scott	Scotland	24 July	2	16NE	
William Scott	Scotland	20 September	1	16NE	
Jacob Smith	Ireland	24 July	3	15NE	
John Smith	Ireland	24 July	3	15SW	
Alexander Snedden	Ireland	20 September	11	26SW	
David Snedden	Ireland	20 September	11	26NE	
George Welby	Ireland	24 July	3	14NE	
James White	Scotland	20 September	11	25SW	
John White	Scotland	20 September	11	27	
William White	Scotland	20 September	11	25NE	

1820

Name	Country	Place	Date		
George Bailey Sr.	Ireland		25 January	12	16NE
George Bailey Jr.	Ireland		30 January	12	16SW
James Carmichael	Scotland	Comrie	23 August	10	23NE
Peter Carmichael	Scotland	Comrie	23 August	10	16NE
Thomas Collins	Ireland		1 May	1	20NE
James Cram	Scotland		23 August	11	20NE
Edward Davis	Ireland		8 January	5	19NE
George Edwards	Ireland		1 May	9	16SW
Richard Edwards	Ireland		20 November	5	20SW
John Garland	Ireland		23 August	6	23SW
John Giff	Ireland		23 August	4	18NE
William Greville	Ireland		28 March	1	16SW
Samuel Kerfoot	Ireland		30 January	4	25 NE
Daniel Mooney	Ireland		25 January	12	17NE
Robert Leech	Ireland		20 August	6	22NE
Samuel Leech	Ireland		20 August	6	22SW
Thomas Moorhouse	Ireland		28 September	1	14NE
Peter McArthur	Scotland	Comrie	2 August	7	15SW	son of James
John McDiarmid	Scotland	Creag Ianaich	29 September	7	26SW
John McEwen	Scotland		30 November	8	23NE
James McFarlane	Scotland	Comrie	23 August	10	24NE	1 child under 12, 1 child 12—17
Colin McLaren	Scotland	Comrie	2 August	5	21NE	2 children under 12
Duncan McLaren	Scotland		30 November	9	25SW
Matthew McNally	Ireland		30 January	12	17SW
John Nowlan	Ireland		2 July	10	14SW
Thomas Ward	Ireland		30 March	5	19SW
William Willis	Ireland		20 August	4	18SW
John Wilson	Ireland		29 March	3	20SW
William Wilson	Ireland		29 March	3	19NE

1821

Name	Country	Place	Date			
Alexander Anderson	Scotland		29 September	8	22NE	
Peter Campbell	Scotland		30 August	10	25SW	
Richard Copeland	Ireland		29 November	2	18NE	
Hugh Coughen	Ireland		30 November	4	24NE	
James Drummond	Scotland		27 February	9	25NE	
Duncan Cram	Scotland		31 January	11	20SW	
Peter Cram Sr.	Scotland		31 January	11	21SW	
Peter Cram Jr.	Scotland		30 August	11	19NE	son of Peter Sr.
James Garland	Ireland		29 November	6	20SW	
Nicholas Garland	Ireland		29 November	6	20NE	
Thomas Glendenning	England		5 July	12	18NE	
				12	19	
				12	20NE	
				12	22SW	
Thomas Kidd	Ireland	Coolcullen	30 August	2	17SW	
William Kidd	Ireland	Coolcullen	30 August	2	17NE	
Francis Kilfoyle	Ireland		29 November	2	18SW	
John Lucas	Ireland		30 August	5	21SW	
William McKeown	Ireland		30 August	6	23NE	
Thomas McKee	Scotland		21 May	10	25NE	
John McKewen	Ireland		9 July	12	20SW	
John McRostie	Scotland		7	7	22NE	
Douglas McTavish	Scotland		30 August	8	15NE	
John McTavish Jr.	Scotland	Dull	30 August	9	16NE	
John Poole	Ireland		30 August	4	24SW	
Christopher Wynn	Ireland		29 November	2	24SW	

1822

Name	Country	Date		
Robert Aitken	Scotland	30 October	7	15NE
Francis Edwards	Ireland	4 September	1	18NE
Nancy Edwards	Ireland	7 September	5	25SW

Name	Country	Date	No.	Lot
Edward Holbrook	Ireland	30 November	2	19SW
Thomas Holbrook	Ireland	30 June	1	18SW
Donald Kennedy	Scotland	30 May	9	23SW
George Kidd	Ireland	13 August	2	20SW
Robert King	Scotland	30 November	12	23SW
Edward Leech	Ireland	30 October	6	18SW
Thomas Leech	Ireland	12 August	5	18NE
William Leslie	Ireland	5 September	5	26NE
Brice McNeely	Ireland	12 July	11	16NE
James McNeely	Ireland	12 July	11	16SW
John McNeely	Ireland	26 November	11	19SW
William Salter	Ireland	26 November	12	22NE
Henry Saunders	Ireland	31 July	2	22NE
James Saunders	Ireland	31 July	2	22SW
John Saunders	Ireland	31 July	2	23SW
James Scott	Scotland	12 August	2	19NE

Source: List compiled by Howard M. Brown, Ottawa, based on 1818 list of immigrants enclosed in 4 July 1818 letter from the Colonial Office to the Duke of Richmond;

Appendix 4

Names of Future Beckwith Inhabitants Selected from Return of Protestant Families Preparing to Emigrate from the Counties of Carlow and Wexford, Ireland in the Ensuing Spring, Compiled by Joseph Elly at Ross, County Wexford, Ireland, November 1817.

Name	No. in Family	Occupation	Printed Folio No.
Tho[ma]s Codd	6	Farmer	178
James Codd	4	Farmer	179
Alexander Kinch	7	Farmer	179
John Kinch	8	Mechanic	179
William Willis	8	Farmer	179
Thomas Kidd	5	Farmer	179
William Pierce	7	Farmer	179
William Davis	6	Farmer	180
Edward Davis	6	Farmer	180
Thomas Kavanagh	9	Farmer	180
Thomas Dowdell	12	Farmer	180
Samuel Pierce	8	Farmer	180
John Pool	11	Farmer	181
William Pool	9	Farmer	181
Matthew Pool	9	Farmer	181
Elizth Pool	8	Farmer	181
Nathaniel Burgess	10	Farmer	181
Luke James	5	Farmer	181
Roger Hawkins	9	Farmer	181
Thomas Walls	5	Farmer	181
Henry Walls	7	Farmer	181
William Burgess	7	Farmer	181
William Burgess Jr.	6	Farmer	182
Thomas Saunders	4	Farmer	182
James Saunders	4	Farmer	182
Hennery May	6	Farmer	182
Charles Kavenagh	7	Farmer	182
James Hawkins	4	Farmer	182
John Rathwell	11	Farmer	182
William Rathwell	7	Farmer	182
James Rathwell	10	Farmer	182
Thomas Rathwell	8	Farmer	182
Samuel Rathwell	8	Farmer	182
John Rathwell Jr.	5	Farmer	182
George Crampton	7	Farmer	182
James Morris	5	Farmer	182
Robert Davis	3	Farmer	183
William Davis	4	Mechanic	183
William Sutton	2	Mechanic	183
Edward Rathwell	4	Farmer	183
Samuel Rathwell	5	Farmer	183
John Rathwell	3	Farmer	183
William Rathwell	7	Farmer	183
Charles Rathwell	6	Farmer	183
Benjamin Rathwell	6	Farmer	183
William Tackaberry	8	Farmer	183
Richard Greville	9	Farmer	183
William James	11	Farmer	183
Richard Tackaberry	4	Farmer	183
Robert Tackaberry	4	Farmer	183
Moague Leech	8	Farmer	183
William Leech	3	Farmer	183

Name	Count	Occupation	Page		Name	Count	Occupation	Page
James Lucas	7	Farmer	183		Richard Garland	4	Farmer	185
Henry Lucas	9	Farmer	183		William May	10	Farmer	185
Edward Lucas	1	Farmer	183		John Bowles	9	Farmer	185
Con Kavenagh	7	Farmer	183		Stephen James	8	Farmer	185
William Sparrow	3	Farmer	183		Thomas Ward	7	Farmer	186
John Willis	10	Farmer	183		Thomas Tomlinson	7	Farmer	186
Stephen Tomlinson	1	Farmer	184		William Tomlinson	5	Farmer	186
Thomas Burrows	4	Farmer	184		Richard Burrows	8	Mechanic	186
George Kerford	3	Farmer	184		George Kidd	1	Farmer	186
John Lummocks	2	Farmer	184		William Kidd	1	Farmer	186
John Whealan	3	Farmer	184		John Nowlan	6	Farmer	186
Patrick Dowling	7	Farmer	185		Alexander Kinch	4	Farmer	186
Richard Dixon	5	Farmer	185		Henry Duck	4	Farmer	186
Jacob James	1	Farmer	185		William Alcock	2	Farmer	186
Edward Johnston	1	Farmer	185		William Tackaberry	6	Farmer	186
William Kerfoot	5	Farmer	185		William McNally	4	Farmer	186
John Garland	14	Farmer	185					

Source: NAC Colonial Office 384, Volumes 1—2, Vol. 3 ff-60 on microfilm reel B-876, pages 178—188.

Appendix 5

A List of Settlers with Numbers of Wives and Children Embarked on Board the Brig *Curlew* of 260 Tons at Greenock, Scotland, Destined for Montreal, 21 July 1818.

Name	Settler	Wives	Children Age 12—17	Children Age Under 12	Name	Settler	Wives	Children Age 12—17	Children Age Under 12
Parish of Blair Athol					Findlay Cameron	1			
John Stewart	1				Jannet Cameron		1		
Ellen Stewart		1			John Kennedy	1			
John Robertson			16		Margaret Kennedy		1		
Isabella Stewart				3 months	James Kennedy				10
Margaret Stewart		1			Mary Kennedy				8
Parish of Dull					Alexander McTavish	1			
Robert Scott	1				Catherin McTavish		1		
Margaret Scott		1			Duncan McTavish				8
Alexander Scott			16		Peter McTavish				6
John Scott	1				Donald Robertson	1			
Margaret Scott		1			Catherin Robertson		1		
Alexander Douglas	1				Donald Robertson 2nd	1			
Elizabeth Douglas		1			Jannet Robertson		1		
Robert Scott 2nd	1				* John Robertson	1			
Nelly Scott		1			Catherin Robertson		1		
Alexander McNaughton		1			Peter Robertson	1			
Elizabeth McNaughton		1			Duncan Robertson	1			
John Stewart	1				Margaret Robertson		1		
Elizabeth Stewart		1			Jannet Robertson				5
Duncan Cameron	1				Mary Robertson				3
Margaret Cameron		1			John McTavish	1			
Isabella Cameron			14		Catherin Robertson		1		
Donald Cameron				5	* Donald Livingston	1			
Hugh McDiarmid	1				Jannet Livingston		1		
Jannet McDiarmid		1			Ann Livingston			13	
Margaret McDiarmid				8	Margaret Livingston			12	
Jannet McDiarmid				6	Catherin Livingston				7

586 APPENDICES

John McTavish 2nd	1		

Parish of Killin

John Robertson	1		
Jannet Robertson		1	
John Robertson			16
Daniel Robertson			14
Duncan McNab	1		
Catherin McNab		1	
Colin McNab			8
Thomas McNab			3
Jannet McNab			6 weeks
* James McLean	1		
Jannet McLean		1	
Margaret McLean			3 months
Jannet Stewart		1	
Duncan Campbell	1		
Catherin Campbell		1	
John Campbell			10
Elizabeth Campbell			8
Jannet Campbell			6
Duncan McKay	1		
Jannet McKay		1	
Ann McKay			3
John McLaren	1		
Catherin McLaren		1	
Christian McLaren			4
Archibald McLaren			2
* Mary McVean		1	
* Archibald McDiarmid	1		
Mary McDiarmid		1	
Donald McDiarmid			4
Catherin McDiarmid			2

Parish of Comrie

James McArthur	1		
Ann McArthur		1	
Peter McArthur			15
Alexander McArthur			11
James McArthur			8
John McArthur	1		
Catherin McArthur		1	
Duncan McArthur			5
Archibald McArthur			2
Robert McGregor	1		
Mary McGregor		1	
James McGregor			12
John McGregor			10
Donald Ferguson	1		
Mary Ferguson		1	
Robert Ferguson	1		
Christine Ferguson		1	
John Ferguson	1		
Mary Ferguson		1	
Duncan Ferguson	1		
Ann Ferguson		1	
James Ferguson	1		
Christine Ferguson		1	
Catherine Ferguson			4
Robert Ferguson			2
John Carmichael	1		
Ann Carmichael		1	
John McLaren	1		
Jannet McLaren		1	
Catherine McLaren			1
* John McLaren 2nd	1		
Jannet McLaren		1	
Isabella McLaren			6
Malcolm McLaren			3
Colin McLaren	1		
Christine McLaren		1	
Elizabeth McLaren			2
John McLaren			6 months
James McCowan	1		
Jannet McCowan		1	
William McEwen	1		
Helen McEwen			8
John McEwen	1		
Christine McEwen			7
Duncan Anderson	1		
Eliza Anderson			9
Peter Anderson			3
Peter McGregor	1		
Christine McGregor		1	
John McGregor	1		
Duncan McCowan	1		
Peter McCowan			6
Duncan McCowan			4
Donald Clark	1		
Margaret Clark		1	
Alexander Clark	1		
Jannet Clark		1	
Mary Clark			9
John McNie	1		
Jannet McNie		1	
Donald McNie			4
Jannet McNie			1
Archibald Dewar	1		
Margaret Dewar		1	
Duncan Dewar			10
Archibald Dewar			7
Malcolm Dewar	1		
Ann Dewar		1	
Ann Dewar			5
Alexander Dewar			2
John Dewar	1		
Peter Dewar	1		
Duncan McCallum	1		
Christine McCallum		1	
Robert McCallum			10
Duncan McCallum 2nd		1	
Angus McCallum			11
Duncan McCallum			6
Duncan McDiarmid	1		
Mary McDiarmid		1	
Catherine McDiarmid			12
John McDiarmid			1
Malcolm Drummond	1		
Christine Drummond		1	
Malcolm Drummond			6
Margaret Drummond			2
John Gow	1		
Margaret Gow		1	
John Cram	1		
Isabella Cram		1	
Mary Cram			3
Peter Comrie	1		
Jane Comrie		1	
Peter Comrie			5
John Comrie			6 months

Parish of Muthil

David Stewart	1		
Catherine Stewart		1	
James Stewart			8

Name	Settler	Wives	Children 12–17	Children Under 12
William Stewart				2
Parish of Callander				
Alexander McGregor	1			
Jannet McGregor		1		
Peter McGregor				4
Alexander McGregor				2
Duncan McGregor				9 months
James McInnes	1			
Marion McInnes		1		
Jannet McInnes				6 months
Parish of Little Dunkeld				
John McEwen	1			
Catherine McEwen		1		
Christine McEwen			13	
Jannet McEwen				9
Parish of Balquhidder				
*Malcolm Fisher	1			
Christine Fisher		1		
Jannet Fisher			14	
John Fisher			13	
Donald Fisher				11
Ann Fisher				9
Malcolm Fisher				4
Mary Fisher		1		
TOTAL	66	59	13	67

Source: NAC RG 7 (G1) volume 10, pp. 67-73.
  * Families that did not settle in Beckwith, but elsewhere in the Bathurst District or what later became known as Lanark County.

Appendix 6

A List of Settlers with Numbers of Wives and Children Embarked on Board the Ship *Sophia* of 230 Tons at Greenock, Scotland, Destined for Montreal, as compiled by Richard Glinn, Agent for Transports, on 26 July 1818.

Name	Settler	Wives	Children Age 12—17	Children Age Under 12	Name	Settler	Wives	Children Age 12—17	Children Age Under 12
Parish of Balquhidder					Hugh McEwen				9
Alexander McGregor	1				Alexander McEwen				5
Mary McGregor		1			James McEwen				3
Jannet McGregor			12		Peter McEwen				½
Archibald McGregor	1				Duncan Ferguson	1			
Jannet McGregor		1			Isabella Ferguson		1		
Duncan McGregor				8	Robert Ferguson				10
Hugh McGregor				6	John Ferguson				8
Peter McGregor	1				John McNie	1			
Catherine McGregor		1			Jannet McNie		1		
Mary McGregor				8	Duncan McNie				10½
Duncan McGregor				6	Isabella McNie				9
Donald McLaren	1				Mary McNie				7
Mary McLaren		1			Catherine McNie				5
John McLaren				11	Malcolm McNie				2
Duncan McLaren				8	John McGregor	1			
Peter McLaren				5	Catherine McGregor		1		
Mary McLaren				3½	John McGregor				11
Donald McLaren				2	Peter McGregor	1			
Archibald McLaren				9 months	Mary McGregor		1		
Donald Munroe	1				John McGregor				6
Mary Munroe		1			Mary McGregor				3
Thomas Munroe				10	**Parish of Kincardine**				
John Munroe				7	Daniel Ferguson	1			
Catherine Munroe				4	Catherine Ferguson		1		
Finley McEwen	1				Alexander Ferguson			15	
Mary McEwen		1			John Ferguson			13	
Catherine McEwen			15		Elizabeth Ferguson				9
Jannet McEwen			14		Ann Ferguson				8
John McEwen				11	Robert Ferguson	1			

Ann Ferguson		1		John Campbell				10
Peter Ferguson	1			Catherine Campbell				7
Jannet Ferguson		1		Susan Campbell				2
Daniel Ferguson	1			* Donald McIntire	1			
Mary Ferguson		1		Isabella McIntire		1		
John Fulford	1			Mary McIntire				9
Jannet Fulford		1		Peter McIntire				7
John Fulford			2	**Parish of Kenmore**				
Elizabeth Fulford			2 months	John Anderson	1			
John King	1			Isabella Anderson		1		
Jannet King		1		Daniel Anderson			13	
Robert King			15	Hugh Anderson				11
Margaret King			13	Margaret Anderson				9
Jannet King			4	Peter Anderson				6
John King			2½	James Anderson				4
John King 2nd	1			Robert Anderson				2
Duncan King	1			Peter Anderson	1			
Christine King		1		Christine Anderson		1		
Christine King		1		Donald Anderson				8
Catherine King		1		James Anderson				7
Parish of Killin				John Anderson				5
* John Campbell	1			Ann Anderson				3
Mary Campbell		1		Peter Anderson				2
Jannet Campbell			16	James Anderson [sic]				6 months
Peter Campbell			14	TOTAL	22	23	11	50
Donald Campbell			12					

Source: NAC RG 7 (G1) volume 10, pp. 67—73.
* Families that did not settle in Beckwith, but elsewhere in the Bathurst District.

Appendix 7

Incomplete List of Settlers Believed to have Embarked on the *Jane* at Greenock, Scotland, Destined for Montreal, on 4 July 1818.

Name	Parish	Name	Parish	Name	Parish
John McNaughtane	Kenmore	James Stewart	Dull	Donald McLaren	Comrie
John McNaughtane	Kenmore	John Stewart	Dull	Donald McLaren	Comrie
Donald Anderson	Kenmore	James Stewart Jr.	Dull	John McOwan	Comrie
Alexander Fisher	Fortingall	John Kennedy	Dull	John Carmichael	Comrie
John Fisher	Fortingall	Margaret Stewart	Dull	Archibald Dewar 2nd	Comrie
Donald Fisher	Fortingall	Peter Scott	Dull	James McFarlan	Comrie
James Fisher	Fortingall	Donald Kennedy	Dull	James McNaughton	Comrie
James McDiarmid	Fortingall	Alexander Kennedy	Dull	Donald McKechnie	Callander
John McDiarmid	Fortingall	John McGregor	Dull	* Peter Fergusson	Dunblane
James McVean	Fortingall	James Carmichael	Comrie	* Archibald McGregor	Kenmore
Janet McVean	Fortingall	Peter Carmichael	Comrie		
Peter McVean	Fortingall	Peter McLaren	Comrie		

Source: This incomplete listing was compiled by Howard M. Brown of Ottawa, by listing those settlers named in Colonial Office parish certificate roll [NAC RG 7 (G1) vol. 10, pp. 67—73] not listed in appendices 7 and 8. The Montreal *Gazette* of 2 September 1818 reported that the ship *Jane* arrived at the port of Quebec on 23 August with 131 settlers.

Appendix 8

Census of Household Heads and Count of Family Members, Beckwith Township, Compiled by Duncan Campbell, Town Clerk, 4 June 1820

Head of Family	Women	Children Male	Female	Total	Head of Family	Women	Children Male	Female	Total
Jonas Albertson				1	Robert Fergusson				1
Joseph Alderson	1		5	7	Daniel Fergusson	1	4	3	9
Austin Allen	1	4	2	8	James Fin[le]y	1			2
Richard Allen				1	Richard Fin[le]y	1	3	4	9
Duncan Anderson				1	Alexander Fisher				1
John Anderson	1	1	5	8	Daniel Fisher				1
Peter Anderson	1	5	1	8	John Fisher	1	1	2	5
George Bailey	1	2	1	5	James Fitzgerald	1			2
George Bailey	1			2	Patrick Fitzgerald	1		1	3
George Bailey				1	John Fulford	1	1	1	4
Alexander Bain				1	Robert Gardiner	1	3		5
William Baker	1	1		3	Dennis Gingley				1
Francis Bennett	1	2	2	6	John Goodfellow	1	1	1	4
John Brown	1	3	2	7	William Goodfellow	1	5	5	12
Thomas Brown				1	John Goth	0	1		2
George Buchanan	1			2	[Janet] Gow				1
William Burgess	1	3	1	6	Robert Greville	1	3	3	8
Donald Cameron				1	Robert Hampton				1
Charles Campbell				1	Henry Hawkins				1
Duncan Campbell	1	4	3	9	Roger Hawkins	1	2	3	7
John Carmichael				1	Henry Hawse	1		1	3
Alexander Clark	1			2	Thomas Hays	1			2
Donald Clark	1		1	3	John Henry				1
George Cliff	1	1	1	4	William Henry				1
William Colbourn				1	Luke James	1	2	1	5
Peter Comrie	1	2	1	5	William Jones	1	1		3
James Connor			1	2	John Kelly				1
Thomas Connor	1		2	4	Alexander Kennedy				1
John Cram	1			2	Donald Kennedy	1	2	3	7
Alexander Dalgety				1	John Kennedy				1
Edward Davis				1	James Kent				1
Robert Davis	1	2	2	6	George Kerfoot	1	1	1	4
William Davis	1		1	3	Thomas Kerfoot				1
John Davison	1		1	3	John King	0	1	3	5
Alexander Dewar				1	John King				1
Archibald Dewar	1			2	James Keys				1
John Dewar				1	Thomas Leach	1		1	3
Malcolm Dewar	1			2	William Leach	1	3	2	7
Patrich Dewar				1	William Leach				1
Alexander Douglas				1	Phineas Lowe				1
Malcolm Drummond	1	4	2	8	Henry Lucas	1	2	3	7
Henry Duncan	1	1		3	James Lucas	1	1	1	4
William Dunn				1	John Lummox	1	3	1	6
George Edwards				1	William Matson				1
James Edwards	1	3	4	9	George Merritt	1	1	3	6
Richard James				1	William Morrett	1	1	3	6
John Fanning				1	James Mildson	1	1	1	4
Duncan Fergusson	1		1	3	John Millage				1
Duncan Fergusson	1	3		5	William Mills				1
James Fergusson	1		1	3	John Moore				1
James Fergusson	1			2	William Moore	1	1	5	8
John Fergusson				1	John Moorhouse				1
Robert Fergusson	1	1		3	Jonathan Morris	1	1	1	4
Peter Fergusson				1	John Mosley				1

Josiah Moss	1	1	1	4	George Perry	1	2		4
Ed[mond] Morphy	1	3	3	8	Philip Philips				1
William Morphy				1	William Philpot				1
Ed Murphy				1	James Pierce	1			2
John Murphy				1	John Pollard				1
James Murphy				1	Stephen Redmond				1
Patrick Murphy	1	3	2	7	William Richardson				1
William Murphy	1		2	4	Thomas Riley				1
Duncan McCuan				1	John Roberts	1	2	2	6
Duncan McCallum				1	John William Roberts				1
John McCallum	1		3	5	Donald Robertson	1		2	4
Charles McCarthy	1			2	Duncan Robertson				1
Duncan McCarthy				1	John Robertson	1			2
Michael McConnell	1		1	3	John Robertson				1
David McCrea	1	1	1	4	Peter Robertson				1
Duncan McDiarmid	1	3	3	8	Patrick Rourke	1	2	1	5
James McDiarmid				1	James Saunders	1		1	3
John McDiarmid	1		2	4	Alexander Scott				1
John McDonald				1	John Scott	1			2
Archibald McDonnell	1	1	1	4	Joseph Scott	1	3	1	6
John McDonnell	1	1	1	4	Peter Scott	1	2	1	5
John McDougall				1	Robert Scott	1		3	5
Peter McDougall	1			2	Robert Scott				1
Duncan McEwen				1	William Scott	1			2
Finlay McEwen	1	4	2	8	Jacob Smith	1	2	2	6
John McEwen	1		4	6	John Smith	1	1	2	5
John McEwen				1	Alexander Snedden	1			2
Alexander McGregor	1	5	3	10	David Snedden				1
John McGregor				1	Hugh Sprat[t]	1		1	3
Patrick McGregor				1	John Stevening?				1
Robert McGregor	1		2	4	Alexander Stewart				1
Alexander McG_____	1		6	8	Charles Stewart	1	1		3
Donald McIntosh				1	David Stewart	1			2
James McKay	0	1	1	3	John Stewart	1		1	3
Thomas McKay	1	5	1	8	James Sutton				1
Donald McKenzie	1		1	3	John Taylor				1
Michael McKenzie	1			2	[Stephen?] Tomlinson				1
Roderick McKenzie				1	William Tomlinson	1	6	1	9
James McKinnon				1	Joseph Vaughan[?]	1			2
Donald McLaren	1	2	1	5	John Wall	1	2	3	7
John McLaren	1		1	3	James Ward	1			2
John McLean	1	2	1	5	Thomas Ward	1			2
Donald [McLellan?]	1	4	1	7	John Webster				1
Duncan McNabb	1	2		4	James Weldon				1
Alexander McNaughton				1	John White	1			2
Malcolm McNaughton				1	William White	1	3	1	5
Donald McNaughton	1	3	3	8	Thomas Wickham	1	1		3
Alexander McTavish				1	Thomas Williams	1			2
John McTavish	1			2	George Willis	1	5	3	10
Duncan McVean	1		1	3	John Willis	1	1	2	5
James Nash	1	2		4	Allen Wilson	1		1	3
John Nowlan				1	John Wilson	1	4	2	7
John Nowlan				1	John Wilson				1
Luke Nowlan				1	William Wilson	1			2
Manny Nowlan				1	William Wilson	1	1		3
Patrick Nowlan	1	2	3	7	Anthony Wiseman	1			2
Dennis O'Loughlin				5	TOTALS				
John O'Neil	1	3	2	7	223 Men	132	179	177	711
Samuel Patterson				1					

Source: OTAR RG 21 (A2), alphabetically revised by Howard M. Brown, Ottawa, 1980.

Appendix 9

Census of Household Heads and Count of Family Members, Beckwith Township, Compiled by John Conboy, Town Clark, 1822.

Head of family	Women	Children Male	Children Female	Total	Female Servants	Head of family	Women	Children Male	Children Female	Total
Joseph Alderson	1		6	8		Robert Ferguson	1	1	1	4
Alexander Anderson	1			2		John Ferguson	1	1		3
Donald Anderson	0		1	2		Richard Fin[le]y	1	3	4	9
Peter Anderson	1	5	2	9		Thomas Fin[le]y				1
George Bailey	1		2	4		Alexander Fisher	0		2	3
George Bailey				1		Donald Fisher				1
Nathaniel Bailey	1			2		Duncan Fisher				1
Alexander Bain				1		John Fisher				1
Philip Bayne				1		James Fitzgerald	1			2
George Buchanan	1			2		John Fulford	1	1	2	5
Francis Bennett	1	2	4	8		Esther Garland	1	3	1	5
John Brown				1		James Garland				1
Thomas Burns				1		John Garland	1	4	1	7
William Burgess	1	3	2	7		Nicholas Garland	1	1	1	4
Donald Cameron				1		Richard Garland	1	3	4	9
John Cameron	1	1		3		John Giff	1	1	1	4
Charles Campbell	1			2		Archibald Gillis	1		5	7
Duncan Campbell	1	3	4	9		Dennis Gingley				1
Peter Campbell	1	1	1	4		Thomas Glendenning	1			2
James Carson	1			2		Robert Goodfellow				1
James Carmichael				1		William Goodfellow	1	4	5	11
Peter Carmichael	1		1	4	1	James Goldrick	1	2	1	5
Baker Castle	1	2		4		John Goth	1			2
John Cavanagh	1	1		3		Jannet Gow	1			1
Alexander Clark	1			2		William Greville				1
Donald Clark				1		Robert Hampton				1
George Cliff	1	1	1	4		Thomas Hatton	1	1		3
William Colbourn				1		Henry Hawkins				1
Peter Comrie	1	2	1	5		Roger Hawkins	1	1	3	6
Thomas Connor	1		2	4		Thomas Hays	1			2
Richard Copeland				1		John James	0	3	2	6
Duncan Cram				1		Luke James	1	1	1	4
James Cram				1		William James				1
John Cram	1		1	3		Robert Johnston				1
Peter Cram	1	2	2	6		Peter Jones	1	2	2	6
Peter Cram				1		William Jones	1	1		3
Alexander Dalgety				1		Alexander Kennedy				1
Edward Davis	1			2		Donald Kennedy	1	2	3	7
Robert Davis	1	1	4	7		John Kennedy				1
William Davis				1		George Kerfoot	1	1	3	6
Alexander Dewar				1		Samuel Kerfoot				1
John Dewar				1		Thomas Kerfoot				1
Malcolm Dewar	1	2		4		William Kerfoot	1		1	3
James Drummond				1		William Kidd	1	1		3
Malcolm Drummond	1	2	3	7		William Kidd	1		1	3
George Edwards				1		Francis Kilfoyle	1	3		5
Richard Edwards				1		John King	1	1	2	5
Thomas Edwards	1	2	4	8		John King				1
John Fallon	1	1		3		John King	1	2	1	5
Alexander Ferguson				1		James Keys	0	2	3	6
Daniel Ferguson	1	2	2	6		Samuel Leech				1
Daniel Ferguson				1		Thomas Leech	1		2	4
Duncan Ferguson	1		2	4		William Leech	1	4	2	8
Duncan Ferguson	1	4		6		William Leech				1
Duncan Ferguson	1	2	2	6		Phineas Lowe	1			2
James Ferguson				1		Andrew Lucas	1	2	2	6

James Lucas	1	2	1	5		Donald McLaren	1	4	1	7
John Lucas	1	1		3		Donald McLaren	1	1		3
John Lummox	1	1		3		Duncan McLaren				1
John Lummox	1	1		3		John McLaren	1		1	3
Eby Martin	1	1	1	4		Donald McLellan?	1	3	2	7
George Merritt	1	1	1	4		Ronald? McLellan?	1		1	3
John Millage				1		Duncan McNabb	1	2		4
David Moffatt				1		Duncan McNaughton				1
John Moore				1		Finlay McNaughton				1
William Moore	1	1	4	7		John McNee?				1
William Moore				1		John McRostie				1
John Moorhouse				1		Bernard McStravock				1
Thomas Moorhouse				1		Alexander McTavish				1
Edmond Morphy	1	3	2	7		Alexander McTavish	1	1		3
James Morphy				1		Douglas McTavish	1	2		4
John Morphy	1			2		John McTavish	1	2	2	6
William Morphy	1			2		John McTavish	1			2
Jonathan Morris	1	2	1	5		James Nash	1		2	4
Josiah Moss	1			2		George Nesbitt				1
James McArthur	1	3	1	6		John Nesbitt				1
Duncan McArthur				1		William Nesbitt	1			2
Duncan McArthur				1		John Nowlan	1			2
John McArthur				1		Luke Nowlan				1
Peter McArthur				1		Manny Nowlan				1
John McCallum	1		3	5		Patrick Nowlan	1	2	3	7
Owen McCarthy	1	1		3		Daniel O'Hare				1
Charles McCarthy	0		1	2		John Pollard				1
Michael McConnell	1	1	1	4		John Poole	1	1		3
David McCrea	1			2		Thomas Pierce	1	1		3
John McCuan				1		Stephen Redmond				1
Duncan McDiarmid	1	3	4	9		Thomas Reily				1
James McDiarmid				1		John Roberts	1	1		3
John McDiarmid	1	2	1	5		John Roberts	1	1	1	4
John McDiarmid	1	2		4		Donald Robertson				1
Donald McDonald	0		1	2		Duncan Robertson				1
Duncan McDonald	1	3	2	7		John Robertson				1
John McDonald				1		Peter Robertson				1
Archibald McDonnell	1	1	1	4		Patrick Rourke				1
John McDonnell	1	3		5		James Saunders	1			2
John McDonnell				1		Alexander Scott				1
John McDougall				1		John Scott	1		1	3
Peter McDougall	1			3	1	Joseph Scott	1	1	2	5
Archibald McEwen	1			2		Robert Scott	1		1	3
Duncan McEwen				1		Robert Scott				1
Duncan McEwen				1		William Scott	1	1	1	4
Finlay McEwen	1	3		5		William Scott				1
John McEwen	1		3	5		Jacob Smith	1	1		3
John McEwen				1		John Smith	1		1	3
John McEwen				1		David Snedden	1	1		3
Peter McEwen				1		James Snedden	1	1	1	4
John McFarlane	1		1	3		John Splane				1
Bernard McGee				1		Samuel Splane	1	2	1	5
Alexander McGregor	0	7	3	11		Alexander Stewart				1
Alexander McGregor	1	2	2	6		Alexander Stewart				1
Archibald McGregor				1		Charles Stewart	1		1	3
John McGregor				1		David Stewart	1	1		3
Peter McGregor				1		John Stewart	1	1	1	4
Peter McGregor	1			2		Andrew [S]ut[t]on?	1	1		3
Robert McGregor	1		2	4		Joseph Sutton				1
James McInnis				1		Stephen Tomlinson				1
Duncan McKay	1		2	4		William Tomlinson	1	2	1	5
Thomas McKee				1		James Wall	1	1	4	7
Alexander McKenzie	1			2		Moses Wall				1
John McKewen				1		Thomas Ward	1			2
William McKowen	1	1		3		Israel Webster				1
Colin McLaren	1	2	6	10		George Welby	1	3	3	8

Isaac Whealey	1	1	1	4	Thomas Willis	1		2	4
James White	1		1	3	William Willis	1		1	3
John White				1	Allen Wilson	1	1	1	4
William White				1	John Wilson	1			2
James Whiting	1	2	3	7	William Wilson	1			2
Thomas Wickham	1			2	Anthony Wiseman	1			2
Thomas Williams	1			2	Richard Wynn	1	5	1	8
George Willis	1	2	3	7	John Wynn?	0	4	2	7
Henry Willis	1	1	2	5	TOTALS				
Richard Willis[?]				1	274 men	152	198	183	810	3

Source: OTAR RG 21 (A2), alphabetically revised by Howard M. Brown, Ottawa, 1980.

Appendix 10

Heads of Families Forming the First Presbyterian Congregation at Beckwith, 1822.

Name	Con.	Lot		Name	Con.	Lot
Donald Anderson	6	11NE		Duncan McDonald	5	3SW
John Anderson	7	10NE		Donald McDougall	8	21NE
Peter Anderson	6	8NE		Peter McDougall	9	19NE
George Buchanan {	6	9 } Clergyman		Duncan McEwen	9	22NE
	6	14		Finlay McEwen	7	23NE
Duncan Campbell	4	11NE		John McEwen	8	14NE
John Carmichael	10	23NE		Alexander McGregor	7	5NE
Peter Carmichael	10	16NE		Donald? McGregor	9	8NE
Peter Comrie	10	19SW		John McGregor	10	15SW
Duncan Cram	11	20SW		Peter McGregor	9	8SW
John Cram	10	20SW		James McInnis	9	20W
Alexander Dewar	9	19SW		Donald McIntosh	8	23SW
Archibald Dewar	7	25SW		Colin McLaren	5	21NE
John Dewar	9	20NE		Donald McLaren	4	4SW
Malcolm Dewar	7	23SW		Duncan McLaren	9	25SW
Peter Dewar	7	25NE		Duncan McNab	4	3NE
Duncan Ferguson	5	10NE		Duncan McNee	6	6SW
James Ferguson	6	24NE		Archibald McPhail	9	18NE
John Ferguson	4	23SW		Alexander McTavish	8	17SW
John Goodfellow	5	8NE		John McTavish	9	16NE
Robert Goodfellow	5	8SW		Duncan Robertson	11	23NE
Alexander Kennedy	6	25NE		Alexander Scott	9	18SW
Donald Kennedy	8	24NE		John Scott	6	25SW
Colin King	10	2NE		Colin Sinclair	9	1SW
Duncan[?] King	6	7NE		Alexander Stewart	8	9NE
James McArthur	7	14SW		Duncan Stewart	9	25SW
Duncan McCuan	10	22SW		James Stewart	6	11SW
Duncan McDiarmid	5	22SW		John Stewart	8	27
James McDiarmid	8	16SW				

Source: Jessie Buchanan Campbell, *The Pioneer Pastor* (Franklin, Pennsylvania, 1905), pp. 33-34 "as nearly as they can be recalled, the register having been burned nearly fifty years ago".

Appendix 11

Roman Catholic Immigrants from the South of Ireland Located in Beckwith by the Honourable Peter Robinson in the Autumn of 1823.

Name	Con.	Lot	Name	Con.	Lot
Daniel Calaghan	1	27	Timothy Mann	12	23E
Jeremiah Cronan	5	15NE	Patrick Fitzgerald	12	24W
Denis Galvin	3	5SW			

Source: NAC Colonial Office 384/12, ff.93—96, cited in Donald E. Read, Donald W. Kelly, James R. Kennedy and Bruce S. Elliott, *St. Michael's Roman Catholic Church Cemetery & Lists of Peter Robinson Settlers: Lot 15, Con. 9, (Corkery) Huntley Twp., Carleton Co.* (Ottawa: Ottawa Branch, Ontario Genealogical Society, 1981), p. 57.

Appendix 12

The Humble Petition of the Inhabitants of Beckwith, [1823], sheweth that we are desirous of a Place of Divine Worship and not having the means to Erect a Suitable Place we Humbly beg of your Excellency [the lieutenant-governor] to take it into your consideration to grant the King's Store[,] Beckwith[,] for a Church of the Established Religion of England and we shall be in Duty bound to Pray your Excellency[']s Humble & Obedient Serv[an]ts

Austin Allen	John Griffin	Samuel Leach	Charles McCarthy	Charles Stewart
George Bailey	William Griffin	Thomas Leach	William McCuan	Joseph Sutton
William Burgess	George Griffith	William Leach Sr.	George Nesbitt	Stephen Tomlinson
Baker Castle	John Griffith	William Leach Jr.	John Nesbitt	William Tomlinson
John Conboy	Robert Griffith	John Lett	John Nowlan	James Wall
Hugh Conn	William Griffith	William Lomax	Luke Nowlan	Moses Wall
Robert Davis	Henry Hawkins	John Lummox	Mana Nowlan	Israel Webster
William Davis	William Hawkins	Thomas Lummox	Patrick Nowlan	Thomas Wickham
George Edwards	James Huatt	Phineas Lowe	Samuel Patterson	William Willis
Francis Edwards	Luke James	Andrew Lucas	John Pool[e]	Allen Wilson
Thomas Edwards	William James	James Lucas	Thomas Riley?	William Wilson
Richard Edwards	Peter Jones	John Lucas	Peter Salter	Anthony Wiseman
Duncan Ferguson	William Kerfoot	George Marriott	William Salter	Christopher Wynne
Richard Finley	James Keys	William Marriott	James Saunders	
James Garland	William Kidd	John Moorehouse	James Saunders	
Edward Griffin	Edward Leach	Jonathan Morris	John Scott	
George Griffin	Samuel Leach	William Murphy	William Scott	

Source: NAC RG 5 (A1) vol. 63, pp. 33790—33791, with names alphabetised by Howard M. Brown.

Appendix 13

Return of Irish Immigrants Settled in the Bathurst District in 1823 by the Honourable Peter Robinson Residing in Beckwith Township in March 1826.

Name	Con.	Lot	No. in Family	No. Acres Cleared	Bushels of Grain Raised Since Arrival	Potatoes	Turnips	Cattle	Hogs
Timothy Mann	12	23	7	12	92	200	100	1	1
David Dooland	12	23	9	14	100	400	50	4	1
Edmund Dooland	12	24	Single	Residing with his Father				1	
John Dooland	12	27	Single	Residing with his Father				1	
TOTAL			18	26	192	600	150	7	2

Source: Report from the Select Committee on Emigration from the United Kingdom cited in Donald E. Read, Donald W. Kelly, James R. Kennedy and Bruce S. Elliott, *St. Michael's Roman Catholic Cemetery & Lists of Peter Robinson Settlers: Lot 1, Con. 9, (Corkery) Huntley Twp., Carleton Co.* (Ottawa: Ottawa Branch, Ontario Genealogical Society, 1981), p. 63.

Appendix 14

Petition of Beckwith Inhabitants to the Lieutenant-Governor of Upper Canada, Advocating that British Born Subjects Only Should be Appointed Magistrates, 15 June 1833.

We the undersigned inhabitants of Beckwith having heard that certain individuals are circulating a paper for Signature, requesting Mr. Morris to recommend to the Lieutenant Governor Mr. C. S. Bellows of Carlton Place as a fit and proper person for a Magistrate in this Township, are of opinion that British born Subjects only should be appointed to that office, out of the many, more, or at least equally qualified with Mr. Bellows.

John Bell	Thomas Hawkins	John Whitby	William James	Thomas May
Wm. More Jnr.	Amable Pappin	William Davis senior	John James	Richard May
Peter Recart	John Whyte	William Salter	Sammule James	John May
James Hunter	William Burgess	William Tomlinson	Charles James	Thomas Armstrong
James Morphy	Alexander Turner	Edward Finlay	William Leech	William Carl
Wm. Moore Snr.	William May	William Moore	Robin Edwards	William Waite
A.H. Wiseman	James Fanning	John Coplin	Patrick Burgess	Thomas Pierce
Edmond Morphy Junr.	Robert Campbell	George Hamilton	John Leech	Thos. Mason
John Morphy	Alexr McTavish	Joseph Boyd	Thos. Griffit	Pinehes Lowe
Hugh Boulton	James McNeely	John Finley	Robt. Griffit	William Jones
Edmd Morphy Senr.	Mathew Macanelly	Thomas Finley	George Nesbitt	Thos. Kidd
John Dinning	William Leech	Thomas Lawford	Richard Wood	Richard Coplan
John Moore	Henry Waite	James Whitting	Richard Douglas	John Conboy
William Sparrow	Richd Finley Jun.	James Whitting Jun.	James Douglas	Thos. Leech
George Willis	Thomas Finley	Thomas Lummox	Thomaz little Burgess	James Floyd
Brice McNeely	James Devlin	Richard Coplin	Isaac Whealey	William Shirley
John McNeely	Samuel Splane	Samule Sutton	Joseph Morris	John Shirley
William Morphy	Peter Goodman	Jacob Smith	George Leech	Henry Hawkins
Simon Roche	Richard Finley	John Smith	John Nasson	William Leach
William Willis	William Linton	Thomas Hawkins	George Codd	John Griffith
Henry Willis	Thomas Splan	Petter Salter	James Dowdle	Charleys Stone
F.W.K. Quinn	Donald McGregor	George Kerfoot	John Dowdle	George Marrit
MannyNowlan Ensign 3rd. Lanark	Nathanial Bearly	William Kerfoot	Luke James	Thomas Williams
	William Merrit	John Scott	Edward Davis	John Mablan
	George Whitby	Henery Griffit	Thomas Morris	Wm. Allen

Patt. Nowlan
James Kent
Christopher Burchill
Christopher Wynn
Willm Salter
John Fennel
William Scott Senior
Robert Davis
Wm. Davis
Peter Jones Senior
Peter Jones Junior
Robert Moore
Peter Fullan

Joseph Scott
William Scott junior
Thomas Sanders
John Camell
John Wilson Sen.
John Griffith
Peter Salter
William Pendergrass
Patt Nowlan Jun.
Edward Wen jun.
George Nowlan
Patrick Redmond
John Campbell

John Wilson
[illegible]
John King
Moses Wall
Samule Bradley
William Bradley
Thimoty Conboy
Henery Sanders
Thomas Poole
John Wilson Jun.
James Hill
Frank Edward
Thomeys Kerfoot

James Kilfoile
James Coplin
Luck Nolen
Dun^n Campbell
Donald Campbell
John Wester
Richard May
Edward Garland
Edwd Davis
John Waite
Edwd Wynn
Duncan Mckether
Thos. Ward

William Wills
James Leech
George Edwards
John Armstrong
James Brown
John Wynne
John Wynne Junr.
Jacob Smith
John Giff Sen.
John Giff
Thos. Leech

Source: NAC RG 5 (A1) vol. 130, p. 71700

Appendix 15

List of Those Desirous of Admission to the Ordinance of the Lord's Supper at the Church of Scotland, Beckwith, Listed by the Reverend John Smith, 14 February 1834.

Duncan McLaren
Mayant McLaren
Duncan Ferguson
Christian Ferguson
Anne Anderson
John Anderson
Alexr McTavish
Anne McTavish
Margaret Fisher
John McTavish
Peter McTavish
Alexr McTavish
John McGregor
Mary McGregor
Catherine McNie
John McArthur
Grace McArthur
Anne McArthur
Jas. Duncan
Mrs. Duncan
Colin McLaren
Mrs. McLaren
John McEwan
Janet McEwan
John McEwan
Christian McEwan
John McEwan Sen.
Catherine McEwan
John McEwan Jun.
Anne McEwan
Catherine McEwan
Peter McFarlane
Hugh McEwan
Catherine McEwan

Peter Dewar
Janet Dewar
Donald Kennedy
Robert Kennedy
John Kennedy
Catherine Kennedy
Catherine Kennedy
Anne Kennedy
Malcolm Dewar
Anne Dewar
John McTavish
Mrs. McTavish
Duncan McEwan
Catherine McEwan
Peter Anderson
George McLaren
John Anderson
Margaret Anderson
Catherine Anderson
William McKenzie
Catherine McKenzie
Peter Carmicael
Margaret Carmicael
John Carmicael
Mary Carmicael
Peter McGregor
Margaret McGregor
Alexr. Dewar
Janet Dewar
Robert Stewart
Helen Stewart
John Ferguson
Mary Ferguson
James McInnes

Margaret McInnes
Duncan Ferguson
Anne Ferguson
James Ferguson
Christian Ferguson
John Scott
Mayant Scott
Donald McDonald
Christena McDougald
Alexr. Scott
Elizabeth Scott
Alexr. McGregor
Mary McGregor
Duncan McGregor
Catherine McDougald
Mary McGregor
Peter Scott
Margaret Scott
Donald Livingston
Janet Livingston
Janet Livingston
John McDiarmid
Mary McDiarmid
Alexr. Stewart
Elizabeth Stewart
Peter Comrie
Janet Comrie
Donald McLaren
Margaret McLaren
Duncan McLaren
Daniel McLaren
Alexr. McLaren

Daniel McLaren
William Muirhead
Agnes McLaren
Mary McLaren
Catherine McLaren
James Stewart
Isabella Stewart
Donald Anderson
Mrs. Anderson
Donald McIntosh
John Campbell, Elder
Mrs. Campbell
Finlay McEwan
Mary McEwan
Hugh McEwan
Christian McEwan
Peter McLaren
Margaret McLaren
Robert Ferguson
Mrs. Ferguson
John Stewart
Helen Stewart
Robert McLaren
David Stewart
Agnes Stewart
Catherine Stewart
John Stewart
John McKenzie
Anne McArthur
James McArthur Sen.
James McArthur Jun.
Douglas McTavish
Elizabeth McTavish
Robert Scott

Isabella Scott
Donald Anderson
Duncan McNee
Janet McNee
Isabella McNee
Duncan McCuan
Catherine McCuan
John McLaren
Elizabeth McLaren
Peter McGregor
David Thomson
Mrs. Thomson
Donald Robertson
Mrs. Robertson
Janet Robertson
Catherine Fisher
Anne Wilson
John Davidson
Anne Davidson
Colin King
Anne King
Mrs. Fisher
Christian Fisher
Elizabeth Scott
John McDonald Elder
Peter Campbell Elder
Isabella Jane Smith

Source: OTAR MS 123 Minutes of the Kirk Session of the Presbyterian Church, Beckwith Township, 1834—1889, pp. 5—7.

Appendix 16

Names of Petitioners Requesting of the Lieutenant-Governor of Upper Canada a Charter for Establishing a Semi-Annual Public Fair at the Village of Franktown in the Township of Beckwith, May 1837.

Frederick Alexander
Austin Allen
John Armstrong
Samuel Bradley
James Brown
Robert Brown
Christopher Burchill
Patrick Burgess
William Burgess Sr.
James Burrows
Duncan Campbell
James Clark
William Clark
John Davis
Thomas Edwards

James Fallon
Richard Fleming
William Gilson
Robert Glendinning
Henry Graham
William Hamilton
Andrew Hughton
John Hughton
Alexander Jackson
James Jackson
Henry James
William James
Francis W.K. Jessop
William Jones
James Kent

George Kerfoot
Anthony Leslie
Phineas Lowe
William Marshall
George Merritt
William Morris
Robert McBride
John McEwan
Alexander McGregor
Archibald McGregor
Peter McGregor
P. McIntosh
John McKenna
Duncan McKercher
James McMaster

John McMaster
George Nesbitt
George Nowlan
Manny Nowlan
Patrick Nowlan
Patrick Nowlan Jr.
Daniel O'Mara
David Pattie
Thomas Pearce
Humphrey Perrin
Peter Salter
William Salter
William Salter Jr.
Duncan Sargeson
William Sargeson

James Saunders
Jonathan Shortt
Charles Stone
Josias Taylor
Michael Walsh
John Webster
John Webster Jr.
M. Williams
John Wynne Sr.
John Wynne Jr.
William Wynne
James Young

Source: NAC RG 1 (E3), vol. 31 Upper Canada State Papers. These names were edited and alphabetised by Howard M. Brown, Ottawa.

Appendix 17

Names of Petitioners in Beckwith and Ramsay Townships Requesting of the Lieutenant-Governor of Upper Canada a Charter for Establishing a Semi-Annual Public Fair at Carlton Place, November 1838.

James Bell
Robert Bell
Edward J. Boswell
Daniel Colvin
John Colvin
Peter Cram
Roger Cunningham
Joseph Dougherty Sr.
Joseph Dougherty Jr.
James Dougherty
John Dewar
Andrew Fitzpatrick

James Fitzpatrick
John Fummerton
John Griffith
William Griffith
William Hawkins
William Henry
Joseph Houston
Francis W.K. Jessop
Jeremiah Kenney
James Kerr
Napoleon Lavallee
William Lummax

Robert Moffatt
James Morphy
John Morphy
William Morton
Michael Murphy
James McAlinden
John McDiarmid
Duncan McEwan
John McEwan
Ewen McEwen
Jacob McFadden
Alexander McLean

James McLean
John McNeiley
John McQuarrie
John Neil
Manny Nowlan
Patrick Parker
David Pattie
Paddy Rahilly
Simon Roche
Edward Rosamond
James Rosamond
Robert Scott

Thomas Sheldon
William Sparrow
Alexander Stewart
John Sumner
John Sykes
James Wallace
John Wethers
Robert Wilkie
William Wilson

Source: NAC RC 1 (E3) vol. 18.

Appendix 18

Names of Inhabitant Freeholders and Householders of the Township of Beckwith Agreeable to Assessment, Compiled by Richard Finlay, assessor, 1841.

Name	Lot	Name	Lot	Name	Lot
1st Concession		Phineas Lowe	8E	*5th Concession*	
Anthony H. Wiseman	1W	Rev. James Padfield	9E	Alexander McLaren	3
Duncan Ferguson	1E	Thomas Williams	9W	Duncan McKay	5E
Colin Ferguson	3W	Dennis McCarthy	10W	William May	7
Archibald Gillis	3E	George Cockle	10E	John Weston	8
Hugh Cameron	4W	Ewen McEwen	10E	Jonathan Moore	10R
Patrick McAlinden	7W	James Burrows		John Moore	10W
Robert McLaughlin	8W	John Smyth	15W	Duncan Ferguson	10E
William Jones	8E	Jacob Smyth	15E	John McDonald	11
Humphrey Perrin	10E		16	John Scott	19W
Patrick Nowlan	11E	William Salter	17W	James Scott	20W
Michael Brennan	14E	Charles Campbell	18W	Alexander Stewart	20E
Patrick Brennan	16W	James Saunders	19E	Colin McLaren	21
Martin Jordan	16E	William Burgess	20E	Robert Ferguson	22W
John Salter	18E	Nathaniel Burgess	20W	Peter McDiarmid	22E
Thomas Holbrook	18W	James Keys	21E	John Ferguson	23W
Thomas Brennan	19E	Robert Saunders	21W	John Poole	24E
		David Stewart	23E	Angus McDiarmid	24W
2nd Concession		Margaret Scott	23W	John McLaren	27
		William James	25		
William Moore	1W	Patrick Dowlan	26	*6th Concession*	
George Hamilton	1E			Archibald Cameron	1
Thomas Finlay	2W	*4th Concession*		John McLellan	3E
Richard Finlay	3W			Donald McDonald	4W
George Stanley	3E	Duncan McLaren	3E	Alexander McKenzie	4E
Donald Cameron	4E	Donald McLaren	4W	Alexander Anderson	5W
Richard Finlay	5W	Duncan McNee	4E	Chrys McNaughton	6W
Thomas Finlay	5E	John Stewart	5	John Brown	6E
Alexander McTavish	6	John McEwan	8E	John Stewart	7W
Thomas Mason	7W	Jeremiah McCarthy	9	John King	7E
William Kidd	7E	Peter McLaren	10	Alexander McGregor	8W
John Cavanah	8E	Duncan Campbell	11E	Peter Anderson	8E
Austin Allen	9E	Archibald Campbell	12W	John Anderson	9W
William Gibson	10E	Nathaniel Bailey	14W	John May	9E
Andrew Hughton	13W	Allan Cameron	14E	Samuel May	10
Duncan McKercher	15W	Richard Fleming	15E	James Stewart	11W
George Kerfoot	15E	Thomas Ward	15W	Daniel Anderson	11E
Widow Shirley	17E	William Davis	16W	James McTavish	12W
John King	24	Robert Davis	16E	Thomas Loma[x]	13
George Buchanan	25E	Peter Jones	17	Duncan Campbell	14
George Edwards	27	Duncan McLaren	18	Robert Scott	20
		Robert Edwards	19R	John Kidd	21E
3rd Concession		Thomas Kidd	20W	Robert Dixon	23E
		Thomas Edwards	20W	George McLaren	24W
James Devillin	1W	Samuel Leech	20E	James Ferguson	24E
Hugh Dewe	1E	Thomas Saunders	21W	John Scott	25W
James Whiting	3W	John Lett	21E	Robert Stewart	25E
Alexander McLaren	3E	Alexander Ferguson	22E	John Tomlinson	27
Thomas Lawford	3E	Samuel Mitchell	24W		
William Allen	6E	William Kerfoot	25W	*7th Concession*	
Peter McLaren	6W	Samuel Kerfoot	25E		
Farlan McFarlan	7	Thomas Alcock	26W	Angus McLellan	2E
Thomas Pierce	8W	Samuel Patterson	27		

Name	Lot	Name	Lot	Name	Lot
Hugh McEwen	3W	William Leech	12E	William Sparrow	17W
Donald McLellan	3E	William Leech	13W	Daniel Cram	20E
Archibald McLellan	4W	Alexander Dalgety	13E	James Cram	2[0]
Alexander McGregor	4E	New Year Watson	14W	Peter Cram	21W
John Cameron	5E	Alexander Stewart	14E	John Goth	22W
John McDonald	6W	Donald Robertson	15W	Peter Robinson	23W
Hugh McGregor	9	John Robertson	16W	Duncan Robertson	23E
Jannet Anderson	10	John McTavish	16E	Peter Campbell	24
Duncan Fisher	11W	Peter McTavish	17W	John McDougall	25
Alexander Fisher	12W	Alexander Scott	18W	Thomas White	25E
Rev. John Smith	12E	Archibald McPhail	18E	Peter McCuan	26
James McArthur	13	Alexander Dewar	19W	John White	26E
Peter McArthur	14W	Widow McDougall	19E		
John McArthur	14E	James McGinnis	20W	12th Concession	
John Campbell	19F	John Dewar	20E		
Peter McFarlane	21W	Duncan McEwen	22	John Dowdall	3R
Ann Dewar	23W	Duncan McLaren	25	William Dowdall	3F
Finlay McEwen	23E	Malcolm Drummond	25	John Swain	4W
Alexander McEwen	24E	Daniel Clark	26W	John Doolin	4
Jannet Dewar	25	Alexander Clark	27	Nicholas Dixon	10W
John McDiarmid	26W			David Moffat	11E
		10th Concession		Robert Hampton	12W
8th Concession				Manny Nowlan	12E
		Peter McLaren	1	Peter Cram	13W
John Willis	3W	John Miller	2W	John McCrosty	13E
John Nesbitt	8W	Colin King	2E	Robert Johnston	13F
Archibald McGregor	8E	Jane Duff	8	James Rosamond	13E
Thomas Burgess	9W	Richard Bolton	8	James Duncan	13E
John Conboy	9E	Elizabeth Burgess	9	John Morphy	15W
James Floyd	10W	James Fanning	10W	James Morphy	15E
Thomas Griffith	10E	Donald Campbell	10E	Michael Morphy	15E
Richard Griffith	11W	John McTavish	11E	George Bailey W	16W
Thomas Armstrong	11E	William Rattray	12W	George Bailey	16E
Thomas Hawkins	12W	James Rattray	12E	William Doherty	18W
Henry Hawkins	12E	Alexander Thompson	13	Daniel Cram	19E
Isaac Whealey	13W	John McGregor	15W	Thomas Glendenning	20W
Samuel Whealey	13E	Peter McGregor	15E	Duncan Cram	21
John McEwen	14	Mary Carmichael	16W	Thomas Cavers	22W
Douglas McTavish	15	Peter Carmichael	16E	Timothy Mann	23W
James McDiarmid	16W	Peter Comrie	19W	Edmond Morphy	23W
Alexander McTavish	17W	John Cram	20W	David Doolin	24W
John Stewart	21	Duncan McCuan	22W		
Donald McDougall	21	John McLaren	23W	Carleton Place	
John McEwen	22	John McCuan	24W		
Donald McIntosh	23W	James McFarlane	24E	Sarah Morphy	14E
Donald Kennedy	24W	Peter McNab	25E	John McEwan	14E
John Kennedy	24E	John McNab	26F	Hugh Boulton	14
Robert Scott	25E			Simon Roche	14
John Stewart	27	11th Concession		David Pattie	14
				Edward Rosamond	14
9th Concession		Alexander Sinclair	1	Michael Walsh	14
		James Morris Sr.	2	Peter Comrie	14
Colin Sinclair	1W	James Morris Jr.	2	Ephraim Tweedy	14W
John Sinclair	1E	George Codd	4	Thomas Morphy	14W
Joseph Morris	5F	Samuel James	5	Orrin Pierce	14
Thomas James	6F	Henry Willis	10F	John Graham	14
James Leach	6W	Duncan Fisher	11W	William Poole	14
Peter McGregor	8	George Willis	12E	William Russell	14
Richard Douglas	9	Francis Jessup	13W	Joseph Bond	14
Alexander Cameron	10	Nathaniel Moore	14E	Henry Fitzpatrick	14
Catherine James	11W	Brice McNeely	16	Jacob Barney	14
Hugh McEwen	11E	John McNeely	16W	Andrew Fitzpatrick	14
Thomas Leech	12W	James McNeely	16E	Rev. Edward Boswell	14

600 APPENDICES

Name	Lot	Name	Lot	Name	Lot
		Franktown		George Nesbitt	12B
Napoleon Lavallee	14			Timothy Conboy	12B
Ephriam Kilpatrick	14	Peter McGregor	1B	James Burrows	14B
		George Nowlan	2B	Thomas Kidd	16B
		James Kent	10B	James Jackson	4B

Source: Beckwith Township Municipal Records, 1840—1849, at Black's Corners, Ontario.

Appendix 19

Beckwith Township Officers, 1841

Town Wardens		John King	2 East
Thomas Kidd		Austin Allen	3 West
Alexander Stewart		Jacob Smith	3 East
Peter McArthur		John McEwen	4 West
Assessor		Alexander Ferguson	4 East
Richard Finlay		William Ferguson	5 West
Collector of Rates		Angus McDiarmid	5 East
Robert Davis		Donald Anderson	6 West
Town Clerk		John Scott	6 East
James Kent		Hugh McGregor	7 West
Poundkeepers for Concessions		Finlay McEwen	7 East
George Stanley	1 & 2	Thomas Burgess	8 West
James Burrows	3 & 4	John McEwen	8 East
Thomas Lomas	5 & 6	John Willis	Parts 8 & 9
Thomas Griffith	7 & 8	William Leech	9 West
Alexander Stewart	9 & 10	John Robertson	9 East
John McEwan	11 & 12	Peter McLaren	Part "over the lake"
Fenceviewers by Concessions		Alexander Thompson	10 West
George Kerfoot	1 & 2	Duncan McCuan	10 East
William Davis	3 & 4	Duncan Fisher	11 West
John Watson	5 & 6	John Goth	11 East
John Conboy	7 & 8	Alexander Sinclair	"over the lake"
New Year Watson	9 & 10	Peter Cram	12 West
Brice McNeely	11 & 12	Thomas Glendinning	12 East
Pathmasters by Concession Areas		James Bell	Carleton Place
Colin Ferguson	Parts 1 & 2	Peter McGregor	Franktown
Donald Cameron	2 West		

Source: Beckwith Township Municipal Records, 1840—1849, at Black's Corners, Ontario.

Appendix 20

Members Joining Carleton Place Library Association and Mechanics Institute, 1846—1851.

James Bell	C.P. merchant	Daniel Cram	Beckwith farmer	Samuel Fuller	C.P. iron founder
Robert Bell	C.P. merchant	David Cram	Beckwith farmer	J.A. Gemmill	C.P. merchant
Joseph Bond	C.P. shoemaker	John Cram	Beckwith farmer	John Gilroy	C.P.
James Boyd	C.P.	Archibald Dewar	C.P.	John Graham	C.P. carpenter
Robert Brown	C.P.	Peter Dewar	Beckwith farmer	Hugh Grady?	
William Cameron	C.P.	Rev. R. Dick	C.P.	William Houston	Ramsay farmer
Duncan Campbell	C.P. merchant	Robert Drynan	C.P.	Napoleon Lavallee	C.P. innkeeper
H.M. Chapman		James Duncan	C.P. blacksmith	Russell Laurence	C.P. clothier
George Codd	Beckwith farmer	George Dunnett	C.P. merchant	David Lawson	C.P. clerk

Robert Lawson	C.P.	William McGee Sr.		James Poole	C.P. publisher
John Masters	C.P.	Alexander McGregor	C.P.	Dr. Gavin Russell	physician
John Mills	C.P.	Duncan McGregor	C.P. blacksmith	William Russell	C.P. currier
William Moffatt	C.P. carpenter	John McIntosh	Beckwith farmer	James Scott	C.P.
John Morphy	C.P. farmer	John McIntyre Sr.	Ramsay farmer	John Sellery	C.P.
John Morphy Jr.	C.P.	John McLaughlan	C.P. carpenter	Thomas Smith	C.P.
Absolem McCaffrey	C.P. cooper	David McNabb	C.P. saddler	Robert Sutherland	C.P. miller
Nathaniel McCaffrey	C.P. carpenter	Peter McRostie	C.P. farmer	Albert Teskey	Ramsay merchant
John McCarton	Ramsay farmer	Johnston Neilson	C.P. schoolmaster	William Wallace	Ramsay farmer
James McDiarmid	C.P. merchant	Thomas Patterson	Ramsay farmer	Thomas Watchorn	C.P. cloth dresser
Allan McDonald	C.P. fuller	David Pattie	C.P. carpenter	John Wethers	Goulbourn
George McEwan	C.P.	William Peden	C.P. merchant	William Wilson	Ramsay farmer
John McEwan	C.P. innkeeper	Samuel Pittard	C.P. farmer	Dr. William Wilson	C.P. physician

Source: Carleton Place Public Library, List of Subscribers to the Carleton Place Library Association and Mechanics' Institute, 1846—1851, as alphabetised and with occupations added by Howard M. Brown.

Appendix 21

Communion Roll of Knox Free Presbyterian Church, Black's Corners, 1847

John MacDonald Elder
Mrs. John MacDonald
Niel Stewart Elder
Mrs. N. Stewart
John MacEwen Elder
Mrs. J. MacEwen
Cathrine MacEwen Widow
James Stewart
Mrs. Jas. Stewart
Alexander Stewart
Christian Stewart
Allan Cameron
Mrs. A. Cameron
Duncan MacNee
Jannet MacNee Widow
Cathrine MacNee
Mrs. Finlay Widow
Mrs. Campbell
Ewen MacEwen Postmaster
Mrs. Ewen MacEwen
John MacEwen
Mrs. John MacEwen
Hugh MacEwen

Mrs. Hugh MacEwen
Alexander Stewart
Mrs. Alexr. Stewart
Mrs. D. Stewart Widow
William Duff
Mrs. W. Duff
Jannet Duff
James Duncan
Mrs. John Black
Allan MacDonald
Mrs. Allan MacDonald
Colin King
Mrs. Colin King
Colin Sinclair
Charles Stewart
John McTavish Jr.
Mrs. John McTavish
Peter McTavish
Mrs. Peter McTavish
Elizabeth McTavish
John Robertson
Donald Robertson
Alexander Dewar

Mrs. A. Dewar
Margaret Dewar
Catherine Dewar
George Dewar
Margaret Dewar
Anne Dewar
Donald MacDougald
Mrs. Donald MacDougald
John MacDougald
Jannet MacDougald
Margaret MacDougald
Christian MacDougald
Mrs. Catherine MacDougall (widow)
Elizabeth MacDougall
Jannet McDougall
Duncan MacEwen
Mrs. Duncan MacEwen
John MacEwen
Mrs. John MacEwen
Findlay MacEwen
Mrs. Finlay MacEwen
Alexander MacEwen

Mrs. R. MacEwen
James MacEwen
Mrs. Peter Dewar (widow)
John MacDougall
Mrs. John MacDougall
Duncan McCallum
Mrs. Colin Sinclair
John Sinclair
Mrs. John Sinclair
John Miller
Mrs. John Miller
William MacDonald
Mrs. Wm. MacDonald
John Macnab Sr.
William Murehead
Alex. MacLaren
Ann MacLaren
John Stewart
Archibald McArthur
Mrs. McArthur

Source: United Church Archives, Toronto, Session Book and Register of Knox Presbyterian Church, Black's Corners.

Appendix 22

Reeves of Beckwith Township, 1850—1991

Name	Term	Religion	Ethnic Origin
Robert Bell	1850—1851	Presbyterian	Scottish
James Burrows	1852—1854	Roman Catholic	Irish
John Conboy	1855	Anglican	Irish
Archibald McArthur	1856—1863	Free Presbyterian	Scottish
James Conn	1864	Church of Scotland	Scottish
Patrick Struthers	1865—1867	Church of Scotland	Irish
Donald Carmichael	1868	Church of Scotland	Scottish
Robert Crampton	1869—1870	Anglican	Irish
James Conn	1871—1877	Church of Scotland	Scottish
Archibald Dewar	1878—1882	Presbyterian	Scottish
William Goth	1883	Anglican	English
Archibald Dewar	1884—1894	Presbyterian	Scottish
Joseph Cram	1895—1896	Presbyterian	Scottish
William Goth	1897—1900	Anglican	English
Joseph Kidd	1901	Methodist	Irish
Archibald Dewar	1902—1916	Presbyterian	Scottish
David B. McLaren	1917	Presbyterian	Scottish
William J. Lightbody	1918—1920	Presbyterian	Irish
Robert O Gardiner	1921—1923	Anglican	Irish
Harold Lowe	1924	Anglican	Irish
Robert J. McEwen	1925—1929	Presbyterian	Scottish
Fred Nesbitt	1930—1945	Anglican	Irish
Adam W. Jones	1946—1950	United Church	Irish
Fred Nesbitt	1951—1954	Anglican	Irish
Stanley Brunton	1955—1966	United Church	Scottish
Clarence McGregor	1967—1968	Presbyterian	Scottish
Stanley Brunton	1969—1985	United Church	Scottish
John Sheil	1986—1991	Baptist	Irish
Stanley Brunton	1992—	United Church	Scottish

Source: Manuscript census returns for Beckwith and Carleton Place, Beckwith municipal records and oral interviews.

Appendix 23

Alphabetical List of Household Heads in Beckwith Township, 1852.

Name	Occupation	Birthplace	Religion	Age	No. in House	House Made of	Lot	Con.
Thomas Alcock	Farmer	Ireland	Wes. Methodist	49	6	Stone	26	4
Austin Allen	Cooper	Ireland	Ch. of England	50	2	Frame		
Austin Allen	Carriage Maker	Ireland	Ch. of England	25	2	Log		
William Allen	Labourer	England	Free Ch. Presby.	50	2	Log	6	3
Donald Anderson	Farmer	Scotland	Free Ch. Presby.	55	4	Log	11	6
Mathew Anderson	Blacksmith	Ireland	Ch. of England	27	5	Shanty	10	3
Peter Anderson	Farmer	Scotland	Ch. of Scotland	74	5	Stone	8	6
Thomas Armstrong	Farmer	Ireland	Ch. of England	57	5	Log	11	8
William Armstrong	Cooper	Canada	Ch. of England	25	6	Log	11	3
George Bailey	Farmer	Ireland	Ch. of England	75	3	Log	16	12
George Bailey	Farmer	Ireland	Wes. Methodist	54	2	Log	17	12
Thomas Bailey	Farmer	Ireland	Ch. of England	24	5	Log	26	1
Alexander Bain	Farmer	Scotland		48	10	Log	13	11
William Barker	Farmer	Ireland	Ch. of England	50	4	Shanty	2	12

Name	Occupation	Origin	Religion	Age	Family	Dwelling	Col 8	Col 9
David Bell	Farmer	Ireland	Ch. of England	35	6	Log	2	2
Margaret Bell		Scotland	Ch. of Scotland	38	5	Frame	14	12
Robert Bell	Merchant	England	Ch. of Scotland	45	8	Frame	15	12
John Berryman	Labourer	Ireland	Ch. of Scotland	34	7	Frame	14	12
Richard Bolton	Farmer	Ireland	Ch. of England	53	11	Log	21	10
Joseph Bond	Shoemaker	Ireland	Ch. of England	40	11	Frame	15	12
Hugh Boulton	Miller	United States	Ch. of England	64	8	Stone	14	12
James Bowles	Carpenter	England	Ch. of England	35	8	Frame	10	3
James Boyle	Cooper	Ireland	Roman Catholic	25	3	Log	14	1
Thomas Bradley	Labourer	Ireland	Ch. of England	35	7	Log	12	6
William Bradley	Weaver	Ireland	Ch. of England	61	2	Log		
John Brennan	Farmer	Ireland	Roman Catholic	43	7	Shanty	19	2
Donald Buchanan	Weaver	Scotland	Baptist	35	8	Log		
George Buchanan	Blacksmith	Scotland		73	2	Shanty	25	2
James Buchanan	Farmer	Ireland	Ch. of England	40	5	Shanty	1	3
Mary Burgess		Ireland	Roman Catholic	64	5	Log		
Patrick Burgess	Farmer	Ireland	Ch. of England	41	6	Log	20	3
Thomas L. Burgess	Farmer	Ireland	Ch. of England	45	12	Stone	9	8
James Burrows	Innkeeper	Ireland	Roman Catholic	40	22	Frame	11	2
John Butler	Tinsmith	Canada	Ch. of England	18	2	Frame	14	12
Alexander Cameron	Farmer	Scotland	Free Ch. Presby.	50	4	Log	10	9
Allan Cameron	Farmer	Scotland	Free Ch. Presby.	40	9	Log	14	4
Archibald Cameron	Farmer	Scotland	Ch. of Scotland	55	9	Log	1	6
Donald Cameron	Farmer	Scotland	Free Ch. Presby.	55	6	Shanty	4	2
John Cameron	Carpenter	Canada	Baptist	28	3	Log	5	7
Widow Cameron		Scotland	Baptist	52	5	Log	5	7
Archibald Campbell	Farmer	Scotland	Free Ch. Preby.	30	6	Log	11	4
Donald Campbell	Farmer	Scotland	Free Ch. Presby.	33	5	Log	10	10
Donald Campbell	Farmer	Scotland		35	9	Stone	24	11
Duncan Campbell	Merchant	Canada	Baptist	26	2	Frame		12
John Campbell	Farmer	Scotland		40	7	Log	6	2
Malcolm Campbell	Weaver	Scotland	Free Ch. Presby.	62	6	Log		
Samuel Carley	Tailor	Ireland		37	7	Log	11	3
Peter Carmichael	Farmer	Scotland	Ch. of Scotland	64	7	Log	17	11
Robert Carmichael	Farmer	Canada	Ch. of Scotland	24	6	Log	16	10
Ann Cashen		Ireland	Ch. of England	56	2	Log		
John Cavanagh	Farmer	Canada	Ch. of England	22	7	Log	8	1
Thomas Cavers	Farmer	Scotland	Ch. of Scotland	40	9	Log	22	12
Thomas Churchill	Cooper	Canada	Wes. Methodist	25	4	Frame	14	12
Alexander Clark	Farmer	Scotland	Free Ch. Presby.	61	4	Log	27	9
Daniel Clark	Tailor	Canada	Free Ch. Presby.	22	1	Frame	14	12
Thomas Clark	Shoemaker	Ireland		35	3	Log	10	3
Daniel Cleary	Farmer	Ireland	Roman Catholic	50	6	Log	24	12
George Code	Farmer	Ireland	Ch. of England	52	12	Log	3	11
Mary Cole		Ireland	Ch. of England	40	3	Shanty		
John Coleman	Shoemaker	Canada	Ch. of England	23	3	Frame	14	12
Peter Comrie	Farmer	Scotland	Ch. of Scotland	62	5	Log	19	10
John Conboy Esq.		Ireland	Ch. of England	54	8	Stone	9	8
Timothy Conboy	Farmer	Ireland	Ch. of England	40	8	Shanty	13	2
James Conn	Clerk	Canada	Wes. Methodist	20	2	Log	26	4
William Copeland	Labourer	Ireland	Ch. of England	30	2	Log		
Elizabeth Craig		Canada	Labourer	29	2	Stone		
Daniel Cram	Farmer	Scotland	Baptist	39	7	Stone	18	12
David Cram	Farmer	Scotland	Free Ch. Presby.	45	8	Frame	21	11
Duncan Cram	Farmer	Scotland	Free Ch. Presby.	51	10	Log	21	12
James Cram	Farmer	Scotland	Free Ch. Presby.	53	10	Log	20	11
John Cram	Farmer	Scotland	Free Ch. Presby.	56	6	Log	20	10
Peter Cram	Farmer	Scotland	Free Ch. Presby.	49	10	Log	13	12
Alexander Dalgatie	Farmer	Scotland	Free Ch. Presby.	66	7	Log	13	9
Robert Davis	Farmer	Ireland	Ch. of England	69	4	Log	16	4
William Davis	Farmer	Ireland	Ch. of England	60	5	Log	16	4
Robert Day	Farmer	Ireland	Wes. Methodist	26	2	Log		
James Devlin	Weaver	Ireland	Ch. of England	60	6	Log	1	3
Janet Dewar		Scotland	Free Ch. Presby.	46	6	Log	25	7
Peter Dewar	Farmer	Canada	Free Ch. Presby.	25	6	Log	22	7

Name	Occupation	Origin	Religion	Age		Dwelling		
Nicholas Dixon	Farmer	Canada	Roman Catholic	32	4	Stone	11	12
Robert Donaldson	Farmer	Scotland	Free Ch. Presby	51	3	Shanty	3	12
William Dougherty	Shoemaker	Canada	Ch. of England	22	2	Frame	14	12
William Dougherty	Farmer	Ireland	Wes. Methodist	73	6	Log	18	12
Thomas Douglas	Farmer	Ireland	Ch. of England	62	8	Log	3	12
William Douglas	Labourer	Ireland	Ch. of England	55	4	Shanty		
George Dowdall	Farmer	Canada	Ch. of England	27	3	Shanty	1	12
John Dowdall	Farmer	Ireland	Ch. of England	77	3	Log	4	12
John Dowdall	Farmer	Ireland	Ch. of England	37	10	Shanty	3	12
David Dowlin	Farmer	Ireland	Roman Catholic	75	8	Log	24	12
Malcolm Drummond	Farmer	Scotland	Free Ch. Presby.	36	1	Log	23	9
Malcolm Drummond	Farmer	Scotland	Free Ch. Presby.	68	5	Log	26	9
James Duff	Farmer	Scotland		36	9	Log	8	10
William Duff	Sawyer	Scotland	Free Ch. Presby.	65	8	Log	10	11
Catherine Duncan		Scotland	Free Ch. Presby.	75	1	Frame		
James Duncan	Blacksmith	Scotland	Free Ch. Presby.	49	7	Frame	14	12
George Dunnet	Merchant	Scotland	Baptist	38	6	Stone		12
George Edwards	Farmer	Ireland	Ch. of England	63	10	Log	27	2
John Edwards	Carpenter	Ireland	Ch. of England	33	10	Frame	11	3
Robert Edwards	Farmer	Ireland	Ch. of England	44	7	Shanty	19	4
Thomas Edwards	Farmer	Canada	Ch. of England	28	5	Log	20	4
Mary Fanning	Farmer	Ireland	Ch. of England	50	7	Log	10	10
Alexander Ferguson	Farmer	Scotland		42	7	Log	22	4
Colin Ferguson	Farmer	Scotland		37	8	Shanty	3	1
Duncan Ferguson	Farmer	Scotland	Ch. of Scotland	59	8	Log	10	5
Duncan Ferguson	Farmer	Scotland	Free Ch. Presby	40	7	Log	22	4
Duncan Ferguson	Farmer	Scotland		33	4	Shanty	2	1
James Ferguson	Farmer	Scotland	Ch. of Scotland	58	10	Log	24	6
John Ferguson	Farmer	Scotland	Ch. of Scotland	60	6	Stone	24	6
Robert Ferguson	Farmer	Scotland	Ch. of Scotland	65	4	Stone	22	5
Thomas Finley	Farmer	Ireland	Ch. of England	38	8	Log	2	2
Duncan Fisher	Farmer	Scotland		63	11	Log	11	11
Andrew Fitzpatrick	Shoemaker	Ireland	Baptist	36	8	Log		
Richard Fleming	Farmer	Ireland	Ch. of England	45	9	Log	15	4
James Floyd	Farmer	Canada	Ch. of England	26	7	Log	10	8
Samuel Fuller	Foundry	United States	Baptist	43	10	Frame	14	12
Patrick Galvin	Tailor	Ireland	Roman Catholic	31	8	Frame	14	12
William Gibson	Farmer	Scotland	Ch. of England	48	11	Log	10	2
Archibald Gillies	Innkeeper	Scotland		64	3	Log	3	1
George Goff	Harness Maker	Ireland	Ch. of England	35	2	Stone	14	12
John Goth	Farmer	England	Ch. of England	63	7	Log	22	11
Alexander Graham	Labourer	Canada	Ch. of Scotland	32	4	Log		
John Graham	Carpenter	Scotland	Free Ch. Presby.	40	13	Frame	14	12
Peter Gray	Clergyman	Scotland	Free Ch. Presby.	35	7	Frame	14	11
Richard Griffith	Farmer	Ireland	Ch. of England	33	7	Log	11	8
Thomas Griffith	Blacksmith	Ireland	Ch. of England	40	9	Log		
Laurence Halcroft	Clergyman	Scotland	Baptist	52	4	Log	14	11
Henry Hawkins	Farmer	Ireland	Ch. of England	51	13	Log	12	8
Thomas Hawkins	Farmer	Ireland	Ch. of England	43	9	Log	12	8
Robert Henderson	Weaver	Scotland	Free Ch. Presby.	26	4	Log	20	8
Hugh Houston	Blacksmith	Ireland	Wes. Methodist	33	5	Log	27	9
John Hughton	Merchant	Ireland	Ch. of England	39	4	Log	11	3
Samuel James	Farmer	Ireland	Ch. of England	37	8	Log	5	12
William James	Farmer	Ireland	Ch. of England	50	14	Stone	25	3
Robert Johnston	Farmer	Ireland	Wes. Methodist	60	4	Log	13	12
Robert Johnston	Merchant	Canada	Ch. of England	32	7	Frame	14	12
John Jones	Farmer	Canada	Ch. of England	30	7	Log	17	4
Martin Jordan	Farmer	Ireland	Roman Catholic	38	8	Log	16	1
Andrew Keeler	Farmer	Ireland	Ch. of England	33	4	Shanty	18	2
John Kelly	Farmer	Ireland	Roman Catholic	30	5	Shanty	27	1
Robert Kennedy	Farmer	Scotland	Free Ch. Presby.	43	10	Log	24	8
George Kerfoot	Farmer	Ireland	Wes. Methodist	52	9	Stone	15	2
Samuel Kerfoot	Farmer	Ireland	Wes. Methodist	48	8	Stone	25	4
William Kerfoot		Ireland	Wes. Methodist	78	2	Stone		
George Kidd	Farmer	Canada	Ch. of England	27	5	Log	17	2

Name	Occupation	Origin	Religion	Age	Col5	Building	Col7	Col8
Margaret Kidd		England	Ch. of England	48	13	Log	21	6
Thomas Kidd	Farmer	Ireland	Ch. of England	60	3	Stone	16	3
Thomas Kidd	Farmer	Ireland	Free Ch. Presby.	32	5	Log	7	1
William Kidd	Farmer	Ireland	Ch. of England	33	8	Log	7	2
Ephriam Kilpatrick	Weaver	Scotland		52	7	Log	14	12
William Kilpatrick	Tailor	Ireland	Ch. of England	70	4	Stone	14	12
Colin King	Farmer	Scotland	Free Ch. Presby.	51	4	Log	2	10
James King	Farmer	Ireland	Ch. of England	66	9	Plank	21	3
John King	Farmer	Scotland	Ch. of Scotland	65	9	Log	7	6
John King	Farmer	Scotland		50	7	Log	24	2
John King	Farmer	Canada	Ch. of England	24	2	Log	30	3
James Kinsella	Farmer	Ireland	Roman Catholic	40	7	Log	13	1
Robert Knox	Labourer	Ireland	Ch. of England	33	8	Log		
Joseph Lateau	Cooper	Canada	Roman Catholic	25	6	Frame	14	12
Francis Lavallee	Cooper	Canada	Roman Catholic	29	6	Frame	14	12
Napoleon Lavallee	Pork Inspector	Canada	Ch. of Scotland	48	6	Stone	18	11
Thomas Lawford	Farmer	England	Wes. Methodist	51	12	Shanty	4	3
David Lawson	Merchant	Scotland	Ch. of Scotland	38	1		14	12
Hanna Leahey		Ireland	Roman Catholic	60	10	Stone		
Robert Leaver	Carpenter	Canada	Ch. of England	34	11	Frame	10	3
James Leech	Farmer	Canada	Ch. of England	26	4	Log	20	4
John Leech	Labourer	Ireland	Ch. of England	52	9	Log		
Samuel Leech	Farmer	Ireland	Ch. of England	50	8	Stone	21	4
Thomas Leech	Farmer	Ireland	Ch. of England	58	6	Log	12	9
William Leech	Farmer	Ireland	Ch. of England	65	5	Stone	12	9
William Leech	Farmer	Ireland	Ch. of England	60	9	Log	13	9
Thomas Lightbody	Weaver	Ireland		53	4	Shanty	4	1
William Lightbody	Farmer	Ireland		27	3	Log	1	2
Andrew Linton	Labourer	Ireland	Free Ch. Presby.	35	10	Log		
John Lyons	Shoemaker	Ireland	Ch. of England	21	3	Log	10	3
Timothy Mann	Farmer	Ireland	Roman Catholic	62	7	Log	23	12
Thomas Mason	Farmer	England	Ch. of England	54	5	Log	7	2
William May		Ireland	Ch. of England	26	3	Log		
Patrick McAlinden	Farmer	Ireland	Roman Catholic	60	5	Log	7	1
Archibald McArthur	Merchant	Scotland	Free Ch. Presby.	34	12	Stone	14	12
James McArthur		Canada	Ch. of Scotland	42	6	Log	13	7
John McArthur	Farmer	Scotland	Ch. of Scotland	51	3	Log	14	7
Peter McArthur	Farmer	Scotland	Ch. of Scotland	49	11	Stone	14	7
Absolom McCaffrey	Cooper	Ireland	Ch. of England	40	6	Frame	14	12
Nathaniel McCaffrey	Carpenter	Ireland	Baptist	35	7	Frame	15	12
Michael McCann	Farmer	Ireland	Roman Catholic	36	8	Log	6	12
James McCarthy	Farmer	Ireland	Ch. of England	20	4	Log	10	3
Duncan McCuan	Farmer	Scotland	Ch. of Scotland	70	9	Log	22	10
Duncan McCuan	Farmer	Scotland	Free Ch. Presby.	50	9	Log	21	9
Peter McCuan	Farmer	Scotland	Free Ch. Presby.	56	9	Shanty	26	11
John McDermot	Farmer	Scotland	Free Ch. Presby.	35	13	Log		
Mary McDermot		Ireland	Roman Catholic	50	6	Log	13	8
Angus McDiarmid	Farmer	Scotland	Free Ch. Presby.	45	11	Log	24	5
Donald McDiarmid	Weaver	Canada	Baptist	26	2	Log	22	4
James McDiarmid	Farmer	Scotland	Baptist	59	11	Log	16	8
James McDiarmid	Merchant	Canada	Ch. of Scotland	38	6	Frame	14	12
John McDiarmid	Farmer	Scotland	Free Ch. Presby.	72	6	Log	26	7
Peter McDiarmid	Farmer	Scotland	Free Ch. Presby.	40	8	Log	22	4
Allan McDonald	Clothier	Scotland	Free Ch. Presby.	41	7	Stone	14	12
Angus McDonald	Shoemaker	Scotland	Free Ch. Presby.	52	3	Frame	14	9
Angus McDonald	Innkeeper	Canada	Roman Catholic	35	4	Frame	14	12
Donald McDonald	Farmer	Canada	Roman Catholic	14	8	Log	4	6
Donald McDonald		Scotland	Ch. of England	50	9	Log		
John McDonald		Scotland	Free Ch. Presby.	56	8	Log	11	5
John McDonald	Farmer	Ireland	Roman Catholic	35	5	Shanty		
Ronald McDonnel	Farmer	Canada	Roman Catholic	35	12	Log	6	7
Donald McDougall	Farmer	Scotland	Free Ch. Presby.	64	8	Stone	21	8
John McDougall	Farmer	Scotland	Free Ch. Presby.	55	6	Log	18	9
John McDougall	Farmer	Canada	Free Ch. Presby.	27	5	Log	19	9
Ewen McEwen	Postmaster	Scotland	Free Ch. Presby.	42	8	Log	10	3

Finley McEwen	Farmer	Scotland	Free Ch. Presby.	74	10	Log	23	7
Hugh McEwen	Lawyer	Scotland	Free Ch. Presby.	61	6	Log	11	9
Hugh McEwen	Farmer	Scotland	Baptist	70	9	Log	2	7
James McEwen	Farmer	Scotland	Free Ch. Presby.	35	5	Log	9	7
John McEwen	Weaver	Scotland	Ch. of Scotland	43	5	Log	14	12
John McEwen	Farmer	Scotland	Roman Catholic	35	5	Log		
John McEwen	Farmer	Scotland	Free Ch. Presby.	46	10	Stone	22	8
John McEwen	Farmer	Scotland	Ch. of Scotland	47	10	Log	18	4
John McEwen	Weaver	Scotland	Ch. of Scotland	71	4	Log		
John McEwen	Foundryman	Scotland		25	4	Stone	14	12
Peter McEwen	Weaver	Scotland	Baptist	34	8	Log		
Donald McFarlane	Innkeeper	Scotland	Ch. of Scotland	53	10	Frame		
James McFarlane	Farmer	Scotland	Ch. of Scotland	60	9	Log	24	10
Mrs. McGovern		Ireland	Roman Catholic	50	2	Shanty		
Alexander McGregor		Scotland	Baptist	50	9	Log	5	7
Duncan McGregor	Blacksmith	Scotland	Ch. of Scotland	33	12	Stone	14	12
Gregor McGregor	Tailor	Scotland	Baptist	38	6	Frame	15	8
John McGregor	Lawyer	Scotland	Ch. of Scotland	55	8	Stone	15	10
Peter McGregor	Farmer	Scotland	Ch. of Scotland	61	6	Stone	15	10
Peter McGregor	Farmer	Scotland	Free Ch. Presby.	57	10	Stone	8	9
James McInnis	Farmer	Scotland	Ch. of Scotland	61	5	Log	20	9
Donald McIntosh	Labourer	Scotland	Wes. Methodist	55	5	Log	23	8
Duncan McKay	Farmer	Scotland	Baptist	66	10	Log	5	5
John McKay	Blacksmith	Scotland	Ch. of Scotland	42	2	Log	14	8
Ellen McKenna		Ireland	Roman Catholic	50	2	Shanty		
Alexander McKenzie	Farmer	Scotland	Ch. of Scotland	62	11	Log	4	6
Duncan McKenzie	Schoolmaster	Scotland	Ch. of Scotland	40	10	Log	11	6
William McKenzie	Weaver	Scotland	Ch. of Scotland	82	3	Log	11	7
Duncan McKercher	Farmer	Scotland	Ch. of England	71	9	Log	15	2
Colin McLaren	Farmer	Canada		28	3	Log	18	4
Collin McLaren	Farmer	Scotland	Ch. of Scotland	65	2	Log	21	5
Donald McLaren	Farmer	Scotland	Ch. of Scotland	35	5	Log	4	4
Donald McLaren		Scotland	Free Ch. Presby.	60	5	Log	4	5
Duncan McLaren		Scotland	Wes. Methodist	50	6	Log	24	4
Duncan McLaren	Farmer	Scotland	Ch. of Scotland	61	12	Log	24	9
Duncan McLaren	Farmer	Canada	Ch. of Scotland	33	1	Log	21	6
Duncan McLaren	Farmer	Scotland	Ch. of Scotland	40	8	Log	3	4
John McLaren	Farmer	Scotland	Free Ch. Presby.	50	8	Log	27	5
John McLaren	Farmer	Scotland	Ch. of Scotland	68	5	Log	23	10
Peter McLaren	Farmer	Scotland	Ch. of Scotland	42	8	Log	22	11
Peter McLaren	Farmer	Scotland	Free Ch. Presby.	40	7	Frame	1	10
Robert McLaren	Carpenter	Scotland	Ch. of Scotland	42	8	Frame	14	12
John McLauchlan	Carpenter	Scotland	Ch. of Scotland	44	6	Frame	14	12
Robert McLauchlan	Farmer	Scotland	Ch. of Scotland	41	10	Log	8	1
Angus McLellan	Farmer	Scotland	Roman Catholic	48	9	Log	2	7
John McLellan	Farmer	Scotland	Roman Catholic	47	7	Log	3	7
David McNabb		Canada	Ch. of Scotland	29	7	Log	14	12
John McNabb	Farmer	Scotland	Free Ch. Presby.	37	5	Log		
Peter McNabb	Farmer	Scotland	Free Ch. Presby.	40	10	Log	26	10
Duncan McNee	Farmer	Scotland	Free Ch. Presby.	40	3	Log	4	4
Brice McNeely	Farmer	Ireland	Ch. of England	58	7	Log	16	11
John McNeely	Farmer	Ireland	Ch. of England	54	5	Log	16	11
Nathaniel McNeely	Blacksmith	Canada	Ch. of England	25	4	Log	17	11
John McRae	Farmer	Scotland	Free Ch. Presby.	40	7	Log	6	3
James McRorie	Weaver	Scotland	Ch. of Scotland	26	4	Log	23	4
John McRostie	Farmer	Scotland	Free Ch. Presby.	54	10	Stone	13	12
John McTavish	Farmer	Scotland	Free Ch. Presby.	40	6	Stone	11	10
John McTavish	Farmer	Scotland	Free Ch. Presby.	81	9	Stone	16	9
Ann McTavish		Scotland	Ch. of Scotland	53	7	Log	16	8
John Miller	Farmer	Scotland	Free Ch. Presby.	63	7	Log	2	10
William Mills	Farmer	England	Ch. of England	59	10	Shanty	7	4
David Moffatt	Farmer	England		70	7	Stone	10	12
William Moffatt	Carpenter	Canada	Ch. of Scotland	30	6	Frame	15	12
Patrick Mooney	Tailor	Ireland	Ch. of England	15	9			
Arthur Moore	Farmer	Ireland	Ch. of England	50	8	Log	14	12

John Moore	Carpenter	Canada	Ch. of England	31	6	Log	10	5
William Moore	Tanner	Canada	Wes. Methodist	25	1	Frame	1	2
William Moore	Farmer	Ireland	Wes. Methodist	54	9	Log	1	2
John Morphy	Farmer	Ireland	Baptist	58	8	Log	15	12
Sarah Morphy		Ireland	Ch. of England	44	3	Log	12	12
Thomas Morphy	Harnessmaker	Ireland	Ch. of England	34	8	Frame		12
George Morris	Farmer	Canada	Ch. of England	28	6	Log		
James Morris	Farmer	Ireland	Free Ch. Presby.	49	7	Log	2	11
James Morris	Blacksmith	Ireland	Ch. of England	22	4	Log	10	3
Sarah Morris		Ireland	Ch. of England	62	9	Log		
Thomas Morris	Farmer	Ireland	Ch. of England	25	50	Log	2	11
Duncan Morrison	Clergyman	Scotland	Ch. of Scotland	35	7	Stone	12	7
John Murdoch	Tanner	Canada	Wes. Methodist	28	3	Frame	13	12
Michael Murray	Shoemaker	Ireland	Roman Catholic	36	5	Lot	11	3
Patrick Nagle	Farmer	Ireland	Roman Catholic	30	2	Log	19	12
Michael Neil	Farmer	Ireland	Roman Catholic	42	8	Log	14	8
Hugh Neilson	Harnessmaker	Ireland	Wes. Methodist	26	6	Frame	14	12
Johnston Neilson	Schoolmaster	Ireland	Ch. of England	54	5	Frame	14	12
Joseph Neilson	Doctor	Ireland		40	3	Log		
George Nesbitt	Doctor	Ireland	Ch. of England	53	10	Log	12	3
John Nesbitt	Farmer	Ireland	Ch. of England	52	5	Log	8	8
William Nesbitt	Cooper	Canada	Ch. of England	22	2	Log		
Patrick O'Donell	Farmer	Ireland	Ch. of England	21	4	Log	14	10
Marice O'Hara		Ireland	Roman Catholic	35	5	Frame	14	12
Michael O'Neil	Labourer	Ireland	Ch. of England	48	10	Shanty	17	11
Rev. James Padfield	Clergyman	England	Ch. of England	50	13	Stone	9	3
David Pattie	Carpenter	Scotland	Ch. of Scotland	44	10	Frame		12
William Peden	Merchant	Scotland	Free Ch. Presby.	36	10	Frame	14	12
Thomas Pierce	Farmer	Ireland	Ch. of England	60	12	Stone	8	3
Joseph Pittard	Carpenter	England	Wes. Methodist	30	2	Frame	14	12
Samuel Pittard	Farmer	England	Ch. of Scotland	26	7	Frame	15	12
Adam Poole	Farmer	Ireland	Wes. Methodist	31	5	Log	24	4
James Poole	Printer	Ireland	Wes. Methodist	26	9	Stone	14	12
John Poole	Farmer	Ireland	Wes. Methodist	62	5	Log	24	4
John Poole	Schoolmaster	Canada	Wes. Methodist	29	2	Frame		
Thomas Prettie	Farmer	Canada	Ch. of England	27	3	Log		
Rev. Alexander Pyne	Clergyman	Ireland	Ch. of England	33	11	Frame	15	12
James Rattray	Farmer	Scotland		33	8	Log	12	10
William Rattray	Sawyer	Scotland		38	6	Stone	12	10
Catherine Roach	Farmer	Ireland	Roman Catholic	40	7	Shanty	19	2
Donald Robinson	Farmer	Canada	Free Ch. Presby.	61	1	Log	15	9
Duncan Robinson	Farmer	Scotland		58	5	Log	23	11
John Robinson	Farmer	Scotland	Free Ch. Presby.	59	10	Log	16	9
Peter Robinson	Farmer	Scotland	Free Ch. Presby.	55	6	Log	23	11
James Rosamond	Manufacturer	Ireland	Ch. of England	47	14	Stone	14	12
William Russell	Farmer	Scotland	Baptist	45	8	Frame	14	12
John Salter	Weaver	Ireland	Wes. Methodist	60	10	Shanty	18	1
Peter Salter	Farmer	Ireland	Ch. of England	34	10	Log	17	3
James Sample	Farmer	Ireland	Ch. of Scotland	40	5	Shanty	5	1
James Saunders	Farmer	Ireland	Ch. of England	50	2	Log	10	3
Robert Saunders	Farmer	Ireland	Ch. of England	50	11	Log	21	3
William Saunders	Farmer	Ireland	Ch. of England	31	8	Log	22	2
Alexander Scott	Farmer	Ireland	Baptist	51	10	Log	18	9
Jane Scott		Scotland	Free Ch. Presby.	37	7	Stone	15	12
John Scott	Farmer	Scotland	Ch. of Scotland	37	60	Log	18	5
John Scott	Sawyer	Canada		21	1	Log	27	3
Margaret Scott		Scotland		60	5	Log	23	3
Margaret Scott		Scotland	Ch. of Scotland	54	5	Log		
Robert Scott	Farmer	Scotland	Free Ch. Presby.	53	2	Log	25	8
Robert Scott	Farmer	Scotland	Ch. of Scotland	77	3	Log	20	6
Walter Scott	Tanner	Scotland	Free Ch. Presby.	29	21	Frame	14	12
William Scott	Tailor	Scotland		22	2	Frame	15	12
Moses Sheil	Tailor	Ireland	Roman Catholic	38	8	Log	10	3
Alexander Sinclair	Farmer	Scotland	Free Ch. Presby.	43	9	Log	2	11
Colin Sinclair	Farmer	Scotland	Free Ch. Presby.	50	8	Log	1	9

Jacob Smyth	Farmer	Ireland	Wes. Methodist	66	6	Log	15	3
John Spencer	Surgeon	Canada	Ch. of England	59	8	Frame	14	12
Alexander Stewart	Farmer	Scotland	Ch. of Scotland	39	7	Log	20	5
Alexander Stewart	Farmer	Scotland	Free Ch. Presby.	55	12	Log	14	9
Alexander Stewart	Shoemaker	Scotland	Ch. of Scotland	27	11	Log		
Alexander Stewart	Farmer	Scotland	Free Ch. Presby.	60	3	Log		
Alexander Stewart	Farmer	Scotland	Baptist	32	4	Log	7	3
David Stewart	Farmer	Canada		30	3	Log	23	3
James Stewart	Farmer	Scotland	Free Ch. Presby.	45	9	Stone	12	6
Janet Stewart		Scotland	Free Ch. Presby.	47	4	Log	15	8
John Stewart	Farmer	Scotland	Ch. of Scotland	59	9	Log	7	6
John Stewart	Farmer	Scotland	Free Ch. Presby.	66	7	Log	29	8
John Stewart	Farmer	Scotland	Free Ch. Presby.	35	2	Log	5	2
John Stewart	Blacksmith	Scotland	Free Ch. Presby.	67	2	Shanty	21	8
John Stewart	Farmer	Scotland	Ch. of Scotland	50	6	Log	5	4
Neil Stewart	Farmer	Scotland	Free Ch. Presby.	40	6	Stone	12	7
Widow Stewart		Scotland	Ch. of Scotland	50	7	Log	26	6
Jane Stuart		Scotland	Free Ch. Presby.	22	9	Log		
Robert Sutherland	Miller	Scotland	Free Ch. Presby.	50	11	Frame	14	12
Edward Sutton	Labourer	Ireland	Ch. of England	25	7			
John Swain	Farmer	Ireland	Ch. of England	39	11	Shanty	4	12
Alexander Thompson	Lawyer	Scotland	Ch. of Scotland	59	6	Shanty	13	10
Anthony Tyndall	Farmer	Ireland	Ch. of England	50	8	Shanty	11	1
Thomas Ward	Farmer	Ireland	Wes. Methodist	57	6	Log	15	4
Thomas Watchorn	Cloth Dresser	Ireland	Ch. of England	22	5	Frame	14	12
New Year Watson	Farmer	England	Ch. of England	70	11	Log	14	9
Samuel Whealey	Farmer	Ireland	Ch. of England	29	4	Log	13	8
James Whiting	Farmer	England	Wes. Methodist	60	6	Log	3	3
James Whyte	Labourer	Scotland	Ch. of England	35	3	Log	17	11
John Whyte	Farmer	Scotland	Free Ch. Presby.	51	6	Log	27	11
Thomas Whyte	Farmer	Scotland	Free Ch. Presby.	42	12	Log	25	11
William Whyte	Labourer	Canada	Free Ch. Presby.	27	3	Log	27	11
Thomas Williams	Beggar	England	Ch. of England	60	1	Shanty		
Hugh Williamson	Weaver	Ireland	Ch. of Scotland	50	6	Shanty	5	1
George Willis	Farmer	Ireland	Ch. of England	74	3	Log	12	11
George Willis	Farmer	Canada	Ch. of England	31	8	Log	12	11
Henry Wilson	Labourer	Ireland	Ch. of England	43	3	Stone	14	12
John Wilson	Weaver	Ireland	Wes. Methodist	50	8	Log	26	4
William Wilson	Surgeon	Scotland	Ch. of Scotland	45	10	Stone	14	12
Michael Wynn	Farmer	Ireland	Ch. of England	42	5	Shanty	10	2

Source: NAC Reel C-11731

Appendix 24

Members of the Carleton Place Rifle Company, August 1863

James C. Poole	William Metcalf	Thomas Scott	James Murphy	Charles Shepherd
Robert Metcalf	William Patterson	William Moore	George Willis	James McFadden
Francis Lavallee	William Pattie	Jones Bell	David McNab	James Moffatt
James Henry	George McPherson	William Beck	John Hogg	Patrick Tucker
Robert Moffatt	Archibald Hamilton	William Neelin	Thomas Garland	Duncan Fisher
John Henry	William Duff	A. McCaffrey	Jacob Leslie	Patrick Struthers

Source: *Carleton Place Herald*, 12 August 1863, p. 2, col. 4.

Appendix 25

Beckwith Members of the 5th Battalion of Lanark Militia, January 1865.

Peter McKay	Neil McEwen	Donald Cameron	John Gillies	James McArthur
William James	Michael Murphy	James Storie	Daniel McCuan	William H. Burrows
Samuel Cram	Alexander Ball	George Burrows	Peter Cram	William Moore
Duncan Robertson	William McCuan	John McDiarmid	James Cram	James Roy
William White	John McEwen	Peter Ferguson	Robert McLachlin	Henry Leaver
John Flemming	William Price	Duncan McLaren	Thomas Salter	William Duff
Maurice Burke	Henry Cram	Alexander McPherson	John McDougall	Daniel McArthur
James McFarlane	Duncan Cameron	Alexander Duff	Duncan Cram	Alexander Dulgatty
Donald Stewart	Peter Mills	William Dack	Malcolm Drummond	Joseph Wilson
Duncan McDermid	John Cameron	Peter McGregor	Robert White	Donald Stewart
Archibald McCallum	John Anderson	John Cameron	Samuel McDonald	Thomas Poole
William House	Edward Willis	Robert Stewart	William Carley	Ronald McDonald
Robert Jordon	Charles Shepherd		John Stewart	William McNeely

Source: *Carleton Place Herald*, 4 January 1865, p. 2, cols. 4—6.

Appendix 26

Businesses and Services in the village of Franktown, 1869.

William Allan, engraver
Matthew Anderson, blacksmith
Joseph Budd, telegraph operator
Dominic Burrows, stock dealer
Robert Cavanagh, general merchant
B. Clarke, druggist
Thomas Clarke, shoemaker
Thomas Clark, hotel keeper
John Edwards, cabinet maker
Duncan Ferguson, auctioneer
Thomas Flegg & Bros., coopers
Miss Forde, milliner
Thomas Griffith, blacksmith
Henry Hawkins, butcher
Edward Huhchback, wood and willow ware manufacturer
James Jackson, soap and candle maker
Thomas James, saddler
George Kidd, Justice of the Peace
John Lawford, sash, door and blind factory
Henry Leaver, cabinet maker
R. McDonnell, stock dealer
EWEN McEWEN, Justice of the Peace, postmaster, commissioner and conveyancer
F. McEwen, insurance agent
Hugh McEwen, telegraph operator
Peter McEwen, real estate agent
D. McGregor, sash, door and blind factory
Hugh McKenna, soap and candle maker
D. McKenzie & Sons, painters
J. McKercher, Justice of the Peace
Robert McLaughlan & Sons, carpenters
J. McMahon, agent B. & O. Railroad
Murray Michael, shoemaker
W. Moore, leather dealer
William Moore, hotel keeper
Joseph Morris, blacksmith
J.A. Neilson, M.D.
M. Neilson, dentist
Rev. A.C. Nesbitt, Church of England
George Nesbitt, M.D.
Thomas Nesbitt, general merchant
George Nowlan, broom maker
Thomas Pierce & Sons, rope makers
Thomas Roach, shoemaker
Thomas Roe & Sons, shingle makers
Rev. Walter Ross (Presbyterian)
Thomas Saunders, wagon maker
Duncan Stewart, tailor
John Stewart, Justice of the Peace

Source: H. McEvoy, ed. and comp., *The Province of Ontario Gazetteer and Directory* (Toronto: Robertson & Cook, 1869), p. 161.

Appendix 27

Businesses and Services in the Village of Ashton, 1869.

George Argue, tanner
Archibald Blair, shoemaker
Rev. C. Brown (Episcopal)
John M. Brown, lime manufacturer
Rev. Caswell (Presbyterian)
C. Church, M.D.
James Cosier, wagon maker
Cosier & Lindsay, shingle manufacturers
James Co[n]n, general merchant
Daniel Fanning, hotel keeper
Miss Ford, dressmaker
Peter Gowe, livery stable
James Hueston, shoemaker
Robert Kennedy, grocer
John Lammond, tailor
James Lindsay & Co., wagon makers
Miss Mary McEwan, teacher
Donald McFarlane, hotel-keeper
John McFarlane, iron founder
Robert McFarlane, liquor dealer
Rev. Mullin (Presbyterian)
JOHN M. MUNRO, editor Ashton Examiner
Hugh Robinson, wagon maker
John Shore, carpenter
Benjamin Stewart, cabinet maker
JOHN SUMNER, Postmaster & general merchant
Hiram Sykes, Justice of the Peace

Source: H. McEvoy, ed. and comp., *The Province of Ontario Gazetteer & Directory* (Toronto: Robertson & Cook, 1869), p. 33.

Appendix 28

Businesses and Services in the hamlet of Prospect, 1869.

WILLIAM BURROWS, Postmaster, hotel keeper
George Craig, general merchant
Thomas Craig, tanner
James Brothers, proprietors of sawmill
Duncan McGregor, proprietor of sawmill
Thomas Moffatt, shoemaker
William Riley, blacksmith
J. Tomlinson, shoemaker

Source: H. McEvoy, ed. and comp., *The Province of Ontario Gazetteer and Directory* (Toronto: Robertson & Cook, 1869), p. 595.

Appendix 29

Businesses and Services in the village of Franktown, 1898.

James Anderson, blacksmith
E.D. Edwards, general store
Robert Loney, hotel
R. McDonnell, grocer
Richard Pierce, general store
William Pierce, hotel
Robert G. White, carriage maker

Source: *Eastern Ontario Gazetteer and Directory, 1898—99* (Ingersoll: Ontario Publishing & Advertising Co., 1898), p. 275.

Appendix 30

Businesses and Services in the village of Ashton, 1898.

George Argue, tanner
W. Cherry, blacksmith
Conn Bros., general store
J. Fleming, boots and shoes

R.W. Lewis, pumps
D.J. McDougall, grocer
Miss McFarlane, fruit
A.A. Mordy, physician

Robert Presley, sawmill
William Presley, carriage maker
S.A. Torrance, blacksmith

Source: *Eastern Ontario Gazetteer and Directory, 1898—99*, (Ingersoll: Ontario Publishing & Advertising Co., 1898), p. 157.

Appendix 31

Businesses and Services in the hamlet of Prospect, 1898.

Mrs. Anderson, tailoress
William Burrows, hotel
Robert Cavanagh, blacksmith

Henry James, harness
James Kettles, saw mill
D.J. McDougall, grocer

A.W. Pool, general store
William Riley, blacksmith
V. Switcher, blacksmith

Source: *Eastern Ontario Gazetteer and Directory, 1898—99* (Ingersoll: Ontario Publishing & Advertising Co., 1898), p. 481.

Appendix 32

Honour Roll of the Township of Beckwith of Those Who Served in the Great War, 1914—1918.

Colonel Dr. George Edward Kidd

Captain J.H. Edwards
Sergeant Major Harold Edwards
Nursing Sister Mrs. C.B. Kidd
Nursing Sister Miss C.B. McLenaghan

Major Clarence B. Kidd
Nursing Sister Mrs. G.E. Kidd
Nursing Sister Mrs. J. Ramsay
Nursing Sister Miss J.M. McDiarmid

Private P.J. Anderson
Private R. Balfour
Private R. Boreland
Private H. Code
Private R.G. Cram
Private A. Dowdall
Private H. Dowdall
Private E.D. Duff
Sergeant L. Edwards
Private F.T. Griffith
Private C. Herald
Private Andrew T. Hughton
Private W. Livingstone Kidd
Private R. Kilfoyle
Private G. Leach (Gunner)
Private S. Lewis

Private J. McDiarmid
Private J.A. McFarlane
Private P. McGowan
Private A. McGreenaugh
Private David McLaren
Private Duncan McLaren
Private J. McLaren
Private A.E. McLenaghan
Private F. McManus
Private H. McMillan
Private Brice McNeely
Private E.P. Monk
Private H. Morris
Private A.A. O'Brien
Private A. Officer
Private J. O'Shea

Private C.E. Payne
Private J.L. Perry
Private M. Perry
Private J. Pierce
Private T. Pressl[e]y
Private F. Reddy
Private J. Ritchie
Private H. Saunders
Private A. Scott
Private C. Smith
Private J. Stanzel
Private W. Symes
Private G. Taylor
Private H. Willis

Source: Honour Roll painted by Charles D. Tinkler, Carleton Place, hanging in the Beckwith municipal chamber.

Appendix 33

For King and Country
Members of the Municipality of Beckwith who Volunteered for Active Service in Canada's Fighting Forces in World War Two.

Bruce Anderson	Sherwood Davies	Clifton McDiarmid	Earl Porteous
Freda Anderson	Clarence Drummond	Elmer McDiarmid	Emmerson Porteous
Muriel Anderson	Floyd Ellis	Leonard McDiarmid	Percy Porteous
Kenneth Bell	Ernest Ford	Ross McDiarmid	Harrison Purdy
Ellen Bennett	Donald Fumerton	Warner McDiarmid	Earl Rathwell
Fred Blaney	Howard Fumerton	Willard McDiarmid	Clarence Rattray
Winston Blaney	Wilfred Garland	Norman McEwen	Howard Rattray
Gordon Boughner	Warner Giff	Marguerite McGratton	Willard Rattray
Wilfred Briscoe	Harry Griffith	Merle McGratton	Lowe Saunders
William Briscoe	Ivan Griffith	Harold McLachlan	Iva Shail
Robert Butterworth	Alexander Hamilton	Donald McLaren	Roy Shail
Ewan Caldwell	Carl Hamilton	Arnold McNeely	Dan Shanks
Edwin Campbell	Eric Hamilton	Bryce McNeely	Kenneth Shanks
Earl Cardiff	Lorne Hamilton	Francis McNeely	Thelma Shirley
Melville Cardiff	Melville Hamilton	Leonard McNeely	Lloyd Simpson
Donald Carmichael	MacDougall Henderson	Norman McRae	Wilfred Simpson
Elvin Coleman	Thomas Hope	Wendell McRae	John Spoor
Orville Cowan	Sidney Irvine	Fred Mears	Gordon Stewart
William Cowan	Alden Jones	Frank Mills	Richard Taylor
Clifford Cox	Wilmer Jones	Harvey Nolan	Gerald Timmins
William Cram	Margaret Lesway	James Nolan	Fred Young
Joseph Currie	Kenneth Lett	Kenneth Nolan	
Hugh Davies	Roy Lett	Clarence O'Brien	
John Davies	Harry Lowe	Vincent O'Brien	

Source: Honour roll hanging in the Beckwith municipal chamber.

Appendix 34

Captions to group photographs.

Plate 205. Carleton Place high school students at Queen's University in 1902. Front row (left to right) T. Spiers, W.S. Cram, S.W.A. Code, Miss K. Teskey, L.B. Code, and C.E. Kidd. Middle row (seated) E.L. Code, Miss J.W. Singleton, W.C. Roberts, Miss F.M. Ewing and W. Moore. Back row (standing) G.F. Cliff, J.H. Code, George Edward Kidd, R.L. McEwen, D.A. Gillies, D.J. Steward, W.J. Kidd, J.R. Steward, Angus J. Kidd, T.W. Cavers and W.J. Knox.

Plate 228. Moulders at Findlay Brothers stove factory, Carleton Place, 1909. (Left to right) Pete Garvin (foreman), Tom Hastings, George Kilpatrick, Jack McPhail, Jim Dunlop, Frank Brazer, Alex McPhee, Pete Milligan, Fred McRostie, Cecil Tetlock, Harris Bennett, Jack McLaren, _____, Abe Powell, Joe Patterson, _____, Jim Ferrill, Frank Donald, Bill Moffatt, Wellie Devlin, Bob Lever, Bill Finner, Hilliard McDaniel and Bill Dow.

Plate 245 Junior war canoe of the Carleton Place Canoe Club ca. 1905. (left to right) Norman Gibson, Bob Green, Bill Sims, Billy Janoe, Jack Virtue, Harry McEwen, _____, Dr. _____, Howard Morphy, _____, _____, Tom Scott, Herb Singleton and Jack Welsh.

Plate 256. Students at S.S. No. 1, Beckwith, Gillies Corners ca. 1920. Front row (left to right) Benson Cameron, Arden Dopson, Ferguson Burns, Arnold Perrin, Hubert Lightbody, Harry Burns, Eldon Perrin, Arthur Burns and Kenneth Bell. Back row (standing, left to right) Jessie Burns, Iva Shirley, Ita Dopson, Jessie Ralph, Helen Kilfoyle, Elma Dopson, Miss Barrigar (teacher), Mabel Ralph, Muriel Perrin and Bessie Burns.

Plate 259. A group of seventh line neighbours raising a log drivesled on the John McEwen farm ca. 1932. Front row (left to right) Billy Green, Dan Carmichael, Earl Henderson, Arthur Hawkins, Harold Buffam and Jim Fitzgerald. Second row (seated) Albert F. McEwen and John McEwen. Third row Lorne McNeely, John McNeely, Jack Hawkins and Cameron Stewart. Back row H.A. Hawkins, Jack Campbell and John Jamieson.

Plate 270 Members of Beckwith Township fire department, 1964. Front row (left to right) Findlay McEwen, Gordon Presley, Herbert Butterworth, fire chief Robert Brooks, Duncan Dakers, Orville Cooke and Warner McDiarmid. Middle row (left to right) Percy Leach, Jack Briscoe, Arthur Nesbitt, Carl Lewis, Cornell B. MacRae, Herb Gardiner, Williard Legree. Back row (left to right) Andrew MacRae, Gary McEwen, Keith Brunton, John Kidd, Howard Bennett, Alex Stewart, Bill McCauley, Howard Shail.

Plate 276. Students at Franktown school posing with bags of milkweed pods ca. 1943. Front row (left to right) Dorothy Burns, Audrey Burns, Margaret Currie, Pauline Phillips, Edith Ford, Jean Saunders, Billy Burns, Earl Ford, Ronnie Butterworth, and John Montgomery. Back row (left to right) Al McLellan, Fred Ford, Robert Hughton, Ronnie Taylor, Ronnie Irvine, Allan Currie, Wilma Saunders, Kathleen Saunders, Vivian Anderson and Anna Ford.

Plate 277. Beckwith township council, October 1985. Sitting, reeve Stanley Brunton. Standing (left to right) Boyd Foster, deputy reeve John Sheil, Chris Tyson and Mervin Devlin.

Abbreviations

A.F. & A.M.	Ancient Free and Accepted Masons
ca.	circa
C.O.	Colonial Office
col.	column
Comp.	compiler
DCB	Dictionary of Canadian Biography
ed.	editor or edition
Ibid.	Same source as the previous reference
Idem	Same author as the previous reference
intro	introduction
I.O.D.E.	Independent Order of Daughters of the Empire
I.O.G.T.	Independent Order of Good Templars
MG	manuscript group
MS	manuscript
NAC	National Archives of Canada, Ottawa
n.d.	no date
n.p.	no pagination
OBCMR	Beckwith township municipal records, Blacks Corners, Ontario
OCP	Carleton Place Public Library
OCPAR	Carleton Place and Beckwith Historical Society Archives
OGS	Ontario Genealogical Society
OKARC	Roman Catholic Archdiocese of Kingston Archives
OKQ	Special Collections, Douglas Library, Queen's University
OKQAR	Queen's University Archives
OOAA	Anglican Diocese of Ottawa Archives
OOARC	Roman Catholic Archdiocese of Ottawa Archives
OOU	Morisset Library, University of Ottawa
OPLCRO	Lanark County Registry Office, Perth, Ontario
OTAR	Archives of Ontario, Toronto
Oxon.	Oxford University
p.	page
pp.	pages
PPA	Protestant Protective Association
RG	Record Group
ROM	Royal Ontario Museum, Toronto
R.R.	Rural route
SPGA	Society for the Propagation of the Gospel Archives, London, England
vol.	volume
WCTU	Women's Christian Temperance Union
W.I.	Women's Institute

INDEX

This is a comprehensive index of the main text. In order to keep the index within a reasonable length, it should be noted that the endnotes for each chapter, the introduction and the appendices have not been indexed. Family names beginning with Mac and Mc are indexed as beginning with Mac. The common occurrence of the same names throughout Beckwith's history make it imperative not to assume that all the page numbers given for a certain name refer to the same individual. Christian names have been given alphabetical precedence over titles such as Mr., Major, and Rev.

Abortions 258, 386, 408, 457, 570
Absentee landowners 54, 198-200, 321-2
Adams, Joshua 93
Admaston Township 282, 296, 412
Adolescence 258, 261, 267, 278, 328, 385, 405-6, 408, 442, 556, 564
Adultery 32, 178-80, 182
Advertising 126, 291, 342-3, 348, 496, 559-60
Age pyramids 254-6, 267
Aging population 266-8
Agitation 108, 212, 358
Agricultural exhibitions 137, 294, 302, 304
Agricultural machinery 298, 301, 346, 400-1, 496, 535
Agricultural markets 361-3
Agricultural societies 124, 130-2, 240-1, 279, 288, 294, 303-4
Agriculture 29-30, 32-4, 38, 46, 52, 54, 64, 69, 78-9, 81-8, 107, 110, 113, 116, 118, 121-5, 136-9, 145, 196-7, 225, 264, 272, 280-2, 284, 286, 288, 293-4, 298-304, 315, 328, 330, 402-10, 500, 515, 561-3, 565
Agriculture, mechanisation of 258, 291, 298, 300-1, 323, 400-1, 404, 407, 418, 458-60, 486-91, 534-8, 540-2
Ainslie, Henry F. 121
Airports 561
Akenson, Donald vii
Alcock family 413, 419
Alcock, Thomas 346
Algonquin College 570
Alien question 198, 230
Allan, James 430

Allan's Point 433, 483, 497 See also Lake Park
Allen, Austin 338
Allen, William H. 499
Almonte 25, 108, 200, 218, 258, 279, 282-3, 286, 288, 299, 304, 310-11, 368-72, 416, 435, 478, 480, 484, 514, 544, 566-8
Alston, John 170, 242
Alwood House 564
Ambrotypes 254-5, 289
American Civil War 505-6, 508-10
American raids 5
American Revolution 2, 24, 56-7
American settlers vii, 2, 4-6, 10, 12, 23-4, 26-7, 72-3, 80-1, 88, 96, 127-8, 144, 146, 166, 198-201, 205, 230, 242-4, 336, 501, 572
Amerindians 14, 80-1
Anasarca 176
Anderson, Captain 240
Anderson, Catharine 463
Anderson, Christina 147
Anderson, Donald 78
Anderson, James 492
Anderson, Matthew 136, 338
Anderson, Peter 154, 241, 243, 245-6, 263
Anderson, Zelda Kathleen 492
"Angel of the House" 261-5
Angels 44
Anglicans 18, 20-1, 26, 52, 54, 56-8, 65-8, 71-3, 79, 93, 97, 100, 109-10, 113, 129, 136, 138, 145-6, 160-1, 172, 184, 187, 194-5, 197-222, 225-30, 236, 241-4, 260, 315-18, 320, 326, 334, 339, 344, 348, 369, 390, 398, 405, 412, 414, 416, 419, 424, 429, 432-7, 439, 443-51, 454, 462, 464, 496, 506, 559, 567
Anglo-Irish 52-74
Anglo-Israel 205
Anniversaries 456
Anti-American feeling 5, 14-15, 23-6
Anti-Catholicism 435, 437, 445-8
Anti-French attitudes 570
Antrim County, Ireland 66, 150, 195
Antrim, Earl of 195
Appleton 119, 258, 361, 372, 416, 532, 564
Appletree Falls 119
Apprentices 64, 194, 227, 356-8, 393, 410, 441
Archer, Sandy 516
Architecture 305-6, 309, 364, 375, 377, 386, 396, 424-5, 440, 443, 448-52, 462, 480
Ard, Scotland 48
Argue, George 344
Argyllshire, Scotland 305
Arklan 348, 373-4
Armagh County, Ireland 56, 66
Armstrong, Alexander 268, 424
Armstrong, Mr. 102
Armstrong, Thomas 19
Armstrong, William 136
Arnprior 120, 283-4, 308-9, 480
Arthur, Sir George 130
Ashes See Potash
Ashton 66, 116, 119, 136, 182-3, 209, 219, 275, 320, 325, 327, 340, 342, 344-7, 349, 410, 414-16, 418, 423, 433, 440, 445, 449, 451, 464, 492, 494, 496, 532, 537, 540, 542, 552, 556-7, 561
Ashton Star Lodge 464

Ashton Station 344, 496, 532, 540
Assimilation 30-2, 45, 56, 197, 242, 334, 438
Asthma 176
Asylums 80, 324, 424-5
Atheism 182
Athletics 47
Athol, Duke of 35
Auctions 362-3, 561
Aughrim, Ireland 339
Augusta Methodist Circuit 72
Augusta Township, 2-3, 210
Australia 129, 308
Automobiles 473, 490, 517, 532, 540, 545, 547, 550-1

Baby boom 3-4, 87-8, 145-6, 551, 558
Bagpipes 47, 113, 216, 247-8, 282, 483, 505
Bailey, George 516
Bailey, George Junior 129
Bain, Elizabeth 296
Bain, Jane 296
Bakers 65
Baldwin, Robert 186, 216
Ballinamore, Ireland 149
Ballyghiblan Riots 96-110, 333-4
Ballygiblon 108
Ballyligpatrick, Ireland 150
Balquhidder, Scotland 30-1, 35-6
Bangs, James S. 361-2
Bangs, John A. 499
Bangs, Raymond 509
Banishment 111
Bank of Ottawa 499
Bankruptcy 281-2, 413, 473, 505, 568
Baptisms 79, 92, 178, 180, 190, 204, 210, 441
Baptists 20, 41-4, 73, 166, 176, 186, 188-90, 210,

225, 260, 325, 353, 429, 432, 441, 444-5, 456, 462, 464, 567
Barbarians 316, 414, 438
Barber, J.W. 552-3
Barclay, Flo 564
Bark marks 359
Barley 30, 125-8, 196, 303, 346, 418, 420, 467-8, 488, 540, 562
Barley mills 346, 376
Barnett, Robert 68, 127
Barns ii, 79, 117, 125, 169, 171-2, 293, 295-8, 310, 377, 401, 403, 407, 414, 469, 565
Barnyards 293, 295, 297, 401
Barry, Dr. Edward M. 130, 218, 267
Barry, Ireland 62
Barry, John 83-4
Barter 139, 225, 327, 344, 355, 474, 545
Bartlett, William H. 83
Bastard Township 4, 412
Bates & Innes 475-6, 479, 482, 520, 527, 550-1, 570
Bates, Charles W. 476, 527
Bathurst District 93, 96-7, 99, 120, 122, 130-1, 146, 152, 213, 226, 230, 232, 234, 236, 239
Bathurst District Agricultural Society 124, 130-3, 241, 304
Bathurst District Temperance Union 243-4
Lord Bathurst 10
Bathurst Township 6, 10, 12, 14, 62, 72-3, 96, 226, 542
Baxter, William 345
Bay of Quinte 4
Baynes, C.H. 439
Beaches 557-8
Beans 126, 488
Beaufort, Rev. Daniel Augustus 53
Beck, Adam 129
Beckwith and Montague Rural Telephone Company 483, 496-8, 539-40, 560
Beckwith colonies 128, 152-64, 288-9, 292, 308
Beckwith, Drummond and Montague Methodist Circuit 451

Beckwith, Montague and Marlborough Methodist Mission 495
Beckwith Patriotic Fund 524
Beckwith Patriotic League 519-20, 526
Beckwith Public School 557, 564, 566-7
Beckwith, Sir Thomas Sydney 7, 12-14
Beckwith Township Agricultural Society 294, 299, 304, 513, 535
Beckwith Township Council ix-x, 315, 317, 324-6, 340, 424-5, 466-7, 548, 564, 571
Beckwith Township Federation of Agriculture 563
Beckwith Township Fire Department 556, 560
Beckwith Township School Area 552-4
Beckwith Village 18, 97, 134, 166-8, 200, 202
Beckwith Women's Institute ix, 542, 548, 563-4
Beef 123-4, 280, 303, 361, 562
Bees 78, 92, 113, 242, 296-8, 438, 469, 539
Begging 145
Belden Historical Atlas ix, 287, 310, 387
Belfast, Ireland 424
Belgian Relief Fund 520
Bell, Andrew 84
Bell, David 147
Bell, Isabella 190
Bell, James 124, 128-9, 176
Bell, John 128, 176, 230
Bell, Margaret 455
Bell, Margaret Nelson 147
Bell, Robert 124, 126, 128-9, 132-3, 136, 176, 190-2, 216, 218-20, 226-8, 231-2, 240-1, 282, 284, 286, 305, 315-20, 322, 342, 356, 358, 366-8, 375, 390, 429, 432, 454-5, 506, 508, 511-12
Bell, Robert Junior 511
Bell Telephone Company 478, 498, 560
Bell, Rev. William 13, 44, 70, 81, 92, 109, 134, 148, 166-8, 170-4, 176-8, 180-

2, 190-2, 197, 200, 209, 220, 233-4, 244, 344, 348, 430
Bell, William 128, 176, 190
Bellcott Post Office 147, 496, 561
Belleville 298
Bellows, Caleb Strong 127-8, 158, 200, 230
Bellowstown 128
Bell's Corners 298
Benefit societies 30
Bennett, Catherine 217
Bennett, David 158
Benson, Mr. 102, 105-6
Beyer, Ferdinand 387, 485
The Bible 65, 168, 195, 204-5, 212, 259, 406, 408, 430, 448, 450, 456, 460
Bilboa, Ireland 64
Bilingualism 44, 168, 172, 174, 569-70, 572
Birthrate 87-8, 145-6, 161, 243, 254-8, 260, 268, 273, 419-20, 422-3, 473, 551-2
Black, John 156, 346
Black's Corners ii, 181-6, 219, 268, 283, 293, 302, 317, 323-5, 327, 346-7, 349, 368, 378, 415-17, 423, 461, 464, 492, 500, 512, 526, 532, 535, 540, 542, 548, 555-7, 560-1, 563, 566, 571, 573
Blacksmiths 68, 127, 132, 136, 138-9, 156, 160, 196, 225, 294, 338, 343-8, 354, 384, 477, 492-4
Blair Athol, Scotland 30-1
Blair Drummond, Scotland 31
Bootlegging 469
Board and batten construction 267
Bobier, George 209
Bond, Joseph 129, 132
Bonussing 474, 476
Books 143-4, 168, 239-41, 310, 326, 332, 335-6, 402, 405, 408-10, 454, 511, 553
Boosterism 284, 286, 308, 338, 368-9, 377, 480, 494
Booth, J.R. 363
Boreland, Robert 526
Boston 281, 344, 478
Boswell, Rev. Edward Jukes 204-6, 212, 232
Bouchette, Joseph 19
Boulton, Henry John 198

Boulton, Hugh 101, 107, 119, 127-9, 356, 367, 381
Bowels, James 338
Bowland, Magistrate 216
Bowles, James 136, 338
Box, James 346, 492
Boxing 79
Boy Scouts 519
Boyne, battle of 54, 339, 436, 438, 445, 507
Bradley, Mr. 302
Bradley, William 126
Braeside 542
Brant County 161-2, 288, 292
Brant Township 292
Brantford 335
Brass bands 384, 390, 414, 520
Breadalbane, Earls of 10-12, 17, 29-30, 39, 45, 92, 184
Bredin, James Henry 359, 373-4
Bredin, Mr. 359
Bredin, William 367, 388, 390
Breweries 128
Brick buildings 271, 306, 321-3, 337, 367, 375, 377, 386, 407, 416-19, 440-1, 445, 460, 468, 478, 488-9, 493, 561, 565
Brickyards 377, 478
Bridges 282
British American Order of Good Templars 336
British Hotel 514
British Israelism 205
Broadsides 279, 299
Brock, Sir Isaac 2, 6
Brockville 12, 23, 60, 62, 64, 80-1, 92, 98, 108, 121, 123, 128, 133-4, 137, 170, 172, 175, 196, 198-9, 202, 208, 214, 219-20, 226, 247, 280, 282, 316, 356, 363, 366, 372, 380, 415, 435, 473, 516
Brockville & Ottawa Railway 133-4, 185, 250, 261, 278, 280-7, 291-2, 302, 308-11, 315, 317, 321-3, 338-45, 350, 354, 364, 366, 368-72, 374-5, 382, 505, 511
Brooke Township 160, 162
Brooks, George 22-3
Brown, A. Roy ix, 519-20

Brown, Howard Morton ix, x, 203
Brown, James Morton 488, 519, 522
Brown, John Horace 367, 478, 488, 521-4
Brown, Lieutenant 514
Brown, Sergeant 102
Bruce County 80, 160-1
Brunton, Keith 562
Brunton, Stanley 554, 562, 566
Buchanan, Ann 167, 173-4, 176-8, 180, 348
Buchanan, Catharine 169
Buchanan, David 177-8
Buchanan, Donald 126
Buchanan, Rev. George viii, ix, 26, 44, 72, 82, 88, 90-2, 112, 134, 146, 167-76, 180, 190, 197, 200, 228, 232-3, 242, 244, 348, 455, 498-9
Buchanan, George Junior 136, 541
Buchanan, Helen 169
Buchanan, Jessie 88, 233
Buchanan, Margaret 180
Buckley, Mr. 102
Buckwheat 125, 302, 404, 420
Budd family 414
Buffalo, New York 335
Building bees 78, 92, 569
Building boom 129, 370-72, 374-5, 387
Building stone 370, 386
Bumsted, J.M. 34
Bungalows 563, 565-6
Burchill, John 159
Burgess family 160
Burgess, George Arthur 478, 525
Burgess Township 4
Burghers 174
Burgoyne, General John 3
Burke, Edmond 389
Burke, Captain George Thew 17-18, 20-2, 55-6, 62, 82, 96, 213
Burnett, Rev. W.H. 407-8, 454, 488
Burns, Rev. Robert 29, 184
Burritt's Rapids viii, 118, 398
Burrowes, Thomas 17, 97
Burrows, Edward 158
Burrows, James 66, 133, 136, 275, 280, 319-20,
322, 324, 334, 336, 338, 340, 342
Burrows, John 345-6, 424
Burrows, William 78, 346, 414
Burwell, Colonel [Mahlon] 36
Bussing 554-6
Butter 122, 124-5, 137, 218, 264, 294, 300, 303-4, 344, 361-2, 372, 430, 458
Byms, Mr. 218
Bytown 17, 19, 66, 71, 99, 118-22, 128, 136, 158, 183, 267, 278, 281, 311, 322, 338, 342, 345, 435 See also Ottawa
Bytown & Prescott Railway 278

Cabinetmakers 294, 338, 354, 376
Cadet training 525
Cadets of Temperance 244, 336
Calaghan, Daniel 74
Caldwell, Alexander 380-2
Caldwell & Brown 374, 376
Caldwell, Boyd Sawmills 292, 364-5, 373-4, 376, 380, 382, 388
Caldwell, Ewan 542
Calendars 479
California 185, 289, 308
Callander, Scotland 30, 234
Cameron, Alexander 295
Cameron, Allan 154
Cameron, Donald 255
Cameron, Ewen 242
Cameron, Rev. James 186
Cameron, John 92, 160, 488
Cameron, Malcolm 132, 160, 186, 191, 200, 218, 226-7, 315-17, 335, 341, 358, 432, 512
Cameron, Mr. 166
Cameronian Presbyterians 175, 186, 190, 260
Camp meetings 208, 219, 412
Campbell, Donald 297
Campbell, Duncan 177
Campbell family 158, 242-3
Campbell, Jessie Buchanan ix, 111, 167, 515
Campbell, John Senior 10, 169
Campbell, John 36, 39, 92-3, 267
Campbell, Mr. 274
Campbell, P. 38
Campbell, Peter 297
Campeau, Mr. 390
Camping 482-6, 495
Canada Central Railway 284, 287, 378, 380, 382, 473
Canada Company 149, 153
Canada Lumber Company 476, 483
Canadian Constitution 570
Canadian Co-operative Wool Growers 546, 551
Canadian Expeditionary Force Grenadier Guards 523
Canadian Fencibles 12
Canadian Pacific Railway 261, 285, 308, 311, 473-5, 477-8, 480, 499, 532, 543, 546, 551
Canadian Women's Auxiliary Corps 547-8, 563
Canadian Woollen Mills 476
Canals 88, 98, 120, 374
Cannadine, David 27
Cannon 282
Canoes 104, 485
Cape Breton 36
Captain Rock 388
Carding 126-7, 132, 356, 372
Cardross, Scotland 184
Careglen, Scotland 143
The Carleton 484
Carleton County 64, 92-3, 96-7, 194, 226, 268, 295-6, 380, 414, 439, 572
Carleton House 357
Carleton Place viii-ix, 14, 37, 65-6, 71-2, 86, 92-3, 114, 118, 133, 183-5, 201, 204-6, 252-6, 258-60, 264-9, 278-84, 286-9, 291-4, 296, 298-304, 307-11, 315-26, 328-31, 333-4, 336, 339-40, 342, 344, 347-50, 353-93, 404, 408, 410-11, 415-16, 424, 429-33, 440-5, 448-56, 458-65, 467-70, 473-87, 489, 491-
3, 495-9, 501-2, 505-6, 508-16, 518-22, 524-7, 530, 532, 534-5, 537-44, 546, 550-69, 572-3, See also Carlton Place and Morphy's Falls
Carleton Place and Beckwith Historical Society ix, 566
Carleton Place Boating Club 483
Carleton Place Canoe Club 485-6, 493, 511
Carleton Place Central Canadian 316, 390-1
Carleton Place Female Association 454
Carleton Place Herald 133, 325, 356
Carleton Place Junction 565
Carleton Place, separation from Beckwith 333, 375-80
Carley, Samuel 136
Carlow County, Ireland 18, 21, 52-4, 62, 64, 71-4, 194, 196
Carlow settlements 60, 62-4, 73
Carlton and Pakenham Methodist Circuit 219
Carlton Place 96-7, 116-17, 120-1, 124-36, 138-9, 146, 149-50, 158, 168, 176-7, 182, 186, 189-90, 194, 200, 204-7, 210-14, 216-21, 225-30, 232-6, 238-44, 246-8
Carlton Place Library Association 240-1
Carlton Place Methodist Circuit 219
Carmichael, Comrie Donald 143
Carmichael, James 143
Carmichael, Jane 459
Carmichael, John 36, 150-2, 168, 176, 326
Carmichael, Peter 242, 297
Carmichael, Robert 152, 297
Carmichael's Grove 464
Carnban, Scotland 45
Carpenters 129, 132, 136, 160, 288, 294, 338, 344-6, 376, 384, 390, 493, 494
Carriagemakers 344, 477
Carsonby 537

617

Carswell, Rev. Mr. 457
Cartes de visites 255
Cash economy 280-2, 417
Castle, Ivor 523
Catholic emancipation 57, 60, 194-5
Cattle fairs 116, 218, 304, 535
Causeways 92, 492
Cavan County, Ireland 65
Cavanaugh, Robert 116
Cavenagh, Robert 338
Cavers, Thomas 265
Cemeteries 18, 56, 65, 73, 111, 161, 176, 204, 242, 273, 280, 287, 310, 417-18, 421, 458, 498
Cenotaphs See War memorials
Censuses 116, 135-6, 156, 228, 232, 252, 266, 269, 275, 292-4, 303, 338, 346, 353-4, 548
Central Canada Machine Works 384, 387, 473, 476, 485
Chain migration 64-6, 156-64, 227, 309
Chair factory 338
Chalmers, Dr. Thomas 183
Chambers, Aaron 116
Change 278, 280, 282-3, 308-11
Charity 154, 379, 387-8, 390, 461-2
Charivaris 182, 244
Chartists 388, 433
Chatham 36, 76
Chaudiere Falls 14, 23, 36
Cheese factories 287, 292, 297, 299, 303, 329, 347, 349, 406-7, 410-12, 415-18, 453, 458, 488, 492-3, 526, 532, 540
Cheese production 125, 137, 218, 264, 294, 297, 299, 303, 377, 412-13, 418, 439, 458, 468, 488, 540-1, 572
Chewett, James G. 25
Child labour 86-7, 382, 385, 390, 393, 398-410, 427, 563
Children 59-60, 79-80, 88, 145-8, 151-5, 158, 232-9, 255-61, 266-8, 273-5, 296, 312, 326-35, 379-80, 382, 393, 398-410, 413, 423, 427, 429, 438, 459, 461,
495, 532-8, 547, 556, 568
The Chimes of Carleton Place 481
Chosen People imagery 205, 209, 396, 458
Christ Church, Ashton 214-15, 344
Christmas 206, 462, 534, 539, 545-6
Christ's Hospital 342
Church architecture 32, 34, 58, 72, 170-5, 177-9, 181, 183, 186-7, 202, 206-7, 209, 212-15, 220-1
Church consolidation 532
Church of England See Anglicans
Church of Ireland 53-4, 56, 58, 212, 448-51
Church of Scotland 24-6, 30, 32-5, 40, 44, 46, 72, 110-12, 138, 166-7, 169, 172-85, 188, 190, 197-8, 213-14, 219, 228, 236-7, 240, 248, 260, 268, 317, 344, 348, 354, 390, 416, 432, 437, 440, 456, 542-4, 564 See also Kirk Session
Circuses 315, 494
Cities 292
Civil servants 569
Civilisation 365-6
Clare County, Ireland 221
Clark, Alexander 143-5
Clark, James M. 447
Clark, Thomas 136
Clarke, Thomas 154
Class feeling 356-8, 388, 392-3, 414, 480-2, 534
Clay houses 54
Clearing land 84-5, 87-8, 91
Clearwater, Montana 308
Clergy 10, 24-6, 32-4, 36, 41, 44, 56, 60, 62, 72, 79, 111-12, 136, 148, 158, 166-90, 197, 208, 212, 232-4, 345, 429, 432, 439, 443-4, 458, 498
Clergy Reserves 4, 6, 17, 26, 62, 86-7, 152-4, 157-9, 161, 184-5, 207-8, 288, 306, 317, 398, 401, 403, 433
Clerical occupations 294, 359-60
Clerk, Thomas 338
Cliff, William W. 316, 390-
1, 482, 492
Cliff's Monthly Journal of Music and General Miscellany 391
Clinjordan, Ireland 64
Clocks 278, 310
Cloth manufacturing 124-7, 303, 356-8, 360, 369-70, 372, 374, 381-5, 550-1
Clothiers 294
Clothing 32, 46, 63, 82, 100, 112, 126, 139, 147, 173-4, 177-8, 248, 255, 268, 310, 344, 355, 357, 385-6, 391, 400, 407, 414, 423-4, 426, 433, 454-5, 461, 490-2, 509, 514, 550-1
Cobourg 154, 175
Cockburn Creek 120
Cockburn, Colonel Francis 18, 20-2, 71
Cockburn, James P. 63, 81, 89
Cockle, George 136
Code, A.B. 519
Code, Abraham 382-4, 441, 473, 551
Code, Elizabeth 498, 522
Code family 160, 402, 519
Colborne, Sir John 190, 206, 212, 228, 230
Coleman, Berton 532
Coleman, James 65-6, 129, 132
Coleman, Smith Esq. 370
Coleman, Rev. William 346
Collegiates 328
Colonial Office 6, 17, 62, 64, 73-4, 94
Communion tokens 169
Communist Party 482
Commuting ix, 551-2, 554-8, 561, 564-6, 568, 571-3
Computers, historical analysis ix, x, 276
Comrie, George 297
Comrie, Jessie 469
Comrie, Margaret 144
Comrie, Peter 124
Comrie, Scotland 30-4, 36, 41, 45-7, 143-4, 344, 546-7
Comrie's Corners 157
Conboy, John 19, 228, 231-2
Conboy, Magistrate 216
Conboy, Timothy 136, 156
Concession lines 14, 91
1, 482, 492
Congregationalism 166
Conn family 288
Conn, James 136, 220, 236, 320, 344-5, 453, 464, 513-14
Connell, Bill 292
Conservatism and Conservatives 2, 38, 46, 52, 57, 60, 110-11, 113, 200, 218-19, 222, 225-31, 241-2, 315-20, 341, 390, 398, 413-14, 416, 432, 434-6, 448, 541-2, 568, 572
Consitt, Francis W. 112
Constables 108, 229, 390
Continuity 289-92, 572-3
Contraception 258
Conversion 221, 435, 448, 456-7, 462
Coogan, Denis 209
Coolcullen, Ireland 64
Coon, Ireland 398
Coopers 68, 127, 129, 132, 136, 294, 338, 393, 494
Copybooks 238-9, 280, 434-5
Corduroy roads 120
Cork County, Ireland 24, 73
Corn 125, 138, 196, 404, 418, 420, 536, 562
Cornwall 5, 10
Cossitt, G.M. & Co. 291, 298
Cottages 473, 486, 497, 499, 532, 557, 570
Cotton mills 370
Council Bluffs, Iowa 162-4
County of Lanark Agricultural Society 124
Court of Quarter Sessions 93
Court of Request 228
Court-houses 96-7
Covenanters 186, 406
Cowan, Donald 143
Cowan, Galech 143
Cox, Rev. Robert G. 326
Craig, George 346
Craig, Russell 553
Craig, William 424
Craigdarrach family 90
Craigelig, Scotland 48
Craigie & Stephenson 372, 374
Cram, Agnes 457
Cram, Andrew 148
Cram, Andrew W. 235
Cram burial ground 242,

545
Cram, Daniel 240, 259, 509
Cram, David 297
Cram, Duncan 11, 148, 444, 456-7, 545
Cram family 160, 177, 546
Cram, George Dunnet 259
Cram, Gertrude 509
Cram, Janet 266
Cram, John 45, 80, 97, 102, 168, 179, 266, 326, 545
Cram, John F. 376
Cram, Joseph 376
Cram, Mr. 170
Cram, Peter 45-6, 126, 547
Cram, Peter Senior 228
Cram, Rev. Peter Wilson 444
Cram, Robert Haldane 499, 509
Cram, William 545
Cram, Wilson D. 546-7
Crampton, Robert 378, 380
Creag Ianaich, Scotland 37-8, 45, 48, 144
Creameries 416, 532
Credit economy 281, 361-2, 367
Crieff, Scotland 30, 546
Crimean War 282, 455, 505, 518
Criminality 238-9, 330, 332-6, 435-6, 438, 572
Croil, James 440
Cronan, Jeremiah 74
Crops 22
Cross Keys 346, 348
Crossley and Hunter 442
Crowe, John 149
Crowe, Mr. Patrick 149
Crown See Monarchy
Crown Lands 158-9, 208, 212
Crown Reserves 4, 6, 10, 17, 26, 62, 86, 144, 152-4, 157, 159, 161, 321-2
Cruickshank, George 57
Cuckoo's Nest 149, 347, 416, 496, 533, 539
Cullen, Louis 54
Culloden, Battle of 310, 427
Cultural baggage 110-13, 198-200, 333-6, 429-30
Cultural paranoia 333-6, 569-73
Cupar-Angus, Scotland 168
Curlew ship 34-6

Curraclone Butler, Ireland 221
Currie, Mrs. 492
Currie, Robert 82
Currin, Mr. 102

Dack, Eliza Ann 266
Dack, William 508
Dairying 79, 138, 264, 279, 292, 297, 299, 303, 400-7, 411, 416, 418, 440, 486-8, 500, 535, 540, 562
Dakota 419
Dalhousie District 97
Dalhousie, Earl of 21-6, 44, 77, 91-2, 134, 166, 200
Dalhousie Township 24, 38, 96, 98, 100, 118, 120
Dancing 47, 384, 406, 408, 412, 438, 485, 494, 552
Darling Township 24, 38, 96, 292
Dart, C. 524
Daughters of Temperance 455
Daverne, Daniel 14-15
Davidson, Mrs. 146
Davies, Josiah 65
Davis, Marjorie 539
Davis, Robert 60, 64-5, 153, 204, 228, 231-2
Davis, Thomas 153
Day Care 564
Death 69-71, 73, 78-80 88, 100, 102-3, 148, 151, 162-4, 176, 178, 185, 188, 242, 244, 255, 258-60, 266-8, 280, 289, 334, 387, 398, 419-20, 424, 435, 456-8, 460, 470, 486, 510, 513, 522, 524, 526
Debating clubs 56
Debt 176, 282-4, 322
Decline 492-6, 501, 517, 532-3, 550, 552-3, 568
Degeneracy 393
Delisle, Benjamin 12
Dell, John 275, 300
DeMeuron Swill regiment 10
Democracy 230
Demographic crisis 153-64, 184, 254, 260-1, 273-4, 288
Denominationalism 209-11, 220
Depressions 542, 550
The Derry ix, 248, 300, 348-9, 396, 398-400, 402, 408,
410, 412-13, 423, 426-7, 442, 492, 496, 516, 540, 562, 565
Derry, Ireland 339
Desertions 4-5, 208
Devils 44
Devine, Patrick 345
Devlin, James 126
Devlin, Mervyn 563
Devonshire, England 66
Dewar, Alexander 97, 102, 105, 111, 168, 176
Dewar & McDonald 372
Dewar, Archibald 40-1, 43, 424
Dewar Cemetery 273, 516
Dewar family 160
Dewar, John 97
DeWatteville Swiss regiment 10
Diaries 122-3, 274-5, 296-8, 300-2, 486-8
Dick, Hon. Paul, MP x
Dickson family 79
Dickson, Margaret 179
Diet 6, 14, 34, 80, 88-90, 123, 173-4, 196, 356, 367, 407, 418, 455-6, 548
Disease 29, 166, 180, 334, 410
Disloyalty 58-9, 111, 198
Disruption of 1843 182-4
Dissenters 198, 210-12, 432
Distilleries 30, 94, 127-9, 132, 136, 156, 242
Divine ordering of Universe 440
Division See localised identities
Division Court 132
Docherty, John 300-2
Docherty, P. 300
Doctors 19, 68, 114, 130, 136, 146, 168-9, 172, 244, 267, 269, 473, 477, 493-4
Doherty, John 216, 300-2
Doherty, Joseph 221
Doherty, Mr. 342
Dolgoy, Leonard 566
Dolgoy, Reva 566
Domestic ghetto 264-5, 296
Dominion Quarries 135, 263, 478-80
Doolan, Patrick 136
Dooland, David 74
Dooland, Edmund 74
Dooland, John 74
Door and sash factory 376

Doran, John 317-18, 441
Douglas, George 342
Douglas, James 209
Dow, James 39
Dowdall, Abraham 490-1
Dowdall, Ann 491
Dowdall, Dora 491
Dowdall, George 491
Dowdall, Herbert 526
Dowdall, Mary 491
Dower 150-2, 266, 290-2, 460
Down County, Ireland 66
Downing, Andrew Jackson 305-5, 309
Drill sheds 324-5, 376, 512-14, 516
Dropsy 176, 268
Drought 98, 110
Drugs, illegal 568, 570
Drummond estates 34
Drummond, Sir Gordon 6
Drummond, Malcolm 297
Drummond, Peter 297
Drummond Township 6, 10, 12, 14, 62, 73, 96-7, 116, 119, 134, 146, 188-9, 205, 219, 226, 228, 347-8, 441, 495, 540, 566
Drummond, William 455
Drysart, Ireland 234
Drysdale, John 230
Drysdale, Mr. 430
Dublin, Ireland 62, 200
Duff, Alexander 274, 292, 492
Duff, Annie Elexey 349, 363, 417, 466, 485-6, 492, 500
Duff, Denysa 466, 492
Duff, James 300-2
Duff, Thomis 302
Duff, William 275, 292, 307, 355, 363, 492, 508
Duff, William Junior 292, 492
Dull, Scotland 30-2
Dunblane, Scotland 30-1
Duncan, Abram 243-4
Duncan, James 124, 132, 275, 320, 353-4
Duncan, Mr. 338
Duncan, Thomas 302
Henry Dundas, Viscount Melville, Baron Dunira 32, 46, 183, 344
Dundurn 348
Little Dunkeld, Scotland 30

Dunkin Act 463-4
Dunlop, Andrew 493
Dunlop, Miss 410
Dunlop, Robert 275
Durham, Lord 213
Dwyer Hill 412, 537

Earthquakes 34
Easter 206-7
Eastern Breeders 562
T. Eaton Company 479, 536
Economic growth 6, 24, 38, 123, 130-2, 286, 366-76
Edey, C. 452
Edey subdivision 558
Edinburgh, Scotland 10, 40, 44, 90, 146, 166, 233, 546
Edwards family 160
Edwards, John 136, 338
Edwards, Robert 154, 160
Edwards, Stearne Tighe 513, 526-7
Edwards, Thomas 154
Edwardsburgh Township 2-3
Elderly people 34-5, 44, 266-8, 424-5, 467
Elders 168, 176, 178, 181-2, 186, 453 See also Kirk session.
Elections 112-13, 133, 149, 190-2, 198, 212, 222, 226, 315-20, 324, 358, 447, 467, 514, 539, 554, 566
Electoral districts 324
Electric railway 485
Electricity 473, 477-8, 547, 550, 552-3
11th Regiment of Foot 84
Lord Elgin 132
Elites 54, 58, 112, 172, 222, 269, 286, 358, 413-14
Elizabethtown Township 2-4, 60
Elliott, Bruce S. 60-1
Elly, Joseph 61-2, 64, 71-2
Elly, Robert 61
Elly, Samuel Junior 61
Elma Township 160
Elmsley Township 4, 134
Elmstone school 335, 348
Emotionally disturbed children 568
Employment 132
English identities 58, 339
English immigrants vii, 3, 12, 18, 22, 24, 38, 53-4, 80, 102, 110, 139, 145, 148, 208-12, 247, 268, 317, 320, 342, 345, 413, 443, 519
English language 30-1, 113, 233, 413, 569-70
Englightenment 434
Enniscorthy, Ireland 57-8, 62, 64, 66, 196, 269
Enough, Stephen 209
The *Enterprise* 374, 483
Entertainment 315, 350, 356, 390-1, 402, 406, 414-15, 464, 478, 482-6, 551
Epileptic seizures 180
Epworth League 407-8, 410-11
Erse language 30-1
Ethnic studies vii
Evil eye 430-2
Exodus 195
Experience meetings 454
Exploitation 358, 441-2
Extended families 270-5

Facades 248
Faction fighting 216-7, 226, 292, 435
Factories 139, 280, 310, 323, 356, 358, 368, 370, 382-3, 408, 439, 474, 530, 550, 565
Fags 226
Fairs 116, 124-5, 130-1, 150, 244, 275, 304, 368, 494, 535
Fallowfield 414, 435
Families 10-12, 34-6, 44, 62, 66, 69-72, 74, 78-9, 82-7, 116, 126, 143-64, 168, 171, 182, 190, 196, 206, 221-2, 225, 258, 260-5, 269-74, 278, 286-8, 292, 296, 298, 330, 377, 403, 408
Family Compact 226, 358
Family Herald 398
Family size 260-2, 271-3, 275, 298
Famine 53, 82-4, 98, 194, 221, 334-5, 438
Fanning, Dan 275
Fanning, James 152
Fanning, Mr. 275
Fanning, Robert 152
Farm consolidation 268, 298-300, 404, 407, 418-19, 421, 492-4, 540, 542, 544, 553-5
Farmers' Advocate 377

Farmer's Co-operative Harvesting Machine Company 541
Farming See Agriculture
Featherston, Euphemia 545
Featherston, Thomas 545
Fences 117-18, 120, 231-2, 241-2, 310, 315, 324-5, 400, 403, 453, 486, 488, 570
Fenians 325, 414, 505, 508, 513-16
Fencible Regiment 62
Fennel, Mrs. 80
Ferguson, Alexander 513
Ferguson, Cathrine 39
Ferguson, Daniel 19, 97, 154-5, 237
Ferguson, Dougald 396, 404
Ferguson, Dougald R. 410
Ferguson, Duncan 160
Ferguson family 44, 158, 166
Ferguson, Hugh 410
Ferguson, James 188-9, 447-8, 486
Ferguson, Jannet 39
Ferguson, Jean 39-40
Ferguson, John 14, 39, 158, 168, 228, 305, 448, 501, 546
Ferguson, Knox 410
Ferguson, Robert 26, 38-40, 86, 97, 126, 154-5, 197, 232, 338, 348, 495
Ferguson, Thomas 179, 236
Ferguson's school 348
Ferries 104, 106
Ferrotypes 255, 345
Fertility rate 87-8, 256-61, 275, 310
Feuds 22
Fiddling 483, 534
5th Battalion of Lanark Militia 506
54th Regiment 22
Filiopietism 320
Findlay, David 372, 474
Findlay, David Junior 474-6
Findlay stove foundry 474-7, 493, 520, 530, 543, 550, 568, 570
Findlay, William 474
Findlay, William F. 482
Finley, Holland 60

Finley, Richard 60, 232
Finley, Thomas 60
Finley, Thomas Senior 60
Finn family 414
Fire-arms 106-8, 385
Fire engines 380
Fire halls 557, 560
Fireplaces 87, 90-1, 107, 135, 145, 163, 179, 203, 245, 247, 265, 307, 493
Fires 36, 172, 174, 241, 346, 367-8, 380, 385, 524, 532, 556, 568, 573
Firewood 77, 152, 247, 274-5, 361, 399, 485, 488, 530, 540-1, 543, 545-6
Fisher, Duncan 97, 102, 105
Fisher, John 41-4
Fitzgerald, Patrick 74
Fitzmaurice, Ulysses 97, 101-3, 106-7, 110
Fitzpatrick, Henry 132
Fitzpatrick, Mr. 130
Fitzpatrick, William 129
Fitzroy Harbour 14
Fitzroy Township 24, 158, 204-5, 288-9, 306, 308-9, 447
Flagg, Samuel 338
Fleming, Andrew 209
Fleming, James 209, 561
Fleming, Richard 154, 203
Flett, John 386
Flood, Rev. John 208
Floods 369
Floorplans 162, 173, 187, 295, 322, 401, 425
Flying aces 526
Food 83, 85-6 See Diet
Forest 76, 78-80, 83-4, 89, 94, 106, 113, 116-17, 120, 133, 139, 158, 225, 231, 241, 246, 280, 348-9, 384, 427, 444
Foresters 486
Forrest, W. 47
Forsyth, Robert 33
Fortingall, Scotland 30-1
Fortune, William 77
Foster, Boyd 562-3
Foster, Greg 563
Foster, Jim 562
Foster, Lynda 562-3
Foster, Vera 563
Foundlings 268
Foundries 132-3, 138, 247, 356, 367, 372, 387, 474, 476, 482

4th Carleton Regiment of Militia 96-7, 101, 107
Fox-Talbot, William Henry 41
Fragmentation of society See Localised identities
Frame buildings 130, 134, 206, 213, 237, 245-6, 267, 297, 301, 305-7, 309-10, 317, 321, 349, 353-4, 357, 368, 384, 386, 389, 419, 437, 565
Framing bees 297
Franchise 222, 315-16, 455, 539
Franktown 18-22, 38, 44, 60, 64, 66, 68, 71-3, 79, 82, 88, 90, 92-4, 100-1, 104-6, 108-9, 116, 118-20, 124-5, 128, 133-6, 138-9, 157-8, 161, 166-8, 197, 200-2, 204, 209, 211-12, 214, 217-18, 234, 237, 240, 242-4, 258, 261, 267-9, 280-2, 284, 286-7, 301, 304, 308, 317, 319-20, 322, 324-5, 327, 336-43, 345-7, 349, 376, 378, 393, 396, 406-7, 415-16, 421, 424, 433, 437, 439-40, 445, 447, 449-53, 458, 461-2, 464, 468-9, 489, 492-6, 498-9, 506-7, 512-13, 519-20, 524-5, 532-3, 537, 539-40, 547, 552, 557, 559, 561
Franktown cemetery 242, 418
Franktown-Numogate Women's Institute 564
Fraser, Alexander 506
Fraser, Donald 97, 225-6, 230, 316
Fraser family 158
Frazer, Alexander 247
Fred Landon award viii
Free Church of Scotland 182-6, 190, 219, 260, 318, 344, 390, 398, 416, 432, 440, 464
Free Schools 236-9, 326, 330-35, 433-4, 436, 572
Freehold tenure 40, 48-9, 149
Freeman, John 182
Freemasonry 242, 246, 486
Freer's Rapids 119
Freethinking 182, 429, 433-4

French people 56, 506
French Canadian Missionary Society 454-5, 462
French Canadians vii, 12, 18, 24, 36, 118, 132, 198, 205, 239, 292, 388, 390, 454-5, 462, 476, 570
French, John 107
French language 569-70
French Revolution 2, 56-7
Frost & Wood 291, 298
Fulford, J.H. 65
Fullan, John 19
Fullan, Peter 19
Fuller, Samuel 133, 356, 367
Fumerton, John 106
Funerals 197, 242, 274, 289, 419, 457-8, 486-7
Furniture 82, 90, 152, 370, 490, 496
Fyfe, Robert 188

Gaelic language 19, 29-31, 36-7, 40-1, 44, 47, 58, 96, 113, 132, 168, 172, 174, 176, 184, 248, 268, 349
Gagan, David viii, 273-4
Galt 382
Galvin, Denis 74
Galvin, Patrick 132
Games 47, 78-9, 243, 408, 438, 477, 486, 534
Gaming 243, 390
Gananoque 244, 484
Gaols 96, 234, 238, 265, 286, 390, 425, 436
Garbage 556
Gardens 17, 190, 300, 461, 488, 565
Garland, Anne 79
Garland, Ellen 79-80
Garland, John 64, 70, 209
Garland, Margaret 64
Garland, Nicholas 64, 79, 209
Garland, Richard 268
Garland, Thomas 64, 79-80, 209
Garner, Mr. 300
Garvey, Mr. 338
Gas warfare 523
Gavazzi riots 435
Gemmill, John A. 124, 132, 240, 244
Genealogy ix
Gentility 88, 280
Gentry 70
George III 2-3, 14, 27, 111

George IV 2-3, 27, 96
George V 426, 511, 521-2
Georgian Bay 49
German principalities 3
Gerrymandering 226-7, 316
Ghosts 430
Gibson, William 153
Gilfillan, Rev. George 34
Gilfillan, Rev. James 149-50
Gilfillan, Rev. Samuel 33-4, 45-7
Gillies, Alexander 387, 476
Gillies and McLaren Sawmill 369, 374, 376, 380, 387-8, 390, 473, 476
Gillies, Archibald M. 136, 451
Gillies, Austin 410, 519
Gillies, Beyer & McLaren 384, 476
Gillies Bros. Co. Ltd. 359, 542
Gillies Corners 120, 136, 147, 210, 287, 292, 325, 346-7, 407, 416, 440, 451, 464, 495-6, 532-3, 540, 561
Gillies, David 325
Gillies, James 359, 375-7, 387-8
Gillies, John 359, 372, 376, 384-5, 387, 473, 476, 485, 487
John Gillies, Son & Company 476, 484
Gillies sawmill 292, 359
Gillies school 464
Gillies woollen mill 385, 473
Gilmour Pollack Company 117
Glasgow Colonial Society 174, 178
Glasgow, Scotland 10, 24, 33, 48, 97-8, 100, 110-11, 150, 166, 172, 233-4, 358, 544
Glebes 44, 207-8, 228
Glen Isle 105, 107, 109, 348, 456, 509, 540
Glendinning, Captain Thomas 97, 102-10, 173-4, 228, 230-1, 244
Glendochart, Scotland 40-1
Glengarry County vii, 2, 10-11, 26, 34, 36-7, 44, 241

Glengarry Fencibles 234
Glengarry Light Infantry regiments 10
Gloucester Township 4, 435
Goad, Charles E. 475
Godfrey's brickyard 377
Gold rushes 185, 308
Goldsmith, Oliver 494
Goodfellow, Mr. 170
Goodwood River See Jock River
Goodwood Rural Telephone Company 483, 496-8, 540, 560
Gordon, Eva 534
Gordon, Miss 390
Gore, Francis 6
Gorey, Ireland 58, 345
Goth family 488
Goth, James 297
Goth, John 80, 297
Gothic Revival architecture 161, 305, 433, 440, 443, 445, 447, 449, 451, 470
Goulbourn Township 6, 15-18, 24, 62, 64, 72, 73, 76, 83, 91-2, 96, 208, 210, 292, 342, 344, 347, 410-11, 496, 540, 552, 556
Gourlay family 414
Gourlay, Rev. John 344
Governor Generals 4, 15, 20-2, 241, 518
Gowan, Ogle R. 198, 214, 219
Gower Township 4
Graham, Catherine 411
Graham, John 132
Graham, Joshua 196
Graham, Samuel 196, 356
Graham Thomas 196-7
Graham, Wiliam H. 411
Grain 116-17, 120, 123, 172, 242, 246, 288, 291-3, 297, 304, 310, 360-2, 367, 404, 418, 420, 468, 474, 535-6, 540, 562
Grammar schools 208, 328, 516
Grand Trunk Railway 317-8
Gravestones 65, 177, 217, 242, 310, 417-18, 421, 427, 458, 498, 516
Gray, Rev. Peter 186
Greek language 233
Greenock, Scotland 35

Grevil, Richard 158
Greville's Corners 157
Grey County 289
Griffeth, Thomas 216
Griffin, Thomas 338
Griffith, Arnold 423
Griffith, Catherine 268
Griffith, Elizabeth 66
Griffith, Fred 512
Griffith, Herb 512
Griffith, Jack 512
Griffith, Mary 85
Griffith, Robert 512
Griffith's Corners 157
Grist mills 118, 127-8, 132, 344, 353, 367, 369-70, 374, 376, 381, 477, 492
Grocery stores 467, 545
Group settlements 38, 40
Guelph 534
Guns See Fire-arms
Gwyn, Julian 276, 296

Haggart, John Graham 318, 437, 441
Halcroft, Lawrence 189-90
Hall, Anna 53-4, 103
Hall, Samuel 53-4, 103
Hamilton viii, 260, 286, 335
Hamilton, Helen 149
Hamilton, Doctor James 146
Hamilton, Mr. 104
Hamilton, Thomas 149
Hamilton, William John 424
Hamlets 347-9
Hammer marks 359
Hammond, J.W. 311
Harkness, Elizabeth 259
Harl 137, 163, 403, 447, 451
Harmoniums 209, 462
Harnessmakers 344, 348
Harris, Rev. Michael 26, 72, 87, 172, 200-2, 207-8, 212, 214
Harte, Rev. Richard 135, 202-4, 212, 228, 234
Harvest excursions 409
Hastey, Lou 426
Havelock 474
Hawkins, Bert 541
Hawkins family 60, 160
Hawkins, Henry 85
Hawkins, Lena 469, 520-1, 538
Hawkins, Nellie 538
Hawkins, Roger 66, 70, 85, 87, 135
Hawthorn, Patrick 342
Hawthorne, Nathaniel xi
Hawthorne woollen mill 383-4, 476
Hay 293, 301-3, 361, 401, 404, 418, 420, 424, 540
Haydon, Andrew 370-2, 416
Head, Sir Francis Bond 116, 212, 226, 230
Healey, Ezra 72
Hebrew language 233
Henderson, James 494
Hendrick, Samuel 196
Henry ship 62
Herrick, Warren 278
High school 402, 404, 410, 412, 473, 525, 538, 553, 568
High technology 568
Highlanders See Scottish highlanders
Highways 540, 547, 552, 565-8, 572
Hill family 160
Hill, Frank 366
Hill, Jane 173
Hill, Mr. 17
Hill, William 150
Hillfield, Mr. 275
Hillview school 348
Hincks, Francis 316, 322
Hired men 275, 296, 300-1, 388, 410, 423-4, 563
Historiography of Beckwith viii-ix
History, sense of 58, 168, 280, 310, 426-7, 498-502, 517, 542-4, 547, 553, 564, 566-8, 573
Hitler 548
Holbrook family 160
Holland 3
Homosexuals 572
Honey 469, 562
Hooliganism 109, 238-9, 386, 432
Hooper, William H. 423, 511, 519
Hope, Thomas 548
Horner, Rev. Ralph 412
Horton, John 60
Horton, Nicholas 60
Horton Township 24, 160
Hospitals 288, 539, 544, 556, 564
Hotels 129, 132-3, 191, 226, 258, 269, 294, 338, 340, 344-5, 347-8, 353, 373, 378, 380, 436, 464, 477, 484-5, 494, 514, 532, 552
Houghton, Andrew 19
Houghton, Mr. 340
Household composition 269-74
"Household of Faith" 459-60, 470
Household size 260-2, 271-3
Housekeeping 262, 264, 490
Housing 22, 36, 40-1, 45, 48, 53-4, 63, 76-7, 85, 87, 90-1, 100, 105, 107, 109, 114, 134-5, 144, 168-70, 188-9, 199, 202-3, 241, 243, 245-6, 263, 265, 267, 269, 271, 273, 286, 293, 301, 303-10, 319, 321-3, 325, 337, 373-4, 377, 381, 386, 407, 414, 416-18, 532, 555, 557, 563, 565, 570
Houston, Hugh 136
Houston, James 132
Houston, Magdalen 132
Houston, Magistrate 216
Houston, Matthew 130-2, 356-7
Howard Temperance Hotel 191
Howes, John 219
Hudson Bay Company 36
Hudson River valley 3
Hughton, Andrew T. 513, 526
Hughton, Donna 561
Hughton, John 136, 258, 269, 338, 340, 345, 552
Hughton, Robert 561
Hull 16, 36, 76
Humanism 434
Hume, James 204, 230
Hunter, Mary 455
Hunting 80-1, 433, 452, 522
Huntley Township 24, 73, 92, 96, 119, 208, 276, 294-5, 493
Hurd, Dr. Willard 510
Hurd, Dr. William H. 320, 380, 462, 510
Huron County 399

Idiots 154
"Idle Wyld" 499
Idleness 218, 238
Illegitimate children 146, 152, 258
Illiteracy 237, 328, 332, 334
Illness 176, 267, 288
Illuminations 282, 505
Immigrants See English immigrants, Irish immigrants, and Scottish immigrants
Immigration 10-12, 17-18, 24, 31, 34-7, 39-40, 47, 60, 62, 70-1, 74, 78, 126, 143-6, 160, 254-5, 261, 285, 288-9, 308-9, 418-20, 434-6, 572
Immorality 328, 336, 416
Imperial sentiment 399, 506, 516-19, 524, 536, 559
Imprisonment 38, 146, 516
Improvement 30, 52, 278, 304, 386, 434
Incest 179
Independent Order of Good Templars 336, 464
Indians See Amerindians
Indigence 267-8
Individual expression 190
Industrial accidents 386-8
Industrialisation 32, 278, 280, 286, 308, 311, 321, 350, 354, 356, 369-70, 372-6, 380-90, 392-3, 440, 573
Infanticide 146, 258, 386, 408
Infidelism 182, 185-6
"Ingle Nook" 499
Inglis, J. 289
Inheritance 56, 124, 150-3, 161-2, 233, 258, 264, 273-4, 289-92, 398-9, 404, 406, 460, 470, 490-2
Innerrich, Scotland 48
Innes, James A. 476
Innisville 119, 382
Inns 20, 22, 66, 71, 127, 129, 132, 134, 136, 166-8, 242-3, 280, 322, 346
Insanity 80, 154, 158, 424-5
Interval House 564
Invasion 199-200, 505-10
I.O.D.E. 483, 486, 524, 526
Iowa 162-4
Irish brogue 342, 413
Irish Catholics vii, 24, 52-3, 57-8, 60, 62-3, 73-4, 98, 100, 106-10, 194, 199, 225, 229-30, 237-8, 246-8, 319, 334-6, 339, 432, 434-

8, 508, 516, 572
Irish identities ii, 58, 108-10, 113, 152-64, 194-222, 225, 243-5, 248, 275, 307-8, 316, 319, 326, 329, 332-6, 339, 342, 375-6, 398, 405, 408, 410, 412-18, 421, 429-32, 443-51, 496, 534, 539, 541-2, 544-7, 559, 566-7, 572-3
Irish immigrants vii, 3, 12, 18, 22, 38, 52-76, 82, 102-5, 145, 154, 156, 158, 176, 194-222, 246-8, 260, 271, 284, 301, 306-8, 315-16, 319, 336, 410, 438
Irish Protestants vii, 17-20, 24, 52-3, 57-9, 62, 64, 73-4, 100, 110, 149, 194, 196-8, 225, 292, 339 See also Anglicans and Methodists
Irish reputation 108, 226, 316-17, 320, 332-6, 416
Irish Yeomanry volunteers 56-8, 64, 76
Irvine, Joan 564
Isolation 76-7, 80, 92-3, 319, 362-8, 408, 410, 413-14, 427, 490, 539, 542, 563, 565-6, 573

Jackson, Catherine 338
Jackson family 160, 338
Jackson, James 340
Jacobins 52
Jacobs, Joseph 124
Jails See Gaols
James family 160, 487
James II 195, 445, 507
James, William H. 62, 86-7, 145, 153-4, 158, 242, 346, 433
Jane ship 34, 36
Jarvis, Rev. Arthur 445, 451, 459, 470
Jasper, Ontario 537
Jeffers, Robert 72
Jehovah's Witnesses 569, 572
Jersey 204
Jessop, Francis W.K. 94, 127, 228
Jinkinson, George 209
Jock River 15-18, 78, 92, 116, 209, 345, 347, 498, 556, 558
Jockbrae farm 562
Johnson, James 486

Johnstown District 2-4, 14, 60, 62, 99, 208
Joiners 196, 294
Jones, John 152
Jones, Lydia 152
Jones, Peter Senior 152
Justices of the Peace See Magistrates

Kanata 568
Katz, Michael B. viii, 260
Kelly, William 514
Kemptville 411-12
Kemptville College of Agricultural Technology 562
Kenmore, Scotland 29-31, 45
Kenmore, Upper Canada 78
Kennedy burial ground 242, 273, 421
Kennedy, Janet 111
Kennedy, Robert 111, 273
Kenny family 160
Kent, James 63, 136, 158-60, 204, 228, 231-2, 234, 236
Keramore, Scotland 48
Kerfoot family 160, 344
Kerfoot, George 72, 149, 158, 163
Kerfoot, J.J. 423
Kerfoot settlement 243
Kerfoot, William 64-6, 72, 149, 162-3, 208, 220, 228
Kerr, James 128-9
Kettles, James 365
Key, Janet 45
Kidd, Andrew 398
Kidd, Angus 398, 400, 402, 404, 410, 412, 425-6
Kidd, Annie 398
Kidd, Rev. Charles 439, 444
Kidd, Edward 398-9
Kidd, Eli 162, 398-9
Kidd, Elizabeth 398, 410
Kidd family 160, 414
Kidd, Fred 402
Kidd, George 62, 64, 152
Kidd, George Edward ix, 398-419, 423-7, 429, 442, 452, 454, 458, 488, 490, 500, 516
Kidd, Harold 398
Kidd, James 398-9, 403, 410, 425-6, 488
Kidd, John 404, 562

Kidd, John Senior 152, 398, 400
Kidd, Joseph 286, 398-410, 414, 416, 442, 444, 467-8, 486-8, 492
Kidd, Margaret 398, 415
Kidd, Thomas 232, 399, 513
Kidd, Wesley 152
Kidd, Rev. William 444
Kidd, William Livingstone 402-3, 413, 427, 532, 562
Kilfoil, James 162
Kilfoil, Martha 163
Kilfoil, Rachel 163
Kilfoyl family 160, 414
Kilkenny County, Ireland 52, 64, 66, 70-1, 196, 234, 398, 400, 419
Killin, Scotland 30-3, 36
Killing 57, 102, 106, 108
Kilmarnock 92, 118, 144 See also Maitland's Rapids
Kilpatrick, Ephraim 126
Kilts 32
Kincardine, Scotland 30
King, Colin 149
King, Donald 566
King, George 480
King, John 303
King's County, Ireland 66, 84
King's Creek 344, 346, 558
King's storehouse 18, 20-3, 38, 64, 72, 81-2, 86, 97-8, 100, 134, 166, 200-2, 208
Kingston xii, 2, 4-6, 10, 23-4, 26, 108, 158, 286, 341-2, 412-13, 426-7, 435, 437, 439, 519
Kippen parish, Scotland 26
Kirk session 178-80, 182 See also Elders
Kitchener, General 522
Kitchens 106, 166, 189, 243, 245, 262, 346, 403, 414, 530
Kitley Township 4, 23, 72
Knights of Labor 480-1
Knockabranar, Ireland 62, 64
Knox Church, Black's Corners 181-3, 185-6, 215, 347, 349, 464, 532, 548
Koch, Christopher W. xii
Kuehn, Fritz 135

Labour 356-8, 370-2, 374, 381-6, 388-90, 441-2, 480-2, 486, 532, 550-1
Labourers 136, 194, 234, 240, 286, 293-4, 342, 356, 358, 366-7, 369, 392, 494
Lachine 14, 36
Ladies Corners 348
Laidlaw, Mr. 132
Lake Park 484-6, 493, 495-7, 499-501, 556
Lake Park Company Limited 484, 486
Lambton County 43, 160-2, 227, 308, 317, 520
Lanark and Carleton Counties Telephone Company 540, 560
Lanark and Ramsay Telephone Company 540, 560
Lanark County 96, 112, 125, 133, 137, 191, 194, 200, 225-8, 230, 278, 284, 287, 312, 322, 342-3, 366, 373, 403, 416, 421, 425, 464, 478, 496, 564, 566, 572
Lanark County Board of Education 564
Lanark County Federation of Agriculture 542
Lanark County Junior Farmers 542
Lanark military settlement 24, 64, 72, 98
Lanark Township 23-4, 38, 73, 96-8, 100, 118, 120, 205, 219, 292, 566
Lanark Village 82, 187, 243, 365, 373, 388, 390, 566
Lanarkshire weavers 24, 38
Lancashire, England 139, 323
Land clearing 72, 94, 113, 241-2
Land consolidation 30, 52 See also Farm consolidation
Land granting 3-4, 8-12, 20-21, 34, 54, 64, 66, 69-70, 76-7, 81, 86, 98, 100, 112-13, 148-9, 152, 512
Land settlement 16-18
Langton, Anne xi
Lard 362

Latin language 233
Laurel, Quebec 412
Lavallee, Napoleon 124, 129, 132, 226, 308, 353, 356-7, 373, 378, 386, 432, 436
Lavallee, Omer 261
Lavant Township 24, 38, 96
Law, Brian 566
Lawford, Janet 464
Lawson, David 239-40, 386
Lawyers 97, 269, 477
Leach family 160
Leach, Samuel 80
Leach, Rev. Thomas 444
Lead mines 29, 366, 470
Leahy, Mr. 106
Leaver, Robert 136, 157, 338
Lectures 240
Leech, Edward 152
Leech, James 152, 288
Leech, Thomas Junior 152
Leech, Thomas Senior 152
Leech, William 64
Leeds and Grenville counties 2-4, 64, 106, 127, 194, 292, 412, 430
Leeds and Lansdowne townships vii, 60
Lees, Thomas 160
Leeson family 414
Leigh Instruments 383, 568
Leighlinbridge parish, Ireland 398
Leitrim County, Ireland 126, 149
Leland Hotel 484, 497
Lelievre, Captain Tito 12
Leslie, John D. 64
Lett family 160
Lett, Janet 151
Letters 38-40, 92, 139, 143-4, 157, 162-4, 174-5, 194, 233-4, 244, 342, 361-2, 519-20
Lever, Robert 338
Lewis, Clarence 565
Lewis, Dorothy 565
Lewis family 160
Libby family 160
Liberals 318, 398, 414, 447-8, 541, 568, 572, See also Reformers and Radicalism
Liberty ideology 98, 216,
226, 435, 444, 568, 570-2
Libraries 90, 132, 190, 239-41, 310, 324, 332, 335-6, 364-6, 408, 427, 481, 518, 534, 556, 568
Licensed Victualler's Association 464
Life expectancy 260-1, 266-8
Lightbody, Jennie 520-1
The *Lillian B.* 484
Lime Kilns 327, 346, 386, 492
Limerick, Ireland 84, 202
Limestone plains 156, 345, 414, 416-18
Lincolnshire, England 65
Lindsay, William 237
Liquor 18, 22-4, 30, 78, 80, 92-4, 102-6, 109-10, 128-9, 132, 136, 148, 156, 170, 174, 176, 190, 216, 218, 242-5, 280, 298, 316, 320, 324, 328, 335-6, 338, 341, 346, 368, 406, 408, 412, 415-16, 424, 436, 438-40, 442, 463-9, 485-6, 494, 500, 523-4, 532, 538, 564, 572
Literacy 278-80, 310
Litigation 146
Little, Rev. Joseph 458
Littleton, Ireland 66
Liturgy 161, 405, 443, 445, 462
Livery stables 357
Livestock 41, 78, 80, 84, 86, 88, 92, 98, 100, 106, 116-19, 124-6, 130-2, 137-9, 150, 152, 170, 173, 176, 204, 231, 264, 275, 279, 294-5, 297-304, 310, 315, 353, 361, 368, 385-6, 400-4, 410, 432, 440, 454, 474, 478, 486-8, 490, 492, 534, 536, 538, 540-2, 546, 562
Local history vii-ix
Localised identities ii, 274-5, 315-20, 323-6, 329, 331, 421, 512-13, 524-6, 533-4, 539-40, 548, 552-5, 556-8, 560-1, 564, 567-8, 570, 572-3
Local option 464-6
Loch Earn, Scotland 48
LochEarnhead, Scotland 144, 234
LochEarnside, Scotland 143
Loch Tay 33, 39
Loch Tayside 24, 29
Log buildings 41, 72, 78-9, 82-3, 85, 87, 90, 100-1, 125, 127, 130, 134-5, 147, 168-72, 199, 203-4, 208, 232-3, 245-6, 273-4, 288, 293, 301, 303-7, 310, 331, 337, 346, 348, 353, 386, 418-19, 425, 453, 467, 493, 534, 539, 565
London 137, 166, 284, 342, 344, 426-7
London Township 36
Loneliness 162-4, 292
Loney, Edward 209
Loney, Elizabeth 494
Long Island 63
Long Sault 36
Lost childdren 79-80
Lost River, Quebec 412
Loucks, William 102-4, 106-7, 109, 127
Lowe, Phineas 139, 153, 159
Lowell, Massachusetts 369-70
Lower classes 328
Lowlanders See Scottish Lowlanders
Loyal Rangers regiment 3
Loyalty ideology 6, 14-15, 23-4, 58-9, 62, 64, 71, 96, 102, 108, 110-11, 198-200, 212, 230, 234, 334, 366, 507-8, 510-11, 525, 571-2
Lucas Andrew 162-3
Lucas family 160
Lucas, Mrs. John 80
Lumax family 160
Lumber camps 264, 292-3, 360, 392, 408, 542 See also Timber Camps
Lumber industry 342, 346-7, 359-61, 363, 372-4, 376, 380-82, 388, 480, 482
Lumsden, Thomas 393
Luxuries 305
Lynch, Thomas 265-6
Lyons, Captain 17
Lyons, John 136
Lyons, Sam 342

Macadamised roads 120, 280, 322
McAlinden, Patrick 66, 158, 218
McAlpine, Mr. 338
McArthur, Archibald 144, 284, 296, 320-1, 357, 368, 376, 381-2, 384-7, 455, 473, 476, 541
McArthur, James 94, 136, 179
McArthur, John 156, 271
McArthur, Margaret 296, 455, 459-60
McArthur, Peter 78, 116, 136, 144, 156, 174, 232, 242
McCaffrey, Absolam 129, 132
McCaffrey's Landing 483
McCallum family 144
McCallum, Margaret 289
McCann's Point 433
M'Caul, Margaret 146
McClenaghan, Caroline 520
McConnell, Bob 426
McCormack, William 146
McCreary's Settlement 416, 532
McCreary's shore 501
McCuan, Alexander 278, 286, 288, 297, 312, 320, 456, 520, 541-2
McCuan, Catherine 90, 145, 278, 288
McCuan, Daniel 122-3, 160, 238-9, 244, 278-80, 284-9, 292, 296-9, 304, 306, 308, 310-12, 340, 342, 434-5, 456-8, 498
McCuan, Duncan 87, 130-1, 135, 143-5, 278, 297, 304
McCuan, Duncan Junior 278, 286, 297, 312
McCuan, Elizabeth 278, 328, 457
McCuan family 158, 286-8, 294, 296, 298, 309
McCuan, James 143-4, 288-9, 308-9, 457
McCuan, John 160, 278, 286, 288, 308, 357
McCuan, Nelly 312
McCuan, Peter 278, 286, 297, 320, 421
McCuan, Thomas 312, 522
McCuan, William 72, 297
McCullough, Elizabeth 65
McDermaid, D.N. 36
McDiarmid, Allan 48-9, 144
McDiarmid, Angus 78-9, 154, 398

McDiarmid, Ann 124
McDiarmid, Bob 377
McDiarmid, Christiana 124
McDiarmid, Christina 111
McDiarmid, Daniel 377
McDiarmid, Donald 126, 136
McDiarmid, Duncan 124, 150
McDiarmid family 158, 492
McDiarmid, J. 38
McDiarmid, James 37-8, 45, 48, 111, 144, 188
McDiarmid, Jessie Mabel 520, 526
McDiarmid, John 78-9, 96, 144, 275, 377
McDiarmid, John M. 526
McDiarmid, Mary 96, 398, 400, 444, 458
McDiarmid, Peter 124
McDiarmid, Susanna 188
McDonald, Allan 126-7, 132, 356, 372, 374, 476
McDonald, Angus 294
McDonald, Donald 152
McDonald, Duncan 168
McDonald family 158, 492
McDonald, John 152
McDonald, Rev. John 218
McDonald, Margaret 180
McDonald, Mr. 188, 372, 376
McDonald, Ronald 117
McDonald, Violet 520
Macdonell, Bishop Alexander 214
McDonell, John 154, 218
McDougall, Dan 275
McDougall, Donald 246, 297
McDougall, John 297
McEwan, Christina 185
McEwan, John 124, 128-9, 132, 230
McEwan, Peter 146
McEwen, Alexander 144
McEwen, Catherine 90
McEwen, Christina 254-5
McEwen, Duncan 297, 463
McEwen, Edie 463
McEwen, Ethel 463
McEwen, Ewen 124, 136, 233, 268, 338, 340, 346
McEwen family 158
McEwen, Findlay 135, 263, 421, 478

McEwen, Finlay 36
McEwen, Helen 39
McEwen, James 297, 308-9
McEwen, Jessie 463
McEwen, John 78, 126, 135, 143-4, 189, 245, 288, 539
McEwen, John S. 404
McEwen, Mabel 463
McEwen, Maggie 520-1
McEwen, Margaret 143
McEwen, Olive 463
McEwen, Ortie 402
McEwen, Peter 144, 233, 494-5
McEwen, Robert 463
McEwen, Robert J. 541
McFadden, Jacob 208
McFadden, Samuel 209
McFarland, William 136
McFarlane, Agnes 490
McFarlane, Archibald 36
McFarlane, Donald 344
McFarlane, Duncan 410-11
McFarlane, Elizabeth 278
McFarlane, Girsal or Grace 318-19
McFarlane, Hasty 410
McFarlane, J. 38
McFarlane, James 36, 304, 318-19, 490
McFarlane, John 490
McFarlane, William 297
McGill, Jean 14
McGilvery, Daniel 302
McGrath, Rev. J. 160
McGrath, Luke 108
McGregor, Alexander 134, 167, 170
McGregor, Dave 423
McGregor, Donald 169
McGregor, Duncan 132, 326, 346
McGregor family 348
McGregor, Hugh 266
M'Gregor, John 40
McGregor, John 326, 421
McGregor, Peter 65, 97, 136, 231, 242, 320, 326
MacGregor, Robert 297
McGuire, Trevor 482
Machine guns 519-20, 524
Machine shops 367, 384, 387, 474-7
McIlquham, Walter 373
McInnis, James 297
McInnis, Marvin viii
McIntosh, Catherine 149

McIntosh, Janet 149
McIntosh, John 288, 372
McIntosh, Mr. 380
McIntyre, A.C. 508
McIntyre, John 242
McIntyre, Peter 143
McKay, John 136
McKay, Mr. 347
McKay, Mrs. 240
McKelligan, Rev. Mr. 36
McKenna, Helen 268
McKenzie, D. 47
McKenzie, Rev. Mr. 457
McKenzie, William 126
Mackenzie, William Lyon 212, 225, 230, 505
McKeown, Elizabeth 162-3
McKeown family 160, 162-4
McKeown, Jane Junior 162-3
McKeown, Jane Senior 162-3
McKeown, William Junior 162-4
McKeown, William Senior 162
McKercher, John 486
McLachlan, Rev. James 186
McLachlin, Daniel 308-9
McLaren, Agnes 185
McLaren, Alexander 136, 185
McLaren, Christina 34, 490
McLaren, Colin 36, 76, 231, 490
McLaren, Daniel 185
McLaren, David 300, 526
McLaren, Donald 275, 297, 490
McLaren, Duncan 3, 143, 490
McLaren family 158
McLaren, George 263, 274-5, 286, 300-3, 361, 490
McLaren, James 144
McLaren, Janet 490
McLaren, John 143, 232, 275, 297, 300
Maclaren, Kate 44
McLaren, Margaret 490
McLaren, Mary 421
McLaren, Mary Ann 490
McLaren, Peter 297, 372, 388, 402, 476, 483, 490, 570

McLaren, Robert 132, 297
McLaren, William 490
McLaughlin, John 129, 132, 346
McLaughlin, Rev. Mr. 175
McLaurin, Rev. John 26, 233, 455
McLean, George 297
McLean, Marianne vii, 11, 34
McLellan, Angus 153-4
McLeod, Hugh 372
McLeod, John 297
McLeod, Kenith 297
MacLeod, Rev. Norman 183-4, 544
McMaster, L. 329
McMillan, Hugh 526
McMillan, James 516
McMillan, Rev. Mr. 184
McNab, Sir Allan 435
McNab, Archibald, Laird of 24, 37, 234
McNab, David 132
McNab family 158, 274
McNab, John 297
McNab, Peter 297
McNab Township 19, 24, 37-8, 234, 327, 346
McNabb, Alexander 232
McNabb, elder Dunacan 44, 126, 176, 188
McNaughton, Duncan 166, 297
McNaughton, Finlay 232
McNaughton, J. 99
McNaughton, James 126, 136
McNaughton, John 150, 244
McNeely, Brice 242
McNeely, Bryce 66, 320, 324
McNeely, Daniel 478
McNeely family 410, 556
McNeely, Elsie 536
McNeely, James 66, 70, 150, 297
McNeely, Rev. John 217, 444
McNeely, William 491, 541
McNeely, William Junior 491
McNie, Duncan 155
McNie family 158
McPhail, Archibald 268
McPhail, Daniel 188-9
Macpherson, Finlay 45
McPherson, John 236

MacQueen, Thomas 86, 152-3
McRae, Audrey 564
McRae, Howard 541
McRae, James 161-2
McRorie, Florence 454
McRorie, James 126, 136, 382
McRostie, John 77
McRostie's grove 464
MacTaggart, John 108
McTavish, Alexander Junior 152, 468-9
McTavish, Alexander Senior 152
McTavish, Ann 152
McTavish, Donald 152
McTavish, Douglas 117
McVean, Bella 538
Madawaska River 37, 288
Magazines 466, 473, 496, 498
Magistrates 64, 92, 94, 108, 216, 218, 228-32, 234, 334, 452
Mail delivery 466
Mail-order catalogues 496
Mains, Raymond 555, 562
Maitland 120
Maitland, Sir Peregrine 71, 108, 202, 214-15
Maitland's Rapids 92, 118
Male camaraderie 392, 408, 432, 468-9, 514, 560
Malloch, Susanna 188
Manitoba 289, 309, 384, 409-10, 412, 419, 439
Mann, Timothy 74
Manse of Beckwith 44, 138, 179-80, 211, 248, 257, 542-4
Mansions 97, 381, 386, 476, 480, 527, 541, 544
Manufacturing 129, 132-3, 144
Maple Grove Temple 464
Maple sugar and syrup 88-90, 404, 430, 501, 540
"Mapleleigh" 375, 377
Maps 5, 8-9, 11, 13, 15, 19-21, 25, 31, 53, 61, 67-9, 71, 93, 99, 155, 159, 219, 253, 281, 287, 301, 329, 343, 347, 354, 371, 475, 537
March Township 24, 96, 208
Marital breakdown 148, 265-6
Marlborough Township 4,
72, 495, 534
Marriage 34, 44, 146-9, 151, 188, 244, 255-6, 258, 262-6, 275
Marshall, William 82, 98
Maryborough Township 292
Masson, Rev. J. 464
Matheson, Alexander 100, 108, 214
Matriarchy 398, 492
May family 160, 288
May, Fleming 345
May, Francis 288, 292
May, John 433
May, Rev. John 234, 341, 439, 444, 450, 489-90, 494, 498, 501
May, Richard 269
May, Samuel 158
Mechanics Institute 132, 240, 310, 481, 518
Melodeons 465
Melville Free Church, Ashton 182-3, 344, 440, 464, 532
Viscount Melville See Dundas, Henry
Memory 309-10, 462
Men's role 148, 459
Mental illness 180-2
Meredith, Colborne P. 447
Merrick, Samuel Starr 488
Merrickville viii, 14, 65, 136, 201, 461
Metcalf, Robert 386
Metcalfe, Governor General 236
Methodists 18, 20, 24-7, 52, 57-9, 66, 68, 71-3, 92, 136, 163, 166, 176-7, 186, 194, 202, 205-6, 208, 210-12, 214, 218-22, 225, 228, 239, 242-3, 260, 317, 325, 334, 344-6, 353-4, 398, 405-8, 410, 413-14, 429, 432-3, 440, 449, 451-6, 458, 462, 464, 467, 495, 532
Metrification 568
Mewburn, H.C. 516
Mewburn, John Hermann 516
Michell, F.L. 404, 496
Middle class 240
Midlands of Ireland 53
Midwives 146
Migration See Immigration and Immigrants

Migration, Trauma of 160
Military settlements ix, xii, 2, 4, 6-11, 20-2, 24, 34, 64, 226, 316, 505-6, 572
Military veterans 2, 4, 6, 11, 19-21, 24, 26-7, 73, 78, 82-4, 105, 143, 152, 200, 225-6, 234, 337, 505-6, 511, 516, 526-7, 548, 564, 572
Militia 56, 64, 84, 96-9, 101-2, 107-8, 110, 130, 216, 229, 246, 267, 322-5, 505-6, 508, 514, 516
Miller, Alexander 232, 234, 237
Miller, Barbara 66
Miller, Cardy 482
Miller, Janet 151
Miller, Rev. Matthew 175
Milligan, Rev. James 186
Mills 32, 40, 70, 82, 97, 101, 107, 119, 127-9, 139, 218, 253, 275, 280, 308-9, 318, 340, 342, 344, 356, 359, 367, 522
Mills family 414
Millwrights 66, 68
Mingas, James 143
Misery 369, 405-6
Missionaries 188-9, 316, 440-2, 462
Mississauga Algonquians 14, 80
Mississippi & Ramsay Branch Temperance Society 243
Mississippi floodplain 111, 134, 217, 265, 289, 301, 537
Mississippi Hotel 373
Mississippi Lake 81, 117, 119-20, 189, 205-6, 218, 305, 347, 361, 441, 483, 495, 522, 540, 557-8
Mississippi Methodist Circuit 219
Mississippi River 13-14, 18-19, 25, 37, 65-6, 69, 100-2, 104, 106, 116-20, 127, 202, 205-6, 282, 292, 311, 350, 353, 356, 359-60, 363, 366, 368-9, 371-4, 376, 380-2, 387-90, 392, 408, 416, 423, 475-6, 501, 525, 543
Mixed farming 288, 292, 295, 298-303, 361, 399, 400-6, 411, 542

Modernisation 30-2, 248, 480, 498
Moffatt, David 66, 68, 186
Moffatt, Elizabeth 66
Moffatt, Robert 70
Moffatt, William 132
Monarchy 2, 4, 27, 44, 52, 54, 58, 70-1, 98, 102, 110-11, 148, 174, 184, 199-200, 212, 216, 218, 247, 339, 398, 426-7, 436-8, 492, 508, 536, 570-1
Montague Township vii-viii, 4, 67, 72, 92, 135-6, 144-5, 156-9, 161, 198, 200-1, 218, 226, 228, 260, 282, 292, 316-17, 321, 332-4, 336, 340, 363, 414-17, 419, 447, 458, 495-6, 526, 534, 540, 542, 554, 561
Montana 308-9
Montmagny, Quebec 568
Montreal 6, 13, 14, 16, 19, 25, 35-6, 64, 96, 108, 143-4, 146, 241, 281, 285, 288-9, 320, 335, 342, 362, 384, 412, 466, 469, 473, 476, 478-9, 496, 517, 551
Montreal River 425-6
Monzievaird, Scotland 30
Moore, Arthur 149
Moore, Catherine 467
Moore, Clara 467
Moore, Ernest 467
Moore, Herbert 467
Moore, Ida 467
Moore, James P. 467
Moore, Jane 66
Moore, William 66, 68, 97, 102, 127, 149
Moorehouse, John 158
Moorhouse, John 19
Moral revolution 258-9, 263-5, 324, 341, 404-8, 410-11, 417-18, 429-70, 481, 492, 525
Morals by-laws 431, 438-40
More, John 242
Morphy, Edmond 66, 68-70, 72, 80, 321
Morphy, James 132
Morphy, John 124
Morphy, Michael 124
Morphy, William 108, 129, 206
Morphy, William Junior 321

Morphy's Falls 14, 18, 25, 37-8, 65-6, 68, 72, 92, 94, 96, 101-9, 113, 116, 119-20, 127, 157, 202, 218
Morris, Alexander (politician) 317-18
Morris, Alexander (tavernkeeper) 94, 96, 101-4, 106-8, 110, 127-8
Morris, Rev. Ebenezer 338
Morris, John 136
Morris, John P.L.S. 371
Morris, Joseph 345
Morris, Hon. William 94, 98, 112-13, 174, 212-14, 225-6, 228, 315-17
Morrison, Rev. Duncan 331, 444
Morrison, Elizabeth 150
Morrison, Mr. 149
Morson, Jane 180
Mortality rate 255, 266-7, 270, 275, 289-90, 419-20, 422
Morton, Rev. A. 488
Moss, Josiah 19
Motels 565
Mother's Catechism 168
Mount Pleasant 136, 182, 209, 242, 342
Mountalexander, Ireland 150
Mourning 163-4
Moving pictures 473, 486
Muirhead, William 185-6, 368
Mullen, R. 524
Mulock, Rev. John A. 210-13
Mulrony, Bernard 221-2
Mulrony, Biddy 221-2
Mulrony, Patrick 221-2
Multiculturalism 572
Municipal Corporations Act 322
Municipal development 228-33, 248, 278, 315, 318-26, 572-3
Municipal Loan Fund Act 322
Municipal officers 325
Munster 410-12
Murder 430, 438
Murdock, William 494
Murphy, Father John 57
Murphy, Michael 132
Murphy's Falls See Morphy's Falls
Murray & Son 415

Murray, J. 247
Murray, James 153
Murray, Michael 136, 338
Museums ix, x, 566
Musgrave, Sir Richard 61
Music 80, 84, 105-6, 108, 168, 181-2, 209, 246-8, 259, 349, 384, 391, 402, 406, 410, 414, 452, 454, 459, 464-6, 481, 483, 494, 534, 536
Muthil, Scotland 30
Mutton 280, 302, 361
Mutuality 288, 292-4, 296-8
Mythology of Beckwith viii-ix, 147, 195-200, 205, 209, 215-16, 248, 308, 338

Nagle, Mr. 546
Nankevill, Rev. Benjamin 210-12
Napanee 390
Napoleonic wars xii, 2, 7, 10, 38, 46, 52, 59-60, 65, 505-6, 512, 516, 527, 570, 572
Nazi Germany 536, 544
Neilson, Johnston 132, 213, 234, 236-42, 264, 324, 454
Nelson, Admiral Horatio 147
Nepean Township 4, 16, 24, 76, 158, 298, 414
Nesbitt, Rev. Andrew C. 450
Nesbitt, Edward 151
Nesbitt, Eva 492
Nesbitt family 275, 302, 424-5
Nesbitt, Frances 151
Nesbitt, Doctor George 19, 68, 97, 101-4, 106, 110, 146, 267, 338, 424
Nesbitt, Rev. George 151, 444
Nesbitt, Hugh 209
Nesbitt, James 151, 275
Nesbitt, John 19, 97, 151, 269, 287, 345
Nesbitt, John Junior 151
Nesbitt, Robert 492
Nesbitt, Thomas 151, 275, 492
Nesbitt, William 338, 393
New Democrats 572
New France 2
New Ontario 426

New Ross, Ireland 58, 62
New York 281, 372, 486
New York state 3, 6, 305, 356
New Zealand 540
Newman, John Henry 448
Newspapers 10, 36, 62, 96, 108, 116-17, 126, 128-30, 132-3, 146-8, 160, 175, 183, 198, 210, 212, 218-19, 227, 258, 261-2, 264, 278, 280, 292, 303, 310, 316, 325, 342, 356, 358, 364-6, 390-1, 406, 415-16, 432, 454, 458, 466, 473, 477, 498, 501-2, 505, 517, 519, 539-40, 558
Newton's Saloon 356
Newtown, Ireland 62
Nichol, John 268
Nichols, W. Abner 361, 363, 478
Nicolson, Murray W. vii
99th Regiment 15-16
Nineveh, Scotland 234
No Surrender Boys 198-9, 201
Nobes, George 554
Nolan, Bob 162
Norman Romanesque Revival Architecture 451-2 See also Scottish Baronial architecture
North Burgess Township 200, 218, 226, 316
North Crosby Township 4
North Elmsley Township 200, 218, 226, 316, 378
North Lanark Agricultural Society 288
North Lanark Highland Games 567-8
North Lanark Museum 564
North Lanark riding 316-18
North Leeds riding 318
North Sherbrooke Township 24, 96, 98
Northumberland, England 66
Nova Scotia Fencibles 10
Nowlan, George 136
Nowlan, John 97, 101-2, 104-6, 110
Nowlan, Manny 97, 128-9, 132, 206, 228
Nowlan, Patrick 19-20, 22-3, 27, 64, 66, 82, 94, 124-5, 158
Nowlan's Corners 157, 496
Nuclear families 270-5
Nuclear Free Zone 566
Numogate 334, 447-8, 564

Oat mills 132, 356, 367, 376
Oats 30, 118, 122-5, 132, 138, 292, 300, 302-4, 402, 417-18, 420, 486, 488, 540, 562
Obscenity 259
Ocean Wave Fire Company 556
O'Connell, Daniel 194
Oddfellows 486
Officer, Arthur 526
Official Languages Act 569-70
Official Plan 566
Old Leighlin, Ireland 62
Old Ross, Ireland 61
Old Sly's Rapids 89
Oliver's Ferry 120
100th Prince Regent's County of Dublin Regiment 16
O'Neil, Nicholas 136
Ontario & Quebec Railway 474
Ontario French language services 569
The Ontario Historical Society viii, x, 498
Ontario Ministry of Natural Resources 569
Ontario Municipal Act viii
Ontario Municipal Board 554
Onzier parish, Scotland 45
Ops Township 160
Orange processions 197, 216, 218, 250-1, 436, 507, 522, 544-5, 567
Orangeism 52, 56-7, 70, 100-1, 108, 191, 194-5, 197-9, 201, 203, 205, 212-20, 222, 225-6, 228, 242, 246, 310, 316, 338-41, 414, 429, 434-8, 445, 448, 486, 567, 572
Orchards 149, 190, 196, 453, 492
Orena Villa 307, 466
Organs 406, 454, 465 See also Harmoniums and Melodeons

Orphans 71-2, 146, 455
Osgoode Township 4, 78, 144, 158, 188
O'Shea, Jeremiah 526
Oswego Canal 88, 98
Ottawa ix, 5, 118, 158, 250, 284-7, 311, 342, 344, 350, 362-3, 370, 373, 378, 380, 412, 452, 466, 478, 484, 488, 494, 498, 500, 519-20, 530, 538, 540, 548, 550-3, 558-60, 562, 566, 568-9, 573 See also Bytown
Ottawa-Carleton, Regional Municipality 552
Ottawa River 6, 13-14, 16, 19, 24-5, 36, 40, 76, 78, 84, 86, 91, 116, 120-2, 128, 158, 208, 280, 284, 288, 312, 322, 362-3, 372, 374, 412, 543
Ottawa Valley 5, 118-19, 133, 227, 250, 292, 303, 308, 356, 392, 473, 478, 500, 572
Ottawa Valley Canoe Association 485
Overpopulation 33, 59-60, 73, 273-4
Oxford Township 4
Oyster suppers 356, 514

Padfield, Rev. James 208, 212, 232, 234, 338
Paganus 360
Paisley, Scotland 76, 97-8, 110-11, 130-2, 149, 307, 357
Paisley, Upper Canada 160
Paisley, William 372
Pakenham 24, 38, 73, 86, 120-1, 134, 152, 204-5, 219, 361-2, 447, 542
Palatine settlers 66
Pamphlets 210
Parlours 243, 454, 460, 465, 492, 517
Passion 258, 412
Paternalism 146, 148, 289
Patriarchy 146, 150-1, 167, 171, 182, 190, 259, 289, 396, 455, 490-2, 572
Patrilineal inheritance 290-2, 490-2, 539
Patronage 227, 545
Patrons of Industry 448, 541

Patterson, Principal 410
Patterson reaping machines 298
Patterson, William 376
Pattie & Rorison 386
Pattie, David 129, 132
Paul, Andrew 242
Pay equity 570
Peace 104, 106, 190, 505, 518, 524, 526
Peale, James Griggs 72
Peas 123, 126, 138, 275, 300, 302-3, 418, 420, 486, 488
Peddie, Rev. James 44
Peden, Archibald 419
Pedlars 278, 362
Peel County viii, 273-4, 286, 288
Pelton, C.C. 463, 512
Pembroke 282-3, 308, 478, 480
Pembroke Township 158
Penal Code 56-7
Pendergast, William 494
Penitentiary 238-9, 265, 436
Penman mill 476
Pensions 105, 177, 228, 290, 511
Perdue, Henry 219
Perth 6, 10, 12-13, 16, 18-20, 22-3, 26-7, 44, 62-4, 69, 71-2, 77-8, 82-4, 86, 91-2, 94, 96-7, 99-101, 108-9, 112, 116, 118-20, 124, 128, 130, 134, 136-7, 146, 154, 162, 166, 168-70, 172, 174, 176, 184, 187-8, 190-1, 199-202, 207, 209, 212-13, 215-16, 218, 220, 222, 225-9, 232, 234, 242-4, 247, 250, 258, 264, 282, 286, 288, 317-18, 329, 340, 344-5, 347, 353, 362-4, 370, 372, 375, 380, 386, 402, 425, 435, 464, 478, 480, 484, 489, 495, 537, 540, 543, 561, 566
Perth County 160-1
Perth military settlement 6, 10, 12, 14, 16-18, 20, 62-4, 71, 82-3, 96-7, 100, 570
Perthshire highland settlers ix, 10-12, 15, 17-18, 21, 24, 29-52, 55, 64-6, 69, 72, 76, 78, 87-8, 91-2, 96, 98,

110-13, 124, 134-5, 137, 143-5, 148, 152, 158, 160, 166-90, 227, 244, 278, 306-7, 319-20, 342, 398, 400, 432, 505, 537, 544, 571-2
Perthshire, Scotland 29-35, 148-50, 183, 288, 305, 310, 315, 348, 429
Perversion 216, 221
Pestilence 170, 292, 334
Peterborough 372
Petitions 65, 68, 124-5, 157, 170, 206, 212-13, 228-30, 236-7, 267-8, 319, 326, 376, 463, 466, 485, 514, 566, 568
Petty & McDonald 376
Philip, Anthony 175
Photographers 255, 519
Photographs 162, 255, 310
Phrenology 130
Pianos 465
Pictures 517
Pierce, Anne 151
Pierce, Jane 269
Pierce, Mary Lena 539
Pierce, Orrin 132
Pierce, Thomas 137
Pierce's Corners 157
The Pinery 414
The Pioneer Pastor ix, 111, 167, 498
Pioneers 310
Pirate merchants 362-4
Pittard, Joseph 132
Planing mills 386, 477-8
Plank roads 241, 280, 322
Playfair, Andrew W. 317
Playing 238-9
Plebiscites 466-7, 500, 554
Plympton Township 43, 160, 308
Poaching 66
Poems 60, 146, 234, 236, 283, 292, 360, 489-90, 493, 517-18
Point Fortune 36
Pointer boats 363
Poisoning 185, 258
Politicians 111-13, 133, 225-28, 230-1, 246, 315-20, 322-3, 414, 429, 432, 435
Polling subdivisions 324
Polls 282, 324
Poole, Adam 346
Poole, Alfred 453
Poole family 413

Poole, James C. 133, 210, 218, 220, 227, 239, 253, 325, 356, 360-8, 372-6, 378-80, 388-90, 393, 430, 432-8, 441-4, 452, 463-4, 468, 505-8, 511-14, 516
Poole, John 72
Poole, John W. 236
Poole, William 68, 70-2, 86-7, 129, 234, 236
Poole, Rev. William H. 205, 220, 444
Poole's Chapel 495
Poole's Corners 157
Poor Law 52
Population growth 125, 139, 252, 254-8, 275, 321, 419-21, 476, 480, 493-5, 532-3, 551-3, 568, 572-3
Pork 122, 124-5, 136, 139, 275, 302-3, 342, 356, 360-2
Port Elmsley 340
Portages 119-20
Porteous, Earl 548
Porter, John 348, 457, 535, 543
Porter, Mary 457
Post Offices 116, 127-8, 136, 147, 230, 253, 268, 337, 340, 342, 344-8, 354, 414, 493, 495-6, 532, 537, 552, 560-1
Potash 116-17, 127, 136-7, 301, 342, 344, 346, 362, 492
Potatoes 30, 59, 122, 124-5, 138, 196, 300-1, 303, 361, 418, 420, 486-8, 509, 536, 540
Poultry 264, 293, 297, 361, 492, 535-6
Poundkeepers 232, 324
Poverty 11, 32, 35, 52, 153, 156, 217, 221, 267-8, 286, 295-6, 303, 307, 330, 390, 415-17, 440, 490
Powell, Colonel James 18, 20, 26, 71, 98, 108
Powell, John A.H. 218, 226
Powell, Sheriff 214
Pratt, Christopher 530
Prayer 168, 171
Presbyterians 20, 24-6, 32-4, 40-4, 54, 56, 58, 66, 72-3, 82, 87, 90, 93, 110, 146, 166-87, 190-2, 194, 197, 202, 208-9, 219, 225-6, 236, 239, 242, 260, 315,

317, 326, 340, 342, 344, 348, 380, 413, 416, 421, 432, 439, 444, 449, 451, 453-6, 461-2, 464, 532, 545
Presbytery of Upper Canada 172
Prescott 66, 100, 210, 244, 253, 343, 347, 354, 435, 473, 516
Presentism 470
Preston, Rev. J.A. 514
Prettie's Island 483, 486
Prevost, Sir George 2
Prince Edward Island 36
Prince of Wales 370, 436-8
Princess Louise Dragoon Guards 484
Princess Patricia's Light Infantry 520
Prisoners 108
Professional occupations 294
Progress ideology 227, 434
Prohibition 466-9, 486
Prospect 66, 68, 71-2, 77, 136, 145, 149, 162-3, 204-5, 208, 210, 217, 220-1, 242-3, 325, 331, 344-9, 364-5, 398, 401, 405-8, 410-16, 418, 423, 433, 437, 440, 445, 451-4, 457-8, 464, 486, 488, 492-3, 496, 515, 532-3, 535, 537, 540, 543, 545, 561
Prospect Banner Temple 464
Prospect Estate, Ireland 345
Prosperity 111, 255, 286, 306-8, 344, 374, 392-3, 416, 418, 421, 440
Prostitutes 146, 258, 369, 386, 408
Protest groups 56
Protestant Protective Association 445-8, 541
Protestant settlements 54
Protestant union 57-9, 434-8, 444-8, 456
Provisioning trade 116, 120-4, 136-8, 225, 292, 360-3, 511, 540-1, 570, 572
Pulp and paper makers' felts 476
Puseyism 210, 212
Putnam, D.P. 253, 343, 347, 354

Putting stones 78

Quakers 32, 61
Quarries 135, 263, 478-80, 488, 566, 570, 572
Quebec 26, 35-6, 40, 61, 70, 78, 118, 200, 202, 207, 335, 373, 511
Queen Caroline 27
Queen Elizabeth II 570-1, 573
Queen Mary 426
Queen Victoria 398-9, 408, 426, 456, 460, 492, 516, 518, 544
Queen's Bush 292
Queen's County, Ireland 66
Queen's Royal Hotel 484, 500
Queen's University 412-13, 425-7, 439, 500, 538, 569
Quinn, Owen 19, 66, 136

Racism 464, 569-70
Radicalism 38, 56, 98, 102, 110-13, 200, 218, 226-9, 240, 357-8, 366, 572
Raftsmen 292, 363
Railroads 133-4, 162, 248, 250, 261, 278, 280-7, 291-2, 302, 308-11, 315, 317, 320-3, 338-45, 350, 354, 358, 363-6, 368-75, 378-82, 387-8, 452, 473, 492, 494, 498, 520, 537, 551
Railway shops 474-5, 546
Raloo, Ireland 66
Ramsay, Jean 520
Ramsay Township 24, 38, 73, 83, 86, 96-8, 100, 106, 108-11, 113, 119-20, 124, 126, 129-30, 133-4, 184, 186, 205, 210, 216-20, 222, 226-30, 242, 246-8, 280, 310, 316, 332-6, 354, 356-8, 361, 366, 386, 413, 416, 438, 455, 482, 492-3, 496, 514, 542, 556, 566
Ramsay Woollen Cloth Manufacturing Company 369
Rath family 160
Rathwell, Earl 548
Rathwell, James 199
Rationing 548
Rattray, Catherine 266
Rattray, Ellen 266

Rattray, James 266
Rattray, William 138, 266
Ray, Miss 455
Rea, William 242
Read, Widow 154
Reade, Dr. George Hume 230
Reaping machines 298
Rebellions 32, 57-61, 64, 194, 196, 198-9, 215-16, 505, 516
Recessions 282, 476, 527
Recluses 425
Recreation 407-8, 556-8
Recruiting soldiers 524, 548
Rectory of Beckwith 138, 202, 207-8, 211, 248, 447, 496
Red Cross 520, 548
Red Deer, Alberta 498
Redmond, Stephen 19
Reeves 284, 319-22, 324-5, 334, 368, 376, 378, 380, 400, 424, 464, 554
Reforestation 29
Reformed Presbyterians 186, 353
Reformers 132, 160, 185-6, 190-1, 197, 200, 216, 218, 222, 225-8, 230, 239, 241-4, 261, 315-18, 322, 335-6, 341, 358, 416, 430, 432-6, 438, 506, 512
Regattas 483-4
Reid family 158, 486
Reid, George A. 171
Reilly, Patrick 342
Reilly, William 346
Relief, municipal 268, 324, 424-5, 460, 516
Religiously mixed households 444, 446
Remembrance Day 526-8, 547, 563
Remittances 149-50
Renfrew 480, 558
Renfrew County 128, 158, 160-1, 194, 246, 250, 254, 288, 292-3, 304, 322, 334, 343, 412, 572
Renfrew Textiles 551
Renfrewshire weavers 24, 38
Republicanism 5, 24, 52, 98, 102, 110, 128, 198-200, 230
Resorts 483-6, 497, 500
Respectability 94, 230, 268,

341, 425, 514
Restaurants 565
Retirement 340
Revivals 188-9, 407-8, 442
Revolutions 227
Reynolds, Mrs. James 563
Rice, Charles 116, 338, 353, 356
Richards, Mr. 318
Richey, James 150
Richey, Josias 18, 20, 71
Richey, Nancy 150
Richmond 15-18, 20-1, 23, 27, 55-6, 62-4, 68-9, 76-8, 82-3, 91-2, 96-7, 118, 134, 179, 204, 208-9, 213, 218, 221, 243, 345, 347
Richmond, Duke of ix, 15, 20-1, 494
Richmond Methodist Circuit 219-20
Richmond military settlement 15-18, 22, 55-6, 62-4, 83, 96, 570
Richthofen, Manfred von ix, 526, 529
Rideau Canal viii, 6, 24-5, 63, 65, 86, 89, 92, 116, 118, 120-2, 145, 156-7, 194, 225-6, 275, 363, 572
Rideau ferry 70, 120
Rideau Methodist Circuit 72
Rideau River 4, 14, 63-4, 73, 152, 156, 158, 198, 201, 228, 430
Rideau settlement 4, 14, 26-7, 36, 99
Ridgeway 516
Riel, Louis 445
Rifle companies 376, 505, 508, 512-14
Riley family 413
Riley, William 346
Riots 102-8, 113, 240-1, 246
Ritual 212, 439, 448-51
Rivalries 78-9, 100, 102-3, 113, 197-8, 209-12, 326, 375-80, 388, 390, 440, 444, 468, 496-8, 520, 524-5
Roads 18, 21-4, 29, 40, 77-8, 91-3, 98-9, 109, 116, 119-21, 133, 136, 170, 228, 232, 235, 241-2, 253, 268, 275, 280, 286, 291, 315, 321, 323-4, 329, 340, 345, 347-9, 360, 362-4, 366, 380, 400, 417, 540, 550,

552, 564
Roberts, John 320, 324, 346
Robertson, David 275, 300
Robertson, Duncan 297
Robertson, Hue 275
Robertson, James 48
Robertson, James W. 349
Robertson, John 34
Robertson, John Junior 305
Robinson, Geraldine 564
Robinson, James 242, 414
Robinson, Sir John Beverley 199-200
Robinson, Margaret 414
Robinson, Mrs. 410
Robinson settlers, Hon. Peter 24, 63, 74, 83-4, 98, 100, 102-11, 129, 194, 438
Roche, Thomas 338
Roche, William 108
Rockcliffe 180
Roe, John 492
Roe, Ronald 551
Roger, Andrew 523
Roller mills 367, 477
Roman Catholics 19, 24-6, 52-7, 62-3, 66, 71-2, 74, 97-8, 100, 103, 108, 184, 194, 199-200, 202, 213-18, 221-2, 225, 260, 317, 334, 414, 432, 434-8, 443-5, 448, 462, 545, 567, 572
Romanesque Revival architecture 451-2, 480
Romanticism 31-2, 38, 321, 480, 498-502, 505, 512, 516-19, 544-7, 567-8
Rorison, Mr. 386
Rorison, William 376
Rosamond, Bennett 149, 455
Rosamond, James 126-9, 132, 216, 218, 231, 356, 358, 360, 367-70, 382, 455
Roscommon, Ireland 149
Rosdelig, Ireland 62
Roseville 540
"Ross Dhu" 325
Ross, Ireland 61
Ross, Scotland 144
Ross Township 158
Ross, Rev. Walter 444
Rothwell, Thomas 77
Roy, Etienne 12
Royal Air Force 546
Royal Artillery 10
Royal Canadian Regiment 519
Royal Marines 10
Royal Military College 519
Royal Naval Air Service 513
Royal Navy 10
Royal Newfoundland Regiment 10
Ruins 492, 498, 517, 544, 553
Runge, D.F. 558
Running water 473, 544, 550, 552-3
Rural Free Mail Delivery 496-8, 561
Russell, Doctor Gavin 130
Russell, Hon. Peter 157
Ryan, John 438
Rye 125, 275, 302, 418, 420, 540
Ryegate, Vermont 186
Ryerson, Egerton 334

Sabbath observance 185, 252, 405-8, 429-30, 432-3, 438, 442, 452, 546, 570
Sabbath schools See Sunday Schools
Sacred relics See Saint Fillan's crozier
Sacrilege 406
Saddlers 129, 294
St. Andrew's Church, Carleton Place 451-2
St. Andrew's Day dinner 244
St. Augustine's Anglican Women's Association 457
St. Augustine's Cemetery 217
St. Augustine's Church, Prospect 433, 437, 440, 532
St. Catharines 202
St. Columba 32
St. Fillan 32
St. Fillan's cemetery 65, 177, 217, 242, 417, 421
St. Fillan's crozier ix, 32, 40-3, 430
St. Fillan's games 47
St. Fillan's, Scotland 31-2, 41, 47
"St. Hellena" 288
St. Hyacinthe, Quebec 476
St. James Church, Carleton Place 206-7, 210-13, 354, 369, 443, 449, 462, 470
St. James Church, Franktown 187, 202-4, 207, 209, 337, 437, 447, 496, 499, 559
St. John's Church, Tennyson 441, 445, 451, 532, 567
St. John's Masonic Lodge 242
St. Lawrence River 2, 4-6, 11, 26, 40, 73, 76, 78, 80, 92, 96, 120, 133, 146, 152, 198, 281, 312, 344, 363, 366, 374
St. Mary's Church, Carleton Place 440, 444
St. Mary's Church, March 208
St. Patrick's Church, Stafford 161
St. Patrick's Day celebration 247-8
St. Patrick's societies 339
St. Paul's Church, Franktown 396, 437, 440, 449, 452-3, 461-2, 524, 532
St. Thomas 473
Salter, John 126, 153, 212
Salter, Peter P. 484-5, 497, 500
Sample, James 306
Sand Point 292, 380
Sanitation 385-6
Sansom, Antwine 268
Sarnia 160
Saskatchewan 421, 426
Saunders family 158, 160
Saunders, James 345
Saunders, Maria 160
Saunders, Robert 149
Saunders, William 419
Savages 108, 316, 334
Sawmills 117, 127-9, 132, 145, 288, 292, 308-9, 327, 342, 344-7, 353, 356, 359, 361, 364-5, 369-70, 372-4, 376, 380, 382, 386, 388-90, 476-8, 480, 540
Sawn lumber industry 372-4 See also lumber industry and sawmills
Schofield, Lancaster 132
School attendance 328-32, 334, 402-4
School consolidation 552-5, 559
School fairs ii, 349, 534-40, 548
School sections 329
Schools 32, 40, 68, 86, 127-8, 132, 136, 158-9, 168-9, 172, 204, 206, 208, 212, 218, 232-9, 242, 246, 253, 264, 280, 282, 287, 315, 320-1, 323-6, 329, 340, 343-4, 346-8, 353-4, 364, 374, 378, 380, 388, 390, 399-400, 402-3, 406, 408, 410, 434, 438, 454-5, 461, 477, 492-3, 496, 511, 514, 532-8, 548, 552-7
Scotch Corners 305, 325, 346-7, 496, 523, 540, 557, 560, 564
Scotch Line 134
Scotland 29-35, 38-40, 177, 179-80, 184, 188, 342
Scott Act 464-6
Scott, Arthur 526
Scott, Benjamin 546
Scott, Donald 346
Scott, Duncan 491
Scott, Fred ii, 293, 349
Scott, Jack 413, 424
Scott, James 337
Scott, John 345-6
Scott, Lizzie 491
Scott, Mary 491
Scott, Mrs. 180-2
Scott, Robert 229, 490
Scott, Robert Junior 403, 553
Scott, Sir Walter 32, 547
Scott, Walter 132
Scottish Baronial architecture 440
Scottish diction 342, 366, 413
Scottish highland clearances 34
Scottish highland games 32, 47
Scottish highland regiments 31-2
Scottish highland revival 31-2, 568
Scottish highland societies 32, 47
Scottish highlanders 10-12, 29-35, 38-41, 44-9, 52, 55, 63, 72, 76, 94, 105, 109-11, 126, 134, 149, 166-90, 197-8, 225, 228-30, 239, 242, 244, 260, 279, 282, 315, 319, 334,

366-7, 375-6, 413, 421, 427, 430, 545, 567-8
Scottish identities ii, 110-13, 134, 152-64, 166-92, 239-41, 245, 275, 307-8, 310, 319, 326, 329, 332-6, 375-6, 398, 406, 412-13, 421, 429-32, 441, 444-8, 451-3, 496, 498, 539, 541-2, 544-7, 561, 566-8, 572-3
Scottish immigrants vii, ix, 3, 10-14, 18, 24, 44-9, 54, 68-9, 76, 78, 81-2, 87-8, 90, 194, 197, 241, 246-8, 260, 271, 278-80, 292, 301, 305-8, 315-16, 318
Scottish lowlanders 10, 31, 38, 72, 97-102, 104-6, 108-11, 113, 126, 129, 134, 191, 200, 210, 217-22, 225-9, 241-2, 246-8, 316, 334-5, 341, 357-9, 389, 416, 542, 572
Scottish reputation 239-41, 336, 362, 366, 416-18
Scrape marks 359
Scullabogue 59-61
Seamstresses 294
Secession Presbyterianism 33-4, 44-7, 72, 110, 167, 172, 174, 190
2nd Carleton Regiment 97
Secret societies 56
Secularisation 434
Sedition 200, 482
Seduction 146, 412
Selkirk, Lord 36
Selkirk Scotland 166
Sentimentality 31-2, 37, 317, 396, 498-502, 509, 516-19, 542-4, 573
Separate schools 334, 434-8, 445
Sermons 47, 180-1, 200, 244, 444, 459
Servants 21-2, 37, 90, 146, 174, 179-82, 221-2, 290, 294-6, 298, 345, 359, 366
Settlement patterns 38, 67-9
79th Highlanders 143-4
77th Regiment 78
Sewing 536
Sex ratios 255-6
Sexual repression 258, 412
Shail, George 468
Shaw, George 316
Shaw, James 226-7, 316-17, 437
Shaw, James Junior 316
Shaw, Richard 316
Sheil, John 532, 540, 563
Sheil, Moses 136
Shepherd's Falls 25
Sherwood, Reuben 12, 14-15, 91
Shillington, Thomas 72
Shingle mills 344, 346, 372-4, 376
Shipman, Daniel 200
Shipman's Falls 218
Shipman's Mills 108, 200
Shirley family 160
Shirley, Richard 407
Shoemakers 36, 65-6, 76, 129, 136, 143, 196, 225, 294, 327, 345-6, 348, 354-5, 493-5
Shopping malls 556, 566-7
Shore, John W. 209, 344
Shortt, Rev. Jonathan 160, 197, 204, 207-8
Simcoe, John Graves 4
Simmons, Bill 346
Simpson, Eliza 414-15
Simpson family 423
Simpson, Irene 414
Simpson, James 119
Simpson, Rev. James 407-8
Simpson, Joshua 414-15, 487
Simpson, Samuel 402
Sinclair, Alexander 305
Sinclair, Colin 376
Sinclair, John 292
Sinclair, Mr. 274
Singing schools 259
Sitting rooms 307
Slaney River 60
Slatich, Scotland 49
Slavery 189-90, 358
Slovenliness 170-1, 173-4, 176-8, 326, 384
Slums 258
Slurs 432
Small, H.C. 511
Smallpox 410
Smith, Cecil 526
Smith, Dorah 146
Smith, Rev. John 174-84, 190, 232, 234, 257, 338, 544
Smith, Mr. 318
Smith, William 305
Smiths Falls viii, 118-21, 133-4, 136, 145, 158, 188, 198, 201-2, 204-5, 218, 222, 226-7, 236, 247, 261, 280, 282, 286, 291, 298, 311, 322, 336, 340, 363, 366, 372, 378, 415-16, 423, 435, 447, 453, 461, 473, 478, 484, 488-9, 496, 537, 540, 543-4, 552, 560-1, 566
Smoking 80, 103, 244, 406, 408, 424, 442, 538
Smuggling 338, 342
Smyth, S.A. 461
Snow clubs 552
Snuff 244
Sobriety 64
Social control 146, 148, 160, 171, 178-82, 190, 225-48, 333-6, 402-10, 429-32, 438-44
Social mobility 392-3
Social structure 254-61, 266-75
Socialising 78, 84, 264-6, 347, 408, 414, 440, 452, 468, 483, 534-8, 564
Society for the Propagation of Christian Knowledge 32
Society for the Propagation of the Gospel 200, 202, 207
Soil quality 288, 416, 492
Soirees 344, 462, 464
Soldiers 38, 57-8, 65-6, 78, 110, 143-4, 215, 234, 315, 327, 455, 505, 514-16, 519-25, 551, 569
Sons of Temperance 244, 336
Sophia ship 34-5
South African War 410, 511, 519
South Crosby Township 4
South Elmsley Township 158
South End, Essex, England 342
South Lanark riding 316-18, 435
South Leeds riding 318
South Sherbrooke Township 24, 96
Soviet Union 568
Spar Aerospace 568
Sparrow, William 157
Speculation 4, 12
Spencer, Dr. John 367
Spies 38
Spinsters 278
Spirituality 444
Sports 244, 298, 350, 402, 412, 483, 486, 518, 525, 536, 556-7
Spratt, Hugh 44, 166
Springside Hall 321, 323
Squatters 26, 64, 117, 144, 153-4, 156-8, 161, 198, 260
S.S. no. 1 329, 533
S.S. no. 2 329
S.S. no. 3 329, 347, 533
S.S. no. 4 326, 329, 331, 496
S.S. no. 5 329, 335, 348, 496
S.S. no. 6 ix, 329, 348, 399, 402-3, 426-7, 496
S.S. no. 7 329, 348, 533
S.S. no. 8 326, 329, 533
S.S. no. 9 326, 329, 348, 496, 533
S.S. no. 10 329
S.S. no. 11 326
S.S. (union) no. 13, 10 and 15 329, 534
Stafford Township 160-1
Stagecoaches 71, 366, 494
Stained glass 405, 450, 462-3
Stamford, Connecticut 466, 469, 521
Stanzel, Benjamin 209
Stanzel, Thomas 209
Star of Beckwith Lodge 464
Starvation 309, 323, 386
Statues 307
Statute labour 153, 235, 268, 275, 325-6, 378, 380, 539, 552, 573
Steam power 342, 344, 365-6, 372-3, 380, 382, 387, 485
Steamboats 35, 374, 483-5
Stephens, Margaret 160
Stereotypes 415-16
Sterns, James 275
Stewart, Alexander 109, 162, 180, 232, 268, 302, 327, 346, 461
Stewart, Alexander F. 421
Stewart, Bishop Charles James 202, 204-7
Stewart, Donald 508
Stewart, Duncan 338
Stewart family 302, 419
Stewart, James 304, 430
Stewart, Janet 344
Stewart, John 179, 461
Stewart, Neil 257, 342

Stewart, Peter 345
Stewart, William 136
Stirling, Alexander 143
Stirling, Scotland 149-50
Stittsville 486
Stone buildings 105, 107, 109, 114, 127, 129-30, 133-4, 136-8, 145, 149, 162-3, 174-5, 178-81, 188-9, 197, 202, 206-9, 211, 220-1, 229, 237, 241, 243, 245-6, 248, 257, 263, 265, 269, 301, 305-7, 310, 317, 319, 321, 325, 327, 331, 333, 335, 338, 340, 344-6, 348-9, 354, 357, 367-8, 373, 381, 383, 386-8, 399, 401, 403, 414, 433, 440, 447, 451, 543, 461, 469, 474, 476, 509, 553
Stone carving 65
Stone crushing 235
Stone, George 154
Stone quarries 135, 263, 478-80, 488
Stonemasons 24, 68, 163, 384
Storehouse See King's storehouse
Stores 344-7, 386, 467, 493-5, 532, 544
Stormont County 10
Story, James 508
Stoves 90-1, 132-3, 245, 247, 265, 362, 372, 474-7, 530, 543
Strachan, Bishop John 134, 210
Strikes 388-9, 477, 480, 570
Strippers 570
Strowan parish, Scotland 45
Subdivisions 558, 570, 572
The sublime 76
Suicide 408, 438, 470
Sullivan, John 83-4
Sumner, Bertha 470
Sumner, John 124, 129, 209, 320, 342, 344, 357, 372
Sumner's Corners 116, 119, 342
Sunday Schools 169, 178, 204, 211, 406-7, 450, 452-4, 456, 461
Supermarkets 467, 565
Superstition 185-6, 366, 430-2, 434-6
Surveys and surveyors 4, 12, 14, 18-20, 68, 77, 82, 91, 93, 136, 153, 158-9
Sutton family 60, 160
Sutton, Joseph 19, 228
Sutton, Mary 153
Sutton, Samuel 64
Swamps 12, 18, 21-2, 69, 76-8, 91-2, 120, 135, 153-4, 158, 160, 169, 199, 208, 235, 242, 248, 258, 286, 301, 303, 306, 345, 349, 398, 408, 411, 414, 419, 488
Swan, Joseph 39, 48
Swearing 200, 211
Switzer, Bella 538
Switzer, Martin 209
Sykes, Hiram 209
Sykes, John 209
Sykes, William 282

Table 1: Numbers of Persons and Land Grants Settled, 1816-1822 16
Table 2: Population Growth of Beckwith and Carleton Place, 1816-1990 252
Table 3: Age Pyramids for Beckwith, 1852-1881 256
Table 4: Mean Size of Household by Birthplace of Head, 1852-1881 262
Table 5: Mean Size of Household by Religion of Head, 1852-1881 262
Table 6: Relative Mortality of Young and Aged, 1852-1881 270
Table 7: Household Composition, 1852-1881 270
Table 8: Nuclear Household Composition, 1852-1881 272
Table 9: Nuclear Household Comparative Size, 1852-1881 272
Table 10: Non-Nuclear Household Composition and Growth, 1852-1881 274
Table 11: Occupation of Household Head by Category, 1852-1881 290
Table 12: Occupation of General Population by Category, 1852-1881 290
Table 13: Number of Servants in Beckwith and Huntley Townships, 1852-1881 296
Table 14: Ratio of Males Aged 20+ to Land Occupied & Improved, 1851-1880 298
Table 15: Land Holdings in Beckwith, 1852-1880 300
Table 16: Agricultural Produce of Beckwith Township, 1851-1890 303
Table 17: Livestock in Beckwith Township, 1851-1890 305
Table 18: House Construction in Beckwith, 1852-1891 306
Table 19: House Construction by Ethnicity of Household Head, 1852 306
Table 20: School Attendance of 10-14 Age Group, 1852-1881 332
Table 21: School Attendance of 5-18 Age Group, 1852-1881 332
Table 22: Carleton Place Major Industries in 1871 376
Table 23: Agricultural Produce of Beckwith, 1890-1920 420
Table 24: Land Holding in Beckwith, 1881-1921 420
Table 25: Birthrate and Rate of Natural Increase for Beckwith Township, 1869-1919 422
Table 26: Mortality Rate for Beckwith Township, 1869-1919 422
Table 27: Religiously Mixed Beckwith Households, 1852-1881 446
Table 28: Manufacturing Industries in Eastern Ontario Towns, 1901-1921 484
Table 29: Land Holdings in Beckwith Township, 1956-1981 542
Table 30: Livestock in Beckwith Township, 1890-1970 542
Table 31: Crop Acreages in Beckwith Township, 1920-1970 544
Tailors 129, 136, 196, 338, 344-5, 376, 494
Talbot, Richard 17
Talbot, Thomas 36
Tanneries 149, 288, 338, 344, 361, 370, 376, 477, 492-3
Tartar, Blade 304
Tartans 32
Taverns 20, 22, 44, 71-2, 82, 94, 96, 101-6, 110, 128, 132, 134, 148, 211, 230, 242-3, 319, 324, 335-8, 344-7, 451, 463-4, 494
Tay Canal 120
Tay River 97, 120
Taylor family 160
Taylor, George 58
Taylor, Josias 12, 97, 226, 229
Taylor, William 289, 292, 308, 478
Taymouth Castle 39, 45
Tea Meetings 455
Teachers 10, 26, 32, 86, 127-9, 132, 136, 145, 158-60, 168-9, 172, 179, 200, 213, 234-9, 288-9, 294, 324, 326-8, 330, 332-3, 345, 347, 400, 402-3, 408-10, 432, 477, 534, 538
Teetotallers 336, 344
Telegraph 286, 294, 344, 366, 453, 477, 505
Telephone 453, 473, 477-8, 483, 490, 496-8, 539-40, 544, 547, 560
Television 558-60, 565, 570
Temperance Movement 132, 148, 185, 190-1, 226-7, 242-6, 259, 335-6, 344, 356, 436, 451, 463-9, 494, 496, 536-8, 572
Templeshanbo parish, Ireland 64
Tennant family 160
Tennyson 120, 325, 329, 347-8, 416, 440-1, 445, 451, 468, 496, 532, 540, 545, 561, 567
Teskey & Bredin 359

Teskey, John 130
Teskey, Mr. 102, 106
Teskey's 361
Theatres 459, 478, 486, 559
Theft 568
3rd Lanark Regiment 246
Thom, Alexander 112
Thompson, Andrew 342
Thomson, John 308
Threshing 117, 302, 424, 442, 545-6
Tierney family 414
Tighe, Rev. Stearne 287
Timber camps 19, 225, 250, 292, 300, 303, 361-3, 408
Timber industry 40, 61, 84-6, 116-19, 121-3, 136-7, 292-4, 485, 526, 540, 570, 572
Timber pirates 117, 154, 158
Timber shanties 116, 118, 124, 211
Timber slides 25, 388
Time 289, 310, 435
Tinkler, Charles D. 526
Tinsmiths 357
Tipperary, Ireland 17-18, 55-6, 62, 66, 342
Tithing 218
Tollman's (Kitley) 23
Tomlinson family 160
Tomlinson, John 345-6
Tooley, Charles 258
Tools 81-4, 100, 291, 298, 300-2, 355
Topography 305
Torbolton Township 24
Toronto vii, 86, 202, 208, 281, 335, 366, 384, 451, 455, 473-4, 480, 487, 496, 516, 536, 539, 541, 552
Toronto Gore Township 286
Torture 57
Town Hall (Carleton Place) 390, 459, 478-80, 483, 489, 496
Town plans 13, 17-18
Town wardens 228
Township hall 317, 323-4, 346-7, 349, 368, 378, 464, 500, 526, 535, 548, 563, 571, 573
Township identity 322-3, 417-18, 539-40, 553-6, 558, 563
Township meetings 228-30, 317, 323-4, 378, 512,
516, 548
Township unity 322-5, 535-40, 554-6, 560, 563-4
Townward migration 453
Tractarians 448-51
Tractor farming 554-5, 562-3
Tramps 416
Treason 105, 110-11, 200, 216, 508
Trenham, N.J. 255
Trespassing 117
Trevor-Roper, Hugh 32
Trial by ordeal 430
Trials 108
Trinity College, Dublin 200
Trinity College, Toronto 217
Triumphal arches 370
Tucker, Patrick 355, 508, 516
Tullimet, Scotland 144
Tully, William 225
Tunnels 282
Turkey fairs 535
Turnips 303, 418, 420, 488
Tweedy, Ephraim 130
Twelfth of July celebrations 216, 250, 340, 412, 445, 507, 522
Tyranny 98, 358

Ulster, Ireland 16, 53-4, 56, 58, 65-6, 234
Underbrushing 275
Unemployment 73, 386, 388, 482, 527
Unions 477, 480
United Church of Canada 532, 548
United Church of England and Ireland See Anglicans
United Counties of Lanark & Renfrew Agricultural Society 279, 299, 304, 370
United Empire Loyalists vii, 2-4, 12, 107, 152, 198-200
United Farmers of Ontario 541-2
United Irishmen 57, 198, 506
United States 2, 10, 24, 61, 98, 100, 158, 188, 198, 254, 261-2, 278, 281, 303, 305-6, 311, 360, 362-3,
412, 426, 476, 506, 573
Universities 146, 166, 177, 186, 233-4, 341, 404, 412-13, 426, 433, 539
University of Ottawa vii-viii, 570
University Rifles 516
Upper Canada College 208
Upton, John 73
Urban ideas 264, 364-6, 375, 377, 379, 458, 460, 466, 473, 477-81, 489-90, 496, 530, 558-60, 564-7
Urban planning 370, 384-6, 566-7
Urbanisation 561-9

Vaccination 29, 59-60
Valcartier 520
Valley Queen Cheese Factory 416, 494
Vancouver 478
Vaughn, Rev. G.F. 62
Vaughn, Sergeant 21
Veal 361
Vermont 186
Victoria Fire Brigade 505
Victoria Macadamised Road 120-1
Victoria Temperance Loyal Orange Lodge 341
Victory Loan Drives 548, 551
Villages 336-47
Vinegar Hill, Ireland 58, 60, 62
Violence 59-60, 73-4, 96, 102-11, 148, 158, 196, 198, 205, 216, 222, 265-6, 292, 316, 334, 369, 388, 390, 392, 408, 435, 438, 494
Virtue 182, 190, 239, 280
Voluntarism 23-4, 44, 57, 109, 184, 186, 236, 247, 331, 390, 432-4, 508, 511, 519-20, 558, 560, 568
Volunteer military companies 23-4, 324-5, 506-8, 514

Waba Creek 288
Waggonmakers 225, 338, 344, 354 See also Carriagemakers
Wakes 103, 458, 572
Walker, Andrew 376
Wall, James 82, 90, 197
Wallace family 160
Walling, Henry F. 253, 343, 347, 354
Walsh, Michael 132
War 31, 196, 262, 282, 410, 420, 476, 509-10, 519-24, 544, 547
War as adventure 516-19
War memorials 526, 548, 563
War of 1812 xii, 2, 4-6, 10, 55
Wardner, George 132
Wards 318-19
Warren families 160
Warwick Township 160, 162-3
Washing machines 300
Waterloo, Battle of xii, 65
Waterloo Hotel 129, 373
Water-power 18, 353, 356, 368-70, 387
Watson, Newyear 347
Watson, Patrick 557, 566
Wealth 185, 286, 306-7, 330, 358, 381
Weavers and weaving 24, 29-30, 38, 46, 88, 100, 102, 111, 116, 126, 130, 136, 225, 228, 258, 294, 348, 356-8, 493
Webster, Israel 132, 228, 230
Weems, Scotland 36
Welfare See Relief, municipal
Wells, Forley 565
Wesley, John 210
Wesleyan Methodists See Methodists
Westmeath Township 128, 158
Westport 412, 435
Westward migration 49, 255, 285, 308-11, 366, 409-10, 412, 418-20, 423-7, 453, 502, 572-3
Wethey, E.J. 525
Wexford bridge 60
Wexford County, Ireland 18, 21, 52-62, 71, 88, 92, 109-11, 113, 144, 148-50, 152, 194, 196-7, 214, 219, 226-7, 269, 310, 315-16, 345, 357, 429, 505, 544, 570-2
Wexford settlements 61-70, 157-64, 537
Wheat crops viii, 118, 122-

3, 128, 138-9, 168, 218, 280, 292, 298, 300, 302-4, 360, 367, 420, 486, 488, 540, 562
Wheelwrights 138
Whigs 56
Whiskey 93, 298, 424, 468
White, Robert 494
White, Thomas 297
Whitehead, Joseph 149
Whyte family 288
Whyte, Helen 304-5, 312
Whyte, John 232, 237, 288
Whyte, Malcolm 322-3
Wickham, Thomas 20, 22-3, 27, 44, 94, 97, 134, 148, 242-3
Wicklow County, Ireland 52-4
Widowed people 87, 150-2, 162-3, 266-8, 271, 273-4, 290, 327, 348, 411, 455, 490-2, 527
Wife beating 148, 244, 265, 457, 564, 570
Wilkie, J.L. 182
William III 195, 339-40, 445, 507
William IV 19
Williams, Mr. 454
Williams, Thomas 153, 159
Williams, William 345
Williamson, Hugh 126
Willing Workers Society 462
Willis, Caton 206
Willis, George E. 129
Willis, Mr. 505

Willoughby family 160
Willoughby, William 478
Wills 124, 150-2, 161, 258, 289-92, 336, 398-9, 460, 465, 490-2
Wilson, Agnes 148
Wilson, Allan 82
Wilson, Edna 454
Wilson, Evelyn M. 469, 521
Wilson family 113, 453
Wilson, George 64
Wilson, John 136
Wilson, Robert 411
Wilson, Sarah Agnes 111
Wilson, Dr. William 114, 130, 258, 464, 521
Wilson, William 92
Winchester, Ian 274
Winnipeg 478
Winter, Rev. D. 458
Wiseman, Douglas MPP x
Witch of Plum Hollow 430
Witches 41, 430-2, 547
Witney, Dudley 295, 297, 401
Wolford Township 4, 14, 72
Wolverine Mills 372
Women 233-4, 244, 275, 289-92, 310, 379, 390, 433, 455, 473, 495, 516, 556, 562-4, 573
Women and religion 180-2, 190, 206, 428, 454-70
Women as "angels of the house" See "Angel of the House"

Women's associations 258, 454-5, 457, 461-2, 483, 486, 520, 539
Women's Christian Temperance Union 336, 466, 536-8
Women's College Hospital 539
Women's domestic sphere 262-5, 466-7, 470, 495, 536-40, 563-4
Women's Foreign Missionary Society 462
Women's Home Missionary Society 462
Women's rights 261-2
Women's role in society xi, 146-8, 167, 173-4, 258-9, 261-5, 289-92, 294-6, 379, 391, 396, 398-400, 429, 538-40, 562-4
Women's separate sphere 458-60, 467, 536, 538-40
Women's work 87-90, 146-8, 234, 258, 262-6, 294-6, 379, 382, 385, 399-400, 402, 408, 455, 458-60, 465-6, 468-70, 492, 501, 515, 520, 534-5, 538, 562-4
Wood market 274-5, 301
Wool 300, 303, 356, 361, 372, 488
Woollen industry 98, 125-7, 132, 279, 356, 360, 550-1
Woollen mills 258, 288, 369-70, 372, 374, 376,

381-5, 473, 475-7, 480, 482, 487, 550
Working class See Labour
World War One 420, 427, 442, 466, 468, 479, 482, 502, 507, 509, 515, 517, 519-25, 541, 544, 546, 548, 563, 569-71
World War Two 519, 547-8, 550, 563-4, 569-71
Wren, Christopher 58
Wright, Philemon 16, 76
Wrightstown (Hull) 16
Wylie, Alexander 128
Wylie, David 380, 382
Wylie, William 382-3, 473, 476
Wynn, Christopher 136, 153
Wynn, Mr. 158

Yeomanry 230-1, 247, 400, 506, 516
Y.M.C.A. 486
York, Upper Canada 36, 86, 108, 154, 170, 202, 208
Young, Archibald M. 237
Young, Arthur 52, 54
Young Ladies Sewing Society 462
Young, Maggie 162
Young, William 162

Zion Church, Carleton Place 440, 462, 480, 532